Sedative, Hypnotic, or Anxiolytic Intoxication
    Delirium
Sedative, Hypnotic, or Anxiolytic Withdrawal
    Delirium

Polysubstance-Related Disorder
Polysubstance Dependence

Schizophrenia and Other Psychotic Disorders

Schizophrenia
    Paranoid Type
    Disorganized Type
    Catatonic Type
    Undifferentiated Type
    Residual Type
Schizophreniform Disorder
Schizoaffective Disorder
Brief Psychotic Disorder
Shared Psychotic Disorder
Psychotic Disorder Due to...
    [Indicate the General Medical Condition]
Substance-Induced Psychotic Disorder
Psychotic Disorder NOS

Mood Disorders

Depressive Disorders
Major Depressive Disorder
Dysthymic Disorder
Depressive Disorder NOS

Bipolar Disorders
Bipolar I Disorder
Bipolar II Disorder
Cyclothymic Disorder
Bipolar Disorder NOS
Mood Disorder Due to...[Indicate the General
    Medical Condition]
Substance-Induced Mood Disorder
Mood Disorder NOS

Anxiety Disorders

Panic Disorder without Agoraphobia
Panic Disorder with Agoraphobia
Agoraphobia without History of Panic
Disorder
Specific Phobia
    Specify type: Animal Type/Natural Environment
    Type/ Blood-Injection-Injury Type/ Situational
    Type/Other Type
Social Phobia
Obsessive-Compulsive Disorder
Posttraumatic Stress Disorder
Acute Stress Disorder
Generalized Anxiety Disorder
Anxiety Disorder Due to...[Indicate the General
    Medical Condition]
Substance-Induced Anxiety Disorder (Refer to
    Substance-Related Disorders for Substance-
    Specific Codes)
Anxiety Disorder NOS

Somatoform Disorders

Somatization Disorder
Undifferentiated Somatoform Disorder
Conversion Disorder
Pain Disorder
Hypochondriasis

Body Dysmorphic Disorder
Somatoform Disorder NOS

Factitious Disorders
Factitious Disorder
Factitious Disorder NOS

Dissociative Disorders
Dissociative Amnesia
Dissociative Fugue
Dissociative Identity Disorder
Depersonalization Disorder
Dissociative Disorder NOS

Sexual and Gender Identity Disorders

Sexual Desire Disorders
Hypoactive Sexual Desire Disorder

Sexual Aversion Disorder

Sexual Arousal Disorders
Female Sexual Arousal Disorder
Male Erectile Disorder

Orgasmic Disorders
Female Orgasmic Disorder
Male Orgasmic Disorder
Premature Ejaculation

Sexual Pain Disorders
Dyspareunia
Vaginismus

Sexual Dysfunction Due to a General Medical
Condition
Sexual Dysfunction NOS

Paraphilias
Exhibitionism
Fetishism
Frotteurism
Pedophilia
Sexual Masochism
Sexual Sadism
Transvestic Fetishism
Voyeurism
Paraphilia NOS

Gender Identity Disorders
Gender Identity Disorder
Gender Identity Disorder NOS
Sexual Disorder NOS

Eating Disorders
Anorexia Nervosa
Bulimia Nervosa
Eating Disorder NOS

Sleep Disorders

Dyssomnias
Primary Insomnia
Primary Hypersomnia
Narcolepsy
Breathing-Related Sleep Disorder
Circadian Rhythm Sleep Disorder
Dyssomnia NOS

Parasomnias
Nightmare Disorder
Sleep Terror Disorder

Parasomnia NOS

Impulse-Control Disorders Not Elsewhere Classified
Intermittent Explosive Disorder
Kleptomania
Pyromania
Pathological Gambling
Trichotillomania
Impulse-Control Disorder NOS

Adjustment Disorders
Adjustment Disorder

Personality Disorders
Note: These are coded on Axis II.
Paranoid Personality Disorder
Schizoid Personality Disorder
Schizotypal Personality Disorder
Antisocial Personality Disorder
Borderline Personality Disorder
Histrionic Personality Disorder
Narcissistic Personality Disorder
Avoidant Personality Disorder
Dependent Personality Disorder
Obsessive-Compulsive Personality Disorder
Personality Disorder NOS

Other Conditions That May Be a Focus of Clinical Intervention

Relational Problems
Relational Problem Related to a Mental
Disorder or General Medical Condition
Parent-Child Relational Problem
Partner Relational Problem
Sibling Relational Problem
Relational Problem NOS

Problems Related to Abuse or Neglect
Physical Abuse of Child
Sexual Abuse of Child
Neglect of Child
Physical Abuse of Adult
Sexual Abuse of Adult

Additional Conditions That May Be a Focus of Clinical Attention
Noncompliance with Treatment
Malingering
Adult Antisocial Behavior
Borderline Intellectual Functioning
Age-Related Cognitive Decline
Bereavement
Academic Problem
Occupational Problem
Identity Problem
Religious or Spiritual Problem
Acculturation Problem
Phase of Life Problem

Essentials of
Abnormal Psychology

Essentials of
Abnormal Psychology

ROBERT E. EMERY
University of Virginia

THOMAS F. OLTMANNS
University of Virginia

PRENTICE HALL, Upper Saddle River, New Jersey 07458

Library of Congress Cataloging-in-Publication Data

Emery, Robert E.
    Essentials of abnormal psychology / Robert E. Emery, Thomas F.
Oltmanns.
        p.   cm.
        Includes bibliographical references and index.
        ISBN 0–13–083330–4
        1. Psychology, Pathological.   I. Oltmanns, Thomas F.   II. Title.
    RC454.E45   1999
    616.89—dc21   99–41291
                                                                   CIP

Editor-in-Chief: Nancy Roberts
Executive Editor: Bill Webber
Development Editor-in-Chief: Susanna Lesan
Development Editor: Leslie Carr
Editorial Assistant: Tamsen Adams
AVP/Director of Production and Manufacturing: Barbara Kittle
Managing Editor: Mary Rottino
Production Editor: Randy Pettit
Manufacturing Manager: Nick Sklitsis
Prepress and Manufacturing Buyer: Lynn Pearlman
Director of Marketing: Gina Sluss
Marketing Manager: Sharon Cosgrove
Creative Design Director: Leslie Osher
Art Director: Maria Lange
Interior and Cover Design: Maria Lange
Portraits: Van Howell
Line Art Supervisor: Guy Ruggerio

For permission to use copyrighted material, grateful
acknowledgment is made to the copyright holders listed
on pages 466–467, which are considered an extension of this
copyright page.

This book was set in 10/12 Minion by Carlisle Communications
and was printed and bound by Courier-Westford. The cover was printed by Phoenix

Printed in the United States of America
10 9 8 7 6 5 4 3 2 1

ISBN 0-13-083330-4

Prentice-Hall International (UK) Limited, *London*
Prentice-Hall of Australia Pty. Limited, *Sydney*
Prentice-Hall Canada Inc., *Toronto*
Prentice-Hall Hispanoamerica, S.A., *Mexico*
Prentice-Hall of India Private Limited, *New Delhi*
Prentice-Hall of Japan, Inc., *Tokyo*
Simon & Schuster Asia Pte. Ltd., *Singapore*
Editora Prentice-Hall do Brasil, Ltda., *Rio de Janeiro*

To Kimberly, Maggie, Jacey, Robert, and Lucy
REE

To Gail, Sara, and Josh
TFO

Brief Contents

Contents

3 Treatment of Psychological Disorders   57

9 Personality Disorders   240

12 Sexual and Gender Identity Disorders

13 Schizophrenic Disorders   352

14 Pervasive Developmental Disorders and Psychological Disorders of Childhood   384

15 | Mental Health and the Law   425

Preface

In this text, as in this course, students will encounter a huge and disturbing range of human behavior. At times students may feel like outsiders peering into a parallel universe of people and problems wholly foreign to their experience. At other times, the topics may feel uncomfortably personal. Emotional disorders are widespread, and although the line between normal and abnormal behavior can be wide, it can be very fine.

REAL PEOPLE

We are interested in making sure readers come away from this course with the sense that above all, abnormal psychology is about people—real people. It is this sense which will help readers see the humanity underlying even the most outlandish of disordered behavior and face their own emotional and psychological difficulties with no less compassion. All of our lives have been touched by emotional disorders, whether personally, through relatives and friends, or in our encounters in everyday life. This book is not about "them;" it is about all of us.

To bring the subject matter of abnormal psychology closer to readers' lives, we open each chapter with an extended case study and include shorter cases studies at various points throughout the text. Most of the case studies are drawn from our own clinical files, but we include a few classic cases from the literature as well. It is the specifics of people's lives, the family life of a person with an eating disorder or the growing loneliness of the person engulfed by depression that make the topics covered in this text both vivid and poignant.

HELPING READERS SEEKING HELP

For those times when the discussion of a mental disorder may strike a reader as uncomfortably close to home, we include a special insert, called Getting Help, in every chapter. These sections give readers empirically-based practical information. Depending on the topic, we offer concrete suggestions for self-help and information on seeking professional assistance. For example, the Getting Help section in Chapter 1 provides several suggestions about how to be an educated consumer when searching for a mental health professional. We offer advice on how to locate a professional who is both an expert in treating a particular disorder and a good "fit" for the person who is seeking therapy. All of the Getting Help sections also include specific self-help suggestions for places to go to learn more about the nature and consequences of various emotional problems and life stresses. The books and web sites they list are not exhaustive, but they are intended to give readers a running start in getting help for themselves or others.

UNDERSTANDING THE FIELD AS A WORK IN PROGRESS AND BECOMING EDUCATED CONSUMERS OF SCIENTIFIC INFORMATION

Of course, for many of the disorders discussed in this book, treatment is not synonymous with cure. Our understanding of the causes of mental disorder is a work in progress, and we present what we know—and what we do not know—about the nature, cause, and treatment of emotional disorders. So even as we refer readers to various sources in the Getting Help sections, the chapters provide a basis for evaluating all the information they may uncover with the informed skepticism of educated consumers of psychological information.

Because there is much that psychological scientists do not yet know about abnormal psychology, it is helpful for students to know how they are going about trying to find answers to the many questions that remain. We include some material in this text on the process of conducting psychological research. We also have carefully reviewed the most recent research in order to offer both the latest information and a sense of where the field is heading in the future.

THE SYSTEMS APPROACH

Twenty-five years ago, psychology could be divided into four or five "schools" of thought (for example; biological, behavioral, cognitive, psychoanalytic, and humanistic psychology). But today these paradigms or theoretical approaches reflect the past, not the future, of abnormal psychology. In looking to the future, we embrace systems theory, the integrative conceptual framework that has revolutionized scientific disciplines ranging from computer science to biology.

In following a systems approach, we integrate research on biological, psychological, and social factors in understanding the causes of abnormal behavior. Our approach not only highlights integration, but also recognizes that biological, psychological, and social theories can be compatible explanations of psychopathology. For example, we note that neurochemical explanations of depression are not necessarily incompatible with explanations that focus on cognitive distortions, gender roles, and other psychosocial factors. The systems approach also calls attention to the essential fact that different psychological disorders have different causes, and no single paradigm can accurately explain all psychological disturbances.

In addition to examining causes, we extend the systems approach to cover treatment in an integrated fashion. We introduce biological, psychological, and social treatments for psychological disorders early in the text (Chapter 3). In this discussion, we emphasize research on psychotherapy outcome and psychotherapy process. Our early introduction to treatment and our empirical focus on psychotherapy allow us in later chapters to highlight only the most promising, empirically based approaches to psychotherapy, medication, and other forms of intervention.

THE LOGIC BEHIND A BRIEFER BOOK

The Essentials of Abnormal Psychology is designed to save students money and to work more comfortably in courses with shorter terms. It also offers students easy access to challenging material. We have pared unnecessary details from every chapter, while including many user-friendly tables and figures to help tie information together concisely and vividly. Every chapter on a major diagnostic category follows a consistent organization, including major sections on typical symptoms and associated features, classification, epidemiology, etiology, and treatment. The consistent organization gives readers a ready framework for learning new material.

SUPPLEMENTS FOR STUDENTS AND INSTRUCTORS

An extensive and useful array of instructor and student supplements are available with this book:

The Instructor's Manual, written by Gordon Atlas of Alfred University and adapted by Jeffrey Aaron at the University of Virginia, contains detailed lecture outlines and teaching suggestions for each chapter, as well as a compendium of handouts and transparency masters and a coordinated list of video segments by chapter.

The Study Guide, written by Shelly Martin of Wesleyan College, provides a chapter review, learning objectives, key concepts and terms (with definitions), self-tests, and activities for each chapter of the text.

The Test Item File, written by Joseph Palladino of the University of Southern Indiana, contains over 1,500 test items.

Prentice Hall Test Manager.   The questions in the Test Item File are available on both Windows and Macintosh platforms and allow instructors complete personal flexibility in building and editing their own customized tests. Advances in the most recent version of this software now allow instructors to load their tests onto a Local Area Network in an on-line testing format.

Instructional Videos.   Two distinct types of videos, providing more than 400 minutes of video material, accompany our text:

ABC News/Prentice Hall Video Library Series III.   provides relevant segments from award-winning ABC News programs, including "Nightline," "20/20," "Prime Time Live," and "American Agenda." A summary of each segment and suggestions on how to incorporate the video into the classroom are included in the Instructor's Manual.

Video Cases in Abnormal Psychology: The Patients as Educators,   James H. Scully, Jr., MD, and Alan M. Dahms, Ph.D., Colorado State University. This exclusive video contains a series of ten patient interviews illustrating a range of disorders. Each interview is preceded by a brief history of the patient and a synopsis of some major symptoms of the disorder and ends with a summary and a brief analysis.

Prentice Hall Color Transparencies for Abnormal Psychology Series III

The New York Times **Abnormal Psychology Supplement.**   *The New York Times* and Prentice Hall are sponsoring Themes of The Times, a program designed to enhance access to current information of relevance in the classroom.

Through this program, the core subject matter provided in the text is supplemented by a collection of time-sensitive articles from one of the world's most distinguished newspapers, *The New York Times*. These articles demonstrate the vital, ongoing connection between what is learned in the classroom and what is happening in the world.

To help you enjoy the wealth of information of *The New York Times* daily, a reduced subscription rate is available. For information, call toll-free: 1-800-631-1222.

Prentice Hall and *The New York Times* are proud to cosponsor Themes of The Times. We hope it will make the reading of both textbooks and newspapers a more dynamic, involving process.

Companion Website.   An interactive website is available for instructors and students who use *Essentials of Abnormal Psychology*. Visitors will find a range of interactive resources, including a free, interactive student study guide, a virtual discussion group/chat area, and related links and resources. The quizzes available in every chapter can be e-mailed to instructors or teaching assistants.

WebCT.   For instructors interested in distance learning, Prentice Hall and WebCT Educational Technologies offer a fully customizable, on-line course with www links, on-line testing, and many other course management features using the popular WebCT on-line course architecture. See your local Prentice Hall representative or visit our special Demonstration Central website at *http://www.prenhall.com/demo* for more information.

Other Features Worth Noting

* We have an *entire chapter on eating disorders*, a separate diagnostic category for the first time in DSM-IV, and one of the most important and prevalent psychological problems, particularly among young adults.
* Posttraumatic stress disorder (PTSD) is featured in a detailed, research-based chapter that also includes a serious consideration of dissociative and somatoform disorders.
* Multicultural issues in abnormal psychology are considered throughout the book. For example, see Further Thoughts on psychotherapy with ethnic minorities (Chapter 3).

- The text grapples with the social issues related to abnormal psychology. We close the text with a timely and engaging chapter on Mental Health and the Law. Students frequently encounter fascinating issues such as the insanity defense in the popular media, and this chapter answers their questions—and raises new ones for them to ponder. Unlike other texts, moreover, the chapter also tackles issues in psychology and law that are more directly relevant to students' lives—child abuse, partner abuse, and divorce and custody disputes.

ACKNOWLEDGMENTS

Years of effort have gone into writing and revising this book, and we are grateful to a number of people who assisted us in this arduous but fruitful task. We would like to start by expressing our appreciation to the following colleagues who reviewed all or parts of the manuscript for this brief edition as well as its more comprehensive parent: Gail Bruce-Sanford, University of Montana; Ann Calhoun-Seals, Belmont Abbey College; Laurie Chassin, Arizona State University; Lee H. Coleman, Miami University of Ohio; Juris G. Draguns, Pennsylvania State University; Marjorie L. Hatch, Southern Methodist University; Jennifer A. Haythornwaite, Johns Hopkins University; Debra L. Hollister, Valencia Community College; Richard D. McAnulty, University of North Carolina–Charlotte; Tracy L. Morris, West Virginia University; William O'Donohue, University of Nevada–Reno; Joseph J. Palladino, University of Southern Indiana; Paul Rasmussen, Furman University; Danny Shaw, University of Pittsburgh; Heather Shaw, American Institutes of Research; Eric Stice, Stanford University; Michael Wierzbicki, Marquette University.

The substance of this book continues to benefit from the feedback provided by reviewers of *Abnormal Psychology*, 2nd Edition:

Pryor Hale, Piedmont Virginia Community College; Pat Slocum, College of DuPage; Sandra Kerr, Westchester University; Stanley Holgate, Fayetteville Technical Community College; Andy Neher, Cabrillo College; Eric Shiraev, Northern Virginia Community College; Thomas Weatherly, Dekalb College, Carol Pandey, Pierce College.

We have been fortunate to work in a stimulating academic environment that has fostered our interests in studying psychopathology and in teaching undergraduate students. We are particularly grateful to our current colleagues Irving Gottesman, Eric Turkheimer, Mavis Hetherington, John Monahan, Joseph Allen, Dan Wegner, and Mary Ainsworth for extended (and ongoing) discussions of the issues that are considered in this book. Close friends and colleagues at Indiana University have also served in this role, especially Richard McFall and Alexander Buchwald. Many undergraduate and graduate students who have taken our courses have helped to shape the viewpoints that are expressed in this book. They are too numerous to identify individually, but we are grateful for the intellectual challenges and excitement that they have provided over the past several years.

Many other people have contributed to the book in various important ways. Kimberly Carpenter Emery did extensive legal research and helped organize Chapter 15; Carol Manning and Charles Vandenberg provided consultation on case study materials; and Linda Christian, Debbie Snow, and Nina Pierce have provided important secretarial support.

The substance of this book continues to benefit from the feedback provided by reviewers of *Abnormal Psychology*, 2nd Edition:

Pryor Hale, Piedmont Virginia Community College; Pat Slocum, College of DuPage; Sandra Kerr, Westchester University; Stanley Holgate, Fayetteville Technical Community College; Andy Neher, Cabrillo College; Eric Shiraev, Northern Virginia Community College; Thomas Weatherly, Dekalb College, Carol Pandey, Pierce College.

In addition, we would like to thank the following people at Prentice Hall:

Leslie Carr, Development Editor
Gina Sluss, Director of Marketing
Susanna Lesan, Editor in Chief
  of Development

Bill Webber, Executive Editor
Nancy Roberts, Editor in Chief
Phil Miller, President
Charlyce Jones Owen, Editorial Director

Mary Rottino, Managing Editor
Randy Pettit, Production Editor
Jennifer Cohen, Assistant Editor
Tamsen Adams, Editorial Assistant

Maria Lange, Art Director, Interior and
  Cover Designer
Lynn Pearlman, Manufacturing Buyer

BOB EMERY

TOM OLTMANNS

About the Authors

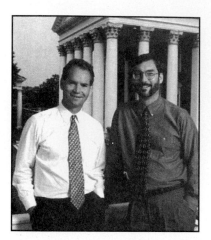

Robert E. Emery (left) is Professor of Psychology and Director of Clinical Training at the University of Virginia. He also is Director of the Center for Children, Families, and the Law and an associate faculty member of the Institute of Law, Psychiatry, and Public Policy at the university. He received a B.A. from Brown University in 1974 and a Ph.D. from SUNY at Stony Brook in 1982. He is on the editorial boards of eight journals and is a member of the Population and Social Sciences study section of NIH. His research focuses on family conflict, children's mental health, and associated legal issues. His 1982 *Psychological Bulletin* paper was designated a "Citation Classic" by the Institute for Scientific Information, and a later *Child Development* paper received the Outstanding Research Publication Award from the American Association for Marriage and Family Therapy in 1989. He is the author of over 75 scientific articles and book chapters and two monographs: *Marriage, Divorce, and Children's Adjustment* (1988; 2nd ed., 1998, Sage Publications) and *Renegotiating Family Relationships: Divorce, Child Custody, and Medication* (1994, Guilford Press).

Thomas F. Oltmanns (right) is Professor of Psychology and Psychiatric Medicine at the University of Virginia, where he was also Director of Clinical Training from 1987 to 1993. He received his B.A. from the University of Wisconsin and his Ph.D. from the State University of New York at Stony Brook. He was on the faculty in the Department of Psychology at Indiana University from 1976 to 1986 before moving to Virginia. He has served as a member of the Psychopathology and Clinical Biology Research Review Committee at NIMH and as Associate Editor of the *Journal of Abnormal Psychology.* He has been elected president of the Society for a Science of Clinical Psychology (1993) and has received the "Outstanding Professor Award" from undergraduate psychology majors at UVA (1997). His current research on the assessment of personality disorders is funded by NIMH. His previous books include *Schizophrenia* (1980), written with John Neale; *Case Studies in Abnormal Psychology* (4th ed., 1995), written with John Neale and Gerald Davison; and *Delusional Beliefs* (1988), edited with Brendan Maher.

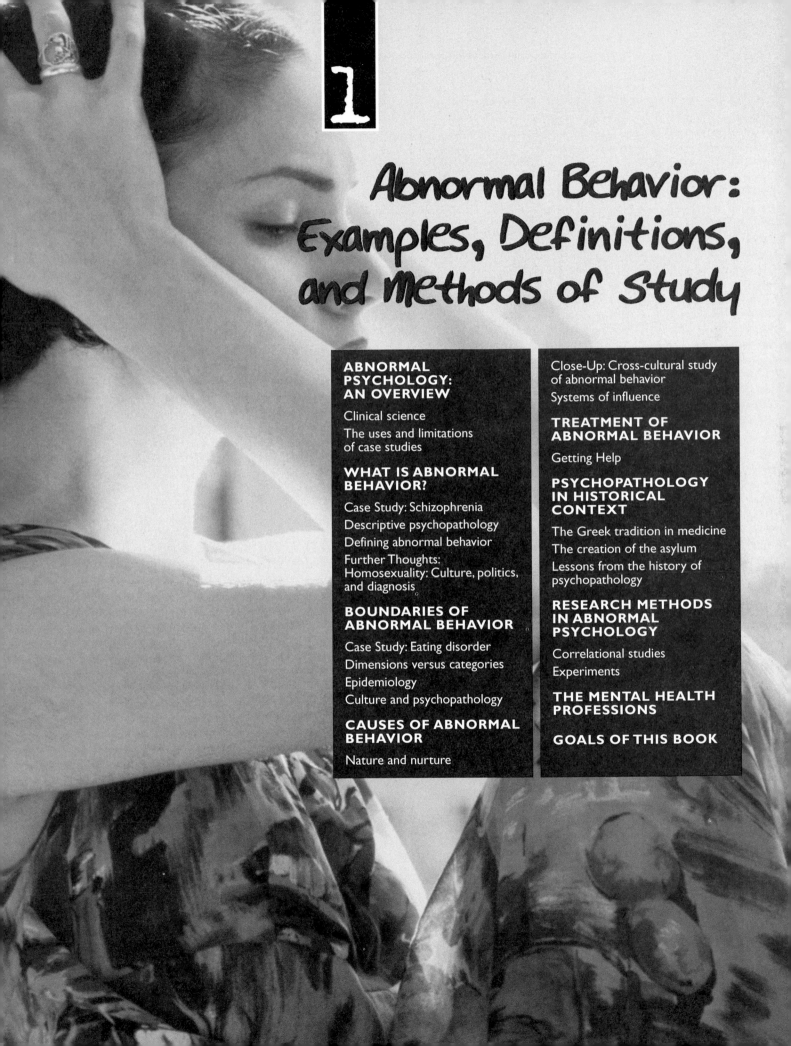

1

Abnormal Behavior: Examples, Definitions, and Methods of Study

Mental disorders touch every realm of human experience. They can disrupt the way people think, the way they feel, and the way they behave. Ultimately, they affect relationships with other people. It would be surprising if you hadn't already heard about most of the problems that will be addressed in this book, such as depression, alcoholism, and schizophrenia. In fact, you are likely to know someone—a friend or family member—who has struggled with one of these disorders. The purpose of this book is to help you become familiar with the nature of these disorders and the various ways in which psychologists are advancing knowledge of their causes and treatment.

Abnormal Psychology: An Overview

psychology   The science, profession, and academic discipline concerned with the study of mental processes and behavior in humans and animals.

abnormal psychology   The application of psychological science to the study of mental disorders. Includes investigation of the causes and treatment of psychopathological conditions.

scientist-practitioner model   A model of training and professional activity, particularly influential in clinical psychology, that emphasizes the integration of science and practice.

The study of mental disorders is often called abnormal psychology. **Psychology** is the scientific study of behavior, cognition, and emotion. Since the late nineteenth century, psychologists have generated an extensive body of knowledge that is concerned with perception, motivation, learning, memory, problem solving, attitudes, emotions, and language—to name only a few of the most general issues that have been studied. That base of knowledge sheds crucial light on the problems that fall under the general heading of mental disorders. **Abnormal psychology** is the application of psychological science to the study of mental disorders.

Clinical Science

Psychologists who treat people with mental disorders are often trained according to the **scientist-practitioner model,** which emphasizes the integration of science and practice (Belar & Perry, 1992). Scientist-practitioners operate simultaneously as behavioral scientists and practicing clinicians. These are two aspects of the same professional role, regardless of whether the person happens to be doing applied clinical work—assessment and therapy with a client—or research on abnormal behavior (McFall, 1991, 1995).

The way in which psychologists collect information about a clinical problem is guided by scientific principles. *Hypotheses*—highly specific and testable predictions about cause and effect—about the causes of the problem, even at the level of the individual client, are based on psychological science, and they are formulated in a testable fashion. In fact, the treatment process parallels the scientific process. Assessment leads to the formulation of a hypothesis, interventions are implemented based on that hypothesis, and the validity of the hypothesis is tested by the success or failure of the treatment. Moreover, most of the important scientific advances in abnormal psychology have been made by researchers who work directly with clinical problems—that is, by people who are familiar with the signs and symptoms of psychopathology and who simultaneously bring to bear the attitudes and methods of scientific inquiry.

We believe that the scientist-practitioner model of training should be applied to the study of abnormal psychology. Descriptions of real clinical problems must be integrated with discussions of more abstract issues. Students should be introduced to the study of abnormal psychology by learning about specific cases—people whose efforts to grapple with various behavioral, emotional, and mental difficulties bring the issues of the field to life. In this way, we hope to convey to our readers our own enthusiasm for this fascinating field.

case study A careful description and analysis of the problems experienced by one person.

psychopathology The manifestations of (and the study of the causes of) mental disorders. Generally used as another term to describe abnormal behavior.

The Uses and Limitations of Case Studies

Before we present our first case, we should consider the ways in which case studies can be helpful in the study of psychopathology, as well as some of their limitations. A **case study** presents a description of the problems experienced by one particular person. Detailed case studies can provide an exhaustive catalog of the symptoms that the person displayed, the manner in which these symptoms emerged, the developmental and family history that preceded the onset of the disorder, and whatever response the person may have shown to treatment efforts. Descriptions of this sort are especially important for conditions that have not received much attention in the literature and for problems that are relatively unusual. Multiple personality disorder and transsexualism are examples of conditions that are extremely infrequent. Much of what we know about these conditions is based on descriptions of individual patients.

Case studies can also be used to generate hypotheses. For example, Freud developed his psychoanalytic theory on the basis of extended case studies (see Chapter 2). His compelling descriptions and insightful analyses of the circumstances under which his patients' problems developed helped make his ideas enormously popular during the first half of the twentieth century.

Case studies also have several drawbacks. The most obvious limitation of case studies is that they can be viewed from many different perspectives. Any case can be interpreted in several ways, and competing explanations may be equally plausible.

The other main limitation of case studies is that it is risky to draw general conclusions about a disorder from a single example. How can we know that this individual is representative of the disorder as a whole? Are his or her experiences typical for people with this disorder? Again, hypotheses generated on the basis of the single case must be tested in research with larger, more representative samples of patients.

What Is Abnormal Behavior?

The cases in this chapter describe the experiences of people whose behavior would be considered abnormal by mental health professionals. Their difficulties illustrate two specific forms of abnormal behavior: schizophrenia and eating disorders. These problems are examples of **psychopathology,** which, literally translated, means "pathology of the mind" and is a term that is generally used to describe abnormal behavior. A *psychopathologist* is a person who studies psychopathology. This term can apply to people with various types of professional training, including psychologists, psychiatrists, and social workers.

We use the cases in this chapter to introduce several fundamental concepts and controversies that are addressed later in this book. The cases allow us to consider definitions of abnormal behavior, processes by which abnormal behaviors are classified, and ways in which psychopathologists think about factors that cause these disorders.

Our first case raises fundamental questions about the definition of abnormal behavior. What is the basis for the distinction between normal and abnormal behavior? What kinds of problems are associated with abnormal behavior, and in what ways do they affect a person's life?

case study

Schizophrenia

Kevin and Joyce Warner (not their real names[†]) had been married for 8 years when they sought help from a psychologist for their marital problems. Joyce was 34 years old, worked full time as a pediatric nurse, and was 6 months pregnant with her first child. Kevin, who was 35 years old, was finishing his third year working as a librarian at a local university. Joyce was extremely worried about what would happen if Kevin lost his job, especially in light of the baby's imminent arrival.

Although the Warners had come for couples therapy, the psychologist soon became concerned about certain eccentric aspects of Kevin's behavior. In the first session, Joyce described one recent event that had precipitated a major argument. One day, after eating lunch at work, Kevin had experienced sharp pains in his chest and difficulty breathing. Fearful, he rushed to the emergency room at the hospital where Joyce worked. The physician who saw Kevin found nothing wrong with him, even after extensive testing. She gave Kevin a few tranquilizers and sent him home to rest. When Joyce arrived home that evening, Kevin told her that he suspected that he had been poisoned at work by his supervisor. He still held this belief.

Kevin's belief about the alleged poisoning raised serious concern in the psychologist's mind about Kevin's mental health. He decided to interview Joyce alone so that he could ask more extensive questions about Kevin's behavior. Joyce realized that the poisoning idea was "crazy." She was not willing, however, to see it as evidence that Kevin had a mental disorder. Joyce had known Kevin for 15 years. As far as she knew, he had never held any strange beliefs before this time, and he had never taken hallucinogenic drugs or smoked marijuana. Joyce said that Kevin had always been "a thoughtful and unusually sensitive guy." She did not attach a great deal of significance to Kevin's unusual belief. She was more preoccupied with the couple's present financial concerns and insisted that it was time for Kevin to "face reality."

Kevin's condition deteriorated noticeably over the next few weeks. He became extremely withdrawn, frequently sitting alone in a darkened room after dinner. On several occasions, he told her that he felt as if he had "lost pieces of his thinking." It wasn't that his memory was failing, but rather he felt as though parts of his brain were shut off.

Kevin's problems at work also grew worse. His supervisor informed Kevin that his contract would definitely not be renewed. Joyce exploded when Kevin indifferently told her the bad news. His apparent lack of concern was especially annoying. She called Kevin's supervisor, who confirmed the news. He told her that Kevin was physically present at the library, but he was only completing a few hours of work each day. Kevin sometimes spent long periods of time just sitting at his desk and staring off into space and was sometimes heard mumbling softly to himself.

Kevin's speech was quite odd during the next therapy session. He would sometimes start to speak, drift off into silence, then reestablish eye contact with a bewildered smile and a shrug of his shoulders. He had apparently lost his train of thought completely. His answers to questions were often off the point, and when he did string together several sentences, their meaning was sometimes obscure. For example, at one point during the session, the psychologist asked Kevin if he planned to appeal his supervisor's decision. Kevin said:

> I'm feeling pressured, like I'm lost and can't quite get here. But I need more time to explore the deeper side. Like in art. What you see on the surface is much richer when you look closely. I'm like that. An intuitive person. I can't relate in a linear way, and when people expect that from me, I get confused.

Kevin's strange belief about poisoning continued to expand. The Warners received a letter from Kevin's mother, who lived in another city 200 miles away. She had become ill after going out for dinner one night and mentioned that she must have eaten something that made her sick. After reading the letter, Kevin became convinced that his supervisor had tried to poison his mother too.

When questioned about this new incident, Kevin launched into a long, rambling story. He said that his supervisor was a Vietnam veteran, but he had refused to talk with Kevin about his years in the service. Kevin suspected that this was because the supervisor had been a member of army intelligence. Perhaps he still was a member of some secret organization. Kevin suggested that an agent from this organization had been sent by his supervisor to poison his mother. Kevin thought that he and Joyce also were in danger. He was particularly wary around men who were about his supervisor's age, because they too might be Vietnam veterans. Kevin also had some concerns about Asians, but he would not specify these worries in more detail. He said that he knew many more things about "what was really going on," but he was not ready to share them.

Kevin's bizarre beliefs and his disorganized behavior convinced the psychologist that he needed to be hospitalized. Joyce reluctantly agreed that this was the most appropriate course of action. She had run out of alternatives. Arrangements were made to have Kevin admitted to a private psychiatric facility, where the psychiatrist prescribed haloperidol (Haldol), a type of antipsychotic medication. Kevin seemed to respond positively to the drug, because he soon stopped talking about plots and poisoning—but he remained withdrawn and uncommunicative. After 3 weeks of treatment, Kevin's psychiatrist thought that he had improved significantly. Kevin was discharged from the hospital in time for the birth of their baby girl. Unfortunately, when the couple returned to consult with the psychologist, Kevin's adjustment was still a major concern. He did not talk with Joyce about the poisonings, but she noticed that he remained withdrawn and showed few emotions, even toward the baby.

When the psychologist questioned Kevin in detail, he admitted reluctantly that he still believed that he had been poisoned.

Slowly, he revealed more of the plot. Immediately after admission to the hospital, Kevin had decided that his psychiatrist, who happened to be from Korea, could not be trusted. Kevin was sure that he too was working for army intelligence or perhaps for a counterintelligence operation. Kevin believed that he was being interrogated by this clever psychiatrist, so he had "played dumb." He did not discuss the suspected poisonings or the secret organization that had planned them. Whenever he could get away with it, Kevin simply pretended to take his medication. He thought that it was either poison or truth serum.

Kevin was admitted to a different psychiatric hospital soon after it became apparent that his paranoid beliefs had expanded. This time, he was given intramuscular injections of antipsychotic medication in order to be sure that the medicine was actually taken. Kevin improved considerably after several weeks in the hospital. He acknowledged that he had experienced paranoid thoughts. Although he still felt suspicious from time to time, wondering whether the plot had actually been real, he recognized that it could not really have happened, and he spent less and less time thinking about it. ♛

†Throughout this text we use fictitious names to protect the identities of the people involved.

Descriptive Psychopathology

Schizophrenia is a form of **psychosis,** a general term that refers to several types of severe mental disorder in which the person is considered to be out of contact with reality. Kevin exhibited several psychotic symptoms. For example, his belief about being poisoned by his supervisor would be called a delusion. A **delusion** is an idiosyncratic belief—one not shared by other members of the society—that is rigidly held in spite of its preposterous nature. In addition, Kevin's speech at times was odd and difficult to understand. This symptom is called *disorganized speech* or *formal thought disorder.* Judgments regarding the presence of disorganized speech depend on the listener's sense that a person's speech is exceedingly vague or difficult to understand. In other words, it involves the form of the person's speech—the way in which a thought is expressed—rather than the content of the speech.

You may also be familiar with other words that are commonly used in describing abnormal behavior. One term is *insanity,* which does not refer to any specific type of psychopathology. In current practice, insanity is actually a legal term that refers to judgments about whether a person should be held responsible for criminal behavior if he or she is also mentally disturbed (see Chapter 15). If Kevin had murdered his Korean psychiatrist, for example, based on the delusional belief that the psychiatrist was trying to harm him, a court of law might consider whether Kevin should be held to be *not guilty by reason of insanity.*

Another old-fashioned term that you may have heard is *nervous breakdown.* If we said that Kevin had "suffered a nervous breakdown," we would be indicating in very general terms that he had developed some sort of incapacitating but otherwise unspecified type of mental disorder. This expression no longer conveys any specific information about the nature of the person's problems. Some people might also say that Kevin was acting *crazy.* This is an informal, pejorative term that does not convey specific information and carries with it many unfortunate, unfounded, and negative implications. Mental health professionals refer to psychopathological conditions as mental disorders or abnormal behaviors. We will define these terms in the pages that follow.

Kevin's situation raises several fundamental questions about abnormal behavior. One of the most difficult issues in the field centers on the processes by which mental disorders are identified. Once Kevin's problems came to the attention of a mental health professional, could he have been tested in some way to confirm the presence or absence of a mental disorder?

At the present time, psychopathology is defined in terms of signs and symptoms—such as delusions and disorganized speech—rather than inferred causes. This approach is sometimes called *descriptive psychopathology.* Psychologists and psychiatrists do not have laboratory tests that can be used to confirm definitively the presence of psychopathology because the processes that are responsible for

psychosis A term that refers to several types of severe mental disorder in which the person is out of contact with reality. Hallucinations and delusions are examples of psychotic symptoms.

delusion An obviously false and idiosyncratic belief that is rigidly held in spite of its preposterous nature.

syndrome A group of symptoms that appear together and are assumed to represent a specific type of disorder.

mental disorders have not yet been discovered. Unlike specialists in other areas of medicine where many specific disease mechanisms have been discovered by advances in the biological sciences, psychologists and psychiatrists cannot test for the presence of a viral infection or a brain lesion or a genetic defect to confirm a diagnosis of mental disorder. Clinical psychologists must depend on their observations of the person's behavior and descriptions of personal experience.

Mental disorders are typically defined by a set of characteristic features. A group of symptoms that appear together and are assumed to represent a specific type of disorder is referred to as a **syndrome.** One problematic behavior is seldom necessary or sufficient to establish a diagnosis. The primary consideration in Kevin's case was his paranoid delusion. Additional problems included his peculiar and occasionally difficult to understand patterns of speech and his flat emotional responses. These are all symptoms of the disorder known as *schizophrenia.* A person must usually exhibit more than one symptom to be diagnosed as having a particular disorder.

The duration of a person's symptoms is also important. Mental disorders are defined in terms of persistent maladaptive behaviors. Many unusual behaviors and inexplicable experiences are short-lived; if we ignore them, they go away. Unfortunately, some forms of problematic behavior eventually interfere with the person's social and occupational functioning. In Kevin's case, he had become completely preoccupied with his suspicions about poison. The magnitude of Kevin's problem was measured, in large part, by its persistence and by the cumulative disruption it caused at work and in the family.

Defining Abnormal Behavior

Why do we consider Kevin's behavior to be abnormal? By what criteria do we decide whether a particular set of behaviors or emotional reactions should be viewed as a mental disorder? These are important questions because they determine, in many ways, how other people will respond to the person, as well as who will be responsible for providing help (if help is required). Many attempts have been made to define abnormal behavior, but none is entirely satisfactory. No one has been able to provide a consistent definition that easily accounts for all situations in which the concept is invoked (Frances, First, & Pincus, 1995; Gorenstein, 1992).

One approach to the definition of abnormal behavior places principal emphasis on the individual's experience of personal distress. We might say that abnormal behavior is defined in terms of subjective discomfort that leads the person to seek help from a mental health professional. This definition is fraught with problems, however. Kevin's case illustrates one of the major reasons that this approach does not work. Before his second hospitalization, Kevin was unable or unwilling to appreciate the extent of his problem or the impact his behavior had on other people. A psychologist would say that he did not have *insight* regarding his disorder (Markova & Berrios, 1992). The discomfort was primarily experienced by Joyce, and she had attempted for many weeks to deny the nature of the problem.

Another approach is to define abnormal behavior in terms of statistical norms—the relative frequency of a specific condition in the general population. By this definition, people with unusually high levels of anxiety or depression would be considered abnormal because their experience deviates from the expected norm. Kevin's paranoid beliefs would be defined as pathological because they are idiosyncratic. Mental disorders are, in fact, defined in terms of experiences that most people do not have.

This approach, however, does not specify *how* unusual the behavior must be before it is considered ab-

In the movie The Fisher King, *actor Robin Williams played a man with schizophrenia. To be diagnosed with a disorder such as schizophrenia, an individual must exhibit a set of symptoms, which are referred to as a* syndrome.

normal. Some conditions that are typically considered to be forms of psychopathology are extremely rare. For example, gender identity disorder, the belief that one is a member of the opposite sex trapped in the wrong body, affects less than 1 person out of every 30,000. In contrast, other disorders are much more common. In the United States, major depression affects 1 out of every 20 women, and alcoholism affects at least 1 out of every 10 men (Robins, Locke, & Regier, 1991).

Another weakness of the statistical approach is that it does not distinguish between deviations that are harmful and those that are not. Some abnormal characteristics, such as exceptional intellectual, artistic, or athletic ability, may actually confer an advantage on the individual. For these reasons, the simple fact that a behavior is statistically rare cannot be used to define psychopathology.

HARMFUL DYSFUNCTION

One useful approach to the definition of mental disorder has been proposed by Jerome Wakefield of Columbia University (Wakefield, 1992a, 1992b). According to Wakefield, a condition should be considered to be a mental disorder if, and only if, it meets two criteria:

1. The condition causes some harm to the person as judged by the standards of the person's culture.
2. The condition results from the inability of some mental mechanism to perform its natural function.

A mental disorder therefore is defined in terms of **harmful dysfunction.** This definition incorporates one element that is based as much as possible on an objective evaluation of performance—dysfunction. The dysfunctions in mental disorders represent disruptions of cognitive, perceptual, emotional, linguistic, and motivational mechanisms.

In Kevin's case, the most apparent dysfunctions involved failures of cognitive, perceptual, and linguistic mechanisms. Disruption of these systems was presumably responsible for his delusional beliefs and his disorganized speech. The *natural function* of cognitive and perceptual processes is to allow the person to perceive the world in ways that are shared with other people and to engage in rational thought and problem solving. The natural function of linguistic mechanisms is to allow the person to communicate clearly with other people. Kevin's abnormal behavior can be viewed as a pervasive dysfunction cutting across several mental mechanisms.

There is, of course, room for argument about the specific nature of these mental mechanisms and the ways in which they are supposed to function naturally. At present, dysfunction is largely inferred on the basis of impaired performance. Some of the confusion and controversy about what is, and what is not, a mental disorder can be traced to our ignorance about the natural functions of cognitive, behavioral, and emotional systems. The connections between these systems and psychopathological symptoms are also unresolved. More precise descriptions of basic mental mechanisms presumably will be provided by scientific research in the psychological and biological sciences.

Wakefield's definition of mental disorder also recognizes that every type of dysfunction does not lead to a disorder. Only dysfunctions that result in significant *harm* to the person are considered to be disorders. This is the second element of his definition. There are, for example, many types of physical dysfunction, such as albinism, reversal of heart position, and fused toes, that clearly represent a significant departure from the way that some biological process ordinarily functions. These conditions are not considered to be disorders, however, because they are not necessarily harmful to the person.

Kevin's dysfunctions were, in fact, harmful to his adjustment. These problems were evident in both his family relationships—his marriage to Joyce and his ability to function as a parent—and his performance at work. His social and occupational performances were clearly impaired. There are, of course, other types of harm that are also associated with mental disorders. These include subjective distress, such as high levels of anxiety or depression, as well as more tangible outcomes, such as suicide.

DSM-IV DEFINITION

The definition of abnormal behavior presented in the official *Diagnostic and Statistical Manual of Mental Disorders,* published by the American Psychiatric Association and currently in its fourth edition—DSM-IV (APA, 1994)—incorporates many of the factors that we have already discussed.

harmful dysfunction A concept used in one approach to the definition of mental disorder. A condition can be considered a mental disorder if it causes some harm to the person and if the condition results from the inability of some mental mechanism to perform its natural function.

TABLE I–I

Summary of the DSM-IV Definition of Mental Disorders

DEFINING CHARACTERISTICS

A behavioral or psychological syndrome (groups of associated features) that is associated with:

1. Present distress (painful symptoms), or
2. Disability (impairment in one or more important areas of functioning), or with
3. A significantly increased risk of suffering death, pain, disability, or an important loss of freedom

CONDITIONS EXCLUDED FROM CONSIDERATION

This syndrome or pattern must not be merely:

1. An expectable and culturally sanctioned response to a particular event (such as the death of a loved one)
2. Deviant behavior (such as the actions of political, religious, or sexual minorities)
3. Conflicts that are between the individual and society (such as voluntary efforts to express individuality)

This definition is summarized in Table 1–1, along with a number of conditions that are specifically excluded from the DSM-IV definition of mental disorders. The DSM-IV definition places primary emphasis on the consequences of certain behavioral syndromes. Accordingly, mental disorders are defined by clusters of persistent, maladaptive behaviors that are associated with personal distress, such as anxiety or depression, or with an impairment in social functioning, such as job performance or personal relationships. The official definition therefore recognizes the concept of dysfunction, and it spells out ways in which the harmful consequences of the disorder might be identified.

In an attempt to avoid becoming a vehicle for social regulation, the DSM-IV definition excludes voluntary behaviors, as well as beliefs and actions that are shared by religious, political, or sexual minority groups. In the 1960s, members of the Yippie Party intentionally engaged in disruptive behaviors, such as throwing money off the balcony at a stock exchange. Their purpose was to challenge traditional values. These were, in some ways, maladaptive behaviors that could have resulted in social impairment if those involved had been legally prosecuted. But they were *not* dysfunctions. They were intentional artistic and political gestures.

In actual practice, abnormal behavior is defined in terms of an official diagnostic system. Mental health, like medicine, is an applied rather than a theoretical field. It draws on knowledge from research in the psychological and biological sciences in an effort to help people whose behavior is disordered. Mental disorders are, in some respects, those problems with which mental

Calvin and Hobbes   by Bill Watterson

further thoughts

Homosexuality: Culture, Politics, and Diagnosis

The influence of political groups on psychiatric classification is perhaps nowhere better illustrated than in the case of homosexuality. The psychiatric community had maintained in the first and second editions of the DSM that homosexuality was, by definition, a form of mental disorder. This position reflected, in large part, the views of psychodynamic therapists and was adopted in spite of the attitudes expressed by scientists such as Alfred Kinsey, who argued that homosexual behavior was not abnormal (see Chapter 12). Toward the end of the 1960s, as the gay and lesbian rights movement became more forceful and outspoken, some of its leaders began to challenge the assumption that homosexuality was pathological. They opposed the inclusion of homosexuality in the official diagnostic system.

Between 1970 and 1974, a dramatic series of events led to important changes in the American Psychiatric Association's classification of sexual disorders, especially homosexuality (see Bayer, 1981, for a detailed description of these events). The first incident took place at an APA meeting in 1970, where gay activists disrupted presentations concerned with psychodynamic theories of sexual deviation. Among the demands presented by gay leaders was a call for the removal of homosexuality from the DSM-II.

Direct discussions between members of the gay community and members of the American Psychiatric Association began in 1972 and continued throughout the following year. A compromise position was eventually presented to the board of trustees of APA at the end of 1973. The trustees voted unanimously to remove homosexuality from DSM-II. In the spring of 1974, the entire membership of the organization participated in a referendum on the board's decision. Approximately 60 percent of the 10,000 votes were cast in favor of the board's decision, thus affirming the removal of homosexuality as a form of mental illness. This sequence of events illustrates quite clearly the ways in which social and political events can influence the classification of mental disorders.

One important consequence of this debate was a shift in the focus on how sexual disorders are classified. The authors of DSM-III came to believe that the classification system should be concerned primarily with subjective distress. They were impressed by the numerous indications, in both personal appeals as well as the research literature, that homosexuality, per se, was not invariably associated with impaired functioning. They decided that, in order to be considered a form of mental disorder, a condition ought to be associated with subjective distress or seriously impaired social or occupational functioning. This emphasis opened the door to a more detailed consideration of problems that centered around impaired sexual performance, such as inability to reach orgasm. Relatively less concern was directed toward the choice of sexual partners or preferred sexual activities, as long as the participants were mutually consenting adults.

Political forces triggered the removal of homosexuality from the diagnostic manual, but the stage was set for these events by gradual shifts in society's attitudes toward several aspects of sexual behavior (Bullough, 1976). For example, more and more people came to believe that reproduction was not the main purpose of sexual behavior. Along with this view came increased tolerance for greater variety in human sexuality. The revision of the DSM's system for describing sexual disorders was therefore the product of several forces, cultural as well as political.

health professionals attempt to deal. As their activities and explanatory concepts expand, so does the list of abnormal behaviors. The practical boundaries of abnormal behavior are defined by the list of disorders that are included in the official *Diagnostic and Statistical Manual of Mental Disorders.* The categories in that manual are listed on the inside of the back cover of this book. The DSM-IV thus provides another simplistic, though practical, answer to our question as to why Kevin's behavior would be considered abnormal: He would be considered to be exhibiting abnormal behavior because his experiences fit the description of schizophrenia, which is one of the officially recognized forms of mental disorder.

SOCIAL AND POLITICAL CONSIDERATIONS

The process by which the *Diagnostic and Statistical Manual* is constructed and revised is necessarily influenced by social and political considerations. The impact of particular behaviors and experiences on an individual's adjustment will, of course, depend on the culture in which the person lives. To use Jerome Wakefield's (1992a) terms, "only dysfunctions that are socially disvalued are disorders" (p. 384). For example, a woman who grew up in a society that discouraged female sexuality might not be distressed or impaired by the absence of orgasmic responses. Because of this lack of discomfort, according to DSM-IV, she would not be considered to have a sexual problem. Therefore this definition of abnormal behavior is not culturally universal and might lead us to consider a particular pattern of behavior to be abnormal in one society and not in another.

There have been many instances in which groups that represent particular political or social values have brought pressure to bear on decisions shaping the diagnostic manual (see Further Thoughts on p. 9). For example, feminist organizations (both within and outside the mental health professions) expressed legitimate concern over the possible inclusion of premenstrual dysphoric disorder in DSM-IV, because they are concerned about the implications of labeling women who have these problems as mentally ill (Caplan, 1995). In a compromise struck by APA's committee on DSM-IV, premenstrual dysphoric disorder appears in an appendix for disorders recommended for further study. These deliberations are a reflection of the practical nature of the manual and of the health-related professions. Value judgments are an inherent part of any attempt to define "disorder" (Sedgwick, 1981).

Boundaries of Abnormal Behavior

Having introduced many of the issues that are involved in the definition of abnormal behavior, we now turn to another clinical example. The woman in our second case study, Mary Childress, suffered from a serious eating disorder known as *bulimia nervosa*. Her problems raise additional questions about the definition of abnormal behavior.

Consider the defining characteristics of mental disorders listed in Table 1–1. As you are reading the case, ask yourself about the impact of Mary's eating disorder on her subjective experience and social adjustment. In what ways are these consequences similar to those seen in Kevin Warner's case? How are they different? This case also introduces another important concept associated with the way that we think about abnormal behavior: How can we identify the *boundary* between normal and abnormal behavior? Is there an obvious distinction between eating patterns that are considered to be part of a mental disorder and those that are not? Or is there a gradual progression from one end of a continuum to the other, with each step fading gradually into the next?

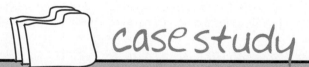

Eating Disorder

Mary Childress was, in most respects, a typical 18-year-old sophomore at a large state university. She was popular with other students and a good student, in spite of the fact that she spent little time studying. She and her boyfriend had been dating for about 2 years. They got along well, cared about each other very much, and planned to get married after they finished college. Everything about Mary's life was relatively normal—except for her bingeing and purging.

Mary's eating patterns were wildly erratic. She preferred to skip breakfast entirely, and often missed lunch as well. By the middle of the afternoon, she could no longer ignore the hunger pangs. At that point, on 2 or 3 days out of the week, Mary would drive her car to the drive-in window of a fast-food restaurant. Her typical order included three or four double cheeseburgers, several orders of french fries, and a large milk shake (or maybe

two). Then she binged, devouring all the food as she drove around town by herself. Later she would go to a private bathroom, where she wouldn't be seen by anyone, and purge the food from her stomach by vomiting. Afterward, she returned to her room, feeling angry, frustrated, and ashamed.

Mary was 5'5" tall and weighed 110 pounds. She was neither fat nor thin, but she believed that her body was unattractive, especially her thighs and hips. She was extremely critical of herself and had worried about her weight for many years. Her weight fluctuated quite a bit, from a low of 97 pounds when she was a senior in high school to a high of 125 during her first year at the university. Her mother was a "full-figured" woman and bought most of her clothes at a special store. Mary swore to herself at an early age that she would never let herself gain as much weight as her mother had.

For the past year Mary had been vomiting at least almost every day and occasionally as many as three or four times a day. The impulse to purge was very strong. Mary felt bloated after having only a bowl of cereal and a glass of orange juice. If she ate a sandwich and drank a diet soda, she began to ruminate about what she had eaten, thinking "I've got to get rid of that!" Before long, she usually found a bathroom and threw up. Her excessive binges were less frequent than the vomiting. Four or five times a week she experienced an overwhelming urge to eat forbidden foods, especially fast food. Her initial reaction was usually a short-lived attempt to resist the impulse. Then she would space out or "go into a zone," becoming only vaguely aware of what she was doing and feeling. In the midst of a serious binge, Mary felt completely helpless and unable to control herself.

There weren't any obvious physical signs that would alert someone to Mary's eating problems, but the vomiting had begun to wreak havoc with her body, especially her digestive system. She had suffered severe throat infections and frequent, intense stomach pains. Her dentist had noticed problems beginning to develop with her teeth and gums, undoubtedly a consequence of constant exposure to strong stomach acids.

Mary's attitudes toward nutrition and health were irrational. Although she sometimes ate 10 or 12 double cheeseburgers a day, Mary insisted that she hated junk food, and she considered herself to be a vegetarian. The meat that she ate didn't count, she reasoned, because she seldom kept it down. For someone who could be described as totally preoccupied with food, she gave little thought to its consumption, never planning her meals. Mary was extremely concerned about the health consequences of obesity. She could cite detailed statistics regarding the increased risk for heart disease that are associated with every additional 5 pounds that a person gains over her ideal body weight. Of course, the physical consequences of repeated bingeing and purging are infinitely more severe than those associated with modest weight gain, but this irony was lost on Mary.

Her eating problem started to develop when Mary was 15. She had been seriously involved in gymnastics for several years but eventually developed a knee condition that forced her to give up the sport. She gained a few pounds in the next month or two and decided to lose weight by dieting. Buoyed by unrealistic expectations about the immediate, positive benefits of a diet that she had seen advertised on television, Mary initially adhered rigidly to its recommended regimen. Six months later, after three of these fad diets had failed, she started throwing up as a way to control her intake of food.

Then her father was diagnosed with bone cancer when she was a junior in high school (only a couple of months after she had starting purging), and he died the next year. Everyone in the family was devastated. Mary's mother became seriously depressed. Her brother dropped out of high school after his sophomore year and continued living at home. Mary's eating problems multiplied. Her grades suffered, but she managed to maintain an adequate record through the remainder of her senior year and to graduate, gaining admission to the state university.

Mary looked forward to leaving home and starting over again at the university, but her problem followed her. She felt guilty and ashamed about her eating problems. She was much too embarrassed to let anyone know what she was doing and would never eat more than a few mouthfuls of food in a public place like the dorm cafeteria. Her roommate, Julie, was from a small town on the other side of the state. They got along reasonably well, but Mary managed to conceal her bingeing and purging, thanks in large part to the fact that she was able to bring her own car to campus. The car allowed her to drive away from campus several times a week so that she could binge.

Mary's boyfriend, Tim, was a freshman at a community college in her hometown. They saw each other one or two weekends each month, usually when she went home. Tim was completely unaware of Mary's eating problems, and she would do anything to keep him from finding out. Mary and Tim had been sexually active since shortly after they met, but they had only had intercourse five times, mostly because Mary had a difficult time enjoying sex. She was frightened by her sexual impulses, which often seemed difficult to control, and she worried about what might happen if she ever let herself go completely. Sexual experiences were a source of great conflict to her. She didn't like her own body, but it made her feel good to know that Tim found her desirable. ♕

Mary's case illustrates many of the characteristic features of bulimia nervosa. As in Kevin's case, her behavior could be considered abnormal not only because it fit the criteria for one of the categories in DSM-IV but also because she suffered from a dysfunction (in this case, of the mechanisms that regulate appetite) that was obviously harmful. The impact of the disorder was greatest in terms of her physical health: Eating disorders can be fatal if they are not properly treated because they affect so many vital organs of the body, including the heart and kidneys. Mary's social functioning and her academic performance were not yet seriously impaired. There are many different ways in which to measure the harmful effects of abnormal behavior.

Mary's case also illustrates the subjective pain that is associated with many types of abnormal behavior. In contrast to the situation described in Kevin's case, Mary was acutely aware of her disorder. She was frustrated and unhappy. In an attempt to relieve this emotional distress, she entered

categorical approach to classification   A view of classification based on the assumption that there are qualitative differences between normal and abnormal behavior as well as between one form of abnormal behavior and other forms of abnormal behavior.

dimensional approach to classification   A view of classification based on the assumption that behavior is distributed on a continuum from normal to abnormal. Also includes the assumption that differences between one type of behavior and another are quantitative rather than qualitative in nature.

threshold model   A perspective on etiology that holds that people can exhibit characteristics of a disorder without experiencing any adverse impact on their adjustment until they pass a critical threshold. Beyond that level, there is presumably a dramatic increase in the number of problems that are encountered.

epidemiology   The scientific study of the frequency and distribution of disorders within a population.

incidence   The number of new cases of a disorder that appear in a population during a specific period of time.

prevalence   An epidemiological term that refers to the total number of cases that are present within a given population during a particular period of time.

psychological treatment. Unfortunately, painful emotions associated with mental disorders can also interfere with, or delay, the decision to look for professional help. Guilt, shame, and embarrassment often accompany psychological problems and sometimes make it difficult to confide in another person.

Dimensions versus Categories

If we accept the argument that Mary's behavior is abnormal, how can we identify the boundaries of this condition? Should we expect to find clear-cut boundaries? It is relatively easy to describe an obvious or typical case of bulimia, where there is no question that the behavior is causing serious problems. There are many borderline cases, however, and borderline cases may outnumber typical cases. What if Mary purged only once a month instead of several times each week? What if she binged but didn't purge, and when she binged she didn't eat such large quantities of food?

If we assume that there is an eating disorder that Mary either has or does not have, we have adopted a **categorical approach to classification.** But it might be more useful to assume that there is a continuous distribution of uncontrolled eating, with the best description of Mary's behavior lying somewhere along that continuum from normal behavior to complete loss of control. This is known as a **dimensional approach to classification.** The distinction between these approaches is one of the central issues involved in the way we think about abnormal behavior. It is always difficult to identify a clear boundary between normal patterns of behavior and psychopathology.

The dimensional and categorical approaches can be combined in the form of a **threshold model** (Gottesman, 1991). According to this approach, the various features of a disorder may be distributed as continuous dimensions. People can presumably exhibit these characteristics in different numbers and combinations and in varying levels of severity without experiencing any adverse impact on their adjustment until they pass a *critical threshold.* Beyond that level, there is presumably a dramatic increase in the number of problems that they encounter. A diagnosis would be assigned only above the threshold, even though the features themselves are continuously distributed.

The DSM-IV follows the categorical approach to classification. Each disorder is defined in terms of specific diagnostic criteria, and the dividing line between normal and abnormal is clearly identified. The clinician's job, in assigning a diagnosis, is to make a *dichotomous decision*—to determine whether a particular individual fits the category, not to determine how much or to what degree the person possesses a particular characteristic. In establishing their diagnostic cutoff points, the committees that wrote DSM-IV obviously made somewhat arbitrary decisions. We discuss the relative merits of the categorical and dimensional approaches to classification in Chapter 4.

Epidemiology

Epidemiology is the scientific study of the frequency and distribution of disorders within a population. Epidemiologists are concerned with questions such as whether the frequency of a disorder has increased or decreased during a particular period of time, whether it is more common in one geographic area than in another, and whether certain types of people—based on factors such as gender, race, and socioeconomic status—are at greater risk than other types for the development of the disorder. Health administrators often use such information to make decisions about the allocation of resources for professional training programs, treatment facilities, and research projects.

Two terms are particularly important in epidemiological research (Zahner, Hsieh, & Fleming, 1995). **Incidence** refers to the number of *new* cases of a disorder that appear in a population during a specific period of time. **Prevalence** refers to the total number of active cases, both old and new, that are present in a population during a specific period of time. The *lifetime prevalence* of a disorder is the total proportion of people in a given population who have been affected by the disorder at some point during their lives.

How prevalent are the disorders listed in DSM-IV? One large-scale study, known as the Epidemiologic Catchment Area (ECA) study, was conducted in the 1980s (Robins & Regier, 1991).

TABLE 1–2

Prevalence Rates for Various Mental Disorders (ECA data)

	WOMEN (%)		MEN (%)	
	1-year	*Lifetime*	*1-year*	*Lifetime*
Phobic disorder	12.9	17.8	6.3	10.4
Alcohol abuse/dependence	2.2	4.6	11.9	23.8
Major depression	4.0	7.0	1.4	2.6
Antisocial personality	0.4	0.8	2.1	4.5
Obsessive–compulsive disorder	1.9	3.2	1.4	2.0
Panic disorder	1.2	2.1	0.6	1.0
Schizophrenia	1.1	1.7	0.9	1.2
Bipolar mood disorder	0.8	0.9	0.6	0.7

Source: *Adapted from L. N. Robins, B. Z. Locke, and D. A. Regier, 1991, An overview of psychiatric disorders in merica. In L. N. Robins and D. A. Regier (Eds.),* Psychiatric Disorders in America: The Epidemiological Catchment Area Study, *pp. 328–366. New York: Free Press.*

Approximately 20,000 people were interviewed in five large metropolitan areas in the United States. Questions were asked pertaining to 30 of the major disorders listed in the DSM. One-year prevalence rates indicated that 20 percent of the people in this sample met diagnostic criteria for at least one type of mental disorder. Table 1–2 lists some more specific results from this study. Notice that gender differences are found in many types of mental disorder: Anxiety disorders (phobias and panic) and depression are more common among women; alcoholism and antisocial personality are more common among men. Other conditions, like schizophrenia and bipolar mood disorder, appear with equal frequency in both women and men. Patterns of this sort raise interesting questions about possible causal mechanisms. What conditions would make women more vulnerable to one kind of disorder and men more vulnerable to another? There are many possibilities, including factors such as hormones, patterns of learning, and social pressures.

Comparisons between 1-year prevalence rates—the number of people with active symptoms during the 12 months prior to the interview—and lifetime prevalence rates are also interesting. In most cases, the lifetime rates are much higher. This discrepancy reflects the fact that mental disorders are not always chronic conditions. Most people experience periods of remission, in which their symptoms improve, in between active episodes of disorder. Many people recover completely. Therefore, although the relatively high lifetime prevalence rates in Table 1–2 are a source of serious concern, the contrast with 1-year prevalence rates is also an indication that mental disorders are not always enduring.

Lee Robins, professor of sociology in psychiatry at Washington University, was principal investigator in the ECA study, which is one extensive base of information regarding the prevalence of mental disorders in the United States.

Culture and Psychopathology

One important aspect of epidemiological studies involves comparison of the frequency of mental disorders in different cultures. Is abnormal behavior more common in certain societies than in others? Is it possible that the social values or living circumstances of some societies are particularly likely to lead to psychopathology? The literature suggests that some disorders, like schizophrenia, show important consistencies in cross-cultural comparisons (see Research Close-Up). Others, like bulimia, are more specifically associated with certain demographic, cultural, and socioeconomic conditions.

There are, for example, dramatic differences between women and men in the frequency of eating disorders. Almost 90 percent of bulimic patients are women (Woodside & Kennedy, 1995). The incidence of bulimia is 5 times higher among university women than among working women,

etiology The causes or origins of a disorder.

nature–nurture controversy The debate that pits genetic and biological factors against life experience as causes of abnormal behavior.

and it is more common among younger women than among older women. Bulimia is relatively rare among African-American women, although it may be increasing among more affluent African Americans who have adopted the attitudes of the dominant culture toward slimness (Dolan, 1991; Hsu, 1989). This pattern suggests that holding particular sets of values related to eating and to women's appearance is an important ingredient in establishing risk for development of an eating disorder.

The strength and nature of the relationship between culture and psychopathology vary from one disorder to the next. Several general conclusions can be drawn from cross-cultural studies of psychopathology (Draguns, 1980, 1994), including the following points:

1. All mental disorders are shaped, to some extent, by cultural factors.
2. No mental disorders can be traced entirely to cultural or social factors.
3. Psychotic disorders are less influenced by culture than are nonpsychotic disorders.
4. The *symptoms* of certain disorders are more likely to vary across cultures than are the disorders themselves (when viewed at the level of a *syndrome*).

We will return to these points as we discuss specific disorders, such as depression, phobias, and alcoholism, throughout the rest of this book.

Causes of Abnormal Behavior

The cases of Kevin Warner and Mary Childress illustrate why it is difficult to define abnormal behavior. They also raise questions about the causes of mental illness. Some people may be born with a predisposition to disorder that will emerge later in their lives. Was Kevin genetically vulnerable to schizophrenia? Did Mary possess a genetic makeup that tended toward binge eating?

Traumatic experiences may set the stage for emotional problems. Did the stress of Kevin's job or Joyce's pregnancy cause Kevin's condition to deteriorate? Was the death of Mary's father responsible for a serious escalation of her eating problems? Finally, what is the role of society in creating psychological problems? Would Mary have begun her frantic efforts to control her weight if our culture didn't place such a high value on thin female figures? These are all questions about the **etiology,** or causes, of psychopathology.

The etiology of most forms of abnormal behavior is poorly understood. This is true both at the level of the individual and at the level of the disorder as a whole. This textbook cannot provide many unequivocal answers about the causes of abnormal behavior. We hope that you will become intrigued rather than frustrated by this uncertainty. The origins of psychopathology represent a compelling mystery that motivates the search for knowledge.

Nature and Nurture

Of all of the questions about the causes of abnormal behavior, the **nature–nurture controversy** is perhaps the most long-standing. This debate pits genetic and biological factors against life experiences as causes of abnormal behavior. Those who argue for nature believe that psychopathology is caused by genes, by infectious diseases, by physical injuries, or by malfunctions of the brain or other parts of the nervous system. The abnormality presumably resides in the person's physical makeup. Life experiences may shape the development of psychological disorders, but their ultimate cause is biological (McGuffin et al., 1994).

The nurture side of the controversy makes the opposite assumption: Experience is the central cause of abnormal behavior. Some proponents of this perspective emphasize how well or how poorly parents care for children during the first years of life. They suggest that these early experiences mold each individual's personality. Others point to the role of learning throughout life in shaping and maintaining abnormal behavior. Some argue that dysfunctional relationships and societal demands cause people to behave in abnormal ways.

Many scientists have come to believe that the nature–nurture controversy is based on a false distinction between the physical and psychological worlds. We agree with this conclusion. Nature and

close-up

Cross-Cultural Study of Abnormal Behavior

Some severe forms of psychopathology have been found in virtually every culture that social scientists have studied. One classic paper that supports this conclusion was written by Jane Murphy (1976), an anthropologist at Harvard University. Murphy studied two groups of non-Western people: the Inuit (or Eskimos) of northwest Alaska and the Yoruba of rural, tropical Nigeria in West Africa.

Murphy discovered that both cultures recognize certain forms of behavior as "being crazy." These behaviors center around aberrant beliefs, feelings, and actions: hearing voices when no one is talking; laughing when there is nothing to laugh at; believing things that are so strange that other people cannot imagine them to be true; talking in strange ways that do not make sense to other people; and behaving in erratic or unpredictable ways. These syndromes bear a striking resemblance to the disorder called schizophrenia in DSM-IV. The specific content of hallucinations and delusions varies from one culture to the next, but the underlying processes appear to be the same. Perhaps most important was the observation that the words that the Inuit and Yoruba use to describe "losing one's mind" refer to a set of problematic behaviors rather than to a single problem.

Murphy also noted that members of both groups viewed "crazy behavior" as being quite different from the behaviors associated with being a shaman or spiritual healer. At certain times, the shaman also behaved in unusual ways, such as responding to voices that other people could not hear or speaking in ways that other people did not understand. This distinction is apparently based primarily on the extent to which these behaviors are controlled (turned on and off voluntarily by the person) and utilized for a socially approved purpose, such as attempting to heal a sick person. One Yoruba villager explained, "When the shaman is healing, he is out of his mind, but he is not crazy."

The Inuit and Yoruba have their own hypotheses concerning the origins of mental disorders, which often involve magic. They also have developed special treatment procedures, or native healing rituals, that they use to help people with these disorders. The prevailing attitudes in both groups appeared to be neither entirely positive nor entirely negative.

Murphy's conclusions have been supported by a large-scale epidemiological study of schizophrenia, sponsored by the World Health Organization (WHO) (Jablensky et al., 1992). This study included 1,200 patients who were admitted to psychiatric hospitals in nine countries: Colombia, Czechoslovakia, Denmark, India, Nigeria, Taiwan, Russia, England, and the United States. In each setting, the investigators found patients who exhibited symptoms of schizophrenia. The frequency of this disorder was approximately the same in each location, in spite of obvious cultural contrasts between sites in developing (India, Nigeria) and developed (Denmark, England) countries.

nurture are not as different as they may seem at first glance (Eisenberg, 1995; Plomin, 1990a). The dominant perspective on the cause of psychological disorders views abnormal behavior as resulting from a combination of nature and nurture. We discuss these issues in more depth in Chapter 2.

Systems of Influence

The consideration of different levels or systems of influence is another way in which we focus on nature *and* nurture, not nature *or* nurture, in this textbook. Abnormal behavior can be studied on many different levels. Psychobiologists and neuroscientists sometimes study abnormal behavior in terms of the various chemicals in the brain. Clinical psychologists frequently focus on characteristics of the individual, such as the tendency to blame oneself or others for life's problems. Other clinical psychologists emphasize social contributions to psychopathology, such as the role of social support or community resources in protecting people against the stresses of everyday life.

The study of biological, psychological, and social systems each offers a valuable perspective on understanding abnormal behavior. Mary Childress provides a good example of the contributions of these different levels of conceptualization. Several biological considerations might be important. Genetic factors may have predisposed Mary toward problems with her weight. Brain mechanisms that are responsible for the regulation of appetite could also be involved. From a psychological point of view, Mary's disturbed pattern of eating could be viewed as one part of a struggle for control—control of her own weight, her feelings, and her relationships

biopsychosocial model   A view of the etiology of mental disorders which assumes that disorder can best be understood in terms of the interaction of biological, psychological, and social systems.

psychopharmacology   The study of the effects of psychoactive drugs on behavior. Clinical psychopharmacology involves the expert use of drugs in the treatment of mental disorders.

psychotherapy   The use of psychological techniques in an attempt to produce change in the context of a special, helping relationship.

with other people. From a social perspective, she had undoubtedly absorbed unrealistic expectations about the ideal female figure from the media and from prevailing community attitudes. These expectations can be especially harmful when coupled with our culture's undue emphasis on the importance of physical appearance, especially for women. Thus Mary's bingeing and purging probably developed and were maintained through some combination of all three systems of influence.

We believe that the task for scientists and for practitioners is to uncover how these different levels of influence interact to cause emotional suffering and psychological disorders. The analytic approach that combines these various levels of influence is called the **biopsychosocial model.**

Treatment of Abnormal Behavior

The case of Kevin Warner allowed us to introduce one of the most common forms of treatment for psychopathology: **psychopharmacology** (medication). Various types of medication are used in the treatment of schizophrenia, depression, anxiety disorders, and other forms of abnormal behavior. **Psychotherapy** is another popular form of treatment, which involves the use of psychological procedures in the context of a special, helping relationship. There are many different approaches to psychotherapy (see Chapter 3). In cognitive therapy, for example, therapists help their patients identify and correct patterns of illogical thinking and maladaptive assumptions about themselves and their environments. Cognitive therapists emphasize replacing self-defeating thoughts with more rational self-statements. In actual practice, it is not unusual for patients to receive medication at the same time that they are engaged in psychotherapy.

Unfortunately, we cannot assume that everyone who needs treatment gets it. The ECA study found that 1 out of every 5 Americans exhibited active symptoms of at least one mental disorder during a particular year (Robins, Locke, & Regier, 1991). That same study also found that only about 1 out of 5 people with an active disorder had received treatment for their condition within

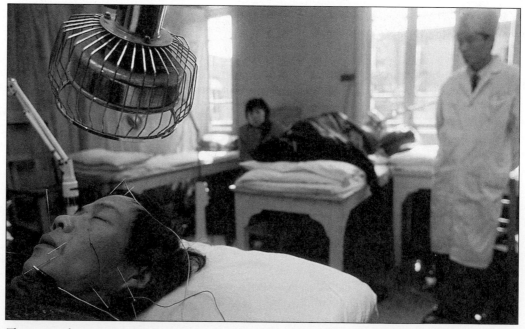

The success of a treatment does not necessarily enlighten us as to the cause of the disorder. In China, for example, acupuncture has been used to treat depression. Regardless of how effective this procedure might be, it is not certain that the results of this therapeutic procedure can teach us much about the origins of depression.

Getting help

Getting Help

Many students take an abnormal psychology class in part to understand more about their own problems or the problems of friends or family members. If you decide you want to get help for yourself or for someone you know, these Getting Help sections should give you a head start in finding good therapists and effective treatments.

Of course, psychology is not just about problems. If you are wondering if you need help, if you are just curious about the problems people can have, or even if you are a little skeptical or disinterested, you will definitely learn more about yourself and others from this course and studying psychology in general. That is what makes the subject so fascinating. But when the topic is abnormal psychology, you should be warned about two risks in advance.

The first is the "medical student's syndrome." As medical students learn about new illnesses, they often "develop" the symptoms of the disease they are studying. The same thing can happen to students of abnormal psychology. In fact, because many symptoms of emotional disorders share much in common with everyday experiences, students of abnormal psychology are even more likely to "discover" symptoms in themselves or others—"Gee, I think maybe I have an anxiety disorder." "He is so self-absorbed; he has a personality disorder." We all are frightened about experiencing illness and abnormality, and this fear can make us suggestible. So try to prepare yourself for bouts of the medical student's syndrome. And remember that it is normal to experience mild versions of many of the symptoms you will read about in this text.

Our second warning is much more serious. If you are genuinely concerned about your own problems or those of a loved one, you probably will consult various self-help resources—books, Web sites, or perhaps groups on- and offline. Do not accept uncritically the treatment programs they may suggest. Your teachers told you that not everything you hear or read is true, and they are right.

Misleading, inaccurate, or simply wrong information is a particular problem in abnormal psychology for three reasons. First, to be honest, as you will learn throughout this course, psychological scientists often simply do not know the causes of, or absolutely effective treatments for, many emotional problems. Much of the time they must piece together treatments based on existing information and the individual characteristics of the client with whom they are working. Second, people who have emotional problems, or who have loved ones who have emotional problems, often are desperate to find a cause and a cure and so will jump at any chance. Third, some well-meaning—and some unscrupulous—people will provide authoritative-sounding "answers" that really are theories, speculations, or distortions.

How can you know what information is accurate and what information is inaccurate? We have worked hard to bring you the most recent scientific information in this text. We also give you practical tips, including recommended self-help books and Web sites in these Getting Help sections. Two general resources you might want to explore now are Martin Seligman's *What You Can Change and What You Can't* and the home page of the National Institute of Mental Health: **www.nimh.nih.gov/**.

But we don't want you to rely only on this text or other authorities. We want you to rely on your own objective and skeptical mind, especially when it comes to getting help for yourself or someone you care about. Remember this: There is an army of scientists out there trying to solve the problems of emotional disorders, because, like us, they want to help. *Breakthrough treatments that really are breakthrough treatments will not be kept secret. They will be announced on the front page of newspapers, not in obscure books or remote Web sites.'* 🌿

---

the past few months. Similar findings have been reported in a more recent survey of 8,000 nationally representative young and middle-aged adults across the United States (Kessler et al., 1994). Many factors may account for this result. Some people who qualified for a formal diagnosis may not have been impaired to such an extent that they were willing to seek treatment. Others may not have recognized their disorder. In some cases, treatment may not have been available, the person may not have had the time or resources to obtain treatment, or the person may have tried treatments in the past that failed. For whatever reason, many people who experience mental disorders do not receive proper treatment.

Much of what we know about psychopathology has been learned in the attempt to help people who are suffering from mental disorders. The connection between etiological speculation and treatment procedures is a two-way street. Theories sometimes spawn new therapies, and successful therapies often spawn new theories. The first antipsychotic drugs were discovered accidentally around 1950. Their dramatic success in relieving symptoms of schizophrenia led quickly to speculation about the neurochemical basis of psychotic disorders.

The success of a treatment does not prove the cause of a problem. After reading Kevin Warner's case, for example, it might be tempting to conclude that Kevin's delusional beliefs were caused by a biochemical imbalance in his brain. His positive response to antipsychotic drugs does not prove, however, that biochemical factors caused his psychotic symptoms in the first place. They may have been caused by a combination of other factors. Aspirin may cure headaches, but this does not mean that headaches are caused by a lack of aspirin. A filling is used to restore a cavity, but this does not mean that cavities are caused by a lack of fillings. When a psychological treatment solves a problem, we often assume that the disorder must have a psychological cause. Similarly, when biological treatments are successful, we often assume that this proves that the cause is biological. Even experienced scientists can fall victim to such errors in reasoning.

Psychopathology in Historical Context

The search for explanations of the causes of abnormal behavior dates to ancient times, as do conflicting opinions about the etiology of emotional disorders. References to abnormal behavior have been found in ancient accounts from Chinese, Hebrew, and Egyptian societies. Many of these records attribute abnormal behavior to the disfavor of the gods or the mischief of demons. In fact, abnormal behavior continues to be attributed to demons in some preliterate societies today.

The Greek Tradition in Medicine

The Greek physician Hippocrates (460–377 B.C.) ridiculed demonological accounts of illness and insanity. Instead, Hippocrates hypothesized that abnormal behavior, like other forms of disease, had natural causes. Health depended on maintaining a natural balance within the body, specifically a balance of four body fluids (which were also known as the four *humors*): blood, phlegm, black bile, and yellow bile. Hippocrates argued that various types of disorder, including psychopathology, resulted from either an excess or a deficiency of one of these four fluids. The specifics of Hippocrates' theories have little value today, but his systematic attempt to uncover natural, biological explanations for all types of illness represented an enormously important departure from previous ways of thinking.

The Hippocratic perspective dominated medical thought in Western countries until the middle of the nineteenth century (Golub, 1994). People trained in the Hippocratic tradition viewed "disease" as a unitary concept. In other words, physicians (and others who were given responsibility for healing people who were disturbed or suffering) did not distinguish between mental disorders and other types of illness. All problems were considered to be the result of an imbalance of body fluids, and treatment procedures were designed in an attempt to restore the ideal balance. They involved bloodletting (intentionally cutting the person to reduce the amount of blood in the body) and purging (the induction of vomiting), as well as the use of heat and cold. These practices continued to be part of standard medical treatments well into the nineteenth century (Starr, 1982).

The Creation of the Asylum

In Europe during the Middle Ages, "lunatics" and "idiots," as the mentally ill and mentally retarded were commonly called, aroused little interest and were given marginal care. Disturbed behavior was considered to be the responsibility of the family rather than the community or the state. Many people were kept at home by their families, and others roamed freely as beggars. Mentally disturbed people who were violent or appeared dangerous often were imprisoned with criminals. Those who could not subsist on their own were placed in almshouses for the poor.

Several factors changed the way that society viewed people with mental disorders and reinforced the relatively new belief that the community as a whole should be responsible for their care

(Grob, 1994). Perhaps most important was a change in economic, demographic, and social conditions. The period between 1790 and 1850 saw rapid population growth and the rise of large cities. The increased urbanization of the American population was accompanied by a shift from an agricultural to an industrial economy. Lunatic asylums—the original mental hospitals—were created to serve heavily populated cities and to assume responsibilities that had previously been performed by individual families.

Early asylums were little more than human warehouses, but as the nineteenth century began, the *moral treatment* movement led to improved conditions in at least some mental hospitals. Founded on a basic respect for human dignity and the belief that humanistic care would help to relieve mental illness, moral treatment reform efforts were instituted by leading mental health professionals of the day, such as Benjamin Rush in the United States, Phillipe Pinel in France, and William Tuke in England. Rather than simply confining mental patients, moral treatment offered support, care, and a degree of freedom. In contrast to the fatalistic, supernatural explanations that had prevailed during the Middle Ages, these reformers touted an optimistic view, arguing that mental disorders could be treated successfully.

Many of the large mental institutions in the United States were built in the nineteenth century as a result of the philosophy of moral treatment. In the middle of the 1800s, mental health advocate Dorothea Dix gave particular impetus to this trend. Dix argued that treating the mentally ill in hospitals was both more humane and more economical than caring for them haphazardly in their communities, and she urged that special facilities be built to house mental patients. In 1830, there were only four public mental hospitals in the United States that housed a combined total of less than 200 patients. By 1880, there were 75 public mental hospitals, with a total population of more than 35,000 residents (Torrey, 1988).

The creation of large institutions for the treatment of mental patients led to the development of a new profession—psychiatry. By the middle of the 1800s, superintendents of asylums for the insane were almost always physicians who had experience caring for people with severe mental disorders. The Association of Medical Superintendents of American Institutions for the Insane (AMSAII), which later became the American Psychiatric Association (APA), was founded in 1844. The large patient populations within these institutions provided an opportunity for these men to observe various types of psychopathology over an extended period of time. They soon began to publish their ideas regarding the causes of these conditions, and they also experimented with new treatment methods (Grob, 1994).

Dorothea Dix (1802–1887) was an early advocate for the humane treatment of the mentally ill. Many mental institutions were built during the late 1800s due in large part to Dix's efforts.

Lessons from the History of Psychopathology

The opinions and procedures that prevailed in psychiatry during the middle of the nineteenth century are, in some very general ways, obvious forerunners of contemporary views. Our etiological theories still focus on a blend of environmental and biological factors, though the specific elements of these theories are now much different. Today's treatment procedures still include the use of medication, as well as efforts to foster personal insight and teach new skills.

The invention and expansion of public mental hospitals set in motion a process of systematic observation and scientific inquiry that led directly to our current system of mental health care. The creation of psychiatry as a professional group, committed to treating and understanding psychopathology, laid the foundation for expanded public concern and financial resources for solving the problems of mental disorders.

There are, of course, many aspects of nineteenth-century psychiatry that, in retrospect, seem to have been naive or misguided. To take only one example, it now seems silly to have thought that masturbation would cause mental disorders. In fact, masturbation is now taught and encouraged as part of treatment for certain types of sexual dysfunction (see Chapter 12). The obvious cultural biases that influenced the etiological hypotheses of those times seem quite unreasonable today.

Our own cultural values continue to influence the ways in which we define, think about, and treat mental disorders. Thomas Szasz (1970), who is perhaps the most eloquent and influential critic of contemporary psychiatric views, has noted that social values still play an important role in our system for classifying mental disorders. Paula Caplan (1995) has drawn attention to the

TABLE 1–3

Somatic Treatments Introduced and Widely Employed in the 1920s and 1930s		
NAME	**PROCEDURE**	**ORIGINAL RATIONALE**
Fever therapy	Blood from people with malaria was injected into psychiatric patients so that they would develop a fever.	Observation that symptoms sometimes disappeared in patients who became ill with typhoid fever.
Insulin coma therapy	Insulin was injected into psychiatric patients to lower the sugar content of the blood and induce a hypoglycemic state and deep coma.	Observed mental changes among some diabetic drug addicts who were treated with insulin.
Lobotomy	A sharp knife was inserted through a hole that was bored in the patient's skull, severing nerve fibers connecting the frontal lobes to the rest of the brain.	Observation that the same surgical procedure with chimpanzees led to a reduction in the display of negative emotion during stress.

Note: *Lack of critical evaluation of these procedures is reflected in the unusual notoriety bestowed upon their inventors. Julius Wagner-Jauregg, an Austrian psychiatrist, was awarded a Nobel Prize in 1927 for his work in developing fever therapy. Egaz Moniz, a Portuguese psychiatrist, was awarded a Nobel Prize in 1946 for introduction of the lobotomy.*

potential influence of gender bias in shaping DSM-IV. One lesson therefore is that the cultural context will determine, in part, which problems are selected for consideration and how they are defined. Learning about the history of psychiatry can make these biases more obvious. We must not let it lull us into thinking, however, that we have outgrown or progressed beyond these difficulties. It seems unlikely that mental disorders can be defined in a cultural vacuum or in a completely objective fashion. The best we can do is to be aware of the problem and include a variety of cultural and social perspectives in thinking about and defining the issues (Manson, 1994).

The other lesson that we can learn from history involves the importance of scientific research. During the nineteenth century, physicians were not trained in scientific research methods. Their optimistic statements about treatment outcome were accepted, in large part, on the basis of their professional authority.

Unfortunately, this type of naive acceptance has become a regrettable tradition. For the past 150 years, mental health professionals and the public alike have repeatedly embraced new treatment procedures that have been hailed as cures for mental disorders. Perhaps most notorious was a group of somatic treatment procedures that was introduced during the 1920s and 1930s (Valenstein, 1986). They included fever therapy, insulin coma, and lobotomy (see Table 1–3). These dramatic procedures, which have subsequently proved to be ineffective, were accepted with the same enthusiasm that greeted the invention of large public institutions in nineteenth-century America. Thousands of patients were subjected to these procedures, which remained widespread until the early 1950s, when more effective pharmacological treatments were discovered. The history of psychopathology teaches us that people who claim that a new form of treatment is effective should be expected to prove it scientifically.

Research Methods in Abnormal Psychology

Scientists have established a basic and extremely important rule for making and testing any new hypothesis: The scientist who makes a new prediction must prove it to be true. Scientists are not obligated to disprove other researchers' assertions. Until a hypothesis is supported by empirical evidence, the community of scientists assumes that the new prediction is false.

The concepts of the experimental hypothesis and the null hypothesis are central to understanding this essential rule of science. An **experimental hypothesis** is any new prediction made by an investigator. Researchers must adopt and state their experimental hypothesis in both correlational studies and experiments. In all scientific research, the **null hypothesis** is the alternative to the experimental hypothesis. The null hypothesis always predicts that the experimental hypothesis is not true. The rules of science dictate that scientists must assume that the null hypothesis holds until research contradicts it. That is, the burden of proof falls on the scientist who makes a new prediction—who offers an experimental hypothesis.

These rules of science are analogous to rules about the burden of proof that have been adopted in trial courts. In U.S. courtrooms, the law assumes that a defendant is innocent until proven guilty. Defendants do not need to prove their innocence; rather, prosecutors need to prove the defendants' guilt. Thus the null hypothesis is analogous to the assumption of innocence, and the burden of proof in science falls on any scientist who challenges the null hypothesis, just as it falls on the prosecutor in a court trial.

These rules in science and in law serve important purposes. Both are conservative principles designed to protect the field from false assertions. Our legal philosophy is that "it is better to let ten guilty people go free than to punish one innocent person." Scientists adopt a similar philosophy—that false "scientific evidence" is more dangerous than undetected knowledge. Because of these safeguards, we can be reasonably confident when an experimental hypothesis is supported or when a defendant is found guilty.

There is one more similarity between the rules of science and the rules of the courtroom. Courtroom verdicts do not lead to a judgment that the defendant is "innocent," but only to a decision that she or he is "not guilty." In theory, the possibility remains that a defendant who is found "not guilty" did indeed commit a crime. Similarly, scientific research does not lead to the conclusion that the null hypothesis is true. Scientists never prove the null hypothesis; they only fail to reject it.

Correlational Studies

Scientists have developed sophisticated methods for conducting research. The most basic scientific tools are the correlational study and the *experiment*. In a **correlational study,** the relation between two factors (their co-relation) is studied in a systematic fashion. For example, you might hypothesize that psychology majors on your campus learn more about research methods than biology majors learn. To support this hypothesis, you might simply argue your point, or you could rely on case studies—"I know more about research than my roommate, and she's a biology major!"

If you were to conduct a correlational study on the question, you would collect a large sample of both psychology and biology majors and compare them on an objective measure of knowledge of research methods. You would then use statistics to test whether research knowledge is *correlated* with academic major.

An important statistic for measuring how strongly two factors are related is the **correlation coefficient.** The correlation coefficient is a number that always ranges between -1.00 and $+1.00$. If all psychology majors got 100 percent correct on your test of research methods and all biology majors got 0 percent correct, the correlation between academic major and research knowledge would be 1.00. If all psychology and biology majors got 50 percent of the items correct, the correlation between major and knowledge would be zero.

Positive correlations (from 0.01 to 1.00) indicate that, as one factor goes up, the other factor also goes up. For example, height and weight are positively correlated, as are years of education and employment income. Taller people weigh more; educated people earn more money. *Negative*

experimental hypothesis A new prediction made by an investigator to be tested in an experiment.

null hypothesis The prediction that an experimental hypothesis is not true. Scientists ust assume that the null hypothesis holds until research contradicts it.

correlational study A scientific research method in which the relation between two factors (their co-relation) is studied in a systematic fashion. Has the advantage of practicality, as correlations between many variables can be studied in the real world, but also has the disadvantage that "correlation does not mean causation."

correlation coefficient A number that always ranges between -1.00 and $+1.00$ and indicates the strength and direction of the relation between two variables. A higher absolute value indicates a stronger relation, while a correlation coefficient of 0 indicates no relation. The sign indicates the direction of the correlation.

reverse causality   Indicates that causation could be operating in the opposite direction: Y could be causing X instead of X causing Y. A threat to interpretation in correlational studies, and a basic reason why correlation does not mean causation.

third variable   An unmeasured factor that may account for a correlation observed between any two variables. A threat to interpretation in correlational studies, and a basic reason why correlation does not mean causation.

hypothesis   A prediction about the expected findings in a scientific study.

independent variable   The variable in an experiment that is controlled and deliberately manipulated by the experimenter (for example, whether or not a subject receives a treatment). Affects the dependent variable.

experimental group   The group of participants in an experiment that receives a treatment that is hypothesized to cause some measured effect. Participants in the experimental group are compared with untreated participants in a control group.

control group   The group of participants in an experiment that receives no treatment or perhaps a placebo treatment. Participants in the control group are compared with participants in the experimental group (who are given an active treatment).

random assignment   Any of several methods of ensuring that each subject has a statistically equal chance of being exposed to any level of an independent variable.

correlations (from −1.00 to −0.01) indicate that, as one number gets bigger, the other number gets smaller. For example, population and open space are negatively correlated. As more people move into an area, the amount of open land diminishes. Two factors are more strongly correlated when a correlation coefficient has a higher absolute value, regardless of whether the relationship is positive or negative.

Self-esteem is negatively correlated with emotional problems. The higher your self-esteem, the fewer problems you have. However, a correlation between two factors must be interpreted cautiously. In particular, you should constantly remember that *correlation does not mean causation*.

In interpreting any correlation, there are always two alternative explanations to making a causal conclusion: reverse causality and third-variable alternative interpretations. We might want to conclude that *X* causes *Y*—that low self-esteem causes depression. However, the concept of **reverse causality** indicates that causation could be operating in the opposite direction: *Y* could be causing *X*. Depression could be causing low self-esteem.

The **third-variable** possibility offers yet another alternative to causal interpretations. A correlation between any two variables could be explained by their joint relation with some unmeasured factor—a third variable. For example, stress might cause both depression *and* low self-esteem.

Let us return to your study of psychology and biology majors to illustrate these issues further. Assume that you did find that psychology majors know more about research methods. Based on this correlational finding, could you conclude that studying psychology *causes* students to learn more about research? No, you could not. A reverse causality interpretation of the correlation might suggest that people who know more about research methods decide to become psychology majors. Knowledge about research causes them to choose this major, not vice versa. A third-variable interpretation of the correlation might suggest that more intelligent people choose to major in psychology, and more intelligent people also know more about the methods of scientific research. According to this interpretation, the correlation between academic major and research knowledge is *spurious*, an artifact of the relation of both of these variables with the third variable of intelligence.

Experiments

Another method of research, the experiment, *does* allow scientists to determine cause and effect relations. However, it often is impractical or unethical to conduct experiments on psychological problems, whereas correlational studies can be conducted with far fewer practical or ethical concerns. Thus the correlational method has the weakness that correlation does not mean causation; it also has the strength that it can be used to conduct research in many real-life circumstances.

The experiment has four essential features. It begins with a **hypothesis**—the experimenter's specific prediction about cause and effect. For example, a researcher might predict that in comparison to no treatment at all, a particular type of medication will reduce certain symptoms of a given emotional disorder. The experimenter might further hypothesize that psychotherapy also will alleviate symptoms more than no treatment, but psychotherapy will cause no more and no less symptom change than will medication.

The second feature of an experiment is the manipulation of an **independent variable.** Independent variables are controlled and deliberately manipulated by the experimenter. The independent variable in the hypothesis just outlined is whether the patients receive medication, psychotherapy, or no treatment. The experimenter controls the independent variable by deciding what specific type of medication or psychotherapy will be made available to the patients in the experiment and by determining who will receive one of these treatments and who will receive no treatment at all. People who receive an active treatment belong to the **experimental group.** Those who receive no treatment or merely a placebo belong to the **control group.** On average, members of the experimental group are hypothesized to improve more than members of the control group.

The third feature of the experiment is **random assignment,** ensuring that each subject has a statistically equal chance of receiving different levels of the independent variable. In the present example, picking the number 1, 2, or 3 out of a hat is one of many possible ways of ensuring random assignment to medication, psychotherapy, or no treatment. Random assignment is essential, because it ensures that any differences among groups are caused by the independent variable and not by biased selection into groups.

The fourth feature of the experiment is the measurement of the **dependent variable.** The dependent variable is the outcome that is hypothesized to vary according to manipulations in the independent variable. The outcome *depends* on the experimental manipulation—thus the term "dependent variable." In the present example, the various symptoms of the disorder make up the dependent variables of the study. The symptoms are expected to change depending on whether the patients receive medication, psychotherapy, or no treatment at all.

Statistical tests typically are conducted to establish whether the independent variable has changed the dependent variable in a predictable manner, or whether the outcome is a result of chance. According to current conventions, a finding is considered to be *statistically significant* if it would occur by chance in less than 1 out of every 20 experiments. That is, the probability of a chance outcome is less than 5 percent, a specification that is often written as $p < .05$. However, a statistically significant result is not the same as a clinically significant finding. A treatment may produce a reliable change in symptoms, for example, but the change may be too small to produce a meaningful difference in the patient's life.

We can conclude that an independent variable *causes* changes in a dependent variable when the experimental method is used correctly and it produces statistically significant results. The ability to establish causation is a powerful strength of the experiment in comparison to the correlational study. The experimental method is limited, however, because many theoretically interesting independent variables cannot be manipulated practically or ethically in real life. We may hypothesize that abusive parenting causes psychological problems, for example, but we obviously cannot randomly assign children to grow up in abusive and nonabusive homes. In fact, practical and ethical limitations make it impossible to use the experiment to test most hypotheses about the causes of abnormal behavior. Thus, when studying the etiology of abnormal behavior, we often must rely on correlational studies or analogue studies.

The effectiveness of various psychological treatments often can be studied using an experiment, because researchers can control whether someone receives a particular medication or form of psychotherapy. Still, it is not easy to completely control the independent variable in treatment outcome research. Some people may drop out of treatment, and others may seek additional help. Clinicians might not conduct psychotherapy according to the design of the experiment, or patients might not take their medication as prescribed.

An experiment has **internal validity** if changes in the dependent variable can be accurately attributed to changes in the independent variable. As we have noted, however, the independent variable can be manipulated poorly, or it can be confounded with other variables. For example, in our hypothetical study it obviously would be wrong to conclude that medication was ineffective if the patients failed to take it, or it would be difficult to draw conclusions about psychotherapy if many of the patients dropped out of the study.

In contrast to internal validity, **external validity** refers to whether the findings of an experiment generalize to other circumstances. A number of questions typically can be raised about an experiment's external validity, because some artificiality needs to be introduced to give the experimenter control over the independent variable. In our hypothetical study, perhaps only a very narrow group of patients would be treated. Thus the findings might not generalize to other people with other problems. Or perhaps psychotherapy might last for exactly 10 sessions in the experiment in order to ensure control of the independent variable. Although this would help the study's internal validity, it might compromise the experiment's external validity. The findings might not apply in the real world, where the length of treatment is tailored to the individual client's needs.

There is no finite list of questions that can be raised about the internal and external validity of experiments. A common trade-off, however, is that the experimenter often must sacrifice one for the other. Recognizing this compromise is essential to conducting and evaluating science. We therefore raise questions throughout this book about the strengths and limitations of the experiment—and of correlational research.

dependent variable   The outcome that is hypothesized to vary according to manipulations in the independent variable in an experiment.

internal validity   Whether changes in the dependent variable can be accurately attributed to changes in the independent variable in an experiment, that is, there are no experimental confounds.

external validity   Whether the findings of an experiment generalize to other people, places and circumstances, particularly real-life situations.

psychiatry   The branch of medicine that is concerned with the study and treatment of mental disorders.

clinical psychology   The profession and academic discipline that is concerned with the application of psychological science to the assessment and treatment of mental disorders.

social work   A profession whose primary concern is how human needs can be met within society.

The Mental Health Professions

Many forms of training prepare people to provide professional assistance to those who suffer from mental disorders. The two professional groups that are mentioned in the cases in this chapter are psychiatrists and clinical psychologists.

Psychiatry is the branch of medicine that is concerned with the study and treatment of mental disorders. Psychiatrists complete the normal sequence of coursework and internship training in a medical school (usually 4 years) before going on to receive specialized residency training (another 4 years) that is focused on abnormal behavior. By virtue of their medical training, psychiatrists are licensed to practice medicine and therefore are able to prescribe medication. Most psychiatrists are also trained in the use of psychosocial intervention.

Clinical psychology is concerned with the application of psychological science to the assessment and treatment of mental disorders (APA, 1991). A clinical psychologist typically completes 5 years of graduate study in a department of psychology, as well as a 1-year internship, before receiving a doctoral degree. Clinical psychologists are trained in the use of psychological assessment procedures and in the use of psychotherapy.

Within clinical psychology, there are two primary types of clinical training programs. One course of study, which leads to the Ph.D. degree (doctor of philosophy), involves a traditional sequence of graduate training with a serious emphasis on research methods. The other approach, which culminates in a Psy.D. degree (doctor of psychology), places greater emphasis on practical skills of assessment and treatment and does not require an independent research project for the dissertation.

Social work is a third major profession that is concerned with helping people achieve an effective level of psychosocial functioning (Hopps & Pinderhughes, 1987). Most practicing social workers have a master's degree in social work. In contrast to psychology and psychiatry, social work is based less on a body of scientific knowledge than on a commitment to action. The practice of social work encompasses a wide range of settings, from courts and prisons to schools and hospitals, as well as other social service agencies. The emphasis tends to be on social and cultural factors, such as the effects of poverty on the availability of educational and health services, rather than individual differences in personality or psychopathology. Psychiatric social workers receive training that is specialized in treatment of mental health problems.

A profession is largely defined in terms of what its members do. In that sense, the mental health professions are similar to one another, and it is not surprising that they are often confused by the public. Clinical psychologists, psychiatrists, and social workers can all be trained to conduct psychotherapy. Some members of all three professions are actively involved in research; others become administrators in hospitals and clinics. All are licensed in their own specialties by state boards of examiners. Table 1–4 gives estimated numbers of mental health professionals currently practicing in the United States.

Clinical psychologists perform many roles. Some provide direct clinical services. Many are involved in research, teaching, and various administrataiave activities.

The distinctions among clinical psychology, psychiatry, and social work have developed gradually over the past 100 years, and it is likely that they will continue to do so in the future. Two landmark court decisions in the early 1970s, *Blue Shield of Virginia* v. *McCready* and *Wyatt* v. *Stickney,* held that licensed clinical psychologists and social workers should be able to treat patients without the supervision of a psychiatrist. Perhaps most importantly, they ruled that these professionals were entitled to receive payments for their services from insurance companies. This ruling essentially established the legal right of patients to freedom of choice in selecting their own practitioners.

At present, many clinical psychologists are pursuing the right to prescribe medication (DeLeon, Sammons, & Sexton, 1995; cf. Klein, 1995). Decisions regarding this issue and related questions will have a dramatic impact on the boundaries that separate the mental health professions. The ongoing conflict over the containment of health care costs suggests that debates over

TABLE 1–4

Estimated Number of Professionals Providing Mental Health Services in the United States, 1996

PROFESSION	NUMBER
Specialty Providers	
Psychiatrists	33,200
Psychologists	42,000
Social workers	45,000
Other Providers	
Family therapists	28,000
Psychiatric nurses	3,000
Primary care physicians	116,600

Source: *K. I. Howard, T. A. Cornille, J. S. Lyons, J. T. Vessey, R. J. Lueger, and S. M. Saunders, 1996,* Patterns of mental health service utilization, Archives of General Psychiatry, *53, 696–703.*

the rights and privileges of patients and their therapists will intensify in the coming years. Therefore it is difficult to say with certainty what the mental health professions will be like in the future.

Goals of This Book

The terms and concepts introduced in this chapter provide a springboard to more detailed discussions of mental disorders. Most of the issues that we have raised are unresolved; many continue to be the focal points of heated controversies that will be considered later.

The application of science to questions regarding abnormal behavior carries with it the implicit assumption that these problems can be studied objectively. We believe that order can be found in the frequently chaotic and puzzling world of mental disorders. This order will eventually allow us to understand the processes by which abnormal behaviors are created and maintained.

Clinical scientists adopt an attitude of open-minded skepticism, tempered by an appreciation for the research methods that are used to collect empirical data. They formulate specific hypotheses, test them, and then refine them based on the results of these tests. This book is, for the most part, an attempt to explain that process. In order to get the most from it, you may have to set aside—at least temporarily—personal beliefs that you have already acquired about mental disorders. Try to adopt an objective, skeptical attitude. We hope to pique your curiosity and share with you the satisfaction, as well as perhaps some of the frustration, of searching for answers to questions about complex behavior problems.

This book has several goals that focus on developing your familiarity with specialized topics within the field of abnormal psychology. The most important are highlighted with headings and features that are consistent from chapter to chapter. We list these goals here:

1. To describe the experiences of a number of individuals who suffer from various types of psychopathology (case studies)

2. To specify more objectively the clinical problems that are associated with mental disorders (typical symptoms)

3. To explain the system that is used to classify these disorders, emphasizing how it has evolved and the criteria by which it is evaluated (classification)

4. To outline current knowledge regarding the frequency and distribution of these problems (epidemiology)

5.   To highlight contemporary hypotheses regarding the causes of abnormal behaviors, focusing in particular on complementary relations among psychological, biological, and environmental systems (etiology)

6.   To provide selected examples of ways in which clinical scientists collect data to test these hypotheses (Research Close-Ups)

7.   To discuss psychological and biological interventions that are used to help people who experience various types of mental disorder (treatment)

We will consider these topics as they apply to each of the major categories of mental disorder. Each chapter will include a summary of current knowledge regarding psychopathology. Keep in mind, however, the preliminary nature of our knowledge. Very little is actually known about the etiology of these problems. Therefore we believe that it is more important for you to understand the principles that guide our ongoing search for knowledge than to digest whatever information is currently available.

Summary

One of our goals in this chapter is to make you more familiar with certain symptoms of **psychopathology.** We have described two relatively common forms of mental disorder: schizophrenia and bulimia nervosa. Schizophrenia is a form of **psychosis.** The symptoms of this disorder include **delusions** and disorganized speech. Bulimia nervosa is an eating disorder that involves recurrent episodes in which the person cannot control what (or how much) he or she eats. These episodes of binge eating are followed by efforts to prevent weight gain, such as self-induced vomiting. These and many other types of mental disorder are described in greater detail in the subsequent chapters of this book.

Mental disorders are defined in terms of typical signs and symptoms rather than identifiable causal factors. A group of symptoms that appear together and are assumed to represent a specific type of disorder is called a **syndrome.** There are no definitive psychological or biological tests that can be used to confirm the presence of psychopathology. At present, the diagnosis of mental disorders depends on observations of the person's behavior and descriptions of personal experience.

No one has been able to provide a universally accepted definition of abnormal behavior. Statistical infrequency and subjective distress cannot be used for this purpose because not all infrequent behaviors are pathological and because some people who exhibit abnormal behaviors do not have insight into their conditions. One useful approach defines mental disorders in terms of **harmful dysfunction.** The official classification system, DSM-IV, defines mental disorders as a group of persistent maladaptive behaviors that result in personal distress or impaired functioning.

Various forms of voluntary social deviance and efforts to express individuality are excluded from the DSM-IV definition of mental disorders. Political and religious actions, and the beliefs on which they are based, are not considered to be forms of abnormal behavior, even when they seem unusual to many other people. We must recognize, however, that the process of defining psychopathology is still influenced by cultural and political values. The categories described in DSM-IV have been appropriately subjected to public debate and criticism.

The boundaries of mental disorders are often difficult to define. They can be classified using either **dimensional** or **categorical** concepts. A **threshold model** incorporates elements of both approaches. DSM-IV has adopted a categorical approach to classification, but we do not have enough information to determine which is the more appropriate.

The scientific study of the frequency and distribution of disorders within a population is known as **epidemiology.** Some severe forms of abnormal behavior, such as schizophrenia, have been observed in virtually every society that has been studied by social scientists. There are also forms of psychopathology—including eating disorders—for which substantial cross-cultural differences have been found. These epidemiological patterns may provide important clues that will help identify factors that influence the etiology of mental disorders.

Some of the best information that is currently available on the epidemiology of mental disorders in the United States was collected in the Epidemiologic Catchment Area (ECA) study. According to this study, the 12-month **prevalence** rate for at least one form of mental disorder was 20 percent. Lifetime prevalence was higher, with 32 percent of adults reporting at least one mental disorder at some point in their lives. The ECA study found significant gender differences for several types of mental disorder, including anxiety disorders, mood disorders, and alcoholism.

Abnormal psychology represents the application of psychological science—its concepts and research tools—to the study of mental disorders. Various forms of professional training prepare people to work with those who suffer from mental disorders. These professions include **clinical psychology, psychiatry,** and **social work.** People who study and treat mental disorders are best trained as **scientist-practitioners.** We want to introduce you to both sides of this process: learning more about the phenomenology of the disorders as well as the methodologies that are used to study them.

The **etiology** of mental disorders is not well understood. It is undoubtedly the product of an interaction among biological, psychological, and social factors. These are complementary systems. The interactive nature of these systems can be described as a **biopsychosocial model** of psychopathology. The resolution of the **nature–nurture controversy** hinges on the recognition that the artificial distinction between biological causes and environmental causes is not helpful in our search for knowledge about mental disorders.

Several types of **psychopharmacology** and **psychotherapy** have been shown to be effective in the treatment of mental disorders. Many important hypotheses about the origins of mental disorders have been derived from efforts to treat these conditions. These hypotheses must then be tested in the context of carefully planned research programs. An individual **case study** does not provide definitive evidence for or against any hypothesis.

Critical Thinking

1. What does it mean for a behavior to be classified as "abnormal"? Why is it so difficult to produce an abstract definition of abnormal behavior? Some people argue that psychopathology is nothing more than the list of disorders presented in the *Diagnostic and Statistical Manual.* Do you agree? Can you provide a better definition?

2. Do you think it is possible to eliminate social values from a definition of abnormal behavior? How would you accomplish this goal? Is there any way of defining mental disorders that would avoid value judgments about which behaviors are adaptive and which are not?

3. Case studies provide interesting descriptions of problems, but they don't help us choose among etiological theories. What kinds of limitations do you see with case studies? Why should we be careful about drawing general conclusions from them?

4. Why is it useful for clinical psychologists to be experts in understanding and conducting research? Does the scientist-practitioner model have any advantages for the training of clinical psychologists?

2

Perspectives on Causes of Abnormal Behavior

Magazine articles explain that depression is caused by a chemical imbalance in the brain, a problem that can be corrected with medication. Television advertisements tell us that alcoholism is a genetic disease that is best treated in a hospital. Books and films often portray emotional disturbances as going back to traumatic childhood experiences that are relived in psychotherapy. Many manuals on parenting tell us that mothers and fathers cause psychological problems when they love their children too little—or indulge them too much. Finally, television shows and newspaper headlines blame violence in our cities on everything from the breakdown of families to the breakdown of schools to the breakdown of society.

Overview

Like the popular media, scientists also may offer different—and often conflicting—explanations concerning the causes, or *etiology*, of psychopathology. Conflicting scientific explanations sometimes confuse the public, but such disagreements may actually be of benefit to science. Scientists pit theories against one another in a competition of research, and the "winner" is the most accurate explanation of psychopathology.

One difficulty, however, is that the traditional biological, psychoanalytic, behavioral, and humanistic approaches are more than alternative theories. They also are alternative *paradigms*. In other words, they conflict not only in their theories of abnormal behavior but also in what they view as acceptable scientific methods, as we discuss shortly.

The more substantial problem, however, is that most forms of psychopathology do not have a single cause or set of causes. Rather, abnormal behavior appears to be determined by *multifactorial causes*, the combination of a variety of different biological, psychological, and social factors. Thus, early childhood experience *and* current life events are important to abnormal behavior, as are individual personality characteristics *and* conflict in close relationships, or inner psychological turmoil *and* societal expectations about gender or ethnicity.

The challenge for science, therefore, is not to identify a single theory that explains the causes of all forms of abnormal behavior. Rather, the challenge is to integrate evidence on the etiologies of different disorders into a coherent whole, a system of contributing factors (Rutter & Rutter, 1993). In this chapter—and throughout the text—we adopt such a systems approach to understanding the etiology of psychopathology. Rather than arguing for or against one theoretical perspective, the systems approach integrates evidence across and among different biological, psychological, and social domains of behavior. Thus the systems approach often is referred to as a *biopsychosocial* perspective. Biological contributions to abnormal behavior range from specific biochemical processes in the brain to broad genetic liabilities passed across generations. Psychological contributions range from unconscious cognitive processes to reinforcement for abnormal behavior. Social and cultural contributions range from conflict in relationships with family members to the broad influences of television and other popular media.

In adopting an integrative systems approach, we must be clear about three issues. First, we do not mean to imply that all theories of the etiology of abnormal behavior are equally valid (1975).

Different types of abnormal behavior also have very different causes, just as different physical diseases are caused by various underlying conditions. In fact, two people may have the same disorder for very different reasons. Third, we must acknowledge that scientists currently do not know what causes most forms of abnormal behavior. You should be suspicious of people who claim to know the cause of psychopathology—they are almost certainly wrong.

In this chapter we explain the systems approach as a general method for understanding abnormal behavior. We also introduce a number of biological, psychological, and social concepts relevant to the etiology of psychopathology. In later chapters we return to these basic concepts when critically reviewing evidence on the multifactorial contributions to the etiology of particular psychological disorders.

Each chapter in this text includes a case study. The case study illustrates key topics from the practitioner side of the scientist-practitioner model. Most cases, including the following one, come from our own therapy files.

case study

Possible Causes of Behavioral Problems

At the age of 14, Meghan B. attempted to end her life by taking approximately 20 Tylenol capsules. Meghan took the pills after an explosive fight with her mother over Meghan's grades and over a boy she was dating. Meghan was in her room when she impulsively took the pills, but shortly afterward she told her mother what she had done. Her parents rushed Meghan to the emergency room, where her vital signs were closely monitored. As the crisis was coming to an end, Meghan's parents agreed that she should be hospitalized to make sure that she was safe and to begin to treat her problems.

Meghan talked freely about many of her problems during the 30 days she spent on the adolescent unit of a private psychiatric hospital. Most of her complaints focused on her mother. Meghan insisted that her mother was always "in her face," telling her what to do and when and how to do it. Her father was "great," but he was too busy with his job as a chemical engineer to spend much time with her.

Meghan also said she had long-standing problems in school. She barely maintained a C average despite considerable efforts to do better. Meghan said she didn't care about school, and her mother's insistence that she could do much better was a major source of conflict between them. Meghan also complained that she had few friends, either in school or outside of school. She described her classmates as "preppy" and "straight," and said she had no interest in them. Meghan was obviously angry as she described her family, school, and friends, but she also showed sadness on a few occasions. She denounced herself as being "stupid" one time, and she cried about being a "reject" when discussing why no friends, including her boyfriend, contacted her while she was in the hospital.

Mrs. B. provided details on the history of Meghan's problems. When Meghan was 2 years old, she had been adopted by Mr. and Mrs. B., who could not have children of their own. According to the adoption agency, Meghan's birth mother was 16 years old when she had the baby. Meghan's biological mother was a drug user, and she haphazardly left the baby in the care of friends and relatives for weeks at a time. Little was known about Meghan's biological father except that he had had some trouble with the law, and Meghan's mother had known him only briefly. When Meghan was 14 months old, her pediatrician reported her mother to a child abuse agency after noting bruises on Meghan's thighs and hips. After a 6-month legal investigation, Meghan's mother decided to give her up for adoption. Meghan came to live with Mr. and Mrs. B. shortly thereafter.

Mrs. B. was eager to give Meghan all the love they both had missed in their lives to that point, and she happily doted on her daughter. Mr. B. also was very loving with Meghan, although Mrs. B., like Meghan, noted that he was rarely at home. Everything seemed fine with Meghan until first grade, when teachers began to complain about her. She disrupted the classroom with her restlessness, and she did not complete her schoolwork. In second grade, Meghan was diagnosed by a school psychologist as a "hyperactive" child who also had a learning disability, and her pediatrician recommended medication as a treatment. Mrs. B. was horrified by the thought of medication or of sending Meghan to a "resource room" for part of the school day. Instead, she decided to redouble her efforts at parenting.

According to Mrs. B., she and Meghan succeeded in getting Meghan through elementary school in reasonably good shape. Meghan's grades and classroom behavior remained acceptable as long as Mrs. B. consulted repeatedly with the school. Mrs. B. noted with bitterness, however, that the one problem that she could not solve was Meghan's relationships with other girls. The daughters of Mrs. B.'s friends and neighbors were well behaved and were excellent students. Meghan did not fit in with them. They were polite when they saw her, but Meghan never got invited to play with the other girls.

Mrs. B. was obviously sad when discussing Meghan's past, but she became agitated and angry when discussing the present. She was very concerned about Meghan, but she wondered out loud if the suicide attempt had been manipulative. Mrs. B.

said that she had had major conflicts with Meghan ever since Meghan started middle school at the age of 12. Meghan would no longer work regularly with her mother on her homework for the usual 2 hours each night. In addition, her mother said that Meghan fought with her about everything from picking up her room to her boyfriend, an 18-year-old whom Mrs. B. abhorred. Mrs. B. complained that she did not understand what had happened to her daughter. She clearly stated, however, that whatever it was, she would fix it. 🌾

biomedical approach A paradigm for conceptualizing abnormal behavior that focuses on biological causation and the analogy between physical and psychological illnesses. Sometimes referred to as the "medical model."

What was causing Meghan's problems? Her case study suggests many plausible alternatives. Some of her troubles seem to be a reaction to a mother whose attentiveness at age 8 seems more like intrusiveness at age 14. Maybe Mrs. B. became more concerned with her own needs for love than with Meghan's changing needs for parenting. Meghan's problems seem bigger than this, however. We could trace some of her troubles to anger over her failures in school or to rejection by her peers. We also can speculate about the effects of Meghan's early childhood experiences. Surely she was affected adversely by the physical abuse, inconsistent love, and chaotic living arrangements during the first, critical years of her life. Finally, we can wonder about possible biological contributions to Meghan's problems. Did Meghan's mother take drugs during pregnancy that affected the developing baby? Was Meghan a healthy, full-term newborn? Given her biological parents' history of troubled behavior, could Meghan's problems be caused by genetic factors?

These searching questions defy a ready answer. Still, psychological theory and research does offer some good leads about etiology. We introduce current psychological approaches to understanding the causes of psychopathology by first considering them in historical perspective.

Brief Historical Perspective on Approaches to Etiology

As we saw in Chapter 1, the search for explanations of the causes of abnormal behavior dates to ancient times. Unfortunately, many of the traditions begun by Hippocrates died away after the fall of the Roman Empire. Although systematic, naturalistic accounts of mental illness were kept alive in Arab cultures (Grob, 1994), the emphasis on objectivity and careful observation faded in Europe. In fact, some scholars have concluded that, during the Middle Ages, mental illness came to be blamed on witchcraft. Advances in the scientific understanding of the etiology of psychopathology were not made until the nineteenth and early twentieth centuries, when three major events occurred. One was the discovery of the cause of general paresis, a severe mental disorder that has a deteriorating course and eventually ends in death. The second was the writing of Sigmund Freud, a thinker who has had a profound influence not only on the field of abnormal psychology but also on Western society as a whole. The third was the creation of a new academic discipline called psychology.

General Paresis and the Biomedical Approach

The **biomedical approach** to abnormal psychology can be traced to the study of the condition we now know as *general paresis* (general paralysis). Prior to 1800, general paresis was not recognized as a distinct disorder and therefore attracted no special attention. In 1798, John Haslam distinguished general paresis from other forms of "lunacy" based on its symptoms. The diagnosis inspired a search for the cause of the new disorder.

The etiological breakthrough began with the observation that people with general paresis had contracted the sexually transmitted disease *syphilis* earlier in their lives. After the turn of

psychoanalytic theory   A paradigm for conceptualizing abnormal behavior based on the concepts and writings of Sigmund Freud. Highlights unconscious processes and conflicts as causing abnormal behavior and emphasizes psychoanalysis as the treatment of choice.

unconscious   Mental processes or contents that reside outside of awareness. In Freudian theory, the seat of many hidden memories, motivations, and defenses.

Sigmund Freud (1856–1939) developed psychoanalytic theory. Freud's approach has been criticized as being unscientific, but the influence of his ideas is unquestionable.

the twentieth century, the spirochete that causes syphilis was discovered. Postmortem examination of the brains of paretic patients proved that the infection had invaded and destroyed parts of the central nervous system. In 1910, Paul Ehrlich, a German microbiologist, developed arsphenamine, an arsenic-containing chemical that destroyed the spirochete and prevented general paresis. Unfortunately, the drug worked only if the patient was treated in the early stages of infection. Later, it was learned that syphilis could be cured by a new discovery, penicillin—the first antibiotic. As a result, general paresis was virtually eliminated when antibiotics became widely available after the end of World War II.

The slow but dramatic discoveries about general paresis gave great impetus to the search for biological causes for other mental disorders. Unfortunately, the causes of most forms of mental illness do not appear to be as straightforward as for general paresis. Like heart disease and cancer, most mental disorders appear to be "lifestyle diseases," problems that have multifactorial causes, including biological, psychological, and social contributions.

Freud and Psychoanalytic Theory

Unlike the biomedical approach, which has been influenced by many notable people, **psychoanalytic theory** owes its origins primarily to the writings of a single individual, Sigmund Freud (1856–1939). Freud introduced many influential ideas, but perhaps his most basic contribution was to provide a counterpoint to the growing biomedical approach. Freud argued that early childhood experiences played a central role in the development of mental illness, even in illnesses that had physical manifestations (see Further Thoughts on p. 34).

Freud was trained in Paris by Jean Charcot (1825–1893), a neurologist who successfully used hypnosis to treat what used to be called *hysteria*. One type of hysteria is characterized by the conversion of psychological conflicts into physical symptoms. It is now called *conversion disorder* (see Chapter 7). "Hysterical blindness," for example, is the inability to see. This dramatic symptom is not caused by a known organic impairment, and the afflicted individual sometimes recovers functioning after resolving an emotional problem.

Patients neither fake conversion symptoms, nor do they consciously associate them with emotional distress. Thus it would seem that psychological conflicts are somehow "converted" into physical symptoms outside conscious awareness. The peculiar problem of hysteria led Freud to emphasize the importance of **the unconscious** in the etiology of emotional disorders. Freud argued that many memories, motivations, and protective psychological processes reside in the unconscious mind, which explains how problems like hysteria might be produced outside conscious awareness.

Freud was derided by many of his contemporaries who favored biological explanations of abnormal behavior, but he proved to have an immense influence on psychiatry and psychology. He can be credited with calling attention to unconscious processes, formulating a stage theory of child development, creating the metaphorical division of the personality into the id, ego, and superego, and identifying numerous intrapsychic defenses (see Table 2–1 and Further Thoughts). However, Freud built his elaborate theory of the development of normal and abnormal behavior on introspection about himself and his past, as well as on several key case histories. His failure to offer more specific hypotheses—and to test them empirically—has been the source of many legitimate criticisms of Freudian theory.

Experimental Psychology and Behaviorism

The nineteenth century witnessed another critical development in approaches to understanding abnormal behavior: the beginning of the science of psychology. At the University of Leipzig, Wilhelm Wundt's (1842–1920) ambitious goal was to understand the nature of human consciousness. He attempted to achieve this end by using a technique called *introspection,* in which his subjects reported systematically and in detail about their inner experiences. Wundt's introspective method proved to be inadequate, and he failed in his attempt to detail the components of human consciousness. Still, Wundt made a profound and lasting contribution by scientifically studying psychological phenomena.

TABLE 2–1

Examples of Some Common Defense Mechanisms

DENIAL	Insistence that an experience, memory, or internal need did not occur or does not exist. For example, you completely block a painful experience from memory as if it never occurred.
DISPLACEMENT	Feelings or actions are transferred from one person or object to another that is less threatening. For example, you kick your dog when you are upset with your boss.
PROJECTION	Attributing one's own feelings or thoughts to other people. For example, a husband argues that his wife is angry at him when, in fact, he is angry at her.
RATIONALIZATION	Intellectually justifying a feeling or especially a disappointment. For example, after not getting the offer, you decide that a job you applied for was not the one you really wanted.
REACTION FORMATION	Converting a painful or unacceptable feeling into its opposite. For example, you "hate" a former lover, but underneath it all you still really love that person.
REPRESSION	Suppressing threatening material from consciousness, although you do not deny the memory when reminded of it. For example, you "forget" about an embarrassing experience.
SUBLIMATION	Diverting id impulses into constructive and acceptable outlets. For example, you study hard to get good grades rather than giving in to desires for immediate pleasure.

classical conditioning   Pavlov's form of learning through association. A conditioned response eventually is elicited by a conditioned stimulus after repeated pairings with an unconditioned stimulus (which produces an unconditioned response).

conditioned stimulus   A neutral stimulus that, when repeatedly paired with an unconditioned stimulus, comes to produce a conditioned response. In Pavlov's experiments, the bell was the conditioned stimulus. Central in classical conditioning.

conditioned response   A response that is elicited by a conditioned stimulus; similar to but weaker than the unconditioned response. Central in classical conditioning.

extinction   The gradual elimination of a response when learning conditions change. In classical conditioning, extinction occurs when a conditioned stimulus no longer is paired with an unconditioned stimulus. In operant conditioning, extinction occurs when the contingent is removed between behavior and its consequences.

operant conditioning   A learning theory asserting that behavior is a function of its consequences. Specifically, behavior increases if it is rewarded, and it decreases if it is punished.

positive reinforcement   Occurs when the onset of a stimulus increases the frequency of behavior (for example, you get paid for your work).

The two most prominent contributors to early learning theory and research were the Russian physiologist Ivan Pavlov (1849–1936) and the U.S. psychologist B. F. Skinner (1904–1990). These psychological scientists articulated, respectively, the principles of classical conditioning and operant conditioning—concepts that continue to be central to contemporary learning theory.

In his famous experiments, Pavlov (1928) rang a bell every time he fed meat powder to dogs. After repeated trials, the salivation that was produced by the sight of food came to be elicited by the sound of the bell alone. Pavlov developed his theory of **classical conditioning** based on these and related experiments. He defined an *unconditioned stimulus* (the meat powder) as a stimulus that automatically produces a reaction, that is, an *unconditioned response* (salivation). A **conditioned stimulus** (the bell) is a neutral stimulus that, when repeatedly paired with an unconditioned stimulus, comes to produce a **conditioned response** (salivation).[†] Finally, **extinction** occurs once a conditioned stimulus no longer is presented together with an unconditioned stimulus. Eventually, the conditioned stimulus no longer elicits the conditioned response.

Skinner's (1953) principle of **operant conditioning** asserts that behavior is a function of its consequences. Specifically, behavior increases if it is rewarded, and it decreases if it is punished. In his numerous studies of rats and pigeons in the famous "Skinner box," Skinner identified four different, crucial consequences of behavior. **Positive reinforcement** occurs when the onset of a

Psychologist B. F. Skinner (1904–1990) outlined the principles of operant conditioning. Skinner's determination to make psychology a science profoundly influenced the discipline in the twentieth century.

[†]*Note that the unconditioned response and the conditioned response are very similar (both involve salivation in this example). One difference, though, is that conditioned responses generally are somewhat weaker than unconditioned responses.*

further thoughts

An Outline of Freudian Theory

Freud divided the mind into three parts: the id, the ego, and the superego. He suggested that the **id** is present at birth and is the source of basic drives and motivations. The id houses biological drives, such as hunger, as well as two key psychological drives: sex and aggression. (Freud's term *libido* can be viewed as a synonym for sexual or life energy.) In Freudian theory, the id operates according to the *pleasure principle*—the impulses of the id seek immediate gratification and create discomfort or unrest until they are satisfied. Thus, in Freud's view, sexual or aggressive urges are akin to biological urges, like hunger.

The **ego** is the part of the personality that must deal with the realities of the world as it attempts to fulfill id impulses as well as perform other functions. Thus the ego operates on the *reality principle*. The ego begins to develop in the first year of life, and it continues to evolve, particularly during the preschool years. Unlike id impulses, which are primarily unconscious, much of the ego resides in conscious awareness.

The third part of the personality is the **superego,** which is roughly equivalent to the *conscience*. The superego contains societal standards of behavior, particularly rules that children learn from trying to be like their parents in their later preschool years. In Freud's view, societal rules are attempts to govern id impulses. For the individual, this means that the three parts of the personality are often in conflict with one another. The ego must constantly mediate between the demands of the id and the prescriptions of the superego. According to Freud, conflict between the superego and the ego produces *moral anxiety,* whereas conflict between the id and the ego produces *neurotic anxiety.*

Freud suggested that the ego protects itself by utilizing various **defense mechanisms,** unconscious processes that reduce conscious anxiety by distorting anxiety-producing memories, emotions, and impulses. For example, the defense of *projection* turns the tables psychologically. When you use projection, you project your own feelings on to someone else: "I'm not mad at you. You're mad at me!" According to Freud, projection and other defense mechanisms protect the ego from the conflict and anxiety produced by unacceptable id impulses. A list of some of the more important and familiar defenses can be found in Table 2–1. One index of Freud's continuing influence is the fact that all these defense mechanisms, and several additional ones, appear in an appendix in DSM-IV on issues requiring further study.

Freud also formulated a stage theory of child development, as we discuss briefly toward the end of this chapter. Freud highlighted sexual conflicts in his theory of *psychosexual development*. The most important psychosexual conflict is the **Oedipal conflict.** Freud reasoned that boys harbor forbidden sexual desires for their mothers. Because these impulses are both overwhelming and impossible to fulfill, boys typically resolve the dilemma between the ages of 4 and 6 by *identifying* with their fathers. In a sense, they fulfill their desire for their mother by adopting the actions and values of her spouse. In Freud's view, girls face a similar dilemma that he termed the *Electra complex.* Freud hypothesized that girls, unlike boys, do not desire their opposite-gender parent sexually as much as they yearn for something their fathers have and they are "missing"—a penis. This is the Freudian notion of "penis envy," which has been roundly criticized for being blatantly sexist.

It is not difficult to criticize other Freudian concepts as well. Many of these criticisms call the theory to task for being too vague, broad, and untestable. We certainly agree with these objections. We also recognize, however, that Freud offered a host of innovative and sometimes penetrating ideas. Some followers of psychoanalytic theory insist on interpreting Freud literally. We believe, however, that Freud would have criticized a literal interpretation of his theories, since he revised them often during the course of his life. In this spirit, we prefer to view Freud's ideas as broad metaphors. Freudian theory has few answers, but it offers many challenging concepts, some of which are worthy of attempts at careful definition and research.

---

negative reinforcement Occurs when the cessation of a stimulus increases the frequency of behavior (for example, a friend's nagging ends when you give in).

stimulus increases the frequency of behavior (for example, you get paid for your work). **Negative reinforcement** occurs when the cessation of a stimulus increases the frequency of behavior (when you give in to a nagging friend, thereby stopping the nagging). *Punishment* occurs when the introduction of a stimulus decreases the frequency of behavior (you spend less money after your parents scold you), and *response cost* is when the removal of a stimulus decreases the frequency of behavior (you no longer stay out late after your parents take away use of the car).[†] *Extinction* results from ending the contingency or association between a behavior and its consequences, similar to the concept of extinction in classical conditioning.

[†]*People frequently use the terms* negative reinforcement *and* punishment *interchangeably, but the two are quite different. With negative reinforcement, behavior becomes more frequent after an aversive stimulus is removed. With punishment, behavior becomes less frequent after an aversive stimulus is introduced.*

TABLE 2–2

Comparing Paradigm

TOPIC	BIOMEDICAL	PSYCHOANALYTIC	BEHAVIORAL	HUMANISTIC
Inborn human nature	Competitive, but some altruism	Aggressive, sexual	Neutral— a blank slate	Basic goodness
Cause of abnormality	Genes, neurochemistry, physical damage	Early childhood experiences	Social learning	Frustrations of society
Type of treatment	Medication, other somatic therapies	Psychodynamic therapy	Cognitive behavior therapy	Nondirective therapy
Paradigmatic focus	Bodily functions and structures	Unconscious mind	Observable behavior	Free will

behaviorism The belief within scientific psychology that observable behaviors, not unobservable cognitive or emotional states, are the appropriate focus of psychological study.

humanistic psychology A paradigm for conceptualizing abnormal behavior that rejects determinism and argues that human behavior is the product of free will—how people choose to act. Also adopts an explicitly positive view of human nature.

The person most responsible for applying learning theory to the study of abnormal behavior was the U.S. psychologist John B. Watson (1878–1958). Watson wanted to promote psychology as a science, and he founded the approach called **behaviorism,** arguing that observable behavior was the only appropriate subject matter for the science of psychology. Watson believed that thoughts and emotions could not be measured objectively; thus he rejected the study of these "internal events." In contrast to Freud, Watson did not offer an elaborate theory of the etiology of abnormal behavior. He did make the very important assumption that abnormal behavior was learned in much the same manner as normal behavior. In his well-known experiment with Little Albert, Watson and Rosalie Rayner (1920) used classical conditioning to induce an 11-month-old boy to fear a rat. They paired the sight of the rat with a loud noise, thus demonstrating that fears could be learned through classical conditioning. Although this was his most famous experiment, Watson and his followers were less concerned with etiology—how people learn abnormal behavior—than with treatment—how people learn new, more adaptive ways of coping with their difficulties.

Free Will and Humanistic Psychology

Abraham Maslow (1908–1970), Fritz Perls (1893–1970), and Carl Rogers (1902–1987) were the major advocates of **humanistic psychology,** a fourth major approach to conceptualizing abnormal behavior that did not emerge until the middle of the twentieth century. In many respects, humanistic psychology was a reaction against biomedical, psychoanalytic, and behavioral theories of abnormal behavior. Humanistic psychologists objected to the *determinism* of these approaches—the assumption that human behavior is caused by predictable and potentially knowable internal and/or external events. To humanistic psychologists, the very essence of humanity is *free will,* the idea that human behavior is *not* determined but is a product of how people choose to act. Humanistic psychology also is distinguished by its explicitly positive view of human behavior. Human nature is assumed to be inherently good, and humanistic psychologists, therefore, blame dysfunctional, abnormal, or aggressive behavior on society instead of on the individual. (See Table 2–2, where the assumptions of the four major approaches are compared.)

The assumption of free will makes it impossible to conduct research on the causes of normal or abnormal behavior, because free will, by definition, is not predictably determined. For this reason, humanistic psychology perhaps is best considered an alternative philosophy of human behavior, not an alternative psychological theory. In this regard, we note that the term *humanistic* must be considered carefully. All attempts to understand the etiology of psychopathology are humanistic in the sense that the ultimate goal is to improve the human condition.

paradigm A set of assumptions both about the substance of a theory and about how scientists should collect data and test theoretical propositions. The term was applied to the progress of science by Thomas Kuhn, an influential historian and philosopher.

systems theory An innovation in the philosophy of conceptualizing and conducting science that emphasizes interdependence, cybernetics, and especially holism—the idea that the whole is more than the sum of its parts. Often attributed to the biologist and philosopher Ludwig von Bertalanffy.

holism The assumption that the whole is more than the sum of its parts. A central tenet of systems theory, and counterpoint to reductionism.

Paradigms and the Causes of Abnormal Behavior

As we have noted, the biomedical, psychoanalytic, behavioral, and humanistic approaches are more than alternative theories of abnormal behavior (see Table 2–2). They are also alternative paradigms. A **paradigm** includes both the substance of a theory and a set of assumptions about how scientists should collect data and test theoretical propositions. The term *paradigm* was applied to the progress of science by Thomas Kuhn (1962), an influential historian and philosopher who argued that paradigms can both direct and misdirect scientists. Paradigms tell the researcher or clinician where and how to look for answers to questions, but sometimes the apparent guidance can be a hindrance. The assumptions made by a paradigm can act as blinders; they can lead an investigator to overlook what otherwise might be obvious. At the same time, however, sometimes paradigms open up new perspectives and avenues for research. For example, the four traditional paradigms of psychopathology make assumptions about the appropriate focus of abnormal psychology that sometimes are too narrow.

Each of these approaches has weaknesses—and strengths. The clash of paradigms has dominated abnormal psychology for half a century, but our concern is not to determine which approach is "right." Rather, our goal is to highlight the scientific understanding of the multifactorial causes of specific emotional disorders. In attempting to understand psychological disorders, we find promise in elements of each of the four traditional paradigms.

Systems Theory

Unlike the traditional paradigms, our approach to etiology begins with **systems theory,** an innovation in understanding and conducting science, not just psychology. The Austrian biologist and philosopher of science Ludwig von Bertalanffy (1901–1972), who taught in universities in Austria, England, Canada, and the United States, has been called the "father of systems theory" (Davidson, 1982). Systems theory, however, has multiple origins; its roots lie not only in psychology but also in engineering, computer science, biology, and philosophy. Systems theory has revolutionized scientific approaches within each of these disciplines and in other scientific fields as well (Davidson, 1982; Ford & Lerner, 1992; Gleick, 1987; Hinde, 1992; von Bertalanffy, 1968).

Holism

The central principle of systems theory is **holism,** the idea that the whole is more than the sum of its parts. This common statement can be illustrated with numerous familiar examples across many disciplines. A water molecule (H_2O) is much more than the sum of two hydrogen atoms and one oxygen atom. A human being is much more than the sum of a nervous system, an organ system, a circulatory system, and so on. Similarly, psychopathology is more than the sum of inborn temperament, early childhood experiences, and learning history. Psychopathology is more than the sum of nature and nurture. We can better appreciate the importance of the principle of holism when we consider its scientific counterpoint, *reductionism*. According to reductionist views, the whole *is* the sum of its parts, and the task for scientists is to divide the world into its smallest components.

The influence of reductionism is pervasive in everyday thinking about the causes of abnormal behavior (Cacioppo & Bernston, 1992). For example, when scientists discover that the depletion of certain chemicals in the brain accompanies depression, the public assumes that brain chemistry is *the* cause of depression. However, it is entirely possible that experiences such as a negative view of the world or living in a prejudiced society cause the changes in brain chemistry that accompany depression (see Chapter 5). That is, the "chemical imbalance in the brain" may be merely a consequence of adverse life experiences. Unfortunately, the public, and many scientists, seem to overlook this possibility, because reductionism assumes that truth comes in smaller and smaller packages.

Subsystems and Levels of Analysis

The principle of holism asserts that it is a mistake to view the smallest cause as *the* cause of something. Rather, smaller units are better conceived as *subsystems* within a larger system. The human circulatory system is an example of a subsystem of the human body, which is also made up of the skeletal, muscular, nervous, digestive, respiratory, and reproductive subsystems.

A far-out example can illustrate some implications of the concept of subsystems for reasoning about causality. Assume for a moment that three Martian scientists are sent to Earth to discover what causes those metallic vehicles to speed, sometimes recklessly and sometimes slowly, across the planet's landmass. One Martian, an ecologist by training, reports back that the vehicles (called "automobiles," the scientist discovers) move at different speeds based on the width of the black paths on which they are set, whether the paths are straight or curved, and the presence of some unexplained phenomenon known as "radar traps." A second Martian, a psychologist, disagrees. This scientist notes that the speed of automobiles is determined by the age, gender, and mood of the individual who sits inside them. Together these factors cause automobiles to move at different speeds. The third scientist, a physicist, derides the other two for their simplistic thinking. This Martian notes that the speed of automobiles is caused by a chemical process that occurs inside an antiquated machine called an internal combustion engine. The process involves oxygen, fuel, and heat and results in mechanical energy.

In this example, it is obvious that the most reductionistic, or *molecular,* explanation is no more (or less) accurate than the most general, or *molar,* one. Reductionist traditions in science often lead us to believe that the most molecular account (biological or biochemical) is the ultimate explanation of causality (Alessi, 1992; Rachlin, 1992). The Martian example, however, demonstrates the potential fallacy of blind reductionism.

The Martian example also suggests an important way of integrating information about multiple influences on the development of psychopathology. Various subsystems can be conceptualized as different *levels of analysis* for conceptualizing causal factors (Hinde, 1992). The biological, psychological, and social approaches to psychopathology are potentially compatible explanations at different levels of analysis. Each approach uses a different lens to analyze the subject; one is a microscope, another a magnifying glass, and the third a telescope. In fact, the various academic disciplines also can be ordered according to levels of analysis (Schwartz, 1982). The use of a different "lens" by different academic disciplines does not make one approach right and the others wrong.

Causality: Multiple Factors and Multiple Pathways

We want you to recognize that the biological, psychological, and social levels of analysis simply can be different ways of conceptualizing the same problem. It is also true, however, that a specific abnormality might occur within any one of these subsystems. In the Martian example, an engine might break down, a driver might be reckless, or a road could be washed out. Similarly, the cause of any one type of abnormal behavior might be located primarily within biological, psychological, or social functioning. Scientists hope to identify such specific causes at one or another level of analysis for at least some psychological problems.

Our caution, however, is that, with current technology, scientists can only rarely attribute *differences* in biological, psychological, or social functioning to *disturbances* or abnormalities within the same level of analysis. When scientists identify a chemical imbalance in the brain that is associated with depression, for example, we cannot yet determine whether the imbalance is an inborn abnormality that causes depression, or whether the imbalance was reaction to a stressful life event. The same cautions about interpretation apply to molar life experiences. For example, genetically determined personality traits may make some people more likely to experience difficult life events (McGue & Lykken, 1992).

Our point is this: It is not enough to focus on one subsystem or level of analysis. Ultimately, we must understand the relations among biological, psychological, and social functioning. In fact,

diatesis   A predisposition to disorder. Also known as *vulnerability*. A diathesis only causes abnormal behavior when it is combined with a stress or challenging experience.

stress   An event that creates physiological or psychological strain for the individual. Stress has been defined differently by various scientists.

many emotional problems apparently are caused by a *combination* of biological, psychological, and social risk factors.

THE DIATHESIS-STRESS MODEL

The *diathesis-stress model* is a useful way of conceptualizing how multiple risk factors may interact to produce a mental disorder. A **diathesis** is a predisposition toward developing a disorder, for example, an inherited tendency toward depression. A **stress** is a difficult life experience, for example, the loss of a loved one through an unexpected death (see Chapter 8). The diathesis-stress model indicates that mental disorders develop only when a stress is added on top of a predisposition; neither the diathesis nor the stress alone is sufficient to cause the disorder.

We commonly think that a diathesis must be a biological risk factor, such as a genetic predisposition. However, a psychological characteristic such as an aggressive personality style can also be a diathesis for a particular disorder. Similarly, a stress need not be a psychological factor. A stress could be a biological experience, such as an injury or an infection.

Although it is a very useful concept, one limitation of the diathesis-stress model is the implication that disorders are caused by the combination of two risk factors. As we have noted, however, some mental disorders may be produced by the combination of several biological, psychological, and/or social risk factors. It also is true, moreover, that a disorder may have several different causes. In some circumstances, many risk factors may be involved in the disorder's etiology. In other cases, a diathesis—or a stress—may be so powerful that the single risk factor produces the disorder.

EQUIFINALITY OR MULTIPLE PATHWAYS

Systems theory articulates the principle of *equifinality,* the idea that the *same* psychological disorder may have *different* causes. For this reason, we also refer to the principle of equifinality in terms of *multiple pathways.*

To help you appreciate the principle of equifinality, let us pose a simple question: What is the cause of automobile accidents? Of course, automobile accidents have many different causes. A car accident may be caused by a single defect, such as faulty brakes or a drunk driver. Or a car accident may be caused by a combination of risk factors, such as excessive speed, a wet road, and worn tires. It would be fruitless to search for *the* cause of automobile accidents, because car accidents have many causes, not one.

Similarly, there may be many different causes for the same psychological disorder. In some cases, depression may be caused primarily by abnormal brain chemistry. In other cases, depression may be caused by a pessimistic style of interpretation. In still other circumstances, a serious personal loss may cause an episode of depression.

Reciprocal Causality and Control Processes

Reciprocal causality, the idea that causality is bidirectional, is one of the most important processes identified by systems theory. According to linear assumptions, causation operates in one direction only: Parents cause their children to behave in a certain way, for example. Both formal reviews of the literature and informal observations by millions of parents indicate, however, that children also change their parents' behavior (Bell, 1968; Maccoby, 1992). Such mutual influences define reciprocal causality, a process that occurs in all types of natural interaction. Psychologists cause rats to press the bar in a Skinner box, but rats also cause scientists to feed them, as the cartoon on this page illustrates.

Cybernetics, another critical control process, uses *feedback loops* to adjust progress toward a goal. The operation of a thermostat is a good example of a simple cybernetic process. Air temperature is monitored continuously to maintain room temperature within a constant range by either turning on or shutting off a heat source.

The concept of cybernetics is essential to understanding *homeostasis*—the tendency to maintain a steady state. The systems concept of homeostasis is familiar in biology, but it is also widely applicable in psychology. For example, people attempt to maintain a balance between too

"Boy, have I got this guy conditioned! Every time I press the bar down he drops a piece of food."

little stimulation and too much stress or anxiety. Some people are thrill seekers. They find that challenging activities like skydiving provide the right balance between the push of boredom and the pull of excitement. Other people are timid, and they find an equilibrium between the need for novelty and fear of the unknown in a limited and carefully controlled world. The setpoints for optimal levels of stimulation differ like the hotter and cooler settings on a thermostat, but all people engage in the homeostatic process of finding an individualized balance between too little and too much stimulation.

Development

Homeostasis maintains equilibrium, but change is also essential in systems. *Development* is the most basic source of change. Over time, people follow a fairly predictable trajectory of change. Children learn to crawl, walk, and run in an established sequence, and their cognitive skills also unfold in a predictable manner. Development, though, is not limited to children or to the physical and intellectual domains. Development continues throughout adult life, and predictable changes occur in both psychological and social experiences.

Because people develop and change over time, knowledge of normal development is essential to understanding psychopathology. *Developmental psychopathology* is a new approach to abnormal psychology that emphasizes the importance of *developmental norms*—age-graded averages—to determining what constitutes abnormal behavior (Cicchetti & Cohen, 1995; Rutter & Garmezy, 1983). Developmental norms tell us that a full-blown temper tantrum is normal at 2 years of age, for example, but that kicking and screaming to get one's own way is abnormal at the age of 22. Similarly, we need to understand the developmental progression of a difficult psychological experience like normal grief in order to recognize when mourning should be considered pathological (too intense) or unresolved (too long-lasting).

For these reasons, we frequently consider questions about normal development in this textbook on abnormal psychology. We also discuss the development of abnormal behavior itself. Many psychological disorders follow unique developmental patterns. Sometimes there is a characteristic *premorbid history,* a pattern of behavior that precedes the onset of the disorder. People with schizophrenia, for example, often are withdrawn and awkward before the onset of their psychosis.

A disorder may also have a predictable course, or *prognosis,* for the future. When schizophrenia is untreated, the condition often deteriorates—psychotic symptoms may improve, but day-to-day coping becomes less adequate (see Chapter 13). By discussing the premorbid adjustment and the course of different psychological disorders, we hope to present abnormal behavior as a moving picture of development and not just as a diagnostic snapshot.

The remainder of this chapter is divided into sections on biological, psychological, and social factors in the development of psychopathology. In each of these sections we focus most of our discussion on normal development. This material forms a basis for our critical consideration of the causes of abnormal behavior in subsequent chapters on specific psychological disorders.

Biological Factors

We begin our discussion of biological factors by considering the smallest anatomic unit within the nervous system, the neuron or nerve cell. Next, we present an overview of the major brain structures and current knowledge of their primary behavioral functions. We then turn to a discussion of psychophysiology, the effect of psychological experience on the functioning of various body systems. Finally, we consider the broadest of all biological influences, the effect of genes on behavior.

In considering biological influences, it is helpful to note the distinction between the study of biological structures and of biological functions. The field of *anatomy* is concerned with the study of biological structures, and the field of *physiology* investigates biological functions. *Neuroanatomy* and *neurophysiology* are subspecialties within these broader fields that focus specifically on brain structures and brain functions.

neuron The nerve cells that form the basic building blocks of the brain. Each neuron is composed of the soma or cell body, the dendrites, the axon, and the terminal buttons.

soma The cell body and largest part of the neuron where most of the neuron's metabolism and maintenance are controlled and performed.

dendrites "Branches" from the soma of the neuron that serve the primary function of receiving messages from other cells.

axon The trunk of the neuron where messages are transmitted outward toward other cells with which a given neuron communicates.

terminal buttons Buds found on the small branches at the end of the axon where messages are sent from one neuron to other neurons.

synapse A small gap filled with fluid that lies between the axon of one neuron and a dendrite or soma of another neuron.

neurotransmitters Chemical substances that are released into the synapse between two neurons and carry signals from the terminal button of one neuron to the receptors of another.

receptors Sites on the dendrites or soma of a neuron that are sensitive to certain neurotransmitters.

reuptake The process of recapturing some neurotransmitters in the synapse before they reach the receptors of another cell and returning the chemical substances to the terminal button. The neurotransmitter then is reused in subsequent neural transmission.

Figure 2–1   The Neuron.   The anatomic structure of the neuron, or nerve cell.

Source: Adapted from *Fundamentals of Human Neuropsychology,* 2nd ed., by Brian Kolb and Ian Q. Whislaw. Copyright © 1980, 1985, by W.H. Freeman and Company. Reprinted with permission.

The Neuron and Neurotransmitters

Billions of tiny nerve cells—**neurons**—form the basic building blocks of the brain. Each neuron has four major anatomic components: the soma or cell body, the dendrites, the axon, and the terminal buttons (see Figure 2–1). The **soma**—the cell body and largest part of the neuron—is where most of the neuron's metabolism and maintenance are controlled and performed. The **dendrites** branch out from the soma; they serve the primary function of receiving messages from other cells. The **axon** is the trunk of the neuron. Messages are transmitted down the axon toward other cells with which a given neuron communicates. Finally, the **terminal buttons** are "buds" found on the small branches at the end of the axon where messages are sent out to other neurons (Barondes, 1993).

Scientists have made great strides in deciphering the neurophysiological processes involved in communication within and among neurons. Within each neuron, information is transmitted as a change in electrical potential that moves from the dendrites and cell body, along the axon, toward the terminal buttons. The terminal buttons are separated from other cells by a **synapse,** a small gap filled with fluid. Neurons typically have synapses with thousands of other cells (see Figure 2–2).

Unlike the electrical communication within a neuron, information is transmitted chemically across a synapse to other neurons. The terminal buttons release chemical substances called **neurotransmitters** into the synapse, which are received at the **receptors** on the dendrites or soma of another neuron. Dozens of different chemical compounds serve as neurotransmitters in the brain, and the functions of particular neurotransmitters vary. Moreover, different receptor sites are more or less responsive to particular neurotransmitters.

Not all neurotransmitters cross the synapse and reach the receptors on another neuron. The process of **reuptake** captures some neurotransmitters in the synapse and returns the chemical substances to the terminal button. The neurotransmitter then is reused in subsequent neural transmission.

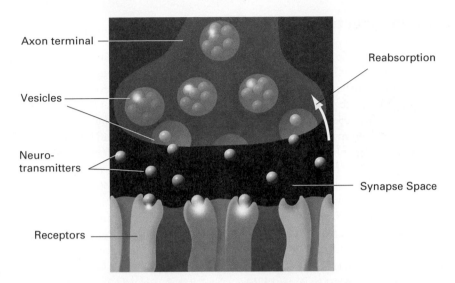

Figure 2–2   Synaptic Transmission.   When an electircal nerve impulse reaches the end of a neuron, synaptic vesicles release neurotransmitters into the synapse. The chemical transmission between cells is complete when neurotransmitters travel to receptor sites on another neuron.

Source: Keith Kasnot, Copyright National Geographic Image Collection.

In addition to the neurotransmitters, a second type of chemical affects communication in the brain. **Neuromodulators** are chemicals that may be released from neurons or from endocrine glands (which we will discuss shortly). Neuromodulators can influence communication among many neurons by affecting the functioning of neurotransmitters, although neuromodulators are not thought to act directly as neurotransmitters (Ciaranello et al., 1995). Neuromodulators often affect regions of the brain that are quite distant from where they were released. The most familiar neuromodulators are the *endorphins*—chemicals that have a structure similar to that of the drug opium (see Chapter 11). Thus they are often referred to as *opioids*. The endorphins were discovered in the 1970s, but active research is still being conducted on their possible role in a number of emotional disorders (Barondes, 1993; Nemeroff & Bissette, 1986).

neuromodulators   Chemicals such as endorphins that may be released from neurons or from endocrine glands. Neuromodulators can influence communication among many neurons, and they often affect regions of the brain that are quite distant from where they were released.

NEUROTRANSMITTERS AND THE ETIOLOGY OF PSYCHOPATHOLOGY

Scientists have found that disrupted communication among neurons, particularly disruptions in the functioning of various neurotransmitters, plays a role in the etiology of several types of abnormal behavior. An oversupply of certain neurotransmitters is found in some mental disorders, an undersupply in other cases, and disturbances in reuptake in other psychological problems. In addition, the density and/or sensitivity of postsynaptic receptors has been implicated as playing a role in some forms of abnormal behavior.

Much research linking mental disorders with neurotransmitters has investigated how drugs affect the symptoms of a disorder and how they alter brain chemistry. For example, medications that alleviate some of the symptoms of schizophrenia are known to affect the availability of the neurotransmitter *dopamine* in the brains of animals (see Chapter 13). (Scientists cannot currently measure neurotransmitters in the living human brain, so neurotransmitter levels must be inferred either from animal studies or from indirect measures in humans.) These and related findings suggest that abnormalities in the dopamine system in the brain may be involved in the development of schizophrenia. Other evidence links disruptions in the functioning of various neurotransmitters with different forms of abnormal behavior, as we discuss throughout the text.

cerebellum Part of the hindbrain that serves as a control center in helping to coordinate physical movements. The cerebellum receives information on body movements and integrates this feedback with directives about desired actions from higher brain structures.

reticular activating system Located in the midbrain, but extending into the pons and medulla as well. Regulates sleeping and waking and sexual behavior.

thalamus A part of the limbic system that is involved in receiving and integrating sensory information both from the sense organs and from higher brain structures.

hypothalamus A part of the limbic system that plays a role in sensation, but more importantly it controls basic biological urges, such as eating, drinking, and sexual activity, as well as much of the functioning of the autonomic nervous system.

cerebral hemispheres The two major structures of the forebrain and the site of most sensory, emotional, and cognitive processes. The functions of the cerebral hemispheres are lateralized. In general, the left cerebral hemisphere is involved in language and related functions, and the right side is involved in spatial organization and analysis.

Major Brain Structures

Neuroanatomists divide the brain into three subdivisions: the hindbrain, the midbrain, and the forebrain. Basic bodily functions are regulated by the structures of the *hindbrain,* which include the medulla, pons, and cerebellum. The *medulla* controls various bodily functions involved in sustaining life, including heart rate, blood pressure, and respiration. The *pons* serves functions in regulating stages of sleep. The **cerebellum** serves as a control center in helping to coordinate physical movements. The cerebellum receives information on body movements and integrates this feedback with directives from higher brain structures about desired actions. Few forms of abnormal behavior are identified with disturbances in the hindbrain, because the hindbrain's primary role is limited to supervising these basic physical functions (Matthysse & Pope, 1986).

The *midbrain* also is involved in the control of some motor activities, especially those related to fighting and sex. Much of the **reticular activating system** is located in the midbrain, although it extends into the pons and medulla as well. The reticular activating system regulates sleeping and waking. Damage to areas of the midbrain can cause extreme disturbances in sexual behavior, aggressiveness, and sleep, but such abnormalities typically result from specific and unusual brain traumas or tumors (Matthysse & Pope, 1986).

Most of the human brain consists of the *forebrain.* The forebrain evolved more recently than the hindbrain and midbrain and therefore is the location of most sensory, emotional, and cognitive processes. These higher mental processes of the forebrain are linked with the midbrain and hindbrain by the limbic system. The *limbic system* is made up of a variety of different brain structures that are central to the regulation of emotion and basic learning processes. Two of the most important components of the limbic system are the thalamus and the hypothalamus. The **thalamus** is involved in receiving and integrating sensory information both from the sense organs and from higher brain structures. The **hypothalamus** also plays a role in sensation, but its more important functions are behavioral ones. The hypothalamus controls basic biological urges, such as eating, drinking, and sexual activity. Much of the functioning of the autonomic nervous system (which we will discuss shortly) also is directed by the hypothalamus.

CEREBRAL HEMISPHERES

Most of the forebrain is composed of the two **cerebral hemispheres**. Many brain functions are *lateralized,* so that one hemisphere serves a specialized role as the site of specific cognitive and emotional activities. In general, the *left cerebral hemisphere* is involved in language and related functions, and the *right cerebral hemisphere* is involved in spatial organization and analysis. The lateralization and localization of certain brain functions often make it possible to pinpoint brain damage based solely on behavioral difficulties.

The two cerebral hemispheres are connected by the *corpus callosum,* which is involved in coordinating the different functions that are performed by the left and the right hemispheres of the brain. When we view a cross section of the forebrain, four connected chambers, or *ventricles,* become apparent. The ventricles are filled with cerebrospinal fluid, and they become enlarged in some psychological and neurological disorders.

Calvin and Hobbes by Bill Watterson

The **cerebral cortex** is the uneven surface area of the brain that lies just underneath the skull. It is the site of the control and integration of sophisticated memory, sensory, and motor functions. The cerebral cortex is divided into four lobes. The *frontal lobe,* located just behind the forehead, is involved in controlling a number of complex functions, including reasoning, planning, emotion, speech, and movement. The *parietal lobe,* located at the top and back of the head, receives and integrates sensory information and also plays a role in spatial reasoning. The *temporal lobe,* located beneath much of the frontal and parietal lobes, processes sound and smell, regulates emotions, and is involved in some aspects of learning, memory, and language. Finally, the *occipital lobe,* located behind the temporal lobe, receives and interprets visual information.

MAJOR BRAIN STRUCTURES AND THE ETIOLOGY OF PSYCHOPATHOLOGY

The brain is incredibly complex, and scientists are only beginning to understand the relations among various anatomic structures and functions. Because of the rudimentary knowledge we have about the brain, only obvious brain injuries and infections and the most severe mental disorders have clearly been linked with abnormalities in neuroanatomy. In most of these cases, brain damage is extensive. For example, during a *stroke,* blood vessels in the brain rupture, cutting off the supply of oxygen to parts of the brain and thereby killing surrounding brain tissue. This in turn disrupts the functioning of nearby healthy neurons because the brain cannot remove the dead tissue.

Scientists have made breakthroughs in observing the anatomic structure of the living brain and in recording some of its global physiological processes. These various imaging procedures are now being used to study psychological disorders ranging from schizophrenia to learning disabilities; they are discussed in Chapter 4, along with several methods of psychological assessment.

At present, the new brain imaging measures are more exciting technically than practically in terms of their contributions to furthering our understanding of the etiology of psychopathology. Scientific advances frequently follow the development of new measures, however, and there is every reason to hope that advances in brain imaging will lead to improvements in understanding abnormalities in brain structure and function.

Psychophysiology

Psychophysiology is the study of changes in the functioning of the body that result from psychological experiences. Some of these physical reactions to environmental provocations are familiar. A pounding heart, a flushed face, tears, sexual excitement, and numerous other reactions are psychophysiological responses. These and other psychophysiological responses reflect a person's psychological state, particularly the degree and perhaps the type of the individual's emotional arousal.

AUTONOMIC NERVOUS SYSTEM

The more familiar and basic system of communication within the body is the *nervous system.* The human nervous system is divided into the *central nervous system,* which includes the brain and the spinal cord, and the *peripheral nervous system.* The peripheral nervous system includes all connections that stem out from the central nervous system and innervate the body's muscles, sensory systems, and organs.

The peripheral nervous system itself has two subdivisions. The *voluntary,* or *somatic nervous, system* governs muscular control, and the *involuntary,* or **autonomic nervous system,** regulates the functions of various body organs, such as the heart and stomach. The somatic nervous system controls intentional or voluntary actions like scratching your nose. The autonomic nervous system is responsible for psychophysiological reactions—responses that occur with little or no conscious control.

The autonomic nervous system can be further divided into two branches, the sympathetic and parasympathetic nervous systems. In general, the **sympathetic nervous system** controls activities associated with increased arousal and energy expenditure, and the **parasympathetic nervous system** controls the slowing of arousal and energy conservation. Thus the two branches work somewhat in opposition to each other as a means of maintaining homeostasis.

cerebral cortex   The uneven surface of the brain that lies just underneath the skull, and controls and integrates sophisticated memory, sensory, and motor functions.

psychophysiology   The study of changes in the functioning of the body that result from psychological experiences.

autonomic nervous system   The division of the peripheral nervous system that regulates the functions of various bodily organs such as the heart and stomach. The actions of the autonomic nervous system are largely involuntary, and it has two branches, the sympathetic and parasympathetic nervous systems.

sympathetic nervous system   The branch of the autonomic nervous system that generally controls psychophysiological activities associated with increased arousal and energy expenditure.

parasympathetic nervous system   The branch of the autonomic nervous system that generally controls the slowing of psychopsysiological arousal and energy conservation.

This cross-sectional image of the brain shows the ventricles, four connected chambers that are filled with cerebrospinal fluid.

genes   Ultramicroscopic units of DNA that carry information about heredity. Located on the chromosomes.

chromosomes   Chainlike structures found in the nucleus of cells that carry genes and information about heredity. Humans normally have 23 pairs of chromosomes.

behavior genetics   The study of broad genetic contributions to the development of normal and abnormal behavior.

monozygotic (MZ) twins   Identical twins produced from a single fertilized egg; thus MZ twins have identical genotypes.

dizygotic (DZ) twins   Fraternal twins produced from separate fertilized eggs. Like all siblings, DZ twins share an average of 50 percent of their genes.

PSYCHOPHYSIOLOGY AND THE ETIOLOGY OF PSYCHOPATHOLOGY

Both psychophysiological overarousal and underarousal have been implicated in various theories of the causes of abnormal behavior. For example, autonomic overactivity is hypothesized to be responsible for excessive anxiety (see Chapter 6). In contrast, some theories suggest that chronic autonomic underarousal is responsible for the indifference to social rules and the failure to learn from punishment that characterize antisocial personality disorder (see Chapter 9).

Other theories of psychophysiology and abnormal behavior do not focus on dysfunctions in the autonomic nervous system. Instead, they emphasize psychophysiological assessment as a way of objectively measuring atypical reactions to psychological events. Scientists have developed numerous methods of measuring psychophysiological activity, ranging from assessments of sexual response to indices of muscle tension. We examine some of these psychophysiological measures in Chapter 4.

Behavior Genetics

The study of genetics is both the most molecular and the most molar approach to examining biological influences on behavior. **Genes** are ultramicroscopic units of DNA that carry information about heredity. Genes are located on **chromosomes,** chainlike structures found in the nucleus of cells. Humans normally have 23 pairs of chromosomes. The field of *genetics* identifies specific genes and their hereditary functions, often by literally focusing at the level of molecules. Geneticists typically have training in biochemistry, not psychology.

Behavior genetics is a much more molar approach that studies genetic influences on the evolution and development of normal and abnormal behavior (Goldsmith, 1988; McGuffin et al., 1994; Plomin, DeFries, & McClearn, 1990; Scarr, 1992). Behavior geneticists study various human characteristics in an attempt to demonstrate that the behavior has a more or less genetic origin. Behavior geneticists seldom posit specific genetic causes of a disorder, however, and they rarely study individual genes.

Behavior geneticists have developed innovative methods for studying broad, genetic contributions to behavior. The most important behavior genetic methods are twin studies, adoption studies, and family incidence studies.

TWIN STUDIES

Identical, or **monozygotic (MZ),** twins are produced from a single fertilized egg. One egg is fertilized by one sperm; thus MZ twins have identical genotypes. *Fraternal,* or **dizygotic (DZ),** twins are produced from separate fertilized eggs. There are two eggs and two sperm. Thus, like all siblings, DZ twins share an average of 50 percent of their genes, whereas MZ twins share 100 percent of their genes. Of course, most MZ and DZ twin pairs are raised in the same family. Thus the two types of twins differ in their degree of genetic similarity, but they are alike in their environmental experiences.

Comparisons between MZ and DZ twin pairs, therefore, can shed light on the genetic and environmental contributions to a disorder. The key comparison involves determining whether MZ twins are more alike than DZ twins are alike. In the case of psychological disorders, the measure of interest is the degree of *concordance* between the twin pairs. A twin pair is concordant when both twins either have the same disorder or are free from the disorder. The twin pair is discordant when one twin has the disorder but the other does not.

If we assume that the environmental effects on a disorder are the same for DZ twin pairs as they are for MZ twin pairs, then any differences between the concordance rates for MZ and DZ twins must be caused by genetics. If a disorder is purely genetic, for example, scientists should find a concordance rate of 100 percent for MZ twins (who are genetically identical) and 50 percent for DZ twins (who share half of the same genes on average).

In contrast, similar concordance rates for MZ and DZ twins rule out genetic contributions and instead implicate environmental causes of a disorder. Environmental causes are implicated regardless of whether the concordance rates for MZ and DZ twins are both 0 percent, both 100 percent, or both anywhere in between. However, the level of concordance does provide information about the nature of the environmental contribution. Higher concordance rates for both MZ and DZ twins point to the etiological role of the *shared environment,* for example, the experience of a parental divorce or growing up in poverty. Because both MZ and DZ pairs have similarly high concordance rates, we know that genes do not explain the high concordance. Instead, the common cause must be found in the environment shared by the twins.

In contrast, similar but low concordance rates for both MZ and DZ pairs point to the influence of the *nonshared environment,* for example, being the favored child. In this case, genetic causes are again ruled out, and the importance of unique experiences is indicated by the fact that only one twin has a psychological disorder (Goldsmith, 1988; Plomin, 1994).

All of this reasoning depends on the assumption that the environment affects DZ twins in the same way that it influences MZ twins. A number of critics have questioned this assumption. One important question is whether MZ twins, because of their striking physical resemblance, are treated more similarly than DZ twins. If so, then higher concordance rates for MZ twins might result from more similar environmental experiences and not from more similar genetic endowments. To address this criticism, many scientists have used another method of behavior genetic research, namely, adoption studies.

ADOPTION STUDIES

Adoption studies also provide evidence on the genetic versus the environmental contributions to the development of a disorder. In this research design, people who have been adopted as infants are compared with their biological versus their adoptive relatives (usually their parents) in terms of concordance for a disorder. If concordance is higher for biological than for adoptive relatives, then genetic factors are involved, because adopted children share their biological relatives' genes but not their environment. On the other hand, if children are more similar to their adoptive than to their biological relatives, then environment must influence the characteristic, because adopted children share their adoptive relatives' environment but not their genes. Adoption studies also have some potential problems, for example, the fact that adoption placement is selective. Still, you can be confident in the findings of behavior genetic research when adoption and twin studies produce similar results (Goldsmith, 1988; Plomin, 1994).

FAMILY INCIDENCE STUDIES

The family incidence study deserves brief mention, if only because findings from these studies are often misinterpreted. Family incidence studies ask whether diseases "run in families." Investigators identify normal and ill *probands,* or index cases, and tabulate the frequency with which other members of their families suffer from the same disorder. If a higher prevalence of illness is found in families where there is an ill proband, this is consistent with genetic causation. The finding also is consistent with environmental causation, however, because families share environments as well as genes. For this reason, no firm conclusions about the relative role of genes or the environment can be reached from family incidence studies alone.

MISINTERPRETING BEHAVIOR GENETICS FINDINGS

The methods of behavior genetics research are powerful, and mounting evidence indicates that genes contribute to a wide variety of psychological disorders. Unfortunately, people often misinterpret findings from behavior genetic research.

One serious misinterpretation is that, if it has a genetic component, the emergence of a psychological disorder is inevitable, even predestined. This conclusion is wrong, in part, because of polygenic inheritance. The probabilities of alternative outcomes are easily identified for simple dominant/recessive inheritance, but predicting the likelihood of a disorder is far more difficult for polygenic transmission. Moreover, genetics alone does not cause the vast majority of emotional

Monozygotic (MZ) twins are identical; they develop from a single fertilized egg. Dizygotic (DZ) twins are fraternal; they develop from two different fertilized eggs.

disorders. Behavior genetics studies of mental illnesses typically find concordance rates for MZ twins that are well below 100 percent. Thus genes may predispose someone toward developing a psychological problem, but the disorder emerges only when the predisposition is combined with environmental stressors.

It also is wrong to think that genetic characteristics cannot be modified or controlled. For example, even in cases where mental retardation has a known genetic cause, certain environmental experiences such as diet or early stimulation have been demonstrated to lead to substantial increases—or decreases—in IQ (Turkheimer, 1991). The conclusion "It's genetic" does not provide an excuse for accepting the status quo. With rare exceptions, society remains responsible for helping people to maximize their genetic potential, and individuals remain personally responsible for their actions.

Finally, it is not clear what mechanism, or *mediating process,* may explain the genetic contribution to a disorder. For example, researchers have found genetic contributions to adult criminality, but there obviously are no genes that predetermine assault, armed robbery, and so on. The critical question is: What partially inherited mediating process accounts for the behavior genetics finding? In the case of criminal behavior, one possible mediating process is the inheritance of a chronically underaroused autonomic nervous system. Thus some people may be more likely to engage in criminal acts because they are less fearful and less likely to learn from experience (see Chapter 9).

GENETICS AND THE ETIOLOGY OF PSYCHOPATHOLOGY

There can be no doubt that genes have very broad effects on abnormal behavior, despite our cautions about interpreting behavior genetics research. Most influences appear to be polygenic; thus psychologists continue to be vexed by the question of where to draw the line between normal and abnormal behavior. Still, a relatively small number of genes may contribute to certain disorders, and the identification of specific genes could lead to breakthroughs in diagnosis and treatment.

Genes partially determine *individual differences,* or why people are different from one another. Genes also are basic to determining *species-typical characteristics*—characteristics that people have in common as a part of all human nature. We consider species-typical characteristics—basic human nature—as part of our next topic, psychological factors in abnormal behavior.

Psychological Factors

Proponents of the psychoanalytic, behavioral, and humanistic paradigms have clashed in theorizing about the etiology of psychopathology. Psychologists are struggling to define common ground, however, and common themes can be found across all approaches. We highlight four such topics in our discussion of psychological factors and the causes of abnormal behavior: basic human motivation, emotion, and temperament; learning and cognition; the sense of self; and stages of psychological development.

Motivation, Emotion, and Temperament

The foundation of any psychological theory is formed in its assumptions about human nature. In fact, we have already compared the traditional paradigms in terms of this essential starting assumption (see Table 2–2). What are our basic psychological motivations—motivations that we may or may not share with other animals?

ATTACHMENT THEORY

A basic psychological need is the need to form close relationships, the focus of detailed theorizing by the influential British psychiatrist John Bowlby (1907–1990). Bowlby was trained in psychoanalysis, but he explicitly rejected Freudian theory by placing the need to form close relationships at the core of his view of development (Bowlby, 1969, 1982). The heart of Bowlby's theory is the observation that infants form **attachments** early in life—that is, they develop special and selective bonds with their caregivers.

Bowlby based attachment theory on findings from *ethology,* the study of animal behavior. Ethologists have documented that close relationships develop between infants and caregivers in many species of animals. In some species, selective relationships develop in the first hours or days of life, a process called *imprinting.* Attachments are far more flexible than imprinting, but like other animals, human infants become distressed when separated from their caregivers. Their displays of distress—long and loud cries—keep caregivers in proximity. Proximity between infants and their caregivers has survival value; thus Bowlby theorized that attachment behavior developed as a result of natural selection.

DOMINANCE RELATIONS

The development of attachments, or more generally of *affiliation,* is only one of two basic social behaviors studied by ethologists. The second is the development of **dominance,** the hierarchical ordering of a social group into more and less powerful members (Sloman, Gardner, & Price, 1989). Dominance hierarchies are easily observed in human as well as animal social groups; thus it would seem that we also share this pattern of behavior with other animals. Note that the development of dominance relations in humans is not inconsistent with Maslow's theory that people need to be esteemed or valued by others.

Thus we conclude that, in addition to more basic biological needs, humans have at least two, sometimes competing, psychological motivations: to form attachments and to compete for dominance. Some contemporary psychoanalytic theorists view the Freudian drives for sex and aggression not as literal instincts but as broad metaphors, much like the contemporary social motivations of affiliation and dominance (Cameron & Rychlak, 1985).

EMOTIONS AND EMOTIONAL SYSTEMS

To this point, we have discussed basic psychological motivations at the level of social behavior—but how are they represented within the individual? Many contemporary theorists assert that key social interactions are motivated by **emotions,** internal feeling states, much like searching for food is motivated by hunger. For example, attachment behavior is motivated both by the fear experienced during separations and by the security felt by infant and caretaker during close contact.

We have hundreds of words for different emotions in the English language, but researchers have used statistical analysis to reduce the list to six basic emotions (National Advisory Mental Health Council, 1995):

- Love
- Joy
- Surprise
- Anger
- Sadness
- Fear

This list can be grouped into the even smaller classifications of *positive emotion* and *negative emotion.* Of course, negative emotions are most relevant to abnormal psychology, and we have separate chapters that focus primarily on sadness (Chapter 5) and fear (Chapter 6); anger is considered in relation to a number of different disorders.

Negative emotions tend to occur together, but somewhat surprisingly, negative emotions also tend to occur together with positive emotions. Apparently, different brain systems process positive and negative emotions. More generally, it is useful to think of emotions in terms of *emotional systems* instead of discrete feelings. That is, experiences may not activate a single isolated feeling, but

attachments   Selective bonds that develop between infants and their caregivers, usually their parents, and are theorized to be related to later development. Analogous to the process imprinting which has been observed in many animals.

dominance   The hierarchical ordering of a social group into more and less powerful members. Dominance rankings are indexed by the availability of uncontested privileges.

emotion   A state of arousal that is defined by subjective feeling states, such as sadness, anger, and disgust. Emotions are often accompanied by physiological changes, such as in heart rate and respiration rate.

temperament   Characteristic styles of relating to the world that are often conceptualized as inborn traits. Generally emphasizes the "how" as opposed to the "what" of behavior.

instead different events may elicit a group of emotions related to a particular social motivation (Panksepp, 1988). For example, fear and security are complementary emotions, not separate feelings, in the attachment system. Together these feelings motivate infants and caretakers to maintain proximity. Other emotional systems may include the rage–fear emotional system associated with fight or flight (see Chapter 8) and the security–anger–sadness emotional constellation linked with grief (see Chapter 15).

The concept of emotional systems is consistent with evolutionary theory and with the biological realities of the brain (Panksepp, 1988). The focus on systems of emotion also holds important implications for understanding human feelings. The same feeling may have a different meaning and a different opposing emotion, depending on its social function or motivation. For example, anger in reaction to a physical threat clearly is different from anger in reaction to loss. In the first case, fear is the emotion opposing anger, but in the second case anger has two opposing emotions: security and sadness.

A final point to note is that emotion may be more "primitive" than cognition (which we consider shortly). Emotions often come to us without intention, effort, or desire, whereas we typically can direct our thoughts. Similarly, we may try to control our feelings with our thoughts, but it often seems difficult to do so. In fact, research indicates that emotions are controlled primarily by subcortical brain structures, whereas more abstract cognitive abilities are localized in the cerebral cortex, a more recent product of evolution. Cognition can shape or modify emotion, but feelings are more "basic": They are not wholly created or controlled by our intellectual interpretations of psychophysiological arousal (Panksepp, 1988).

TEMPERAMENT

Basic motivations and emotions are species-typical characteristics, but there are wide individual differences in how people relate to the social and physical worlds. An important approach to research on individual differences is the study of **temperament,** characteristic styles of relating to the world. Some theorists assert that temperament is the expression of inborn characteristics (Goldsmith, 1988), whereas other psychologists equate temperament with the broader construct of personality (Zuckerman, 1991). In all cases, however, research on temperament focuses on the "how" of behavior, not the "what."

For decades, psychologists have debated which elements make up the basic *temperamental styles,* but recently researchers have reached a consensus at least about the dimensions of adult temperament (Goldberg, 1993; Zuckerman, 1991). Based on extensive analysis of subjects' responses to structured questionnaires, researchers have identified five bipolar dimensions of personality, sometimes called "the big five." These are (1) *neuroticism*—nervous and moody versus calm and pleasant; (2) *extraversion*—active and talkative versus passive and reserved; (3) *openness to experience*—imaginative and curious versus shallow and imperceptive; (4) *agreeableness*—trusting and kind versus hostile and selfish; and (5) *conscientiousness*—organized and reliable versus careless and negligent.

Individual differences in temperamental styles have been hypothesized to play a role in the development of a number of psychological disorders, particularly the development of personality disorders, as we discuss in Chapter 9. Temperament also holds a special place in research on the etiology of behavior problems among children, a topic we take up in Chapter 14. Specifically, researchers have focused on the *goodness of fit* between children's temperament and their environment. A "difficult" temperament may increase the risk for the subsequent development of abnormal behavior, but experience determines whether problems emerge (Chess & Thomas, 1984).

Learning and Cognition

Emotions, motivations, and temperamental styles can be modified, at least to some degree, by the higher processes of learning and cognition. In our historical review, we have already discussed two

critical learning processes: classical and operant conditioning. These modes of learning are essential to normal development. As you will see in later chapters, classical and operant conditioning also play an important role in the etiology or maintenance of several psychological disorders.

MODELING

A third method of learning, known as modeling, was originally identified by the U.S. psychologist Albert Bandura of Stanford University (Bandura & Walters, 1963). The concept of **modeling** suggests that people learn much of their behavior by imitating others, a process that you surely have observed many times.

A similar but more complex concept is the process of learning through identification. The concept of *identification* was introduced by Freud (1940/1969), who asserted that children identify strongly with one adult, normally the same-gender parent. The process of identification suggests that children not only imitate an adult's behavior but also adopt his or her values.

SOCIAL COGNITION

The field of *social cognition*—the study of how humans process information about themselves and others—also has shed light on psychopathology. The concept of attribution illustrates the social cognition approach. **Attributions** are perceived causes—people's beliefs about cause–effect relations. In evaluating a friend's hostility toward you, for example, you rarely examine it scientifically. Instead, you attribute his or her actions to some reasonable cause, perhaps a tendency to overreact. Attribution theorists suggest that humans are "intuitive scientists" who routinely draw such conclusions about causality. We use shorthand calculations instead of more detailed methods in attributing causes because the quick assessments are efficient—they require little cognitive processing. Attributions can be inaccurate, however, in part because they are made intuitively rather than scientifically (Nisbett & Wilson, 1977). Moreover, errors in making attributions, and other cognitive biases, have increasingly been suggested to play a role in the development of abnormal behavior (Peterson & Seligman, 1984).

LEARNING, DISTORTED COGNITION, AND THE ETIOLOGY OF PSYCHOPATHOLOGY

At least some abnormal behavior apparently is learned. Fears can be classically conditioned, antisocial behavior often is rewarded, and some children imitate or identify with an alcoholic parent, to cite a few examples. Abnormal behavior also may be learned through more complex cognitive processes, particularly as a result of systematic errors or distortions in information processing.

Learned helplessness theory, for example, suggests that depression is caused by wrongly attributing negative events to internal, global, and stable causes (Peterson & Seligman, 1984; see Chapter 5). According to this theory, you are at risk for depression if you conclude that the reason for your bad grade on a calculus exam is: "I'm stupid." The "stupid" attribution blames the grade on internal, global, and stable causes, a cognition that makes you feel more helpless and ultimately more depressed. According to learned helplessness theory, healthier attributions are "the teacher was unfair," "I'm lousy at math," or "I didn't work hard enough," because each attribution is, respectively, external, specific, and unstable in quality.

Another theory suggests that depression is caused by automatic and distorted perceptions of reality, particularly negative *cognitive errors* (Beck, Rush, Shaw, & Emery, 1979). For example, people prone to depression may conclude that they are inadequate based on a single unpleasant experience. It is interesting to note that a treatment based on this theory encourages depressed people to be more scientific and less intuitive in evaluating their conclusions (see Chapter 5).

The Sense of Self

We share emotions and motivations with other animals, and we share some information-processing strategies with computers. Still, our sense of self seems to be a uniquely human quality.

modeling   A social learning concept describing the process of learning through imitation. Contrasts with the broader concept of identification.

attribution   Perceived causes; people's beliefs about cause–effect relations.

Stanford University psychologist Albert Bandura extensively studied modeling, the process of learning through imitation.

identity   Erikson's term for the broad definition of self; in his view, identity is the product of the adolescent's struggle to answer the question "Who am I?"

self-control   Appropriate behavior guided by internal (rather than external) rules.

self-efficacy   Albert Bandura's central cognitive concept, the belief that one can achieve desired goals.

The exact definition of our sense of self is elusive. This often is true personally, and the definition of self clearly is elusive in its numerous psychological conceptualizations.

One important and influential conceptualization is Erik Erikson's (1968) concept of **identity.** Erikson viewed identity as the product of the adolescent's struggle to answer the question "Who am I?" In his view, the conflict caused by this persistent question eventually produces an enduring identity, an integrated sense of individuality, wholeness, and continuity.

Some theorists have countered that identity is not a unitary construct. Instead, they argue that there are many "selves." The psychologist George Kelly (1905–1966), for example, emphasized the many different roles that people play in life. These include such obvious roles as being a daughter, a student, and a friend, and they also include less obvious roles, like being a "caretaker," a "jock," or "the quiet one." Thus, rather than having a single identity, Kelly argued, people develop many different *role identities,* various senses of oneself that correspond with actual life roles.

Even more specific views on the individual's sense of self are found in cognitive conceptualizations that discuss specific *self-schema*—cognitions about oneself. Albert Ellis (1970), the most prominent advocate of rational emotive therapy (see Chapter 3), provides one example of this approach. He points to people's irrational beliefs as the source of much of their psychological distress. *Irrational beliefs* are impossible, absolute standards, such as "Everyone must love me all of the time." According to Ellis, failure and psychological distress are the inevitable consequences of irrational beliefs, because nobody can live up to such impossible standards.

SELF SYSTEMS AND THE ETIOLOGY OF PSYCHOPATHOLOGY

There is no commonly accepted definition of self in psychology. Still, two ideas—self-control and self-esteem—are frequently found in theorizing and research on psychopathology.

The idea that children and adults must develop **self-control**—internal rules for guiding appropriate behavior—is commonly accepted in research on abnormal behavior. Self-control is learned through the process of *socialization,* wherein parents, teachers, and peers use discipline, praise, and their own example to teach children prosocial behavior and set limits on their antisocial behavior. Over time, these standards are *internalized*—that is, the external rules become internal regulations. The result is self-control (Maccoby, 1992).

A sense of self-worth is a different aspect of the self. Various discussions of the importance of high self-esteem have been emphasized by psychoanalytic, behavioral, and humanistic theorists. Sigmund Freud (1940/1969) discussed the importance of a healthy ego, a strong and confident inner reserve (see Further Thoughts earlier in this chapter). Carl Rogers (1961) highlighted a healthy *self-concept*—feeling worthy and capable—as the core structure of personality in his humanistic approach. Finally, the social learning theorist Albert Bandura (1977) argued for the primacy of **self-efficacy,** the belief that one can achieve desired goals.

Each theorist highlights the importance of the individual's sense of self-worth for mental health. You should consider, however, that low self-esteem could be a *result* rather than a cause of abnormal behavior. High self-esteem grows from success and fulfillment, whereas anxiety and depression—and low self-esteem—result from failure, loss, conflict, and rejection. In short, low self-esteem may only be an index of emotional problems, not a cause of them.

Social Factors

The broadest perspective for understanding the causes of abnormal behavior is at the level of the social system. There are an almost endless number of potential social influences on behavior, including many aspects of interpersonal relationships, social institutions, and cultural values. Therefore we must be selective in reviewing social contributions to psychopathology. In this section we begin with a focus on relationships and then move on to a consideration of gender roles, ethnicity, poverty, and broad societal values.

Relationships and Psychopathology

social support The emotional and practical assistance received from others.

Much evidence links abnormal behavior with distressed or conflicted relationships. Obvious difficulties like anger and conflict in relationships are linked with a number of emotional disorders ranging from schizophrenia to conduct problems among children (Emery, 1982). Still, often it is impossible to determine if troubled relationships actually *cause* abnormal behavior. In many cases, it seems equally or more likely that relationship distress is the *effect* of individual problems.

MARITAL STATUS AND PSYCHOPATHOLOGY

The relationship between marital status and psychopathology is a good example of the cause–effect dilemma we have just discussed. The demographics of the U.S. family have changed greatly over the last few decades. Cohabitation before marriage is frequent, many children are born outside of marriage, and half of all marriages end in divorce (Cherlin, 1992). In part because of the uncertainty created by these rapid changes, researchers have frequently examined the psychological consequences of alternative family structures for children and for adults (Amato & Keith, 1991a, 1991b; Emery, 1988, 1994; Gotlib & McCabe, 1990).

The findings of this large body of research must be interpreted with caution and care. On the one hand, marital status and psychological problems clearly are *correlated*. Somewhat more emotional problems are found among children and adults from divorced or never-married families than among people living in always-married families (see Chapter 15). On the other hand, despite common assumptions to the contrary, it is not clear that marital status is a direct *cause* of the emotional problems. Alternative explanations of the correlation include suggestions that common genetic factors cause both emotional disorders and marital disruption (McGue & Lykken, 1992), as well as the likelihood that marital status can be a consequence, not a cause, of some psychological problems among adults (Gotlib & McCabe, 1990). Thus marital status may cause psychopathology, but abnormal behavior also can create dysfunctional families.

SOCIAL RELATIONSHIPS

In addition to relationships within the family, key relationships outside the family can also affect mental health. For example, research indicates that a good relationship with an adult outside the family can buffer children from the effects of troubled family circumstances (National Advisory Mental Health Council, 1995; Werner & Smith, 1982, 1992). Close relationships also provide protection against the development of psychopathology (Cohen & Wills, 1985).

Research suggests that a few things are critical about **social support**—the emotional and practical assistance received from others. Significantly, one close relationship can provide as much support as being involved in many relationships. The greatest risk comes from having no social support. In addition, it is much worse to be actively rejected than to be neglected (Coie & Kupersmidt, 1983). Especially among children, it is far worse to be "liked least" than not to be "liked most" by your peers.

The association between abnormal behavior and the lack of supportive peer relationships may have several different causes. In

Social isolation and especially active rejection by peers are linked with an increased prevalence of psychological disorders.

gender roles Roles associated with social expectations about gendered behavior, for example, "masculine" or "feminine" activities.

some circumstances, peer rejection may be the cause of emotional difficulties. Being made an outcast surely can cause much distress. In other cases, the lack of a close relationship may be a consequence of psychopathology, as when a disturbed individual is extremely awkward in social relationships. Finally, social support—having someone to talk to and feeling cared for, for example—may help people cope more successfully with emotional problems. The presence or absence of a close relationship might not cause a psychological problem, but once the problem emerges, social support may be the difference between successful and failed coping.

Gender and Gender Roles

Gender roles may influence the development, expression, or consequences of psychopathology. Some theorists have suggested, for example, that women's traditional roles foster dependency and helplessness, which accounts for the considerably higher rates of depression among women (Nolen-Hoeksema, 1990; see Chapter 5). Others have suggested that gender roles are not responsible for the etiology of abnormal behavior, but they do influence how psychopathology is expressed. According to this view, each gender may experience helplessness, but women are allowed to be depressed, whereas men's gender roles dictate that they "carry on" as if nothing were wrong. Instead of becoming depressed, men may express their inner turmoil as a psychosomatic disorder (see Chapter 8). In other cases, gender roles may shape the course and consequences of abnormal behavior. For example, women's but not men's gender roles may allow them to avoid feared circumstances following a panic attack, and this avoidance may help determine whether the difficulty develops into the generalized problem of agoraphobia (see Chapter 6). We repeatedly consider evidence on epidemiological differences between men and women in the prevalence of psychological disorders. When appropriate, we interpret this evidence in terms of the roles played by men and women in U.S. society.

Race and Poverty

Race and poverty are broad social influences on psychological well-being in the United States today. We consider these two factors together because they are so commonly linked in American life. In 1993, 13 percent of white children were living below the poverty level, compared with 46 percent of black children and 40 percent of Latino children. Race and poverty also are closely linked to marital status. Among African-American children who lived with married parents, 15 percent lived in poverty, in comparison to 57 percent of children who lived with a single mother. Comparable figures among whites were 8 percent and 39 percent (Zill & Nord, 1994).

Evidence indicates that various psychological disorders are related to race and poverty (National Advisory Mental Health Council, 1995). In examining this evidence, one task is to disentangle the separate consequences of race and poverty. Poverty potentially may play several roles in the development of psychopathology. Children from poor inner-city neighborhoods witness and are victims of an incredible amount of violence in their communities. For example, one researcher found that 12 percent of school-aged children living in a Washington, D.C., neighborhood reported having seen a dead body in the streets outside their homes (Richters, 1993). Poverty also increases exposure to chemical toxins, such as to the lead found in old, chipping paint and automotive exhaust fumes. When ingested at toxic levels, lead can cause damage to the central nervous system.

The conditions of poverty are more likely to affect blacks, because more blacks live in poverty. However, the experiences of American blacks and whites differ in many more ways than socioeconomic status. African Americans have endured a history of slavery and discrimination, and broad racial prejudices can undermine social opportunities and self-image. Moreover, distinctive aspects of African-American culture have too readily been labeled as deficits

Getting help

Because we hope you will seek and find meaningful help for any type of psychological problems, the Getting Help sections at the end of the chapters on various kinds of psychological disorders offer psychological resources for dealing with specific types of difficulties. Those in these opening chapters are concerned with general issues that involve the initial decision to seek help.

As you read in this chapter, there can be a number of influences causing the psychological problems described in this textbook, from genes to early childhood experiences to parental models; and there are a number of points of view regarding how best to treat them. So how do you go about getting help if you decide you need it? How do you choose?

If you are curious about the possibility of seeking therapy, a good place to start is to talk frankly with someone you trust—either a friend, a family member, or a mental health professional. If you are interested in talking to a mental health professional, there are several things that you can do to be sure that you find the best person to help you with your problem. Jack Gorman, professor of psychiatry at Columbia University and deputy director of the New York State Psychiatric Institute, has written a good book—*The Essential Guide to Mental Health*—that provides excellent information on all sorts of important issues, including how to select among mental health professionals of various points of view. Gorman describes cognitive, behavioral, and psychodynamic approaches to psychotherapy as well as recent advances in psychopharmacology. His guide includes extensive practical suggestions about how to prepare for the first visit with a mental health professional and what should be accomplished in that meeting. Other steps in selecting a therapist are covered in the next Getting Help section.

What should you realistically expect as a *result* of treatment? How can you expect to feel if treatment is successful? You will not achieve eternal calmness, wisdom, or total happiness! Remember that negative emotions are part of everyday experience. Mild to moderate levels of anxiety, sadness, and anger are normal responses to events that we all encounter on a regular basis. In fact, as we will see, these emotions are often adaptive, helping to organize and energize our efforts to cope with challenging events. Therefore, you should not expect that, after successful treatment, you will always feel "on top of the world." You can expect, however, that these negative emotions will no longer be as intense, persistent, or overwhelming as they may have been in the past. They should no longer seriously interfere with your ability to get along with other people or do your work. A successful outcome should be measured in terms of your ability to function on a day-to-day basis and to adjust to the demands of your life, as well as improving your sense of your own subjective well-being.

One of the advantages of having various treatment approaches available is that if you try one approach to making a change and it doesn't work, don't lose hope. Try something else. Remember that none of the disorders that are described in this book are irreversible. Psychotherapy works for some people and some problems. Others, again depending on the kind of psychological distress they have, find medication more beneficial. Many use both. Some people are able to change on their own (perhaps guided by self-help books) while others benefit most from professional treatment. It often takes time and repeated effort to find the approach to treatment that will work best for you. 👑

instead of differences. For example, the maternal grandmother often fulfills the role of a supportive second parent among African-American single-mother families, but these families are sometimes viewed by psychologists and policy makers as flawed nevertheless (Wilson, 1989). Some differences among ethnic groups are adaptive, some are maladaptive, and some are merely differences.

Broad Societal Values

Broad social values also may influence the nature and development of abnormal behavior. For example, humanistic psychologists have questioned the conflict between the requirements for healthy psychological development and societal demands in our frenzied and competitive culture of materialism (Szasz, 1961). Other people, however, find great value in the material, technological, and scientific gains that accompany industrialization. From this perspective, concerns about society's frustration of personal growth are, in fact, luxuries of the very success that commentators deride.

paradigm   A set of assumptions both about the substance of a theory and about how scientists should collect data and test theoretical propositions. The term was applied to the progress of science by Thomas Kuhn, an influential historian and philosopher.

Our personal lives, our education, and even our science are deeply embedded within contemporary U.S. culture. The broad practices, beliefs, and values of our society play a role in the definition and development of abnormal behavior and in shaping the scientific enterprise that attempts to uncover the roots of psychopathology.

The **biomedical, psychoanalytic, behavioral,** and **humanistic** approaches to understanding the causes of abnormal behavior are alternative **paradigms,** and not just alternative theories.

Summary

Biological approaches emphasize causes that occur "within the skin." Psychoanalytic theory highlights unconscious processes and detailed case histories. Behavioral viewpoints focus on observable, learned behavior. Finally, humanistic psychology argues that behavior is not determined but, instead, is a product of free will. In short, these approaches conflict not only in their explanations of abnormal behavior but also in what they view as acceptable scientific methods.

Although science benefits from competition, the conflict between these broad paradigms has outlived its usefulness, because none of these approaches offers the "right" explanation. Rather, abnormal behavior is determined by the combination of different biological, psychological, and social factors. The current challenge for scientists is to integrate evidence on the etiology of different psychological disorders into a coherent whole, a system of contributing factors.

Systems theory is an innovation in understanding and conducting science that offers assistance in this integration. Its central principle is **holism,** the idea that the whole is more than the sum of its parts—a scientific counterpoint to *reductionism*. In systems theory, smaller units are not "ultimate" causes but subsystems of the larger whole. Other important systems principles include *reciprocal causality*—the idea that causality is bidirectional—and **cybernetic** processes—the use of feedback loops to adjust progress toward a goal. Systems theory also emphasizes *equifinality,* the idea that there are multiple pathways to the development of any one disorder.

Biological factors relevant to abnormal behavior begin with the smallest anatomic unit within the nervous system, the **neuron,** or nerve cell. Each neuron has four major anatomic components: the **soma,** or cell body, the **dendrites,** the **axon,** and the **terminal buttons.** Communication between neurons occurs when the terminal buttons release chemical substances called **neurotransmitters** into the **synapse** between nerve cells. Disrupted communication among neurons, particularly disruptions in the functioning of various neurotransmitters, is implicated in the etiology of several types of abnormal behavior. We must not equate a neurophysiological explanation of a psychological disorder with a biological abnormality, however.

Neuroanatomists commonly divide the brain into three subdivisions: the hindbrain, the midbrain, and the forebrain. Basic bodily functions are regulated by the structures of the hindbrain, which is rarely implicated in abnormal behavior. The midbrain controls some motor activities, especially those related to fighting and sex. Damage to the midbrain can cause extreme disturbances, but such abnormalities typically result from specific and unusual brain traumas or tumors. The forebrain is the location of most sensory, emotional, and cognitive processes. Most of the forebrain is composed of the two *cerebral hemispheres,* and many brain functions are *lateralized,* so that each hemisphere is the site of specific cognitive and emotional activities. Finally, the **cerebral cortex** is the uneven surface area of the brain that lies just underneath the skull. It is the site of the control and integration of sophisticated memory, sensory, and motor functions. Because of the rudimentary state of our knowledge about the brain, only the most severe mental disorders have been clearly linked with abnormalities in neuroanatomy. In most of these cases, brain damage is extensive and obvious.

Psychophysiology is the study of changes in the functioning of the body that result from psychological experiences. The **autonomic nervous system** is the part of the central nervous system that is responsible for psychophysiological reactions. It has two branches, the **sympathetic** and the **parasympathetic nervous systems.** In general, the sympathetic nervous system controls arousal, and the parasympathetic nervous system controls energy conservation. Psychophysiological overarousal and underarousal both have been implicated in theories of the causes of abnormal behavior.

Behavior genetics is the study of genetic influences on the development of behavior. Comparisons of **monozygotic (MZ)** and **dizygotic (DZ) twins** can yield information about polygenic contributions, as can adoption studies. It is important to understand that the fact that a psychological disorder has a polygenic component does not mean that the disorder will inevitably appear, and that genetically influenced behavior is influenced by the environment. Moreover, it is not clear what mechanism may account for behavior genetic findings. Few single genes directly affect abnormal behavior; thus genetic effects probably occur at some more basic level—for example, by affecting psychophysiological arousal.

Psychology has not reached a consensus about its core constructs, but certain commonalties found across theories include issues of motivation and temperament, learning and cognition, a sense of self, and stages of psychological development. In addition to biological needs, humans apparently have at least two basic psychological motivations: to form **attachments** and to compete for **dominance. Emotion** drives these basic motivations, and recent observations suggest that organized systems of emotion may be activated by certain social needs or challenges. **Temperament** is the individual's characteristic style of relating to the world. Researchers recently have agreed on consistencies in temperamental styles—the "how" of behavior.

Learning mechanisms include **classical conditioning, operant conditioning, modeling,** and information processing. At least some abnormal behavior is learned, and in the last two decades researchers have highlighted systematic cognitive biases that relate to some psychological disorders.

The sense of self is a uniquely human quality that would seem to play a role in causing emotional problems. It is possible, however, that self-esteem merely is another index of mental health. Finally, the idea of *developmental stages* not only charts the course of normal development, against which abnormal behavior must be compared, but it also highlights the important issue of developmental transitions.

Social roles influence the definition and development of psychopathology. Evidence links abnormal behavior with distressed or conflicted family relationships, and **social support** from people other than family members can be an important buffer against stress. **Gender roles** may influence the development, expression, or consequences of psychopathology. Some theorists suggest, for example, that women's traditional roles foster dependency and helplessness. Race and poverty, which are often related, also are broad social influences on psychological well-being in the United States today. Finally, humanistic psychologists have pointed out that there may be conflict between the demands of our competitive society and the requirements for healthy psychological development.

Critical Thinking

1. What are your beliefs about the causes of abnormal behavior? Do you adhere to one of the paradigms described here? Are your reasons for preferring a particular approach personal or scientific? Has the information in this chapter changed your thinking?

2. Think about your social groups—your family, friends, clubs or organizations, or the people you live with. Consider the relationships between people in these groups, and try to understand them better by using concepts from systems theory—for example, reciprocal causality, cybernetics, homeostasis, subsystems.

3. Some people believe that we blame too many social and personal problems on biology. What are your thoughts? Do you think biological abnormalities cause (most) mental disorders? If so, what are the implications for personal responsibility for change? What are our societal responsibilities to people with emotional problems?

4. In what ways do social roles contribute to your behavior (e.g., your gender, ethnicity, or more subtle roles like being the "smart one" or the "responsible one" in your family)? What roles do you see friends and family playing? Do any of these roles encourage maladaptive or abnormal behavior?

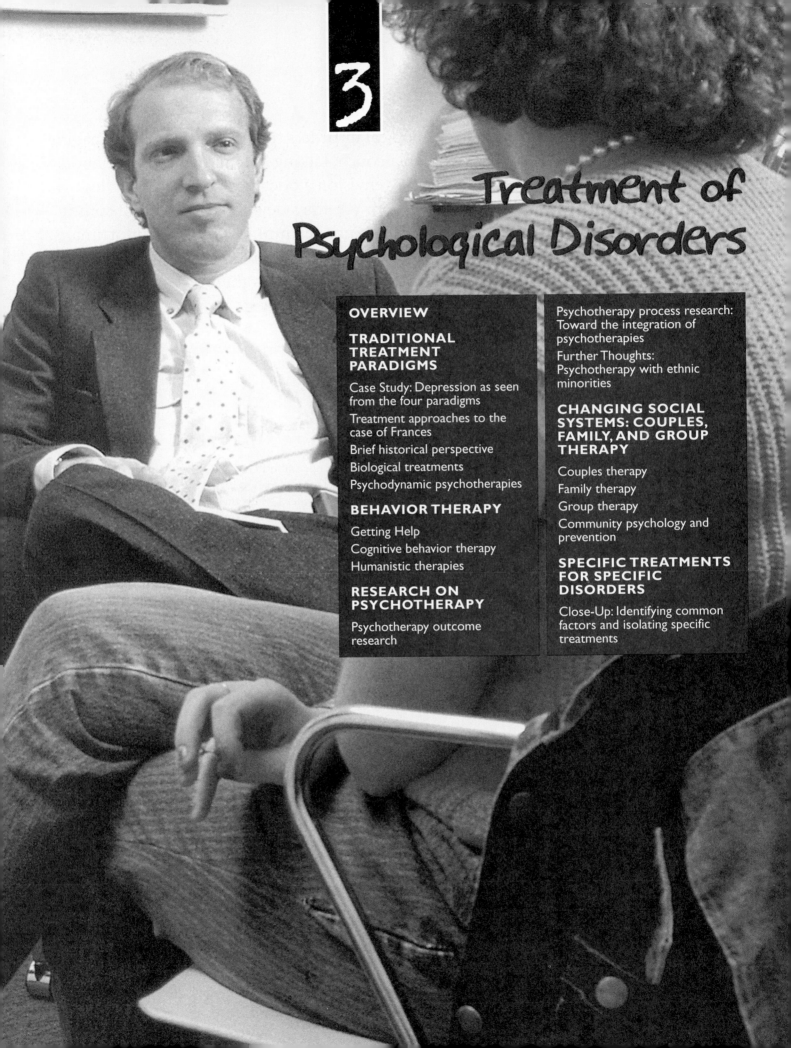

3

Treatment of Psychological Disorders

How are psychological disorders treated? Perhaps you imagine someone lying on a couch, talking at length about childhood memories. You may envision a doctor sitting behind a desk and writing a prescription. You may view the treatment of some mental disorders as inhumane, thinking of some unfortunate individual locked up and forgotten inside a dreary mental hospital. Or maybe you conceive of a therapist as a kind and wise elder—someone who listens, who cares, and who knows just the right things to say.

Overview

One reason for these conflicting images is our ambivalence about the treatment of psychological disorders. Emotional problems are widely misunderstood, as are the professions of clinical psychology, psychiatry, and social work (see Chapter 1). Less than 30 percent of people with a diagnosable mental disorder receive treatment, including many people with severe disturbances (Howard et al., 1996). Policy debates about health insurance coverage reflect the controversy about whether psychological treatments are used too little or too much. On the one hand, mental health advocates are fighting for parity in the coverage of mental and physical disorders. On the other hand, managed care organizations often drop or restrict mental health coverage, for example, by limiting reimbursed visits to 10 or even fewer therapy sessions.

"He's in an H.M.O. Get some of the King's horses and a few of the King's men."
Courtesy *The New Yorker*

Another reason for our conflicting stereotypes about psychological treatment is the wide variety of approaches to therapy. According to one review, there are more than 400 different "schools" of psychotherapy for adults and 200 for children (Kazdin, 1994a). The number of different therapies creates practical as well as intellectual quandaries. How do you choose a good therapist? How do you know whether you are receiving the most effective treatment?

We can greatly simplify the overwhelming array of psychological treatments by grouping them according to the four paradigms: the biomedical, psychoanalytic, behavioral, and humanistic approaches (see Chapter 2). Advocates of each paradigm have developed very different treatments. In fact, mental health professionals often ask one another, "What is your theoretical orientation?" and the answer to the question is supposed to be "biological," "psychoanalytic," "behavioral," or "humanistic."

Though we reject the paradigms approach, the first section of this chapter elaborates on the contrasting biomedical, psychoanalytic, behavioral, and humanistic treatments of psychological disorders. We focus on the paradigms because each theory has had an important historical influence on contemporary treatments. You need to be familiar with the general approach so you can better understand the specific treatments for specific disorders that we discuss in subsequent chapters. We also highlight differences among paradigms, because researchers have not yet identified the most promising treatment for many psychological disorders. Thus clinicians often must rely on a more general theory for guidance in planning treatments.

In the second section of the chapter, we emphasize the similarities rather than the differences across the four paradigms. One basic similarity is that three of the paradigms—the psychoanalytic, behavioral, and humanistic approaches—are forms of **psychotherapy:** Each of these three approaches uses psychological techniques to produce change in the context of a special, helping relationship. We highlight this basic similarity in reviewing research on psychotherapy outcome and on psychotherapy process. *Psychotherapy outcome research* compares the effectiveness of alternative forms of treatment. One major finding from outcome research is that all three major schools of psychotherapy produce significantly more benefit than does no treatment at all. This finding suggests that there may be more similarities among alternative treatments in practice than is apparent in theory. *Psychotherapy process research* investigates similarities in practice by studying aspects of the therapist–client relationship. For example, psychotherapy process research indicates that all treatments are more effective when there is a positive relationship between therapist and client.

Although we discuss research and theory on traditional paradigms, the chapter also follows the biopsychosocial model. Our overview of biological treatments early in the chapter highlights efforts to produce psychological change through physiological means. The detailed discussion of psychotherapy process and outcome research highlights intervention at the psychological level. Toward the end of the chapter, we discuss treatments that focus on social relationships and societal institutions.

At the end of the chapter we highlight the most important finding about the treatment of psychological disorders: Different therapies vary in their effectiveness for treating different problems. The most promising advances have come from the development and evaluation of specific treatments for specific disorders. In fact, the majority of therapists identify their approach as being **eclectic** (Garfield & Kurtz, 1976; Zook & Walton, 1989). Eclectic therapists do not adhere to any one paradigm; rather, they tailor their treatment for individual disorders and clients. In subsequent chapters we are eclectic in discussing alternative treatments. We focus only on specific treatments that, based on research evidence, hold particular promise for the psychological disorder under discussion.

Traditional Treatment Paradigms

Biomedical (biological) therapies approach mental illness by drawing an analogy to physical illness. Changing psychological experience through biological means is the goal of these treatments. Medication is by far the most common biomedical treatment for psychological disorders. Other biological techniques include convulsive therapy and psychosurgery.

psychotherapy   The use of psychological techniques in an attempt to produce change in the context of a special, helping relationship.

eclectic   An approach of picking different treatments according to the needs of individual disorders and individual clients.

Freudian psychoanalysis has spawned a number of related treatments that generally are referred to as *psychodynamic psychotherapy*. Like psychoanalysis, psychodynamic psychotherapy begins with an exploration of the client's past, unconscious motivations, and defense mechanisms. Psychodynamic therapy also shares the psychoanalytic goal of promoting insight, the heightened awareness of unconscious conflicts and motivations. According to the psychodynamic tradition, conscious awareness of what was formerly unconscious—insight—is sufficient for a cure.

Behavior therapists believe that both normal and abnormal behavior are learned, and therapy is seen as a form of education. Promoting change, and not insight, is the major goal of behavior therapy, although the target for change may be behavior, cognition, or emotion. In fact, many behavior therapists prefer to call themselves "cognitive behavior therapists" or simply "cognitive therapists." These terms underscore the increasing importance of cognition in psychological science and in therapy.

Unlike other approaches, humanistic psychotherapists do *not* act as experts who diagnose and solve problems. Instead, humanistic therapy tries to help people to make their own life choices. In order to help clients make choices, humanistic therapists encourage their clients to become more aware of their emotions. In exploring emotions, humanistic therapists focus on present feelings, not past experiences, and they urge clients to take responsibility for their feelings and ultimately for their actions.

The following case history and discussion illustrate some of the contrasting ways in which biological, psychodynamic, behavioral, and humanistic therapists conceptualize treatment.

Depression as Seen from the Four Paradigms

Frances was a 23-year-old woman who sought psychotherapy for depression. Frances reported having been depressed for almost 3 years, with intermittent periods of relative happiness or deeper despair. When she came into therapy, her depression was quite severe. She had little appetite and had lost 10 pounds over the previous 6 weeks, and her erratic sleeping patterns were worse than usual. She awoke around 2 or 3 A.M. every night, tossed in bed for several hours, and finally fell asleep again near dawn.

Frances reported feeling profoundly depressed about herself, her new marriage, and life in general. She freely admitted to frequent thoughts of suicide. She once sat in her bathroom holding a razor blade for over an hour, contemplating whether to slash her wrists. But she decided she could never commit the act. Now, she often wished she was dead, but she felt that she "lacked the courage" to take her own life.

Frances also noted that she found herself without motivation. She withdrew from her husband and the few friends she had, and she frequently called in sick at work when she felt blue. Frances's reports of depression were underscored by her careless dress, frequent bouts of crying, and slowed speech and body movements.

Frances reported that she had experienced a happy childhood. She had not known depression until the current episode began in her senior year in college. At first, she convinced herself that she was only suffering from "senior year syndrome." She wasn't sure what to do with her life. Secretly, she longed to move to New York and finally break out and do something exciting. But when she told her parents about her plans, her mother begged Frances to return home. She insisted the two of them needed to have fun together again after 4 long years with Frances away at college. After graduation, Frances returned home to live with her parents.

It was shortly after moving home that Frances realized that her difficulties were much more serious than she had thought. She found herself intermittently screaming at her anxious and doting mother and being "super-nice" to her after feeling guilty about losing her temper. Frances described her mother as "a saint." Frances thought that her erratic behavior toward her mother was all her fault. Her mother apparently agreed. In Frances's mind, she was a failure as a daughter.

Frances described both her mother and her father as loving and giving, but some of her comments about them were far from glowing. She said she was her mother's best friend. When asked if her mother was her best friend, Frances began to cry. She felt like her mother's infant, her parent, or even her husband, but not her friend and certainly not like her grown daughter. Frances had little to say about her father. She pictured him drinking beer, eating meals, and falling asleep in front of the television.

Throughout the time she lived at home, Frances's depression only seemed to deepen. After a year of living with her parents, she married her high school sweetheart. Frances felt pressured to get married. Both her future husband and her mother insisted that it was time for her to settle down and start a family. At the time, she had hoped that marriage would be the solution to her problems. The excitement of the wedding added to this hope. But after the marriage, Frances said that things were worse—if that were possible. Still, she insisted that her marriage problems were all her fault.

Frances's husband was a young accountant who she said reminded her more and more of her father. He didn't drink, but he spent most of his brief time at home working or reading in his study. She said they had little communication, and she felt no warmth in her marriage. Her husband often was angry and sullen, but Frances said she couldn't blame him for feeling that way. His problem was being married to her. She wanted to love him, but she never had. She was a failure as a wife. She was a failure in life.

The theme of self-blame pervaded Frances's descriptions of her family. She repeatedly noted that, despite their flaws, her parents and her husband were good and loving people. She was the one with the problem. She had everything that she could hope for, yet she was unhappy. One reason she wanted to die was to ease the burden on them. How could they be happy when they had to put up with her foul moods? When she talked about these things, however, Frances's tone of voice often made her sound more angry than depressed. ₩

Treatment Approaches to the Case of Frances

Biological, psychodynamic, behavioral, and humanistic therapists all would note Frances's depressed mood, her self-blame, and her troubled close relationships. However, therapists working within these different theoretical frameworks would approach treatment with Frances in very different ways. See Table 3-1, on page 62.

A BIOLOGICAL APPROACH

A biologically oriented psychiatrist or psychologist would focus first on making a diagnosis of Frances's problems. This would not be difficult in Frances's case, because her symptoms paint a clear picture of depression. The therapist surely would take note of Frances's description of her father, who seems chronically depressed. Perhaps a genetic predisposition toward depression runs in her family.

A biologically oriented therapist would sympathize with Frances's interpersonal problems, but the therapist would not blame either Frances or her family for their troubles. Rather, he or she would blame a problem that neither Frances nor her family members could control: depression. It is exhausting to deal with someone who is constantly agitated and depressed. In the end, the therapist probably would explain that depression can be caused by a chemical imbalance in the brain. Medication would be recommended, and follow-up appointments would be scheduled to monitor the effects of the medication on Frances's mood and on her life.

A PSYCHODYNAMIC APPROACH

In contrast, a psychodynamic therapist would take note of Frances's *defensive style*. For example, the therapist would see Frances's justification of her parents' and husband's behavior as a form of *rationalization*. Perhaps the therapist would also see a pattern of *denial* in Frances's refusal to acknowledge the imperfections of her loved ones and their failure to fulfill her needs. In Frances's seeing herself as a burden on her family, the therapist also might wonder if she was *projecting* onto them her own sense of feeling burdened by her mother's demands and her husband's indifference. Some psychodynamic theorists view depression as "anger turned inward" (see Chapter 5). Thus, getting Frances to express her anger directly toward her family rather than toward herself might be a goal in overcoming her defenses.

Although a psychodynamic therapist would note her unexpressed anger, he or she would not challenge Frances's defenses early in therapy. Instead, the first part of treatment would be more exploratory, focusing largely on Frances's past and her hopes, feelings, and frustrations. The exploration would be directed minimally by the therapist, who would encourage Frances to talk about issues she wanted to discuss. The goal of the unstructured discussions would be to illuminate Frances's unconscious motivations, intrapsychic conflicts, and defenses to the therapist and,

TABLE 3–1

Some Comparisons among Biomedical, Psychodynamic, Behavioral, and Humanistic Treatments				
TOPIC	**BIOMEDICAL**	**PSYCHODYNAMIC**	**BEHAVIORAL**	**HUMANISTIC**
Goal of treatment	Alter biology to relieve psychological distress	Gain insight into defenses/unconscious motivations	Learn more adaptive behaviors/cognitions	Increase emotional awareness and make life choices
Primary treatment methods	Diagnosis, medications	Discussion and interpretation of defenses	Instruction, guided, learning, homework	Empathy, support, exploring emotions
Role of therapist	Active, directive, diagnostician	Passive, nondirective, interpreter (may be aloof)	Active, directive, nonjudgmental, teacher	Passive, nondirective, but warm, accepting, supporter
Length of treatment	Very brief initially, occasional visits to manage medication	Usually long term; some new short-term treatments	Mostly short term; may include later "booster" sessions	Varies; length not typically structured

over time, to Frances herself. To facilitate therapy, the psychodynamic therapist gradually would confront Frances's defenses in order to help her gain insight into her hidden resentment toward her mother, longing for a relationship with her father, and unfulfilled fantasies about marriage.

A COGNITIVE-BEHAVIORAL APPROACH

A cognitive behavior therapist would note many of the same issues in Frances's life but would approach therapy quite differently. Rather than focusing on defense mechanisms, a behavior therapist would note Frances's cognitive and behavioral patterns. Frances's self-blame—her pattern of attributing all of her interpersonal difficulties to herself—would be seen as a cognitive error. Her withdrawal from pleasing activities and her apparent unassertiveness also would be seen as contributing to her depression. In comparison to a psychodynamic therapist, a behavior therapist would be far more directive in discussing these topics. For example, he or she likely would tell Frances that her thinking was distorted and her cognitive errors were contributing to her depression.

Learning new ways of thinking and acting in the present would be the focus of behavior therapy. For example, the therapist probably would encourage Frances to appropriately blame others, not just herself, for her relationship problems, and the psychologist or psychiatrist might urge her to try out new ways of relating to her mother, father, and husband. The behavior therapist would want Frances to play an active role in this learning process by completing *homework*—activities designed to continue her treatment outside the therapy session. Homework might include careful monitoring of specific conflicts with her family in an attempt to help Frances understand that she is not the cause of *all* family disputes. A behavior therapist also might teach Frances how to assert herself more with family members. The therapist would expect Frances's depressed mood to begin to lift once she learned to assert her rights and no longer blamed herself for everything that went wrong in her life.

A HUMANISTIC APPROACH

A humanistic therapist also would note Frances's depression, her self-blame, and her unsatisfactory relationships with loved ones. A more prominent focus, however, would be her lack of emotional *genuineness*—her inability to "be herself" with other people and within herself. Frances's tendencies to bury her true feelings would be explored as they related to the emotions she expressed in the therapy session. The humanistic therapist would want Frances to recognize her inner feelings and would encourage her to make life choices based on her heightened emotional awareness.

In conducting therapy, the humanistic therapist probably would be nondirective in terms of specific topics for discussion but would continually focus therapy on emotional issues. Initially, the therapist might simply empathize with Frances's feelings of sadness, loneliness, and isolation. Over time, he or she likely would suggest that Frances had other feelings that she did not express. These might include frustration and guilt over her mother's controlling yet dependent style, and anger at her husband's and her father's self-centeredness. The humanistic therapist would tell Frances that her feelings were legitimate and might encourage Frances to "own" her feelings. The humanistic therapist would not directly encourage Frances to act differently, but Frances would be expected to make some changes in her life as a result of her increased emotional awareness.

These approaches to treating Frances are very different, but they may not be as different as they seem. All three approaches to psychotherapy focus on Frances's distorted thoughts and feelings, and each hones in on her self-blame for her troubled close relationships. Even a biologically oriented therapist might recommend psychotherapy in addition to medication, in order to help Frances cope with some aspects of her depression and family troubles. We discuss such integrated approaches to treatment in more detail later in this chapter. First, we elaborate further on the differences among the four approaches. The contrasts among them can best be understood by examining the treatments from a historical perspective.

Brief Historical Perspective

If we use a broad definition of "treatment," practices that date back to ancient times must be included in a history of the treatment of psychological disorders. In searching back through time, we can trace the roots of psychotherapy to two broad traditions of healing: the spiritual/religious tradition and the naturalistic/scientific tradition (Frank, 1973).

The spiritual/religious tradition attributes both physical and mental ailments to supernatural forces. This tradition dates back through ancient times, and it continues today both inside and outside formal religions. An ancient practice called *trephining* is one of the earliest examples of the spiritual/religious tradition. From skulls unearthed by archaeologists, researchers have concluded that tribal healers performed a primitive form of surgery as a treatment for mental disorders. Trephining involved chipping a hole through the unfortunate sufferer's skull with a crude stone tool. Presumably, the purpose of trephining was to allow evil spirits to escape.

Still, the influence of spiritual beliefs and rituals cannot be ignored. Believing is a powerful part of healing. Spiritual beliefs influence how people cope with all sorts of life difficulties.

Naturalistic/scientific approaches to helping the mentally disturbed also have ancient roots. Hippocrates recommended treatments such as rest, exercise, and a healthy diet (see Chapter 1). Later, "insane asylums" were developed as a new treatment for the mentally ill. One rationale for these institutions was to remove disturbed individuals from society, but another was the hope that rest and isolation would alleviate their bizarre behavior.

Although their beginnings can be traced to ancient times, contemporary biological, psychodynamic, behavioral, and humanistic treatments are tied much more directly to developments in the nineteenth and twentieth centuries.

Trephining was a primitive attempt to treat psychological problems by cracking a hole in the skull of the sufferer. Presumably, evil spirits could escape through the hole, thereby curing the problem.

Biological Treatments

The scientific beginnings of biological treatments can be traced to the nineteenth century and the discovery of the diagnosis, cause, and cure for general paresis (see Chapter 2). This remarkable achievement paralleled other medical advances in its course of discovery. As the first step, an increasingly refined and accurate diagnosis is developed. Next, information pertaining to causal factors is put together like pieces of a puzzle to form a complete picture of the specific etiology of the disease. Finally, scientists develop treatments by experimenting with various methods for preventing or curing the disorder. These are far from simple tasks, of course, as is evident in the span of over a century between the diagnosis of general paresis, the discovery of syphilis as its cause, and the development of antibiotics as a treatment for the disease.

electroconvulsive therapy (ECT) A treatment that involves the deliberate induction of a convulsion by passing electricity through one or both hemispheres of the brain. Modern ECT uses restraints, medication, and carefully controlled electrical stimulation to minimize adverse consequences. Can be an effective treatment for severe depression, especially following the failure of other approaches.

psychosurgery A controversial treatment that involves the surgical destruction of specific regions of the brain. Modern psychosurgery involves relatively little destruction of brain tissue, unlike the discredited prefrontal lobotomy.

prefrontal lobotomy A psychosurgery technique introduced in 1935 by Egas Moniz in which the two hemispheres of the brain were severed. Moniz won a Nobel Prize for the treatment, which now is discredited.

A similar success story cannot be told about the development of biological treatments for many other mental disorders. Uncovering specific causes has proved to be difficult. As a result, many efforts to develop biological treatments have attempted to skip the middle step in the process of discovery; that is, they experiment with alternative treatments before discovering a specific etiology. These treatments focus on *symptom alleviation,* reducing the dysfunctional symptoms of a disorder but not eliminating its root cause.

Experimentation has produced mixed results in the biological treatment of emotional problems. Bleeding, forced hot baths, the use of various physical restraints, and the surgical removal of sexual organs are some of the unhappy experimental treatments that were used in the not-so-distant past. In contrast, the second half of the twentieth century has witnessed the discovery of numerous medications, many of which are remarkable in their effectiveness at symptom alleviation. Before presenting an overview of these new drugs, we briefly consider two controversial biological treatments: electroconvulsive therapy and psychosurgery.

ELECTROCONVULSIVE THERAPY

Electroconvulsive therapy (ECT) involves the deliberate induction of a seizure by passing electricity through the brain. The technique was developed in 1938 by Ugo Cerletti and Lucio Bini, two Italian physicians who were seeking a treatment for schizophrenia (see Chapter 13). At the time, schizophrenia was erroneously thought to be rare among people who had epilepsy. This led to speculation that epileptic seizures somehow prevented the disorder.

Approximately 100 volts of electric current was passed through the patients' brains in what is now termed *bilateral ECT.* Electrodes are placed on the left and right temples, and the current passes through both brain hemispheres. In *unilateral ECT,* the electric current is passed through only one side of the brain, the nondominant hemisphere. Both procedures induce brief unconsciousness and seizures, but unilateral ECT apparently produces less memory loss—a common side effect of ECT (Squire & Slater, 1978). Unfortunately, unilateral ECT may not be as effective as bilateral ECT. Thus some experts now recommend unilateral ECT only when bilateral ECT leads to severe memory impairments (Weiner & Krystal, 1994). In any case, the dangerous, jerking body movements that occur during a convulsion—and often resulted in broken bones and other physical injuries—are now controlled by restraints and the administration of a muscle relaxant. Typically, ECT involves a series of 6 to 12 sessions scheduled over the course of a few weeks (Weiner & Krystal, 1994).

As we will see in Chapter 5, evidence indicates that ECT is quite effective in treating severe depressions that do not respond to other treatments (see Chapter 5). Because of its potential side effects, however, ECT must be used cautiously even when other treatments fail (NIMH, 1985). Nevertheless, estimates indicate that about 36,000 courses of ECT are administered in the United States each year, and interest in ECT—and possibly the frequency of using it—have increased in recent years (Weiner & Krystal, 1994).

PSYCHOSURGERY

Psychosurgery is an even more controversial biological treatment, as it involves the surgical destruction of specific regions of the brain. Psychosurgery was introduced in 1935 by Egas Moniz (1874–1953), a Portuguese neurologist. **Prefrontal lobotomy** was the technique refined by Moniz—a procedure in which the frontal lobes of the brain are surgically and irrevocably severed. The technique was widely adopted throughout the world, and thousands of prefrontal lobotomies were performed throughout the middle of this century—between 10,000 and 20,000 in the United States alone. In fact, Moniz won a Nobel Prize in 1949 for his discovery of this treatment.

Prefrontal lobotomy was subsequently discredited because of its limited effectiveness and its frequent and severe side effects, which included a 25 percent mortality rate, excessive tranquillity, and the absence of emotional responsiveness. Ironically, Moniz himself was shot and paralyzed by one of his lobotomized patients, a sad testament to the unpredictable outcome of the procedure (Snaith, 1994; Swayze, 1995).

Although prefrontal lobotomies are no longer performed, some forms of highly circumscribed psychosurgery are used today to treat severe disorders. For example, a form of limited psychosurgery called *cingulotomy* may be effective in treating some very severe cases of obsessive–compulsive disorder when all other treatments have failed (Baer, Rauch, Ballantine et al., 1995; Mindus & Jenike, 1992; see Chapter 6).

PSYCHOPHARMACOLOGY

Psychopharmacology—the study of the use of medications to treat psychological disturbances—has been the most promising avenue of biological treatment. In recent years, scientists have developed new medications that have increasingly refined effects on emotional states and mental disorders.

You may be familiar with the effects of some **psychoactive drugs,** chemical substances that affect psychological state. Alcohol, for example, produces rapid and notable changes in thinking, mood, and behavior. Some psychoactive medications produce similarly obvious changes. Many antianxiety agents, such as Xanax or Librium, have effects that become apparent soon after the medication is taken (see Chapter 6). Others have more subtle influences that build up gradually over time. The antidepressant medications are an example of this type of effect (see Chapter 5). Other psychoactive drugs affect people with mental disorders very differently from the way they affect someone who is functioning normally. Antipsychotic medications help to eliminate delusions and hallucinations among people suffering from schizophrenia (see Chapter 13), but the same medications would disorient most people and send them into a long, groggy sleep.

The success of psychopharmacology is evident in the proliferating discovery and use of psychoactive medications in recent years. For example, in the 1990s the antidepressant medication Prozac outsold *every* prescription medication, including any medications used to treat physical ailments. (In the 1970s, the antianxiety medication Valium held this distinction.)

There are a few general points that you should note about psychopharmacology. First, much evidence indicates that various medications are effective and safe treatments for particular mental disorders. Psychopharmacology lies well within the realm of modern medicine. A second point, however, is that psychoactive medications typically offer symptom relief, not a cure of underlying pathology. Symptom alleviation is extremely important. Where would we be without aspirin, another drug that treats symptoms but not causes? Still, some commentators worry that medication is given too readily to address psychological or social problems (Breggin, 1994). Third, all medications have side effects, some of which are very unpleasant. Partly as a result of unpleasant side effects, many patients do not take their medication as prescribed, and they often experience a relapse as a result. Finally, many psychoactive drugs must be taken for long periods of time. Because the medications alleviate symptoms but do not produce a cure, it may be necessary to keep taking the drug—for months, years, or sometimes for a lifetime (Klerman et al., 1994).

psychopharmacology   The study of the effects of psychoactive drugs on behavior. Clinical psychopharmacology involves the expert use of drugs in the treatment of mental disorders.

psychoactive drugs   Various drugs—ranging from alcohol, tobacco, and caffeine to controlled substances—that affect the individual's psychological state.

free association   A basic technique in Freudian psychoanalysis in which patients are encouraged to speak freely about whatever thoughts cross their mind; presumed to give insight into the unconscious.

psychoanalysis   Freud's orthodox form of psychotherapy that is practiced rarely today because of its time, expense, and questionable effectiveness in treating mental disorders. Freud viewed the task of psychoanalysis as promoting insight by uncovering the unconscious conflicts and motivations that cause psychological difficulties.

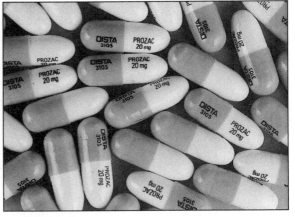

Prozac is an effective antidepressant that is the bestselling medication for treating psychological problems.

Psychodynamic Psychotherapies

Psychodynamic approaches to treatment were first developed during the nineteenth and early twentieth centuries. Joseph Breuer's (1842–1925) pioneering technique known as the "cathartic method" was one of the earliest influences.

FREUDIAN PSYCHOANALYSIS

Breuer's contemporary and collaborator, Sigmund Freud (1856–1939), adopted the cathartic method for a time, but he soon concluded that hypnosis was not necessary to encourage open expression. Instead, Freud simply told his patients to speak freely about whatever thoughts crossed their mind. This method, called **free association,** became a cornerstone of Freud's famous treatment, **psychoanalysis.**

Unlike Breuer, Freud did not see catharsis as an end in itself. The true benefit of free association, in Freud's view, was that it revealed aspects of the unconscious mind. Freud found clues to

insight   Self-understanding; the extent to which a person recognizes the nature (or understands the potential causes) of his or her disorder. In psychoanalysis, insight is the ultimate goal, specifically, to bring formerly unconscious material into conscious awareness.

interpretation   A tool in psychotherapy and psychoanalysis in which the therapist suggests new meanings about a client's accounts of his or her past and present life.

his patients' intrapsychic lives in their unedited speech. Freud also believed that dreams (during which intrapsychic defenses presumably are weaker) and slips of the tongue (known commonly as "Freudian slips") provided especially revealing information about the unconscious. Thus, according to Freud, free association, dreams, and slips of the tongue are valuable, because they serve as "windows into the unconscious."

According to Freud, the psychoanalyst's task is to uncover the unconscious conflicts and motivations that cause psychological difficulties. However, this discovery is only the first step in treatment. In order to overcome their dysfunctions, patients must come to share the psychoanalyst's understanding of their intrapsychic life. The ultimate goal of psychoanalysis is to bring formerly unconscious material into conscious awareness. This is what Freud called **insight.** Freud asserted that insight is sufficient for curing psychological disorders.

The analyst's main tool for promoting insight is **interpretation.** In offering an interpretation, the analyst suggests hidden meanings to patients' accounts of their past and present life. Typically, interpretations relate to past experiences, especially experiences with loved ones. Recall from Chapter 2, however, that according to Freudian theory, the ego defense mechanisms keep intrapsychic conflicts from conscious awareness. Thus psychoanalysts must overcome defenses like denial and projection as patients resist their interpretations. Timing is everything in overcoming *resistance.* The patient must be on the verge of discovering the hidden meaning himself or herself; otherwise, the interpretation will be rejected. For example, return to the case history and consider the dilemma of convincing Frances that deep resentment lies beneath her professed, unwavering love for her mother. Given her long history of subjugating her own needs to those of her mother, Frances would be unlikely to accept such an interpretation if it were made too early in her treatment.

The analyst remains distant in order to encourage *transference,* the process whereby patients transfer the feelings about some key figure in their life onto the shadowy figure of the analyst. For psychoanalysis to succeed, the analyst must not respond to transference in a manner that the patient views as critical or threatening. Psychoanalysts particularly must guard against *countertransference,* or letting their own feelings influence their responses to their patients. Analysts also must avoid reacting to their patients in the same way as the transference figure had reacted. Otherwise, the past will be repeated, and patients' fears will be confirmed. Instead, the analyst's job is to interpret the patient's actions and motivations in order to promote insight about the transference.

A common misconception about psychoanalysis is that the ultimate goal of insight is to rid the patient of all defenses. This is not the case. According to Freud, defenses are essential for the functioning of a healthy personality. Thus, rather than ridding the patient of defenses, one goal of psychoanalysis is to replace them. Defenses such as denial and projection are confronted because they distort reality dramatically, whereas "healthier" defenses, such as rationalization and sublimation, are left unchallenged. A second goal of psychoanalysis is to help patients become more aware of their basic needs or drives so that they may find socially and psychologically appropriate outlets for them (Maddi, 1980). A goal for Frances, for example, would be to admit that anger is a legitimate and acceptable part of her personality.

CURRENT STATUS OF FREUDIAN PSYCHOANALYSIS

Patients meet with psychoanalysts for 45–50 minutes several times each week, and psychoanalysis often lasts for years. Because psychoanalysis requires substantial time, expense, and self-exploration, it is accessible only to people who are relatively well functioning, introspective, and financially secure. In many respects, psychoanalysis now is construed more as a process of self-understanding than as a treatment for specific emotional disorders. This view is bolstered by the fact that very little therapy outcome research has been conducted on classical psychoanalysis. Freud believed that not every patient would benefit from the treatment—a belief shared by many contemporary practitioners. Those suffering from psychotic and personality disorders are thought to be especially unlikely to benefit, whereas people suffering from "neurotic" disorders, especially excessive anxiety, have been thought to benefit most.

Although it is still practiced, the expense and time involved, and the limited amount of data available on outcome, have made Freudian psychoanalysis less popular. However, variations on Freudian theory have led to the development of new forms of insight-oriented therapy. These revisionist approaches are termed **psychodynamic** rather than psychoanalytic. Psychodynamic psychotherapists often are more engaged and directive in therapy, and treatment may be relatively brief in comparison to psychoanalysis.

EGO ANALYSTS AND PSYCHODYNAMIC PSYCHOTHERAPY

The development of **ego analysis** is the most important innovation in Freudian theory and therapy. Ego analysis originated in the work of a number of therapists who were trained in Freudian psychoanalysis but who independently developed innovations in theory and technique. Whereas Freud emphasized the paramount role of the id in personality and psychopathology, these new theorists focused much more on the ego. The major function of the ego, according to Freudian theory, is to mediate between the conflicting impulses of the id and the superego (see Chapter 2). Of equal importance to ego analysts, however, is the ego's role in dealing with reality (Hartmann, Kris, & Loewenstein, 1947). Ego analysts therefore are concerned with unconscious motivations, but they also consider the patient's dealings with the external world. They attend to the role of society and culture in producing emotional disturbance, as well to the effects of current life circumstances and the patient's reactions to them.

Of greatest importance in ego analysis are the patient's past and present interpersonal relationships. The ego analyst Harry Stack Sullivan (1892–1949) was extremely influential in highlighting this paramount role of relationships. Like many interpersonal theorists, Sullivan saw two basic dimensions of interpersonal relationships. One dimension reflects interpersonal power, ranging from dominance to submission. A second dimension concerns interpersonal closeness, with affiliation on one end of the continuum and hostility at the opposite pole.

Other especially influential ego analysts include Erik Erikson (1902–1994) and Karen Horney (1885–1952). Horney's (1939) most lasting contribution has been her suggestion that people have conflicting ego needs. Essentially, Horney argued that there are competing human (ego) needs for closeness, for dominance, and for autonomy. She viewed people with interpersonal or intrapsychic conflicts as being too rigid in fulfilling only one of these needs. In her view, the key to a healthy personality is finding a balance among the three styles of relating to others. Frances's characteristic style and her conflicting needs come across pretty clearly.

Erikson's stage theory of development, as with other ego analysts, was a critical departure from Freud and focused on the interpersonal context. This can be seen in his emphasis on the externally oriented psycho*social* stages of development rather than the internally oriented psycho*sexual* stages. Erikson also introduced the argument that an individual's personality is not fixed by early experience but continues to develop as a result of predictable psychosocial conflicts throughout the life span (see Chapter 17). In contrast, Freud viewed personality patterns as being fixed by intrapsychic conflicts that occurred primarily during the first few years of life.

John Bowlby's (1907–1991) attachment theory (see Chapter 2) perhaps has had the greatest effect on contemporary thought about interpersonal influences on personality and psychopathology. Freud viewed closeness in relationships as merely an outgrowth of the reduction of primary drives, such as hunger and sex. In contrast, Bowlby emphasized the need for close relationships as essential for healthy functioning.

SHORT-TERM PSYCHODYNAMIC PSYCHOTHERAPY

Psychodynamic psychotherapists are more actively involved with their patients than are classically Freudian analysts. They are more ready to direct the patient's recollections, to focus on current life circumstances, and to offer interpretations quickly and directly. Most psychodynamic psychotherapists are also much more "human" in conducting therapy. They may be distant and reflective at times, but they also are willing to offer appropriate emotional support (Garfield, 1989).

Short-term psychodynamic psychotherapy is a form of treatment that uses many psychoanalytic techniques. Therapeutic neutrality is typically maintained, and transference remains a central issue, but the short-term psychodynamic therapist actively focuses on a particular emotional issue rather than relying on free association (Garfield, 1989; Sifneos, 1988). The short-term approach is gaining increased attention because it typically is limited to 25 sessions

psychodynamic   A variation on the Freudian approach that searches for unconscious conflicts and motivations, but does not adhere to Freud literally as in psychoanalysis.

ego analysis   Originated in the work of different therapists trained in Freudian psychoanalysis, but who focus much more on the ego than on the id. Ego analysts are concerned with the patient's dealings with the external world.

Harry Stack Sullivan (1892–1949) was a U.S. psychiatrist and ego analyst. Sullivan suggested that personality could be conceptualized in interpersonal terms and not just in intrapsychic ones.

or less and therefore is less expensive and more amenable to research (Garfield, 1989; Luborksy, 1984; Luborsky, Barber, & Beutler, 1993). Current research on psychodynamic psychotherapy generally supports Freud's observation that psychodynamic therapy is ineffective in treating more severe disorders, although it may be effective in treating milder anxiety (Luborsky et al., 1993). There still is a pressing need for further evidence on the technique, however.

behavior therapy An approach to psychotherapy that focuses on behavior change in the present; includes a diverse array of techniques, many of which were developed from basic, psychological research.

behaviorism The belief within scientific psychology that observable behaviors, not unobservable cognitive or emotional states, are the appropriate focus of psychological study.

systematic desensitization A treatment for overcoming fears and phobias developed by Joseph Wolpe. Involves learning relaxation skills, developing a fear hierarchy, and systematic exposure to imagined, feared events while simultaneously maintaining relaxation.

Behavior Therapy

Behavior therapy focuses on behavior change in the present, not on insight about the past. The approach includes a diverse array of techniques, many of which were developed on the basis of psychological research findings.

The beginnings of behavior therapy can be traced to John B. Watson's (1878–1958) writings in the early part of the twentieth century. Watson was the key figure in developing **behaviorism** in American psychology—the belief that observable behaviors, not unobservable cognitive or emotional states, are the appropriate focus of psychological study. Watson maintained that abnormal behavior was learned and could be unlearned, just like normal behavior. He viewed the behavior therapist's job as analogous to that of a teacher.

Unlike psychoanalysis, behavior therapy does not offer a substantive theoretical core concerning the composition of the human personality. Rather, it is an outcome-oriented approach relying on empirical evaluation. This empirical emphasis is evident in the behavior therapist's application of psychological science to clinical problems and in the hundreds of treatment outcome experiments that have been conducted on behavior therapy.

The behavior therapist's focus on present behavior, learning processes, and empirical evaluation can be seen in the diverse treatment techniques that are part of the approach. In the following sections we consider some of the most common techniques: classical conditioning, operant conditioning, and cognitive behavior therapy techniques.

CLASSICAL CONDITIONING TECHNIQUES

A number of behavior therapy techniques have been developed from Pavlov's theory of classical conditioning (see Chapter 2). All classical conditioning techniques use *counterconditioning,* altering existing responses by pairing new responses with old stimuli.

Joseph Wolpe developed the most influential counterconditioning technique. Wolpe, a South African psychiatrist, has concentrated his research and therapy efforts on eliminating phobias. Wolpe (1958) assumed that at least some phobias were learned through classical conditioning. He reasoned that if fears could be learned, they could be unlearned. The key was to break the association between stimulus and response. The technique he developed to do so is called **systematic desensitization.**

Joseph Wolpe is a leading behavior therapist. Wolpe developed systematic desensitization, a pioneering technique that uses classical conditioning to eliminate fears.

Systematic Desensitization Systematic desensitization has three key elements. The first is relaxation training. Wolpe believed that in order to replace anxiety as a response to a feared stimulus, the new conditioned response, relaxation, must be easily elicited. He focused on the technique of *progressive muscle relaxation,* a method of inducing a calm state through the contraction and subsequent relaxation of all of the major muscle groups. The second component of systematic desensitization is the construction of a *hierarchy of fears* ranging from very mild to very frightening stimuli. Because anxiety initially is a stronger response to the feared stimulus than is relaxation, Wolpe thought that exposure to fears must be gradual, or the relaxation would be overwhelmed by the anxiety. The third part of systematic desensitization is the pairing of the feared stimulus with the relaxation response. Wolpe had his clients carry out this pairing in their imagination. Thus systematic desensitization involves imagining increasingly fearful events while simultaneously maintaining a state of relaxation.

Getting help

How can you find the right therapist? Our basic advice is to be a good consumer. Find out more about the nature of the psychological problem and about treatments that work. To the extent that you feel comfortable discussing your interest in finding a therapist, talk to people or professionals you know and ask who they recommend in your community. You will find a lot of useful information in later chapters in this textbook on treatments for specific disorders, including the many practical suggestions in the Getting Help sections.

As a good consumer, you should consider carefully what type of treatment you think you prefer and who you prefer to see. A good fit between you and any therapist is an important part of effective therapy. For example, you may be more or less comfortable seeing a man or a woman. Many therapists offer, or even expect you to have, an initial interview before deciding about beginning therapy with them. If you are not comfortable, you should feel free to shop around until you find a therapist who not only offers well-supported treatments but who also seems to understand you well. In fact, you may want to consult briefly with a few professionals before starting therapy, so you can pick the one who seems best for you.

People from a lot of professional backgrounds offer psychotherapy. The person usually is more important than the profession, but we recommend that you see a professional from one of the three major mental health professions—a clinical psychologist, a psychiatrist, or a clinical social worker.

If you feel you may need medication, you will need to see a medical doctor in order to obtain a prescription. Your family physician may be willing to prescribe antidepressants or some other commonly used medications. You might need to talk to a psychiatrist, a physician specializing in mental disorders, if your family physician is uncomfortable offering you a particular type of medication or if you also feel you would benefit from discussions with someone trained as a therapist.

If you are considering psychotherapy, read about different types of therapy, particularly those that research shows to be more helpful for certain disorders. In addition to consulting the relevant Getting Help and treatment sections of this book, you might also want to explore some resources on the Internet. The Web site of the National Institute of Mental Health http://www.nimh.nih.gov contains a lot of useful, up-to-date information on disorders and treatments. We refer you to Web sites on specific disorders and specific treatments in later Getting Help sections. ♛

Most investigators agree that *exposure* is the key to fear reduction. This observation has led to the development of variations on desensitization techniques, the most notable of which is in vivo desensitization. In vivo desensitization involves gradually being exposed to the feared stimulus in real life while simultaneously maintaining a state of relaxation. Research on in vivo desensitization indicates that the way to overcome fears is to confront them.

OPERANT CONDITIONING TECHNIQUES

A second set of behavior therapy techniques is based on Skinner's work on operant conditioning (see Chapter 2). The major assumption of these approaches is straightforward: Behaviors that are reinforced will increase, and those that are punished will diminish.

Contingency Management   The goal of *contingency management* is to reward desirable behavior systematically and to extinguish or punish undesirable behavior. In order to achieve this goal, the therapist must control relevant rewards and punishments. Thus contingency management is used primarily in circumstances where the therapist has considerable direct or indirect control over the client's environment, such as in institutional settings or when children are brought for treatment by their parents.

The **token economy** is an example of contingency management that has been adopted in many institutional settings. For example, in a group home for juvenile offenders, a token economy may specify that residents earn tokens for completing schoolwork and household chores, while they lose tokens for arguing or fighting. Each resident's behavior is monitored and recorded, and tokens are "paid" accordingly. The key to the success of the program is that tokens can be exchanged for rewards desired by the residents—for example, going out unescorted on a Saturday night.

Research shows that contingency management successfully changes behavior for diverse problems such as institutionalized clients with schizophrenia (Paul & Lentz, 1977) and juvenile offenders

token economy   A type of contingency management program that has been adopted in many institutional settings. Desired and undesired behaviors are identified, contingencies are defined, behavior is monitored, and rewards or punishments are given according to the rules of the economy.

social skills training   A behavior therapy technique in which clients are taught new skills that are desirable and likely to be rewarded in the everyday world.

cognitive behavior therapy   The expansion of the scope of behavior therapy to include cognition and research on human information processing. Includes various general techniques, such as Beck's cognitive therapy and Ellis's RET.

cognitive therapy   A psychotherapy technique and important part of cognitive behavior therapy that was developed specifically as a treatment for depression by Aaron Beck. Beck's cognitive therapy involves challenging negative cognitive distortions through a technique called collaborative empiricism.

living in group homes (Phillips, Phillips, Wolf, & Fixsen, 1973). The evidence for success must be interpreted carefully, however. Improvements that occur in the setting where the operant program is in place often do not generalize to real-life situations (Emery & Marholin, 1977). In the real world, undesirable behavior often is rewarded, and punishments for inappropriate behavior—and rewards for appropriate behavior—often are inconsistent or delayed. Thus contingency management programs work in controlled environments, but generalization to other settings is limited.

Social Skills Training   Another behavior therapy technique based on operant conditioning principles is **social skills training.** The goal of social skills training is to teach clients new ways of behaving that are both desirable and likely to be rewarded in the everyday world (McFall, 1982). Two commonly taught skills are assertiveness (Lange & Jakubowski, 1976) and social problem solving (D'Zurrilla & Goldfried, 1971; Spivack & Shure, 1974).

The goal of *assertiveness training* is to teach clients to be direct about their feelings and wishes. The training may involve a variety of levels of detail in social skills, from learning to make eye contact to asking a boss for a raise. In teaching assertiveness, therapists frequently use *role playing,* an improvisational acting technique that allows clients to rehearse new social skills. Clients try out new ways of acting, while the therapist assumes the role of some person in their life. Later, the therapist offers feedback and suggests different approaches to the client. In addition to teaching new social skills, assertiveness training seeks to produce cognitive change, such as learning to recognize personal "rights." Returning to the case history, for example, a behavior therapist might teach Frances that she has a right to express her feelings. She does not necessarily have the right to get everything that she wants, however. Thus assertiveness would be defined in terms of her actions, not in terms of her success in changing her mother.

Social problem solving is a multistep process that has been used to teach children and adults ways to go about solving a variety of life's problems (D'Zurrilla & Goldfried, 1971; Spivack & Shure, 1974). The first step in social problem solving involves assessing and defining the problem in detail. This step is important, as we often see problems as being more manageable when they are defined specifically. "Brainstorming" is the second step in social problem solving. In order to encourage creativity, therapists ask clients to come up with as many alternative solutions as they can imagine—even wild and crazy options—without evaluating these alternatives. The third step in social problem solving involves carefully evaluating each of the options that has been generated. Finally, one alternative is chosen and implemented, and its success in solving the problem is evaluated objectively. If the solution is unsuccessful, the entire process can be repeated until an effective solution is found.

We consider the effectiveness of social skills training in treating specific problems in subsequent chapters.

Cognitive Behavior Therapy

Many practitioners have expanded the scope of behavior therapy into the cognitive realm, a broader approach called **cognitive behavior therapy.** Cognitive behavior therapy departs from Watson's exclusive focus on observable behavior and recognizes that many unobservable cognitive processes, such as forming impressions or making judgments, are central to human learning.

Cognitive behavior therapy has been strongly influenced by the clinical work of Aaron Beck (1976). Beck's **cognitive therapy**—the most famous form of cognitive behavior therapy—was developed specifically as a treatment for depression (Beck et al., 1979; see Chapter 5). Beck suggested that depression is caused by errors in thinking. These hypothesized distortions lead depressed people to draw incorrect, negative conclusions about themselves, thus creating and maintaining the depression. Simply put, Beck hypothesized that depressed people see the world through gray-colored glasses (as opposed to the rose-colored variety). According to Beck's analysis, this negative filter makes the world appear much bleaker than it really is.

Beck's cognitive therapy involves challenging these negative distortions. Cognitive therapists gently confront their clients' cognitive fallacies in therapy, but they ask clients to decide for themselves whether their thinking is distorted based on their analysis of their own life (Beck et al., 1979).

TABLE 3–2

Some Treatment Variations within the Major Paradigms of Psychotherapy

PARADIGM OR VARIATION	DISTINGUISHING FEATURES
Psychoanalytic/Psychodynamic Therapy	
Psychoanalysis	Freud's classic treatment focuses on childhood memories and unconscious conflicts; techniques include free association, dream analysis, transference, and interpretation; several meetings a week for several years; therapist aloof.
Ego analysis	Psychodynamic treatments developed by Sullivan, Horney, Erikson, and other followers of Freud; insight is goal but the present, the conscious mind, and social relationships (the ego) considered by more active, warm therapist. Long term but shorter than psychoanalysis.
Psychodynamic psychotherapy	Many variations of this short-term, insight-oriented treatment; therapist is more directive or confrontational in interpreting defenses; treatment focuses on single issue or theme.
Behavior Therapy	
Radical behaviorism	Adheres to Watson's and Skinner's focus on behavior and eschews consideration of "internal events"; many treatments offered but therapies focus on operant and classical conditioning; short-term treatment.
Cognitive behavior therapy	Recognizes or emphasizes cognition in human learning; many techniques in addition to operant and classical conditioning, including cognitive therapy, rational–emotive therapy, self-instruction training, and attribution retraining; short-term treatment.
Humanistic Therapy	
Client-centered therapy	Rogers' nondirective therapy emphasizes warmth, genuineness, and empathy as necessary and sufficient conditions for treatment success. Length not typically structured.

For example, a cognitive therapist might ask Frances to keep a record of her various family conflicts, including a brief description of the disputes and of the circumstances that preceded and followed each episode. Together with Frances, the cognitive therapist would use this information to challenge Frances's tendency to blame herself for the troubled relationships, a tendency that presumably results from a cognitive distortion rather than an accurate appraisal of her interactions.

Humanistic Therapies

Humanistic psychotherapy originally was promoted as a "third force" to counteract what were seen as the overly mechanistic and deterministic views of both the psychodynamic and behavioral approaches to psychotherapy (see Table 3–2). Humanists argue that psychodynamic, behavioral, and biomedical therapists overlook the most essential of all human qualities: the individual's ability to make choices and freely determine his or her future.

Humanistic therapists believe that emotional distress results from the frustrations of human existence, particularly from alienation from the self and others. They also argue that each individual has the responsibility for finding meaning in her or his own life. Unlike the behavior

humanistic psychotherapy An approach that assumes that the most essential human quality is the ability to make choices and freely act on them (free will). Promoted as a "third force" to counteract the deterministic views of psychodynamic and behavioral approaches to psychotherapy.

client-centered therapy   Carl Rogers's humanistic therapy that follows the client's lead. Therapists offer warmth, empathy, and genuineness, but clients solve their own problems.

empathy   Emotional understanding. Empathy involves understanding others' unique feelings and perspectives. Highlighted by Rogers but basic to most forms of psychotherapy.

Carl Rogers (1902–1987) was a U. S. psychologist who developed client-centered therapy. Rogers asserted that therapeutic warmth, empathy, and genuineness were the necessary and sufficient conditions for successful psychotherapy

therapist, the humanistic therapist does not believe that treatment can solve problems. Rather, treatment is seen only as a way to help individuals make their own life choices and resolve their own dilemmas (Rogers, 1961).

To help clients make choices, humanistic therapists strive to increase *emotional awareness.* They encourage clients to recognize and experience their true feelings. Like psychodynamic approaches, this involves "uncovering" hidden emotions, and some psychologists therefore classify the two treatments together as insight therapies (London, 1964). However, humanistic therapists are more concerned with how their clients are feeling than with why they are feeling that way. They focus on experiencing life, not on the structure of the personality. Thus, like behavior therapy, humanistic therapy is much more oriented to the present than is psychodynamic treatment.

One unique aspect of humanistic psychotherapy is the paramount importance placed on the therapist–client relationship. Humanistic therapists view a genuine and reciprocal relationship between therapist and client as the central means of producing therapeutic change. Therapists from other schools also place importance on the therapist–client relationship, but the relationship is viewed primarily as a means of delivering the treatment. In humanistic therapy, the relationship *is* the treatment.

CLIENT-CENTERED THERAPY

Carl Rogers (1902–1987) and his **client-centered therapy** provide the clearest example of the humanistic focus on the therapeutic relationship. Rogers (1951) wrote extensively about the process of fostering a warm and genuine relationship between therapist and client. He particularly noted the importance of **empathy,** or emotional understanding. Empathy involves "putting yourself in someone else's shoes" as a way of understanding the other person's unique feelings and perspectives. In order to demonstrate empathy, the therapist must communicate this emotional understanding. Empathy is conveyed by reflecting the client's feelings and, at a deeper level, by sharing an understanding of emotions that remain unexpressed.

In forming an empathic relationship, the client-centered therapist does not act as an "expert" who knows more about the client than the client knows about himself or herself. Rather, the humanistic therapist endeavors to share in another human's experience. In fact, Rogers encouraged *self-disclosure* on the part of the therapist. In contrast to the psychoanalyst's distance, client-centered therapists may intentionally reveal aspects of their own feelings and experiences to their clients. The ability to share another's perspective can come from many life experiences, not just from professional training. For this reason, Rogers felt that client-centered therapists did not need to be professionals. Rather, they could be ordinary people who had faced life difficulties similar to those of their clients.

Rogers also felt that client-centered therapists must be able to demonstrate *unconditional positive regard* for their clients. This involves valuing the clients for who they are and refraining from judging them. Because of this basic respect for the client's humanity, client-centered therapists avoid directing the therapeutic process. According to Rogers, if clients are successful in experiencing and accepting themselves, they will achieve their own resolution to their difficulties. Thus client-centered therapy is *nondirective.*

HUMANISTIC PSYCHOTHERAPY: A MEANS, NOT AN END?

Little research supports the effectiveness of client-centered therapy in treating abnormal behavior (Greenberg, Elliott, & Lietaer, 1994). One problem in evaluating effectiveness is that clients who seek humanistic treatments often are functioning rather well in their lives. They view therapy as a growth experience, not as a treatment for an emotional problem. Another problem is that few investigators have conducted psychotherapy outcome research on humanistic therapy.

We should note, however, that Rogers and his colleagues were strongly committed to psychotherapy *process* research. As we discuss in more detail shortly, research on psychotherapy processes indicates that therapists who are humanistic in style are more effective when using virtually any treatment technique. Empathy and other relationship factors have been empirically documented to predict successful outcome across different approaches to psychotherapy (Rogers, 1957; Truax & Carkhuff, 1967).

Research on Psychotherapy

Now that we have an introduction to the major treatments for psychological disorders, we can begin to ask some basic and important questions about psychotherapy. Does psychotherapy work? Many people claim not to "believe" in psychotherapy. Is their skepticism founded? And if therapy is helpful, what approach to psychotherapy works best? Which is more effective, psychotherapy or medication? These questions are straightforward, but psychotherapy research does not offer simple answers.

Based on our own evaluation of the extensive research on psychotherapy, we have reached three major conclusions about psychotherapy. First, psychotherapy *does work*—for many people and for many problems. Second, the major approaches to psychotherapy share basic similarities that are often overlooked (e.g., the therapist–client relationship), and these common factors contribute to the success of therapy in important ways. Third, different treatments, including medication, are more or less effective for different disorders. We discuss evidence pertaining to the first conclusion in reviewing psychotherapy *outcome* research. We address the second conclusion when we consider psychotherapy *process* research. We focus on the third conclusion throughout subsequent chapters of the text where we discuss specific biological, psychological, and social interventions that are most effective in preventing or treating specific disorders.

"*So, while extortion, racketeering, and murder may be bad acts, they don't make you a bad person.*"

Courtesy *The New Yorker*

Psychotherapy Outcome Research

Psychotherapy outcome research examines the outcome, or result, of psychotherapy—that is, its effectiveness for relieving symptoms, eliminating disorders, and/or improving life functioning. Hundreds of studies have compared the outcome of psychotherapy with the results of alternative treatments or with the effect of receiving no treatment at all.

Treatment outcome researchers widely accept that about two-thirds of clients improve as a result of psychotherapy. Some skeptics have suggested, however, that far more than one-third of untreated emotional disorders have a *spontaneous remission.* That is, many people with psychological problems may improve without any treatment at all. In fact, the British psychologist Hans Eysenck—who wrote one of the earliest and most famous criticisms of psychotherapy—concluded that treatment was totally ineffective for this very reason. In reviewing early evidence on psychotherapy, Eysenck (1952/1992) agreed that about 2 out of 3 people were helped by therapy. However, he asserted that *two-thirds,* not one-third, of people with emotional problems improve without treatment. Thus he concluded that psychotherapy offered little in the way of extra help.

Who is right? How many people improve without treatment? This is a complicated question to answer, because most people in distress seek help informally if they cannot get professional treatment. For example, if they cannot see a mental health professional, emotionally distraught people are like to seek counseling and advice from family members, friends, or religious leaders. Thus "treatment" can be difficult to define, and researchers face numerous practical and ethical problems trying to ensure that clients assigned to "no treatment" control groups actually do not receive treatment.

Informal counseling often is helpful, as you surely know from your own life experiences. Thus some experts argue that "no treatment" controls actually receive some form of "treatment." If so, at least some people in "no treatment" control groups improve as a result of the support they receive and not because of a spontaneous remission. Other people argue that informal help is *not* psychotherapy (Lambert, Shapiro, & Bergin, 1986).

Is the estimate that one-third of people improve without treatment too high or too low? We think it is about right. We believe that social support *is* an important element of psychotherapy, but, in any case, improvement rates following psychotherapy exceed improvement rates following unstructured meetings with a therapist (e.g., Borkovec & Costello, 1993; see Research Close-Up on p. 000). Thus we conclude that psychotherapy does, indeed, work for many people with many problems (Lambert, Shapiro, & Bergin, 1986).

EFFICACY AND EFFECTIVENESS: THE *CONSUMER REPORTS* STUDY

We have been discussing the most basic type of psychotherapy outcome research, that is, the *efficacy study*, in which researchers conduct experiments in which they randomly assign patients to alternative treatments or to no treatment at all. The best efficacy studies are tightly controlled. Not only do efficacy studies assign patients to treatments at random, but they also select patients with clearly defined problems and offer carefully controlled treatments (Seligman, 1995). For example, an efficacy study may treat only clients who are clinically depressed but suffer from no other disorder. Therapy may be restricted to 12 sessions of Beck's cognitive therapy, and therapists may not be allowed to depart from restrictions about what should and should not be discussed in treatment—typically as spelled out in a lengthy "treatment manual."

Efficacy studies tell us if psychotherapy *can* work under prescribed circumstances, but efficacy studies do not tell us whether psychotherapy *does* work as it is actually practiced. In everyday psychotherapy, most clients have multiple problems and choose therapists with care, not at random. Moreover, most therapists are eclectic and tailor the type and length of treatment to the perceived needs of individual clients (Seligman, 1995). How does psychotherapy fare under these circumstances? This question is examined by a second type of psychotherapy outcome research, the *effectiveness study*.

Effectiveness studies do not use random assignment; thus they are correlational studies that cannot inform us about cause and effect (see Chapter 1). Correlational studies can provide valuable descriptive information, however. In fact, the magazine *Consumer Reports* (1995, November) conducted an effectiveness study of psychotherapy by surveying readers who had seen a mental health professional in the past 3 years. The nearly 3000 respondents generally rated their experiences in psychotherapy highly. Among the major findings of the *Consumer Reports* study were the following (1995, November; Seligman, 1995):

- Therapy helped. Of the 426 people who were feeling "very poor" at the beginning of treatment, 87 percent reported feeling "very good," "good," or at least "so-so" when they were surveyed.
- The major mental health professionals were equally effective. The clients of psychologists, psychiatrists, and social workers reported no differences in treatment outcome, but all three professions were *more* effective than marriage counselors.
- Medication added little to psychotherapy. People who received psychotherapy alone improved no more or less than people who received psychotherapy plus medication.

Because the *Consumer Reports* study was a correlational study, you can and should question the interpretation of these findings. It is possible, for example, that people who had good experiences in psychotherapy were more likely to respond to the survey than were people who had bad experiences. Nevertheless, the findings of this survey bolster our conclusion that psychotherapy works for many people and many problems, because they are broadly consistent with the results of numerous carefully controlled efficacy studies.

TWO PREDICTORS OF TREATMENT OUTCOME: TREATMENT LENGTH AND THE YAVIS CLIENT

Research indicates that if therapy is going to be effective, it usually will be effective rather quickly. As Figure 3–1 indicates, most people who improve in psychotherapy do so in the first several months of treatment. Improvement continues with longer term therapy but at a notably slower rate (Howard et al., 1986). The *Consumer Reports* study revealed a similar pattern, although the rate of improvement did not slow as dramatically after 6 months of treatment (Seligman, 1995). Other evidence suggests that 1 year, and not 6 months, may be a more realistic trial period for clients who do not respond earlier in treatment (Kopta, Howard, Lowry, & Beutler, 1994).

Significantly, clients' background characteristics also predict outcome in psychotherapy. The acronym *YAVIS* was coined to indicate that clients improve more in psychotherapy when they are "young, attractive, verbal, intelligent, and successful." This finding has caused considerable concern, for it seems to indicate that psychotherapy works best for the most advantaged members of our society (Lorion & Felner, 1986).

What about the disadvantaged and those who are discriminated against? Research on psychotherapy with ethnic minorities is limited in scope, but a recent review of the literature

Figure 3–1 Relation between Number of Psychotherapy Sessions and Percentage of Clients Improved

Source: K.I. Howard, S.M. Kopta, M.S. Krause, and D.E. Orlinsky, 1986, The dose–effect relationship in psychotherapy, *American Psychologist, 41,* 159–164.

concluded that there is not enough evidence to decide whether psychotherapy is effective or ineffective for minority group members (Sue et al., 1994). Some evidence suggests that psychotherapy is more effective when client and therapist share a similar cultural background and when the treatment is tailored to the specific culture. Therapy also may be more effective when therapists are trained to be sensitive to minority issues (Casas, 1995; Sue et al., 1994; see Further Thoughts on page 76).

Psychotherapy Process Research: Toward the Integration of Psychotherapies

Psychotherapy process research studies qualities of the therapist–client relationship that predict successful outcome irrespective of the theoretical orientation of the therapist. Much interest in common factors and psychotherapy integration was prompted by Jerome Frank, an American trained both in psychology and psychiatry, who has spent most of his career at the Johns Hopkins Medical School. Frank's analysis begins with his very broad definition of psychotherapy as involving

(1) a trained, socially sanctioned healer, whose healing powers are accepted by the sufferer and by his social group or an important segment of it

(2) a sufferer who seeks relief from the healer

(3) a circumscribed, more or less structured series of contacts between the healer and the sufferer, through which the healer, often with the aid of a group, tries to produce certain changes in the sufferer's emotional state, attitudes, and behavior. All concerned believe these changes will help him. Although physical and chemical adjuncts may be used, the healing influence is primarily exercised by words, acts, and rituals in which sufferer, healer and—if there is one—group, participate jointly." (Frank, 1973, pp. 2–3)

Frank goes on to point out, "These three features are common not only to all forms of psychotherapy as the term is generally used, but also to methods of primitive healing" (p. 3).

It is easy to misunderstand Frank's argument. Is he saying that psychotherapy is little more than voodoo? No, Frank's point is just the opposite. He argues that psychotherapists should attempt to harness the powerful psychological tools used intuitively by both primitive and modern healers.

Jerome Frank is a U.S. psychologist and psychiatrist. Frank has analyzed psychotherapy as a process of persuasion and healing, drawing broad analogies between therapy and healing rituals in both industrialized and nonindustrialized cultures.

further thoughts

Psychotherapy with Ethnic Minorities

More than 25 percent of people living in the United States today are members of ethnic minority groups, and demographers predict that during the twenty-first century the number of ethnic minorities will surpass the number of white Americans of European descent. Among the dozens of ethnic minority groups in the United States, the most numerous are African Americans, Latinos, Asian Americans, and Native Americans. Treating people from such diverse backgrounds represents a major challenge to the psychology profession. Indeed, critics have questioned the sensitivity, appropriateness, and the effectiveness of mainstream psychotherapy in meeting the mental health needs of ethnic groups (Casas, 1995; Sue et al., 1994).

One basic concern is that mental health professionals recognize the unique cultural values and societal experiences of members of different ethnic minority groups. Psychotherapists must be aware of both commonalities and diversity in experience. Minority groups share experiences, such as the historical and ongoing racism faced by African Americans, but members of minority groups also are heterogeneous in terms of their societal, political, and cultural backgrounds. For example, the experience of Asian Americans, who have come to the United States voluntarily, is very different from the experience of Native Americans, who were driven from their homeland and confined to reservations. Wide individual differences in experience are also found *within* minority groups. For example, peoples designated as "Latino" are actually a diverse group with origins in Mexico, the Caribbean, and Central and South America. Similarly, the experiences of African Americans differ widely based on socioeconomic status, religion, and region of upbringing.

A second basic concern is that mental health professionals recognize that many of the emotional and adjustment problems faced by ethnic minorities stem from social and cultural experiences and not from individual psychological problems. A general challenge faced by all ethnic minorities is *acculturation,* the process of learning or adopting the cultural patterns of the majority group (Casas, 1995; Sue et al., 1994). The acculturation of diverse ethnic groups into the mainstream is a political goal of the American "melting pot." However, the process of acculturation taxes individual coping resources, as people's prior beliefs and actions may not be supported by the dominant culture. In fact, ethnic values and social customs may be undermined or even derided by the majority culture, and acculturation pressures often disrupt adaptive ethnic traditions and relationships. Yet another problem is that our society makes acculturation more difficult for the members of some ethnic minority groups who are not readily accepted by members of the dominant culture unless—or even if—the individual minority member wholly adopts the majority culture. In particular, African Americans and Native Americans have faced tremendous challenges in acculturation. Unlike immigrants, the members of these ethnic groups did not choose to become Americans, and historically both groups have faced discrimination in mainstream society and repeated attempts to obliterate their cultural heritage.

Acculturation and other social forces often challenge and change *ethnic identity,* the ethnic minority members' understanding of self in terms of their own culture. Atkinson, Morten, and Sue (1993) have proposed a five-stage model of the development of ethnic identity. The stages include (1) *conformity,* a time of self-depreciation and discrimination; (2) *dissonance,* a period of conflict between self-depreciation and appreciation of one's ethnicity; (3) *resistance and immersion,* a stage of self-appreciation and ethnocentrism, accompanied by depreciation of the majority group; (4) *introspection,* a phase of questioning the basis of self-appreciation, as well as the basis for depreciation of the majority group; and (5) *synergetic articulation and awareness,* including both self-appreciation and appreciation of the basis for majority group values. The model of ethnic identity development can be viewed as analogous to how the group process of acculturation proceeds at the level of the individual. Although researchers have only begun to study this model of ethnic identity development, recognition of the influence of acculturation pressures on the development of individual identity is essential both to assessing individual well-being and to establishing a strong therapeutic relationship (Casas, 1995).

Frank (1961, 1973) notes that, like primitive healers, psychotherapists and other helping professionals are imbued with powers that stem from culturally sanctioned roles. The power comes from the mystery of the unconscious mind, incomprehensible medical treatments, or even from science itself. In the United States today, we strongly believe in the effectiveness of science, and we often treat science as if it were a mystical force. In short, even in modern societies part of the professional helper's healing power comes from the belief that doctors can heal.

THE PLACEBO EFFECT

The **placebo effect** is one important and dramatic illustration of the healing power of beliefs in medicine and in psychotherapy. In medicine, *placebos* are pills that are pharmacologically inert; that is, they have no medicinal value. More broadly, placebos are any type of treatment that contains no known "active ingredients" for treating the condition being evaluated. But the absence of active ingredients does not prevent placebos from healing. Placebos have powerful influences on both physical and psychological ailments. In medicine, potent placebo effects have been demonstrated in dentistry, optometry, cancer treatment, and even surgery (Shapiro & Morris, 1978). Some psychiatric outpatients who are given placebo medications report greatly improved comfort that lasts over an extended period of time (Frank, 1973). The power of placebos also lies behind the common wisdom to "use new treatments quickly before they lose their power to heal." All helping professionals know that the latest treatment owes part of its effectiveness to its being the latest treatment (Shapiro & Morris, 1978).

The ultimate goal of treatment research is to identify therapies that produce change above and beyond placebo effects, that is, to find interventions that contain one or more active ingredients for treating a particular disorder. Thus many investigations in medicine and psychotherapy include **placebo control groups**—groups of patients who are given treatments that are intentionally designed to have no active ingredients.

Placebos apparently work because they create an *expectation* of change. They work because the patient expects them to work. Placebos also work because the healer expects them to work, thus making double-blind placebo control studies necessary. In a **double-blind study,** neither the physician nor the patient knows whether the prescribed pill is the real medication or a placebo. These double precautions are necessary because the expectations of both the patient and the physician repeatedly have been found to influence the success of all kinds of biomedical treatments (Rosenthal & Rosnow, 1969).

Unfortunately, it is impossible to conduct double-blind studies of psychotherapy because researchers cannot disguise from therapists whether a particular psychological intervention is a placebo. Thus it is important to be aware of *allegiance effects* in psychotherapy research. That is, psychotherapy researchers typically find that their favorite treatment—the one to which they hold an allegiance—is the most effective treatment. Allegiance effects tell us that, as with other treatments, the therapist's expectations influence the effectiveness of different forms of psychotherapy.

Heightened expectations for change are created by different approaches to psychotherapy; thus they are one common factor in psychotherapy. There are many more important common factors in therapy, however, most of which involve aspects of the therapist–client relationship (Mahoney, 1991; see Table 3–3 on page 78). Different schools of therapy construe the therapist–client relationship in various ways, but they all recognize its importance (Strupp, 1986). We consider some essential components of this unique relationship—basic issues if diverse approaches to psychotherapy are to be integrated—in the two brief sections that follow.

PSYCHOTHERAPY AS SOCIAL SUPPORT

All major schools of psychotherapy emphasize the importance of warmth in the therapist–client relationship. Research on psychotherapy process indicates that a therapist's supportiveness is related to positive outcomes across approaches to treatment (Parloff, Waskow, & Wolfe, 1978). Significantly, objective indicators of a therapist's support are less potent predictors of successful outcome than are a client's rating of the therapist. A supportive relationship is not defined simply by a therapist's behavior but by a therapist's behavior in relation to a particular client. Some, perhaps most, people feel that they are understood by a therapist who makes empathic statements, but others may be more comfortable with a therapist who is somewhat detached (Beutler, Crago, & Arizmendi, 1986). Thus clients may perceive different therapeutic stances as supportive, depending on the particular types of relationships with which they are most comfortable.

A supportive therapeutic relationship is important, but is therapy more than this? Research indicates that therapist supportiveness is neither necessary nor sufficient for therapeutic success, despite the fact that supportiveness predicts a more successful outcome (Beutler, Crago, & Arizmendi, 1986). Many other factors influence treatment effectiveness.

placebo effect   The improvement in a condition produced by a placebo (sometimes a substantial change). An overriding goal of scientific research is to identify treatments that exceed placebo effects.

placebo control group   A group of subjects given a treatment with no known specific ingredients for the purpose of comparison with alternative treatments that are thought to contain specific, therapeutic benefits.

double blind, placebo-controlled study   A study in which neither the therapist nor the patient knows whether the patient receives the real treatment (for example, a medication) or a placebo.

TABLE 3–3

Common Characteristics of Effective Brief Psychotherapies

1. Treatment is offered soon after the problem is identified.
2. Assessment of the problem is rapid and occurs early in treatment.
3. A therapeutic alliance is established quickly, and it is used to encourage change in the client.
4. Therapy is designed to be time-limited, and the therapist uses this to encourage rapid progress.
5. The goals of therapy are limited to a few specified areas.
6. The therapist is directive in managing the treatment sessions.
7. Therapy is focused on a specific theme.
8. The client is encouraged to express strong emotions or troubling experiences.
9. A flexible approach is taken in the choice of treatment techniques.

Source: *Adapted from M. P. Koss and J. M. Butcher, 1986. Research on brief psychotherapy. In S. L. Garfield and A. E. Bergin (Eds.),* Handbook of Psychotherapy and Behavior Change, *3rd ed., pp. 627–670. New York: Wiley.*

PSYCHOTHERAPY AS SOCIAL INFLUENCE

Psychotherapy is a process of social influence as well as one of social support. The three major schools of therapy clearly differ in terms of the degree to which therapists directly attempt to influence clients. Beyond their explicit theoretical stance, however, all therapists influence clients in ways that are both obvious and subtle, intentional and unintentional.

One social influence is the nonjudgmental attitude found in all major approaches to psychotherapy. People often fear that their secret fears and failures will be met with criticism or ridicule, and the therapist's acceptance can come as a welcome relief. Whether construed as catharsis, extinction, or a corrective emotional experience, a common change process found in all psychotherapies is the provision of a safe forum for secret revelations (Pennebaker, 1990; Strong, 1978).

All therapists also influence their clients by pointing out discrepancies to them, that is, by offering interpretations. For example, a therapist may note inconsistencies between Frances's professed beliefs and her actions: "You talk about being sad, but you sound angry." Such an interpretation can create *dissonance* or internal conflict for Frances. As a way of resolving dissonance, we all alter our beliefs to be more consistent. Thus Frances may be forced to grapple with the inconsistency between her avowed sadness and her angry tone. For example, she might decide that she *is* angry—justifiably so—or perhaps she may instead recognize that she is uncomfortable showing genuine sadness. Of course, a therapist must be a credible source if interpretations are to be effective (Strong, 1978). If a therapist is not credible, a client can resolve dissonance not by challenging personal beliefs but by discounting the therapist's perspective.

Process research clearly demonstrates the social influence of psychotherapy. For example, researchers have found that clients tend to adopt beliefs similar to those of their therapists. In fact, treatment is more effective when, over time, clients' beliefs become more similar to those of their therapists (Beutler, Crago, & Arizmendi, 1986; Kelly, 1990). Positive outcomes are more likely when the changed beliefs relate directly to psychotherapy—for example, the importance of expressing emotions—than when they reflect broad social and religious values (Beutler, Machado, & Neufeldt, 1994).

Nevertheless, recognition of social influence raises questions about values in psychotherapy. Psychotherapy is not value-free. There are values inherent in the nature of therapy itself—for example, the belief that expressing emotions is good. Moreover, the values of individual therapists about such topics as love, marriage, work, and family necessarily influence clients. Like the rest of the human race, psychotherapists cannot transcend their own beliefs and values. All we can do is to recognize our biases and inform our clients about them. Because psychotherapy is a process of social influence, values invariably enter into therapy.

couples therapy Partners who are involved in an intimate relationship are seen together in psychotherapy; sometimes called marital therapy or marriage counseling. Improving communication and negotiation are common goals.

Changing Social Systems: Couples, Family, and Group Therapy

Biomedical approaches and psychotherapy are not the only treatments for individual psychological problems. Returning to the case of Frances, we realize that her family relationships should improve if we successfully treat her depression with medication or psychotherapy. Therapy with her parents and/or husband also might alleviate Frances's depression. More broadly, some theorists would argue that Frances would be less depressed if women were encouraged to assume more independent roles in society.

In fact, social interventions for psychological disorders include treatments for couples and entire families, group therapy, and even broader efforts at preventing emotional disorders through improving society. As is true of individual psychotherapy, there are different "schools" of couples, family, and group therapy, and the goals of alternative social interventions vary widely. For these reasons, we must be selective in our overview of social approaches to treatment.

Couples Therapy

Couples therapy involves seeing intimate partners together in psychotherapy. This approach is sometimes called *marital therapy* or *marriage counseling*, but the reference to couples captures the range of partners who may seek treatment together. Dating pairs, prospective mates, live-in partners, and gay and lesbian couples also may seek couples therapy.

The goal of couples therapy typically is to improve the relationship, and not to treat the individual. However, couples treatment also may be used to help both partners function more adequately when one member suffers from a psychological problem. In treating relationships, all couples therapists focus on resolving conflicts and promoting mutual satisfaction. Couples therapists do not tell their clients what compromises they should accept or how they should change their relationship. Instead, they typically help partners to improve their *communication* and *negotiation* skills (Baruth & Huber, 1984; Fincham & Bradbury, 1990; Margolin, 1987).

A couples therapist might suggest to Frances that she had a problem with "mind reading" in her marriage. Frances may be hoping (or expecting) that her husband would know what she wanted without telling him directly. She might want more attention, for example, but perhaps she never told her husband that lack of attention was a problem. She may want him to "figure it out for himself." Couples therapists point out that it is impossible to read another person's mind, and they encourage partners in close relationships to communicate their wishes directly (Gottman et al., 1976). This may sound simple, but learning to be direct can be tricky for many people. Frances may have felt selfish when making requests, for example, or perhaps she wanted to be "surprised" with her husband's attention. She may have thought that his attention would be less meaningful if she asked for it.

Another component of most couples therapies is negotiation or *conflict resolution* (Heitler, 1992). Negotiation is the imprecise art of give and take. Most approaches to negotiation emphasize the importance of clearly defining problems, considering a wide range of solutions, uncovering "hidden agendas" (unstated issues), and experimenting with alternative solutions. These strategies are similar to the social problem-solving model discussed earlier, and this approach has been effectively applied to work with couples (Emery, 1994). Polite communication also is an essential component of negotiation, and setting ground rules can be essential to encouraging polite communication. Examples of ground rules include not raising your voice, not interrupting the other person, and speaking about your own feelings—that is, not telling your partner how he or she feels (Gottman et al., 1976).

family therapy Treatment that might include two, three, or more family members in the psychotherapy sessions. Improving communication and negotiation are common goals, although family therapy also may be used to help well members adjust to a family member's illness.

group therapy The treatment of three or more people in a group setting, often using group relationships as a central part of therapy.

Research has documented that couples therapy can improve satisfaction in marriages (Baucom & Epstein, 1990; Holtzworth-Munroe & Jacobson, 1991). However, some people view marital problems as stemming from broader social forces, such as financial pressures or the roles assumed by men and women. In contrast, others view many societal problems as a result of the breakdown of marriage in the United States today. From the former perspective, couples therapy faces many obstacles and may help preserve a problematic status quo. From the latter perspective, couples therapy holds the promise of improving marital happiness and promoting marriage.

Couples therapy also has been used in the treatment of specific disorders, including depression, anxiety, substance abuse, and child behavior problems. This typically is done either as a supplement or an alternative to individual therapy. When couples therapy is used in conjunction with individual treatment, the combined approach often is more effective than individual therapy alone, as we discuss in subsequent chapters on specific disorders (Barlow, O'Brien, & Last, 1984; Beach, Sandeen, & O'Leary, 1990; Dadds, Schwartz, & Sanders, 1987; Jacobson, Holtzworth-Monroe, & Schmaling, 1989).

Family Therapy

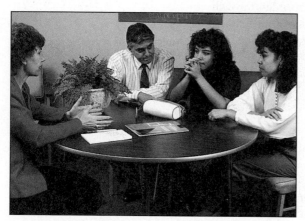

Family therapy includes at least two or perhaps more or all family members in treatment. Family therapists strive to improve mental health by altering family relationships.

Family therapy might include two, three, or more family members in the psychotherapy sessions. Family therapy shares many features in common with couples therapy, for example, improving communication and negotiation. Including children in family therapy can add complexity to this treatment approach, however, as does the obvious fact that relationships and treatments get more complicated when more people are involved.

Like couples therapy, family therapy has the general goal of improving satisfaction with relationships. Some forms of family therapy also are designed to resolve specific conflicts, such as disputes between adolescents and their parents (Robin, Koepke, & Nayar, 1986). *Parent management training* is an approach that teaches parents new skills for rearing troubled children (Forehand & McMahon, 1981; Patterson, 1982; see Chapter 15). Moreover, some important forms of family therapy are designed to educate families about how best to cope with the serious psychopathology of one family member (Falloon et al., 1985; see Chapter 13).

Many approaches to family therapy differ from other treatments in their long-standing emphasis on the application of systems theory. In applying systems theory, family therapists emphasize interdependence among family members and the paramount importance of the family within the larger social system. For example, family systems therapists often call attention to the pattern of *alliances* or strategic loyalties among family members (P. Minuchin, 1985). In well-functioning families, the primary alliance is between the two parents, even when the parents do not live together. In contrast, dysfunctional families often have alliances that cross generations—that is, "teams" that include one parent and some or all of the children opposing the other parent or another child. Like a poorly organized business, families function inadequately when their leaders fail to cooperate. Thus a common goal in systems approaches to family therapy is to strengthen the alliance between the parents, to get parents to work together and not against each other (S. Minuchin, 1974).

Early family therapists overemphasized the role of the family in causing individual psychopathology, particularly severe psychological disorders. Many contemporary approaches to family therapy have a much broader view of etiology. Irrespective of etiology, however, troubled relationships often intensify individual psychopathology, and individual psychopathology commonly strains relationships. It is not surprising therefore that family therapy may serve as an effective alternative or adjunct to individual treatment (Alexander, Holtzworth-Munroe, & Jameson, 1994).

Group Therapy

Like couples therapy and family therapy, **group therapy** involves the treatment of more than one person at one time. Therapy groups may be as small as 3 or 4 people or as large as 20 or more.

Group therapy has numerous variations in terms of paradigmatic approaches and targets for treatment (Yalom, 1985). These variations are far too numerous to discuss here, so we highlight only a few facets of the group approach.

Psychoeducational groups are designed to teach group members specific information or skills relevant to psychological well-being. The term *psychoeducational* aptly conveys the goals of this type of group. Teaching is the primary mode of treatment, but the content of the "course" focuses on psychological issues. For example, assertiveness might be taught in a group format.

There are at least two basic reasons for offering therapy in a psychoeducational group instead of in individual psychotherapy. Lower expense is one obvious justification. A second rationale is the support, encouragement, and practice that group members can offer to one another. Many people who have psychological problems feel isolated, alone, and sometimes "weird." Thus the simple act of coming to a group can be part of the therapeutic process (Bloch & Crouch, 1987).

Group therapy gives clients the opportunity to meet with and learn from other people who have similar problems.

The *self-help group*, such as Alcoholics Anonymous, has grown tremendously in popularity. Self-help groups bring together people who share a common problem. Self-help group members share information and experiences in an attempt to help themselves and one another.

Technically, self-help groups are not therapy groups, and typically are not led by a professional. The popularity of self-help groups attests to their perceived benefits. Moreover, available evidence suggests that self-help groups and other treatments can be quite effective even when they are delivered by *paraprofessionals*—people who do have limited professional training but who have personal experience with the problem (Christensen & Jacobson, 1994). However, the lack of research on process and outcome is a notable shortcoming for self-help groups and for group therapy in general (Kaul & Bednar, 1986).

Community Psychology and Prevention

Social influences on psychopathology extend far beyond interpersonal relationships. Social institutions such as child-care centers, schools, and work environments are important contributors to mental health, as are such broad societal concerns as poverty, racism, and sexism. Of course, the goal of improving society is hardly the exclusive domain of psychologists. Still, *community psychology* is one approach within clinical psychology that attempts to improve individual well-being by promoting social change.

The concept of prevention is an important consideration in promoting social change. Community psychologists often distinguish among three levels of prevention (Kaplan, 1964). *Primary prevention* tries to improve the environment in order to prevent new cases of a mental disorder from developing. The goal of primary prevention is to promote health, not just treat illness. Efforts at primary prevention range from offering prenatal care to impoverished pregnant women to teaching schoolchildren about the dangers of drug abuse.

Secondary prevention focuses on the early detection of emotional problems in the hope of preventing them from becoming more serious and difficult to treat. The screening of "at-risk" schoolchildren is one example of an effort at secondary prevention. Crisis centers and hot lines are other examples of efforts to detect and treat problems before they become more serious.

Finally, *tertiary prevention* may involve any of the treatments discussed in this chapter, because the intervention occurs after the illness has been identified. In addition to providing treatment, however, tertiary prevention also attempts to address some of the adverse, indirect consequences of mental illness. Helping the chronically mentally ill to find adequate housing and employment is an example of a tertiary prevention effort.

No one can doubt the importance of prevention, whether directed toward biological, psychological, or social causes of abnormal behavior. Unfortunately, many prevention efforts face an insurmountable obstacle: We simply do not know the specific cause of most psychological disorders. Prevention efforts directed at broader social change face another obstacle that also seems

Identifying Common Factors and Isolating Specific Treatments

A study by Thomas Borkovec and Ellen Costello (1993) illustrates how psychotherapy outcome research can account for some common factors across treatments while also isolating specific effects. These psychologists at Pennsylvania State University wanted to identify the effectiveness of different approaches to behavior therapy in treating generalized anxiety disorder, an emotional problem characterized by excessive anxiety that is experienced in a variety of circumstances (see Chapter 6).

Borkovec and Costello compared two types of behavior therapy. *Applied relaxation (AR)* involved training clients in the use of relaxation techniques to cope with thoughts, feelings, or situations that provoked anxiety. Most of the 12-session treatment involved discussions of how to anticipate and deal with stressful events, including practice at using relaxation techniques. *Cognitive behavior therapy (CBT)* began with the same types of discussions and relaxation training as AR did. Most of the sessions, however, involved elements of Beck's cognitive therapy as well as other cognitive techniques designed to alter anxiety-producing thoughts. Finally, a third group of clients received *nondirective therapy (ND)* in order to test and control for the contributions of common factors to treatment outcome. The 12 sessions of nondirective therapy consisted of offering support and empathy in response to issues the clients chose to explore in therapy.

Borkovec and Costello randomly assigned 55 clients carefully diagnosed as suffering from generalized anxiety disorder to one of the three treatments. All treatments were offered by the same therapists, thus ensuring that differences in outcome would not be due to differences in therapists. This raised a new problem, however. The therapists generally held a cognitive behavioral orientation, and their low expectations about ND might have affected the success of the treatment. To help control for this possibility, an expert nondirective therapist helped to supervise the ND cases. Finally, audiotapes of a portion of the sessions were coded to ensure that what was supposed to happen during the therapy sessions actually occurred.

A number of measures of the clients' anxiety were administered prior to treatment, immediately after treatment, and 6 months and 1 year after treatment. No differences were found among groups prior to treatment, but statistically significant differences were found immediately after treatment. The AR and CBT groups both were functioning significantly better than the ND clients at this time, but they were not significantly different from each other. Both the AR and CBT groups also improved significantly from the beginning to the end of treatment. The anxiety of the ND group did not change during this time. Finally, evidence indicated that differences among groups were clinically significant—and they favored CBT. A year after treatment, 58 percent of the CBT group was functioning within a normal range, in comparison with 37 percent of the AR clients and 28 percent of ND participants.

These findings indicate that specific treatment effects can be obtained beyond the influence of common factors. In the treatment of generalized anxiety disorders, cognitive behavior therapy has specific benefits both in the short term and in the long run, and these benefits exceed the general improvement associated with seeking psychotherapy. Still, the study also demonstrated the importance of common factors despite the "active ingredients" in cognitive behavior therapy. The best predictor of a successful outcome across all three groups was the clients' expectations for success, which were measured after the first therapy appointment. ⚼

---

insurmountable at times. Poverty, racism, and sexism defy easy remedies. We do not wish to blame the victim of social injustice, but blaming the system can be equally problematic. Each individual must take personal responsibility for changing his or her own life, even as we collectively work to shape a world that promotes mental health.

Specific Treatments for Specific Disorders

The field of psychotherapy began with the development of treatments based solely in theory and case histories. It progressed as researchers documented the superiority of some form of psychotherapy over no treatment at all. Contemporary psychotherapy researchers are advancing knowledge by recognizing and studying factors common to all therapies and by using these common factors to predict successful outcome across different approaches to therapy.

These efforts are important, and scientists can point with increasing pride to research on psychotherapy, which has grown both in volume and in quality. The ultimate goal of treatment research, however, is to discover more than the common factors across paradigmatic approaches to psychotherapy. Researchers must continue to work to identify different therapies that have specific ingredients for treating specific disorders (see Research Close-Up). Consistent with this goal, in subsequent chapters we discuss only treatments that either are promising or have proved to be effective for alleviating the symptoms of specific disorders.

The identification of specific, effective treatments for specific disorders is necessary if clinical psychology is to fulfill its scientific promise. Still, we must not overlook the importance of establishing a human, helping relationship in psychotherapy. Individual people, not diagnostic categories, seek treatment for psychological disorders. The challenge for the mental health professional is to approach treatment both as a scientist and as a practitioner. Awareness of diagnostic categories is essential for applying scientific knowledge, but sensitivity to the individual is also essential to maximizing the effectiveness of clinical practice.

Summary

A tremendous number of different treatments have been developed for psychological disorders, but the various forms of **psychotherapy** can be roughly classified into four broad groups. Biomedical approaches alter the functioning of the body in an attempt to improve psychological well-being, primarily by using **psychopharmacology** or medication that has psychoactive effects. **Psychodynamic psychotherapies** encourage the exploration of the past in order to obtain insight into unconscious motivations. **Cognitive behavior therapy** focuses on present experience in helping clients overcome maladaptive behaviors and learn adaptive ones. **Humanistic psychotherapy** offers clients warmth, empathy, and unconditional positive regard in helping them to heighten emotional awareness and make life choices.

Psychotherapy "works" in that research indicates that approximately two-thirds of outpatient clients benefit from treatment, whereas about one-third of the same population improves without treatment. However, psychotherapy outcome researchers have documented only small differences in the effectiveness of the alternative paradigmatic approaches to treatment. **Behavior therapy** is somewhat more effective in treating some disorders, but there is a clear need to establish the effectiveness of different treatments for different disorders.

A renewed interest in psychotherapy process research and the integration of diverse approaches is one consequence of evidence that different psychotherapies produce similar outcomes (Goldfried & Castonguay, 1993). Dimensions of the therapist–client relationship that are related to improved outcome include increasing the client's expectations of help, forming a warm therapist–client relationship, encouraging the experience of emotions in therapy, offering new learning experiences, and persuading clients to accept new, more adaptive explanations for their problems.

Another area of innovation in psychotherapy is the development of effective treatments that extend into the social system. These interventions include **couples therapy, family therapy,** and **group therapy.** They also include efforts to change dysfunctional aspects of the broader society. Thus consistent with the systems approach, intervention for psychological problems may be directed toward biological, psychological, or social systems.

The future of psychotherapy outcome research involves developing therapies that have effectiveness beyond the "common factors" found across different approaches to psychotherapy. The task is to identify specific therapies for specific disorders. In subsequent chapters of this text, we review progress toward this goal, as we highlight those treatments that have demonstrated success or promise in alleviating the symptoms of a particular disorder.

Critical Thinking

1. What are your personal beliefs about the treatment of psychological disorders? Were your beliefs changed by the ideas or evidence presented in this chapter? Why or why not? What research evidence would convince you that treatments for psychological disorders do (or do not) "work"?

2. Do you prefer one of the major paradigms discussed in this chapter? If you were looking for a therapist for yourself, would you pick one based on her or his "theoretical orientation"? We argue that mental health professionals should offer treatments based on proven effectiveness rather than on theoretical orientation. Do you agree?

3. Some critics have argued that psychotherapy is "the purchase of friendship." What do you think? How are "common factors" found across different schools of psychotherapy similar to, and different from, friendship?

4. What is the appropriate level for intervention with psychological disorders? Do you favor medication, psychotherapy, family treatment, or social change? In what ways do your views about the nature and causes of abnormal behavior influence your thoughts about treatment?

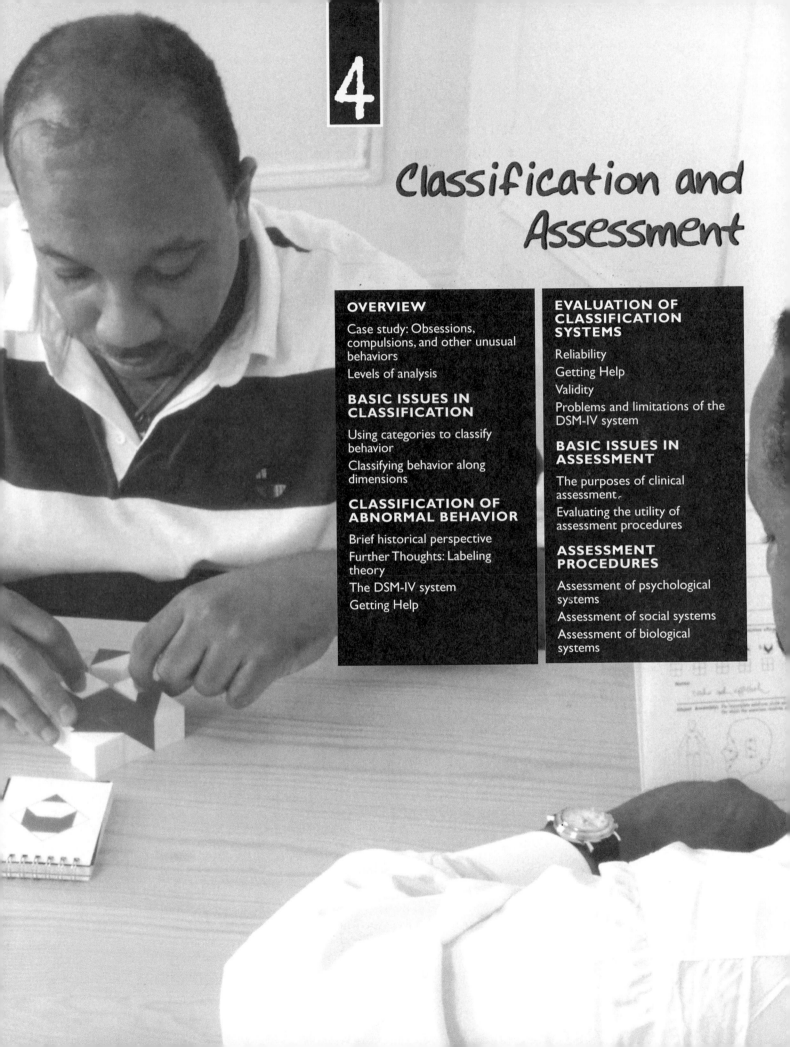

4

Classification and Assessment

Mental disorders are seldom easy to understand. Psychologists need extensive information before they can make decisions about the nature of a person's problems and formulate plans for treatment. The process of gathering this information is called **assessment.** Psychologists use many different assessment tools to generate information about their clients. Interviews, observations, questionnaires, and psychological tests are among the most frequently used procedures. These measures are often supplemented by information from other sources, including formal records from schools and clinics, as well as informal reports from people who are well acquainted with the person. Psychologists must organize and integrate this information before it can be useful. Therefore the assessment process also involves judgments and decisions.

Overview

assessment The process of gathering and organizing information about a person's behavior.

diagnosis The process of determining the nature of a person's disorder. In the case of psychopathology, deciding that a person fits into a particular diagnostic category, such as schizophrenia or major depressive disorder.

One important part of the assessment process is making a diagnostic decision based on the official classification system—the set of categories in DSM-IV that describe mental disorders. **Diagnosis** refers to the identification or recognition of a disorder on the basis of its characteristic symptoms. In psychopathology, a clinician assigns a diagnosis if the person's behavior meets the specific criteria for a particular type of disorder, such as schizophrenia or major depressive disorder. This decision is important because it tells the clinician that the person's problems are similar to those that have been experienced by some other people. The diagnosis enables the clinician to refer to the base of knowledge that has accumulated with regard to the disorder. For example, it will provide clues about associated symptoms and treatments that are most likely to be effective.

There is another way to interpret the meaning of the word "diagnosis." In some fields, diagnosis refers to *causal* analysis. If your car doesn't start, you expect that your mechanic's "diagnosis" will explain the origins of the problem. Has the battery lost its charge? Is the fuel line blocked? In the field of psychopathology, assigning a diagnosis does *not* mean that we understand the etiology of the person's problem (see Chapter 2). Specific etiologies have not been identified for mental disorders. Psychologists can't "look under the hood" in the same way that a mechanic can examine your car. In the case of a mental disorder, assigning a diagnostic label simply identifies the nature of the problem without implying exactly how the problem came into existence.

Our consideration of the assessment enterprise and diagnostic issues will begin with an example from our own clinical experience. In the following pages we will describe one person's problems and the social context in which they appeared. The case study on pages 88–89 illustrates the kinds of decisions that psychologists have to make about ways to collect and interpret information.

case study

Obsessions, Compulsions, and Other Unusual Behaviors

Michael was an only child who lived with his mother and father. He was 16 years old, a little younger than most of the other boys in the 11th grade, and he looked even younger. From an academic point of view, Michael was an average student, but he was not a typical teenager in terms of social behavior. He felt completely alienated from other boys, and he was extremely anxious when he talked to girls. He hated being at school; he despised everything about school. His life at home was not much more pleasant than his experience at school. Michael and his parents argued frequently. His relationship with his father was especially volatile.

One awful incident seemed to sum up Michael's bitter feelings about school. As a sophomore, he decided to join the track team. Michael was awkward and somewhat clumsy, hardly an athlete; when he worked out with the other long-distance runners at practice, he soon became the brunt of their jokes. One day, a belligerent teammate forced Michael to take off his clothes and run naked from the bushes to a shelter in the park. When he got there, Michael found an old pair of shorts, which he put on and wore back to the locker room. The experience was humiliating. Later that night, Michael started to worry about those shorts. Who had left them in the park? Were they dirty? Had he been exposed to some horrible disease? Michael quit the track team the next day, but he couldn't put the experience out of his mind. Every time he saw the other boys in school, he became enraged.

Although he knew it was irrational, Michael began to fear that he would catch AIDS from those shorts. He couldn't get the thought out of his mind. He read everything he could find regarding early symptoms of the disease. These fears progressed to the point where every time he coughed, he thought he was getting a respiratory infection. If he lost his balance, he thought he had a neurological complication. The list of "symptoms" went on and on.

In the following year, Michael became more and more consumed by anxiety. He was constantly obsessed about "contamination," which he imagined to be spreading from his books and school clothes to the furniture and other objects in his house. When the clothes that he had worn to school rubbed against a chair or a wall at home, he felt as though that spot had become contaminated. He didn't believe this was literally true; it was more like a reminder by association. When he touched something that he had used at school, he was more likely to think of school. That triggered unpleasant thoughts and the negative emotions with which they were associated (anger, fear, sadness).

Michael tried in various ways to minimize the spread of contamination. For example, he took a shower and changed his clothes every evening at 6 o'clock immediately after he finished his homework. After this "cleansing ritual" he was careful to avoid touching his books or dirty clothes as well as anything that they had touched. If he bumped into one of these contaminated objects by accident, he would go into the bathroom and wash his hands. Michael washed his hands 10 or 15 times in a typical evening. He also paced back and forth watching television without sitting down so that he would not touch contaminated furniture.

Whenever he was not in school, Michael preferred to be alone at home. Being with other people made him very uncomfortable. If he spent more than a few minutes with other people, he felt drained, and he had to recuperate by withdrawing to his room to play games on his computer. He did not enjoy sports, music, or outdoor activities. The only literature that interested him was fantasy and science fiction. Dungeons and Dragons was the only game that held his attention. It had, in fact, become an important escape for Michael. He read extensively about the magical powers of fantastic characters and spent hours dreaming up new variations on themes described in books about this imaginary realm. When Michael talked about the Dungeons and Dragons characters and their adventures, his speech would sometimes become vague and difficult to follow. He would begin to speak more rapidly and his thoughts would jump from one topic to the next in an excited and confused manner. Although other students at Michael's school shared his interest in Dungeons and Dragons, he didn't want to play the game with them. Michael said he was different from the other students. He expressed disdain and contempt for other teenagers, as well as for the city in which he lived and for his own neighborhood.

Michael and his parents had been working with a family therapist for more than 2 years. Although the level of interpersonal conflict in the family had been reduced, Michael's anxiety seemed to be getting worse. He had become even more isolated from other boys his own age, and was actually quite suspicious about their motives. He said that he sometimes felt that they were talking about him, and that they were planning to do something else to him in order to humiliate him again.

His worries about contamination had become almost unbearable to his parents, who were deeply confused and frustrated by his behavior. They could obviously see that he had become socially isolated and extremely unhappy. They believed that he would never be able to resume a more normal pattern of development until he gave up these "silly" ideas. Michael's fears also disrupted his parents' own activities in several ways. They weren't allowed to touch him or his things after being in certain rooms of the house. His peculiar movements and persistent washing were troublesome to them. Michael's father usually worked at home, and he and Michael when Michael ran water in the bathroom next to his father's

continued

frequently ended up quarreling with each other, especially study. The conflict became so severe that Michael's father once asked his wife to make a choice: "Is it me or Michael? One of us has to go!"

Michael and his mother had always been very close. In fact, he was quite dependent on her, and she was devoted to him. They spent a lot of time together while his father was working. Although they still supported each other, his mother had begun to find it difficult to be close to Michael. He shunned physical contact. When she touched him, he sometimes cringed and withdrew. Once in a while he would shriek, reminding her that she was contaminated by her contact with

reminding her that she was contaminated by her contact with chairs and other objects like his laundry. Recently, Michael had also become aloof intellectually. His mother felt that he was shutting her out as he seemed to withdraw further into his world of Dungeons and Dragons fantasy and obsessional thoughts about contamination.

Michael's parents eventually decided to seek individual treatment for him. They talked with their family therapist and asked her whether anything could be done to help Michael deal with his fear of contamination. Could he stop his repeated washing? Would he be able to develop normal friendships? ✹

classification system   A system for grouping together objects or organisms that share certain properties in common. In psychopathology, the set of categories in DSM-IV that describes mental disorders.

Levels of Analysis

Michael's situation raises several fundamental issues with regard to assessment and classification. The first is the level of analysis at which a psychologist should think about the problem. Is this primarily Michael's problem, or should we consider this problem in terms of all members of the family? One possibility is that Michael has a psychological disorder that is disrupting the life of his family. It may be the other way around, however: Perhaps the family system as a whole is dysfunctional, and Michael's problems are only one symptom of this dysfunction.

Another set of choices involves the type of data that a psychologist will employ to describe Michael's behavior. One type of data is Michael's own report. Another is the report of his parents. A psychologist may also decide to employ psychological tests. Although biological tests have not achieved definitive status in psychopathology, there are some intriguing suggestions that biochemical tests and images of the brain may shed light on the distinctions among different forms of abnormal behavior.

Given the information that the psychologist has obtained, the two most likely diagnostic alternatives are obsessive–compulsive disorder (OCD) and schizotypal personality disorder (see Chapters 6 and 9). These conditions can be difficult to tell apart. Because they respond to different forms of treatment, the distinctions are extremely important. In the next section we will review the development and modification of classification systems for abnormal behavior.

Basic Issues in Classification

A **classification system** is used to subdivide or organize a set of objects. The objects of classification can be inanimate things, such as rocks or books; living organisms, such as plants, insects, or primates; or abstract concepts, such as numbers, religions, or historical periods. Formal classification systems are essential for the collection and communication of knowledge in all sciences and professions.

There are many ways to subdivide any given class of objects. Classification systems can be based on different principles. Some systems are based on descriptive similarities. For example, both a diamond and a ruby may be considered jewels because they are valuable stones. Other systems are based on less obvious characteristics, such as structural similarities. A diamond and a piece of coal, for example, may belong together because they are both made of carbon.

The point is simple. Classification systems can be based on various principles, and their value will depend primarily on the purpose for which they were developed (Clementz & Iacono, 1993). Different classification systems are not necessarily right or wrong; they are simply more or less useful for a particular purpose. In the following section we will consider several fundamental principles that affect all attempts to develop a useful classification or typology of human behavior.

Using Categories to Classify Behavior

Classification is often based on "yes or no" decisions (Hempel, 1961). After a category has been defined, any object is either a member of the category or it is not. A **categorical approach to classification** assumes that distinctions between members of different categories are qualitative. In other words, the differences reflect a difference in kind (quality) rather than a difference in amount (quantity). In the classification of living organisms, for example, we usually consider species to be qualitatively distinct; they are different kinds of living organisms. Human beings are different from other primates; an organism is either human or it is not. Many medical conditions are categorical. Pregnancy is one clear example. A woman is either pregnant or she is not. It doesn't make sense to talk about "how pregnant" a woman might be.

Classifying Behavior along Dimensions

Although categorically based classification systems are often useful, they are not the only kind of system that can be used to organize information systematically. As an alternative, scientists often employ a **dimensional approach to classification**—that is, one that describes the objects of classification in terms of continuous dimensions. Rather than assuming that an object either has, or does not have, a particular property, it may be useful to focus on a specific characteristic and determine how much of that characteristic the object exhibits. This kind of system is based on an ordered sequence or on quantitative measurements rather than on qualitative judgments.

For example, in the case of intellectual ability, psychologists have developed sophisticated measurement procedures. Rather than asking whether or not a particular person is intelligent (a "yes or no" judgment), the psychologist sets out to determine *how much* intelligence the person exhibits on a particular set of tasks. This process offers some advantages over categorical distinctions. It allows scientists to record subtle distinctions that would be lost if they were forced to make all-or-none decisions. It also provides for more powerful quantitative measurements.

Classification of Abnormal Behavior

A classification system is useful to clinicians who must match their clients' problems with the form of intervention that is most likely to be effective. Second, a classification system must be used in the search for new knowledge. The history of medicine is filled with examples of problems that were recognized long before they could be treated successfully. The definition of a specific set of symptoms has often laid the foundation for research that eventually identified a cure or a way of preventing the disorder.

Brief Historical Perspective

There have been many attempts to classify personality and psychopathology throughout history. The oldest written descriptions can be traced to the Egyptians, Greeks, and Romans, but these bear little resemblance to contemporary perspectives. Progress toward the adoption of a single, internationally accepted system began during the nineteenth century, when cities in Europe and the United States established large asylums for people with major mental disorders. The physicians who presided over these institutions had an unprecedented opportunity to observe the behavior of many patients over an extended period of time. Many different classification systems were introduced during the ensuing years. In some areas, each hospital or university clinic developed and used its own unique system (Kendell, 1975).

Emil Kraepelin (1856–1926), a German psychiatrist, is generally regarded as the father of the categorical classification system that currently prevails in psychopathology. He believed that

Although a person's height clearly lies on a continuous dimension, it is sometimes convenient and useful to describe people in categorical terms. Basketball players are often described as inside players (like Manute Bol, who at 7' 7" is one of the tallest players ever to play in the National Basketball Association) and perimeter players (like Mugsy Bogues, who at 5' 3" is one of the shortest players ever to play in the NBA).

further thoughts

Labeling Theory

Labeling theory is a perspective on mental disorders that is primarily concerned with the social context in which abnormal behavior occurs and the ways in which other people respond to this behavior. It assigns relatively little importance to specific behaviors as symptoms of a disorder that resides within the person. Labeling theory is more interested in social factors that determine whether a person will be given a psychiatric diagnosis than in psychological or biological reasons for the abnormal behaviors (Levine & Perkins, 1987). In other words, it is concerned with events that take place after a person has behaved in an unusual way rather than with factors that might explain the original appearance of the behavior itself.

Thomas Scheff, a sociologist at the University of California at Santa Barbara, is one of the leading figures in labeling theory. According to Scheff (1966, 1984), it is useful to think of mental disorders as maladaptive social roles, with the process of diagnostic labeling being the most important factor in establishing that role for a particular person. Scheff suggests that the symp-

toms of mental disorders are best viewed as violations of residual rules: showing too much emotion; not showing enough emotion; or talking too much or in strange ways. These behaviors create situations in which a person might be labeled as mentally disturbed.

Scheff maintains that people break residual rules frequently and for many different reasons. These behaviors are usually ignored or dismissed as unimportant. Scheff assumes that in such cases the behaviors will be relatively brief. Persistent abnormal behaviors develop only after someone has been brought to the attention of the mental health system and assigned an official diagnostic label. That process sets in motion a number of other events that ensure that the person will accept the social role associated with the diagnosis and will continue to exhibit abnormal behaviors that are expected from people in that role. We all presumably learn the role of "mental patient" through cultural stereotypes, such as the negative images of people with mental disorders that are repeatedly displayed in the media (Signorielli, 1989).

According to labeling theory, the probability that a person will receive a diagnosis is determined by several factors. These include the extent of the rule breaking and its visibility, as well

---

labeling theory   A perspective on mental disorders that is primarily concerned with the social context in which abnormal behavior occurs. Labeling theory is more interested in social factors that determine whether or not a person will be given a psychiatric diagnosis than in psychological or biological reasons for the behaviors.

Robert Spitzer, professor of psychiatry at Columbia University, chaired the committee that produced DSM-III. Spitzer's vision and forceful leadership helped the committee to accomplish one of the most important changes in psychiatric classification of the twentieth century.

mental illness could be understood in terms of a finite number of specific disorders. Each disorder was presumed to have an identifiable set of symptoms and a unique course and was the product of a yet to be determined form of cerebral pathology (Berrios & Hauser, 1988). Kraepelin's views were widely influential, but they did not lead directly to a formal, universally adopted classification system.

Currently, two diagnostic systems for mental disorders are widely recognized. One—the *Diagnostic and Statistical Manual* (DSM)—is published by the American Psychiatric Association. The other—the *International Classification of Diseases* (ICD)—is published by the World Health Organization. Both systems were developed shortly after World War II, and both have been revised several times. Because the American diagnostic manual is now in its fourth edition, it is called DSM-IV. The World Health Organization's manual is in its tenth edition and is therefore known as ICD-10.

During the 1950s and 1960s, psychiatric classification systems were widely criticized. One major criticism focused on the lack of consistency in diagnostic decisions (Spitzer & Fleiss, 1974). Independent clinicians frequently disagreed with one another about the use of diagnostic categories as they were listed in the first two editions of the American classification system, DSM-I and DSM-II. Objections were also raised from philosophical, sociological, and political points of view. Some critics charged that diagnostic categories in psychiatry would be more appropriately viewed as "problems in living" than as medical disorders (Szasz, 1960). Others were concerned about *self-fulfilling prophesies*. In other words, once a psychiatric label had been assigned, the person so labeled might be motivated to continue behaving in ways that were expected from someone who is mentally disturbed (see Further Thoughts). For all of these reasons, many mental health professionals paid less and less attention to the formal process of diagnosis during these years.

Renewed interest in the value of psychiatric classification grew steadily during the 1970s, culminating in the publication of the third edition of the DSM in 1980. This version of the manual represented a dramatic departure from previous systems. It was clearly a major turn-as the tolerance level of the community. The most important considerations are the social status of the person who breaks the rules and the social distance between that person and mental health professionals. People from disadvantaged groups, such as racial and sexual minorities and women, are presumably more likely to be labeled than are white males.

The merits and limitations of labeling theory have been hotly debated since the mid-1960s. The theory has inspired research on a number of important questions. Some studies have found that people from lower-status groups are indeed more likely to be assigned severe diagnoses (Holman & Caston, 1987). On the other hand, it would also be a great exaggeration to say that the social status of the patient is the most important factor influencing the diagnostic process. In fact, clinicians' diagnostic decisions are determined primarily by the form and severity of the patient's symptoms rather than by such factors as gender, race, and social class (Farmer & Griffiths, 1992; Gove, 1990).

Another focus of the debate regarding labeling theory is the issue of stigma. Is a diagnosis of mental disorder a sign of disgrace or discredit? Do people avoid those who have mental disorders? Labeling theory assumes that negative attitudes toward mental disorders prevent patients from obtaining jobs, finding housing, and forming new relationships. Negative attitudes are undoubtedly associated with many types of mental disorder, such as alcoholism, schizophrenia, and sexual disorders (Fabrega, 1991; Fink & Tasman, 1992).

Research studies have also found, however, that stigma is a complicated issue. Critics of labeling theory have argued that the effects of stigma are generally short-lived (Gove, 1970, 1990). Furthermore, some patients maintain positive attitudes about their own difficulties and about the mental health systems in which they are treated (Weinstein, 1983). The impact of stigma on a person's self-esteem is difficult to predict (Major & Crocker, 1993).

Although labeling theory has drawn needed attention to a number of important problems associated with the classification of mental disorders, it does not provide an adequate explanation for abnormal behavior. It is clearly an exaggeration to think of mental disorders as nothing more than social roles. Many factors other than the reactions of other people contribute to the development and maintenance of abnormal behavior. Furthermore, a diagnosis of mental illness can have positive consequences, such as encouraging access to proper treatment. Many patients and their family members are relieved to learn that their problems are similar to those experienced by other people and that help may be available. The effects of diagnostic labeling are not always harmful. ᴡ

ing point in the history of psychiatric classification (Kendell, 1991; Sabshin, 1990). The committee that was responsible for developing DSM-III was chaired by Robert Spitzer, a psychiatrist at the New York State Psychiatric Institute. Spitzer and his colleagues made several bold changes in the manual. One broad consideration was their commitment to the production of a classification system that was based on clinical description rather than on theories of psychopathology that had not been empirically validated. Other major changes included the introduction of a multiaxial system, discussed below, and the production of specific, detailed criterion sets for each disorder.

All these changes have been retained in both DSM-IV and ICD-10. These features will be described in the following section. The two manuals are very similar in most respects. Deliberate attempts were made to coordinate the production of DSM-IV and ICD-10. Most of the categories listed in the manuals are identical, and the criteria for specific disorders are usually similar."[†]

multiaxial classification system A classification system in which the person is rated with regard to several separate aspects of behavior or adjustment.

The DSM-IV System

The DSM-IV employs a **multiaxial classification system;** that is, the person is rated on five separate axes. Each axis is concerned with a different domain of information. Two are concerned with diagnostic categories, and the other three provide for the collection of additional relevant data. The rationale for this approach is that to manage individual cases, the clinician must consider several important factors besides specific symptoms. These supplementary factors include the environment in

[†]There are some interesting differences between DSM-IV and ICD-10. There are, for example, differences in the ways in which they subdivide mood disorders and personality disorders. The U.S. system also devotes more attention to eating disorders and sexual disorders, which appear to be less prevalent in other cultures (Kendell, 1991).

TABLE 4–1

Major Axes in DSM-IV	
AXIS I	Clinical Syndromes
AXIS II	Personality Disorders and Mental Retardation
AXIS III	General Medical Conditions
AXIS IV	Psychosocial and Environmental Problems
AXIS V	Global Assessment of Functioning

which the patient is living, aspects of the person's health that might affect psychological functions, and fluctuations in the overall level of the patient's adjustment. Table 4–1 lists the five specific axes from DSM-IV.

DIAGNOSTIC AXES

The first two axes are concerned with clinical disorders that are defined largely in terms of symptomatic behaviors. Most diagnoses appear on Axis I, which includes conditions such as schizophrenia and mood disorders that are the topics of most chapters in this text. Many of the diagnoses that are described on Axis I are characterized by episodic periods of psychological turmoil. Axis II is concerned with more stable, long-standing problems, such as personality disorders and mental retardation. The separation of disorders on Axis I and Axis II is designed to draw attention to conditions that might be overlooked in the presence of a more dramatic symptomatic picture, such as the hallucinations and delusions frequently found in schizophrenia. Clinicians are encouraged to list both types of problems when they are present. A person can be assigned more than one diagnosis on either Axis I or Axis II (or on both axes) if he or she meets criteria for more than one disorder.

More than 200 specific diagnostic categories are described in DSM-IV. These are arranged under 18 primary headings. A complete list appears inside the covers of this book. Disorders that present similar kinds of symptoms are grouped together. For example, conditions that include a prominent display of anxiety are listed under "Anxiety Disorders," and conditions that involve a depressed mood are listed under "Mood Disorders."

The manual lists specific criteria for each diagnostic category. We can illustrate the ways in which these criteria are used by examining the diagnostic decisions that would be considered in Michael's case. The criteria for obsessive–compulsive disorder (OCD), which is an Axis I disorder, and schizotypal personality disorder, which is an Axis II disorder, are listed in Table 4–2.

First, let's consider obsessive–compulsive disorder. Michael would meet all of the criteria in "A" for both obsessions and compulsions. His repetitive hand-washing rituals were performed in response to obsessive thoughts regarding contamination. He also meets criterion "C" in that these rituals were time-consuming and interfered with his family's routine. His relationships with friends were severely limited because he refused to invite them to his house, fearing that they would spread contamination.

On Axis II, Michael would also be coded as meeting criteria for schizotypal personality disorder. He exhibited five of the nine symptoms listed under criterion "A": odd speech, suspiciousness, eccentric behavior, no close friends, and excessive social anxiety. This pattern illustrates an important feature of DSM-IV. For many disorders, a patient must exhibit a certain number of symptoms, but the specific pattern is not determined. Michael exhibited symptoms 4, 5, 7, 8, and 9. Another person who happened to exhibit a different combination could also be classified as having schizotypal personality disorder. The specific items are not weighted in terms of their importance for making the diagnosis. These are, of course, somewhat arbitrary diagnostic standards. Little evidence suggests that five symptoms is a better cutoff point than four or six.

A diagnosis can also be ruled out if certain conditions prevail. For example, in the case of schizotypal personality disorder, the diagnosis would not be made if the symptoms occurred only during the course of a schizophrenic disorder (criterion "B").

TABLE 4–2

DSM–IV Criteria for Obsessive–Compulsive Disorder

A. **EITHER OBSESSIONS OR COMPULSIONS:**
   OBSESSIONS as defined by (1), (2), (3), and (4):

1. Recurrent and persistent thoughts, impulses, or images that are experienced, at some time during the disturbance, as intrusive and inappropriate, and that cause marked anxiety or distress

2. The thoughts, impulses, or images are not simply excessive worries about real-life problems

3. The person attempts to ignore or suppress thoughts, impulses, or images or to neutralize them with some other thought or action

4. The person recognizes that the obsessional thoughts, impulses, or images are a product of his or her own mind (not imposed from without as in thought insertion)

COMPULSIONS as defined by (1) and (2):

1. Repetitive behaviors (such as hand washing, ordering, checking) or mental acts (such as praying, counting, repeating words silently) that the person feels driven to perform in response to an obsession, or according to rules that must be applied rigidly

2. The behaviors or mental acts are aimed at preventing or reducing distress or preventing some dreaded event or situation; however, these behaviors or mental acts either are not connected in a realistic way with what they are designed to neutralize or prevent, or are clearly excessive

B. **AT SOME POINT DURING THE COURSE OF THE DISORDER, THE PERSON HAS RECOGNIZED THAT THE OBSESSIONS OR COMPULSIONS ARE EXCESSIVE OR UNREASONABLE.**

C. **THE OBSESSIONS OR COMPULSIONS CAUSE MARKED DISTRESS; ARE TIME-CONSUMING (TAKE MORE THAN ONE HOUR A DAY); OR SIGNIFICANTLY IN-TERFERE WITH THE PERSON'S NORMAL ROUTINE, OCCUPATIONAL (OR ACA-DEMIC) FUNCTIONING, OR USUAL SOCIAL ACTIVITIES OR RELATIONSHIPS WITH OTHERS.**

D. **IF ANOTHER AXIS I DISORDER IS PRESENT, THE CONTENT OF THE OBSESSIONS OR COMPULSIONS IS NOT RESTRICTED TO IT (FOR EXAMPLE, PREOCCUPA-TION WITH FOOD IN THE PRESENCE OF AN EATING DISORDER; PREOCCUPA-TION WITH DRUGS IN THE PRESENCE OF A SUBSTANCE USE DISORDER; OR GUILTY RUMINATIONS IN THE PRESENCE OF MAJOR DEPRESSIVE DISORDER).**

continued

In certain instances, the duration of a problem is considered as well as the clinical picture. Criterion "C" for obsessive–compulsive disorder specifies that the patient's compulsive rituals must take more than 1 hour each day to perform.

OTHER DOMAINS FOR ASSESSMENT

Axis III is concerned with general medical conditions that are outside the realm of psychopathology but may be relevant to either the etiology of the patient's abnormal behavior or the patient's treatment program. Examples include thyroid conditions, which may lead to symptoms of psychosis. In Michael's case, there were no known physical disorders that were relevant to his psychological problems.

TABLE 4–2 *CONTINUED*

DSM-IV Criteria for Schizotypal Personality Disorder

A. A PERVASIVE PATTERN OF SOCIAL AND INTERPERSONAL DEFICITS MARKED BY ACUTE DISCOMFORT WITH, AND REDUCED CAPACITY FOR, CLOSE RELATIONSHIPS AS WELL AS BY COGNITIVE OR PERCEPTUAL DISTORTIONS AND ECCENTRICITIES OF BEHAVIOR, BEGINNING BY EARLY ADULTHOOD AND PRESENT IN A VARIETY OF CONTEXTS, AS INDICATED BY FIVE (OR MORE) OF THE FOLLOWING:

1. Ideas of reference (excluding delusions of reference)
2. Odd beliefs or magical thinking that influence behavior and are inconsistent with subcultural norms—for example superstitiousness, belief in clairvoyance, telepathy, or "sixth sense"
3. Unusual perceptual experiences, including bodily illusions
4. Odd thinking and speech (for example, vague, circumstantial, metaphorical, overelaborate, or stereotyped)
5. Suspiciousness or paranoid ideation
6. Inappropriate or constricted affect
7. Behavior or appearance that is odd, eccentric, or peculiar
8. Lack of close friends or confidants other than first-degree relatives
9. Excessive social anxiety that does not diminish with familiarity and tends to be associated with paranoid fears rather than negative judgments about self

B. DOES NOT OCCUR EXCLUSIVELY DURING THE COURSE OF SCHIZOPHRENIA, A MOOD DISORDER WITH PSYCHOTIC FEATURES, ANOTHER PSYCHOTIC DISORDER, OR A PERVASIVE DEVELOPMENTAL DISORDER.

Axis IV is concerned with psychosocial and environmental problems that may affect the diagnosis or treatment of a mental disorder. The clinician is asked to indicate specific factors that are present in the person's life (see Chapter 8 for a more complete discussion). The clinician is asked to record those problems that were present during the year prior to the current assessment. Problems that occurred prior to the previous year may be noted if the clinician is convinced that they made a significant contribution to the development of the person's current problems or if they have become a focus of treatment.

Michael's therapist noted the presence of three psychosocial problems: frequent arguments within the family, social isolation, and discord with classmates at school. Stressful circumstances may be the products as well as the causes of mental disorders. In Michael's case, for example, many of the family's arguments were precipitated by his hand-washing rituals. In deciding whether to list social stresses on Axis IV, psychologists need not determine whether the stresses primarily arose from or contributed to the condition. They are all listed if they are relevant to treatment planning, and these were all important considerations in Michael's case.

Finally, Axis V provides for a global rating of adaptive functioning (Goldman, Skodol, & Lave, 1992). This rating is made on a scale that ranges from 1 to 100, with higher numbers representing better levels of adjustment. The scale applies to psychological, social, and occupational functioning. Ratings are typically made for the person's current level of functioning. In some circumstances, the clinician might also consider the person's highest level of functioning during the past year.

Michael's psychologist assigned a rating of 50 for his current level of functioning. Michael was performing at an adequate level academically, but his social life was clearly impaired as a consequence of his rituals.

Evaluation of Classification Systems

The *Diagnostic and Statistical Manual* is an evolving document. An enormous effort was devoted to the revision process that resulted in the publication of DSM-IV in 1994. The work extended over a period of more than 5 years. Final decisions about the manual were made by the Task Force on DSM-IV, which was composed of 30 distinguished mental health professionals (26 psychiatrists and 4 psychologists) and chaired by Allen Frances, a psychiatrist at Duke University. Work groups were appointed to examine each of the major diagnostic categories, such as anxiety disorders, mood disorders, and so on. The work groups made recommendations to the task force on the basis of reviews of the existing literature on the problem, new analyses performed on already-collected sets of data, and large-scale, issue-focused field trials.

How can we evaluate a system like DSM-IV? Is it a useful classification system? Utility can be measured in terms of two principal criteria: reliability and validity.

Reliability

Reliability refers to the consistency of measurements, including diagnostic decisions. If a diagnostic category is to be useful, it will have to be used consistently. One important form of reliability, known as *inter-rater reliability,* refers to agreement among clinicians. Suppose, for example, that two psychologists interview the same patient and that each psychologist independently assigns a diagnosis using DSM-IV. If both psychologists decide that the patient fits the criteria for a major depressive disorder, they have used the definition of that category consistently. Of course, one or two cases would not provide a sufficient test of the reliability of a diagnostic category. The real question is whether the clinicians would agree with each other over a large series of patients. Several formal procedures have been developed to evaluate diagnostic reliability. Most studies of psychiatric diagnosis in the past 20 years have employed a measure known as **kappa.** Instead of measuring the simple proportion of agreement between clinicians, kappa indicates the proportion of agreement that occurred *above and beyond that which would have occurred by chance.* Negative values of kappa indicate that the rate of agreement was less than that which would have been expected by chance in this particular sample of people. Thus kappa of zero indicates chance agreement, and kappa of +1.0 indicates perfect agreement between raters.

How should we interpret the kappa statistic? There is no easy answer to this question (Grove et al., 1981; Kirk & Kutchins, 1992). It would be unrealistic to expect perfect consistency, especially in view of the relatively modest reliability of other diagnostic decisions that are made in medical practice (Cameron & McGoogan, 1981; Koran, 1975). On the other hand, it isn't very encouraging simply to find that the level of agreement among clinicians is somewhat better than chance. We expect more than that from a diagnostic system, especially when it is used as a basis for treatment decisions. One convention suggests that kappa values of .70 or higher indicate relatively good agreement (Matarazzo, 1983; Spitzer, Foreman, & Nee, 1979). Values of kappa below .40 are often interpreted as indicating poor agreement.

The reliability of many diagnostic categories has improved since the publication of DSM-III. Increased reliability can be attributed, in part, to the use of more detailed diagnostic criteria for specific disorders. Still, most studies also indicate that there is considerable room for improvement. The reliability of some diagnostic categories remains well below acceptable standards. Consider, for example, evidence from field trials that were conducted by the World Health Organization when ICD-10 was being prepared (Sartorius et al., 1993). Data were collected at more than 100 clinical centers in 39 countries around the world. Assessment interviews were conducted with 2,460 psychiatric patients by more than 700 clinicians. Each person was interviewed separately by two clinicians who independently arrived at a diagnosis.

Using the standard of .70 or higher, good agreement was found for many specific categories, especially obsessive–compulsive disorder, bipolar mood disorder, and paranoid schizophrenia. For some other categories, such as phobic disorder and depressive episode, diagnostic reliability

getting help

Getting Help

Only one in five people who need and could benefit from treatment actually get it. One reason for this sad statistic is that some people are reluctant to seek help because they fear that a stigma is attached to having "mental problems," despite the fact that seeking therapy is now commonplace. Those 4 out of 5 who don't seek help, even when it might help them lead happier and more productive lives, are evidence that negative stereotypes regarding mental disorders persist. We hope that you will not allow these antiquated views to delay or interfere with efforts to improve your life.

If you have concerns about this issue, it may help to read about stigma and mental health, a problem that has been addressed by Rosalynn Carter, a leading advocate on behalf of people with mental disorders. The wife of former president Jimmy Carter, her book, *Helping Someone with Mental Illness,* contains an excellent discussion of these issues. She also heads The Carter Center, which is actively involved in issues that affect public policies regarding mental disorders. The URL for the center's Web Page is www.CarterCenter.org/mentalhealth.html. The site contains information relevant to the struggle to correct biased and inaccurate views of people with mental disorders.

Another reason why people may not get help is that they fail to recognize the presence of a serious problem. Your read-ing this text may help in that regard. You will get care more promptly and make better treatment choices if you understand your problems and their relation to formal diagnostic criteria used by mental health professionals. Allen Frances, chairperson of the DSM-IV Task Force, and Michael First have written a useful book called *Your Mental Health: A Layman's Guide to the Psychiatrist's Bible.* This book is written as a primer for consumers of mental health services and covers many types of adult and childhood disorders. Each chapter includes a concise, readable description of the typical symptoms and course of the disorder, followed by a discussion (Am I Okay?) designed to help you decide whether your problems warrant professional help. Finally, the authors review treatment options and where to go for help for each problem.

We can all help to promote accurate portrayals of mental disorders and to eliminate discrimination against those who suffer from (or have recovered from) mental disorders. Advice for positive action is presented on several Web sites, including the National Mental Health Association's Stigma Watch home page: www.nmha.org/newsroom/stigma/index.cfm. This site includes, for example, a sample letter that can be mailed to legislators, as well as instructions that encourage people to report media events that depict mental disorders in an unfair light. People will find it easier to seek help when they recognize the symptoms of mental disorders and when they no longer need to worry about the potential effects of distorted, negative views of their problems. ⚜

---

validity   The meaning or systematic importance of a construct or a measurement.

was acceptable while clearly leaving room for improvement. Reliability for generalized anxiety disorder was only fair, and the reliability for diagnosing personality disorders was very low. In the case of schizotypal personality disorder, for example, the kappa coefficient was only .37, a poor level of agreement. Therefore we should not accept uncritically the assumption that DSM-IV and ICD-10 are always used reliably (Kirk & Kutchins, 1992).

Validity

The ultimate issue in the evaluation of a diagnostic category is whether it is useful. By knowing that a person fits into a particular group or class, do we learn anything *meaningful* about that person? Does the diagnosis tell us anything about the factors or circumstances that might have contributed to the onset of this problem?

These questions are concerned with the validity of the diagnostic category. The term **validity** refers to the meaning or importance of a measurement—in this case, a diagnostic decision (Hempel, 1961; Kendell, 1989). After a clinical description has been established, these phases may occur in any order. Diagnostic categories are refined and validated through this process of scientific exploration. Diagnostic categories are more or less useful, and their validity (or utility) can be determined in several ways.

A lawyer presenting a case to a court of appeals. Just as judges sometimes disagree in their assessment of evidence presented during trial, psychologists and psychiatrists do not always agree on how various disorders should be diagnosed and classified. Of course, both judges and mental health professionals attempt to be reliable, that is, consistent.

Validity is, in a sense, an index of the success that has been achieved in understanding the nature of a disorder. Have important facts been discovered? Systematic studies aimed at establishing the validity of a disorder often proceed in a sequence of phases (Robins & Guze, 1989), which are listed in Table 4–3. The overall utility or validity of a diagnostic category depends on the body of evidence that accumulates as scientists seek answers to these questions.

The list of categories included in DSM-IV is based heavily on conventional clinical wisdom. Each time the manual is revised, new categories are added and old categories are dropped, presumably because they are not sufficiently useful. Up to the present time, clinicians have been more willing to include new categories than to drop old ones. It is difficult to know when we would decide that a particular diagnostic category is not valid. At what point in the accumulation of knowledge are clinical scientists willing to conclude that a category is of no use and to recommend that the search for more information should be abandoned? This is a difficult question that the authors of DSM-IV have confronted, and it will become increasingly important in the production of future revisions.

comorbidity The simultaneous manifestation of more than one disorder.

Problems and Limitations of the DSM-IV System

Although DSM-IV represents a clear improvement over the early versions of APA's classification system, it is also hampered by a number of problems (Clark, Watson, & Reynolds, 1995). One of the most thorny issues involves **comorbidity,** which is defined as the simultaneous appearance of two or more disorders in the same person. Comorbidity rates are very high for mental disorders as they are defined in the DSM system. For example, in the National Comorbidity Survey, among those people who qualified for at least one diagnosis at some point during their lifetime, 56 percent met the criteria for two or more disorders (Kessler, 1995; Kessler et al., 1994). A small subgroup, 14 percent of the sample, actually met the diagnostic criteria for *three or more* lifetime disorders. That group of people accounted for almost 90 percent of the severe disorders in the study.

The real problem associated with comorbidity arises when a person with a mixed pattern of symptoms, usually of a severe nature, simultaneously meets the criteria for more than one disorder. Consider, for example, a client who was treated by one of the authors of this text. This man

TABLE 4–3

Types of Studies Used to Validate Clinical Syndromes

Identification and description of the syndrome, either by clinical intuition or by statistical analyses.

Demonstration of boundaries or "points of rarity" between related syndromes.

Follow-up studies establishing a distinctive course or outcome.

Therapeutic trials establishing a distinctive treatment response.

Family studies establishing that the syndrome "breeds true."

Demonstration of association with some more fundamental abnormality—psychological, biochemical, or molecular.

Source: *Adapted from R. E. Kendell, (1989), Clinical validity,* Psychological Medicine, 19, 47.

experienced a large number of diffuse problems associated with anxiety, depression, and interpersonal difficulties. According to the DSM-IV system, he would have met the criteria for major depressive disorder, generalized anxiety disorder, and obsessive–compulsive disorder, as well as three types of personality disorder listed on Axis II. It might be said therefore that he suffered from at least six types of mental disorder. But is that really helpful? Is it the best way to think about his problems? Would it be more accurate to say that he had a complicated set of interrelated problems that were associated with worrying, rumination, and the regulation of high levels of negative emotion, and that these problems constituted one complex and severe type of disorder?

Such questions must be faced by clinicians when they use the DSM-IV system, and are another reason why we can expect the classification system to continue to be revised. As before, these changes will be driven by the interaction of clinical experience and empirical evidence.

Basic Issues in Assessment

Up to this point, we have discussed the development and use of classification systems. But we haven't talked about the way in which a psychologist might collect the information that is necessary to arrive at a diagnostic decision. Furthermore, we have looked at the problem only in relatively general terms. The diagnostic decision is one useful piece of information. It is not, however, a systematic picture of the specific person's situation. It is only a starting point. In the following section we extend our discussion to consider methods of collecting information. In so doing, we discuss a broad range of data that may be useful in understanding psychopathological behavior.

The Purposes of Clinical Assessment

Psychological assessment is the process of collecting and interpreting information that will be used to understand another person. Numerous data-gathering techniques can be used in this process. Several of these procedures are described in the following pages. We must remember, however, not to confuse the process of assessment with this list of techniques. Assessment procedures are tools that can be used in many ways. They cannot be used in an intellectual vacuum. Interviews can be used to collect all sorts of information for all sorts of reasons. Psychological tests can be interpreted in many different ways. The value of assessment procedures can be determined only in the context of a specific purpose (McFall & McDonel, 1986).

Three primary goals guide most assessment procedures: making predictions, planning interventions, and evaluating interventions. The practical importance of predictions should be obvious: Many crucial decisions are based on psychologists' attempts to determine the probability of future events. Will a person engage in violent behavior? Can a person make rational decisions? Is a parent able to care for his or her children? Assessment is also commonly used to evaluate the likelihood that a particular form of treatment will be helpful for a specific patient and to provide guideposts by which the effectiveness of treatment programs can be measured (Hayes, Nelson, & Jarrett, 1987). Different assessment procedures are likely to be employed for different purposes. Those that are useful in one situation may not be helpful in another.

Psychologists typically employ more than one source of information when conducting a formal assessment. Because we are trying to compose a broad, integrated picture of the person's adjustment, we must collect information from several sources and then attempt to integrate these data. Each piece of information may be considered to be one sample of the person's behavior. One way of evaluating the possible meaning or importance of this information is to consider the consistency across sources. Do the conclusions drawn on the basis of a diagnostic interview agree with those that are suggested by a psychological test? Do the psychologist's observations of the client's behavior and the client's self-report agree with observations that are reported by parents or teachers?

Evaluating the Utility of Assessment Procedures

The same criteria that are used to evaluate diagnostic categories are used to evaluate the utility of assessment procedures: reliability and validity. We have already discussed inter-rater reliability with regard to diagnostic decisions. In the case of assessment procedures, reliability can refer to various types of consistency. For example, the consistency of measurements over time is known as *test–retest reliability*. Will a person receive the same score if an assessment procedure is repeated at two different points in time? The internal consistency of items within a test is known as *split-half reliability*. If a test with many items measures a specific trait or ability, and if the items are divided in half, will the person's scores on the two halves agree with each other? Assessment procedures must be reliable if they are to be useful in either clinical practice or research.

The validity of an assessment procedure refers to its meaning or importance (Foster & Cone, 1995). Is the person's score on this test or procedure actually a reflection of the trait or ability that the test was designed to measure? And does the score tell us anything useful about the person's behavior in other situations? Knowing that the person has achieved a particular score on this evaluation, can we make meaningful predictions about the person's responses to other tests, or about the person's behavior in future situations? These are all questions about the validity of an assessment procedure. In general, the more consistent the information provided by different assessment procedures, the more valid each procedure is considered to be.

Assessment Procedures

An enormous array of assessment tools is available to clinicians who are interested in treating or studying abnormal behavior. Many of these procedures are commonly employed in clinical practice, and they are also used in the process of research. Our purpose in the rest of this chapter is to outline a range of assessment procedures. This is a selective sampling of measures rather than an exhaustive review of assessment procedures.

We begin our discussion with measures that are typically concerned with psychological variables—characteristic traits and behaviors that are associated with abnormal behavior. From there, we move to a consideration of the assessment of social systems, such as families and institutional environments (schools and hospitals). The last section of this chapter will be concerned with measures used in biological systems—the neurological and biochemical underpinnings of mental disorders. In many cases, the assessment of psychopathology is based on the combined use of measures that cover selective aspects of all of these systems.

At the end of each section, we have provided a quick summary of the advantages and limitations of each type of procedure. These are intended only as general guides and not as definitive critiques. Please keep in mind our earlier comment: The true value of the tool can be determined only in light of the specific purpose for which it is used.

Assessment of Psychological Systems

"Person variables" are typically the first thing that comes to mind when we think about the assessment of psychopathology. What did the person do or say? How does the person feel about his or her current situation? What skills and abilities does the person possess, and are there any important cognitive or social deficits that should be taken into consideration? These questions about the individual person can be addressed through a number of procedures, including interviews, observations, and various types of self-report instruments and psychological tests.

INTERVIEWS

Often, the best way to find out about someone is to talk with that person directly. The clinical interview, which has been described as "a conversation with a purpose" (Bingham & Moore, 1924), is the most commonly used procedure in psychological assessment. Most of the categories that are defined in DSM-IV are based on information that can be collected in an interview. These data are typically supplemented by information that is obtained from official records (previous hospital admissions, school reports, court files) and interviews with other informants (for example, family members), but the clients' own direct descriptions of their problems are the primary basis for diagnostic decisions. Except for mental retardation, none of the diagnostic categories in DSM-IV is defined in terms of psychological or biological tests.

Interviews provide an opportunity to ask people for their own descriptions of their problems. Many of the symptoms of psychopathology are subjective, and an interview can provide a detailed analysis of these problems. Consider, for example, Michael's problems with anxiety. The unrelenting fear and revulsion that he experienced at school was the central feature of his problem. His obsessive thoughts of contamination were private events that could only be known to the psychologist on the basis of Michael's self-report, which was quite compelling. His family could observe Michael's peculiar habits with regard to arranging his schoolbooks, changing his clothes, and washing his hands, but the significance of these behaviors to Michael was not immediately apparent without the knowledge that they were based on an attempt to control or neutralize his anxiety-provoking images of taunting classmates.

Interviews also allow clinicians to observe important features of a person's appearance and nonverbal behavior. In Michael's case, the psychologist noticed during their initial interview that the skin on Michael's hands and lower arms was red and chafed from excessive scrubbing. He was reluctant to make eye contact, and his speech was soft and hesitant. His obvious discomfort in this social situation was consistent with his own descriptions of the anxiety that he felt during interactions with peers. These nonverbal aspects of Michael's behavior provided useful information about the nature of his distress.

The psychologist asked Michael to describe the sequence of events in a typical day. How did he spend his time when he was at school? What were his interests outside of school? How did his rituals and obsessive thoughts interfere with these activities? Taken together, this information provides a broader context in which the specific symptoms can be understood.

Structured Interviews   Assessment interviews vary with regard to the amount of structure that is imposed by the clinician. Some are relatively open-ended, or nondirective. In this type of interview, the clinician follows the train of thought supplied by the client. One goal of nondirective interviews is to help people clarify their subjective feelings and to provide general empathic support for whatever they may decide to do about their problems. In contrast to this open-ended style, some interviews follow a more specific question-and-answer format. Structured interviews, in which the clinician must ask each patient a specific list of detailed questions, are frequently employed for collecting information that will be used to make diagnostic decisions and to rate the extent to which a person is impaired by psychopathology.

Several different structured interviews have been developed for the purpose of making psychiatric diagnoses in large-scale epidemiological and cross-national studies. Other forms of structured diagnostic interviews have been designed for use in the diagnosis of specific types of problems, such as personality disorders, anxiety disorders, dissociative disorders, and the behavior problems of children.

Structured interviews list a series of specific questions that lead to a detailed description of the person's behavior and experiences. As an example, consider the Structured Interview for DSM-IV Personality Disorders (SIDP-IV; Pfohl, Blum, & Zimmerman, 1995), which could have been used as part of the assessment process in Michael's situation. The SIDP is a widely adopted semistructured interview that covers all of the DSM-IV personality disorder categories. Selected questions from the SIDP-IV are presented in Table 4–4. We have included in this table several of the questions that are specifically relevant to a diagnosis of schizotypal personality disorder.

Structured interview schedules provide a systematic framework for the collection of important diagnostic information, but they don't eliminate the need for an experienced clinician. If the interviewer is not able to establish a comfortable rapport with the client, then the interview might not elicit useful information. Furthermore, it is difficult to specify in advance all the questions that should be asked in a diagnostic interview. The client's responses to questions may require clarification. The interviewer must determine when it is necessary to probe further and in what ways to probe. Having lists of specific questions and clear definitions of diagnostic criteria will make the clinician's job easier, but clinical judgment remains an important ingredient in the diagnostic interview.

Advantages   The clinical interview is the primary tool employed by clinical psychologists in the assessment of psychopathology. There are a number of reasons for this:

1. The interviewer can control the interaction and can probe further when necessary.
2. By observing the patient's nonverbal behavior, the interviewer can detect areas of resistance.
3. An interview can provide a lot of information in a short period of time. It can cover past events and many different settings.

Limitations   Several limitations in the use of clinical interviews as part of the assessment process must be kept in mind. These include the following considerations:

1. Some patients, such as young children or psychotic patients, may be unable or unwilling to provide a rational account of their problems.
2. People may be reluctant to admit experiences that are embarrassing or frightening. They may feel that they should report to the interviewer only those feelings and behaviors that are socially desirable.
3. Subjective factors play an important role in the interpretation of information provided in an interview. The person's responses to questions are not scored objectively, and the situation is not entirely structured and depends heavily on the training and experience of the interviewer.
4. Information provided by the client may be influenced or distorted by errors in memory and by selective perception.
5. Interviewers can influence their clients' accounts by the ways in which they phrase their questions and respond to the clients' responses, possibly suggesting symptoms or problems.

OBSERVATIONAL PROCEDURES

In addition to the information that we gain from what people are willing to tell us during interviews, we can also learn a lot by watching their behavior. Observational skills play an important part in most assessment procedures. Sometimes the things that we observe confirm the person's self-report, and at other times the person's overt behavior appears to be at odds with what he or she says.

Observational procedures may be either informal or formal. *Informal observations* are primarily qualitative. The clinician observes the person's behavior and the environment in which it occurs without attempting to record the frequency or intensity of specific responses. Michael's

TABLE 4–4

Sample Items from the Structured Interview for DSM-IV Personality (SIDP-IV)

Scoring Guidelines:

0 = not present or limited to rare isolated examples.

1 = subthreshold—some evidence of the trait but it is not sufficiently pervasive or severe to consider the criterion present.

2 = present—criterion is clearly present for most of the last 5 years (i.e., present at least 50% of the time during the last 5 years).

3 = strongly present—criterion is associated with subjective distress or some impairment in social or occupational functioning, or intimate relationships.

CLOSE RELATIONSHIPS

This part of the interview asks about your relationships with friends and family. Remember that I'm interested in the way you are when you are your usual self.

1. Neither desires nor enjoys close relationships, including being part of a family   0   1   2   3

   Do you have close relationships with friends or family?

   (IF YES): What do you enjoy about these relationships?

   (IF NO): Do you wish you had some close relationships?

2. Lacks close friends or confidants other than first-degree relatives   0   1   2   3

   Not counting your immediate family, do you have close friends you can confide in?

PERCEPTION OF OTHERS

The questions in this section ask about experiences you may have had with other people. Remember that I'm interested in knowing how you feel about these situations when you are your usual self, not during an episode of illness or hospitalization.

1. Suspects, without sufficient basis, that others are exploiting, harming, or deceiving him or her   0   1   2   3

   Have you had experiences where people who pretended to be your friends took advantage of you?

   (IF YES): What happened?

   How often has this happened?

   Are you good at spotting someone who is trying to deceive or con you?

   (IF YES): Examples?

2. Ideas of reference (excluding delusions of reference)   0   1   2   3

   Have you ever found that people around you seem to be talking in general, but then you realize their comments are really meant for you?

   (IF YES): How do you know they're talking about you?

   Have you felt like someone in charge changed the rules specifically because of you, but they wouldn't admit it?

   Do you sometimes feel like strangers on the street are looking at you and talking about you?

   (IF YES): Why do you think they notice you in particular?

Source: *Pfohl, Blum, & Zimmerman, Department of Psychiatry, University of Iowa, Iowa City.*

Direct observations can provide one of the most useful sources of information about a person's behavior. In this case, the children and their teacher are being observed from behind a one-way mirror in order to minimize reactivity, the effect that the observer's presence might have on their behavior.

case illustrates the value of informal observations in the natural environment. When the therapist visited Michael and his parents at their home, he learned that the ritualistic behaviors were more extreme than Michael had originally described. This was useful but not particularly surprising, as patients with OCD are often reluctant to describe in an interview the full extent of their compulsive behavior. The therapist also learned that the parents themselves were quite concerned with rules and order. Everything in their home was highly polished and in its place. This observation helped the therapist understand the extent to which Michael's parents might contribute to, or reinforce, his rigid adherence to a strict set of rules.

Although observations are often conducted in the natural environment, there are times when it is useful to observe the person's behavior in a situation that the psychologist can arrange and control. Sometimes it isn't possible to observe the person's behavior in the natural environment because the behavior in question occurs infrequently or at times when an observer cannot be present; at other times the environment is inaccessible; and sometimes the behavior that is of interest is inherently a private act. In these cases, the psychologist may arrange to observe the person's behavior in a situation that in some ways approximates the real environment. These artificial situations may also allow for more careful measurements of the person's problem than could be accomplished in a more complex situation.

Rating Scales   Various types of procedures can be used to provide quantitative assessments of a person's behavior that are based on observations. One alternative is to use a **rating scale** in which the observer is asked to make judgments that place the person somewhere along a dimension. For example, a clinician might observe a person's behavior for an extended period of time and then complete a set of ratings that are concerned with dimensions such as the extent to which the person exhibits compulsive ritualistic behaviors. Ratings can also be made on the basis of information collected during an interview.

Rating scales provide abstract descriptions of a person's behavior rather than a specific record of exactly what the person has done. They require social judgments on the part of the observer, who must compare this person's behavior with an ideal view of other people (Cairns & Green, 1979). How does this person compare to someone who has never experienced any difficulties in this particular area? How does the person compare to the most severely disturbed patients? In

rating scale An assessment tool in which the observer is asked to make judgments that place the person somewhere along a dimension.

many cases, that is a difficult judgment. The value of these judgments will depend, in large part, on the experience of the person who makes the ratings. They are useful to the extent that the observer is able to synthesize accurately the information that has been collected and then rate the frequency or severity of the problem relative to the behavior of other people.

Behavioral Coding Systems   Another approach to quantifying observational data depends on recording the person's actual activities. Rather than making judgments about where the person falls on a particular dimension, **behavioral coding systems**—also known as *formal observation schedules*—focus on the frequency of specific behavioral events (Foster & Cone, 1986). This type of observation therefore requires fewer inferences on the part of the observer. Coding systems can be used with observations that are made in the person's natural environment as well as with those that are performed in artificial, or contrived, situations that are specifically designed to elicit the problem behavior under circumstances in which it can be observed precisely. In some cases, the observations are made directly by a therapist, and at other times the information is provided by people who have a better opportunity to see the person's behavior in the natural environment, including teachers, parents, spouses, and peers.

Some approaches to systematic observation can be relatively simple. Consider, once again, the case of Michael. After the psychologist had conducted several interviews with Michael and his family, he asked Michael's mother to participate in the assessment process by making detailed observations of his hand-washing over a period of several nights. The mother was given a set of forms—one for each day—that could be used to record each incident, the time at which it occurred, and the circumstances that preceded the washing. The day was divided into 30-minute intervals starting at 6:30 A.M., when Michael got out of bed, and ending at 10:30, when he usually went to sleep. On each line (one for each time interval), his mother indicated whether he had washed his hands, what had been going on just prior to washing, and how anxious (on a scale from 1 to 100) Michael felt at the time that he washed.

Some adult clients are able to complete this kind of record by keeping track of their own behavior—a procedure known as *self-monitoring*. In this case, Michael's mother was asked to help because she was considered a more accurate observer and because Michael did not want to touch the form that would be used to record these observations. He believed that it was contaminated because it had touched his school clothes, which he wore to the therapy session.

Two weeks of observations were examined prior to the start of Michael's treatment. They indicated several things, including the times of the day when Michael was most active with his washing rituals (between 6 and 9 o'clock at night) and those specific objects and areas in the house that were most likely to trigger a washing incident. This information helped the therapist to plan the treatment procedure, which would depend on approaching his problem at the level that could most easily be handled and moving toward those situations that were the most difficult for him. The observations provided by Michael's mother were also used to mark his progress after treatment began.

Advantages   Observational measures, including rating scales and more detailed behavioral coding systems, can provide an extremely useful supplement to information that is typically collected in an interview format. Their advantage lies primarily in the fact that they can provide a more direct source of information than interviews can, because clinicians observe behavior directly rather than relying on patients' self-reports (Foster & Cone, 1986; Gottman, 1985).

Limitations   Observations are sometimes considered to be similar to photographs: They provide a more direct or realistic view of behavior than do people's recollections of their actions and feelings. But just as the quality of a photograph is influenced by the quality of the camera, the film, and the process that is used to develop it, the value of observational data depends on the procedures that are used to collect them (Nietzel, Bernstein, & Milich, 1994).

Observational procedures can be time-consuming and therefore expensive. Observers can make errors. Their perception may be biased, just as the inferences of an interviewer may be biased. People may alter their behavior, either intentionally or unintentionally, when they know that they are being observed. In addition, observational measures tell us only about the particular situation that was selected to be observed. Finally, there are some aspects of psychopathology that cannot be observed by anyone other than the person who has the problem (Jacobson, 1985).

PERSONALITY TESTS AND SELF-REPORT INVENTORIES

Personality tests are another important source of information about an individual's adjustment. Tests provide an opportunity to collect samples of a person's behavior in a standardized situation. These samples of behavior presumably reflect underlying abilities or personality traits. In any psychological test, the person who is being tested is presented with some kind of standard stimuli. The stimuli may be specific questions that can be answered "true" or "false." They might be problems that require solutions, or they can be completely ambiguous inkblots. Exactly the same stimuli are used every time that the test is given. In that way, the clinician can be sure that differences in performance can be interpreted as differences in abilities or traits rather than differences in the testing situation.

The psychologist observes people's responses in the test situation and draws inferences or makes predictions about how they will behave in other situations. For example, achievement tests present students with a series of mathematical and verbal problems. Performance on these standardized problems is taken as a reflection of the amount the student has learned and is also used to predict how well he or she will do in future academic situations.

Personality Inventories   Because of their structure, **personality inventories** are sometimes referred to as "objective tests." They consist of a series of straightforward statements; the person being tested is typically required to indicate whether each statement is true or false in relation to himself or herself. Several types of personality inventories are widely used. Some are designed to identify personality traits in a normal population, and others focus more specifically on psychopathological problems. We have chosen to focus on the most extensively used personality inventory—the Minnesota Multiphasic Personality Inventory (MMPI)—to illustrate the characteristics of these tests as assessment devices.

The original version of the MMPI was developed in the 1940s at the University of Minnesota by Starke Hathaway (1903–1984) and his colleagues. For the past 30 or 40 years, it has been the most widely used psychological test. Thousands of research articles have been published on the MMPI (Archer, 1992). The current version of the MMPI is known as the MMPI-2, (Graham, 1990; Greene, 1991).

The MMPI and the MMPI-2 are based on a series of more than 500 statements that cover topics ranging from physical complaints and psychological states to occupational preferences and social attitudes. Examples are statements such as "I sometimes keep on at a thing until others lose their patience with me"; "My feelings are easily hurt"; and "There are persons who are trying to steal my thoughts and ideas." After reading each statement, the person is instructed to indicate whether it is true or false. Scoring of the MMPI is objective. After totaling the responses to all questions, the person receives a numerical score on each of 10 clinical scales as well as 4 validity scales.

Before considering the possible clinical significance of a person's MMPI profile, the psychologist will examine a number of *validity scales,* which reflect the patient's attitude toward the test and the openness and consistency with which the questions were answered. The L (Lie) Scale is sensitive to unsophisticated attempts to avoid answering in a frank and honest manner. For example, one statement on this scale says, "At times I feel like swearing." Although this is perhaps not an admirable trait, virtually all normal subjects indicate that the item is true. Subjects who indicate that the item is false (does not apply to them) receive one point on the L scale. Several responses of this sort would result in an elevated score on the scale and would indicate that the person's overall test results should not be interpreted as a true reflection of his or her feelings. Other validity scales reflect tendencies to exaggerate problems, carelessness in completing the questions, and unusual defensiveness.

If the profile is considered valid, the process of interpretation will be directed toward the 10 clinical scales, which are described in Table 4–5 on page 107. Some of these scales carry rather obvious meaning, whereas others are associated with a more general or mixed pattern of symptoms.

personality inventory   Sometimes called an *objective personality test,* it consists of a series of straightforward statements that the person is required to rate or endorse as being either true or false in relation to himself or herself.

Starke Hathaway, professor of psychology at the University of Minnesota, created the Minnesota Multiphasic Personality Inventory (MMPI), which has become the most widely employed objective test of personality.

For example, Scale 2 (Depression) is a relatively straightforward index of degree of depression. Scale 7 (Psychasthenia), in contrast, is more complex and is based on items that measure anxiety, insecurity, and excessive doubt. There are many different ways to obtain an elevated score on any of the clinical scales, because each scale is composed of many items. The schizophrenia scale, for example, is based on 78 items, and a person who endorses any 20 of these statements in a deviant direction will receive an elevated score. Therefore even the more obvious scales can indicate several different types of problems, and the pattern of scale scores is more important than the elevation of any particular scale.

Rather than depending only on their own experience and clinical judgment, which may be subject to various sorts of bias and inconsistency, many clinicians analyze the results of a specific test on the basis of an explicit set of rules that are derived from empirical research. This is known as an *actuarial interpretation*. Actuarial descriptions are probability statements. They indicate that a certain proportion of the people who produce this pattern of scores will be associated with a certain characteristic or behavior.

Advantages   The MMPI is seldom used by itself, but, for the following reasons, it can serve as a useful supplement to other methods of collecting information.

1.   The MMPI provides information about the person's test-taking attitude, which alerts the clinician to the possibility that clients are careless, defensive, or exaggerating their problems.
2.   The MMPI covers a wide range of problems in a direct and efficient manner. It would take a clinician several hours to go over all of these topics using an interview format.
3.   Because the MMPI is scored objectively, the initial description of the person's adjustment is not influenced by the clinician's subjective impression of the client.
4.   The MMPI can be interpreted in an actuarial fashion, using extensive banks of information regarding people who respond to items in a particular way.

Limitations   The MMPI also has a number of limitations. Some of its problems derive from the fact that it has been used for many years. When the MMPI-2 was developed in the late 1980s, its authors decided to maintain the same clinical scales (see Table 4–5). New standardization data were obtained, and some old-fashioned items were replaced, but the underlying structure of the MMPI-2 is still based on diagnostic concepts and dimensions of psychopathology that were used 40 years ago (Helmes & Reddon, 1993). More specific limitations of the MMPI are listed below.

1.   The test is not particularly sensitive to certain forms of psychopathology, especially those that have been added with the publication of DSM-III and DSM-IV.
2.   Some people cannot complete the rather extensive list of questions. These include many people who are acutely psychotic, intellectually impaired, or poorly educated.
3.   Some studies have found that profile types are not stable over time. It is not clear whether this instability should be interpreted as lack of reliability or as sensitivity to change in the person's level of adjustment.

Other Self-Report Inventories   Sophisticated personality inventories like the MMPI are not the only approach to the measurement of subjective psychological states. Many other questionnaires and checklists have been developed to collect information about adjustment problems including subjective mood states such as depression and anxiety; patterns of obsessive thinking; and attitudes about drinking alcohol, eating, and sexual behavior. One example is the Beck Depression Inventory (BDI), which is used extensively in both clinical and research settings as an index of severity of depression.

The format of most *self-report inventories* is similar to that employed with objective personality tests like the MMPI. The primary difference is the range of topics covered by the instrument. Tests like the MMPI are designed to measure several dimensions that are related to abnormal behavior, whereas a self-report inventory is aimed more specifically at a focal topic or at one aspect

TABLE 4–5

Clinical Scales for the MMPI

SCALE NUMBER	SCALE NAME	INTERPRETATION OF HIGH SCORES
1	Hypochondriasis	Excessive bodily concern; somatic symptoms
2	Depression	Depressed; pessimistic; irritable; demanding
3	Hysteria	Physical symptoms of functional origin; self-centered; demands attention
4	Psychopathic Deviate	Asocial or antisocial; rebellious; impulsive, poor judgment
5	Masculinity–Femininity	Male: aesthetic interests Female: assertive; competitive; self-confident
6	Paranoia	Suspicious, sensitive; resentful; rigid; may be frankly psychotic
7	Psychasthenia	Anxious; worried; obsessive; lacks self-confidence; problems in decision making
8	Schizophrenia	May have thinking disturbance, withdrawn; feels alienated and unaccepted
9	Hypomania	Excessive activity; lacks direction; low frustration tolerance; friendly
0	Social Introversion	Socially introverted; shy; sensitive; over-controlled; conforming

of the person's adjustment. Self-report inventories may not be standardized on large samples of normal subjects prior to their use in a clinical setting.

Self-report inventories offer many advantages as supplements to information that is collected during clinical interviews. They are an extremely efficient way to gather specific data regarding a wide range of topics. They can also be scored objectively and therefore provide a specific index that is frequently useful in measuring change from one period of time to the next—for example, before and after treatment.

Despite their many advantages, self-report inventories can lead to serious problems if they are used carelessly. The BDI, for example, was designed as an index of change. Unfortunately, many investigators and clinicians have erroneously used it for diagnostic purposes. It is a serious mistake to assume that anyone who appears to be depressed on the basis of a self-report inventory would necessarily be diagnosed as being depressed after a clinical interview (Myers & Weissman, 1980; Oliver & Simmons, 1984). Self-report scales sometimes fail to identify patients who are considered depressed on the basis of a clinical interview. One reason for this discrepancy is the fact that some depressed patients consider themselves to be less depressed than they appear to a clinician when they are interviewed (Sayer et al., 1993).

projective tests   Personality tests, such as the Rorschach inkblot test, in which the person is asked to interpret a series of ambiguous stimuli.

PROJECTIVE PERSONALITY TESTS

In **projective tests,** the person is presented with a series of ambiguous stimuli. The best-known projective test, introduced in 1921 by Hermann Rorschach (1884–1922), a Swiss psychiatrist, is based on the use of inkblots. The *Rorschach test* consists of a series of 10 inkblots. Five contain various shades of gray on a white background, and five contain elements of color. The person is asked to look at each card and indicate what it looks like or what it appears to be. There are, of course, no correct answers. The instructions are intentionally vague in order to avoid influencing the person's responses through subtle suggestions.

Projective techniques such as the Rorschach test were originally based on psychodynamic assumptions about the nature of personality and psychopathology. Considerable emphasis was placed on the importance of unconscious motivations—conflicts and impulses of which the person is largely unaware. In other words, people being tested presumably *project* hidden desires and conflicts when they try to describe or explain the cards. In so doing, they may reveal things about themselves of which they are not consciously aware or that they might not be willing to admit if they were asked directly. The cards are not designed or chosen to be realistic or representational; they presumably look like whatever the person wants them to look like.

Michael did not actually complete any projective personality tests. We can illustrate the way in which these tests might have been used in his case, however, by considering a man who had been given a diagnosis of obsessive–compulsive disorder on Axis I, as well as showing evidence of two types of personality disorder, dependent and schizotypal features. This patient was 22 years old, unemployed, and living with his mother. His father had died in an accident 4 years earlier. Like Michael, this man was bothered by intrusive thoughts of contamination, and he frequently engaged in compulsive washing (Hurt, Reznikoff, & Clarkin, 1991). His responses to the cards on the Rorschach frequently mentioned emotional distress ("a man screaming"), interpersonal conflict ("two women fighting over something"), and war ("two mushrooms of a nuclear bomb cloud"). He did not incorporate color into any of his responses to the cards.

The original procedures for scoring the Rorschach were largely impressionistic and placed considerable emphasis on the content of the person's response. Responses given in the example above might be taken to suggest a number of important themes. Aggression and violence are obvious possibilities. Perhaps the man was repressing feelings of hostility, as indicated by his frequent references to war and conflict. These themes were coupled with a guarded approach to emotional reactions, which is presumably reflected by his avoidance of color. The psychologist might have wondered whether the man felt guilty about something, such as his father's death. This kind of interpretation, which depends heavily on symbolism and clinical inference, provides intriguing material for the clinician to puzzle over. Unfortunately, the reliability and validity of this intuitive type of scoring procedure are very low (Shontz & Green, 1992).

More recent approaches to the use of projective tests view the person's descriptions of the cards as a sample of his or her perceptual and cognitive styles. The psychologist John Exner has developed an objective scoring procedure for the Rorschach that is based primarily on the form rather than the content of the subject's responses (Exner, 1986; Kleiger, 1992). According to Exner's system, interpretation of the test depends on the way in which the descriptions take into account the shapes and colors on the cards. Does the person see movement in the card? Does she focus on tiny details, or does she base her descriptions on global impressions of the entire form of the inkblot? These and many other considerations contribute to the overall interpretation of the Rorschach test. The reliability of this scoring system is better than would be achieved by informal, impressionistic procedures. The validity of the scores, however, remains open to question (Davis, 1978; Shontz & Green, 1992).

Projective tests require a person to respond to ambiguous stimuli. Here, a woman is taking the Thematic Apperception Test (TAT), in which she will be asked to make up a story about a series of drawings of people.

There are many different types of projective tests. Some employ stimuli that are somewhat less ambiguous than the inkblots in the Rorschach. The Thematic Apperception Test (TAT), for example, consists of a series of drawings that depict human figures in various ambiguous situations. Most of the cards portray more than one person. The figures and their poses tend to elicit stories with themes of sadness and violence. The person is asked to describe the identities of the people in the cards and to make up a story about what is happening. These stories presumably reflect the person's own ways of perceiving reality.

Advantages   The advantages of projective tests center on the fact that the tests are interesting to give and interpret and they sometimes provide a way to talk to people who are otherwise reluctant or unable to discuss their problems. Projective tests are more appealing to psychologists who adopt a psychodynamic view of personality and psychopathology because to whatever extent a person's relationships with other people are governed by unconscious cognitive and emotional events, projective tests may provide information that cannot be obtained through direct interviewing methods or observational procedures (Stricker & Healey, 1990).

Limitations   There are many serious problems with the use of projective tests. The popularity of projective tests has declined considerably since the 1970s, even in clinical settings, primarily because research studies have found little evidence to support their reliability and validity (Wierzbicki, 1993; Wood, Nezworski, & Stejskal, 1996). Lack of standardization in administration and scoring is a serious problem, even though Exner's system for the Rorschach has made some improvements in that regard. Also, little information is available to use as norms for either adults or children. Finally, some projective procedures, such as the Rorschach, can be very time-consuming, particularly if the person's responses are scored with a standardized procedure such as Exner's system.

Assessment of Social Systems

The same range of procedures that we have discussed for the assessment of person variables (psychological systems) can also be used to examine situation variables (social systems). For example, clinical interviews can be used to describe the client's family and social environment, both past and present. These are obviously important considerations in planning a treatment program.

In Michael's case, the psychologist was interested in Michael's social relationships with classmates as well as his interactions with his parents. His father indicated that he was quite concerned about Michael's problems and that he was willing to help as they planned a treatment procedure that would allow Michael to learn to cope more effectively with his obsessive thoughts about contamination. Michael's mother also told the psychologist that arguments between Michael and his father often seemed to trigger an increase in the frequency of his compulsive washing rituals. This information convinced the psychologist that Michael's treatment should focus on improving his relationship with his father and not just on his compulsive washing. He made this decision knowing that family conflict and negative family attitudes have a negative impact on the results of treatment for obsessive–compulsive disorder (Leonard et al., 1993; Steketee, 1993).

Many self-report inventories, rating scales, and behavioral coding systems have also been designed for the assessment of marital relationships and family systems. One popular self-report inventory is the Family Environment Scale (FES), which is composed of 90 true–false items and was designed to measure the social characteristics of families (Moos, 1974, 1981). The scale is composed of 10 subscales that are aimed at three dimensions of the family: *relationships* (cohesion, expressiveness, and conflicts); *personal growth* (independence, achievement orientation, intellectual-cultural orientation, active-recreational orientation, and moral-religious emphasis); and *system maintenance* (organization and control). Extensive testing with large numbers of families has been used to establish norms on the FES for distressed and nondistressed families. The FES has been used widely in clinical settings and in research studies. Unfortunately, evidence regarding test–retest reliability and the validity of the subscales is not impressive (L'Abate & Bagarozzi, 1993).

Direct observations can also be used to assess the social climate within a family. The Family Interaction Coding System (FICS) was developed by Gerald Patterson and John Reid, clinical psychologists at the Oregon Research Institute, to observe interactions between parents and children in their homes (Jones, Reid, & Patterson, 1975; Reid, 1978). A trained observer visits the family's home and collects information for at least 70 minutes just prior to lunch or dinner. Everyone in the family must be present during this time period, and they must stay in a two-room area. For each 5-minute block of time, the observer focuses on two members of the family and describes their behavior, using the coding system. The observer rotates his or her attention from one "target" to the next throughout the observation period.

Trained raters can achieve high levels of reliability with the FICS. In addition, a number of research studies have demonstrated that it is a valid measure of aggressive behaviors in children, as well as a useful way to assess the family context in which these behaviors occur. It can distinguish between the families of children with antisocial behavior or conduct disorders and nondisturbed families. The FICS is also a useful clinical tool that is sensitive to changes that occur during the course of family treatment (Grotevant & Carlson, 1989). The main disadvantages of this coding system are that the process of training observers is expensive and the collection of data is time-consuming.

Assessment of Biological Systems

In addition to psychological and social factors, biological factors affect human behavior. Clinicians have developed a number of techniques for measuring the behavioral effects of biological systems. These techniques are seldom used in clinical practice (at least for the diagnosis of psychopathology), but they have been employed extensively in research settings, and it seems possible that they will one day become an important source of information on individual patients.

PSYCHOPHYSIOLOGICAL ASSESSMENT

Changes in physiological response systems, such as heart rate, respiration rate, and skin conductance, are another important source of information regarding a person's psychological adjustment. The basic components of the human nervous system (reviewed in Chapter 2) include the central nervous system (CNS) and the peripheral nervous system (PNS). The PNS is divided into two parts: the somatic nervous system and the autonomic nervous system. The *somatic nervous system* is responsible for communication between the brain and external sense receptors, as well as regulation of voluntary muscle movements. The *autonomic nervous system* is responsible for body processes that occur without conscious awareness, such as heart rate. It maintains equilibrium in the internal environment.

The autonomic nervous system is highly reactive to environmental events and can provide useful information about a person's internal states, such as emotion (Miller & Kozak, 1993). Recording procedures have been developed to measure variables such as respiration rate, heart rate, and skin conductance. As the person becomes aroused, the activity of these systems changes. Psychophysiological measures can therefore provide sensitive indices of the person's internal state.

It must be emphasized, however, that all of these measures do not act together. The concept of general arousal was abandoned many years ago (for example, see Lacey, 1967). If several physiological responses are measured at the same time, they may not all demonstrate the same strength, or even direction, of response. Moreover, physiological measures frequently disagree with the person's own subjective report. Therefore, as with other assessment procedures, physiological recordings should be used in conjunction with other measures. They represent supplements to, rather than substitutes for, the other types of measures that we have already considered (Iacono, 1991).

Anxiety disorders are one type of problem in which psychophysiological measurements have been used (Turpin, 1991). Consider Michael's case. He was afraid to touch contaminated objects in his house. If he had been forced to do so, it is likely that his heart rate would have increased dramatically. Psychophysiological events of this sort can be monitored precisely. To the extent that the clinician might be in need of information that would confirm data from other sources (observation, self-report) or that could be used to measure changes in the person's response to particular stimuli in the environment, physiological measurements may be very useful.

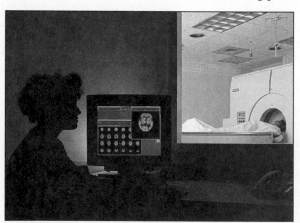

Position emission topography (PET scan) can provide useful images of dynamic brain functions. Areas that appear red or yellow indicate areas of the brain that are active (consuming the labeled glucose molecules), whereas those that are blue or green are relatively inactive. Different areas of the brain become active depending on whether the person is at rest or engaged in particular activities when the image is created.

Advantages   Psychophysiological recording procedures do not depend on self-report and therefore may be less subject to voluntary control. People may be less able to make the assessment show what they want it to show. Some of these measures can also be obtained while the subject is sleeping or while the subject is actively engaged in some other activity.

Limitations   In addition to the fact that they require relatively sophisticated equipment and a technician who is trained in their use, physiological measures have a number of drawbacks.

1. The recording equipment and electrodes may be frightening or intimidating to some people.

2. There are generally low correlations between different autonomic response systems. It is not wise to select arbitrarily one specific physiological measure, such as heart rate, and assume that it is a direct index of arousal.

3. Physiological reactivity and the stability of physiological response systems vary from person to person. The measures may be informative for some people but not for others.

4. Physiological responses can be influenced by many other factors. Some are person variables, such as age and medication, as well as psychological factors, such as being self-conscious or fearing loss of control (Anderson & McNeilly, 1991). Other important considerations are situational variables, such as extraneous noise and electrical activity.

BRAIN IMAGING TECHNIQUES

The past several decades have seen a tremendous explosion of information and technology in the neurosciences. We now understand in considerable detail how neurons in the central nervous system communicate with one another, and scientists have invented sophisticated methods to create images of the living human brain (Daniel, Zigun, & Weinberger, 1994; Posner, 1993). Some of these procedures provide static pictures of various brain structures at rest, just as an X-ray provides a photographic image of a bone or some other organ of the body. Other methods can be used to create dynamic images of brain functions—reflecting the rate of activity in various parts of the brain—while a person is performing different tasks.

Static Brain Imaging   Many investigations of brain structure in people with various forms of psychopathology have employed an imaging technique called *computerized tomographic (CT) scanning*. In CT scanning, X-ray beams are passed through the brain to a series of detectors that measure the density of the tissues through which the beams have passed. A series of two-dimensional images are created at sequential slices or planes of the brain by rotating the scanner around the body for the full 360 degrees.

A much more precise measure of brain structure can be obtained with *magnetic resonance imaging (MRI)*. In MRI, images are generated using electromagnetic phenomena rather than X-rays (Andreasen, 1989). Both CT scanning and MRI provide a static image of specific brain structures. MRI provides better images than CT scans and is able to identify smaller parts of the brain. For this reason, and because it lends itself more easily to the creation of three-dimensional pictures of the brain, MRI is replacing CT scanning where it is available.

Dynamic Brain Imaging   In addition to CT scanning and MRI, which provide a static view of brain structures, advances in the neurosciences have also produced techniques that create images of brain functions (Raichle, 1994a, 1994b). Unlike CT scanning, which is available at most hospitals, the dynamic imaging procedures are very expensive, and they are currently available only to a few investigators.

Positron emission tomography (PET) is one scanning technique that can be used to create dynamic brain images. This procedure is much more expensive than the other imaging techniques because it requires a nuclear cyclotron to produce special radioactive elements. PET scans are capable of providing relatively detailed images of the brain. In addition, they can reflect changes in brain activity as the person responds to the demands of various tasks.

A second functional imaging procedure is *single photon emission computed tomography,* or *SPECT.* SPECT is more widely available than PET because single-photon-emitting compounds have relatively long physical half-lives. Therefore they can be manufactured in one location and transported to another, distant location where the imaging procedure is being conducted. On the other hand, the resolution of SPECT images is not as good as that obtained using PET.

Dynamic brain imaging procedures have been used extensively to study possible neurological underpinnings of various types of mental disorder. For example, in the case of obsessive–compulsive disorder (OCD), considerable research has focused on the *basal ganglia,* a complex set of nuclei connecting structures in the cerebral cortex with the thalamus (Insel, 1992). Studies using SPECT (Edmonstone et al., 1994) and PET (Perani et al., 1995) have suggested that increased metabolic rates in the basal ganglia may be correlated with the presence of obsessions and compulsions.

These results are intriguing because they suggest that this circuit in the brain may somehow be associated with the presence of obsessive–compulsive symptoms. We must emphasize, however, that the results of such imaging procedure are not useful diagnostically with regard to an individual person. In other words, some people with OCD do not exhibit increased metabolism rates in the basal ganglia, and some people who do not have OCD do show increased levels of activity in their basal ganglia.

Advantages   Brain imaging techniques provide detailed information regarding the structure of brain areas and activity levels in the brain that are associated with the performance of particular tasks. They have important uses, primarily as research tools, but in clinical practice, imaging techniques can be used to rule out various neurological conditions, such as brain tumors, that might explain behavioral or cognitive deficits. More commonly, procedures such as MRI and PET can help research investigators explore the relation between brain functions and specific mental disorders. This type of information will be considered in several chapters later in this book.

Limitations   Brain imaging procedures have little clinical importance outside the assessment and treatment of disorders such as Alzheimer's disease. Since norms have not been established for any of these measures, it is not possible to use brain imaging procedures for diagnostic purposes. Finally, these procedures are relatively expensive—especially PET scans—and some procedures must be used cautiously because the patient may be exposed to radioactive substances.

Summary

Formal **classification systems** for mental disorders have been developed in order to facilitate communication, research, and treatment planning. The current official system published by the American Psychiatric Association is the fourth edition of the *Diagnostic and Statistical Manual of Mental Disorders,* or DSM-IV. It is based on a **categorical approach to classification.** The categories that are defined in DSM-IV are based primarily on descriptive principles rather than on theoretical knowledge regarding the etiology of the disorders. Five axes are included in this system. Axes I and II are employed for describing mental disorders (personality disorders and mental retardation on Axis II). The remaining three axes are concerned with supplementary information that may also be useful in treatment planning.

The utility of a classification system depends on several criteria, especially **reliability** and **validity.** The reliability of many categories in DSM seems to have improved with the introduction of specific inclusion criteria and exclusion criteria. Nevertheless, serious questions remain about this issue. The reliability of some categories, such as the personality disorders, is still marginal in many studies. Reliability is also likely to be diminished in clinical settings where clinicians are not experts in a particular disorder and reliability is not being monitored. The validity, or systematic meaning, of most categories is still under active investigation.

The general process of collecting and interpreting information is called **assessment.** Many different assessment tools can be used to generate information systematically. Interviews, observations, and tests are among the most frequently used procedures. Assessments can be directed toward biological, psychological, and social systems. In many cases, information is collected and integrated across more than one system, but it is never possible to learn everything about a particular person. Choices have to be made, and some information must be excluded from the analysis.

Psychological systems are typically assessed using interviews, observations, or self-report inventories. Structured diagnostic interviews are used extensively in conjunction with the DSM-IV classification system. They can also form the basis for ratings of the person's adjustment on a number of dimensions. Interviews can be used to collect additional information that is relevant to planning treatment. Their main advantage is their flexibility. Their primary limitation lies in the inability or unwillingness of some clients to provide a rational description of their own problems, as well as the subjective factors that influence the clinician's interpretation of data collected in an interview.

Psychological tests are also used in the assessment of psychological systems. **Personality inventories,** like the MMPI, offer several advantages as supplements to interviews and observations. They can be scored objectively, they often contain validity scales that reflect the person's attitude and test-taking set, and they can be interpreted in reference to well-established standards for people with and without specific types of adjustment problems. Some psychologists use projective personality tests, like the Rorschach, to acquire information that might not be obtained from direct interviews or observations. Unfortunately, research studies have found little evidence to support the reliability and validity of projective tests. The continued use of these tests is therefore controversial.

Social systems, including marital relationships and families, can also be evaluated using interviews, observations, and self-report inventories. Although the instruments that are used for this purpose have not been developed as extensively as those that address psychological systems, they represent an important consideration in thinking about mental disorders and their treatment.

Many different tools are available for assessing biological systems related to mental disorders. These include psychophysiological recording procedures as well as brain imaging techniques, such as MRI and PET scans. Biological assessment procedures are used extensively in research studies. They do not have diagnostic value in clinical situations, except for the purpose of ruling out certain conditions, such as brain tumors and vascular disease.

Critical Thinking

1. Do we need a classification system in the field of psychopathology? If so, how should it be evaluated? What are the characteristics of a useful classification system? Should we expect that such a system will be based solely on scientific considerations?

2. What are some of the inherent limitations of a classification system? What are the advantages and disadvantages associated with the process of psychiatric diagnosis? If there are problems, how can they be resolved, or at least minimized?

3. How will your choice of an assessment procedure be influenced by the conceptual frame of reference that you adopt in thinking about a clinical problem? How will it be influenced by the nature of the specific problem that you are trying to address? Why isn't it possible to have a universal assessment battery that could be used consistently for all clinical problems?

5

Mood Disorders

Some of the simplest emotions require little description. We all know how it feels to be angry or sad. Most of our feelings are momentary—like the apprehension that grips us when we are watching a frightening movie, or the amusement we experience when listening to a comedian. Others can be relatively enduring, like the grief we may suffer when a close friend moves away. Most emotional fluctuations, including many that are unpleasant, are part of normal experience. Unfortunately, some people experience extreme fluctuations in emotion that become persistent and severely debilitating. In this chapter we will consider emotional disorders that involve prolonged periods of severe depression.

Overview

emotion A state of arousal that is defined by subjective feeling states, such as sadness, anger, and disgust. Emotions are often accompanied by physiological changes, such as in heart rate and respiration rate.

affect The pattern of observable behaviors that are associated with subjective feelings. People express affect through changes in their facial expressions, the pitch of their voices, and their hand and body movements.

mood A pervasive and sustained emotional response that, in its extreme, can color the person's perception of the world.

depression Can refer to a *symptom* (subjective feelings of sadness), a *mood* (sustained and pervasive feelings of despair), or to a clinical *syndrome* (in which the presence of a depressed mood is accompanied by several additional symptoms, such as fatigue, loss of energy, sleeping difficulties, and appetite changes).

mania A disturbance in mood characterized by such symptoms as elation, inflated self-esteem, hyperactivity, and accelerated speaking and thinking. An exaggerated feeling of physical and emotional well-being.

Psychopathologists use several terms to describe problems that are associated with emotional response systems. This language can become confusing because most of us already use these words in our everyday vocabulary. We must define these terms as they are used in psychopathology so that our discussion will be clear. **Emotion** refers to a state of arousal that is defined by subjective states of feeling, such as sadness, anger, and disgust. Emotions are often accompanied by physiological changes, such as changes in heart rate and respiration rate. **Affect** refers to the pattern of observable behaviors that are associated with these subjective feelings. People express affect through changes in their facial expressions, the pitch of their voices, and their hand and body movements. **Mood** refers to a pervasive and sustained emotional response that, in its extreme form, can color the person's perception of the world (APA, 1994). The disorders that are discussed in this chapter are primarily associated with two specific moods: depression and elation.

Depression can refer either to a mood or to a clinical syndrome—a combination of emotional, cognitive, and behavioral symptoms. The feelings associated with a *depressed mood* often include disappointment and despair. Although sadness is a universal experience, profound depression is not. People who are in a severely depressed mood describe the feeling as overwhelming, suffocating, or numbing. In the syndrome of depression, which is also called *clinical depression*, a depressed mood is accompanied by several other symptoms, such as fatigue, loss of energy, difficulty in sleeping, and changes in appetite. Clinical depression also involves a variety of changes in thinking and overt behavior. The person may experience cognitive symptoms, such as extreme guilt, feelings of worthlessness, concentration problems, and thoughts of suicide. Behavioral symptoms may range from constant pacing and fidgeting to extreme inactivity. Throughout the rest of this chapter, we will use the term *depression* to refer to the clinical syndrome rather than the mood.

Mania, the flip side of depression, also involves a disturbance in mood that is accompanied by additional symptoms. Euphoria or elated mood is the opposite emotional state from a depressed mood: It is characterized by an exaggerated feeling of physical and emotional well-being (APA, 1994). Manic symptoms that frequently accompany an elated mood include inflated self-esteem, decreased need for sleep, distractibility, pressure to keep talking, and the subjective

mood disorders   A broad category of psychopathology that includes depressive disorders and bipolar disorders. These conditions are defined in terms of episodes in which the person's behavior is dominated by either clinical depression or mania.

unipolar mood disorder   A form of mood disorder in which the person experiences episodes of depression but has never experienced an episode of mania or hypomania.

bipolar mood disorder   A form of mood disorder in which the person experiences episodes of mania as well as episodes of depression.

feeling of thoughts racing through the person's head faster than they can be spoken. Mania is therefore a syndrome in the same sense that clinical depression is a syndrome.

Mood disorders are defined in terms of episodes—discrete periods of time in which the person's behavior is dominated by either a depressed or manic mood. Unfortunately, most people with a mood disorder experience more than one episode. The case studies printed here illustrate the way that numerous symptoms combine to form syndromes that are used to define mood disorders. They also provide examples of the two primary types of mood disorders: (1) those in which the person experiences only episodes of depression, known as **unipolar mood disorder,** and (2) those in which the person experiences episodes of mania as well as depression, known as **bipolar mood disorder.** A small number of patients have only manic episodes with no evidence of depression; they are included in the bipolar category. Years ago, bipolar mood disorder was known as *manic–depressive disorder*. Although this term has been replaced in the official diagnostic manual, some clinicians still prefer to use it because it offers a more direct description of the patient's experience (Jamison, 1995).

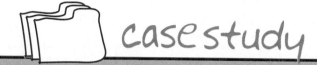

Unipolar Mood Disorder: Major Depressive Episode

Cathy was a 31-year-old attorney who had been promoted to the rank of partner the previous year and was considered one of the brightest, most promising young members of her firm. In spite of her apparent success, she was plagued by doubts about her own abilities and was convinced that she was unworthy of her promotion. Cathy decided to seek treatment because she was profoundly miserable. Beyond being depressed, she felt numb. She had been feeling unusually fatigued and irritable for a period of several months, but her mood took a serious swing for the worse after one of the firm's clients, for whom Cathy was primarily responsible, decided to switch to another firm. Although the decision was clearly based on factors that were beyond her control, Cathy blamed herself. She interpreted this event as a reflection of her professional incompetence, in spite of the fact that virtually all of her other clients had praised her work and the senior partners in her firm had given her consistently positive reviews.

Cathy had always looked forward to going to the office, and she truly enjoyed her work. After she lost this client, however, going to work had seemed like an overwhelming burden.

She found it impossible to concentrate and instead brooded about her own incompetence. Soon she started calling in sick. She began to spend her time sitting in bed staring at the television screen, without paying attention to any program, and she never left her apartment. She felt lethargic all the time, but she wasn't sleeping well. Her appetite disappeared. Her best friend tried repeatedly to get in touch with her, but Cathy wouldn't return her calls. She listened passively as her friend left messages on the answering machine. She just didn't feel like doing anything or talking to anyone.

Cathy considered her social life to be a disaster, and it didn't seem to be getting any better. She had been separated from her husband for 5 years, and her most recent boyfriend had started dating another woman. She had tried desperately for several weeks to force herself to be active, but eventually she stopped caring. The situation seemed completely hopeless. Although she had often gone to parties with other members of her law firm, she usually felt as though she didn't fit in. Everyone else seemed to be part of a couple, and Cathy was usually on her own. Other people didn't appreciate the depth of her loneliness. Sometimes it seemed to Cathy that she would be better off dead. She spent a good deal of time brooding about suicide, but she feared that if she tried to harm herself she might make things worse than they already were. ♛

Cathy's problems would be classified as a unipolar mood disorder because she had experienced at least one episode of major depression and she had never had a manic episode. Our next case illustrates the symptoms of mania, which often appear after a person has already experienced at least one episode of depression. People who experience episodes of both depression and mania are given a diagnosis of bipolar mood disorder. The symptoms of a full-blown manic episode are not subtle. People who are manic typically have terrible judgment and may get into considerable trouble as a result of their disorder. The central feature of mania is a persistently elevated or irritable mood that lasts for at least 1 week.

case study

Bipolar Mood Disorder: Manic Episode

Debbie, a 21-year-old single woman, was admitted to a psychiatric hospital in the midst of a manic episode. She had been in psychotherapy for depression for a period of several months while she was in high school but had not received any type of treatment since that time. After she completed two semesters at a community college, Debbie found a well-paying job in the advertising office of a local newspaper, where she had been working for 2 years.

Debbie's manic episode could be traced to experiences that began 3 or 4 months prior to her admission to the hospital. Debbie had been feeling unusually good for several weeks. At first she didn't think anything was wrong. In fact, her impression was quite the opposite. Everything seemed to be going right for her. Her energy level was up, and she felt a renewed confidence in herself and her relationships with other people, especially with her boyfriend, who had recently moved to a distant city. Debbie initially welcomed these feelings, especially because she had been so lethargic and also tended to be reserved interpersonally.

One day when she was feeling particularly exhilarated, Debbie impulsively quit her job and went to visit her boyfriend. Giving up her job without careful consideration and with no prospect for alternative employment was the first indication that Debbie's judgment was becoming impaired. Although she left home with only enough money to pay for her airplane ticket, she stayed for several weeks, mostly engaged in leisure activities. It was during this time that she started having trouble sleeping. The quality of her mood also began to change. It was less often cheerful and frequently irritable. She was extremely impatient and would become furious if her boyfriend disagreed with her. On one occasion, they had a loud and heated argument in the parking lot of his apartment complex. She took off her blouse and angrily refused to put it on again in spite of his demands and the presence of several interested bystanders. Shortly after the fight, she packed her clothes and hitchhiked back home.

After returning to her parents' home, Debbie argued with them almost continuously for several days. Her moods shifted constantly. One moment she would be bubbling with enthusiasm, gleefully throwing herself into new and exciting activities. If her plans were thwarted, she would fly into a rage. She phoned an exclusive tennis club to arrange for private lessons, which she obviously could not afford, especially now that she was unemployed. Her mother interrupted the call and canceled the lessons. Debbie left the house in a fury and set off to hitch a ride to the tennis club. She was picked up by two unknown men, who persuaded her to accompany them to a party rather than go to the club. By the time they arrived at the party, her mood was once again euphoric. She stayed at the party all night and had intercourse with three men whom she had never met before.

The following day, Debbie borrowed money from a friend and took a train home. Another argument ensued when she arrived at home. Debbie struck her father and took the family car. Angry and frightened by her apparently irrational behavior, her parents phoned the police, who found her and brought her home. When another argument broke out, even more hostile than the first, the police took Debbie to their precinct office, where she was interviewed by a psychiatrist. Her attitude was flippant, and her language was abusive and obscene. On the basis of her clearly irrational and violent mood as well as her marked impairment in judgment, the psychiatrist arranged for her to be committed to a psychiatric hospital.

Debbie's behavior on the ward was belligerent, provocative, and demanding. Although she hadn't slept a total of more than 4 hours in the previous 3 days, she claimed to be bursting with energy. Her affect vacillated quickly and frequently. The slightest provocation could change an elated, expansive mood into a furious burst of anger. She behaved seductively toward some of the male patients, sitting on their laps, kissing them, and occasionally unfastening her clothing. Although her speech was coherent, it was rapid and pressured. She expressed several grandiose ideas, including the boast that she was an Olympic swimmer and skier and that she was a premed student in college. She had no insight into the severity of her mental condition. Failing to recognize that her judgment was impaired, she insisted that she had been brought to the ward so that she could help the other patients ("I am a psychic therapist").

Typical Symptoms and Associated Features

The cases of Cathy and Debbie illustrate many of the most important symptoms and signs of mood disorders, which can be divided into four general areas: emotional symptoms, cognitive symptoms, somatic symptoms, and behavioral symptoms. Each area is typically involved in episodes of major depression and mania.

dysphoria   Unpleasant mood, often associated with depression.

euphoria   An exaggerated feeling of physical and emotional well-being, typically associated with manic episodes in bipolar mood disorder.

Emotional Symptoms

Depressed, or **dysphoric** (unpleasant), mood is the most common and obvious symptom of depression. Most people who are depressed describe themselves as feeling utterly gloomy, dejected, or despondent. There is no clear-cut line dividing normal sadness from the depressed mood that is associated with clinical depression. Clinicians use several features to help guide this diagnostic distinction, including the severity, the quality, and the pervasive impact of the depressed mood.

The severity of a depressed mood can reach painful and overwhelming proportions. William Styron, a Pulitzer Prize–winning author, has described the feeling as "despair beyond despair." Styron's account of his own experience with profound depression, which took him to the brink of suicide, provides a compelling description of the disorder. He says that the sensation most closely resembled drowning or suffocation. Styron wrote about the unique quality of his depressed mood:

> What I had begun to discover is that, mysteriously and in ways that are totally remote from normal experience, the gray drizzle of horror induced by depression takes on the quality of physical pain. But it is not an immediately identifiable pain, [and] . . . comes to resemble the diabolical discomfort of being imprisoned in a fiercely overheated room. And because no breeze stirs this caldron, because there is no escape from this smothering confinement, it is entirely natural that the victim begins to think ceaselessly of oblivion. (1990, p. 50)

In contrast to the unpleasant feelings associated with clinical depression, manic patients like Debbie experience periods of inexplicable and unbounded joy known as **euphoria**. Debbie felt extremely optimistic and cheerful—"on top of the world"—in spite of the fact that her inappropriate behavior had made a shambles of her current life circumstances. Bursting with energy, she exhibited boundless enthusiasm, even after she was admitted to the psychiatric hospital. In bipolar mood disorders, periods of elated mood tend to alternate with phases of depression. The duration of each episode and the frequency of the cycle vary from one patient to the next.

Kay Jamison, professor of psychiatry at Johns Hopkins University School of Medicine, has written an eloquent and moving description of her own experiences with mania and depression. The symptoms of mania are initially quite pleasant. The person may experience periods of increased energy that are accompanied by feelings of enhanced productivity and creativity. Unfortunately, as these feelings become more intense and prolonged, they may become ruinous. It may not be clear when the person's experience crosses the unmarked boundary between being productive and energetic to being out of control and self-destructive. Jamison described this subtle transition in the following way:

> There is a particular kind of pain, elation, loneliness, and terror involved in this kind of madness. When you're high it's tremendous. The ideas and feelings are fast and frequent like shooting stars, and you follow them until you find better and brighter ones. Shyness goes, the right words and gestures are suddenly there, the power to captivate others a felt certainty. There are interests found in uninteresting people. Sensuality is pervasive, and the desire to seduce and be seduced irresistible. Feelings of ease, intensity, power, well-being, financial omnipotence, and euphoria pervade one's marrow. But, somewhere, this changes. The fast ideas are far too fast, and there are far too many; overwhelming confusion replaces clarity. Memory goes. Humor and absorption on friends' faces are replaced by fear and concern. Everything previously moving with the grain is now against—you are irritable, angry, frightened, uncontrollable, and enmeshed totally in the blackest caves of the mind. You never knew those caves were there. It will never end, for madness carves its own reality. (1995, p. 67)

Many depressed and manic patients are irritable. Their anger can be directed either at themselves or at others, and frequently at both. Even when they are cheerful, people

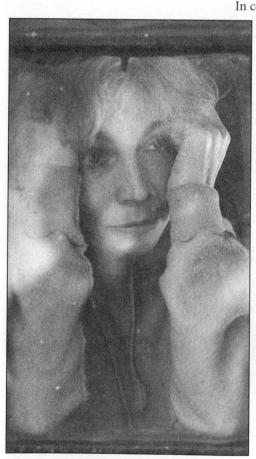

The quality of a depressed mood is often different from the sadness that might arise from an event such as the loss of a loved one. Some depressed people say that they feel like they are drowning or suffocating.

in a manic episode, like Debbie, are easily provoked to anger. Debbie became extremely argumentative and abusive, particularly when people challenged her grandiose statements about herself and her inappropriate judgment.

Anxiety is also common among people with mood disorders, just as depression is a common feature of some anxiety disorders (see Chapter 6). Two out of every 3 depressed patients also report feeling anxious (Kendall & Watson, 1989). People who are depressed are sometimes apprehensive, fearing that matters will become even worse than they already are or that others will discover their inadequacy. They sometimes report that they are chronically tense and unable to relax.

somatic symptoms   Symptoms of mood disorders that are related to basic physiological or bodily functions, including fatigue, aches and pains, and serious changes in appetite and sleep patterns.

Cognitive Symptoms

In addition to changes in the way people feel, mood disorders also involve changes in the way people think about themselves and their surroundings. People who are clinically depressed frequently note that their thinking is slowed down, that they have trouble concentrating, and that they are easily distracted. Cathy's ability to concentrate was so disturbed that she became unable to work. She had extreme difficulty making even the simplest decisions. After she started staying home, she sat in front of the television set but was unable to pay attention to the content of even the simplest programs. Her thought processes were almost completely shut down.

Guilt and worthlessness are common preoccupations. Depressed patients blame themselves for things that have gone wrong, regardless of whether they are in fact responsible. They focus considerable attention on the most negative features of themselves, their environments, and the future—a combination that A. T. Beck (1967) has labeled the "depressive triad."

In contrast to the cognitive slowness associated with depression, manic patients commonly report that their thoughts are speeded up. Ideas flash through their minds faster than they can articulate their thoughts. Manic patients can also be easily distracted, responding to seemingly random stimuli in a completely uninterpretable and incoherent fashion. Grandiosity and inflated self-esteem are also characteristic features of mania.

SUICIDAL IDEAS

Many people experience self-destructive ideas and impulses when they are depressed. Interest in suicide usually develops gradually and may begin with the vague sense that life is not worth living (Hamilton, 1982). Such feelings may follow directly from the overwhelming fatigue and loss of pleasure that typically accompany a seriously depressed mood. In addition, feelings of guilt and failure can lead depressed people to consider killing themselves. Over a period of time, depressed people may come to believe that they would be better off dead or that their family would function more successfully and happily without them. Preoccupation with such thoughts then leads to specific plans and may culminate in a suicide attempt.

Somatic Symptoms

The **somatic symptoms** of mood disorders are related to basic physiological or bodily functions. They include fatigue, aches and pains, and serious changes in appetite and sleep patterns. People, like Cathy, who are clinically depressed often report feeling tired all the time. The simplest tasks, which she had previously taken for granted, seemed to require an overwhelming effort. Taking a shower, brushing her teeth, and getting dressed in the morning became virtually impossible.

Sleeping problems are also common, particularly trouble getting to sleep. This disturbance frequently goes hand in hand with cognitive difficulties mentioned earlier. Worried about her endless problems and unable to relax, Cathy found that she would toss and turn for hours before finally falling asleep. Some people also report having difficulty staying asleep throughout the night, and they awaken 2 or more hours before the usual time. Early-morning waking is often associated with particularly severe depression. A less common symptom is for a depressed individual to spend more time sleeping than usual.

psychomotor retardation A generalized slowing of physical and emotional reactions. The slowing of movements and speech; frequently seen in depression.

comorbidity The simultaneous manifestation of more than one disorder.

Depressed people frequently experience a change in appetite. Although some patients report that they eat more than usual, most reduce the amount that they eat; some may eat next to nothing. Food just doesn't taste good any more.

People who are severely depressed commonly lose their interest in various types of activities that are otherwise sources of pleasure and fulfillment. One common example is a loss of sexual desire. Depressed people are less likely to initiate sexual activity, and they are less likely to enjoy sex if their partners can persuade them to participate.

Various ill-defined somatic complaints can also accompany mood disorders. Some patients complain of frequent headaches and muscular aches and pains. These concerns may develop into a preoccupation with bodily functions and fear of disease.

Behavioral Symptoms

The symptoms of mood disorders also include changes in the things that people do and the rate at which they do them. The term **psychomotor retardation** refers to several features of behavior that may accompany the onset of serious depression. The most obvious behavioral symptom of depression is slowed movement. Patients may walk and talk as if they are in slow motion. Others become completely immobile and may stop speaking altogether. Some depressed patients pause for very extended periods—perhaps several minutes—before answering a question.

In marked contrast to periods when they are depressed, manic patients are typically gregarious and energetic. Debbie's behavior provided many examples, even after her admission to the psychiatric hospital. Her flirtatious and provocative behavior on the ward was clearly inappropriate. She found it impossible to sit still for more than a moment or two. Virtually everything was interesting to her, and she was easily distracted, flitting from one idea or project to the next. Like other manic patients, Debbie was full of plans that were pursued in a rather indiscriminate fashion.

Other Problems Commonly Associated with Depression

Many people with mood disorders suffer from some clinical problems that are not typically considered symptoms of depression. Within the field of psychopathology, the simultaneous manifestation of a mood disorder and other syndromes is referred to as **comorbidity,** suggesting that the person exhibits symptoms of more than one underlying disorder.

Alcoholism and depression are clearly related phenomena. Many people who are depressed also drink heavily, and many people who are dependent on alcohol—between 33 and 59 percent—eventually become depressed (Merikangas & Gelernter, 1990; Schuckit & Monteiro, 1988). There is also an association between these disorders within families. Alcohol abuse is common among the immediate families of patients with mood disorders. Eating disorders and anxiety disorders are also more common among first-degree relatives of depressed patients than among people in the general population.

Classification

Psychopathologists have proposed hundreds of systems for describing and classifying mood disorders (Grove & Andreasen, 1992). Two primary issues have been central regarding definitions of mood disorders. First, should these disorders be defined in a broad or narrow fashion? Table 5–1 presents a list of considerations that can be used to distinguish clinical depression from normal sadness. Definitions of depression that incorporate all these criteria tend to be more narrow than those that include only some of them.

The second issue concerns heterogeneity. All depressed patients do not have exactly the same set of symptoms, the same pattern of onset, or the same course over time. Some patients have manic episodes, whereas others experience only depression. Some exhibit psychotic symptoms,

TABLE 5–1

Important Considerations in Distinguishing Clinical Depression from Normal Sadness	
INTENSITY	The mood change pervades all aspects of the person and impairs social and occupational functions.
ABSENCE OF PRECIPITANTS	The mood may arise in the absence of any discernible precipitant or may be grossly out of proportion to those precipitants.
QUALITY	The mood change is different from that experienced in normal sadness.
ASSOCIATED FEATURES	The change in mood is accompanied by a cluster of signs and symptoms, including cognitive and somatic features.
HISTORY	The mood change may be preceded by a history of past episodes of elation and hyperactivity.

Source: *P. C. Whybrow, H. S. Akiskal, and W. T. McKinney, Jr., 1984,* Mood Disorders: Toward a New Psychobiology. *New York: Plenum.*

Freud's view of depression was built on a consideration of the relation between grief and clinical depression. His observations were concerned particularly with psychological mechanisms in response to loss.

such as delusions and hallucinations, in addition to their symptoms of mood disorder; others do not. In some cases, the person's depression is apparently a reaction to specific life events, whereas in others the mood disorder seems to come out of nowhere. Are these qualitatively distinct forms of mood disorder, or are they different expressions of the same underlying problem? Is the distinction among the different types simply one of severity?

dysthymia One of the mood disorders; a form of mild depression characterized by a chronic course (the person is seldom without symptoms).

Contemporary Diagnostic Systems

The DSM-IV (APA, 1994) approach to classifying mood disorders recognizes several subtypes of depression, placing special emphasis on the distinction between unipolar and bipolar disorders. The overall scheme includes two types of unipolar mood disorder and three types of bipolar mood disorder.

UNIPOLAR DISORDERS

The unipolar disorders include two specific types: major depressive disorder and dysthymia. In order to meet the criteria for major depressive disorder, a person must experience at least one major depressive episode in the absence of any history of manic episodes. Table 5–2 lists the DSM-IV criteria for a major depressive episode. Although some people experience a single, isolated episode of major depression followed by complete recovery, most cases of unipolar depression follow an intermittent course with repeated episodes.

Dysthymia differs from major depression in terms of both severity and duration. Dysthymia represents a chronic mild depressive condition that has been present for many years. In order to fulfill DSM-IV criteria for this disorder, the person must, over a period of at least 2 years, exhibit a depressed mood for most of the day on more days than not. Two or more of the following symptoms must also be present:

1. Poor appetite or overeating
2. Insomnia or hypersomnia
3. Low energy or fatigue

TABLE 5–2

Symptoms Listed in DSM-IV for Major Depressive Episode

A. FIVE OR MORE OF THE FOLLOWING SYMPTOMS HAVE BEEN PRESENT DURING THE SAME 2-WEEK PERIOD AND REPRESENT A CHANGE FROM PREVIOUS FUNCTIONING; AT LEAST ONE OF THE SYMPTOMS IS EITHER (1) DEPRESSED MOOD, OR (2) LOSS OF INTEREST OR PLEASURE.

1. Depressed mood most of the day, nearly every day, as indicated either by subjective report (for example, feels sad or empty) or observation made by others (for example, appears tearful). Note: in children and adolescents, can be irritable mood.
2. Markedly diminished interest or pleasure in all, or almost all, activities most of the day, nearly every day (as indicated either by subjective account or observation by others).
3. Significant weight loss when not dieting or weight gain (for example, a change of more than 5 percent of body weight in a month), or decrease or increase in appetite nearly every day. Note: in children, consider failure to make expected weight gains.
4. Insomnia or hypersomnia nearly every day.
5. Psychomotor agitation or retardation nearly every day (observable by others, not merely subjective feelings of restlessness or being slowed down).
6. Fatigue or loss of energy nearly every day.
7. Feelings of worthlessness or excessive or inappropriate guilt (which may be delusional) nearly every day (not merely self-reproach or guilt about being sick).
8. Diminished ability to think or concentrate, or indecisiveness, nearly every day (either by subjective account or as observed by others).
9. Recurrent thoughts of death (not just fear of dying), recurrent suicidal ideation without a specific plan, or a suicide attempt or a specific plan for committing suicide.

4. Low self-esteem
5. Poor concentration or difficulty making decisions
6. Feelings of hopelessness

hypomania An episode of increased energy that is not sufficiently severe to qualify as a full-blown manic episode.

These symptoms must not be absent for more than 2 months at a time during the 2-year period. If, at any time during the initial 2 years, the person met criteria for a major depressive episode, the diagnosis would be major depression rather than dysthymia. As in the case of major depressive disorder, the presence of a manic episode would rule out a diagnosis of dysthymia.

The distinction between major depressive disorder and dysthymia is somewhat artificial because both sets of symptoms are frequently seen in the same person. In such cases, rather than thinking of them as separate disorders, it is more appropriate to consider them as two aspects of the same disorder, which waxes and wanes over time (Frances, First, & Pincus, 1995).

BIPOLAR DISORDERS

All three types of bipolar disorders involve manic or hypomanic episodes. Table 5–3 lists the DSM-IV criteria for a manic episode. The mood disturbance must be severe enough to interfere with occupational or social functioning. A person who has experienced at least one manic episode would be assigned a diagnosis of bipolar I disorder. The vast majority of patients with this disorder have episodes of major depression in addition to manic episodes.

Some patients experience episodes of increased energy that are not sufficiently severe to qualify as full-blown mania. These episodes are called **hypomania.** A person who has experienced at least one major depressive episode, at least one hypomanic episode, and no full-blown manic episodes would be assigned a diagnosis of bipolar II disorder. The symptoms that are used in DSM-IV to identify a hypomanic episode are the same as those for manic episode (at least three of the seven symptoms listed in Table 5–3). The differences between manic and hypomanic episodes involve duration and severity. The symptoms need to be present for a minimum of only 4 days to meet the threshold for a hypomanic episode (as opposed to 1 week for a manic episode). The mood change in a hypomanic episode must be noticeable to others, but the disturbance must not be severe enough to impair social or occupational functioning or to require hospitalization.

TABLE 5–3

Symptoms Listed in DSM-IV for Manic Episode

A. A DISTINCT PERIOD OF ABNORMALLY AND PERSISTENTLY ELEVATED, EXPANSIVE, OR IRRITABLE MOOD, LASTING AT LEAST 1 WEEK (OR ANY DURATION IF HOSPITALIZATION IS NECESSARY).

B. DURING THE PERIOD OF MOOD DISTURBANCE, THREE OR MORE OF THE FOLLOWING SYMPTOMS HAVE PERSISTED (FOUR IF THE MOOD IS ONLY IRRITABLE) AND HAVE BEEN PRESENT TO A SIGNIFICANT DEGREE:

1. Inflated self-esteem or grandiosity.
2. Decreased need for sleep—for example, feels rested after only 3 hours of sleep.
3. More talkative than usual, or pressure to keep talking.
4. Flight of ideas or subjective experience that thoughts are racing.
5. Distractibility—that is, attention too easily drawn to unimportant or irrelevant external stimuli.
6. Increase in goal-directed activity (either socially, at work or school, or sexually) or psychomotor agitation.
7. Excessive involvement in pleasurable activities that have a high potential for painful consequences—for example, the person engages in unrestrained buying sprees, sexual indiscretions, or foolish business investments.

cyclothymia A chronic, less severe form of bipolar disorder. The bipolar equivalent of dysthymia.

seasonal affective disorder A type of mood disorder (either unipolar or bipolar) in which there has been a regular temporal relation between onset (or disappearance) of the person's episodes and a particular time of the year. For example, the person might become depressed in the winter.

Cyclothymia is considered by DSM-IV to be a chronic but less severe form of bipolar disorder. It is therefore the bipolar equivalent of dysthymia. In order to meet criteria for cyclothymia, the person must experience numerous hypomanic episodes and numerous periods of depression (or loss of interest or pleasure) during a period of 2 years. There must be no history of major depressive episodes and no clear evidence of a manic episode during the first 2 years of the disturbance.

FURTHER DESCRIPTIONS AND SUBTYPES

The DSM-IV includes several additional ways of describing subtypes of the mood disorders. These are based on two considerations: (1) more specific descriptions of symptoms that were present during the most recent episode of depression (known as *episode specifiers*) and (2) more extensive descriptions of the pattern that the disorder follows over time (known as *course specifiers*).

One episode specifier allows the clinician to indicate the presence of *psychotic features*—hallucinations or delusions—during the most recent episode of depression or mania. The psychotic features can be either consistent or inconsistent with the patient's mood. For example, if a depressed man reports hearing voices that tell him he is a worthless human being who deserves to suffer for his sins, the hallucinations would be considered "mood congruent psychotic features." Depressed patients who exhibit psychotic features are more likely to require hospitalization and treatment with a combination of antidepressant and antipsychotic medication.

Another episode specifier applies to women who become depressed or manic following pregnancy. A major depressive or manic episode can be specified as having a *postpartum onset* if it begins within 4 weeks after childbirth. Because the woman must meet the full criteria for an episode of major depression or mania, this category does not include minor periods of postpartum "blues," which are relatively common.

Researchers refer to a mood disorder in which the onset of episodes is regularly associated with changes in seasons as **seasonal affective disorder.**[†] The episodes most commonly occur in winter, presumably in response to fewer hours of sunlight. Seasonal disorders have attracted considerable interest among mental health professionals since the 1980s (Blehar & Rosenthal, 1989). Seasonal depression is usually characterized by somatic symptoms, such as overeating, carbohydrate craving, weight gain, fatigue, and sleeping more than usual. One study found that, among outpatients who had a history of at least three major depressive episodes, 16 percent met criteria for the seasonal pattern (Thase, 1989). Most patients with seasonal affective disorder have a unipolar disorder, but many would meet criteria for bipolar II disorder. People in the latter group typically become depressed in the winter followed by a mood reversal to hypomania in the spring. Relatively few have bipolar I disorder (Oren & Rosenthal, 1992).

Course and Outcome

To consider the typical course and outcome of mood disorders, it is useful to study unipolar and bipolar disorders separately. Most studies point to clear-cut differences between these two conditions in terms of age of onset and prognosis (Perris, 1992).

UNIPOLAR DISORDERS

Data regarding the onset and course of unipolar mood disorders must be viewed with some caution because virtually all studies have focused exclusively on the people who have sought treatment for their depression. Very little is known about untreated depressions, but it seems reasonable to assume that they are likely to remit spontaneously in a short period of time.

People with unipolar mood disorders typically have their first episode in middle age; the average age of onset is in the mid-forties. The length of episodes varies widely. DSM-IV sets the minimum duration at 2 weeks, but they can last much longer. In one large-scale follow-up study, 10

[†]*"Affect" and "mood" are sometimes used interchangeably in psychiatric terminology. Depression and mania were called "affective disorders" in DSM-III.*

percent of the patients had depressive episodes that lasted more than 2 years (Thornicroft & Sartorius, 1993). Most unipolar patients will have at least two depressive episodes. The mean number of lifetime episodes is five or six.

The results of long-term follow-up studies of treated patients indicate that major depressive disorder is frequently a chronic and recurrent condition, in which episodes of severe symptoms may alternate with periods of full or partial recovery (Keller, 1994; Thornicroft & Sartorius, 1993). When a person's symptoms are diminished or improved, the disorder is considered to be in *remission,* or a period of recovery. *Relapse* is a return of active symptoms in a person who has recovered from a previous episode.

Approximately half of all unipolar patients recover within 6 months of the beginning of an episode. The probability that a patient will recover from an episode goes down after 6 months, and 10 to 20 percent have not recovered after 5 years. Among those who recover, 40 percent relapse within 1 year. The risk of relapse goes down as the period of remission increases. In other words, the longer the person remains free of depression, the better his or her chance of avoiding relapse. Older patients tend to relapse more quickly than younger patients, and females relapse more quickly than males.

BIPOLAR DISORDERS

Onset of bipolar mood disorders usually occurs between the ages of 28 and 33 years, which is younger than the average age of onset for unipolar disorders. The first episode is just as likely to be manic as depressive in nature (Coryell & Winokur, 1992). The average duration of a manic episode runs between 2 and 3 months. Bipolar II patients tend to have shorter and less severe episodes (Coryell et al., 1985; Keller, 1987).

The long-term course of bipolar disorders is most often episodic, and the prognosis is mixed (Winokur et al., 1994). Most patients have more than one episode, and bipolar patients tend to have more episodes than unipolar patients. The length of intervals between episodes is difficult to predict. The long-term prognosis is mixed for patients with bipolar mood disorder. Although some patients recover and function quite well, others experience continued impairment. Several studies that have followed bipolar patients over periods of up to 10 years have found that 40 to 50 percent of patients are able to achieve a sustained recovery from the disorder. Many patients, however, remain chronically disabled. Rapid cycling patients are less likely to recover from an episode and are more likely to relapse after they do recover (Keller et al., 1993).

Epidemiology

Questions about the frequency and distribution of mood disorders are difficult to answer precisely. One problem is the widespread variation in the definition of clinical depression. Some investigators have adopted a broad approach to diagnosis, whereas others have focused on a narrow range of severely disturbed patients. The procedure used to identify potential cases is also important. Many of the early epidemiological studies focused on patients treated at hospitals and mental health centers. Unfortunately, large numbers of people experience serious depression without wanting, or being able to seek, professional help. Formal statistics must therefore be considered with caution.

Several large epidemiological studies providing detailed information regarding mood disorders have been completed in recent years. Perhaps most notable among these is the Epidemiologic Catchment Area (ECA) Study, in which nearly 20,000 residents of five U.S. communities were interviewed (Robins & Regier, 1991).

Incidence and Prevalence

Unipolar depression is one of the most common forms of psychopathology. Among people who were interviewed for the ECA study, approximately 6 percent of the population in this sample was suffering from a diagnosable mood disorder during a period of 6 months. Unipolar disorders are much more common than bipolar disorders. The ratio of unipolar to bipolar disorders is at least 5:1 (Smith & Weissman, 1992).

Myrna Weissman, a professor of psychiatry at Columbia University, is one of the leading investigators in the study of the epidemiology of depression.

Lifetime risk for major depressive disorder was approximately 5 percent: The lifetime risk for dysthymia was approximately 3 percent, and the lifetime risk for bipolar I disorder was close to 1 percent. Almost half the people who met diagnostic criteria for dysthymia had also experienced an episode of major depression at some point in their lives. At each of the sites examined by Robins and her colleagues, the lifetime prevalence of all types of mood disorders combined (about 8 percent) ranked third behind substance use disorders (about 17 percent) and anxiety disorders (about 12 percent). When you consider the magnitude of these numbers, you should also know that other, more recent studies have produced even higher figures for the lifetime prevalence of mood disorders (see Kessler et al., 1994). Therefore the prevalence estimates for mood disorders in the ECA study are probably conservative.

Because the ECA study identified a representative sample of community residents rather than patients already in treatment, it also allows some insight regarding the proportion of depressed people who seek professional help for their problems. Slightly more than 30 percent of those people who met DSM-III criteria for a mood disorder made contact with a mental health professional during the 6 months prior to their interview. These data indicate that a substantial proportion of people who are clinically depressed do not receive professional treatment for their disorders. Finding ways to help these people represents an important challenge for psychologists and psychiatrists who treat mood disorders.

Gender Differences

Women are 2 or 3 times more vulnerable to depression than men are (Nolen-Hoeksema, 1990). This pattern has been reported in study after study, using samples of treated patients as well as community surveys, and regardless of the assessment procedures employed. The increased prevalence of depression among women is apparently limited to unipolar disorders. In the ECA program, for example, the lifetime prevalence rates for major depression were 7 percent in women but only 2.6 percent in men. Relatively large gender differences were also observed for dysthymia, with lifetime prevalence rates of 4.1 percent in women and 2.2 percent in men. Gender differences were not observed, however, for bipolar mood disorders. The lifetime prevalence rates for bipolar I disorder were 0.9 percent for women and 0.7 percent for men (Weissman et al., 1991).

Some observers have suggested that the high rates for unipolar mood disorders in women reflect shortcomings in the data-collection process. Women might simply be more likely than men to seek treatment or to be labeled as being depressed. Another argument holds that culturally determined sanctions make it more difficult for men to admit to subjective feelings of distress such as hopelessness and despair. None of these alternatives has been substantiated by empirical evidence (Nolen-Hoeksema, 1990). Research studies clearly indicate that the higher prevalence of depression among women is genuine.

Cross-Cultural Differences

Comparisons of emotional expression and emotional disorder across cultural boundaries encounter a number of methodological problems. One problem involves vocabulary. Each culture has its own ways of interpreting reality, including different styles of expressing or communicating symptoms of physical and emotional disorder (Good & Kleinman, 1985b; Katschnig & Amering, 1990). Words and concepts that are used to describe illness behaviors in one culture might not exist in other cultures. For example, some African cultures have only one word for both anger and sadness. Interesting adaptations are therefore required to translate questions that are supposed to tap experiences such as anxiety and depression. One investigation, which employed a British interview schedule that had been translated into Yoruba—a language spoken in Nigeria—used the phrase "the heart goes weak" to represent depression (Leff, 1988).

We must remember that our own diagnostic categories have been developed within a specific cultural setting; they are not culture-free and are not necessarily any more reasonable than the ways in which other cultures describe and categorize their own behavioral and emotional disorders. One illustration of this principle comes from the study of *neurasthenia,* which is a relatively common problem in China but is rarely diagnosed in Western societies. Although the diagnostic term was not introduced to Chinese physicians until the twentieth century, the concept fits closely with ancient traditions in Chinese folk medicine. Neurasthenic patients present many different complaints that focus primarily on physical symptoms: headaches, insomnia, dizziness, pain, weakness, loss of energy, poor appetite, tingling in the head, and so on. Related psychological symptoms include memory problems, anxiety, disturbing dreams, and poor concentration.

Arthur Kleinman, a psychiatrist and anthropologist at Harvard University, and a group of Chinese psychiatrists studied 100 neurasthenic patients at an outpatient clinic associated with a Chinese medical school (Kleinman, 1982). Interviews were conducted using a translation of an American diagnostic interview schedule, and diagnoses were assigned using DSM-III criteria. In all, 87 of the 100 patients received a diagnosis of major depressive disorder, and 69 received a diagnosis of anxiety disorder. Thus most of the patients fit the criteria for both depression and anxiety.

The cross-cultural differences suggested by Kleinman's study have been confirmed by a number of large-scale research projects, including the World Health Organization's Collaborative Study on Depression (WHO, 1983), which examined cultural variations in symptomatology among depressed patients in Canada, India, Iran, Japan, and Switzerland. The WHO study found comparable overall frequencies of mood disorders across all five countries, but the specific symptoms expressed by the patients varied considerably from one culture to the next. For example, depressed patients in Europe and North America were more likely to express feelings of guilt and suicidal ideas, while patients in non-Western countries were more likely to exhibit somatic symptoms.

Contrary to popular views, older people are actually less likely to be depressed than are younger people. Some subgroups of elderly people, however, are at high risk for depression. For example, among the 5 percent of elderly people who live in nursing homes, rates of depression can be as high as 50 percent.

These cross-cultural comparisons suggest that, at its most basic level, clinical depression is a universal phenomenon that is not limited to Western or urban societies. They also indicate that a person's cultural experiences, including linguistic, educational, and social factors, may play an important role in shaping the manner in which different people express and cope with the anguish of depression. Cross-cultural variations should also be kept in mind when clinicians attempt to identify central or defining features of depression. We will return to this point later in the chapter when we discuss the rationale behind studies that rely on animal models of depression.

Risk for Mood Disorders Across the Life Span

Age is an important consideration in the epidemiology of mood disorders. Some readers might expect that the prevalence of depression would be higher among older people than among younger people. This was, in fact, what many clinicians expected prior to large-scale epidemiological investigations, such as the ECA study. This belief may stem from the casual observation that many older people experience brief episodic states of acute unhappiness, often precipitated by changes in status (for example, retirement, relocation) and loss of significant others (for example, children moving away, deaths of friends and relatives). But brief episodes of sadness and grief are not the same thing as clinical depression.

Although many people mistakenly identify depression with the elderly, data from the ECA project suggest that mood disorders actually are most frequent among young and middle-aged adults. Prevalence rates for major depressive episodes and dysthymia were significantly lower for people over the age of 65. The frequency of bipolar disorders was also low in the oldest age groups. These data are illustrated in Figure 5–1. Notice that rates of both major depression and bipolar I disorder are lowest in the oldest age group. When unipolar and bipolar mood disorders are combined to examine gender differences and age, the lowest rates are found in the oldest age group for both men and women.

Several explanations have been offered for this pattern. People who are in their 70s and 80s may have more trouble remembering, and therefore may fail to report, episodes of depression that occurred several months before the research interview is conducted. Also, because mood

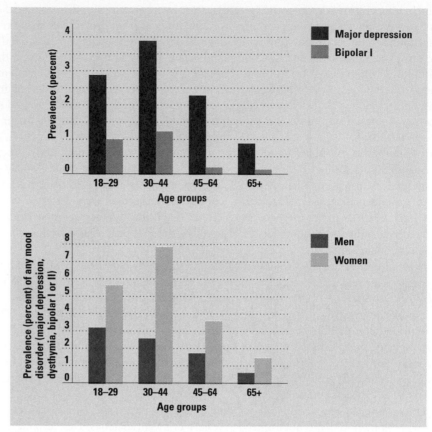

Figure 5–1 (*top*) Twelve-month prevalence for unipolar and bipolar mood disorders in different age groups. (*bottom*) Twelve-month prevalence for mood disorder in men and women in different age groups.

Source: M. M. Weissman, M. L. Bruce, P. J. Leaf, L. P. Florio, and C. Holzer, 1991, Affective disorders. In L. N. Robins and D. A. Regier (Eds.), *Psychiatric Disorders in America: The Epidemiologic Catchment Area Study.* New York: Free Press, p. 60.

disorders are associated with increased mortality (for example, suicide), many severely depressed people might not have survived into old age. These are both plausible hypotheses that may have influenced the results of the ECA study and related investigations. Nevertheless, the same pattern has been observed in several studies, and most investigators now believe that the effect is genuine: Clinical depression is less common among elderly people than it is among younger adults (Lewinsohn et al., 1993; Wittchen, Knauper, & Kessler, 1994). However, the prevalence of depression is particularly high among those who are about to enter residential care facilities in comparison to a random sample of elderly people living in the community. One study found that approximately 1 out of 3 elderly applicants for community social services would meet criteria for a clinical depressive disorder (Goldberg, 1970).

Comparisons Across Generations

The ECA findings on age and depression also raise another important question: Has the frequency of depression increased in recent years? The answer is apparently yes. People born after World War II seem to be more likely to develop mood disorders than were people from previous generations. In fact, several studies have reported a consistent trend toward higher lifetime rates of depression in successively younger generations (Lavori et al., 1987; Wittchen, Knauper, & Kessler, 1994). The average age of onset for clinical depression also seems to be younger in people who were born more recently. This kind of pattern is sometimes called a *birth cohort trend.*

Etiological Considerations and Research

In the next few pages we turn our attention to current speculation and knowledge about causes of mood disorders. Rather than presenting separate discussions for unipolar and bipolar mood disorders, we have organized the information on etiology according to social, psychological, and biological considerations. Most research on the etiology of bipolar mood disorders has focused on biological factors, especially genetics and neurochemistry. Our discussion of psychological factors will focus exclusively on the etiology of unipolar depression.

Social Factors

It should not be surprising that much of the literature on depression focuses on interpersonal loss and separation. From birth to death, our lives are intertwined with those of other people. We are fundamentally social organisms, and we feel sad when someone close to us dies. Similar feelings occasionally follow major disappointments, such as failure to win acceptance to the school of our choice or being fired from a job. In these cases, rather than losing other people, some clinicians have suggested that we may be losing "social roles" or ways in which we think about ourselves.

Various theories of depression have been built around a consideration of the impact of stressful life events. Beginning around the turn of the century, psychodynamic theories emphasized the central role played by interpersonal relationships and loss of significant others in setting the stage for depression as well as in bringing about a depressive episode.

FREUD'S THEORY OF DEPRESSION

Freud's classic paper on the etiology of depression focused on a comparison of clinical depression with the normal process of grieving (Freud, 1917/1961). Among the various symptoms of depression, Freud was particularly interested in self-reproach and guilt. The fundamental assumption of Freud's view was that depressed people are, in fact, not so much complaining about themselves as they are angry with someone else. The other person is presumably someone with whom the patient has had a very close relationship and who has either died or been lost in some other way—either in reality or figuratively by withdrawing his or her affection. Instead of recognizing and dealing with this anger consciously, depressed people identify with the other person and direct their anger toward themselves.

Freud further argued that the distinction between people who mourn the loss of another and those who become clinically depressed is reflected in the types of interpersonal relationships they form. People predisposed to depression tend to form "narcissistic" relationships in which they depend on the other person to maintain their self-esteem. This dependence invariably leads to negative as well as positive emotions, resulting in an intense ambivalence. The depressed individual cannot express this ambivalence openly for fear of alienating and perhaps losing the other person. When the other person is no longer available, the anger is turned inward and directed toward the self; this expression of inwardly directed anger is presumably depression.

Freud's theory laid the intellectual foundation for many subsequent studies of psychological and social factors in the development and maintenance of unipolar depression. He focused interest on the possibility that stressful life events may precipitate the onset of mood disorders. Freud's notion of narcissistic relationships also anticipated subsequent studies of social skills in depression and the importance of interpersonal relationships over the course of mood disorders. We will review these considerations in a later section on psychological factors.

Stressful life events and depression are clearly correlated, but the direction of this relationship is not always clear. For example, does the loss of a job lead a person to become depressed? Or does the onset of depression interfere with the person's ability to perform the job, thereby increasing the risk of losing it?

STRESSFUL LIFE EVENTS AND UNIPOLAR DISORDERS

Several investigations have explored the relationships between stressful life events and the development of unipolar mood disorders. Do people who become clinically depressed actually experience an increased number of stressful life events? The answer is yes. The experience of stressful life events is associated with an increased probability that a person will become depressed. This correlation has been demonstrated many times (Paykel & Cooper, 1992).

Once the relatively strong relationship between stressful life events and depression was found, difficult methodological issues had to be faced before it could be interpreted. One particularly difficult problem involves the direction of the relationship between life events and mood disorders. For example, being fired from a job might lead a person to become depressed. On the other hand, the onset of a depressive episode, with its associated difficulties in energy and concentration, could easily affect the person's job performance and lead to being fired. Therefore, if depressed people experience more stressful events, what is the direction of effect? Does failure lead to depression, or does depression lead to failure?

The use of prospective research designs, in which subjects are followed over time, has allowed investigators to address the question of cause and effect. Prospective studies have found that stressful life events are useful in predicting the subsequent onset of unipolar depression (Lewinsohn, Hoberman, & Rosenbaum, 1988). This evidence supports the argument that, in many cases, stressful life events contribute to the onset of mood disorders.

Although many kinds of negative events are associated with depression, a special class of circumstances—those involving major losses of important people or roles—seems to play a crucial role in precipitating unipolar depression (Monroe & Simons, 1991). This conclusion is based, in large part, on a series of studies reported by George Brown and his colleagues. Their studies have compared the living circumstances and life experiences of depressed and nondepressed women, regardless of whether they are receiving treatment for their problems.

Brown and Harris (1978) found that "severe" events—those that are particularly threatening and have long-term consequences for the woman's adjustment—increased the probability that a woman would become depressed. The frequency of nonsevere events was roughly equivalent for depressed and nondepressed women. Only 16 percent of the events that were reported by all of the women in the study were considered severe by these standards. Most cases of depression appeared after a single severe event. Brown's data suggest that depression is not caused by an accumulation of ordinary hassles and difficulties to which most of us are exposed on a daily basis (Monroe & Simons, 1991).

The relationship between stressful life events and depression is not entirely one-way; it runs in both directions. Independent stressors, which are not caused by the person's own behavior, contribute to the onset of depression. The depressed person then behaves in a maladaptive fashion, leading to even higher levels of stress and perhaps a further deterioration in his or her mood. We will return to our consideration of interpersonal behaviors later in the section on psychological factors.

SOCIAL FACTORS AND BIPOLAR DISORDERS

Most investigations of stressful life events have been concerned with unipolar depression. Considerably less attention has been paid to bipolar mood disorders, but some evidence suggests that the weeks preceding the onset of a manic episode are marked by an increased frequency of stressful life events (Johnson & Roberts, 1995). Stressful life events are also likely to trigger a relapse in bipolar patients who have recovered from previous episodes. Some people with bipolar disorder are less sensitive to stress than others. One study found that bipolar patients whose personality style was extroverted were less likely to relapse, even if they were exposed to a high level of stress (Swendsen, Hammen, Heller, & Gitlin, 1995).

Aversive patterns of emotional expression and communication within the family can also have a negative impact on the adjustment of people with bipolar mood disorders. Patients living with family members who are hostile toward or critical of the patient are more likely to relapse shortly after being discharged from the hospital (Miklowitz et al., 1988). This evidence indicates that the course of bipolar mood disorder can be influenced by the social environment in which the person is living.

schema   A general cognitive pattern that guides the way a person perceives and interprets events in his or her environment.

Psychological Factors

Severe events are clearly related to the onset of depression, but they do not provide a complete account of who will become depressed. Many women who do not become depressed also experience severe events. In the study reported by Brown and Harris (1978), only 1 out of every 5 women who reported a severe event in the preceding year became depressed. Therefore the investigators looked for characteristics that might identify women who were more likely than others to become depressed if they experienced a severe event. They found four such features, which they called "vulnerability factors." These included (1) absence of an intimate, confiding relationship, (2) having several young children at home, (3) lacking employment away from home, and (4) loss of her mother at an early age. Vulnerability factors of this sort presumably reduce the woman's self-esteem and her sense that she will be able to cope successfully in the face of adversity (Brown, Bifulco, & Andrews, 1990). If a threatening event occurs at a time when a woman is less able to be hopeful and to persevere, the probability of serious depression is increased.

Several psychological factors may contribute to a person's vulnerability to stressful life events. In the following pages, we will consider two principal areas that have received attention in the research literature: cognitive factors and social skills. These studies have focused almost exclusively on unipolar mood disorders, so we will not discuss bipolar disorders in this section.

COGNITIVE RESPONSES TO FAILURE AND DISAPPOINTMENT

Cognitive theories concerning the origins of unipolar depression are based on the recognition that humans are not only social organisms; they are also thinking organisms. Cognitive therapists assume that the ways in which people think about and perceive their world have an important influence on the way that they feel. Two people may react very differently to the same event, in large part because they may interpret the event differently.

Beck's Cognitive Model   Aaron Beck, a psychiatrist at the University of Pennsylvania, has been one of the most influential proponents of a cognitive view of depression (see, for example, Beck, 1967, 1974, 1984). Like Freud, Beck began with a primary interest in the things that depressed people say, particularly their self-critical thoughts and their extremely pessimistic views of their environment. In contrast to the psychodynamic position, however, Beck has not chosen to view depressed people's critical self-statements as a reflection of their anger toward others. He argues instead that the negative things that depressed people say represent direct manifestations of fundamental cognitive distortions or erroneous ways of thinking about themselves. According to Beck's theory, pervasive and persistent negative cognitions play a central role in the onset of depression.

Beck has described various types of distortions, errors, and biases that characterize the thinking of depressed people. These include tendencies to assign global, personal meaning to experiences of failure; to overgeneralize conclusions about the self based on negative experiences; to draw arbitrary inferences about the self in the absence of supporting evidence (often in spite of contradictory evidence); to selectively recall events with negative consequences; and to exaggerate the importance of negative events while simultaneously discounting the significance of positive events.

How might these self-defeating biases eventually lead to the onset of depression? Why aren't they evident prior to the onset of an episode? According to Beck's theory, cognitive distortions and "depressogenic premises" (for example, "I should be able to endure any hardship with grace," "I should be smart and capable all the time") combine to form a general pattern or cognitive **schema** that guides the ways in which people perceive and interpret events in their environment. Schemas are described as enduring and highly organized cognitive structures—representations

hopelessness theory A theory regarding the role of cognitive events in the etiology of depression; depression is associated with the expectation that very desirable events probably will not occur and that aversive events probably will occur regardless of what the person does.

of prior experience. Although schemas may be latent—that is, not prominently represented in the person's conscious awareness at any given point in time—they are presumably reactivated when the person experiences a similar event. Depressive schemas increase the probability that the person will overreact to similar stressful events in the future.

Hopelessness Theory Another, related view of the role played by cognitive events has been proposed by Lynn Abramson, Gerald Metalsky, and Lauren Alloy, clinical psychologists at the University of Wisconsin, Lawrence University, and Temple University, respectively. Their perspective has most recently been described in terms of *hopelessness* (Abramson, Metalsky, & Alloy, 1989). According to this view, depression may be associated with the expectation that very desirable events probably will not occur or that aversive events probably will occur regardless of what the person does. Hopelessness refers to the person's negative expectations about future events and the associated belief that these events cannot be controlled. After a negative life event has occurred, the probability that the person will become depressed is a function of the explanations and importance that the person ascribes to these events. These explanations are known as *causal attributions*.

Abramson, Metalsky, and Alloy argue that some people exhibit a general "depressogenic" attributional style that is characterized by a tendency to explain negative events in terms of internal, stable, global factors. For example, after failing an important exam, the person who possesses a depressogenic attributional style would be likely to think that her poor performance was the result of her own inadequacies (internal), which she has recognized for a long time and which will persist into the future (stable), and which are also responsible for her failure in many other important tasks, both academic and otherwise (global). As in Beck's description of negative schemas, attributional style represents an important predisposition to depression. People with a generalized depressogenic attributional style are more likely to develop hopelessness if they experience a negative life event.

Research studies provide some support for the argument that attributional style is useful in predicting people's responses to negative events (Metalsky et al., 1993). Furthermore, people who make the type of cognitive errors that are characteristic of depression are also more likely to generate high levels of stress in their own environments (Simons, Angell, Monroe, & Thase, 1993).

INTERPERSONAL FACTORS AND SOCIAL SKILLS

In addition to how we think about negative or stressful experiences, the ways in which we actually respond to these events may also influence the probability that we will become depressed. This focus on overt behavior has been stimulated, in part, by the application of learning theory to the study of depression.

Lewinsohn's Behavioral Model Peter Lewinsohn (1974), a psychologist at the University of Oregon, proposed an influential behavioral model in which depressed people presumably become less active because their behavior is not followed by positive reinforcement. The decrease in adaptive behavior, which is produced by this prolonged "extinction schedule," presumably has a negative impact on the person's mood. Thus a vicious cycle is set in motion: Reduced rate of response-contingent positive reinforcement leads to reduced activity, which is followed by a further reduction in reinforcement, and so on.

The role of interpersonal relationships is perhaps the most important aspect of this model. According to Lewinsohn, some "depressed behaviors," such as crying, complaining, and criticizing oneself, may be initially reinforced by other people in their attempts to provide comfort and support. By making these social contacts contingent upon the expression of a depressed mood, significant others may unintentionally increase the frequency and stability of their friend's depression. Lewinsohn proposed further that the continued manifestation of depressed behaviors has an aversive impact on other people. Thus the depressed person's few remaining sources of social support will eventually be driven away.

Peter Lewinsohn, whose behavioral model of depression inspired much of the research on interpersonal factors in depression. His longitudinal studies have contributed important information regarding the role of cognitive factors and social skills in the development of depression.

The behavioral model has stimulated interest in the role played by social skills and interpersonal relationships in mood disorders. How does the depressed person cope with stressful events and respond to other people? What types of responses does the patient elicit from others? What are the extent and form of social resources that are available to help support the person during a crisis? Notice that in many ways these questions bring us back to the issue of intimacy, which Brown and Harris identified as one vulnerability factor in their model of depression, as well as the notion of interpersonal dependency, which has been an important consideration in psychodynamic views of depression.

Research on Interpersonal Factors   James Coyne, a psychologist at the University of Pennsylvania, has studied the ways in which depressed people interact with those around them (Coyne, 1976; Coyne, Downey, & Boergers, 1993). This interpersonal perspective, which emphasizes the active, reciprocal nature of our social environments, has produced some interesting findings regarding factors that contribute to depression. The assumptions behind this model are quite different from those incorporated in more cognitively oriented theories. For example, Beck might argue that faulty processing of information from their environment leads those who are depressed to believe (erroneously) that their relationships with other people are inadequate. Coyne suggests that depressed people may actually behave in ways that have a genuinely negative effect on other people, thus alienating themselves from friends and family members.

Several research studies have demonstrated that depressed people do indeed have a negative impact on other people's moods and on their nonverbal behavior (Joiner & Metalsky, 1995; Segrin & Abramson, 1994). In addition, depressed people have smaller and less supportive social networks than do people who are not depressed. They know fewer people, interact with them less often, and consider them to be less supportive. Family interactions are generally more negative and argumentative. Perhaps most importantly, these maladaptive patterns of interpersonal relationships are ongoing characteristics of the individual's behavior that persist into periods of symptomatic remission. They are not evident only during active episodes of major depression (Gotlib & Hammen, 1992).

Response Styles and Gender   A slightly different aspect of coping behavior may help to explain gender differences in the frequency of depression. Susan Nolen-Hoeksema (1990, 1994), a psychologist at the University of Michigan, has proposed that the manner in which a person responds to the onset of a depressed mood will influence the duration and the severity of the mood. The model emphasizes two different response styles. Some people respond to feelings of depression by turning their attention inward, contemplating the causes and implications of their sadness. Nolen-Hoeksema refers to this as a *ruminative style*. Writing in a diary or talking extensively with a friend about how one feels are indications of a ruminative style. Other people employ a *distracting style* to divert themselves from their unpleasant mood. They work on hobbies, play sports, or otherwise become involved in activities that draw their attention away from symptoms of depression.

The first hypothesis of Nolen-Hoeksema's model is that people who engage in ruminative responses have longer and more severe episodes of depression than do people who engage in distracting responses. Her second hypothesis is that women are more likely to employ a ruminative style in response to depression, whereas men are more likely to employ a distracting style. Because the ruminative style leads to episodes of greater duration and intensity, women are more susceptible to depression than men are.

Research evidence provides some support for both of Nolen-Hoeksema's hypotheses. A ruminative response style tends to be associated with longer and more severely depressed moods, and women are more likely than men to exhibit a ruminative style in response to depressed mood (Butler & Nolen-Hoeksema, 1994; Nolen-Hoeksema, Morrow, & Frederickson, 1993). The model has been tested most extensively with analogue subjects, normal subjects who were experiencing a dysphoric mood. Relatively little information is available regarding its applicability with clinically depressed subjects.

Stressful life events that lead to the onset of depression often involve interpersonal relationships. Women may be more vulnerable to depression than men are because they are likely to respond empathically when something bad happens to their friends or family members.

INTEGRATION OF COGNITIVE AND INTERPERSONAL FACTORS

Ian Gotlib, a clinical psychologist at Stanford University, and Constance Hammen, a clinical psychologist at UCLA, have proposed a conceptual framework for understanding unipolar disorders (Gotlib & Hammen, 1992). Their model is especially interesting because it considers depression in terms of several stages: vulnerability, onset, and maintenance. Cognitive factors and interpersonal skills play an important role within each stage. The model emphasizes the importance of ongoing transactions between the person and his or her environment. Adverse events influence a person's mood, but people also play an active role in selecting and shaping their own environments.

Vulnerability to depression is influenced by experiences during childhood, including events such as the loss of a parent. Negative ways of thinking about the world and dysfunctional interpersonal skills are presumably learned early in life. Gotlib and Hammen argue that the combination of cognitive schemas and deficits in interpersonal skills affects the person's social environment in several ways: It increases the likelihood that the person will enter problematic relationships; it diminishes the person's ability to resolve conflict after it occurs; and it minimizes the person's ability to solicit support and assistance from other people.

The *onset* of depression is most often triggered by life events and circumstances. The stressful life events that precipitate an episode frequently grow out of difficult personal and family relationships. Gotlib and Hammen note, at this point, another factor that may make women more likely than men to develop depression. Women are more likely to respond empathically to life events that happen to friends and family members. Men, in contrast, are affected only by things that happen directly to them (Kessler & McLeod, 1984). The impact of these experiences depends on the meanings that people assign to them. People become depressed when they interpret events in a way that diminishes their sense of self-worth.

Depression is *maintained* over an extended period of time, and can escalate to clinical proportions, as a result of persistent interpersonal and cognitive problems. Depressed people behave in ways that elicit negative reactions and rejection from others. They are also more likely to be acutely aware of criticism and rejection. Their negative cognitive schemas remain activated, accentuating the impact of stressful circumstances.

Biological Factors

We have considered a number of social and psychological factors that contribute to the etiology of mood disorders. Biological factors are also influential in the regulation of mood. Research conducted since the 1970s has established that certain biological factors are associated with both unipolar and bipolar mood disorders. Various studies suggest that genetic factors are somehow involved, that the process of neural transmission in the brain is dysfunctional in some patients, and that hormonal abnormalities are regularly associated with depression.

GENETICS

In Kraepelin's early writings on manic–depressive psychoses, he noted the presence of a "hereditary taint" in the majority of cases. This inference was based on his observation that many of the patients' relatives exhibited symptoms of the same disorder. Subsequent studies have confirmed his impression that genetic factors are involved in the transmission of mood disorders. They have also provided useful insights regarding the utility of the unipolar/bipolar distinction.

Family Studies   If the development of mood disorders is influenced by genetic factors, these disorders should show a familial pattern of transmission. In other words, first-degree relatives (siblings, parents, and children) of patients with mood disorders should be more vulnerable to the disorder because they share 50 percent of their genes with an affected individual. Several carefully controlled studies have confirmed this hypothesis. Family studies begin with the identification of an individual who has been diagnosed as having a mood disorder, who is known as the *proband*. Researchers obtain as much information as possible about the proband's relatives, either through personal interviews, family informants, or mental health records. They use this information to decide whether each relative fits criteria for mood disorders. They can then compare the lifetime morbid risk among patients' relatives with those figures already established for the general population.

Table 5–4 presents a summary of data from several family studies of mood disorder. An interesting pattern distinguishes unipolar and bipolar mood disorders. Remember that the lifetime risk for major depressive disorder was approximately 5 percent in the ECA study, whereas the lifetime risk for bipolar disorder was approximately 1 percent. With these figures in mind, consider the frequency of disorder among the relatives of unipolar probands. The risk for bipolar disorder among their relatives is close to that seen in the general population, but the risk for unipolar disorder is almost doubled. Among the relatives of bipolar probands, the risk for both bipolar and unipolar disorder is much higher than that seen in the general population. The combined risk for both types of mood disorder is about 19 percent, almost double the combined risk of 10 percent found among the relatives of unipolar probands. Both types of mood disorder are therefore

TABLE 5–4

Average Morbid Risk for Mood Disorders in First-Degree Relatives of Unipolar and Bipolar Patients

TYPE OF PROBAND	RELATIVES' DISORDER (% WITH DISORDER)	
	UNIPOLAR	BIPOLAR
Unipolar	9.1	0.6
Bipolar	11.4	7.8

Based on 7 studies of relatives of unipolar probands and 12 studies of relatives of bipolar probands.
Source: R. Katz and P. McGuffin, 1993, The genetics of affective disorders. In L. J. Chapman, J. P. Chapman, and D. Fowles (Eds.), Progress in Experimental Personality and Psychopathology Research. New York: Springer.

markedly familial. Family studies support the conclusion that bipolar mood disorders should be considered a separate type of mood disorder because the risk for bipolar disorder is elevated only among the families of probands who have bipolar disorders themselves (Winokur et al., 1995).

Twin Studies   The comparison of monozygotic (MZ) and dizygotic (DZ) twin pairs provides a more stringent test of the possible influence of genetic factors (see Chapter 2). Several twin studies of mood disorders have reported higher concordance rates among MZ than among DZ twins (Katz & McGuffin, 1993; Moldin, Reich, & Rice, 1991).

One classic study was reported by Axel Bertelson, a Danish psychiatrist, and his colleagues (1977). They used national twin and psychiatric registers in Denmark to identify 110 pairs of same-sexed twins in which at least one member was diagnosed as having a mood disorder. The concordance rates for bipolar disorders in MZ and DZ twins were .69 and .19, respectively. For unipolar disorders, concordance rates for MZ and DZ twins were .54 and .24, respectively. The fact that the concordance rates were significantly higher for MZ than for DZ twins indicates that genetic factors are involved in the transmission of both bipolar and unipolar mood disorders. The fact that the difference between the MZ and DZ rate was somewhat higher for bipolar than for unipolar disorders may suggest that the effects of genes are more important in the case of bipolar disorders. Similar patterns of MZ and DZ concordance rates have been reported subsequently from twin studies of mood disorders conducted in Sweden (Torgersen, 1986) and in England (McGuffin, Katz, Watkins, & Rutherford, 1996).

Twin studies also indicate that environmental factors mediate the expression of a genetically determined vulnerability to depression. The best evidence for the influence of nongenetic factors is the concordance rates in MZ twins, which consistently fall short of 100 percent. If genes told the whole story, MZ twins would always be concordant. Mathematical analyses have been used to estimate the relative contributions of genetic and environmental events to the etiology of mood disorders. The results of these analyses are expressed in terms of *heritability,* which can range from 0 percent (meaning that genetic factors are not involved) to 100 percent (meaning that genetic factors alone are responsible for the development of the trait in question). These analyses indicate that genetic factors are particularly influential in bipolar mood disorders, for which the heritability estimate is 80 percent. Genes and environment contribute about equally to the etiology of major depressive disorder, in which the heritability estimate is 52 percent. The genetic contribution may be relatively minor for dysthymia or neurotic depression, where the heritability estimate is only 10 percent (Katz & McGuffin, 1993).

Genetic Risk and Sensitivity to Stress   How do genetic factors and stressful life events interact to bring about depression? The combined effects of genetic and environmental factors can be evaluated by incorporating the investigation of stressful life events into the traditional twin design. One important study that followed this procedure employed approximately 1,000 pairs of female same-sexed twins (590 MZ and 440 DZ pairs) in a study of unipolar mood disorder (Kendler et al., 1995). At two points in time, each separated from the next by approximately a year and a half, the investigators collected information regarding symptoms of depression and the experience of stressful life events.

They divided their sample into four groups, based on levels of genetic risk:

- Highest genetic risk: women with a depressed MZ co-twin
- High genetic risk: women with a depressed DZ co-twin
- Low genetic risk: women with a nondepressed DZ co-twin
- Lowest genetic risk: women with a nondepressed MZ co-twin

These groups were further subdivided into those who had experienced a severe life event (death of a close relative, assault, serious marital problems, divorce/breakup) during the follow-up period and those who had not. The data from these comparisons are illustrated in Figure 5–2. Two primary conclusions can be drawn from these results. First, severe life events increase the probability that a person will become depressed, even among those who presumably have a rela-

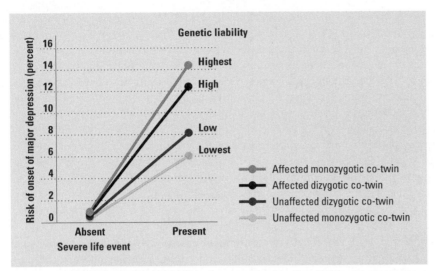

Figure 5–2   Risk of onset of major depression as a function of genetic liability and the presence or absence of a severe life event.

Source: K. S. Kendler, R. C. Kessler, E. E. Walters, C. MacLean, M. C. Neale, A. C. Heath, and L. J. Eaves, 1995, Stressful life events, genetic liability, and onset of an episode of major depression in women, *American Journal of Psychiatry, 152,* 838–842.

tively low genetic risk for the disorder. Second, the magnitude of the environmental effect is much larger for people who are genetically predisposed to the development of unipolar depression. Therefore the effects of the environment and genetic factors are not independent. Genetic factors apparently control the person's sensitivity to environmental events.

Mode of Transmission and Linkage Studies   The family and twin studies indicate that genetic factors play an important role in the development of mood disorders. They have not, however, established the operation of a particular mode of inheritance. Most investigators view mood disorders as being polygenic—they are influenced by several different genes.

In contrast, some investigators favor the single-locus model of inheritance, which holds that one gene at a particular location, or *locus,* on a particular chromosome is responsible for mood disorders. To support their arguments they have searched for evidence of chromosomal linkage between the locus of a known gene and the locus for a gene that is responsible for mood disorders. Two loci are said to be *linked* when they occupy positions that are close together on the same chromosome. Linkage is usually detected by examining the degree of association between two or more traits within specific families.

Linkage studies of mood disorders have focused on bipolar patients because the effects of genetic factors appear to be greater in bipolar than in unipolar disorders. With the introduction of new gene-mapping techniques, our knowledge in this area is expanding dramatically. Thus far, the results are mixed (Berrettini, 1993; Craddock & McGuffin, 1993).

NEUROTRANSMITTERS AND DEPRESSION

Chemical activity in the brain is another important biological factor that is undoubtedly involved in the etiology of mood disorders (Delgado, Price, Heninger, & Charney, 1992; Mann & Kupfer, 1993). Our knowledge in this area initially was based on the accidental discovery during the late 1940s and the 1950s of several drugs that have the ability to alter people's moods.

Iproniazid was being used to treat people suffering from tuberculosis. Clinicians observed that some patients who took this drug experienced inappropriate mood elevation. Neuroscientists soon determined that iproniazid inhibits the action of monoamine oxidase (MAO), one of the enzymes that break down monoamines, such as norepinephrine and serotonin, in the nerve terminal. Psychiatrists found that this general class of drugs, known as monoamine oxidase (MAO) inhibitors, could be used successfully to treat depressed patients.

A related discovery was made by scientists working for a pharmaceutical company. They were looking for a variant of the phenothiazines, a class of drugs shown to have beneficial effects for people with schizophrenia (see Chapter 13). Imipramine was tested with a variety of psychiatric patients, and although it did not prove useful with schizophrenia, it did appear to have mood-elevating properties and was subsequently shown to be effective with depressed patients. Imipramine and several related compounds form the group of drugs that are known as tricyclic antidepressants (TCAs) because their molecular structures include three rings.

Based on this evidence, Schildkraut (1965) and Bunney and Davis (1965) proposed a simple biochemical theory—the *catecholamine hypothesis*—to explain the etiology of depression.[†] According to this theory, depression was associated with a decrease in the levels of brain catecholamines, especially norepinephrine. Mania, on the other hand, was presumably associated with an excess of norepinephrine. Shortly thereafter, and based largely on the same pharmacological data, other investigators suggested that serotonin, another neurotransmitter in the central nervous system, might also be related to depression because MAO inhibitors and TCAs affect this neurotransmitter in the same way that they affect norepinephrine. This second theory came to be known as the *indolamine hypothesis*.

Two important considerations have recently led to a somewhat different perspective on neurochemistry and mood disorders. First, several new drugs have different physiological effects than the classic antidepressant drugs. More specifically, they do not affect the reuptake of monoamines (norepinephrine or serotonin), and they do not inhibit MAO. The second consideration involves the distinction between short-term and long-term drug effects. Antidepressants typically must be taken for 1 to 3 weeks before they have a clinical effect.

If depression is associated with a low level of norepinephrine in certain brain areas, and if TCAs block the uptake of norepinephrine right away, why don't these antidepressants have *immediate* beneficial effects on the patient's mood? Studies of the *long-term* effects of antidepressants on membrane receptors suggest that the original notions presented in the catecholamine and indolamine hypotheses—that depression was produced by a simple reduction in the amount of norepinephrine or serotonin—were much too simple. Current theories tend to place a greater emphasis on the interactive effects of several neurotransmitter systems, including dopamine (Depue & Iacono, 1989; Kapur & Mann, 1992), as well as serotonin, norepinephrine, and neuropeptides—short chains of amino acids that exist in the brain and appear to modulate the activity of the classic neurotransmitters. These theories focus more on the role of postsynaptic receptor sensitivity and density rather than on a simple deficiency in the amount of neurotransmitter substances that are available (Charney et al., 1991; Potter, Grossman, & Rudorfer, 1993). In essence, they propose that postsynaptic receptors are both more sensitive and more dense in depressed patients. These theories are based in part on animal studies that have demonstrated that treatment with antidepressants decreases the sensitivity and density of these receptors (McNeal & Cimbolic, 1986).

THE NEUROENDOCRINE SYSTEM

The endocrine system plays an important role in regulating a person's response to stress. As we saw in Chapter 2, endocrine glands, such as the pituitary, thyroid, and adrenal glands, are located at various sites throughout the body. In response to signals from the brain, these glands secrete hormones into the bloodstream. One important pathway in the endocrine system that may be closely related to the etiology of mood disorders is called the *hypothalamic–pituitary–adrenal (HPA) axis*. Signals from the hypothalamus cause the pituitary gland to secrete a hormone called ACTH, which in turn modulates hormone secretion by the adrenal glands.

[†]*One general class of neurotransmitters in the central nervous system is known as the monoamines, which are organic compounds containing nitrogen in one amino group. The monoamine neurotransmitters contain two important subtypes: catecholamines, which have a catechol portion (such as norepinephrine and dopamine), and indolamines, which have an indole portion (such as serotonin and tryptamine).*

Interest in the relation between mood disorders and the endocrine system was stimulated in part by descriptions of Cushing's syndrome, a disease associated with the adrenal glands that results in abnormally high concentrations of the hormone cortisol in the bloodstream. Approximately half of all patients with Cushing's syndrome are also clinically depressed. After Cushing's syndrome is corrected, most patients also recover from their depression. This pattern suggests that abnormally high levels of cortisol may lead to the onset of depression (Checkley, 1992).

In what ways might endocrine problems be related to other etiological factors we have already discussed? At a more general level, hormone regulation may provide a process through which stressful life events interact with a genetically determined predisposition to mood disorder. Stress causes the release of adrenal steroids, such as cortisol, and steroid hormones play an active role in regulating the expression of genes (Checkley, 1992; Haskett, 1993).

Treatment

Several procedures, both psychosocial and biological, have proved to be useful in the treatment of mood disorders. We have already mentioned that MAO inhibitors and TCAs can be effective with some depressed patients. Alternative forms of antidepressant medication have also been developed. Current psychological interventions emphasize cognitive patterns and interpersonal skills that are related to the etiological perspectives we have just reviewed. In the following pages we will examine some of the more prominent contemporary approaches to the treatment of unipolar and bipolar mood disorders, as well as the research evidence on their usefulness.

Unipolar Disorders

Most psychological approaches to the treatment of depression owe some debt to psychodynamic procedures and Freud's emphasis on the importance of anger and interpersonal dynamics. According to Freud's view, the primary goal of therapy should be to help the patient understand and express the hostility and frustration that are being directed against the self. These negative emotions are presumably rooted in dysfunctional relationships with other people. Freud also placed considerable emphasis on the apparently irrational beliefs that depressed people hold about themselves and their world. These cognitive factors are also emphasized by cognitive therapists.

COGNITIVE THERAPY

Cognitive therapy has been developed and promoted by Aaron Beck and his colleagues (e.g., Beck et al., 1979). His cognitive model assumes that emotional dysfunction is influenced by the ways in which people interpret events in their environments and the things that they say to themselves about those experiences. Cognitive treatments are based on the assumption that the patient's depression will be relieved if these irrational beliefs are changed. Cognitive therapists focus on helping their patients replace self-defeating cognitions with more rational self-statements.

A specific example may help to illustrate this process. Consider the case of Cathy, the depressed attorney whom we introduced at the beginning of the chapter. Cathy focused a great deal of attention on relatively minor negative events at work, blaming herself for anything other than a perfect performance. Her therapist helped her to recognize that she was engaging in a pattern of cognitive distortion that Beck has labeled "selective abstraction." Taking a detail out of context, she would invariably ignore those aspects of her performance that refuted the conclusion that she was professionally incompetent. Her therapist helped her overcome these tendencies by teaching her to question her conclusions and to develop more objective ways of evaluating her experiences.

Cathy also tended to think about herself in absolute and unvarying terms. During the course of therapy, she learned to recognize this pattern and to substitute more flexible self-statements. Instead of saying to herself, "I am a hopeless introvert and will never be able to change," she learned to substitute, "I am less comfortable in social situations than some other people, but I can learn to be more confident."

Aaron Beck has developed an influential cognitive theory of depression, emphasizing the importance of distorted ways of thinking about the self. He has pioneered the use of cognitive therapy for the treatment of depression.

Although Beck's approach to treatment emphasizes the importance of cognitive events, it shares many features with behavioral approaches to intervention. Cognitive therapists are active and directive in their interactions with clients, and they focus most of their attention on their clients' current experience. They also assume that people have conscious access to cognitive events: Our thinking may not always be rational, but we can discuss private thoughts and feelings. Another important aspect of Beck's approach to treatment, and a characteristic that it shares with the behavioral perspective, is a serious commitment to the empirical evaluation of the efficacy of treatment programs. Several studies have found that cognitive therapy is effective in the treatment of nonpsychotic, unipolar depression (Hollon, Shelton, & Davis, 1993). Two direct comparisons of cognitive therapy and behavioral therapy in the treatment of major depressive disorder have found that both types of treatment were effective, with neither being superior to the other (Hollon et al., 1993; Murphy et al., 1984).

INTERPERSONAL THERAPY

Interpersonal therapy is another contemporary approach to the psychological treatment of depression (Klerman et al., 1984). Based originally on traditional psychodynamic notions regarding dependent personality traits and depression, interpersonal therapy focuses primarily on current relationships, especially those involving family members. The therapist helps the patient develop a better understanding of the interpersonal problems that presumably give rise to depression (Gotlib & Hammen, 1992) and attempts to improve the patient's relationships with other people by building communication and problem-solving skills. Therapy sessions often include nondirective discussions of social difficulties and unexpressed or unacknowledged negative emotions as well as role playing to practice specific social skills.

ANTIDEPRESSANT MEDICATIONS

The types of medication that are used most frequently in the treatment of unipolar mood disorders fall into three general categories: tricyclics (TCAs), monoamine oxidase inhibitors (MAO-Is), and selective serotonin reuptake inhibitors (SSRIs).

Tricyclics   The **tricyclics,** such as imipramine (Tofranil) and amitriptyline (Elavil), have been in relatively widespread use since the 1950s. They affect brain functions by blocking the uptake of neurotransmitters (for example, norepinephrine and dopamine) from the synapse. There are several different kinds of tricyclic medication that vary in potency and side effects, but they are generally equal in terms of effectiveness.

Monoamine Oxidase Inhibitors   The antidepressant effects of **monoamine oxidase (MAO) inhibitors** were discovered at about the same time as those of the tricyclic drugs. These drugs have not been used as extensively as tricyclics, however, primarily for two reasons. First, patients who use MAO inhibitors and also consume foods containing large amounts of the compound tyramine, such as cheese and chocolate, often develop very high blood pressure. Second, some early empirical evaluations of antidepressant medications suggested that MAO inhibitors are not as effective as tricyclics (see, for example, British Medical Research Council, 1965).

More recent studies have shown that MAO inhibitors are indeed useful in the treatment of depressed patients (Larsen, 1991). They can be used safely when the patient takes the necessary precautions regarding his or her diet. In addition, MAO inhibitors are now widely used in the treatment of certain anxiety disorders, especially agoraphobia and panic attacks (see Chapter 6).

Selective Serotonin Reuptake Inhibitors   The **selective serotonin reuptake inhibitors (SSRIs)** are a comparatively new class of antidepressant medication that was developed in the early 1980s (Silverstone, 1992). Unlike the original forms of antidepressant medication, which were discovered by accident, SSRIs were synthesized in the laboratories of pharmaceutical companies on the basis of theoretical speculation regarding the role of serotonin in the etiology of mood disorders. The SSRIs inhibit the reuptake of serotonin into the presynaptic nerve ending and therefore promote neurotransmission in serotonin pathways by increasing the amount of serotonin in the synaptic cleft. They are called "selective" because they seem to have little if any effect on the uptake of other neurotransmitters.

The SSRIs have fewer side effects (such as weight gain, constipation, and drowsiness) than TCAs or MAO inhibitors do, and they are less dangerous if the patient takes an overdose. This does not mean, of course, that they are completely without side effects. Some patients experience nausea, headaches, fatigue, restlessness, and insomnia, although these symptoms are usually mild and short term.

The best known of the SSRIs is fluoxetine (Prozac). Prozac is now a popular form of treatment that is prescribed by psychiatrists more than twice as often as the next most common type of antidepressant drug. Controlled outcome studies indicate that Prozac and other SSRIs are about as effective as traditional forms of antidepressant medication (Greenberg et al., 1994; Stokes, 1993).

THE EFFICACY OF PSYCHOTHERAPY AND TCAS

The Treatment of Depression Collaborative Research Program (TDCRP) was a large-scale study that compared the effectiveness of two types of psychotherapy—cognitive and interpersonal therapy—with that of antidepressant medication (Elkin et al., 1989; Elkin et al., 1996). The study was sponsored by the National Institute of Mental Health (NIMH) and was conducted at three different sites. Unipolar depressed outpatients were assigned to one of four treatment groups: cognitive therapy, interpersonal therapy, antidepressant medication (imipramine, a standard TCA), or placebo plus "clinical management." Patients in the latter group met regularly with a therapist to receive pills that they believed to be antidepressants and also received extensive support and encouragement. Treatment lasted approximately 16 weeks in all conditions.

The results of the TDCRP are extensive and complex, given the large number of measures that were collected on all patients, differences across the three treatment sites, and variability in dropout rates in the different types of treatment. A few major findings stand out. First, all three types of active treatment were superior to the placebo plus clinical management condition in terms of their ability to reduce depression and improve overall levels of functioning. Second, there were no significant differences between cognitive and interpersonal therapy, and both were generally as effective as antidepressant medication. Third, patients improved somewhat more rapidly if they were receiving imipramine, but the rate of improvement in both psychotherapy groups caught up to the drug condition by the end of treatment. Fourth, contrary to expectations, patients who received different forms of psychotherapy did not exhibit improvements in specific psychological domains that were addressed in therapy. In other words, patients who received interpersonal therapy showed as much improvement on measures of cognitive distortion as did the patients who received cognitive therapy.

The three active forms of treatment in the TDCRP appeared to be roughly equivalent on the basis of initial comparisons of all the patients in the study. Subsequent analyses, however, found differences among treatments when the patient sample was subdivided based on how severe their depression was when they entered the study. Among severely depressed patients, those who received imipramine and those who received interpersonal treatment still showed more improvement than the placebo group. Severely depressed patients who received cognitive therapy, however, were not better off than those who received placebo. This result suggests that antidepressant medication and interpersonal therapy are more effective with certain types of depressed patients (Elkin et al., 1996; Jacobson & Hollon, 1996; Klein & Ross, 1993).

The results of the TDCRP were positive over the short run. Unfortunately, follow-up evaluations conducted 18 months after the completion of treatment were less encouraging. By that time, patients in the three active treatment groups were no longer functioning at a higher level than those who received only the placebo and clinical management. Less than 30 percent of the patients who were considered markedly improved at the end of treatment were still nondepressed at follow-up. This aspect of the study's results points to the need for continued efforts to improve currently available treatment methods.

Bipolar Disorders

Lithium   In 1949, the Australian psychiatrist John Cade discovered that the salt *lithium carbonate* was effective in treating bipolar mood disorders. An extensive literature indicates that lithium carbonate is an effective form of treatment in the alleviation of manic episodes (Abou-Saleh, 1992; Keck & McElroy, 1993). It is also useful in the treatment of bipolar patients who are experiencing a depressive episode. Perhaps most importantly, bipolar patients who continue to take lithium between episodes are significantly less likely to experience a relapse.

Unfortunately, there are also some limitations associated with the use of lithium. Some bipolar patients—perhaps 20 to 25 percent—do not improve when they take lithium (O'Shea, 1993). Nonresponse is particularly common among rapid cycling patients and those who exhibit a mixture of manic and schizophrenic symptoms. Compliance with medication is also a frequent problem: At least half the people for whom lithium is prescribed either fail to take it regularly or stop taking it against their psychiatrist's advice (Goodwin & Jamison, 1990). The main reasons that patients give for discontinuing lithium are negative side effects, including memory problems, weight gain, and impaired coordination.

Anticonvulsant Medications   Often, bipolar patients who do not respond positively to lithium are prescribed anticonvulsant drugs, particularly carbamazepine (Tegretol) or valproic acid (Depakene) (McElroy et al., 1992; O'Shea, 1993). Outcome data suggest that slightly more than 60 percent of bipolar patients respond positively to these drugs (Gerner & Stanton, 1992). Like lithium, carbamazepine and valproic acid can be useful in reducing the frequency and severity of relapse, and they can be used to treat acute manic episodes.

Psychotherapy   Although medication is the most important method of treatment for bipolar disorders, psychotherapy can be an effective supplement to biological intervention. Both interpersonal therapy and cognitive therapy have been adapted for use with bipolar disorders. In interpersonal therapy with bipolar patients, special emphasis is placed on monitoring the interaction between symptoms (especially the onset of hypomanic or manic episodes) and social interactions. Regulation of sleep and work patterns is also important (Klerman & Weissman, 1992). Cognitive therapy can be used to address both the patient's reactions to stressful life events and his or her reservations about taking medication (Haaga & Beck, 1992).

Relatively little research has been done to evaluate the utility of psychological treatments for bipolar mood disorders. Support for their use hinges, in large part, on clinical intuition and compelling testimonials from grateful patients. Unfortunately, enthusiastic endorsements based on personal experience do not constitute strong evidence in favor of a treatment procedure (see Chapter 1). There is an obvious need for more extensive research on the effectiveness of various types of psychosocial treatment for bipolar mood disorders (Goldstein & Miklowitz, 1994; Solomon et al., 1995).

Electroconvulsive Therapy

The procedure known as *electroconvulsive therapy* (or *ECT*) has proved beneficial for many patients suffering from unipolar or bipolar mood disorders (see Chapter 3 for a review of the background of ECT). Electroconvulsive therapy is typically administered in an inpatient setting and consists of a series of treatments given two or three times a week (Abrams, 1993). Many patients show a dramatic improvement after six to eight sessions, but some require more. In current clinical practice, muscle relaxants are always administered before a patient receives ECT. This procedure has eliminated bone fractures and dislocations that were unfortunate side effects of earlier techniques.

Although the mode of action in ECT remains largely a mystery (Kapur & Mann, 1993), empirical studies have demonstrated that it is an effective form of treatment for severely depressed patients (Consensus Conference, 1985). Legitimate reservations regarding the use of ECT center around widely publicized, although apparently infrequent, cases of pervasive and persistent memory loss. No one denies that ECT is an invasive procedure that should usually be reserved for patients who

In 1938, two Italian psychiatrists introduced a technique for inducing convulsions through electrical, rather than chemical, methods. In this procedure, electrodes were placed on either side of the patient's head, and an alternating current of 110 volts was passed through the brain for approximately half a second.

have been resistant to other forms of intervention such as medication and cognitive therapy. Nevertheless, it remains a viable and legitimate alternative for some severely depressed patients, especially those who are so suicidal that they require constant supervision to prevent them from harming themselves. Rapid cycling bipolar patients and depressed patients with psychotic symptoms may also be more responsive to ECT than to medication (Fink, 1993). As always, the risks of treatment must be carefully weighed against those associated with allowing the disorder to follow its natural course.

Seasonal Mood Disorders

The observation that fluctuations in seasons can help bring on episodes of mood disorder leads to the relatively obvious implication that some patients might respond to manipulations of the natural environment. For centuries, physicians have prescribed changes in climate for their depressed clients (Wehr, 1989). The prominent French psychiatrist Jean Esquirol (1772–1840) reportedly advised a patient whose depression appeared when the days grew shorter to move from Belgium to Italy during the winter.

Modern light therapy was introduced in the 1980s (Oren & Rosenthal, 1992; Rosenthal et al., 1984). Typical treatment involves exposure to bright (2,500 lux), broad-spectrum light for 1 to 2 hours every day. Some patients respond positively to shorter periods (30 minutes) of high-intensity (10,000 lux) light (Hill, 1992). This high-intensity light is roughly equivalent to the amount of light that would be generated by a 750-watt spotlight focused on a surface 1 square meter in area. The light source—most often a rectangular box containing fluorescent ceiling fixtures—must be placed close (90 cm) to the patient at eye level. Improvement in the person's mood is often seen within 2 to 5 days.

Outcome studies have found that light therapy is an effective form of treatment for seasonal affective disorder (Terman et al., 1989). The most difficult issue in evaluating this type of treatment has been to control for placebo effects. It is not possible to conduct a true double-blind study because patients know that they are being exposed to light, and they often believe that light will be helpful. The general conclusion is that light therapy is not simply a placebo effect. It is not clear, however, how or why it works (Hill, 1992).

getting help

The distinction between severe depression and the ups and downs of everyday life provides an important guide to the need for treatment. If you have been seriously depressed for several weeks, and if depression is interfering with your ability to function, you should seek professional help. Fortunately, you have already taken the first step toward improvement. By reading this chapter, you can learn to recognize the symptoms of mood disorders.

Several effective forms of treatment are available for mood disorders. The first step in getting help is to find someone with whom you can talk. This might be your family physician, someone at your school's counseling center, or a therapist in private practice. It is important that you feel comfortable with the person you choose and with the form of treatment that he or she will provide.

Depression is not uncommon, but people who are depressed often feel lonely and alienated, as though they were the only ones who feel as they do. A number of good books and Internet sites may help make it easier to find the right treatment. Various antidepressant medications are described in *The Essential Guide to Psychiatric Drugs,* by Jack Gorman. Other self-help books may be useful to people whose depression is not debilitating but who still want to feel happier. We recommend two books based on treatment procedures that have been evaluated empirically. The cognitive approach to therapy is described with exceptional clarity in *Feeling Good: The New Mood Therapy,* by David Burns, a psychiatrist who had worked extensively with Aaron Beck. *Control Your Depression,* written by Peter Lewinsohn and his colleagues, provides a thoughtful, layperson's description of a psychological treatment program that places emphasis on interpersonal behaviors and social skills.

Several sites on the Internet provide useful information to people who are suffering from mood disorders (as well as their family and friends). The National Institute of Mental Health has established a public and professional educational program called Depression: Awareness, Recognition, and Treatment. The URL for its Web site is **webtest.nimh.nih.gov/dart.** Patient-run organizations can also be helpful, particularly in organizing local support groups and sharing information about treatment alternatives. One outstanding example is the National Depressive and Manic–Depressive Association, which was founded by and for people with mood disorders. The URL for its Web site is **www.ndmda.org./.** Finally, for a list of sensible answers to frequently asked questions about bipolar mood disorder, you should visit **moodswing.org,** a site maintained by the Bipolar Disorder Online Support Group.

People who are depressed need support and encouragement to seek treatment. Families and friends of depressed people find themselves in a very difficult and challenging situation. Mood disorders interfere with the person's ability to get along with other people and deplete the person's energy and motivation for seeking treatment. If they don't follow through with therapy or make noticeable improvements after several sessions, their friends can easily become discouraged or frustrated. Don't feel guilty if your efforts appear to go unrewarded. And don't blame the depressed person if he or she doesn't get better right away. Mood disorders are serious problems that require professional help. More detailed advice for families and friends can be found at the Web sites listed here.

Suicide

Although many people who commit suicide do not appear to be depressed, and psychopathology doesn't explain all suicidal behavior, there is undoubtedly a strong relationship between depression and self-destructive acts. The available evidence suggests that at least 50 percent of all suicides occur as a result of, or in the context of, a primary mood disorder (Whybrow, Akiskal, & McKinney, 1984). Moreover, the risk of completed suicide is much higher among people who are clinically depressed than it is among people in the general population. Follow-up studies consistently indicate that 15 to 20 percent of all patients with mood disorders will eventually kill themselves (Goodwin & Jamison, 1990). Thus it seems reasonable to conclude that there is a relatively close link between suicide and depression.

Epidemiology of Suicide

In the United States and Canada, the annual rate of completed suicide across all age groups has averaged 12 people per 100,000 population during the twentieth century. More than 30,000 people in the United States kill themselves every year. Suicide rates vary as a function of many factors, including age, gender, and socioeconomic status (see Figure 5–3). The suicide rate among adoles-

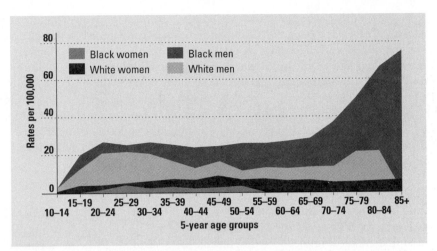

Figure 5–3   Suicide Rates Across the Lifespan. Suicide rates per 100,000 population by 5-year age group, race, and gender, United States, 1991.

Source: Moscicki, E. K., 1995, Epidemiology of suicidal behavior, *Suicide and Life-Threatening Behavior, 25,* 22–35.

cents has increased alarmingly in recent decades. Between 1955 and 1980 (years in which "baby boomers" became adults), the suicide rate tripled for young men between the ages of 15 and 24. The rate for young women in the same age range doubled during the same period (Garland & Zigler, 1993). Rates among other age groups have either fallen or remained steady. Suicide has become the third leading cause of death for people between the ages of 15 and 24, and it is the eighth leading cause of death in the general population (Moscicki, 1995).

Suicide attempts are much more common than are completed suicides. The ratio of attempts to completed suicides in the general population is approximately 10 to 1; among adolescents, the ratio is closer to 100 to 1 (Hendin, 1995). There are important gender differences in rates of attempted suicide versus rates of completed suicide. Females aged 15 to 19 years make 3 times as many suicide attempts as males. Completion rates, however, are 4 times higher among males (Tsuang, Simpson, & Fleming, 1992). The difference in fatalities may be due, in part, to the methods employed. Men and boys are more likely to use violent and lethal methods such as firearms and hanging, whereas women and girls are more likely to take an overdose of drugs, which may allow time for discovery and interventions by other people.

The risk of fatal suicide is highest among older people. Suicide rates have increased dramatically among young adults in recent years, but the highest rates are still found among older people, especially older white men. Although suicide attempts are most common among younger people, with most being made by those younger than 30, the proportion of suicide attempts that end in death is particularly high among the elderly. It is not clear whether this pattern should be attributed to a difference in method or to decreased physical resilience. Rates of suicide in the United States—broken down by age, race, and gender—are illustrated in Figure 5–3. In 1991, more than 70 percent of all suicides were committed by white men, with the highest rate being among those over the age of 80. The pattern for women is somewhat different. Their risk for suicide increases steadily with age until midlife and then tends to level off.

Etiology of Suicide

Many factors contribute to the etiology of suicide. William Eaton (1994), a distinguished epidemiologist at Johns Hopkins University, offered the following example to illustrate the multiple levels of analysis that can be employed to examine factors leading to suicide:

Consider a truck driver who commits suicide after finishing a long run. The suicide is at the behavioral level. The depletion of dopamine, which contributed to the suicide, resulted from the rebound effect of taking amphetamines during the run (biological level). At the psychological level, the individual driver may be saddened by a recent death in his family. The drug is available, and regarded as normative, in the driver's peer group (social-psychological level). The driver is able to take the illegal drug because the work is not supervised (social structural). The driver needs to make the run, and take the drug, because the union is less effective in protecting workers from exploitive labor practices (political) which reward drivers for long runs in the face of declining standards of living (economic). (pp. 27–28)

PSYCHOLOGICAL FACTORS

Many experts have argued that psychological events lie at the core of suicidal behavior (Schneidman, 1996). Social factors may set the stage for self-destructive acts, but events taking place within the person's mind are most immediately responsible for determining whether a particular individual will attempt to end his or her own life. Prominent among these events are the experience of intense emotional distress and hopelessness. An outline of several psychological variables that are commonly associated with suicide is presented in Further Thoughts.

Personality theorists have identified a number of fundamental human needs or motives—needs for achievement, esteem, belongingness, and safety. Frustration in meeting these needs can lead to prolonged, intense, negative emotional states, such as shame, guilt, anger, and grief. Most people who experience these emotions do not attempt suicide. But for some people, suicide appears to offer a solution or a way to end their intolerable distress.

BIOLOGICAL FACTORS

Studies of the connection between neurotransmitters and suicide have focused primarily on reduced levels of serotonin, which might be related to poor impulse control as well as increased levels of violent and aggressive behavior (Asberg, 1994; Hengeveld, 1994; Siever & Trestman, 1993). Dysregulation of serotonin systems has been found among people who attempted suicide, and it has also been found among people who have shown other types of violent and aggressive behavior, such as criminals convicted of murder (Garza-Trevino, 1994).

Serotonin dysfunction has also been linked to depressive disorders. It seems reasonable to wonder whether that connection might explain the findings regarding serotonin and suicide. People who attempt suicide may exhibit abnormal serotonin levels because they are depressed. That might be a reasonable interpretation for some of the data, but the results of other studies indicate that the link to suicide is more direct.

Consider, for example, a follow-up study of 92 people who were hospitalized following a suicide attempt (Nordstrom et al., 1994). All of the participants met the criteria for a major depressive disorder. The investigators measured levels of a particular serotonin by-product, 5-HIAA (5-hydroxyindoleacetic acid), in each patient's cerebrospinal fluid (CSF) shortly after admission to the hospital. The patients were divided into two groups on the basis of these measurements: those below the median for CSF 5-HIAA and those above the median. In the first year after their attempted suicide, 11 of the 92 patients committed suicide, and 8 of the 11 who died were from the low CSF 5-HIAA group. This result suggests that biochemical measures might be useful for predicting risk for suicide within groups of depressed patients.

Twin studies and adoption studies have found that genetic factors are involved in the transmission of major mood disorders. Do genes contribute to the risk for suicide indirectly by increasing the risk for mental disorders, such as depression, schizophrenia, and substance abuse? Is there a more direct contribution of genetic factors to self-destructive behavior? The answer appears to be yes (Mitterauer, 1990; Roy, 1992; Roy et al., 1991). One important investigation examined cases of depression and suicide in a group of large Amish families over a period of 100 years (Egeland & Sussex, 1985). Each family included at least one person who suffered from a mood disorder. Within this sample, there were 26 documented instances of suicide. The vast majority of the suicides (92 percent) occurred in people who had been diagnosed as having a mood

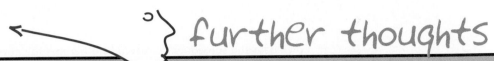

Common Elements of Suicide

Most people who kill themselves are suffering from some form of mental disorder, such as depression, substance dependence, or schizophrenia (Caldwell & Gottesman, 1992). No single explanation can account for all self-destructive behavior. Edwin Shneidman (1996), a clinical psychologist who is a leading authority on suicide, described 10 characteristics commonly associated with completed suicide. Schneidman's list includes features that occur most frequently and may help us understand many cases of suicide:

1. **The common purpose of suicide is to seek a solution.** Suicide is not a pointless or random act. To people who think about ending their own lives, suicide represents an answer to an otherwise insoluble problem or a way out of some unbearable dilemma. If someone else whom the person admired or cared for has committed suicide, then the person is more likely to do so.

2. **The common goal of suicide is cessation of consciousness.** People who commit suicide seek the end of conscious experience, which to them has become an endless stream of distressing thoughts with which they are preoccupied.

3. **The common stimulus (or information input) in suicide is unbearable psychological pain.** Excruciating negative emotions—including shame, guilt, anger, fear, and sadness—frequently serve as the foundation for self-destructive behavior. These emotions may arise from any number of sources.

4. **The common stressor in suicide is frustrated psychological needs.** People with high standards and expectations are especially vulnerable to ideas of suicide when progress toward these goals is suddenly frustrated. Family turmoil is an especially important source of frustration to adoles-

cents. Occupational and interpersonal difficulties frequently precipitate suicide among adults. For example, rates of suicide increase during periods of high unemployment (Yang et al., 1992).

5. **The common emotion in suicide is hopelessness-helplessness.** The suicidal person is convinced that absolutely nothing can be done to improve his or her situation; no one else can help.

6. **The common cognitive state in suicide is ambivalence.** Most people who contemplate suicide, including those who eventually kill themselves, have ambivalent feelings about this decision. They are sincere in their desire to die, but they simultaneously wish that they could find another way out of their dilemma.

7. **The common perceptual state in suicide is constriction.** The suicidal person is temporarily unable or unwilling to engage in effective problem-solving behaviors and may see his or her options in extreme, all-or-nothing terms.

8. **The common action in suicide is escape.** Suicide provides a definitive way to escape from intolerable circumstances, which include painful self-awareness (Baumeister, 1990).

9. **The common interpersonal act in suicide is communication of intention.** Most people who commit suicide have told other people about their plans. Many have made previous suicidal gestures. Schneidman estimates that in at least 80 percent of committed suicides, the people provide verbal or behavioral clues that indicate clearly their lethal intentions.

10. **The common pattern in suicide is consistency of lifelong styles.** During crises that precipitate suicidal thoughts, people generally employ the same coping responses that they have used throughout their lives. For example, people who have refused to ask for help in the past are likely to persist in that pattern, increasing their sense of isolation.

disorder. Furthermore, most of the suicides occurred in a small subset of four families. The investigators suggested that this pattern might be best explained by the existence of a genetic factor that is associated with suicidal behavior, independent of risk for major depression. This factor might be associated with impulsive personality characteristics. Suicide appears to be an especially likely outcome when a person inherits a predisposition to both psychopathology and impulsive or violent behavior.

SOCIAL FACTORS

The French sociologist Emile Durkheim (1858–1917) believed that suicide rates had increased during the nineteenth century because of an erosion of the influence of traditional sources of social integration and regulation, such as the church and the family (1897/1951). Durkheim's own data and subsequent research by other investigators have provided support for the notion that social structures do represent one important consideration with regard to suicide. For example, Pescosolido and Georgianna (1989) found that religious affiliation is significantly related to suicide rates; lowest rates were found among Catholics and Evangelical Baptists, whereas higher rates were found among mainstream Protestant denominations, such as Episcopalians, Presbyterians, and Lutherans. This pattern can be explained in terms of social networks. People who belong to Catholic or conservative Protestant groups are more likely to participate in the various rituals and activities of the church community. These networks become an important source of emotional support during difficult times, protecting the person from the potential influence of self-destructive impulses.

Social policies regulating access to firearms, especially handguns, also have an effect on suicide rates. Guns are a particularly lethal method of suicide, accounting for more than 60 percent of the 30,000 deaths that occur in the United States each year (Hendin, 1995). In states with restrictive gun laws, the suicide rate usually drops, particularly among adolescents (Loftin, McDowall, Wiersma, & Cottey, 1991). Of course, people who have definitely decided to end their own lives can inevitably find a way to accomplish that goal, but many people who attempt suicide are ambivalent in their intent. Many attempts are made impulsively. Ready access to guns increases the chance that a person who does engage in an impulsive suicide attempt will die, because gunshot wounds are very likely to be fatal.

Prominent television and newspaper coverage of suicidal deaths, especially those of well-known celebrities, can have disastrous consequences by unintentionally encouraging other people to kill themselves. Young people are especially vulnerable to this effect, which is sometimes called *contagious suicide* or a *suicide cluster*. There was, for example, an increase in rates of suicide in both the United States and England in the months immediately after Marilyn Monroe committed suicide (Hendin, 1996). Imitation of this sort may represent a misdirected attempt to lend meaning to a person's life through association with the death of a celebrity. It might also be inspired by the attention that results with increased media coverage that invariably follows in the wake of multiple or sequential suicides. Descriptions of someone else's death may simply reduce some people's resistance to impulsive action.

Treatment of Suicidal People

Efforts to avoid the tragic consequences of suicidal behavior can be organized at several levels. The social factors that we have just considered suggest some changes that could be made in contemporary Western societies in an effort to reduce the frequency of suicide. For example, more restrictive gun control laws might minimize access to the most lethal method of self-destruction. More cautious reporting by the media of suicidal deaths might reduce the probability of cluster suicides. These are, of course, controversial decisions, in which many other considerations play an important role. The media, for example, are motivated to report stories in a way that will maximize their popularity with the public. And many people oppose gun control legislation for reasons that have nothing to do with suicide rates. Therefore it may be unrealistic to hope that these measures, aimed broadly at the level of an entire population, will be implemented widely. Most treatment programs that are concerned with suicidal behavior have been directed toward individual persons and their families.

CRISIS CENTERS AND HOT LINES
Many communities have established crisis centers and telephone hot lines to provide support for people who are distraught and contemplating suicide. Sponsored by various agencies, including community mental health centers, hospitals, and religious groups, these services are often staffed by nonprofessionals, frequently volunteers. They offer 24-hour-a-day access to people who have been trained to provide verbal support for those who are in the midst of a crisis and who may have nowhere else to turn. Most crisis centers and hot lines help the person through the immediate crisis and then refer him or her to mental health professionals.

Public and professional enthusiasm for suicide prevention centers peaked during the 1960s and 1970s. Unfortunately, creation of crisis centers and hot lines does not seem to reduce suicide rates in communities (Frankish, 1994; Hendin, 1995). Why don't hot lines reduce suicide rates? The challenges faced by these programs are enormous. Think about the characteristics of people who are driven to contemplate suicide. They are often socially isolated, feeling hopeless, and unable to consider alternative solutions. Many people with the most lethal suicidal ideation will not call a hot line or visit a drop-in crisis center. The primary problem faced by suicide prevention programs is this: The people who they are trying to serve are, by definition, very difficult to reach.

It might be hard to justify the continued existence of crisis centers and hot lines if they are viewed solely in terms of suicide prevention. Only a small proportion of people who call hot lines are seriously suicidal. Most are people who are experiencing serious difficulties and who need to talk to someone about those problems. The value of contact with these individuals should not be underestimated. Crisis centers and hot lines provide support and assistance to very large numbers of people in distress. These services are undoubtedly valuable in their own right, even if serious questions remain about their impact on suicide rates.

PSYCHOTHERAPY WITH SUICIDAL CLIENTS

Psychological interventions with people who are suicidal can take many forms. These include all the standard approaches to psychotherapy, such as cognitive, behavioral, psychoanalytic, and family therapy. These methods address underlying problems that have set the stage for the person's current problems. The following recommendations cover special considerations that are particularly important when clients have expressed a serious intent to harm themselves (adapted from Berman & Jobes, 1994):

1. *Reduce lethality.* The most important task is to reduce the person's experience of psychological pain (see Further Thoughts), from which the person is seeking escape. At a more concrete level, this also involves reducing access to means that could be used to commit suicide, such as guns and pills.

2. *Negotiate agreements.* Therapists frequently ask clients who have threatened to kill themselves to sign a contract, in which the client agrees to postpone self-destructive behavior for at least a short period of time. The process of negotiating the agreement can also help the clinician determine the severity of the client's suicidal intentions.

3. *Provide support.* Friends and family members are alerted and asked to be available so that the person is not alone. The presence of others allows the person to discuss his or her problems (if he or she chooses to do so) and also provides supervision that may inhibit dangerous behaviors.

4. *Replace tunnel vision with a broader perspective.* Death may strike others as an irrational choice, but to people contemplating suicide, in the midst of the crisis, it seems perfectly logical. The therapist must help potential suicide victims develop or recover a more flexible and adaptive pattern of problem solving.

MEDICATION

Treatment of mental disorders, especially depression and schizophrenia, is an important element of intervention with suicidal clients. The use of various types of medication is often an important part of these treatment efforts. Antidepressant drugs are frequently given to patients who are clinically depressed, and antipsychotic medication is useful with those who meet the diagnostic criteria for schizophrenia (see Chapter 13).

Considerable attention has recently been devoted to the use of selective serotonin reuptake inhibitors (SSRIs), such as fluvoxamine (LuVox) and fluoxetine (Prozac), because of the link between suicide and serotonin dysregulation. Extensive clinical reports suggest that the use of SSRIs in treating depression actually lowers suicide rates (Banki, 1995; Wagner, Zaborny, & Gray, 1994). It should also be noted, however, that placebo-controlled outcome studies have not addressed this specific question. Furthermore, cases have been reported in which treatment with SSRIs has been followed by the developmental of new suicidal ideation (King, Segman, & Anderson, 1994). This pattern suggests that the relation between serotonin and suicide is neither direct nor simple and that caution is warranted in the use of SSRIs in treating suicidal clients.

INVOLUNTARY HOSPITALIZATION

People who appear to be on the brink of committing suicide are often hospitalized, either with their permission or involuntarily (see Chapter 15 for a discussion of the legal issues involved in this process). The primary consideration in such cases is safety. In many cases, commitment to a hospital may be the best way to prevent people from harming themselves. The person's behavior can be monitored continuously, access to methods of harming oneself can be minimized (though perhaps not entirely eliminated), and various types of treatment can be provided by the hospital's professional staff.

Summary

Mood disorders are defined in terms of emotional, cognitive, behavioral, and **somatic symptoms.** In addition to a feeling of pervasive despair or gloom, people experiencing an episode of major **depression** are likely to show a variety of symptoms, such as diminished interest in their normal activities, changes in appetite and sleep, fatigue, and problems in concentration. In contrast, a person in a manic episode feels elated and energetic. Manic patients also exhibit related symptoms, such as inflated self-esteem, rapid speech, and poor judgment.

DSM-IV lists two major categories of **mood disorders.** People with **unipolar mood disorders** experience only episodes of depression. People with **bipolar mood disorders** experience episodes of **mania,** which are most often interspersed with episodes of depression. There are two specific types of unipolar mood disorder in DSM-IV. Major depressive disorder is diagnosed if the person has experienced at least one episode of major depression without any periods of mania. **Dysthymia** is a less severe, chronic form of depression in which the person has been depressed for at least 2 years without a major depressive episode.

A person who has experienced at least one manic episode would receive a diagnosis of bipolar I disorder, regardless of whether he or she has ever had an episode of depression. One episode of major depression combined with evidence of at least one period of **hypomania** would qualify for a diagnosis of bipolar II disorder. **Cyclothymia** is a less severe, chronic form of bipolar mood disorder in which the person has experienced numerous periods of hypomania interspersed with periods of depressed mood.

The validity of the distinction between unipolar and bipolar mood disorders is supported by several types of evidence. Bipolar disorders tend to have an earlier age of onset and a worse prognosis than unipolar disorders.

Mood disorders are among the most common forms of psychopathology. Epidemiological studies have found that the lifetime risk for major depressive disorder is approximately 5 percent and the lifetime risk for dysthymic disorder is approximately 3 percent. Rates for both of these disorders are 2 or 3 times higher among women than among men. The lifetime risk for bipolar I disorder is close to 1 percent. Women and men are equally likely to develop bipolar mood disorder.

The etiology of mood disorders can be traced to the combined effects of social, psychological, and biological factors. Social factors include primarily the influence of stressful life events, especially severe losses that are associated with significant people or significant roles. Some studies show that people who are clinically depressed help to create some of the stressful events that they experience, especially those involving interpersonal relationships.

Two types of psychological factors play an important role in the development of mood disorders: cognitive responses to disappointment and failure and interpersonal skills. Cognitive theories are primarily concerned with the way in which depressed people experience a severe event. Beck's **schema** model places principal emphasis on cognitive distortions or the erroneous ways in which some people think about themselves and their environments. The **hopelessness** model holds that depression is associated with the expectation that desirable events will not occur or aversive events will occur regardless of what the person does. Furthermore, people will be more likely to become depressed if they attribute negative events to internal, stable, global factors.

Interpersonal theories focus on the ways in which individuals respond to people and events in their environments. Depressed people behave in ways that have a negative impact on other people. In this way they contribute to the stressful nature of their social environment. Coping behaviors may help to explain gender differences in the prevalence of unipolar depression. A ruminative style, in which the person's attention is turned inward, may be associated with longer and more severe episodes of depression. Women may be more likely than men to employ a ruminative style of response to the onset of a depressed mood.

Family and twin studies indicate that genetic factors play an important role in the etiology of both unipolar and bipolar mood disorders. They also indicate that genetic factors may play a stronger role in the development of bipolar than unipolar disorders. Genes may contribute to the development of depression directly through an effect on the central nervous system and indirectly by influencing the person's sensitivity to environmental events, such as severe stress.

Neurochemical messengers in the brain also play a role in the regulation of mood and the etiology of mood disorders. Current thinking is focused on serotonin, norepinephrine, and dopamine, although many other neurotransmitter substances may also be involved in depression. Evidence regarding the long-term effects of antidepressant medications points to the importance of sensitivity and density of postsynaptic receptors as well as the interactive effects of multiple neurotransmitter systems.

Several types of psychological and biological treatment have been shown to be effective for mood disorders. Two types of psychotherapy, cognitive therapy and interpersonal therapy, are beneficial for unipolar patients. Three types of antidepressant medication are also useful in the treatment of major depressive disorder: **selective serotonin reuptake inhibitors, tricyclic antidepressants,** and **monoamine oxidase inhibitors.** Medication and psychotherapy are frequently used together. Outcome studies do not consistently favor either psychological or psychopharmacologic treatment.

Three other types of biological treatment are beneficial for specific types of mood disorder. Lithium carbonate and certain anticonvulsant drugs are useful for patients with bipolar mood disorders. Electroconvulsive therapy has been shown to be effective in the treatment of certain depressed patients, and it may be especially useful for patients who are severely suicidal or have failed to respond to other types of treatment. Light therapy seems to be effective for managing seasonal affective disorders.

People commit suicide for many different reasons. Most people who kill themselves are suffering some form of mental disorder, such as depression, substance abuse, or schizophrenia. For some people, suicide represents an escape from unbearable negative emotions or painful self-awareness, which are often the result of frustrated psychological needs. Suicidal ideas are often accompanied by narrow patterns of perception and cognitive activity that make suicide seem like a reasonable solution to an otherwise unbearable dilemma. Serotonin dysfunction and genetic factors seem to contribute to the etiology of suicidal behavior. Social factors that have been studied in relation to suicide include religious affiliation, gun control laws, and media coverage of suicidal deaths. Efforts to prevent suicide include the use of hot lines and crisis centers, as well as the provision of psychotherapy and medication for people who are willing or able to seek professional treatment.

Critical Thinking

1. Women are more likely to become depressed at some point during their lives than men are. Can you think of any explanations for this difference? Some data from epidemiological studies suggest that depression is more prevalent among young adults than among elderly persons. Can you explain this fact?

2. Imagine that you're talking to a psychiatrist. She tells you that depression is nothing more than a biochemical imbalance in the brain because certain medications are effective with depressed people. Is she right? What else do we know about the etiology of depression? Suppose a drug changes a neurotransmitter. Does taking that drug eliminate the cause of depression? How do biological factors (neurotransmitters and neurohormones) interact with stress to cause depression? What is the connection?

3. Contemporary psychological views of depression focus on cognitive reactions to negative experiences as well as interpersonal behaviors. Do these theories owe any debt to Freudian theory? How are they similar to Freudian theory? How are they different?

4. What are the relative risks and benefits of (a) medication and (b) cognitive therapy in the treatment of depression? If you were going to be treated, which would seem more useful to you? Imagine that somebody close to you is severely depressed and is threatening suicide. Medication doesn't work. The psychiatrist recommends electroconvulsive therapy but wants your consent. What would you decide? Why?

6

Anxiety Disorders

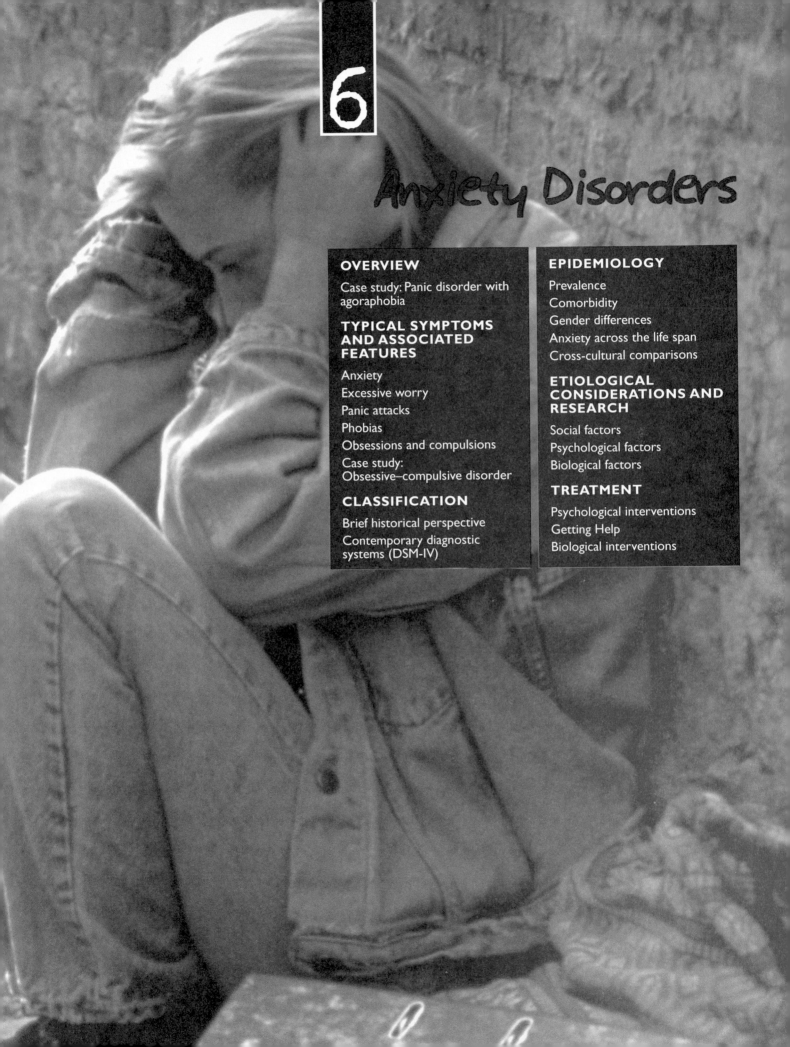

Taken together, the various forms of anxiety disorders—including phobias, obsessions, compulsions, and extreme worry—represent the most common type of abnormal behavior. The National Comorbidity Study found that 17 percent of adults in the U.S. population have at least one type of anxiety disorder in any given year (Kessler et al., 1994). In addition to being relatively common, the anxiety disorders have played a crucial role in the history of psychopathology research and treatment. This influence cuts across theoretical perspectives, from Freud and his followers to learning theorists and proponents of biological hypotheses.

Overview

Anxiety disorders share several important similarities with mood disorders. From a descriptive point of view, both categories are defined in terms of negative emotional responses. Feelings such as guilt, worry, and anger frequently accompany anxiety and depression. There is also considerable overlap between anxiety disorders and depression. Many patients who are anxious are also depressed, and similarly, many patients who are depressed are also anxious.

The close relationship between symptoms of anxiety and those for depression suggests that these disorders may share common etiological features. Stressful life events seem to play a role in the onset of both depression and anxiety. Cognitive factors are also important in both types of problems. From a biological point of view, certain neurotransmitters, such as serotonin, are involved in the etiology of various types of anxiety disorders as well as mood disorders. This chapter employs many of the concepts that you studied in our discussion of mood disorders in an effort to understand the onset and maintenance of anxiety disorders.

The following case study illustrates the kinds of problems that are included under the heading of anxiety disorders. One feature that should become obvious is the overlap among different features of anxiety disorders, including panic, worry, avoidance, and a variety of alarming somatic sensations. This narrative was written by Johanna Schneller (1988), a freelance writer who has been treated for panic disorder. Her vivid description of her own problems highlights the remarkable clarity of insight that is typical of people with anxiety disorders. *Agoraphobia* refers to an exaggerated fear of being in situations from which escape might be difficult, such as being caught in a traffic jam on a bridge or in a tunnel.

case study

Panic Disorder with Agoraphobia

"Three years have passed since my first panic attack struck, but even now I can close my eyes and see the small supermarket where it happened. I can feel the shoppers in their heavy coats jostling me with their plastic baskets, and once again my stomach starts to drop away.

"It was November. I had just moved to New York City and completed a long search for a job and an apartment. The air felt
continued

close in that checkout line, and black fuzz crept into the corners of my vision. Afraid of fainting, I began to count the number of shoppers ahead of me, then the number of purchases they had. The overhead lights seemed to grow brighter. The cash register made pinging sounds that hurt my ears. Even the edges of the checkout counter looked cold and sharp. Suddenly I became nauseated, dizzy. My vertigo intensified, separating me from everyone else in the store, as if I were looking up from underwater. And then I got hot, the kind of hot you feel when the blood seems to rush to your cheeks and drain from your head at the same time.

"My heart was really pounding now, and I felt short of breath, as if wheels were rolling across my chest. I was terrified of what was happening to me. Would I be able to get home? I tried to talk myself down, to convince myself that if I could just stay in line and act as if nothing was happening, these symptoms would go away. Then I decided I wasn't going to faint—I was going to start screaming. The distance to the door looked vast and the seconds were crawling by, but somehow I managed to stay in the checkout line, pay for my bag of groceries and get outside, where I sat on a bench, gulping air. The whole episode had taken ten minutes. I was exhausted.

"At home, I tried to analyze what had happened to me. The experience had been terrifying, but because I felt safe in my kitchen, I tried to laugh the whole thing off—really, it seemed ridiculous, freaking out in a supermarket. I decided it was an isolated incident; I was all right, and I was going to forget it ever happened.

"Two weeks later, as I sat in a movie theater, the uncomfortable buzz began to envelop me again. But the symptoms set in faster this time. I mumbled something to my friends about feeling sick as I clambered over them. It was minutes before I caught my breath, hours before I calmed down completely.

"A month full of scattered attacks passed before they started rolling in like Sunday evenings, at least once a week. I tried to find a pattern: They always hit in crowded places,

places difficult to escape. My whole body felt threatened, primed to run during an attack. Ironically, my attacks were invisible to anyone near me unless they knew what to look for—clenched neck muscles, restless eyes, a shifting from foot to foot—and I was afraid to talk to anyone about them, to perhaps hear something I wouldn't want to hear. What if I had a brain tumor? And I was embarrassed, as if it were my fault that I felt out of control. But then one night I had an attack alone in my bed—the only place I had felt safe. I gave in and called a doctor.

"As the weeks passed and the attacks wore on, I began to think maybe I was crazy. I was having attacks in public so often I became afraid to leave my house. I had one on the subway while traveling to work almost every morning—but, luckily, never panicked on the job. Instead, I usually lost control in situations where I most wanted to relax: on weekend trips, or while visiting friends. I felt responsible for ruining other people's good time. One attack occurred while I was in a tiny boat deep-sea fishing with my family; another hit when I was on a weekend canoe trip with my boyfriend. I also suffered a terrifying attack while on my way to see friends, stuck in traffic, merging into a tunnel near Boston's Logan Airport, with no exit ramp or emergency lane in sight.

"I began declining offers I wanted to accept: all I could think was, "What if I panic in the middle of nowhere?" The times I did force myself to go out, I sat near the doors of restaurants, in aisle seats at movie theaters, near the bathroom at parties. For some reason, I always felt safe in bathrooms, as if whatever happened to me there would at least be easy to clean up.

"On days when I didn't have an actual attack, I could feel one looming like a shadow over my shoulder; this impending panic was almost worse than the real thing. By remembering old episodes, I brought on new ones, and each seemed to pull me closer to a vision I had of my mind snapping cleanly in half, like a stalk of celery." ♛

This case illustrates many of the most important features of a panic attack, as well as the manner in which agoraphobia sometimes develops. Johanna's description of her problems also raises a number of interesting questions, to which we will return later in the chapter. Was it just a coincidence that her first attack occurred shortly after the difficult experience of moving to a new city, starting a new job, and finding a new apartment? Could the stress of those experiences have contributed to the onset of her disorder? Was there a pattern to her attacks? Why did she feel safe in some situations and not in others? She mentions feeling out of control, as if she were responsible for her attacks. Could she really bring on another attack by remembering one from the past?

Typical Symptoms and Associated Features

People with anxiety disorders share a preoccupation with, or persistent avoidance of, thoughts or situations that provoke fear or anxiety. Anxiety disorders frequently have a negative impact on various aspects of a person's life. Johanna found that anxiety and its associated problems constrained

fear An unpleasant emotional reaction experienced in the face of real, immediate danger. It builds quickly in intensity and helps to organize the person's responses to threats from the environment.

anxiety A diffuse emotional reaction that is out of proportion to threats from the environment. Rather than being directed toward the person's present circumstances, anxiety is typically associated with the anticipation of future problems.

both her ability to work and her social relationships. In spite of these problems, most people who knew her probably did not know that she suffered from a mental disorder. In spite of the private terrors that she endured, she was able to carry on most aspects of her life.

In addition to these general considerations, the diagnosis of anxiety disorders depends on several specific types of symptoms, which we discuss in the following sections. We begin by discussing the nature of anxiety, which should be distinguished from more discrete emotional responses, like fear and panic.

Anxiety

Like depression, the term *anxiety* can refer to either a mood or a syndrome. Here, we use the term to refer to a mood. Specific syndromes associated with anxiety disorders are discussed later in the chapter.

Anxious mood is often defined in contrast to the specific emotion of fear, which is more easily understood. **Fear** is experienced in the face of real, immediate danger. It usually builds quickly in intensity and helps organize the person's behavioral responses to threats from the environment (escaping or fighting back). Classic studies of fear among normal adults have often focused on people in combat situations, such as airplane crews during bombing missions over Germany in World War II (Rachman, 1991). In contrast to fear, **anxiety** involves a more general or diffuse emotional reaction—beyond simple fear—that is out of proportion to threats from the environment (Roth & Argyle, 1988). Rather than being directed toward the person's present circumstances, anxiety is associated with the anticipation of future problems.

Anxiety can be adaptive at low levels, because it serves as a signal that the person must prepare for an upcoming event (Costello, 1976). When you think about final exams, for example, you may become somewhat anxious. That emotional response may help to initiate and sustain your efforts to study. In contrast, high levels of anxiety become incapacitating by disrupting concentration and performance.

A pervasively anxious mood is often associated with pessimistic thoughts and feelings ("If something bad happens, I probably won't be able to control it"). The person's attention turns inward, focusing on negative emotions and self-evaluation ("Now I'm so upset that I'll never be able to concentrate during the exam!") rather than on the organization or rehearsal of adaptive responses that might

Anxiety is not associated with an immediate threat from the environment. People with anxiety disorders anticipate future negative events, even in situations that are not actually dangerous.

be useful in coping with negative events. Taken together, these factors can be used to define maladaptive anxiety, or what David Barlow, a psychologist at Boston University, has called *anxious apprehension*, which consists of (1) high levels of diffuse negative emotion, (2) a sense of uncontrollability, and (3) a shift in attention to a primary self-focus or a state of self-preoccupation (Barlow, 1991).

Excessive Worry

Worrying is a cognitive activity that is associated with anxiety. In recent years psychologists have studied this phenomenon carefully because they consider it to be critical in the subclassification of anxiety disorders (DSM-IV). **Worry** can be defined as a relatively uncontrollable sequence of negative, emotional thoughts and images that are concerned with possible future threats or danger. This sequence of worrisome thoughts is usually self-initiated or provoked by a specific experience or ongoing difficulties in the person's daily life. When excessive worriers are asked to describe their thoughts, they emphasize the predominance of verbal, linguistic material rather than images (Borkovec, 1994). In other words, worriers are preoccupied with "self-talk" rather than unpleasant visual images.

Because everyone worries at least a little bit, you might wonder whether it is possible to distinguish between pathological and normal worry. The answer is yes. The distinction hinges in part on quantity—how often the person worries and about how many different topics the person worries. But it also depends on the quality of worrisome thought. Excessive worriers are more likely than other people to report that the content of their thoughts is negative, that they have less control over the content and direction of their thoughts, and that in comparison to other adults, their worries are less realistic (Craske et al., 1989). This evidence suggests that the crucial features of pathological worrying may be lack of control and negative affect rather than simply the anticipation of future events.

Panic Attacks

A **panic attack** is a sudden, overwhelming experience of terror or fright, like the attack that was experienced by Johanna as she waited in the checkout line. Whereas anxiety involves a blend of several negative emotions, panic is more focused. Some clinicians think of panic as a normal fear response that is triggered at an inappropriate time (Barlow, Brown, & Craske, 1994). In that sense, panic is a "false alarm." Descriptively, panic can be distinguished from anxiety in two other respects: It is more intense, and it has a sudden onset.

Panic attacks are defined largely in terms of a list of somatic or physical sensations, ranging from heart palpitations, sweating, and trembling to nausea, dizziness, and chills. Table 6–1 lists the DSM-IV criteria for a panic attack. A person must experience at least 4 of these 13 symptoms in order for the experience to qualify as a full-blown panic attack. The symptoms must develop suddenly and reach a peak intensity within 10 minutes. The actual numbers and combinations of panic symptoms vary from one person to the next, and they may also change over time within the same person.

People undergoing a panic attack also report a number of cognitive symptoms. They may feel as though they are about to die, lose control, or go crazy. Some clinicians believe that the misinterpretation of bodily sensations lies at the core of panic disorder. Patients may interpret heart palpitations as evidence of an impending heart attack, or racing thoughts as evidence that they are about to lose their minds.

Panic attacks are further described in terms of the situations in which they occur, as well as the person's expectations about their occurrence. An attack is said to be situationally bound, or *cued*, if it occurs only in the presence of a particular stimulus. For example, someone who is afraid of public speaking might have a cued panic attack if forced to give a speech in front of a large group of people. Unexpected panic attacks, like Johanna's experience in the grocery checkout line, appear without any warning or expectation, as if "out of the blue."

Phobias

In contrast to both diffuse anxiety, which represents a blend of negative emotions, and panic attacks, which are frequently unexpected, **phobias** are persistent, irrational, narrowly defined fears

worry A relatively uncontrollable sequence of negative, emotional thoughts and images that are concerned with possible future threats or danger.

panic attack A sudden, overwhelming experience of terror or fright. While anxiety involves a blend of several negative emotions, panic is more focused.

phobia A persistent and irrational narrowly defined fear that is associated with a specific object or situation.

agoraphobia An exaggerated fear of being in situations from which escape might be difficult. Literally means "fear of the marketplace," and is sometimes described as fear of public spaces.

TABLE 6–1

Diagnostic Criteria for Panic Attack in DSM-IV

A DISCRETE PERIOD OF INTENSE FEAR OR DISCOMFORT, IN WHICH FOUR (OR MORE) OF THE FOLLOWING SYMPTOMS DEVELOPED ABRUPTLY AND REACHED A PEAK WITHIN 10 MINUTES:

1. Palpitations, pounding heart, or accelerated heart rate
2. Sweating
3. Trembling or shaking
4. Sensations of shortness of breath or smothering
5. Feeling of choking
6. Chest pain or discomfort
7. Nausea or abdominal distress
8. Feeling dizzy, unsteady, light-headed, or faint
9. Derealization (feelings of unreality) or depersonalization (being detached from oneself)
10. Fear of losing control or going crazy
11. Fear of dying
12. Paresthesias (numbness or tingling sensations)
13. Chills or hot flushes

that are associated with a specific object or situation. Avoidance is an important component of the definition of phobias. A fear is not considered phobic unless the person avoids contact with the source of the fear or experiences intense anxiety in the presence of the stimulus. Phobias are also irrational or unreasonable. Avoiding only snakes that are poisonous, or only guns that are loaded, would not be considered phobic.

The most straightforward type of phobia involves fear of specific objects or situations. Different types of specific phobias have traditionally been named according to the Greek words for these objects. Examples of typical specific phobias include fear of heights (acrophobia); fear of enclosed spaces (claustrophobia); fear of small animals (zoophobia); fear of blood or injury; and fear of traveling on airplanes.

Some people experience marked fear when they are forced to engage in certain activities, such as public speaking, initiating a conversation, eating in restaurants, or using public rest rooms, which might involve being observed or evaluated by other people (Liebowitz et al., 1985). Attempts to avoid these feared situations cause serious impairment in the person's social and occupational activities.

AGORAPHOBIA

The most complex and incapacitating form of phobic disorder is known as **agoraphobia,** which literally means "fear of the marketplace (or places of assembly)" and is usually described as fear of public spaces. The case of Johanna provides a brief description of the types of problems experienced by a person suffering from agoraphobia. The fear usually becomes more intense as the distance between the person and his or her familiar surroundings increases, or as avenues of escape are closed off. In that sense, agoraphobia is somewhat different from the other phobias because it is not so much a fear of being close to one specific object or situation (for example, animals, public speaking) as it is of being separated from signals associated with safety.

Typical situations that cause problems include crowded streets and shops, enclosed places like theaters and churches, traveling on public transportation, and driving an automobile on bridges, in tunnels, or on crowded expressways. In any of these

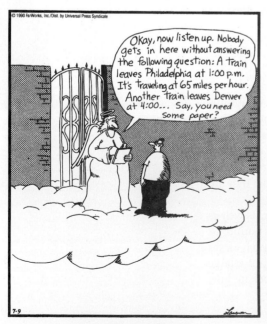

THE FAR SIDE   By GARY LARSON

Math phobic's nightmare

People with agoraphobia are afraid of crowded places from which they might not be able to escape. They also frequently experience panic attacks that are not cued by particular environmental circumstances.

obsession   A repetitive, unwanted, intrusive cognitive event that may take the form of thoughts, images, or impulses. Obsessions intrude suddenly into consciousness and lead to an increase in subjective anxiety.

compulsion   A repetitive, ritualistic behavior that is aimed at the reduction of anxiety and distress or the prevention of some dreaded event. Compulsions are considered by the person to be senseless or irrational. The person feels compelled to perform the compulsion; he or she attempts to resist but cannot.

situations, the presence of a trusted friend may help the person with agoraphobia feel more comfortable. In the most extreme form of the disorder, agoraphobic patients are unable to venture away from their own homes.

The uncomfortable sensations experienced by people with agoraphobia are similar to those that have already been described for other anxiety disorders. People with agoraphobia are frequently afraid that they will experience an "attack" of these symptoms that will be either incapacitating or embarrassing, and that help will not be available to them. Many patients report that they are afraid of becoming dizzy, fainting, losing bladder or bowel control, or having heart problems. In some cases, previous experiences of this sort may have triggered persistent fear of repeated episodes.

Some clinicians have suggested that "fear of fear" is the central feature of agoraphobia (e.g., Goldstein & Chambless, 1978; Klein, 1981). The crucial event that triggers subsequent fears is often a terrifying, unexpected panic attack. Following such an experience, the person may become acutely aware of all internal bodily sensations that may signal the onset of another attack.

Obsessions and Compulsions

Obsessions are repetitive, unwanted, intrusive cognitive events that may take the form of thoughts or images or impulses. They intrude suddenly into consciousness and lead to an increase in subjective anxiety. Obsessive thinking can be distinguished from worry in two primary ways: (1) obsessions are usually experienced as coming from "out of the blue," whereas worries are often triggered by problems in everyday living; and (2) the content of obsessions most often involves themes that are perceived as being socially unacceptable or horrific, such as sex, violence, and disease/contamination, whereas the content of worries tends to center around more acceptable, commonplace concerns, such as money and work (Turner, Beidel, & Stanley, 1992).

Compulsions are repetitive behaviors or mental acts that are used to reduce anxiety. These actions are considered by the person who performs them to be senseless or irrational. The person attempts to resist performing the compulsion but cannot. The following case study illustrates many of the most common features of obsessions and compulsions.

case study

Obsessive–Compulsive Disorder

Ed, a 38-year-old lawyer, lived with his wife, Phyllis. Most aspects of Ed's life were going well, except for the anxiety-provoking thoughts that lurked beneath his relatively easygoing exterior. One focus of Ed's anxiety was handwriting. He became so tense that his eyes hurt whenever he was forced to write. Feeling exhausted and overwhelmed, Ed avoided writing whenever possible. The problem seemed utterly ridiculous to him, but he couldn't rid himself of his obsessive thoughts.

Sinister meanings had somehow become linked in Ed's imagination to the way in which letters and numbers were formed. The worst letters were *P* and *T* (the first letters in "Phyllis" and in "Tim," his younger brother's name). "Improperly" formed letters reminded Ed of violent acts, especially decapitation and strangulation. If the parts of a letter, such as the two lines in the letter *T*, were not connected, an image of a head that was not attached to its body might pop into his mind. Closed loops reminded him of suffocation, like a person whose throat had been clamped shut. These images were associated with people whose names began with the malformed letter. As a result of these concerns, Ed's handwriting had become extremely awkward and difficult to read.

These writing problems made it very difficult for Ed to complete his work, especially when he was under time pressure. In one particularly upsetting incident, Ed was responsible for completing an important official form that had to be mailed that day. He came to a section in which he needed to write a capital *P* and became concerned that he hadn't done it properly. The loop seemed to be closed, which meant that Phyllis might be strangled! He tore up the first copy and filled it out again. When it was finally done to his satisfaction, Ed sealed the form in an envelope and put it in the box for outgoing mail. After returning to his desk, he was suddenly overwhelmed by the feeling that he had indeed made a mistake with that *P*. If he allowed the form to be mailed, the evil image would be associated forever with his wife. Consumed by fear, Ed rushed back to the mailbox, tore up the envelope, and started a new form. Twenty minutes later, he had the form filled out and back in the mailbox. Then the cycle repeated itself. Each time, Ed became more distraught and frustrated, until he eventually felt that he was going to lose his mind.

In addition to his problems with writing, Ed was also afraid of axes. He would not touch an ax, or even get close to one. Any situation in which he could possibly encounter an ax made him extremely uncomfortable. He refused to shop in hardware stores because they sell axes, and he would not visit museums because their exhibits often contain artifacts such as medieval armor. His fear of axes was quite specific. Ed wasn't afraid of knives, guns, or swords.

One frightening experience seemed to trigger the pervasive anxiety that had plagued Ed for 20 years. When he was 17 years old, some friends persuaded Ed to try smoking marijuana. They told him that it would make him feel high—relaxed, sociable, and perhaps a bit giddy. Unfortunately, Ed didn't react to the drug in the same way that the others had. The physical effects seemed to be the same, but his psychological reaction was entirely different. After sharing two joints with his friends, Ed began to feel light-headed. Then things around him began to seem unreal, as though he were watching himself and his friends in a movie. The intensity of these feelings escalated rapidly, and panic took over. Frightening thoughts raced through his head. Was he losing his mind? When would it stop? This experience lasted about 2 hours.

The marijuana incident had an immediate and lasting impact. Ed became preoccupied with a fear of accidentally ingesting any kind of mind-altering drug, especially LSD. Every spot on his skin or clothing seemed as though it might be a microscopic quantity of this hallucinogen. He felt compelled to clean his hands and clothes repeatedly to avoid contamination. Intellectually, Ed knew that these concerns were silly. How could a tiny spot on his hand be LSD? It didn't make any sense, but he couldn't keep the thought out of his mind.

The most horrifying aspect of the drug experience was the sensation of being totally out of control of his actions and emotions. The fear of returning to that state haunted Ed. He struggled to resist impulses that he had never noticed before, such as the temptation to shout obscenities out loud in church. He also began to worry that he might hurt his younger brother. He resisted the impulses with all his might. He never acted on them, but they pervaded his consciousness and absorbed his mental energy.

The thoughts were so persistent and unshakable that Ed began to wonder if he might, in fact, be a pathological killer. Could he be as deranged and evil as Richard Speck, who had brutally murdered eight nurses in a Chicago apartment building in 1966? Ed spent many hours reading articles about Speck and other mass murderers. The number 8 came to have special meaning to him because of the number of Speck's victims. Over time, Ed's fears and worries became focused on numbers and letters. The violent images and impulses became a less prominent part of his everyday life, but the writing difficulties escalated proportionately. ♦

It is not just the intrusive quality of the thought but also the unwanted nature of the thought that makes it an obsession. Some scientists and artists, for example, have reported experiencing intrusive thoughts or inspirational ideas that appear in an unexpected, involuntary way, but these thoughts are not unwanted. Obsessions are unwelcome, anxiety-provoking thoughts. In spite of the recognition that these thoughts do not make sense, the person with full-blown obsessions is unable to ignore or dismiss them.

Examples of typical obsessive thoughts include the following: "Did I kill the old lady?" "Christ was a bastard!" "Am I a sexual pervert?" Examples of obsessive impulses include "I might expose my genitals in public," "I am about to shout obscenities in public," "I feel I might strangle a child." Obsessional images might include mutilated corpses, decomposing fetuses, or a family member being involved in a serious car accident. Although obsessive impulses are accompanied by a compelling sense of reality, obsessive people seldom act upon these impulses.

Ed's constricted style of forming letters and his habitual pattern of going back to check and correct his writing illustrate the way in which compulsions are used to reduce anxiety. If he did not engage in these ritualistic behaviors, he would become extremely uncomfortable. His concern about someone being strangled or decapitated if the letters were not properly formed was not delusional, because he readily acknowledged that this was a "silly" idea. Nevertheless, he couldn't shake the obsessive idea that some dreadful event would occur if he was not excruciatingly careful about his writing. This paradox is extremely frustrating to obsessive–compulsive patients, and it is one of the most common and interesting aspects of the disorder.

Although some clinicians have argued that compulsive rituals are associated with a complete loss of voluntary control, it is more accurate to view the problem in terms of *diminished control*. For example, Ed could occasionally manage to resist the urge to write in his compulsive style. The behavior was not totally automatic. But whenever he did not engage in this ritualistic behavior, his subjective level of distress increased dramatically, and within a short period of time he returned to the compulsive writing style.

The two most common forms of compulsive behavior are cleaning and checking. Compulsive cleaning is often associated with an irrational fear of contamination, and in that respect it bears a strong resemblance to certain phobias (Rachman & Hodgson, 1980). There are passive as well as active features of compulsive cleaning. Compulsive cleaners go out of their way to avoid contact with dirt, germs, and other sources of contamination. Then, when they believe that they have come into contact with a source of contamination, they engage in ritualistic cleaning behavior, such as washing their hands, taking showers, cleaning kitchen counters, and so on. These rituals typically involve a large number of repetitions. Some people may wash their hands 50 times a day.

Compulsive checking frequently represents an attempt to ensure the person's safety or the safety and health of a friend or family member. The person checks things over and over again in an attempt to prevent the occurrence of an imagined, unpleasant, or disastrous event (for example, accidents or sickness).

Classification

To understand the way in which anxiety disorders are currently classified, we must briefly consider the history of these concepts. This general set of problems has been the topic of considerable diagnostic controversy throughout the twentieth century.

Brief Historical Perspective

Anxiety and abnormal fears did not play a prominent role in the psychiatric classification systems that began to emerge in Europe during the second half of the nineteenth century (see Chapter 4). Anxiety disorders were probably left out of these descriptions because the authors were primarily superintendents of large asylums. Their patients were people who were psychotic or so disorganized

neurosis A traditional term, often associated with psychoanalytic theory, that describes maladaptive behavior resulting from the ego's failure to control anxiety resulting from unconscious conflicts. In DSM-I and DSM-II, neurotic disorders were defined as those in which anxiety is the chief characteristic. Anxiety presumably could be felt and expressed directly, or it could be controlled unconsciously by defense mechanisms.

that they could no longer reside in the larger community (Jablensky, 1985; Klerman, 1990a). People with anxiety problems seldom came to the attention of psychiatrists during the nineteenth century because very few cases of anxiety disorder require institutionalization.

Freud and his followers were responsible for some of the first extensive clinical descriptions of pathological anxiety states. Working primarily with patients who were not hospitalized, Freud had an opportunity to treat and study a variety of anxiety-related problems. He described cases of phobia, generalized anxiety, and obsessive–compulsive behavior. His approach emphasized etiological similarities among the various manifestations of anxiety disorders. The form of specific symptoms (a phobia as compared to a compulsion) was considered to be less important than the underlying causes, which were presumably similar.

PSYCHOANALYTIC THEORY

Freud's psychological explanations for the origins of anxiety disorders have been extremely influential throughout the twentieth century. Freud focused primarily on the importance of mental conflicts and innate biological impulses (primarily sexual and aggressive instincts) as the sources of anxiety (see Chapter 2). This perspective played a central role in the way that anxiety disorders were classified in early versions of the DSM. They were grouped with several other types of problems under the general heading of **neurosis,** a term used to describe persistent emotional disturbances, such as anxiety and depression, in which the person is aware of the nature of the problem. Neurotic disorders are distinguished from psychotic disorders, in which the person is often out of touch with reality and unaware of the nature of his or her problems. According to Freud, all the neuroses share a common etiological process.

The basic outline of Freud's theory of anxiety hinges on the notion that the person's ego can experience a small amount of anxiety as a *signal* indicating that an instinctual impulse that has previously been associated with punishment and disapproval is about to be acted on. This usually means that the person is about to do something aggressive or sexual that is considered inappropriate. *Signal anxiety* triggers the use of ego defenses—primarily repression—that prevent conscious recognition of the forbidden impulse, inhibit its expression, and thereby reduce the person's anxiety. When the system works as it should, anxiety is adaptive, and the person's behavior is regulated to conform with social expectations.

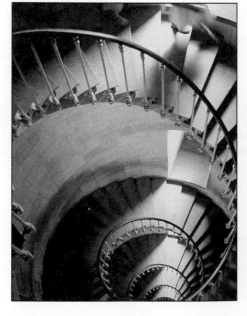

Specific phobias are irrational fears associated with specific situations that the person avoids. Acrophobia is the name given to fear of heights.

Unfortunately, people can still experience pathological levels of anxiety if the system is overwhelmed. Traumatic events or circumstances can lead to extreme levels of free-floating anxiety. The ego is then forced to resort to additional defensive maneuvers that can produce symptoms such as phobias and compulsions. The specific form of overt symptoms is determined by the defense mechanisms that are employed by the ego, but the underlying process is presumably the same across all of the anxiety neuroses.

Consider, for example, a Freudian explanation for the etiology of Ed's obsessive–compulsive disorder. According to this model, the instinctual drive that is most problematic in OCD is aggression. Problems that Ed encountered during early childhood must have left him with serious difficulties in dealing with aggressive impulses, which are coupled with resentment harbored toward his younger brother, Tim. Violent aggressive impulses are unacceptable to the ego, and they have to be dealt with using reaction formation, which is presumably the primary defense in obsessive–compulsive disorder. Rather than attempting to harm his brother (decapitating him or strangling him, as in his violent images), Ed was obliged to spend his time correcting printing errors in order to "protect" Tim or ensure that Tim's name is not forever associated with the image of a violent act. The compulsive rituals are viewed as the product of the defense mechanism that was unconsciously employed to fend off anxiety associated with aggression.

Freud's conceptual model for the anxiety neuroses incorporated several important features, including the importance of biologically based impulses, learning experiences based on interactions with other people, and cognitive (or intrapsychic) events that play an important role in mediating between current and past experience. It was firmly grounded in Freud's observations of his own patients' experiences. Although it served as a useful stimulus to future clinicians and identified many important factors in the etiology of anxiety disorders, his model suffered from a number of weaknesses. Perhaps the major problem was that of measurement. Because Freud's concepts were not linked directly to observable behaviors, his theory of anxiety could not be tested empirically (outside of case studies).

Contemporary Diagnostic Systems (DSM-IV)

The DSM-IV (APA, 1994) approach to classifying anxiety disorders recognizes several specific subtypes. It includes panic disorder, three types of phobic disorders, obsessive–compulsive disorder, and generalized anxiety disorder, as well as posttraumatic stress disorder (PTSD) and acute stress disorder. (The last two conditions are discussed in Chapter 7.)

To meet the diagnostic criteria for panic disorder, a person must experience recurrent, *unexpected* panic attacks. At least one of the attacks must have been followed by a period of 1 month or more in which the person has either persistent concern about having additional attacks, worry about the implications of the attack or its consequences, or a significant change in behavior related to the attacks. Panic disorder is divided into two subtypes, depending on the presence or absence of agoraphobia.

DSM-IV defines agoraphobia in terms of anxiety about being in situations from which escape might be either difficult or embarrassing. This approach is based on the view that agoraphobia is typically a complication that follows upon the experience of panic attacks (Frances, First, & Pincus, 1995). In order to meet the DSM-IV criteria, the person must either avoid agoraphobic situations, such as traveling away from his or her own home; endure the experience with great distress; or insist on being accompanied by another person who can provide some comfort or security. In most cases, the person avoids a wide variety of situations rather than just one specific type of situation.

People who fit this description of agoraphobia without meeting the criteria for panic disorder would be assigned a diagnosis of agoraphobia without history of panic disorder. This category has been the topic of considerable debate. Recent analyses of data from the Epidemiologic Catchment Area study suggest that agoraphobia seldom occurs without panic attacks (Horwath et al., 1993), but the National Comorbidity Study results indicated a 12-month prevalence of 2.8 percent (men and women combined) for this disorder. These discrepancies will undoubtedly be addressed in future research studies.

A *specific phobia* is defined in DSM-IV as "a marked and persistent fear that is excessive or unreasonable, cued by the presence or anticipation of a specific object or situation." Exposure to the phobic stimulus must be followed by an immediate fear response. Furthermore, the person must appreciate the fact that the fear is excessive or unreasonable, and the person must avoid the phobic situation. DSM-IV also provides a severity threshold: The avoidance or distress associated with the phobia must interfere significantly with the person's normal activities or relationships with others.

The DSM-IV definition of **social phobia** is almost identical to that for specific phobia, but it includes the additional element of performance. A person with a social phobia is afraid of (and avoids) social situations. These situations fall into two broad headings: doing something in front of unfamiliar people (performance anxiety) and interpersonal interactions (such as dating and parties). Fear of being humiliated or embarrassed presumably lies at the heart of the person's discomfort. Some people have a circumscribed form of social phobia that is focused on one particular type of situation. Examples include giving a speech, playing a musical instrument, urinating in a public rest room, or eating in a restaurant. In other cases, the fear is more generalized, and the person is intensely anxious in almost any situation that involves social interaction. This type of person might be described as being extremely shy. The extensive overlap between generalized social phobia and avoidant personality disorder (see Chapter 9) has created some confusion and has been the topic of numerous research studies (Tran & Chambless, 1995).

Generalized anxiety disorder (GAD) is defined in terms of excessive anxiety and worry that the person finds difficult to control and that lead to significant distress or impairment in occupational or social functioning. The worry must occur more days than not for a period of at least 6 months, and it must be about a number of different events or activities. In order to distinguish GAD from other forms of anxiety disorder, DSM-IV notes that the person's worries should not be focused on

social phobia   A type of phobic disorder in which the person is persistently fearful of social situations that might expose him or her to scrutiny by others, such as fear of public speaking.

generalized anxiety disorder   One of the anxiety disorders, which is characterized by excessive and uncontrollable worry about a number of events or activities (such as work or school performance) and associated with symptoms of arousal (such as restlessness, muscle tension, and sleep disturbance).

Donald Klein, a psychiatrist at Columbia University, suggested that panic disorder should be classified separately from generalized anxiety disorder on the basis of his clinical experience, which indicated that panic attacks could be treated successfully with medication.

Social phobias involve a performance element. The person is afraid of being embarrassed in front of other people. Singer Carly Simon has suffered from performance anxiety throughout her successful career.

having a panic attack (as in panic disorder), being embarrassed in public (as in social phobia), or being contaminated (as in obsessive–compulsive disorder). Finally, the person's worries and "free-floating anxiety" must be accompanied by at least three of the following symptoms: (1) restlessness or feeling keyed up or on edge, (2) being easily fatigued, (3) difficulty concentrating or mind going blank, (4) irritability, (5) muscle tension, and (6) sleep disturbance.

Generalized anxiety disorder remains one of the most controversial anxiety disorders for several reasons. The diagnostic reliability of GAD is often substantially lower than that observed for other types of anxiety disorder (DiNardo et al., 1993; Wittchen, Kessler, Zhao, & Abelson, 1995). The validity of GAD as a separate diagnostic category is therefore open to serious question.

DSM-IV defines *obsessive–compulsive disorder* in terms of the presence of either obsessions or compulsions. Most people who meet the criteria for this disorder actually exhibit both of these symptoms. The person must recognize that the obsessions or compulsions are excessive or unreasonable. Obsessions are described as "recurrent and persistent thoughts, impulses, or images that are experienced, at some time during the disturbance, as intrusive and inappropriate, and cause marked anxiety or distress." The diagnostic manual specifies further that these thoughts must not be simply excessive worries about real problems. Intrusive thoughts about overdue bills, for example, would not qualify as obsessions. The DSM-IV definition also requires that the person must attempt to ignore, suppress, or neutralize the unwanted thoughts or impulses. Compulsions are defined as "repetitive behaviors or mental acts that the person feels driven to perform in response to an obsession, or according to rules that must be applied rigidly." These behaviors or mental acts must be aimed at reducing or avoiding distress or anxiety.

The line of demarcation between compulsive rituals and normal behavior is often difficult to define. How many times should a person wash her hands in a day? How long should a shower last? Is it reasonable to check more than one time to be sure that the door is locked or the alarm clock is set? DSM-IV has established an arbitrary threshold that holds that rituals become compulsive if they cause marked distress, take more than an hour per day to perform, or interfere with normal occupational and social functioning.

Epidemiology

Some epidemiological studies focus exclusively on treated cases of a disorder, but that strategy can provide a distorted view of the distribution of the disorder within the general population. Recent evidence indicates that only about 25 percent of people who qualify for a diagnosis of anxiety disorder ever seek psychological treatment. Therefore our estimates of the frequency and severity of these problems must be based on community surveys.

Prevalence

The National Comorbidity Survey (NCS), which included approximately 8,000 people aged 15 to 54 throughout the United States, found that anxiety disorders are more common than any other form of mental disorder (Kessler et al., 1994). The same conclusion had been reached previously in the ECA study (see Table 1–3). Specific phobias are the most common type of anxiety disorder, with a 1-year prevalence of about 9 percent of the adult population (men and women combined). Social phobia is almost as common, with a 1-year prevalence of 8 percent. Agoraphobia without panic disorder and GAD both affect approximately 3 percent of the population, and 2 percent of adults meet the criteria for panic disorder in any given year. Obsessive–compulsive disorder affects another 2 percent of the population.

Comorbidity

The symptoms of various anxiety disorders overlap considerably. Many people who experience panic attacks develop phobic avoidance, and many people with obsessive thoughts would also be considered chronic worriers. One study found that 50 percent of people who met the criteria for one anxiety disorder also met the criteria for at least one other form of anxiety disorder or mood disorder (Brown & Barlow, 1992). The highest rates of comorbidity were found for generalized anxiety disorder (82 percent) and severe cases of panic disorder with agoraphobia (72 percent). The lowest rate was found for cases of specific phobia; only 20 percent of the people with this diagnosis met the criteria for an additional type of anxiety disorder. The most common secondary diagnosis was generalized anxiety disorder (23 percent of the cases). Given this pattern of results, it is not surprising that some clinical scientists have argued that the distinction between GAD and other anxiety disorders is not particularly clear (Andrews, 1996).

Given the emotional bases of both anxiety and depression, it is not surprising that considerable overlap also exists between anxiety disorders and mood disorders. Sixty-one percent of the people who received a primary diagnosis of major depression also qualified for a secondary diagnosis of some type of anxiety disorder (Brown, 1996). This extensive overlap raises interesting questions about the relation between these general diagnostic categories. Do people who meet the criteria for both depression and an anxiety disorder really suffer from two distinct syndromes? Or should we think about the existence of three types of disorder: "pure" anxiety disorders, "pure" mood disorders, and a third type of disorder that represents a mixture of anxiety and depression? Reasonable arguments have been made on both sides of this debate, which remains unresolved (Reich et al., 1993).

Substance dependence is another problem that is frequently associated with anxiety disorders. In one sample of alcoholic patients, Chambless and her colleagues found that 40 percent would have met diagnostic criteria for at least one anxiety disorder at some point during their lives (Chambless et al., 1987). In situations such as these, questions of cause and effect are not clear. Did the person use alcohol in an attempt to control abnormal anxiety, or did the person become anxious after drinking excessively? It can work both ways. Chambless concluded that, in most cases, anxiety was the more long-standing problem. This is especially true for phobic disorders and panic disorder with agoraphobia (Kushner, Sher, & Beitman, 1990).

Gender Differences

There are significant gender differences in several types of anxiety disorders. Pertinent data from the National Comorbidity Survey are summarized in Figure 6–1. The gender difference is particularly large for specific phobias, where women are 3 times as likely as men to experience the disorder. Women are about twice as likely as men to experience panic disorder, agoraphobia (without panic disorder), and generalized anxiety disorder. Social phobia is also more common among women than among men, but the difference is not as striking as it is for other types of phobia. The only type of anxiety disorder for which there does not appear to be a significant gender difference is OCD (Karno & Golding, 1991).

The significant gender differences in panic disorder, generalized anxiety disorder, specific phobias, and social phobias must be interpreted in the light of etiological theories, which are considered in the next section. Several explanations remain plausible. Psychological speculation has focused on such factors as gender differences in child-rearing practices or differences in the way in which men and women respond to stressful life events (Cameron & Hill, 1989). Gender differences in hormone functions or neurotransmitter activities in the brain may also be responsible (Yonkers & Gurguis, 1995).

Anxiety Across the Life Span

Data from the ECA study indicate that the prevalence of anxiety disorders is lower among elderly men and women than it is among people in other age groups. Some scientists speculate that something about the aging process may reduce the probability that stressful or threatening life events will lead to the onset of an anxiety disorder (Flint, 1994; Gurian & Goisman, 1993).

Most elderly people with an anxiety disorder have had the symptoms for many years. It is relatively unusual for a person to develop a new case of panic disorder, specific phobia, social phobia, or obsessive–compulsive disorder at an advanced age. The only type of anxiety disorder that

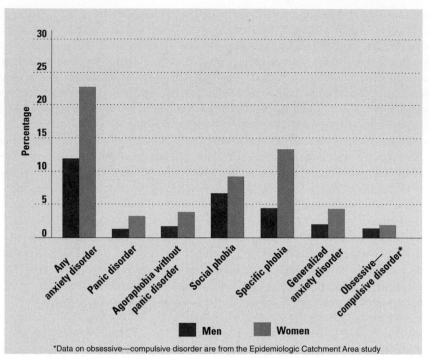

Figure 6–1 Gender Differences in the 12-Month Prevalence of Anxiety Disorders

*Data on obsessive–compulsive disorder are from the Epidemiologic Catchment Area study (Karno & Golding, 1991) because the National Comorbidity Survey did not ask about obsessions and compulsions.
Source: R. C. Kessler, K. A. McGonagle, S. Zhao, C. B. Nelson, M. Hughes, S. Eshleman, H. Wittchen, & K. S. Kendler, 1994; Lifetime and 12-month prevalence of DSM-III-R psychiatric disorders in the United States: Results from the National Cormorbidity Survey, *Archives of General Psychiatry, 51,* 8–19.

begins with any noticeable frequency in late life is agoraphobia, and this is also subject to question (Flint, 1994). A frail elderly person who falls down on the street may become afraid to leave home alone, but this may be a reasonable concern rather than a symptom of agoraphobia. For reasons such as these, the diagnosis of anxiety disorders must be done with extra caution in elderly men and women.

Cross-Cultural Comparisons

Peoples in many kinds of cultures experience anxiety disorders. Population surveys suggest that between 1 and 4 people out of 100 experience various types of anxiety disorders in different cultures (Good & Kleinman, 1985a). The focus of typical anxiety complaints can vary dramatically across cultural boundaries, however. People in Western societies often experience anxiety in relation to their work performance, whereas in other societies people may be more concerned with family issues or religious experiences. In the Yoruba culture of Nigeria, for example, anxiety is frequently associated with fertility and the health of family members.

Anxiety disorders have been observed in preliterate as well as Westernized cultures. Of course, the same descriptive and diagnostic terms are not used in every culture, but the basic psychological phenomena appear to be similar. Cultural anthropologists have recognized many different culture-bound syndromes that, in some cases, bear striking resemblance to anxiety disorders listed in DSM-IV.

In the Cross-National Collaborative Panic Study (1992), panic disorder occurred in all the countries that were included. Nevertheless, some important differences were found among panic patients from different regions. Choking or smothering and fear of dying were more common among patients from southern countries in both the Americas and in Europe. Phobic avoidance was much more common among panic patients seen at clinics in the United States and Canada—9 out of every 10—compared to patients seen at clinics in Latin American countries.

Etiological Considerations and Research

Current theories regarding the etiology of anxiety disorders often focus on the evolutionary significance of anxiety and fear. These emotional response systems are clearly adaptive in many situations. They mobilize responses that help the person survive in the face of both immediate dangers and long-range threats. Anxiety disorders can be viewed as problems that arise in the regulation of these response systems (Barlow, 1988; Marks & Nesse, 1994). In order to understand the etiology of anxiety disorders, we must consider a variety of psychological and biological systems that have evolved for the purpose of triggering and controlling these alarm responses.

Should we expect to find unique etiological pathways associated with each of the types of anxiety disorder listed in DSM-IV? This seems unlikely, particularly in light of the extensive amount of overlap among the various subtypes. Should we expect that all the different types of anxiety disorders are produced by the same causes? This also seems unlikely. Isaac Marks and Randolph Nesse (1994) have proposed a broad evolutionary perspective for the etiology of anxiety disorders that suggests a middle ground between these two extremes. They suggest that generalized forms of anxiety probably evolved to help the person prepare for threats that could not be identified clearly. More specific forms of anxiety and fear probably evolved to provide more effective responses to certain types of danger. For example, fear of heights is associated with a freezing of muscles rather than running away, which could lead to a fall. Social threats are more likely to provoke responses such as shyness and embarrassment that may increase acceptance by other people by making the individual seem less threatening. Each type of anxiety disorder can be viewed as a mechanism that has evolved to deal with a particular kind of danger. This model leads us to expect that the etiological pathways leading to various forms of anxiety disorders may be partially distinct but not completely independent.

Social Factors

Stressful life events, particularly those involving danger and interpersonal conflict, can trigger the onset of certain types of anxiety disorders. Various aspects of parent–child relationships may leave some people more vulnerable to the development of anxiety disorders when they become adults. Taken together, the evidence bearing on these issues helps explain the relationship between, and the overlap among, anxiety disorders and mood disorders.

STRESSFUL LIFE EVENTS
Common sense might suggest that people who experience high stress levels are likely to develop negative emotional reactions. In Chapter 5 we reviewed the literature concerning stressful life events and depression. Several investigations suggest that stressful life events can influence the onset of anxiety disorders as well as depression (Blazer, Hughes, & George, 1987; Monroe & Wade, 1988).

Why do some negative life events lead to depression while others lead to anxiety? The nature of the event may be an important factor in determining the type of mental disorder that appears. This possibility was initially reported by Finlay-Jones and Brown (1981), who interviewed women attending a general medical clinic. This group included women who were depressed, women with anxiety disorders, and women who qualified for a dual diagnosis of anxiety and depression.

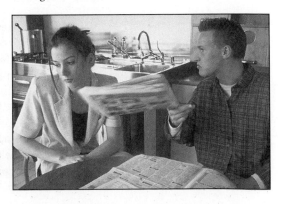

Negative life events can precipitate the appearance of anxiety disorders. The onset of agoraphobia is sometimes preceded by serious interpersonal conflicts, including marital discord.

The women with anxiety symptoms were much more likely to have experienced an event involving *danger* (lack of security), whereas the women who were depressed were more likely to have experienced a severe *loss* (lack of hope). Mixed cases frequently reported both types of events. This pattern of results has also been found in more recent investigations (Brown, 1993).

Serious interpersonal conflicts seem to be especially common prior to the onset of agoraphobia. Consider, for example, the following list of life events, which were all reported with greater frequency by patients being treated for agoraphobia when they were compared to people visiting a general practice physician (Franklin & Andrews, 1989):

* Increase in serious arguments with partner or parents
* Serious problems with a close friend, neighbor, or relative
* Broke off a steady relationship

Each of these events was at least 4 times more common in the agoraphobic group. The relatively high frequency of stressful life events was accompanied by a rather remarkable lack of insight on the part of the agoraphobic patients. When they were asked about their understanding of the development of their disorder, 90 percent said that they found the onset of agoraphobic symptoms "totally baffling and incomprehensible."

CHILDHOOD ADVERSITY

If recent dangers and conflicts can precipitate the full-blown symptoms of an anxiety disorder, do past experiences—those that took place years ago—set the stage for this experience? Further research by George Brown and his colleagues indicates that they can (Brown & Harris, 1993). Their studies of these phenomena focus on measures of *childhood adversity*.

Within a community sample of approximately 400 working-class women, G.W. Brown and Harris (1993) found that 25 percent met diagnostic criteria for at least one type of anxiety disorder. The relationship between childhood adversity and the presence of these anxiety disorders is illustrated in Figure 6–2. Women who were suffering from most types of anxiety disorder were more likely than women with no disorder to report having been exposed to parental indifference and physical abuse during childhood or adolescence. This pattern was particularly striking for the women with panic disorder. In contrast, women with specific phobias or only mild symptoms of agoraphobia could not be distinguished from the control group on the basis of childhood adversity. This result is consistent with the notion that somewhat different etiological pathways may be associated with specific phobias than with other, frequently more severe forms of anxiety disorder.

Psychological Factors

Research suggests that stressful life events and childhood adversity contribute to the development of anxiety disorders. But what are the mechanisms that link these experiences to specific emotional difficulties such as intense fears, panic attacks, and excessive worry? This question brings our discussion of etiology to a different level of analysis. A number of psychological mechanisms undoubtedly play an important role in helping to shape the development and maintenance of anxiety disorders. These processes include learning and cognitive events.

LEARNING PROCESSES

Since the 1920s, experimental psychologists working in laboratory settings have been interested in the possibility that fears might be learned through classical (or Pavlovian) conditioning (see Eysenck, 1979; Mineka, 1985; Mineka & Zinbarg, 1995). The central mechanism in the classical conditioning process is the association between an unconditioned stimulus (UCS) and a conditioned stimulus (CS). The UCS is able to elicit a strong unconditioned emotional response (UR), such as fear. Examples of potential UCSs are painfully loud and unexpected noises, the sight of dangerous animals, and sudden, intense pain. According to psychologists' original views of the classical conditioning process, the CS could be any neutral stimulus that happened to be present when an intense fear reaction was provoked. Through the process of association, the CS would subsequently elicit a conditioned response (CR), which was similar in quality to the original UCR (see Chapter 2).

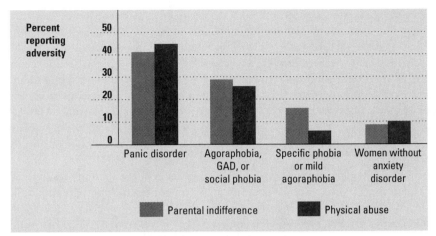

preparedness theory   The notion that organisms are biologically prepared, on the basis of neural pathways in their central nervous systems, to learn certain types of associations (also known as *biological constraints on learning*).

Figure 6–2   Parental Indifference and Physical Abuse are Frequently Reported by Women who Later Develop Panic Disorder.   They do not seem to be related to specific phobias.

Source: G. W. Brown and T. O. Harris, 1993, Aetiology of anxiety and depressive disorders in an inner-city population. I. Early adversity, *Psychological Medicine, 23,* 143–154.

This explanation for the development of specific phobias fits easily with common sense as well as with clinical experience. Many intense, persistent, irrational fears seem to develop after the person has experienced a traumatic event (Öst & Hugdahl, 1981). An enormous body of research has been conducted on the process of fear acquisition and extinction in laboratory animals and in humans (Eysenck, 1979; Rachman, 1991). Evidence from these studies indicates that certain constraints, which appear to be biologically based and may be the result of evolutionary pressures, are associated with the process by which fears are learned. We review these considerations in the next few pages.

Preparedness   Learning theories do not explain why conditioned fear responses that are learned in a laboratory situation are typically easy to extinguish, while phobic responses are extremely persistent and difficult to change; or why phobias that develop after traumatic experiences are typically learned in one trial, while very few laboratory studies have been able to demonstrate one-trial conditioning with fear responses. Finally, the original conditioning model held that any neutral stimulus could be used as the CS. If that model is correct, why are phobias associated only with certain types of objects and situations, such as animals, heights, and small enclosed spaces? It is quite unusual for people to develop phobic responses to other types of objects, such as guns, cars, and electrical outlets, even though they are at least as likely to be associated with danger and pain.

In order to account for these difficulties, Martin Seligman, a psychologist at the University of Pennsylvania, proposed that conditioning is governed by a process called **preparedness.** Organisms are assumed to be biologically "prepared," on the basis of neural pathways in their central nervous systems, to learn certain types of associations more quickly than others (1971). Rats, for example, can learn to associate the sensation of nausea (UCS) with the taste of food (CS). They can learn this association in one trial, and once they have developed an aversion to a particular taste, that aversion is highly resistant to extinction. Because it protects animals from poisoning, it serves an adaptive, evolutionary function.

Seligman argued that human fears that reach phobic proportions may be similar to the taste aversion phenomenon. Fear of certain stimuli may have conferred a selective advantage upon those people—hundreds of thousands of years ago—who were able to develop fears and consequently avoid certain kinds of dangerous stimuli, such as heights, snakes, and storms. This is not to say that the fears are innate or present at birth, but rather that they can be learned and maintained very easily.

In Chapter 2 we argued that most disorders arise from the interaction of biological, social, and psychological factors. The preparedness model of phobias offers another example of the way in which these factors may combine and interact in the production of specific phobias. The key biological factor is the neurological system, which is prepared to associate quickly certain types of stimuli with intense fear responses. The psychological and social factors in this model involve the nature of the person's developmental history and environmental experience, through which he or she actually learns to associate fear with specific stimuli. Many investigations have been conducted to test various facets of Seligman's preparedness conditioning model (McNally, 1987; Öhman, 1996). The results of these studies support certain features of the model.

The process of prepared conditioning may play an important role in the etiology of both social phobias and specific phobias. In specific phobias, the prepared stimuli are things like snakes, heights, storms, and small enclosed places. The prepared stimulus in social phobias might involve other people's faces. Öhman (1986, 1996) has argued that we are prepared to fear faces that appear angry, critical, or rejecting if they are directed toward us. This process is presumably an evolutionary remnant of factors involved in establishing dominance hierarchies, which maintain social order among primates. Animals that are defeated in a dominance conflict are often allowed to remain as part of the group if they behave submissively. The responses of people with social phobias may be similar in the sense that they are afraid of directly facing, or being evaluated by, other people.

Observational Learning We all learn many behaviors through imitation. Albert Bandura's early work on modeling, for example, demonstrated that children who observe a model hitting a doll are more likely to behave aggressively themselves when given the opportunity (see Chapter 2). Similar processes may also affect the etiology of intense fear, because some phobias develop in the absence of any direct experience with the feared object. People apparently learn to avoid certain stimuli if they observe other people showing a strong fear response to those stimuli (Rachman, 1990). In other words, the traumatic event does not have to happen to you; it may be enough for you to witness a traumatic event happening to someone else or to watch someone else behave fearfully.

Susan Mineka, a psychologist at Northwestern University, and Michael Cook have conducted a series of intriguing experiments that combine observational learning with the preparedness formulation (e.g., Mineka & Cook, 1993). Rhesus monkeys that were raised in their natural environment are markedly afraid of certain kinds of stimuli, such as snakes. Most monkeys reared in the laboratory do not initially react fearfully when they are presented with a toy snake. They quickly acquire this fear, however, after watching a monkey reared in the wild exhibit intense fear in the presence of snakes. The greater the fear exhibited by the wild monkey, the more intense the fears developed by the observer monkey. Further, live observation is not necessary. Monkeys can learn to fear snakes by watching videotapes of other monkeys exhibiting fear reactions.

Fear of snakes is clearly adaptive, because snakes represent a threat to rhesus monkeys in their natural environment. In Seligman's terms, this could be seen as a prepared association. Will monkeys also learn to avoid nonthreatening and presumably *unprepared* stimuli if they observe a model reacting with intense fear? Is the association between fear and particular stimuli random, or is it selective? Mineka and Cook conducted a series of investigations that proved that the relationship is, in fact, selective: Monkeys are prepared to learn to avoid fear-relevant stimuli (such as snakes and crocodiles) but are not prepared to learn to avoid fear-irrelevant stimuli (such as rabbits or kittens) (Cook & Mineka, 1991).

Learning experiences are clearly important in the etiology of phobias, but their impact often depends on the existence of prepared associations between stimuli. Furthermore, vicarious learning is often as important as direct expe-

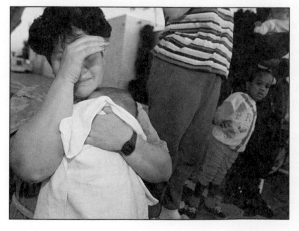

Vicarious learning can influence the development of strong fear responses. Children who observe adults demonstrating strong emotional responses, like this child in the aftermath of the California earthquakes in 1994, may be likelier to develop phobias.

rience. The importance of the latter factor can be illustrated by considering the development of children's fears during the bombing of London in World War II. When civilian areas were subjected to prolonged and terrifying attacks, families sought safety in underground shelters. If intense fear could be conditioned to any originally neutral stimulus, most of the people subjected to this traumatic experience would develop specific phobic responses in association with whatever stimuli happened to be present during the worst moments of a raid (fear of tunnels, fear of the dark).

In fact, it didn't work that way. Although people showed short-term emotional reactions, very few developed persistent, irrational phobic responses as a result of these terrifying experiences. Anecdotal evidence suggested that children were more likely to become fearful if they had observed their parents exhibiting strong emotional responses during the raids (Rachman, 1990).

COGNITIVE FACTORS

Up to this point, we have talked about the importance of life events and specific learning experiences—variables that can be measured outside the organism. But cognitive events also play an important role as mediators between experience and response. Perceptions, memory, and attention all influence the ways that we react to events in our environments. It is now widely accepted that these cognitive factors play a crucial role in the etiology and maintenance of various types of anxiety disorders.

Perception of Control   Cognitive theories of emotion have, for many years, emphasized the important relationship between anxiety and the perception of control (for example, Mandler, 1966). People who believe that they are able to control events in their environment are less likely to show symptoms of anxiety than are people who believe that they are helpless.

An extensive body of evidence supports the conclusion that people who believe that they are less able to control events in their environment are more likely to develop global forms of anxiety (Andrews, 1996), as well as various specific types of anxiety disorder (McNally, 1994). Laboratory research indicates that feelings of lack of control contribute to the onset of panic attacks among patients with panic disorder. The perception of uncontrollability has also been linked to the submissive behavior frequently seen among people with social phobias (Mineka & Zinbarg, 1995), as well as the chronic worries of people with generalized anxiety disorder (Brown, Barlow, & Liebowitz, 1994).

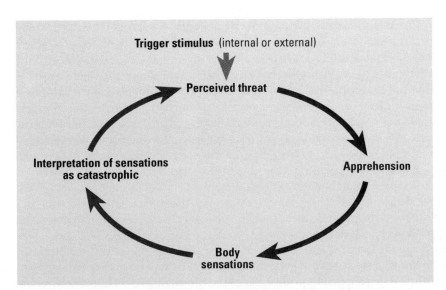

Figure 6–3   Diagram of Clark's Cognitive Model of Panic Attacks.

Source: D.M. Clark, 1986, A cognitive approach to panic, *Behavior Research and Therapy, 24,* 461–470.

Thomas Borkovec, a clinical psychologist at Penn State University, has conducted extensive research on characteristics of uncontrollable worry and the treatment of anxiety disorders.

Catastrophic Misinterpretation   A somewhat different type of cognitive dysfunction has been described by David Clark, a psychologist at Oxford University in England. According to this view, panic disorder may be caused by the *catastrophic misinterpretation* of bodily sensations or perceived threat (Clark, 1986b; Clark & Ehlers, 1993). This process is illustrated in Figure 6–3 on page 171. For example, a person who believes that there is something wrong with his heart might misinterpret a slight acceleration in heart rate as being a sign that he is about to have a heart attack. This reaction ensures the continued operation of this feedback loop, with the misinterpretation enhancing the person's sense of threat, and so on until the process spirals out of control. Thus both cognitive misinterpretation and biological reactions associated with the perception of threat are necessary for a panic attack to occur.

Many research studies have found that the subjective experience of body sensations is, in fact, closely associated with maladaptive self-statements among patients with panic disorder (McNally, 1994). However, catastrophic misinterpretations cannot account for all instances of panic attacks. For example, patients with panic disorder sometimes experience panic attacks in their sleep (Klein & Klein, 1989). How could that happen if the escalation to panic requires catastrophic misinterpretation of physical sensations? Clearly other factors are also involved.

Attention to Threat and Shifts in Attention   Earlier in the chapter we saw that worry involves negative thoughts and images that anticipate some possible future danger. In recent years, several lines of research have converged to clarify the basic cognitive mechanisms involved in worry. Experts now believe that attention plays a crucial role in the onset of this process. People who are prone to excessive worrying are unusually sensitive to cues that signal the existence of future threats (Mathews, 1990; Rapee, 1991; Williams, Mathews, & MacLeod, 1996). They attend vigilantly to even fleeting signs of danger, especially when they are under stress. At such times, the recognition of danger cues triggers a maladaptive, self-perpetuating cycle of cognitive processes that can quickly spin out of control.

The threatening information that is generated in this process is presumably encoded in memory in the form of elaborate schemas (see Chapter 5), which are easily reactivated. In comparison with the depressed person, who is convinced that failure will definitely occur, the anxious person is afraid of failure that may occur as a future event, the outcome of which remains uncertain (Beck & Emery, 1985). The threat schemas of anxious people contain a high proportion of "What if" questions, such as "What am I going to do if I don't do well in school this semester?" (Kendall & Ingram, 1989; Vasey & Borkovec, 1992).

Once attention has been drawn to threatening cues, the performance of adaptive, problem-solving behaviors is disrupted, and the worrying cycle launches into a repetitive sequence in which the person rehearses anticipated events and searches for ways to avoid them. The readily accessed network of threat-related schemas then activates an additional series of "What if" questions that quickly leads to a dramatic increase in negative affect.

If worriers are preoccupied with the perception of threat cues and the rehearsal of dangerous scenarios but are unable to reach satisfactory solutions to their problems, why do they continue to engage in this vicious, maladaptive cycle? Thomas Borkovec, a clinical psychologist at Pennsylvania State University, and his students have studied the uncontrollable nature of the worry process. Two of Borkovec's conclusions are particularly important in explaining the self-perpetuating nature of worry: (1) Worry is primarily a verbal-linguistic event (as opposed to visual images), and (2) worry serves the function of avoiding unpleasant somatic activation through the suppression of imagery (Borkovec & Inz, 1990; Roemer & Borkovec, 1993). In other words, some people apparently continue to worry, even though it is not productive, because worrying is reinforced by an immediate (though temporary) reduction in uncomfortable physiological sensations.

Attentional mechanisms also seem to be involved in the etiology and maintenance of social phobias. People who are capable of performing a particular task when they are alone (in practice) cannot perform it in front of an audience. Barlow (1988) has argued that this deterioration in skill is caused by anxious apprehension, which is similar to Borkovec's description of the process of worrying. An increase in negative affect presumably triggers a shift toward self-focused attention

("Oh, no, I'm getting really upset") and activates threat schemas ("What if I make a mistake?"). The person becomes distracted by these thoughts, and performance deteriorates. In a sense, the person's fearful expectations become a self-fulfilling prophesy.

Biological Factors

Several pieces of evidence indicate that biological events play an important role in the development and maintenance of the anxiety disorders. In the following pages we review the role of genetic factors and the use of chemicals to induce symptoms of panic. These factors undoubtedly interact with the social and psychological variables that we have considered in the preceding sections.

GENETIC FACTORS

Some of the most useful information about the validity of anxiety disorders comes from studies aimed at identifying the influence of genetic factors. These data address the overlap, as well as the distinctions, among various types of anxiety disorder. They also shed additional light on the relationship between anxiety and depression.

Family Studies   Several studies have focused specifically on the risk for panic disorder among relatives of panic patients. All these studies have found a relatively high rate of panic disorder—between 8 and 21 percent—among the patients' relatives (Weissman, 1993). The patients' relatives are also more likely to experience major depression, even if the probands in the study were originally selected because they had panic disorder without comorbid depression (Maier et al., 1993). These results are consistent with two conclusions: (1) Some people inherit a genetic predisposition to developing panic disorder, and (2) panic disorder and unipolar mood disorders may share some etiological factors.

A family study of social phobia has demonstrated that the *generalized form* of this disorder (where the person is fearful in most types of social situations) is also familial in nature and etiologically distinct from other types of anxiety disorder. The investigators studied first-degree relatives of probands with "pure" social phobia (Fyer et al., 1993; Mannuzza et al., 1995). Probands in the control group were people who had never had a mental disorder. The results indicated that the rate of social phobia was particularly high (16 percent) in the relatives of probands whose social phobia was generalized. In contrast, only 5 percent of the relatives in the control group met the diagnostic criteria for social phobia.

Data regarding obsessive–compulsive disorder suggest that a more general vulnerability to anxiety disorders is genetically transmitted through the family. The predisposition can apparently be expressed in different ways, with OCD being only one of them. The relatives of OCD probands apparently do not inherit a specific predisposition to this disorder, but they do inherit a more global tendency toward anxiety disorders (Black et al., 1992). The expression of that tendency is presumably influenced by subsequent experience.

The results of the family studies all point toward the potential influence of genetic factors in anxiety disorders. Most of the evidence also supports the validity of the DSM-IV subtypes. Comparisons of panic and GAD support the movement toward splitting these disorders apart in the diagnostic manual. The generalized form of social phobia also seems to be at least somewhat distinct from the other anxiety disorders. On the other hand, data regarding relatives of OCD probands are more consistent with the traditional preference in psychiatric classification for lumping anxiety disorders together.

Twin Studies   Family studies do not prove the involvement of genes, because family members also share environmental factors (for example, diet, culture, and so on). Twin studies provide a more stringent test of the genetic hypothesis (see Chapter 2). Kenneth Kendler, a psychiatrist at the Medical College of Virginia, and his colleagues have studied anxiety disorders in a sample of more than 2,000 female–female twin pairs (Kendler, Neale et al., 1992a, 1992b). The people who participated in this study were not psychiatric patients; they were living in the community and were identified through a state-wide registry of twins. Diagnoses were assigned following structured diagnostic interviews conducted by the research team.

Statistical estimates indicated that anxiety disorders are modestly heritable, with genetic factors accounting for somewhere between 20 and 30 percent of the variance in the transmission of GAD. Although all types of phobias appear to be influenced by genetic factors in this study, the greatest genetic influence was found for agoraphobia. The etiology of specific phobias was relatively more influenced by specific environmental factors. Social phobias fell between the other types.

Kendler and his colleagues subsequently examined the influence of both genetic and environmental factors on the etiology of several types of panic disorder, phobia, GAD, and major depression in this same large sample of female twins (Kendler et al., 1995). Their statistical procedures led them to several important conclusions:

1. Genetic risk factors for these disorders are neither highly specific (a different set of genes being associated with each disorder) nor highly nonspecific (one common set of genes causing vulnerability for all disorders).
2. Two genetic factors were identified: one associated with GAD and major depression, and the other with panic disorder and phobias.
3. Environmental risk factors that would be unique to individuals also played an important role in the etiology of all of the disorders that were examined. Environmental factors that would be shared by all members of a family did not appear to be influential.
4. Some environmental risk factors appear to be "disorder-specific." This was especially true for phobias.

NEUROCHEMISTRY

If some people inherit a predisposition that makes them vulnerable to the development of an anxiety disorder, what form does this predisposition take? Considerable speculation has focused on the role of neurochemical factors in this regard, especially in the case of panic disorder. Some clinical scientists have suggested that the central noradrenergic system might be "hyperactive" in people with panic disorder (Ballenger, 1989).

Pharmacological challenge procedures have played a very important role in exploring the neurochemistry of panic disorder. The logic behind this method is simple: If a particular brain mechanism is "challenged" or stressed by the artificial administration of chemicals, and if that procedure leads to the onset of a panic attack, then the neurochemical process that mediates that effect may also be responsible for panic attacks that take place outside the laboratory.

One laboratory procedure that is capable of inducing panic attacks in people who suffer from panic disorder involves the infusion of lactate.[†] The discovery of this effect was inspired by a few clinical studies, reported in the 1940s and 1950s, that noted that patients with "anxiety neurosis" sometimes experienced an increase in subjective anxiety following vigorous physical exercise. This change in subjective symptoms appeared to be associated with an extremely rapid and excessive increase in lactic acid in the blood.

A large number of studies have demonstrated that lactate infusions can provoke panic attacks in anywhere from 50 to 90 percent of patients with anxiety or panic disorders, as compared to only between 0 and 25 percent of normal control subjects (Barlow, 1988). Several other procedures can also be used to induce panic in the laboratory. These include the infusion of other chemicals, such as caffeine, as well as the inhalation of air that has been enriched with carbon dioxide. Some investigators discovered that the administration of certain types of medication, such as MAO inhibitors, could prevent the experience of lactate-induced panic attacks.

The *locus ceruleus,* a small area located in the brain stem, has been the focus of considerable emphasis in research on panic disorder. This area contains a large percentage of the brain's nor-

---

[†]*Lactic acid is formed during anaerobic respiration, the phase of cellular respiration that occurs in the absence of oxygen. The respiratory and circulatory systems are usually able to support aerobic respiration when a person is resting. These systems become overloaded when skeletal muscles are used strenuously. Muscle fibers then need to depend on anaerobic respiration to generate energy (Hole, 1984). This process converts glucose to pyruvic acid. As the oxygen supply becomes depleted, pyruvic acid is converted to lactic acid, which accumulates in the bloodstream and is later converted back to glucose by the liver.*

epinephrine. Neural projections from the locus ceruleus extend to the cerebral cortex as well as the limbic system, which is located in the temporal lobes. Research with monkeys has demonstrated that the firing rate of neurons in the locus ceruleus increases dramatically when a monkey is frightened. Furthermore, electrical stimulation of the locus ceruleus triggers a strong fear response that resembles a panic attack (Redmond, 1985). Several studies of people with panic disorder have pointed toward a dysregulation of the norepinephrine system in some patients, but the evidence is mixed. It does not seem to account for all cases of the disorder (McNally, 1994).

Panic induction procedures allow investigators to monitor brain activities that occur during a panic attack. For example, positron emission tomography, or PET scans, have been used to compare blood flow to various areas of the brain before and after anxiety disorder patients experienced lactate-induced panic attacks. One study found that panic is associated with increased blood flow in the temporal lobes (Reiman et al., 1989), an area that is generally considered to be associated with fear and other emotions (Gray, 1990).

As brain imaging procedures improve, enhancing our ability to isolate anatomic regions, these methods may lead to the localization of specific areas of the brain that mediate symptoms of anxiety. This is an exciting possibility. Information of this sort would tell us where neurological underpinnings of panic are located in the brain. That knowledge, coupled with data regarding social and psychological factors, will help us understand why people experience panic attacks.

Treatment

In the following discussion, we review some of the treatment procedures that have been demonstrated to be useful with anxiety disorders. This is one of the areas of psychopathology in which clinical psychologists and psychiatrists are best prepared to improve the level of their clients' functioning. We begin by describing procedures that were used in an effort to help Ed, the person with obsessive–compulsive disorder whose problems were described at the beginning of this chapter.

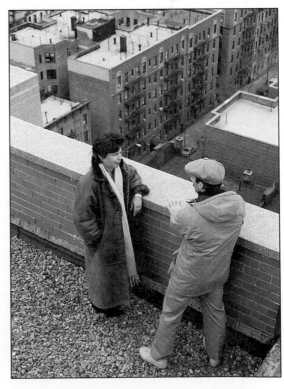

Exposure treatments can be administered in imagination or in the person's natural environment. In this photograph, a patient with acrophobia is accompanied to the top of a tall building by a therapist who is conducting exposure therapy.

Ed's psychiatrist gave him a prescription for clomipramine (Anafranil), an antidepressant drug that is also used to treat people with severe obsessions. Weekly psychotherapy sessions continued as the dose was gradually increased. The medication had a beneficial impact after 4 weeks. Ed said that he had begun to feel as though he was trapped at the bottom of a well. After the medication, he no longer felt buried. His situation still wasn't great, but it no longer seemed hopeless or unbearable. He was also less intensely preoccupied by his obsessive violent images. They were still there, but they weren't as pressing. The drug had several annoying, though tolerable, side effects. His mouth felt dry, and he was occasionally a bit dizzy. He also noticed that he became tired more easily. Although Ed was no longer feeling seriously depressed, and the intensity of his obsessions was diminished, they had not disappeared, and he was now avoiding writing altogether.

Because the obsessions were still a problem, Ed's psychiatrist referred him to a psychologist who specialized in behavior therapy for anxiety disorders. He continued seeing the psychiatrist every other week for checks on his medication, which he continued to take. The new therapist told Ed that his fears of particular letters and numbers would be maintained as long as he avoided writing. Ed agreed to begin writing short essays every day, for a period of at least 30 minutes. The content could vary from day to day—anything that Ed felt like writing about—but he was encouraged to include the names of his wife and brother as often as possible. Furthermore, he was instructed to avoid his compulsive writing style, intentionally allowing the parts of letters to be separated or loops to be closed. At the beginning and end of each essay, Ed was required to record his anxiety level so that the therapist could monitor changes in his subjective discomfort. Over a period of 8 to 10 weeks, Ed's handwriting began to change. It was less of a struggle to get himself to write, and his handwriting became more legible.

The final aspect of behavioral treatment was concerned with his fear of axes. Ed and his therapist drew up a list of objects and situations related to axes, arranging them from those that were the least anxiety-provoking through those that were most frightening. They began with the least frightening. In their first exposure session, Ed agreed to meet with the psychologist while a relatively dull, wood-splitting maul was located in the adjoining room. Ed was initially quite anxious and distracted, but his anxiety diminished considerably before the end of their 2-hour meeting. Once that had been accomplished, the therapist helped him to confront progressively more difficult situations. These sessions were challenging and uncomfortable for Ed, but they allowed him to master his fears in an orderly fashion. By the end of the twelfth session of exposure, he was able to hold a sharp ax without fear.

Psychological Interventions

Psychoanalytic psychotherapy has been used to treat patients with anxiety disorders since Freud published his seminal papers at the turn of the century. The emphasis in this type of treatment is on fostering insight regarding the unconscious motives that presumably lie at the heart of the patient's symptoms (such as Ed's feelings about his brother). Although many therapists continue to employ this general strategy, it has not been shown to be effective in controlled outcome studies.

EXPOSURE: SYSTEMATIC DESENSITIZATION AND FLOODING

Like psychoanalysis, behavior therapy was initially developed for the purpose of treating anxiety disorders, especially specific phobias. The first widely adopted procedure was known as systematic desensitization (see Chapter 3). In desensitization, the client is first taught progressive muscle relaxation. Then the therapist constructs a hierarchy of feared stimuli, beginning with those items that provoke only small amounts of fear and progressing through items that are most frightening. Then, while the client is in a relaxed state, he or she imagines the lowest item on the hierarchy. The item is presented repeatedly until the person no longer experiences an increase in anxiety when thinking about the object or situation. This process is repeated several times as the client moves systematically up the hierarchy, sequentially confronting images of stimuli that were originally rated as being more frightening.

In the years since systematic desensitization was originally proposed (Wolpe, 1958), many different variations on this procedure have been employed. The crucial feature of the treatment involves systematic maintained exposure to the feared stimulus (Marks, 1987; Rachman, 1990). Positive outcomes have been reported, regardless of the specific manner in which exposure is accomplished. Some evidence indicates that direct ("in vivo") exposure works better than imaginal exposure. A few prolonged exposures can be as effective as a larger sequence of brief exposures. Another variation on exposure procedures, known as *flooding*, begins with the most frightening stimuli rather than working up gradually from the bottom of the hierarchy. All of these variations on the basic procedure have been shown to be effective in the treatment of phobic disorders. Several research studies have demonstrated that exposure therapy leads to clinically meaningful improvement when compared to placebo treatments. Positive results are typically maintained several months after the end of treatment (O'Sullivan & Marks, 1991). Exposure is often accomplished in the presence of the therapist, but the treatment can be just as effective when the client directs his or her own systematic exposure in the natural environment (Al-Kubaisy et al., 1992).

EXPOSURE AND RESPONSE PREVENTION

The most effective form of psychological treatment for obsessive–compulsive disorder combines exposure to the situation that increases the person's anxiety with prevention of the person's typical compulsive response (Turner & Beidel, 1988). Neither component is effective by itself. The combination of exposure and response prevention is necessary because of the way in which people with obsessive–compulsive disorder use their compulsive rituals to reduce anxiety that is typically stimulated by the sudden appearance of an obsession. If the compulsive behavior is performed, exposure is effectively cut short.

Consider, for example, the treatment program employed with Ed. His obsessive thoughts and images, which centered around violence, were associated with handwriting. By the time he entered behavior therapy, Ed had avoided writing altogether for several months. The therapist arranged for him to begin writing short essays to be sure that he was exposed, for at least 30 minutes each day, to the situation that was most anxiety-provoking. In their sessions Ed was also required to write long sequences of the letter *T* in which he deliberately failed to connect the two lines. He was not allowed to go back and correct this "mistake." The combination represents exposure to an anxiety-provoking stimulus and response prevention.

Controlled-outcome studies indicate that this approach is effective with OCD patients (Rachman & Hodgson, 1980). One review of 18 outcome studies found that 51 percent of the OCD patients who had been treated with prolonged exposure and response prevention were either free of symptoms or much improved at the end of treatment; another 39 percent were considered moderately improved. Only 10 percent did not benefit at all (Foa, Steketee, & Ozarow, 1985).

APPLIED RELAXATION

Behavior therapists have used relaxation procedures for many years. Relaxation training usually involves teaching the client alternately to tense and relax specific muscle groups while breathing slowly and deeply (Bernstein & Borkovec, 1973). This process is often described to the client as an active coping skill that can be learned through consistent practice and used to control anxiety and worry.

Outcome studies indicate that relaxation is a useful form of treatment for generalized anxiety disorder. Borkovec and Costello (1993) compared applied relaxation and cognitive behavior therapy to nondirective psychotherapy for the treatment of patients with generalized anxiety disorder (see Close-Up in Chapter 3). Patients who received relaxation training and those who received cognitive therapy were more improved at the end of treatment than those who received only nondirective therapy.

COGNITIVE THERAPY

Cognitive therapy is used extensively in the treatment of anxiety disorders. Cognitive treatment procedures for anxiety disorders have been developed by Aaron Beck (Beck & Emery, 1985) and Albert Ellis (1962). They are similar to those employed in the treatment of depression. Therapists help clients identify cognitions that are relevant to their problem; recognize the relation between these cognitions and maladaptive emotional responses (such as prolonged anxiety); examine the evidence that supports or contradicts these beliefs; and teach more useful ways of interpreting events in their environments (Schuyler, 1991).

In the case of anxiety disorders, cognitive therapy is usually accompanied by additional behavior therapy procedures, such as applied relaxation and exposure (Barlow & Cerny, 1988). One aspect of the cognitive component involves an analysis of errors in the ways in which people think about situations in their lives. Typical examples of faulty logic include jumping to conclusions before considering all of the evidence, overgeneralizing (basing negative predictions about future performance on a very limited set of previous experiences), all-or-none thinking (assuming that one mistake means total failure), and so on.

A second aspect of Barlow's cognitive component for panic patients is called *decatastrophisizing*. In this procedure, the therapist asks the client to imagine what would happen if his or her worst-case scenario actually happened. The same principles that are used in examining faulty logic are then applied to this situation. The therapist might say, "I don't think that you will fail the exam. But what would happen if you did fail the exam?" The client's initial reaction might be catastrophic ("I would die." "My parents would kill me." "I would flunk out of school."). Upon more careful analysis, however, the client might agree that these negative predictions actually represent gross exaggerations that are based on cognitive errors. Discussions in the therapy session are followed by extensive practice and homework assignments during the week. As one way of evaluating the accuracy of their own hypotheses, clients are encouraged to write down predictions that they make about specific situations and then keep track of the actual outcomes.

getting help

Most people suffering from anxiety disorders can be treated successfully. Several forms of intervention are beneficial, primarily behavior therapy, cognitive therapy, and medication. If you plan to work with a professional therapist, do some research before you begin working with a specific person. Read about treatments that have been evaluated empirically, and look for someone who uses one of these procedures. Some excellent Internet sites may help you to find the best therapist for you. Patient-run organizations have established support groups in many communities and share information about treatment alternatives. One outstanding example is the Anxiety Disorders Association of America. The URL for its Web site is: **www.adaa.org.** The site includes a consumer's guide to treatment alternatives that is organized by specific types of anxiety disorders. More detailed information about obsessive–compulsive disorder and related problems can be obtained from the Obsessive–Compulsive Foundation, a not-for-profit organization composed of people with obsessive–compulsive disorder, their families,

and professionals. The foundation's web address is: **www.ocfoundation.org.**

Some people may be able to make improvements on their own with the advice of a useful self-help book. There are a lot of good books to choose from in the area of anxiety disorders. We recommend two books that describe a combination of cognitive and behavioral approaches to treatment. *Triumph over Fear,* by Jerilyn Ross and Rosalynn Carter, describes the successful experiences of people who have recovered from various types of anxiety disorders, including phobias, panic, and generalized anxiety disorder. Practical self-help strategies are also summarized in *Panic, Anxiety, and Phobias: New Strategies to Free Yourself from Worry and Fear,* written by Shirley Babior and Carol Goldman. This book includes simple instructions in progressive muscle relaxation, cognitive techniques to master anxiety, and exposure procedures for overcoming avoidance. Finally, more specific information about dealing with obsessive–compulsive disorder can be found in *When Once Is Not Enough* by Gail Steketee and Kerrin White. ♥

Several controlled outcome studies attest to the efficacy of cognitive therapy in the treatment of various types of anxiety disorder, including panic disorder, agoraphobia, social phobia, generalized anxiety disorder, and obsessive–compulsive disorder (Chambless & Gillis, 1993; Clark et al., 1994; Margraf et al., 1993; Zinbarg et al., 1992).

Biological Interventions

Medication is the most effective and most commonly used biological approach to the treatment of anxiety disorders. Several types of drugs have been discovered to be useful. They are often used in conjunction with psychological treatment.

ANTIANXIETY MEDICATIONS

The most frequently used types of minor tranquilizers are from the class of drugs known as benzodiazepines, which includes diazepam (Valium) and alprazolam (Xanax). These drugs reduce many symptoms of anxiety, especially vigilance and subjective somatic sensations, such as increased muscle tension, palpitations, increased perspiration, and gastrointestinal distress. They have relatively less effect on a person's tendency toward worry and rumination (Hoehn-Saric & McLeod, 1991). Benzodiazepines were the most widely prescribed form of psychiatric medication until the 1990s.

Benzodiazepines bind to specific receptor sites in the brain that are ordinarily associated with a neurotransmitter known as gamma-aminobutyric acid (GABA). Benzodiazepines, which inhibit the activity of GABA neurons, fall into two types, based on their rate of absorption and elimination from the body. Some, such as alprazolam and lorazepam (Ativan), are absorbed and eliminated quickly, whereas others, such as diazepam, are absorbed and eliminated slowly.

Benzodiazepines have been shown to be effective in the treatment of generalized anxiety disorders and social phobias (Davidson, Tupler, & Potts, 1994). They are not typically beneficial for patients with phobic disorders or obsessive–compulsive disorder.

Certain high-potency benzodiazepines are also useful for treating panic disorder (Rosenberg, 1993). Alprazolam (Xanax) is considered by some psychiatrists to be the drug of choice for patients with this condition because it produces clinical improvement within 1 to 3 weeks and because it has fewer side effects than antidepressants.

The results of most placebo-controlled outcome studies have been positive. The Cross-National Collaborative Panic Study (CNCPS), which was conducted in two phases, provides some of the best evidence in this regard. The first phase compared alprazolam to a placebo in 500 patients (Ballenger et al., 1988). Among the patients who received alprazolam, 30 percent were markedly improved after 8 weeks of treatment, and another 52 percent were moderately improved. Only 10 percent of the patients who received the placebo were markedly improved after treatment, and another 43 percent in this group were moderately improved.

The second phase of the CNCPS compared alprazolam, imipramine, and placebo treatment in a sample of 1,100 panic disorder patients. The investigators found that alprazolam and imipramine were equally effective in comparison to a placebo. Fewer patients dropped out of the alprazolam group, because the drug had fewer side effects than imipramine. Patients improved faster on alprazolam, but there were no differences between the two drugs after 6 to 8 weeks of treatment.

Some studies have found that many patients with panic disorder and agoraphobia relapse if they discontinue taking medication. Exposure may be a preferable form of treatment for patients with a diagnosis of panic disorder with agoraphobia, because of the high relapse rate that was observed after alprazolam was withdrawn (Marks et al., 1993).

Common side effects of benzodiazepines include sedation accompanied by mild psychomotor and cognitive impairments. These drugs can, for example, increase the risk of automobile accidents, because they interfere with motor skills. They can also lead to problems in attention and memory, especially among elderly patients.

The most serious adverse effect of benzodiazepines is their potential for addiction. Approximately 40 percent of people who use benzodiazepines for 6 months or more will exhibit symptoms of withdrawal if the medication is discontinued (Sussman & Chou, 1988). Withdrawal reactions include the reappearance of anxiety, somatic complaints, concentration problems, and sleep difficulties. They are most severe among patients who abruptly discontinue using them. The risk for becoming dependent on benzodiazepines is greatest among people who have a history of abusing other substances, like alcohol.

ANTIDEPRESSANT MEDICATIONS

In the early 1960s, Donald Klein and his research group discovered that tricyclic antidepressant drugs, especially imipramine, can be effective in treating panic attacks in patients with agoraphobia. They recommended that psychological intervention be used to eliminate anticipatory anxiety and avoidant behavior after the medication eliminated the threat of further panic attacks. Some psychiatrists still consider imipramine to be the preferred medication for panic disorder (Agras, 1993; Noyes, 1991) because patients are less likely to become dependent on the drug than they are to high-potency benzodiazepines like alprazolam. In addition, patients experience fewer problems when imipramine is withdrawn. The usual duration of treatment is 6 months. Relapse may occur after medication is withdrawn.

The tricyclic antidepressants produce several unpleasant side effects, including weight gain, dry mouth, and overstimulation (sometimes referred to as an "amphetamine-like" response). Some of the side effects, like palpitations, sweating, and light-headedness, are upsetting to patients because they resemble symptoms of anxiety. Side effects often lead patients to discontinue treatment prematurely. In one study of patients who received long-term treatment with imipramine, 50 percent experienced distressing side effects, including 17 percent who found the effects intolerable (Noyes, Garvey, & Cook, 1989).

The selective serotonin reuptake inhibitors (SSRIs) have also been employed with anxiety disorders, but they have not been evaluated extensively in double-blind, placebo-controlled studies. Panic disorder and OCD have been treated with SSRIs such as fluvoxamine (Boyer, 1992).

In actual practice, anxiety disorders are often treated with a combination of psychological and biological procedures. The selection of specific treatment components depends on the specific group of symptoms that the person exhibits. Table 6–2 summarizes various types of psychological treatment and specific types of medication that are effective with anxiety disorders. These are not the only types of treatment that are available, but they include those that have been subjected to empirical validation.

TABLE 6–2

Treatments of Choice for Anxiety Disorders

DISORDER	DRUG TREATMENT		PSYCHOLOGICAL TREATMENT
	Generic Name	*Trade Name*	
Panic Disorder	Imipramine	Tofranil	Cognitive therapy
	Alprazolam	Xanax	
Agoraphobia	Imipramine	Tofranil	Exposure in vivo
			Cognitive therapy
Generalized Anxiety Disorder	Alprazolam	Xanax	Applied relaxation
	Diazepam	Valium	Cognitive therapy
Specific Phobias	Medication not typically recommended		Exposure in vivo
Social Phobia	Propranolol	Inderal	Cognitive therapy
			Social skills training
Obsessive– Compulsive Disorder	Clomipramine	Anafranil	Exposure plus
	Fluoxetine	Prozac	response prevention

Source: *Adapted from R. Noyes, Jr., 1991, Treatments of choice for anxiety disorders. In W. Coryell and G. Winokur (Eds.),* The Clinical Management of Anxiety Disorders. *New York; Oxford University Press.*

Summary

Anxiety disorders are defined in terms of a preoccupation with, or persistent avoidance of, thoughts or situations that provoke **fear** or anxiety. **Anxiety** involves a diffuse emotional reaction that is associated with the anticipation of future problems and is out of proportion to threats from the environment. A pervasive anxious mood is typically associated with pessimistic thoughts and feelings. The person's attention may also turn inward, focusing on negative emotions and self-evaluation rather than on the organization or rehearsal of adaptive responses that might be useful in coping with negative events.

A **panic attack** is a sudden, overwhelming experience of terror or fright. Panic attacks are defined largely in terms of a list of somatic sensations, ranging from heart palpitations, sweating and trembling, to nausea, dizziness, and chills.

Phobias are persistent and irrational narrowly defined fears that are associated with avoidance of a specific object or situation. The most complex and incapacitating form of phobic disorder is **agoraphobia,** which is usually described as fear of public spaces. It is not so much a fear of being close to one specific object or situation as it is a fear of being separated from signals associated with safety.

Obsessions are repetitive, unwanted, intrusive cognitive events that may take the form of thoughts or images or impulses. They intrude suddenly into consciousness and lead to an increase in subjective anxiety. **Compulsions** are repetitive behaviors, considered by the person to be senseless or irrational, that reduce the anxiety associated with obsessions. The person attempts to resist but cannot. The two most common forms of compulsive behavior are cleaning and checking.

DSM-IV recognizes several specific subtypes of anxiety disorders: panic disorders (with or without agoraphobia), phobic disorders (specific phobia, social phobia, and agoraphobia without panic attacks), obsessive–compulsive disorder, and generalized anxiety disorder, as well as post-traumatic stress disorder and acute stress disorder.

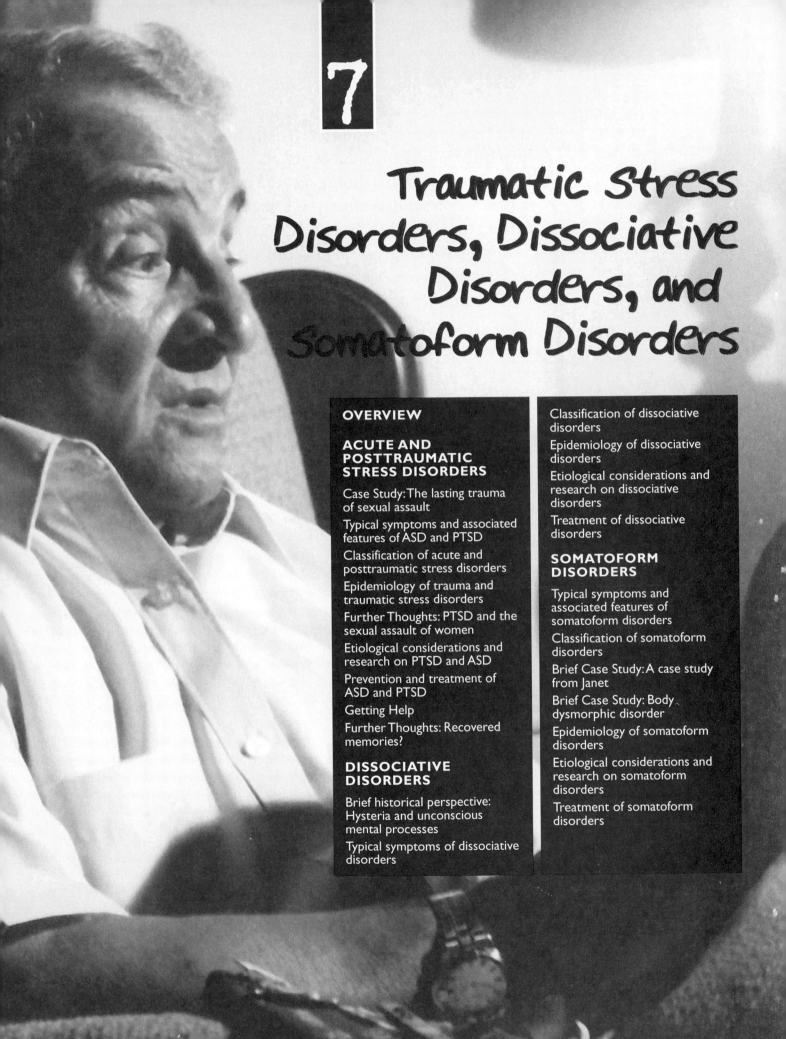

7

Traumatic Stress Disorders, Dissociative Disorders, and Somatoform Disorders

At times in your life, you may briefly have felt cut off or detached from your usual experience of yourself and the world around you. Perhaps things seemed unreal for a few moments, or you may have had an out of body experience where you seemed to be watching yourself from above. Psychological theorists have long speculated and argued about the meaning of these everyday experiences, as well as the meaning of far more severe examples of **dissociation**—the disruption of the normally integrated mental processes involved in memory or consciousness (Spiegel & Cardena, 1991). To a greater or lesser extent, dissociative symptoms characterize all of the intriguing disorders we consider in this chapter: acute and posttraumatic stress disorders, dissociative disorders, and somatoform disorders.

Overview

dissociation The separation of mental processes such as memory or consciousness that normally are integrated. Normal dissociative experiences include fleeting feelings of unreality and *déjà vu* experiences—the feeling that an event has happened before. Extreme dissociative experiences characterize dissociative disorders

acute stress disorder (ASD) A new category of mental disorder in DSM-IV that is defined as a reaction occurring within 4 weeks following a traumatic experience and is characterized by dissociative symptoms, reexperiencing, avoidance, and marked anxiety or arousal. Contrasts with posttraumatic stress disorder, which either lasts longer or has a delayed onset.

posttraumatic stress disorder (PTSD) A psychological disorder characterized by recurring symptoms of numbing, reexperiencing, and hyperarousal following exposure to a traumatic stressor.

dissociative disorders A category of psychological disorders characterized by persistent, maladaptive disruptions in the integration of memory, consciousness, or identity. Examples include dissociative fugue and dissociative identity disorder (multiple personality).

Acute stress disorder and posttraumatic stress disorder are reactions to *traumatic stress,* exposure to some event that involves actual or threatened death or serious injury to self or others and creates intense fear, helplessness, or horror. Rape, military combat, and exposure to man-made or natural disasters are examples of traumatic stressors. **Acute stress disorder** (**ASD**) occurs within 4 weeks after exposure to a trauma and is characterized by dissociative symptoms, reexperiencing of the event, avoidance of reminders of the trauma, and marked anxiety or arousal. Like acute stress disorder, **posttraumatic stress disorder** (**PTSD**) is defined by symptoms of reexperiencing, avoidance, and arousal, but in PTSD the symptoms either are lasting (they persist longer than 1 month) or delayed (the onset of symptoms is 6 months or longer after the traumatic event).

As we noted in Chapter 6, the DSM-IV classifies posttraumatic stress disorder and acute stress disorder with the anxiety disorders. However, we discuss these disorders separately in this chapter, for two main reasons. First, the symptoms of acute and posttraumatic stress disorders include *both* anxiety and dissociation; thus we place them between the two disorders they most resemble—anxiety disorders in Chapter 6 and dissociative disorders in this chapter. In fact, when DSM-IV was being developed, some experts argued that ASD and PTSD should be classified as dissociative disorders (Brett, Spitzer, & Williams, 1988), and others suggested ASD and PTSD should be placed in a separate diagnostic category (Davidson & Foa, 1991). Second, and perhaps more importantly, our separate treatment of acute and posttraumatic stress disorders calls attention to the growing body of research on these very important and all-too-common psychological problems.

Case histories of dissociative and somatoform disorders are fascinating, because they challenge many ordinary assumptions about the psyche. **Dissociative disorders** are characterized by persistent, maladaptive disruptions in the integration of memory, consciousness, or identity. You may be familiar with the actual case histories of *multiple personality disorder* (now called *dissociative identity disorder*) explored in the book *Sybil* and in the movie *The Three Faces of Eve.*

Equally intriguing are **somatoform disorders**—problems characterized by unusual physical symptoms that occur in the absence of a known physical illness. The sudden onset of paralysis or blindness without a clear biological cause is a dramatic example of a somatoform disorder. There is no demonstrable physical cause for the symptoms of somatoform disorders. They are somatic in form only—thus their name.[†]

We already have discussed numerous problems in objectively measuring people's reports about their conscious experience. Imagine, then, the difficulties involved in developing objective, scientific measures of unconscious processes. Our inability to assess unconscious mental processes adequately challenges clinicians as well as research scientists. For skeptical clinicians, one pressing diagnostic question is *malingering:* Could the patient be pretending to have a dissociative, somatoform, or posttraumatic stress disorder in order to achieve some gain, such as a disability payment or avoidance of a legal responsibility? A related diagnostic concern is *factitious disorder,* a feigned condition that, unlike malingering, is motivated primarily by a desire to assume the sick role rather than by a desire for external gain.

Because of the limited assessment and research on dissociative and somatoform disorders, we must be cautious in attempting to explain these problems. At the same time, we cannot help but be captivated and challenged by unusual case studies of the disorders. Throughout the chapter we consider both long and brief case studies, as well as the difficult scientific and clinical questions raised by these intriguing problems. We begin by considering the less controversial and more adequately researched problems of acute and posttraumatic stress disorders.

> **somatoform disorders**   A category of psychological disorders characterized by unusual physical symptoms that occur in the absence of a known physical pathology. Examples include hypochondriasis and conversion disorder. Somatoform disorders are somatic in form only, thus their name (note the distinction from psychosomatic disorders, which do involve real physical pathology).

Acute and Posttraumatic Stress Disorders

Stress is an inevitable, and in some cases a desirable, fact of everyday life. Some stressors, however, are so catastrophic and horrifying that they can cause serious psychological harm. Examples of these *traumatic stressors* include rape, bombings, airplane crashes, earthquakes, major fires, and devastating automobile wrecks. Both the survivors of and witnesses to traumatic stressors are expected to be greatly distressed as a part of their normal response. For some victims, the trauma continues long after the event itself has ended. The horrifying experience leads to general increases in anxiety and arousal, avoidance of emotionally charged situations, and the frequent reliving of the traumatic event. When these symptoms occur in the first 4 weeks after a traumatic stressor, the individual is said to be suffering from *acute stress disorder (ASD).* When symptoms persist for more than a month or have a delayed onset, the condition is referred to as *posttraumatic stress disorder (PTSD).* The following case study is a dramatic illustration of the horrors and lasting effects of exposure to traumatic stress.

case study

The Lasting Trauma of Sexual Assault

Stephanie Cason was a bright, attractive, and well-adjusted 27-year-old graduate student when she suffered a highly traumatic experience. One spring evening, Stephanie ran outside to investigate a major fire in another building in her apartment complex. While she was outside, Stephanie chatted amiably about the scene with a man who she assumed was a neighbor. After talking with a few other people, Stephanie returned to her apartment. The fire had caused a power outage, but Stephanie

continued

[†] *The absence of demonstrable physical impairment in somatoform disorders distinguishes them from psychosomatic illnesses, stress-related physical disorders that do involve real, organic pathology (see Chapter 8). In everyday language, we sometimes say "his problems are psychosomatic" to indicate that an illness is "all in his head." However, it is somatoform disorders, not psychosomatic disorders, that are purely psychological problems.*

found her way upstairs and changed into her nightclothes. When she came back downstairs to check on things, she found the very large man she had met outside standing in the shadows of her darkened apartment. Without saying a word, he raised a tire iron and struck Stephanie across the top of her head—repeatedly, until she fell to the floor and stopped screaming. Stephanie was cut deeply and stunned by the vicious blow, but she attempted to resist as the man began to grab at her breasts and rip at her clothes. He began to mutter obscenities and told Stephanie he wanted to have sex with her. All Stephanie could think was, "I'm going to be killed."

Somehow Stephanie remained strong enough to think keenly despite the shock of the assault and the blood pouring from her head. She decided she would "agree" to have sex with her assailant, but she told him that she needed to "freshen up" first. Eventually, Stephanie convinced him to let her go to clean up, and as soon as she reached her room, she shoved a bureau in front of the door and screamed frantically out the window for help. Her screams frightened her attacker and brought help to Stephanie. Later, she learned that one of the firefighters tackled and captured the assailant as he tried to run away from the apartment complex.

Stephanie saved herself from being raped, but she could not protect herself from the emotional fallout of her sexual assault. She was tortured by the fear of almost being killed. For days, eventually weeks, she felt intermittently terrified, dazed, and grateful to be alive. She replayed the horror of the evening in her mind repeatedly, and when she managed to fall asleep, she often was wakened by frightening nightmares. Stephanie was terrified to be alone, especially at night but even at many times during the day. She relied on the unwaivering support of her boyfriend and friends to stay nearby and help her cope.

Shortly after the assault, Stephanie sought help from a skilled clinical psychologist, but she fell into a depression despite the therapy. Antidepressant medication helped somewhat with her mood and lethargy, but for months after the trauma she continued to be hypervigilant, to have difficulty concentrating, and to have intermittent feelings of numbness or unreality. In addition, she frequently reexperienced the images and emotions surrounding the dreaded event. She was able to resume her studies at a reduced pace after about 3 months and, within 6 or 8 months she was working fairly regularly, but with considerably less confidence and concentration than formerly. As the anniversary of her assault approached, however, Stephanie grew increasing upset. The calendar and the spring weather—usually a welcome change—reminded her of the terror of the previous spring. Her feelings of unreality returned, and she had flashbacks

where she suddenly found herself reliving the dreaded night in her mind. In addition, the nightmares and her fears about being alone reappeared. She again needed the company of friends, especially at night, and she found herself unable to concentrate. Once again, she fell into a depression, although she did not take medication this time. As the dreaded date passed, her reactions eased slowly. After about 2 or 3 months of great emotional disruption, she was able to renew her normal life—as normal as her life could be—with fewer struggles than earlier.

Stephanie found it painful but also helpful to talk about her assault with friends and, over time, more publicly. After the passing of the 1-year anniversary, she actually gave a few lectures about her experiences to classes and to women's groups. She found that talking about the event gave her some relief, and perhaps more importantly, it gave her a sense that some good might come from her trauma. Stephanie also was willing and able to testify at the trial of her assailant, who was convicted of his crimes and sent to prison for 20 years. Although she appeared strong in the courtroom, the trial renewed many of Stephanie's previous symptoms of posttraumatic stress disorder. She again relived the terror of the assault, avoided being alone at night, and became fearful and hypervigilant about potential dangers in her world.

Once the trial was finished and her assailant was sent to prison, Stephanie felt a degree of relief and resolution about the trauma. She also felt some satisfaction and pride in the strength it took to share her experiences with others. Still, she could not fully banish the demons of the traumatic sexual assault. She was disgusted and distressed by thoughts of sexual violation, but Stephanie was most traumatized by the persistent thought that she was almost killed. She again experienced intensely distressing episodes of PTSD for a couple of months surrounding the second and third anniversaries of the sexual assault. In her heart, she knew the trauma would be with her forever, and she also knew her distress would be most intense near the anniversary of the event. Even at other times, however, Stephanie could unexpectedly fall victim to the terror of her assault. For example, more than 3 years after the assault, her boyfriend (now her husband) silently entered her room after returning home unexpectedly one night. Frightened by his sudden appearance, Stephanie first screamed in terror, then sobbed in uncontrollable fear, and felt numb and unreal for several days afterwards.

Stephanie did not behave like a victim from the moment of the assault, throughout the trial, or in her public discussions of her trauma. But despite her admirable strength, Stephanie could not prevent or control the recurrent terror of PTSD brought on by a violent sexual assault. ♛

Typical Symptoms and Associated Features of ASD and PTSD

As illustrated in Stephanie's terrifying experience, acute and posttraumatic stress disorder both are characterized by (1) reexperienced trauma; (2) marked avoidance of stimuli associated with the trauma; and (3) persistent arousal or increased anxiety. In addition, ASD is characterized by a fourth cluster of problems, namely, dissociative symptoms.

REEXPERIENCING

Like Stephanie, people who have been confronted with a traumatic stressor *reexperience* the event in a number of different ways. Some people experience repeated, distressing images or thoughts of the incident. For example, they visualize the trauma over and over or repeatedly question how they might have acted differently. Other people relive the trauma in horrifying dreams like those that haunted Stephanie. Many people with ASD or PTSD have repeated and intrusive *flashbacks,* sudden memories during which the trauma is replayed in images or thoughts—often at full emotional intensity. In rare cases, reexperiencing occurs as a *dissociative state,* and the person feels and acts as if the trauma actually is recurring in the moment. A combat veteran in a dissociative state might act as if he believes he is back in battle, and he may even take dangerous actions like gathering weapons or barricading himself in his residence.

AVOIDANCE

Marked or persistent avoidance of stimuli associated with the trauma is a second symptom of ASD and PTSD. Trauma victims with these disorders may attempt to avoid thoughts or feelings related to the event, or like Stephanie, they may avoid people, places, or activities that remind them of the trauma. In PTSD, the avoidance also may manifest itself as a general numbing of responsiveness. People suffering from PTSD often complain that their feelings seem dampened or even nonexistent, and they frequently withdraw from others, particularly from close relationships. Alternative terms for numbing of responsiveness, such as "psychic numbing" or "emotional anesthesia," convey more dramatically a sense of the nature of the symptom.

AROUSAL OR ANXIETY

Despite their general withdrawal from feelings, people, and painful situations, individuals with ASD and PTSD also experience symptoms that indicate increased arousal and anxiety in comparison to what they felt before the trauma. Stephanie's hypervigilance in searching for dangers in her world is a common symptom of PTSD. Like Stephanie, many trauma victims also have trouble falling or staying asleep or difficulty maintaining their concentration. Other trauma victims feel restless and agitated, and they may be irritable and subject to angry outbursts. A number of people with PTSD or ASD also have an exaggerated startle response, excessive fear reactions to unexpected stimuli, such as loud noises. These various symptoms of anxiety and arousal are the reason why traumatic stress disorders are grouped with the anxiety disorders in DSM-IV.

DISSOCIATIVE SYMPTOMS

In addition to reexperiencing, avoidance, and increased arousal, acute stress disorder (but not necessarily PTSD) is characterized by explicit dissociative symptoms. Many people become less aware of their surroundings following a traumatic event. Like Stephanie, they report feeling dazed, and they may seem "spaced out" to other people. Other people experience *depersonalization,* feeling cut off from themselves or their environment. *Derealization* is a related dissociative experience—people feel a marked sense of unreality about themselves or the world around them. ASD also may be characterized by features of *dissociative amnesia,* specifically the inability to recall important aspects of the traumatic experience. (We discuss depersonalization, derealization, and dissociative amnesia in more detail when we review the dissociative disorders later in this chapter.) Finally, the DSM-IV lists a sense of numbing or detachment from others as a dissociative symptom that characterizes acute stress disorder. You might note that a very similar symptom is listed as an indicator of avoidance, not dissociation, in the diagnosis of PTSD (see Table 7–1). This discrepancy in diagnostic criteria reflects some of the broader controversy about whether acute and posttraumatic stress disorders should be classified as dissociative or anxiety disorders (van der Kolk & McFarlane, 1996).

TABLE 7–1

DSM-IV Diagnostic Criteria for Posttraumatic Stress Disorder (PTSD)

A. THE PERSON HAS BEEN EXPOSED TO A TRAUMATIC EVENT IN WHICH BOTH OF THE FOLLOWING WERE PRESENT:

1. The person experienced, witnessed, or was confronted with an event or events that involved actual or threatened death or serious injury, or a threat to the physical integrity of self or others.
2. The person's response involved intense fear, helplessness, or horror.

B. THE TRAUMATIC EVENT IS PERSISTENTLY REEXPERIENCED IN ONE (OR MORE) OF THE FOLLOWING WAYS:

1. Recurrent and intrusive distressing recollections of the event including images, thoughts, or perceptions
2. Recurrent distressing dreams of the event
3. Acting or feeling as if the traumatic event were recurring
4. Intense psychological distress at exposure to internal or external cues that symbolize or resemble an aspect of the traumatic event
5. Physiologic reactivity upon exposure to internal or external cues that symbolize or resemble an aspect of the traumatic event

C. PERSISTENT AVOIDANCE OF STIMULI ASSOCIATED WITH THE TRAUMA AND NUMBING OF GENERAL RESPONSIVENESS, AS INDICATED BY THREE (OR MORE) OF THE FOLLOWING:

1. Efforts to avoid thoughts, feelings, or conversation associated with the trauma
2. Efforts to avoid activities, places, or people that arouse recollections of the trauma
3. Inability to recall an important aspect of the trauma
4. Markedly diminished interest or participation in significant activities
5. Feeling of detachment or estrangement from others
6. Restricted range of affect
7. Sense of a foreshortened future

D. PERSISTENT SYMPTOMS OF INCREASED AROUSAL, AS INDICATED BY TWO (OR MORE) OF THE FOLLOWING:

1. Difficulty falling or staying asleep
2. Irritability or outbursts of anger
3. Difficulty concentrating
4. Hypervigilance
5. Exaggerated startle response

E. DURATION OF THE DISTURBANCE IS MORE THAN 1 MONTH

Specify if:

Acute: If duration of symptoms is less than 3 months

Chronic: If duration of symptoms is 3 months or more

Specify if:

With delayed onset: If onset of symptoms is at least 6 months after the stressor

victimization   A pattern of responses often observed among victims of violent crimes, particularly rape, that includes fear, guilt, self-blame, powerlessness, and lowered self-esteem.

Classification of Acute and Posttraumatic Stress Disorders

BRIEF HISTORICAL PERSPECTIVE

Maladaptive reactions to traumatic stress have long been of interest to the military, where "normal" performance is expected in the face of the trauma of combat. Historically, most of the military's concern has focused on battle dropout, that is, men who leave the field of action as a result of what was called "combat neurosis" (Frances et al., 1995). During the Vietnam War, however, battle dropout was less frequent than in earlier wars, but delayed reactions to the trauma of combat were much more frequent (Figley, 1978). This outcome prompted much interest in posttraumatic stress disorder, a condition first listed in the DSM in 1980 (DSM-III).

CONTEMPORARY CLASSIFICATION

The basic diagnostic criteria for PTSD—reexperiencing, avoidance, and arousal—have remained more or less the same in revisions of the DSM. (See Table 7–1 for a list of DSM-IV diagnostic criteria.) However, the DSM-IV included two significant changes in the classification of traumatic stress disorders: Acute stress disorder was included as a separate diagnostic category and the definition of trauma was altered.

Acute Stress Disorder   The diagnosis of acute stress disorder (ASD) was introduced for the first time in DSM-IV. The symptoms of ASD and PTSD are essentially the same, except that ASD describes reactions occurring in the first 4 weeks after a traumatic stressor, whereas PTSD includes problems extending or beginning at least 1 month subsequent to the traumatic experience. (See Table 7–2 for the diagnostic criteria.) Not surprisingly, many people suffer from psychological troubles immediately after a trauma, and the severity of their immediate impairment is a fairly good predictor of whether or not they will have subsequent troubles. The diagnosis of ASD is an attempt to recognize this fact and to prevent the development of PTSD with early treatment. The dissociative symptoms were included in the diagnosis of ASD, but not PTSD, because dissociative symptoms are particularly likely to occur in the immediate aftermath of a trauma (Frances et al., 1995).

Traumatic Events   Earlier versions of the DSM defined trauma as an event "outside the range of usual human experience," but as we will discuss shortly, research has revealed that, unfortunately, many traumatic stressors are a *common* part of human experience in the United States today. The DSM-IV revised the definition of trauma to reflect this fact, and the manual also attempted to define trauma more precisely (Frances et al., 1995). Thus the DSM-IV developed the two-part definition of trauma that includes (1) the experience of an event involving actual or threatened death or injury to self or others and (2) a response of intense fear, helplessness, or horror in reaction to the event (see Tables 7–1 and 7–2).

Although we can define traumatic stress disorders in general terms, different traumatic stressors can dramatically influence how people experience PTSD or ASD. Delayed stress reactions to combat experience, particularly among Vietnam War veterans, were the first focus of research on PTSD, but valuable recent efforts have extended research to such traumatic events as rape (Kilpatrick et al., 1989), child sex abuse (Deblinger et al., 1989), spouse abuse (Astin, Ogland-Hand, Coleman, & Foy, 1995), and witnessing disasters (Rubonis & Bickman, 1991). Each of these traumas may result in ASD or PTSD, but, as illustrated by the case of Stephanie, diagnosis and treatment must be extremely sensitive to the unique consequences of different traumatic events (see Further Thoughts).

A particular concern is the experience of **victimization.** Like Stephanie, the victims of violent crimes, particularly sexual assault, have been found to suffer from a number of emotional difficulties, including fear, guilt, self-blame, powerlessness, and lowered self-esteem (see Further Thoughts). Crime victims also have an increased risk for developing affective and anxiety disorders, and as many as one-quarter may develop PTSD. Among rape victims, the rate of PTSD may climb to 50 percent or more (Breslau et al., 1991; Kessler et al., 1995; Kilpatrick et al., 1989).

TABLE 7–2

DSM-IV Diagnostic Criteria for Acute Stress Disorder (ASD)

A. **THE PERSON HAS BEEN EXPOSED TO A TRAUMATIC EVENT IN WHICH BOTH OF THE FOLLOWING WERE PRESENT:**

1. The person experienced, witnessed, or was confronted with an event or events that involved actual or threatened death or serious injury, or a threat to the physical integrity of self or others.
2. The person's response involved intense fear, helplessness, or horror.

B. **EITHER WHILE EXPERIENCING OR AFTER EXPERIENCING THE DISTRESSING EVENT, THE INDIVIDUAL HAS THREE (OR MORE) OF THE FOLLOWING DISSO-CIATIVE SYMPTOMS:**

1. A subjective sense of numbing, detachment, or absence of emotional responsiveness
2. A reduction in awareness of his or her surroundings (e.g., "being in a daze")
3. Derealization
4. Depersonalization
5. Dissociative amnesia (i.e., the inability to recall an important aspect of the trauma)

C. **THE TRAUMATIC EVENT IS PERSISTENTLY REEXPERIENCED IN AT LEAST ONE OF THE FOLLOWING WAYS: RECURRENT IMAGES, THOUGHTS, DREAMS, ILLU-SIONS, FLASHBACK EPISODES, OR A SENSE OF RELIVING THE EXPERIENCE; OR DISTRESS ON EXPOSURE TO REMINDERS OF THE TRAUMATIC EVENT.**

D. **MARKED AVOIDANCE OF STIMULI THAT AROUSE RECOLLECTIONS OF THE TRAUMA (E.G., THOUGHTS, FEELINGS, CONVERSATIONS, ACTIVITIES, PLACES, PEOPLE).**

E. **MARKED SYMPTOMS OF ANXIETY OR INCREASED AROUSAL (E.G., DIFFICULTY SLEEPING, IRRITABILITY, POOR CONCENTRATION, HYPERVIGILANCE, EXAG-GERATED STARTLE RESPONSE, MOTOR RESTLESSNESS).**

F. **THE DISTURBANCE CAUSES CLINICALLY SIGNIFICANT DISTRESS OR IMPAIR-MENT IN SOCIAL, OCCUPATIONAL, OR OTHER IMPORTANT AREAS OF FUNC-TIONING OR IMPAIRS THE INDIVIDUAL'S ABILITY TO PURSUE SOME NECES-SARY TASK, SUCH AS OBTAINING NECESSARY ASSISTANCE OR MOBILIZING PERSONAL RESOURCES BY TELLING FAMILY MEMBERS ABOUT THE TRAU-MATIC EXPERIENCE.**

G. **THE DISTURBANCE LASTS FOR A MINIMUM OF 2 DAYS AND A MAXIMUM OF 4 WEEKS AND OCCURS WITHIN 4 WEEKS OF THE TRAUMATIC EVENT.**

Epidemiology of Trauma and Traumatic Stress Disorders

Only in recent years have experts begun to study the epidemiology of trauma and traumatic stress disorders. Several studies support the importance of assault and combat exposure in causing PTSD in women and men, respectively, but recent research has documented that the prevalence of PTSD is much higher than previously thought.

A study of a random sample of 1,200 adults living in the Detroit area was the first to offer important details about how many people are exposed to traumatic stress and how many of these people develop PTSD (Breslau et al., 1991). Consistent with the change in the DSM-IV defini-

further thoughts

PTSD and the Sexual Assault of Women

The diagnosis of posttraumatic stress disorder is helpful because it highlights many basic similarities in the reactions of victims to different types of traumatic events. Moreover, it calls attention to the fact that extreme distress is a normal response to being a victim of abnormal events. Still, in focusing on the common features of reactions to traumatic stressors, we must not forget that each individual's reaction to particular forms of trauma has certain unique elements as well. (Goodman, Koss, & Russo, 1993b).

Like many other traumatic stressors, sexual assault is not outside the realm of normal human experience in the United States today. Several surveys have found that approximately 20 percent of U.S. women have been victims of rape. More than 80 percent of these rapes are *acquaintance rapes:* assaults committed by people known to the victim, rather than by strangers (Goodman, Koss, & Russo, 1993a).

The physical consequences of rape cannot be ignored. Thirty-nine percent of rape victims are physically injured on parts of their bodies other than the genitals. A significant proportion of rape victims are infected with a sexually transmitted disease, and about 5 percent of rapes result in pregnancy. Finally, many victims of sexual assault suffer from subsequent gastrointestinal problems, such as nausea.

Most victims of sexual assault show the symptoms of PTSD. Victims may reexperience the horrors of the assault; they may feel numbed in reacting to others, particularly sexual partners; they may avoid any potentially threatening situation; and they may maintain both autonomic hyperarousal and hypervigilance against possible victimization. At the same time, victims of sexual assault also may experience profound relief and fears about simply being alive. They are grateful to be alive, yet fearful that their life could be so threatened. Depression is also common. Sadness, crying, and withdrawal from others often are coupled with sleep and appetite disturbances. Loss of interest in sex, insecurities about sexual identity, sexual dysfunction, and negative feelings toward men also are common.

Another frequent psychological problem is that many victims of sexual assault blame themselves despite the fact that they are the victims. Women may wonder if they unwittingly encouraged their assailant, or they may chastise themselves for not being more cautious in avoiding dangerous circumstances. This irrational self-blame is abetted by cultural myths that women provoke rape or that they actually enjoy it. These myths also may explain why as many as two-thirds of stranger rapes and four-fifths of acquaintance rapes are not reported to authorities. In fact, many women feel that they cannot discuss the sexual assault with anyone, which surely impedes recovery of more normal functioning.

Because sexual assault is difficult to discuss, Goodman, Koss, and Russo (1993a) recommend that all mental and physical health care providers routinely ask their patients whether they have been victims of physical or sexual violence. This is critical information for making a diagnosis of both physical and mental conditions, and questions may encourage some victims to open up about their experiences. There also is the hope that the prevalence of sexual assault can be reduced by increasing awareness of its frequency and its devastating consequences.

---

tion of trauma, a high number of adults in this study—39 percent—reported that they had experienced a traumatic stressor. About 25 percent of those exposed to such a stressor later developed PTSD. The disorder was more likely following rape in comparison to other traumas and was less likely following a sudden injury or serious accident. Figure 7–1 on page 192 illustrates the results of this study, which have been supported by the findings of the National Comorbidity Survey (Kessler et al., 1995).

The Detroit study also documented factors that increased the risk for experiencing trauma and conditions that made PTSD more likely among the trauma victims. Trauma was more likely to be experienced by men, by those with less education, and by people who were more "neurotic" (anxious) or extroverted, who had a history of conduct problems during childhood, and who had a family history of mental disorder. Among victims of traumatic stress, PTSD was more likely to be found among women, the more "neurotic," those with a family history of mental disorder, and people who themselves previously suffered from an emotional problem (Breslau et al., 1991). The same team of investigators replicated many of these findings in a prospective longitudinal study (Breslau, Davis, & Andreski, 1995). Thus, people with a history of emotional problems are more likely both to experience trauma and to suffer PTSD as a consequence.

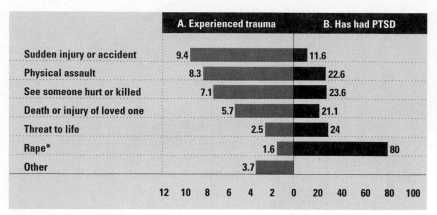

Figure 7–1   These Bar Graphs Highlight the Prevalence of Trauma and the Risk for Posttraumatic Stress Disorder.   Part (A) illustrates the percentage of the overall population who had experienced a particular trauma (based on a study of 1,200 adults in Detroit between the ages of 21 and 30). Part (B) shows the percentage of people exposed to those traumas who developed PTSD. Note that the rape victims were by far the most likely to experience PTSD.

*The prevalence of rape as reported in this study was much lower than that reported in other studies. We assume that this statistic reflects only the most violent rapes.
Source: Adapted from N. Breslau, G. C. Davis, P. Andreski, and E. Peterson, 1991, Traumatic events and posttraumatic stress disorder in the urban population of young adults, *Archives of General Psychiatry, 48,* 216–222.

These findings, and those from other research, raise questions about the role of premorbid personality in experiencing trauma and PTSD. Findings suggest that premorbid maladjustment is not necessary for the development of PTSD, but preexisting psychological problems increase the risk for the disorder in two ways: They increase the likelihood of experiencing trauma, and they diminish the individual's ability to cope with that trauma.

Etiological Considerations and Research on PTSD and ASD

By definition, traumatic experience causes ASD and PTSD, and this identification of a precise etiological agent distinguishes these problems from most disorders listed in the DSM-IV. However, the fact that not everyone who experiences trauma develops ASD or PTSD indicates that the etiology of the disorder is more complex. That is, a given trauma is a necessary but not a sufficient cause of ASD or PTSD.

In general, there are three alternative ways to explain the imperfect relation between the experience of trauma and the development of traumatic stress disorders. *Threshold models* suggest that "everyone has a breaking point." Thus, from this perspective, anyone will develop ASD and/or PTSD when exposed to a sufficiently intense trauma. From the threshold perspective, the most relevant etiological issues concern the nature of the traumatic event and the individual's exposure to it. In contrast, *diathesis-stress models* indicate that trauma is necessary for the development of a traumatic stress disorder, but the disorder will emerge only when combined with other risk factors, such as premorbid personality characteristics. The interaction between risk and trauma is most important from the diathesis-stress perspective. Finally, *illness models* hold that, in many cases, emotional problems found *after* the experience of a trauma actually were present *before* the event occurred. From the illness point of view, the trauma merely leads to the identification or emergence of a preexisting condition. It is important to keep in mind these three general models when examining research on specific biological, psychological, and social risk factors.

BIOLOGICAL FACTORS IN TRAUMATIC STRESS DISORDERS

Behavior genetic researchers have found that biological factors increase the risk of both experiencing trauma and developing PTSD. A twin study of more than 4,000 Vietnam-era veterans found that MZ twins had a higher concordance rate than DZ twins for experiencing trauma, specifically exposure to combat, and for developing PTSD symptoms (True et al., 1993). Of particular note was the finding that the magnitude of genetic effects differed across symptoms of the disorder. Genetic contributions were greatest in accounting for arousal/anxiety symptoms and least for symptoms of reexperiencing. Conversely, level of exposure to combat predicted symptoms of reexperiencing and avoidance of activities, but exposure did not predict other symptoms of PTSD (True et al., 1993). Thus, consistent with the diathesis-stress model, it appears that genetic factors contribute to PTSD. However, a preexisting diathesis may contribute more to arousal/anxiety symptoms than to symptoms of reexperiencing, which may be more direct reactions to trauma.

Several different psychological characteristics may account for the increased risk for trauma exposure and for PTSD that has been identified in research in behavior genetics and other areas. Psychological risk factors include antisocial behavior (Helzer, Robins, & McEvoy, 1987; King, King, Foy, & Gudanowski, 1996), depression (Frank et al., 1981), and neuroticism (McFarlane, 1988). One study found that premorbid personality (specifically, a positive family history of psychopathology) was related to PTSD among veterans with low exposure to combat, but it was unrelated to PTSD when combat exposure is high (Foy et al., 1987). This evidence supports both the threshold and the diathesis-stress models. People subjected to intense levels of stress may develop PTSD even in the absence of premorbid personality risk factors, but the risk factors become central in contributing to PTSD when the trauma is less intense.

Biological Effects of Exposure to Trauma   A very different biological approach focuses on the biological *consequences* of exposure to trauma and how these consequences may play a role in the maintenance of PTSD (van der Kolk, 1996; Watson, Hoffman, & Wilson, 1988; Yehuda & McFarlane, 1995). One group of investigators has suggested that trauma alters the activity of particular neurotransmitters in the brain (van der Kolk et al., 1984). According to this theory, trauma increases the production of the neurotransmitter norepinephrine. This excess production of norepinephrine in turn causes the increased arousal and anxiety that are symptoms of the disorder. This hypothesis further suggests that excess norepinephrine causes the normal stress response to be activated more intensely and by milder stressors. (See Chapter 8 for a discussion of norepinephrine and the normal stress response.)

Another hypothesis suggests that exposure to traumatic stress increases the production of endogenous (internally produced) *opioids,* chemicals manufactured by the body that have similar effects to exogenous (produced outside the body) opioids like morphine (see Chapter 11). According to this hypothesis, the increase in internally produced opioids causes the numbing that characterizes PTSD (van der Kolk et al., 1984). One interesting study of the hypothesis found that Vietnam veterans with PTSD showed *decreased* pain sensitivity following exposure to a film of combat. No change in pain threshold was found when the veterans were administered naloxone, a chemical that blocks the effects of the opioids, and no changes in pain tolerance—either with or without naloxone—were found among veterans without PTSD (Pitman et al., 1990). The findings of this study are open to several alternative interpretations, but they provide justification for further study of this intriguing hypothesis.

We must remember that biological explanations can be perfectly consistent with psychological and social hypotheses about the development of the disorder. Because every psychological experience has an underlying biological counterpart, ASD and PTSD *must* be accompanied by changes in brain structure or function. The task for psychobiologists and biochemists who wish to understand the effects of psychological trauma is to identify specific brain sites and biochemical actions that are linked with traumatic stress disorders.

PSYCHOLOGICAL FACTORS IN TRAUMATIC STRESS DISORDERS

In addition to the role of premorbid personality, several hypotheses have been offered about how psychological reactions to trauma may play a part in the development of ASD and PTSD.

Psychodynamic formulations emphasize the role of the defenses in protecting the individual against the anxiety created by trauma. Psychodynamic theorists suggest that massive repression plays a role in numbing and withdrawal, a result of the need for strong intrapsychic defenses to cope with intense trauma. Conversely, reexperiencing is thought to result from a breakdown of repression (Oei, Lim, & Hennessy, 1990).

Edna Foa is a psychologist at the Eastern Pennsylvania Psychiatric Institute in Philadelphia. Foa has done extensive research on the etiology and treatment of PTSD.

The psychologist Edna Foa, a leading researcher on social learning causes and treatments for PTSD, has used *two-factor theory* to explain the development of symptoms following a number of traumas (Foa, Steketee, & Rothbaum, 1989). Two-factor theory involves a combination of classical conditioning and operant conditioning. According to Foa and other two-factor theorists, classical conditioning *creates* a number of fears when the terror inherent in trauma is paired with the cues associated with the traumatic event. Operant conditioning, in turn, *maintains* these fears. Specifically, when fear-producing situations are avoided, the avoidance behavior is negatively reinforced by the reduction of aversive anxiety (Keane, Zimering, & Caddell, 1985). For example, Stephanie's fears of being alone at night are understandable both intuitively and from the perspective of classical conditioning. Her avoidance of fearful circumstances, such as being alone, probably helped to maintain her fear in the short run. More importantly, Stephanie's courage in confronting her fears—and her attacker—and her willingness to discuss her experiences surely helped her to learn to overcome her fears, as we discuss in more detail shortly.

Learning theorists suggest that such cognitive processes as self-blame and expectancies of further trauma are also important in the etiology of traumatic stress disorders (Foa, Steketee, & Rothbaum, 1989; Jones & Barlow, 1990). In practice, however, it is difficult to determine whether such factors as self-blame or expectancies are causes of or reactions to (symptoms of) ASD and PTSD. Research indicates that expectancies can be important in that people cope with traumatic stress more adequately when they are able to anticipate its onset. For example, pilots with prior training appear to cope more successfully with subsequent helicopter crashes than pilots who have received no training preparing them for emergency crashes. At the same time, evidence indicates that more severe short-term reactions to trauma—more severe ASD—predicts more severe PTSD in the long term (Shalev, 1996). In fact, research has demonstrated that, among Israeli trauma victims, the degree of dissociation reported within 1 week following a trauma predicted more severe PTSD 6 months later (Shalev et al., 1996). This finding suggests that dissociation may be better conceived as a symptom of traumatic stress disorders and not a (unconscious) coping mechanism. By extension, the finding raises questions about whether other cognitive or emotional processes (e.g., self-blame, anger) are better viewed as reactions to, rather than mediating causes of, ASD and PTSD.

SOCIAL FACTORS IN TRAUMATIC STRESS DISORDERS

Researchers recently have documented that the risk for PTSD among Vietnam combat veterans increases if they have had a history of family instability or of exposure to prior traumas (King et al., 1996). Thus the predisposition in the diathesis-stress model sometimes may be a past social experience and not just a biological or psychological vulnerability. Most research on social factors in ASD and PTSD has not focused on past events, however, but instead has investigated the role of social factors that occur during or following the trauma. In particular, scientists have studied the extent to which the risk for PTSD is affected by (1) the nature of the traumatic event and the individual's level of exposure to it and (2) the availability of social support following the traumatic event.

Consistent with the threshold model, researchers have found that more intense and life-threatening traumatic events are more likely to result in PTSD. For example, victims of attempted rape are more likely to develop PTSD if the rape is completed, if they are physically injured during the assault, and if they perceive the sexual assault as life-threatening (Kilpatrick et al., 1989). The importance of the experience of trauma is dramatically underscored by evidence from the same twin study we discussed earlier. Among MZ twin pairs during the Vietnam era, the prevalence of PTSD was found to be 9 times higher for co-twins who served in Vietnam than for their identical twin who did not serve (Goldberg, True, Eisen, & Henderson, 1990). Thus twin research clearly documents the importance of *both* genes *and* experience in causing PTSD.

As with less severe stressors, the availability of social support after the occurrence of the trauma appears to play a crucial role in alleviating long-term psychological damage. Many victims of rape mistakenly feel guilty and somehow responsible for being attacked. Rape crisis centers and rape support groups offer social support that helps women recognize that they are not at fault—they are victims of a heinous crime. A lack of social support also is thought to have contributed to the high prevalence of PTSD found among Vietnam veterans (Oei, Lim, & Hennessy, 1990). Rather than being praised as heroes, returning veterans often were treated with disdain. This absence of support made it difficult for many veterans to justify the trauma that they had suffered, and it likely increased the number of cases of PTSD as a result.

INTEGRATION AND ALTERNATIVE PATHWAYS

The combination of evidence suggests some support for all three models, and, in fact, there likely are alternative pathways to the development of ASD and PTSD. In some cases, the threshold model probably is true: Anyone could develop a traumatic stress disorder given a critical level of exposure and a trauma of sufficient intensity. In other cases, the illness model also is likely to be true: A trauma may call attention to or exacerbate preexisting disorders or maladaptive personality characteristics. Notwithstanding these possibilities, evidence indicates that a diathesis-stress model best explains most cases. Although trauma is a necessary cause of PTSD, the specific etiology of PTSD typically involves a complex interaction of risk factors that are present before the trauma, during the trauma, and after its occurrence.

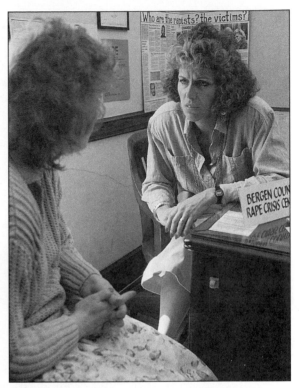

Rape crisis centers offer women support in dealing with sexual assault.

Future research should clarify which biological, psychological, and social factors increase the risk for ASD and PTSD, and hopefully scientists also will identify *protective factors.* For example, researchers recently have documented that increased *hardiness*—a personal sense of commitment, control, and challenge in facing stress—predicted lower rates of PTSD among troops in the Persian Gulf War (Sutker, Davis, Uddo, & Ditta, 1995).

Prevention and Treatment of ASD and PTSD

In most cases, the symptoms of traumatic stress disorders begin immediately or shortly after a traumatic event. However, the symptoms of PTSD can begin months or years after the trauma, and the reexperiencing of the trauma can continue for long periods of time. In addition to situations that are reminiscent of the trauma, reminders such as anniversary dates often cause the horror to be relived, as we saw with the case of Stephanie. Because of the variability in onset and duration of symptoms, it is important to distinguish emergency attempts to help trauma victims from longer-term treatment efforts.

EMERGENCY TREATMENT OF TRAUMA VICTIMS

Trauma is a known cause of ASD and PTSD, and this knowledge makes prevention the first consideration in the treatment of the disorders. Early intervention with trauma victims holds the hope of both easing the pain of coping with a horrific event and of preventing the subsequent development of PTSD.

Psychologists and other mental health professionals frequently offer emergency assistance to individual victims of trauma or to groups of people who have experienced a disaster. These emergency treatments range from intensive individual counseling sessions with rape victims to group discussions with children whose school has been destroyed by a tornado. There are many differences in the therapeutic approaches used across such prevention efforts, but offering immediate social support to trauma victims is a common goal of all early interventions (Raphael, Wilson, Meldrum, & McFarlane, 1996).

Little systematic research has been conducted on the effectiveness of most emergency interventions with the victims of trauma (Raphael et al., 1996). The treatment of soldiers in combat

Getting help

Getting Help

The disorders discussed in this chapter are fascinating, and the controversies about them are intellectually exciting—unless you or someone you know is suffering from PTSD or a dissociative or somatoform disorder. In this case, the unusual symptoms of these disorders can be extremely frightening, the lack of knowledge and acceptance can be isolating, and the controversy surrounding the disorders can seem callous, manipulative, or both.

The controversies and limited scientific information about these disorders make it difficult to make clear recommendations for getting help. However, we can readily offer one strong suggestion: If you have been the victim of trauma, for example, rape, abuse, or a victim or witness of some other form of violence, talk to someone about it. You may find it difficult to trust anyone, but trying to "forget about it" is exactly the wrong thing to do. Confronting fear, embarrassment, or others' lack of understanding is far better than keeping it all inside. If you are not willing to consider therapy, confide in someone.

We are particularly concerned about the trauma of rape, an all-too-frequent occurrence among college students. If you or someone you know has been raped, the first step may be to get to a hospital emergency room or to call the police. You also may want to contact a rape crisis center in your area. The Rape Abuse and Incest Network National hotline, 800-656-4673, can provide you with the telephone number of the rape crisis center closest to you. Two excellent websites about rape and other forms of intimate violence are *http://www.victimservices.org/*,

Victim Services, and *http://www.worldchat.com/public/asarc/*, Anonymous Sexual Abuse Recovery. A good self-help book is *Free of the Shadows: Recovering from Sexual Violence,* by Caren Adams and Jennifer Fay.

There are many other resources for victims of rape and other types of trauma. A helpful, general website is *http://www.dartmouth.edu/dms/ptsd/*, the National Center for PTSD. This site focuses particularly on PTSD following combat exposure. A website that is more focused on the legal system and the rights of crime victims than on the psychological aspects of trauma is *http://www.nvc.org/*, the National Center for Victims of Crime. Finally, the Sidran Foundation, *http://www.sidran.org/*, is a nonprofit organization promoting information and awareness on PTSD and dissociative disorders.

Unfortunately, we have to close with a strong word of caution about getting help for PTSD, dissociative, and somatoform disorders. The controversies discussed in this chapter are not just theoretical. There are many self-help resources—and professionals—who claim that one side or the other of a given controversy is fact, not theory or opinion. We urge you to be extremely cautious if a professional or resource fails to acknowledge the uncertain state of scientific information and the range of opinion about such things as the long-term consequences of childhood trauma, the prevalence of multiple personality disorder, or the nature of recovered memories. A dramatic illustration of the havoc that can be created by those who are supposed to help can be found in the book *Remembering Satan,* Lawrence Wright's journalistic account of the consequences of one episode of false "recovered memories" of Satanic ritual abuse. 🌿

is one of the few exceptions where empirical evidence is available. Since World War I, the treatment of soldiers who experience combat stress has been based on the three principles of offering (1) immediate treatment in the (2) proximity of the battlefield with the (3) expectation of return to the front lines upon recovery. The effectiveness of these treatment principles has been long assumed, but they were not studied systematically until 1982, when the Israeli army implemented the practices during the Lebanon war. Evaluation of the emergency services indicated that 60 percent of soldiers who were treated near the front recovered sufficiently to return to battle within 72 hours. Soldiers who expected to return to the front experienced lower rates of PTSD than did those who did not expect to return to battle. In addition, those soldiers who were treated on the front lines were less likely to develop PTSD subsequently when compared to soldiers who were treated in civilian facilities away from the battlefield (Oei, Lim, & Hennessy, 1990).

It seems reasonable to generalize these principles to the treatment of victims of many, but not all (e.g., rape victims), forms of trauma. For example, we would expect that victims of a natural disaster would benefit from immediate treatment near their communities with the expectation of a rapid return to normal life. Perhaps the key to this intervention strategy is the creation of the expectation that extreme distress in the face of trauma is normal, as is recovery from the trauma. This expectation may become a reality when combined with successful, subsequent coping.

TREATMENT OF PTSD

Psychotropic medication is frequently used in the treatment of PTSD, but there is no single medication that has specific effects on the disorder. Rather, various antidepressant and antianxiety medications sometimes are used to treat particular symptoms associated with PTSD (Davidson & van der Kolk, 1996; Marshall & Klein, 1995).

Psychotherapists who specialize in PTSD have suggested some general principles for the psychological treatment of the disorder. In the order in which they are likely to be addressed in therapy, these include (1) establishing a trusting therapeutic relationship, (2) providing education about the process of coping with trauma, (3) stress-management training, (4) encouraging the reexperience of the trauma, and (5) integrating the traumatic event into the individual's experience (Scurfield, 1985).

Therapeutic Reexposure to Trauma   Reexposure to the traumatic event is perhaps the least obvious but most important of these strategies (Frueh, Turner, & Beidel, 1995; Rothbaum & Foa, 1996). Perhaps because the terrifying and uncontrollable reliving of trauma is one of the most distressing symptoms of PTSD, reexperiencing in a controlled treatment setting becomes basic to the therapeutic process. Therapeutic approaches differ widely in how this reexperience is encouraged, yet all treatments encourage the recounting of trauma in some form. The most direct method is *trauma desensitization,* a variation of the well-researched treatment for phobias, systematic desensitization (see Chapter 6). Initially, the client is taught a basic relaxation technique. He or she then relives the traumatic event through discussions with the therapist or through imagining the experience. Exposure to the trauma is gradual, so that the client can maintain a state of relaxation. The client confronts increasingly distressing details only after he or she can relive less upsetting events while remaining calm.

Little research had been conducted on the effectiveness of trauma desensitization or other treatments for PTSD until recent years, when a few investigations have been completed (Frueh, Turner, & Beidel, 1995; Rothbaum & Foa, 1996). A study conducted in the Netherlands compared the effectiveness of trauma desensitization, hypnotherapy, and psychodynamic therapy in the treatment of people suffering from the effects of a variety of traumatic experiences (Brom, Kleber, & Defares, 1989). Trauma desensitization followed the procedures described above. Hypnotherapy was similar to trauma desensitization, except that hypnosis was used to facilitate the reliving of the traumatic experience. Psychodynamic therapy focused on the intrapsychic conflicts caused by the trauma rather than on the trauma itself.

All treatments produced significantly more positive outcomes in comparison with an untreated control group. The most notable improvements were that subjects were less likely to avoid difficult situations and experienced intrusive thoughts less frequently. Overall, however, there were no statistically significant differences among the three alternative treatments (Brom, Kleber, & Defares, 1989).

The similarities in treatment effectiveness may be another indication of the common factors found across different types of psychotherapy (see Chapter 3). In this study, the common factor may have been the reliving of the trauma, whether through desensitization, hypnosis, or discussion of its effects on intrapsychic life. This conclusion is supported by a treatment outcome study of rape victims (Foa et al., 1991). Prolonged exposure involving repeated reliving of the trauma over nine therapy sessions produced more long-term reductions in PTSD symptoms than did three alternatives: (1) stress inoculation training (focusing on relaxation and stress management), (2) supportive counseling (which explicitly omitted exposure procedures), and (3) a wait list control group. Also of interest was the finding that stress inoculation training produced more short-term benefits, whereas prolonged exposure was more effective in the long run.

COURSE AND OUTCOME

Relatively little is known about the long-term course of ASD or PTSD. Evidence indicates, however, that PTSD can be chronic and can interfere with many areas of life functioning. One study of World War II prisoners of war who suffered from PTSD (as diagnosed by retrospective report) found that only about 30 percent were fully recovered, whereas 60 percent continued to have mild to moderate symptoms of the disorder. Another 10 percent either showed no recovery or had a deteriorating course (Kluznik et al., 1986). Given that the follow-up study was conducted 40 years after the imprisonment, these data suggest a poor prognosis, at least for those subjected to the extreme and prolonged trauma of being prisoners of war.

further thoughts

Recovered Memories?

In 1990, George Franklin was convicted of the brutal murder of an 8-year-old girl. The crime had occurred over 20 years earlier, and the major evidence was the "recovered memory" of Franklin's daughter Eileen. Eileen claimed to have witnessed the rape and murder of her friend by her father, but dissociation pushed the memory of the horrid experience into her unconscious mind. Twenty years later, according to the daughter, the memory returned. In fact, Eileen provided both verifiable and inconsistent accounts of the horrifying event. She recalled a smashed ring on her friend's finger as she raised her hand to protect herself from a blow with a rock. Case records corroborated the memory. On the other hand, Eileen changed her story about the presence of her sister in the van she was riding in that day, and she changed the time of day from morning to afternoon. George Franklin was convicted of murder in 1990, but his conviction was overturned in 1995, and he was released from prison. A U.S. District Court judge did not bar Eileen Franklin's testimony about her recovered memories, but he ruled that the lower court erred in excluding evidence that Eileen could have learned details about the 1969 murder from news articles. Thus the question remains: Was Eileen's memory accurate?

Recovered memories have become an important and controversial issue. Popular books and earnest therapists urge people to unearth past traumas, particularly remembrances of physical and sexual abuse, and an increasing number of people have claimed that they have recovered horrible memories from the past. Many parents faced with accusations about the past suggest, however, that they are being caused to suffer unnecessary pain. They suggest that false memories are being created by misguided, overeager therapists. Are recovered memories examples of dissociation, or are they merely examples of the power of suggestion?

This question has been considered in detail by the psychologist Elizabeth Loftus (1993), a specialist in memories of painful events who has served as an expert witness in numerous trials. Although it is impossible to verify—or disprove—many memories from the distant past, Loftus suggests numerous reasons for skepticism, or at least caution. One area of recovered memories that Loftus clearly disputes are recollections that date to very early childhood. A number of people have claimed to recall trauma dating from infancy or toddlerhood, but such memories are inconsistent with current knowledge of memory in early childhood. Most memories prior to school age are forgotten, and few people can report memories dating back before age 3 or 4. One study found, for example, that few subjects who were under the age of 3 at the time could recall where they were when President Kennedy was assassinated. In contrast, most subjects who had been at least 8 years old at the time of the assassination reported at least some memory of being told about the tragedy (Winograd & Killinger, 1983).

recovered memories Dramatic recollections of long-forgotten traumatic experiences; a controversial topic because the "memories" often are impossible to validate and many such memories may be created rather than recovered.

Recovered Memories?   A final issue in consideration of the course and outcome of traumatic stress disorders is the very controversial topic of **recovered memories,** dramatic recollections of a long-forgotten traumatic experience (see Further Thoughts). Is it possible that some traumatic experiences are so overwhelming that the mind blocks them from conscious awareness? If so, could some experience—perhaps psychotherapy—cause accurate memories of such experiences to resurface into the conscious mind many years later?

We believe that proponents have greatly exaggerated the extent and accuracy of recovered memories, although we have no doubt that many memories, including traumatic ones, can become inaccessible over time. In reaching these conclusions, we note three facts (also see Further Thoughts). First, evidence indicates that some people fail to recall traumatic experiences such as childhood sexual abuse that have been documented to occur long ago (Williams, 1994). Second, evidence also indicates that some people report *false memories* of events that are known *not* to have occurred in the past (Loftus, Garry, & Feldman, 1994). Third, psychologists have no reliable and valid method for determining whether, in any given individual case, a "recovered memory" is accurate or false. In any case, the dissociation between traumatic experience and memory provides another link between PTSD and our next topic, dissociative disorders.

Dissociative Disorders

Until recent years, *dissociative disorders*—characterized by persistent, maladaptive disruptions in the integration of memory, consciousness, or identity—were of more interest to theorists and novelists than to empirically oriented mental health professionals. However, there has been an explosion of

More suspicions emerge from an examination of some case histories of recovered memories. Studies indicate that therapists rarely doubt their clients' recovered memories of the past (Loftus, 1993; Loftus & Ketcham, 1994), but the concern embraces much more than a lack of skepticism. Many therapists and popular books encourage people to search for (create?) memories that they do not recall. Symptoms as common and mild as low self-esteem are sometimes interpreted as indications of past, forgotten trauma. Gaps in memory are also interpreted as a sign of dissociated memories. One example of this approach is noted in the popular book *The Courage to Heal.* The authors state:

> You may think you don't have memories, but often as you begin to talk about what you do remember, there emerges a constellation of feelings, reactions, and recollections that add up to substantial information. To say "I was abused," you don't need the kind of recall that would stand up in a court of law.
>
> Often the knowledge that you were abused starts with a tiny feeling, an intuition. It's important to trust that inner voice and work from there. Assume your feelings are valid. So far, no one we've talked to thought she might have been abused and then later discovered that she hadn't been. (Bass & Davis, 1988, p. 22)

Could such suggestions lead some people to create memories about events that never happened? We think the answer is yes. Determining the truth in any one case is difficult, sometimes impossible. Nevertheless, several studies supply evidence that memories, even of highly dramatic events, can be inaccurate (Loftus, 1993; Loftus & Ketcham, 1994). In one such study, subjects were interviewed the day after the explosion of the space shuttle *Challenger* and described the circumstances of how they learned of the tragedy. Three years later, the same subjects again were asked how they had learned about the explosion. About one-third of the subjects reported vivid—and grossly inaccurate—memories of what they were doing and how they learned about the *Challenger* tragedy (Neisser & Harsch, 1992).

These observations do not prove that memories of trauma are false. In fact, evidence indicates that memories for emotion-laden events are more accurate than memories for ordinary experiences (Koss, Tromp, & Tharan, 1995). Still, the malleability of memory suggests grounds for skepticism, particularly when a memory is "recovered" after a therapist encourages a client to search for it. A therapist's unwillingness to believe a patient can damage the therapeutic relationship, but false memories also can produce great harm to the client—and to anyone who is falsely accused. Skepticism and clinical sensitivity are not incompatible. There is dramatic and apparently accurate evidence to suggest that traumatic memories sometimes are repressed. Dissociation between experience and memory should not be dismissed merely because it is difficult to demonstrate. At the same time, psychologists must not be overzealous in assuming certain knowledge about topics that inherently involve much uncertainty. ❦

---

interest in dissociative disorders since the 1980s. This bodes well for future research. Currently, however, clinical and theoretical approaches to dissociative disorders are controversial, and as you will soon discover, sound empirical evidence on dissociative disorders remains sharply limited.

If the dissociative symptoms found in acute and posttraumatic stress disorders are dramatic, the symptoms of dissociative disorders verge on the unbelievable. The person with a dissociative disorder may be unable to remember many seemingly familiar details about the past; he or she may wander far from home and perhaps assume a new identity; or in extreme cases, two or more personalities may coexist within the same person.

hysteria An outdated but influential diagnostic category that included both somatoform and dissociative disorders. Attempts to treat hysteria had a major effect on Charcot, Freud, and Janet, among others. In Greek, *hysteria* means "uterus," a reflection of ancient speculation that hysteria was restricted to women and caused by frustrated sexual desires.

Brief Historical Perspective: Hysteria and Unconscious Mental Processes

Dissociative disorders (and somatoform disorders, which we discuss later in the chapter) once were viewed as expressions of **hysteria,** a term that dates to ancient Greece. In Greek, *hystera* literally means "uterus," and the term *hysteria* reflects ancient speculation that these disorders were caused by frustrated sexual desires, particularly the desire to have a baby. According to the theory, the uterus became detached from its normal location and moved about the body, causing a problem in the location where it eventually lodged. Variants of this fantastic view continued throughout Western history, and as late as the nineteenth century many physicians erroneously believed that hysteria occurred only among women (van der Hart & Friedman, 1989).

New speculation about the etiology of hysteria emerged toward the end of the nineteenth century. The work of Jean Charcot, who used hypnosis both to treat and to induce hysteria, was

The French neurologist Jean Charcot (1825–1893) demonstrating a case of hysteria at the Salpetriere, a famous hospital in Paris. Charcot's work with hysteria and hypnosis greatly influenced the thinking of both Sigmund Freud and Pierre Janet.

Pierre Janet (1859–1947) conducted psychological experiments as a professor in Paris, and he later trained as a physician in Jean Charcot's clinic. Janet's views on dissociation were much more circumscribed than those of his rival, Sigmund Freud.

particularly important. Charcot greatly influenced the thinking of Freud, who observed Charcot's hypnotic treatments early in his training (see Chapter 2). Charcot also had a strong influence on the work of Freud's contemporary and rival, Pierre Janet (1859–1947). Janet was a French philosophy professor who conducted psychological experiments on dissociation and who later trained as a physician in Charcot's clinic (see Chapter 6).

Both Janet and Freud were eager to explain and treat hysteria, and the problem led both of them to develop theories about unconscious mental processes. The two competitors differed in the specifics of their views about dissociation and the unconscious mind. Janet viewed dissociation as an abnormal process. To him, detachment from conscious awareness occurred only as a part of psychopathology. Thus Janet defined unconscious processes narrowly, consistent with what he observed in dissociative and somatoform disorders. In contrast, Freud viewed dissociation as a normal process, a routine means through which the ego defended itself against unacceptable unconscious thoughts. Freud saw dissociation and repression as similar processes, and, in fact, he often used the two terms interchangeably (Erdelyi, 1990; Perry & Laurence, 1984). Thus Freud considered dissociative and somatoform disorders to be merely one of many expressions of unconscious conflict.

Janet's work became increasingly obscure as Freudian theory dominated the mental health professions throughout much of the twentieth century. As Freudian influences have declined in recent years, scholars have rediscovered Janet's contributions and his more narrow conception of dissociation and unconscious mental processes.

Contemporary psychologists continue to raise important and controversial questions about dissociation and unconscious processes, but they generally agree about two things. First, unconscious processes do exist, and they play a role in both normal and abnormal emotion and cognition (Wegner, 1994). Second, contemporary cognitive scientists distinguish their more restricted view of unconscious processes from Freud's elaborate view of *the* unconscious.

Freud postulated a global unconscious mind, comprising an intricate set of processes (for example, the defenses) and contents (e.g., id impulses). Contemporary cognitive scientists also recognize unconscious contents (e.g., inaccessible memories) and processes (e.g., memory search strategies). In contrast to Freud, however, contemporary scientists view unconscious events as being much less influential in shaping both normal and abnormal behavior (Bowers & Meichenbaum, 1984; Singer, 1990). In the words of one cognitive scientist, the unconscious mind is "dumb," not "smart"; that is, it has a limited influence on human behavior (Loftus & Klinger, 1992).

Typical Symptoms of Dissociative Disorders

We cannot observe unconscious processes, but scientists note that, like many ordinary cognitive procedures, the symptoms of dissociative disorders apparently involve mental processing that occurs outside of conscious awareness. Extreme cases of dissociation include a split in the functioning of the individual's entire sense of self. In dissociative identity disorder, two or more personalities coexist within a single individual, and one or both of the personalities may be unaware of the existence of the other. Unless we assume that the symptom is feigned, dissociative identity disorder would seem to demonstrate the existence of multiple levels of mental functioning.

Depersonalization is a less dramatic form of dissociation wherein people feel detached from themselves or their social or physical environment. Examples of depersonalization include feeling like a stranger or a "robot" in social interactions, and out-of-body experiences—feelings of detachment from one's physical being.

Another dramatic example of dissociation is *amnesia*—the partial or complete loss of recall for particular events or for a particular period of time. Brain injury or disease can cause amnesia (see Chapter 14), but *psychogenic* (psychologically caused) amnesia results from traumatic stress or other sources of emotional distress. Psychogenic amnesia may occur alone or in conjunction with other dissociative experiences. For example, in dissociative identity disorder one personality may not remember the actions—or even the existence—of another (Spiegel & Cardena, 1991).

Classification of Dissociative Disorders

BRIEF HISTORICAL PERSPECTIVE

For centuries, theorists considered dissociative and somatoform disorders together as alternative forms of hysteria. However, Freudian proponents, who defined dissociation broadly, classified hysteria as a subtype of *neurosis*—a diagnostic category that also included anxiety and depressive disorders. The category "neurosis" reflected the Freudian view that unconscious conflict was the common cause of each of these apparently different disorders. Still, the historical link between somatoform and dissociative disorders was preserved in many classification systems.

The descriptive approach to classification led to the separation of dissociative and somatoform disorders into discrete diagnostic categories. The distinction is preserved in DSM-IV (1994), because the symptoms of the two disorders clearly differ greatly, as we discuss shortly. Consistent with DSM-IV, we review the two problems separately. We nevertheless discuss both problems in a single chapter because of their historical relationship and because both apparently involve unconscious processes.

CONTEMPORARY CLASSIFICATION

The DSM-IV distinguishes four major subtypes of dissociative disorders: dissociative fugue, dissociative amnesia, depersonalization disorder, and dissociative identity disorder. *Dissociative fugue* is characterized by sudden and unexpected travel away from home, an inability to recall the past, and confusion about identity or the assumption of a new identity.

Dissociative amnesia involves a sudden inability to recall extensive and important personal information that exceeds normal forgetfulness. The memory loss in dissociative amnesia is not attributable to substance abuse, head trauma, or a cognitive disorder, such as Alzheimer's disease. As with fugue, dissociative amnesia typically is characterized by a sudden onset in response to trauma or extreme stress and by an equally sudden recovery of memory. The most common form of amnesia in dissociative disorders is *selective amnesia,* in which patients do not lose their memory completely but instead are unable to remember only selected personal events and information, often events related to a traumatic experience. (See Chapter 13 for a discussion of other types of amnesia found in cognitive disorders.) In one study of 25 patients in a dissociative disorders clinic, 76 percent had selective amnesia (Coons & Milstein, 1988, cited in Spiegel & Cardena, 1991).

dissociative amnesia A type of dissociative disorder characterized by the sudden inability to recall extensive and important personal information. The onset often is sudden and may occur in response to trauma or extreme stress.

depersonalization disorder   A type of dissociative disorder characterized by severe and persistent feelings of being detached from oneself (depersonalization experiences). For example, the repeated and profound sensation of floating above your body and observing yourself act.

dissociative identity disorder   An unusual dissociative disorder characterized by the existence of two or more distinct personalities in a single individual (also known as multiple personality disorder). At least two personalities repeatedly take control over the person's behavior, and some personalities have limited or no memory of the other.

multiple personality disorder   An unusual dissociative disorder characterized by the existence of two or more distinct personalities in a single individual (called *dissociative identity disorder* in DSM-IV).

Depersonalization disorder is a less dramatic problem that is characterized by severe and persistent feelings of being detached from oneself. Depersonalization experiences include such sensations as feeling as though you are in a dream, or the sensation of floating above your body and observing yourself act. Occasional depersonalization experiences are normal and are reported by about half the population. In depersonalization disorder, however, such experiences are persistent or recurrent, and they cause marked personal distress. The onset of the disorder commonly follows a new or disturbing event, such as drug use. All depersonalization experiences are "as if" feelings, not rigid, delusional beliefs. Some experts question whether depersonalization should be considered a type of dissociative disorder. Unlike other dissociative disorders, depersonalization disorder involves only limited splitting between conscious and unconscious mental processes, and no memory loss occurs (Spiegel & Cardena, 1991).

To many people, the most fascinating subtype of dissociative disorder is **dissociative identity disorder,** a condition that was known as **multiple personality disorder** before DSM-IV. This unusual mental disorder is characterized by the existence of two or more distinct personalities in a single individual. At least two of these personalities repeatedly take control over the person's behavior, and the individual is unable to recall information that is too extensive to be explained by ordinary forgetfulness. The original personality especially is likely to have amnesia for subsequent personalities, which may or may not be aware of the "alternates" (Aldridge-Morris, 1989).

THE THREE FACES OF EVE: THE CASE OF CHRIS SIZEMORE

Perhaps the best-known case history of multiple personality disorder was detailed in Thigpen and Cleckley's (1957) book, *The Three Faces of Eve,* which was made into a motion picture. Thigpen and Cleckley described the case of Eve White, a young mother with a troubled marriage who sought psychotherapy for severe headaches, feelings of inertia, and "blackouts." Eve White was seen for several therapy sessions and was hypnotized during this time as a treatment for her amnesia. Then, during what proved to be a remarkable session, Eve White became agitated and complained of hearing an imaginary voice. As Thigpen and Cleckley wrote, "after a tense moment of silence, her hands dropped. There was a quick, reckless smile and, in a bright voice that sparkled, she said, 'Hi there, Doc!' " (p. 137). Eve Black had emerged—a carefree and flirtatious personality who insisted upon being called "Miss" and who scorned Eve White, the wife and mother.

Therapy with Eve White, Eve Black, and a third, more calm and mature personality, Jane, lasted over a period of 2 1/2 years. Thigpen used hypnosis to bring out the different personalities in an attempt to understand and reconcile them with one another. He eventually adopted the goal of fading out the two Eves and allowing Jane to take control. Therapy appeared to be successful. According to the psychiatrists' account, treatment ended with one integrated personality in control. This personality was much like Jane, but she decided to call herself "Mrs. Evelyn White."

The end of therapy with Thigpen and Cleckley was not the end of therapy for "Eve." Eve, whose real name is Chris Sizemore, claims to have had a total of 22 different personalities, some of which developed before her treatment with Thigpen and Cleckley and some of which developed afterwards. The personalities always occurred in groups of three, and they always included a wife/mother image, a party girl, and a more normal, intellectual personality (Sizemore & Pittillo, 1977). Sizemore has written several books about her life, and as a well-functioning, unified personality, she has become a spokesperson for mental health concerns. In her book, *A Mind of My Own,* she offers the following observations on her personalities:

Chris Sizemore is "Eve," the patient from the book and movie The Three Faces of Eve. *Sizemore is now cured and is an advocate for the mentally ill.*

Among these twenty-two alters, ten were poets, seven were artists, and one had taught tailoring. Today, I paint and write, but I cannot sew. Yet these alters were not moods or the result of role-playing. They were entities that were totally separate from the personality I was born to be, and am today. They were so different that their tones of voice changed. What's more, their facial expressions, appetites, tastes in clothes, handwritings, skills, and IQs were all different, too. (Sizemore, 1989, p. 9)

The case of Chris Sizemore dramatically illustrates the characteristics of dissociative identity disorder. Sizemore's words also foreshadow controversies about the condition. Some professionals argue that dissociative identity disorder is nothing more than role playing; others assert that multiple personalities are very real and very common.

Epidemiology of Dissociative Disorders

The prevalence of dissociative disorders is difficult to establish. The conditions generally have been considered to be extremely rare. For example, only about 200 case histories of dissociative identity disorder were reported in the entire world literature prior to 1980 (Greaves, 1980). A number of clinicians have diagnosed dissociative identity disorder with much greater frequency in recent years, however. This increase in diagnosis has occurred in conjunction with the recognition of the distressingly high prevalence of child sexual abuse, a traumatic experience that is hypothesized to play a role in the etiology of many dissociative disorders (Kluft, 1987). Thus, in comparison to the 1980 survey, a 1986 report suggested that approximately 6,000 cases of dissociative identity disorder had been diagnosed in North America (Coons, 1986).

Clearly, either some investigators have been overzealous in defining dissociative disorders or diagnosticians have been highly inaccurate for years. In fact, a small but vocal and apparently growing group of professionals has argued that most clinicians commonly overlook dissociative disorders. According to this analysis, many patients who are truly suffering from dissociative disorders are misdiagnosed as having schizophrenia, borderline personality disorder, depression, panic disorder, or substance abuse (Gleaves, 1996; Ross, Norton, & Wozney, 1989).

Despite such claims, the majority of mental health professionals remain skeptical about the prevalence of dissociative disorders. Although cases have been identified in many cultures (Gleaves, 1996), the diagnosis remains extremely rare in Europe and Japan, perhaps reflecting a North American diagnostic "fad" (Mersky, 1992; Piper, 1994). Some professionals have even raised doubts about the very existence of dissociative identity disorder, arguing that this phenomenon was created by the power of suggestion (Mersky, 1992).

Given the current status of research, we reach a cautious conclusion about the epidemiology of dissociative disorders. True dissociative disorders appear to be rare, and although some cases no doubt are misdiagnosed, a much greater problem is the creation of the diagnosis in the minds of clinicians and clients (Mersky, 1992; Piper, 1994). At the same time, we do not doubt the existence of the dissociative disorders. These real but apparently rare psychological problems raise probing questions not only about the disorders themselves but about the very nature of the human psyche.

Etiological Considerations and Research on Dissociative Disorders

Little systematic research has been conducted on the etiology of dissociative disorders. Thus theory and outright speculation dominate discussions of the etiology.

BIOLOGICAL FACTORS

Very little evidence and not much more speculation has been offered about the role of biological factors in the etiology of dissociative disorders (Brown, 1994). Some researchers have theorized that disturbances of the temporal lobe of the brain, including seizure disorders, play a role in dissociative identity disorder (Mesulam, 1981), but this possibility has not been systemically investigated (Brown, 1994). Still, it is known that dissociative states or permanent dissociation can result from biological causes. Examples include the dramatic personality changes that sometimes

TABLE 7–3

Features Associated with Dissociative Identity Disorder in Two Large-Scale Surveys of Clinicians' Case Histories

ITEM	ROSS[1] N = 236	PUTNAM[2] N = 100
Average age	30.8	35.8
Percentage of females	87.7%	92.0%
Average years of treatment before diagnosis	6.7	6.8
Average number of personalities	15.7	13.3
Opposite-sex personality present	62.6%	53.0%
Amnesia between personalities	94.9%	98.0%
Past suicide attempt	72.0%	71.0%
History of child physical abuse	74.9%	75.0%
History of child sexual abuse	79.2%	83.9%

[1]Based on data from C. A. Ross, G. R. Norton, and K. Wozney, 1989, Multiple personality disorder: An analysis of 236 cases, Canadian Journal of Psychiatry, 34, 413–418.
[2]Based on data from F. W. Putnam, J. J. Curoff, et al., 1986, The clinical phenomenology of multiple personality disorder: Review of 100 recent cases. Journal of Clinical Psychiatry, 47, 285–293.

accompany substance use or abuse (see Chapter 11) and the amnesia that is found in various cognitive disorders associated with aging (see Chapter 14).

PSYCHOLOGICAL FACTORS

As we noted earlier, professionals agree that trauma can produce dissociative amnesia and fugue, because the onset of the dissociation often can be traced to a specific traumatic experience. A more controversial question is the extent to which trauma plays a role in the etiology of dissociative identity disorder. Many case histories suggest that multiple personalities develop in response to trauma, particularly the trauma of child abuse.

In support of this observation, some researchers have compiled large numbers of case histories from surveys of practitioners. As Table 7–3 indicates, a history of childhood sexual abuse was noted in 79 percent of 236 cases of dissociative identity disorder, according to the results of one survey. Physical abuse was reported in 75 percent of the same cases. Other surveys of clinicians have reported similar results (Gleaves, 1996; Kluft, 1987; Putnam, Curoff, et al., 1986; see Table 7–3). When interpreting these findings, however, be aware that these case observations are based on patients' memories and clinicians' evaluations. They are not objective assessments of the past.

Researchers have raised many concerns about the validity of such *retrospective reports*—evaluations of the past from the vantage point of the present. A particular concern is that memories may be selectively recalled, may be distorted, or may even be created to conform with subsequent experiences. An adequate test of the hypothesized relation between child abuse and dissociative disorders requires prospective research following trauma victims from childhood into adult life—and objective assessments of dissociation throughout development.

Other speculation has focused on hypnosis as both a cause of, and a treatment for, dissociative disorders. Janet and Freud both were impressed by the similarity in the dissociation experienced during hypnotic states and in hysteria, and at least one contemporary writer has suggested that multiple personality disorder is caused by self-hypnosis (Bliss, 1986). The same questions that have been raised about dissociation can be asked about hypnosis, however. In particular, there is debate about whether hypnosis represents an independent state of consciousness or whether different individuals merely are more or less susceptible to suggestion and only appear to be "hypnotized" (Frankel, 1990). Obviously, the possible etiological role of hypnosis in the development of dissociation depends on accurate answers to this question.

iatrogenesis   A creation of a disorder by an attempt to treat it.

SOCIAL FACTORS

Few interpersonal or societal factors have been suggested to play a role in the development of dissociative disorders. One exception is that some clinicians have pointed to the risk posed by relationships that are simultaneously abusive and loving. For example, dissociation has been hypothesized to be more common when children are abused by parents. In this circumstance, the child obviously cannot seek parental support in coping with the trauma. Instead, she or he must rely on internal coping mechanisms. According to this speculation, if the conflict between the terror of the abuse and the need for love is great, the child may cope by dissociating these two experiences (Braun, 1989).

A sociological view offers a very different perspective on the etiology of dissociative disorders. At least one theorist has suggested that dissociative disorders are produced by **iatrogenesis,** the manufacture of the dissociative disorders by their treatment. Mersky (1992) reviewed classic case histories of dissociative identity disorder and concluded that many "cases" were created by the expectations of therapists. Mersky does not doubt the pain experienced by the patients in these cases. He argues, however, that the patients developed multiple personalities in response to leading questions asked by their therapists, not as a result of their own defense mechanisms. Thus, Mersky asserts that dissociative identity disorder is little more than a social role. A twist on this reasoning is that perhaps highly hypnotizable people are convinced that they have a dissociative disorder because of their susceptibility to suggestion (Kihlstrom, Glisky, & Angiulo, 1994).

Treatment of Dissociative Disorders

Dating from the time of Janet and Freud, perhaps the central aspect of the treatment of dissociative disorders has been uncovering and recounting past traumatic events. A basic assumption of this approach is that dissociation occurs as a response to unacceptable and overwhelming trauma. Thus it is presumed that if the trauma can be expressed and accepted, then the need for dissociation will disappear (Horevitz & Loewenstein, 1994).

As we have already noted, many clinicians use hypnosis to help patients explore and relive traumatic events. The painful experience is assumed to be more easily recalled while the patient is under hypnosis. These recollections, in turn, are thought to facilitate the integration of the trauma into conscious experience. Unfortunately, no research is available either on *abreaction,* the emotional reliving of a past traumatic experience, or on hypnosis as a treatment for dissociative disorders (Horevitz & Loewenstein, 1994).

In addition to helping patients reexperience trauma, clinical experts emphasize the need to win the trust of the dissociative patient (Braun, 1989; Kluft, 1987), establishing rapport with each of the personalities of patients who suffer from dissociative identity disorder. The difficulty of this task can be readily recognized if you recall that, in theory, each personality has developed as a protection against the others.

The goal of treatment is not to have one personality triumph over the others. Rather, the objective is to reintegrate the different personalities into a whole. This is not unlike the far less difficult task faced by all of us as we struggle to integrate the different life roles we play into a coherent sense of self.

Antianxiety, antidepressant, and antipsychotic medications also may be used to treat dissociative disorders. The objective in prescribing these medications is to reduce distress, not to cure the disorder. The ultimate goal of reintegrating the dissociated states, memories, or personalities is considered to be more of a psychological than a pharmaceutical task (Horevitz & Loewenstein, 1994).

Figure 7–2   Conversion Disorders Are Expressed as Physical Symptoms, but Their Psychological Nature Sometimes can Be Detected When the Symptom Makes no Anatomical Sense.   As illustrated in this figure, for example, pain insensitivity may be limited to one side of the face in a conversion disorder. However, the nerves involved in pain sensation do not divide the face neatly in half. This symptom thus makes no anatom-ical sense, suggesting the numbness has a psychogenic origin.

Source: Adapted from D. M. Kaufman, 1985, *Clinical Neurology for Psychiatrists,* 2nd ed., p. 28. Orlando FL: Grune and Stratton.

conversion disorder   A type of somato-form disorder characterized by physical symptoms that often mimic those found in neurological dis-eases, such as blindness, numbing, or paralysis. The symptoms often make no anatomic sense.

At this time, little research has been conducted on the effectiveness of any treatment for dis-sociative disorders, let alone on the comparison of alternative treatments. Advances in therapy await a more accurate description of the disorders and, more generally, a better understanding of the split between conscious and unconscious cognitive processes.

Somatoform Disorders

In addition to dissociative disorders, the ancient diagnostic category hysteria included what we now know as *somatoform disorders*—somatic symptoms in the absence of a physical illness. In-deed, somatoform disorders are synonymous with hysteria in the eyes of many people, because Janet and Freud frequently wrote case histories about patients with unusual and unexplained physical symptoms. For our purposes, we link somatoform disorders with dissociative disorders, because of their historical connection and because somatoform disorders apparently involve a de-gree of dissociation. In some cases of somatoform disorder, the dissociation is relatively minor; in other cases, it is dramatic.

Typical Symptoms and Associated Features of Somatoform Disorders

All somatoform disorders involve complaints about physical symptoms. In contrast to psychoso-matic disorders (see Chapter 8), the symptoms of somatoform disorders cannot be explained by an underlying organic impairment. There is nothing physically wrong with the patient. The symp-toms are not feigned, however, as the physical problem is very real in the mind of the person with a somatoform disorder.

The physical symptoms can take a number of different forms. In some dramatic cases, the symptom involves substantial impairment of a somatic system, particularly a sensory or muscular system. The patient will be unable to see, for example, or will report a paralysis in one arm. In other types of somatoform disorder, patients experience multiple physical symptoms rather than a single, substantial impairment. In these cases, patients usually have numerous, constantly evolving complaints about such problems as chronic pain, upset stomach, and dizziness. Finally, some types of somatoform disorder are defined by a preoccupation with a particular part of the body or with fears about a particular illness. The patient may constantly worry that he or she has contracted some deadly disease, for example, and the anxiety persists despite negative medical tests and clear reassurance by a physician.

Classification of Somatoform Disorders

The DSM-IV lists five major subcategories of somatoform disorders: (1) conversion disorder, (2) somatization disorder, (3) hypochondriasis, (4) pain disorder, and (5) body dysmorphic disorder.

CONVERSION DISORDER

In many respects, the classic type of somatoform disorder is **conversion disorder.** The symptoms of conversion disorder often mimic those found in neurological diseases, and they can be dramatic. "Hysterical" blindness or "hysterical" paralysis are examples of conversion symptoms. Although conversion disorders often resemble neurological impairments, they sometimes can be distinguished from these disorders because they make no anatomic sense. The patient may complain about anesthesia (or pain) in a way that does not correspond with the innervation of the body part. In some facial anesthesias, for example, numbness begins at the middle of the face; but the nerves involved in sensation do not divide the face into equal halves (see Figure 7–2).

The term *conversion disorder* accurately conveys the central assumption of the diagnosis—the idea that psychological conflicts are converted into physical symptoms. Conversion disorders were the problems that particularly captivated the attention of Charcot, Freud, and Janet and that led them to develop theories about dissociation and unconscious mental processes. The following case is from Janet's writings, and it illustrates his view of hysteria.

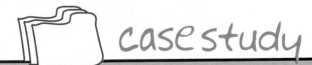

Brief Case Study:
A Case Study from Janet

A girl of nineteen years of age suffered, at the time of her monthly period, convulsive and delirious attacks which lasted several days. Menstruation began normally, but a few hours after the commencement of the flow the patient complained of feeling very cold and had a characteristic shivering; menstruation was immediately arrested and delirium ensued. In the interval of these attacks the patient had paroxysms of terror with the hallucination of blood spreading out before her, and also showed various permanent stigmata, among others anesthesia of the left side of the face with amaurosis of the left eye.

During a careful study of this patient's history, and particularly of the memories she had conserved of various experiences of her life, certain pertinent facts were ascertained. At the age of thirteen years she had attempted to arrest menstruation by plunging into a tub of cold water with resulting shivering and delirium; menstruation was immediately arrested and did not recur for several years; when it did reappear the disturbance I have just cited took place. Later on she had been terrified by seeing an old woman fall on the stairs and deluge the steps with her blood. At another time, when she was about nine years old, she had been obliged to sleep with a child whose face, on the left side, was covered with scabs, and during the whole night she had experienced a feeling of intense disgust and horror. (Janet, 1914/1915, pp. 3–4)

somatization disorder A type of somatoform disorder characterized by multiple, somatic complaints in the absence of organic impairments.

This case describes symptoms that are consistent with conversion disorder. The numbness on the left side of the face of Janet's young patient is a clear example of a conversion symptom. At the same time, we wonder about other aspects of this classic case. The frightening hallucinations of blood might suggest another diagnosis, perhaps psychotic depression (see Chapter 5) or schizophrenia (see Chapter 13), with the conversion symptom as a secondary aspect of the case. Many alternative diagnoses were not available during the time of Charcot, Janet, and Freud, and this might explain why conversion disorders once were thought to be quite prevalent but are uncommon today.

SOMATIZATION DISORDER

Today, a far more common somatoform disorder is **somatization disorder,** characterized by a history of multiple, somatic complaints in the absence of organic impairments. The extent of the health concerns in somatization disorder is apparent from a cursory examination of the DSM-IV diagnostic criteria. In order to be diagnosed with somatization disorder, the patient must complain of at least eight physical symptoms, as listed in Table 7–4. The complaints must involve multiple somatic systems, moreover, including symptoms of pain, gastrointestinal symptoms (for example, nausea and diarrhea), sexual symptoms (sexual dysfunction, menstrual difficulties), and pseudoneurologic symptoms. Pseudoneurologic symptoms are complaints that mimic neurological diseases—for example, double vision, numbness, seizures, and amnesia (see Table 7–4).

Patients with somatization disorders sometimes present their symptoms in a *histrionic* manner—a vague but dramatic, self-centered, and seductive style (see Chapter 9). Patients also occasionally exhibit *la belle indifference* ("beautiful indifference"), a flippant lack of concern about the physical symptoms. For example, a patient may list a long series of somatic complaints in an

---

TABLE 7–4

DSM-IV Diagnostic Criteria for Somatization Disorder

A. A HISTORY OF MANY PHYSICAL COMPLAINTS BEGINNING BEFORE AGE 30 THAT OCCUR OVER A PERIOD OF SEVERAL YEARS AND RESULT IN TREATMENT BEING SOUGHT OR SIGNIFICANT IMPAIRMENT IN SOCIAL, OCCUPATIONAL, OR OTHER IMPORTANT AREAS OF FUNCTIONING.

B. EACH OF THE FOLLOWING CRITERIA MUST HAVE BEEN MET, WITH INDIVIDUAL SYMPTOMS OCCURRING AT ANY TIME DURING THE COURSE OF THE DISTURBANCE.

1. Four pain symptoms: A history of pain related to at least four different sites or functions (for example, head, abdomen, back, joints, extremities, chest, rectum, during sexual intercourse, during menstruation, or during urination)
2. Two gastrointestinal symptoms: A history of at least two gastrointestinal symptoms other than pain (for example, nausea, diarrhea, bloating, vomiting other than during pregnancy, or intolerance of several different foods)
3. One sexual symptom: A history of at least one sexual or reproductive symptom other than pain (for example, sexual indifference, erectile or ejaculatory dysfunction, irregular menses, excessive menstrual bleeding, vomiting throughout pregnancy)
4. One pseudoneurologic symptom: A history of at least one symptom or deficit suggesting a neurological disorder not limited to pain (conversion symptoms such as blindness, double vision, deafness, loss of touch or pain sensation, hallucinations, aphonia, impaired coordination or balance, paralysis or localized weakness, difficulty swallowing or lump in throat, difficulty breathing, urinary retention, seizures; dissociative symptoms such as amnesia; or loss of consciousness other than fainting)

offhanded and cheerful manner. Although some clinicians have viewed either or both of these styles as defining characteristics of somatization disorders, research indicates that they are found in only a minority of cases (Lipowski, 1988).

HYPOCHONDRIASIS

Hypochondriasis is a problem characterized by a fear or belief that the individual is suffering from a physical illness. Aspects of this mental disorder surely are familiar to you. The pejorative term *hypochondriac* is a part of everyday language. We all worry about our health, and even unrealistic worries sometimes are normal. Medical students often fear that they have contracted each new disease they encounter in their studies. Many students in abnormal psychology worry that each problem they read about is a perfect description of themselves.

Hypochondriasis is much more serious than these normal and fleeting worries. The preoccupation with fears of disease extends over long periods of time. The worries must last for at least 6 months according to DSM-IV criteria. In addition, in hypochondriasis, a thorough medical evaluation or examination does not alleviate the fear of the disease. The person still worries that the illness may be emerging or that a test was overlooked. Still, the anxiety of hypochondriasis falls short of being delusional. For example, a person may worry excessively about contracting AIDS and therefore may repeatedly go for blood tests. When faced with negative results, however, the person does not delusionally believe that he or she actually has contracted the illness. Nevertheless, the persistent worries that characterize hypochondriasis are severe and preoccupying, and they often lead to substantial impairment in life functioning.

PAIN DISORDER

As its name implies, **pain disorder** is a subtype of somatoform disorder that is characterized by preoccupation with pain. Although there is no objective way to evaluate pain, psychological factors are judged to be significant in creating or intensifying the chronic pain in pain disorder. Complaints seem excessive and apparently are motivated at least in part by psychological factors. Some pain disorder patients may seem to relish the attention their illness brings to them. The DSM-IV distinguishes between pain disorder that occurs with associated problems in general medical conditions and pain disorder that appears in the absence of such problems. For example, low back pain that begins after a physical injury would be differentiated from back pain that cannot be traced to any physical cause.

As with hypochondriasis and somatization disorder, pain disorder can lead to the repeated, unnecessary use of medical treatments. People who experience chronic pain are at a particular risk for developing a dependence on minor tranquilizers or painkillers. The disorder also frequently disrupts social and occupational functioning.

BODY DYSMORPHIC DISORDER

Body dysmorphic disorder is a quite different type of somatoform disorder in which the patient is preoccupied with some imagined defect in appearance. The preoccupation typically focuses on some facial feature, such as the nose or mouth, and in some cases may lead to repeated visits to a plastic surgeon. Preoccupation with the body part far exceeds normal worries about physical imperfections. The endless worry causes significant distress, and in extreme cases, it may interfere with work or social relationships.

Little research has been conducted on body dysmorphic disorder. The problem has received more attention among European and Asian mental health professionals than in the United States, but systematic research has not been conducted anywhere. One controversy is whether the diagnosis should be grouped with other somatoform disorders. In Japan and Korea, body dysmorphic disorder is classified as a type of social phobia (Phillips, 1991). The following brief case history illustrates this unusual type of somatoform disorder.

hypochondriasis A type of somatoform disorder characterized by a person's preoccupying fear or belief that he or she is suffering from a physical illness.

pain disorder A type of somatoform disorder characterized by preoccupation with pain, and complaints are motivated at least in part by psychological factors.

body dysmorphic disorder A type of somatoform disorder characterized by constant preoccupation with some imagined defect in physical appearance.

Felix Unger, a character from The Odd Couple, *played here by Jack Lemmon, had numerous hypochondriacal complaints—much to the annoyance of his roommate, Oscar (portrayed by Walter Matthau).*

case study

Brief Case Study: Body Dysmorphic Disorder

A 28-year-old single white man became preoccupied at the age of 18 with his minimally thinning hair. Despite reassurance from others that his hair loss was not noticeable, he worried about it for hours a day, becoming "deeply depressed," socially withdrawn, and unable to attend classes or do his schoolwork. Although he could acknowledge the excessiveness of his preoccupation, he was unable to stop it. He saw four dermatologists but was not comforted by their reassurances that his hair loss was minor and that treatment was unnecessary. The patient's preoccupation and subsequent depression have persisted for 10 years and have continued to interfere with his social life and work, to the extent that he avoids most social events and has been able to work only part-time as a baker. He only recently sought psychiatric referral, at the insistence of his girlfriend, who said his symptoms were ruining their relationship. (Phillips, 1991, pp. 1138–1139).

Epidemiology of Somatoform Disorders

No one knows how prevalent conversion disorders were during the time of Charcot, Janet, and Freud, but the literature of the period suggests that they were common (Shorter, 1992). Today, conversion disorders are rare. For example, one investigation found only a 0.4 percent prevalence of conversion symptoms in an urban community sample (Weissman, Meyers, & Harding, 1978), a figure that probably overestimates the prevalence in the general population.

Ironically, the unusual disorders treated by Freud and Janet appear to have been less enduring than the theories they developed to explain them. This change in prevalence across time may be a result of improved diagnostic practices, as we have suggested, or it may reflect the role of society in the etiology of conversion disorder, a theory that we discuss shortly.

Other somatoform disorders appear to be equally rare, although sound epidemiological research has not been conducted on hypochondriasis, body dysmorphic disorder, or pain disorder. According to the Epidemiologic Catchment Area study, the lifetime prevalence of somatization disorder within the 50 states is only 0.13 percent (Swartz et al., 1987). On the other hand, physical complaints that do not meet all of the diagnostic criteria for somatization disorder are very common. In the same study, 11.6 percent of people were found to suffer from four to six physical symptoms with no identifiable organic cause (fewer than the eight required for the diagnosis of somatization disorder; see Table 7–4) (Swartz et al., 1990).

Hypochondriasis is equally common among men and women, but all other forms of somatoform disorder are more common among women. This is particularly true of somatization disorder, which is 10 times more common among females than among males (Swartz et al., 1990).

Somatization disorder also is more common among lower socioeconomic groups and among people who have less than a high school education. It is 4 times as common among African Americans as among Americans of European heritage, and a considerably higher rate of somatization disorder (0.7 percent) has been reported for Puerto Rico than for the U.S. mainland (Canino, Bird, et al., 1987). Finally, more somatic symptoms are found among people who have lost a spouse through divorce, separation, or death. Never-married adults actually have lower rates than the married population, suggesting that loss may play a role in the etiology of the disorder (Swartz et al., 1990).

Etiological Considerations and Research on Somatoform Disorders

Little systematic research has been conducted on the etiology of somatoform disorders. Few contemporary hypotheses have been offered about these problems, moreover, despite their historical significance in Janet's and Freud's theories about unconscious psychological processes. We consider perspectives on the etiology of somatoform disorders in the context of the biopsychosocial model. However, the limited evidence prohibits us from offering a complete, systemic model of contributing factors.

BIOLOGICAL FACTORS

An obvious—and potentially critical—biological consideration in somatoform disorders is the possibility of misdiagnosis. A patient may be incorrectly diagnosed as suffering from a somatoform disorder when, in fact, he or she actually has a real physical illness that is undetected or is perhaps unknown. The diagnosis of a somatoform disorder requires that no organic cause of the symptom can be identified. This is very different from the positive identification of a psychological cause of the symptom.

Diagnosis by Exclusion   Because mental health professionals cannot demonstrate psychological causes of physical symptoms objectively and unequivocally, the identification of somatoform disorders involves a process called *diagnosis by exclusion*. The physical complaint is assumed to be a part of a somatoform disorder only when various known physical causes are excluded or ruled out. The possibility always remains, however, that an incipient somatic disease has been overlooked. Some of the problems with diagnosis by exclusion can be appreciated by way of analogy. Consider the difference in certainty between two police lineups, one in which a victim positively identifies a criminal—"That's him!"—versus a second in which an identification is made by ruling out alternatives; "It isn't him or him or him, so it must be that one."

The possibility of misdiagnosis is more than a theoretical concern. Follow-up studies of patients diagnosed as suffering from conversion disorders indicate that somatic illnesses are later detected in some cases (Shalev & Munitz, 1986). Typically, a neurological disease such as epilepsy or multiple sclerosis is the eventual diagnosis. In one classic study, about a quarter of patients diagnosed as having a conversion symptom later were found to develop a neurological disease (Slater, 1965). Thus a significant number of cases of "somatoform disorder" eventually may prove to be real, neurological diseases. This possibility poses a dilemma for diagnosticians. They must weigh the consequences of an incorrect diagnosis of somatoform disorder against the consequences of incorrectly diagnosing a psychological problem as a physical illness.

PSYCHOLOGICAL FACTORS

Both Janet and Freud developed psychological theories in an attempt to explain the dissociation between emotional conflicts and physical symptoms. Both theorists initially assumed that a traumatic experience was the starting point for conversion disorder. According to their reasoning, the trauma overwhelmed normal coping efforts, and unconscious coping processes were called into action as a result. Janet viewed this dissociation of experience as an abnormal process. His explanation of conversion disorder followed his account of dissociative disorders, as we discussed earlier in this chapter.

In contrast, Freud came to view dissociation—a term that he used synonymously with repression—as a normal psychological process. He initially viewed traumatic stress as a necessary precondition for conversion disorders. Later, however, Freud suggested that normal id impulses (particularly sexual urges) were unacceptable to the conscious mind and therefore required unconscious coping efforts—that is, the use of intrapsychic defenses.

Primary and Secondary Gain   Freud came to believe therefore that "normal" unconscious processes could lead to the development of hysteria. He assumed that the unacceptable impulse or intolerable memory was unconsciously converted into a physical symptom by intrapsychic defenses (Freud, 1924/1962). The symptom thus served the function of protecting the conscious mind by expressing the psychological conflict unconsciously. In psychoanalytic terminology, this is referred to as the *primary gain* of the symptom. Freud thought that clues about the nature of the primary gain might be found in the symbolism of the specific physical symptom that was expressed. For example, hysterical blindness might result from witnessing some horrifying event.

Freud also recognized that hysterical symptoms could help a patient to avoid work or responsibility or to gain attention and sympathy. He referred to this as the *secondary gain* of the symptom. Cognitive behavioral theorists agree that secondary gain contributes to somatoform disorders, but they use a more direct term to describe the process: reinforcement. More generally, cognitive behaviorists suggest that *learning the sick role* is a part of the etiology of somatoform disorders. In addition to positive reinforcement (extra attention) or negative reinforcement (avoidance of work), social learning theorists suggest that modeling may be involved in learning the sick role (Lipowski, 1988).

Other perspectives on the etiology of somatoform disorders highlight cognitive and social influences in addition to reinforcement and modeling (Kirmayer, Robbins, & Paris, 1994). Key additional factors that contribute to etiology include (1) a tendency to amplify somatic symptoms, (2) *alexithymia*—a deficit in the individual's capacity to recognize and express the emotions signaled by physiological arousal—and (3) the misattribution of normal somatic symptoms.

The sick role and other social learning accounts may partially explain the etiology of pain disorder, hypochondriasis, and somatization disorder. However, they generally fail to account for conversion disorder and the fascinating question of how psychological distress may be converted into physical symptoms. Although the specifics of Freud's or Janet's accounts can be readily criticized, the etiology of conversion disorder seems to require theorizing about unconscious processes. Thus these disorders pose a theoretical challenge for cognitive scientists as well as for neuroscientists.

SOCIAL FACTORS

Social and cultural theorists offer a more straightforward explanation of the physical symptoms of somatization disorder, hypochondriasis, and pain disorder. Theorists assume that patients with these disorders are experiencing some sort of underlying psychological distress. However, the patients describe their problems as physical symptoms, and to some extent experience them that way, because of limited insight into their emotional distress and/or the lack of social tolerance of psychological complaints. Thus sociocultural theorists assume that people with somatoform disorders really are fearful, sad, or uncertain about their life, but they experience, or at least express, these emotional concerns in terms of physical complaints. A simple analogy for this theorizing is a child who complains about an upset stomach, not about fear of failure, before giving a piano recital.

Sociocultural theories of somatoform disorders are based on prevalence data. Somatoform disorders are more common in nonindustrialized countries, and they are more frequent among less educated people in the United States (Kirmayer, 1984; Kirmayer et al., 1994; Mechanic, 1986). The hypothesized explanation for this is that people with less education or financial security do not have the opportunity to learn to describe their inner turmoil in detailed psychological terms (Lipowski, 1988). Similarly, it has been suggested that the apparent reduction in the prevalence of conversion disorders today as compared with 100 years ago is a result of the increased social acceptance of inner feelings (Shorter, 1992).

Treatment of Somatoform Disorders

The sociocultural view of the etiology of somatoform disorders is consistent with the approaches to treatment developed by Charcot, Janet, and Freud. These therapists encouraged their patients to recall and recount psychologically painful events as a way of treating the disorder.

The exploration and uncovering of past or present traumas may free some patients of conversion symptoms, as it apparently did in some classic cases. Nevertheless, no research has been conducted on any "uncovering" therapies for somatoform disorders, and very little systematic research has been conducted on other treatments. The one exception is behavior therapy. Some evidence suggests that cognitive behavior therapy is effective in treating body dysmorphic disorder (Rosen, Reiter, & Orosan, 1995), and researchers have conducted fairly extensive studies of both operant and cognitive behavioral treatments of pain disorders. Operant approaches to chronic pain attempt to alter contingencies that reward "pain behavior" and the sick role. The goal is to reward successful coping and life adaptation instead (Fordyce, 1976). Cognitive behavior therapy typically incorporates operant techniques but also uses cognitive restructuring to address the emotional and cognitive components of pain. Research demonstrates the effectiveness of both variations on behavior therapy in treating chronic lower back pain (Blanchard, 1994).

One reason for the limited research on the psychological treatment of somatoform disorders is that primary care physicians treat most of these patients. Patients with somatoform disorders typically consult physicians about their ailments, and they often insist that their problems are physical even after extensive testing. They are likely to refuse a referral to a mental health professional. Thus primary care physicians often must learn how to manage hypochondriasis, somatization disorder, and related problems in the medical setting.

Summary

To a greater or lesser extent, all the intriguing disorders we consider in this chapter involve **dissociation,** the disruption of the normally integrated mental processes involved in memory or consciousness. Many of the disorders also are known or hypothesized to be reactions to exposure to some event that involves actual or threatened death or serious injury to self or others—and creates intense fear, helplessness, or horror. Sources of traumatic stress include rape, bombings, airplane crashes, earthquakes, major fires, and devastating automobile wrecks.

Traumatic stress disorders include acute stress disorder and posttraumatic stress disorder. **Acute stress disorder (ASD)** is a short-term reaction to trauma that is characterized by symptoms of dissociation, reexperiencing, avoidance, and increased anxiety or arousal. **Posttraumatic stress disorder (PTSD)** is characterized by very similar symptoms—reexperiencing, numbed responsiveness or avoidance, and increased autonomic arousal—but the symptoms either last for longer than 1 month or have a delayed onset in PTSD. Trauma may be reexperienced as a *flashback*—a dissociative state in which the person relives the trauma in the moment. The diminished responsiveness has been referred to as psychic numbing or emotional anesthesia. The increased arousal in ASD or PTSD may include excessive fear, anxiety, or irritability, as well as general psychophysiological arousal.

Scientists have only begun to study the epidemiology of PTSD. Current evidence points to the surprisingly high frequency that people experience some traumatic events. Epidemiology also calls attention to the particularly devastating consequences of rape for women and combat exposure for men.

By definition, the experience of trauma is the central cause of PTSD, but other factors appear to be important in its etiology. Genetic factors increase the risk both for experiencing trauma and for experiencing PTSD following trauma, probably as a result of genetic influences on personality characteristics or psychological disorders. A number of adverse reactions may be produced by classical conditioning during the experience of trauma, and the reactions can be maintained by operant conditioning as people continue to avoid stressful circumstances. Some short-term reactions may be better conceived as symptoms of ASD, however, and more severe ASD seems to be a fairly good predictor of subsequent PTSD. Finally, the nature and level of exposure to a traumatic event, as well as social support after the occurrence of the trauma, appear to be crucial to facilitating long-term adjustment.

Early intervention with trauma victims can contribute to easing the pain of coping with a horrific event and to preventing the subsequent development of PTSD. Reliving the traumatic event is perhaps the least obvious but most important strategy for subsequent treatment. According to research that is being conducted on therapy outcome, recounting and reexperiencing the trauma in a controlled treatment setting appears to be basic to the therapeutic process. Still, PTSD can have a chronic course in over one-third of all cases. Evidence suggests skepticism, however, that the course of PTSD may include **recovered memories,** the sudden remembering of long-forgotten traumatic experiences.

Dissociative disorders are characterized by persistent, maladaptive disruptions in the integration of memory, consciousness, or identity. **Somatoform disorders** are identified by unusual physical symptoms that occur in the absence of a known physical illness. Memories become inaccessible in dissociative disorders; psychological distress is converted into physical symptoms in somatoform disorders. Thus these unusual emotional problems involve unconscious processes by definition, and they challenge psychological theorists to explain those psychological events that occur outside of awareness. In fact, both Freud and Janet developed their influential theories about unconscious processes when attempting to explain these disorders.

The DSM-IV distinguishes four major subtypes of dissociative disorders: fugue, amnesia, depersonalization disorder, and dissociative identity disorder. *Dissociative fugue* is characterized by sudden and unexpected travel away from home, an inability to recall the past, and confusion about identity or the assumption of a new identity. **Dissociative amnesia** involves a sudden inability to recall extensive and important personal information that exceeds normal forgetfulness. As with fugue, dissociative amnesia typically is characterized by a sudden onset in response to trauma or extreme stress and an equally sudden recovery of memory.

Depersonalization disorder is a less dramatic problem that is characterized by severe and persistent feelings of being detached from oneself—sensations such as feeling as if you are in a dream, or as though you are floating above your body and observing yourself act. Occasional depersonalization experiences are normal, but depersonalization disorder involves persistent or recurrent symptoms. Finally, **dissociative identity disorder,** also known as **multiple personality disorder,** is characterized by the existence of two or more distinct personalities in a single individual. At least two of these personalities repeatedly take control over the person's behavior, and some of the personalities have limited or no memory of the others.

Although some investigators suggest that the conditions are pervasive, dissociative disorders appear to be quite rare. A growing body of evidence links the conditions with traumatic experiences, particularly with child abuse. Evidence is weak or nonexistent on other factors that may contribute to the development of the disorder. Similarly, there is no systematic research on the treatment of dissociative disorders, although clinical tradition emphasizes reliving trauma as a way of reintegrating experience.

The DSM-IV lists five major subcategories of somatoform disorders. In many respects, the classic type of somatoform disorder is **conversion disorder.** The term *conversion disorder* accurately conveys the central assumption of the diagnosis—the idea that psychological conflicts are converted into physical symptoms. "Hysterical" blindness or "hysterical" paralysis are examples of conversion symptoms. **Somatization disorder** is characterized by a history of multiple, somatic complaints in the absence of organic impairments. The complaints involve multiple somatic systems, including symptoms of pain, gastrointestinal symptoms, sexual symptoms, and pseudoneurologic symptoms. **Hypochondriasis** is characterized by a fear or belief that the individual is suffering from a physical illness. The persistent worries that characterize hypochondriasis are severe and preoccupying and often result in substantial impairment in life functioning. **Pain disorder** is characterized by preoccupation with pain. Although there is no objective way to evaluate pain, psychological factors are judged to be significant in creating or exacerbating the chronic pain in pain disorder. In **body dysmorphic disorder** the patient is preoccupied with some imagined defect in appearance—a preoccupation that typically focuses on some facial feature, such as the nose or mouth.

The etiology of somatoform disorders has not been the subject of much research. Etiological concerns include the misdiagnosis of incipient neurological diseases as somatoform disorders; secondary gain or reinforcement for the sick role; cognitive factors, such as a tendency to amplify somatic symptoms; alexithymia—a deficit in the individual's capacity to recognize and express the emotions signaled by physiological arousal; and cultural influences.

Treatment research on somatoform disorders is sorely lacking. Some evidence indicates that behavior therapy is effective in the treatment of body dysmorphic disorder and especially chronic pain. Investigators also are beginning to identify aspects of effective medical management of somatoform disorders. Still, in many ways, these disorders continue to pose as much of a challenge now as they did at the turn of the twentieth century when they attracted the attention of leading figures in the history of abnormal psychology.

Critical Thinking

1. Based on what you have read in this chapter and in Chapter 6, do you think that traumatic stress disorders are more similar to anxiety disorders or to dissociative disorders—or do you see ASD and PTSD as being separate from these two diagnostic categories?

2. Because both are reactions to traumatic stress, ASD and PTSD would seem to be purely "psychological" problems. However, the disorders are best explained by the systems perspective. What biological, psychological, and social risk factors might combine to cause the disorders? What *protective* factors would you hypothesize to lower the likelihood of ASD or PTSD following exposure to trauma?

3. There is much controversy about several of the topics in this chapter, including such issues as recovered memories, dissociative identity disorder, hypnosis, and conversion reactions. These elusive ideas are difficult to evaluate empirically and require a certain amount of "believing" as opposed to "knowing." If you believe in the existence of these phenomena, how could you prove your beliefs to skeptics? If you are a skeptic, what evidence would convince you that the psychic phenomena are "real"?

4. Do you know people who seem to express their psychological concerns through somatic complaints? How do you explain this? Did you express your feelings in this way as a child? Do you still experience or express your emotions in terms of physical sensations or symptoms?

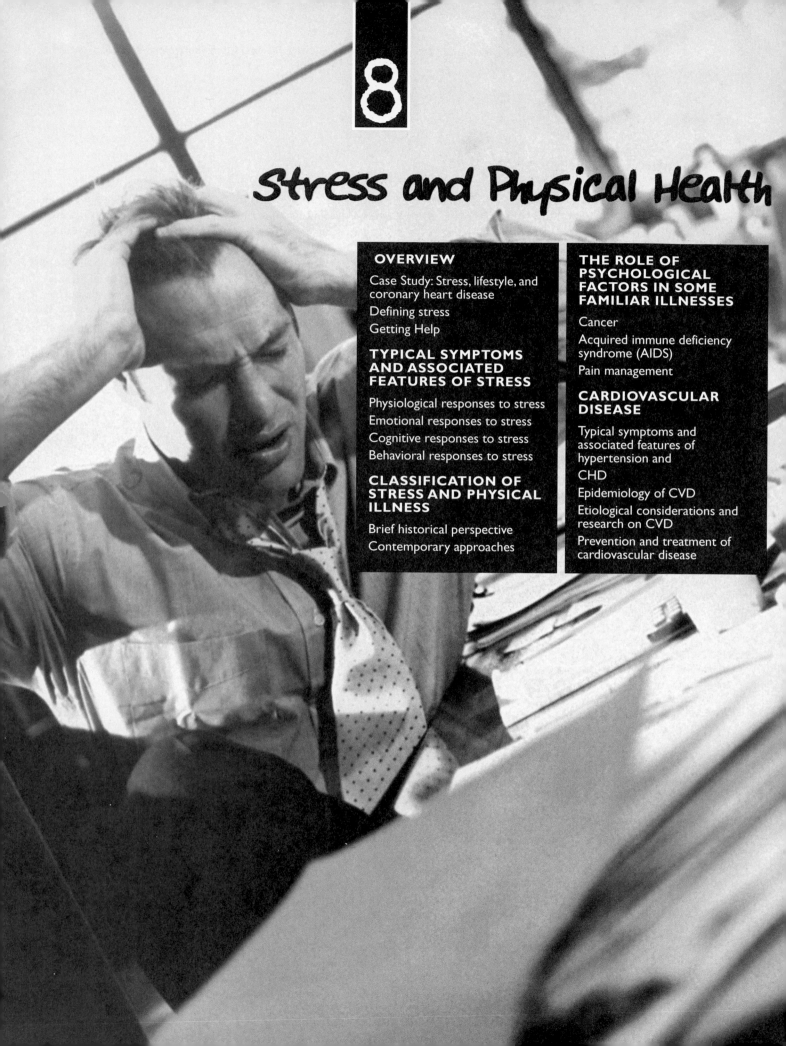

8

Stress and Physical Health

Newspaper stories and magazine articles regularly warn us about the dangers of stress. We are cautioned that stress not only can cause psychological problems but can also lead to physical illnesses ranging from the common cold to heart attacks. Scientific studies support many of the popular concerns about the role of stress in physical illness. As we will see in this chapter, however, scientific evidence is not nearly as clear-cut as is popular belief. In fact, evidence suggests that, under the right conditions, stress can promote "toughness" or *resilience* rather than disorder. A certain amount of stress is adaptive. The key is to maintain a balance between being challenged and being overloaded by stress.

stress An event that creates physiological or psychological strain for the individual. Stress has been defined differently by various scientists.

psychosomatic disorder A term indicating that a physical disease is a product both of the psyche (mind) and the soma (body).

Stress can be broadly defined as a challenging event that requires physiological, cognitive, or behavioral adaptation. As we discuss shortly, however, scientists disagree about how stress should be defined more precisely for research purposes. Stress may be produced by minor, daily hassles, like the frustration of being trapped in a traffic jam, as well as by major events, such as getting fired from a job or going through a divorce. *Traumatic stress* is caused by exposure to some catastrophic event that involves actual or threatened death or serious injury to oneself or others and creates intense fear, helplessness, or horror (see Chapter 7).

For many years, scientists thought that psychological stress was irrelevant to most physical (or *somatic*) illnesses. Instead, the causes of most physical illnesses were thought to lie "within the skin." This viewpoint was fueled by the discovery of bacteria as a cause of illness and the subsequent development of immunization and antibiotics as successful treatments for bacterial disease. Despite the dominance of "germ theory" throughout much of the twentieth century, some scientists argued that psychological stress contributed to a limited number of illnesses termed **psychosomatic disorders** (sometimes also called *psychophysiological disorders*). The term *psychosomatic* indicates that a given physical disease is a product of both the *psyche* (mind) and the *soma* (body). Ulcers, migraine headaches, hypertension (high blood pressure), and asthma are examples of physical illnesses that were once called psychosomatic disorders.[†]

The DSM no longer contains a list of psychosomatic disorders, because medical scientists now view *every* physical illness as a product of the interaction between the psyche and soma, mind and body. Contemporary researchers have found that stress plays a role in the onset or exacerbation of all physical illnesses—from a cold to cancer to AIDS. Moreover, evidence indicates that learning more adaptive ways of *coping* can limit the recurrence or improve the course of many

[†]*In everyday language, we sometimes misuse the term* psychosomatic *to imply that an illness is imagined or not real in a physical sense; for example, "His problems are psychosomatic." Unlike conversion disorders (see Chapter 7), psychosomatic disorders are very real physical illnesses that involve clear damage to the body.*

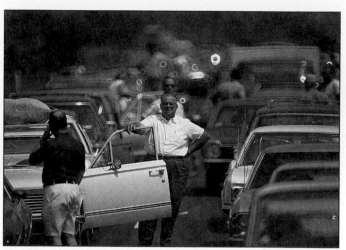

Stress is a part of everyday life. Stress cannot be avoided, but some ways of coping with life's challenges are more effective than others.

behavioral medicine A multidisciplinary field concerned with studying and treating the behavioral components of physical illness.

physical illnesses. In short, medical scientists now recognize that the distinction between mind and body is a false dualism (see Chapter 2). Theories of the etiology of physical illnesses have adopted—and in many ways have promoted—the systems approach.

This holistic view of disease and health has brought about major changes in both psychology and medicine. Of particular note is the rapid development of **behavioral medicine,** a multidisciplinary field that includes both medical and mental health professionals who investigate psychological factors in the symptoms, etiology, and treatment of physical illness and chronic disease. Psychologists who specialize in behavioral medicine often are called *health psychologists.*

Experts in behavioral medicine and health psychology emphasize health rather than just disease. They define disease as "dis-ease," indicating that illness is a departure not only from adaptive biological functioning but also from adaptive social and psychological functioning. In turn, experts view health as successful adaptation to the environment, not merely the absence of somatic illness (Weiner & Fawzy, 1989). Behavioral medicine specialists and health psychologists therefore study and encourage such healthy behaviors as stress management, proper diet, regular exercise, and avoidance of tobacco use in order to promote positive health among the general public. Examples of treatments for the physically ill include providing education and support to parents of chronically ill children, helping patients cope with chronic pain, and even offering support groups to people with terminal cancer.

In this chapter we discuss a number of innovations in behavioral medicine and health psychology, and we review evidence on the link between stress and a number of different physical illnesses. We also include an extended discussion of hypertension and coronary heart disease in order to illustrate the challenges in studying stress and physical illness. We begin our discussion with a case history of coronary heart disease from our files.

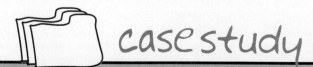

case study

Stress, Lifestyle, and Coronary Heart Disease

One Thursday afternoon, Bob Carter, a salesman for a beer and liquor wholesaler, was completing his regular route, calling on customers. Throughout the morning, he had felt a familiar dis-

comfort in his chest and left arm. As had been happening on occasion for at least a year, that morning he experienced a few fleeting but sharp pains in the center and left side of his chest. This was followed by a dull ache in his chest and left shoulder and a feeling of congestion in the same areas. Breathing deeply made the pain worse, but Bob could manage it as long as he took shallow breaths. The discomfort was not bad enough to interfere with Bob's work, although this time the pain lasted longer than usual. Still, he continued on his route, alternately vowing to see a doctor soon and cursing his aging body for not performing up to his expectations.

After grabbing a hamburger and a beer for lunch, Bob called on a customer who was behind in his payments to the wholesaler. At first, Bob shared a cigarette with the customer and chatted with him in a friendly way. He was a salesman after all. Soon it was time to pressure him about the bill. As Bob was raising his voice in anger, a crushing pain returned to his chest and radiated down his left arm. This was much worse than anything he had experienced before. The pain was so intense that Bob was unable to continue speaking. He slumped forward against the table, but with his right arm he waved away any attempts to help him. After sitting still for about 10 minutes, Bob was able to drag himself to his car and drive to his home 30 miles away. When his wife saw him shuffle into the house looking haggard and in obvious pain, she called for an ambulance. The Carters soon discovered that Bob had suffered a myocardial infarction (a heart attack).

Bob was 49 years old at the time. He was married and the father of three children. His home life was normal and happy, but it also put a lot of pressures on him. His 24-year-old daughter was living at home while her husband was serving in combat duty overseas. Naturally, the entire family was anxious about the son-in-law's well-being. More stress came from Bob's 21-year-old daughter, who had just graduated from college and was getting married in 3 weeks. Finally, Bob's 19-year-old son was home from his first year of college, full of rebellion and ideas that challenged Bob's authority. There was no shortage of family stress.

Bob also put plenty of stress on himself. A former high school athlete, he had always been competitive and hard-driving. He wanted to be the best at whatever he did, and right now his goal was to be the best salesman in his company. Bob worked hard selling beer and liquor. He used his charm, humor, and some not-so-gentle pressure to sell his products, and it worked. But once he had become the best salesman in his wholesaling company, Bob wanted to be the best salesman for the producers whose products he sold. No matter what he accomplished, Bob drove himself hard to meet a new goal.

Bob maintained his drive and competitiveness from his youthful days as a star athlete, but he had not maintained his physical condition. The only exercise he got was playing golf, and he usually rode in a cart instead of walking the course. He was at least 30 pounds overweight, smoked a pack and a half of cigarettes a day, ate a lot of fatty red meat, and drank heavily. If he had seen a physician earlier, Bob would have been told that he was a good candidate for a heart attack. As it was, he heard this from a cardiologist only after his heart attack.

Bob recuperated quickly in the hospital. He was tired and in considerable pain for a couple of days, but he was telling jokes before the end of a week. His cardiologist explained what had happened to him and gave Bob a stern lecture about how he needed to change his lifestyle. He wanted Bob to quit smoking, lose weight, cut down on his drinking, and gradually work himself back into shape with a careful program of exercise. He urged Bob to slow down at work and told him to quit worrying about his children—they were old enough to take care of themselves.

To underscore these messages, the cardiologist asked a psychologist from the hospital's behavioral medicine unit to consult with Bob. The psychologist reviewed information on coronary risk with Bob and gave him several pamphlets to read on risk factors. The psychologist also explained that the hospital ran several programs that might interest Bob after discharge. These included workshops on stress management, weight reduction groups, and exercise classes. The fees for these programs were minimal, because the hospital ran them primarily as a community service. The psychologist asked Bob if he had other concerns that he wanted to discuss, but Bob said there were none. The psychologist suggested that some issues might come up in the future, and Bob should feel free to raise them with the psychologist or with his cardiologist. The psychologist noted that cardiac patients and their families sometimes had trouble adjusting to the illness and the sudden reminder of the patient's mortality. Bob thanked the psychologist for the information but waved off the professional's offer of assistance much as he had waved off help in the middle of his heart attack.

Bob was discharged from the hospital 10 days after being admitted. Against his doctor's advice, he walked his daughter down the aisle at her wedding the following weekend, and he was back to work within a month. At his 6-week checkup, Bob admitted to his cardiologist that he was smoking again. His weight was unchanged, and his exercise and drinking were only a "little better," according to Bob. When the cardiologist chastised Bob for not following medical advice, Bob promised to renew his efforts. He belied his assertion of commitment, however, by commenting that giving up these small pleasures might or might not make him live any longer, but life surely would seem longer without any indulgences. Clearly, one heart attack was not going to get Bob Carter to slow down. ◣

The case of Bob Carter illustrates a number of critical issues and questions about the potential link between stress and physical illness. Most basically, the case strongly suggests that life stress is a factor in the onset of coronary heart disease.

The case of Bob Carter also raises a number of questions about the link between stress and coronary heart disease. What is the physiological mechanism that transforms psychological stress into coronary risk? Is stress the problem, or is the real culprit the unhealthy behaviors that result from stress—smoking, drinking, and overeating? What is more important to the experience of stress—a single major life change, such as the marriage of Bob's daughter, or ongoing hassles like Bob's fighting with his son? What is the role of personality in stress? Bob constantly put pressure on himself, whereas another person might have been more likely to "roll with the punches" on the job and at home. Can someone like Bob be helped to change his lifestyle, and if so, does this lower the risk for future heart attacks? We consider these and related questions in this chapter. First, though, we need to consider more carefully exactly what we mean by "stress."

Defining Stress

In the introduction to this chapter, we defined *stress* as a challenging event that requires physiological, cognitive, or behavioral adaptation. We stand by this definition, but we also note that questions arise when we examine it closely. Is stress the event itself? Some people would relax after becoming the top salesman, but this achievement only produced another, more difficult challenge for Bob Carter. This suggests that perhaps stress should be defined in terms of the individual's reactions to the event. However, our theories indicate that stress causes adverse reactions. Defining stress in terms of these reactions runs the risk of becoming an exercise in circular logic. In fact, scientists continue to debate whether stress is best defined in terms of a life event (a stimulus), an adverse reaction (a response), or a stimulus-response combination.

STRESS AS A STIMULUS

Various efforts to quantify stressful life events have attempted to define stress in terms of a stimulus or *stressor*—a difficult event regardless of the individual's reaction to it. The early work of Holmes and Rahe (1967) was particularly influential. Holmes and Rahe developed the Social Readjustment Rating Scale (SRRS), a list of various troublesome life events. They assigned stress values to life events, basing these ratings on the judgments of a large group of normal adults. Their attempts to measure the amount of stress caused by various life events was both provocative and controversial. Holmes and Rahe concluded that different stressors cause more or less stress, as indexed by what they called *life change units*. Thus an individual's total stress is the sum of the life change units for each item that is checked on the scale.

The SRRS and similar instruments have been used frequently in research (Miller, 1989). Not surprisingly, investigators have repeatedly found that more life stress as measured by life change units is associated with a wide variety of physical and psychological disorders. This method of defining stress has been subjected to several criticisms, however. Some critics suggest that people who experience physical or psychological disorders are simply more likely to recall difficult life events than are people who are doing well. Another concern is the limited number of life stressors that are compiled on such scales and the appropriateness of these limited listings for subjects of different ages and ethnic backgrounds. For example, the SRRS includes many life events that are irrelevant to most college students—getting divorced, receiving a jail term, obtaining a mortgage. At the same time, the measure omits many of the most relevant stressors that might be experienced by this age group, such as moving away from home, considering abortion, or changing career plans.

Another objection is that the SRRS includes both positive and negative events as stressors. People may rate getting married and getting fired from a job as being similar in terms of life change units, but the (presumably) positive event of getting married would seem to differ in many important ways from the negative event of being dismissed from a job. Still another objection is the failure to distinguish between transient and chronic life events. Most of the items on the SRRS are not isolated events. Events such as marital separation or beginning college are major life transitions that have consequences extending into many realms of life and lasting over long periods of time.

The most important objection to instruments like the SRRS is that a given stressor does not always produce the same number of life change units for all individuals in all situations. Different life events have different consequences for different people at different points in their lives. For example, getting pregnant has a very different meaning for an unwed teenager who failed to use birth control than it has for a married couple in their 30s who are eager to conceive a baby.

STRESS AS A RESPONSE

The Canadian physiologist Hans Selye (1907–1982) was an extremely influential stress researcher who defined stress as a response. More precisely, Selye (1956) defined stress in terms of his concept of the **general adaptation syndrome (GAS),** a specific response to a variety of (nonspecific) stressors. The GAS consists of three stages: alarm, resistance, and exhaustion (see Figure 8–1). The stage of *alarm* involves the mobilization of the body in reaction to perceived threat. The stage of *resistance* is a period of replenishment during which the body becomes physiologically prepared to deal with new threats. *Exhaustion* is the final stage, which occurs if the body's resources are depleted by chronic stress, making further adaptation impossible.

Much of Selye's research was devoted to animal analogue studies of the GAS, and this is one reason why he focused his definition of stress on a response rather than a stimulus. Stressors administered in the laboratory (such as an unpredictable electric shock) are independent variables that are controlled and manipulated by the experimenter (see Research Methods in Chapter 2). Stressful events are clearly defined in a laboratory experiment, where the major interest is the dependent variable—the animal's response to stress.

The laboratory analogue approach to studying stress has tremendous value, and we discuss the biological findings of Selye and other laboratory researchers in more detail shortly. However, by its very nature, the laboratory artificially controls events that are uncontrolled in the real world. As we have noted, all life events do *not* have the same meaning or impact in the everyday, human world, and this fact has forced researchers who study naturalistic stress among people to seek broader definitions of stress.

STRESS AS A STIMULUS-RESPONSE COMBINATION

Richard Lazarus (1966) argues that stress arises not from life events themselves but from the individual's *primary appraisal* or cognitive evaluation of the challenge, threat, or harm posed by a particular event (Lazarus & Folkman, 1984). Lazarus asserts that any given life event is a stressor only when it is considered stressful by the individual. For example, an impending exam causes stress when a student feels inadequate in his or her knowledge, but not when he or she feels confident about the subject matter. Lazarus also theorizes that *secondary appraisal,* the assessment of one's abilities and resources for coping with a difficult event, is critical to defining stress. Thus, even if a student believes his or her knowledge is inadequate, the stress caused by an impending exam will be minimized if the student has the time and the ability to study adequately.

general adaptation syndrome (GAS)
Selye's three stages in reaction to stress: alarm, resistance, and exhaustion.

Figure 8–1   Stress as a Response: Selye's General Adaptation Syndrome (GAS).   Hans Selye defined stress in terms of a response. He assumed that the three stages of the GAS are activated in the same way by different stressors.

Source: Adapted from A. Baum, L.M. Davidson, J.E. Singer, and S.W. Street, 1987, Stress as a psychophysiological response. In A. Baum and J.E. Singer (Eds.), *Handbook of Psychology and Health. Stress,* vol. 5, p. 4. Hillsdale, NJ: Erlbaum.

getting help

Stressed out? We all are at times—when we face exams, have to deal with difficult relationships, or just have too much to do and not enough time to do it.

If there is too much stress in your life, a helpful first step is to analyze it. One great way to begin is to write about the situations that stress you out, your responses, and your attempts at coping. You could start a journal; you could write someone a letter (that you may or may not mail); or you could just jot down a few notes. Writing can help you get some things off your chest—(and off your mind)—but it can also help you to sort things out. Writing takes thoughts and feelings from the inside and puts them out there, in the world, where you can look at them. Sometimes just putting your thoughts into words can help: "Whew! I don't have to think about that any more!" Another benefit is that you can always go back and read what you wrote and correct and organize your thoughts and feelings. An engaging, research-based account of the benefits of writing is James Pennebaker's *Opening Up: The Healing Power of Expressing Emotions.*

Another way you may want to analyze stress in your life is to complete some stress-rating forms. You can find some interesting resources on the Internet, including a very detailed form at the home page of the Biobehavioral Institute of Boston

(http://www.bbinst.org/) and a much simpler one at a commercial Web site (http://www.teachhealth.com/), where you also will find a lot of useful information presented with some fun and humor.

What about coping with stress? If your usual strategies aren't working, a useful general resource is Herbert Benson's *The Relaxation Response.* If you have troubling physical symptoms linked with stress, you should first consult with your family physician. A mental health professional may be appropriate to contact if your stress responses are more emotional.

Finally, if you are suffering from the stress of a physical illness and want to know about the latest research, the place to start on-line is the home page of the National Institutes of Health (http://www.nih.gov/). If your illness is chronic, particularly difficult, or rare, you might find it helpful to communicate on-line with others who suffer from the same disease. Because there are so many resources on the Internet, most search engines contain a category specifically for "health." As you browse, remember to be skeptical and cautious in evaluating information. If a treatment really is a breakthrough, you should be able to find it discussed and evaluated on sites like that of the National Institutes of Health. ♛

Lazarus thus defines stress as the combination of a difficult event and a cognitive appraisal of the event as being potentially harmful and exceeding the individual's coping resources. Lazarus's approach solves many of the problems with stimulus or response definitions of stress, but it runs the risk of being *tautological,* or circular. What is stress? An event that causes us to feel threatened and overwhelmed. What causes us to feel threatened and overwhelmed? Stress. We agree with Lazarus that, in naturalistic studies of humans, stress must be defined in terms of both a stimulus and a response (note our definition given earlier). Because of the potential for circularity, however, great caution must be exercised in distinguishing independent variables (stressors) from dependent variables (adverse outcomes) in research on stress.

Typical Symptoms and Associated Features of Stress

In this section we consider short-term physiological, emotional, cognitive, and behavioral responses to stress. We distinguish these immediate reactions from the physical illnesses that stress may cause over longer periods of time.

Physiological Responses to Stress

Hans Selye (1907–1982) was a physiologist and prolific stress researcher. Selye's concept of the general adaptation syndrome continues to influence contemporary research on the stress response.

The American physiologist Walter Cannon (1871–1945) was one of the first researchers to conduct systematic studies of stress, and his profound influence on the field continues to the present day. Cannon (1935) was primarily interested in what he called the *emergency response,* the mobilization of the body in reaction to a perceived threat. According to Cannon, physical or psychological threats produce generalized emotional reactions accompanied by psychophysiological responses, specifically the general arousal of the sympathetic nervous system (see Figure 8–2). When

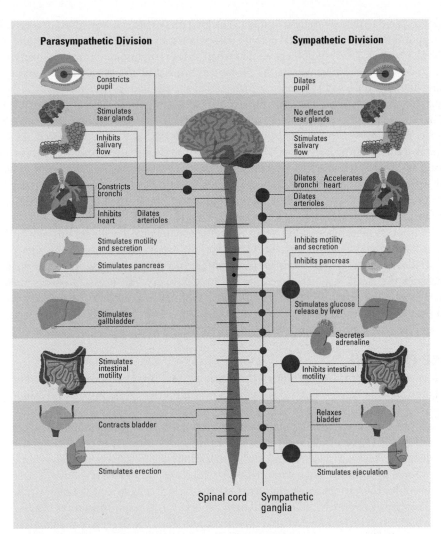

Figure 8–2   Sympathetic and Parasympathetic Divisions of the Autonomic Nervous System.   The sympathetic nervous system is activated by stress and generally increases arousal. The parasympathetic nervous system typically calms the individual and returns the body to homeostatis.
Source: From *Biology,* 4th ed., by Willis H. Johnson, Louis E. Delanney, Thomas A. Cole, and Austin E. Brooks. Copyright © 1972 by Holt, Rinehart and Winston, Inc.

fight or flight response   A response to a threat in which psychophysiological reactions mobilize the body to take action against danger.

the sympathetic nervous system is aroused, heart and respiration rates increase; blood pressure rises; the pupils dilate; blood sugar levels elevate; and blood flow is redirected in preparation for muscular activity (Baum et al., 1987; Koranyi, 1989).

Cannon argued that these reactions prepare humans (and other animals) for fight or flight in response to threat. Cannon's **fight or flight response** is the reaction you witness when a cat is surprised by a barking dog. At the behavioral level of analysis, the cat can either flee to safety or turn to scratch at the dog. Physiologically, the cat's body becomes prepared for either action. Attention is heightened, energy is provided for sudden action, and its body prepares for the possibility of injury (Sapolsky, 1992).

The fight or flight response has obvious survival value when we are confronted with a physically dangerous threat. However, fight or flight seems to be a maladaptive response to many psychological threats that characterize the modern world, such as being reprimanded by your boss, giving a speech before a large audience, or getting caught in a traffic jam. Behavioral fight or flight obviously is inappropriate in such circumstances, and the physiology of the response may be similarly maladaptive. In fact, our physiological reactions to stress may be prolonged precisely because

Walter Cannon (1871–1945) was one of the first scientists to conduct systematic research on stress. Cannon focused on the emergency response, the body's physiological preparation for fight or flight.

psychoneuroimmunology (PNI) Research on the effects of stress on the functioning of the immune system.

we cannot respond to them with fight or flight. The load on the heart is less, for example, when people can respond to stress with physical activity than when they cannot respond physically (Charvat et al., 1964). Cannon (1935) hypothesized that when stress is intense or chronic, it overwhelms the body's homeostatic mechanisms, and the prolonged arousal of the sympathetic nervous system eventually damages the body. (Cannon, in fact, coined the familiar term *homeostasis.*)

Much like Cannon, Selye identified the stage of exhaustion in his GAS as responsible for converting stress into physical illness (refer back to Figure 8–1). There are subtle differences between the two theories, however. In Selye's view, if stress is sufficiently intense or prolonged, the body can no longer respond appropriately to it. The stress response is exhausted, and the body is damaged by continuous, failed attempts to activate it. An analogy for Cannon's theory is a car in which the engine continues to race instead of idling down after running fast. In contrast, an analogy for Selye's theory is a car that has run out of gas and is damaged because stress keeps turning the key, trying repeatedly and unsuccessfully to restart the engine.

Contemporary researchers suggest that stress may create physical illness through both mechanisms, but a third explanation may be even more important. According to this viewpoint, the problem is that the body cannot perform routine functions such as storing energy or repairing injuries because the stress response demands too much energy and uses the energy inefficiently (Sapolsky, 1992). The result is greater susceptibility to illness. An automotive analogy for the demands of stress in this third model is constantly running a car at high speeds, thus preventing the cooling and lubricant systems from performing their functions.

IMMUNE FUNCTION

Research on stress and the functioning of the immune system is an important illustration of this third theoretical perspective. Numerous studies have found that stress impairs functioning of the immune system, thus weakening the body's ability to fight off infectious disease (Maier, Watkins, & Fleshner, 1994). In fact, research in this area has spawned a new field of study called **psychoneuroimmunology (PNI),** research on the effects of stress on the functioning of the immune system.

Scientists are beginning to document the physiology of how stress weakens immune functioning. Adrenal hormones called *glucocorticoids,* which are secreted in response to stress, inhibit and may even destroy various immune agents, particularly *T cells,* one of the major types of *lymphocytes,* a category of white blood cells that fight off *antigens,* foreign substances like bacteria that invade the body. Experts hypothesize that *immunosuppression,* the decreased production of T cells and other immune agents, makes the body more susceptible to infectious diseases. For example, researchers have found that among medical students during exam periods, T-cell activity diminishes, and rates of various infectious diseases increase (Glaser et al., 1987).

Immunosuppression has also been found among people who are depressed (Herbert & Cohen, 1993), and researchers now link immunosuppression directly to the experience of stress. In one fascinating study, 90 newly married couples were admitted to a hospital research ward where they engaged in a 30-minute discussion of marital problems. Partners who were more hostile or negative during the interaction showed greater immunosuppression over the next 24 hours in comparison to newlyweds who had more positive conversations. (Blood pressure also remained elevated longer following hostile interactions than following friendly interactions.) This research demonstrates that stress has a direct effect on immune functioning.

Why does stress inhibit immune function? As we noted earlier, stress mobilizes the body for fight or flight, and from an evolutionary perspective, it may seem that *heightened* rather than impaired immune function is a more adaptive physiological response to threat. That is, heightened immune functioning might prepare the body for the injury or infection that often follows fight or flight. Maier, Watkins, and Fleshner (1994) argue, however, that the immune response actually impairs action, for example, it creates inflammation, maintains fever, and intensifies pain. Therefore inhibited immune function may be an adaptive reaction to immediate threat from an evolutionary point of view. Consistent with the "energy drain" model discussed at the beginning of this section, Maier and colleagues view fight or flight as competing with the immune response for the body's resources. Thus they argue that stress causes immunosuppression by diverting energy from the immune system to the fight or flight response.

Emotional Responses to Stress

In general, the emotions aroused by stress are negative ones (Baum et al., 1987). Anxiety, depression, and anger are the primary affective responses to stressors, although different individuals may experience these emotions as tension, sadness, frustration, numbness, or simply as a somatic symptom like an upset stomach.

Consideration of emotional responses to stress brings us back to the vital topic of coping. A distinction is often made between problem-focused and emotion-focused coping (Lazarus & Folkman, 1984). **Problem-focused coping** is externally oriented and involves attempts to change a stressor. If your job is too stressful, you can look for a new one. In contrast, **emotion-focused coping** is an attempt to alter internal distress. When a romance ends, you may tell yourself that you really don't care.

Emotion-focused coping may involve a deliberate effort to relax or to reevaluate a stressor. Before taking a big exam, you might sit quietly and breathe deeply for several minutes. Other forms of emotion-focused coping may involve unconscious or automatic methods for dampening emotional experience. For example, various intrapsychic defense mechanisms, particularly *repression,* have been hypothesized to alter emotional responses to stress—sometimes with maladaptive consequences.

Not surprisingly, the repression hypothesis is difficult to test empirically. Some evidence suggests that people who do not acknowledge their experience of anxiety show exaggerated psychophysiological reactions to stress (Schwartz, 1989). Similar findings have been reported for "defensive-deniers"—subjects who report positive mental health but whom clinicians judge to have emotional problems (Shedler, Mayman, & Manis, 1993). Other research indicates that when people are encouraged to recount very stressful experiences, they show reductions in various psychophysiological indicators of the stress response (Pennebaker, 1990; Petrie et al., 1995). Although the repression hypothesis is difficult to test, talking about your feelings clearly is healthy.

Cognitive Responses to Stress

In addition to the important issues of primary and secondary appraisal, findings from animal and human research indicate that other aspects of cognition can dramatically alter responses to stress. Two critical issues are the *predictability* of stressors and *control* over them. A rat has a smaller physiological response to a shock that is signaled by the flash of a light than to an unsignaled shock of the same magnitude (Sapolsky, 1992). In a sense, predictability allows us to begin to cope even *before* the onset of a stressor.

The importance of control has been documented in much research with animals and humans. Rats who are able to stop a shock by pressing a bar have a smaller stress response than rats exposed to exactly the same shock but who have no opportunity of stopping it through their own actions (Sapolsky, 1992). Even the illusion of control can help to alleviate stress in humans (Mineka & Kihlstrom, 1978), but the perception of being able to control a stressor is not always a good thing. The perception of control can *increase* stress when people believe they can exercise control but are unable to do so, or when they lose control over a formerly controllable stressor (Mineka & Kihlstrom, 1978). Thus control alleviates stress when it can be exercised or even when it is illusory, but failed attempts at control intensify stress.

Behavioral Responses to Stress

As we have noted, responding to stress with physical activity reduces the physiological reactions of the fight or flight response. In fact, the response need not be directed at the stressor itself, but may include other *outlets for frustration.* For example, rats secrete fewer glucocorticoids if they can attack another rat or run on a running wheel after the administration of an electric shock (Sapolsky, 1992).

As suggested by the literature on control, however, there is a problem with responding to stressors directly: It is often unclear which coping response will be effective, or even whether a stressor can be changed. A difficult class may cause you great stress because you cannot maintain your usual

problem-focused coping Externally oriented coping in an attempt to change or otherwise control a stressor.

emotion-focused coping Internally oriented coping in an attempt to alter one's emotional or cognitive responses to a stressor.

health behavior A wide range of activities that are essential to promoting good health, including positive actions such as proper diet and the avoidance of negative activities such as cigarette smoking.

Calvin and Hobbes   by Bill Watterson

grades. What is the most effective response to this situation? Should you redouble your efforts, drop the course, or accept that this is not your best subject? Problem-focused (behavioral) coping is the appropriate way to conquer many actual stressors, but attempts to change some stressors are doomed to failure. In such cases, efforts at problem-focused coping will increase, not reduce, distress. Thus the only alternative is to accept the stressor for what it is and to use emotion-focused coping to alter your response to it. In short, there is much truth in Reinhold Niebuhr's (1951) "Serenity Prayer":

> God, give us the serenity to accept what cannot be changed;
> Give us the courage to change what should be changed;
> Give us the wisdom to distinguish one from the other.

HEALTH BEHAVIOR

Stress may cause illness indirectly, by affecting health behaviors, rather than directly, by altering our physiology (Cohen & Williamson, 1991; see Figure 8–3). **Health behavior** involves activities that are essential to promoting good health. Proper health behavior includes positive actions like eating, sleeping, and exercising adequately, as well as the avoidance of unhealthy activities such as cigarette smoking, excessive alcohol consumption, and drug use. Stress can lead people to engage in less positive and more negative health behavior, and these poor health habits, and not stress, per se, may be responsible for much of the relation between stress and illness (Cohen & Williamson, 1991). In considering the importance of health behavior, you should note that over the last 2 centuries basic health behaviors—personal hygiene, maintaining sanitation, and eating an adequate diet—are more responsible for our vastly increased health and life expectancy than are scientific advances like the discovery of penicillin (Starr, 1982).

Stress may also be related to the very important positive health behavior of following medical advice. (Recall that Bob Carter discounted his cardiologist's recommendations to alter his lifestyle.) In fact, as many as 93 percent of all patients *fail* to adhere fully to medical advice (Taylor, 1990). This is a particular problem for illnesses like hypertension (high blood pressure) that usually have no obvious symptoms. In such cases patients may discontinue their medication because it produces no noticeable relief, although it may be controlling a dangerous condition. Stressors such as family conflict also can interfere with adherence to treatments that *do* have clear symptoms. For example, children with insulin-dependent diabetes are less likely to adhere to medical recommendations concerning exercise, diet, testing blood sugars, and the timing and frequency of insulin injections when family conflict is high (Miller-Johnson et al., 1994).

Illness behavior—behaving as if you are sick—also appears to be stress-related. Considerable research indicates that increased stress is correlated with such illness behaviors as making more frequent office visits to physicians or allowing chronic pain to interfere with everyday activities (Taylor, 1990). On the positive side, a happier, less stressful life may motivate people to cope successfully with chronic illness, where effective coping may involve ignoring physical discomfort and living life as normally as possible.

Finally, the fact that many people consult physicians for psychological rather than physical concerns underscores the value of *social support* in coping with stress. Social support can encour-

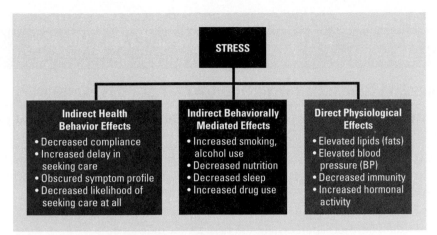

Figure 8–3   Indirect and Direct Effects of Stress on Illness.   Stress can promote illness both directly through adverse physiological effects and indirectly by undermining positive health behaviors and increasing negative health behaviors.

Source: A. Baum, 1994, Behavioral, biological, and environmental interactions in disease processes. In S. Blumenthal, K. Matthews, and S. Weiss (Eds.), *New Research Frontiers in Behavioral Medicine: Proceedings of the National Conference,* p. 62. Washington, DC: NIH Publications.

age adaptive coping with illness, but research suggests that social support also has direct, physical benefits. For example, one investigation found that stressed monkeys exhibited less immunosuppression when they interacted more often with other monkeys (Cohen et al., 1992). Other findings indicate that increased social support is associated with adaptive functioning of the immune, cardiovascular, and endocrine systems (Uchino, Cacioppo, & Kiecolt-Glaser, 1996).

Classification of Stress and Physical Illness

Now that we have discussed short-term responses to stress, we can consider the relation between stress and more general physical health. We begin with an overview of classification of stress-related physical illnesses.

Brief Historical Perspective

Scientific interest in the link between life experience and physical illness was first pursued with vigor by psychoanalytically oriented psychiatrists who helped to establish the field of psychosomatic medicine in the middle of the twentieth century. These early theorists developed a classification of psychosomatic illnesses based on what has become known as the *specificity hypothesis*—the idea that specific personality types cause specific psychosomatic diseases. Specificity theorists (e.g., Alexander, 1950) attempted to classify various psychosomatic illnesses, such as asthma, ulcer, and so on, according to the unique personality type that presumably caused the specific illness.

Contemporary Approaches

Research does not support the specificity hypothesis, and a more generalized view of stress has come to dominate modern science. As we have noted, contemporary approaches also reject the psychosomatic medicine view that only certain physical illnesses have psychological causes. Psyche and soma are now considered to play a role in all physical illnesses; thus a list of "psychosomatic disorders" would contain every known physical illness.

The DSM-IV highlights the essential role of stress in illness by including two separate diagnostic axes, Axis III and Axis IV (see Chapter 4). Physical illnesses that are judged to be

TABLE 8–1

DSM-IV Diagnostic Criteria for Psychological Factors Affecting Medical Condition

A. A GENERAL MEDICAL CONDITION (CODED ON AXIS III) IS PRESENT.

B. PSYCHOLOGICAL FACTORS ADVERSELY AFFECT THE GENERAL MEDICAL CONDITION IN ONE OF THE FOLLOWING WAYS:

1. The factors have influenced the course of the general medical condition as shown by a close temporal association between the psychological factors and the development or exacerbation, or delayed recovery from, the general medical condition.
2. The factors interfere with the treatment of the general medical condition.
3. The factors constitute additional health risks for the individual.
4. Stress-related physiological responses precipitate or exacerbate symptoms of the general medical condition.

relevant to understanding or treating an emotional disorder are coded on Axis III, *general medical conditions*. The only criteria for coding a physical illness on this axis are (1) the disorder involves organic pathology (that is, it is not a somatoform disorder), and (2) the physical illness is related to the Axis I diagnosis in a meaningful way. When the physical illness is the focus of the treatment, the Axis I diagnosis of *psychological factors affecting medical condition* is used in conjunction with the Axis III medical disorder (see Table 8–1). You should note that it is *not* necessary for an Axis I mental disorder to be present in order to use the diagnosis of psychological factors affecting medical condition. In fact, the diagnosis may be used whether the patient has a mental disorder or simply exhibits psychological symptoms, personality traits, maladaptive health behaviors, or stress-related physiological responses that might affect his or her medical condition.

The DSM-IV also has a separate axis for coding stressors, Axis IV, *psychosocial and environmental problems*. The DSM makes no attempt to offer an exhaustive listing of potential life stressors for Axis IV. Instead, it simply includes categories of stressors with specific examples under each heading.

As we have noted, scientists have not yet reached consensus about how "stress" should be defined or rated. Perhaps the only certainty for the future is that the DSM definition of stress will change as researchers continue to refine methods of categorizing and quantifying life stressors.

The Role of Psychological Factors in Some Familiar Illnesses

In addition to the emerging medical discoveries of the era, there is a good reason why germ theory dominated medicine at the beginning of the twentieth century. Infectious diseases, specifically influenza, pneumonia, and tuberculosis, were the most common causes of death in the United States in 1900 (Taylor, 1995). Thanks to advances in medical science, and especially in public health, far fewer people die of infectious disease today compared to 100 years ago. As you can see from Figure 8–4, infectious disease is no longer at the top of the list of killers. In fact, lifestyle plays a central role in 7 of the top 10 causes of death in the United States today (Human Capital Initiative, 1996).

In the following sections we briefly review evidence on psychological factors in the etiology, course, and treatment of cancer, HIV infection, and chronic pain. Later, we review research in some detail on the relation between stress and today's number one killer, cardiovascular disease. Our goal is to convey a sense of both the breadth and the depth of research in behavioral medicine.

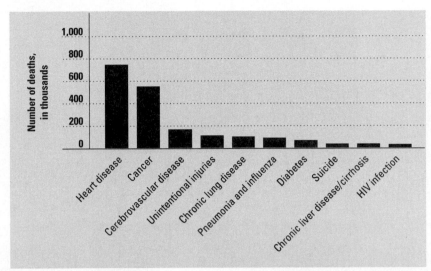

Figure 8–4   The 10 Leading Causes of Death in the United States in 1996.
Stess and health behavior play a central role in most of the major causes of death in the United States today.

Source: K. D. Peters, K. D. Kochanek, and S. L. Murphy, (1998). Deaths: Final data for 1996. *National Vital Statistics Reports, 47,* 9. (Hyaltsville, MD: National Center for Health Statistics).

Cancer

Cancer is the second leading cause of mortality in the United States today, accounting for 23 percent of all deaths. In contrast to the declining rate of death due to cardiovascular disease, moreover, cancer deaths have risen by 20 percent over the last 30 years (American Cancer Society, 1994). At first glance, cancer would seem to be the paramount example of a purely biological illness, but the importance of stress and health behavior becomes apparent upon closer examination. To some degree, for example, our actions determine the extent to which we are exposed to various *carcinogens,* cancer-causing agents, such as cigarette smoking.

Stress and health behavior also appear to affect the course of cancer. Not surprisingly, cancer patients often are anxious or depressed, and their negative emotions can lead to increases in negative health behavior (e.g., alcohol consumption) and decreases in positive health behavior (e.g., exercise). Stress or the absence of social support also can undermine compliance with unpleasant but vitally important medical treatments for cancer (Anderson, Kiecolt-Glaser, & Glaser, 1994). Finally, some research indicates that stress *directly* affects the course of cancer. In animal analogue studies, for example, rats exposed to inescapable shock are less able to reject implanted cancer tumors than rats exposed to escapable shock or no stress at all (Visintainer, Seligman, & Volpicelli, 1982). The adverse effects of stress on the immune system may explain how stress may exacerbate the course of cancer. Evidence indicates that immunity plays an important role in limiting the spread of cancerous tumors, and immunosuppression due to stress may disrupt this protective function (Anderson et al., 1994).

A cause and effect relationship between stress and the course of cancer also is implied by some exciting treatment research. Various psychological treatments have been offered to cancer patients in an attempt to improve their quality of life. The type of intervention varies widely, but treatments often include a structured, self-help group. Many of these interventions are successful in improving the quality of life among cancer patients, and a few of the psychological interventions appear to have beneficial *physical* effects (Anderson et al., 1994). For example, one study found that 6 years after treatment, significantly fewer patients who participated in a support group died (9 percent) in comparison to patients who received no psychosocial treatment (29 percent) (Fawzy et al., 1993).

Any number of factors may explain this striking outcome, including lower stress, increased social support, and improved health behavior. We must be cautious not to overinterpret the result,

acquired immune deficiency syndrome (AIDS) A disease caused by the human immunodeficiency virus (HIV) that attacks the immune system and leaves the patient susceptible to unusual infections.

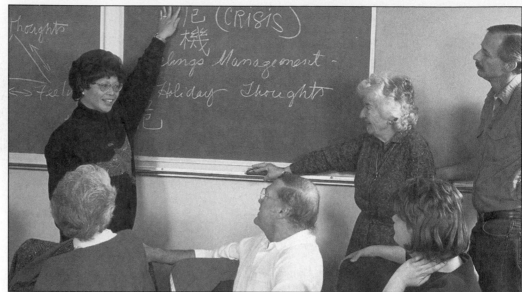

A self-help group for patients with cancer. Some evidence suggests that cancer support groups not only improve quality of life, but they may actually help extend the lives of the terminally ill.

especially until the finding is replicated widely. Cancer *is* a physical illness. We are hardly arguing that psychological factors alone are responsible for causing cancer, nor are we asserting that the disease should be treated psychologically instead of medically. Still, intervention research dramatically illustrates that psychological factors contribute to the course of one of our most dreaded physical illnesses.

Acquired Immune Deficiency Syndrome (AIDS)

Acquired immune deficiency syndrome (AIDS) is caused by the *human immunodeficiency virus (HIV),* which attacks the immune system and leaves the patient susceptible to unusual infections. However, people who are HIV positive vary widely in how rapidly they develop AIDS. Some people develop AIDS quickly after HIV infection, whereas others remain symptom-free for 10 years or more. In fact, scientists disagree about whether people who are HIV positive will inevitably develop AIDS, or whether some will escape the dreaded disease (U.S. Department of Health and Human Services, 1993).

We do know that the virus is transmitted through contact with the bodily fluids of an infected individual, particularly blood and semen. Researchers have isolated a number of high-risk behaviors, including anal sex between homosexual men and heterosexual vaginal intercourse. The use of condoms greatly reduces the risk of the sexual transmission of HIV, as you undoubtedly have learned from public service announcements in various popular media. Other behaviors that increase the risk for HIV infection include sharing hypodermic needles, and transmission from an infected mother to her unborn child (U.S. Department of Health and Human Services, 1993).

Although the public has become much more knowledgeable about AIDS, changing behavior is very difficult. For example, practices such as condom use that reduce the risk of infection are now more common among members of high-risk groups such as homosexual men or heterosexual young people with multiple sexual partners. However, unprotected sex is still very common even among members of high-risk groups, and researchers have detected some backsliding in recent years (Taylor, 1995).

Stress causes immunosuppression, but evidence is inconsistent as to whether the course of AIDS is exacerbated by exposure to stress. Similarly, research is contradictory about the benefits of psychological intervention in altering the progression of AIDS. It is clear, however, that social support is extremely important to the AIDS patient's *psychological* well-being. Unfortunately, misunderstanding and fear cause many people, including many health professionals, to distance themselves from AIDS victims rather than offering them understanding, acceptance, and support.

hypertension   High blood pressure.

coronary heart disease (CHD)   A group of diseases of the heart that includes angina pectoris (chest pains) and myocardial infarction (heart attack).

Pain Management

Pain is associated with a number of acute injuries and illnesses, and it often serves the useful functions of alerting people to a problem and motivating them to seek treatment. Pain is not always adaptive, however, and in many cases, pain is *not* a signal of an underlying condition that can be controlled with treatment. Problematic pain can take the form of recurrent acute pain, or pain can be chronic. Headaches are an example of recurrent acute pain, and lower back problems are a common form of chronic pain.

Pain can take a huge toll not only on the sufferer but also on family members—and on the family's and the society's economy. Repeated attempts to treat chronic pain quickly become expensive, and chronic pain can greatly impair work performance. The adverse personal, social, and economic consequences of pain are even more important, because pain is pervasive. In fact, some estimates indicate that as many as 90 million people in the United States suffer from recurrent or chronic pain (Taylor, 1995).

Basketball superstar Ervin (Magic) Johnson became a spokesman for increasing awareness of HIV and AIDS after he tested HIV positive.

Pain is subjective, and this makes it difficult to evaluate or compare patients' reports about the extent or nature of their pain. Evaluation is especially difficult when pain is not associated with an identifiable injury or illness, as is commonly the case with headaches and lower back pain. Some evidence links reports of increased pain with depression and anxiety (Taylor, 1995). Researchers commonly interpret this finding as indicating that people who are anxious or depressed are more sensitive to pain, less able to cope with it, and more willing to complain than are people who apparently have similar levels of suffering.

Psychologists have tried a number of treatments designed to directly reduce patients' experience of pain. Treatments include a wide range of techniques, such as hypnosis, biofeedback, relaxation training, and cognitive therapy. Researchers report a degree of success with each of these various approaches, but pain reduction typically is modest at best (Taylor, 1995). As a result, most current efforts focus on the *pain management,* not pain reduction. The goal of pain management programs is to help people to cope with pain in a way that minimizes its impact on their lives, even if the pain cannot be eliminated or controlled entirely.

Researchers have reported that pain management programs are successful in treating a wide variety of pain problems stemming from various underlying conditions, including headaches, lower back pain, and facial pain. Following treatment, patients report greater satisfaction with their life and relationships, improved employment status, and less reliance on medication. Moreover, patients commonly report that their pain has lessened once they are better able to function in their lives (Taylor, 1995). It is not clear whether improved life functioning actually reduces pain or just reduces patients' awareness of discomfort. In either case, however, these positive results offer strong justification for using behavioral medicine in the treatment of chronic pain.

Cardiovascular Disease

In order to illustrate the complexities of research and treatment relating stress to physical illness, we focus on the very important problem of cardiovascular disease in considerable detail. *Cardiovascular disease (CVD)* is a group of disorders that affect the heart and circulatory system. The most important of these illnesses are **hypertension** (high blood pressure) and **coronary heart disease (CHD).** Hypertension increases the risk for CHD, as well as for other serious disorders, such as stroke. The most deadly and well-known form of coronary heart disease is *myocardial infarction (MI),* commonly called a heart attack.

Cardiovascular disorders are the leading cause of mortality in most industrialized countries, including the United States, where they account for almost half of all deaths. About two-thirds of the deaths due to cardiovascular disorders are caused by coronary heart disease (Jenkins, 1988). Mortality due to CHD is of particular concern because about half of all Americans with CHD and about a quarter of all stroke victims are under the age of 65.

An individual's risk for developing CVD, and particularly CHD, is associated with a number of health behaviors, including weight, diet, exercise, and cigarette smoking, as we saw in the case of Bob Carter. This link between CVD and lifestyle is one reason why health psychology is so important in preventing and treating these disorders. Psychology also is important in understanding hypertension and heart disease, because behavioral and physical risk indicators account for only about half of all cases of CHD (Jenkins, 1988). In addition to health behavior, personality styles, behavior patterns, and forms of emotional expression appear to contribute directly to the development of CVD.

Typical Symptoms and Associated Features of Hypertension and CHD

Hypertension is often referred to as the "silent killer" because it produces no obvious symptoms. For this reason, high blood pressure often goes undetected, and routine blood pressure monitoring is extremely important.

The most notable symptom of CHD is chest pain. Typically, the pain is centralized in the middle of the chest, and it often extends through the left shoulder and down the left arm. In less severe forms of the disorder, the pain that accompanies CHD is mild, or it may be sharp but brief. The pain during more severe forms of CHD such as myocardial infarction typically is so intense that it is crippling. Two-thirds of all deaths from CHD occur within 24 hours of a coronary event (Kamarck & Jennings, 1991). In over half of these sudden deaths, the victim received no previous treatment for CHD, an indication that either there were no warning symptoms or the symptoms were mild enough to have been ignored.

CLASSIFICATION OF CVD

Myocardial infarction and angina pectoris are the two major forms of coronary heart disease. *Angina pectoris* involves intermittent chest pains that are usually brought on by some form of exertion. Attacks of angina do not damage the heart, but the chest pain can be a sign of underlying pathology that puts the patient at risk for a myocardial infarction. MI (heart attack) does involve damage to the heart, and as noted, it often causes death within 24 hours of a coronary episode.

Hypertension can be primary or secondary. *Secondary hypertension* results from a known problem such as a diagnosed kidney or endocrine disorder. It is called secondary hypertension because the high blood pressure is secondary to—that is, a consequence of —the principal physical disorder. Primary or *essential hypertension* is the major concern of behavioral medicine and health psychology. In the case of essential hypertension, the high blood pressure is the principal disorder. There is no single, identifiable cause of essential hypertension, which accounts for approximately 85 percent of all cases of high blood pressure. Instead, multiple physical and behavioral risk factors are thought to contribute to elevated blood pressure.

Epidemiology of CVD

Cardiovascular disease is the major cause of death in most industrialized countries, but some important differences among nations have emerged in recent years. The rate of death due to CVD has declined by 25 percent or more in the United States, Japan, and many West European countries, whereas mortality rates attributed to CVD have increased in many East European countries. The increased awareness of the negative effects of stress in the West—and the increased industrialization that may raise maladaptive stress levels in Eastern Europe—may be part of the explanation.

RISK FACTORS FOR CHD

Epidemiological studies have identified several risk indicators for CHD. Men are twice as likely to suffer from CHD as are women; these sex differences are even greater with more severe forms of the disorder. Age is another major risk factor. For men, risk for CHD increases in a linear fashion with increasing age after 40. For women, risk for CHD accelerates more slowly until they reach menopause and increases sharply afterwards. Rates of CHD also are higher among low-income groups, a finding that likely accounts for the higher rates of CHD among black than among white Americans. Finally, a positive family history is also linked to an increased risk for CHD, due at least in part to genetic factors (Jenkins, 1988).

In addition to these background factors, several health behaviors have been linked to CHD. Hypertension increases the risk for CHD by a factor of 2 to 4. The risk for CHD also is 2 to 3 times greater among those who smoke a pack or more of cigarettes a day. Obesity, a fatty diet, elevated serum cholesterol levels, heavy alcohol consumption, and lack of exercise are also related to an increased risk for CHD. Specific risk ratios are difficult to identify for each of these factors, however, because weight, diet, cholesterol, alcohol consumption, and exercise all are closely interrelated (Jenkins, 1988).

Also, it is difficult to calculate the specific risk for CHD associated with psychological characteristics other than health behaviors. This is because of difficulties in measuring some relevant behavioral styles and because of conflicting findings in epidemiologic research. For example, a great deal of research on the psychological contributions to CHD has focused on what is known as the Type A behavior pattern, which is a highly driven, competitive personality type. In 1981, the National Heart, Lung, and Blood Institute officially concluded that Type A behavior increased the risk for CHD independently of other health behaviors. However, recent research has challenged this conclusion, as we discuss shortly.

RISK FACTORS FOR HYPERTENSION

About 30 percent of all U.S. adults suffer from hypertension, and many of the same risk factors that predict CHD also predict high blood pressure, including genetic factors, a high salt diet, health behavior, and lifestyle factors. Hypertension is more common in industrialized countries, and in the United States, high blood pressure is found with greater frequency among men, African Americans, low-income groups, and people exposed to high levels of chronic life stress. Although many of these risk factors are interrelated, they appear to have independent effects in increasing the prevalence of hypertension. For example, one study found that hypertension was twice as common among blacks as whites, but among black men who lived in high-stress neighborhoods, the risk was 4 times as great (Roberts & Rowland, 1981).

Etiological Considerations and Research on CVD

BIOLOGICAL FACTORS IN CVD

The immediate cause of CHD is the deprivation of oxygen to the heart muscle. No permanent damage is caused by the temporary oxygen deprivation *(myocardial ischemia)* that accompanies angina pectoris, but part of the heart muscle dies in cases of myocardial infarction. Oxygen deprivation can be caused by temporarily increased oxygen demands on the heart, for example, as a result of exercise. More problematic is when atherosclerosis causes the gradual deprivation of the flow of blood (and the oxygen it carries) to the heart. *Atherosclerosis* is the thickening of the coronary artery wall that occurs as a result of the accumulation of blood lipids (fats) with age. The most dangerous circumstance is when the oxygen deprivation is sudden, as occurs in a *coronary occlusion.* Coronary occlusions result either from arteries that are completely blocked by fatty deposits or from blood clots that make their way to the heart muscle.

The immediate biological causes of hypertension are less well understood, as are the more distant biological causes of both hypertension and CHD. As we noted, a positive family history is a risk factor for both hypertension and CHD, and most experts interpret this association as indicating a genetic contribution to CVD. However, the specific mediating mechanism has yet to be identified. Moreover, research on animal models of CVD suggests that heritable risk interacts with environmental risk. For example, rats prone to develop hypertension do so only when exposed to salty diets or environmental stress (Schneiderman, Chesney, & Krantz, 1989). Other biological risk factors for CVD, such as obesity and elevated serum cholesterol, involve health behaviors, and therefore we consider them as a part of psychological contributions to the disease.

PSYCHOLOGICAL FACTORS IN CVD

CVD is a *lifestyle disease,* a clear example of the inextricable link between behavior and physical health. Avoiding or quitting smoking, maintaining a proper weight, following a low-cholesterol diet, exercising frequently, monitoring blood pressure regularly, and taking antihypertensive medication as prescribed can all reduce the risk of heart disease. Our bodies need routine maintenance, much as any machinery does.

Stress also contributes to CVD, in two different ways. First, stress increases blood pressure and heart rate, thus taxing the cardiovascular system and sometimes precipitating immediate symptoms or broader episodes of CHD. As in the case of Bob Carter, many people report that stress sets off both the minor symptoms of angina pectoris and the major problem of a myocardial infarction. Second, some theories suggest that over the long run the heart can be worn out by constant stress—much like a car that is chronically abused by its driver, especially when routine maintenance is ignored. In the following sections, we consider three areas of research linking stress to cardiovascular disease: (1) cardiovascular reactivity to stress, (2) actual exposure to life stress, and (3) characteristic styles of responding to stress (Krantz et al., 1988).

Cardiovascular Reactivity to Stress   Increased blood pressure and heart rate are normal reactions to stress, but researchers have long observed that different people exhibit different **cardiovascular reactivity** to stress—greater or lesser increases in blood pressure and heart rate when they are exposed to stress in the laboratory. Are people who show greater cardiovascular reactivity to stress more likely to develop CVD?

The cardiovascular reactivity hypothesis is increasingly supported by research on patients with CHD (Krantz et al., 1988). Patients with coronary disease show greater cardiovascular reactivity to stress than nonpatients (Corse et al., 1982), and diastolic blood pressure reactivity predicted the subsequent development of CHD in one study (Keys et al., 1971). In a recent study of patients with coronary artery disease, mental stress was a better predictor of subsequent cardiac events than was physical stress (exercise testing) (Jiang et al., 1996).

In many respects, it is impressive that cardiovascular reactivity in the laboratory predicts subsequent heart disease, because people are exposed to different degrees of stress in their real life. A high-level cardiovascular reactivity will have little effect on an individual if he or she experiences little stress. Thus actual life stress must also be considered in the equation that predicts cardiovascular disease.

Life Stressors and CVD: Job Strain as an Example   Exposure to chronic stress increases risk for cardiovascular disease (Krantz et al., 1988). Researchers have linked increased rates of coronary heart disease with high-stress occupations. A stressful job is more than just a demanding job. What appears to be most important is *job strain,* a situation that pairs high psychological demands with a low degree of decisional control (Karasek et al., 1982). A waitress has relatively high demands and low control, for instance, whereas a forest ranger has relatively few demands and a high degree of control. Figure 8–5 portrays a number of occupations and how they vary in terms of psychological demands and decisional control.

Several studies have found a relationship between job strain and CHD (Krantz et al., 1988). For example, among women who participated in the Framingham Heart Study—a major longitudinal study of the development of coronary heart disease—the risk for CHD was 1½ times higher among those who were rated as having high job strain based on objective evaluations of their occupations. The risk was 3 times higher among women whose self-reports indicated high job strain (LaCroix & Haynes, 1987).

Such strains are not limited to employment, but include work that is performed in other life roles. In an earlier analysis of women in the Framingham study, women who were employed for more than half of their adult lives were no more likely to develop CHD than were homemakers.

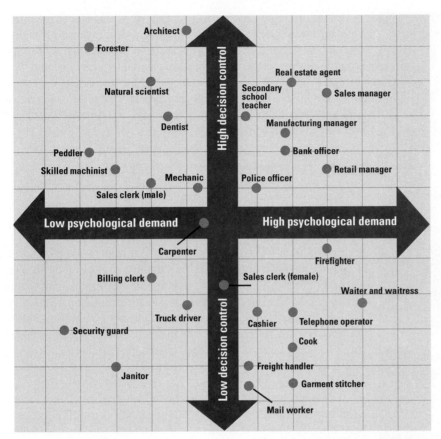

Figure 8–5   Occupational Control and Demand and Cardiovascular Risk.
Occupations classified according to the degree of demand and control that are associated with them. Jobs with low control and high demands are associated with increased cardiovascular risk.

Source: From R.A. Karasek, 1988. Cited in D.S. Krantz, R.J. Contrada, D.R. Hill, and E. Friedler,
Environmental stress and biobehavioral antecedents of coronary heart disease, *Journal of
Consulting and Clinical Psychology, 56,* 334.

However, working women with children were more likely to suffer from heart disease. In fact, the
risk for CHD increased with the number of children for working women but not for homemakers (Haynes & Feinleib, 1980). This finding echoes the dilemma of contemporary women who feel
strains not only within their occupation but also among their various family roles.

Type A Behavior and Hostility   Characteristic styles of responding to stress may also increase
the risk for CVD. In particular, much research has focused on the increased risks associated with
the **Type A behavior pattern**—a competitive, hostile, urgent, impatient, and achievement-striving
style of responding to challenge. As originally identified by cardiologists Meyer Friedman and Ray
Rosenman (1959), the *Type A* individual is a "superachiever" who knows no obstacle to success
and who may sacrifice everything for the sake of achievement (Jenkins, 1988). *Type B* individuals,
in contrast, are more calm and content. The case of Bob Carter is an example of someone who is
Type A; Bob Carter would not allow anything to beat him, including a heart attack.

It now appears that only certain elements of Type A behavior increase the risk for CHD. In
particular, *hostility* is a more consistent predictor of future heart disease than other aspects of
Type A behavior or the pattern as a whole (Booth-Kewley & Friedman, 1987; Matthews, 1988;
Miller et al., 1996; Schneiderman, Chesney, & Krantz, 1989). For example, a Finnish investigation found that three items reliably predicted death among men who had a history of CHD or
hypertension: ease with which anger was aroused, argumentativeness, and irritability (Koskenvuo et al., 1988).

These stock traders illustrate the Type A behavior pattern. Type A is a personality style characterized by competitiveness, hostility, urgency, impatience, and achievement striving in response to challenge.

We should note that hostility and Type A behavior likely interact with both cardiovascular reactivity and exposure to life stress in increasing the risk for heart disease. Evidence indicates that hostile, Type A people are more physiologically reactive to stress (as measured by heart rate and blood pressure) than are their Type B counterparts (Lyness, 1993). We can safely assume that hostile, competitive people also are more likely to create and perhaps seek added stress in their lives, as well as to have less social support available to them (Miller et al., 1996).

SOCIAL FACTORS IN CVD

The research we already have reviewed makes it clear that CVD is affected by both interpersonal relations and broader societal influences. As you may recognize from your own life, social support from friends and family members, as well as from professionals, can encourage a healthy—or an unhealthy—lifestyle (Rook & Dooley, 1985). Interpersonal conflict obviously is a source of much of the anger and hostility that can increase the risk for coronary heart disease. In fact, research demonstrates that economic resources, being married, and/or having a close confidant all predict a more positive prognosis among patients with coronary artery disease (Williams et al., 1992). Finally, the cross-cultural differences in the epidemiology of CVD surely are influenced by a range of societal values, such as attitudes about health behaviors like smoking and cultural norms about competition in the workplace.

Experts recognize the importance of interpersonal and societal influences on CVD and on physical health in general. A multitude of efforts have been directed toward structuring the *social ecology*—the interrelations between the individual and the social world—in such a way as to promote health (Stokols, 1992).

INTEGRATION AND ALTERNATIVE PATHWAYS

Much progress has been made in identifying biological, psychological, and social risk factors for CVD, a prime example of a physical illness that is best explained by the systems approach. An important goal for future research is to integrate knowledge across risk factors. Numerous questions need to be addressed. For example, how do cardiovascular reactivity and the experience of life stress interact in producing risk? How do we distinguish the effects of stress as an immediate, precipitating cause of CHD from its cumulative effects on health over long periods of time? To what extent are the risks associated with stress caused by poor health behavior and not by stress itself? What are the alternative pathways to the development of CHD? What protects those individuals who do not become ill even when they are exposed to multiple risk factors?

In considering these questions, we return to the analogy between the functioning of the cardiovascular system and an automobile. Some cars are built for high performance, some for economy. Some are defective when they leave the factory. Whatever the original condition of the new automobile, its state of repair is affected by how it is driven and how it is maintained. Like make and the wear and tear on different automobiles, the multiple pathways and multiple risk factors that cause CVD combine genetic makeup, an occasional structural defect, maintenance in the form of health behavior, and how hard the heart is driven by stress, coping, and societal standards. Even though some cars and some hearts operate well after being abused, routine maintenance is prudent in all cases. We should attempt to minimize each risk factor associated with CVD. As we noted at the beginning of the chapter, however, avoidance of life's challenges is *not* the way to avoid heart disease. A moderate amount of use is healthy for a car, and a moderate amount of stress may be healthy for the heart.

Prevention and Treatment of Cardiovascular Disease

Because many of the risk factors for CVD are linked with health behavior, it may be possible to reduce or prevent heart disease with psychological intervention. In the following sections, we consider efforts to alter lifestyle and to lower the risk for heart disease in terms of the three levels of intervention introduced in Chapter 3: primary, secondary, and tertiary prevention.

As we have noted, numerous public service advertisements attempt to prevent CVD by encouraging people to quit smoking, eat well, exercise, monitor their blood pressure, and otherwise improve their health behavior. Most of these familiar efforts at primary prevention have not been evaluated systematically.

The treatment of essential hypertension is one of the most important attempts at the secondary prevention of CHD, because hypertension is a significant risk factor for heart disease. Treatments of hypertension fall into two categories. One focuses on improving health behavior, and the other emphasizes **stress management,** attempts to teach more effective coping skills.

Improvements in health behavior—including weight reduction, decreased alcohol consumption, and reduced intake of dietary salt—can help lower blood pressure. For many patients these behavioral changes eliminate the need for taking antihypertensive medication (Johnston, 1989). What is less clear is the extent to which psychological intervention brings about improvements in health behavior. Available evidence suggests that psychological intervention is minimally effective at best, in part because many attempts to change health behavior are weak or poorly constructed. For example, physicians may simply encourage their patients to lose weight or give them educational pamphlets to read. More intensive treatments appear to be more effective in changing health behavior, although more research is needed on their effectiveness (Johnston, 1989).

The major form of stress management used with hypertensives is behavior therapy, particularly relaxation training (see Chapter 3) and biofeedback. **Biofeedback** uses laboratory equipment to monitor physiological processes that generally occur outside conscious awareness and to provide the patient with conscious feedback about these processes. Blood pressure may be displayed on a video screen, for example, so that increases or decreases are readily apparent to the patient.

Both relaxation training and biofeedback produce reliable, short-term reductions in blood pressure. Unfortunately, the reductions are small, are often temporary, and are considerably less than those produced by antihypertensive medications (Andrews et al., 1984). Although these stress management treatments occasionally may be a useful adjunct to medication, they are not an alternative at this point in time. In particular, the viability of biofeedback has not been supported by empirical evidence (Johnston, 1989).

The Trials of Hypertension Prevention (TOHP) is the most important ongoing study of whether stress management and health behavior interventions succeed in lowering high blood pressure (TOHP Collaborative Research Group, 1992). In this investigation, more than 2,000 women and men with hypertension were randomly assigned to one of seven different treatments. Treatments included three lifestyle interventions—weight reduction, sodium (salt) reduction, and stress management—plus four nutritional supplement conditions. Results from Phase I of the study indicated that only the weight reduction and the salt reduction programs were successful in lowering blood pressure over a follow-up period of up to 1 1/2 years. Neither stress management nor any of the dietary supplements produced beneficial effects on blood pressure. The TOHP currently is examining the effects of combined treatments and long-term outcomes, but data from this Phase II of the investigation are not yet available.

Tertiary prevention of CHD targets patients who have already had a cardiac event, typically a myocardial infarction. The hope is to reduce the incidence of recurrence of the illness. Exercise programs are probably the most common treatment recommended for cardiac patients, but evidence of their effectiveness is limited (Johnston, 1989). Some evidence suggests that carefully implemented exercise training programs can reduce the risk for cardiovascular death for up to 3 years (O'Connor et al., 1989). Other researchers have found that treatment programs may dramatically reduce death rates if they are individualized and target multiple health behaviors (Frasure-Smith & Prince, 1985). One patient may benefit from entering a smoking reduction program, a second may be helped by a stress reduction workshop, and a third may be assisted by

stress management A treatment used in behavioral medicine and health psychology to teach more effective coping skills, reduce adverse reactions to stress, and improve health behavior.

biofeedback Behavioral medicine treatment that uses laboratory equipment to monitor physiological processes (that generally occur outside of conscious awareness) and provide feedback about them. Hypothesized to help patients to gain conscious control over problematic physiological processes such as hypertension.

exercise classes. Together, the findings on successful programs underscore the need to offer behavioral medicine programs that are both highly structured and carefully tailored to the individual (see Blanchard, 1992). Handing out educational pamphlets or delivering stern lectures in the physician's office does little to alter health behavior, as we saw in the case of Bob Carter.

As a final note, we should mention that some important psychological treatments focus on the *effects* of heart disease on life stress rather than the other way around. Several investigators have helped cardiac patients cope more successfully with the anxiety and depression that often result from having a heart attack, as well as with the effects of a myocardial infarction on their everyday life. Coronary patients frequently report difficulties with depression, sexuality, marriage and family relationships, and accepting the necessary restrictions on normal activities (Johnston, 1985). In turn, researchers recently have identified depression as a risk factor for subsequent cardiac illness (Carney, Freeland, Rich, & Jaffe, 1995). Psychological treatment can help patients with CHD and their families adjust to the illness. In turn, treating depression and family distress may improve the patient's physical health. The link between stress and physical health clearly is reciprocal, as the systems theory would lead us to expect.

Summary

Stress can be defined broadly as a challenging event that requires physiological, cognitive, or behavioral adaptation. The DSM no longer contains a list of **psychosomatic disorders,** because medical scientists now view every physical illness as a product of the interaction between the psyche and soma, mind and body. This holistic view has influenced both psychology and medicine, as is evidenced by the rapid development of **behavioral medicine,** a multidisciplinary field that investigates psychological factors in physical illness.

Scientists disagree about whether stress is best defined in terms of a life event (a stimulus), an adverse reaction (a response), or a stimulus-response combination. Each approach has advantages and disadvantages for research purposes. Despite this controversy, much is known about people's reactions to stress. The **fight or flight response** is a reaction to a threat that is activated by stress and is characterized by intense arousal of the sympathetic nervous system. The **general adaptation syndrome (GAS)** is a more global response to stress that includes the stages of alarm, resistance, and exhaustion. Both responses are mediated by the secretion of hormones from the adrenal gland, including epinephrine/norepinephrine and glucocorticoids. Recent research on **psychoneuroimmunology (PNI)** has identified yet another physiological consequence of stress, less adequate functioning of the immune system.

Emotional responses to stress are especially likely to include increased anxiety, depression, and anger. Coping with these reactions may involve **problem-focused coping,** which is an attempt to change the stressor, or **emotion-focused coping,** which is an attempt to alter distress internally. Critical cognitive processes include *primary appraisal,* the individual's evaluation of the threat posed by a stressor, and *secondary appraisal,* the evaluation of one's ability to cope with a stressor. Predictability and control are other key cognitive evaluations that can greatly facilitate coping.

Behavioral responses to stress include not only attempts to avoid or alter a stressor but also the search for other outlets for frustration. Poor *health behavior* can be another behavioral consequence of stress, including a decrease in positive actions (e.g., exercise) or an increase in negative actions (e.g., alcohol consumption). Illness behavior, behaving as if you were sick, also is stress-related. Finally, it is clear that illness can cause stress, as well as stress causing illness.

The DSM-IV has no list of stress-related or psychosomatic illnesses, because psychological factors are deemed important in all physical illnesses. The essential role of stress in illness is highlighted by the inclusion of two separate diagnostic axes. Physical illnesses that are relevant to mental condition are coded on Axis III, general medical conditions, often in association with the Axis I diagnosis of psychological factors affecting medical condition. The DSM-IV also contains a separate axis for coding stressors, Axis IV.

Infectious diseases were the most common causes of death in the United States in 1900, but lifestyle plays a central role in seven of the top 10 causes of death in the United States today. Cancer would seem to be a purely biological illness, but behavior contributes to cancer through exposure to some carcinogens, health behavior, social support in coping with the illness, and perhaps through effects on immune functioning. **Acquired immune deficiency syndrome (AIDS)** is caused by the human immunodeficiency virus (HIV), which is transmitted through risky behaviors, such as unprotected sex and shared hypodermic needles. Psychologists also work to help people cope with chronic pain, most notably through pain management.

The complexities of research on stress and physical illness are illustrated by evidence on the number-one killer in the United States today, cardiovascular disease (CVD), disorders that affect the heart and circulatory system. Cardiovascular diseases include *essential hypertension* (high blood pressure) and **coronary heart disease (CHD),** particularly myocardial infarction (MI), or heart attack. Several health behaviors have been linked to CVD, and other psychological factors may also contribute to CVD. These include **cardiovascular reactivity,** responses to stressors presented in a laboratory; chronic stressors in real life (for example, job strain); and the **Type A behavior pattern,** a characterological response to challenge. Recent evidence suggests that hostility may be the central Type A characteristic related to CHD.

The primary prevention of CHD includes attempts to encourage people to improve their health behaviors. The treatment of hypertension through improved health behaviors or **stress management** is one of the more important attempts at the secondary prevention of CHD. Tertiary prevention of CHD targets patients who have already had a cardiac event, for example, attempting to modify their Type A behavior.

Critical Thinking

1. How do you define stress in your own life? Based on your own experiences, what dimensions of stress do you think are critical for physical and mental health? What about coping? How do you cope with life's struggles? What are your theories about effective and ineffective coping?

2. Like a moderate amount of physical exercise, exposure to a moderate amount of stress may be adaptive. Why might this be the case? How can people find the balance between being challenged and being "stressed-out"?

3. Many of today's most deadly illnesses are "lifestyle diseases," and this raises the issue of responsibility for lifestyle contributions to physical illnesses. For example, cigarette companies increasingly are being sued by people with lung cancer. Is the company responsible, or is the smoker? What about other illnesses like AIDS? What is society's responsibility for altering lifestyle or treating people whose unhealthy lifestyle contributes to their illness?

4. Pause to think about your lifestyle. How has research on stress and health behavior affected your life? Are pressures to live a healthier lifestyle helpful? Stressful? How much have you been influenced by public service campaigns or other messages to lead a healthier life?

9

Personality Disorders

Personality is an elusive concept that is based largely on our observations of interpersonal behaviors. The combination of traits or characteristics that, taken as a whole, describe a person's behavior is considered to be his or her personality. The DSM-IV defines **personality** as "enduring patterns of perceiving, relating to, and thinking about the environment and oneself, which are exhibited in a wide range of important social and personal contexts" (APA, 1994). Without these presumed consistencies in others' behaviors, we would find it difficult to think about and organize our social worlds.

personality   The combination of persistent traits or characteristics that, taken as a whole, describe a person's behavior.

personality disorder   Inflexible and maladaptive patterns of personality that begin by early adulthood and result in either social or occupational problems or distress to the individual.

When a person's traits bring him or her into repeated conflict with others, that person's personality may be considered disordered. According to the DSM-IV definition of **personality disorder,** the problems must be part of "an enduring pattern of inner experience and behavior that deviates markedly from the expectations of the individual's culture" (APA, 1994). The pattern must be evident in two or more of the following domains: cognition (such as ways of thinking about the self and other people), emotional responses, interpersonal functioning, or impulse control. This pattern of maladaptive experience and behavior must also be:

- Inflexible and pervasive across a broad range of personal and social situations
- The source of clinically significant distress or impairment in social, occupational, or other areas of functioning
  Stable and of long duration, with an onset that can be traced back at least to adolescence or early adulthood

The impairment associated with most forms of personality disorder causes less personal distress than that found in other types of mental disorder. Some studies estimate that as many as 80 percent of people with personality disorders have never sought professional help for these problems (Samuels et al., 1994).

The personality disorders are among the most controversial categories in the diagnostic system for mental disorders. They are difficult to identify reliably, their etiology is poorly understood, and there is relatively little evidence to indicate that they can be treated successfully. There are important discrepancies between DSM-IV and ICD-10, its European counterpart, in their descriptions of these problems. One type of personality disorder in the U.S. system—narcissistic—is not even included in ICD-10. For all of these reasons, you should think critically about the validity of these categories.

Most clinical disorders are listed on Axis I of DSM-IV, whereas the personality disorders are listed on Axis II. The authors of DSM-IV have organized 10 specific forms of personality disorder into three clusters on the basis of broadly defined characteristics. The specific disorders in each cluster are listed in Table 9–1. The first cluster includes socially isolated people who are odd or eccentric. The second cluster includes flamboyant people, who appear to be excessively dramatic,

TABLE 9–1

Personality Disorders Listed in DSM-IV	
CLUSTER A	**CHARACTERISTIC FEATURES**
Paranoid	Distrust and suspiciousness of others
Schizoid	Detachment from social relationships and restricted range of expression of emotions
Schizotypal	Discomfort with close relationships; cognitive and perceptual distortions; eccentricities of behavior
CLUSTER B	
Antisocial	Disregard for and frequent violation of the rights of others
Borderline	Instability of interpersonal relationships, self-image, emotions, and control over impulses
Histrionic	Excessive emotionality and attention seeking
Narcissistic	Grandiosity, need for admiration, and lack of empathy
CLUSTER C	
Avoidant	Social inhibition, feelings of inadequacy, and hypersensitivity to negative evaluation
Dependent	Excessive need to be taken care of, leading to submissive and clinging behavior
Obsessive–compulsive	Preoccupation with orderliness and perfectionism at the expense of flexibility

emotional, or erratic. The third cluster includes people who tend to be anxious and fearful. All of the personality disorders are based on exaggerated personality traits that are frequently annoying or disturbing to other people.

The following cases illustrate several of the most important features of personality disorders. Our first case is an example of antisocial personality disorder, which is defined in terms of a pervasive and persistent disregard for, and frequent violation of, the rights of other people. This 21-year-old man was described by Hervey Cleckley in his classic treatise on this topic (Cleckley, 1976). The man had been referred to Cleckley by his parents and his lawyer after his most recent arrest for stealing. The parents hoped that their son might avoid a long prison sentence if Cleckley decided that he was suffering from a mental disorder. Notice that the fundamental features of this man's problems were clearly evident by early adolescence, and they were exhibited consistently over an extended period of time. The stable, long-standing nature of personality disorders is one of their most characteristic features. In this way, they are distinguished from many other forms of abnormal behavior, which are episodic in nature (Hirschfeld, 1993).

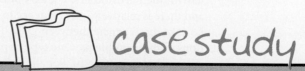

case study

Antisocial Personality Disorder

Tom looks and is in robust physical health. His manner and appearance are pleasing. In his face a prospective employer would be likely to see strong indications of character as well as high incentive and ability. He is well informed, alert, and entirely at ease, exhibiting a confidence in himself that the observer is likely to consider amply justified. This does not look like the sort of man who will fail or flounder about in the tasks of life but like someone incompatible with all such thoughts.

Evidence of (Tom's) maladjustment became distinct in childhood. He appeared to be a reliable and manly fellow but could never be counted upon to keep at any task or to give a straight account of any situation. He was frequently truant from school. No advice or persuasion influenced him in his acts, despite his excellent response in all discussions. Though he was generously provided for, he stole some of his father's chickens from time to time, selling them at stores downtown. Pieces of table silver would be missed. These were sometimes recovered from those to whom he had sold them for a pittance or swapped them for odds and ends which seemed to hold no particular interest or value for him. He resented and seemed eager to avoid punishment, but no modification in his behavior resulted from it. He did not seem wild or particularly impulsive, a victim of high temper or uncontrollable drives. There was nothing to indicate he was subject to unusually strong temptations, lured by definite plans for high adventure and exciting revolt.

He lied so plausibly and with such utter equanimity, devised such ingenious alibis or simply denied all responsibility with such convincing appearances of candor that for many years his real career was poorly estimated. Among typical exploits with which he is credited stand these: prankish defecation into the stringed intricacies of the school piano, the removal from his uncle's automobile of a carburetor for which he got 75 cents, and the selling of his father's overcoat to a passing buyer of scrap materials.

At 14 or 15 years of age, having learned to drive, Tom began to steal automobiles with some regularity. Often his intention seemed less that of theft than of heedless misappropriation. A neighbor or friend of the family, going to the garage or to where the car was parked outside an office building, would find it missing. Sometimes the patient would leave the stolen vehicle within a few blocks or miles of the owner, sometimes out on the road where the gasoline had given out. After he had tried to sell a stolen car, his father consulted advisers and, on the theory that he might have some specific craving for automobiles, bought one for him as a therapeutic measure. On one occasion while out driving, he deliberately parked his own car and, leaving it, stole an inferior model which he left slightly damaged on the outskirts of a village some miles away.

Private physicians, scoutmasters, and social workers were consulted. They talked and worked with him, but to no avail. Listing the deeds for which he became ever more notable does not give an adequate picture of the situation. He did not every day or every week bring attention to himself by major acts of mischief or destructiveness. He was usually polite, often considerate in small, appealing ways, and always seemed to have learned his lesson after detection and punishment. He was clever and learned easily. During intervals in which his attendance was regular, he impressed his teachers as outstanding in ability. Some charm and apparent modesty, as well as his very convincing way of seeming sincere and to have taken resolutions that would count, kept not only the parents but all who encountered him clinging to hope. Teachers, scoutmasters, the school principal, and others, recognized that in some very important respects he differed from the ordinary bad or wayward youth. (They) made special efforts to help him and to give him new opportunities to reform or readjust.

When he drove a stolen automobile across a state line, he came in contact with federal authorities. In view of his youth and the wonderful impression he made, he was put on probation. Soon afterward he took another automobile and again left it in the adjoining state. It was a very obvious situation. The consequences could not have been entirely overlooked by a person of his excellent shrewdness. He admitted that the considerable risks of getting caught had occurred to him but he felt he had a chance to avoid detection and would take it. No unusual and powerful motive or any special aim could be brought out as an explanation.

Tom was sent to a federal institution in a distant state where a well-organized program of rehabilitation and guidance was available. He soon impressed authorities at this place with his attitude and in the way he discussed his past mistakes and plans for a different future. He seemed to merit parole status precociously and this was awarded him. It was not long before he began stealing again and thereby lost his freedom (Cleckley, 1976, pp. 64–67). ♛

This case provides an excellent example of the senseless nature of the illegal and immoral acts committed by people who meet the diagnostic criteria for antisocial personality disorder. Another puzzling feature of this disorder is the apparent lack of remorse and the inability to learn from experience that accompany such a history of delinquent behavior. It is difficult to understand why someone would behave in this manner.

Most other forms of mental disorder, such as anxiety disorders and mood disorders, are *ego-dystonic;* that is, people with these disorders are distressed by their symptoms and uncomfortable with their situations. Personality disorders are usually *ego-syntonic*—the ideas or impulses with which they are associated are acceptable to the person. People with personality disorders frequently do not see themselves as being disturbed. Tom did not believe that his repeated antisocial behavior represented a problem. The other people for whom he created problems were suffering, but he was not. Many forms of personality disorder are defined primarily in terms of the problems that these people create for others rather than in terms of their own subjective distress.

The person described in the case study below illustrates one of the most important characteristics of personality disorders as they are defined in DSM-IV: overlap among categories. Most people who meet the criteria for one type of personality disorder will also meet the criteria for at least one more. The person in this case met the diagnostic criteria for narcissistic personality disorder and also exhibited some features of histrionic personality disorder. According to DSM-IV, the former is characterized by "grandiosity, lack of empathy, and hypersensitivity to the evaluation of others." The latter is associated with attention seeking and excessive emotionality.

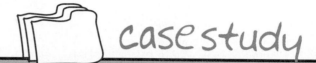

Narcissistic Personality Disorder with Histrionic Traits

Lawrence was a 34-year-old professor of English literature at an exclusive private university. He was clever, engaging, and ambitious. The chairperson of the English Department and the university administration considered him to be one of their brightest academic stars, even though he was much younger than most other distinguished faculty members. They treated him with considerable deference, but their efforts were never sufficient to fulfill Lawrence's own expectations for the special consideration that he felt he deserved.

Not surprisingly, Lawrence's colleagues came to view him as pompous and unbearably self-centered. He had a successful record of scholarship for a person of his age, but most of his colleagues in the English Department were similarly productive, and were highly regarded by their peers at other universities. Lawrence refused to acknowledge the accomplishments of his colleagues, and behaved as though he were the only eminent professor in the entire university. Instead of being grateful for the special position he had attained after a series of rapid promotions, Lawrence complained constantly that the university did not know how to treat someone as famous as he. He argued that he was entitled to special privileges. For example, he adamantly refused to teach undergraduate students after he was granted tenure, arguing that undergraduates were not intelligent enough to benefit from the things that he could teach them.

Although Lawrence held an inflated opinion of himself, he also appeared at times to be remarkably insecure. He bombarded colleagues with copies of everything he wrote. His critical reviews and short stories were distributed widely shortly after their publication. His intent was clearly to seek the approval and praise of his peers, who had learned that it was not wise to engage Lawrence by attempting to offer constructive criticism.

Lawrence's personal appearance was also distinctive. Most of his colleagues dressed casually when they were teaching or working in their offices, but Lawrence always insisted on wearing expensive tailored suits. His shirts were carefully pressed and starched, and he wore expensive ties and shoes. His hair was always carefully trimmed and blown dry in a contemporary style that also minimized the effect of his slightly receding hairline and the barely visible thinning patch at the crown of his head. Lawrence was exceedingly sensitive, and responded with surprisingly intense anger if he was teased about these hints that he might be going bald at an early age. He was completely unable to laugh at himself. At the same time, however, he frequently chastised colleagues for the casual way in which they dressed.

Lawrence was married for 10 years before being separated from his wife, Kathleen, and their two young children. The separation had seemed inevitable to everyone who knew the family. Kathleen had always been responsible for all the household chores and for caring for the children, because Lawrence worked at least 12 hours a day, every day of the week. He maintained that this was an eminently fair arrangement because it was Kathleen who had wanted to have children. Given the importance of his academic work, and his unique intellectual talents, he did not believe that his time should be wasted on pedestrian tasks, such as raising his children, that could be accomplished by anyone. He also noted that Kathleen should be happy to have married as handsome and successful a person as he, and that she should be fulfilled simply in being the mother of his children.

One of Lawrence's most annoying characteristics was his complete insensitivity to the feelings of other people. He could be charming and witty, particularly when he was trying to impress someone whom he considered to be (almost) as important as he, but he was also known for his sharp remarks that seemed designed to put other people down. He was particularly likely to say rude things when someone else had become the center of attention and he felt he was being ignored. Parties and celebrations that were called in someone else's honor were particularly difficult for him to handle, especially if the recipient was being honored for an academic achievement. ▼

Classification

In the following pages we give brief descriptions of the personality disorder subtypes included in DSM-IV. These brief descriptions provide an overview that will be useful when we review the epidemiology of personality disorders. Later in the chapter we describe in considerably more detail three disorders that are relatively frequent and have been studied extensively: schizotypal, borderline, and antisocial personality disorders.

Cluster A: Paranoid, Schizoid, and Schizotypal Personality Disorders

Cluster A includes three disorders: paranoid, schizoid, and schizotypal forms of personality disorder. The behavior of people who fit the subtypes in this cluster is typically odd, eccentric, or asocial. All three types share similarity with the symptoms of schizophrenia (see Chapter 13). One implicit assumption in the DSM-IV system is that these types of personality disorder may represent behavioral traits or interpersonal styles that precede the onset of full-blown psychosis. Because of their close association with schizophrenia, they are sometimes called *schizophrenia spectrum* disorders.

Paranoid personality disorder is characterized by the pervasive tendency to be inappropriately suspicious of other people's motives and behaviors. People who fit the description for this disorder are constantly on guard. They expect that other people are trying to harm them, and they take extraordinary precautions to avoid being exploited or injured. Relationships with friends and family members are difficult to maintain because these people don't trust anyone. They frequently overreact in response to minor or ambiguous events to which they attribute hidden meaning.

When they overreact, people with paranoid personality disorder often behave aggressively or antagonistically. These actions can easily create a self-fulfilling prophesy. In other words, thinking (incorrectly) that he or she is being attacked by others, the paranoid person strikes. The other person is, naturally, surprised, annoyed, and perhaps frightened by this behavior, and begins to treat the paranoid person with concern and caution. This response serves to confirm the original suspicions of the paranoid individual, who does not comprehend how his or her own behavior affects others.

Paranoid personality disorder must be distinguished from psychotic disorders, such as schizophrenia and delusional disorder. The pervasive suspicions of people with paranoid personality disorder do not reach delusional proportions. In other words, they are not sufficiently severe to be considered obviously false and clearly preposterous. In actual practice, this distinction is sometimes quite subtle and difficult to make.

Schizoid personality disorder is defined in terms of a pervasive pattern of indifference to other people, coupled with a diminished range of emotional experience and expression. These people are loners; they prefer social isolation to interactions with friends or family. Other people see them as being cold and aloof. By their own report, they do not experience strong subjective emotions, such as sadness, anger, or happiness.

Schizotypal personality disorder centers around peculiar patterns of behavior rather than on the emotional restriction and social withdrawal that are associated with schizoid personality disorder. Many of these peculiar behaviors take the form of perceptual and cognitive disturbance. People with this disorder may report bizarre fantasies and unusual perceptual experiences. Their speech may be slightly difficult to follow because they use words in an odd way or because they express themselves in a vague or disjointed manner. Their affective expressions may be constricted in range, as in schizoid personality disorder, or they may be silly and inappropriate.

In spite of their odd or unusual behaviors, people with schizotypal personality disorder are not psychotic or out of touch with reality. Their bizarre fantasies are not delusional, and their unusual perceptual experiences are not sufficiently real or compelling to be considered hallucinations.

paranoid personality disorder   An enduring pattern of thinking and behavior characterized by a pervasive tendency to be inappropriately suspicious of other people's motives and behaviors. People who fit the description for this disorder expect that other people are trying to harm them, and they take extraordinary precautions to avoid being exploited or injured.

schizoid personality disorder   An enduring pattern of thinking and behavior characterized by pervasive indifference to other people, coupled with a diminished range of emotional experience and expression. People who fit this description prefer social isolation to interactions with friends or family.

schizotypal personality disorder   An enduring pattern of discomfort with other people coupled with peculiar thinking and behavior. The latter symptoms take the form of perceptual and cognitive disturbances. Considered by some experts to be part of the schizophrenic spectrum.

antisocial personality disorder A pervasive and persistent disregard for, and frequent violation of, the rights of other people. Also known as *psychopathy*. In DSM-IV, it is defined in terms of a persistent pattern of irresponsible and antisocial behavior that begins during childhood or adolescence and continues into the adult years.

borderline personality disorder An enduring pattern of thinking and behavior whose essential feature is a pervasive instability in mood, self-image, and interpersonal relationships. Manifestations of this disorder include frantic efforts to avoid real or imagined abandonment. People who fit this description frequently hold opinions of significant others that vacillate between unrealistically positive and negative extremes.

In The Treasure of the Sierra Madre, *Humphrey Bogart played a prospector whose pervasive paranoia culminated in his murdering his partner and stealing their gold.*

Cluster B: Antisocial, Borderline, Histrionic, and Narcissistic Personality Disorders

Cluster B includes four specific types: antisocial, borderline, histrionic, and narcissistic personality disorders. According to DSM-IV, these disorders are characterized by dramatic, emotional, or erratic behavior, and all are associated with marked difficulty in sustaining interpersonal relationships. The rationale for grouping these disorders together is less compelling than that for Cluster A. In particular, antisocial personality disorder clearly involves something more than just a dramatic style or erratic behavior.

Antisocial personality disorder is defined in terms of a persistent pattern of irresponsible and antisocial behavior that begins during childhood or adolescence and continues into the adult years. The case study of Tom, with which we opened this chapter, illustrates this pattern of behavior. The DSM-IV definition is based on features that, beginning in childhood, indicate a pervasive pattern of disregard for, and violation of, the rights of others. Once the person has become an adult, these difficulties include persistent failure to perform responsibilities that are associated with occupational and family roles. Conflicts with others, including physical fights, are also common. These people are irritable and aggressive with their spouses and children as well as with people outside the home. They are impulsive, reckless, and irresponsible.

We have all read newspaper accounts of famous examples of antisocial personality disorder. These often include people who have committed horrendous crimes against other people, including serial murders. One such person who attracted considerable attention in the national media was Westley Allan Dodd, who was executed after being found guilty of raping, torturing, and killing three young boys. His apparent indifference to the boys' suffering, and his insistence that he would commit similar crimes if he were ever released from prison, led many observers to believe that he fit the criteria for antisocial personality disorder. You should not be misled, however, into thinking that only serious criminals meet the criteria for this disorder. Many other forms of persistently callous and exploitative behavior could lead to this diagnosis.

Borderline personality disorder is a diffuse category whose essential feature is a pervasive pattern of instability in mood and interpersonal relationships. People with this disorder find it very difficult to be alone. They form intense, unstable relationships with other people and are often seen by others as being manipulative. Their opinions of significant others frequently vacillate between unrealistically positive and negative extremes. They also exhibit emotional instability.

Their mood may shift rapidly and inexplicably from depression to anger to anxiety over a pattern of several hours. Intense anger is common and may be accompanied by assault or suicidal threats and gestures.

Many clinicians consider identity disturbance to be the diagnostic hallmark of borderline personality disorder. People with this disturbance presumably have great difficulty maintaining an integrated image of themselves that incorporates their positive and negative features. They frequently express uncertainty about such issues as personal values, sexual preferences, and career alternatives. Chronic feelings of emptiness and boredom may also be present.

Histrionic personality disorder is characterized by a pervasive pattern of excessive emotionality and attention-seeking behavior. People with this disorder thrive on being the center of attention. They are self-centered, vain, and demanding, and they constantly seek approval from others. When interacting with other people, their behavior is often inappropriately sexually seductive or provocative. Their emotions tend to be shallow and may vacillate erratically. They frequently react to situations with inappropriate exaggeration.

The concept of histrionic personality is rooted in clinical tradition rather than systematic empirical research (Pfohl, 1995). It overlaps extensively with other types of personality disorder, especially those in Cluster B. From a psychodynamic perspective, histrionic personality disorder has been described as being a less severe form of borderline personality (Kernberg, 1988). People with both disorders are intensely emotional and manipulative. Unlike people with borderline personality disorder, however, people with histrionic personality disorder have an essentially intact sense of their own identity and a better capacity for stable relationships with other people.

There may also be an etiological link between histrionic and antisocial personality disorders. Both may reflect a common tendency toward lack of inhibition. People with both types of disorder form shallow, intense relationships, and they can be extremely manipulative. Family history studies indicate that this predisposition to disinhibition may be expressed as histrionic personality disorder in women and as antisocial personality disorder in men (Pfohl, 1995).

The essential feature of **narcissistic personality disorder** is a pervasive pattern of grandiosity, need for admiration, and inability to empathize with other people. The case of Lawrence, described earlier in this chapter, illustrates this disorder. Narcissistic people have a greatly exaggerated sense of their own importance. They are preoccupied with their own achievements and abilities. Because they consider themselves to be very special, they cannot empathize with the feelings of other people and are often seen as being arrogant or haughty.

There is a considerable amount of overlap between narcissistic personality disorder and borderline personality disorder. Both types of people feel that other people should recognize their needs and do special favors for them. They may also react with anger if they are criticized. The distinction between these disorders hinges on the inflated sense of self-importance that is found in narcissistic personality disorder and the deflated or devalued sense of self found in borderline personality disorder (Ronningstam & Gunderson, 1991).

histrionic personality disorder An enduring pattern of thinking and behavior that is characterized by excessive emotionality and attention-seeking behavior. People with this disorder are self-centered, vain, and demanding. Their emotions tend to be shallow and may vacillate erratically.

narcissistic personality disorder An enduring pattern of thinking and behavior that is characterized by pervasive grandiosity. Narcissistic people are preoccupied with their own achievements and abilities.

avoidant personality disorder An enduring pattern of thinking and behavior that is characterized by pervasive social discomfort, fear of negative evaluation, and timidity. People with this disorder tend to be socially isolated outside of family circles. They want to be liked by others, but they are easily hurt by even minimal signs of disapproval from other people.

Westley Allan Dodd was hanged in 1991 in the state of Washington for the sadistic rape and murder of three small boys.

Cluster C: Avoidant, Dependent, and Obsessive–Compulsive Personality Disorders

Cluster C includes three subtypes: avoidant, dependent, and obsessive–compulsive personality disorders. The common element in all three disorders is presumably anxiety or fearfulness. This description fits most easily with the avoidant and dependent types. In contrast, obsessive–compulsive personality disorder is more accurately described in terms of preoccupation with rules and with lack of emotional warmth than in terms of anxiety.

Avoidant personality disorder is characterized by a pervasive pattern of social discomfort, fear of negative evaluation, and timidity. People with this disorder tend to be socially isolated

dependent personality disorder An enduring pattern of dependent and submissive behavior. These people are exceedingly dependent on other people for advice and reassurance. Often unable to make everyday decisions on their own, they feel anxious and helpless when they are alone.

obsessive–compulsive personality disorder An enduring pattern of thinking and behavior that is characterized by perfectionism and inflexibility. These people are preoccupied with rules and efficiency. They are excessively conscientious, moralistic, and judgmental.

when outside their own family circles because they are afraid of criticism. Unlike people with schizoid personality disorder, they want to be liked by others, but they are extremely shy—easily hurt by even minimal signs of disapproval from other people.

Avoidant personality disorder is often indistinguishable from generalized social phobia (see Chapter 6). In fact, some experts have argued that they are probably two different ways of defining the same condition (Frances, First, & Pincus, 1995). Others have argued that people with avoidant personality disorder have more trouble than people with social phobia in relating to other people (Millon & Martinez, 1995). People with avoidant personality disorder are presumably more socially withdrawn and have very few close relationships because they are so shy. People with social phobia may have a lot of friends, but they are afraid of performing in front of them. This distinction is difficult to make, however, if the social phobia becomes more generalized.

The essential feature of **dependent personality disorder** is a pervasive pattern of submissive and clinging behavior. People with this disorder are afraid of separating from other people on whom they are dependent for advice and reassurance. Often unable to make everyday decisions on their own, they feel anxious and helpless when they are alone. Like people with avoidant personality disorder, they are easily hurt by criticism, extremely sensitive to disapproval, and lacking in self-confidence. One difference between avoidant and dependent personality disorders involves the point in a relationship at which they experience the most difficulty. People who are avoidant have trouble *initiating* a relationship (because they are fearful); people who are dependent have trouble *separating* after the relationship has gone on for some time.

Obsessive–compulsive personality disorder is defined by a pervasive pattern of orderliness, perfectionism, and mental and interpersonal control, at the expense of flexibility, openness, and efficiency. People with this disorder set ambitious standards for their own performance that frequently are so high as to be unattainable. Many would be described as "workaholics." They are so preoccupied with details and rules that they lose sight of the main point of an activity or project. Intellectual endeavors are favored over feelings and emotional experience. These people are excessively conscientious, moralistic, and judgmental, and they tend to be intolerant of emotional behavior in other people. At modest levels, these traits can represent an adaptive coping style, particularly in the face of the demands of our complex, technological society. Very high levels of these characteristics begin to interfere with a person's social and occupational adjustment.

Obsessive–compulsive personality disorder should not be confused with obsessive–compulsive disorder (OCD), which is a type of anxiety disorder (see Chapter 6). A pattern of intrusive, unwanted thoughts accompanied by ritualistic behaviors is used to define OCD. The definition of obsessive–compulsive personality disorder, in contrast, is concerned with personality traits, such as excessively high levels of conscientiousness. People who meet the criteria for obsessive–compulsive personality disorder seem to be at risk for *various* kinds of anxiety disorders, including generalized anxiety disorder and panic disorder as well as OCD. Obsessive–compulsive personality disorder may be more closely related to the form of OCD that involves checking rituals than to the form of OCD that involves washing and cleaning rituals (Gibbs & Oltmanns, 1995).

Epidemiology

Personality disorders are generally considered to be one of the most common forms of psychopathology, but it is difficult to provide empirical support for that claim (Maier et al., 1992; Weissman, 1993). With the exception of antisocial personality, these disorders did not receive close scrutiny until after the publication of DSM-III, and they have not been included in large-scale epidemiological studies, such as the Epidemiologic Catchment Area study and the National Comorbidity Study.

Prevalence in Community and Clinical Samples

How many people in the general population will meet the criteria for at least one personality disorder? In studies that have examined community-based samples of adults, the overall lifetime prevalence for having any type of Axis II disorder varies between 10 and 14 percent (Weissman, 1993).

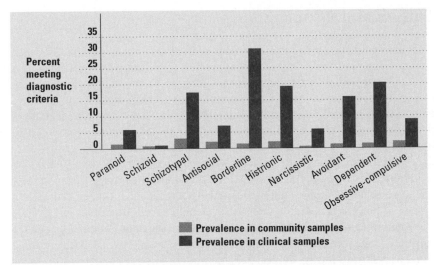

Figure 9–1 Prevalence of Personality Disorders in Community and Clinical Samples. These estimates of prevalence are based on the median rate for each disorder that has been reported across several different studies.

Source: M.J. Lyons, 1995, Epidemiology of personality disorders. In M.T.Tsuang, M.Tohen, and G.E.P. Zahner (Eds.), *Textbook in Psychiatric Epidemiology*, p. 423. New York: Wiley.

Evidence regarding the prevalence of specific types of personality disorder in community samples is summarized in Figure 9–1. This figure presents summary data that have been averaged across a number of studies (Lyons, 1995). Among community samples, the highest prevalence rates are found for schizotypal, histrionic, antisocial, obsessive–compulsive, and dependent personality disorders. Narcissistic personality disorder seems to be the least common form, affecting only 0.2 percent of the population.

The most precise information that is available regarding the prevalence of personality disorders in community samples is concerned specifically with the antisocial type. In both the ECA study and NCS, structured interviews relating to this disorder were conducted with several thousand participants. The overall lifetime prevalence rate for antisocial personality disorder (men and women combined) was 2.6 percent in the ECA study (Robins et al., 1991) and 3.5 in the NCS (Kessler et al., 1994).

Notice that the prevalence rates from the ECA study and NCS are higher than the rate reported in Figure 9–1, which reflects an average across several studies. One rigorous investigation of 11,000 people in Taiwan found that only 0.2 percent met the criteria for antisocial personality disorder (Compton et al., 1991). This result might be taken to indicate that antisocial personality disorder is more common in our individualistic society than it is in a society that places greater emphasis on collectivism. But this is only one interpretation. More information is clearly needed before strong conclusions can be drawn.

There is considerable overlap among categories in the personality disorders. Most people who meet the diagnostic criteria for one personality disorder also meet the criteria for another disorder (Shea, 1995). Some changes in specific diagnostic criteria that were introduced with the publication of DSM-IV in 1994 were intended to reduce the extent of overlap among the various types of personality disorder, but it is too early to tell whether this effect was achieved.

The prevalence of personality disorders is much higher among people who are being treated for another mental disorder listed on Axis I of DSM-IV. These data are also summarized in Figure 9–1. Borderline personality disorder appears to be the most common disorder in both inpatient and outpatient settings. Averaged across studies, the evidence suggests that this disorder is found among slightly more than 30 percent of all patients who are treated for psychological disorders.

The four basic personality types

Culture and Personality

Personality disorders are presumably defined in terms of behavior that "deviates markedly from the expectations of the individual's culture." In setting this guideline, the authors of DSM-IV recognized that judgments regarding appropriate behavior vary considerably from one society to the next. Some cultures encourage restrained or subtle displays of emotion, whereas others promote visible, public displays of anger, grief, and other emotional responses. Behavior that seems highly extraverted (or histrionic) in the former cultures might create a very different impression in the latter cultures. Cultures also differ in the extent to which they value *individualism* (the pursuit of personal goals) as opposed to *collectivism* (sharing and self-sacrifice for the good of the group) (Triandis, 1994). Someone who seems exceedingly self-centered and egotistical in a collectivist society might appear to be normal in an individualistic society like the United States.

A number of studies have been conducted regarding normal personality in cross-cultural perspective (Berry, Poortinga, Segall, & Dasen, 1992). These studies emphasize comparisons of *average* or typical personality styles in one society with those in another. Relatively less information is available regarding the extent of *individual differences* within various types of non-Western cultures.

The personality disorders may be more closely tied to cultural expectations than any other kind of mental disorder (Frances, First, & Pincus, 1995). Some investigators have wondered whether borderline personality disorder and narcissistic personality disorder are unique to Western societies (Lewis-Fernandez & Kleinman, 1994; Tyrer, 1995). More information is needed before we can determine whether the DSM-IV system for describing these problems will be useful in other societies. The World Health Organization is sponsoring a large study of personality disorders in 11 countries spanning North America, Europe, Africa, and Asia (Loranger et al., 1994). The results of that study will answer many important questions about the cross-cultural validity of the personality disorders.

Gender Differences

The *overall* prevalence of personality disorders is approximately equal in men and women (Weissman, 1993). There are, however, consistent gender differences with regard to at least one specific disorder: Antisocial personality disorder is unquestionably much more common among men than among women. The ECA study found rates of 4.5 percent for men and 0.8 percent for women (Robins, Tipp, & Przybeck, 1991). The NCS reported rates of 5.8 percent for men and 1.2 percent for women (Kessler et al., 1994). Thus antisocial personality disorder is actually an alarmingly common problem among adult males in the United States.

Epidemiological evidence regarding gender differences for the other types of personality disorder is much more ambiguous. Very few community-based studies have been done using standardized interviews as a basis for diagnosis. In one community sample of more than 3,400 adults, the prevalence of histrionic personality disorder was found to be 2.2 percent in both men and women (Nestadt et al., 1990). Almost nothing is known about the extent of potential gender differences for the other types of personality disorder. Borderline personality disorder and dependent personality disorder may be somewhat more prevalent among women than men (Zimmerman & Coryell, 1989). There has been some speculation that paranoid and obsessive–compulsive personality disorders may be somewhat more common among men than women (Bernstein, Useda, & Siever, 1995; Funtowicz & Widiger, 1995).

Members of different societies have different rules and norms regarding expected social behaviors. Would the DSM-IV descriptions of personality disorders be meaningful for the members of this society in New Guinea?

GENDER BIAS AND DIAGNOSIS

One of the controversies that has surrounded the diagnosis of personality disorders involves the issue of gender bias. Critics contend that the definitions of some

Vivien Leigh won Academy Awards for her performances as Scarlett O'Hara in Gone with the Wind *(1940) and Blanche DuBois in* A Streetcar Named Desire *(1952). Both characters exhibit blends of histrionic and narcissistic features that fit stereotyped views of female personality traits.*

categories are based on sex-role stereotypes and therefore are inherently sexist. The dependent type, for example, might be viewed as a reflection of certain traditionally feminine traits, such as being unassertive or putting the needs of others ahead of one's own. It has been suggested that, in DSM-IV, these traits are arbitrarily labeled as being maladaptive. Therefore these definitions may turn traditional sex-role behaviors into "disorders" and minimize the extent to which women may simply be trying to cope with unreasonable or oppressive environmental circumstances, including discrimination and sexual abuse (Brown, 1992; Caplan, 1995).

If the criteria for certain categories are based on stereotypes of feminine traits, is it relatively easy for a woman to meet the criteria for that diagnosis even if she is not experiencing significant distress of impairment in other areas of her life? The answer to that question is tentatively "no" (Funtowicz & Widiger, 1995). In other words, the threshold for assigning a diagnosis of personality disorder does not appear to be lower for those types that are based largely on traits that might be considered traditionally feminine (dependent, histrionic, borderline) than for those that are based on traits that might be considered traditionally masculine (antisocial, paranoid, compulsive).

Are clinicians more likely to assign diagnoses such as dependent and borderline personality disorder to a woman than to a man, if both people exhibit the same set of symptoms? The answer to this question is tentatively "yes." One study found that both male and female mental health professionals were significantly (though not overwhelmingly) more likely to describe a person as exhibiting symptoms of borderline personality disorder if that person was female rather than male (Becker & Lamb, 1994).

Stability over Time

Temporal stability is one of the most important assumptions about personality disorders. Evidence for the assumption that personality disorders appear during adolescence and persist into adulthood has, until recently, been limited primarily to antisocial personality disorder. A classic follow-up study by Lee Robins (1966) began with a large set of records describing young children treated for adjustment problems at a clinic during the 1920s. Robins was able to locate and interview almost all of these people, who by then were adults. The people who were most likely to be considered antisocial as adults were boys who had been referred to the clinic on the basis of serious theft or aggressive behavior; who exhibited such behaviors across a variety of situations; and whose antisocial behaviors created conflict with adults outside their own homes. More than half of the boys in Robins's study who exhibited these characteristics were given a diagnosis of antisocial personality disorder as adults.

Another longitudinal study has collected information regarding the prevalence and stability of personality disorders among adolescents (Bernstein et al., 1993). This investigation is particularly important because it did not depend solely on subjects who had been referred for psychological treatment and because it was concerned with the full range of personality disorders. The rate of personality disorders was relatively high in this sample: 17 percent of the adolescents received a diagnosis of at least one personality disorder. While many of these people continued to exhibit the same problems over time, fewer than half of the adolescents who were originally considered to have a personality disorder qualified for that same diagnosis 2 years later. This evidence suggests that maladaptive personality traits are frequently transient phenomena among adolescents.

Schizotypal Personality Disorder (SPD)

Now that we have reviewed some of the important general issues for the entire set of personality disorders, we consider three specific types of disorder in greater detail. We have decided to focus on schizotypal, borderline, and antisocial types because they have been the subject of extended research and debate in the scientific literature.

We begin each of the three sections with a brief case study. We have chosen cases that are prototypes for each disorder. In other words, these are people who exhibit most, if not all, of the features of the disorder. You should not infer from these descriptions that everyone who meets the criteria for these disorders would represent this type of typical case. Remember, also, that many people simultaneously meet the criteria for more than one personality disorder; these cases are relatively simple examples.

The description of the following case, taken from J. Walsh, illustrates some of the most important features of schizotypal personality disorder (SPD).

Brief Case Study

Leslie was a 43-year-old unemployed widow fighting to retain custody of her two adolescent children. Shortly after her husband's death from cancer 8 years ago, her parents-in-law accused her of being an unfit mother and successfully acquired temporary custody of the children through the county children's service bureau. Leslie wanted her children with her, and after many appeals the children's bureau was preparing to return them to her. At this time a casual friend suggested to Leslie that getting counseling for herself would further impress the bureau, and this is why she set up her initial appointment. For some unclear reason, however, Leslie chose to keep her counseling experience a secret.

During her early sessions Leslie was quiet, suspicious, and ill at ease. She had no particular agenda for her counseling, only noting in vague terms that she wanted to "get out to the pool." Her affect was constricted, her communications terse and obscure, and her vocabulary rather primitive. Her grooming was haphazard; on some summer days she came dressed in a fur coat, shorts, and hiking boots. Most sessions lasted only 15 to 20 minutes. Leslie would abruptly announce that she had to leave, sometimes to get to work, and quickly walk out, although she always made a point of rescheduling for the following week. Eventually I learned that her work involved collecting tin cans for recycling. Otherwise she spent her time taking long walks in her small town of residence.

Despite her presentation, it eventually became clear that Leslie was not psychotic and in fact was a college graduate with an impressive athletic background. She had married shortly after college when she became pregnant, but had done little since then aside from raising her children as best she could and tolerating an irresponsible husband. Leslie actually felt relieved when he died, saying "Being married never did me any good." She had functioned marginally ever since leaving college (Walsh, 1990, pp. 45–46). ▼

Brief Historical Perspective

The concept of schizotypal personality disorder is closely tied to the history of schizophrenia as a diagnostic entity (Gottesman, 1987). These maladaptive personality traits are presumably seen among people who possess the genotype that makes them vulnerable to schizophrenia. The symptoms of schizotypal personality disorder represent early manifestations of the predisposition to develop the full-blown disorder. It has been recognized for many years that a fairly large proportion of the family members of schizophrenic patients exhibit strange or unusual behaviors that are similar to, but milder in form than, the disturbance shown by the patient.

TABLE 9–2

DSM-IV Criteria for Schizotypal Personality Disorder

A. A PERVASIVE PATTERN OF SOCIAL AND INTERPERSONAL DEFICITS MARKED BY ACUTE DISCOMFORT WITH, AND REDUCED CAPACITY FOR, CLOSE RELATIONSHIPS AS WELL AS BY COGNITIVE OR PERCEPTUAL DISTORTIONS AND ECCENTRICITIES OF BEHAVIOR, BEGINNING BY EARLY ADULTHOOD AND PRESENT IN A VARIETY OF CONTEXTS, AS INDICATED BY FIVE (OR MORE) OF THE FOLLOWING:

1. Ideas of reference (excluding delusions of reference)
2. Odd beliefs or magical thinking that influences behavior and is inconsistent with subcultural norms (such as superstitiousness, belief in clairvoyance, or telepathy)
3. Unusual perceptual experiences, including bodily illusions
4. Odd thinking and speech (vague, circumstantial, metaphorical, overelaborate, or stereotyped)
5. Suspiciousness or paranoid ideation
6. Inappropriate or constricted affect*
7. Behavior or appearance that is odd, eccentric, or peculiar
8. Lack of close friends or confidants other than first-degree relatives
9. Excessive social anxiety that does not diminish with familiarity and tends to be associated with paranoid fears rather than with negative judgments about self

B. DOES NOT OCCUR EXCLUSIVELY DURING THE COURSE OF SCHIZOPHRENIA, A MOOD DISORDER WITH PSYCHOTIC FEATURES, ANOTHER PSYCHOTIC DISORDER, OR A PERVASIVE DEVELOPMENTAL DISORDER.

Inappropriate affect refers to emotional responses that appear to be inconsistent with the social context—for example, uncontrollable giggling at a wake or funeral. Constricted affect refers to the absence of emotional responsiveness, such as lack of facial expressions. See Chapter 13 for a more detailed discussion.

Clinical Features and Comorbidity

The DSM-IV criteria for schizotypal personality disorder are listed in Table 9–2. These criteria represent a blend of those characteristics that have been reported among the relatives of schizophrenic patients and those symptoms that seem to characterize nonpsychotic patients with schizophrenic-like disorders (Siever, Bernstein, & Silverman, 1995). In addition to social detachment, emphasis is placed on eccentricity and cognitive or perceptual distortions.

People who meet the criteria for schizotypal personality disorder frequently meet the criteria for additional Axis II disorders. There is a considerable amount of overlap between schizotypal personality disorder and other personality disorders in Cluster A (paranoid and schizoid), as well as with avoidant personality disorder. In one study, 33 percent of the patients with schizotypal personality disorder also met the criteria for borderline personality disorder (Morey, 1988).

Etiological Considerations

Most of the interest in the etiology of schizotypal personality disorder has focused on the importance of genetic factors. Is schizotypal personality disorder genetically related to schizophrenia? Family and adoption studies indicate that the answer is "yes" (Thapar & McGuffin, 1993).

Twin studies have examined genetic contributions to schizotypal personality disorder from a dimensional perspective in which schizotypal personality traits are measured with questionnaires. This evidence also points to a significant genetic contribution (Nigg & Goldsmith, 1994).

The first-degree relatives of schizophrenic patients are considerably more likely than people in the general population to exhibit schizotypal personality disorder (Kendler et al., 1993). The diagnostic specificity of this finding remains open to question; some studies have reported that schizotypal personality disorder is also found with increased frequency among the children of parents with mood disorders (Erlenmeyer-Kimling et al., 1995).

The relationship among schizotypal personality disorder, schizophrenia, and major depression can be better understood through an examination of the specific criteria that are used to define schizotypal personality. One study compared the nonpsychotic first-degree relatives of schizophrenic patients with the first-degree relatives of depressed patients (Torgersen et al., 1993). Some of the features, such as lacking close friends and ideas of reference, were actually more common among the relatives of the depressed patients. Only three features of schizotypal personality disorder were significantly more common among the relatives of the schizophrenic patients than among the relatives of the depressed patients:

- Odd thinking and speech
- Inappropriate or constricted affect
- Excessive social anxiety

The investigators concluded that these three features may represent the core of "true" schizotypal personality disorder, if that disorder is viewed as a form of personality that is genetically related to schizophrenia.

Treatment

Two important considerations complicate the treatment of people with personality disorders and make it difficult to evaluate the effectiveness of various forms of intervention (Gorton & Akhtar, 1990). The first consideration involves the ego-syntonic nature of many personality disorders. Many people with these disorders do not seek treatment for their problems because they do not see their own behavior as being the source of distress. A related difficulty involves premature termination: A relatively high proportion of personality disorder patients drop out of treatment before it is completed.

When people with personality disorders appear at hospitals or clinics, it is often because they are also suffering from another type of mental disorder, such as depression or substance abuse. This comorbidity is the second consideration that complicates treatment. "Pure forms" of personality disorder are relatively rare. There is tremendous overlap between specific personality disorder categories and other forms of abnormal behavior, including disorders that would be listed on both Axis I and Axis II. Treatment is seldom aimed at problem behaviors that are associated with only one type of personality disorder, and the efficacy of treatment is therefore difficult to evaluate.

The literature regarding treatment of schizotypal personality disorder mirrors efforts aimed at schizophrenia. A few studies have focused on the possible treatment value of antipsychotic drugs, which are effective with many schizophrenic patients. Some studies have found that low doses of antipsychotic medication are beneficial in alleviating cognitive problems and social anxiety in patients who have received a diagnosis of schizotypal personality disorder (for example, Goldberg et al., 1986). There is also some indication that patients with schizotypal personality disorder may respond positively to antidepressant medication (Markovitz et al., 1991). In general, the therapeutic effects of medication are positive, but they tend to be modest (Gitlin, 1993).

Clinical experience seems to suggest that these patients do not respond well to insight-oriented psychotherapy, in part because they do not see themselves as having psychological problems and also because they are so uncomfortable with close personal relationships (Hoch & Polatin, 1949). Some clinicians have suggested that a supportive, educational approach that is focused on fostering basic social skills may be beneficial if the goals of treatment are modest (Stone, 1985; Walsh, 1990). Unfortunately, controlled studies of psychological forms of treatment with schizotypal personality disorder have not been reported.

Borderline Personality Disorder (BPD)

People who meet the criteria for borderline personality disorder (BPD) are typically involved in intense, chaotic relationships. This pattern of interpersonal behavior is reflected in their vacillating attitudes about people. They alternate frequently between viewing themselves and others as all good (*idealizing*) or all bad (*devaluing*). The following case, written by A. Krohn, illustrates many of the features associated with this disorder.

case study

Brief Case Study

Miss L. was a 21-year-old, reasonably attractive, slightly overweight woman of medium height who walked with a brusque gait, held herself very erect, seemed aloof, and appeared to know just where she was going. She had a high, loud, and shaky voice that was experienced by many as grating and demanding. Though she did not deliberately behave dramatically, her body movements and speech habits seemed a bit larger than life, like postures or poses, and tended to draw attention to herself.

Following puberty, the patient had developed interests in music and writing that quickly became all-consuming preoccupations. She began to ruminate interminably about her future, became preoccupied with what others thought of her, and became extremely sensitive to the most subtle slights, real or imagined. A fantasy of herself as a great artist alternated with an image of herself as completely worthless. Disgusted by the prospect of a drab, workaday life, she dreamed of living on an exalted plane, continuously achieving and creating—fantasizing inside herself founts of dazzling creativity that would permit her to write, sing, and perform effortlessly.

People often initially experienced the patient as pushy and obnoxious. Her manner made others feel that she was blaming them for her difficulties, that she felt she had been treated unfairly and that she deserved and needed more. What came through in her manner was a gnawing hunger, a sense of being deprived, a demand for recompense, and a haughty demand to be looked up to and respected. The patient initially felt that she was shy, modest, and unnoticed. In consciously trying to compensate for this, she often struck others as trying to impress and boast.

Though she had some friends, she had very few who felt capable of gratifying her intense and continuous needs for support, reassurance, and maternal comfort. She grew enraged even at those who befriended her, because they could not do enough. At moments when she felt people were actually depriving her, she felt a "white-hot rage," involving impulses to murder, smash windows, or throw herself out a window. These rageful episodes frightened her greatly and would make her feel she should kill herself. Alternately, she deprecated herself, feeling like a loathsome, ugly, fat person who contributed nothing to the world, who was a parasite and therefore deserved to be hated.

She would develop clinging, dependent relationships characterized by intense wishes to have the qualities of the other (person), often including intense envy of the (person). (Krohn, 1980, pp. 344–345)

Brief Historical Perspective

The intellectual heritage of borderline personality disorder is quite diverse, and it is more difficult to trace than is the case with schizotypal personality disorder. It is, in fact, rather confusing. Several traditions are important, and in some cases they represent conflicting points of view (Leichtman, 1989).

Otto Kernberg (1967, 1975), a psychiatrist at Cornell University, has developed an explanation of borderline personality that is based on psychodynamic theory. According to Kernberg, borderline disorder is not a specific syndrome. Rather, it refers to a set of personality features or deficiencies that can be found in individuals with various disorders.

Kernberg's emphasis on a broadly defined level of pathology, rather than on discrete clinical symptoms, resulted in a relatively expansive definition of borderline personality. Viewed from this

further thoughts

Impulse Control Disorders

Failure to control harmful impulses is associated with several of the disorders listed in DSM-IV. People who meet the criteria for borderline personality disorder and antisocial personality disorder engage in various types of impulsive, maladaptive behaviors (most often self-mutilation in the case of BPD and theft and aggression in the case of ASPD). People in the midst of a manic episode frequently become excessively involved in pleasurable activities that can have painful consequences, such as unrestrained buying or sexual indiscretions. These are examples of impulse control problems that appear as part of a more broadly defined syndrome or mental disorder.

The DSM-IV includes several additional problems under a heading called **impulse control disorders.** Relatively little is known about these problems (Wise & Tierney, 1994). They are defined in terms of persistent, clinically significant impulsive behaviors that are not better explained by other disorders in DSM-IV. They include the following:

- *Intermittent explosive disorder:* Aggressive behaviors resulting in serious assaultive acts or destruction of property. The level of aggression is grossly out of proportion to any precipitating psychosocial stressors.

- *Kleptomania:* Stealing objects that are not needed for personal use or for their financial value. The theft is not motivated by anger or vengeance.
- *Pyromania:* Deliberate and purposeful setting of fires, accompanied by fascination with or attraction to fire and things that are associated with it. The behavior is not motivated by financial considerations (as in arson), social or political ideology, anger, vengeance, or delusional beliefs.
- *Trichotillomania:* Pulling out one's own hair, resulting in noticeable hair loss as well as significant distress or impairment in social or occupational functioning.
- *Pathological gambling:* Repeated maladaptive gambling that is associated with other problems, such as repeated, unsuccessful efforts to stop gambling, restlessness or irritability when trying to stop gambling, lying to family members and friends to conceal the extent of gambling, and committing crimes to finance gambling.

In most cases, the impulsive behavior is preceded by increasing tension and followed by a feeling of pleasure, gratification, or relief. The motivation for these impulsive behaviors is therefore somewhat different than the motivation for *compulsive behavior* (see Chapter 6). Impulsive and compulsive behaviors can be difficult to distinguish. Both types of behavior are repetitive and difficult to resist. The primary difference is that the original goal for impulsive behavior is to experience

John Gunderson, a psychiatrist at Harvard University, has played a central role in the development of diagnostic criteria for borderline personality disorder.

perspective, borderline disorder can encompass a great many types of abnormal behavior, including paranoid, schizoid, and cyclothymic personality disorders, impulse control disorders (see Further Thoughts), substance use disorders, and various types of mood disorder. It should not be surprising therefore that the DSM-IV category of borderline personality disorder has been shown to overlap extensively with other forms of personality disorder and with a number of Axis I disorders.

In an effort to foster research on borderline disorders, these psychodynamic views regarding personality organization were translated into more reliable, descriptive terms by several prominent clinicians. John Gunderson (1984, 1994), a psychiatrist at Harvard University, identified a number of descriptive characteristics that are commonly associated with Kernberg's concept of borderline personality. Gunderson and his colleagues developed a structured interview that would allow clinicians to diagnose the condition reliably. Their definition of the concept depends heavily on the presence of intense, unstable interpersonal relationships, manipulative suicide attempts, unstable sense of the self, negative affect, and impulsivity.

The psychiatrist Hagop Akiskal (1992, 1994) maintains a very different view of borderline personality disorder. He has argued that borderline personality disorder is not a valid or meaningful diagnostic concept. According to his view, the borderline personality concept includes a heterogeneous collection of symptoms that are associated with mild forms of brain dysfunction (for example, epilepsy, attention deficit disorder, pregnancy and birth complications), schizophrenic-like conditions, and typical as well as subclinical mood disorders. Akiskal favors the separation of these various conditions into more homogeneous categories. This point of view is shared by some other experts in the field of personality disorders who believe that the boundaries of the borderline concept are too vague and fuzzy for it to be useful diagnostically (Tyrer, 1994).

pleasure, and the original goal for compulsive behavior is to avoid anxiety (Frances, First, & Pincus, 1995).

The most prevalent type of impulse control disorder is pathological gambling, which may affect as many as 9 million people in the United States (McElroy et al., 1995). Men are more likely than women to become pathological gamblers. They tend to be intelligent, well-educated, competitive people who enjoy the challenges and risks involved in betting.

Most gambling is obviously not associated with a mental disorder. Social gambling is a form of recreation that is accepted in most cultures. Professional gambling is an occupation pursued by people whose gambling is highly disciplined. Pathological gambling, in contrast, is out of control, takes over the person's life, and leads to horrendous financial and interpersonal consequences.

The tragic life of Art Schlichter provides a vivid illustration of the devastating impact that persistent, uncontrolled, impulsive gambling can have on a person and his family (Keteyian, 1986; Valente, 1996). Schlichter, an All-American quarterback at Ohio State University, was the first player drafted by the National Football League in 1982. He had been gambling since high school, but the problem became worse after he started playing professional football. His career was disappointing. As the pressures mounted, so did his gambling debts, which eventually reached $1 million. He was cut from several teams in the National Football League and the Canadian Football League, and was ultimately banned from the NFL for betting on professional games. He entered treatment for his compulsive gambling on several occasions, but the results were unsuccessful. His repeated promises to stop gambling went unfulfilled. Schlichter was arrested four times between 1987 and 1994 and served 2 years in jail. The charges against him included unlawful gambling, bank fraud, and writing bad checks. His promising football career was ruined, and his young family was torn apart by his uncontrolled gambling.

The impulse control disorders occupy an interesting and controversial niche in DSM-IV. The implication of impulse control disorders is that people who repeatedly engage in dangerous, illegal, or destructive behaviors *must* have a mental disorder. If they do not, why do they do these things? Unfortunately, this reasoning quickly becomes circular. Why does he gamble recklessly? Because he has a mental disorder. How do you know he has a mental disorder? Because he gambles recklessly. This logical dilemma is particularly evident in the case of impulse control disorders because these problem behaviors do not appear as part of a broader syndrome in which other symptoms of disorder are also present. In other words, the problem behavior *is* the disorder. Until we can step outside this loop, validating the utility of the diagnostic concept by reference to other psychological or biological response systems, we are left with an unsatisfying approach to the definition of these problems. 〰

Clinical Features and Comorbidity

The DSM-IV criteria for borderline personality disorder are presented in Table 9–3. The overriding characteristic of borderline personality disorder is a pervasive pattern of instability in self-image, in interpersonal relationships, and in mood. Identity disturbance may be manifested by indecision in such areas as career goals, sexual orientation, and personal values. Chaotic interpersonal relationships are also common.

Borderline personality disorder overlaps with several other categories on Axis II, including the histrionic, narcissistic, paranoid, dependent, and avoidant types. There is also a significant amount of overlap between borderline personality disorder and Axis I disorders, especially depression (Trull, 1995; Widiger & Trull, 1993). Many patients with other types of impulse control problems, such as substance dependence and eating disorders, also qualify for a diagnosis of borderline personality disorder.

Follow-up studies suggest many similarities between borderline personality disorder and mood disorders. Akiskal and his colleagues studied a group of 100 outpatients with a diagnosis of borderline personality disorder. During follow-up, 29 percent of the sample developed severe depression. A longitudinal study of patients who were discharged from a private psychiatric hospital is also interesting in this regard. Of the patients with a pure diagnosis of borderline personality disorder (that is, those who did not receive any other diagnosis on Axis I or II), 23 percent developed major depressive episodes in the course of the 15-year follow-up (McGlashan, 1986).

Etiological Considerations

Genetic factors do not seem to play a central role in the etiology of borderline personality disorder, when it is viewed in terms of the syndrome that is defined in DSM-IV (Torgersen, 1994). It is

impulse control disorder   A disorder characterized by failure to resist an impulse or a temptation to perform some pleasurable or tension-releasing act that is harmful to oneself or others; examples are pathological gambling, setting fires, and stealing.

TABLE 9–3

DSM-IV Criteria for Borderline Personality Disorder

A. A PERVASIVE PATTERN OF INSTABILITY OF INTERPERSONAL RELATIONSHIPS, SELF-IMAGE, AND AFFECTS, AND MARKED IMPULSIVITY BEGINNING BY EARLY ADULTHOOD AND PRESENT IN A VARIETY OF CONTEXTS, AS INDICATED BY FIVE (OR MORE) OF THE FOLLOWING:

1. Frantic efforts to avoid real or imagined abandonment.
2. A pattern of unstable and intense interpersonal relationships characterized by alternating between extremes of idealization and devaluation.
3. Identity disturbance: markedly and persistently unstable self-image or sense of self.
4. Impulsiveness in at least two areas that are potentially self-damaging (for example, spending, sex, substance abuse, reckless driving, binge eating).
5. Recurrent suicidal behavior, gestures, or threats, or self-mutilating behavior.
6. Affective instability due to a marked reactivity of mood (such as intense episodic dysphoria, irritability, or anxiety usually lasting a few hours and only rarely more than a few days).
7. Chronic feelings of emptiness.
8. Inappropriate, intense anger or difficulty controlling anger (for example, frequent displays of temper, constant anger, recurrent physical fights).
9. Transient, stress-related paranoid ideation or severe dissociative symptoms.

premature to conclude that genes are irrelevant to the development of this set of problems because neuroticism (one of the personality traits that is clearly related to the borderline concept) is influenced by genetic factors (Nigg & Goldsmith, 1994). Nevertheless, most of the discussion regarding causes of borderline personality disorder has focused on environmental events.

Akiskal elaborated on Kernberg's psychodynamic theory and proposed a similar model for the development of "residual" borderline conditions, those that remain after the exclusion of brain disorders, mood disorders, and schizotypal disorders. He argued that borderline patients suffer from the negative consequences of parental loss during childhood (Davis & Akiskal, 1986). The model is supported by studies of the families of borderline patients and by comparisons with the literature on social development in monkeys that examined the effects of separating infants from their mothers.

Studies of patients with borderline personality disorder point toward the influence of widespread problematic relationships with their parents (Guzder et al., 1996). Separation appears to be only one aspect of this complicated picture. Adolescent girls with borderline personality disorder report pervasive lack of supervision, frequent witnessing of domestic violence, and being subjected to inappropriate behavior by their parents and other adults, including verbal, physical, and sexual abuse (Norden et al., 1995; Weaver & Clum, 1993). The extent and severity of abuse vary widely across individuals. Many patients describe multiple forms of abuse by more than a single individual.

We must be careful, however, when we interpret the evidence regarding the relationship between borderline personality disorder and environmental factors, such as separation and abuse. With the exception of the data from primate models, all the evidence is correlational. It is therefore risky to draw causal inferences. What is the direction of effect? It seems likely that this type of family conflict represents the result of a dynamic, transactional process in which children and parents influence each other over an extended period of time (Crowell et al., 1993).

Treatment

Given that the concept of borderline personality disorder is rooted in psychodynamic theory, it should not be surprising that many clinicians have advocated the use of psychotherapy for the treatment of these conditions (Freeman & Gunderson, 1989; Shea, 1991). In psychodynamically based treatment, the transference relationship, defined as the way in which the patient behaves toward the therapist, is used to increase patients' ability to experience themselves and other people in a more realistic and integrated way.

Personality disorders have traditionally been considered to be hard to treat from a psychological perspective, and borderline conditions are among the most difficult. Close personal relationships form the foundation of psychological intervention, and it is specifically in the area of establishing and maintaining such relationships that borderline patients experience their greatest difficulty. Their persistent alternation between overidealization and devaluation leads to frequent rage toward the therapist and can become a significant deterrent to progress in therapy. Not surprisingly, between one-half and two-thirds of all patients with borderline personality disorder discontinue treatment, against their therapists' advice, within the first several weeks of treatment (Kelly et al., 1992).

Some people with borderline personality disorders engage in recurrent suicidal gestures or self-mutilating behaviors.

One promising approach to psychotherapy with borderline patients, called *dialectical behavior therapy (DBT)*, has been developed and evaluated by Marsha Linehan (1993), a clinical psychologist at the University of Washington. This procedure combines the use of broadly based behavioral strategies with the more general principles of supportive psychotherapy. Traditional behavioral and cognitive techniques, such as skill training, exposure, and problem solving, are employed to help the patient improve interpersonal relationships, tolerate distress, and regulate emotional responses. Considerable emphasis is also placed on the therapist's acceptance of patients, including their frequently demanding, manipulative, and contradictory behaviors. This factor is important, because borderline patients are extremely sensitive to even the most subtle signs of criticism or rejection by other people.

A controlled study of dialectical behavior therapy produced encouraging results with regard to some aspects of the patients' behavior (Linehan et al., 1993, 1994). Patients were randomly assigned to receive either DBT or treatment as usual, which was essentially any form of treatment that was available within the community. The adjustment of patients in both groups was measured after 1 year of treatment and over a 1-year period following termination. One of the most important results involved the dropout rate. Almost 60 percent of the patients in the treatment-as-usual group terminated prematurely, whereas the rate in the DBT group was only 17 percent. The patients who received DBT also showed a significant reduction in the frequency and severity of suicide attempts, spent fewer days in psychiatric hospitals over the course of the study, and rated themselves higher on a measure of social adjustment. The groups did not differ, however, on other important measures, such as level of depression and hopelessness.

Psychotropic medication is also used frequently in the treatment of borderline patients. Unfortunately, no disorder-specific drug has been found. Psychiatrists employ the entire spectrum of psychoactive medication with borderline patients, from antipsychotics and antidepressants to lithium and anticonvulsants (Gitlin, 1993; Stein, 1992). Different types of drugs are recommended to treat individual symptoms, but there is no systematic proof that a specific drug is effective for any of the borderline features (Soloff, 1994).

Antisocial Personality Disorder (ASPD)

Antisocial personality disorder (ASPD) has been studied more thoroughly and for a longer period of time than any of the other personality disorders (Blashfield & McElroy, 1989). One case study involving this disorder was presented at the beginning of this chapter. Tom, the man in that case, illustrated the pattern of repeated antisocial behavior that is associated with the disorder. Emotional and interpersonal problems also play an important role in the definition of antisocial personality disorder. The case study on page 260, written by Robert Hare, a clinical psychologist at the University of British Columbia, illustrates the egocentricity that is a central feature of the disorder. It also demonstrates the stunning lack of concern that such people have for the impact of their behavior on other people, especially those who are close to them.

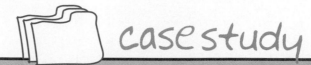

Brief Case Study

Terry is 21, the second of three boys born into a wealthy and highly respected family. His older brother is a doctor, and his younger brother is a scholarship student in his second year of college. Terry is a first-time offender, serving 2 years for a series of robberies committed a year ago.

By all accounts, his family life was stable, his parents were warm and loving, and his opportunities for success were enormous. His brothers were honest and hardworking, whereas he simply "floated through life, taking whatever was offered." His parents' hopes and expectations were less important to him than having a good time. Still, they supported him emotionally and financially through an adolescence marked by wildness, testing the limits, and repeated brushes with the law—speeding, reckless driving, drunkenness—but no formal convictions. By age 20 he had fathered two children and was heavily involved in gambling and drugs. When he could no longer obtain money from his family he turned to robbing banks, and he was soon caught and sent to prison. "I wouldn't be here if my parents had come across when I needed them," he said. "What kind of parents would let their son rot in a place like this?" Asked about his children, he replied, "I've never seen them. I think they were given up for adoption. How the hell should I know!" (Hare, 1993, p. 167)

---

psychopathy Another term for antisocial personality disorder. Usually associated with Cleckley's definition of that concept, which included features such as disregard for the truth, lack of empathy, and inability to learn from experience.

The contrast between Terry's willingness to blame his own problems on his parents and his apparent inability to accept responsibility for his own children is striking. It illustrates clearly the callous indifference and shallow emotional experience of the person with antisocial personality disorder.

Brief Historical Perspective

Current views of antisocial personality disorder have been greatly influenced by two specific books. These books have inspired two different approaches to the definition of the disorder itself. The first book, *The Mask of Sanity,* was written by Hervey Cleckley, a psychiatrist at the University of Georgia, and was originally published in 1941. It included numerous case examples of impulsive, self-centered, pleasure-seeking people who seemed to be completely lacking in certain primary emotions, such as anxiety, shame, and guilt. Cleckley used the term **psychopathy** to describe this disorder. According to Cleckley's definition, the *psychopath* is a person who is intelligent and superficially charming but also chronically deceitful, unreliable, and incapable of learning from experience. This diagnostic approach places principal emphasis on emotional deficits and personality traits. Unfortunately, Cleckley's definition was difficult to use reliably because it relied on such elusive features as "incapacity for love" and "failure to learn from experience."

The second book that influenced the concept of antisocial personality disorder was a report by Lee Robins of her follow-up study of children who had been treated many years earlier at a child guidance clinic. The book, *Deviant Children Grown Up* (1966), demonstrated that certain forms of conduct disorder that were evident during childhood, especially among boys, were reliable predictors of other forms of antisocial behavior when these same people became adults. The diagnostic approach inspired by this research study was adopted by DSM-III (APA, 1980). It places principal emphasis on observable behaviors and repeated conflict with authorities, including failure to conform to social norms with respect to lawful behavior. This approach can be used with greater reliability because it is focused on concrete consequences of the disorder, which are often documented by legal records, rather than subjectively defined emotional deficits, such as lack of empathy.

Psychopathy and ASPD are two different attempts to define the same disorder. Yet they are sufficiently different that they certainly do not identify the same people, and they are no longer used interchangeably. Critics argued that DSM-III had blurred the distinction between antisocial personality and criminality. Cleckley's approach had been relatively clear on this point; all criminals are not psychopaths, and all psychopaths are not convicted criminals. The DSM-III definition made it difficult to diagnose antisocial personality disorder in a person who did not already have a criminal record, such as an egocentric, manipulative, and callous busi-

getting help

Personality Disorders

As we mention in this chapter, most people who would meet the diagnostic criteria for a personality disorder do not enter treatment, at least not voluntarily. Although their interpersonal problems are pervasive and deeply ingrained, these maladaptive tendencies are part of a tightly woven pattern of beliefs that, they believe, justify their actions. If you are reading this because you feel you don't have the friends you want or that you are driving people away somehow, but you also feel that there are good reasons for your actions, you might look into therapy with an eye to uncovering the reasons why you have had to develop a personality style that is not helping you get what you want.

The negative way in which personality disorders are sometimes portrayed may make some people reluctant to acknowledge that they have a personality disorder. We prefer to discuss these problems in terms of *personality limitations* or *maladaptive response styles*. No one is perfect. Being able to recognize your own weaknesses is a sign that you are open-minded and willing to change. This is the first important step toward improvement.

It also helps to have a little compassion for yourself, along with the determination to work toward a lasting change in the way you relate to the people and events of your life. *Lost in the Mirror: An Inside Look at Borderline Personality Disorder* by Richard Moskovitz provides an insightful and sympathetic guide to the painful emotional experiences associated with borderline personality disorder and the ways in which these symptoms affect the lives of patients, their families, and their friends.

If you are interested in help because you have to deal with someone who you think may have a personality disorder, you probably feel confused, frustrated, and angry. You may also feel extremely guilty if you blame yourself for problems in the relationship or for the other person's unhappiness. This may be particularly the case if you are involved romantically with the person or work closely with him or her. Fortunately, it is possible to adapt to such interactions. Several self-help guides provide advice about getting along with difficult people. Most recommend that you begin by learning about the predictable nature of the other person's style. Recognize the presence of personality weaknesses and learn how to adapt to them. You must also accept the limits of your own ability to control the other person or to get him or her to change. One useful Web site, called BPD Central, is located at the following URL: members.aol.com/BPDCentral. It is a collection of resources for people who care about someone with borderline personality disorder, including advice about caring for yourself as well as information regarding programs and therapists who treat people with BPD.

Sometimes the only solution is to end the relationship. At their most extreme, people with personality disorders cannot form reciprocal, mutually satisfying relationships with other people. This is particularly true in the case of antisocial personality disorder. Some people repeatedly abuse, exploit, and cheat others. We all may run across such people from time to time, and we need to learn how to protect ourselves. Robert Hare, an expert on psychopathy, concludes his book, *Without Conscience* with a brief "survival guide" that may help you minimize your risk. He notes, for example, that we should be aware of the symptoms and interpersonal characteristics of psychopathy. We should be cautious in high-risk situations, and know our own weaknesses. Hare's advice may be extremely helpful to someone who finds himself or herself trapped in a relationship with someone who is a psychopath. In fact, you may want to speak to a therapist or counselor to figure out why you have become involved in such an unequal, nonreciprocal relationship.

nessperson. It also moved in the direction of including a much larger proportion of criminals within the boundaries of antisocial personality disorder. (Hare, Hart, & Harpur, 1991). The true meaning of the concept might have been sacrificed in DSM-III for the sake of improved reliability.

Clinical Features and Comorbidity

Table 9–4 lists the DSM-IV criteria for antisocial personality disorder. One prominent feature in this definition is the required presence of symptoms of conduct disorder (see Chapter 14) prior to the age of 15, which reflects the impact of Robins's work. The definition also requires the presence of at least three out of seven signs of irresponsible and antisocial behavior after the age of 15. One of these criteria, "lack of remorse," did not appear in DSM-III but was one of Cleckley's original criteria. Its inclusion in DSM-IV clearly signals an attempt to move the definition back toward the original concept.

Some investigators and clinicians prefer the concept of psychopathy to the DSM-IV definition of antisocial personality. Robert Hare has developed a systematic approach to the assessment

TABLE 9–4

DSM-IV Criteria for Antisocial Personality Disorder

A. THERE IS A PERVASIVE PATTERN OF DISREGARD FOR AND VIOLATION OF THE RIGHTS OF OTHERS OCCURRING SINCE AGE 15, AS INDICATED BY THREE (OR MORE) OF THE FOLLOWING:

1. Failure to conform to social norms with respect to lawful behavior as indicated by repeatedly performing acts that are grounds for arrest.
2. Deceitfulness, as indicated by repeated lying, use of aliases, or conning others for personal profit or pleasure.
3. Impulsivity or failure to plan ahead.
4. Irritability and aggressiveness, as indicated by repeated physical fights or assaults.
5. Reckless disregard for safety of self or others.
6. Consistent irresponsibility, as indicated by repeated failure to sustain consistent work behavior or honor financial obligations.
7. Lack of remorse, as indicated by being indifferent to or rationalizing having hurt, mistreated, or stolen from another.

B. THE INDIVIDUAL IS AT LEAST 18 YEARS OLD.

C. EVIDENCE OF CONDUCT DISORDER WITH ONSET BEFORE AGE 15.

Robert Hare, a psychologist at the University of British Columbia, is a leading expert on psychopathy. He developed the Psychopathy Checklist, which has become the standard assessment instrument for this disorder.

of psychopathy, known as the *Psychopathy Checklist (PCL)*, that is based largely on Cleckley's original description of the disorder. The PCL includes two major factors (groups of symptoms): (1) emotional/interpersonal traits and (2) social deviance associated with an unstable or antisocial lifestyle. Key symptoms for both factors are summarized in Table 9–5. The major difference between this definition of psychopathy and the DSM-IV definition of antisocial personality disorder involves the list of emotional and interpersonal traits (although DSM-IV does include being deceitful and failure to experience remorse). Extensive research with the PCL indicates that, contrary to previous experience with Cleckley's criteria, the emotional and interpersonal traits can be used reliably (Hare, Hart, & Harpur, 1991).

The ultimate resolution of this prolonged dispute over the best definition of antisocial personality disorder will depend on systematic comparisons of the two approaches (Lilienfeld, 1994; Widiger & Corbitt, 1995). This situation is a classic example of the issues involved in studying the *validity* of a diagnostic concept (see Chapter 4). How different are these definitions? Which definition is most useful in predicting events such as repeated antisocial behavior following release from prison? The field trial that was conducted when DSM-IV was being prepared represents one large-scale effort of this type (Widiger et al., 1996). That project did not find any major differences in validity between the DSM-based definition of antisocial personality disorder and a PCL-based definition of psychopathy.

Etiological Considerations

Psychologists have studied etiological factors associated with antisocial personality disorder more extensively than for any of the other personality disorders. Research studies on this topic fall into three general areas. One is concerned with the biological underpinnings of the disorder, especially the possible influence of genetic factors. The second focus of investigation is social factors. The relationship between familial conflict and the development of antisocial behavior in children falls under this general heading. The third group of studies has addressed the nature of the psychological factors that might explain the apparent inability of people with antisocial personality disorder to learn from experience.

TABLE 9–5

Key Symptoms of Psychopathy	
EMOTIONAL/INTERPERSONAL TRAITS	**SOCIAL DEVIANCE (ANTISOCIAL LIFESTYLE)**
Glib and superficial	Impulsive
Egocentric and grandiose	Poor behavior controls
Lack of remorse or guilt	Need for excitement
Lack of empathy	Lack of responsibility
Deceitful and manipulative	Early behavior problems
Shallow emotions	Adult antisocial behavior

Source: R. D. Hare, 1993, *Without Conscience: The Disturbing World of the Psychopaths Among Us.* New York: Pocket Books.

BIOLOGICAL FACTORS

Several investigators have employed adoption methods to evaluate the relative contributions of genetic and environmental factors to the development of antisocial personality disorder, and of criminal behavior more generally (Carey & Gottesman, 1996). This strategy is based on the study of *adoptees*: people who were separated from their biological parents at an early age and raised by adoptive families (see Chapter 2).

Several different adoption studies have found that the development of antisocial behavior is determined by an *interaction* between genetic factors and adverse environmental circumstances (Cadoret et al., 1995). In other words, both types of influence are important. The highest rates of conduct disorder and antisocial behavior are found among the offspring of antisocial biological parents who are raised in an adverse adoptive environment.

SOCIAL FACTORS

Adoption studies indicate that genetic factors interact with environmental events to produce patterns of antisocial and criminal behavior. The combination of a biological predisposition toward antisocial behavior and environmental adversity is particularly harmful. What kinds of events might be involved in this process? One obvious candidate is family conflict.

Robins (1966) found that children raised in families characterized by inconsistent discipline or the complete absence of discipline were more likely to receive a diagnosis of antisocial personality disorder when they reached adulthood. She also found that subjects who received a diagnosis of antisocial personality disorder as adults were likely to have had fathers who exhibited antisocial behavior themselves. Her study suggests that parental behaviors can have an important influence on the development of antisocial behavior in their children.

How can the interaction between genetic factors and family processes be explained? There may be multiple, interacting pathways or systems (Moffitt, 1993). One pathway involves the concept of children's temperament and the effect that their characteristic response styles may have on parental behavior. Children with a "difficult" temperament—whose response style is characterized by high levels of negative emotion or excessive activity—may be especially irritating to their parents and caretakers (Bates, Wachs, & Emde, 1994). They may be clumsy, overactive, inattentive, irritable, or impulsive. Their resistance to disciplinary efforts may discourage adults from maintaining persistent strategies in this regard. This type of child may be most likely to evoke maladaptive reactions from parents who are poorly equipped to deal with the challenges presented by this kind of behavior. Parents may be driven either to use unusually harsh punishments or to abandon any attempt at discipline. This interaction between the child and the social environment fosters the development of poorly controlled behavior. Antisocial behavior is perpetuated when the person selects friends who share similar antisocial interests and problems.

The best predictor of adult antisocial personality disorder in Lee Robins's study was conduct disorder characterized by physical aggression and other rule violations.

After a pattern of antisocial behavior has been established during childhood, many factors lock the person into further antisocial activities. Moffitt's theory emphasizes two sources of continuity. The first is a limited range of behavioral skills. The person does not learn social skills that would allow him or her to pursue more appropriate responses than behaviors such as lying, cheating, and stealing. Once the opportunity to develop these skills is lost during childhood, they may never be learned. The second source of continuity involves the results of antisocial behavior during childhood and adolescence. The person becomes progressively ensnared by the aftermath of earlier choices. Many possible consequences of antisocial behavior, including being addicted to drugs, becoming a teenaged parent, dropping out of school, and having a criminal record, can narrow the person's options.

PSYCHOLOGICAL FACTORS

Adoption, twin, and family studies provide clues to the types of etiological factors that may cause antisocial personality disorder. Another series of studies, beginning in the 1950s and extending to the present, has been concerned with the psychological mechanisms that may mediate this type of behavior. These investigations have attempted to explain several characteristic features of psychopathy, such as lack of anxiety, impulsivity, and failure to learn from experience, using various types of laboratory tasks.

Subjects in these tasks are typically asked to learn a sequence of responses in order either to receive a reward or avoid an aversive consequence, such as electric shock or loss of money. Although the overall accuracy of psychopaths' performance on these tasks is generally equivalent to that of nonpsychopathic subjects, their behavior sometimes appears to be unaffected by the anticipation of punishment (Kosson & Newman, 1986; Lykken, 1957). Two primary hypotheses have been advanced to explain the poor performance of psychopaths on these tasks.

One point of view is based on Cleckley's argument that psychopaths are emotionally impoverished. Their lack of anxiety and fear is particularly striking. Research support for this hypothesis is based in large part on an examination of physiological responses while subjects are performing laboratory tasks. For example, psychopaths' startle responses follow a different pattern than those observed in normal subjects (Patrick, 1994); they do not show the exaggerated startle response that is indicative of fear in the presence of aversive stimuli. This emotional deficit may explain why psychopaths are relatively insensitive to, or able to ignore, the effects of punishment (Hare, 1993).

The other hypothesis holds that psychopaths have difficulty shifting their attention to consider the possible negative consequences of their behavior after a response pattern has been well established (Newman, Kosson, & Patterson, 1992; Patterson & Newman, 1993).

Critics of this line of research have noted some problems with existing psychological explanations for the psychopath's behavior. One limitation is the implicit assumption that most people conform to social regulations and ethical principles because of anxiety or fear of punishment. It might be argued that the most crucial features are not low anxiety and failure to learn from experience but lack of shame and pathological egocentricity. According to this perspective, the psychopath is simply a person who has chosen, for whatever reason, to behave in a persistently selfish manner that ignores the feelings and rights of other people. "Rather than moral judgment being driven by anxiety, anxiety is driven by moral judgment" (Levenson, 1992).

Treatment

People with antisocial personalities seldom seek professional mental health services unless they are forced into treatment by the legal system. When they do seek treatment, the general consensus among clinicians is that it is seldom effective (Quality Assurance Project, 1991). This widely held impression is based, in part, on the traits that are used to define the disorder; like people with borderline personality disorder, people with antisocial personality disorder are typically unable to establish intimate, trusting relationships, which obviously form the basis for any treatment program.

The research literature regarding the treatment of antisocial personality disorder is rather sparse (Dolan & Coid, 1993). Very few studies have identified cases using official diagnostic criteria for antisocial personality disorder. Most of the programs that have been evaluated have focused on juvenile delinquents, adults who have been imprisoned, or people otherwise referred by the criminal justice system. Outcome is often measured in terms of the frequency of repeated criminal offenses rather than in terms of changes in behaviors more directly linked to the personality traits that define the core of antisocial personality. The high rate of alcoholism and other forms of substance dependence in this population is another problem that complicates planning and evaluating treatment programs aimed specifically at the personality disorder itself.

Although no form of intervention has proved to be effective for antisocial personality disorder, psychological interventions that are directed toward specific features of the disorder might be useful (Doren, 1993). Examples are behavioral procedures that were originally designed for anger management and deviant sexual behaviors. Behavioral treatments can apparently produce temporary changes in behavior while the person is closely supervised, but they may not generalize to other settings (Freeman & Gunderson, 1989).

Personality disorders are defined in terms of rigid, inflexible, maladaptive ways of perceiving and responding to oneself and one's environment that lead to social or occupational problems or subjective distress. This pattern must be pervasive across a broad range of situations, and it must be stable and of long duration. Among the hallmark features of personality disorders are major problems in interpersonal relationships. Many people with personality disorders do not see themselves as being disturbed.

Personality disorders are controversial for a number of reasons, including their low diagnostic reliability, the tremendous overlap among specific personality disorder categories, and the relative absence of effective forms of treatment. They are presumably defined in terms of behaviors that deviate markedly from the expectations of the person's culture. Unfortunately, little information is currently available to indicate whether the DSM-IV system for personality disorders will be useful in societies other than the United States, Canada, and Western Europe.

DSM-IV lists 10 types of personality disorder, arranged in 3 clusters. There is considerable overlap among and between these types. Cluster A includes **paranoid, schizoid,** and **schizotypal personality disorders.** These categories generally refer to people who are seen as being odd or eccentric. Cluster B includes **antisocial, borderline, histrionic,** and **narcissistic personality disorders.** People who fit into this cluster are generally seen as being dramatic, unpredictable, and overly emotional. Cluster C includes **avoidant, dependent,** and **obsessive–compulsive personality disorders.** The common element in these disorders is presumably anxiety or fearfulness.

The lifetime prevalence of personality disorders among adults in the general population is between 10 and 14 percent. The overall lifetime prevalence rate for antisocial personality disorder (men and women combined) was 2.6 percent in the ECA study and 3.5 percent in the NCS, with rates being at least 4 times higher in men than in women.

The disorders listed in Cluster A, especially schizoid and schizotypal personality disorders, have been viewed as possible antecedents or subclinical forms of schizophrenia. They are defined largely in terms of minor symptoms that resemble the hallucinations and delusions seen in the full-blown disorder, as well as peculiar behaviors that have been observed among the first-degree relatives of schizophrenic patients. Research on the etiology of schizotypal personality disorder has focused primarily on studies of its genetic relationship to schizophrenia.

The most important features of borderline personality disorder revolve around a pervasive pattern of instability in self-image, in interpersonal relationships, and in mood. Some investigators believe that borderline personality disorder is an extremely heterogeneous category that should be further subdivided. Research regarding the etiology of borderline personality disorder has focused on two primary areas. One involves the impact of chaotic and abusive families. The other is concerned with the premature separation of children from their parents. Both sets of factors can presumably lead to problems in emotional regulation.

Psychopathy and ASPD are two different attempts to define the same disorder. The DSM-IV definition of antisocial personality disorder (ASPD) places primary emphasis on social deviance in adulthood (repeated lying, physical assaults, reckless and irresponsible behavior). The concept of psychopathy places greater emphasis on emotional and interpersonal deficits, such as lack of remorse, lack of empathy, and shallow emotions. Adoption studies indicate that the etiology of antisocial behavior is determined by an interaction between genetic factors and adverse environmental circumstances. Laboratory studies of people who meet the criteria for psychopathy have focused on two hypothesis. One suggests that psychopaths are emotionally impoverished. The other holds that psychopaths have difficulty shifting their attention in order to avoid punishment.

Treatment procedures for people with personality disorders are especially difficult to design and evaluate, for three principal reasons. First, people with these disorders frequently don't have insight into the nature of their problems. They are therefore unlikely to seek treatment, and if they do, they frequently terminate prematurely. Second, pure forms of personality disorder are relatively rare. Most people with a personality disorder who are in treatment also exhibit comorbid forms of personality disorder and/or comorbid Axis I disorders, such as depression or drug addiction. Third, people with personality disorder have difficulty establishing and maintaining meaningful, stable interpersonal relationships of the sort that are required for psychotherapy.

Treatment for schizotypal and borderline personality disorders often involves the use of antipsychotic medication or antidepressant medication. A few controlled studies indicate that these drugs can be beneficial. Long-term outcome tends to be better for patients with borderline than schizotypal personality disorder. Various types of psychological intervention, including psychodynamic procedures as well as dialectical behavior therapy, have frequently been employed with borderline patients. People with antisocial personality disorder seldom seek treatment voluntarily. When they do, the general consensus among clinicians is that it is seldom effective.

Critical Thinking

1. The DSM-IV lists the personality disorders on a separate axis from the other types of mental disorder. In what ways are these problems different from disorders like depression, schizophrenia, and alcoholism? How are they similar?

2. Imagine that you are a clinical psychologist who is treating a client who is depressed. How would your treatment plan change if you knew that, in addition to a diagnosis of unipolar mood disorder on Axis I, the person also met the DSM-IV criteria for borderline personality disorder? What if the Axis II diagnosis was dependent personality disorder?

3. Imagine that you are a judge who must decide the fate of a 17-year-old male juvenile delinquent who has just been convicted of his first felony offense (theft). You know that he has a long history of truancy from school and of running away from home. His attorney asks you to place him on probation contingent on his entering into psychological treatment, on the grounds that he is suffering from a mental disorder. What would you do? Does that seem like a plausible alternative to jail? Would you respond differently if the man were 40 years old?

10

Eating Disorders

Popular culture in the United States today is obsessed with physical appearance. We are told that "beauty is only skin deep," but the cosmetic, fashion, and diet industries are eager to convince young people that "looks are everything." In fact, women's thinness is equated with beauty, fitness, success, and ultimately with happiness. Given our national obsession with appearance, weight, and diet, is it surprising that many young people, especially young women, become obsessed with food to the point where they develop eating-related disorders?

Overview

eating disorders   A category of psychological disorders characterized by severe disturbances in eating behavior, specifically anorexia nervosa and bulimia nervosa.

anorexia nervosa   A type of eating disorder characterized by the refusal to maintain a minimally normal body weight along with other symptoms related to eating and body image.

bulimia nervosa   A type of eating disorder characterized by repeated episodes of binge eating followed by inappropriate compensatory behaviors (such as self-induced vomiting) together with other symptoms related to eating and body image.

Eating disorders are severe disturbances in eating behavior that result from the sufferer's obsessive fear of gaining weight. Some experts have suggested that "dieting disorder" is a more accurate term for these behaviors (Beumont, Garner, & Touyz, 1994), because dread of weight gain and obsession with weight loss are central features of eating disorders. The DSM-IV lists two major subtypes of eating disorders: anorexia nervosa and bulimia nervosa. The most obvious characteristic of **anorexia nervosa** is extreme emaciation, or more technically, the refusal to maintain a minimally normal body weight. The term *anorexia* literally means "loss of appetite," but this is a misnomer. People with anorexia nerovsa *are* hungry, yet they starve themselves nevertheless. Some unfortunate victims literally starve themselves to death.

Bulimia nervosa is characterized by repeated episodes of binge eating, followed by inappropriate compensatory behaviors such as self-induced vomiting, misuse of laxatives, or excessive exercise. The literal meaning of the term *bulimia* is "ox appetite," but people with bulimia nervosa typically have a normal appetite and maintain a normal weight. In fact, most sufferers view their binge eating as a failure of control, not as an indulgence of their excessive appetites or as a relief from the pressures of dieting. Thus people with bulimia nervosa commonly are ashamed and secretive about their binge eating and purging. Princess Diana is one famous woman who has publicly admitted to struggling with bulimia.

Both anorexia and bulimia are about 10 times more common among females than males, and they develop most commonly among women in their teens and early twenties. The increased incidence among young people reflects both the intense focus on young women's physical appearance and the difficulties many adolescent girls encounter in adjusting to the rapid changes in body shape and weight that begin with puberty (Hsu, 1990). According to the National Centers for Disease Control and Prevention, at any point in time 44 percent of high school females are attempting to lose weight compared with 15 percent of males. In fact, many adolescent boys want to *gain* weight in order to look bigger and stronger (Serdula et al., 1993). Moreover, a recent national survey found that almost half of American women have a negative body image, particularly concerning their waist, hips, and/or thighs (Cash & Henry, 1995; see Figure 10–1). Clearly, cultural attitudes about weight, thinness, and appearance play a central role in causing eating disorders.

Because the symptoms of anorexia nervosa differ considerably from those of bulimia nervosa, we consider the typical symptoms of the two disorders sep-

Images of women in advertising and the popular media often equate thinness with beauty, success, and happiness.

Figure 10–1   Women's Dissatisfaction with Their Physical Attributes.   Percentage of females reporting that they were "very or mostly dissatisfied" with specific physical attributes in a national sample of women aged 18 to 70 interviewed in 1993.

Source: T.F. Cash and P.E. Henry, 1995, Women's body images: The results of a national survey in the U.S.A., *Sex Roles, 33,* 19–28.

arately in this chapter. We combine the two disorders when discussing classification, prevalence, and etiology, however, because they share many developmental similarities. For example, many people with anorexia nervosa also binge and purge on occasion; many people with bulimia nervosa have a history of anorexia nervosa. When discussing treatment, we again discuss the two disorders separately, reflecting the important differences in the focus and effectiveness of therapy for each disorder. We begin our consideration of eating disorders with a case study.

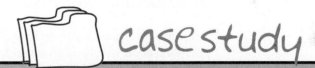

case study

Anorexia Nervosa

Seritta was an attractive, well-dressed, and polite 15-year-old high school sophomore who was living in a friendly joint-custody arrangement. She spent alternating weeks living with each of her successful, middle-class parents. Serrita was an excellent student whom her mother described as a "sweet girl who never gave me an ounce of worry—until now." When she was first seen by a clinical psychologist for the treatment of anorexia nervosa, Seritta was 5 feet 2 inches tall and weighed 81 pounds. Seritta's gaunt appearance was painfully obvious to the psychologist and to anyone else who looked at her. However, Seritta firmly denied that she was too thin. Instead, she asserted that she looked "almost right." She was still on a diet, and every day she carefully inspected her stomach, thighs, hips, arms, and face for any signs of fat. Although Seritta was generally pleased with the image she saw in her bathroom mirror, she remained deathly afraid of gaining weight. She monitored her food intake with incredible detail, and she could recite every item of food

she had consumed recently, as well as discuss its caloric and fat content.

Seritta had begun her diet 9 months earlier after visiting her family doctor. At the time, Seritta weighed 108 pounds, a normal weight for her age, height, and body type, although her physician told her that she could stand to lose a pound or two. Seritta claimed that the doctor's comment had motivated her to begin a diet. Previously, Seritta's weight had ranged between 102 and 108 pounds, and she set a goal of getting back to 102. The doctor's suggestion was not the only motivation for Seritta. She said that she also decided to diet because she wanted to look more attractive. Seritta admitted that she secretly hoped that having a "great body" would help compensate for her perceived inadequacies and make her beautiful in her own eyes and in the eyes of her classmates.

Seritta's diet began normally enough. She was very bright and began to read extensively about food, weight, and diet. She quickly lost the 6 pounds she wanted to lose, and her success was reinforced by her parents' and girlfriends' positive comments. To her knowledge, however, the boys in her school did
continued

not notice the change in her appearance, and her social life did not improve. Without really planning to do so, Seritta simply continued her diet. By then, she had developed the habit of scouring her image in the mirror, and she invariably found some spot that was just a bit "too fat." As a result, she was continually setting a new goal to lose another couple of pounds. She weighed herself constantly and said that the bathroom scale became her "best friend." Although her friends and family soon were telling her that she looked too thin, privately Seritta was exhilarated by their comments. To her, the concerned remarks only proved that her diet was working. At last, she had mastered her hunger, eating, and weight.

Seritta's diet was extreme and rigid. She ate breakfast and lunch on her own and adhered obsessively to her routine. Breakfast consisted of one slice of dry wheat toast and a small glass of orange juice. Lunch was either an apple or a small salad without dressing. In between meals, Seritta drank several diet colas, which helped her control her constant, gnawing appetite. Dinner typically was a family meal whether Seritta was at her mom's or her dad's house. During these meals, Seritta picked at whatever she was served. Often her parents would lecture her or plead with her to eat more, and Seritta typically would eat a bit in an attempt to appease them. On occasion, perhaps once a week, Seritta would force herself to vomit after dinner if she felt that she had been made to eat too much.

In talking with the psychologist, Seritta agreed that she understood why everyone was concerned about her health. She knew about anorexia nervosa, which she realized was a serious problem. Seritta even hinted that she recognized that she herself was suffering from anorexia nervosa. Nevertheless, Seritta steadfastly denied that she needed to gain weight. Although she was happy to talk with the psychologist, she was not prepared to change her eating habits. Seritta was deathly afraid that eating even a little more normally would cause her to "lose control" and "turn into a blimp." Perhaps more importantly, she was *proud* of her mastery of her hunger. She was not about to give up the control she had fought so hard to obtain. ₩

Typical Symptoms and Associated Features of Anorexia Nervosa

Seritta showed all the classic symptoms that define anorexia nervosa: extreme emaciation, a disturbed perception of her own body, an intense fear of gaining weight, and the cessation of menstruation (in women). Seritta also exhibited a number of problems that are commonly associated with anorexia nervosa but are not defining symptoms. These include her obsessive preoccupation with food, her occasional purging, and her central and "successful" struggle for control over her persistent hunger. Finally, Seritta did not suffer from a few important problems that are sometimes associated with anorexia nervosa, particularly mood disturbance, sexual difficulties, a lack of impulse control, and medical problems secondary to the weight loss. The core symptoms of anorexia nervosa are generally the same, but the symptoms and associated features can vary from person to person. Eating disorders among men are especially likely to include unique features, as we examine in Further Thoughts on page 271.

Refusal to Maintain a Normal Weight

The most obvious and most dangerous symptom of anorexia nervosa is *a refusal to maintain a minimally normal body weight.* Many instances of anorexia nervosa begin with a diet designed to lose just a few pounds. In anorexia nervosa, however, the diet goes awry, and losing weight eventually becomes the key focus of the individual's life. Weight falls below the normal range for age, height, and body type, and it often plummets to dangerously low levels. Another pattern is when a developing adolescent fails to make expected weight gains as a result of dieting.

The DSM-IV contains no formal cutoff as to how thin is too thin, but it suggests 85 percent of expected body weight as a rough guideline. Unlike Seritta, who was fortunate in this sense, some people with anorexia nervosa are not treated until their weight loss becomes life-threatening. In fact, experts estimate that over 10 percent of people admitted to university hospitals with anorexia nervosa die of starvation, suicide, or medical complications stemming from their extreme weight loss (APA, 1994; Hsu, 1995).

further thoughts

Eating Disorders in Males

Both anorexia nervosa and bulimia nervosa are approximately 10 times more common among females than males, but eating disorders *do* occur among males. What do psychologists know about eating disorders among males? For both females and males, the disorders typically begin during adolescence or young adulthood, but men who develop eating disorders deviate far from the expected cultural norm. Peers, therapists, and even females with eating disorders may reject and stigmatize a male who develops an eating problem precisely because his appearance differs so much from the standard for men. The social isolation of a man with an eating disorder can become an important issue in treatment, and it greatly affects one common symptom of anorexia nervosa. As we have discussed, females with anorexia nervosa typically view their appearance and disorder positively, perhaps even with a degree of pride. In contrast, anorexia nervosa is much more likely to have a negative effect on the self-esteem of a male, because weight and/or eating struggles are "unmanly," that is, different from the cultural image of the ideal male (Andersen, 1995).

Eating disorders are more common among certain subgroups of males than in the general population. Male wrestlers have a particularly high prevalence of eating disorders, a result of the intense pressure to "make weight"—to weigh below the weight cutoffs used to group competitors in a wrestling match. Eating disorders also are more common among gay than heterosexual men, although only about 20 percent of men with eating disorders are gay. Finally, men with eating disorders are likelier to have a history of obesity in comparison to women with eating disorders (Andersen, 1995).

Other aspects of eating disorders appear to be similar for males and females, including the age of onset. Attempts to predict risk among adolescent boys have not been as successful as among teenage girls, however, in part because prediction is made difficult by the relatively small number of boys with eating problems (Leon et al., 1995). Still, more research is needed, even though eating disorders are comparatively infrequent among boys. It would be particularly interesting to study the influence of cultural standards and personal ideals for body weight and shape in males. Such research might shed light on the development of eating disorders not only among boys but also among girls. ⚜

Disturbance in Perceiving or Evaluating Weight or Shape

distorted body image A perceptual inaccuracy in evaluating body size and shape that sometimes is found in anorexia nervosa.

A second defining symptom of anorexia nervosa involves a perceptual, cognitive, or affective disturbance in evaluating one's weight and shape. Like Seritta, many individuals with anorexia nervosa steadfastly *deny problems with their weight*. Even when confronted with the possibility of medical complications or with their own withered image in a mirror, some people with anorexia nervosa nevertheless insist that their weight is not a problem.

Other people with the disorder apparently suffer from a *disturbance in the way body weight or shape is experienced*. Some experts claim that this symptom stems from a **distorted body image,** an inaccuracy in how people with anorexia nervosa actually perceive their body size and shape. However, many people without the disorder inaccurately estimate the size of their body (Garfinkel, Kennedy, & Kaplan, 1995; Thompson, 1996).

Thus not all people with anorexia nervosa have a distorted body image or deny problems with their weight. At a minimum, however, all people with the disorder are *unduly influenced by their body weight or shape in self-evaluation*. Experts agree that, whatever its specific form, a defining characteristic of anorexia nervosa is a disturbance in the way one's body or weight is perceived or evaluated. People with anorexia nervosa do not recognize their emaciation for what it is, a misrepresentation that may continue to perplex victims who have recovered from the disorder. After returning to a more normal weight, many former sufferers recognize their past distortions but can't explain the reasons for their misperception.

Fear of Gaining Weight

An intense fear of becoming fat is a third central characteristic of anorexia, as Seritta also demonstrated. The fear of gaining weight presents particular problems for treatment. A therapist's encouragement to eat more can terrify a client with anorexia nervosa. The client fears that relaxing

amenorrhea The absence of at least three consecutive menstrual cycles; a defining symptom of anorexia nervosa in females.

control, even just a little, will lead to a total loss of control. Ironically, the fear of gaining weight is not soothed by the tremendous weight loss. In fact, the fear may grow more intense as the individual loses more weight (APA, 1994).

Cessation of Menstruation

Amenorrhea, the absence of at least three consecutive menstrual cycles, is the fourth and final defining symptom of anorexia nervosa in females. Many people with anorexia nervosa also have sexual difficulties, particularly a lack of interest in sex. The amenorrhea and sexuality symptoms have led to much speculation concerning the role of sex and sexual maturation in the etiology of anorexia nervosa. However, evidence indicates that amenorrhea typically is a *reaction* to the physiological changes produced by anorexia nervosa, specifically a low level of estrogen secretion, and not a symptom that precedes the disorder (APA, 1994). Sexual disinterest also is a common reaction to severe weight loss (Keys et al., 1950).

Medical Complications

Anorexia nervosa can cause a number of *medical complications.* People with anorexia commonly complain about constipation, abdominal pain, intolerance to cold, and lethargy. Some of these complaints stem from the effects of semistarvation on blood pressure and body temperature, both of which may fall below normal. In addition, the person's skin can become dry and cracked, and some people develop *lanugo,* a fine, downy hair, on their face or trunk of their bodies. Broader medical difficulties that can result from anorexia nervosa include anemia, impaired kidney functioning, cardiovascular difficulties, dental erosion, and osteopenia (bone loss) (Pomeroy, 1996). A particularly dangerous medication complication is an *electrolyte imbalance,* a disturbance in the levels of potassium, sodium, calcium, and other vital elements found in bodily fluids that can lead to cardiac arrest or kidney failure. Anorexia nervosa may begin with the seemingly harmless desire to be a bit thinner or more attractive, but the eating disorder can lead to serious health problems and even death.

Struggle for Control

Although some people with eating disorders act impulsively, clinical accounts and some research indicate that people suffering from anorexia nervosa are likelier to exhibit *excessive conformity* and a paramount *struggle for control.* In one sense, anorexia nervosa is the height of "success" in self-control. The individual with anorexia nervosa has all but conquered one of our most basic biological needs. Consistent with this view, people with anorexia nervosa often take great pride in their self-denial. They feel like masters of control. As we discuss in considering the etiology of the disorder, some theorists speculate that the disorder develops out of a desperate pursuit for control. Excessively compliant "good girls" may find that they can govern at least one area of their lives by obsessively regulating their eating behaviors (Bruch, 1982).

Comorbid Psychological Disorders

Anorexia nervosa may be associated with other psychological problems, particularly obsessive–compulsive disorder (Kasvikis et al., 1986), obsessive–compulsive personality disorder (Gillberg, Rastam, & Gillberg, 1995), and depression (Braun, Sunday, & Halmi, 1994). In many cases, however, these comorbid psychological problems may be reactions to anorexia, not causes or associated features of the disorder.

People with anorexia nervosa *are* obsessed with food and diet, and they often follow compulsive rituals around eating. However, a unique study found that obsessive–compulsive behavior can result from starvation rather than cause it. In this study, 32 World War II conscientious objectors fulfilled their military obligation by voluntarily undergoing semistarvation for 24 weeks. (The researchers wanted to learn about the effects of starvation on military personnel in the field.) As the men reduced their food intake and lost more and more weight, they developed extensive obsessions about food and compulsive eating rituals. For many of the men, in fact, the obsessions and compulsions continued long after they returned to their normal weight (Keys et al., 1950). Thus obsessive–compulsive personality disorder may sometimes contribute to anorexia nervosa, but some obsessive–compulsive *behavior* may be a reaction to starvation.

We also need to consider cause and effect carefully when considering the depressive symptoms that commonly accompany anorexia nervosa. Most people with anorexia nervosa show symptoms of mild depression, such as sad moods, irritability, insomnia, social withdrawal, and diminished interest in sex (Braun, Sunday, & Halmi, 1994). Like obsessive–compulsive behavior, however, depression has been found to be a common secondary reaction to starvation. Although mood disturbances sometimes seem to play a role in the development of anorexia nervosa, depression also can be a reaction to the eating disorder (Cooper, 1995; Hsu, 1990).

Finally, we should note that anorexia often co-occurs with the symptoms of bulimia, as we discuss in the following section.

Typical Symptoms and Associated Features of Bulimia Nervosa

Olympic-class gymnast Christy Heinrich with her boyfriend in 1993. After a 5-year struggle with anorexia nervosa, she died of multiple organ failure in 1994. She weighed less than 50 pounds at the time.

Bulima nervosa and anorexia nervosa share many other similarities in addition to the overlap in the symptoms of binge eating and purging. One important connection is that many people with bulimia nervosa have a history of anorexia nervosa, as was the circumstance in the following case study.

Michelle's frequent struggles with binge eating and purging, her sense of lost control during a binge, and her undue focus on her weight and figure are the core symptoms that define bulimia nervosa. Depression also is commonly associated with the disorder, as it was for Michelle despite her continual struggle to hide her unhappiness from those around her. In addition to depression, substance abuse (see Chapter 11) and personality disorders frequently are comorbid with bulimia nervosa.

case study

Bulimia Nervosa

Michelle was a sophomore at a state university when she first sought help for a humiliating problem. Several times a week, she fell into an episode of uncontrollable binge eating followed by self-induced vomiting. The episodes were particularly likely to occur on "bad days," of which Michelle had many. Michelle had enough control to limit her binge eating to periods when her roommate was away. But when Michelle was alone and feeling badly, she typically would buy a half-gallon of ice cream and perhaps a bag of cookies, and bring the food back to her room where she secretly gorged herself. The binge brought her some comfort when she first started eating, but when she was finished, she felt physically uncomfortable, sickened by her lack of control, and terrified of gaining weight. To compensate, she would walk across the street to an empty bathroom in the psychology department. There, she forced herself to vomit by sticking her finger down her throat.

The vomiting brought relief from the physical discomfort and fear of gaining weight, but it did not relieve her shame. Michelle decided to seek treatment only when a friend from her psychology class discovered her purging in the bathroom. The friend also had a history of bulimia nervosa, but she had gotten her eating under control. She convinced Michelle to try therapy.

Michelle's eating problems actually began when she was in high school. She had studied ballet since she was 8 years old, and with the stern encouragement of her instructor she had struggled to maintain her willowy figure as she became an adolescent. At first she dieted openly, but her parents constantly criticized her inadequate eating. In order to appease them, Michelle occasionally would eat a normal meal but force herself to vomit shortly afterwards. When she was a junior in high school, Michelle's parents confronted her and brought her to a psychologist, who treated her for anorexia nervosa. She was 5 feet 6 inches tall at the time, but she weighed only 95 pounds. Michelle was furious at her parents and refused to talk in any

continued

depth with the therapist. She allowed herself to gain a few pounds—to about 105—only to convince her parents that she did not need treatment.

Throughout most of her college years, she starved herself all week so she could eat normally on dates during the weekend. Occasionally, she forced herself to vomit after eating too much, but she did not see this as a big problem. Until the previous summer, she had maintained her weight near her goal of 105 pounds. Over the summer, however, Michelle relaxed her diet considerably as she "partied" with old friends. She gained about 15 pounds, a healthy weight for her height and body type. When she returned to college, however, Michelle became disgusted with her appearance and fearful of gaining even more weight.

When she started her current school year, Michelle started to purge more frequently in an increasingly desperate attempt to lose weight, but she soon found herself binge eating more frequently too. Michelle was extremely frustrated by her "lack of self-control" over her binge eating/purging and her inability to lose weight. Although she now recognized her past problems

with anorexia nervosa, Michelle openly longed for the discipline she had once achieved over her hunger and diet.

By all outward appearances, Michelle was a bright, attractive, successful, and happy young woman. Nevertheless, she admitted to her new therapist that she felt like a failure and a "fake." She longed to have a long-term dating relationship, but although she dated a lot, she had never had a real boyfriend. She also was intensely if privately competitive with her girlfriends. She wanted to be more beautiful and intelligent than other girls, but she inevitably felt inferior to one classmate or another. She had been determined at least to be thinner than her girlfriends, but she felt that she had lost all control over this goal. Michelle also was furious with her parents. Their constant questions about her well-being caused her to feel angry and resentful instead of loved and supported. Michelle viewed her parents as intrusive in their concerns but emotionally distant at the same time. In her mind, they asked all the right questions, but they cared more about the family's image than about Michelle as a person. Michelle pretended to be happy and normal, but inside she felt as though she was going to explode. ₩

binge eating   Eating an amount of food in a fixed period of time that is clearly larger than most people would eat under similar circumstances. One part of the eating disorder of bulimia nervosa.

Binge Eating

Binge eating is defined in DSM-IV as eating an amount of food in a fixed period of time (e.g., less than 2 hours) that is clearly larger than most people would eat under similar circumstances. Variations in normal eating complicate these alternative definitions, however, as eating a very large number of calories may be normal under certain circumstances and having two cookies may be considered a "binge" by other people. Thus the present DSM-IV definition relies on a clinician's judgment about normal eating patterns (Garfinkel et al., 1995).

Sadly, many of the inappropriate eating behaviors that are symptoms of bulimia nervosa border on being statistically normal—and clearly unhealthy—in our food- and weight-obsessed society. Over 35 percent of people report occasional binge eating. Distressingly large numbers of people also report that they fast (29 percent) and use self-induced vomiting (8 percent) or laxatives (over 5 percent) in an attempt to compensate for their eating (Fairburn & Beglin, 1990).

Binges may be planned in advance, or they may begin spontaneously. In either case, binges typically are secret. Most people with bulimia nervosa are ashamed of their eating problems and often go to elaborate efforts to conceal their binge eating. During a binge, the individual typically eats very rapidly and soon feels uncomfortably full. Although the types of foods that are consumed can vary widely, the person often selects ice cream, cookies, or other foods that are high in calories. Foods also may be selected for smooth texture to make vomiting easier (e.g., ice cream).

Binge eating is commonly triggered by an unhappy mood, which may begin with an interpersonal conflict, self-criticism about weight or appearance, or intense hunger following a period of fasting. The binge initially is comforting and alleviates some of the person's unhappy feelings, but physical discomfort and fear of gaining weight soon override the positive aspects of binge eating (Garfinkel et al., 1995).

Some individuals experience a binge as a "feeding frenzy," where they lose all control and eat compulsively and rapidly. Others describe the *lack of control* as a dissociative experience, as if they were watching themselves gorge. It should be noted, however, that people with the disorder do not experience the lack of control as absolute. For example, they can stop if someone unexpectedly interrupts them during an episode of binge eating. In fact, as the disorder progresses, some people feel more in control of their eating during a binge. Nevertheless, they are still unable to stop the broader cycle of binge eating and compensatory behavior.

Inappropriate Compensatory Behavior

The inappropriate compensatory behaviors that follow binge eating can take a number of forms. Almost all people with bulimia nervosa engage in **purging**, designed to eliminate the consumed food from the body. The most common form of purging is self-induced vomiting; as many as 90 percent of people with bulimia nervosa engage in this behavior (APA, 1994). Vomiting brings immediate relief from the physical discomfort caused by a binge, and it reduces morbid fears of gaining weight. Other less common forms of purging include the misuse of laxatives, diuretics (which increase the frequency of urination), and most rarely, enemas. Vomiting prevents the absorption of only about half the calories consumed during a binge, and laxatives, diuretics, and enemas have few lasting effects on calories or weight (Kaye et al., 1993).

Compensatory behaviors other than purging include extreme exercise or rigid fasting following a binge. The extent to which these actions actually compensate for binge eating also is questionable, given what we know about the body's biological regulation of weight, a topic we discuss later in this chapter (Brownell & Fairburn, 1995).

Excessive Emphasis on Weight and Shape

The self-esteem and much of the daily routine of people with bulimia nervosa center around weight and diet. Some people with bulimia nervosa are exhilarated by positive comments or interest in their appearance, but their esteem crashes and burns if a negative comment is made or if someone else draws more attention. Other people with the disorder constantly criticize their appearance, and the struggle with binge eating and purging only adds to their self-denigration.

Comorbid Psychological Disorders

Not surprisingly, depression is common among individuals with bulimia nervosa, especially those who self-induce vomiting (APA, 1994). Some individuals clearly become depressed prior to developing the eating disorder, and the bulimia may be a reaction to the depression in some of these cases. In many instances, however, depression begins at the same time as or follows the onset of bulimia nervosa (Braun et al., 1994). In such circumstances, the depression may be a reaction to the bulimia rather than a cause of it. In support of this view, evidence indicates that depression often lifts following successful treatment of bulimia nervosa, as we discuss in more detail when considering treatment (Mitchell et al., 1990).

Other psychological disorders that may co-occur with bulimia nervosa include anxiety disorders, personality disorders (particularly borderline personality disorder), and substance abuse, particularly excessive use of alcohol and/or stimulants. Although each of these psychological difficulties presents special challenges in treating bulimia, the comorbidity with depression is the most common and most significant clinical concern (Brewerton et al., 1995).

Medical Complications

A number of medical complications can result from bulimia nervosa. Repeated vomiting can erode dental enamel, particularly on the front teeth, and in severe cases teeth can become chipped and ragged-looking. Repeated vomiting can also produce a gag reflex that is triggered too easily and perhaps unintentionally. One consequence of the sensitized gag reflex—one that is just beginning to be reported in the scientific literature—is *rumination,* the regurgitation and rechewing of food (Parry-Jones, 1994). Another possible medical complication is the enlargement of the salivary glands, a consequence that has the ironic effect of making the sufferer's face appear puffy. As in anorexia nervosa, potentially serious medical complications can result from electrolyte imbalances. Finally, rupture of the esophagus or stomach has been reported in rare cases, sometimes leading to death (Pomeroy, 1996).

purging   An intentional act designed to eliminate consumed food from the body. Self-induced vomiting is the most common form.

Classification of Eating Disorders

Brief Historical Perspective

Isolated cases of eating disorders have been reported throughout history. In fact, the term *anorexia nervosa* was coined in 1874 by a British physician, Sir William Withey Gull (1816–1890). Still, the history of professional concern with the disorders is very brief. References to eating disorders were rare in the literature prior to 1960, and the disorders have received scientific attention only in recent decades (Hsu, 1990; Yates, 1989). In fact, the term *bulimia nervosa* was used for the first time only in 1979 (Russell, 1979).

The diagnoses of anorexia nervosa and bulimia nervosa first appeared in the DSM in 1980 (DSM-III), and although the diagnostic criteria have changed somewhat, the same eating behaviors remain as the central features of these disorders. The only major change in DSM-IV was the creation of a separate diagnostic category for eating disorders. They previously had been listed as a subtype of the Disorders Usually First Diagnosed in Infancy, Childhood, or Adolescence (see Chapter 14), because most eating disorders begin during the teenage years. The new, separate diagnostic grouping reflects the fact that eating disorders sometimes begin during adult life, as well as a more general recognition of the importance of these psychological problems.

Contemporary Classification

ANOREXIA NERVOSA

The DSM-IV contains only two subtypes of eating disorders: anorexia nervosa and bulimia nervosa. Anorexia nervosa is defined by four symptoms: (1) a refusal to maintain weight at or above minimally normal weight for age and height; (2) an intense fear of gaining weight; (3) a disturbance in the way weight or body shape is experienced, undue influence of weight or body shape on self-evaluation, or denial of the seriousness of low body weight; and (4) amenorrhea, the absence of menstruation, in postmenarcheal females (see Table 10–1).

The DSM-IV includes two subtypes of anorexia nervosa. The *restricting type* includes people who rarely engage in binge eating or purging behavior. In contrast, the *binge-eating/purging type* is defined by regular binge eating and purging during the course of the disorder. People with the binge-eating/purging type make up approximately half of those people with anorexia nervosa, and, in comparison to the restricting type, they are likelier to have weighed more before the illness began, to come from families where obesity is more common, to show various problems with impulse control such as substance abuse or impulsive sexual behavior, and to have more personality disorders (Agras, 1987; Garfinkel et al., 1995).

As we noted earlier, however, many people with anorexia nervosa purge following normal or even restricted eating, not following a binge. Should these people be considered the restricting type or the binge-eating/purging type? Evidence suggests that purging, not binge eating, is the key to distinguishing the subtypes. In a study that compared a sample of 116 pure restricters with both binge-purge ($N = 190$) and purge only ($N = 74$) subjects, both of the groups who purged were found to be older, to have had a longer history of anorexia nervosa, to have more obesity in their families, to engage in more impulsive behavior, and to suffer from more psychopathology in comparison to the pure restricters (Garner, Garner, & Rosen, 1993). Thus it is appropriate that the DSM-IV defines the binge-eating/purging subtype in terms of either binge eating *or* purging (see Table 10–1).

BULIMIA NERVOSA

Bulimia nervosa is defined by five symptoms: (1) recurrent episodes of binge eating over which the individual feels a lack of control; (2) recurrent inappropriate compensatory behavior; (3) an average frequency of at least two episodes per week over a period of at least 3 months; (4) undue influence of weight and body shape on self-evaluation; and (5) the disturbance does not occur solely during episodes of anorexia nervosa (see Table 10–2 on page 278).

TABLE 10–1

DSM-IV Diagnostic Criteria for Anorexia Nervosa

A. **REFUSAL TO MAINTAIN BODY WEIGHT AT OR ABOVE A MINIMALLY NORMAL WEIGHT FOR AGE AND HEIGHT (E.G., WEIGHT LOSS LEADING TO MAINTENANCE OF BODY WEIGHT LESS THAN 85 PERCENT OF THAT EXPECTED; OR FAILURE TO MAKE EXPECTED WEIGHT GAIN DURING PERIOD OF GROWTH, LEADING TO BODY WEIGHT LESS THAN 85 PERCENT OF THAT EXPECTED)**

B. **INTENSE FEAR OF GAINING WEIGHT OR BECOMING FAT, EVEN THOUGH UNDERWEIGHT.**

C. **DISTURBANCE IN THE WAY IN WHICH ONE'S WEIGHT OR SHAPE IS EXPERIENCED, UNDUE INFLUENCE OF BODY WEIGHT OR SHAPE ON SELF-EVALUATION, OR DENIAL OF THE SERIOUSNESS OF THE CURRENT LOW BODY WEIGHT.**

D. **IN POSTMENARCHEAL FEMALES, AMENORRHEA, THAT IS, THE ABSENCE OF AT LEAST THREE CONSECUTIVE MENSTRUAL CYCLES.**

Specify type:

Restricting type: During the current episode, the person has not regularly engaged in binge eating or purging behavior.

Binge-eating/purging type: During the current episode, the person has regularly engaged in binge eating or purging behavior.

Bulimia nervosa also is divided into two subtypes in the DSM-IV. The *purging type* is characterized by the regular use of self-induced vomiting or the misuse of laxatives, diuretics, or enemas. The individual with the *nonpurging type* of bulimia nervosa does not regularly purge but instead attempts to compensate for binge eating with fasting or excessive exercise. The purging subtype of bulimia nervosa is more common and is associated with more frequent binge eating, more psychopathology (particularly depression), and more family dysfunction, including parental discord and child sexual abuse (Agras, 1991; Garfinkel, Lin, & Goering, in press; McCann et al., 1991).

BINGE EATING DISORDER AND OBESITY

There has been some debate about whether other eating problems should be included in the DSM-IV list of eating disorders. **Binge eating disorder** is one problem that was given extensive consideration. In fact, provisional diagnostic criteria for binge eating disorder are included in an appendix of DSM-IV for diagnostic categories requiring further study. The proposed disorder involves episodes of binge eating much like those found in bulimia nervosa but without compensatory behavior.

Research has demonstrated that binge eating is associated with a number of psychological and physical difficulties other than anorexia nervosa and bulimia nervosa (Fairburn & Wilson, 1993). Among these problems is **obesity,** or excess body fat, a circumstance that roughly corresponds with a body weight 20 percent *above* the expected weight. A cutoff of 40 percent above normal is a rough marker of severe overweight (Brownell, 1995). Like binge eating, the DSM-IV committee considered classifying obesity as an eating disorder, but too little information was available to justify this move (Garfinkel et al., 1995). Calling obesity a "mental disorder" is controversial, moreover, especially given the high prevalence of overweight individuals in the United States and throughout the world.

Epidemiology of Eating Disorders

Estimates of the epidemiology of anorexia and bulimia vary, but it is clear that the prevalence of both disorders has increased dramatically since the 1960s and 1970s (Hoek, 1995; Kendler et al., 1991). Figure 10–2 illustrates the surge in the number of new cases of anorexia nervosa based on

binge eating disorder A controversial diagnosis defined by repeated episodes of binge eating but in the absence of compensatory behavior; included in an appendix of DSM-IV.

obesity Excess body fat, a circumstance that roughly corresponds with a body weight 20 percent above the expected weight.

cohort   A group that shares some feature in common, particularly their date of birth.

TABLE 10–2

DSM-IV Diagnostic Criteria for Bulimia Nervosa

A. **RECURRENT EPISODES OF BINGE EATING. AN EPISODE OF BINGE EATING IS CHARACTERIZED BY BOTH OF THE FOLLOWING:**
   1. Eating, in a discrete period of time (e.g., within any 2-hour period), an amount of food that is definitely larger than most people would eat during a similar period of time and under similar circumstances.
   2. A sense of lack of control over eating during the episode (e.g., a feeling that one cannot stop eating or control what or how much one is eating).

B. **RECURRENT INAPPROPRIATE COMPENSATORY BEHAVIOR IN ORDER TO PREVENT WEIGHT GAIN, SUCH AS SELF-INDUCED VOMITING; MISUSE OF LAXATIVES, DIURETICS, ENEMAS, OR OTHER MEDICATIONS; FASTING; OR EXCESSIVE EXERCISE.**

C. **THE BINGE EATING AND INAPPROPRIATE COMPENSATORY BEHAVIORS BOTH OCCUR, ON AVERAGE, AT LEAST TWICE A WEEK FOR 3 MONTHS.**

D. **SELF-EVALUATION IS UNDULY INFLUENCED BY BODY SHAPE AND WEIGHT.**

E. **THE DISTURBANCE DOES NOT OCCUR EXCLUSIVELY DURING EPISODES OF ANOREXIA NERVOSA.**

Specify type:

Purging type: During the current episode, the person has regularly engaged in self-induced vomiting or the misuse of laxatives, diuretics, or enemas.

Nonpurging type: During the current episode, the person has used other inappropriate compensatory behaviors, such as fasting or excessive exercise, but has not regularly engaged in self-induced vomiting or the misuse of laxatives, diuretics, or enemas.

one investigator's compilation of evidence from a number of different studies (Hoek, 1995). According to this summary, the annual *incidence* (i.e., number of new cases each year) of anorexia nervosa rose from 1 case per million people in 1930–1940 to over 50 cases per million people in 1980–1990. Figure 10–2 also suggests that anorexia nervosa is rare in the general population. It is far more common among certain segments of the population, however, particularly among young women. The DSM-IV indicates that anorexia nervosa is found among 0.5 to 1.0 percent of females in adolescence or early adulthood, a figure that is consistent with empirical estimates of the prevalence of the disorder (Hoek, 1995).

Recent decades also seem to have witnessed a torrent of new cases of bulimia nervosa. Changes in the incidence of bulimia nervosa are difficult to document, however, because the diagnostic term was introduced only in 1979.

Figure 10–3 (page 280) portrays lifetime prevalence rates of bulimia nervosa among a large sample of American women who were born either before 1950, between 1950 and 1959, or in 1960 or after. The lifetime prevalence of bulimia nervosa was far greater among the **cohort** (a group that shares some feature in common, particularly time of birth) of women born after 1960 than it was for the cohort of women born before 1950. The risk for women born between 1950 and 1959 was intermediate between these two extremes (Kendler et al., 1991). Thus the recent surge of cases of bulimia nervosa is not due to a general increase among all women but instead results from a flood of cases—some say an epidemic—among women born after 1960.

Figure 10–3 also shows that new cases of bulimia nervosa develop among women in their twenties and their thirties. Still, the risk of developing the disorder declines with increasing age, at least among older cohorts. The curve flattens at older ages, an indication of the discovery of fewer and fewer new cases among older women.

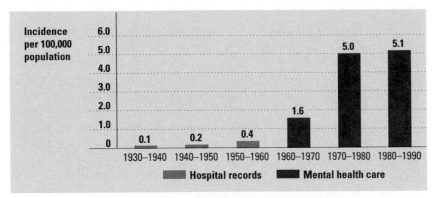

Figure 10–2   Incidence of Anorexia Nervosa, 1930–1990.   Anorexia nervosa has increased dramatically in recent decades. This figure portrays the annual incidence per 100,000 people in the general population based on data pooled from studies of hospital records and outpatient mental health care. Considerably higher rates are found among population subgroups, particularly young women.

Source: H.W. Hoek, 1995, The distribution of eating disorders. In K.D. Brownell and C.G. Fairbanks (Eds.), *Eating Disorders and Obesity: A Comprehensive Handbook,* p. 209. New York: Guildford.

Although the frequency of both disorders has increased dramatically since the 1960s and 1970s, experts agree that bulimia nervosa is far more common than anorexia nervosa (Fairburn, Hay, & Welch, 1993; Hoek, 1995). According to DSM-IV, bulimia nervosa occurs among 1 to 3 percent of adolescent and young adult women, a rate that is 2 or 3 times the number of cases of anorexia nervosa in the same age group. As we noted earlier, moreover, the prevalence of subclinical bulimia—occasional binge eating and/or purging—is far greater than the number of cases that meet DSM-IV criteria for bulimia nervosa. Finally, we should note again that there is considerable overlap between anorexia nervosa and bulimia nervosa. About 50 percent of all people with anorexia nervosa engage in episodes of binge eating and purging (Agras, 1987; Garfinkel et al., 1995), and perhaps 30 percent of cases of bulimia nervosa have a history of anorexia nervosa (Yates, 1989).

Gender Differences and Standards of Beauty

Both anorexia and bulimia nervosa are approximately 10 times more common among women than among men. Many commentators and scientists propose that this huge difference is explained by gender roles and standards of beauty (Hsu, 1990; Striegel-Moore, 1995). Popular attitudes about women in the United States often convey the notion that "looks are everything," and thinness is essential to our dominant cultural image of good looks—and happiness. In contrast, young men are valued as much for their achievements as for their appearance, and in any case, the ideal body type for men is considerably larger than for women (Hsu, 1990; Striegel-Moore, 1995).

The growing prevalence of eating disorders in recent decades also may be explained by changing standards of beauty, as beauty increasingly has been equated with thinness. The cultural ideal of beauty is not fixed; it changes over time. For example, Marilyn Monroe, the movie idol of the 1950s, may seem rather chunky by today's standards. In fact, researchers have demonstrated the shift toward thinness in the American view of the "beautiful woman" by examining changes in the dimensions of *Playboy* centerfolds and Miss America Beauty Pageant contestants—cultural icons but dubious models for young women. Between 1959 and 1988, the ratio of weight to height of these "ideal women" has declined dramatically.

Standards of beauty are relative, not absolute. Today, eating disorders are found almost exclusively in North America, Western Europe, and Japan and other industrialized Asian countries; in other cultures, women who are more rounded are considered to be more beautiful (Hsu, 1990; Striegel-Moore, 1995; Yates, 1989). This may reflect a relationship between wealth and standards of beauty. In Third World countries where food is scarce, wealth is positively correlated with body

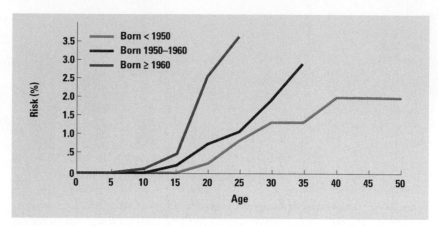

Figure 10–3   Bulimia Nervosa Among Three Cohorts of Women.   The lifetime cumulative risk for developing bulimia nervosa is far greater for women born after 1960 than for women born before 1950. The risk for developing the disorder decreases with age, at least among the earlier birth cohort. Later birth cohorts have not yet moved through the entire age of risk.

Source: K.S. Kendler, C. MacLean, M. Neale, R. Kessler, A. Heath, and L. Eaves, 1991, The genetic epidemiology of bulimia nervosa, *American Journal of Psychiatry, 148,* 1631.

weight. Being larger is a symbol of beauty and success. In industrialized nations where food is plentiful, wealth is negatively correlated with weight (Hsu, 1989). As the Western saying goes, "You can never be too rich or too thin."

Age of Onset

Both anorexia and bulimia nervosa typically begin in late adolescence or early adulthood. A significant minority of cases of anorexia nervosa begin during early adolescence, particularly as young girls approach puberty. The adolescent onset of eating disorders has provoked much speculation about their etiology. Certain characteristics of adolescence have been speculated to cause eating disorders; these include hormonal changes (Garfinkel & Garner, 1982), autonomy struggles (Minuchin, Rosman, & Baker, 1978), and problems with sexuality (Coovert, Kinder, & Thompson, 1989). Other theorists have noted that the young adolescent girl is the most idealized cultural image of beauty (Hsu, 1990; Striegel-Moore, 1995). Weight gain is normal during adolescence, but the addition of a few pounds can trouble a young woman who is focused on the numbers on her scale. Breast and hip development not only change body shape, but they also affect self-image, social interaction, and the fit of familiar clothes. As we shall see, each of these explanations may have some value in explaining the age of onset of eating disorders.

Etiological Considerations and Research

The regulation of normal eating and body weight results from a combination of biological, psychological, and social factors, and researchers have focused on each of these levels of analysis in attempting to explain the etiology of anorexia and bulimia (see Brownell & Fairburn, 1995). Scientists agree, however, that sociocultural factors are central contributors to the high rate of eating disorders found among young women today. Of course, not every young woman in the United States or other industrial countries develops an eating disorder. Even within a culture obsessed with weight, diet, and appearance, other social, psychological, and biological risk factors determine who develops anorexia nervosa or bulimia nervosa and who does not.

Social Factors

The image of the ideal woman as extremely thin and the overriding value placed on young women's appearances are basic starting points in searching for the causes of eating disorders. This statement is supported by the epidemiological evidence we have already reviewed, as well as by related findings:

- Eating disorders are even more common among young women working in fields that especially emphasize weight and appearance, such as models, ballet dancers, and gymnasts (Yates, 1989).
- Eating disturbances are more common among young women who report greater exposure to popular media, endorse more gender-role stereotypes, or internalize societal standards towards appearance (Heinberg, Thompson, & Stormer, 1995; Stice et al., 1994).
- Eating disorders are considerably more common among middle- and upper-class whites, who are especially likely to equate thinness with beauty in women. Eating disorders also are increasing among well-to-do African Americans, who increasingly hold to the thinness ideal (Hsu, 1990; Thompson, 1996; Yates, 1989).
- The prevalence of eating disorders is higher among Arab and Asian women who are living or studying in Western countries than among women living in their native country (Mumford, Whitehouse, & Platts, 1991; Nasser, 1986).

Together, these facts make it clear that adolescent girls and young women are at risk for developing eating disorders in part because they attempt to shape themselves, quite literally, to fit the image of the ideally proportioned, thin woman. Our culture needs to do a better job of teaching young women that who you are is much more important than how you look.

Rounded bodies once were the ideal of beauty for women, as illustrated in Turkish Bath, *painted by Jean Auguste Dominique Ingres in 1859–1863 (Louvre, Paris).*

enmeshed family   Families whose members are overly involved in one another's lives.

TROUBLED FAMILY RELATIONSHIPS

Other stressors must interact with the cultural diathesis to produce eating disorders. Troubled family relationships may be one such contributing factor. Researchers have documented family problems in a number of studies, but the typical patterns differ for anorexia nervosa and bulimia nervosa. Young people with bulimia nervosa report considerable conflict and rejection in their families, difficulties that also may contribute to their depression. In contrast, young people with anorexia generally perceive their families as cohesive and nonconflictual (Vandereycken, 1995; Yates, 1989).

Although the families of young people with anorexia nervosa appear to be well functioning, some theorists see the families as being too close—that is, they are **enmeshed families,** or families whose members are overly involved in one another's lives. Young people with anorexia nervosa are obsessed with controlling their eating, and according to the enmeshment hypothesis, this is because eating is the *only* thing they can control in their intrusive families (Minuchin et al., 1978). A relation between measures of conflictual but controlling parent–child relationships and anorexia nervosa has been found in some research (Humphrey, 1987), but it may be that the parents of an adolescent with anorexia nervosa become "enmeshed" as a worried reaction to their daughter's obviously emaciated appearance, not as a cause of it.

A number of clinical observers have noted that a disproportionate number of women with eating disorders report a history of sexual abuse, a terrible experience that may explain many of their concerns. (See Chapter 15 for a general discussion of child abuse and child sexual abuse.) Recent evidence indicates that sexual abuse does not play a *specific* role in the development of eating disorders. Instead, child sexual abuse apparently increases the risk for a variety of psychological problems during adult life including but not limited to eating disorders (Palmer 1995; Welch & Fairburn, in press).

Finally, we should note that there are many direct ways in which parents may influence children toward developing eating disorders (Pike & Rodin, 1991). Many parents struggle with diet

introceptive awareness Recognition of internal cues including various emotional states as well as hunger.

and thinness themselves, and they are models of overconcern for their children; other parents directly encourage their children to be extra thin as a part of the general push to compete with their peers. Parents also may help to shape personality patterns that increase the risk of eating disorders, an issue we discuss in the next section.

Psychological Factors

Researchers have suggested a number of psychological concerns as etiologic factors in eating disorders, including dissatisfaction with body image, various problems with control (including having too little and wanting too much), difficulties with sexuality, fear of autonomy, low self-esteem, perfectionism, reactions to dieting, and a number of comorbid psychological disorders, including various mood disorders, anxiety disorders, and personality disorders. It is likely that there will prove to be many alternative pathways to the development of eating disorders, not just one. Here we highlight four of the most promising approaches: control issues, depression/dysphoria, body image dissatisfaction, and reactions to dietary restraint.

A STRUGGLE FOR CONTROL

Hilde Bruch (1904–1984), a physician who fled her native Germany in 1933 to escape the Nazi regime and subsequently settled and studied psychiatry in the United States, was one of the first and most prolific clinical observers of eating disorders. Bruch strongly asserted that a *struggle for control* is the central psychological issue in the development of eating disorders (Bruch, 1982). Bruch observed that girls with eating disorders seem to be exceptionally "good"—conforming and eager to please. She further suggested that these exceptionally "good girls" give up too much of the normal adolescent struggle for autonomy, and instead they attempt to please others, particularly their parents. Bruch thus viewed their obsessive efforts to control eating and weight as a way that overly compliant "good girls" control themselves further. At the same time, she also saw their dieting as an attempt to wrest at least a little control from their parents—control over what they eat. In this struggle for control, young people with anorexia nervosa "succeed" and take considerable pride in their extreme self-control. In contrast, people with bulimia nervosa continually strive—and fail—to gain complete control over eating and weight. The success or failure of control, in turn, may explain the denial that characterizes anorexia nervosa and the humiliation that accompanies bulimia nervosa.

Researchers often use the term *perfectionism* to describe the endless pursuit of control described by Bruch and other clinicians. Perfectionists set unrealistically high standards, are self-critical, and demand a performance from themselves that is higher than is required by a given situation. Research demonstrates that young women with eating disorders endorse perfectionist goals both about eating and weight and about general expectations for themselves (Bastiani et al., 1995; Garner, Olmstead, & Polivy, 1983). Moreover, some evidence indicates that unrealistically high standards persist among women with anorexia nervosa even after they return to a more normal weight (Bastiani et al., 1995).

Young people with eating disorders may also try to control their own emotions excessively, perhaps as a result of their constant attempt to please others instead of themselves (Bruch, 1982). The result may be a lack of **introceptive awareness,** recognition of internal cues including various emotional states as well as hunger. Simply put, people with eating disorders may be unaware of their own needs and feelings. In fact, one of the largest studies of the development of eating disorders found that a measure of lack of introceptive awareness not only predicted the presence of concurrent eating disorders but also predicted the development of eating disorders 2 years in the future (Leon et al., 1993; Leon et al., 1995). Thus excessive external control, perfectionism, and a lack of introceptive awareness appear to be one cluster of psychological contributions to the development of eating disorders.

DEPRESSION, LOW SELF-ESTEEM, AND DYSPHORIA

Depression is another psychological factor that may contribute to eating disorders, particularly to bulimia nervosa. Researchers have found an increased prevalence of depression not only among

Caraline, 28 years old, told a reporter, "I'm not telling you how much I weigh because I'm ashamed I don't weigh less." She later died of complications due to anorexia nervosa.

people with eating disorders but also among the members of their families (Strober, 1995). This has led some experts to speculate that the two problems are etiologically related. In support of this theory, research indicates that antidepressant medications are effective in reducing some symptoms of bulimia nervosa (Mitchell, Raymond, & Specker, 1993).

Other experts suggest, however, that depression may be a reaction to developing bulimia nervosa and especially a reaction to the onset of anorexia nervosa (Hsu, 1990; Yates, 1989). In support of this alternative view, research indicates that depression improves markedly following successful group psychotherapy for bulimia (Mitchell et al., 1990). Moreover, in one large study a measure of depression failed to predict either concurrent or future eating disorders (Leon et al., 1995). Another study of anorexia nervosa found considerable depression at the time of the original diagnosis but not at a 6-year follow-up (Rastam, Gillberg, & Gillberg, 1995). Thus clinical depression may contribute to the development of eating disorders in a subset of cases, but in most eating disorders, depression appears to be a secondary problem and not the primary issue.

Despite these conclusions, many researchers and clinicians suggest that depressive *symptoms,* and not necessarily clinical depression, are central factors in various specific aspects of eating disorders. Low self-esteem is a particular concern. More specifically, many observers note that women with eating disorders are preoccupied with their *social self* (Jones, 1985; Striegel-Moore, Silberstein, & Rodin, 1993). The social self includes both how we present ourselves in public and how other people perceive and evaluate us. Lacking the confidence and esteem to "be yourself," young people instead may present a facade to the world. Such people may be happy when they get positive reactions from others but distraught when they get negative reactions or no response at all. They may act like "fakes," feel like "frauds," and depend on others' reactions for self-esteem.

Researchers are just beginning to examine these intuitively appealing ideas. Evidence indicates that women with bulimia nervosa or a negative body image report more public self-consciousness, social anxiety, and perceived fraudulence in comparison to other women (Striegel-Moore et al., 1993).

Depressive symptoms also clearly play a role in maintaining problematic eating behaviors. Dysphoria or negative mood states commonly trigger episodes of binge eating in bulimia nervosa and in the binge-eating/purging subtype of anorexia nervosa. The dysphoria may be brought on by social criticism or conflict, dissatisfaction with eating and diet, or an ongoing depressive episode.

Psychiatrist Hilde Bruch (1904–1984) was an early and prolific clinical observer who viewed the young woman's struggle for control as a central issue in the development of eating disorders.

NEGATIVE BODY IMAGE

A *negative body image,* a highly critical evaluation of one's weight and shape, is another psychological factor that has long been thought to contribute to the development of eating disorders (Bruch, 1962). Psychologists have used a number of techniques to evaluate a negative body image, including self-report measures, callipers or other devices used to directly estimate the size of various body parts (Thompson, 1996).

Early studies of body image in eating disorders focused on a *distorted* body image, a perceptual inaccuracy in judging one's size, particularly in cases of anorexia nervosa. Current research focuses on *dissatisfaction* with one's body image, a negative evaluation of one's body that includes cognitive and affective elements and not just perceptual distortions. Thus one way to assess a negative body image is to compare people's ratings of their "current" and "ideal" size. Several longitudinal studies have found negative evaluations of weight, shape, and appearance to predict the subsequent development of disordered eating (Attie & Brooks-Gunn, 1989; Cattarin & Thompson, 1994; Striegel-Moore et al., 1989).

DIETARY RESTRAINT

Some of the symptoms of eating disorders are likely to be effects of *dietary restraint,* that is, direct consequences of restricted eating (Heatherton & Polivy, 1992; Herman & Polivy, 1988). This is ironic, because many of the "out-of-control" symptoms of eating disorders appear to be caused by inappropriate efforts to control eating. These symptoms include binge eating, preoccupation with food, and perhaps out-of-control feelings of hunger.

Inappropriate dieting appears to contribute directly to subsequent binge eating. An overly restrictive diet increases hunger, frustration, and lack of attention to internal cues, all of which make

weight set point Fixed weights or small ranges of weight around which the body regulates weight, for example, by increasing or decreasing metabolism.

binge eating more likely. Moreover, because "quick-fix" diets rarely work, dieters are likely to be left with a sense of failure, disappointment, and self-criticism. The negative affect, in turn, makes further binge eating likely and further lowers the self-esteem of people who already have perfectionistic standards or a negative body image (Heatherton & Polivy, 1992; Herman & Polivy, 1988).

Dietary restraint also may directly cause some of the symptoms of anorexia nervosa. As we noted earlier, military studies during World War II found that obsessive thoughts about food and compulsive eating rituals were one direct consequence of semistarvation (Keys et al., 1950). The same studies also found that during refeeding, many men felt intense, uncontrollable hunger even after eating a considerable amount of food. Perhaps a similar reaction explains some of the intense fear of losing control and gaining weight found in anorexia nervosa.

Biological Factors

Scientists conceptualize normal eating and weight regulation in systems terms, specifically as a result of the interplay among behavior (e.g., energy expenditure, eating), peripheral physiological activity (e.g., digestion, metabolism), and central physiological activity (e.g., neurotransmitter release) (Blundell, 1995). Evidence indicates that homeostatic mechanisms govern the regulation of weight. Specifically, the body maintains weight around certain **weight set points,** fixed weights or small ranges of weight. Maintaining weight near a set point is biologically adaptive. Thus, if weight declines, hunger increases, food consumption goes up, and metabolism slows in an attempt to return weight to its set point (Keesey, 1995). The process is very much like the way a thermostat regulates heating and cooling to maintain air temperature near a given setting.

From this systems perspective, it is clear that, even though they can be conceptualized in psychological terms, the effects of dietary restraint also are biological contributors to the development of eating disorders. The motivations (e.g., hunger) and behaviors (e.g., binge eating) that follow dietary restraint are a part of the body's attempts to maintain weight at a set point through behavioral actions. The body also attempts to maintain weight at a set point through physiological actions. In particular, when food intake is reduced, there is a slowing in the *metabolic rate,* the rate at which the body expends energy, and movement toward *hyperlipogenesis,* the storage of abnormally large amounts of fat in fat cells throughout the body (Brownell & Fairburn, 1995). The body does not distinguish between intentional attempts to lose weight and potential starvation.

Other evidence suggests that biological factors contribute to eating disorders through genetic mechanisms. The most extensive twin study of bulimia nervosa conducted to date found a concordance rate of 23 percent for MZ twins and 9 percent for DZ twins (Kendler et al., 1991). Higher MZ than DZ concordance rates for dysfunctional eating attitudes have also been reported (Rutherford et al., 1993).

It is important to note, however, that MZ–DZ twin differences could be explained by several different heritable mechanisms. It is unlikely that eating disorders are directly inherited, especially given the historically recent surge in prevalence rates. Rather, genetics may influence some personality characteristic that, in turn, increases the risk for bulimia nervosa (Strober, 1995). Or a certain body type or weight set point may be inherited, and this may account for the higher concordance rates found among MZ twins. If so, the well-established genetic contributions to determining weight and body type (Price & Gottesman, 1991) contribute to the development of eating disorders only when combined with cultural expectations about thinness—and with individual concerns about living up to these expectations. Genes clearly affect weight set points and body type, but we cannot mindlessly conclude that eating disorders are "genetic."

Finally, we should note that several measures of neurophysiology have been found to be linked with eating disorders, including elevations in endogenous opioids, low levels of serotonin, and diminished neuroendocrine functioning (Yates, 1990). In extremely rare cases, eating disorders have been linked with a specific biological abnormality, such as a hormonal disturbance or a lesion in the *hypothalamus,* the area of the brain that regulates routine biological functions, including appetite (see Chapter 2). The weight of current evidence suggests, however, that most biological abnormalities associated with eating disorders are either reactions to or indirect contributors to eating disorders.

getting help

Eating Disorders

Eating disorders are very common, so it is not unlikely that you or someone close to you may well be struggling with eating issues. What can help?

One step is to get more information—but you need to be careful. Some self-help books and Web sites on eating disorders offer misleading or inaccurate information. One Web site that we recommend is http://members.aol.com/edapinc, the home page of Eating Disorder Awareness & Prevention, Inc., a non-profit organization dedicated to increasing the awareness and prevention of eating disorders. The Web page of the National Institute of Mental Health, http://www.nimh.nih.gov, also contains helpful information about eating disorders, as well as other mental health problems. An excellent self-help book is *Overcoming Binge Eating* by Christopher Fairburn whose treatment research is discussed in this chapter. *Living with Anorexia and Bulimia* by James Moorey is another good book that deals with a broader range of eating issues.

If you are seriously concerned about your own eating, weight, or body shape, you should talk with a professional. Colleges and universities often have special information and treat-

ments for eating disorders. Call your student health service for information and referral. If no student health resources are available to you, another option is to talk with your family physician. You should have a physical exam to explore possible medical complications caused by your abnormal eating, and your physician also should know of a mental health professional who specializes in eating disorders. As indicated by the research we review in this chapter, some of the treatment options you should consider and discuss include cognitive behavior therapy, interpersonal therapy, family therapy, and antidepressant medication. Hospitalization may be another option, but only for very serious problems like severe weight loss.

If you are concerned about a friend's eating, you should make a plan and talk to her or him. Bring some information on local resources for treating eating disorders. And be prepared to listen as well as to talk! Your friend probably has not confided about his or her problems with many people. If your friend denies a problem, there is no point in arguing. You have done your job by raising the issue. It will be up to him or her to admit to the problems and get help. A good resource before and after talking with a friend is *Surviving an Eating Disorder: Strategies for Friends and Families* by Michele Siegel, Judith Brisman, and Margot Weinshel. ♛

Integration and Alternative Pathways

Clearly, eating disorders are best understood in terms of a systems approach. Social and cultural values that emphasize thinness, beauty, and appearance over personality are the starting point in understanding eating disorders, particularly among young women.

Although a majority of young women in the United States today are concerned with weight and shape, only a minority actually develop anorexia nervosa or bulimia nervosa. Direct risk factors that distinguish people who develop eating disorders include familial and social pressures to be thin, a negative body image, direct behavioral and biological reactions to dietary restraint, and genetic influences on body weight and shape. Less obvious risk factors include preoccupation with external evaluation, lack of awareness of internal desires, and preoccupation with conformity and self-control. In some cases, family difficulties may contribute to eating disorders, but in others, parental conflict and concern are better viewed as reactions to a child's frightening loss of weight. Similarly, comorbid mood and anxiety disorders sometimes may cause, but seemingly more often result from, eating disorders.

These latter observations underscore an important point we have emphasized throughout the text: there is no one pathway to developing any given emotional problem; rather there are many. Some women who develop eating disorders are naturally thin, but they have perfectionistic standards that drive them to be even thinner. Other women with the disorders may have genetically determined body types that are at or above normal weight, and their eating disorder is a reaction to the social criticism they feel as a result. For some people, an eating disorder is an expression of depression. Other people may develop an eating disorder because they focus too much on outward appearance instead of inner standards.

In considering the development of eating disorders, a key issue that remains unanswered is why some women develop anorexia nervosa and others develop bulimia nervosa. Many social, psychological, and biological elements of the two disorders are similar, although the symptoms and treatment (as we will soon see) of the two conditions differ widely. Future research should help uncover answers to the important question of what factors determine whether a young woman masters her appetite—and becomes emaciated as a result—or whether she continually struggles with frequent binge eating and compensatory behavior.

Treatment of Eating Disorders

The treatments for anorexia nervosa and bulimia nervosa differ in approach and effectiveness. Anorexia nervosa, particularly in severe cases, is more likely to require inpatient treatment, and the initial goal in treating anorexia nervosa is to encourage the sufferer to gain weight. Treatment of bulimia nervosa rarely requires such extreme intervention. Most effective approaches to treating bulimia nervosa focus on directly changing eating patterns. Recent evidence about the treatment of bulimia nervosa is encouraging, but attempts to treat anorexia nervosa have met with less success. For all these reasons, in the following sections we consider the treatment and course of anorexia nervosa and bulimia nervosa separately.

Treatment of Anorexia Nervosa

The treatment of anorexia nervosa usually focuses on two goals. The first goal is to help the patient gain at least a minimal amount of weight. If weight loss is severe, the patient may be treated in an inpatient setting, where clinicians may use coercive methods, such as tube or intravenous feeding, or introduce strict behavior therapy programs in which rewards (for example, social activities) are contingent on weight gain. Hospitalization also may be needed to prevent suicide, to address severe depression or medical complications, or to remove the patient temporarily from a dysfunctional social circumstance (Garner & Needleman, 1996).

The second goal in treating anorexia nervosa is more general—to address the broader difficulties that may have caused or are maintaining the disorder. Many different forms of treatment may be used to achieve this goal. The clinical literature commonly advocates family therapy. There are many different forms of family therapy, but perhaps the most common is *structural family therapy,* which views parents' interference with adolescent autonomy—and avoidance of their own disagreements—as the central problems in anorexia nervosa. Structural family therapists attempt to redefine the eating disorder as an interpersonal problem, to get the young person with anorexia nervosa out of the sick role, and to encourage parents to confront their own conflicts directly and not through their children (Minuchin et al., 1978). Some evidence indicates that family therapy for anorexia nervosa is more effective than individual treatment, at least when the client is an adolescent (Russell et al., 1987).

Clinicians have also tried a number of different individual therapies for anorexia nervosa. Three approaches of note are (1) Bruch's (1982) modified psychodynamic therapy designed to increase introceptive awareness and correct distorted perceptions of self; (2) cognitive behavioral approaches that aim to alter the belief that "weight, shape, or thinness can serve as the sole or predominant referent for inferring personal value or self-worth" (Garner & Bemis, 1982, p. 142); and (3) *feminist therapies,* which encourage young women to pursue their own values rather than blindly adopting prescribed social roles (Fallon, Katzman, & Wooley, 1994). There is currently little, if any, evidence to show that any of these treatments is effective. Similarly, medication seems to offer no relief for victims of anorexia nervosa (Garner & Needleman, 1996). Keep in mind, however, that the three approaches to individual therapy share the common goal of basing self-esteem more on internal standards and less on external evaluations. Working toward this end is a logical goal in treating and, we believe, in preventing anorexia nervosa.

Course and Outcome of Anorexia Nervosa

Evidence on the course and outcome of anorexia nervosa demonstrates that contemporary treatments are not very effective. At posttreatment follow-up assessments, 50 to 60 percent of patients have a weight within the normal range, 10 to 20 percent remain significantly below their healthy body weight, and the remainder are intermediate in weight (Hsu, 1990; Steinhausen, 1996). Perhaps as many as 10 percent starve themselves to death or die of related complications.

Although important, weight gain is not the only measure of the course of anorexia nervosa. In fact, more than half the women with a history of anorexia nervosa continue to have difficulties with eating notwithstanding gains in weight. Predictors of a better prognosis include an early age of onset, conflict-free parent–child relationships, early treatment, less weight loss, and the absence of binge eating and purging (Steinhausen, 1996).

Treatment of Bulimia Nervosa

In recent years, researchers have uncovered promising evidence of the effectiveness of several approaches to treating bulimia nervosa. The most effective forms of treatment include antidepressant medication, cognitive behavior therapy (delivered both individually and in groups), and interpersonal psychotherapy.

ANTIDEPRESSANT MEDICATIONS

All classes of antidepressant medications (see Chapter 5) have been shown to be somewhat effective in treating bulimia nervosa; however, medication is *not* the treatment of choice. Binge eating and compensatory behavior improve only among a minority of people treated with antidepressants, and relapse appears to be common when medication is stopped. Moreover, initial depression or improvement in mood state does not predict improvement in the symptoms of bulimia (Walsh, 1995). Most importantly, medication is not the treatment of choice because several studies have shown psychotherapy to be more effective.

COGNITIVE BEHAVIOR THERAPY

The most thoroughly researched psychotherapy for bulimia nervosa is cognitive behavior therapy. As developed by the British psychiatrist Christopher Fairburn, the cognitive behavioral approach views bulimia as stemming from several maladaptive tendencies, including an excessive emphasis on weight and shape in determining self-esteem; perfectionism; and dichotomous "black or white" thinking (Fairburn, 1996). Overall, cognitive behavior therapy leads to a 70 percent reduction in binge eating and purging across people in treatment. Between one-third and one-half of all clients are able to cease these patterns completely. The majority of individuals maintain these gains at 6-month to 1-year follow-up (Fairburn et al., 1993).

Group psychotherapy proved to be an effective treatment that resulted in a 90 percent reduction in episodes of binge eating. Antidepressant medication also reduced binge eating (by 65 percent), but medication was significantly less effective than psychotherapy, and women on medication also were likelier to drop out of the study. Finally, the addition of antidepressant medication (group therapy plus medication versus group therapy plus placebo) did not add significantly to the effectiveness of the group treatment for bulimia nervosa, although it led to some improvement in depression (Mitchell et al., 1990). These results and similar findings indicate that cognitive behavior therapy, not antidepressant medication, is the treatment of choice for bulimia nervosa (Fairburn, 1995; Walsh, 1995).

INTERPERSONAL PSYCHOTHERAPY

Interpersonal psychotherapy, which was originally developed for the treatment of depression (see Chapter 5), may also be an effective treatment for bulimia nervosa. This is surprising because interpersonal therapy does not address eating disorders directly but instead focuses on difficulties in close relationships. Interpersonal therapy for bulimia was initially studied when the treatment

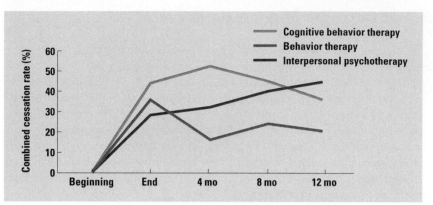

Figure 10–4   Effectiveness of Treatments for Bulimia Nervosa over Time.
Percentage of patients who no longer purged or had episodes of bulimia according to objective or subjective reports. Note the decline for the behavior therapy group and continued improvement for the interpersonal therapy group over the 1-year follow-up interval.

Source: C.G. Fairburn, R. Jones, R.C. Peveler, R.A. Hope, and M. O'Connor, 1993, Psychotherapy and bulimia nervosa: Longer-term effects of interpersonal psychotherapy, behavior therapy, and cognitive behavior therapy, *Archives of General Psychiatry, 50,* 423.

was included as a placebo control group in a study of cognitive behavior therapy. Fairburn and colleagues (1991, 1993) planned to evaluate whether cognitive behavior therapy had specific treatment effects above and beyond the nonspecific, general benefits of receiving psychotherapy (see Chapter 3). The investigators picked interpersonal therapy as a credible placebo treatment because interpersonal problems often are associated with bulimia nervosa. However, they hypothesized that cognitive behavior therapy would outperform the interpersonal approach. The study also included a third condition, a behavior therapy alone group, which essentially was cognitive behavior therapy without the cognitive elements.

When Fairburn and his colleagues (1991) evaluated outcome shortly after treatment, they found that cognitive behavior therapy was more effective than interpersonal therapy in changing dieting behavior, self-induced vomiting, and attitudes about weight and shape. Cognitive behavior therapy also was more effective than behavior therapy alone when attitude change was the outcome measure; however, the results of the two behavioral treatments were similar in other respects.

A very different picture emerged at 12-month follow-up (Fairburn et al., 1993) (see Figure 10–4). The improvements brought about by behavior therapy alone deteriorated over time, and a large number of patients dropped out of this group, perhaps reflecting their dissatisfaction with the treatment. In comparison, the improvements in the cognitive behavior therapy group remained fairly stable. Most surprising, however, members of the interpersonal therapy group *continued to improve* in the 12 months following the end of treatment. At 1-year follow-up, in fact, the improvements for interpersonal therapy equaled the improvements for cognitive behavior therapy and outdistanced the behavior therapy alone group.

The continued improvement for the interpersonal therapy group was surprising and impressive, for at least two reasons. First, the interpersonal treatments explicitly excluded direct discussions of eating, diet, and related topics. Second, the investigators had lower expectations for the interpersonal therapy group, and the expectations of experimenters, therapists, and clients often affect treatment outcome. Some other researchers also have found that interpersonal therapy can be effective in treating bulimia nervosa (Wilfley et al., 1993). Thus interpersonal therapy is emerging as a promising alternative or supplement to cognitive behavior therapy for treating bulimia nervosa.

Course and Outcome of Bulimia Nervosa

Researchers are just beginning to publish findings on the course and long-term outcome of bulimia nervosa. At this point the evidence suggests that the outcome for bulimia nervosa is generally more positive than for anorexia nervosa. About half of clients are free of all symptoms of the disorder following treatment, about one in five continue to meet the diagnostic criteria for bulimia nervosa, and the remainder have occasional relapses or subclinical levels of binge eating and compensatory behavior. Most clients manage to maintain a weight that is generally in the normal range, and—in contrast to anorexia nervosa—mortality is rare. Although data are insufficient, it also appears that comorbid psychological disorders tend to improve with improvements in bulimia nervosa (Hsu, 1995). Few predictors of better or worse outcome have been identified, other than obvious indicators; for example, more frequent purging at the time of diagnosis predicts a less positive outcome (Olmstead, Kaplan, & Rockert, 1994). In closing, we should note that all these findings on outcome are derived from studies following treatment; essentially no evidence is available on the natural course of bulimia nervosa.

Summary

Eating disorders are severe disturbances in eating behavior that result from the sufferer's obsessive fear of gaining weight. The DSM-IV lists two major subtypes of eating disorders: anorexia nervosa and bulimia nervosa. The defining symptoms of **anorexia nervosa** include extreme emaciation, a disturbed perception of one's body, an intense fear of gaining weight, and the cessation of menstruation (in women). Concerns that commonly characterize anorexia nervosa but are not defining symptoms include obsessive preoccupation with food and an exaggerated struggle for control. Other problems that may be associated with anorexia nervosa include mood disturbance, sexual difficulties, a lack of impulse control, and medical problems secondary to the weight loss. The defining symptoms of **bulimia nervosa** are **binge eating** and compensatory behavior (**purging** or excessive exercise), a sense of lost control during a binge, and undue focus on weight and shape. Depression is commonly associated with bulimia nervosa; substance abuse and personality disorders are to a much lesser degree.

The DSM-IV includes two subtypes of anorexia nervosa. The restricting type includes people who rarely engage in binge eating or purging behavior, whereas the binge-eating/purging type is characterized by regular binge eating and purging. Bulimia nervosa also is divided into two subtypes. The purging type is characterized by the regular use of self-induced vomiting or the misuse of laxatives, diuretics, or enemas. The nonpurging type compensates for binge eating with fasting or excessive exercise. There has been debate about adding to the DSM-IV list of eating disorders. **Binge eating disorder** is included in a special appendix. **Obesity** has been considered for inclusion but rejected.

The prevalence of both anorexia nervosa and bulimia nervosa has increased dramatically in recent years, particularly among young women. Both anorexia and bulimia nervosa are approximately 10 times more common among women than among men, and many scientists blame our society's gender roles and standards of beauty for encouraging eating disorders.

The regulation of normal eating and weight results from a combination of biological, psychological, and social factors. Epidemiological evidence highlights the role of social factors. Adolescent girls and young women are at risk, in part, because they attempt to shape themselves to fit the image of the ideal woman. The emphasis on appearances also lessens the value of other roles filled by girls and women. To a lesser extent, family relationships also may influence eating disorders. Four of the most prominent psychological factors in the development of eating disorders are issues of control and perfectionism, dysphoria combined with a lack of **introceptive awareness**, body image dissatisfaction, and reactions to dietary restraint. Biological contributions include the body's attempts to maintain **weight set points,** genetic influences on body weight and shape, and in rare cases a dysfunction of the hypothalamus.

Treatments for anorexia nervosa and bulimia nervosa differ in approach and effectiveness. Anorexia nervosa is likelier to require inpatient treatment with the initial goal of gaining weight, even through the use of coercive methods if necessary. Following treatment, 50 to 60 percent of people with anorexia nervosa have a normal weight, and 10 to 20 percent have weights well below normal (the remainder are in between these two groups). About 10 percent of people with the disorder die of starvation, suicide, or medical complications.

Treatments for bulimia nervosa are more promising, particularly cognitive behavior therapy and interpersonal psychotherapy and to a lesser extent antidepressant medication. About half of clients with bulimia nervosa are free of all symptoms following treatment.

Critical Thinking

1. Many psychologists believe that young women develop eating disorders in part because the popular media portray extremely thin women as beautiful, fit, happy, and successful. Is this perspective consistent with your experience? What changes would you like to see in these images of women?

2. What roles are young women expected to play in their families and in social relationships (including relationships with men and with other women), and how might these roles contribute to the development of eating disorders?

3. What roles are young men expected to play in their families and in social relationships (including relation-

ships with women and with other men), and how might these roles protect men against (or sometimes contribute to) the development of eating disorders?

4. If you had an eating disorder, would you want to be treated with cognitive behavior therapy, interpersonal therapy, or antidepressant medication? What are the reasons for your choice? Why might people who received interpersonal therapy continue to improve over time, whereas people who received behavior therapy often regress?

11

Substance Use Disorders

The abuse of alcohol and other drugs is one of the most serious problems facing our society. Research efforts, treatment priorities, and national publicity have all helped transform national attitudes toward the abuse of chemical substances. The picture of the drug addict as a homeless derelict whose personality defects and lack of motivation are largely responsible for the problem is being replaced by a new view in which substance abuse is seen to affect people from all walks of life. Treatment is increasingly included within mainstream health care programs and health insurance (Roman & Blum, 1987).

Overview

substance dependence   The more severe form of substance use disorder listed in DSM-IV. Refers to a pattern of repeated self-administration that results in tolerance, withdrawal, or compulsive drug-taking behavior.

substance abuse   The less severe form of substance use disorder listed in DSM-IV. Describes a pattern of drug use that is defined in terms of interference with the person's ability to fulfill major role obligations, the recurrent use of a drug in dangerous situations, or the experience of repeated legal difficulties that are associated with drug use.

addiction   A term used to describe substance use problems such as alcoholism. Replaced in official terminology by the term *substance dependence,* with which it is synonymous.

The costs of substance abuse are astronomical. Alcohol abuse costs the United States $99 billion each year, and abuse of other drugs costs an additional $67 billion. One obvious cost is medical treatment, both for substance use disorders and for the other medical conditions that are associated with these disorders. Substance abuse exacts many other costs to society, including lost productivity, aid to families of individuals with substance use disorders, and enforcement of drug laws.

The impact of drug abuse is even more compelling when viewed in terms of its devastation of human lives. More than 75 percent of all foster children are products of alcohol- and/or drug-addicted parents (Children's Defense Fund, 1994). Approximately 15 percent of all deaths in the United States can be attributed to alcohol and drug use (McLellan, Woody, & Metzger, 1996). Tobacco-related diseases (such as cancer and heart disease) kill more than 400,000 people in the United States each year (Kessler et al., 1996). The health problems associated with alcohol use and abuse are also severe. Cirrhosis of the liver, which is frequently the product of chronic alcoholism, is the ninth leading cause of death in the United States. In addition, alcohol plays a prominent role in many suicides, homicides, and motor vehicle accidents. If all of these problems were combined, alcohol would be the fourth leading cause of death in the United States (Merikangas, 1990).

The habitual use of various kinds of drugs or chemical substances can create problems that interfere with a person's social and occupational functioning. The DSM-IV uses two terms to describe substance use disorders, which reflect two different levels of severity. **Substance dependence,** the more severe of the two forms, refers to a pattern of repeated self-administration that often results in tolerance, the need for increased amounts of the drug to achieve intoxication; withdrawal, unpleasant physical and psychological effects that the person experiences when he or she tries to stop taking the drug; or compulsive drug-taking behavior. **Substance abuse** describes a more broadly conceived, less severe pattern of drug use that is defined in terms of interference with the person's ability to fulfill major role obligations at work or at home, the recurrent use of a drug in dangerous situations, or the experience of repeated legal difficulties that are associated with drug use. People with a substance use disorder frequently abuse several types of drugs; this condition is known as *polysubstance abuse.*

Addiction is another, older term that is often used to describe problems such as alcoholism. The term has been replaced in official terminology by the term *substance dependence,* with which it is synonymous, but it is still used informally by many laypeople. Most people have two principal things in mind when they use the word *addiction:* craving and lack of control. A person who is addicted to something presumably has a compelling need for it and also experiences considerable difficulty regulating behaviors that are associated with it.

When used in this fashion, the notion of addiction can be applied to many forms of behavior that extend well beyond the use of drugs. Many people feel that they are addicted to food. Others have difficulty controlling impulsive behaviors, such as gambling and sex (see Further Thoughts in Chapter 9). In fact, the list could probably be expanded to include such things as watching television, shopping, working, and running. For the sake of our discussion, however, we will focus on problems that center on the abuse of chemical substances.

A **drug of abuse**—sometimes called a *psychoactive substance* is a chemical substance that alters a person's mood, level of perception, or brain functioning (Schuckit, 1989). All drugs of abuse can be used to increase a person's psychological comfort level (make you feel "high") or to alter levels of consciousness. The list of chemicals on which people can become dependent is long and seems to be growing longer. It includes drugs that are legally available in our society, whether over the counter or by prescription only, as well as many that are illegal (see Table 11–1).

drug of abuse   (also called a *psychoactive substance*) A chemical substance that alters a person's mood, level of perception, or brain functioning.

TABLE 11–1

Classification of Psychoactive Drugs

CLASS	EXAMPLES
CNS DEPRESSANTS	Alcohol
	Hypnotics (barbiturates)
	Anxiolytics (antianxiety drugs)
CNS STIMULANTS	Amphetamine ("speed")
	Cocaine
	Caffeine
	Nicotine
	Methylphenidate (Ritalin)
	Weight-loss products
OPIATES	Heroin
	Morphine
	Methadone
	Prescription painkillers (almost all)
CANNABINOIDS	Marijuana
	Hashish
HALLUCINOGENS	Lysergic acid diethylamide (LSD)
	Mescaline
	Psilocybin
SOLVENTS	Aerosol sprays
	Glues
	Paint thinner
OVER-THE-COUNTER DRUGS	Sedatives (sleep aids)
	Weak stimulants
OTHERS	Phencyclidine (PCP)

Source: *Adapted from M. A. Schuckit, 1989,* Drug and Alcohol Abuse: A Clinical Guide to Diagnosis and Treatment *(3rd ed.). New York: Plenum.*

The central nervous system (CNS) depressants include alcohol as well as types of medication that are used to help people sleep, called *hypnotics,* and those for relieving anxiety, known as *sedatives* or *anxiolytics.* The CNS stimulants include illegal drugs like amphetamine and cocaine, as well as nicotine and caffeine. The opiates, also called *narcotic analgesics,* can be used clinically to decrease pain. The cannabinoids, such as marijuana, produce euphoria and an altered sense of time. At higher doses, they may produce hallucinations.

One basic question we must address is whether we should view each type of addiction as a unique problem. Experts who answer "yes" to this question point out that each class of abused substance seems to affect the body in distinct ways. For example, the long-term use of opiates such as heroin does not seem to cause many chronic physical health problems (Brecher, 1972; Room, 1987), whereas alcohol and tobacco can have a devastating impact on a person's physical health.

Despite these differences, the various forms of substance abuse share many common elements. The psychological and biochemical effects on the user are often similar, as are the negative consequences for both social and occupational behaviors. At the most fundamental level, all forms of abuse represent the inherent conflict between immediate pleasure and longer term harmful consequences (Lang, 1983). The reasons for initial experimentation with a drug, the factors that influence the transition to dependence, and the processes that lead to relapse after initial efforts to change are all similar in many respects. For these reasons, many clinicians and researchers have moved toward a view of substance abuse that emphasizes common causes, behaviors, and consequences (Marlatt et al., 1988; Miller, 1987). In fact, DSM-IV employs a single set of diagnostic criteria that defines dependence for all types of drugs.

The variety of problems associated with substance use disorders can be illustrated using a case study of alcohol abuse. Ernest Hemingway (1899–1961), a Nobel Prize–winning writer, was a chronic alcohol abuser. The following paragraphs, quoted from an article by Paul Johnson (1989), describe the progression of Hemingway's drinking and the problems that it created. They illustrate many typical features of substance dependence, as well as the devastating impact that alcohol can have on various organs of the body. These paragraphs also raise a number of interesting questions about the etiology of this disorder. Most men and women consume alcoholic beverages at some point during their lives. Why do some people become dependent on alcohol while others do not? What factors influence the transition from social drinking to abuse?

 case study

Ernest Hemingway's Alcohol Dependence

Hemingway began to drink as a teenager, the local blacksmith, Jim Dilworth, secretly supplying him with strong cider. His mother noted his habit and always feared he would become an alcoholic. In Italy he progressed to wine, then had his first hard liquor at the officers' club in Milan. His wound [from World War I] and an unhappy love affair provoked heavy drinking: in the hospital, his wardrobe was found to be full of empty cognac bottles, an ominous sign. In Paris in the 1920s, he bought Beaune by the gallon at a wine cooperative, and would and did drink five or six bottles of red at a meal.

Hemingway particularly liked to drink with women, as this seemed to him, vicariously, to signify his mother's approval. Hadley [the first of his four wives] drank a lot with him, and wrote: "I still cherish, you know, the remark you made that you almost worshipped me as a drinker." The same disastrous role was played by his pretty 1930s companion in Havana, Jane Mason, with whom he drank gin followed by champagne chasers and huge jars of iced daiquiris; it was indeed in Cuba in this decade that his drinking first got completely out of hand. One bartender there said he could "drink more martinis than any man I have ever seen." On safari, he was seen sneaking out of his tent at 5 A.M. to get a drink. His brother Leicester said that, by the end of the 1930s, at Key West, he was drinking seventeen Scotch-and-sodas a day, and often taking a bottle of champagne to bed with him at night.

At this period, his liver for the first time began to cause him acute pain. He was told by his doctor to give up alcohol completely, and indeed tried to limit his consumption to three whiskeys before dinner. But that did not last. During World War II his drinking mounted steadily and by the mid-1940s he was reportedly pouring gin into his tea at breakfast. A. E. Hotchner, interviewing him for *Cosmopolitan* in 1948, said he dispatched seven double-size Papa Doubles (the Havana drink named after him, a mixture of rum, grapefruit and maraschino), and when he left for dinner took an eighth with him for the drive. And on top of it all, there was constant whiskey: His son Patrick said his father got through a quart of whiskey a day for the last 20 years of his life.

Hemingway's ability to hold his liquor was remarkable. Lillian Ross, who wrote his profile for the *New Yorker*, does not seem to have noticed he was drunk a lot of the time he talked to her. Denis Zaphior said of his last safari: "I suppose he was drunk the whole time but seldom showed it." He also demonstrated an unusual ability to cut down his drinking or even to eliminate it altogether for brief periods, and this, in addition to his strong physique, enabled him to survive.

But despite his physique, his alcoholism had a direct impact on his health beginning with his damaged liver in the late 1930s. By 1959, following his last big drinking bout in Spain, he was experiencing both kidney and liver trouble and possibly hemochromatosis (cirrhosis, bronzed skin, diabetes), edema of the ankles, cramps, chronic insomnia, blood-clotting and high blood uremia, as well as his skin complaints. He was impotent and prematurely aged. Even so, he was still on his feet, still alive; and the thought had become unbearable to him. His father had committed suicide because of his fear of mortal illness. Hemingway feared that his illnesses were not mortal: On July 2, 1961, after various unsuccessful treatments for depression and paranoia, he got hold of his best English double-barreled shotgun, put two canisters in it, and blew away his entire cranial vault.

Why did Hemingway long for death [and why did he drink]? . . . He felt he was failing his art. . . . He knew when he wrote below his best, and the knowledge was intolerable to him. He sought the help of alcohol, even in working hours. He was first observed with a drink, a "Rum St. James," in front of him while writing in the 1920s. This custom, rare at first, became intermittent, then invariable. The effect on his work was exactly as might be expected, disastrous. (Johnson, 1989, pp. 58–59) ⚜

Typical Symptoms and Associated Features

Substance use disorders are associated with a host of problems, many of which are illustrated in the life of Ernest Hemingway. Nevertheless, substance dependence is difficult to define. Alcoholism is one important example. George Vaillant (1995), a psychiatrist at Dartmouth Medical School and the author of an important longitudinal study of alcoholic men, notes that it is difficult to say that one specific problem or set of problems represents the core features of this disorder:

Not only is there no single symptom that defines alcoholism, but often it is not who is drinking but who is watching that defines a symptom. A drinker may worry that he has an alcohol problem because of his impotence. His wife may drag him to an alcohol clinic because he slapped her during a blackout. Once he is at the clinic, the doctor calls him an alcoholic because of his abnormal liver-function tests. Later society labels him a drunk because of a second episode of driving while intoxicated. (p. 24)

The number of problems that a person encounters seems to provide the most useful distinction between people who are dependent on a substance and those who are not. These problems can be sorted loosely into two general areas: (1) patterns of pathological consumption, including psychological and physiological dependence, and (2) consequences that follow a prolonged pattern of abuse, including social and occupational impairment, legal and financial difficulties, and deteriorating medical condition.

It might seem that the actual amount of alcohol that a person consumes would be the most useful index of an alcohol problem. Hemingway, for example, clearly consumed enormous quantities of alcohol over a period of many years. In fact, though, this measure turns out to be of little use in defining alcoholism, because people vary significantly in the amount of alcohol they can consume. Factors such as age, gender, activity level, and overall physical health have a great impact on a person's ability to metabolize alcohol. Some people can drink a lot without developing problems; others drink very little and encounter difficulties.

The Concept of Substance Dependence

Many psychological features or problems are associated with dependence on chemical substances. One such feature involves *craving*. This word is frequently used to describe a forceful urge to use drugs, but the relationship between craving and drug use is actually very complex (Kassel & Shiffman, 1992). People who are dependent on drugs often say that they take the drug to control how they are feeling.

psychological dependence A term used to describe forceful, subjective urges to use drugs, often as a means of relieving negative mood states. Contrasts with the term "physiological dependence," which involves symptoms of tolerance and withdrawal.

tolerance The process through which the nervous system becomes less sensitive to the effects of a psychoactive substance. As a result, the person needs to consume increased quantities of the drug to achieve the same subjective effect.

withdrawal The constellation of symptoms that are experienced shortly after a person stops taking a drug after heavy or prolonged use.

They need it to relieve negative mood states or to avoid withdrawal symptoms from previous episodes. They may feel compelled to take the drug as a way to prepare for certain activities, such as public speaking, writing, or sex. Some clinicians refer to this condition as **psychological dependence.** One useful index of craving is the amount of time that the person spends planning to take the drug. Is access to drugs or alcohol a constant preoccupation? If the person is invited to a party or is planning to eat at a restaurant, does he or she always inquire about the availability of alcoholic drinks?

As the problem progresses, it is not unusual for the person who abuses drugs to try to stop. In the case of alcoholism, for example, it is possible for even heavy drinkers to abstain for at least short periods of time (Fingarette, 1988). Most clinicians and researchers agree that diminished control over drinking is a crucial feature of the disorder. Some experts have described this issue as "freedom of choice." When a person first experiments with the use of alcohol, his or her behavior is clearly voluntary; the person is not compelled to drink. After drinking heavily for a long period of time, most people with a drinking disorder try to stop. Unfortunately, efforts at self-control are typically short-lived and usually fail.

TOLERANCE AND WITHDRAWAL

Two particularly important features of substance dependence are the phenomena known as tolerance and withdrawal. These symptoms are usually interpreted as evidence of *physiological dependence.* **Tolerance** refers to the process through which the nervous system becomes less sensitive to the effects of alcohol or any other substance. A person who has been regularly exposed to alcohol will need to drink increased quantities to achieve the same subjective effect ("buzz," "high," or level of intoxication). The specific mechanisms that are responsible for the development of tolerance are unknown.

Some drugs are much more likely than others to produce a buildup of tolerance (APA, 1994). The most substantial tolerance effects are found among people who are heavy users of opioids, such as heroin, and CNS stimulants, such as amphetamine and cocaine. Pronounced tolerance is also found among people who use alcohol and nicotine. The evidence is unclear regarding tolerance effects and prolonged use of marijuana and hashish. Most people who use cannabinoids are not aware of tolerance effects, but these effects have been demonstrated in animal studies. Hallucinogens (LSD) and phencyclidine (PCP) may not lead to the development of tolerance.

Withdrawal refers to the symptoms experienced when a person stops using a drug. They can go on for several days. For example, alcohol is a CNS depressant, and the heavy drinker's system becomes accustomed to functioning in a chronically depressed state. When the person stops drinking, the system begins to rebound within several hours, producing many unpleasant side effects—hand tremors, sweating, nausea, anxiety, and insomnia. The most serious forms of withdrawal include convulsions and visual, tactile, or auditory hallucinations. Some people develop delirium, a sudden disturbance of consciousness that is accompanied by changes in cognitive processes such as lack of awareness of the environment or inability to sustain attention. This syndrome is called *alcohol withdrawal delirium* in DSM-IV (more traditionally known as *delirium tremens,* or *DTs*) if it is induced by withdrawal from alcohol.

The symptoms of withdrawal vary considerably for different kinds of substances. Unpleasant reactions are most evident during withdrawal from alcohol, opioids, and the general class of sedatives, hypnotics, and anxiolytics (such as Valium). Withdrawal symptoms are also associated with stimulants, such as amphetamine, cocaine, and nicotine, though they are sometimes less pronounced than those associated with alcohol and opioids.

The symptoms of substance use disorders fall along a continuum. It is convenient to consider these problems in terms of qualitative distinctions: people who can control their drinking and those who cannot; people who crave alcohol and those who do not; people who have developed a tolerance to the drug and those who have not; and so on. In fact, there are no clear dividing lines on any of these dimensions. For this reason it is extremely difficult to define the nature of substance dependence disorders.

In the next few pages we briefly review some of the most important classes of drugs. For each group, we will describe short-term effects on physiology and behavior as well as the consequences of long-term abuse. Unless otherwise specified, these descriptions are based on information presented by William McKim in his textbook on drugs and behavior (1997).

Alcohol

Alcohol affects virtually every organ and system in the body (Yi, 1991). After alcohol has been ingested, it is absorbed through membranes in the stomach, small intestine, and colon. The rate at which it is absorbed is influenced by many variables, including the concentration of alcohol in the beverage (for example, distilled spirits are absorbed more rapidly than beer or wine), the volume and rate of consumption, and the presence of food in the digestive system. After it is absorbed, alcohol is distributed to all the body's organ systems. Almost all the alcohol that a person consumes is eventually broken down or metabolized in the liver. The rate at which alcohol is metabolized varies from person to person, but the average person can metabolize about 1 ounce of 90-proof liquor or 12 ounces of beer per hour (Nathan, 1993). If the person's consumption rate exceeds this metabolic limit, then blood alcohol levels will rise.

Blood alcohol levels are measured in terms of the amount of alcohol per unit of blood. There is a relatively strong correlation between blood alcohol levels and CNS intoxicating effects (Verebey, 1991). According to DSM-IV, the symptoms of alcohol intoxication include slurred speech, lack of coordination, an unsteady gait, nystagmus (involuntary to-and-fro movement of the eyeballs induced when the person looks upward or to the side), impaired attention or memory, and stupor or coma.

SHORT-TERM EFFECTS

Some people become intoxicated after drinking relatively small quantities of alcohol, with blood levels less than 10 to 30 mg percent. In most states, the legal limit of alcohol concentration for driving is 100 mg percent. Some state legislatures are considering lowering this limit, because slowed reaction times and interference with other driving skills may occur at lower blood alcohol levels. People with levels of 150 to 300 mg percent will almost always act intoxicated. Neurological and respiration complications begin to appear at higher levels. There is an extreme risk of coma leading to toxic death when blood alcohol levels go above 400 mg percent (Slaby & Martin, 1991).

CONSEQUENCES OF PROLONGED USE AND ABUSE

The long-term abuse of alcohol can have a devastating impact on many areas of a person's life. The disruption of relationships with family and friends can be especially painful. The impact of Hemingway's drinking on his writing career and his family life is clearly evident. Most critics agree that his literary accomplishments were confined primarily to the early stages of his career, before his alcoholism began to interfere with his ability to write. Drinking also took its toll on his marriages, which were characterized by frequent and occasionally furious conflict in public and by repeated episodes of verbal and physical abuse in private (Johnson, 1989).

Many people who abuse alcohol experience blackouts. In some cases, abusers may continue to function without passing out, but they will later be unable to remember their behavior. An example is the person who drives home drunk from a party and in the morning finds a dent in the car bumper but can't remember how it got there. Sometimes problem drinkers will be told by a friend about how they behaved at the previous night's party, but they cannot remember what they did.

Regular heavy use of alcohol is also likely to interfere with job performance. Coworkers and supervisors may complain. Attendance at work may become sporadic. Eventually the heavy drinker may be suspended or fired. Related to job performance is the problem of financial difficulties. Losing one's job is clearly detrimental to one's financial stability, as are the costs of divorce, health care, liquor, and so on.

Many heavy drinkers encounter problems with legal authorities. These problems may include arrests for drunken driving and public intoxication, as well as charges of spouse and child abuse. Many forms of violent behavior are more likely to be committed when a person has been drinking. The association between crime and alcohol is rather strong. In Vaillant's longitudinal study, 61 percent of the men who were dependent on alcohol had been arrested more than twice for alcohol-related offenses (Vaillant, 1995).

barbiturates Drugs that depress activities of the central nervous system; mostly for sedation.

benzodiazepines Group of drugs that have potent hypnotic, sedative, and anxiolytic action (also called antianxiety drugs).

On a biological level, prolonged exposure to high levels of alcohol can disrupt the functions of several important organ systems, especially the liver, pancreas, gastrointestinal system, cardiovascular system, and endocrine system. The symptoms of alcoholism include many secondary health problems, such as cirrhosis of the liver, heart problems (in part, the result of being overweight), and various forms of cancer, as well as severe and persistent forms of dementia and memory impairment, or amnestic disorders, such as Korsakoff's syndrome. Alcoholism is also associated with nutritional disturbances of many types, because chronic abusers often drink instead of eating balanced meals. Alcohol can suppress a person's appetite, and it can also interfere with normal eating patterns as a result of its effects on the gastrointestinal system. In fact, over an extended period of time, alcohol dependence has more negative health consequences than does abuse of almost any other drug.

Barbiturates and Benzodiazepines

The families of drugs known as barbiturates and benzodiazepines are also known informally as tranquilizers, hypnotics, and sedatives. *Tranquilizers* are used to decrease anxiety or agitation. *Hypnotics* are used to help people sleep. *Sedative* is a more general term that describes drugs that calm people or reduce excitement (other than the relief of anxiety). The **barbiturates,** such as phenobarbital (Nembutal) and amobarbital (Amytal), were discovered in the early twentieth century. They were used widely for many years and for a variety of purposes, ranging from the treatment of chronic anxiety to the prevention of seizures and to relieve pain. The **benzodiazepines** are synthetic drugs whose therapeutic effects were discovered in the 1950s. Some are used in the treatment of anxiety disorders (see Chapter 6), and others are used to relieve sleeping problems. The benzodiazepines, which include diazepam (Valium), alprazolam (Xanax), and triazolam (Halcion), have replaced the barbiturates in medical practice. This is in large part because of their lower potential for producing a lethal overdose.

SHORT-TERM EFFECTS

The barbiturates and benzodiazepines are most often taken orally. They can be used occasionally to achieve a brief period of relaxation or mild euphoria. They can also be used on a regular basis, as prescribed by a physician, to relieve chronic anxiety or to help a person sleep. Speed of action varies considerably among the specific types of benzodiazepines and barbiturates. The faster-acting drugs tend to have a shorter duration of effect. When the drugs are taken orally, they are absorbed from the digestive system much more quickly if the person has also been drinking alcohol. More rapid effects are also achieved if these drugs are injected rather than taken orally. This method of self-administration is more dangerous than oral use, leading to more profound tolerance and withdrawal effects, as well as increased risk of exposure to the human immunodeficiency virus (HIV).

Sedatives and hypnotics can lead to a state of intoxication that is identical to that associated with alcohol. It is characterized by impaired judgment, slowness of speech, lack of coordination, a narrowed range of attention, and disinhibition of sexual and aggressive impulses. Intravenous use of barbiturates can lead quickly to a pleasant, warm, drowsy feeling. The anxiolytics (benzodiazepines) can also produce intoxication. Although their main effect is to reduce tension, they sometimes lead to an increase in hostile and aggressive behavior. Some clinicians call this a "rage reaction" or aggressive dyscontrol.

The barbiturates and benzodiazepines seem to work by enhancing the effects of GABA, an inhibitory neurotransmitter in the central nervous system. Their effect therefore is to reduce arousal in many areas of the brain. Higher doses of barbiturates can be used to induce unconsciousness and anesthesia.

CONSEQUENCES OF PROLONGED USE AND ABUSE

People who abruptly stop taking high doses of benzodiazepines may experience a return—and, in some cases, a worsening—of the original anxiety symptoms, if the medication was being used to treat an anxiety disorder. The person may also develop new symptoms that are directly associated with drug withdrawal. These include irritability, paranoia, sleep disturbance, agitation, muscle tension, restlessness, and perceptual disturbances. Withdrawal symptoms are less likely to occur if the medication is discontinued gradually rather than abruptly.

Tolerance and withdrawal can develop after using barbiturates for several weeks. Symptoms of withdrawal include anxiety, insomnia, anorexia, and motor tremors. People who have been taking very high doses of barbiturates are likely to experience motor seizures on the second or third day after they stop taking the drug. They may also develop *delirium,* a cognitive disorder that is characterized by impairment in consciousness, attention, and other cognitive abilities. Lethal overdose—either accidental or as an intentional means of suicide—is a very serious risk associated with the use of barbiturates because they can induce respiratory failure.

Opiates

The **opiates** (sometimes called *opioids*) are drugs that have properties similar to *opium.* The main active ingredients in opium are *morphine* and *codeine.* Morphine was first isolated from opium in the early nineteenth century. Morphine and codeine are still widely used in medicine, particularly to relieve pain. They are available legally only by prescription in the United States. *Heroin* is a synthetic opiate that is made by modifying the morphine molecule. It was originally marketed as an alternative to morphine when physicians believed, erroneously, that heroin is not addictive.

The opiates can be taken orally, injected, or inhaled. Opium is sometimes eaten or smoked. When morphine is used as a painkiller, it is taken orally so that it is absorbed slowly through the digestive system. Heroin can be injected, inhaled through the nose in the form of snuff, or smoked and inhaled through a pipe or tube.

SHORT-TERM EFFECTS

The opiates can induce a state of dreamlike euphoria, which may be accompanied by increased sensitivity in hearing and vision. People who inject morphine or heroin also experience a rush—a brief, intense feeling of pleasure that is sometimes described as being like an orgasm in the entire body.

Laboratory studies of mood indicate that the positive, emotional effects of opiates do not last. They are soon replaced by long-term negative changes in mood and emotion. These unpleasant experiences are relieved for 30 to 60 minutes after each new injection of the drug, but they eventually color most of the rest of the person's waking experience.

The opiates can induce nausea and vomiting among novice users, constrict the pupils of the eye, and disrupt the coordination of the digestive system. Continued use of opiates decreases the level of sex hormones in both women and men, resulting in reduced sex drive and impaired fertility.

High doses of opiates can lead to a comatose state, severely depressed breathing, and convulsions. The number of people admitted to hospital emergency rooms for treatment of heroin overdoses increased substantially between 1990 and 1995. Between 3,000 and 4,000 people die from accidental overdoses of heroin in the United States each year (Leland, 1996).

CONSEQUENCES OF PROLONGED USE AND ABUSE

The effects of opiates on occupational performance and health depend in large part on the amount of the drug that the person takes. At high doses, people who are addicted to opiates become chronically lethargic and lose their motivation to remain productive. At low to moderate doses, people who use opiates for an extended period of time can remain healthy and work productively in spite of their addiction. This finding is, of course, dependent on the person having easy and relatively inexpensive access to opiates. One possibility is being maintained by a physician on *methadone,* a synthetic opiate that is sometimes used therapeutically as an alternative to heroin.

People who are addicted to opiates become preoccupied with finding and using the drug, in order to experience the rush and to avoid withdrawal symptoms. Tolerance develops rather quickly, and the person's daily dose increases regularly until it eventually levels off and remains steady.

Most of the severe health consequences of opiate use are the result of the lifestyle of the addict rather than the drug itself. The enormous expenses and difficulties associated with obtaining

opiates (sometimes called opioids) Drugs that have properties similar to opium. The main active ingredients in opium are morphine and codeine.

further thoughts

Governmental Regulation of Tobacco Products

On August 23, 1996, the U.S. Food and Drug Administration (FDA) issued a regulation prohibiting the sale and distribution of tobacco products to children and adolescents (Kessler et al., 1996). Previous efforts to limit smoking focused more narrowly on restricting smoking in public places, eliminating cigarette advertisements on television, and increasing sales taxes. The new rule was much more threatening to the tobacco industry because it asserted that, as a drug, nicotine should be controlled by the government. The decisions behind this regulation raise a number of critical issues with regard to substance use disorders. How does the FDA decide whether a product is a drug? What type of evidence is required to demonstrate that a drug is addicting? Should the government control people's access to addicting drugs? If so, what is the best way to control access?

The FDA invoked the Food, Drug, and Cosmetic Act to justify its jurisdiction over cigarettes and smokeless tobacco. This act authorizes the FDA to regulate drugs, which are defined as "articles (other than food) intended to affect the structure or any function of the body." The agency had conducted an extensive investigation to determine whether tobacco products were *intended* by their manufacturers to deliver nicotine to consumers. Independent research studies, documents from the tobacco industry's own research laboratories, and testimony from former tobacco company scientists and executives pointed to three main conclusions (Dreyfuss, 1996):

1. Nicotine is addictive and has other pharmacological effects on the structure and function of the body. This conclusion was based on overwhelming evidence indicating that people who use tobacco products clearly develop symptoms of dependence, including tolerance, withdrawal, and a pattern of compulsive use. Heavy smokers consume cigarettes in a manner that serves to maintain a relatively constant level of nicotine in their system.

2. Tobacco manufacturers have known for at least 30 years that consumers use tobacco because of the pharmacological effects of nicotine (Hilts, 1996).

3. Nicotine meets the legal definition of a "drug" because the companies designed their products to have these effects, and they intentionally manipulated nicotine levels to ensure that they did. The agency decided, on the basis of this evidence, that cigarettes are "drug-delivery systems" designed to dispense nicotine in a way that the smoker can readily absorb.

The FDA could have chosen to regulate tobacco products as either a *drug* or as a *medical device* (drug-delivery system)

---

illegal opiates almost invariably consume all the person's resources. The person typically neglects housing, nutrition, and health care in the search for another fix. Heroin addicts are much more likely than other people in the general population to die from AIDS, violence, and suicide.

Nicotine

Nicotine is the active ingredient in tobacco, which is its only natural source. Nicotine is almost never taken in its pure form because it can be toxic. Very high doses have extremely unpleasant effects. Controlled doses are easier to achieve by smoking or chewing tobacco, which provides a diluted concentration of nicotine. Another way of ingesting nicotine is to inhale snuff into the nostrils. When tobacco smoke is inhaled, nicotine is absorbed into the blood through the mucous membranes of the lungs. This route of administration results in the highest concentrations of nicotine because it is carried directly from the lungs to the heart and from there to the brain.

SHORT-TERM EFFECTS

The effects of nicotine on the peripheral nervous system (see Chapter 2) include increases in heart rate and blood pressure. In the central nervous system, nicotine has pervasive effects on a number of neurotransmitter systems. It stimulates the release of norepinephrine from several sites, producing CNS arousal. Nicotine also causes the release of dopamine and norepinephrine in the mesolimbic dopamine pathway, also known as the reward system of the brain. The serotonin system, which also mediates the effects of antidepressant medication, is influenced by nicotine. In fact, some people have suggested that nicotine mimics the effects of antidepressant drugs.

Top executives from seven tobacco companies testified at a congressional hearing that they did not beleive that cigarettes were addictive.

markets would spring up immediately, similar to those involved with other illegal drugs. An outright ban on nicotine would fail, just as efforts to ban other drugs have failed (Baum, 1996; Brecher, 1972).

The FDA decided instead to approach the nicotine problem by invoking its authority to regulate *medical devices*. The new tobacco regulations imposed by the FDA are prevention efforts designed to break the cycle of addiction to nicotine. The new rule prohibits the sale of tobacco products to anyone less than 18 years old. It also severely restricts advertising, on which the tobacco industry had previously spent $4 billion a year (Cooper, 1994), eliminating attractive, colorful images that are likely to appeal to children and adolescents. These restrictions are intended to reduce the rate at which young people are recruited to become new smokers and to minimize future health casualties from tobacco use.

The FDA policy on nicotine represents a middle-of-the-road approach to this particular drug problem. It is a compromise between two extreme alternatives: allowing completely open access to a dangerous drug or attempting to ban it completely. Public policy will not be able to determine whether adults in our society will use harmful drugs like nicotine. The FDA's new regulation represents one attempt to minimize the risk that children and adolescents will become addicted before they are old enough to make informed decisions about their own health. ⚘

(Arno et al., 1996). If it had chosen to pursue its drug-regulation authority, the FDA could have required tobacco companies to demonstrate that cigarettes and smokeless tobacco are safe products. In the absence of such information, these products could have been banned entirely. The FDA did not consider this option to be practical or politically viable. Because so many adults are already addicted to nicotine, extensive black

Nicotine has a complex influence on subjective mood states. Many people say that they smoke because it makes them feel more relaxed. Some believe that it helps them control their subjective response to stress. This phenomenon is somewhat paradoxical in light of the fact that nicotine leads to increased arousal of the sympathetic nervous system. Various explanations may account for this apparent inconsistency. One involves differences in dosage levels; low doses of nicotine may lead to increased arousal while higher doses lead to relaxation. Another alternative involves withdrawal. Regular smokers may feel relaxed when they smoke a cigarette because it relieves unpleasant symptoms of withdrawal.

CONSEQUENCES OF PROLONGED USE AND ABUSE

Nicotine is one of the most harmful addicting drugs. Considerable evidence points to the development of both tolerance and withdrawal symptoms among people who regularly smoke or chew tobacco (see Further Thoughts, pages 300–301). The physiological symptoms of withdrawal from nicotine include drowsiness, lightheadedness, headaches, muscle tremors, and nausea. People who are attempting to quit smoking typically experience sleeping problems, weight gain, concentration difficulties, and mood swings ranging from anxiety to anger and depression. From a psychological point of view, withdrawal from nicotine is just as difficult as withdrawal from heroin. Many people report that these symptoms disappear after a few months, but some report serious cravings for several years after they quit.

People who smoke tobacco increase their risk of developing many fatal diseases, including heart disease, lung disease (bronchitis and emphysema), and various types of cancer. Eighty percent of all deaths caused by lung cancer can be attributed to smoking tobacco. More than

psychomotor stimulants Drugs such as amphetamine and cocaine that produce their effect by simulating the effects of certain neurotransmitters, specifically epinephrine, norepinephrine, dopamine, and serotonin.

400,000 people in the United States die prematurely each year as a result of tobacco. Large numbers of people are also killed or injured in fires caused by careless smoking. Women who smoke are also more likely to become infertile. Babies born to mothers who smoked during pregnancy are also likely to weigh less than those born to mothers who do not smoke, and they may be more vulnerable to certain types of birth defects.

Amphetamine and Cocaine

Members of the class of drugs known as **psychomotor stimulants** produce their effects by simulating the actions of certain neurotransmitters, specifically epinephrine, norepinephrine, dopamine, and serotonin. *Cocaine* is a naturally occurring stimulant drug that is extracted from the leaf of a small tree that grows at high elevations, as in the Andes Mountains. The *amphetamines* (such as dexedrine and methamphetamine, also known as "speed," or "ice" in its crystallized form) are produced synthetically.

The stimulants can be taken orally, injected, or inhaled. It is easier to maintain a constant blood level when the drugs are taken orally. They are absorbed more slowly through the digestive system, and their effects are less potent. For many centuries, Indians in the Andes have used cocaine by rolling coca leaves into a ball that can be tucked in the cheek and sucked for an extended period of time. More dramatic effects are achieved by injecting the drug or sniffing it.

Cocaine can also be smoked, using various procedures that have been popularized in the past several years. Some people employ a particularly dangerous procedure called "freebasing," in which the drug is heated and its vapors are inhaled. Many people have been seriously burned when these highly combustible chemicals are accidentally ignited. *Crack* is produced by mixing salt cocaine hydrochloride with a solution of baking soda. The resulting crystallized chunks can be heated in pipes, and the vapors are inhaled. Like freebasing, this process leads to more rapid absorption and a much stronger drug effect.

SHORT-TERM EFFECTS
Cocaine and amphetamines are called stimulants because they activate the sympathetic nervous system. They increase heart rate and blood pressure and dilate the blood vessels and the air passages of the lungs. Stimulants also suppress the appetite and prevent sleep. These effects have been among the reasons for the popularity and frequent abuse of stimulants. They have been used, for example, by truck drivers who want to stay awake on long trips and by students who want to stay awake to study for exams. Unfortunately, in addition to their addicting properties, large doses of amphetamines can also lead to dizziness, confusion, and panic states, which clearly interfere with activities such as driving and studying.

Many people use (and abuse) stimulants because they induce a positive mood state. When they are injected, amphetamines and cocaine produce very similar subjective effects, but the effects of cocaine do not last as long. Low doses of amphetamines make people feel more confident, friendly, and energetic. This effect is most noticeable for a period of 3 to 6 hours after taking the drug. At higher doses, the person is likely to experience a brief, intense feeling of euphoria. The rushes associated with snorting or injecting cocaine are frequently described in sexual terms. Although many people believe that cocaine enhances sexual arousal and pleasure, most of the evidence suggests that prolonged use leads to sexual dysfunction (Jaffe, 1995). Tolerance develops quickly to the euphoric effects of stimulant drugs. The feelings of exhilaration and well-being are typically followed, several hours later, by the onset of lethargy and a mildly depressed or irritable mood.

Acute overdoses of stimulant drugs can result in irregular heartbeat, convulsions, coma, and death. The highly publicized overdose deaths of several prominent athletes, such as that of All-American basketball star Len Bias in 1986, indicate that the intense cardiovascular effects of cocaine can be fatal, even among people who are otherwise strong and healthy. The lethal consequences of cocaine seem to stem from a rapid increase in drug levels in the brain. Individual differences in sensitivity to the subjective effects of cocaine may play a role in cocaine-related deaths. In other words, people who are resistant to cocaine-induced euphoria may consume unusually large quantities of the drug while trying to achieve the rush that others have described.

CONSEQUENCES OF PROLONGED USE AND ABUSE

High doses of amphetamines and cocaine can lead to the onset of psychosis. The risk of a psychotic reaction seems to increase with repeated exposure to the drug. This syndrome can appear in people who have no prior history of mental disorder, and it usually disappears a few days after the drug has been cleared. Stimulants can also increase the severity of symptoms among people who have already developed some type of psychotic condition. The symptoms of *amphetamine psychosis* include auditory and visual hallucinations, as well as delusions of persecution and grandeur. The similarity between amphetamine psychosis and paranoid schizophrenia is quite striking.

As in the case of other forms of addiction, the most devastating effects of stimulant drugs frequently center around the disruption of occupational and social roles. The compulsion to continue taking cocaine can lead to physical exhaustion and financial ruin. People who are dependent on cocaine must spend enormous amounts of money to support their habit. They may have to sell important assets, such as their homes and cars, in order to finance extended binges.

Prolonged use of amphetamines has also been linked to an increase in violent behavior, but it is not clear whether this phenomenon is due to the drug itself or to the lifestyles with which it is frequently associated. Some violence might be related to a drug-induced increase in paranoia and hostility. Statistics concerning drugs and violent crime are very difficult to interpret. The direct effects of the drug on human behavior are confounded with various economic and social factors that are associated with buying, selling, and using an expensive, illegal drug like cocaine. Other dangers associated with chronic use of psychomotor stimulants, such as an increased risk of exposure to the HIV virus, may be attributed to promiscuous sexual behavior and the exchange of needles that are not sterile.

People who discontinue taking stimulant drugs do not typically experience severe withdrawal symptoms. The most common reaction is depression. Long-term exposure to high doses of amphetamine can lead to a profound state of clinical depression, which is often accompanied by ideas of suicide.

Cannabis

Marijuana and hashish are derived from the hemp plant, *Cannabis sativa*. The most common active ingredient in cannabis is a compound called delta-9-tetrahydro-cannabinol (delta-9-THC, or THC). Because every part of the plant contains THC, cannabis can be prepared for consumption in several ways. **Marijuana** refers to the dried leaves and flowers, which can be smoked in a cigarette or pipe. It can also be baked in brownies and ingested orally. **Hashish** refers to the dried resin from the top of the female cannabis plant. It can be smoked or eaten after being baked in cookies or brownies.

When it is smoked, the effects of marijuana and hashish can be felt within a few minutes and may reach a maximum within 30 to 60 minutes. Most of the drug is metabolized in the liver. Blood levels of THC diminish quickly, but traces of its by-products can be detected as long as 30 days after ingestion.

SHORT-TERM EFFECTS

The subjective effects of marijuana are almost always pleasant. "Getting high" on marijuana refers to a pervasive sense of well-being and happiness. Laboratory research has shown that marijuana can have variable effects on a person's mood. Many people begin to feel happy, whereas a few become anxious and paranoid. The mood of other people seems to be especially important. After smoking marijuana, a person's mood may become more easily influenced by the way in which other people are behaving.

Cannabis intoxication is often accompanied by *temporal disintegration,* a condition in which people have trouble retaining and organizing information, even over relatively short periods of time. Conversations may become disjointed because the drug interferes with the people's ability to recall what they have said or planned to say. Lapses in attention and concentration problems are frequent.

marijuana   The dried leaves and flowers of the female cannabis plant. "Getting high" on marijuana refers to a pervasive sense of well-being and happiness.

hashish   The dried resin from the top of the female cannabis plant. Ingestion of hashish leads to a feeling of being "high" (see marijuana).

hallucinogens   Drugs that produce
hallucinations.

CONSEQUENCES OF PROLONGED USE AND ABUSE

The issue of the addictive properties of cannabis remains controversial (Grinspoon & Bakalar, 1993). Some tolerance effects to THC have been observed in laboratory animals. Tolerance effects in humans remain ambiguous. Most evidence suggests that people do not develop tolerance to THC unless they are exposed to high doses over an extended period of time. Some people actually report that they become *more* sensitive (rather than less sensitive) to the effects of marijuana after repeated use. This phenomenon is called *reverse tolerance*. Although reverse tolerance has been reported casually by frequent users, it has not been demonstrated in a laboratory situation, where dosage levels can be carefully controlled. Experienced smokers may believe that they have become more sensitive to the effects of the drug when in fact they have learned to inhale more efficiently (and therefore need to smoke fewer joints to get high).

Withdrawal symptoms are unlikely to develop among people who smoke marijuana occasionally. One investigation found no withdrawal symptoms in a group of people who were required (for the purpose of the study) to smoke one joint a day for 28 days. People who have been exposed to continuous, high doses of THC may experience withdrawal symptoms, such as irritability, restlessness, and insomnia.

Prolonged heavy use of marijuana may lead to certain types of performance deficits on neuropsychological tests, especially those involving sustained attention, learning, and decision making (Pope & Yurgelun-Todd, 1996). These effects should be interpreted cautiously. They might indicate that exposure to high doses of marijuana can have toxic effects on the brain, but they also may be a reflection of residual drug action seen in people who last smoked the drug several hours before taking the tests. Performance deficits may also be an indication of cognitive symptoms of withdrawal rather than permanent intellectual impairment.

Hallucinogens

Drugs that are called **hallucinogens** cause people to experience hallucinations. Although many other types of drugs can lead to hallucinations at toxic levels, hallucinogens cause hallucinations in relatively low doses. There are many different types of hallucinogens, and they have very different neurophysiological effects. The molecular structure of many hallucinogens is similar to the molecular structure of neurotransmitters, such as serotonin and norepinephrine. The most common hallucinogen is a synthetic drug called *LSD* (D-lysergic acid diethylamide), which bears a strong chemical resemblance to serotonin. It acts by blocking serotonin receptors in the brain. *Psilocybin* is another type of hallucinogen whose chemical structure resembles that of serotonin. It is found in different types of mushrooms, which grow primarily in the southern United States and Mexico. *Mescaline* is a type of hallucinogen that resembles norepinephrine. It is the active ingredient in a small, spineless cactus called *peyote*. Mescaline and psilocybin have been used in religious ceremonies by various Native American peoples for many centuries.

Phencyclidine (PCP; also known as *crystal* or *angel dust)* is another synthetic drug that is often classified with the hallucinogens, although its effects are quite different than those associated with LSD and mescaline. It was originally developed as a painkiller. Small doses of PCP lead to relaxation, warmth, and numbness. At higher doses, PCP can induce psychotic behavior, including delusional thinking, catatonic motor behavior, manic excitement, and sudden mood changes. The drug is typically sold in a crystallized form that can be sprinkled on leaves, such as tobacco, marijuana, or parsley, and then smoked.

SHORT-TERM EFFECTS

The effects of hallucinogenic drugs are difficult to study empirically because they are based primarily in subjective experience. They typically induce vivid, and occasionally spectacular, visual images. During the early phase of this drug experience, the images often take the form of colorful geometric patterns. The later phase is more likely to be filled with meaningful images of people, animals, and places. The images may change rapidly, and they sometimes follow an explosive pattern of movement.

Although these hallucinatory experiences are usually pleasant, they are occasionally frightening. "Bad trips" are a decidedly unpleasant experience that can lead to panic attacks and the fear of losing one's mind. Some people believe that hallucinogenic drugs can facilitate the process of self-exploration. People who are "tripping" on hallucinogens sometimes report achieving deep insights about their own thoughts and feelings. For this reason, LSD and related chemicals have also been known as *psychedelic* (mind-expanding) drugs.

CONSEQUENCES OF PROLONGED USE AND ABUSE

The use of hallucinogens follows a different pattern than that associated with most other drugs. Hallucinogens—with the possible exception of PCP—are used sporadically and on special occasions rather than continuously. Tolerance develops very quickly to hallucinogens such as LSD, psilocybin, and mescaline (but not to PCP). If these drugs are taken repeatedly within 2 or 3 days, their effects disappear. Most people do not increase their use of hallucinogens over time. People who stop taking hallucinogens after continued use do not experience problems; there seem to be no withdrawal symptoms associated with the hallucinogens that resemble serotonin and norepinephrine.

Most hallucinogens are not particularly toxic. People do not die from taking an overdose of LSD, psilocybin, or mescaline. However, PCP is much more toxic. High doses can lead to coma, convulsions, respiratory arrest, and brain hemorrhage. Death is more likely to occur if the person has also been drinking alcohol and taking barbiturates in addition to using PCP.

The perceptual effects of hallucinogenic drugs almost always wear off after several hours. There are cases, however, in which these drugs have induced persistent psychotic behavior. Most experts interpret these examples as an indication that the drug experience can trigger the onset of psychosis in people who were already vulnerable to that type of disorder. PCP is more likely than the other hallucinogens to produce persistent psychotic behavior.

Some people who have taken hallucinogens experience *flashbacks*—brief visual aftereffects that can occur at unpredictable intervals long after the drug has been cleared from the person's body. Scientists do not understand the mechanisms that are responsible for flashbacks. Flashbacks may be more likely to occur when the person is under stress or after the person has used another drug, such as marijuana.

Classification

The problems that we have reviewed in the preceding pages indicate that substance dependence represents an extremely diverse set of problems. Everyone—clinicians and researchers, as well as those who abuse drugs and their families—seems to recognize the existence of a serious psychological disorder. But does it have a core? What is the best way to define it? In the following pages we briefly review some of the ways in which alcoholism and drug abuse have been defined. We must begin with the recognition that alcoholism and other types of addiction have not always been viewed as medical conditions that require treatment.

Brief History of Legal and Illegal Substances

One of the most widely recognized facts about alcohol consumption is that drinking patterns vary tremendously from one culture to the next and, within the same culture, from one point in time to another. For example, heavy drinking was not generally considered to be a serious problem in the colonial United States (Levine, 1978). The average amount of alcohol consumed per person each year was much higher in those days than it is today (Fingarette, 1988). Drunkenness was not considered to be either socially deviant or symptomatic of medical illness.

Public attitudes toward alcohol changed dramatically in the United States during the first half of the nineteenth century. Members of the temperance movement preached against the consumption of alcohol in any form. Temperance workers ardently believed that anyone who drank alcohol would become a drunkard. Their arguments were largely moral and religious rather than medical or scientific, and many of their publications included essays on the personality weaknesses that were associated with such morally reprehensible behaviors (Levine, 1978).

The movement finally succeeded in banning the manufacture and sale of alcoholic beverages when Congress approved the Eighteenth Amendment to the Constitution in 1919. During the following years, known as the Prohibition era, the average consumption of alcohol fell substantially, and the incidence of associated medical illnesses, such as cirrhosis of the liver, also declined. Nevertheless, these laws were extremely difficult to enforce, and Prohibition was repealed in 1933.

DSM-IV

The DSM-IV divides addictions into two categories: substance abuse and substance dependence, with the latter being the more severe and advanced form of disorder. This distinction is based, in part, on the recognition that many people who suffer serious impairment from substance abuse do not progress to the level of dependence. The manual lists 11 types of drugs that can lead to problems of abuse and dependence. Rather than including separate definitions of dependence and abuse for each class of substance, the manual provides one generic set of criteria for substance dependence and another for substance abuse. These criterion sets can be applied to any type of drug.

TABLE 11–2

DSM-IV Criteria for Substance Dependence

A. **A MALADAPTIVE PATTERN OF SUBSTANCE USE, LEADING TO CLINICALLY SIGNIFICANT IMPAIRMENT OR DISTRESS, AS MANIFESTED BY THREE (OR MORE) OF THE FOLLOWING, OCCURRING AT ANY TIME IN THE SAME 12-MONTH PERIOD:**

1. Tolerance, as defined by either of the following:
   a. A need for markedly increased amounts of the substance to achieve intoxication or desired effect.
   b. Markedly diminished effect with continued use of the same amount of the substance.
2. Withdrawal, as manifested by either of the following:
   a. The characteristic withdrawal syndrome for the substance (criteria sets for withdrawal are listed separately for specific substances).
   b. The same (or a closely related) substance is taken to relieve or avoid withdrawal symptoms.
3. The substance is often taken in larger amounts or over a longer period than was intended.
4. There is a persistent desire or unsuccessful efforts to cut down or control substance use.
5. A great deal of time is spent in activities necessary to obtain the substance (for example, visiting multiple doctors or driving long distances), use the substance (for example, chain-smoking), or recover from its effects.
6. Important social, occupational, or recreational activities are given up or reduced because of substance use.
7. The substance use is continued despite knowledge of having a persistent or recurrent physical or psychological problem that is likely to have been caused or exacerbated by the substance (for example, current cocaine use despite recognition of cocaine-induced depression, or continued drinking despite recognition that an ulcer was made worse by alcohol consumption).

The DSM-IV criteria for *substance dependence* are presented in Table 11–2. The person has to exhibit at least three of the seven criteria for a diagnosis of substance dependence to be made. Tolerance and withdrawal are not required for the person to meet this definition of dependence. Their importance is recognized with a subtype designation. If there is evidence of either tolerance or withdrawal (or both), the additional specification of *physiological dependence* is made.

However, a single definition of dependence may conceal differences between the kinds of problems that are associated with various classes of drugs (Frances, First, & Pincus, 1995). For example, dependence on opiates almost always involves physiological symptoms of tolerance and withdrawal, whereas dependence on cannabis or hallucinogens almost never does.

Substance abuse is defined in terms of harmful consequences that appear in the absence of tolerance, withdrawal, or a pattern of compulsive use (dependence). The DSM-IV definition of substance abuse is presented in Table 11–3. One difficult issue in defining this condition involves the identification of a boundary between substance abuse and the recreational use of drugs. The diagnostic manual emphasizes the terms *recurrent* and *maladaptive pattern* for this purpose. The problem must be persistent before this diagnosis would be considered.

Proposed Subtypes

DSM-IV does not recognize any systems for subtyping substance dependence, other than the presence or absence of physiological symptoms (tolerance or withdrawal). Nevertheless, procedures for subdividing alcoholism have been employed extensively in research studies (Sher, 1991, 1994). One system that is currently influential was proposed by Robert Cloninger (1987), a psychiatrist at Washington University in St. Louis. Cloninger proposed two prototypical varieties of alcoholism. According to this system, Type 1 alcoholism is characterized by a somewhat later onset, prominent psychological dependence (loss-of-control drinking), and the absence of antisocial personality traits. It is found in both men and women. Type 2 alcoholism, which is found almost exclusively among men, typically has an earlier onset and is associated with the co-occurrence of persistent antisocial behaviors. This proposed distinction has been useful in many research studies. On the other hand, the difference between Type 1 and Type 2 alcoholism may be more quantitative than qualitative in nature (Vaillant, 1994). We return to a discussion of these two types when we consider the influence of genetic factors on the etiology of alcoholism.

TABLE 11–3

DSM-IV Criteria for Substance Abuse

A. A MALADAPTIVE PATTERN OF SUBSTANCE USE LEADING TO CLINICALLY SIGNIFICANT IMPAIRMENT OR DISTRESS, AS MANIFESTED BY ONE (OR MORE) OF THE FOLLOWING, OCCURRING WITHIN A 12-MONTH PERIOD:

   1. Recurrent substance use resulting in a failure to fulfill major role obligations at work, school, or home.
   2. Recurrent substance use in situations in which it is physically hazardous.
   3. Recurrent substance-related legal problems.
   4. Continued substance use despite having persistent or recurrent social or interpersonal problems caused or exacerbated by the effects of the substance.

B. THE SYMPTOMS HAVE NEVER MET THE CRITERIA OF SUBSTANCE DEPENDENCE FOR THIS CLASS OF SUBSTANCE.

Course and Outcome

It is impossible to specify a typical course for substance dependence, especially alcoholism. Age of onset varies tremendously, ranging from childhood and early adolescence throughout the life span. Although we can roughly identify stages that intervene between initial exposure to a drug and the eventual onset of tolerance and dependence, the timing with which a person moves through these phases can vary enormously. The best available information regarding the course of substance use disorders comes from the study of alcoholism. The specific course of this problem varies considerably from one person to the next. The only thing that seems to be certain is that periods of heavy use alternate with periods of relative abstinence, however short-lived they may be.

In an effort to examine the natural history of alcoholism, George Vaillant (1996) studied the lives of 456 inner-city adolescents from Boston and 268 former undergraduate students from Harvard University. Initial information was collected in 1940, when the participants were adolescents. Follow-up information was collected every other year by questionnaire and every fifth year by physical examination. The college group has been followed until 70 years of age, and the core city group has been followed to age 60. At some point during their lives, 21 percent of the college men and 35 percent of the core city men met diagnostic criteria for alcohol abuse, which Vaillant defined as the presence of four or more problems in such areas as employer complaints, marital and family difficulties, medical complications, and legal problems. Most of the alcoholic men went through repeated cycles of abstinence followed by relapse.

As expected, the mortality rate was higher among men who abused alcohol than among those who did not. Heart disease and cancer were twice as common among the alcohol abusers, perhaps in part because they were also more likely to be heavy cigarette smokers.

Many men spent the previous 20 years alternating between periods of controlled drinking and alcohol abuse. The proportion of men who continued to abuse alcohol went down after the age of 40. The proportion of alcoholic men in both groups who became completely abstinent went up slowly but consistently during the follow-up period. The longer a man remained abstinent, the greater the probability that he would continue to be abstinent. Vaillant's data indicated that relapse to alcohol abuse was unlikely among men who were able to remain abstinent for at least 6 years.

The relapse process is an important problem for all types of substance dependence. Some evidence suggests that this process may include certain common elements across various types of drugs (Brownell et al., 1986). Most people who have quit using drugs like alcohol or tobacco describe a sequence of circumstances, beginning with cognitive events (contemplating change, making a commitment to change) leading to behavioral outcomes (initial cessation, long-term maintenance).

Many important questions remain to be answered about the relapse process. Is there a "safe point" that separates a period of high risk for relapse from a period of more stable change? Vaillant's data suggest that the 6-year mark may be important for men who abuse alcohol. Will this suggestion be replicated in other studies? And does it generalize to other drugs? Do relapse rates stabilize over time? Is an addicted person more likely to succeed on a later attempt to quit than on an early attempt? Answers to these questions will be useful in the development of more effective treatment programs.

Other Disorders Commonly Associated with Addictions

People who abuse alcohol often exhibit other forms of mental disorder as well. Most prominent among these are antisocial personality disorder, mood disorders, and anxiety disorders (Kushner, Sher, & Beitman, 1990; Merikangas & Gelernter, 1990; Weissman, 1988). The complexity of the association among these problems makes them difficult to untangle. In some cases, prolonged heavy drinking can result in feelings of depression and anxiety. The more the person drinks, the more guilty the person feels about his or her inability to control the drinking. In addition, increased

George Vaillant's longitudinal study of alcoholic men indicated that the disorder follows an unpredictable, episodic course in which periods of abstinence are often followed by relapse.

drinking often leads to greater conflict with family members, coworkers, and other people. Sometimes the depression and anxiety precede the onset of drinking. In fact, some people seem to use alcohol initially in a futile attempt to self-medicate for these other conditions. Ultimately, the alcohol makes things worse.

Epidemiology

Drug-related problems are found in most countries around the world. There are interesting variations, however, in patterns of use for specific types of drugs. The maps in Figure 11–1 indicate global variations in the use of opium, cocaine, and cannabis. The use of specific drugs is determined, in part, by their availability. Opium (Figure 11–1) is used most heavily in Southeast Asia, as well as in some Middle Eastern countries, where the opium poppy is cultivated. Cocaine (Figure 11–1b) is used frequently in certain countries of South America where coca trees grow; it is also imported into North America, particularly the United States. Use of cannabis (Figure 11–1c) is very widespread, in part because the plants can grow in many different climates. In contrast, in Japan, where the amount of land available for cultivation is severely limited, the largest drug problem involves amphetamine, a synthetic drug.

When we consider the epidemiology of drug addiction, we must keep in mind the distinction between use and dependence. People have to use the drug before they can become dependent on it. Patterns of increased use can therefore be alarming. The percentage of eighth-grade students who have tried certain kinds of drugs, particularly cocaine, heroin, and marijuana, went up during the early 1990s. These increases are obviously a reason for serious concern; however, most people who occasionally use alcohol and illicit drugs, such as marijuana and cocaine, do not become addicted. Dependence almost always develops slowly after extended exposure to a drug. The average time between initial use of illicit drugs and the onset of symptoms of dependence is between 2 and 3 years (Anthony & Helzer, 1991). The distinction between people who eventually become addicted and those who use drugs without becoming addicted is an important consideration in this field.

Prevalence of Alcohol Abuse and Dependence

Approximately two out of every three males in Western countries drink alcohol regularly, at least on a social basis; less than 25 percent abstain from drinking completely. Among all men and women who have ever used alcohol, roughly 20 percent will develop serious problems at some point in their lives as a consequence of prolonged alcohol consumption (Anthony, Warner, & Kessler, 1994).

The Epidemiologic Catchment Area (ECA) study provides one detailed picture of the prevalence of alcoholism. The investigators found a lifetime prevalence rate of 13.8 percent for alcoholism (either alcohol abuse or dependence). The 12-month prevalence rate was 6.3 percent. Alcohol-related disorders were the second most common type of mental disorder in the United States—second only to phobias—when men and women were considered together.

GENDER DIFFERENCES
Approximately 60 percent of women in the United States drink alcohol at least occasionally, but, in comparison to men, relatively few develop alcoholism. Among people who chronically abuse alcohol, men outnumber women by a ratio of approximately 5 to 1 (Robins & Regier, 1991). Recent information suggests that this disparity may be narrower today than it was 20 years ago, especially among younger people. The National Comorbidity Survey (NCS) found a 12-month prevalence rate for alcohol dependence of 11 percent for men and 4 percent for women (Kessler et al., 1994). Although the rate of alcoholism among younger women appears to be increasing, prevalence is still much higher in men, and the rates do not seem likely to converge. Persistent differences can probably be attributed to biological variables, including the fact that women are, on

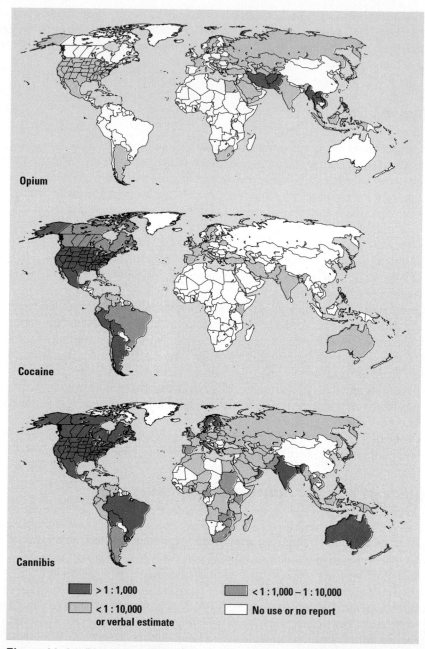

Opium

Cocaine

Cannibis

■ > 1 : 1,000   ■ < 1 : 1,000 – 1 : 10,000

□ < 1 : 10,000   □ No use or no report
or verbal estimate

Figure 11–1   Global Patterns of Drug Use.   These maps illustrate the prevalence of the use of opium, cocaine, and cannabis around the world. Each drug is used most heavily in regions in which it is most accessible.

Source: J. C. Anthony and J. E. Helzer, 1995, Epidemiology of drug dependence. In M. T. Tsuang, M. Tohen, and G. E. P. Zahner (Eds.), *Textbook in Psychiatric Epidemiology,* pp. 362–64. New York: Wiley.

average, less physically tolerant of alcohol, as well as social variables, such as negative attitudes toward intoxication in women (Gomberg, 1988).

There are also important gender differences in alcohol metabolism. A single standard dose of alcohol, measured in proportion to total body weight, will produce a higher peak blood alcohol level in women than in men (Jones & Jones, 1976). One explanation for this difference lies in the fact that men have a higher average content of body water than women do. A standard dose

TABLE 11–4

Lifetime Prevalence for Drug Dependence Syndromes (NCS Data)

DRUG GROUP	PERCENT
Tobacco	24.1
Alcohol	14.1
Cannabis	4.2
Cocaine	2.7
Amphetamines	1.7
Barbiturates and benzodiazepines	1.2
Hallucinogens	0.5
Heroin	0.4
Inhalants	0.3

Source: *J. C. Anthony, L. A. Warner, and R. C. Kessler, 1994, Comparative epidemiology of dependence on tobacco, alcohol, controlled substances, and inhalants: Basic findings from the national Comorbidity Survey,* Experimental Clinical Psychopharmacology, 2, 1–24.

of alcohol will be less diluted in women because alcohol is distributed in total body water. This may help to explain the fact that women who drink heavily for many years are more vulnerable to liver disorders.

Prevalence of Drug and Nicotine Dependence

The National Comorbidity Study (NCS) surveyed more than 8,000 household residents in the United States between 1990 and 1992. Lifetime prevalence rates generated by this study for specific types of drug dependence are listed in Table 11–4. The combined lifetime prevalence in the NCS for dependence on any type of controlled substance (those that are illegal or available only by prescription) was 7.5 percent. This is approximately half the rate for alcohol dependence. The NCS found a lifetime prevalence of 24 percent for nicotine dependence.

The percentage of people in the United States who smoke tobacco has actually declined since 1964, when the U.S. Surgeon General's Report announced it had found a definite link between smoking and cancer and other diseases. The rate of decline has been greatest among men, who traditionally have smoked more than women. Among teenagers, smoking rates may have stabilized at approximately 10 percent for both males and females (Figure 11–2, page 312), but there has been some indication that smoking prevalence among high school seniors had begun to increase again in 1994 and 1995 (Davis, 1996). Furthermore, although tobacco consumption has declined in industrialized countries, it has increased dramatically in the developing countries, where people may be less educated about the health risks associated with smoking (McKim, 1997).

Approximately 32 percent of those people who have ever used tobacco eventually meet the criteria for dependence (Anthony et al., 1994). This statistic might be considered an index of the addicting properties of a drug. In other words, if you use a drug repeatedly, will you develop symptoms of dependence? When viewed from this perspective, nicotine may be among the most addicting drugs that are used in our society (see Further Thoughts, page 300). Comparable figures (percentage of users who develop dependence) for other drugs were anxiolytics and hypnotics, 25 percent; alcohol, 20 percent; heroin, 20 percent; cocaine, 15 percent; marijuana, 15 percent; amphetamines, 10 percent; and hallucinogens, less than 10 percent.

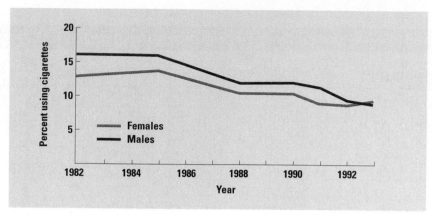

Figure 11–2 **Cigarette Use Among Teenagers.** Rates of cigarette use in 1 month reported by females and males between the ages of 12 and 17, according to the 1993 U.S. National Household Survey.

Source: W. A. McKim, 1997, *Drugs and Behavior*, p. 169. Upper Saddle River, NJ: Prentice Hall.

Etiological Considerations and Research

Our discussion of etiology will focus primarily on alcohol dependence and abuse. We have chosen this approach because clinical scientists know more about alcohol and its abuse than about any of the other drugs. Research on alcohol abuse illustrates many factors that are also important in the etiology of other forms of substance dependence.

Most contemporary investigators approach the development of alcoholism in terms of multiple systems. Biological factors obviously play an important role. The addicting properties of certain drugs are crucial: People become addicted to drugs like heroin, nicotine, and alcohol, but they do not become addicted to drugs like the antidepressants or to food additives like Nutrasweet. We must therefore understand how addicting drugs affect the brain in order to understand the process of dependence. At the same time, we need to understand the social and cultural factors that influence how and under what circumstances an individual first acquires and uses drugs. Our expectations about the effects of drugs are shaped by our parents, our peers, and the media. These are also important etiological considerations.

The etiology of alcoholism is best viewed within a developmental framework that views the problem in terms of various stages: (1) initiation and continuation, (2) escalation and transition to abuse, and (3) development of tolerance and withdrawal (Marlatt & Baer, 1988; Vaillant, 1995). In the following pages we review some of the social, psychological, and biological factors that explain why people begin to drink, how their drinking behaviors are reinforced, and how they develop tolerance after prolonged exposure.

Social Factors

People who don't drink obviously won't develop alcoholism. Therefore one important link in the chain of causal events is the process of initiation. Which people will expose themselves to addictive substances, and why? Among those young people who choose to drink alcohol (or smoke cigarettes, or consume other addictive substances), which ones will eventually develop problems? The development of drug dependence requires continued use, and it is influenced by the manner in which the drug is consumed. In other words, with regard to alcohol, will the person's initial reaction to the drug be pleasant, or will the person become sick and avoid alcoholic beverages in the future? If the person continues drinking, will he or she choose strong or weak drinks, with or without food, with others or alone, and so on?

Initial experimentation with drugs is most likely to occur among those individuals who are rebellious and extroverted and whose parents and peers model or encourage use (Chassin, 1984). The relative influence of parents and friends varies according to the gender and age of the adolescent as well as the drug in question. For example, parents may have a greater influence over their children's decision to drink alcohol, whereas peers seem to play a more important role in the initial exposure to marijuana.

Parents can influence their children's drinking behaviors in many ways. They can serve as models for using drugs to cope with stressful circumstances. They may also help promote attitudes and expectations regarding the benefits of drug consumption, or they may simply provide access to licit or illicit drugs (Lang & Stritzke, 1993). Adolescents with alcoholic parents are more likely to drink alcohol than those whose parents do not abuse alcohol. This increased risk seems to be due to several factors, including the fact that alcoholic parents monitor their children's behavior less closely, thereby providing more opportunities for illicit drinking. The level of negative affect is also relatively high in the families of alcoholic parents. This unpleasant emotional climate, coupled with reduced parental monitoring, increases the probability that an adolescent will affiliate with peers who use drugs (Chassin et al., 1993). Taken together, these considerations indicate that parents' drinking has a definite influence on their children's use of alcohol and that the mechanisms involved in this relationship are quite complex.

The circumstances in which an adolescent is initially exposed to alcohol can influence the person's pattern of drinking as well as his or her response to the drug. Drinking small amounts of wine with meals on a regular basis may be less likely to lead to alcohol dependence than the sporadic consumption of hard liquor for the purpose of becoming intoxicated.

Biological Factors

Initial physiological reactions to alcohol can have a dramatic negative influence on a person's early drinking experiences. For example, millions of people are unable to tolerate even small amounts of alcohol. These people develop flushed skin, sometimes after only a single drink. They may also feel nauseated, and some experience an abnormal heartbeat. This phenomenon is most common among people of Asian ancestry and may affect 30 to 50 percent of this population. Not coincidentally, the prevalence of alcoholism is unusually low among Asian populations. Research studies indicate a link between these two phenomena. For example, Japanese Americans who experience the fast-flushing response tend to drink less than those who do not flush (Nakawatase et al., 1993). The basic evidence suggests that in addition to looking for factors that make some individuals especially vulnerable to the addicting effects of alcohol, it may also be important to identify protective factors that reduce the probability of substance dependence.

A person's initial use of addictive drugs is obviously one important step toward the development of substance dependence, but the fact remains that most people who drink alcohol do not develop alcoholism. What accounts for the next important phase of the disorder? Why do some people abuse the drug while others do not? In the following pages we outline several additional biological variables. We begin by examining genetic factors, and then we consider the neurochemical effects of the drugs themselves.

GENETICS OF ALCOHOLISM

An extensive literature attests to the fact that patterns of alcohol consumption, as well as psychological and social problems associated with alcohol abuse, tend to run in families. The lifetime prevalence of alcoholism among the parents, siblings, and children of people with alcoholism is at least three to five times higher than the rate in the general population (Merikangas, 1990; Schuckit, 1987). Of course, this elevated risk among first-degree relatives could reflect the influence of either genetic or environmental factors, because families share both types of influence. Therefore we must look to the results of twin and adoption studies in an effort to disentangle these variables.

Twin Studies Several twin studies have examined patterns of alcohol consumption in nonalcoholic twins. The evidence indicates that both genetic factors and shared environmental factors influence the quantity and frequency of social drinking in normal men and women (Heath, Jardine, & Martin, 1989; Merikangas, 1990; Prescott et al., 1994).

Other studies have examined twin concordance rates for alcoholism when the proband is identified through a treatment program. Here the focus is on severely disabling drinking problems rather than simply the consumption of alcohol. Several studies have found that concordance rates are higher among MZ than among DZ twin pairs, but in some studies this finding is limited to male subjects (McGue, Pickins, & Svikis, 1992). Different etiological pathways may be responsible for alcoholism in men and women. The possibility is particularly interesting in light of the marked gender differences in the prevalence of alcohol abuse and dependence.

Adoption Studies The strategy followed in an adoption study allows the investigator to separate relatively clearly the influence of genetic and environmental factors. The probands in this type of study are individuals who meet two criteria: (1) they had a biological parent who was alcoholic, and (2) they were adopted away from their biological parents at an early age and raised by adoptive parents.

Two major adoption studies have examined the possible role of genetic factors in the etiology of alcoholism. One investigation was conducted in Denmark by the psychiatrist Donald Goodwin of the University of Kansas and his colleagues (Goodwin et al., 1994). This study revealed that by the age of 30, 18 percent of the male offspring of alcoholic biological parents had developed alcoholism, compared to only 5 percent of the control adoptees. The results were quite different for the daughters of alcoholic parents; the risk for alcoholism among female offspring was only 4 percent among both the index cases and the control sample. These data are consistent with the results of McGue's twin study. Genetic factors apparently influence the development of alcoholism among men, but their influence is more ambiguous among women.

A pair of adoption studies was conducted in Sweden by Robert Cloninger and his colleagues (Cloninger, 1987; Sigvardsson, Bohman, & Cloninger, 1996). The results of these investigations are consistent with Goodwin's adoption study in pointing toward the influence of genetic factors in the etiology of alcohol abuse and dependence. They also indicate, however, that the manner in which genetic and environmental events combine probably differs from one type of alcoholism to another. Using Cloninger's subtyping system, genetic factors may play a role in the etiology of Type 1 alcoholism in women. The daughters of people with Type 2 alcoholism, on the other hand, are at risk for the development of certain types of anxiety disorders, but they are not more likely to develop alcoholism themselves. Studies that lump together these different types of drinking problems will probably produce less consistent results for women than for men.

What can we conclude from the adoption studies? McGue (1993) conducted a comprehensive review of the adoption study evidence and reached the following general conclusions:

- The offspring of alcoholic parents who are reared by nonalcoholic adoptive parents are more likely than people in the general population to develop drinking problems of their own. Thus the familial nature of alcoholism is at least partially determined by genes.
- Being reared by an alcoholic parent, in the absence of other etiological factors, does not appear to be a critical consideration in the development of the disorder.
- The etiology of alcoholism is probably heterogeneous in nature; that is, there are several pathways to the disorder.
- There is an association between antisocial personality traits, or "behavioral undercontrol," and alcohol abuse or dependence. The exact nature of this relation and the direction of effect have not been determined.

NEUROCHEMICAL MODES OF ACTION

Assuming that some people are genetically more vulnerable to the addicting effects of alcohol than others, what genetic mechanisms are involved, and how do they function? Considerable speculation has focused on brain mechanisms, especially those involving neural transmission (Schuckit, 1994). All of the addicting psychoactive drugs produce changes in the chemical processes by which messages are transmitted in the brain.

Endogenous Opioid Receptors   One promising research area in the neurosciences involves the discovery of the endogenous opioids known as **endorphins.** These relatively short chains of amino acids, or neuropeptides, are naturally synthesized in the brain and are closely related to morphine in terms of their pharmacological properties. Endorphins possess a chemical affinity for specific receptor sites, in the same way that a key fits into a specific lock. More than a dozen endorphins are distributed widely throughout the brain. They appear to be especially important in the activities associated with systems that control pain, emotion, stress, and reward, as well as such biological functions as feeding and growth (Cohen, 1988).

Research studies have demonstrated many interesting features of the endorphins. Laboratory animals can develop tolerance to injections of endorphins, just as they develop tolerance to addicting drugs like morphine, and they also exhibit symptoms of withdrawal if the injections are suddenly discontinued. These studies confirm the pharmacological similarity between endogenous and exogenous opioids, but one crucial difference remains: We don't become addicted to endorphins in normal brain functioning.

Some theorists associate alcoholism with excessive production of endogenous opioids (Blum & Payne, 1991; Gianoulakis, 1993). This hypothesis suggests that common neurochemical mechanisms might account for addiction to alcohol and to opioids such as heroin and morphine. It is based on several observations that indicate that the behavioral and pharmacological effects of alcohol are similar to those of the opioids. For example, laboratory animals that have received injections of small amounts of morphine will increase their consumption of alcohol. Although the relationship between endorphins and alcoholism is intriguing, the hypothesis is also inconsistent with some other facts. The experiences of alcoholics during withdrawal differ markedly from those of heroin addicts (APA, 1994). The endorphin hypothesis would predict that the reactions should be similar because they are caused by common neurochemical processes (Cohen, 1988).

The Serotonin Hypothesis   Addicting drugs probably have widespread effects on the process of neural transmission in the brain, including systems that involve catecholamines (for example, dopamine, norepinephrine, and serotonin) as well as the neuropeptides. Although alcohol does not bind directly to any receptor sites in the brain, it does alter the permeability of neuronal membranes (Yi, 1991). Channels for potassium and chlorine ions are opened, and corresponding channels for sodium and calcium are closed, thus depressing the central nervous system. Concentrations of neurotransmitters, such as serotonin and dopamine, are initially increased. If the person continues to drink heavily over an extended period of time, the drinking produces many effects that are opposite to those of short-term intoxication: The central nervous system becomes excited rather than depressed, and the ion channel events are reversed.

The serotonin theory of the etiology of alcoholism assumes that alcohol dependence is caused by a genetically determined deficiency in serotonin activity in certain areas of the limbic system of the brain (Ferreira & Soares da Silva, 1991; Wallis, Rezazadeh, & Lal, 1993). The serotonin theory suggests that some people begin with a deficiency in serotonin, and the consumption of alcohol initially helps to correct for this deficiency. Unfortunately, prolonged consumption further depletes the system. Therefore the person initially drinks to feel good—alcohol stimulates activity in the reward systems of the brain—but after a while he or she must drink more to avoid feeling worse when serotonin levels are reduced below their initial point.

Evidence supporting this theory comes from several kinds of investigation. First, animals that are bred to exhibit high and low preferences for alcohol exhibit differences in serotonin levels. Those with a high preference for alcohol have lower levels of serotonin in areas of the brain that regulate emotional responses (McBride et al., 1993). Second, alcohol abusers with an early onset

endorphin   The term is a contraction formed from the words *endogenous* (meaning "within") and *morphine*. Endorphins are relatively short chains of amino acids, or neuropeptides, that are naturally synthesized in the brain and are closely related to morphine (an opioid) in terms of their pharmacological properties.

Attitudes and expectations about the effects of drugs are shaped, in part, by the beliefs of peers. Many people believe that alcohol makes them more sociable.

and a family history for the disorder have lower serotonin activity than those with a later onset and no family history for the disorder (Buydens-Branchey et al., 1989). Third, drugs that enhance serotonin transmission (such as selective serotonin reuptake inhibitors or SSRIs; see Chapter 5) can decrease voluntary alcohol consumption in human subjects.

Psychological Factors

Extensive research over the past several decades has found that the progression of substance dependence depends on an interaction between environmental and biological events. One time-honored perspective on the development of alcoholism is the tension-reduction hypothesis. At its most general level, this viewpoint holds that people drink alcohol in an effort to reduce the impact of a stressful environment.

The tension-reduction hypothesis became the focal point for scientific investigation when Conger (1956) adapted formal learning theory to the problem and proposed that alcohol consumption is reinforced by its ability to relieve unpleasant emotional states, especially fear and anxiety. As we will see in the following pages, the relation between stress and alcohol has turned out to be more complex than this theory suggests. Drug effects interact with the person's beliefs and attitudes as well as with the social context in which the drugs are taken.

Placebo effects demonstrate that expectations are an important factor in any study of drug effects (see Chapter 3). During the 1970s, several research studies sought to evaluate the influence of alcohol on various facets of behavior using the *balanced placebo design*. This procedure allows the investigator to separate the direct, biological effects of the drug from the subjects' expectations about how the drug should affect their behavior. The results indicated that expectations can account for many effects that have often been attributed to the drug itself. For example, subjects who believed that they had ingested alcohol but who had actually consumed only tonic water displayed exaggerated aggression and reported enhanced feelings of sexual arousal (Goldman, Brown, & Christiansen, 1987; Goldman et al., 1991; Hull & Bond, 1986). Much less is known about expectancies for drugs other than alcohol, but there is good reason to believe that these cognitive factors also influence the ways in which people respond to cannabis, nicotine, stimulants, anxiolytics, and sedatives (Brandon, Wetter, & Baker, 1996; Brown, 1993).

The results of experiments using the balanced placebo design stimulated considerable thought about the role that alcohol expectancies may play in the etiology of drinking problems. These studies do not manipulate expectancies directly, however. They only lead subjects to believe that they have consumed alcohol when, in fact, they have not. The investigators infer that the subjects believed that alcohol would make them aggressive.

But is that really the case? Subsequent investigations began to examine alcohol expectancies directly (Brown et al., 1980). Investigators asked people, Why do you drink? What do you expect to happen after you have consumed a few beers or a couple of glasses of wine? Answers that subjects provided to these questions fit into six primary categories:

1. Alcohol transforms experiences in a positive way (for example: Drinking makes the future seem brighter).
2. Alcohol enhances social and physical pleasure (for example: Having a few drinks is a nice way to celebrate special occasions).
3. Alcohol enhances sexual performance and experience (for example: After a few drinks, I am more sexually responsive).
4. Alcohol increases power and aggression (for example: After a few drinks it is easier to pick a fight).

5.   Alcohol increases social assertiveness (for example: Having a few drinks makes it easier to talk to people).
6.   Alcohol reduces tension (for example: Alcohol enables me to fall asleep more easily).

These expectations may constitute one of the primary reasons for continued and increasingly heavy consumption of alcoholic beverages. In fact, expectancy patterns can help predict drinking behaviors. Longitudinal studies have found that adolescents who are just beginning to experiment with alcohol and who initially have the most positive expectations about the effects of alcohol go on to consume greater amounts of alcoholic beverages (Goldman et al., 1991; Smith et al., 1995). This type of demonstration is important because it indicates that, in many cases, the expectations appear before the person begins to drink heavily. Therefore, they may play a role in the onset of the problem rather than being consequences of heavy drinking.

These expectations may be influenced by parental and peer attitudes and by the portrayal of alcohol in the mass media. Follow-up studies have demonstrated that adolescents' expectations about the effects of alcohol are useful in predicting which individuals will later develop drinking problems (Christiansen et al., 1989; Stacy, Newcomb, & Bentler, 1991). Positive expectancies about alcohol—which are likely to encourage people to drink—are especially influential. Negative expectancies are associated with diminished use but seem to be less powerful (Leigh & Stacy, 1993; Stacy, Widaman, & Marlatt, 1990).

Integrated Systems

Alcoholism clearly results from an interaction among several types of systems. Various social, psychological, and biological factors influence the person's behavior at each stage in the cycle, from initial use of the drug through the eventual onset of tolerance and withdrawal. The process seems to progress in the following way. Initial experimentation with drugs is influenced by the person's family and peers, who serve as models for the use of drugs. Other people also influence the person's attitudes and expectations about the effects of drugs. Access to drugs, in addition to the patterns in which they are originally consumed, are determined, in part, by cultural factors.

For many people, drinking alcohol leads to short-term positive effects that reinforce continued consumption. The exact psychological mechanisms that are responsible for reinforcing heavy drinking may take several different forms. They may involve diminished self-awareness, stress reduction, or improved mood. These effects of alcohol on behavior and subjective experience are determined, in part, by the person's expectations about the way in which the drug will influence his or her feelings and behavior (Goldman, 1994).

There are most likely several different types of genetic influence, as illustrated by the results of the Swedish adoption studies. Genes interact strongly with environmental events for certain types of the disorder. A genetic predisposition to alcohol dependence probably causes the person to react to alcohol in an abnormal fashion. It is not clear whether those who are vulnerable to alcoholism are initially more or less sensitive than other people to the reinforcing effects of alcohol. Research studies have demonstrated both patterns of response (Sher, 1993).

The biological mechanisms responsible for abnormal reactions to alcohol may involve a deficiency in serotonin activity in certain areas of the limbic system. Drinking alcohol initially corrects this problem and increases serotonin activity, but the person eventually begins to feel worse after tolerance develops. Another point of view holds that people who are biologically insensitive to the adverse effects of alcohol are more likely to become alcoholics (Goodwin, 1988).

Drinking gradually becomes heavier and more frequent. The person becomes tolerant to the effects of alcohol and must therefore drink larger quantities to achieve the same reinforcing effects. After the person becomes addicted to alcohol, attempts to quit drinking are accompanied by painful withdrawal symptoms. Prolonged abuse can lead to permanent neurological impairment as well as the disruption of many other organ systems.

detoxification The process of short-term medical care (medication, rest, diets, fluids, and so on) during removal of a drug upon which a person has become dependent. The aim is to minimize withdrawal symptoms.

Treatment

The treatment of alcoholism and other types of substance use disorders is an especially difficult task. Many people with these problems do not acknowledge their difficulties, and only a relatively small number seek professional help. When they do enter treatment, it is typically with reluctance or on the insistence of friends, family members, or legal authorities. Compliance with treatment recommendations is often low, and dropout rates are high. The high rate of comorbidity with other forms of mental disorder presents an additional challenge, complicating the formulation of a treatment plan. Treatment outcome is likely to be least successful with those people who have comorbid conditions.

The goals of treatment for substance use disorders are a matter of controversy. Some clinicians believe that the only acceptable goal is total abstinence from drinking or drug use. Others have argued that, for some people, a more reasonable goal is the moderate use of legal drugs. Important questions have also been raised about the scope of improvements that might be expected from a successful treatment program. Is the goal simply to minimize or eliminate drug use, or should we expect that treatment will also address the social, occupational, and medical problems that are typically associated with drug problems? If these associated problems are the result of the person's prolonged abuse of alcohol or other drugs, the problems may improve on their own if the person becomes abstinent. However, to the extent that family problems or interpersonal difficulties contribute to the person's use of drugs, it may be necessary to address these difficulties before the drug problem can be resolved (McLellan et al., 1992).

Detoxification and Pharmacotherapy

Treatment of alcoholism and related forms of drug abuse is often accomplished in a sequence of stages, beginning with a brief period of **detoxification**—the removal of a drug on which a person has become dependent—lasting between 3 and 6 weeks (Dackis & Gold, 1991). This process is often extremely difficult, as the person experiences marked symptoms of withdrawal and gradually adjusts to the absence of the drug. For many types of CNS depressants, such as alcohol, hypnotics, and sedatives, detoxification is accomplished gradually. Stimulant drugs, in contrast, can be stopped abruptly (Cohen, 1988). During the detoxification period, medical staff closely monitor the patient's vital signs to prevent seizures and delirium. Although detoxification usually takes place in a hospital, some evidence indicates that it can be accomplished with close supervision on an outpatient basis.

People who are going through alcohol detoxification are often given various types of medication, including anxiolytics, primarily as a way of minimizing withdrawal symptoms (Weddington, 1992). This practice is controversial, in part because many people believe that it is illogical to use one form of drug—especially one that can be abused itself—to help someone recover from dependence on another drug.

Psychiatrists have also used SSRIs, such as Prozac, for the long-term treatment of alcoholic patients. This treatment is based, in part, on evidence from animal studies indicating that the increased availability of serotonin in the brain suppresses alcohol consumption. The effectiveness of this type of pharmacotherapy has not been extensively evaluated (Litten & Allen, 1991).

DISULFIRAM (ANTABUSE)

Disulfiram (Antabuse) is a drug that can block the chemical breakdown of alcohol. If a person who is taking Antabuse consumes even a small amount of alcohol, he or she will become violently ill. The symptoms include nausea, vomiting, profuse sweating, and increased heart rate and respiration rate. People who are taking Antabuse will stop drinking alcohol in order to avoid this extremely unpleasant reaction.

Unfortunately, voluntary compliance with this form of treatment is poor. Many patients discontinue taking Antabuse, usually because they want to resume drinking or because they believe that they can manage their problems without the drug (Børup, Kaiser, & Jensen,

1992). People can drink alcohol without experiencing an unpleasant reaction about 2 or 3 days after they stop taking Antabuse. Treatment therefore requires close medical supervision (Brewer, 1992).

Studies that have employed placebo control groups have found that patients who receive Antabuse are no more likely to remain sober than are those receiving a placebo (Fuller & Roth, 1979). Although most patients eventually relapse, those who are taking Antabuse may be able to stay sober for longer periods of time.

Self-Help Groups: Alcoholics Anonymous

One of the most widely accepted forms of treatment for alcoholism is Alcoholics Anonymous (AA). Organized in 1935, this self-help program is maintained by alcohol abusers for the sole purpose of helping other people who abuse alcohol become and remain sober. Because it is established and active in virtually all communities in North America and Europe as well as many other parts of the world, AA is generally considered to be "the first line of attack against alcoholism" (Nathan, 1993). Surveys conducted by AA indicate that its membership increased considerably during the 1970s and 1980s. In 1989, there were approximately 1 million members of AA in the United States and Canada (Chappel, 1993). Many members of AA are also involved in other forms of treatment offered by various types of mental health professionals, but AA is not officially associated with any other forms of treatment or professional organizations. Similar self-help programs have been developed for people who are dependent on other drugs, such as opioids (Narcotics Anonymous) and cocaine (Cocaine Anonymous).

The viewpoint espoused by AA is fundamentally spiritual in nature. AA is the original "12-step program." In the first step, the person must acknowledge that he or she is powerless over alcohol and unable to manage his or her drinking. The remaining steps involve spiritual and interpersonal matters such as accepting "a Power greater than ourselves" that can provide the person with direction; recognizing and accepting personal weaknesses; and making amends for previous errors, especially instances in which the person's drinking caused hardships for other people. One principal assumption is that people cannot recover on their own (Bean, 1975; Chappel, 1992).

The process of working through the 12 steps to recovery is facilitated by regular attendance at AA meetings, as often as every day of the first 90 days after the person stops drinking (Chappel, 1992). Most people choose to attend less frequently if they are able to remain sober throughout this initial period. Meetings provide chronic alcohol abusers with an opportunity to meet and talk with other people who have similar problems. New members are encouraged to call older members for help at any time if they experience an urge to drink. There is enormous variability in the format and membership of local AA meetings (Montgomery, Miller, & Tonigan, 1993).

It is difficult to evaluate the effectiveness of AA, for a number of reasons. Long-term follow-up is difficult, and it is generally impossible to employ some of the traditional methods of outcome research, such as random assignment to groups and placebo controls. Early dropout rates are relatively high: About half of all the people who initially join AA drop out in less than 3 months. On the other hand, survival rates (defined in terms of continued sobriety) are much higher for those people who remain in AA. About 80 percent of AA members who have remained sober for between 2 and 5 years will remain sober in the next year (Mäkelä, 1994).

Although the format of AA presents several obstacles to research, some studies indicate that AA does provide important help to many people. In his longitudinal study of alcoholic men, Vaillant (1995) found that attendance at AA meetings was an important predictor of positive outcomes. More recent outcome studies that have examined the effects of AA in combination with other forms of treatment indicate that participation in AA makes a significant positive contribution to treatment outcome (Pisani et al., 1993; Walsh et al., 1991).

Group therapy, like this session from the movie Clean and Sober, *is an important part of most inpatient treatment programs. It offers an opportunity for patients to acknowledge and confront openly the severity of their problems.*

getting help

If you have been looking for help in the area of substance dependence, you have probably noticed two things: (1) there are so many different sources of advice and information that the situation can quickly become quite confusing, and (2) the field is sharply divided on a number of crucial issues. Whose advice should you follow? Of all the self-help books dealing with drugs and alcohol, one stands out for its strong link to the research literature as well as the extensive clinical experience of the author. Marc Schuckit's *Educating Yourself about Alcohol and Drugs: A People's Primer* provides sensible answers to the questions asked by people who are wondering about their own, or someone else's, substance use problems.

Denial is a prominent feature of most substance use disorders. It is usually easier to dismiss suggestions that you have begun to use alcohol or drugs in a self-destructive pattern than it is to face the problem directly. Schuckit's book includes a perceptive chapter titled "Is There Really a Problem?" The bottom line is this: "If you repeatedly have returned to substance use even though that substance has caused a disruption in your life, you *do* have a problem." Subsequent chapters in Schuckit's book provide thoughtful and practical guidance with regard to such topics as the symptoms of withdrawal, the process of detoxification, the relative merits of self-help groups, outpatient therapy, and hospitalization, and how to find a specific treatment program in your area.

The Internet also provides an enormous amount of information regarding substance use disorders. For information about problems associated with the use of alcohol and drugs, you might want to visit Web pages that are maintained by the National Institute on Alcohol Abuse and Alcoholism: www.niaaa.nih.gov and by the National Institute on Drug Abuse: www.nida.nih.gov. These Web sites are primarily concerned with information about federally funded research programs, but they also include answers to frequently asked questions, as well as treatment referral information.

Most people who enter treatment for substance use problems become involved, at least temporarily, with self-help groups, such as Alcoholics Anonymous (AA) and Narcotics Anonymous (NA). Related groups, like Alanon and Alateen, are designed for families and children of people who are dependent on alcohol. You can contact these groups through the Internet. The URL for Alcoholics Anonymous is www.alcoholics-anonymous.org. Many people believe, often passionately, that AA is the most beneficial program for helping people to recover from alcoholism. Others disagree. If you want to consider alternative points of view, you should visit the Web site maintained by Stanton Peele, who is one of AA's most persistent, enthusiastic, and articulate critics. The URL for this home page is www.peele.net. Peele challenges the popular argument that alcoholism is an entirely biological problem and emphasizes the importance of psychological factors in the continuation of heavy drinking. He also promotes approaches to treatment that do not rely exclusively on total abstinence from drinking.

Evidence regarding the long-term outcome of serious substance use disorders can be discouraging, but it is important to remember that a substantial minority of people with these problems do manage to achieve an extended, stable recovery. The research literature does not point to one form of treatment as being clearly superior to another. Therefore, you should consider several alternatives to treatment and select the one that makes most sense in terms of your own life and your own view of the world. ₩

Controlled Drinking

One psychological approach to the treatment of alcoholism, known as Individualized Behavior Therapy for Alcoholics (IBTA), was developed by psychologists Mark and Linda Sobell (Sobell & Sobell, 1973, 1976). It employed a wide range of therapeutic procedures in an effort to address abusive drinking patterns as well as other types of maladaptive behavior that are associated with alcohol dependence. The latter included training in the use of social skills, which might be used to resist pressures to drink heavily, and problem-solving procedures, which might help the person both to identify situations that lead to heavy drinking and to formulate alternative courses of action.

The most controversial aspect of IBTA was its consideration of controlled drinking as a potential goal for people who are dependent on alcohol. This concept refers to the moderate consumption of alcohol in a pattern that avoids drinking to the point of intoxication. The Sobells set out to teach chronic alcohol abusers to drink in more appropriate ways. Their procedures encouraged patients to choose mixed drinks rather than straight liquor and to take small, intermittent sips rather than gulping drinks quickly. Results suggested that patients who were trained to drink in a controlled fashion had a better outcome, on average, than those in a control group for whom the goal was total abstinence.

The results of the Sobells' IBTA study were subjected to close scrutiny, and they ignited an intense controversy that has lasted for several years (Maltzman, 1989; Peele, 1992; Pendery, Maltzman, & West, 1982; Sobell & Sobell, 1989). Critics claimed, based on their own follow-up assessments, that the patients who had received IBTA did not return successfully to controlled drinking. The general consensus seems to be that, due to methodological problems with the IBTA study, researchers cannot reach definitive conclusions one way or the other.

Relatively few mental health professionals currently consider controlled drinking to be a realistic goal for people who are dependent on alcohol. However, a substantial minority of people who are dependent on alcohol apparently return to alcohol use on a moderate basis. For example, one follow-up study found that approximately 20 percent of a group of people with alcohol use disorders had returned to nonproblem drinking 10 years after receiving inpatient treatment (Finney & Moos, 1991). Therefore treatment aimed at reduced levels of drinking rather than total abstinence may be successful for some people with drinking problems. This approach is perhaps most reasonable with patients who have only recently begun to experience problems associated with alcohol consumption, especially young adults (Donovan & Marlatt, 1993; Kivlahan et al., 1990).

Relapse Prevention

Most people who have been addicted to a drug will say that quitting is the easy part of treatment. The most difficult challenge is to maintain this change after it has been accomplished. Unfortunately, most people will "slip up" and return to drinking soon after they stop. The same thing can be said for people who stop smoking or using any other drug of abuse. These slips often lead to a full-scale return to excessive and uncontrolled use of the drug. Successful treatment therefore depends on making preparations for such incidents.

Alan Marlatt, a clinical psychologist at the University of Washington, and his colleagues have proposed a cognitive behavioral view of the relapse process (Marlatt, 1985, 1996). The relapse prevention model addresses several important issues that confront the addict in trying to deal with the challenges of life without drugs. The model emphasizes increasing people's belief that they will be able to control their own behavior and events in their lives. The therapist also helps patients learn more adaptive coping responses, such as applied relaxation and social skills, that can be used in situations that formerly might have triggered drug use.

Another important feature of the relapse prevention model is concerned with the *abstinence violation effect,* which refers to the guilt and perceived loss of control that the person feels whenever he or she slips and finds himself or herself having a drink (or a cigarette or whatever drug is involved) after an extended period of abstinence. People typically blame themselves for failing to live up to their promise to quit. They also interpret the first drink as a signal that further efforts to control their drinking will be useless. Marlatt's approach to relapse prevention teaches patients to expect that they may slip occasionally and to interpret these behaviors as a temporary "lapse" rather than a total "relapse."

General Conclusions

Comprehensive reviews of the research literature regarding treatment of alcoholism and drug abuse point to several general conclusions (McLellan et al., 1992):

- People who enter treatment for various types of substance abuse and dependence typically show improvement in terms of reduced drug use that is likely to persist for several months following the end of treatment. Unfortunately, relapse is also relatively common.
- There is little if any evidence to suggest that one form of treatment (inpatient or outpatient, professional or self-help, individual or group) is more effective than another (Project Match Research Group, 1997).
- Among those people who are able to reduce their consumption of drugs, or abstain altogether, improvements following treatment are usually not limited to drug use alone but extend to the person's health in general as well as to the person's social and occupational functioning.

Long-term outcome for the treatment of alcoholism is best predicted by the person's coping resources (social skills and problem-solving abilities), the availability of social support, and the level of stress in the environment. These considerations appear to be more important than the specific type of intervention that people receive (Finney & Moos, 1992). Those individuals who are in less stressful life situations, whose families are more cohesive, and who are themselves better equipped with active coping skills are most likely to sustain their improvement for a period of several years.

We must also remember that the vast majority of people with substance use disorders do not receive treatment from professionals or self-help organizations (Kessler et al., 1994). Nevertheless, many people manage to recover on their own. By studying the process of "natural recovery," clinicians may find clues that can be used to develop more effective forms of treatment. For example, the Sobells have compared people who were able to recover from alcohol dependence without the aid of treatment or AA to untreated drinkers who had not recovered. More than half of all recoveries were initiated by cognitive events, primarily as a result of a reappraisal of the benefits and problems associated with continued drug use. They were not triggered by negative life events, which were frequent in the lives of both groups (Sobell et al., 1993).

Summary

DSM-IV uses two terms to describe substance use disorders. **Substance dependence,** the more severe of the two forms, refers to a pattern of repeated self-administration that often results in **tolerance, withdrawal,** or compulsive drug-taking behavior. **Substance abuse** describes a more broadly conceived, less severe pattern of drug use that is defined in terms of interference with the person's ability to fulfill major role obligations at work or at home, recurrent use of a drug in dangerous situations, or the experience of repeated legal difficulties that are associated with drug use.

A **drug of abuse**—sometimes called a psychoactive substance—is a chemical substance that alters a person's mood, level of perception, or brain functioning. The list of chemicals on which people become dependent includes drugs that are legally available in the United States as well as many that are illegal. Although patterns of dependence are similar in some ways for all drugs, each type of drug also has some unique features.

Prolonged abuse of alcohol can have a devastating impact on social relationships and occupational functioning while disrupting the functions of several important organ systems. Alcohol dependence has more negative health consequences than does abuse of almost any drug, with the possible exception of nicotine.

Barbiturates and **benzodiazepines** can be used, as prescribed by a physician, to decrease anxiety (tranquilizers) or help people sleep (hypnotics). They can also lead to a state of intoxication that is identical to that associated with alcohol. People who abruptly stop taking high doses of benzodiazepines may experience withdrawal symptoms, including a return of the original anxiety symptoms. Tolerance and withdrawal can develop after using barbiturates for several weeks.

Opiates have properties similar to opium and can induce a state of dreamlike euphoria. Tolerance develops quickly to opiates. After repeated use, their positive emotional effects are replaced by long-term negative changes in mood and emotion. Most of the severe health consequences of opiate use are the result of the lifestyle of the addict rather than the drug itself.

Nicotine is one of the most harmful addicting drugs. Recognizing the serious long-term health consequences of exposure to nicotine, the U.S. Food and Drug Administration has prohibited the sale and distribution of tobacco products to children and adolescents. This policy attempts to prevent the development of nicotine addiction rather than trying to ban use of the drug completely.

The **psychomotor stimulants,** such as amphetamine and cocaine, activate the sympathetic nervous system and induce a positive mood state. High doses of amphetamines and cocaine can lead to the onset of psychosis. The most devastating effects of stimulant drugs center around the disruption of occupational and social roles.

Marijuana and **hashish** can induce a pervasive sense of well-being and happiness. People do not seem to develop tolerance to THC (the active ingredient in marijuana and hashish) unless they are exposed to high doses over an extended period of time. Withdrawal symptoms are unlikely to develop among people who smoke marijuana occasionally.

Hallucinogens induce vivid visual images that are usually pleasant, but occasionally frightening. Unlike other drugs of abuse, hallucinogens are used sporadically rather than continuously. Most people do not increase their use of hallucinogens over time, and withdrawal symptoms are not observed.

It is impossible to specify a typical course for substance dependence. The specific pattern varies from one person to the next. In the case of alcoholism, the only thing that seems certain is that periods of heavy use alternate with periods of relative abstinence. Among alcoholic men in one long-term follow-up study, the proportion who become completely abstinent went up slowly but consistently over a period of many years. Relapse to alcohol abuse was unlikely among men who were able to remain abstinent for at least 6 years.

Alcohol dependence and abuse are the most common forms of mental disorder among men, with a lifetime prevalence of 13.8 percent in the ECA study. Among people with alcohol use disorders, men outnumber women by a ratio of approximately 5 to 1. Prevalence rates for alcohol dependence are highest among young adults and lowest among the elderly. According to the NCS, the combined lifetime prevalence for dependence on any type of controlled substance (those that are illegal or available only by prescription) was 7.5 percent.

Research on the etiology of alcoholism illustrates the ways in which various systems interact to produce and maintain drug dependence. There are several pathways to the disorder. Social factors are particularly influential in the early phases of substance use. Initial experimentation with drugs is most likely to occur among those adolescents whose parents and peers model or encourage drug use. The culture in which a person lives influences the types of drugs that are used, the purposes for which they are used, and the expectations that people hold for the ways in which drugs will affect their experiences and behavior.

Twin studies indicate that genetic factors influence patterns of social drinking as well as the onset of alcohol dependence. Adoption studies indicate that the offspring of alcoholic parents who are raised by nonalcoholic parents are more likely than people in the general population to develop drinking problems of their own. Genetic factors may be more influential in the development of alcoholism among men than among women.

The influence of genetic factors may vary in different subtypes of alcoholism. The combination of a genetic predisposition to alcoholism and environmental circumstances that encourage heavy drinking may lead to the onset of Type 1 alcoholism (late onset, no antisocial personality). In the case of Type 2 alcoholism (early onset, accompanied by antisocial personality), a genetic contribution increases risk for the disorder regardless of the type of environment in which the person is raised.

One focus of neurochemical research has been the role of endogenous opioids known as **endorphins.** Some theorists have argued that alcoholism is associated with excessive production of endorphins. Another neurochemical hypothesis suggests that alcohol dependence is caused by a genetically determined deficiency in serotonin activity in certain limbic areas of the brain.

Psychological explanations for the etiology of substance use disorders have often focused on the ability of drugs to relieve unpleasant emotional states. Expectations about drug effects have an important influence on the ways in which people respond to alcohol and other drugs. People who believe that alcohol enhances pleasure, reduces tension, and increases social performance are more likely than other people to drink frequently and heavily.

Treatment of substance use disorders is an especially challenging and difficult task in light of the fact that many people with these problems do not recognize or acknowledge their own difficulties. Recovery begins with a process of detoxification. Self-help programs, such as Alcoholics Anonymous, are the most widely used and probably one of the most beneficial forms of treatment.

Critical Thinking

1. What is the difference between the rituals characteristic of obsessive–compulsive disorders and the compulsive drug-taking behaviors associated with substance dependence? Are there any similarities? Do you think that these disorders should be classified together?

2. Some drugs of abuse are illegal in the United States, whereas others are legally available. What impact does this legal policy have on the definition of substance dependence as well as the probability that a person will receive a DSM-IV diagnosis?

3. Most adults in Western countries drink alcohol on a fairly regular basis, yet relatively few develop alcoholism. Why? There are gender differences and age differences in the prevalence of alcohol dependence. Why would women be less likely than men to become dependent on alcohol?

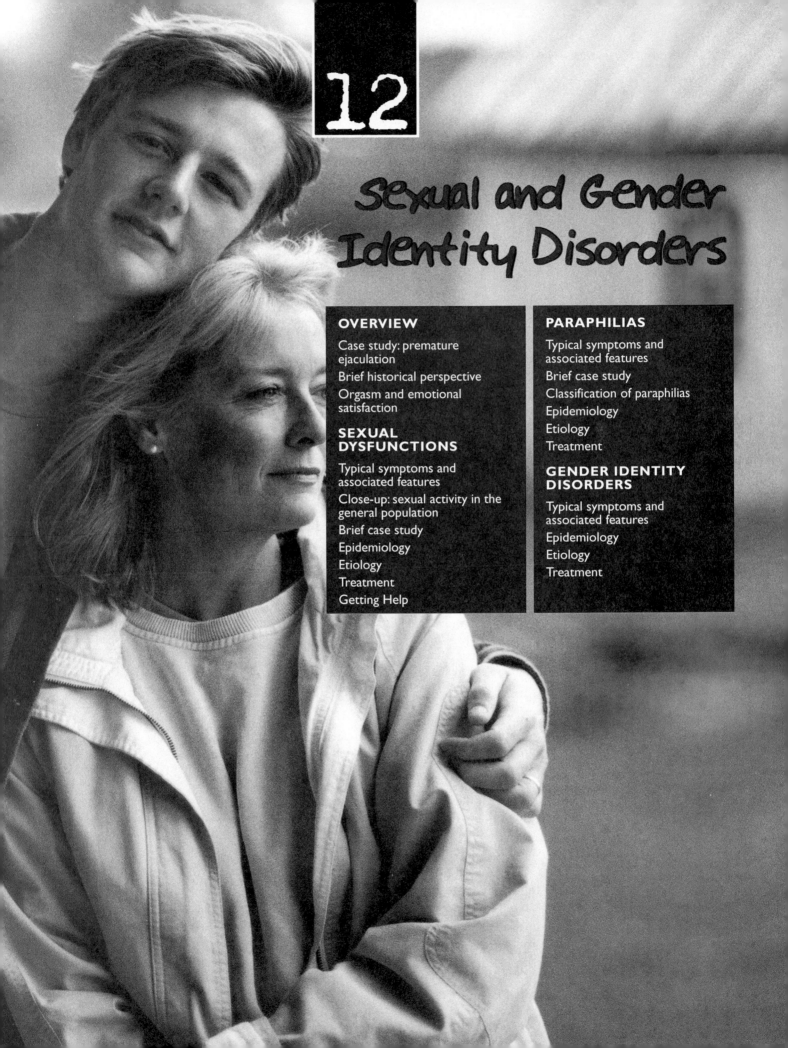

12

Sexual and Gender Identity Disorders

Sexual behavior is considered abnormal when it results in personal distress or when it involves nonconsenting partners. Inhibitions of sexual desire and interference with the physiological responses leading to orgasm are called **sexual dysfunctions.** These experiences often lead to anxiety and depression, and they are frequently associated with interpersonal problems, especially marital distress. Another group of sexual disorders is known as the **paraphilias.** This term applies to people who are sexually aroused by unusual things and situations, such as inanimate objects, sexual contact with children, exhibiting their genitals to strangers, and inflicting pain on another person.

Overview

sexual dysfunctions Forms of sexual disorder that involve inhibitions of sexual desire or interference with the physiological responses leading to orgasm.

paraphilias Forms of sexual disorder that involve sexual arousal in association with unusual objects and situations, such as inanimate objects, sexual contacts with children, exhibiting their genitals to strangers, and inflicting pain on another person.

Any discussion of sexual disorders requires some frank consideration of normal sexuality. Such openness has been encouraged and promoted by mental health professionals who specialize in the study and treatment of sexual behavior.

William Masters, a physician, and Virginia Johnson, a psychologist, undoubtedly have been the best-known sex therapists and researchers in the United States since the late 1960s (Masters, Johnson, & Kolodny, 1994). Their first book, *Human Sexual Response,* published in 1966, was based on their studies of nearly 700 normal men and women. Observations and physiological recordings were made in a laboratory setting while these individuals engaged in sexual activities, including masturbation and intercourse. Masters and Johnson's research received widespread attention in the popular media and helped make laboratory studies of sexual behavior acceptable.

On the basis of their data, Masters and Johnson described the human sexual response cycle in terms of a sequence of overlapping phases: excitement, orgasm, and resolution. Analogous processes occur in both men and women, but the timing may differ.

Sexual *excitement* increases continuously from initial stimulation up to the point of orgasm. It may last anywhere from a few minutes to several hours. Among the most dramatic physiological changes during sexual excitement are those associated with vasocongestion—engorgement of the blood vessels of various organs, especially the genitals. The male and female genitalia become swollen, reddened, and warmed. Sexual excitement also increases muscular tension, heart rate, and respiration rate. These physiological responses are accompanied by subjective feelings of arousal, especially at more advanced stages of excitement.

The experience of *orgasm* is usually distinct from the gradual buildup of sexual excitement that precedes it. This sudden release of tension is almost always experienced as being intensely pleasurable, but the specific nature of the experience varies from one individual to the next. The female orgasm occurs in three stages, beginning with a "sensation of suspension or stoppage," which is associated with strong genital sensations. The second stage involves a feeling of warmth spreading throughout the pelvic area. The third stage is characterized by sensations of throbbing or pulsating, which are tied to rhythmic contractions of the vagina, the uterus, and the rectal sphincter muscle.

The male orgasm occurs in two stages, beginning with a sensation of ejaculatory inevitability. This is triggered by the movement of seminal fluid toward the urethra. In the second stage, regular contractions propel semen through the urethra, and it is expelled through the urinary opening.

During the *resolution* phase, which may last 30 minutes or longer, the person's body returns to its resting state. Men are typically unresponsive to further sexual stimulation for a variable period of time after reaching orgasm. This is known as the *refractory period.* Women, on the other hand, may be able to respond to further stimulation almost immediately. They are capable of experiencing a series of distinct orgasmic responses that are not separated by a period of noticeably lowered excitement (Andersen & Cyranowski, 1995).

Sexual dysfunctions can involve a disruption of any stage of the human sexual response cycle. The following case study, which was described by Barry McCarthy, is concerned with a man who had difficulty controlling the rate at which he progressed from excitement to orgasm. It illustrates some of the most important features of sexual dysfunction.

 case study

Premature Ejaculation

Margaret and Bill, both in their late twenties, had been married for 2 years, and they had intercourse frequently. Margaret seldom reached orgasm during these experiences, but she was orgasmic during masturbation. The central feature of their problem was the fact that Bill was unable to delay ejaculation for more than a few seconds after insertion.

Unbeknownst to Margaret, Bill had attempted a "do-it-yourself" technique to gain better control [of ejaculation]. He had bought a desensitizing cream he'd read about in a men's magazine and applied it to the glans of his penis 20 minutes before initiating sex. He also masturbated the day before couple sex.

During intercourse he tried to keep his leg muscles tense and think about sports as a way of keeping his arousal in check. Bill was unaware that Margaret felt emotionally shut out during the sex. Bill was becoming more sensitized to his arousal cycle and was worrying about erection. He was not achieving better ejaculatory control, and he was enjoying sex less. The sexual relationship was heading downhill, and miscommunication and frustration were growing.

Margaret had two secrets that she had never shared with Bill. Although she found it easier to be orgasmic with manual stimulation, she had been orgasmic during intercourse with a married man she'd had an affair with a year before meeting Bill. Margaret expressed ambivalent feelings about that relationship. She felt that the man was a very sophisticated lover, and she had been highly aroused and orgasmic with him. Yet, the relationship had been a manipulative one. He'd been emotionally abusive to Margaret, and the relationship had ended

when he accused Margaret of giving him herpes and berated her. In fact, it was probably he who gave Margaret the herpes. Margaret was only experiencing herpes outbreaks two or three times a year, but when they did occur, she was flooded with negative feelings about herself, sexuality, and relationships. She initially saw Bill as a loving, stable man who would help rid her of negative feelings concerning sexuality. Instead, he continually disappointed her with the early ejaculation. Bill knew about the herpes but not about her sexual history and strong negative feelings.

Bill was terribly embarrassed about his secret concerning masturbation, which he engaged in on a twice-daily basis. From adolescence on, Bill had used masturbation as his primary means of stress reduction. For him, masturbation was a humiliating secret (he believed married men should not masturbate). The manner in which he masturbated undoubtedly contributed to the early ejaculation pattern. Bill focused only on his penis, using rapid strokes with the goal of ejaculating as quickly as he could. This was both to prevent himself from being discovered and from a desire to "get it over with" as soon as he could and forget about it.

When it came to his personal and sexual life, Bill was inhibited, unsure of himself, and had particularly low sexual self-esteem. As an adolescent, Bill remembered being very interested sexually, but very unsure around girls. Bill's first intercourse at 19 was perceived as a failure because he ejaculated before he could insert his penis in the woman's vagina. He then tried desperately to insert because the young woman urged him to, but he was in the refractory period (a phenomenon Bill did not understand), and so he did not get a firm erection and felt doubly humiliated. (McCarthy, 1989, pp. 151–159)

Sexual dysfunctions are best defined in terms of the couple rather than individual persons. They are frequently associated with marital distress.

The case of Bill and Margaret illustrates several important points. First, sexual problems are best defined in terms of the couple rather than the individual persons involved. Second, although problems in sexual behavior clearly involve basic physiological responses and behavioral skills, mental scripts regarding the meaning of sexual behavior are also extremely important. Sexual behavior usually takes place in the context of a close, personal relationship. The partners need to talk to each other about the things they enjoy as well as about their worries. Failure to communicate is often motivated by feelings of guilt and frustration, which can easily escalate over time.

The classification of sexual disorders has changed dramatically during the twentieth century. Before describing the disorders that are included in DSM-IV, we outline briefly some of the clinical and scientific views on sexuality that laid the foundation for our current system.

Brief Historical Perspective

Early medical and scientific approaches to sexual behavior were heavily influenced by religious doctrines and by prevailing cultural values. The exclusive purpose of sexual behavior was assumed to be biological reproduction; anything that varied from that narrow goal was considered to be a form of psychopathology and was usually subject to severe moral and legal sanctions.

The period between 1890 and 1930 saw many crucial changes in the ways in which society viewed sexual behavior (D'Emilio & Freedman, 1988). A significant number of people were beginning to think of sex as something other than a simple procreative function. If the purpose of sexual behavior was to foster marital intimacy or to provide pleasure, then interference with that goal might become a legitimate topic of psychological inquiry. Over the course of the twentieth century, there has been a trend toward greater tolerance of sexual variation among consenting adult partners and toward increased concern about impairments in sexual performance and experience.

The work of Alfred Kinsey (1894–1956), a biologist at Indiana University, was especially significant. In keeping with his conscious adherence to scientific methods, Kinsey adopted a behavioral stance, focusing specifically on those experiences that resulted in orgasm. His research largely ignored subjective experience. In their efforts to describe human sexual behavior, Kinsey and his colleagues (1948, 1953) interviewed 18,000 men and women between 1938 and 1956.

The incredible diversity of experiences reported by his subjects led Kinsey to reject the distinction between normal and abnormal sexual behavior (Robinson, 1976). He argued that differences among people are quantitative rather than qualitative. For example, Kinsey argued that the distinction between heterosexual and homosexual persons was essentially arbitrary and fundamentally meaningless. His comments regarding sexual dysfunction reflected a similar view. Kinsey believed that low sexual desire was simply a reflection of individual differences in erotic capacity rather than a reflection of psychopathology (Kinsey et al., 1948).

Orgasm and Emotional Satisfaction

How do people evaluate the quality of their sexual relationships? Subjective judgments obviously have an important impact on each person's commitment to a partnership. Dissatisfaction sometimes leads the couple to seek help from a mental health professional. It is therefore useful to know something about the ways in which normal couples evaluate their own sexual activities before we consider specific types of sexual dysfunction.

The National Health and Social Life Survey (NHSLS) collected extensive information about patterns of sexual activity and satisfaction in the general population (see Close-Up, page 330). Several aspects of these data are worth mentioning. First, there is a very large difference between men and women with regard to the experience of orgasm (see Table 12–1). Only 29 percent of women reported that they always have an orgasm with this specific partner, compared to 75 percent of men. Second, notice that 44 percent of men reported that their partners always had orgasms during sex.

On the basis of his extensive interviews, Alfred Kinsey argued that the distinction between normal and abnormal sexual behavior was not useful.

TABLE 12–1

Sexual Satisfaction in Self-Reported Primary Partnership During the Previous Year		

RESPONSE CATEGORY	MEN (%)	WOMEN (%)
R always had an orgasm with P	75.0	28.6
P always had an orgasm with R	43.5	78.0
R extremely physically satisfied with P	46.6	40.5
R extremely emotionally satisfied with P	41.8	38.7

R = respondent; P = partner.
Source: *E.O. Laumann, J.H. Gagnon, R.T. Michael, S. Michaels, 1994,* The Social Organization of Sexuality: Sexual Practices in the United States. *Chicago: University of Chicago Press.*

This figure is much higher than the rate reported by women themselves. There are several plausible explanations for this discrepancy. Because female orgasm is sometimes less clearly defined than male orgasm, men may misinterpret some events as signs that their partners have had an orgasm. It may also be the case that women sometimes mislead their partners into thinking that they have reached orgasm so that their partners will feel better about their own sexual prowess.

Perhaps the most important aspect of the data in Table 12–1 involves the participants' ratings of physical and emotional satisfaction. A relationship may be considered intimate and satisfying simply because sexual activity occurs, regardless of whether it always results in orgasm. In fact, a large proportion of both men and women indicated that they were extremely satisfied with their partners, on both the physical and emotional dimensions. Notice in particular that, although only 29 percent of women indicated that they always have an orgasm with their partner, 41 percent of women said that they were extremely physically satisfied with their partners. This pattern suggests that the experience of orgasm is only one aspect of sexual satisfaction, especially for women. Other aspects of the relationship, including tenderness, intimacy, and affection, are also critically important (Tiefer, 1988).

Sexual Dysfunctions

Sexuality represents a complex behavioral process that can easily be upset. These problems can arise anywhere, from the earliest stages of interest and desire through the climactic release of orgasm.

Negative emotions, such as anger, fear, and resentment, are often associated with sexual problems. In some cases, these emotional states appear before the onset of the sexual problem, and sometimes they develop later. Given the connection that many cultures make between virile sexual performance and "manhood," it is not surprising that men with erectile difficulties are often embarrassed and ashamed. Their humiliation can lead to secondary problems such as anxiety and depression. Similar feelings frequently accompany premature ejaculation and the recognition that a partner's sexual impulses have not been fulfilled. Women who have trouble becoming aroused or reaching orgasm also frequently experience profound frustration and disappointment. The emotional consequences of sexual problems can be devastating for both partners.

The following sections describe the DSM-IV system for classifying various types of sexual dysfunction.

Typical Symptoms and Associated Features

The DSM-IV subdivides sexual dysfunctions into several types (see Table 12–2). Failure to reach orgasm is not considered a disorder unless it is persistent or recurrent and results in marked distress or interpersonal difficulty. The DSM-IV criteria also require that the sexual dysfunction is not

TABLE 12–2

Sexual Dysfunctions Listed in DSM-IV

Hypoactive Sexual Desire Disorder: Persistently or recurrently deficient (or absent) sexual fantasies and desire for sexual activity.

Sexual Aversion Disorder: Persistent or recurrent extreme aversion to, and avoidance of, all (or almost all) genital sexual contact with a sexual partner.

Female Sexual Arousal Disorder: Persistent or recurrent inability to attain, or to maintain until completion of the sexual activity, an adequate lubrication-swelling response of sexual excitement.

Male Erectile Disorder: Persistent or recurrent inability to attain or maintain until completion of the sexual activity, an adequate erection.

Female Orgasmic Disorder: Persistent or recurrent delay in, or absence of, orgasm following a normal sexual excitement phase.

Male Orgasmic Disorder: Persistent or recurrent delay in, or absence of, orgasm following a normal sexual excitement phase during sexual activity.

Premature Ejaculation: Persistent or recurrent ejaculation with minimal sexual stimulation before, on, or shortly after penetration and before the person wishes it.

Dyspareunia: Recurrent or persistent genital pain associated with sexual intercourse in either a male or a female.

Vaginismus: Recurrent or persistent involuntary spasm of the musculature of the outer third of the vagina that interferes with sexual intercourse.

---

hypoactive sexual desire Diminished desire for sexual activity and reduced frequency of sexual fantasies.

better explained by another Axis I disorder (such as major depression) and is not the direct result of a chemical substance (such as alcohol) or a general medical condition. For many types of disorders, the clinician must decide whether the person has engaged in sexual activities that would normally be expected to produce sexual arousal or orgasm. Diagnostic judgments must take into consideration the person's age, as well as the circumstances in which the person is living, such as the presence of a partner, access to privacy, and so on.

Sexual dysfunction can be characterized with regard to pattern of onset. The problem can be either *lifelong*, meaning that the problem has been present since the person's first sexual activities, or it can be *acquired*, meaning that the problem developed only after a period of normal functioning. With regard to context of occurrence, the problem can either be *generalized*, meaning that the dysfunction is not limited to certain situations or partners, or *situational*, meaning that the dysfunction is limited to certain situations or partners.

HYPOACTIVE SEXUAL DESIRE DISORDER

Sexual desire sets the stage for sexual arousal and precedes the phases of the sexual response cycle outlined by Masters and Johnson. Some clinicians refer to sexual desire as the person's willingness to approach or engage in those experiences that will lead to sexual arousal. Inhibited or **hypoactive sexual desire** is defined in terms of subjective experiences, such as lack of sexual fantasies and lack of interest in sexual experiences. The absence of interest in sex must be both persistent and pervasive to be considered a clinical problem.

The absolute frequency with which a person engages in sex cannot be used as a measure of inhibited sexual desire because the central issue is interest—actively seeking out sexual experiences—rather than participation. For example, some people acquiesce to their partners' demands, even though they would not choose to engage in sexual activities if it were left up to them. In the absence of any specific standard, the identification of hypoactive sexual desire must depend on a clinician's subjective evaluation of the level of desire that is expected given the person's age, gender, marital status, and many other relevant considerations.

Sexual Activity in the General Population

What kinds of sexual behavior do adults in our society typically practice? Many critical public health issues, including plans for preventing the spread of sexually transmitted diseases, such as AIDS, hinge on answers to this question. Information about the sexual experiences of other people also helps us understand our own feelings and impulses. The most comprehensive information on this topic was collected by a team of investigators headed by Robert Michael, an economist, and Edward Laumann, a sociologist, who are both at the University of Chicago, and John Gagnon, a sociologist at the State University of New York at Stony Brook (Laumann, Gagnon, Michael, & Michaels, 1994). Their study, known as the National Health and Social Life Survey (NHSLS), was the first large-scale follow-up to the Kinsey reports.

The NHSLS research team conducted detailed, face-to-face interviews with nearly 3,500 men and women between the ages of 18 and 59 throughout the United States. Several elements of research design contribute to the overall value of the NHSLS data. Perhaps most important, the investigators used a procedure known as *probability sampling*—sampling in which every member of a clearly specified population has a known probability of selection—to identify their participants. This procedure is absolutely essential in survey research. Without it, conclusions cannot be generalized to the population as a whole.

The results of the survey paint a somewhat more conservative picture of sexual activity than some people may have expected. For example, monogamy is by far the most common pattern. In the year of the survey, only 16 percent of the participants had more than one sexual partner; 73 percent had only one partner, and 11 percent had no partner. Among the other key findings are the following:

- Married couples have sex more often than single people.
- Married couples reported more physical pleasure and emotional satisfaction from sex than single people did.
- People in younger generations were more likely than people in older generations to have had premarital sex (84 percent for men and 80 percent for women born between 1963 and 1974).
- One-third of the overall sample said they had sex with a partner at least twice a week; another third had sex with a partner a few times a month; and the remaining third had sex with a partner a few times a year or didn't have sexual partners at all.

Lifetime prevalence rates for specific forms of sexual activity are presented in Figure 12–1.

Masturbation is relatively common among both men and women. Approximately 1 out of every 4 men and 1 out of every 10 women reported masturbating at least once a week. Approximately half of the men and women who masturbated indicated that they felt guilty about it. People without religious affiliations reported less guilt than people with strong religious connections. This pattern provides support for the argument that social factors play a role in shaping normal sexual activities and experiences.

The NHSLS questionnaire also asked about four basic sexual techniques involving partners—vaginal intercourse, fellatio, cunnilingus, and anal intercourse. The lifetime prevalence of these techniques for sexual activities with an opposite-gender partner are illustrated in Figure 12–1 (data for same-gender sexual partnerships were analyzed separately). Virtually all of the men (95 percent) and women (97 percent) had experienced vaginal intercourse at some time during their lives. The investigators concluded that the vast majority of heterosexual encounters focus on vaginal intercourse.

Most of the men and women also reported that they had engaged in oral sexual activities (as both the person giving and receiving oral-genital stimulation). However, the percentage of men and women who indicated that their *most recent* sexual

continued

Figure 12–1   Lifetime Prevalence of Sexual Activities (with an opposite-gender partner).   This graph illustrates the prevalence of various types of sexual activities, based on responses to the NHSLS questionnaire. Note that vaginal intercourse is the most frequent activity, although masturbation and oral sex are also common.

Source: E. O. Laumann, J. H. Gagnon, R. T. Michael, and S. Michaels, 1994, *The Social Organization of Sexuality: Sexual Practices in the United States.* Chicago: University of Chicago Press.

activity involved oral sex was much lower. This pattern suggests that although most people have some experience with oral sex, it is not sufficiently common to be considered a defining feature of sexual encounters between men and women (such as kissing and vaginal intercourse).

Regarding anal intercourse, most men and women in the study reported that they had never engaged in this activity. Anal sex has become a source of concern because it presents a relatively high risk for transmission of HIV. Among those people who had experimented with anal sex, relatively few had incorporated it into their usual sexual experiences.

The use of condoms was more frequent among younger, better-educated people. Men and women who had more than one sexual partner in the past year used condoms more frequently than people involved in stable, monogamous relationships. Nevertheless, some people still engaged in relatively high-risk behaviors. Only 40 percent of the people who had sex with four partners in the past year said that they used a condom during their most recent experience with vaginal intercourse. Many people were reluctant to use condoms during the initial stages of a new sexual relationship, even though this is a time when they are more vulnerable to exposure to sexually transmitted diseases. ☙

---

sexual aversion disorder   A form of sexual dysfunction in which a person has an extreme aversion to, and avoids, genital sexual contact with a partner.

Almost everyone recognizes that sexual desire fluctuates in intensity over time, sometimes dramatically and frequently, for reasons that we do not understand (Levine, 1987). The fact that hypoactive sexual desire is listed in DSM-IV as a type of disorder should not lead us to believe that it is a unitary condition with a simple explanation. It is, in fact, a collection of many different kinds of problems. People who suffer from low levels of sexual desire frequently experience other mental and medical disorders. Perhaps as many as 85 percent of males and 75 percent of females seeking treatment for hypoactive sexual desire report other forms of sexual dysfunction (Donahey & Carroll, 1993). Men and women with low sexual desire also have high rates of mood disorders (Schreiner-Engel & Schiavi, 1986). The mood disorder typically appears before the onset of low sexual desire. It therefore appears likely that many cases of low sexual desire develop after the person has experienced other forms of psychological distress.

SEXUAL AVERSION DISORDER

Some people develop an active aversion to sexual stimuli and begin to avoid these situations altogether. Some people avoid only certain aspects of sexual behavior, such as kissing, intercourse, or oral sex. This reaction is stronger than simple lack of interest. Fear of sexual encounters can occasionally reach intense proportions, at which point it may be better characterized as **sexual aversion disorder.** This problem might be viewed as a form of panic disorder because it extends well beyond anxiety about sexual performance. Consider, for example, the following case from our files. The couple sought help at a psychological clinic in the hope that they might improve their sexual relationship.

Brief Case Study: Sexual Aversion Disorder

Doug and Jennifer were both 32 years old. They had been married for 5 years, but they had never had sexual intercourse. They cared for each other very much and described themselves as being like brother and sister. Their inability to have intercourse was upsetting to them both for many reasons. Most important was their mutual desire to have children. Doug also felt that their marriage would be stronger and more enjoyable if they were sexually intimate. Jennifer wasn't interested in sexual

activity; she never experienced sexual fantasies or erotic thoughts. She did view sex as her duty, however, and she felt guilty about not fulfilling that part of her "marital obligation." Jennifer's primary concern about the relationship involved a different kind of intimacy; she wished that Doug would spend more time with her—talking, taking walks, and doing things together that did not involve sex.

Neither Doug nor Jennifer had been experienced sexually at the time of their marriage. Jennifer was clearly anxious in the presence of stimuli that were sexual in nature, such as movies or books with a sexual theme, but she did not avoid these situations or sexual interactions altogether. She and Doug had engaged in kissing and gentle touching early in their marriage. Jennifer masturbated Doug to orgasm several times, but she felt disgusted at the sight of semen when he ejaculated. Doug had persuaded her to engage in oral sex on a few occasions. She found it unpleasant and was unable to continue long enough for Doug to reach orgasm. They attempted intercourse once, but Jennifer was unable to become aroused and insertion had been impossible.

Doug and Jennifer gradually lost interest in sexual activities. He was extremely busy with his work and said that he no longer thought about sex very often, although he continued to masturbate. Since their failed attempt at intercourse, Doug had also begun to feel less sexually attracted to Jennifer. They even-

tually entered treatment in order to explore their feelings for each other and to see if they could do anything to salvage their sexual relationship, primarily in the hope that they would be able to have children.

Several weeks after entering therapy, Jennifer reluctantly confided in her therapist that she had been sexually abused by an uncle with whom she had lived for 2 years as a child. He had forced her to perform oral sex several times when she was about 9 years old. She had never told anyone about the abuse—her parents, her aunt, or Doug—for many reasons. She was ashamed of the experience and frightened of what her uncle might do to her. The memories of this experience were still vivid, especially when she attempted to have sex with her husband. ♛

Jennifer's aversion to sexual activity was easily understandable in the context of previous abuse. The symptoms of sexual aversion disorder are often more pronounced than those that were exhibited by Jennifer. In some people, full-blown symptoms of panic attack may be triggered by exposure to sexual stimuli.

MALE ERECTILE DISORDER

Many men experience difficulties either obtaining an erection that is sufficient to accomplish intercourse or maintaining an erection long enough to satisfy themselves and their partners during intercourse. Both problems are examples of **erectile dysfunction.** Men with this problem may report feeling aroused, but the vascular reflex mechanism fails and sufficient blood is not pumped to the penis to make it erect. These difficulties can appear at any time prior to orgasm. Some men have trouble achieving an erection during sexual foreplay, whereas others lose their erection around the time of insertion or during intercourse. This phenomenon used to be called *impotence,* but the term has been dropped because of its negative implications.

Erectile dysfunctions can be relatively transient, or they can be more chronic. Occasional experiences of this type are not considered unusual. When they persist and become a serious source of distress to the couple, however, erectile difficulties can lead to serious problems.

erectile dysfunction Difficulty experienced by a man in obtaining an erection that is sufficient to accomplish intercourse or maintaining an erection long enough to satisfy himself or his partner during intercourse.

inhibited sexual arousal Difficulty experienced by a woman in achieving or maintaining genital responses, such as lubrication and swelling, that are necessary to complete sexual intercourse.

FEMALE SEXUAL AROUSAL DISORDER

Sexual arousal can also be impaired in women, but it is somewhat more difficult to describe and identify than is erectile dysfunction in men. Put simply, a woman is said to experience **inhibited sexual arousal** if she cannot either achieve or maintain genital responses, such as lubrication and swelling, that are necessary to complete sexual intercourse. The desire is there, but the physiological responses that characterize sexual excitement are inhibited.

Investigators who have studied sexual responses in normal women have reported that women's self-reports of subjective arousal and physiological measures, such as the amount of vaginal lubrication or vasocongestion, do not always correlate (Morokoff, 1989). Therefore inhibitions in sexual arousal must be defined in terms of this self-report dimension as well as in terms of specific genital responses.

Sexual arousal is somewhat more difficult to measure for women than for men. Women's subjective feelings of arousal are not always directly connected to physiological responses.

PREMATURE EJACULATION

Some men experience problems with the control of ejaculation. They are unable to prolong the period of sexual excitement long enough to complete intercourse. Once they become intensely sexually aroused, they reach orgasm very quickly.

premature ejaculation A type of sexual disorder, in which a man is unable to delay ejaculation long enough to accomplish intercourse.

orgasmic disorder A sexual disorder in which the person has recurrent difficulties reaching orgasm after a normal sexual arousal.

dyspareunia Persistent genital pain during or after sexual intercourse. The problem can occur in either men or women.

vaginismus A form of sexual dysfunction in which the outer muscles of the vagina snap tightly shut when penetration is attempted, thus preventing insertion of any object.

There have been many attempts to establish specific, quantitative criteria for this condition, known as **premature ejaculation.** None of the attempts has been entirely satisfactory, but certain boundaries identify conditions that can be problematic. If the man ejaculates before or immediately upon insertion, or after only three or four thrusts, almost all clinicians will identify his response as premature ejaculation (Grenier & Byers, 1995; McCarthy, 1989).

Another way to think about premature ejaculation places emphasis on the couple's satisfaction rather than on the amount of time required to reach orgasm. Masters and Johnson (1970) suggested that premature ejaculation might be present if the man is unable to delay ejaculation until his partner reaches orgasm at least 50 percent of the time. Kaplan (1974) concluded that if progression to orgasm is beyond the man's voluntary control once he reaches an intense level of sexual arousal, he has a problem with premature ejaculation.

FEMALE ORGASMIC DISORDER

Some women are unable to reach orgasm even though they apparently experience uninhibited sexual arousal. Women who experience orgasmic difficulties may have a strong desire to engage in sexual relations, they may find great pleasure in sexual foreplay, and they may show all the signs of sexual arousal. Nevertheless, they cannot reach the peak erotic experience of orgasm. Women whose orgasmic impairment is generalized have never experienced orgasm by any means. Situational orgasmic difficulties occur when the woman is able to reach orgasm in some situations but not in others. That might mean that she is . . . orgasmic during masturbation but not during intercourse, or perhaps she is orgasmic with one partner but not with another.

Orgasmic disorder is somewhat difficult to define in relation to inhibited sexual arousal because the various components of female sexual response are more difficult to measure than are erection and ejaculation in the male. One experienced researcher has described this issue in the following way:

> In my experience, many women who have never reached orgasm present the following set of symptoms: They report that when engaging in intercourse they do not have difficulty lubricating and experience no pain. However, they report no genital sensations . . . and do not appear to know what sexual desire or arousal is . . . and often have never masturbated. . . . Most of these women seek therapy because they have heard from others or have read that they are missing something, rather than because they themselves feel frustrated. (Morokoff, 1989, p. 74)

PAIN DURING SEX

Some people experience persistent genital pain during or after sexual intercourse, which is known as **dyspareunia.** The problem can occur in either men or women, although it is considered to be much more common in women (Quevillon, 1993). The severity of the discomfort can range from mild irritation following sexual activities to searing pain during insertion of the penis or intercourse (Lazarus, 1988). The pains may be sharp and intense, or they may take the form of a dull, aching sensation; they may be experienced as coming from a superficial area near the barrel of the vagina or as being located deep in the lower abdominal area; they may be intermittent or persistent.

The experience of severe genital pain is often associated with other forms of sexual dysfunction. Not surprisingly, many women with dyspareunia develop a lack of interest in, or an aversion toward, sexual activity.

Access to the vagina is controlled by the muscles surrounding its entrance. Some women find that whenever penetration of the vagina is attempted, these muscles snap tightly shut, preventing insertion of any object. This involuntary muscular spasm, known as **vaginismus,** prevents sexual intercourse as well as other activities, such as vaginal examinations and the insertion of tampons. Women with vaginismus may be completely sexually responsive in other respects, fully capable of arousal and orgasm through manual stimulation of the clitoris. Women who seek therapy for this condition often report that they are afraid of intercourse and vaginal penetration (Beck, 1993). The problem can be severe or partial in nature. Some couples report that a mild form of vaginismus occurs from time to time, making intercourse difficult and sometimes painful.

Epidemiology

Surveys conducted among the general population indicate that various forms of sexual dysfunction are relatively common (Ernst et al., 1993; Rosen et al., 1993). We must keep in mind, however, that this impression is based on self-report questionnaires and judgments made by laypersons, which are less precise than those made by experts. Diagnoses made by experienced therapists would take into account the person's age, the context of the person's life, and whether the person had experienced stimulation that would ordinarily be expected to lead to sustained arousal and orgasm. Clinicians would also take into consideration the amount of distress and interpersonal difficulty associated with the problem before arriving at a diagnosis of sexual dysfunction. We must therefore be cautious in our interpretations of these survey data.

The most extensive set of information regarding sexual problems among people living in the community comes from the National Health and Social Life Survey (NHSLS; see Research Close-Up, page 330). Each participant was asked whether, during the past 12 months, he or she had experienced "a period of *several months or more* when you lacked interest in having sex; had trouble achieving or maintaining an erection or (for women) had trouble lubricating; were unable to come to a climax; came to a climax too quickly; or experienced physical pain during intercourse." For each item, the person was asked for a simple yes or no response. Figure 12–2 indicates the overall percentage of men and women who indicated that they had experienced each of these specific problems. Premature ejaculation is the most frequent form of male sexual dysfunction, affecting almost 1 out of every 3 adult men. All the other forms of sexual dysfunction are reported more often by women. One-third of women said that they lacked interest in sex, and almost one-quarter indicated that they experienced a period of several months during which they were unable to reach orgasm.

Figure 12–2   Prevalence of Sexual Dysfunctions.   This graph shows the percentage of NHSLS respondents who reported having sexual difficulties at some time during the previous 12 months. Note the differences in the problems reported by men and women.

Survey data can be supplemented with information on the prevalence of specific types of sexual dysfunction among people who seek professional treatment for sexual problems (Benet & Melman, 1995; Spector & Carey, 1990). These reports indicate several trends:

- Orgasmic and erectile dysfunction have become more frequent complaints among people seeking treatment.
- Premature ejaculation has become less common as the presenting problem among people seeking treatment for sexual dysfunction.
- The frequency of desire disorders as presenting problems in sex clinics has increased.
- Recently, males have outnumbered females as the person with the presenting problem when couples seek treatment.

SEXUAL BEHAVIOR ACROSS THE LIFE SPAN

Sexual behavior changes with age. Masters and Johnson devoted considerable attention to this topic in their original studies. Their data challenged the myth that older adults are not interested in, or capable of performing, sexual behaviors. The NHSLS data also indicate that many people remain sexually active later in life. Gender differences become marked in the late fifties, when rates of inactivity increase dramatically for women. Between the ages 70 to 74, 65 percent of men are still sexually active, compared to only 30 percent of women. These differences may be, at least partially, the result of biological factors that are part of the aging process. They may also reflect the influence of a cultural prejudice against sexual activity among older women.

Differences between younger and older people are mostly a matter of degree. As men get older, they tend to achieve erections more slowly, but they can often maintain erections for longer periods of time. Older men find it more difficult to regain an erection if it is lost before orgasm. As women get older, vaginal lubrication may occur at a slower rate, but the response of the clitoris remains essentially unchanged. The intensity of the subjective experience of orgasm is decreased for older men and women. For both men and women, healthy sexual responsiveness is most likely to be maintained among those who have been sexually active as younger adults.

The relation between sexual experience and aging is closely related to other health problems, which increase with age. People who rate their health as being excellent have many fewer sexual problems than people who rate their health as being only fair or poor (Laumann et al., 1994).

Etiology

At each stage of the sexual response cycle, a person's behavior is determined by the interaction of many biological and psychological factors, ranging from vasocongestion in the genitals to complex cognitive events involving the perception of sexual stimuli and the interpretation of sexual meanings.

BIOLOGICAL FACTORS

The experience of sexual desire is partially controlled by biological factors. Among males, sexual desire is influenced by sex hormones, especially testosterone (Davidson, 1990). The influence of male sex hormones on sexual behavior is thought to be on sexual appetite rather than on sexual performance. This process probably involves a threshold level of circulating testosterone (Bancroft, 1989). The reduction of male sex hormones over the life span probably explains, at least in part, the apparent decline in sexual desire among elderly males.

Among the various types of sexual problems, erectile dysfunction is most often biologically based. We must remember, however, that the distinction between psychological and biological causes is often arbitrary. It is not clear that this simple dichotomy is useful, and in many cases the etiology involves some combination or interaction of many factors (LoPiccolo, 1985).

Erection is the direct result of a threefold increase in blood flow to the penis. Thus it is not surprising that vascular diseases, which may affect the amount of blood reaching the penis, are likely to result in erectile difficulties. Neurological diseases, such as epilepsy and multiple sclerosis, can also produce erectile difficulties, because erection depends on spinal reflexes. Diabetes may be the most common neurologically based cause of impaired erectile responsiveness (Wincze & Carey, 1991).

Other factors that can influence a man's erectile response include various drugs (McCabe et al., 1996). One interesting set of results indicates that men who smoke cigarettes are more likely to experience erectile difficulties than are men in the general population (see Mohr & Beutler, 1990). Many other drugs, including alcohol and marijuana, may have negative effects on sexual arousal. Medication used to treat hypertension can impair erectile responsiveness, and so can various types of antipsychotic and antidepressant drugs. For example, many people who take Prozac (fluoxetine) for the treatment of depression experience delayed ejaculation and orgasmic dysfunction as a side effect (Rothschild, 1995; Segraves, 1988).

Various types of neurological disorder, pelvic disease, and hormonal dysfunction can interfere with the process of vaginal swelling and lubrication in women. Unfortunately, relatively little research has been conducted on problems of sexual arousal in women (Andersen & Cyranowski, 1995). These mechanisms are therefore not well understood.

SOCIAL FACTORS

Although sexual desire is rooted in a strong biological foundation, social variables also play an important role in the determination of which stimuli a person will find arousing. John Gagnon, Edward Laumann, and William Simon have argued that sexual desire and arousal are determined by mental scripts that we learn throughout childhood and adolescence (Gagnon & Simon, 1973; Laumann & Gagnon, 1995). According to this view, the social meaning of an event is of paramount importance in releasing the biological process of sexual arousal. Both members of the potential couple must recognize similar cues, defining the situation as potentially sexual in nature, before anything is likely to happen.

Beliefs and attitudes toward sexuality, as well as the quality of interpersonal relationships, have an important influence on the development of low sexual desire, especially among women. The quality of the relationship is an important factor to consider with regard to low sexual desire (Stuart, Hammond, & Pett, 1987).

Some societies openly encourage female sexuality; others foster a more repressive atmosphere. Within U.S. culture, there are tremendous variations with regard to women's ability to experience and express their sexuality, and some studies have found that different attitudes are associated with different levels of sexual responsiveness. For example, many women feel guilty about having sexual fantasies, in spite of the fact that such fantasies are extremely common. Women who feel guilty about fantasizing while they are having intercourse are more likely to be sexually dissatisfied and to encounter sexual problems, including arousal difficulties (Cado & Leitenberg, 1990).

Social factors are also related to orgasmic difficulties. For example, women who were born in more recent decades are more likely to reach orgasm successfully than are women born in previous decades (Morokoff, 1978). This pattern reflects the fact that public attitudes toward female sexuality, and especially the expectation that women can and should experience orgasm, have changed progressively over the past several decades (Kelly, Strassberg, & Kircher, 1990). The most important factors contributing to failure to reach orgasm involved negative attitudes, feelings of guilt, and failure to communicate effectively.

PSYCHOLOGICAL FACTORS

Among the psychological factors contributing to impaired sexual arousal, Masters and Johnson (1970) gave primary emphasis to *performance anxiety,* or fear of failure. People who have experienced inhibited sexual arousal on one or two occasions may be likely to have further problems to the degree that these difficulties make them more self-conscious or apprehensive regarding their ability to become aroused in future sexual encounters. And men who have sexual arousal disorders are more likely to report feeling high levels of performance anxiety (Ackerman & Carey, 1995).

Recent evidence suggests that anxiety disrupts sexual performance to the extent that it alters certain perceptual and attentional processes. These cognitive factors have been studied by David Barlow and his colleagues, who have examined the relation between performance concerns and interfering thoughts in men with erectile difficulties. Men who experience erectile failure are less

sensate focus A procedure for the treatment of sexual dysfunction that involves a series of simple exercises in which the couple spends time in a quiet, relaxed setting, learning to touch each other.

sexually responsive when they are confronted with demands to become sexually aroused; sexually functional men show the opposite effect (Cranston-Cuebas et al., 1993). Dysfunctional men also tend to be less aware of their level of sexual arousal, and they are more likely to experience negative emotions in the presence of erotic stimuli. Studies suggest that sexual arousal problems may be mediated by a feedback process in which unpleasant feelings lead to self-distraction and avoidance of erotic stimuli (Barlow, 1986; Cranston-Cuebas & Barlow, 1990).

Relationship factors represent another important consideration in the etiology of sexual dysfunction. Couples who experience communication problems, power conflicts, and an absence of intimacy and trust are more likely than others to experience sexual problems. Lack of assertiveness and lack of comfort while talking about sexual activities and pleasures are associated with various types of female sexual dysfunction (Rosen & Leiblum, 1995).

Finally, previous harmful or traumatic experiences can also have an important effect on various aspects of sexual interests and arousal. As we have already discussed in the case of Jennifer, a previous history of sexual abuse can lead to sexual aversion, and it can interfere with a woman's ability to become sexually aroused (Becker, 1989). Premature ejaculation and low sexual desire in men have also been linked to long-lasting, adverse relationships with adults during childhood (Kinzl et al., 1996).

Treatment

Masters and Johnson were pioneers in developing and popularizing a short-term, skills-based approach to treatment of sexual dysfunctions. Hundreds of couples who visited their clinic in St. Louis went through a 2-week course of assessment and therapy in which they became more familiar with their bodies, learned to communicate more effectively with their partners, and received training in procedures designed to help them diminish their fears about sexuality. The results of this treatment program were very positive and quickly spawned a burgeoning industry of psychosocial treatment for sexual dysfunction.

William Masters and Virginia Johnson conducted groundbreaking research on the human sexual response cycle. They have also been pioneers in the field of treatment for sexual dysfunction.

PSYCHOLOGICAL PROCEDURES

The cornerstone of sex therapy is known as **sensate focus,** a procedure developed by Masters and Johnson. Sensate focus involves a series of simple exercises in which the couple spends time in a quiet, relaxed setting, learning to touch each other. They may start with tasks as simple as holding hands or giving each other back rubs. The rationale for sensate focus hinges on the recognition that people with sexual problems must learn to focus on erotic sensations. The goal is to help them become more comfortable with this kind of physical sharing and intimacy, to learn to relax and enjoy it, and to talk to each other about what feels good and what does not.

A related facet of psychological approaches to treating sexual dysfunction is *scheduling* time for sex. Couples need a quiet, relaxed, and private environment in order to engage in pleasurable and satisfying sexual behavior.

The second major aspect of sex therapy involves education and cognitive restructuring—changing the way in which people think about sex. In many cases the therapist needs to help the couple correct mistaken beliefs and attitudes about sexual behavior. Examples are the belief that intercourse is the only true form of sex, that foreplay is an adolescent interest that most adults can ignore, and that simultaneous orgasm is the ultimate goal of intercourse. Providing information about sexual behaviors in the general population can often help alleviate people's guilt and anxiety surrounding their own experiences. Some people are relieved to know that they are not the only ones who fantasize about various kinds of sexual experiences, or that the fact that they fantasize about these things does not mean that they are going to be compelled to behave in deviant ways.

The final element of treatment for sexual dysfunction is communication training. Many different studies have indicated that people with sexual dysfunction often find it difficult to talk to

getting help

Sexual Disorders

Many sexual problems can be traced to the absence of information about the nature of sexual attitudes, feelings, preferences, and behaviors. In other words, they are based on ignorance and nothing more. Fortunately, access to these data and public attitudes toward their discussion have improved dramatically in recent years. The Sexuality Information and Education Council of the United States (SIECUS) collects and disseminates information and promotes education about sexuality. Its Internet home page—www.siecus.org—contains an extensive list of resources, including books and links to other Web sites, that deal with topics that range from reproduction, women's health, gender identity, and sexual orientation to sexually transmitted diseases and various types of sexual disorders.

If you have been troubled by problems with sexual arousal, inhibited orgasm, or premature orgasm, behavioral procedures can be very helpful. This is one area in which the research literature justifies true optimism. Most of these problems can be treated successfully using procedures that were originally developed by Masters and Johnson. Before you seek professional therapy, you may want to try some self-help techniques that have grown out of this treatment tradition. Two exceptionally well-written and practical books describe how these procedures can be used by people who want to enhance the pleasure that they experience in their sexual relationships. They are *Becoming Orgasmic: A Sexual and Personal Growth Program for Women*, by Julia Heiman and Joseph LoPiccolo, and *The New Male Sexuality*, by Bernie Zilbergeld.

If you are still experiencing problems after trying self-help procedures, you should seek treatment with a professional sex therapist. The person's professional background is less important than her or his training for treatment of these specific problems. When you contact potential therapists, ask them whether their treatment methods are similar to those developed by Masters and Johnson. Information regarding counseling, therapy, medical attention, and other sexuality resources for people with sexual problems is available from the Sexual Health Network: www.sexhealth.org. Concise, readable descriptions of various forms of sexual dysfunction and treatments used to address them can be found at the Sexual Health InfoCenter: www.sexualhealth.com. These sites can help you to increase your knowledge of sexuality, suggest ways in which its expression can be inhibited, and present procedures that can be used to improve sexual performance and experience. ♛

their partners about what kinds of things they find sexually arousing and what kinds of things turn them off. Therefore sex therapists often employ structured training procedures aimed at improving the ways in which couples talk to each other.

The outcome results of psychological treatment programs for sexual disorders have been quite positive. While this initial optimism has subsequently been tempered by other studies that have reported less positive results (such as Bancroft et al., 1986), the overall conclusion is still that psychological treatments for sexual dysfunction are frequently successful (see LoPiccolo & Stock, 1986; O'Donohue & Geer, 1993).

BIOLOGICAL TREATMENTS

Biological treatments are also useful in the treatment of sexual dysfunctions. This is especially true for severe forms of erectile disorder, the most frequent sexual problem for which men seek professional help. One procedure involves surgically inserting a penile implant (or prosthesis), which can be used to make the penis rigid during intercourse (Melman & Tiefer, 1992).

Various kinds of medication have been used successfully in the treatment of sexual dysfunction, especially erectile disorder. Sildenafil citrate (Viagra) was the first oral drug approved in the United States for use in treating erectile dysfunction. Introduced in 1998, it quickly became one of the most popular drugs on the market. Taken 1 hour before sexual activity, Viagra facilitates erection by increasing blood flow to certain areas of the penis. It facilitates the man's ability to respond to stimuli that he would ordinarily find sexually arousing, but it does not influence overall sexual desire.

Double-blind, placebo-controlled studies have evaluated the use of Viagra in men with erectile problems associated with various conditions, including hypertension, diabetes, and coronary artery disease. It is effective, increasing the number of erections for approximately two-thirds of men with severe erectile dysfunction (Mitka, 1998). Men taking Viagra were also more likely than those on placebo to accomplish successful vaginal penetration during intercourse (46 percent compared to 8 percent). Unfortunately, some men experience negative side effects, such as headaches, facial flushing, nasal congestion, and altered vision. Perhaps most important, Viagra can lead to sudden drops in blood pressure if taken together with various forms of medication known as "nitrates," which are used in the treatment of heart disease. Some deaths were reported after Viagra was introduced because of this misuse.

Viagra is an important new option for men with erectile problems, but it may not produce a complete solution to sexual dysfunction in the absence of additional treatment factors. Couples that have experienced sexual problems have often struggled with a number of difficult issues for several years. Increasing the man's capacity for erection may address only one part of the problem. Therapists may need to work with couples to improve intimacy and communication while also helping them to overcome frustrations and anxiety that have accumulated over recent years (Lamberg, 1998).

Paraphilias

In certain extreme forms of unusual sexual behavior, called *paraphilias,* sexual arousal is associated with atypical stimuli, and the person is preoccupied with or consumed by these activities. Literally translated, paraphilia means "love" *(philia)* "beyond the usual" *(para).* According to DSM-IV, the central features of all paraphilias are persistent sexual urges and fantasies that are associated with (1) nonhuman objects, (2) suffering or humiliation of oneself or one's partner, or (3) children or other nonconsenting persons. In the following pages we summarize a few of the most common types of paraphilias, and we consider some of the factors that might influence the development of unusual sexual preferences.

Typical Symptoms and Associated Features

One hundred years ago, many psychiatrists considered any type of sexual behavior other than heterosexual intercourse to be pathological. Contemporary researchers and clinicians have expanded the boundaries of normal behavior to include a much broader range of sexual behavior. A large proportion of men and women engage in sexual fantasies and mutually consenting behaviors such as oral sex. These experiences enhance their relationships without causing problems (Laumann et al., 1994).

Problems with sexual appetites arise when a pattern develops involving a long-standing, unusual erotic preoccupation that is highly arousing, coupled with a pressure to act on the erotic fantasy. The diagnosis of paraphilia is made only if the person has acted on the urges or is distressed by them.

It is actually somewhat misleading, or imprecise, to say that paraphilias are defined in terms of reactions to unusual stimuli. The central problem is that sexual arousal is dependent on images that are detached from reciprocal, loving relationships with another adult (Levine, Risen, & Althof, 1990; McConaghy, 1994). Themes of aggression, violence, and hostility are common in paraphilic fantasies, as are impulses involving strangers or unwilling partners. Rather than focusing on whether the stimuli are common or uncommon, some experts place principal emphasis on the lack of human intimacy that is associated with many forms of paraphilias (Marshall et al., 1996).

Compulsion and lack of flexibility are also important features of paraphilic behaviors. Paraphilias may occupy large amounts of time and consume much of the person's energy. In that sense, they are similar to addictions. People with paraphilic disorders are not simply aroused by unusual images or fantasies. They feel *compelled* to engage in certain acts that may be personally degrading or harmful to others, in spite of the fact that these actions are often repulsive to others and are sometimes illegal. The study on page 341 describes some of the central features of paraphilias.

This case illustrates the way in which paraphilias can interfere with a person's life, especially relationships with other people. Jon's preoccupation with fantasies of women wrestling led him to

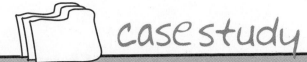

case study

Brief Case Study: Paraphilia

For the past 40 years, Jon has masturbated to images of barely clad women violently wrestling each other. Periodically throughout his marriage, he has tried to involve his wife in wrestling matches with her friends and, eventually, with their adolescent daughter. When Jon was drunk, he occasionally embarrassed his wife by trying to pick fights between her and other women. On summer vacations, he sometimes jokingly suggested that the women wrestle. During much of his sober life, however, his daydreams of women wrestling were private experiences that preoccupied only him. He amassed a collection of magazines and videotapes depicting women wrestling, to which he would resort when driven by the need for excitement.

Jon presented for help with his inability to maintain his erection with his wife for intercourse. With the exception of procreational sex, he was not able to consummate his long marriage. He was able to (become) erect if his wife described herself wrestling other women while he stimulated his penis in front of her, but he always lost his erection when intercourse was attempted. (Levine, Risen, & Althof, 1990) ⩙

say and do things that disrupted his marriage and his friendships with other people. Many people with paraphilias experience sexual dysfunction involving desire, arousal, or orgasm during conventional sexual behavior with a partner. The wives of men with paraphilias frequently protest that their husbands are not interested in their sexual relationship. In fact, the husband may be engaged in frequent masturbation to paraphilic fantasies.

Several researchers have noted that men with paraphilias can typically be described as timid, low in self-esteem, and lacking in social skills (Blair & Lanyon, 1981; Bradford, Bloomberg, & Bourget, 1988). It is, of course, difficult to know whether these characteristics are traits that set the stage for the development of paraphilias or whether they are consequences associated with the performance of sexual behaviors that are considered repugnant by society.

Some gay men who dress in women's clothes refer to themselves as "drag queens." This is different from transvestic fetishism, which applies only to heterosexual men whose cross-dressing is associated with intense, sexually arousing fantasies or urges.

fetishism The use of nonliving objects as a focus of sexual arousal.

transvestic fetishism A form of paraphilia in which sexual pleasure is derived from dressing in the clothing of the opposite gender.

sexual masochism A form of paraphilia in which sexual arousal is associated with the act of being humiliated, beaten, bound, or otherwise made to suffer.

Classification of Paraphilias

Although they are listed as distinct disorders, it might be more useful to think of paraphilia as one diagnostic category, with the variations listed in DSM-IV representing subtypes of this single disorder (Frances, First, & Pincus, 1995). The types of paraphalias described below are the ones most often seen in clinics that specialize in the treatment of sexual disorders. Not surprisingly, they are also the ones that frequently lead to a person being arrested.

FETISHISM

Anthropologists use the word *fetish* to describe an object that is believed to have magical powers to protect or help its owner. In psychopathology, **fetishism** refers to the association of sexual arousal with nonliving objects. The range of objects that can become associated with sexual arousal is virtually unlimited, but fetishism most often involves women's underwear, shoes and boots, or products made out of rubber or leather (Junginger, 1997; Mason, 1997). The person may go to great lengths, including burglary, to obtain certain kinds of fetish objects.

People who fit the description of fetishism typically masturbate while holding, rubbing, or smelling the fetish object. Particular sensory qualities of the object—texture, visual appearance, and smell—can be very important in determining whether or not the person finds it arousing. In addition to holding or rubbing the object, the person may wear, or ask his sexual partner to wear, the object during sexual activity. The person may be unable to become sexually aroused in the absence of the fetish object.

An intense sexual attraction to specific body parts(most often legs or feet, and excluding genitals, breasts, and buttocks) is known as *partialism*. Many experts believe that partialism is a form of fetishism (de Silva, 1993). In DSM-IV, partialism is excluded from fetishism and listed in a miscellaneous category called "paraphilias not otherwise specified."

TRANSVESTIC FETISHISM

A *transvestite* is a person who dresses in the clothing of the other gender. In DSM-IV, **transvestic fetishism** is defined as cross-dressing for the purpose of sexual arousal. It has been described almost exclusively among heterosexual men and should not be confused with the behavior of some gay men known as *drag queens* (for whom cross-dressing has a very different purpose and meaning). People who engage in transvestic fetishism usually keep a collection of female clothes that are used to cross-dress. Some wear only a single article of women's clothing, such as female underwear, covered by male clothing. Others dress completely as women, including makeup, jewelry, and accessories. Cross-dressing may be done in public or only in private. The person masturbates while he is cross-dressed, often imagining himself to be a male as well as the female object of his own sexual fantasy. Aside from their interest in cross-dressing, men with transvestic fetishism are unremarkable masculine in their interests, occupations, and other behaviors. Most of these men marry and have children (Schott, 1995). For some men, transvestism may eventually lead to feelings of dissatisfaction with being male. They may eventually want to live permanently as women. These men, who develop persistent discomfort with their gender role or identity, would be assigned a subtype diagnosis of *transvestic fetishism with gender dysphoria*.

SEXUAL MASOCHISM

People who become sexually aroused when they are subjected to experiencing pain or embarrassment are called masochists. The DSM-IV defines **sexual masochism** as recurrent, intense sexually arousing fantasies, urges, or impulses involving being humiliated, beaten, bound, or otherwise made to suffer. (The experience must be real, not simulated.) People may act on these impulses by themselves or with a partner. In some large cities, clubs cater to the sexual interests of masochistic men and women, who pay people to punish and abuse them.

The person may become aroused by being bound, blindfolded, spanked, pinched, whipped, verbally abused, forced to crawl and bark like a dog, or in some other way made

THE FAR SIDE   By GARY LARSON

Popeye! No!

I yam what I yam!

to experience pain or feelings of shame and disgrace. One relatively common masochistic fantasy takes the form of being forced to display one's naked body to other people. Masochists desire certain types of pain (which are carefully controlled to remain within specified limits, usually unpleasant but not agonizing), but they also go to great lengths to avoid injury during their contrived, often ritualized experiences (Stoller, 1991). They do not enjoy, and are not immune to, painful experiences that lie outside these limited areas of their lives.

Many people who engage in masochistic sexual practices are highly educated and occupationally successful (Levitt, Moser, & Jamison, 1994). Masochists tend to be disproportionately represented among the privileged groups in society. This pattern leads to the suggestion that masochism may be motivated by an attempt to escape *temporarily* from the otherwise constant burden of maintaining personal control and pursuing self-esteem (Baumeister & Butler, 1997).

SEXUAL SADISM

Someone who derives pleasure by inflicting physical or mental pain on other people is called a *sadist*. The term is based on the writings of the Marquis de Sade, whose novels described the use of torture and cruelty for erotic purposes. The DSM-IV defines **sexual sadism** in terms of intense, sexually arousing fantasies, urges, or behaviors that involve the psychological or physical suffering of a victim. Sadistic fantasies often involve asserting dominance over the victim; the experience of power and control may be as important as inflicting pain (Hucker, 1997). Some people engage in sadistic sexual rituals with a consenting partner (who may be a sexual masochist) who willingly suffers pain or humiliation. Others act on sadistic sexual urges with nonconsenting partners. In some cases, the severity of the sadistic behaviors escalates over time.

EXHIBITIONISM

The DSM-IV defines **exhibitionism** in the following way: "Over a period of at least 6 months, recurrent, intense sexually arousing fantasies, sexual urges, or behaviors involving exposure of one's genitals to an unsuspecting stranger" (p. 526). This behavior is also known as *indecent exposure*. About half of these men have erections while exposing themselves, and some masturbate at the same time. The others usually masturbate shortly after the experience while fantasizing about the victim's reaction. Their intent usually involves a desire to shock the observer, but sometimes they harbor fantasies that the involuntary observer will become sexually aroused. They rarely attempt to touch or otherwise molest their victims, who are usually women or children (Maletzky, 1997; Murphy, 1997).

Exhibitionism is almost exclusively a male disorder. Most exhibitionists begin to expose themselves when they are teenagers or in their early twenties. As adults, most are either married or living with a sexual partner. Exhibitionism is seldom an isolated behavior; men who engage in this type of behavior tend to do it quite frequently (Abel & Osborn, 1992).

VOYEURISM

The focus of sexual arousal in **voyeurism** is the act of observing an unsuspecting person, usually a stranger, who is naked, in the process of disrobing, or engaging in sexual activity. Many people, especially men, are sexually aroused by the sight of people who are partially clad or naked. Voyeurs are not aroused by watching people who know that they are being observed. The process of looking ("peeping") is arousing in its own right. The person might fantasize about having a sexual relationship with the people who are being observed, but direct contact is seldom sought. The voyeur reaches orgasm by masturbating during observation or later while remembering what he saw. Most keep their distance from the victim and are not dangerous, but there are exceptions to this rule (King, 1996).

FROTTEURISM

In **frotteurism,** a person who is fully clothed becomes sexually aroused by touching or rubbing his genitals against other, nonconsenting people. The frotteur usually chooses crowded places, such as sidewalks and public transportation, so that he can easily escape arrest. He either rubs his genitals against the victim's thighs and buttocks or fondles her genitalia or breasts.

sexual sadism A form of paraphilia in which sexual arousal is associated with desires to inflict physical or psychological suffering, including humiliation, on another person.

exhibitionism One of the paraphilias, characterized by distress over, or acting on, urges to expose one's genitals to an unsuspecting stranger.

voyeurism A form of paraphilia (also known as *peeping*) in which a person becomes sexually aroused by observing unsuspecting people (usually strangers) while they are undressing or engaging in sexual activities.

frotteurism One of the paraphilias, characterized by recurrent, intense sexual urges involving touching and rubbing against a nonconsenting person; it often takes place in crowded trains, buses, and elevators.

pedophilia One of the paraphilias, characterized by marked distress over, or acting on urges involving, sexual activity with a prepubescent child.

incest Sexual activity between close blood relatives, such as father-daughter, mother-son, or siblings.

rape Acts involving nonconsensual sexual penetration obtained by physical force, by threat of bodily harm, or when the victim is incapable of giving consent by virtue of mental illness, mental retardation, or intoxication.

Like exhibitionism, frotteurism is a high-frequency form of paraphilia; interviews with people being treated for frotteurism indicate that they may engage in hundreds of individual paraphilic acts (Abel et al., 1987). People who engage in frotteurism seek to escape as quickly as possible after touching or rubbing against the other person. They are not seeking further sexual contact.

PEDOPHILIA

People who persistently engage in sexual activities with children exhibit what is undoubtedly the most alarming, damaging, and objectionable form of paraphilic behavior: pedophilia. One large-scale survey found that 27 percent of women and 16 percent of men reported that they had experienced some form of sexual abuse as children (Finkelhor et al., 1990). The harmful, long-term consequences of sexual abuse include elevated risk for many of the disorders that we have already considered in this book, including anxiety disorders, mood disorders, personality disorders, substance use disorders, and sexual dysfunction.

Pedophilia entails recurrent, intense, sexually arousing fantasies, sexual urges, or behaviors involving sexual activity with a prepubescent child (generally age 13 years or younger). In order to qualify for a diagnosis of pedophilia in DSM-IV, the person must be at least 16 years of age and at least 5 years older than the child. The terms *pedophile* and *child molester* are sometimes used interchangeably, but this practice confuses legal definitions with psychopathology. A child molester is a person who has committed a sexual offense against a child victim. In many locations, a child might be anyone under the age of consent, even if that person has reached puberty. All child molesters are not pedophiles. Furthermore, some pedophiles may not have molested children, because the diagnosis can be made on the basis of recurrent fantasies in the absence of actual behavior (Barbaree & Seto, 1997).

Pedophilia includes a great variety of behaviors and sexual preferences (Bradford et al., 1988). Some pedophiles are attracted only to children, whereas others are sometimes attracted to adults. Most pedophiles are heterosexual, and the victims of pedophilia are more often girls than boys. Some offenders are attracted to both girls and boys. Sexual contact with children typically involves caressing and genital fondling. Vaginal, oral, and anal penetration are less common, and physical violence is relatively rare. In many cases, the child willingly and naively complies with the adult's intentions. In most cases, the child knows the person who molests him or her. More than half of all offenses occur in the home of either the child or the offender.

Incestuous relationships, in which the pedophile molests his own children, should perhaps be distinguished from those in which the offender is only casually acquainted with the victim. **Incest** refers to sexual activity between close blood relatives, such as father–daughter, mother–son, or between siblings. The definition may also be expanded to include stepchildren and their stepparents in reconstituted families. Most reported cases of incest involve fathers and stepfathers sexually abusing daughters and stepdaughters (Cole, 1992). Many incest perpetrators would not be considered pedophiles, either because their victims are postpubescent adolescents or because they are also young themselves (such as male adolescents molesting their younger sisters). Perhaps as many as half of the men who commit incest have also engaged in sexual activity with children outside their own families (Abel & Osborn, 1992). This subgroup of pedophilic incest perpetrators may be the most harmful and the most difficult to treat. Their personality style is typically passive and dependent. They are unable to empathize with the plight of their victims, perhaps in part because they were absent or uninvolved in early child-care responsibilities (Williams & Finkelhor, 1990).

RAPE AND SEXUAL ASSAULT

The legal definition of **rape** includes "acts involving nonconsensual sexual penetration obtained by physical force, by threat of bodily harm, or when the victim is incapable of giving consent by virtue of mental illness, mental retardation, or intoxication" (Goodman et al., 1993a). One conservative estimate of rape prevalence based on a national survey indicated that 14 percent of adult women had been raped (National Victims Center, 1992). The actual rate is probably higher—perhaps in the vicinity of 20 percent (Koss, 1992, 1993).

The frequency of coercive sex was studied as part of the NHSLS (Laumann et al., 1994). The 3,500 participants were asked whether they had ever been forced to do something sexually that they did not want to do. The question was focused broadly and did not necessarily focus only on acts involving penetration or threats of violence. Slightly more than one out of every five women in the sample reported that they had been forced by a man to engage in some kind of sexual activity against their will. Among those women who had experienced forced sex, 30 percent said that they had been forced sexually by more than one person.

Some rapes are committed by strangers, but many others—known as *acquaintance rapes*—are committed by men who know their victims. Most female victims know the person who raped them (Wiehe & Richards, 1995). Consider, for example, evidence from women in the NHSLS who had been victims of forced sex (excluding those who had been forced by more than one person). Most reported that the person was either someone with whom they were in love or their spouse. Only 4 percent were forced to do something sexual by a stranger.

Rapes are committed by many different kinds of people for many different reasons (Newcomb, 1993). The feminist perspective on rape emphasizes male aggression and violence. The traditional clinical perspective has been concerned with sexual deviance. The authors of DSM-IV considered including rape as a type of paraphilia. This proposal was rejected, primarily because it might imply that rape is always motivated by sexual arousal, and it is not. Nevertheless, the behavior of some rapists does include essential features of paraphilias: recurrent, intense sexually arousing fantasies and urges that involve the suffering of nonconsenting persons. Half the convicted rapists in one study reported a history of other types of paraphilia: pedophilia (24 percent), exhibitionism (19 percent), and voyeurism (17 percent) (Abel & Gouleau, 1990). Current efforts to classify sexual offenders attempt to distinguish between those for whom deviant sexual arousal contributes to the act and those whose behavior is motivated primarily by anger or violent impulses.

Epidemiology

There is very little evidence regarding the frequency of various types of unconventional sexual behavior. This is especially true for victimless or noncoercive forms of paraphilia, such as fetishism, transvestic fetishism, and sexual masochism, because most of these people seldom seek treatment or come to the attention of law enforcement officials. Furthermore, the fact that these forms of behavior are considered deviant or perverse makes it unlikely that people who engage in them will readily divulge their secret urges and fantasies.

With the exception of masochism, paraphilias are almost always male behaviors. Some 95 percent of the people who seek treatment for paraphilic disorders are men (Kaplan, 1989; Levine, Risen, & Althof, 1990).

Paraphilias are seldom isolated phenomena. People who exhibit one type of paraphilia often exhibit others (Gosselin & Wilson, 1980). This pattern has been called crossing of paraphilic behaviors.

Etiology

Those experiences and conditions that predispose an individual to one form of paraphilia are apparently also likely to lead to another. In the following pages we review a number of proposals regarding the etiology of paraphilias. Some of these have been associated with specific types of paraphilia. For the most part, however, they are concerned more generally with many forms of paraphilias.

The epidemiological evidence suggests another important pattern that must be explained by any theory of paraphilias: They are more prevalent among men than among women. The exception to this rule seems to be masochism, which may be equally common in both genders. We might conclude therefore that the development of masochism may be governed by different factors than those that account for the etiology of other types of paraphilias.

BIOLOGICAL FACTORS

Most of the evidence regarding the role of biological factors in the etiology of paraphilias has focused on the endocrine system, the collection of glands that regulates sexual responses through the release of hormones (Collaer & Hines, 1995). Some studies of convicted sexually violent offenders have found evidence of elevated levels of testosterone. These reports must be viewed with some skepticism, however, for two reasons. First, the participants in these studies are invariably convicted sexual offenders. It is therefore not clear that the findings can be generalized to all people with paraphilias. Second, there is a high rate of alcoholism and drug abuse among men convicted of sexual crimes. For that reason, we do not know whether biological abnormalities that are observed in these men are causes of their deviant sexual behavior or, instead, consequences of prolonged substance abuse (Langevin, 1992).

Neurological abnormalities may also be involved in the development of paraphilias. Structures located in the temporal lobes of the brain, especially the amygdala and the hippocampus, appear to play an important role in the control of both aggression and sexual behavior. These limbic structures, in conjunction with the hypothalamus, form a circuit that regulates biologically significant behaviors that sometimes are whimsically called the four F's—feeding, fighting, fleeing, and sexual behavior (Valenstein, 1973). In 1937, two scientists reported that, after extensive bilateral damage to the temporal lobes, rhesus monkeys showed a dramatic increase in sexual activity, as well as a number of related behavioral and perceptual abnormalities.

Some reports indicate that men with pedophilia and exhibitionism show subtle forms of left temporal lobe dysfunction, as evidenced by abnormal patterns of electrophysiological response and impaired performance on neuropsychological tests (Flor-Henry, 1987; Murphy, 1997). Some men with fetishism exhibit diffuse signs of neurological impairment, but these are also focused predominantly in the left temporal lobe. Similar findings have been reported for sexually sadistic criminals (Gratzer & Bradford, 1995). Before these results are interpreted too broadly, however, it should also be noted that most people who suffer from temporal lobe epilepsy do not engage in paraphilic behaviors. In fact, the most frequent result of temporal lobe epilepsy is a reduction in sexual activity (Huws, Shubsachs, & Taylor, 1991; Murphy, 1997). It seems reasonable to conclude that some cases of paraphilia are caused, at least in part, by endocrine and neurological abnormalities, but the relations among these factors are not entirely clear.

SOCIAL FACTORS

Some types of paraphilias seem to be distortions of the normal mating process when viewed in a broad, evolutionary context. For male primates, sexual behavior involves a sequence of steps: location and appraisal of potential partners; exchange of signals in which partners communicate mutual interest; and tactile interactions that set the stage for sexual intercourse. Voyeurism, exhibitionism, and frotteurism may represent aberrant versions of these social processes. Kurt Freund and Ray Blanchard, both at the University of Toronto, have described the paraphilias as "courtship disorders" (Freund & Blanchard, 1986, 1993). Something has apparently gone wrong, disrupting whatever mechanisms facilitate the identification of a sexual partner and govern behaviors used to attract a partner.

If people with paraphilias have somehow failed to learn more adaptive forms of courtship behavior, what sort of childhood experiences might have produced such unexpected results? Several background factors have been observed repeatedly among people who engage in atypical sexual behaviors (Wincze, 1989). These include the following:

- Early crossing of normative sexual boundaries through a direct experience (for example, sexual abuse by an adult) or an indirect experience (hearing about a father's atypical sexual behavior)
- Lack of a consistent parental environment in which normative sexual behavior and values were modeled
- Lack of self-esteem
- Lack of confidence and ability in social interactions
- Ignorance and poor understanding of human sexuality

All these factors may increase the probability that a person might experiment with unusual types of sexual stimulation or employ maladaptive sexual behaviors.

Although the most notable feature of paraphilias is sexual arousal, the paraphilias are ultimately problems in social relationships. Interpersonal skills may therefore play as important a role as sexual arousal. William Marshall, a psychologist at Queen's University in Canada, has argued that the core feature of unusual sexual behavior is a failure to achieve intimacy in relationships with other adults (Marshall, 1989; Seidman, Marshall, Hudson, & Robertson, 1994). According to this perspective, people with paraphilias are lonely, insecure, and isolated and have significant deficits in social skills. Offensive sexual behaviors, such as those observed in pedophilia, are maladaptive attempts to achieve intimacy through sex. These efforts are invariably unsuccessful and self-defeating in the sense that they serve to isolate the person further from the rest of the community. Paradoxically, the pattern may become deeply ingrained because it results in the momentary pleasure associated with orgasm and because it offers the illusory hope of eventually achieving intimacy with another person.

PSYCHOLOGICAL FACTORS

John Money (1984), a psychologist at Johns Hopkins University, has described the development of paraphilias in somewhat different terms, using a geographic metaphor that he calls a *lovemap*. A lovemap is a mental picture representing a person's ideal sexual relationship. It might also be viewed as the software that encodes his or her sexual fantasies and preferred sexual practices. These "programs" are written early in life, and they are quite persistent. Children learn their lovemaps during sexual play, by imitation of their parents and other adults, and through messages that they digest from the popular media. The child learns that love—romantic attachment to another adult—and lust—erotic attraction—can be directed toward the same person.

John Money, a psychologist at Johns Hopkins University, has written extensively about the etiology of paraphilias. His concept of distorted lovemaps provides an interesting view of their development.

The lovemap can be distorted, according to Money's metaphor, if the child learns that romantic attachment and sexual desire are incompatible—that these feelings cannot be directed toward the same person. The inability to integrate these aspects of the lovemap lies at the heart of Money's explanation of paraphilias. One solution to this dilemma would be to avoid or deny sexual expression altogether. That might explain the development of lack of sexual desire. Sexual impulses are powerful, however, and they are not easily denied. In some cases, they are rerouted rather than being shut off completely. Various types of paraphilias represent alternative strategies through which the person finds it possible to express sexual feelings outside of an intimate, loving relationship with another adult. Exhibitionism, voyeurism, and fetishism are therefore partial solutions to the perceived incompatibility of love and lust.

The etiological mechanisms that we have considered thus far seem most applicable to paraphilias that are found predominantly among men, such as fetishes, voyeurism, and exhibitionism. A different story may be necessary to explain masochism, the association of sexual arousal with pain and suffering, because this condition is equally common among women and men.

One intriguing clue regarding the origins of masochism has been reported by Robert Stoller (1991), a psychoanalyst at UCLA who wrote extensively about unusual erotic behaviors. Stoller spent several months conducting detailed interviews with people who were seriously involved in sadomasochistic behaviors with consenting partners. Those who were most committed to physical sadism and masochism had, as children, experienced traumatic physical disease followed by frightening forms of medical treatment. These people described to Stoller how they had "consciously forced themselves to master what at first, in infancy and childhood, was uncontrollable physical agony and terror by taking the pain and working with it in their heads, eventually via daydreams, altered states of consciousness, or genital masturbation, until it was converted into pain-that-is-pleasure" (Stoller, 1991, p. 25). In other words, a strong positive emotion like sexual arousal can be actively employed to control intolerable physical pain. The unfortunate consequence is the development of a persistent association between pain and arousal.

Treatment

The treatment of paraphilias is different from the treatment of sexual dysfunctions in several ways. Perhaps most important is the fact that most people with paraphilias do not enter treatment on a voluntary basis. They are often referred to a therapist by the criminal justice system after they have been arrested for exposing themselves, peeping through windows, or engaging in sexual behaviors with children. Their motivation to change is therefore open to question (Wincze, 1989). Participation in treatment may help them receive reduced sentences or avoid other legal penalties. In

aversion therapy A classical conditioning technique for attempting to eliminate unwanted behavior by pairing an unpleasant (aversive) stimulus with the behavior—for example, inducing nausea when alcohol is consumed.

many cases, they are being asked to abandon highly reinforcing behaviors in which they have engaged for many years. Their families and other members of society may be much more concerned about change than they are. We mention this issue at the beginning of our discussion because the results of outcome studies in this area are typically less positive than are those concerning the treatment of sexual dysfunctions (Furby, Weinrott, & Blackshaw, 1989; McConaghy, 1990).

AVERSION THERAPY

For the past several decades, the most commonly used form of treatment for paraphilias has been **aversion therapy.** In this procedure, the therapist repeatedly presents the stimulus that elicits inappropriate sexual arousal—such as slides of nude children—in association with an aversive stimulus, such as repulsive smells, electric shock, or chemically induced nausea. Revolting cognitive images are sometimes used instead of tangible aversive stimuli. Whatever the exact procedure, the rationale is to create a new association with the inappropriate stimulus so that the stimulus will no longer elicit sexual arousal. Several research studies have suggested that aversion therapy does produce some positive effects (Kilmann et al., 1982). It has more recently fallen into disfavor, however, because the studies that were used to evaluate it suffered from design flaws.

COGNITIVE-BEHAVIORAL TREATMENT

There is considerable reason to believe that paraphilias are based on a variety of cognitive and social deficits (Marshall, 1989; McFall, 1990). Broad-based cognitive and social treatment procedures may ultimately be most useful in the treatment of paraphilias and sexual disorders (Marshall et al., 1996).

Encouraging results have been reported from the Sex Offender Treatment and Evaluation Project (Marques et al., 1993), which was designed for men convicted of either rape or child molestation. Men selected for the treatment program are transferred to a special hospital unit, where they remain for several months. They receive education in human sexuality as well as cognitive behavior therapy, including applied relaxation and social skills training and stress and anger management. Treatment also includes a relapse prevention component that is based on procedures used in the treatment of alcoholism (see Chapter 11). Relapse prevention procedures help the men confront personal, social, and sexual difficulties that may increase their risk of relapse after they are released from prison.

Men in the treatment group were significantly less likely than were men in the control groups to commit new sex offenses during their first 5 years after release (Marques et al., 1994). Results were somewhat more encouraging with men convicted of rape than with those who had molested children.

The number of people who had been treated by the time of these reports was still relatively small, so the results should be interpreted with caution. Nevertheless, the data from this program indicate that broadly based behavioral programs that focus on education, social skills, and relapse prevention procedures may be more promising than more traditional forms of therapy.

HORMONES AND MEDICATION

Another approach to the treatment of paraphilias involves the use of drugs that reduce levels of testosterone, on the assumption that male hormones control the sexual appetite (Bradford, 1997). One study reported that treatment of paraphilic men with cyproterone acetate, a drug that blocks the effects of testosterone, produced a significant reduction in some aspects of sexual behavior, especially sexual fantasies (Bradford & Pawlak, 1993). Among men with pedophilia, the study found a greater reduction of sexual fantasies of children than for images of sex between consenting adults.

Antidepressants and antianxiety drugs have also been used to treat paraphilias. One study found that three patients with paraphilias responded positively to Prozac (Perilstein, Lipper, & Friedman, 1991). The process by which these drugs manage to alter sexual behavior is open to question. For example, medication may reduce social anxiety, which interferes with the ability to enjoy an intimate sexual relationship with another adult (Golwyn & Sevlie, 1992). This hypothesis is consistent with the approach taken by Marshall and his colleagues, whose psychological treatment program is aimed at similar types of social deficits.

Gender Identity Disorders

Our sense of ourselves as being either male or female is known as **gender identity.** Gender identity almost always reflects the child's physical anatomy: Toddlers who possess a penis learn that they are boys, and those with a vagina learn that they are girls. Gender identity is usually fixed by the time a child reaches 2 or 3 years of age (Serbin & Sprafkin, 1987).

Gender identity must be distinguished from **sex roles,** which are characteristics, behaviors, and skills that are defined within a specific culture as being either masculine or feminine. In our own culture, masculine and feminine sex roles have changed considerably in recent years, and they overlap to a degree.

Typical Symptoms and Associated Features

Some people are firmly convinced that they are living in the wrong kind of body. In males, this means that they feel strongly that they are women trapped in a man's body. For females, the opposite pattern holds. The DSM-IV categorizes this sense of discomfort with one's anatomical sex as **gender identity disorder.** It has also been called *transsexualism* (Satterfield, 1988) or *gender dysphoria* (Blanchard, 1989). People with gender identity disturbances do not literally believe that they are members of the other gender. Rather, they feel that, with the exception of their physical anatomy, they are more like the other gender.

Most transsexuals report that they were aware of these feelings very early in childhood. Many report that they dressed in clothing and adopted sex-role behaviors of the other gender during childhood and adolescence. The intensity of the person's discomfort varies from one individual to the next. Invariably it becomes more intense during adolescence, when the person develops secondary sexual characteristics, such as breasts and wider hips for girls, and facial hair, voice changes, and increased muscle mass for boys. These characteristics make it more difficult for a person to pass for the other gender. Many transsexuals become preoccupied with the desire to change their anatomical sex through surgical procedures.

Gender identity disorders should be distinguished from transvestic fetishism, which is a form of paraphilia in which a heterosexual man dresses in the clothing of the other gender in order to achieve sexual arousal. These are, in fact, very different conditions. Transvestic fetishists do not consider themselves to be women, and transsexuals are not sexually aroused by cross-dressing.

Epidemiology

Gender identity disorders are quite rare in comparison to most of the other disorders that we have considered in this book. Male-to-female transsexuals are apparently more common than female-to-male transsexuals, at least based on the numbers of people who seek treatment at clinics. One study estimated the prevalence figures to be 1 person with gender identity disorder for every 18,000 males and 54,000 females (Eklund, Gooren, & Bezemer, 1988).

Deeply ingrained cross-gender behaviors and attitudes among children occur infrequently in the general population (Zucker, 1985). Mild forms of cross-gender behavior, such as dressing up in the clothes of the other gender or expressing a desire to be a member of the other sex, are relatively common during the preschool years. Extreme forms of these behaviors are relatively rare, however, especially among boys (Achenbach & Edelbrock, 1981).

Transsexual Christine Jorgenson (right) in 1952 and the former George Jorgenson (left), an Army veteran from New York. Jorgenson's sex-reassignment surgery, performed in Denmark, attracted worldwide attention.

Etiology

Very little is known about the origins of gender identity in normal men and women, so it is not surprising that the etiology of gender identity disorders is also poorly understood. There is some reason to believe that gender identity is

gender identity A person's sense of himself or herself as being either male or female.

sex roles Characteristics, behaviors, and skills that are defined within a specific culture as being either masculine or feminine.

gender identity disorder A strong and persistent identification with the opposite sex coupled with a sense of discomfort with one's anatomic sex.

strongly influenced by sex hormones, especially during the prenatal period (LeVay, 1993; Swaab & Gofman, 1995). Much of the research in this area has been done with animals, but an interesting set of data comes from studies of people with a condition that is sometimes called *pseudohermaphroditism*. Individuals with this condition are genetically male, but they are unable to produce a hormone that is responsible for shaping the penis and scrotum in the fetus. Therefore the child is born with external genitalia that are ambiguous in appearance—thus the term *pseudohermaphrodite*.[†]

Many of these children are raised as girls by their families. When they reach the age of puberty, a sudden increase in testosterone leads to dramatic changes in the appearance of the adolescent's genitals. The organ that had previously looked more like a clitoris becomes enlarged and turns into a penis, and testicles descend into a scrotum. The child's voice becomes deeper, muscle mass increases, and the child quickly begins to consider himself to be a man (Imperato-McGinley et al., 1974). The speed and apparent ease with which people with these conditions adopt a masculine gender identity suggest that their brains had been prenatally programmed for this alternative (Hoenig, 1985).

Treatment

There are two obvious solutions to problems of gender identity: Change the person's identity to match his or her anatomy, or change the anatomy to match the person's gender identity. Various forms of psychotherapy have been used in an effort to alter gender identity, but the results have been fairly negative.

One alternative to psychological treatment is *sex-reassignment surgery*, in which the person's genitals are changed to match the gender identity (Hage, 1995). Medical science can construct artificial male and female genitalia. The artificial penis is not capable of becoming erect in response to sexual stimulation, but structural implants can be used to obtain rigidity. These surgical procedures have been used with thousands of patients over the past 50 or 60 years. Clinics that perform these operations employ stringent selection procedures, and patients are typically required to live for several months as a member of the other gender before they can undergo the surgical procedure.

The results of sex-reassignment surgery have generally been positive. Interviews with patients who have undergone surgery indicate that most are satisfied with the results, and the vast majority believe that they do not have any trouble passing as a member of their newly assumed gender. Psychological tests obtained from patients who have completed surgery indicate reduced levels of anxiety and depression (Bodlund & Kullgren, 1996; Snaith, Michael, & Russell, 1993).

The DSM-IV recognizes two major forms of sexual disorders. **Sexual dysfunctions** involve an inhibition of sexual desire or disruption of the physiological responses leading to orgasm. **Paraphilias** are defined in terms of extreme forms of unusual sexual behavior, in which sexual arousal is associated with atypical stimuli. The central problem in paraphilias is that sexual arousal has become detached from a reciprocal, loving relationship with another adult.

Sexual dysfunctions are subdivided into several types, based on the stages of the sexual response cycle. These include problems related to sexual desire, sexual arousal, and orgasm. Related difficulties include sexual aversion disorder and **premature ejaculation. Dyspareunia** is defined in terms of persistent genital pain during or after sexual intercourse. **Vaginismus** is an involun-

---

[†]*A hermaphrodite has both male and female reproductive organs.*

tary spasm of the muscles surrounding the entrance to the vagina. All forms of sexual dysfunction can lead to personal distress, including anxiety and depression, as well as interpersonal and marital difficulties.

Sexual behavior is dependent on a complex interaction among biological, psychological, and social factors. These factors include cognitive events related to the perception of sexual stimuli, social factors that influence sexual meanings or intentions, and physiological responses that cause vasocongestion of the genitals during sexual arousal.

Biological factors that contribute to sexual dysfunction include inadequate levels of sex hormones, which can contribute to diminished sexual desire, and a variety of medical disorders. Vascular and neurological diseases are important factors in many cases of **erectile dysfunction.** The effects of alcohol, illicit drugs, and some forms of medication can also contribute to erectile dysfunction in men and to **orgasmic disorder** in men and women.

Several psychological factors are involved in the etiology of sexual dysfunction. Prominent among these are performance anxiety and guilt. Communication deficits can also contribute to sexual dysfunction. Previous experiences, including sexual abuse, play an important role in some cases of sexual dysfunction.

Psychological treatments for sexual dysfunction are quite successful. They focus primarily on negative attitudes toward sexuality, failure to engage in effective sexual behaviors, and deficits in communication skills.

Common characteristics of paraphilias include lack of human intimacy and urges toward sexual behaviors which the person feels compelled to perform. Many people with paraphilias experience sexual dysfunctions during conventional sexual behavior with an adult partner. The diversity and range of paraphilic behavior is enormous. DSM-IV describes a few of the most prominent forms, such as **exhibitionism, fetishism, frotteurism, pedophilia, sexual masochism, sexual sadism, transvestic fetishism,** and **voyeurism.** These are not typically isolated preferences or patterns of behavior; people who exhibit one form of paraphilia often exhibit others.

Treatment outcome is generally less successful with paraphilias than with sexual dysfunction. The most promising approaches to the treatment of paraphilias currently use a combination of cognitive and behavioral procedures to address a broad range of etiological factors, including deficits in social skills and stress and anger management as well as knowledge and attitudes regarding sexuality.

Gender identity disorder represents a disturbance in the person's sense of being either a man or a woman. People with this problem, which is also known as transsexualism, have developed a **gender identity** that is inconsistent with their physical anatomy. These disorders are extremely rare. Very little is known about their etiology. Gender identity seems to be strongly influenced by sex hormones, perhaps during the process of fetal development. Treatment of gender identity disorders may involve sex-reassignment surgery.

Critical Thinking

1. Suppose that you are a therapist who has been contacted by a couple who are concerned that the woman is unable to reach orgasm. What are the first things that you would want to know? Would you want to see each partner alone?

2. Drag queens are gay men who dress up in women's clothing. Their masquerade balls are typically a source of pride and enjoyment. Why wouldn't this type of behavior be considered a sexual disorder? How is their behavior different from transvestic fetishism?

3. Do you think that rape—or some specific subtype of rape—should have been included in DSM-IV under paraphilias? Why or why not?

13

Schizophrenic Disorders

Schizophrenia encompasses what most of us have come to know as "madness." People with schizophrenia exhibit many different symptoms. They may hear voices that aren't there, express absurd ideas and beliefs, or make comments that are difficult, if not impossible, to understand. Their symptoms follow different patterns over time. Some recover fairly quickly, whereas others deteriorate progressively. In the face of this marked diversity, many clinicians believe that schizophrenia, or "the group of schizophrenias," may actually include several forms of disorder that have different causes. Others contend that schizophrenia is a single pathological process and that variations from one patient to the next in symptoms and course of the disorder reflect differences in the expression or severity of this process.

Overview

schizophrenia   A type of (or group of) psychotic disorders characterized by positive and negative symptoms and associated with a deterioration in role functioning. The term was originally coined by Eugen Bleuler to describe the *splitting of mental associations*, which he believed to be the fundamental disturbance in schizophrenia (previously known as *dementia praecox*).

positive symptoms   (of schizophrenia) Include hallucinations, delusions, disorganized speech, inappropriate affect, and disorganized behavior.

negative symptoms   (of schizophrenia) Include flat or blunted affect, avolition, alogia, and anhedonia.

disorganization   A type of symptom, such as disorganized speech and bizarre behavior, found in schizophrenic disorders that does not fit easily into either the positive or negative category of symptoms.

The most common symptoms of schizophrenia include changes in the way a person thinks, feels, and relates to other people and the outside environment. No single symptom or specific set of symptoms is characteristic of all schizophrenic patients. All of the individual symptoms of schizophrenia can also be associated with other psychological and medical conditions. Schizophrenia is defined by various combinations of psychotic symptoms in the absence of other forms of disturbance, such as mood disorders (especially manic episodes), substance dependence, delirium, or dementia.

The symptoms of schizophrenia can be divided into three dimensions: positive symptoms, negative symptoms, and disorganization (Andreasen et al., 1995; Thompson & Meltzer, 1993). **Positive symptoms,** also called *psychotic symptoms,* are assumed to indicate a *distortion of normal functions.* Hallucinations and delusions are considered positive symptoms of schizophrenia. In contrast, **negative symptoms** presumably reflect the *loss of normal functions*—symptoms such as lack of initiative, social withdrawal, and deficits in emotional responding. Some additional symptoms of schizophrenia, such as disorganized speech, do not fit easily into either the positive or negative type. Verbal communication problems and bizarre behavior represent a third symptom dimension, which is sometimes called **disorganization.** Note that these symptom dimensions overlap and combine in various ways within individual patients.

The DSM-IV definition of schizophrenia requires that the person exhibit symptoms of the disorder for at least 6 months before he or she is considered to meet the diagnostic criteria. If the person displays psychotic symptoms for at least 1 month but less than 6 months, the diagnosis would be *schizophreniform disorder.* The diagnosis would be changed to schizophrenic disorder if the person's problems persisted beyond the 6-month limit.

In the following case studies (page 354 and 355) we describe the experiences of two people who exhibited symptoms of schizophrenia. The DSM-IV divides schizophrenic disorders into several subtypes, based primarily on the type of symptoms that the patient exhibits. Our first case illustrates the paranoid subtype of schizophrenia, which is characterized by a preoccupation with one or more delusions or by frequent auditory hallucinations, most often persecutory.

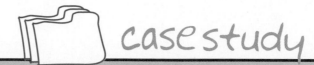

Paranoid Schizophrenia

Ann was 21 years old the first time that she was admitted to a psychiatric hospital. She had completed business college and had worked as a receptionist until she became pregnant with her son, who was born 6 months prior to her admission. She and her husband lived in a small apartment with his 5-year-old daughter from a previous marriage. This was her first psychotic episode.

The first signs of Ann's disturbance appeared during her pregnancy, when she accused her husband of having an affair with her sister. The accusation was based on a conversation that Ann had overheard on a bus. Two women (who were neighbors in Ann's apartment building) had been discussing an affair that some woman's husband was having. Ann believed that this might have been their way of telling her about her husband's infidelity. Although her husband and her sister denied any romantic interest in each other, Ann clung to her suspicions and began to monitor her husband's activities closely. She also avoided talking with her neighbors and friends.

Before this period of time, Ann had been an outgoing and energetic person. Now she seemed listless and apathetic and would often spend days without leaving their apartment. Her husband at first attributed this change in her behavior to the pregnancy, believing that she would "snap out of it" after the baby was born. Unfortunately, Ann became even more socially isolated following the birth of her son. She seldom left her bedroom and would spend hours alone, mumbling softly to herself.

Ann's behavior deteriorated markedly 2 weeks prior to her hospital admission, when she noticed that some photographs of herself and her baby were missing. She told her husband that they had been stolen and were being used to cast a voodoo spell on her. Ann became increasingly preoccupied with this belief in subsequent days. She called her mother repeatedly, insisting that something would have to be done to recover the missing photographs. Her friends and family tried to reassure Ann that the photographs had probably been misplaced or accidentally discarded, but she was totally unwilling to consider alternative explanations.

Ann finally announced to everyone who would listen that someone was trying to kill her and the children. Believing that all the food in the house had been poisoned, she refused to eat and would not feed the children. She became increasingly suspicious, hostile, and combative. Her husband and parents found it impossible to reason with her. She was no longer able to care for herself or the children. The family sought advice from their family physician, who recommended that they contact a psychiatrist. After meeting with Ann briefly, the psychiatrist recommended that she be hospitalized for a short period of time.

After admission, Ann argued heatedly with the hospital staff, denying that she was mentally disturbed and insisting that she must be released so that she could protect her children from the conspiracy. She had no insight into the nature of her problems.

The onset of schizophrenia typically occurs during adolescence or early adulthood. The period of risk for the development of a first episode is considered to be between the ages of 15 and 35. The number of new cases drops off slowly after that, with few people experiencing an initial episode after the age of 55 (Gottesman, 1991).

The subsequent course of the disorder can follow many different patterns. The problems of most patients can be divided into three phases of variable and unpredictable duration: prodromal, active, and residual. Symptoms such as hallucinations, delusions, and disorganized speech are characteristic of the *active phase* of the disorder. The *prodromal phase* precedes the active phase and is marked by an obvious deterioration in role functioning as a student, employee, or homemaker. The person's friends and relatives often view the beginning of the prodromal phase as a change in the person's personality. Prodromal signs and symptoms are similar to those associated with schizotypal personality disorder (see Chapter 9). They include peculiar behaviors (such as talking to one's self in public), unusual perceptual experiences, outbursts of anger, increased tension, and restlessness. Social withdrawal and avolition (indecisiveness and lack of willpower) are often seen during the prodromal phase.

The *residual phase* follows the active phase of the disorder and is defined by signs and symptoms that are similar in many respects to those seen during the prodromal phase. At this point, the positive symptoms of psychosis have improved, but the person continues to be impaired in various ways.

After the onset of schizophrenia, many people do not return to expected levels of social and occupational adjustment. The man in our second case illustrates this pattern. He is also an example of the disorganized type of schizophrenia. Patients who fit criteria for this category exhibit disorganized speech and behavior and flat or inappropriate expression of emotion.

case study

Disorganized Schizophrenia

Edward was 39 years old and had lived at home with his parents since dropping out of school after the 10th grade. Edward worked on and off as a helper in his father's roofing business prior to his first psychotic episode at the age of 26. After that time, he was socially isolated and unable to hold any kind of job. He was hospitalized in psychiatric facilities 10 times in the next 14 years. When he was not in the hospital, most of his time at home was spent watching television or sitting alone in his room.

The tenth episode of psychosis became evident when Edward told his mother that he had seen people arguing violently on the sidewalk in front of their house. He believed that this incident was the beginning of World War II. His mother tried to persuade him that he had witnessed an ordinary, though perhaps heated, disagreement between two neighbors, but Edward could not be convinced. He continued to mumble about the fight and became increasingly agitated over the next few days. When he wasn't pacing back and forth from his bedroom to the living room, he could usually be found staring out the front window. Several days after witnessing the argument, he took curtains from several windows in the house and burned them

in the street at 2 A.M. A neighbor happened to see what Edward was doing and called the police. When they arrived, they found Edward wandering in a snow-covered vacant lot, talking incoherently to himself. Recognizing that Edward was psychotic, the police took him to the psychiatric hospital.

Although his appearance was somewhat disheveled, Edward was alert and cooperative. He knew the current date and recognized that he was in a psychiatric hospital. Some of his speech was incoherent, and his answers to questions posed by the hospital staff were frequently irrelevant. His expressive gestures were severely restricted. Although he said that he was frightened by the recent events that he reported to his mother, his face did not betray any signs of emotion. He mumbled slowly in a monotonous tone of voice that was difficult to understand. He said that he could hear God's voice telling him that his father was "the Master of the universe" and he claimed that he had "seen the shadow of the Master." Other voices seem to argue with one another about Edward's special calling and whether he was worthy of this divine power. The voices told him to prepare for God's return to earth. At times Edward said that he was a Nazi soldier and that he was born in Germany in 1886. He also spoke incoherently about corpses frozen in Greenland and maintained that he was "only half a person." 👑

Typical Symptoms and Associated Features

In this section we describe in greater detail various types of positive and negative symptoms that are commonly observed among schizophrenic patients and that are currently emphasized by official diagnostic systems, such as DSM-IV. Remember that all these symptoms can fluctuate in severity over time. Some patients exhibit persistent psychotic symptoms. Others experience symptoms during acute episodes and are better adjusted between episodes.

hallucination A perceptual experience in the absence of external stimulation, such as hearing voices that aren't really there.

delusion An obviously false and idiosyncratic belief that is rigidly held in spite of its preposterous nature.

Hallucinations

Our senses provide us with fundamental information that is vital to our notions of who we are, what we are doing, and what others think of us. Many people with schizophrenia experience perplexing and often frightening changes in perception. The most obvious perceptual symptoms are **hallucinations,** or sensory experiences that are not caused by actual external stimuli. Although hallucinations can occur in any of the senses, those experienced by schizophrenic patients are most often auditory. Many patients hear voices that comment on their behavior or give them instructions. Others hear voices that seem to argue with one another. Edward heard the voice of God talking to him. Although Edward's voices were frightening, in some cases hallucinations can be pleasing to the patient. Patients who experience auditory hallucinations often hear the voice (or voices) speaking to them throughout the day and for many days at a time.

Delusional Beliefs

Many schizophrenic patients express **delusions,** or idiosyncratic beliefs that are rigidly held in spite of their preposterous nature. Delusions have sometimes been defined as false beliefs based

Many of the symptoms of schizophrenia, including hallucinations and delusions, can be extremely distressing.

disorganized speech (also known as *formal thought disorder*) Severe disruptions of verbal communication, involving the form of the person's speech.

on incorrect inferences about reality. This definition has a number of problems, including the difficulty of establishing the ultimate truth of many situations. Ann's accusation that her husband was having an affair, for example, could easily become a choice between her word and his. This suspicion would not, on its own, be considered a delusion. The judgment that her beliefs were delusional depended to a large extent on their expansion to more absurd concerns about stolen photographs, voodoo spells, and alleged plots to kill her children.

Several additional characteristics are important in identifying delusions (Harrow, Rattenbury, & Stoll, 1988). In the most obvious cases, delusional patients express and defend their beliefs with utmost conviction, even when presented with contradictory evidence. For example, Ann's belief that the stolen photographs were being used to cast a spell on her was totally fixed and resistant to contradiction or reconsideration. Preoccupation is another defining characteristic of delusional beliefs. During periods of acute psychosis, many patients like Ann find it difficult, if not completely impossible, to avoid thinking or talking about these beliefs (see Further Thoughts on page 360). Finally, delusional patients are typically unable to consider the perspective that other people hold with regard to their beliefs. Ann, for example, was unable to appreciate the fact that other people considered her paranoid beliefs to be ridiculous.

Although delusional beliefs can take many forms, they are typically personal. They are not shared by other members of the person's family or cultural group. Common delusions include the belief that thoughts are being inserted into the patient's head, that other people are reading the patient's thoughts, or that the patient is being controlled by mysterious, external forces. Many delusions focus on grandiose or paranoid content. For example, Edward expressed the grandiose belief that his father was the Master of the universe. Ann clung persistently to the paranoid belief that someone was trying to kill her and her children.

Disorganized Speech

Another set of schizophrenic symptoms, known as **disorganized speech,** involves the tendency of some patients to say things that don't make sense. Signs of disorganized speech include making irrelevant responses to questions, expressing disconnected ideas, and using words in peculiar ways (Berenbaum & Barch, 1995; Marengo & Harrow, 1993). This symptom is sometimes called *thought disorder* because clinicians have assumed that the failure to communicate successfully reflects a disturbance in the thought patterns that govern verbal discourse. The following excerpt from an interview with a patient illustrates an extreme form of disorganized speech.

Interviewer: Have you been nervous or tense lately?
Patient: No, I got a head of lettuce.
Interviewer: You got a head of lettuce? I don't understand.
Patient: Well, it's just a head of lettuce.
Interviewer: Tell me about lettuce. What do you mean?
Patient: Well, . . . lettuce is a transformation of a dead cougar that suffered a relapse on the lion's toe. And he swallowed the lion and something happened. The . . . see, the . . . Gloria and Tommy, they're two heads and they're not whales. But they escaped with herds of vomit, and things like that. (Neale & Oltmanns, 1980, p. 102)

When speech becomes this disrupted, it is considered *incoherent.* Notice that this patient did not string words together in a random fashion. His speech followed grammatical rules. He was placing nouns and verbs together in an appropriate order, but they didn't make any sense. His speech conveyed little, if any, meaning, and that is the hallmark of disorganized speech.

Several types of verbal communication disruption contribute to clinical judgments about disorganized speech (Docherty, DeRosa, & Andreasen, 1996). Common features of disorganized speech in schizophrenia include shifting topics too abruptly, called *loose associations* or *derailment;* replying to a question with an irrelevant response, called *tangentiality;* or persistently repeating the same word or phrase over and over again, called *perseveration.* We all say things from time to time that fit these descriptions. It is not the occasional presence of a single feature but, rather, the accumulation of a large number of such features that defines the presence of disorganized speech.

Another type of speech disturbance is called *alogia,* which literally means "speechlessness." The term *alogia* refers to impoverished thinking, which is inferred on the basis of nonfluent or barren speech. In one form of alogia, known as *poverty of speech,* patients show remarkable reductions in the amount of speech. In another form, referred to as *thought blocking,* the patient's train of speech is interrupted before a thought or idea has been completed.

Motor Disturbances

Schizophrenic patients may exhibit various forms of unusual motor behavior. *Catatonia* most often refers to immobility and marked muscular rigidity, but it can also refer to excitement and overactivity. For example, some patients engage in apparently purposeless pacing or repetitious movements, such as rubbing their hands over each other in a special pattern for hours at a time. Many catatonic patients exhibit reduced or awkward spontaneous movements. In more extreme forms, patients may assume unusual postures or remain in rigid standing or sitting positions for long periods of time. For example, some patients will lie flat on their backs in a stiff position with their heads raised slightly off the floor as though they were resting on a pillow. Catatonic patients typically resist attempts to alter their position, even though maintaining their awkward postures would normally be extremely uncomfortable or painful.

Catatonic posturing is often associated with a *stuporous state,* or generally reduced responsiveness. The person seems to be unaware of his or her surroundings. Unlike people with other stuporous conditions, however, catatonic patients seem to maintain a clear state of consciousness. Many patients report, after the end of a catatonic episode, that they were perfectly aware of events that were taking place around them, in spite of their failure to respond appropriately.

blunted affect A flattening or restriction of the person's nonverbal display of emotional responses. Blunted patients fail to exhibit signs of emotion or feeling.

anhedonia The inability to experience pleasure. In contrast to blunted affect, which refers to the lack of outward expression, anhedonia is a lack of positive subjective feelings.

inappropriate affect A form of emotional disturbance seen in schizophrenia. The central features of inappropriate affect are incongruity and lack of adaptability in emotional expression.

Affective and Emotional Disturbances

Schizophrenic patients demonstrate emotional changes of various kinds. One of the most characteristic phenomena involves a flattening or restriction of the person's nonverbal display of emotional responses that has sometimes been called **blunted affect,** or *affective flattening.* This symptom was clearly present in Edward's case. Blunted patients fail to exhibit signs of emotion or feeling. They are neither happy nor sad, and they appear to be completely indifferent to their surroundings. The faces of blunted patients are apathetic and expressionless. Their voices lack the typical fluctuations in volume and pitch that other people use to signal changes in their mood. Events in their environment hold little consequence for them. They may demonstrate a complete lack of concern for themselves and for others.

Another type of emotional deficit is called **anhedonia,** which refers to the inability to experience pleasure. Whereas blunted affect refers to the lack of outward expression, anhedonia is a lack of positive subjective feelings.

Although many schizophrenic patients appear to be emotionally blunted, others exhibit affective responses that are obviously inconsistent with their situation. This symptom is particularly difficult to describe in words. The most remarkable features of **inappropriate affect** are incongruity and lack of adaptability in emotional expression. For example, when one patient described the private terror that she felt in the presence of her family, she giggled in a silly fashion. The content of her speech was inconsistent with her facial expression, her gestures, and her voice quality.

Social Withdrawal and Avolition

One of the most important and seriously debilitating aspects of schizophrenia is a malfunction of interpersonal relationships (Meehl, 1993). This is, of course, not surprising in light of

These dementia praecox patients, treated by Emil Kraepelin in the late nineteenth century, display "waxy flexibility," a feature of catatonic motor behavior. "They were put without difficulty in the peculiar positions and kept them, some with a sly laugh, others with rigid seriousness."

the extensive cognitive and emotional difficulties that we have considered in the preceding pages. In many cases, however, social isolation develops before the onset of symptoms, such as hallucinations, delusions, and disorganized speech. It can be one of the earliest signs that something is wrong. This was certainly true in Ann's case. She became socially isolated from her family and friends many weeks before she started to talk openly about the stolen pictures and the plot to kill her children. Social withdrawal appears to be both a symptom of the disorder and a strategy that is actively employed by some patients to deal with their other symptoms. They may, for example, attempt to minimize interactions with other people in order to reduce levels of stimulation that can exacerbate perceptual and cognitive disorganization (Walker, Davis, & Baum, 1993).

The withdrawal seen among many schizophrenic patients is accompanied by indecisiveness, ambivalence, and a loss of willpower. This symptom is known as **avolition** (lack of volition or will). A person who suffers from avolition becomes apathetic and ceases to engage in purposeful actions.

avolition   (lack of volition or will) A negative symptom of schizophrenia involving a loss of willpower, indecisiveness, and ambivalence. The person becomes apathetic and ceases to engage in purposeful actions.

dementia praecox   Kraepelin's original term for the disorder now known as schizophrenia. It referred to psychotic disorders that ended in severe intellectual deterioration (dementia) and that had an early or premature (praecox) onset, usually during adolescence.

Classification

The broad array of symptoms outlined in the previous section have all been described as being part of schizophrenic disorders. The specific organization of symptoms has been a matter of some controversy for many years. Schizophrenic disorders have been defined in many different ways. In the following pages we briefly review some of the trends that led up to the DSM-IV description of these disorders.

Brief Historical Perspective

Descriptions of schizophrenic symptoms can be traced far back in history, but they were not considered to be symptoms of a single disorder until late in the nineteenth century (Gottesman, 1991). At that time, Emil Kraepelin, a German psychiatrist, suggested that several types of problems that previously had been classified as distinct forms of disorder should be grouped together under a single diagnostic category called **dementia praecox.** This term referred to psychoses that ended in severe intellectual deterioration (dementia), had an early or premature (praecox) onset, usually during adolescence, and progressed over time.

In 1911, Eugen Bleuler (1857–1939), a Swiss psychiatrist and a contemporary of Kraepelin, published an extremely influential monograph in which he agreed with most of Kraepelin's suggestions about this disorder. He did not believe, however, that the disorder always ended in profound deterioration or that it always began in late adolescence. Kraepelin's term *dementia praecox* was therefore unacceptable to him. Bleuler suggested a new name for the disorder—*schizophrenia.* This term referred to the *splitting of mental associations,* which Bleuler believed to be the fundamental disturbance in schizophrenia. One unfortunate consequence of this choice of terms has been the confusion among laypeople of schizophrenia with dissociative identity disorder (also known as multiple personality), a severe form of dissociative disorder (see Chapter 7). The two disorders actually have very little in common.

The Swiss psychiatrist Eugen Bleuler coined the term *schizophrenia* in his 1911 monograph on the disorder.

DSM-IV

The current U.S. approach to the diagnosis of schizophrenic disorders gives primary consideration to three types of symptoms: positive (psychotic) symptoms, negative symptoms, and disorganized speech and behavior. The DSM-IV lists several specific criteria for schizophrenia (see Table 13–1 on page 361). The first requirement (Criterion A) is that the patient must exhibit

further thoughts

First-Person Accounts of Schizophrenia

"At the beginning of my last year at (the university), 'feelings' began to descend on me. I felt distinctly different from my usual self. I would sit for hours on end staring at nothing, and I became fascinated with drawing weird, disconnected monsters. I carefully hid my drawings, because I was certain I was being watched. Eventually I became aware of a magical force outside myself that was compelling me in certain directions. The force gained power as time went on, and soon it made me take long walks at 2 or 3 o'clock in the morning down dark alleys in my high-crime neighborhood. I had no power to disobey the force. During my walks I felt as though I was in a different, magical, four-dimensional universe. I understood that the force wanted me to take those walks so that I might be killed.

"I do not clearly understand the relationship between the force and the Alien Beings (alas, such a name!), but my universe soon became populated with them. The Alien Beings were from outer space, and of all the people in the world, only I was aware of them. The Alien Beings soon took over my body and removed me from it. They took me to a faraway place of beaches and sunlight and placed an Alien in my body to act like me. At this point I had the distinct impression that I did not really exist, because I could not make contact with my kidnapped self. I also saw that the Aliens were starting to take over other people as well, removing them from their bodies and putting Aliens in their place. Of course, the other people were unaware of what was happening; I was the only person in the world who had the power to know it. At this point I determined that the Aliens were involved in a huge conspiracy against the world.

"The Alien Beings were gaining strength and had given me a complex set of rules. The rules were very specific and governed every aspect of my behavior. One of the rules was that I could not tell anyone else about the Aliens or the rules, or else the Aliens would kill me. Another of the rules was that I had to become utterly, completely mad. So now I was living in a world of great fear.

"I had a number of other symptoms as well. I felt as though I had been pushed deep within myself, and I had little or no re- action to events or emotions around me. Almost daily the world became unreal to me. Everything outside of me seemed to fade into the distance; everything was miles away from me. I came to feel that I had the power to influence the behavior of animals; that I could, for instance, make dogs bark simply by hooking up rays of thought from my mind to theirs. Conversely, I felt that certain people had the capacity to read my mind. I became very frightened of those people and tried my best to avoid them. Whenever I saw a group of two or three people, I was sure they were talking about me. Paranoia is a very painful emotion! But when I saw crowds of people (as in a shopping mall), I felt an acute longing to wander among them, singing hymns and nursery rhymes" (Payne, 1992, pp. 726–727).

The long-term emotional impact of this disorder on parents and families has been described by a woman whose daughter, then in her mid-thirties, had exhibited symptoms of schizophrenia for 17 years. Her statement also indicates that even the most severely disturbed patients may eventually show signs of improvement.

"The saddest thing of all is to realize that the stories of family life and previous achievements that were a part of the past lives of each of these people are no longer important to them. Nothing in (our daughter's) growing up years could have prepared us for the shock and devastation of seeing this normal, happy child become totally incapacitated by schizophrenia. Coming to grips with the thought of your child living in a mental hospital, possibly for many years, leaves you with a gnawing sense of helplessness that never really dissipates.

"In the past year, a new Cindy has emerged. Where once there was a rather unfriendly, often unpleasant girl, there is now an amiable, more responsive person. Cindy smiles more these days, something a person with schizophrenia doesn't do very often. For years her face was a solemn mask, and she could neither give nor receive affection. She knew something terrible had happened to her and could not understand why no one would rescue her from the hell in her head. In the past few months she has become quite loving, and the smiles that now light her face light mine as well" (Smith, 1991, pp. 690–691).

two (or more) active symptoms for at least 1 month. Notice that only one of the characteristic symptoms is required if that symptom is a bizarre delusion or hallucination. Negative symptoms, such as blunted affect, avolition, and social withdrawal, play a relatively prominent role in the DSM-IV definition of schizophrenia, although some concern has been expressed about the reliability with which they are measured. The work group that developed DSM-IV considered negative symptoms vital both to determining the causes of the disorder and to treating it successfully (Andreasen & Carpenter, 1993).

The DSM-IV definition requires evidence of a decline in the person's social or occupational functioning as well as the presence of disturbed behavior over a continuous period of at least

TABLE 13–1

DSM-IV Diagnostic Criteria for Schizophrenia

A. CHARACTERISTIC SYMPTOMS: TWO (OR MORE) OF THE FOLLOWING, EACH PRESENT FOR A SIGNIFICANT PORTION OF TIME DURING A 1-MONTH PERIOD (OR LESS IF SUCCESSFULLY TREATED):

1. Delusions
2. Hallucinations
3. Disorganized speech (such as frequent derailment or incoherence)
4. Grossly disorganized or catatonic behavior
5. Negative symptoms, such as affective flattening, alogia, or avolition

(Note: Only one A symptom is required if delusions are bizarre or hallucinations consist of a voice keeping up a running commentary on the person's behavior or thoughts, or two or more voices conversing with each other.)

B. SOCIAL/OCCUPATIONAL DYSFUNCTION: FOR A SIGNIFICANT PORTION OF THE TIME SINCE THE ONSET OF THE DISTURBANCE, ONE OR MORE MAJOR AREAS OF FUNCTIONING SUCH AS WORK, INTERPERSONAL RELATIONS, OR SELF-CARE IS MARKEDLY BELOW THE LEVEL ACHIEVED PRIOR TO THE ONSET.

C. DURATION: CONTINUOUS SIGNS OF THE DISTURBANCE PERSIST FOR AT LEAST 6 MONTHS. THIS 6-MONTH PERIOD MUST INCLUDE AT LEAST 1 MONTH OF SYMPTOMS THAT MEET CRITERION A (ACTIVE PHASE SYMPTOMS), AND MAY INCLUDE PERIODS OF PRODROMAL OR RESIDUAL SYMPTOMS. DURING THESE PRODROMAL OR RESIDUAL PERIODS, THE SIGNS OF THE DISTURBANCE MAY BE MANIFESTED BY ONLY NEGATIVE SYMPTOMS OR TWO OR MORE SYMPTOMS LISTED IN CRITERION A PRESENT IN AN ATTENUATED FORM (SUCH AS ODD BELIEFS, UNUSUAL PERCEPTUAL EXPERIENCES).

6 months (Criteria B and C). Active phase symptoms do not need to be present for this entire period. The total duration of disturbance is determined by adding together continuous time during which the person has exhibited prodromal, active, and residual symptoms of schizophrenia.

The final consideration in arriving at a diagnosis of schizophrenia involves the exclusion of related conditions, especially mood disorders. If symptoms of depression or mania are present, their duration must be brief relative to the duration of the active and residual symptoms of schizophrenia.

Subtypes

Schizophrenia is a heterogeneous disorder with many different clinical manifestations and levels of severity. The title of Bleuler's classic text referred to "the group of schizophrenias" in an effort to draw attention to the varied presentations of the disorder. It is not clear, however, how best to think about the different forms of schizophrenia. Many clinicians and investigators believe that schizophrenia is a general term for a group of disorders, each of which may be caused by a completely different set of factors. Other clinicians believe that the numerous symptoms of schizophrenia are most likely varying manifestations of the same underlying condition (Gottesman, 1991). Given the current state of evidence, it is not possible to choose between these conceptual options. Nevertheless, most investigators agree that we should at least consider the possibility that there are distinct forms.

DSM-IV SUBCATEGORIES

Five subtypes are recognized in DSM-IV. The subtypes are used to describe the clinical state of the patient during the most recent examination. Only one subtype can be assigned at any point in time. The five subtypes are arranged in a hierarchy so that patients who exhibit symptoms of

catatonic type A subtype of schizophrenia that is characterized by symptoms of motor immobility (including rigidity and posturing) or excessive and purposeless motor activity.

disorganized type A subtype of schizophrenia (formerly known as hebephrenia) that is characterized by disorganized speech, disorganized behavior, and flat or inappropriate affect. If delusions or hallucinations are present, their content is not well organized.

paranoid type A subtype of schizophrenia that is characterized by systematic delusions with persecutory or grandiose content. Preoccupation with frequent auditory hallucinations can also be associated with the paranoid type.

undifferentiated type A subtype of schizophrenia that includes patients who display prominent psychotic symptoms and either meet the criteria for several subtypes or otherwise do not meet the criteria for the catatonic, paranoid, or disorganized types.

residual type A subtype of schizophrenia that includes patients who no longer meet the criteria for active phase symptoms but nevertheless demonstrate continued signs of negative symptoms or attenuated forms of delusions, hallucinations, or disorganized speech.

schizoaffective disorder A disorder defined by a period of disturbance during which the symptoms of schizophrenia partially overlap with a major depressive episode or a manic episode.

delusional disorder Describes persons who do not meet the full symptomatic criteria for schizophrenia, but they are preoccupied for at least 1 month with delusions that are not bizarre.

different subtypes can be diagnosed. The catatonic type is at the top of the hierarchy. Patients who fit this description are diagnosed as catatonic even if they show additional symptoms that are characteristic of other subtypes. The remaining subtypes, in descending order, are the disorganized subtype, the paranoid subtype, the undifferentiated subtype, and the residual subtype.

The **catatonic type** is characterized by symptoms of motor immobility (including rigidity and posturing) or excessive and purposeless motor activity. In some cases, the person may be resistant to all instructions or refuse to speak, for no apparent reason. Catatonic patients may also show a decreased awareness of their environment and a lack of movements and activity.

The **disorganized type** of schizophrenia is characterized by disorganized speech, disorganized behavior, and flat or inappropriate affect. All three features must be present to make this diagnosis. Social impairment is usually quite marked in these patients. The patient's speech is frequently incoherent, and, if delusions or hallucinations are present, their content is usually not well organized. Consider, for example, the delusions expressed by Edward. At various times, he talked about Nazi soldiers and World War II, frozen corpses in Greenland, being "half a person," and having special powers because he was the son of God. These fragmented and bizarre ideas were clearly delusional, but they were not woven into a coherent framework.

The most prominent symptoms in the **paranoid type** are systematic delusions with persecutory or grandiose content. Preoccupation with frequent auditory hallucinations can also be associated with the paranoid type. Ann would have received a diagnosis of schizophrenic disorder, paranoid type, because of her preoccupation with the systematic delusion about the photographs that had been stolen and the attempt to harm her children. Patients who exhibit disorganized speech, disorganized behavior, flat or inappropriate affect, or catatonic behavior are excluded from a diagnosis of paranoid schizophrenia and would fall into one of the other subtypes.

Two additional subtypes are described in DSM-IV, presumably to cover those patients who do not fit one of the traditional types. The **undifferentiated type** of schizophrenia includes schizophrenic patients who display prominent psychotic symptoms and either meet the criteria for several subtypes or otherwise do not meet the criteria for the catatonic, disorganized, or paranoid types. They often exhibit some disorganized symptoms together with hallucinations and/or delusions.

The **residual type** includes patients who no longer meet the criteria for active phase symptoms but nevertheless demonstrate continued signs of negative symptoms or attenuated forms of delusions, hallucinations, or disorganized speech. They are in "partial remission."

Related Disorders

The U.S. concept of schizophrenia is relatively narrow. The boundaries of the disorder have been refined by excluding patients with certain types of psychotic symptoms from a diagnosis of schizophrenic disorder. The DSM-IV lists three disorders other than schizophrenia that are characterized by prominent psychotic symptoms.

Schizoaffective disorder is an ambiguous and somewhat controversial category (Frances, First, & Pincus, 1995). It describes the symptoms of patients who fall on the boundary between schizophrenia and mood disorder with psychotic features. This diagnosis applies only to the description of a particular episode of disturbance; it does not describe the overall lifetime course of the person's disorder. Schizoaffective disorder is defined by an episode in which the symptoms of schizophrenia partially overlap with a major depressive episode or a manic episode. The key to making this diagnosis is the presence of delusions or hallucinations for at least 2 weeks in the absence of prominent mood symptoms. If the delusions and hallucinations are present only during a depressive episode, for example, the diagnosis would be major depressive episode with psychotic features. Schizoaffective disorder will continue to be a vague diagnostic category until progress is made in unraveling the etiological distinction between mood disorders and schizophrenia.

People with **delusional disorder** do not meet the full symptomatic criteria for schizophrenia, but they are preoccupied for at least 1 month with delusions that are not bizarre. These are beliefs about situations that could occur in real life, such as being followed or poisoned. Ann's delusion, for example, might have fit this description. She believed that someone was trying to kill her and her children and that someone was trying to cast a voodoo spell on them. Ann would not be assigned a diagnosis of delusional disorder, however, because she also displayed negative symptoms, such as avolition. The presence of hallucinations, disorganized speech, catatonic behavior, or negative symptoms rules out a diagnosis of delusional disorder. The definition of delusional disorder also holds that the person's behavior is not bizarre and that social and occupational functioning are not impaired except for those areas that are directly affected by the delusional belief.

Brief psychotic disorder is a category that includes those people who exhibit psychotic symptoms—delusions, hallucinations, disorganized speech, or grossly disorganized or catatonic behavior—for at least 1 day but no more than 1 month. An episode of this sort is typically accompanied by confusion and emotional turmoil, often (but not necessarily) following a markedly stressful event. After the symptoms are resolved, the person returns to the same level of functioning that had been achieved prior to the psychotic episode. This diagnosis is not assigned if the symptoms are better explained by a mood disorder, schizophrenia, or substance abuse. This category is used infrequently, and very little research has been conducted with people who have this disorder.

People with schizophrenia sometimes exhibit disorganized behavior, like this hospitalized woman.

brief psychotic disorder A diagnostic category in DSM-IV that includes people who exhibit psychotic symptoms for at least 1 day but no more than 1 month. After the symptoms are resolved, the person returns to the same level of functioning that had been achieved prior to the psychotic episode.

Course and Outcome

Traditionally, schizophrenia has been considered a severe, progressive disorder that most often begins in adolescence and typically has a poor outcome. Recent evidence suggests that this view may be unnecessarily pessimistic. Many patients in fact experience a good outcome (Harding, Zubin, & Strauss, 1992). For example, Manfred Bleuler (1978) studied a sample of 208 schizophrenic patients who had been admitted to his hospital in Switzerland during 1942 and 1943. After a follow-up period of 23 years, 53 percent of the patients were either recovered or significantly improved.

Follow-up studies of schizophrenic patients have found that the description of outcome can be a complicated process. Many factors must be taken into consideration other than whether the person is still in the hospital. Is the person still exhibiting symptoms of the disorder? Does he or she have any other problems, such as depression or anxiety? Is the person employed? Does she have any friends? How does he get along with other people? The evidence indicates that different dimensions of outcome, such as social adjustment, occupational functioning, and symptom severity, are only loosely correlated. As in most situations where psychologists attempt to predict future behavior, the outcome data regarding schizophrenia suggest that the best predictor of future social adjustment is previous social adjustment. Similarly, the best predictor of symptom severity at follow-up is severity of psychotic symptoms at initial assessment (Carpenter & Strauss, 1991; Strauss & Carpenter, 1978, 1981).

Epidemiology

One of the most informative ways of examining the frequency of schizophrenia is to consider the *lifetime morbid risk*—that is, the proportion of a specific population that will be affected by the disorder at some time during their lives. Most studies in Europe and the United States have reported lifetime morbid risk figures of approximately 1 percent (Jablensky, 1986). In other words, approximately 1 out of every 100 people will experience or display schizophrenic symptoms at some time during their lives. Of course, prevalence rates depend on the diagnostic criteria that are used to define schizophrenia in any particular study, as well as the methods that are used to identify cases in the general population. Investigators who have used more narrow or restrictive criteria for the disorder typically report lower morbid risk figures.

Data from the Epidemiologic Catchment Area (ECA) study are consistent with figures reported earlier (Keith, Regier, & Rae, 1991). Using DSM-III criteria for the disorder, the investigators found a lifetime prevalence of 1.3 percent for schizophrenia and 0.2 percent for schizophreniform disorder. The mean age of onset was 20 years, and 71 percent of the people who met criteria for schizophrenia had experienced their first symptoms by the age of 25. For those persons who no longer exhibited active symptoms at the time of the interview, the mean duration of the disorder was 15 years.

Gender Differences

Most epidemiological studies have reported that, across the life span, men and women are equally likely to be affected by schizophrenia (Gottesman, 1991; Keith, Regier, & Rae, 1991). This conclusion has been challenged in recent years, however, by studies that suggest that, among new cases of schizophrenia, men may outnumber women by a ratio of at least 2:1 (e.g., Iacono & Beiser, 1992).

The controversy surrounding gender differences in incidence may reflect, at least in part, gender differences in more specific aspects of schizophrenia. There are some interesting and widely recognized differences between male and female patients with regard to patterns of onset, symptomatology, and course of the disorder. For example, the average age at which schizophrenic males begin to exhibit overt symptoms is younger by about 4 or 5 years than the average age at which schizophrenic women first experience problems (Hafner et al., 1994). A summary of proposed gender differences in schizophrenia is presented in Table 13–2. Male patients are more likely than female patients to exhibit negative symptoms, and they are also more likely to follow a chronic, deteriorating course.

Gender differences in the age of onset and symptomatic expression of schizophrenia can be interpreted in several ways (Castle et al., 1995; Goldstein, 1995b; Lewine & Seeman, 1995). One approach assumes that schizophrenia is a single disorder and that its expression varies in men and women. A common, genetically determined vulnerability to schizophrenia might be expressed differently in men than in women. An alternative approach suggests that there are two qualitatively distinct subtypes of schizophrenia: one with an early onset that affects men more often than women, and another with a later onset that affects women more often than men. Both approaches fit the general diathesis-stress model. The available evidence does not allow us to favor one of these explanations over the other.

Cross-Cultural Comparisons

Schizophrenia has been observed in virtually every culture that has been subjected to careful scrutiny. Of course, the formal term *schizophrenia* is not used in all societies, but the symptoms of the disorder are nevertheless present (see Research Close-Up in Chapter 1).

Two large-scale epidemiological studies, conducted by teams of scientists working for the World Health Organization (WHO), indicate that the incidence of schizophrenia is relatively constant across different cultural settings. The International Pilot Study of Schizophrenia (IPSS) be-

TABLE 13–2

Typical Gender Differences in Schizophrenia		
VARIABLE	**MEN**	**WOMEN**
Age of onset	Earlier (18–25)	Later (25–35)
Premorbid adjustment	Poor social functioning; more schizotypal traits	Good social functioning; fewer schizotypal traits
Typical symptoms	More negative symptoms; more withdrawn and passive	More hallucinations and paranoia; more emotional and impulsive
Course	More often chronic; poorer response to treatment	Less often chronic; better response to treatment

Source: *Based on J. M. Goldstein, 1995, The impact of gender on understanding the epidemiology of schizophrenia. In M. V. Seeman (Ed.),* Gender and Psychopathology, *pp. 159–199. Washington, DC: American Psychiatric Press.*

gan in the 1960s and was conducted in nine countries in Europe, North America, South America, Africa, and Asia. The Collaborative Study on the Determinants of Outcome of Severe Mental Disorders (DOS) was conducted a few years later in six of the same countries that had participated in the IPSS, plus four others. Both the IPSS and DOS projects examined rural and urban areas in both Western and non-Western countries.

The IPSS results indicated that patients who exhibited characteristic signs and symptoms of schizophrenia were found in all of the study sites. Comparisons of patients across research centers revealed more similarities than differences in clinical symptoms at the time of entry into the study, which was always an active phase of disorder that required psychiatric treatment. Using a relatively narrow set of diagnostic criteria, scientists found that the incidence of schizophrenia did not differ significantly among the research centers. The IPSS investigators also found that clinical and social outcomes at 2- and 5-year follow-up were significantly better for schizophrenic patients in developing countries than in developed countries, such as the United States, England, and Russia (Leff et al., 1992). The DOS study confirmed those results (Jablensky et al., 1992). Taken together, the WHO studies provide compelling support for the conclusion that schizophrenia occurs with similar frequency and presents with similar symptoms in different cultures.

Etiological Considerations and Research

Having considered the defining characteristics of schizophrenia, ways in which it has been classified, and some basic information regarding its distribution within the general population, we now review the evidence regarding factors that might contribute to the development of the disorder, as well as its course and outcome.

Biological Factors

Research in the areas of molecular genetics and the neurosciences has progressed at an explosive rate in the past decade. Much of what we know today about the biological substrates of schizophrenia has emerged from advances that have taken place in other sciences.

GENETICS

The role of genetic factors has been studied more extensively with regard to schizophrenia than with any other type of mental disorder. The existing data are based on sophisticated methods that have been refined over many years. The cumulative weight of this evidence points clearly toward some type of genetic influence in the transmission of this disorder (Gottesman & Moldin, 1997).

Family Studies   Figure 13–1 illustrates the lifetime risk for schizophrenia for various types of relatives of a person with schizophrenia. Irving Gottesman, a psychologist at the University of Virginia, created this figure by pooling data from 40 European studies that were published between 1920 and 1987 (Gottesman, 1991). All of the studies employed conservative diagnostic criteria for the disorder.

Irving Gottesman, Sherrell J. Aston Professor of Psychology at the University of Virginia, is one of the world's leading experts on genetic factors and schizophrenia.

Consider the data for first-degree relatives and second-degree relatives. On average, siblings and children share 50 percent of their genes with the schizophrenic proband; nieces, nephews, and cousins share only 25 percent. The lifetime morbid risk for schizophrenia is much greater among first-degree relatives than it is among second-degree relatives. The risk in the second-degree relatives is greater than the 1 percent figure that is typically reported for people in the general population. As the degree of genetic similarity increases between an individual and a schizophrenic patient, the risk to that person increases. The family history data are consistent with the hypothesis that the transmission of schizophrenia is influenced by genetic factors. They do not prove the point, however, because family studies do not separate genetic and environmental events (see Chapter 2).

Twin Studies   Several twin studies have examined concordance rates for schizophrenia. The results of these studies are also summarized in Figure 13–1. The average concordance rate for MZ twins is 48 percent, whereas the comparable figure for DZ twins is 17 percent. One study from

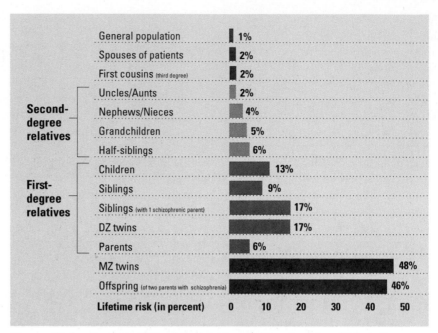

Figure 13–1   Average Risk of Developing Schizophrenia.   Risk applies among biological relatives of a schizophrenic proband.

Source: I. I. Gottesman, 1991, *Schizophrenia Genesis: The Origins of Madness,* p. 96. New York: Freeman.

Norway, published after Gottesman computed average rates for his figure, found a concordance rate of 48 percent among MZ twins and only 4 percent among DZ twins (Onstad et al., 1991). Although the specific rates vary somewhat from study to study, all of the published reports have found that MZ twins are significantly more likely than DZ twins to be concordant for schizophrenia. This pattern suggests strongly that genetic factors play an important role in the development of the disorder.

It should also be pointed out, however, that none of the twin studies of schizophrenia has found a concordance rate that even approaches 100 percent, which would be expected if genetic factors were entirely responsible for schizophrenia. Thus the twin studies also provide compelling evidence for the importance of environmental events. Some people apparently inherit a predisposition to the development of schizophrenia. Among that select group of vulnerable individuals, certain environmental events must determine whether a given person will eventually exhibit the full-blown symptoms of the disorder.

Adoption Studies   Studies of children who were adopted away from their biological parents and reared by foster families provide this type of clear distinction between genetic and environmental influence. The first adoption study of schizophrenia was reported by Leonard Heston (1966), a psychiatrist at the University of Washington. He began by identifying records for a group of 49 children who were born between 1915 and 1945 while their mothers were hospitalized for schizophrenia. All the children were apparently normal at birth and were separated from their mothers within 3 days of birth. To rule out possible exposure to the environment associated with the mother's psychosis, any child who had been in contact with maternal relatives was excluded from the study. A control group of children was selected using the admission records of foundling homes where many of the target children had originally been placed. These children were matched to the patients' children on a number of variables, including age, sex, type of eventual placement, and length of institutionalization.

Heston was able to locate and interview most of the offspring, the majority of whom were then in their mid-thirties. Five of the adult offspring of schizophrenic mothers received a diagnosis of schizophrenia. Correcting for the fact that most of the participants were still within the period of risk for the disorder, this resulted in a lifetime morbidity risk for schizophrenia of 16.6 percent in the target group, which is almost exactly the rate observed among children of schizophrenic parents who were raised by their biological parents (see Figure 13–1). In contrast, none of the adult offspring in the control group received a diagnosis of schizophrenia. Because the only difference between the two groups was the genetic relationship between the target offspring and their schizophrenic biological mothers, Heston's data indicate that genetic factors play a role in the development of the disorder. Several other adoption studies have been concerned with schizophrenia, and all reach the same conclusion as Heston's original report (see Gottesman, 1991, and Kendler & Diehl, 1993, for reviews of this literature).

Linkage Studies   The combined results from twin and adoption studies indicate that genetic factors are involved in the transmission of schizophrenia. This conclusion does not imply, however, that the manner in which schizophrenia develops is well understood. We know little beyond the fact that genetic factors are involved in some way. The mode of transmission has not been identified. Some clinical scientists believe that a single dominant gene is involved. Others believe that schizophrenia is a polygenic characteristic, which means that it is the product of a reasonably large number of genes rather than a single gene (see Chapter 2).

One of the most exciting areas of research on genetics and schizophrenia focuses on the search for genetic linkage. Studies of this type are designed to identify the location of a specific gene that is responsible for the disorder (or some large component of the disorder). Linkage analysis has not yet produced any firm conclusions or replicable findings. Kendler and Diehl (1993) reviewed more than 30 genetic linkage studies of schizophrenia. None of the subsequent studies has found strong support for linkage to any genetic locus. Supporters of linkage analysis contend that the absence of definitive discoveries is not necessarily surprising when we consider that there are probably tens of thousands of genes that influence activities in the brain. They feel that the search for a particular gene that causes schizophrenia will take much time. Critics respond that schizophrenia is a polygenic disorder, and therefore we will never trace its etiology to a single gene. There is good reason to believe that polygenic models provide the best explanation for the distribution of the disorder within families (Gottesman & Moldin, 1997; Vogler et al., 1990).

PREGNANCY AND BIRTH COMPLICATIONS

People with schizophrenia are more likely than the general population to have been exposed to various problems during pregnancy and to have suffered birth injuries. Problems during pregnancy include the mother's contracting various types of diseases and infections. Birth complications include extended labor, breech delivery, forceps delivery, and the umbilical cord wrapped around the baby's neck. These events may be harmful, in part, because they impair circulation or otherwise reduce the availability of oxygen to developing brain regions. Birth records indicate that the mothers of people who later develop schizophrenia experienced more complications at the time of labor and delivery (McNeil, Cantor-Graae, Sjostrom, et al., 1994; McNeil, Cantor-Graae, Torrey, Sjostrom, et al., 1994).

It is not clear whether the effects of pregnancy and birth complications interact with genetic factors (Gottesman, 1991). They may produce neurodevelopmental abnormalities that result in schizophrenia regardless of family history for the disorder. Conversely, a fetus that is genetically predisposed to schizophrenia may be more susceptible to brain injury following certain kinds of obstetric difficulties.

Dietary factors may also play a role in the etiology of the disorder. Severe maternal malnutrition in the early months of pregnancy leads to an increased risk of schizophrenia among the offspring. This conclusion is based on a study of medical and psychiatric records of people who were born in the western part of the Netherlands between 1944 and 1946 (Susser et al., 1996). The Nazi blockade of ports and other supply routes in this area led to a severe famine at the end of World War II. People who were conceived during the worst months of the famine were twice as likely to develop schizophrenia as were people whose mothers became pregnant at other times, including the early months of the famine. These results suggest that prenatal nutritional deficiencies may disrupt normal development of the fetal nervous system.

VIRAL INFECTIONS

Some speculation has focused on the potential role that viral infections may play in the etiology of schizophrenia (Gupta, 1993; Torrey & Yolken, 1995). One indirect line of support for this hypothesis comes from studies indicating that people who develop schizophrenia are somewhat more likely than other people to have been born during the winter months (Bradbury & Miller, 1985; Huttunen, Machon, & Mednick, 1994; Pulver et al., 1992). Some clinicians interpret this pattern to mean that, during their pregnancies, the mothers were more likely to develop viral infections, which are more prevalent during the winter. Support for the hypothesis remains indirect. No evidence has yet been found to confirm a direct link between viral infections and schizophrenia (Kirch, 1993).

NEUROPATHOLOGY

One important step toward understanding the etiology of schizophrenia would be to identify its neurological underpinnings. If people with schizophrenia suffer from a form of neurological dysfunction, shouldn't it be possible to observe differences between the structure of their brains and those of other people? This is a very challenging task. Scientists have invented methods to create images of the living human brain (see Chapter 4). Some of these procedures provide static pictures of various brain structures at rest, just as an X ray provides a photographic image of a bone or some other organ of the body. More recently, sophisticated methods have enabled us to create functional images of the brain while a person is performing different tasks. Studies using these techniques have produced evidence indicating that a number of brain areas are involved in schizophrenia (Gur & Pearlson, 1993; Van Horn, Berman, & Weinberger, 1996). You may want to review the description of brain structures in Chapter 2 (Figure 2–4) and consult Figure 13–2 before reading the next sections of this chapter.

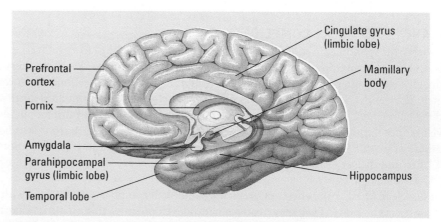

Figure 13–2   Areas of the Brain Implicated in Schizophrenia.   Brain imaging studies have suggested that specific components of the limbic system, including the hippocampus and the amydala, may be dysfunctional in schizophrenia.

Source: Adapted from F. Martini and M. Timmons, 1995, *Human Anatomy*, p. 318. Upper Saddle River, NJ: Prentice Hall.

The Danish High-Risk Project

Our ability to understand the etiology of schizophrenia is limited by a lack of information regarding patients' developmental histories. Once a person has become psychotic, it is difficult to reconstruct events from previous years. Furthermore, comparisons between schizophrenic patients and other groups are difficult to interpret because the patients have already been exposed to treatment. For these reasons, it would be extremely useful if systematic data could be collected before the onset of the disorder.

In 1962, Sarnoff Mednick, now a psychologist at the University of Southern California, and Fini Schulsinger, a Danish psychiatrist, began in Denmark a longitudinal study of biological children of parents with schizophrenia (Mednick & Schulsinger, 1968). These people were selected because, in comparison to members of the general population, they are at *high risk* for schizophrenia. Roughly 13 percent of the high-risk group would be expected to develop the disorder as adults (see Figure 13–1). The project included 207 high-risk children whose biological mothers had been diagnosed as schizophrenic and 104 low-risk children to serve as a comparison group. The families of the low-risk children had been free of mental illness for at least three generations. When the study was begun, none of the children had exhibited any overt signs of psychological disorder. The family environments (for example, social class, rural or urban residence) were similar in both groups.

Mednick and his colleagues have collected an enormous amount of information in order to describe the developmental histories of children in both groups, from birth to adulthood. They relied on hospital records to determine the frequency of pregnancy and delivery complications associated with each subject's birth. The investigators conducted follow-up assessments, including structured diagnostic interviews, with each person at two principal times: in the early 1970s and again in

the late 1980s, when the participants' average age was 42 years. The latter assessment included the use of CT scans to detect structural brain pathology.

It has been more than 30 years since the Danish study began, and 31 of the high-risk offspring have developed schizophrenia (Parnas et al., 1993). Age-corrected morbid risk rates for schizophrenia in the high- and low-risk groups are 17 percent and 3 percent, respectively. The high-risk offspring were also more likely than the low-risk offspring to meet the criteria for schizotypal personality disorder (18 percent compared to 5 percent). Rates of mood disorders were similar in both groups, suggesting that the high-risk group was predisposed to schizophrenia-spectrum disorders in particular rather than to serious mental disorders in general.

The most important data in this project involve factors that may precede the onset of schizophrenic symptoms. Several intriguing findings have been reported. For example, researchers noted a correlation between delivery complications and enlarged ventricles among people in the high-risk group but not among people in the low-risk group (Cannon et al., 1993). In addition, an earlier report indicated that, in comparison to members of the high-risk group who did not become schizophrenic, those high-risk individuals who did develop schizophrenia had experienced more pregnancy and birth complications (Cannon, Mednick, & Parnas, 1990). This was especially true for people who developed negative symptoms of the disorder. Thus far, the overall pattern of results suggests that vulnerability to schizophrenia may be associated with a pattern of fetal brain development that is especially sensitive to disruptions caused by delivery complications. The combination of genetic risk and problems in delivery seems to be especially relevant. Data from the Danish high-risk project are also consistent with the hypothesis that neurodevelopmental problems in schizophrenia are antecedents rather than consequences of the disorder. ⚜

Structural Brain Imaging   Many investigations of brain structure in people with schizophrenia have employed computerized tomographic (CT) scanning, which produces a series of two-dimensional images at sequential slices or planes of the brain (see Chapter 4 for an explanation of this process). The most consistent result across a large number of CT-scan studies has been the finding that some people with schizophrenia have mildly to moderately enlarged *lateral ventricles,* the cavities on each side of the brain that are filled with cerebrospinal fluid (Kotrla & Weinberger, 1995; Raz & Raz, 1990). These differences seem to reflect a natural part of the disorder rather than a side effect of treatment with antipsychotic medication. In fact, some studies have found enlarged ventricles in young schizophrenic patients before they have been exposed to any form of treatment. One important study has also found enlarged ventricles prior to the onset of symptoms (see

Close-Up on page 369). Significantly, these differences do not appear to become more marked as time goes on. The structural changes seem to occur early in the development of the disorder and therefore may play a role in the onset of symptoms.

Many questions remain to be answered regarding the relation between enlarged ventricles and schizophrenia. Does the pattern reflect a generalized deterioration of the brain, or is it the result of a defect in specific brain sites? We don't know. Is the presence of enlarged ventricles consistently found in some subset of schizophrenic patients? Some investigators have reported an association between this type of neuropathology and other factors, such as negative symptoms, poor response to medication, and absence of family history of the disorder. These are all interesting possibilities, but none has been firmly established (Torrey et al., 1994).

With *magnetic resonance imaging (MRI),* investigators are able to identify clearly many specific smaller structures within the brain that were not clearly visible using CT scans. The temporal lobes have been studied rather extensively using MRI scans. Several studies have reported decreased size of the hippocampus, the amygdala, and the thalamus, which are all parts of the limbic system (Buchsbaum et al., 1996; Gur & Pearlson, 1993). These areas of the brain (located in the temporal lobes; see Figure 13–2) play a crucial role in the regulation of emotion as well as the integration of cognition and emotion. Decreased size of these structures in the limbic area of the temporal lobes may be especially noticeable on the left side of the brain, which plays an important role in the control of language. One interesting study found that schizophrenic patients who exhibited the greatest degree of disorganized speech were most likely to show a decrease in the size of left temporal lobe structures (Shenton et al., 1992).

Functional Brain Imaging   In addition to CT- and MRI-scan procedures, which provide static pictures of brain structures, clinical scientists are also using techniques that provide dynamic images of brain functions. One of these procedures involves the measurement of *regional cerebral blood flow (rCBF).* Images can be generated while the subject is at rest or performing a specific task. Visual stimulation will produce increased cerebral blood flow in the visual cortex; people performing a simple motor task exhibit increased flow in the motor cortex.

Studies using the measurement of rCBF have found differences between people with schizophrenia and others, particularly in the frontal regions of the brain (Weinberger & Lipska, 1995). Daniel Weinberger, a psychiatrist at the National Institute of Mental Health, and his colleagues have measured rCBF in the prefrontal cortex while participants perform an abstract problem-solving task that presumably requires cognitive abilities that are mediated in the frontal lobes. Normal people show an increase in blood flow to the frontal regions of the brain when they are engaged in this task. Many schizophrenic patients, in contrast, do not show this same increase. Studies of brain metabolism and blood flow have also identified functional changes in the temporal lobes and basal ganglia in many persons with schizophrenia.

Another dynamic brain imaging technique is *positron emission tomography (PET)* scanning. Like rCBF, it can reflect changes in brain activity as the person responds to various task demands. The results of PET-scan studies are consistent with rCBF results and suggest dysfunction in the frontal cortex as well as the temporal lobes (Goldman-Rakic, 1996; Gur et al., 1995). These problems are also observed among patients with major mood disorders.

The role of neurological abnormalities in schizophrenia has been highlighted by a study of identical twins conducted by a group of investigators at the National Institute of Mental Health (NIMH). Participants included 27 pairs of twins discordant for schizophrenia and 13 pairs that were concordant for the disorder. Changes in brain structure, measured by MRI, and changes in brain function, measured by cerebral blood flow, were prominent in the twins who had developed schizophrenia. Their well co-twins also exhibited more neurological impairment than a group of normal control participants, but these abnormalities were less marked than those found in the probands. Among discordant monozygotic pairs, the schizophrenic twin typically had the smaller hippocampus and smaller amygdala. The schizophrenic twins always showed reduced frontal lobe rCBF activity compared with their unaffected co-twins. Results for enlarged ventricles were less consistent. In general, neurological dysfunction seemed to be associated with the overall severity of the disorder rather than being indicative of an etiologically distinct subgroup of patients (Torrey et al., 1994).

General Conclusions   The primary conclusion that can be drawn from existing brain imaging studies is that schizophrenia is associated with diffuse patterns of neuropathology. The most consistent findings point toward structural as well as functional irregularities in the limbic areas of the temporal lobes, which play an important role in cognitive and emotional processes. The neural network connecting these areas with the frontal cortex may be fundamentally disordered in schizophrenia.

Speculation regarding disruptions in neural circuitry must also be tempered with caution. Evidence of neuropathology does not seem to be unique to schizophrenic patients. Many patients with other psychiatric and neurological disorders show similar changes in brain structure and function. Furthermore, a specific brain lesion has not been identified, and it is unlikely that one will be found. As Paul Meehl (1990) has argued, it is unlikely that a disorder as complex as schizophrenia will be traced to a single site in the brain. The various symptoms and cognitive deficits that have been observed in schizophrenic patients may be linked to a host of subtle disruptions in neurological functions (M. Strauss, 1993).

It should also be emphasized that brain imaging procedures are not diagnostically meaningful tests for mental disorders. For example, a CT scan showing enlarged ventricles does not prove that a patient has schizophrenia. Brain imaging procedures have identified interesting *group* differences, but they do not predict the presence of schizophrenia for *individuals*. The group differences that have been observed are quite subtle in comparison to the levels of neuropathology found in disorders such as Alzheimer's disease and Huntington's disease. Some schizophrenic patients do not show abnormalities in brain structure or function.

A dramatic example of this point was found in the NIMH study of discordant MZ twins. In one pair, the well twin was a successful businessman who had never had any problems with mental disorder. His twin brother had been severely impaired with schizophrenia for 20 years. The well twin had ventricles that were five times larger than those of the schizophrenic twin. Thus we should approach all these hypotheses with caution and skepticism.

NEUROCHEMISTRY

The neurological underpinnings of schizophrenia may not take the form of changes in the size or organization of brain structures. They may be even more subtle, involving alterations in the functioning of particular parts of the brain. As we saw in Chapter 2, the process of chemical transmission in the brain is an active, dynamic system. Neurons regulate the synthesis and release of neurotransmitters as they monitor levels of these chemicals in the system. Too much dopamine in the synapse can result in decreased synthesis in the cell body. Similarly, insufficient amounts of dopamine can result in the synthesis of extra postsynaptic receptors. These dynamic properties are important in understanding the way in which antipsychotic drugs affect abnormal behavior.

The Dopamine Hypothesis of Schizophrenia   Scientists have proposed various neurochemical theories to account for the etiology of schizophrenia (Iqbal & van Praag, 1995; Kahn & Davidson, 1995). The most influential theory, known as the *dopamine hypothesis,* focuses on the function of specific dopamine pathways in the limbic area of the brain. The original version of the dopamine hypothesis proposed that the symptoms of schizophrenia are the product of excessive levels of dopaminergic activity. This hypothesis grew out of attempts to understand how antipsychotic drugs, also known as *neuroleptics,* improve the adjustment of many schizophrenic patients. Animals who receive doses of neuroleptic drugs show a marked increase in the production of dopamine. In 1963, Arvid Carlsson, a Swedish pharmacologist, suggested that neuroleptics block postsynaptic dopamine receptors. The presynaptic neuron recognizes the presence of this blockade and increases its release of dopamine in a futile attempt to override it (Carlsson & Lindqvist, 1963).

Further support for the dopamine hypothesis came from two additional observations. First, patients who receive neuroleptic medication for an extended period of time often develop motor side effects that resemble the symptoms of Parkinson's disease, which is produced by the destruction of dopamine in certain brain pathways. It therefore seemed likely that schizophrenia was associated with an initially overactive dopamine system and that treatment with antipsychotic medication corrected this problem.

The second observation involves the effect of chronic amphetamine use. Amphetamine is able to stimulate firing by dopamine neurons. People who take amphetamines for an extended period of time often develop a form of paranoid psychosis that is very similar to schizophrenia. This suggests that the natural form of schizophrenia may also be associated with overactivity in these neural pathways.

If the dopamine system is dysfunctional in schizophrenic patients, what is the specific form of this problem? One possibility that has received a great deal of attention in the past few years is concerned with the number of postsynaptic dopamine receptors. The potency of various types of antipsychotic drugs is specifically related to their ability to block one type of dopamine receptor, known as D_2 *receptors* (Creese, Burt, & Snyder, 1976). Autopsy studies of schizophrenic patients' brains have found that some patients have an excessive number of D_2 receptors in the striatum, while the number of D_1 receptors is apparently normal (Kornhuber et al., 1989).

With regard to etiology, the most important question is whether an increased number of D_2 receptors is present before schizophrenic patients are treated with neuroleptic medication. The results of autopsy studies may simply reflect the fact that treatment with antipsychotic drugs produces an increase in the number of D_2 receptors. The density of dopamine receptors can be measured in the brains of living patients using PET scanning procedures. One laboratory has reported that untreated, first-episode schizophrenic patients have significantly more D_2 receptors when compared to a group of normal volunteers, but other studies have failed to replicate this result (Farde et al., 1995).

Current Neurochemical Models   The original dopamine hypothesis stimulated an enormous amount of research, and it has been an extremely useful model from that point of view. At least for some patients, a dysfunction of certain dopamine tracts in the brain is somehow involved in the disorder. On the other hand, biologically minded investigators now generally agree that this model was too simple. It failed to account for many different aspects of the disorder, including the following: Some patients do not respond positively to drugs that block dopamine receptors; the effects of antipsychotic drugs require several days to become effective, but dopamine blockage begins immediately; research studies that examined the by-products of dopamine in cerebrospinal fluid were inconclusive at best.

Current neurochemical hypotheses regarding schizophrenia focus on a broad array of neurotransmitters, including GABA, acetylcholine, serotonin, and neuropeptides. Special interest has been focused on serotonin pathways since the introduction of a new class of antipsychotic drugs such as clozapine (Clozaril) that are useful in treating patients who were resistant to traditional neuroleptic drugs. (See the section on treatment.) These "atypical" antipsychotics apparently work by producing a strong blockade of serotonin receptors and only a weak blockade of D_2 receptors. This pattern leads to speculation that the neurochemical substrates of schizophrenia may involve a complex interaction between serotonin and dopamine pathways in the brain (Kapur & Remington, 1996; Meltzer, 1993).

Social Factors

There is little question that biological factors play an important role in the etiology of schizophrenia, but twin studies also provide compelling evidence for the importance of environmental events. The disorder is expressed in its full-blown form only when vulnerable individuals experience some type of environmental event, which might include anything from nutritional variables to stressful life events (Fowles, 1992). What sorts of nongenetic events interact with genetic factors to produce schizophrenia? Specific answers are not available at the present time. We can, however, review some of the hypotheses that have been studied.

SOCIAL CLASS
People from different social classes are presumably exposed to different levels of environmental stress, with those people in the lowest class being subjected to the most hardships. More than 50 years ago, social scientists working in Chicago found that the highest prevalence of schizophrenia

was found in neighborhoods of the lowest socioeconomic status (Faris & Dunham, 1939). Many research studies have subsequently confirmed this finding in several other geographic areas (Neale & Oltmanns, 1980). The evidence supporting an inverse relationship between social class and schizophrenia is substantial.

There are two ways to interpret the relationship between social class and schizophrenia. One holds that harmful events associated with membership in the lowest social classes, which might include many factors ranging from stress and social isolation to poor nutrition, play a causal role in the development of the disorder. This is often called the *social causation hypothesis*. It is also possible, however, that low social class is an outcome rather than a cause of schizophrenia. Those people who develop schizophrenia may be less able than others to complete a higher-level education or hold a well-paying job. Their cognitive and social impairments may cause downward social mobility. In other words, regardless of the social class of their family of origin, many schizophrenic patients may gradually drift into the lowest social classes. This view is sometimes called the *social selection hypothesis*. Research studies have found evidence supporting both views.

In general, the evidence regarding socioeconomic status and schizophrenia indicates that the disorder is, to a certain extent, influenced by social factors. Adverse social and economic circumstances may increase the probability that persons who are genetically predisposed to the disorder will develop its clinical symptoms (Cohen, 1993; Freeman, 1994). The literature on social class has identified this relationship in very general terms. Some of the specific details have been examined in studies that are considered in the next section of this chapter.

Psychological Factors

Psychodynamic views of psychopathology encouraged the consideration of family interactions and patterns of interpersonal communication in the etiology of schizophrenia. Several clinicians proposed that schizophrenia was caused by deviant patterns of interaction between patients and their parents, typically while the patient was still a small child. These hypotheses were particularly popular in the United States during the 1950s and 1960s.

FAMILY INTERACTION

Hypotheses regarding family communication and the etiology of schizophrenia were tested extensively during the 1960s and 1970s. Some investigators approached the problem by bringing young patients and their parents into a laboratory and directly observing the manner in which they communicated with one another (Mishler & Waxler, 1968). Results typically indicated that the families of schizophrenic patients communicated less effectively than did the families of control participants.

Do these difficulties play a causal role in the onset of the disorder? Most of the data are correlational in nature: Schizophrenic patients tend to have parents who perform in unusual ways on psychological tasks and communicate less effectively than other parents. The direction of this relationship is not clear (Onstad, Skre, Torgersen, & Kringlen, 1994). Figure 13–3 illustrates several possible explanations. Some clinicians have argued that subtle communication impairment among the parents eventually cause their children to develop schizophrenia (Model 1 in Figure 13–3). Studies have found, however, that parents of schizophrenic patients do not communicate in an unusual way when they are observed interacting with their offspring who did not become schizophrenic. Furthermore, parents whose offspring are all normal will also begin to exhibit communication problems if they interact with a schizophrenic patient in a laboratory setting (Liem, 1974). This pattern suggests that the children influence their parents, rather than the other way around (Model 2 in Figure 13–3).

A third explanation suggests that problems in verbal communication are symptoms of the genetically transmitted predisposition to schizophrenia. If that is the case, many of the patients' parents would speak in a disorganized or confusing way because they are predisposed to schizophrenia, even though they have not developed the full-blown disorder (Model 3 in Figure 13–3). According to this interpretation, the parents' communication problems may not directly influence the development of their children's disorder.

Model 1: Parent problems cause children's disorder.
         Parental Communication Problems ⟶ **Child's Schizophrenia**

Model 2: Child's adjustment problems cause parents' problems.
         Child's Schizophrenia ⟶ **Parental Communication Problems**

Model 3: Both the child's disorder and the parents' communication problems reflect the common genetic influence.

                                      Parental Communication Problems
      Genotype for Schizophrenia ⟨
                                        Child's Schizophrenia

Figure 13–3   Causal Pathways Involving Communication Problems and Schizophrenia.   Research has indicated that communication problems between parents are related to schizophrenia among their children, but the nature of this relationship remains unclear. This figure illustrates three possible explanations for this relationship.

A large adoption study that is being conducted in Finland is concerned with issues of this sort. Pekka Tienari, Lyman Wynne, and their colleagues have identified 155 people, called *index cases,* who were adopted away at an early age from parents with schizophrenia. All were born between 1960 and 1979. Their comparison group is composed of 186 people, called *control cases,* who were adopted away from parents who never had a psychotic disorder.

Preliminary reports from the Finnish Adoptive Family Study indicate that 14 of the adoptees have some type of psychosis: 13 of these people are the offspring of mothers with schizophrenia, and 1 is in the control group[†] (Tienari et al., 1994). This pattern is consistent with earlier adoption studies, reflecting a genetically determined predisposition to the disorder. Tienari also found that, among those who were genetically predisposed, the people who became psychotic were most often those whose adoptive families were also rated as being disturbed. Very few cases of severe psychopathology were found among the people who were raised by healthy adoptive families, regardless of whether their biological mothers had schizophrenia. In other words, the *combination* of genetic and environmental factors seems to be especially harmful.

These results must be viewed with caution. By the time the investigators conducted their initial assessments of the adoptive families, some of the index cases had already become psychotic. In these cases, either of the first two models in Figure 13–3 provides a plausible explanation of the relation between family disturbance and mental disorders in their offspring. Tienari's data cannot be explained in terms of the third model in the figure because the adoptive parents were no more genetically predisposed to the disorder than were people in the general population.

The most important part of the Finnish Adoptive Family Study remains to be completed. The youngest adoptees had not entered the primary age of risk for schizophrenia when the family assessments were completed. These people are now being followed prospectively. The longitudinal data from this part of the study will address the distinction between Models 1 and 2 in Figure 13–3 because the investigators will be able to determine whether the parents' communication problems appeared *before* the onset of psychopathology in their adoptive children.

EXPRESSED EMOTION

A related body of research indicates that the family environment has a significant impact on the course (as opposed to the etiology) of schizophrenia. These studies are concerned with the post-treatment adjustment of patients who have already exhibited schizophrenic symptoms.

[†]*Within the group of 13 index cases who had become psychotic, 7 were diagnosed with schizophrenia, 2 with schizophreniform disorder, 2 with delusional disorder, and 2 with bipolar mood disorder with psychotic features.*

Figure 13–4   Expressed Emotion, Interpersonal Contact, and Relapse Rates.   Close contact increases the risk of relapse for schizophrenic patients living with a high-EE relative. In low-EE families, increased contact has a protective effect.

Source: P. Bebbington and L. Kuipers, 1994, The predictive utility of expressed emotion in schizophrenia: An aggregate analysis, *Psychological Medicine, 24,* 707–718.

George Brown, John Wing, and their colleagues at the University of London found that men with schizophrenia were much more likely to return to the hospital within the next 9 months if they went to live with their wives or parents than if they went to live in other lodgings or with their siblings. Furthermore, patients who returned to live with their mothers were particularly likely to relapse if both they and their mothers were unemployed. Although these results could be interpreted in a number of ways, the investigators hypothesized that many of the patients who relapsed were reacting negatively to some feature of their close relationship with their wives or mothers. The data suggested that the family environment had an effect on the course of the patient's disorder.

Subsequent research by the same group confirmed this initial impression (Brown, Birley, & Wing, 1972; Vaughn & Leff, 1976). The investigators interviewed relatives of schizophrenic patients prior to the patients' discharge from the hospital. Many of the relatives expressed hostility toward the patient or repeatedly criticized the patient's behavior. Others appeared to be overprotective or too closely identified with the patient. This general collection of negative or intrusive attitudes was referred to as **expressed emotion (EE).** If at least one of a patient's relatives was hostile, critical, or emotionally overinvolved, the family environment was considered *high in expressed emotion.* Patients who returned to live in a home with at least one member who was high in EE had a 51 percent relapse rate in the first 9 months after discharge. Only 13 percent of the patients from low EE homes relapsed during the same period of time. This result has been replicated many times as investigators have gradually expanded our understanding of this phenomenon. More than 25 studies have been conducted in several different countries.

Another interesting result that has emerged from the studies of high EE families is concerned with the effect of face-to-face contact between patients and other family members. Most investigators divide patients into two groups for this purpose. Those who spend more than 35 hours per week with a high EE relative are placed in the "high-contact" category; less than 35 hours per week is considered "low contact." The relationship between family contact and patients' relapse rates is illustrated in Figure 13–4. This figure is based on a reanalysis of data from 25 studies, with a combined sample of more than 800 patients (Bebbington & Kuipers, 1994). Close contact with relatives increases the risk of relapse for schizophrenic patients living with a high EE relative. The opposite pattern is seen in low EE families, where increased contact with relatives seems to have a protective influence.

The influence of expressed emotion is not unique to schizophrenia. Patients with unipolar and bipolar mood disorders are also more likely to relapse following discharge if they are living with a high EE relative (Hooley & Teasdale, 1989; Miklowitz et al., 1988). The extension of this phenomenon to

expressed emotion (EE)   A concept that refers to a collection of negative or intrusive attitudes sometimes displayed by relatives of patients who are being treated for a disorder. If at least one of a patient's relatives is hostile, critical, or emotionally overinvolved, the family environment typically is considered high in expressed emotion.

schizotaxia According to Paul Meehl's theoretical model for schizophrenia, a subtle neurological defect of unknown form that is inherited by all individuals who are predisposed to schizophrenia.

Paul Meehl, Regents Professor Emeritus of Psychology at the University of Minnesota, is the only clinical psychologist ever elected to the National Academy of Science. His theory of schizophrenia has guided research efforts to discover signs of vulnerability to the disorder.

other disorders should not be taken to mean that it is unimportant or that the social context of the family is irrelevant to our understanding of the maintenance of schizophrenia. It may indicate, however, that this aspect of the etiological model is shared with other forms of psychopathology. The specific shape of the person's symptoms may hinge on the genetic diathesis.

High EE seems to be related, at least in part, to relatives' knowledge and beliefs about their family member's problems. Relatives find it easier to accept positive symptoms as being the product of a mental disorder (Brewin et al., 1991). They show less tolerance toward negative symptoms, such as avolition and social withdrawal, perhaps because the patient may appear to be simply lazy or unmotivated. Fortunately, relatives' negative attitudes can change. Ratings of relatives' EE can fluctuate over time and are often highest while the patient is hospitalized. Six months after the patient's discharge, roughly half of the people who were originally rated as being high EE are considered to be low EE (Leff et al., 1990).

We must be cautious to avoid a narrow view of this phenomenon. The EE studies raise extremely sensitive issues for family members, who have too frequently been blamed for the problems of people with schizophrenia. Expressed emotion is not the only factor that can influence the course of a schizophrenic disorder. Some patients relapse in spite of an understanding, tolerant family environment. Furthermore, research studies have shown that the relationship between patients' behavior and relatives' expressed emotion is a transactional or reciprocal process. In other words, patients influence their relatives' attitudes at the same time that relatives' attitudes influence patients' adjustment. Persistent negative attitudes on the part of relatives appear to be perpetuated by a negative cycle of interactions in which patients play an active role (Cook et al., 1989; Miklowitz et al., 1989).

The EE concept has stimulated a great deal of research on the family and schizophrenia (Hooley & Richters, 1995; Kuipers, 1992). Interest in EE has inspired innovative psychosocial treatment programs aimed at the family context in which schizophrenia is treated (see later section on treatment). It is not clear that the emotional climate of the family contributes to the original onset of schizophrenic symptoms, but it is clearly one factor that can influence the course of the disorder.

Integrated Systems and Multiple Pathways

The combined results of many twin and adoption studies point strongly toward the influence of genetic factors in the etiology of schizophrenia. It is also clear, however, that these genetic factors do not provide a complete explanation for the disorder, because MZ twins are not always concordant for schizophrenia. In fact, the concordance rate for MZ twins is approximately 50 percent. A useful etiological model must therefore provide for the interaction of genetic factors and environmental events.

The heterogeneous nature of the disorder, in terms of symptoms as well as course, also suggests that schizophrenia should be explained in terms of multiple pathways. Some forms of the disorder may represent the product of a strong genetic predisposition acting in combination with relatively common psychosocial experiences, such as stressful life events or disrupted communication patterns. For other people, relatively unusual circumstances, such as severe malnutrition during pregnancy, may be responsible for neurodevelopmental abnormalities that eventually lead to the onset of psychotic symptoms in the absence of genetic vulnerability.

Paul Meehl has proposed a theory of schizophrenia that provides a useful guide to investigators who are trying to understand this complex disorder. According to Meehl (1962, 1990, 1993), individuals who are predisposed to schizophrenia inherit a subtle neurological defect of unknown form. Meehl referred to this condition as **schizotaxia.** As a result of the interaction between this defect and inevitable learning experiences, schizotaxic individuals develop odd or eccentric behaviors, which he called *schizotypic signs.* Most prominent among these behaviors are "associative loosening," which is similar to the cognitive symptoms emphasized by Bleuler, and "aversive drift," in which the individual withdraws from interpersonal relationships because they are associated with negative affect. These are relatively subtle behaviors in comparison to the full-blown symptoms of psychosis. Only a small proportion of schizotypic persons will eventually become overtly schizophrenic.

Various kinds of environmental events have been linked to the etiology of schizophrenia. Some may operate in interaction with the genotype for schizophrenia; others may be sufficient to produce the disorder on their own. Considerable speculation has focused recently on biological factors, such as viral infections and nutritional deficiencies. Psychosocial factors, such as adverse economic circumstances and dysfunctional patterns of family communication, may also be involved. These events may be particularly harmful to those individuals who are genetically predisposed to the disorder.

neuroleptic   A type of antipsychotic medication that also induces side effects that resemble the motor symptoms of Parkinson's disease.

Treatment

Schizophrenia is a complex disorder that often must be treated over an extended period of time. Clinicians must be concerned about the treatment of acute psychotic episodes as well as the prevention of future episodes. A multifaceted approach to treatment is typically required. Neuroleptic medication is the primary mode of treatment for this disorder. Because many patients remain impaired between episodes, long-term care must often involve the provision of housing and social support. People with impaired occupational and social skills need special types of training. The treatment of schizophrenia requires attention on all of these fronts and is necessarily concerned with the cooperative efforts of many types of professionals.

Neuroleptic Medication

The antipsychotic properties of a class of drugs known as the phenothiazines were discovered quite accidentally in the early 1950s by a French neurosurgeon who was using them as a supplement to anesthesia. They were not effective for the purpose he intended, but they did have a calming effect on the patients. This experience prompted psychiatrists to try using the same drugs with their patients. Early reports of success in treating chronic psychotic patients quickly led to the widespread use of phenothiazines, such as chlorpromazine (Thorazine), in psychiatric hospitals throughout Europe and the United States. The discovery of these drugs quickly changed the way in which schizophrenia was treated. Many patients who had previously been institutionalized could be discharged to community care (but see Chapter 15 on the effects of deinstutionalization).

Several related types of drugs have been developed in subsequent years. They are called *antipsychotic drugs* because they have a relatively specific effect—to reduce the severity of, and sometimes eliminate, psychotic symptoms. Antipsychotics are also known as **neuroleptic** drugs because they induce side effects that resemble the motor symptoms of Parkinson's disease. Traditional forms of neuroleptic medication act by blocking D_2 dopamine receptors in the cortical and limbic areas of the brain (Marder et al., 1993). The antipsychotic efficacy of various types of neuroleptic drugs is directly proportional to their ability to block D_2 receptors.

Beneficial effects are sometimes noticed within a week after the patient begins taking neuroleptics, but it often takes several weeks before improvement is seen. Among the traditional or standard types of neuroleptic medication, there is no convincing evidence to indicate that one is more effective than another (Kane & Marder, 1993). The possible exception to this conclusion involves clozapine (Clozaril), an atypical form of antipsychotic medication, which we will discuss after a brief review of the traditional neuroleptics.

Most studies find that about half of the patients who receive neuroleptic medication are rated as being much improved after 4 to 6 weeks of treatment. Further improvements may continue beyond that point for some patients. In contrast, patients treated with placebos exhibit much smaller rates of improvement, and many of them actually deteriorate.

Lionel Aldridge was a defensive lineman for the Green Bay Packers when they won the first Super Bowl in 1965. He later developed schizophrenia. With the help of antipsychotic medication, his disorder went into remission. Until his death in 1998, Aldridge was a spokesman for the needs of people who suffer from schizophrenia.

Neuroleptic drugs may be more useful for certain types of symptoms than for others (Kane, 1995). Positive symptoms, such as hallucinations, seem to respond better to medication than negative symptoms, such as alogia and blunted affect. This differential effect is not entirely clearcut, however. For example, some patients who are socially withdrawn become less isolated when taking neuroleptics.

Unfortunately, a substantial minority of schizophrenic patients, perhaps 25 percent, do not improve on neuroleptic medication (Lewander, 1992). Another 30 to 40 percent might be considered partial responders: Their condition improves, but they do not show a full remission of symptoms. Investigators have been unable to identify reliable differences between patients who improve on medication and those who do not. Some experts have suggested that the more severe the symptoms, the less the improvement brought about by medication (Farmer & Blewett, 1993).

SIDE EFFECTS

Most neuroleptic drugs produce several unpleasant side effects. Consequently, patients frequently dislike taking these medications, and some discontinue using them, against their psychiatrist's advice. Side effects come in varying degrees and affect different patients in different ways. The most obvious and troublesome are called *extrapyramidal symptoms (EPS)* because they are mediated by the extrapyramidal neural pathways that connect the brain to the motor neurons in the spinal cord. These symptoms include an assortment of neurological disturbances, such as muscular rigidity, tremors, restless agitation, peculiar involuntary postures, and motor inertia. EPS may diminish spontaneously after 3 or 4 months of continuous treatment. Additional drugs, such as benztropine (Cogentin), can be used to minimize the severity of EPS during the first few months of treatment. Unfortunately, some patients exhibit persistent signs of EPS in spite of these efforts.

Prolonged treatment with neuroleptic drugs frequently leads to the development of *tardive dyskinesia (TD)*. This syndrome consists of abnormal involuntary movements of the mouth and face, such as tongue protrusion, chewing, and lip puckering, as well as spasmodic movements of the limbs and trunk of the body. The latter include writhing movements of the fingers and toes and jiggling of the legs, as well as jerking movements of the head and pelvis. Taken as a whole, this problem is distressing to patients and their families. The TD syndrome is induced by neuroleptic treatment, and it is irreversible in some patients, even after neuroleptics have been discontinued. In fact, in some patients, TD becomes worse if neuroleptic medication is withdrawn.

The incidence of TD increases steadily with continued use of neuroleptic medication. Roughly 5 percent of patients will develop TD during the first year of neuroleptic treatment. Approximately 20 percent of patients develop TD after long-term treatment with neuroleptic drugs (Kane, 1995).

MAINTENANCE MEDICATION

After patients recover from acute psychotic episodes, there is a high probability that they will have another episode. The relapse rate may be as high as 65 to 70 percent in the first year after hospital discharge if patients discontinue medication. Continued treatment with neuroleptic drugs can reduce this rate to approximately 40 percent (Hogarty, 1993). Therefore the great majority of schizophrenic patients continue to take medication after they recover from psychotic episodes, although usually at lower dosages. The need for maintenance medication is less clearly defined among patients who have had only one episode of schizophrenia. The relapse rate for these patients is lower than among those who have had multiple episodes.

Some patients who have had more than one psychotic episode can also avoid relapse without taking medication on a maintenance basis. Approximately 20 percent of chronic schizophrenic patients can avoid rehospitalization without taking neuroleptics and can function at least as well as they would on medication (Johnstone & Geddes, 1994). Unfortunately, we do not know how to distinguish these patients from those who need continued pharmacological treatment, other than through trial and error.

ATYPICAL ANTIPSYCHOTICS

Some relatively new forms of antipsychotic medication are known as **atypical antipsychotics** because they do not produce EPS and may not be associated with increased risk of TD. In addition, at least 30 percent of schizophrenic patients who were previously treatment resistant improve after taking atypical antipsychotic drugs (Buchanan, 1995). Treatment resistance is usually defined as failure to improve on at least three different types of classic neuroleptic medication after 6 weeks on moderate to high doses.

The best known of the atypical drugs, clozapine (Clozaril), was first manufactured in the 1950s and has been used extensively throughout Europe since the 1970s. Use of clozapine was delayed for several years in the United States because it can produce a lethal blood condition known as agranulocytosis in about 1 percent of patients. It was approved for use by the U.S. Food and Drug Administration in 1990, with the requirement that patients receive weekly monitoring of their white-blood-cell levels. Controlled-outcome studies indicate that clozapine has beneficial effects on positive symptoms of schizophrenia without inducing unpleasant motor side effects. Some reports have also noted improvements in negative symptoms among previously treatment-resistant patients, but other studies have not found this effect. Clozapine would probably be the treatment of choice for all schizophrenic patients if it were not for the risk of agranulocytosis (Buchanan, 1995; N. Carpenter et al., 1995).

Risperidone (Risperdal) is another atypical antipsychotic drug, which was first marketed in the United States in 1994. Several double-blind studies indicate that risperidone is at least as effective as classic neuroleptics in the treatment of schizophrenic patients who are in the active phase of the disorder (Umbricht & Kane, 1995). Like clozapine, risperidone is associated with a very low rate of adverse motor side effects. Some studies have reported that risperidone may be more effective than classic neuroleptics in treating patients with prominent negative symptoms. Relatively little empirical evidence is available regarding the effectiveness of risperidone during maintenance treatment or in use with treatment-resistant patients.

Clozapine and risperidone produce different neurochemical actions in the brain than do the classic neuroleptic drugs. Clozapine produces a relatively strong blockade of serotonin receptors and a relatively weak blockade of D_2 dopamine receptors (Lieberman, 1994; Meltzer, 1993). Its reduced affinity for dopamine receptors is presumably the reason for its failure to produce significant EPS. The fact that clozapine has well-documented beneficial effects for schizophrenic patients and that its site of action in the brain involves serotonin pathways has required important revisions to the original dopamine hypothesis. Risperidone resembles the classic neuroleptic drugs in terms of its ability to block D_2 receptors. Like clozapine, however, it also produces a relatively strong blockade of serotonin receptors. Further progress in the pharmacological treatment of schizophrenia will undoubtedly produce new drugs that have varying mechanisms of neurochemical action.

Psychosocial Treatment

Several forms of psychological treatment have proved to be effective for schizophrenic patients. These procedures address a wide range of problems that are associated with the disorder. In contrast to pharmacological approaches, psychological approaches place relatively little emphasis on the treatment of acute psychotic episodes. Instead, they concentrate on long-term strategies (Bellack & Mueser, 1993).

FAMILY-ORIENTED AFTERCARE

Studies of expressed emotion have inspired the development of innovative family-based treatment programs (Goldstein, 1994). Family treatment programs attempt to improve the coping skills of family members, recognizing the burdens that people often endure while caring for a family member with a chronic mental disorder. Patients are maintained on antipsychotic medication on an outpatient basis throughout this process. There are several different approaches to this type of family intervention. Most include an educational component that is designed to help family members understand and accept the nature of the disorder. One goal of this procedure is to eliminate unrealistic expectations for the patient, which may lead to harsh criticism. Behavioral family management also places considerable emphasis on the improvement of communication and problem-solving skills, which may enhance the family members' ability to work together and thereby minimize conflict.

Schizophrenia can be a devastating condition for patients and their families. Fortunately, the past two decades have seen many important advances in treatment for this disorder. Perhaps no other form of disorder requires such an extensive array of services, ranging from medication and short-term inpatient care to long-term residential facilities and psychosocial help for family members. An extremely useful book, *Coping with Schizophrenia: A Guide for Families*, written by Kim Mueser and Susan Gingrich, offers sound advice on a variety of crucial topics. For example, the authors discuss various forms of antipsychotic drugs, their side effects, their use in preventing relapse, and ways to respond to a patient's reluctance to continue taking necessary medication. They outline community resources that are available to help patients and their families deal with acute episodes, as well as the long-term challenges of residual symptoms, occupational difficulties, and housing needs.

Another excellent resource is *The Family Face of Schizophrenia*, by Patricia Backlar, who is a mental health ethicist and also the mother of a son who suffers from schizophrenia. This book includes a series of seven stories about people who have struggled with this disorder and the often confusing and sometimes inadequate array of mental health services that are available in many communities. Each story is followed by a commentary that includes advice for patients and their families (such as how to obtain insurance benefits for treatment, how to find a mentally ill family member who is missing, how to cope with suicidal risks, and how to navigate legal issues that can arise in caring for someone with a serious mental disorder). Patients and family members coping with a psychotic disorder will benefit from reading these books carefully.

The National Alliance for the Mentally Ill (NAMI) is an extremely influential grassroots support and advocacy organization that has worked tirelessly to improve the quality of life for patients and their families. It has more than 1,000 state and local affiliates throughout the 50 states. Among various items on NAMI's public policy agenda is a commitment to increasing access to community-based services such as housing and rehabilitation for people with severe mental disorders. Its Web site is www.nami.org—a comprehensive source of information regarding all aspects of severe mental disorders (especially schizophrenia and mood disorders), including referral to various support groups and professional service providers. The NAMI Web page includes a "Helpline Online," which can provide direct answers to questions about severe mental disorders, as well as a copy of its own *Consumer and Family Guide to Schizophrenia Treatment.*

Several empirical studies have evaluated the effects of family interventions. Most have found dramatic reductions in relapse rates for people receiving family treatment. Family-based treatment programs can delay relapse, but they do not necessarily prevent relapse in the long run. The beneficial effects of treatment may be lost shortly after treatment ends (Hogarty, 1993). In the case of a disorder such as schizophrenia, which is often chronic, treatment programs must be available to patients and their family members on a continuous basis.

SOCIAL SKILLS TRAINING

Many patients who avoid relapse and are able to remain in the community continue to be impaired in terms of residual symptoms. They also experience problems in social and occupational functioning. For these patients, drug therapy must be supplemented by psychosocial programs that address residual aspects of the disorder. The need to address these problems directly is supported by evidence that shows that deficits in social skills are relatively stable in schizophrenic patients and relatively independent of other aspects of the disorder, including both positive and negative symptoms (Mueser et al., 1991).

Social skills training (SST) is a structured, educational approach to these problems that involves modeling, role playing, and the provision of social reinforcement for appropriate behaviors (Liberman, DeRisi, & Mueser, 1989). Controlled-outcome studies indicate that, in combination with neuroleptic medication, SST leads to improved performance on measures of social adjustment. It is not clear, however, that SST has any beneficial effects on relapse rates (Penn & Mueser, 1996). This may not be surprising in light of evidence regarding the course of this disorder, which suggests that various aspects of outcome, including symptom severity and social adjustment, tend to be relatively independent.

Gordon Paul, a clinical psychologist at the University of Houston, has developed behavioral assessment and treatment procedures for psychotic behaviors. His research demonstrated that social learning programs can significantly improve the adjustment of seriously disturbed patients.

INSTITUTIONAL PROGRAMS

Although schizophrenic persons can be treated with medication on an outpatient basis, various types of institutional care continue to be important. Most patients experience recurrent phases of active psychosis (Eaton et al., 1992). Brief periods of hospitalization (usually 2 or 3 weeks) are often beneficial during these times.

Some patients are chronically disturbed and require long-term institutional treatment. Social learning programs, sometimes called *token economies,* can be useful for these patients. In these programs, specific behavioral contingencies are put into place for all of the patients on a hospital ward. The goal is to increase the frequency of desired behaviors, such as appropriate grooming and participation in social activities, and to decrease the frequency of undesirable behaviors, such as violence or incoherent speech. Staff members monitor patients' behavior throughout the day. Each occurrence of a desired behavior is praised and reinforced by the presentation of a token, which can be exchanged for food or privileges, such as time to watch television. Inappropriate behaviors are typically ignored, but occasional punishment, such as loss of privileges, is used if necessary.

Gordon Paul, a clinical psychologist at the University of Houston, and his colleagues conducted an extensive evaluation of behavioral treatment with chronic schizophrenic patients (Paul & Lentz, 1977). They compared two inpatient programs in the treatment of severely disturbed patients who had been continuously hospitalized for many years. One program followed a carefully designed and closely supervised social learning model, and the other followed a more traditional approach. These experimental treatments were compared to a group of similar patients who continued to reside in their original hospital wards. The patients' adjustment was evaluated at 6-month intervals over a period of approximately 6 years.

Both groups of patients who received treatment showed significant improvement, especially during the first 6 months of the study. This finding highlights the possibility for improvement, even among chronically disturbed patients. Patients in the social learning program showed even more improvement than those in the traditional group, especially with regard to social functioning and self-care. These benefits were maintained throughout the duration of the treatment program. Perhaps most impressive was the fact that, by the end of the first 4 years of active treatment, 11 percent of the patients in the social learning program were discharged to independent living in the community without being readmitted to the hospital. In contrast, none of the patients in the standard hospital comparison group was released to independent living. This study indicates that carefully structured inpatient programs, especially those that follow behavioral principles, can have important positive effects for chronic schizophrenic patients.

Summary

People who meet the diagnostic criteria for **schizophrenia** exhibit many types of symptoms that represent impairments across a broad array of cognitive, perceptual, and interpersonal functions. These symptoms can be roughly divided into three types. **Positive symptoms** include hallucinations and delusions. **Negative symptoms** include **blunted affect,** alogia, **avolition,** and social withdrawal. Symptoms of **disorganization** include verbal communication problems and bizarre behavior.

The onset of schizophrenia is typically during adolescence or early adulthood. The disorder can follow different patterns over time. Some people recover fairly quickly from schizophrenia, whereas others deteriorate progressively after the initial onset of symptoms.

The disorder was originally defined by Emil Kraepelin, who emphasized the progressive course of the disorder. Eugen Bleuler coined the term *schizophrenia,* proposing that disturbances in speech and emotion are the fundamental symptoms of the disorder. Many clinicians believe that schizophrenia actually includes several types of disorder with different causes. Others believe that it is a single pathological process with variations in symptomatic expression and course.

The negative symptoms of schizophrenia have been given increased emphasis in DSM-IV. The manual requires evidence of a decline in the person's social or occupational functioning, as well as the presence of disturbed behavior over a continuous period of at least 6 months. The DSM-IV recognizes several subtypes of schizophrenia, such as **paranoid, catatonic,** and **disorganized types,** that are based on prominent symptoms.

The lifetime prevalence of schizophrenia is approximately 1 or 2 percent in virtually all areas of the world. Men and women are equally likely to be affected, although the onset of the disorder appears at an earlier age in males. Male patients are more likely than female patients to exhibit negative symptoms, and they are also more likely to follow a chronic, deteriorating course. Two large cross-cultural studies found patients who exhibited characteristic signs and symptoms of schizophrenia in all of the study sites. Comparisons of patients across centers revealed more similarities than differences in clinical symptoms.

Genetic factors clearly play a role in the development of schizophrenia. Risk for developing the disorder is between 10 and 15 percent among first-degree relatives of schizophrenic patients. Concordance rates are approximately 48 percent in MZ twins compared to only 17 percent in DZ pairs. Adoption studies have found that approximately 15 percent of the offspring of a schizophrenic parent will eventually develop the disorder themselves, even if they are separated from their biological parent at an early age and are raised by adoptive families. Linkage studies have not found consistent evidence for a specific gene of major influence.

Advances in brain imaging technology have allowed extensive study of structural and functional brain abnormalities in schizophrenia. A specific brain lesion has not been identified, and it is unlikely that a disorder as complex as schizophrenia will be traced to a single site in the brain. Structural images of schizophrenic patients' brains reveal enlarged ventricles as well as decreased size for parts of the limbic system. Studies of brain metabolism and blood flow have identified functional changes in the frontal lobes, temporal lobes, and basal ganglia in many persons with schizophrenia. Current evidence points toward a subtle and diffuse type of neuropathology in schizophrenia.

The discovery of antipsychotic medication stimulated interest in the role of neurochemical factors in the etiology of schizophrenia. The dopamine hypothesis provided the major unifying theme in this area for many years, but it is now considered too simple to account for the existing evidence. Current neurochemical hypotheses regarding schizophrenia focus on a broad array of neurotransmitters, with special emphasis on serotonin.

The importance of environmental events in the etiology of schizophrenia is evident in the results of twin studies, which show that concordance rates in MZ twins do not approach 100 percent. Several social and psychological factors have been shown to be related to the disorder. Social class is inversely related to the prevalence of schizophrenia. In some cases, low levels of socioeconomic achievement represent a consequence of the disorder. Several kinds of research studies have also found, however, that social factors appear to make a causal contribution to the disorder. Disturbed patterns of family communication have been presumed to be related to the etiology of schizophrenia for many years. There is no evidence to indicate that the behavior of family members contributes to the original onset of schizophrenic symptoms. Recent efforts on this topic have examined the relation between the social context of the family and the long-term course of the disorder. Patients from families that are high in **expressed emotion** are more likely to relapse than those from low EE families. Expressed emotion is the product of an ongoing interaction between patients and their families, with patterns of influence flowing in both directions. The evidence regarding etiology supports a diathesis-stress model.

The central aspect of treatment for schizophrenia is antipsychotic medication. These drugs help to resolve acute psychotic episodes. They can also delay relapse and improve the level of patients' functioning between episodes. Unfortunately, they often produce troublesome side effects, and a substantial minority of schizophrenic patients are resistant to classic types of antipsychotic medication. The **atypical antipsychotics** are able to help some patients who do not respond to other drugs, and they produce fewer unpleasant motor side effects.

Various types of psychosocial treatment also provide important benefits to schizophrenic patients and their families. Prominent among these are family-based treatment for patients who have been stabilized on medication following discharge from the hospital. Social skills training can also be useful in improving the level of patients' role functioning.

Critical Thinking

1. The typical course of schizophrenia may be less chronic in developing countries than in developed countries. How would you explain these differences? Why would the disorder tend to be more long-lasting among people living in the United States than in people living in rural India, for example?

2. Clinical scientists have been unable to identify a specific type of environmental event that is responsible for triggering the original onset of symptoms of schizophrenia. Where would you look if you were conducting research on the "stress" end of the diathesis-stress model?

3. Imagine that you are the director of a large mental health center that provides services for all types of disorders. If you have limited resources, which aspects of schizophrenia would receive highest priority in your programs? Medication for the resolution of acute psychotic episodes? Support to family members? Alternative housing? Social skills training?

14

Pervasive Developmental Disorders and Psychological Disorders of Childhood

Is it normal to lie on the floor, kick, scream, and cry if you don't get your way? Not for a 19-year-old college student. However, it is normal, though sometimes obnoxious, for a 2-year-old child to throw a temper tantrum. Similarly, fears of monsters are developmentally normal at the age of 4, but not at the age of 14. We judge abnormal behavior by making comparisons with normal behavior, but what is considered normal changes rapidly during the first 20 years of life. Thus, in evaluating whether a child's behavior is normal or abnormal, the first question we must ask is: How old is the child?

Overview

externalizing disorders   An empirically derived category of disruptive child behavior problems that create problems for the external world (for example, attention-deficit/hyperactivity disorder).

internalizing disorders   An empirically derived category of psychological problems of childhood that affect the child more than the external world (for example, depression).

learning disorders   A heterogenous group of educational problems characterized by academic performance that is notably below academic aptitude.

pervasive developmental disorders   A category of unusual psychological problems that begin early in life and involve severe impairments in a number of areas of functioning. Autistic disorder is one example.

Children and adolescents may suffer from most of the disorders we have covered in earlier chapters. For example, children sometimes develop mood disorders, anxiety disorders, or schizophrenia. However, all of the psychological disorders we have discussed so far are far more prevalent among adults than among children. An important implication of this epidemiological fact is that children who do suffer from an "adult" disorder depart considerably from developmental norms. Thus their disorder may be especially severe.

Psychological problems that arise more commonly among children than adults are listed in the DSM-IV category Disorders Usually First Diagnosed in Infancy, Childhood, or Adolescence. The most important disorders in this category are the various **externalizing disorders.** Externalizing disorders create difficulties for the child's external world. They are characterized by children's failure to control their behavior according to the expectations of others—parents, siblings, peers, teachers, and legal authorities.

Internalizing disorders are psychological problems that primarily affect the child's internal world—for example, excessive anxiety or sadness. The DSM-IV does not list internalizing disorders as separate psychological disorders of childhood; rather, it notes that children may qualify for many "adult" diagnoses, such as anxiety or mood disorders. However, we think it is important to take a *developmental psychopathology* approach (see Chapter 2) and highlight children's unique experience of anxiety and depression. Children do not interpret events or express emotions in the same manner as adults; developmental norms change rapidly with age; and the family, peer, and school contexts typically affect children more dramatically than they affect adults. Thus we suggest that children's mood and anxiety disorders are not simply miniature versions of adult diagnoses.

In this chapter we also introduce many of the 26 *additional* diagnoses included in the DSM-IV's list of disorders usually first diagnosed during childhood. An important and familiar example of these psychological problems are **learning disorders,** substantial discrepancies between academic achievement and intellectual ability. Our coverage of many of these other childhood disorders is necessarily limited, not only by their sheer number but also by questions we have about the appropriateness of several of these diagnostic categories.

The **pervasive developmental disorders** are unusual problems that begin early in life and involve severe impairments in a number of areas of functioning. People with pervasive developmental disorders exhibit profound disturbances in relationships, engage in repetitive, stereotyped activities, and typically have substantial communication difficulties. These difficulties are pronounced in

autistic disorder   A severe form of pervasive developmental disorder characterized by oddities in social interaction (autistic aloneness), communication impairments, and stereotyped behavior, interests, and activities.

autistic disorder (also know as **autism**), the most carefully researched form of pervasive developmental disorder. The dictionary definition of the word *autism* is "absorption in one's own mental activity," but the term understates the profound social disturbances that accompany the disorder.

Few children or adolescents identify themselves as having a psychological problem. Instead, some adult, often a parent or teacher, decides that a child is emotionally troubled. Not surprisingly, children often disagree with the parent's or teacher's evaluation. Some children are unable to recognize or admit to their disturbed feelings. In other cases, however, the child may be right, and the adult may be wrong. In a sense, children sometimes serve as "projective tests" for adults—depressed parents may overinterpret the significance of children's normal moodiness, or intolerant teachers may see normal misbehavior as a sign of an externalizing disorder. Not only do children and adults often see things differently, but different adults also frequently disagree in their evaluation of a child's behavior. Such conflicting perceptions on the normality or abnormality of children's behavior challenge the assessment and classification of childhood disorders, because it is often unclear who is objective and who is biased, as illustrated in the following case study.

case study

Conflicts about Externalizing Behavior

Jeremy W., an 8-year-old boy, was brought to a clinical psychologist by his mother following the recommendations of his second-grade teacher and a school counselor. Mrs. W. came to the psychologist reluctantly, because she was not sure if she agreed with the suggestions of the school personnel. In fact, Mrs. W. wasn't sure if she agreed with her husband about what was going on with Jeremy.

According to Mrs. W., Jeremy was constantly in trouble at school. His teacher reprimanded Jeremy daily for disrupting the class, not paying attention, and failing to finish his work. The teacher felt that her attempts at discipline had little effect. Sometimes Jeremy would listen for awhile, but soon he was pestering another child, talking out of turn, or simply staring off into space. Lately, Jeremy had begun to talk back when he was disciplined, and his teacher had sent him to the principal's office several times in the past month.

The psychologist confirmed this information in a subsequent telephone call to the school. At that time, the teacher also noted that Jeremy had no real friends in school, and that other kids thought of him as a "pain." The teacher had referred Jeremy to a school counselor, who gave him several academic tests. According to an individualized intelligence test, Jeremy had an IQ of 108. However, his achievement test scores indicated that he was achieving at a first-grade level, almost a year behind his current grade level. The school counselor suspected that Jeremy might have a learning disorder, but she also thought that his behavior problems were interfering with his learning. She concluded that Jeremy should remain in his regular classroom for the present. As a first step, the counselor recommended therapy for Jeremy and perhaps for his parents. After treatment, she would reevaluate him for possible placement in a "resource room," a special class for students with learning problems.

Mrs. W. was frightened by the counselor's suggestion that Jeremy might be "emotionally disturbed" or "learning disordered." According to his mother, Jeremy was somewhat difficult to manage at home, but she had never considered the possibility that he needed psychological help. Jeremy had been a handful ever since the "terrible twos," but in her view, he had never been a bad child. Instead, Mrs. W. thought that Jeremy expressed himself better through actions than words. In this respect, he was the opposite of his 11-year-old sister, who was an A and B student. Mrs. W. was not convinced that Jeremy's teacher was the best person to work with him, but she did agree that he was having problems in school. In her mind, Jeremy was developing low self-esteem, and many of his actions were attempts to get attention.

According to Mrs. W., Jeremy's father spent very little time with him. Mr. W. worked long hours on his construction job, and he often was off with his friends on weekends. Mrs. W. said that her husband was of little help even when he was home. He would tell his wife that it was her job to take care of the kids— he needed his rest. With tears in her eyes, Mrs. W. said that she needed a rest, too.

In any case, Mr. W. was not concerned about Jeremy's behavior or his schoolwork. Instead, he thought that Jeremy was just "all boy" and not much of a student—just like Mr. W. was as a child. He refused to take time off from work to see a psychologist.

In confidence, Mrs. W. said that she too saw a lot of his father in Jeremy—too much of him, in fact. She got no support from her husband in disciplining Jeremy or in encouraging him in his schoolwork. She blamed her husband for Jeremy's problems, and she was secretly furious with him. She knew that Jeremy had to do well in school in order to live a better life, and she felt like a failure as a mother. She was willing to try anything to help Jeremy, but she doubted that there was anything she could do without her husband's support. 🦋

The case of Jeremy W. illustrates many of the complicated issues that arise in assessing and treating children's psychological problems. Is Jeremy a disobedient child, as his teacher thinks? A learning-disordered child, as suggested by the school counselor? An emotionally disturbed child, as his mother fears? Or is he simply "all boy," as his father claims? What about Jeremy? How does he feel about himself, about his family, and about his schoolwork and his friendships at school?

Mental health professionals who treat children are constantly vexed by such difficult questions, and treatment often begins with an attempt to achieve consensus about the nature of a child's problem. The overriding goal is to reach an accurate diagnosis, but another goal is to reduce the conflicts between adults that often contribute to a child's misbehavior. In Jeremy's case, Mr. and Mrs. W. may need to learn to support each other and to present a "united front" to Jeremy, and to do so they may need to resolve issues in their marriage. Because it is so important for adults to work together, many psychologists prefer to see children in *family therapy* rather than treat children alone. Many psychologists also work to coordinate treatment between the home and the school and to establish better communication and cooperation between parents and teachers.

Of course, Jeremy is also at least part of the problem. If we can trust his teacher's report—and experienced child clinical psychologists do trust teachers—Jeremy clearly has some type of externalizing problem. The question is: What is the problem, and why does he have it? Perhaps Jeremy's behavior is simply a reaction to his parents' conflicts, and he will get better if they work out their differences. Or perhaps Jeremy is a troubled child who is causing some of these conflicts, not just reacting to them. Mr. and Mrs. W. both felt that Jeremy and his father were a lot alike. Could Jeremy have learned or inherited some of his father's characteristics?

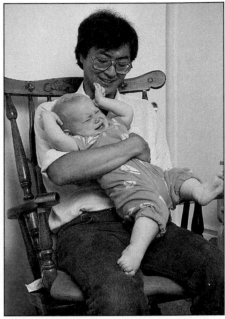

Temper tantrums are a normal part of child development during the "terrible twos." Awareness of developmental norms is essential for evaluating abnormal behavior in children.

Typical Symptoms: Externalizing Disorders

Externalizing disorders may be characterized by a broad range of specific transgressions ranging from defying rules at home to daydreaming and earning poor grades in school to committing very serious criminal acts like robbery, rape, or murder. Psychologists organize these many, specific problem behaviors into broader categories of symptoms, including rule violations; negativity, anger, and aggression; impulsivity; hyperactivity; and attention deficits. Rule violations and negativity, anger, and aggression are more characteristic of oppositional defiant disorder and related conduct problems. Impulsivity, hyperactivity, and attention deficits are symptoms of attention-deficit/hyperactivity disorder.

Rule Violations

Many externalizing symptoms are characterized by violations of age-appropriate social rules. Rule violations may include disobeying parents or teachers, violating social or peer group norms (e.g., annoying others), and perhaps violating the law. All children violate at least some social rules, of course, and we often admire an innocent and clever rule breaker. For example, Mark Twain's fictional character Tom Sawyer broke all kinds of rules, but we still view Tom as the prototypical "all-American boy." Tom Sawyer decidedly was not a candidate for psychotherapy! Similarly, we see Calvin of the Calvin and Hobbes cartoons as devilish, but he is not really "bad," and we certainly do not view him as "sick."

SERIOUSNESS OF CHILDREN'S RULE VIOLATIONS

Some misconduct is normal, perhaps even healthy, for children. However, the rule violations found in externalizing disorders are not trivial and are far from "cute." Many schoolteachers lament that they spend far too much time disciplining children—a circumstance that is frustrating to teachers and unfair to well-behaved youngsters in the classroom. Even more serious, the FBI reports that 29 percent of arrests for index offenses—major crimes including murder, forcible

Calvin and Hobbes   by Bill Watterson

CALVIN AND HOBBES © Watterson. Dist. by UNIVERSAL PRESS SYNDICATE.
Reprinted with permission. All rights reserved.

rape, and robbery—are of juveniles under the age of 18 (FBI, 1992). Other evidence indicates that the worst 5 percent of juvenile offenders account for about half of all juvenile arrests (Farrington, Ohlin, & Wilson, 1986).

Several factors influence how we evaluate the seriousness of children's rule violations. Externalizing behavior is a far greater concern when it is frequent, intense, lasting, and pervasive. That is, externalizing behavior is more problematic when it is part of a *syndrome,* or cluster of problems, than when it is a *symptom* that occurs in isolation. The existence of an externalizing syndrome has been demonstrated consistently by statistical analysis (factor analysis) of checklists on which parents or teachers rate children's psychological symptoms. Moreover, agreement among adult raters typically is fairly high for this externalizing dimension (Achenbach, McConaughy, & Howell, 1987).

CHILDREN'S AGE AND RULE VIOLATIONS

Children of different ages are likely to violate very different rules. A preschooler with an externalizing problem is likely to be disobedient to his parents and uncooperative with other children. During the school years, he or she is more likely to be disruptive in the classroom, uncooperative on the playground, or defiant at home. By adolescence, the problem teenager may be failing in school, ignoring all discipline at home, hanging out with delinquent peers, and perhaps violating the law.

Children's age is also important to consider in relation to the timing as well as the nature of rule violations. All children violate rules, but children with externalizing problems violate rules at a younger age than is developmentally normal (Loeber, 1988). For example, most young people experiment with smoking, alcohol, or sexuality, but children with externalizing disorders do so at a notably younger age.

ADOLESCENCE-LIMITED VERSUS LIFE-COURSE-PERSISTENT EXTERNALIZING BEHAVIOR

We must be especially aware of the developmental norms for committing rule violations during the teen years, as adolescence is a stage of normal development that borders on the abnormal—at least from the perspective of adults. Teenagers often violate the rules laid down by parents, teachers, and society as a means of asserting their independence and perhaps of conforming to the rules of their peer group (see Figure 14–1). Because of this normative increase in externalizing behavior, it is essential to distinguish between externalizing behavior that is *adolescent-limited*—that ends along with the teen years—and *life-course-persistent* antisocial behavior that continues into adult life (Moffitt, 1993).

In fact, externalizing problems that begin *before* adolescence are more likely to persist over the individual's life course than are problems that begin *during* adolescence. It is counterintuitive, but true, that scientists are better able to predict adult antisocial behavior from information obtained during childhood than from information obtained during adolescence (Farrington, Ohlin, & Wilson, 1986; Loeber, 1988; Moffitt, 1993).

The vast majority of antisocial adults do have a history of adolescent social and legal rule violations (see Chapter 9). However, so many teenagers violate at least some rules that, in order to distinguish life-course-persistent antisocial behavior, scientists need to look back in time to a stage of development (childhood) when conformity, not rebellion, was the norm (Moffitt, 1993).

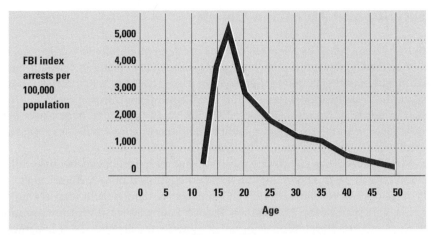

Figure 14–1   Arrest Rates for FBI Index Offenses at Different Ages.   Arrest rates across age for the Federal Bureau of Investigation's index offenses in 1980, which include homicide, forcible rape, robbery, aggravated assault, burglary, larceny, and auto theft.

Source: A. Blumstein, J. Cohen, and D. P. Farrington, 1980, Criminal career research: Its value for criminology, *Criminology, 26*,11.

Negativity, Anger, and Aggression

Negativity, anger, and aggression also are symptoms of oppositional defiant disorder and related externalizing problems. These symptoms range from oppositional behavior, stubbornness, and uncooperativeness, particularly among younger children, to hostility, threats, and causing physical injury to others, particularly among adolescents. In addition to the harmful effects of interpersonal aggression, these symptoms are important because they shed light on the motivations of a child with an externalizing disorder. We may chuckle at the innocent adventures of a Calvin or a Tom Sawyer, but we judge externalizing behavior harshly if the perpetrator is uncaring, angry, and callous.

The reason for this is that children's negativity, anger, and aggression strongly influence our judgments about their *intent* and *remorse*. As in our legal system, we judge externalizing behavior more harshly when the actions are selfishly motivated and when perpetrators express little regret about the consequences of their actions. You might wonder about Jeremy W.'s private motivations, for example, and judge him differently based on whether he is an angry child who cares little about being "bad" or an impulsive child who tries but just cannot consistently be "good." Externalizing behavior that is motivated by anger is very different from externalizing behavior that is more innocent or impulsive, not only for rendering social judgments but also in distinguishing between attention-deficit/hyperactivity disorder and oppositional defiant disorder.

Impulsivity

Impulsivity is acting before thinking, and it is a symptom that characterizes **attention-deficit hyperactivity disorder (ADHD)** rather than **oppositional defiant disorder (ODD).** Children with ADHD often fail, and seem unable, to control many of their impulses. They may have trouble waiting their turn, blurt out answers in class, intrude into the activities of other children, or cause accidents around the house, school, or playground. Such actions certainly are annoying and disruptive to others, but the impulsive behavior in ADHD is more innocent than the negativity and anger in ODD. In fact, the impulsive behavior of the youngster with ADHD is much the opposite of intentional aggression. Children with ADHD generally want to be "good," not "bad," but they seem unable to control their behavior according to situational demands.

hyperactivity A symptom of attention-deficit/hyperactivity disorder (ADHD), often manifested as squirming, fidgeting, or restless behavior. Found across situations but particularly notable in structured settings.

attention deficit Inattention characterized by distractibility, frequent shifts from one uncompleted activity to another, careless mistakes, and/or poor organization or effort. A key symptom of attention-deficit/hyperactivity disorder.

Hyperactivity and Attention Deficits

Hyperactivity, the most obvious symptom of ADHD, often is manifested as squirming, fidgeting, or restless behavior. Children with this symptom are described as being in constant motion, and they have difficulty engaging in quiet activities, even leisure ones like watching television. Hyperactivity is found across situations, even during sleep, but it is much more notable in structured settings than in unstructured ones (Barkley, 1988, 1990). In particular, hyperactive behavior is much more noticeable in the classroom than in other circumstances, and this is one reason why ADHD typically is diagnosed for the first time during the early school years.

Situational influences can complicate the evaluation of hyperactivity, because children who are extremely active in the classroom may be relatively controlled in the pediatrician's or the psychologist's office (Sleator & Ullmann, 1981). Consequently, reports from teachers are critical in identifying hyperactive behavior. The Conners Teacher Rating Scale is a measure commonly used by pediatricians and other professionals in order to assess teacher ratings of hyperactivity and other symptoms of ADHD in the classroom (see Figure 14–2).

Attention deficit, or inattention, is the third classic symptom of attention-deficit/hyperactivity disorder. Attention deficits are characterized by distractibility, frequent shifts from one uncompleted activity to another, careless mistakes, poor organization or effort, and general "spaciness," for example, not listening well or responding to questions. A particular attentional problem is "staying on task," or what has been termed difficulties with *sustained attention* (Douglas & Pe-

Observation	Degree of Activity			
CLASSROOM BEHAVIOR	**(0)** **Not** **At All**	**(1)** **Just a** **Little**	**(2)** **Pretty** **Much**	**(3)** **Very** **Much**
Constantly fidgeting				
Demands must be met immediately— easily frustrated				
Restless or overactive				
Excitable, impulsive				
Inattentive, easily distracted				
Fails to finish things he starts— short attention span				
Cries often and easily				
Disturbs other children				
Mood changes quickly and drastically				
Temper outbursts; explosive and unpredictable behavior				

Figure 14–2 Brief Conners Teacher Rating Scale for Attention-Deficit/ Hyperactivity Disorder. Psychologists often ask teachers to complete this ten-item scale as a screening device for ADHD. A total score of 15 (mean of 1.5) of greater suggests that a child may have ADHD.

Source: C. K. Conners, 1969, A teacher rating scale for use with drug studies with children, *American Journal of Psychiatry, 126,* 884-888.

ters, 1979). Numerous studies have documented that children with ADHD perform poorly on the *continuous performance test,* a laboratory task that requires the subject to monitor and respond to numbers or letters presented on a computer screen. As with impulsivity, the ADHD child's inattention is not intentional or oppositional; rather, it reflects an inability to maintain a focus despite an apparent desire to do so.

Typical Symptoms: Internalizing Disorders

Children's *internalizing symptoms* include sadness, fears, and somatic complaints, as well as other indicators of mood and anxiety disorders—for example, feeling worthless or tense. As we have noted, the DSM-IV does not have a separate category for children's internalizing disorders, but the manual does identify some unique ways in which children experience the symptoms of mood and anxiety disorders. When diagnosing major depressive episodes among children and adolescents, for example, the manual allows the clinician to substitute "irritable mood" for "depressed mood." The manual's authors realized that children sometimes act angry when they are feeling sad, and, more generally, that children may express their feelings in unique ways, or they may hide their true emotions, especially when talking to adults.

Another example of how the DSM deals with symptoms in children involves the diagnosis of phobia. In contrast to adults, children are not required to recognize that their fears are unreasonable. This suggests that children may have limited insight into their problems. More generally, young children may lack the *cognitive capacity* to experience some of the internalizing symptoms found among adults with the same or similar disorder.

Internalizing Symptoms and Normal Development: A Challenge for Research

These provisions in the DSM-IV recognize that children's capacity to recognize emotions emerges over the course of development, as does their ability to express—and to mask—their own feelings (Lewis & Michalson, 1983). Unfortunately, the course of children's normal emotional development is not well charted, because it is extremely difficult to assess children's feelings. Children, especially at younger ages, typically are not reliable or valid informants about their internal life, and it is much more difficult for adults to evaluate children's inner experiences than it is to observe their externalizing behavior.

Research on depressed children illustrates some of the problems in assessing internalizing symptoms. In one study of children hospitalized for depression, for example, clinicians found a correlation of *zero* between children's and parents' ratings on identical measures of the children's depression (Kazdin, French, & Unis, 1983). In another study, children's and parents' ratings of depression were correlated with very different associated features. Children linked depression with other indices of their internal distress—feelings of hopelessness, low self-esteem, internal attributions for negative events, and external locus of control. In contrast, parents' ratings of children's depression were correlated with ratings of children's externalizing behavior—not with measures of children's internal distress (Kazdin, 1989). Finally, and perhaps of greatest concern, evidence indicates that parents systematically underestimate the extent of depression reported by their children and adolescents (Kazdin & Petti, 1982; Rutter, 1986).

Given parents' and children's widely differing perceptions, psychologists are rightly concerned about a child's depression if *either* a parent *or* a child notes problems. In assessing children's internalizing problems, mental health professionals must obtain information from *multiple informants*—parents, teachers, and the children themselves. More generally, our understanding of children's internalizing symptoms would be aided greatly by better evidence on the normal course of emotional development, a future challenge for developmental psychopathology research.

Depression becomes much more common during adolescence, especially among teenage girls.

separation anxiety disorder A psychological disorder of childhood characterized by persistent and excessive worry for the safety of an attachment figure and related fears such as getting lost, being kidnapped, nightmares, and refusal to be alone. Distinct from normal separation anxiety, which typically develops shortly before an infant's first birthday.

school refusal *(school phobia)* Extreme reluctance to go to school, accompanied by various symptoms of anxiety such as stomachaches and headaches. May be a fear of school or an expression of separation anxiety disorder.

Calvin and Hobbes   by Bill Watterson

Children's Fears in Developmental Perspective

Evidence on children's fears offers an example of how research on normal development could improve our understanding of internalizing symptoms in children. Although children cannot identify many of their inner feelings, they are often able to identify their fears, and adults also can observe much of children's fearful behavior. Thus research on the development of children's fears is more advanced than it is for other internalizing symptoms.

Three findings from fear research are especially helpful. First, children develop different fears for the first time at different ages, and the onset of new fears may be sudden and have no apparent cause in the child's environment. For example, infants typically develop a fear of strangers in the months just before their first birthday; preschoolers develop fears of monsters and the dark between the ages of 2 and 4; and children between ages 5 and 8 often develop fears related to school. (To cite one curious example, if you ever dreamed of going to school in your underwear or partially dressed, you are not alone. Such dreams are surprisingly common among school-aged children.) In short, many fears, even those that seem odd or arise suddenly, are developmentally normal, a conclusion that can be reassuring to parents and perhaps to children. A second finding of importance is that some fears, particularly fears of uncontrollable events, are both common and relatively stable across different ages. Third, many other fears, especially specific ones, decline in frequency as children grow older (King et al., 1989). Apparently, children "outgrow" many of their fears, probably by gradually confronting them in everyday life.

Separation Anxiety Disorder and School Refusal

Separation anxiety is a normal fear that typically develops just before a baby's first birthday. Toddlers and preschoolers continue to show a degree of distress even during routine separations from their attachment figures.

We can illustrate the importance of these three findings by considering the special case of separation anxiety. *Separation anxiety* is distress expressed following separation from an attachment figure, typically a parent or other close caregiver. It is a normal fear that begins to develop around 8 months and peaks around 15 months (Kagan, Kearsley, & Zelazo, 1978). An infant who has tolerated separations in the past may suddenly start to cling, cry, and scream whenever a parent tries to leave, even for a brief separation. Children's upset lessens over time, but even toddlers and preschoolers typically experience distress upon separation, particularly when left in an unfamiliar circumstance.

Although it is a normal response at younger ages, excessive separation anxiety can become a serious problem at older ages if children fail to "outgrow" the reaction. In fact, the DSM-IV contains a diagnosis for **separation anxiety disorder,** which is defined by symptoms such as persistent and excessive worry for the safety of an attachment figure, fears of getting lost or being kidnapped, nightmares with separation themes, and refusal to be alone. For a child to be diagnosed with this disorder, he or she must exhibit three or more of these symptoms for at least 4 weeks.

Separation anxiety disorder is especially problematic when it interferes with school attendance. **School refusal,** also known as *school phobia,* is characterized by an extreme reluctance to go to school and is accompanied by various symptoms of anxiety, such as stomachaches and headaches. Some children are literally school phobic—they are afraid of school or specific aspects of attending school. But in many cases, school refusal can be traced to separation anxiety disorder (Last & Strauss, 1990). Whatever its origins, school refusal is a serious problem that has been reported to account for more than two-thirds of referrals to an anxiety disorders clinic for children.

attention-deficit/hyperactivity disorder A psychological disorder of childhood characterized by hyperactivity, inattention, and impulsivity. Typically has an onset by the early school years.

Classification of Psychological Disorders of Childhood

Brief Historical Perspective

The beginnings of child clinical psychology as a discipline can be traced to 1896. In that year, the psychologist Lightner Witmer (1867–1956) of the University of Pennsylvania established the first psychological clinic for children in the United States. Prior to the nineteenth century, life was harsh for children, who were expected to act and work (beginning around the age of 7) like little adults (Aries, 1962). Beginning in the latter half of the nineteenth century, however, child labor laws were passed, schooling became mandatory, and special juvenile courts were created. In short, U.S. society began to recognize that children require special protection and nurturance.

Contemporary Classification: Some Strengths and Weaknesses in DSM-IV

Table 14–1 (page 394) summarizes the childhood disorders contained in DSM-IV (1994). Many of the DSM-IV diagnoses in Table 14–1 may be unfamiliar to you, in part, because some of them are rare and unusual problems. Another reason some of the disorders listed may be unfamiliar is the questionable nature of their status as "mental disorders." A number of commentators believe that, beginning with DSM-III, the manual became overinclusive in its listing of childhood disorders. That is, the manual included too many "disorders" that are not in fact mental disorders (Garmezy, 1978). Many disorders were dropped from DSM-III and DSM-III-R, but there seem to be other ways in which the list should be shortened.

"Developmental coordination disorder" is perhaps the most obvious example of overinclusion in DSM-IV. The manual defines this problem as follows: "Performance in daily activities that require motor coordination is substantially below that expected given the person's chronological age and measured intelligence" (p. 54). In poking fun at such diagnostic overzealousness, two pediatricians proposed a new diagnostic category they called "sports deficit disorder." The major diagnostic criterion for this "disorder" is always being the last one chosen for a sports team (Burke & McGee, 1990).

The "learning disorders" and "communication disorders" are more controversial examples of possible overinclusion in DSM-IV. Educators call these childhood problems learning disabilities (see Further Thoughts, page 396–397) and speech and hearing problems, respectively. Learning disabilities and speech and hearing problems both are common and serious difficulties experienced by children, but we question their status as mental disorders. We view both problems as involving educational more than mental health concerns.

SUBCLASSIFICATION OF EXTERNALIZING DISORDERS

DSM-IV lists three major subtypes of disruptive behavior disorders: attention-deficit/hyperactivity disorder (ADHD), oppositional defiant disorder (ODD), and conduct disorder (CD). The appropriate subclassification of externalizing disorders is an important, controversial, and frequently studied issue. The distinction between attention-deficit/hyperactivity disorder and oppositional defiant disorder is particularly important.

Attention-Deficit/Hyperactivity Disorder   Attention-deficit/hyperactivity disorder is characterized by hyperactivity, attention deficit, and impulsivity (see Table 14–2, p. 395).

TABLE 14–1

DSM-IV Disorders Usually First Diagnosed in Infancy, Childhood, or Adolescence[a]

Attention-Deficit and Disruptive Behavior Disorders
  Attention-deficit/hyperactivity disorder
    Combined type
    Predominantly inattentive type
    Predominantly hyperactive-impulsive type
  Conduct disorder
  Oppositional defiant disorder

Learning Disorders
  Reading disorder
  Mathematics disorder
  Disorder of written expression

Motor Skills Disorder
  Developmental coordination disorder

Communication Disorders
  Expressive language disorder
  Mixed receptive-expressive language disorder
  Phonological disorder
  Stuttering

Mental Retardation
  Mild mental retardation
  Moderate mental retardation
  Severe mental retardation
  Profound mental retardation

Pervasive Developmental Disorders
  Autistic disorder
  Rett's disorder
  Childhood disintegrative disorder
  Asperger's disorder

Feeding and Eating Disorders of Infancy or Early Childhood
  Pica
  Rumination disorder
  Feeding disorder of infancy or early childhood

Tic Disorders
  Tourette's disorder
  Chronic motor or vocal tic disorder
  Transient tic disorder

Elimination Disorders
  Encopresis
    With constipation and overflow incontinence
    Without constipation and overflow incontinence
  Enuresis

Other Disorders of Infancy, Childhood, and Adolescence
  Separation anxiety disorder
  Selective mutism
  Reactive attachment disorder of infancy or early childhood
  Stereotypic movement disorder

[a]Note: *This listing does not include "Not Otherwise Specified" (NOS) subtypes of the diagnoses. NOS subtypes exist for many of the disorders listed here, and they are used when a child meets many but not all of the diagnostic criteria for the specific disorder.*

TABLE 14–2

DSM-IV Diagnostic Criteria for Attention-Deficit/Hyperactivity Disorder

A. EITHER (I) OR (II):

(I) **Inattention:** Six (or more) of the following symptoms of inattention have persisted for at least 6 months to a degree that is maladaptive and inconsistent with developmental level:

1. Often fails to give close attention to details or makes careless mistakes in schoolwork, work, or other activities.
2. Often has difficulty sustaining attention in tasks or play activities.
3. Often does not seem to listen when spoken to directly.
4. Often does not follow through on instructions and fails to finish schoolwork, chores, or duties in the workplace.
5. Often has difficulty organizing tasks and activities.
6. Often avoids, dislikes, or is reluctant to engage in tasks that require sustained mental effort.
7. Often loses things necessary for tasks or activities.
8. Is often easily distracted by extraneous stimuli.
9. Is often forgetful of daily activities.

(II) **Hyperactivity and Impulsivity:** Six (or more) of the following symptoms of hyperactivity-impulsivity have persisted for at least 6 months to a degree that is maladaptive and inconsistent with developmental level:

Hyperactivity

1. Often fidgets with hands or feet or squirms in seat.
2. Often leaves seat in classroom or in other situations in which remaining seated is expected.
3. Often runs about or climbs excessively in situations in which it is inappropriate.
4. Often has difficulty playing or engaging in leisure activities quietly.
5. Is often "on the go" or often acts as if "driven by a motor."
6. Often talks excessively.

Impulsivity

7. Often blurts out answers before questions have been completed.
8. Often has difficulty awaiting turn.
9. Often interrupts or intrudes on others.

B. SOME HYPERACTIVE-IMPULSIVE OR INATTENTIVE SYMPTOMS THAT CAUSED IMPAIRMENT WERE PRESENT BEFORE AGE 7 YEARS.

C. SOME IMPAIRMENT FROM THE SYMPTOMS IS PRESENT IN TWO OR MORE SETTINGS.

D. THERE MUST BE CLEAR EVIDENCE OF CLINICALLY SIGNIFICANT IMPAIRMENT IN SOCIAL, ACADEMIC, OR OCCUPATIONAL FUNCTIONING.

Code Based on Type

Combined Type: Criteria for I and II are met for past 6 months.

Predominantly Inattentive Type: Criteria for I are met but Criteria for II are not met for past 6 months.

Predominantly Hyperactive-Impulsive Type: Criteria for II are met but Criteria for I are not met for past 6 months.

further thoughts

Learning Disorders

The classification *learning disorder* (or *learning disability*) refers to a heterogeneous group of problems in which academic performance differs noticeably from academic aptitude. There are numerous ways of defining learning disabilities more specifically, but each method presents difficulties (Lyon, 1996; Wicks-Nelson & Israel, 1991). The most common definition compares scores on intelligence tests, which measure academic aptitude, with scores on *academic achievement tests*—measures of performance in some academic subject area. Typically, a learning disorder is defined as a difference of one or two standard deviations between aptitude and achievement. Thus, according to this definition, a child would be considered to have a learning disorder if he or she scored a standard deviation above the mean on an intelligence test (an IQ of 115) but a standard deviation below the mean in reading (scoring well below the average for his or her grade level).

The DSM-IV includes learning disorders in its list of mental disorders. The DSM-IV also includes subcategories of learning disorders in reading, arithmetic, and written expression. Learning disorders typically are diagnosed by school professionals, however, and they almost always are treated in aca-

demic settings. Thus mental health professionals typically work with children with learning disorders only when the problems co-occur with other psychological disorders. In fact, there is a high degree of comorbidity between learning disabilities and both attention-deficit/hyperactivity disorder and oppositional defiant disorder (Barkley, 1990).

The origins of learning disorders have been traced to a number of problems, including perceptual distortions, attentional problems, language difficulties, and poor cognitive strategies. Typically, etiology is attributed to some biological cause, and considerable research has been conducted on brain functions in learning disorders. This research, however, has not identified any psychological deficit or biological cause that is common to all learning disorders (Wicks-Nelson & Israel, 1991).

Tremendous efforts have gone into attempts to treat learning disorders. Interventions in schools were given great impetus in 1975 when Congress passed the Education for All Handicapped Children Act. This law mandated that local school systems must provide special resources for educating handicapped children, including children with learning disorders. The federal legislation dramatically increased the number of children identified as having a learning disorder (see Figure 14–3). However, this increase has led some commentators to question whether we are using

---

oppositional defiant disorder A psychological disorder of childhood characterized by persistent but relatively minor transgressions, such as refusing to obey adult requests, arguing, and acting angry.

Although they have been given equal billing in DSM-IV, at earlier points in time the symptoms of hyperactivity and attention deficit each have been viewed as the central characteristic of ADHD. In fact, DSM-II called the disorder *hyperkinesis*, a synonym for "hyperactivity," whereas DSM-III referred to it as *attention-deficit disorder*, or *ADD*. We are not concerned whether "attention deficit" or "hyperactivity" gets top billing in labeling a condition with an ever-changing series of names, but we are concerned about two facts. First, contrary to what has been asserted by some professionals, hyperactivity is not merely a consequence of inattention or vice versa (Barkley, 1990). Each is an independent symptom. Second, some children have problems primarily with only one of the two symptoms, as is evident in the subtypes of ADHD listed in DSM-IV (see Table 14–2).

Oppositional Defiant Disorder **Oppositional defiant disorder** is defined as a pattern of negative, hostile, and defiant behavior. The rule violations in ODD typically involve rather minor transgressions, however, such as refusing to obey adult requests, arguing, and acting angry (see Table 14–3, page 397). Such behavior may be developmentally normal among adolescents, but it is a cause for concern among school-aged children. Childhood ODD may foreshadow the development of much more serious antisocial behavior during adolescence and adult life.

ADHD versus ODD Professionals have long debated whether oppositional defiant disorder is distinct from attention-deficit/hyperactivity disorder. Some professionals have argued that the two conditions are distinct not only in symptomatology but also in terms of etiology and effective treatment. Others have asserted that the distinction between ADHD and ODD is false and is wrongly used to justify treating troubled children with medication. Researchers have struggled to test these widely opposing overly broad definitions of learning disorders (Lyon, 1996). Even more critically, it is not clear that the identification of students with learning problems has led to more effective education for these students. Numerous interventions have been attempted, including intensive tutoring, individually or in small groups; behavior therapy programs in which academic success is systematically rewarded; psychostimulant medication; counseling for related problems (for example, low self-esteem); and various special efforts such as training in visual-motor skills. Unfortunately, no treatment has demonstrated consistent success (Lyon, 1996; Wicks-Nelson & Israel, 1991).

We can conclude that a substantial number of children in the United States—perhaps 5 percent of all schoolchildren—do not achieve at a level consistent with their abilities (Lyon, 1996). Learning disorders are "real" in the sense that these children seem to have the ability and motivation to perform better in school, yet they still perform well below their abilities. Nevertheless, the identification of the discrepancy between ability and performance has not solved the puzzle of learning disor-

Figure 14–3   Children with Learning Disorders: 1976–1993. Federal legislation greatly increased the diagnosis of learning disorders. Some commentators attribute the increase to social, economic, and political factors—not to better intervention with children.

Source: Office of Special Education Programs, 1993, *Implementation of the Individuals with Disabilities Education Act: Fifteenth Annual Report to Congress.* Washington, DC: U.S. Department of Education.

ders. Controversy and uncertainty remain about their definition, cause, and treatment. 🐾

TABLE 14–3

DSM-IV Diagnostic Criteria for Oppositional Defiant Disorder

A. A PATTERN OF NEGATIVISTIC, HOSTILE, AND DEFIANT BEHAVIOR LASTING AT LEAST 6 MONTHS, DURING WHICH FOUR (OR MORE) OF THE FOLLOWING ARE PRESENT:

1. Often loses temper.
2. Often argues with adults.
3. Often actively defies or refuses to comply with adults' requests or rules.
4. Often deliberately annoys people.
5. Often blames others for his or her mistakes or misbehavior.
6. Is often touchy or easily annoyed by others.
7. Is often angry and resentful.
8. Is often spiteful and vindictive.

B. THE DISTURBANCE IN BEHAVIOR CAUSES CLINICALLY SIGNIFICANT IMPAIRMENT IN SOCIAL, ACADEMIC, OR OCCUPATIONAL FUNCTIONING.

conduct disorder (CD)   A psychological disorder of childhood that is defined primarily by behavior that is illegal as well as antisocial.

juvenile delinquency   A legal term that refers to a minor who has violated the law and been judged responsible for the lawbreaking.

Boys breaking into school lockers. Juveniles commit many minor and many very serious illegal acts.

viewpoints, but they have been hampered by diagnostic difficulties. Differential diagnosis cannot be easily made with a high level of reliability; thus it is difficult or impossible to determine whether investigators are studying subjects with ADHD, ODD, or both disorders (Hinshaw, 1987, 1994).

The current consensus is that the two disorders are best conceived as separate but overlapping problems (Barkley, 1990; Hinshaw, 1987, 1994). Oppositional defiant disorder and attention-deficit/hyperactivity disorder can be differentiated, but they are highly comorbid conditions. As many as half of all children with one disorder also have the other problem (Hinshaw, 1994).

ADHD with and without Hyperactivity   The subtyping of ADHD into cases with and without hyperactivity is another important and sometimes controversial distinction. Consistent with the DSM-IV, researchers generally accept the distinction between ADHD with and without hyperactivity, but confusion arises when we consider all subtypes together. For example, are there cases of ADHD with hyperactivity *and* comorbid ODD, and are there other cases of ADHD with hyperactivity but *no* comorbid ODD? We cannot answer this question definitively, but evidence suggests that ADHD *with* hyperactivity might be akin to—or the same thing as—ADHD with comorbid oppositional defiant disorder. Note that ADHD with hyperactivity is linked with many of the same factors associated with ODD, such as antisocial behavior and rejection by peers (Hinshaw, 1994).

Conduct Disorder   Conduct disorder (CD) is similar to oppositional defiant disorder, except the aggression and rule violations are far more serious in conduct disorder. Conduct disorder is defined primarily by rule violations that are illegal as well as antisocial, for example, assault or robbery (see Table 14–4). Consistent with research we reviewed earlier, the DSM-IV notes that the ODD and CD often are developmentally related. Oppositional defiant disorder is diagnosed primarily among school-aged children, and may develop into a more serious conduct disorder during preadolescence or adolescence (Loeber, Lahey, & Thomas, 1991). You should note that the DSM-IV also includes a notation for age of onset in defining conduct disorders—a distinction between the adolescent-limited versus life-course patterns of antisocial behavior, as we discussed earlier (see Table 14–4).

You may think of what DSM-IV calls conduct disorder as being equivalent to juvenile delinquency. However, **juvenile delinquency** is a legal classification, not a mental health term. Technically, youths are not classified as delinquent until they are found to be delinquent by a judge. In the United States, juvenile court judges may find a youth to be delinquent for committing either criminal or status offenses, although adjudication for status offenses is increasingly rare.

Epidemiology of Psychological Disorders of Childhood

A panel of experts assembled by the National Academy of Sciences (1989) concluded that at least 12 percent of the 63 million children living in the United States suffer from a mental disorder. The panel found that a minimum of $1.5 billion was spent annually for the direct mental health treatment of children—and this figure excluded the additional costs of treating children's emotional problems in general medical settings, schools, welfare agencies, and juvenile courts. Clearly, children's mental health is a major national problem, but epidemiological evidence is valuable for reasons other than documenting the extent of children's psychological difficulties. Factors correlated with higher prevalence rates identify subgroups of children at risk, and this information suggests possible causes of children's psychological disorders.

Gender Differences in Externalizing and Internalizing Problems

Gender is one risk factor for psychological problems, but the risk associated with gender reverses across the course of development. More boys than girls are treated for psychological problems, but

TABLE 14–4

DSM-IV Diagnostic Criteria for Conduct Disorder

A. **A REPETITIVE AND PERSISTENT PATTERN OF BEHAVIOR IN WHICH THE BASIC RIGHTS OF OTHERS OR MAJOR AGE-APPROPRIATE SOCIETAL NORMS OR RULES ARE VIOLATED, AS MANIFESTED BY THE PRESENCE OF THREE (OR MORE) OF THE FOLLOWING CRITERIA IN THE PAST 12 MONTHS, WITH AT LEAST ONE CRITERION PRESENT IN THE PAST 6 MONTHS:**

Aggression to People and Animals

1. Often bullies, threatens, or intimidates others.
2. Often initiates physical fights.
3. Has used a weapon that can cause serious physical harm to others.
4. Has been physically cruel to people.
5. Has been physically cruel to animals.
6. Has stolen while confronting a victim.
7. Has forced someone into sexual activity.

Destruction of Property

8. Has deliberately engaged in fire setting with the intention of causing serious damage.
9. Has deliberately destroyed others' property.

Deceitfulness or Theft

10. Has broken into someone else's house, building, or car.
11. Often lies to obtain goods or favors to avoid obligations.
12. Has stolen items of nontrivial value without confronting a victim.

Serious Violations of Rules

13. Often stays out at night despite parental prohibitions, beginning before age 13 years.
14. Has run away from home overnight at least twice while living in parental or parental surrogate home.
15. Is often truant from school, beginning before age 13 years.

B. **THE DISTURBANCE IN BEHAVIOR CAUSES CLINICALLY SIGNIFICANT IMPAIRMENT IN SOCIAL, ACADEMIC, OR OCCUPATIONAL FUNCTIONING.**

Specify Type Based on Age at Onset

Childhood-Onset Type: Onset of at least one criterion characteristic of Conduct Disorder prior to age 10 years.

Adolescent-Onset Type: Absence of any criteria characteristic of Conduct Disorder prior to age 10 years.

more women than men enter into therapy. Where is the turning point, and what is the explanation for this phenomenon? We can begin to answer this question by examining gender differences in externalizing and internalizing problems.

Epidemiological studies consistently find that, after the first few years of life, boys have far more externalizing disorders than girls (Keenan & Shaw, in press; National Academy of Sciences, 1989; Rutter, 1989). From 3 to 5 percent of children are estimated to have attention-deficit/hyperactivity disorder, and anywhere from 5 to 15 percent of youths may have oppositional defiant disorder and/or conduct disorder. These problems are 2 to 10 times more common among boys than among girls.

The prevalence of externalizing behavior generally declines with age, although it declines at much earlier ages for girls (age 4 or 5) than for boys (Keenan & Shaw, in press). In contrast, the

Mourners at the wake of three teenagers who committed suicide together.

prevalence of internalizing problems increases with age. In particular, depression begins to emerge in preadolescence and adolescence (Achenbach & Edelbrock, 1981; Fleming & Offord, 1990; National Academy of Sciences, 1989; Rutter, 1989), and mood disorders become one of the most common psychological problems of adult life (see Chapter 5). Thus we can offer this explanation for the changing status of gender as a risk factor across age: Parents, teachers, and other adults seek treatment for younger boys' externalizing behavior, but the increase in depression among teenagers, especially adolescent girls, begins to balance the relationship between gender and the prevalence of psychological problems (Lewinsohn et al., 1994). By early adult life, more females than males report psychological problems.

Family Risk Factors

The prevalence of psychological disorders among children is related to several factors in addition to gender. Family adversity is a particularly important risk factor, as has been highlighted by the British psychiatrist Michael Rutter. Rutter's family adversity index (1978b, 1989) includes six family predictors of behavior problems among children: (1) low income, (2) overcrowding in the home, (3) maternal depression, (4) paternal antisocial behavior, (5) conflict between the parents, and (6) removal of the child from the home. Rutter found that the risk for externalizing problems did not increase substantially when only one family risk factor was present. However, the risk increased fourfold when two family adversity factors were present. The risk for children's antisocial behavior increased even further with three or more sources of family adversity.

Other epidemiological findings underscore the relationship between children's psychological problems and social disadvantage. For example, psychological disorders are found among over 20 percent of children living in inner-city neighborhoods (National Academy of Sciences, 1989) and are associated with divorce and single parenting. Family dysfunction and stressful life events are associated with both internalizing and externalizing problems (Fleming & Offord, 1990). For these reasons, family adversity is a substantial concern in the etiology of children's psychological problems.

Suicide among Children and Adolescents

Michael Rutter, a British psychiatrist, is an international authority on child psychopathology. Rutter was knighted by the queen of England in recognition of his many contributions.

Because of their prevalence and disruptiveness, externalizing problems are the focus of much psychological attention. Adults also need to be sensitive to children's internal distress, however, as the evidence on suicide underscores in a dramatic fashion. Suicide is the third leading cause of death among teenagers, trailing only automobile accidents and natural causes. Teenage suicide is of special concern because adolescent suicide rates have tripled since the 1960s. Suicide is extremely rare among children under the age of 10, but the rate of suicide also has increased among younger age groups (Hawton, 1986).

In comparison to adult suicide attempts, suicide attempts among adolescents are more impulsive, are more likely to follow a family conflict, and are more often motivated by anger rather than depression (Hawton, 1986). Cluster suicides are also more common among teenagers than among adults (Spirito et al., 1989). When one teenager commits suicide, his or her peers are at an increased risk for suicide attempts. The risk sometimes stems from suicide pacts, but in addition, the death may make suicide seem more acceptable to other teenagers. As suggested by some accounts of reactions to the 1994 suicide of rock star Kurt Cobain, some adolescents may view a peer's suicide as understandable, even romantic.

Etiological Considerations and Research

We begin our review of the etiology of childhood disorders with a discussion of parenting, family relationships, and other social factors, because parenting and the family context are critical to children's psychological adjustment. As we have noted repeatedly throughout the text, however, bear in mind that families share genes as well as the family environment. Also bear in mind that, as with other topics we have reviewed, the preponderance of research focuses on the development of externalizing disorders. Most research on the causes of mood and anxiety disorders among children is based on the same theories of etiology we have discussed in relation to adults (Puig-Antich, 1986; see Chapters 5 and 6). Evidence simply is lacking or inadequate on the development of many other psychological problems of childhood. In discussing etiology, we follow our developmental psychopathology approach and begin each section with a brief consideration of normal development. In discussing social factors, we highlight the development of attachments and the socialization of children as central issues in normal development and in developmental psychopathology.

Social Factors

ATTACHMENT RELATIONSHIPS

The major task of social development during the first year of life is the formation of a close bond, an *attachment,* between an infant and his or her caregivers (see Chapter 2). The British psychiatrist and theorist John Bowlby (1969, 1973, 1980) and the Canadian-American psychologist and empiricist Mary Ainsworth (1979) together have developed *attachment theory,* a set of proposals about the normal development of attachments and the adverse consequences of troubled attachment relationships.

Attachment theory also predicts that variations in the quality of early attachments are associated with normal or maladjustment among children. Attachment quality can be broadly divided into secure (healthy) and anxious attachments. Infants with *secure attachments* separate easily and explore away from their attachment figures, but they quickly seek proximity and comfort when they are threatened or distressed. Infants with **anxious attachments** are fearful about exploration and are not easily comforted by their attachment figures, who respond inadequately or inconsistently to the child's needs (Ainsworth et al., 1978; Carlson & Sroufe, 1995). Anxious attachments are further subcategorized into (1) *anxious avoidant attachments,* where the infant is generally unwary of strange situations and shows little preference for the attachment figure over others; (2) *anxious resistant attachments,* where the infant is wary of exploration, not easily soothed by the attachment figure, and angry or ambivalent about contact; and (3) *disorganized attachments,* where the infant responds inconsistently because of conflicting feelings toward an inconsistent caregiver who is the potential source of either reassurance or fear (Carlson & Sroufe, 1995).

A number of longitudinal studies have demonstrated that secure versus anxious attachments during infancy foreshadow difficulties in children's social and emotional adjustment throughout childhood. However, an insecure attachment does not seem to result in the development of any particular emotional disorder. Rather, insecure attachments predict a number of internalizing and social difficulties, including lower self-esteem, less competence in peer interaction, and increased dependency on others (Carlson & Sroufe, 1995; Cassidy, 1988; Sroufe & Fleeson, 1986). Recent research demonstrates, moreover, that stable, anxious attachments during infancy also predict externalizing behavior at 3 years of age (Shaw & Vondra, 1995). Thus, anxious attachments appear to be a general rather than a specific risk factor for children's subsequent psychological problems.

SOCIALIZATION

Socialization is the process of shaping children's behavior and attitudes to conform to the expectations of parents, teachers, and society as a whole (Hetherington & Parke, 1986). Many psychologists believe that parental explanation, example, and appropriate discipline are most important in socializing children, but other influences cannot be ignored. Peer groups exert strong if sometimes subtle conformity pressures that increase as children grow older. School and television also are powerful socialization agents.

Ineffective Discipline and Parenting Styles   Parental discipline, a major socialization tool, is sometimes mistakenly viewed as the polar opposite of attachment or loving children. In fact, parents need not choose between being strict and loving. Secure attachments facilitate parenting by making

anxious attachment   An insecure relationship in which an infant or child shows ambivalence about seeking reassurance or security from an attachment figure.

socialization   The process of shaping children's behavior and attitudes to conform to the expectations of parents, teachers, and society.

The Canadian-American psychologist Mary Ainsworth (1913–1999) was an internationally reknowned expert on infant-caregiver attachments. Her empirical studies grounded and expanded attachment theory.

Together with Mary Ainsworth the British psychiatrist John Bowlby (1907–1990) can be credited with developing attachment theory, a set of proposals about the importance of close parental relationships to children's psychological development.

authoritative parenting A style of parenting that is both loving and firm and is often used by parents of well-adjusted children.

coercion A pattern of interaction in which unwitting parents positively reinforce children's misbehavior (by giving in to their demands), and children negatively reinforce parents' capitulation (by ending their obnoxious behavior).

time-out A discipline technique that involves briefly isolating a child as a punishment for misbehavior.

Clinical psychologist Gerald Patterson is a leader in studying children's aggression from a social learning perspective.

discipline both less necessary and more effective (Shaw & Bell, 1993). For example, attachment research indicates that babies are not "spoiled" when they are picked up, cuddled, and loved in other ways. Such natural interactions make infants easier, not more difficult, to manage (Ainsworth, 1979).

But love alone is not enough as children grow older. **Authoritative parenting,** parenting that is both loving and firm, is most effective in rearing well-adjusted children. In fact, developmental psychologists classify parenting into four styles by combining the two dimensions of warmth and control. In contrast to authoritative parents, *authoritarian* parents lack warmth, and while their discipline is strict, it is often harsh and undemocratic. Children of authoritarian parents generally are compliant, but they also may be anxious. *Indulgent* parents are the opposite of authoritarian parents—affectionate but lax in discipline. The children of indulgent parents tend to be impulsive and noncompliant, but they are not extremely antisocial. Finally, *neglectful* parents are unconcerned either with their children's emotional needs or with their needs for discipline. Children with serious conduct problems often have neglectful parents (Baumrind, 1971; Loeber & Dishion, 1983; Maccoby & Martin, 1983).

Coercion More specific problems in parenting also appear to contribute to the development of children's externalizing problems. The psychologist Gerald Patterson's (1982) concept of coercion is one of the most important examples of this line of research. **Coercion** occurs when parents *positively* reinforce children's misbehavior by giving in to their demands. The children, in turn, *negatively* reinforce their parents by ending their obnoxious behavior as soon as their parents capitulate. Thus coercion describes a system of interaction in which parents and children reciprocally reinforce child misbehavior and parent capitulation. The concept is illustrated in the following brief case study.

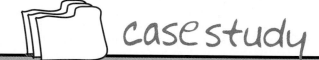

Brief Case Study

Ms. B. finally admitted that she had lost all control of her 4-year-old son, Billy. Ms. B. was a single parent who was exhausted by her routine of working from 8 to 5:30 every day and managing Billy and the household in the evenings and on weekends. She had no parenting or financial support from Billy's father or anyone else, and Ms. B. was worn down. When it came time to discipline Billy, she usually gave in—either because this was the easiest thing to do, or because she felt too guilty to say no.

Ms. B. described many difficult interactions with Billy. One example stood out in the mind of the psychologist she consulted. Ms. B. would often stop at the grocery store with Billy after work, and he inevitably gave her trouble while they were shopping. Dealing with the candy aisle was a recent problem. Billy had asked for some candy when they first approached the aisle. Ms. B. told him no, but in an increasingly loud voice Billy protested, "I WANT CANDY!" Ms. B. attempted to stick to her guns, but soon she was embarrassed by the disapproving looks on the faces of other mothers. Feeling both resentful and resigned, she grabbed a bag of M&Ms and gave it to Billy. This gave her a few minutes of peace and quiet while she completed her shopping. ♛

Clearly, Ms. B. rewarded Billy for his misbehavior in this interaction. As suggested by the coercion construct, Billy also negatively reinforced his mother by quieting down when she gave in to his demands. Because both parties were reinforced, the coercive interaction is predicted to continue over time (Patterson, 1982).

The coercion concept is appealing, in part, because it has direct, practical implications. Parents need to break the pattern of interaction by ignoring the misbehavior (extinction), punishing it, or rewarding more positive actions (Forehand & McMahon, 1981). We discuss such treatments of noncompliant behavior later in the chapter. In Billy's case, the psychologist recommended the use of **time-out,** the technique of briefly isolating a child following misbehavior. The next time Billy acted up in the grocery store, Ms. B. left her shopping cart, and she and Billy sat in the car until he quieted down. She then completed her shopping. Several trips to the car were needed the first day, but Billy's behavior improved so that soon no time-outs were needed. He quickly was earning rewards for being good—not for being bad—while shopping.

Conflict and Inconsistent Discipline   Inconsistent discipline is another frequent correlate of children's externalizing problems (Patterson, DeBaryshe, & Ramsey, 1989). Inconsistency can involve frequent changes in the style and standards of one parent, or two parents may be inconsistent in their differing expectations and rules for a child. For example, inconsistency between mothers and fathers often becomes a problem when parents have conflicts in their own relationship—as when they are unhappily married, divorced, or experience other forms of family adversity (Shaw & Emery, 1988; Shaw et al., 1994). In these circumstances, parents may deliberately undermine each other's discipline.

Yet another problem occurs when parents' actions are inconsistent with their words. For example, consider the contradiction inherent in angry and harsh physical punishment. On the one hand, such discipline teaches children to follow the rules. On the other hand, it teaches children that anger and aggression are acceptable means of solving problems. Parents socialize children by modeling appropriate behavior as well as by disciplining them, and children often imitate what their parents do, not what they say (Bandura, 1973).

Broader Social Influences: Peers, Neighborhoods, Television, and Society   Parents are not solely responsible for socializing children. Violence is continually modeled on television, for example, and longitudinal evidence indicates that children learn aggression from television programs (Eron, 1982). Peer groups also can teach antisocial behavior. In fact, some researchers have suggested that socialized delinquency, in which criminal acts occur in the company of others, is an important subtype of externalizing disorders (Kazdin, 1995).

As we noted earlier, more psychological problems are found among children who grow up in poor inner-city neighborhoods (Rutter, 1978b, 1989; Shaw & Emery, 1988; Shaw et al., 1994).

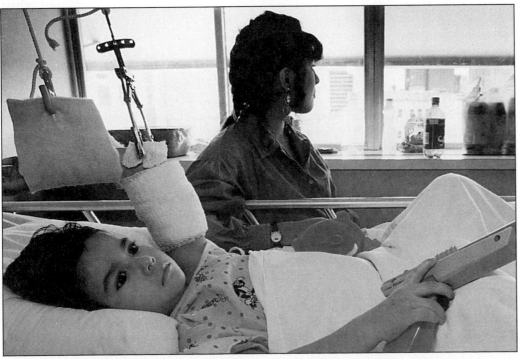

Societal influences on children's behavior are pervasive. This 3-year-old boy suffered a gunshot wound during a drive-by shooting. Note the toy pistol he holds while recuperating in his hospital bed.

temperament   Characteristic styles of relating to the world that are often conceptualized as inborn traits. Generally emphasizes the "how" as opposed to the "what" of behavior.

Professionals who wish to promote children's mental health therefore need to be concerned about poverty, inadequate schooling, and violence (Caspi & Moffitt, 1995; Dishion, French, & Patterson, 1995).

Cross-cultural evidence also points to broad societal influences on externalizing behavior. Citizens of other countries often are horrified and puzzled by the extent of teenage crime in the United States, and there is good reason for their shock and fear. Robbery, sexual offenses, assault, and burglary are far more common in the United States than in Europe or Japan. As we have noted, many of these crimes are committed by juveniles. According to many politicians, crime is widespread because the United States is "soft on crime." In fact, far *more* people are imprisoned in the United States than in Europe, Canada, or Japan. This suggests that other aspects of U.S. culture, such as higher poverty rates or lack of gun control, may account for the societal influences on juvenile crime (Jones & Krisberg, 1994).

Social Factors in Attention-Deficit/Hyperactivity Disorder   There are essentially no theories of how social factors might play a unique role in the development of attention-deficit/hyperactivity disorder (Hinshaw, 1994). Some researchers have found that the parents of children with ADHD are less effective than other parents. For example, mothers of children with ADHD have been observed to be more critical, demanding, and controlling when compared to the mothers of normal children (Mash & Johnston, 1982). However, problems in parenting may be a reaction to the children's troubles and not a cause of them.

In fact, children with ADHD become more attentive and compliant while on medication, and their mothers' behavior "improves" as well. In comparison to the placebo group, mothers become less negative and less controlling when their children are medicated (Barkley et al., 1984; Danforth, Barkley, & Stokes, 1991). Children with ADHD make social interactions more difficult. Still, troubled parenting surely intensifies their problems.

Biological Factors

All children require some socialization to control their selfish or aggressive behavior (Caspi & Moffit, 1995; Dishion et al., 1995). All children do not come into the world with the same behavioral tendencies, however, as any parent of two children will attest. In this section we consider four biological influences on individual differences related to the development of psychological disorders among children: temperament, behavior genetics, neuropsychological abnormalities, and the ingestion of food additives and sugar.

TEMPERAMENT

Temperament refers to a child's inborn behavioral characteristics, such as activity level, emotionality, and sociability (Buss, 1991). Temperament researchers disagree about exactly what qualities comprise children's temperamental characteristics (Goldsmith et al., 1987), but Thomas and Chess's (1977) grouping into easy, difficult, and slow-to-warm-up categories is one clear and enduring categorization of temperamental styles. *Easy* children quickly form social relationships and follow discipline; *difficult* children challenge parental authority; *slow-to-warm-up* children tend to be shy and withdrawn. Many theorists have argued that a difficult temperament is a risk factor for later externalizing disorders, an assertion that has been supported by some recent research on infants and toddlers (Shaw, Keenan, & Vondra, 1994).

Some of the most exciting recent research on children's temperament has been conducted by the psychologist Jerome Kagan and colleagues (Kagan & Snidman, 1991), who have studied a temperamental style that they call *inhibited to the unfamiliar,* which is similar to the slow-to-warm-up grouping. As opposed to uninhibited infants, infants who are inhibited to the unfamiliar cry easily and often in response to novel toys, people, or circumstances, and their psychophysiological responses (e.g., heart rate acceleration) also indicate their fearfulness. About 10 percent of babies consistently show inhibition to unfamiliar circumstances during the first 2 years of life (Kagan & Snidman, 1991). Most important for present purposes, researchers have linked behavioral inhibition with an increased risk for anxiety disorders among children and their parents or other relatives. More specifically, the prevalence of anxiety disorders is higher among parents and biological relatives of children who have been identified as inhibited than it is among the general population (Biederman, Rosenbaum, Chaloff, & Kagan, 1995).

BEHAVIOR GENETIC RESEARCH

Genes not only affect general temperamental characteristics, but they also may contribute more specifically to the development of children's psychological disorders. Few behavior genetic studies have been conducted on internalizing disorders, except for some recent research documenting genetic influences on childhood onset obsessive–compulsive disorder (March, Leonard, & Swedo, 1995).

Many scientists believe that genetics plays an especially important role in the etiology of attention-deficit/hyperactivity disorder (Barkley, 1990). Researchers recently have identified a specific genetic disorder (that produces generalized resistance to thyroid hormone) that is strongly related to ADHD but not to other mental disorders (Hauser et al., 1993). However, only a tiny proportion of children with ADHD has this genetic disorder; thus it accounts for very few cases. In broader samples, researchers have found a 51 percent concordance rate for ADHD among MZ twins, compared with a 33 percent concordance rate for DZ pairs (Goodman & Stevenson, 1989). These data demonstrate that genes contribute to ADHD, but the moderate concordance for MZ twins indicates that nongenetic factors must be involved as well (Hinshaw, 1994).

Evidence also indicates that genetic factors influence the development of antisocial behavior. It is important to note, however, that genetic factors are much more important in the development of life-course-persistent than adolescent-limited antisocial behavior. Presumably, this is because of the strong social pressures to violate rules during the teen years (Gottesman & Goldsmith, 1994).

We noted earlier in the chapter that conventional wisdom views ADHD as a biological problem and ODD and conduct disorder as psychological problems. However, there are two basic problems with this conventional view. First, it oversimplifies etiology by pitting genes against the environment. In contrast, the systems approach acknowledges multiple contributions and multiple pathways to the development of externalizing disorders. Second, conventional wisdom confuses etiology with some basic symptoms of ADHD and ODD. Children with ADHD try but fail to control their behavior; they are impulsive. Children with ODD or CD seem like they are not trying to control their behavior; they have aggressive intentions and show lack of remorse. Such symptoms may seem to be related to biological versus psychological causation, but the relationship is only a superficial one.

If genes contribute to the development of externalizing disorders, an essential question is: What is the inherited mechanism? Hyperactivity or inattention may be directly inherited but rule violations surely are not. No one has suggested that there is a "crime gene," let alone an "argue with your teacher gene!" One inherited tendency that may contribute to ODD or CD is chronic underarousal of the autonomic nervous system. That is, children with externalizing problems may be less emotionally reactive than other children. As a result, they may be more likely to engage in stimulation-seeking and less likely to learn from punishment (Quay, 1965, 1993).

Psychological Factors

SELF-CONTROL AND EXTERNALIZING DISORDERS

Child development proceeds from the external to the internal control of emotion and behavior. For example, parents initially control children's behavior with discipline, but *self-control,* the internal regulation of behavior, is the ultimate goal of this socialization. Not surprisingly, several investigators have found problems with self-control among children with externalizing disorders.

One area of research on self-control has focused on *delay of gratification*—the adaptive ability to defer smaller but immediate rewards for larger long-term benefits. (An example of delay of gratification is studying for an exam rather than going out with friends.) In general, children with externalizing problems have been found to be lacking in the ability to delay gratification. They are more oriented to the present than are other children. They opt for immediate rewards rather than for long-term goals, a maladaptive characteristic for achieving educational and career goals (Mischel, 1983).

Children with externalizing problems also may fail to exert self-control because they misinterpret the intentions of others, particularly in ambiguous social situations. Several studies by the psychologist Ken Dodge and his colleagues have indicated that aggressive children overinterpret the aggressive intentions of their peers (Crick & Dodge, 1994; Dodge & Frame, 1982). In a sense, some children with externalizing problems seem to believe that they need to "get you before you get me."

EMOTION REGULATION AND INTERNALIZING BEHAVIOR

Although less obvious than the regulation of behavior, the regulation of children's emotions also progresses from external to internal control across the course of development. For example, attachment relationships offer security and soothe anxiety for infants and toddlers. As children grow older, however, they develop internal *working models* or expectations about relationships as extensions of their early attachment experiences (Carlson & Sroufe, 1995). *Emotion regulation* is a more general process as children learn to identify, evaluate, and control their feelings based on the reactions, attitudes, and advice of their parents and others in their social world.

As noted earlier, our understanding of children's emotional development is far from complete, and only scattered efforts have attempted to link troubles with emotion regulation to children's internalizing disorders. One exciting example comes from the research of the psychologist Carolyn Zahn-Waxler, who has conducted several studies of children of depressed mothers. Children of depressed mothers are at an increased risk for depression themselves, and Zahn-Waxler hypothesizes that troubled parenting is one contributing cause. More specifically, she believes these children take excessive responsibility in caring for their mothers, rather than being cared for by them. One problematic result of this role reversal can be excessive feelings of guilt on the part of the children. In fact, Zahn-Waxler and colleagues (1990) found excessive guilt among 5- to 6-year-old children of depressed mothers and indications of defensiveness against excessive guilt among 7- to 9-year-olds. Studies have not determined whether children's feelings of responsibility and guilt increase the risk for subsequent childhood depression, but future research should address this question. More generally, research should focus on how children are socialized to regulate various emotions and the extent to which problems in emotion regulation contribute to the development of internalizing disorders.

Integration and Alternative Pathways

How can we integrate evidence on the diverse contributions to the development of psychological disorders of childhood? Two conclusions seem clear. First, childhood disorders have many etiological pathways, not one. Obviously, different factors contribute to causing internalizing versus externalizing disorders or to causing subtypes of disorders such as ADHD versus ODD. However, there also are different pathways to the development of the *same* disorder. An example is the different pathways to externalizing behavior during adolescence. Life-course-persistent and adolescent-limited antisocial behavior cannot be distinguished based on their appearance, but the two problems clearly reflect different etiological pathways: long-standing biological and socialization problems in the former cases, and short-term rebellion and peer influences in the latter cases (Moffitt, 1993).

Second, biological, psychological, and social factors clearly interact in causing children's psychological disorders. Temperament theorists note, for example, that the *goodness of fit* between a child's temperament and the family environment may be of greatest importance to healthy psychological development (Shaw & Bell, 1993). A difficult child should benefit from firm, consistent, patient, and loving discipline, whereas the combination of a difficult temperament and family adversity may result in ODD and eventually conduct disorder (Kasen, Cohen, Brook, & Hartmark, 1996).

Future research may succeed in identifying specific subtypes of childhood disorders, some of which may have very specific causes such as the thyroid resistance already identified among a very small proportion of children with ADHD (Hauser et al., 1993). We believe, however, that multifactorial causality and equifinality—the systems approach—will continue to be the best explanations of the etiology of most childhood disorders.

Treatment

Treatment of Internalizing Disorders

psychostimulants Medications that heighten energy and alertness when taken in small dosages, but lead to restless, even frenetic, behavior when misused. Often used in the treatment of attention-deficit/hyperactivity disorder.

Until recently, children were expected to "outgrow" most of their internalizing problems. Thus few treatments for anxiety or mood disorders have been developed or studied specifically as they apply to children (Kazdin, 1994a). Recent findings indicate, however, that the disorders are not "outgrown"—they persist across time, sometimes into adult life (Harrington et al., 1990). Children's internalizing problems therefore require treatment, and treatments need to be developed and modified to meet children's unique needs.

Some findings are beginning to emerge on the treatment of children's internalizing disorders. For example, it may surprise you to learn that antidepressant medications are no more effective than placebos in treating depression among children and adolescents (DeVane & Sallee, 1996; Geller et al., 1992). More optimistically, children with obsessive–compulsive disorders respond positively to clomipramine, the same medication that is effective with adults (Leonard et al., 1989). Moreover, some forms of cognitive behavior and family therapy for children's internalizing problems show promise (Barrett, Dadds, & Rapee, 1996; Kendall, 1994). Still, the most accurate conclusion about the treatment of children's internalizing disorders is that research is needed on the effects of psychological and psychopharmacological interventions.

Treatment of Externalizing Disorders

In contrast to internalizing disorders, numerous treatments have been developed for children's externalizing disorders. Unfortunately, however, these problems are difficult to change (Kazdin, 1987, 1995). The most promising treatments include psychostimulants for attention-deficit/hyperactivity disorder, behavioral family therapy for oppositional defiant disorder, and various family and residential programs for treating conduct disorders and delinquent youth.

PSYCHOSTIMULANTS AND ADHD

Every year more than 600,000 children in the United States—between 1 and 2 percent of the school-age population—are treated with **psychostimulants** for attention-deficit/hyperactivity disorder (Safer & Krager, 1988). These numbers may startle you, but medication is an inexpensive, carefully researched, and effective treatment for the disorder (Barkley, 1990; Henker & Whalen, 1989). Psychostimulants produce immediate and noticeable improvements in the behavior of about 75 percent of children with ADHD. Still, these conclusions must be qualified on several grounds. Psychostimulants have only limited effects on learning; it is not clear whether they produce long-term benefits; and they have several side effects.

Usage and Effects The most commonly prescribed psychostimulants are known by the trade names of Ritalin, Dexedrine, and Cylert. Each medication has the effect of increasing alertness and arousal. Psychostimulants usually are prescribed by pediatricians, who typically are consulted following a child's difficulties in the early years of school. The central nature of school-related problems is evident in the fact that psychostimulants typically are prescribed around the school day. A pill is taken before school in the morning, and because the effects of most medications last only 3 or 4 hours, another pill is taken at the lunch hour. A third pill may or may not be taken after school, but the medication typically is not taken on weekends or during school vacations because of concerns about side effects.

Children take psychostimulants for years, not days or weeks. Traditionally, medication was discontinued in early adolescence, because it was believed that the problem was "outgrown" by that age. However, follow-up studies indicate that problems with inattention, impulsivity, and hyperactivity continue through adolescence and into adult life (Thorley, 1984; Weiss et al., 1985). Thus the current trend is to continue psychostimulants through the teen years and perhaps into adulthood (Barkley, 1991; Campbell, Green, & Deutsch, 1985).

dose-response effects Different treatment responses to different dosages of a medication.

Psychostimulants indisputably improve children's attentiveness and decrease their disruptiveness (Barkley, 1991; Pelham et al., 1993). These benefits have been demonstrated in numerous double-blind, placebo-controlled studies, but they also are demonstrated more informally. Many teachers who are unaware of the new treatment send notes home about the improved behavior of one of their "problem" pupils. The benefits of psychostimulants for learning are less certain. On the one hand, psychostimulants lead to improved schoolwork, evident in more accurate completion of reading, spelling, and arithmetic assignments (Pelham et al., 1993). On the other hand, grades and achievement test scores do not improve dramatically, if they improve at all (Henker & Whalen, 1989; O'Leary, 1980).

Research on **dose-response effects,** the response to different dosages of medication, was once thought to explain the different effects on behavior and learning. Sprague and Sleator (1977) found that a lower dosage of psychostimulants produced maximum gains in learning, but the medication *interfered* with learning at higher dosages. These same higher doses produced maximum improvements in behavior, suggesting that some children received too much medication, because medication typically is increased gradually or *titrated* until maximum behavioral improvements are reached.

Dose-response effects have been inconsistent in subsequent research, however, and different children often respond uniquely to different dosages of medication (Tannock, Schachar, & Logan, 1995). Although more research is needed on dose-response effects, it is uncertain why improved attention and behavior in the classroom do not translate into notably improved grades and achievement. An even more troubling and puzzling fact is that psychostimulants have not been found to lead to long-term improvements in behavior, learning, or other areas of functioning (Barkley, 1990; Dulcan, 1986; Hinshaw, 1994).

Side Effects The side effects of psychostimulants also are somewhat troubling. Some side effects are relatively minor, such as decreased appetite, increased heart rate, and sleeping difficulties. Evidence that psychostimulants can slow physical growth is of much greater concern. Children maintained on psychostimulants fall somewhat behind expected gains in height and weight, although rebounds in growth occur when the medication is stopped. This is one reason why the medication often is discontinued when children are out of school. Still, careful monitoring of cases is necessary because of possible individual differences in growth effects (Campbell, Green, & Deutsch, 1985).

Another side effect that concerns some psychologists is that parents, teachers, and children often credit the pills, not the child, for the improved behavior (Whalen et al., 1991). When they are having an "off" day, for example, many children with ADHD are asked, "Did you take your pill today?" Some research indicates that ADHD children on psychostimulants do not credit "the pill"; they make internal attributions for their positive behavior (Hoza et al., 1993). Still, the question about attributions may reflect a more general concern: Should children's misbehavior be corrected with medication?

This is an important and reasonable question to ask, especially considering that the effects of psychostimulants are not specific to attention-deficit/hyperactivity disorder. Medication improves oppositional and defiant behavior as well (Klorman et al., 1994). ADHD has not been proved to be a unique biological problem with a specific biological treatment. At the same time, psychostimulants are an inexpensive and effective treatment, especially in comparison with the alternatives. Many parents and professionals identify medication as the treatment of choice for ADHD; others are fearful that we are overmedicating schoolchildren.

Antidepressant Medication for ADHD Psychostimulants clearly are the medication of choice for treating ADHD. However, a number of children with ADHD have been treated with antidepressant medication in recent years. Although depression and ADHD often do co-occur, this is not the rationale for the treatment. Rather, the antidepressants are thought to affect ADHD symptoms directly for reasons that are not yet clear. What is clear, however, is that antidepressants are a second-line treatment for ADHD. Their use is justified only following the failure of psychostimulants (Biederman et al., 1989; DeVane & Sallee, 1996).

BEHAVIORAL FAMILY THERAPY

Behavioral family therapy is the major alternative treatment for ADHD, as well as a common treatment for other externalizing problems. There are several variations of behavioral family therapy, but all approaches train parents and perhaps teachers to use the principles of operant conditioning to improve discipline in children's daily life.

Behavioral family therapy typically begins with *parent training.* Parents are taught to identify specific problematic behaviors, list preferred alternative behaviors, and set consequences for appropriate and inappropriate behavior. Parents also may be told to make a "star chart" for recording children's progress and perhaps to develop a "daily report card" that the child will carry home from school as a way of coordinating discipline in both settings.

Other aspects of parent training may include teaching parents about punishment strategies, such as the time-out technique. Conventional wisdom in parent training holds that punishment should be firm but not angry, and that rewards should far outweigh punishments as a strategy of discipline. These are reasonable goals, but some experts feel that parent training should directly emphasize increasing warmth as well as discipline in parent–child relationships. From this perspective, the goal of parent training is to teach parents to be authoritative.

Research with younger (Forehand, Wells, & Griest, 1980) and older (Patterson, 1982) children with oppositional defiant disorders supports the short-term effectiveness of behavioral family therapy. Some evidence also indicates that improvements are sustained over the course of a year (Patterson & Fleischman, 1979). A comprehensive review concluded that parent training was "one of the more promising treatments for conduct disorders" (Kazdin, 1987, p. 191). The same reviewer argued, however, that conduct disorders are chronic diseases that require intensive and repeated treatment. Behavior therapy leads to short-term improvements, but because externalizing problems are often chronic, treatment may need to be repeated over time.

A positive evaluation of behavioral family therapy is tempered further by several studies that have compared the treatment with psychostimulants in working with children with ADHD. Medication has consistently been found to be more effective, although a combination of medication and behavior therapy may be better than either alone (Henker & Whalen, 1989; Pelham et al., 1993). In considering the challenges for behavioral family therapy, you should recall that the parents of children with externalizing problems are often living in adverse circumstances that make it difficult to alter their parenting (Emery, Fincham, & Cummings, 1992). In fact, parent training has been found to be less effective when family troubles are greater (Kazdin, 1995). Parents can be effective in changing children's behavior, but psychologists need to develop more effective ways of helping parents to cope with difficult family environments.

TREATMENT OF CONDUCT DISORDERS AND JUVENILE DELINQUENCY

Numerous programs have been developed to treat conduct disorders and juvenile delinquency. In fact, exciting claims about the effectiveness of new programs for difficult youth commonly are reported in the popular media. You should be cautious as you learn about these new approaches. Research indicates that conduct disorders among adolescents are even more resistant to treatment than are externalizing problems among younger children (Kazdin, 1994a, 1995).

Some behavioral family therapy approaches have shown promise in treating young people with family or legal problems (Alexander & Parsons, 1982). These treatments are based on principles similar to those in programs for younger children, such as parent training. An important difference is that *negotiation*—a process in which young people are actively involved in defining rules—is central to behavioral family therapy with adolescents. An obvious reason for the negotiation strategy is that parents have less direct control over adolescents than over younger children. Because of diminishing parental control, many mental health professionals also advocate treating externalizing problems prior to adolescence.

Multisystemic therapy is another approach to family intervention that has received increasing attention (Henggeler & Borduin, 1990). In recognition of the diverse causes of externalizing behavior, multisystemic therapy combines family treatment with coordinated interventions in other important contexts of the troubled child's life, including peer groups, schools, and neighborhoods. Multisystemic therapy has not yet been adequately evaluated by independent

recidivism Repeat offending in violating the law.

diversion A practice of directing problem youth away from the juvenile justice system and into some alternative treatment or program. For example, a juvenile offender may be referred to counseling instead of having a hearing held in court.

research groups, but initial evidence is promising for improving family relationships and school attendance while reducing arrest rates among youth with conduct disorders (Borduin et al., 1995; Henggeler, 1994).

Residential Programs and Juvenile Courts   A significant number of adolescents are treated in residential programs outside the home, because their conduct problems are severe, their families are dysfunctional, or they have been determined by the courts to be juvenile delinquents. One of the most actively researched residential programs is *Achievement Place,* a group home that operates according to highly structured behavior therapy principles. Achievement Place homes, like many similar residential programs, are very effective in improving aggression and noncompliance while the adolescent is living in the treatment setting. For this reason, professionals working in residential or inpatient settings are wise to adopt similar behavioral strategies. Unfortunately, the programs do not prevent **recidivism,** or repeat offending, once the adolescent leaves the residential placement (Emery & Marholin, 1977; Kazdin, 1987, 1995). Delinquent adolescents typically return to family, peer, and school environments that do not consistently reward prosocial behavior or monitor and punish antisocial behavior.

In theory, juvenile courts are designed to help troubled youth, not to punish them. This lofty goal is belied by research indicating that **diversion**—keeping problem youths out of the juvenile justice system—is a promising "treatment" (Davidson et al., 1987). The juvenile justice system often seems to create delinquency instead of curing it, and evidence indicates that recidivism is lower when delinquents are diverted away from the courts.

Our overview of the treatment of externalizing disorders is realistic, but we do not intend it to be pessimistic. Externalizing disorders are of vast importance for children, families, and society, and the difficulties in treating antisocial youth should be seen as a challenge and not a defeat. Perhaps the best hope is to prevent some of these problems from developing in the first place by helping to ease some of the sources of family adversity that help to create them.

Course and Outcome

Until recently, psychologists believed that children outgrew internalizing problems. Prospective research demonstrates, however, that certain internalizing disorders often persist over time. Specific fears tend to be relatively short-lived, but more complex disorders, such as depression (Harrington et al., 1990; Kovacs et al., 1984) and obsessive–compulsive disorder (March, Leonard, & Swedo, 1995), are likely to continue from childhood into adolescence and adult life. Thus the prognosis is not optimistic for a child who has a full-blown mood or anxiety disorder.

Externalizing disorders also are stable over the course of development, but the pattern is much the opposite as it is for internalizing disorders. Roughly half of all children with externalizing disorders continue to have problems with antisocial behavior into adulthood, but antisocial behavior rarely begins during adult life (Hinshaw, 1994; Kazdin, 1995). Somewhat different patterns of continuity hold for various subtypes of externalizing disorders. As we noted earlier, antisocial behavior that begins during adolescence has a *better* adult prognosis than antisocial behavior that begins during childhood (Moffit, 1993). Similarly, the prognosis of attention-deficit/hyperactivity disorder depends on whether there is comorbid oppositional-defiant disorder or conduct disorder. In such cases, the patients are more likely to develop problems with substance abuse, criminality, and other forms of antisocial behavior (Hinshaw, 1994).

The continuity of childhood disorders clearly underscores the need for more and better research on the etiology and effective treatment of psychological disorders of childhood. If we can do better in helping children, we will succeed in preventing a number of psychological disorders among adults.

Autistic Disorder and Pervasive Developmental Disorders

Children who suffer from autistic disorder, as well as other pervasive developmental disorders, have severe impairments in a number of areas of functioning. The impairments begin early in life, and they are long-lasting despite notable improvements among a minority of people with the disorder. Even those adults who achieve exceptionally good outcomes continue to show severely disturbed behavior. Consider the remarkable case of Temple Grandin, a woman who achieved what may be the most successful outcome of autism on record.

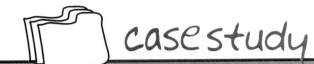

Temple Grandin: An Anthropologist on Mars

Temple Grandin, a woman who is now in her forties, suffered from the classic symptoms of autism as a child. She had not developed language by the age of 3, and she threw wild tantrums in response to social initiations, even gentle attempts to give her a hug. Grandin spent hours staring into space, playing with objects, or simply rocking or spinning herself. She also engaged in other unusual behaviors, such as repeatedly smearing her own feces. With the extensive help of her parents and teachers, and with her own determination, however, Grandin developed complex strategies to help her compensate for, and cope with, her severe psychological impairments. Remarkably, she even earned a Ph.D. in animal science and has developed widely used techniques for managing cattle. In stark contrast to Grandin, the majority of people with autism spend most of their adult life in institutions.

One of Grandin's most complex coping strategies is "computing" how other people feel and how she should react in social circumstances. Like the characters of Data or Mr. Spock from the "Star Trek" series—with whom she identifies—Grandin does not experience normal human emotions and motivations. Rather, she describes herself as "an anthropologist on Mars." Like an anthropologist in a strange culture, she has had to learn how to relate to the human species through careful ob-

servation of "their" behavior. Grandin details her struggles with social situations and other aspects of autism in two autobiographies, *Emergence: Labelled Autistic* and *Thinking in Pictures*.

Although she feels that she lacks even children's understanding of social motivations, Grandin apparently has residual traces of human needs, such as the need for physical contact. Still, she finds human touch—hugging—overwhelming. As a result, Grandin developed another remarkable strategy to compensate for her deep-seated aversion to human touch. She developed a "squeeze machine," a device that gives her a soothing, mechanical hug. 👑

Temple Grandin, who suffers from autism, has achieved remarkable success both as an advocate for autistic disorder and as an animal scientist who has developed more humane methods of slaughtering cattle.

We have numerous descriptions of the unusual behavior of people with autistic disorder. But social and communicative impairments of autism typically prevent us from learning about the inner world of autism. Temple Grandin offers us a compelling exception to the rule. Throughout the remainder of this chapter, we quote from *Thinking in Pictures* in an attempt to offer some insight into autism from the inside.

Typical Symptoms and Associated Features

Autism begins early in life, and in retrospect many parents recall abnormalities that seem to date back to birth. Because many infants with autism make few demands and have a normal physical appearance, the condition may not be accurately diagnosed for a few years. In the majority of cases, however, parents become aware that their child is profoundly disturbed by the age of 3 (Short & Schopler, 1988). By this time, parents have noted the child's impaired communication abilities, one of the three classic symptoms of autism. The other two central symptoms are impairments in social interaction and stereotyped patterns of behavior, interests, and activities. In the following sections we discuss disturbances in terms of these three defining symptoms. We also discuss other notable symptoms commonly found among people with autism and other pervasive developmental disorders, specifically apparent sensory deficits, self-injurious behavior, and savant performance—highly specialized abilities found in some rare but fascinating cases.

IMPAIRED SOCIAL INTERACTION

Many mental health professionals view the inability to relate to others as the central feature of autistic disorder. Social impairments range from relatively mild oddities, such as a lack of social or emotional reciprocity, to extreme difficulties in which there is little awareness of the existence of others, let alone of their perspective. Some children and adults with pervasive developmental disorders treat other people as if they were confusing and foreign objects rather than as sources of protection, comfort, and reciprocal stimulation.

Many people with pervasive developmental disorders appear to be missing the basic, inborn tendency to form attachments with other people. As infants, they do not show the attachment behaviors that help normal children form a special bond with their caregivers. In retrospect, many parents remember that their children did not seek them out in times of distress, nor were they comforted by physical contact. Many children with autism find normal hugs and kisses disturbing, even painful, rather than reassuring.

Social impairments continue as the infants become toddlers and preschoolers. Children with pervasive developmental disorder show little interest in their peers. They do not engage in spontaneous social play, and they fail to develop friendships as they grow older. They also exhibit *gaze aversion;* that is, they actively avoid eye contact.

IMPAIRED COMMUNICATION

In addition to their dramatic social isolation, people with pervasive developmental disorders suffer from a variety of impairments in communication. (The one exception is Asperger's disorder.) The communication problems often are severe, but there can be a range of difficulties. Some children fail to speak at all between the ages of 1 and 2, the time when normal children typically learn their first words. Others learn a few rudimentary words such as "Mama" and then suddenly lose their language abilities. Still other children progress further in acquiring language, but they either lose their abilities or stop progressing at the normal rate of language acquisition (Schreibman, 1988). Many children with autism remain mute, and about half never acquire functional language (Rutter, 1978a; Volkmar et al., 1994). According to field studies conducted for DSM-IV, 54 percent of patients with autism remain mute, compared with 35 percent of patients with other pervasive developmental disorders (Volkmar et al., 1994).

The speech difficulties found in autism and other pervasive developmental disorders are not the products of auditory or other sensory problems, nor are they simply disturbances in the mechanics of speech. Rather, the difficulties stem from basic disturbances in the ability to communicate, and even more basically, in the ability to imitate or reciprocate interactions. Unlike infants and toddlers who are deaf or mute, children with autism do not use gestures as substitutes for speech. In fact, some children do not engage in the social imitation that is essential for learning basic skills, let alone for building relationships. In many respects, children with autism seem to lack the essential motivation for communicating with others. Their communication difficulties convey the failure to appreciate the perspective—or even the existence—of other minds (Tager-Flusberg, 1996).

Even high-functioning people with pervasive developmental disorders who imitate others and have relatively well-developed language skills nevertheless demonstrate a limited ability to communicate about or understand abstractions. They may fail to generate unique or imaginative speech, and they have difficulty comprehending abstractions like metaphors. Thus the language problems in the pervasive developmental disorders apparently involve restrictions in thinking, not just in expression. Here is how Temple Grandin describes her struggles with language and abstraction:

> I can remember the frustration of not being able to talk at age three. This caused me to throw many a tantrum. I could understand what people said to me, but I could not get my words out. It was like a big stutter, and starting words was difficult. My first few words were very difficult to produce and generally had only one syllable, such as "bah" for "ball." (p. 45)

Autistics have problems learning things that cannot be thought about in pictures. The easiest words for an autistic child to learn are nouns, because they directly related to pictures. . . . Spatial words such as "over" and "under" had no meaning for me until I had a visual image to fix them in my memory. Even now, when I hear the word "under" by itself, I automatically picture myself getting under the cafeteria tables at school during an air-raid drill, a common occurrence on the East Coast during the early fifties.

STEREOTYPED BEHAVIOR, INTERESTS, AND ACTIVITIES

The third major symptom of autism and other pervasive developmental disorders is restricted, repetitive, and stereotyped patterns of behavior, interests, and activities. Many children with autistic disorder literally spend hours spinning a top or flapping a string in front of their eyes. Others might become uncontrollably agitated if the arrangement of furniture in a room is changed even slightly. Compulsively rigid adherence to daily routines is yet another aspect of these restricted activities and interests.

Not surprisingly, these odd preoccupations and rituals create social complications. People unfamiliar with the disorder are likely to find such behavior bizarre and perhaps frightening. The ritualistic behavior also causes numerous problems for those who are trying to manage and educate children with autism. How do you educate a child who is totally preoccupied with flapping a string in front of his or her face for hours?

What purpose does such stereotyped behavior serve for the disturbed individual? Rituals such as flapping a string or spinning a top seem to serve no other function than to provide sensory feedback. Thus they are often referred to as *self-stimulation*. The common interpretation of self-stimulation is that the child with autism receives too little sensory input, and that the ritual self-stimulation increases sensation to a more desirable level. We prefer an alternative interpretation. The stimulation of everyday environments has been described as overwhelming by several high-functioning people with pervasive developmental disorders. Perhaps self-stimulation reduces rather than increases sensory input by making the stimulation monotonously predictable. This alternative interpretation suggests, in fact, that all of the stereotyped behavior found in pervasive developmental disorders can be viewed as a form of compulsive ritual. The repetitive actions may serve the function of making a terrifying world more constant and predictable and therefore less frightening. Again, here are some comments by Temple Grandin on the topic:

When left alone, I would often space out and become hypnotized. I could sit for hours on the beach watching sand dribbling through my fingers. I'd study each individual grain of sand as it flowed between my fingers. Each grain was different, and I was like a scientist studying the grains under a microscope. As I scrutinized their shapes and contours, I went into a trance which cut me off from the sights and sounds around me.

Rocking and spinning were other ways to shut out the world when I became overloaded with too much noise. Rocking made me feel calm. It was like taking an addictive drug. The more I did it, the more I wanted to do it. My mother and my teachers would stop me so I would get back in touch with the rest of the world. (pp. 44–45)

APPARENT SENSORY DEFICITS

Some people with autism or other pervasive developmental disorders respond to auditory, tactile, or visual sensations in highly unusual and idiosyncratic manners. For example, some people with autistic disorder occasionally respond as if they were deaf, even though their hearing is intact. This unresponsiveness is an example of an *apparent sensory deficit* (Lovaas et al., 1971). There is no impairment in the sense organ, but the individual's responding makes it appear otherwise. Even more puzzling is that the same person who fails to be startled by a sudden crack of thunder may scream in apparent pain in reaction to a small sound like the scratch of chalk on a blackboard (Schreibman, 1988). This inconsistency suggests that the problem lies at some higher level of perception rather than at a lower level of sensation. The sensory apparatus is intact, but some cortical abnormality in integrating and perceiving sensory input creates these unusual and varied

savant performance An exceptional ability in a highly specialized area of functioning typically involving artistic, musical, or mathematical skills.

reactions to sounds, sights, and touches. Temple Grandin has argued that psychological researchers have not paid sufficient attention to this aspect of autistic disorder. Here are some of her comments on her own experience:

> When I was little, loud noises were also a problem, often feeling like a dentist's drill hitting a nerve. They actually caused pain. I was scared to death of balloons popping, because the sound was like an explosion in my ear. Minor noises that most people can tune out drove me to distraction. When I was in college, my roommate's hair dryer sounded like a jet plane taking off. (p. 67)

SELF-INJURY

Self-injurious behavior is one of the most bizarre and dangerous difficulties that can accompany autism and other pervasive developmental disorders. The most common forms of self-injury are repeated head banging and biting of the fingers and wrists (Rutter, Greenfield, & Lockyer, 1967). The resultant injuries may involve only minor bruises, or they can be severe enough to cause broken bones, brain damage, and even death. It is important that this self-injury not be misinterpreted as suicidal behavior. The child with autism does not have enough self-awareness to be truly suicidal. Instead, self-injury seems to have several possible causes, the most widely accepted of which is self-stimulation (Carr, 1977). Fortunately, self-injury can be treated effectively with behavior modification techniques, as we discuss later.

SAVANT PERFORMANCE

Nadia, a girl with autism, drew this picture of a horse and rider when she was 5 1/2 years old. Nadia's savant drawing ability diminished as she began to learn to communicate and relate to others.

One of the most intriguing characteristics of autism and pervasive developmental disorders is the occasional child who shows **savant performance**—an exceptional ability in a highly specialized area of functioning. Savant performance typically involves artistic, musical, or mathematical skills. The image on this page portrays the savant artistic abilities of Nadia, a girl with autism who drew numerous, highly sophisticated pictures during her preschool and early school-aged years. Nadia's artistic abilities are impressive and fascinating, especially if you pause to consider the usual drawings of a 5-year-old child. Even more puzzling is that Nadia's artistic abilities deteriorated as her symptoms improved following intensive therapy (Selfe, 1977).

No one has an adequate theory, let alone an explanation, for savant performance. Unfortunately, one thing does seems clear. Despite what many people had hoped, the existence of savant performance does not indicate that children with autistic disorder have superior intelligence. Most children with autism do not exhibit these special abilities, and savant performance sometimes is observed among people with mental retardation or brain injury. More specifically, approximately a quarter of children with autism have IQs below 55, about half have IQs between 55 and 70, and only one-fourth have IQs over 70 (Volkmar et al., 1994; see Table 14–5). Moreover, the IQ scores of children with autistic disorder behave like the IQs of normal children: They are stable over time, and they predict future educational attainment (Schreibman, 1988). We should note, however, that people with Asperger's disorder generally have normal intelligence.

Classification

BRIEF HISTORICAL PERSPECTIVE

The history of the classification of the pervasive developmental disorders is very brief. The syndrome of "early infantile autism" was first described in 1943 by the psychiatrist Leo Kanner (1894–1981) of Johns Hopkins University. Kanner reported on 11 children whose unusual symptoms were strikingly similar and whose difficulties were dramatically different from those of other emotionally disturbed children. Among the characteristics that Kanner noted were an inability to form relationships with others, delayed or noncommunicative speech, a demand for sameness in the environment, stereotyped play activities, and lack of imagination (Kanner, 1943). To Kanner's credit, contemporary diagnostic criteria are very similar to the symptoms he described.

Whereas Kanner's contributions are well known, mental health professionals have only recently recognized that the Viennese psychiatrist Hans Asperger (1944/1991) identified a very sim-

TABLE 14–5

IQ Scores for Patients with Autism and Other Pervasive Developmental Disorders Based on DSM-IV Field Trials

IQ SCORE	AUTISM		OTHER PERVASIVE DEVELOPMENTAL DISORDER	
	N	PERCENT	N	PERCENT
>70	118	26.0	122	50.8
55–69	197	43.4	61	25.4
<20–54	114	25.1	53	22.1
Unspecified	25	5.5	4	1.7

Source: *Based on F. R. Volkmar et al., 1994, Field trial for autistic disorder in DSM-IV,* American Journal of Psychiatry, *151, 1361–1367.*

Asperger's disorder A subtype of pervasive developmental disorder (new in DSM-IV) that is identical to autism (oddities in social interaction, stereotyped behavior), with the exception that there is no clinically significant delay in language.

ilar condition to autism at virtually the same time as Kanner. One important difference, however, was that Asperger's patients exhibited higher intellectual functioning. The distinction between Kanner's and Asperger's patients has been introduced into the formal diagnostic nomenclature in DSM-IV. **Asperger's disorder** is now listed as a subtype of pervasive developmental disorder. Descriptively, it is identical to autism, with the exception that the disorder involves no clinically significant delay in language.

CONTEMPORARY CLASSIFICATION
The diagnostic criteria for autistic disorder have evolved somewhat in the DSM, but the basic symptoms of the disorder have remained the same. The major change in the DSM-IV criteria, which are summarized in Table 14–6, was to define the symptoms more narrowly in order to reduce the high rate of false-positive diagnoses produced by earlier DSM criteria (Volkmar, 1996).

Epidemiology

Autism is an extremely rare disorder. Traditional estimates indicated that only 4–5 of every 10,000 children qualify for the diagnosis, although some recent statistics suggest 1 in 1,000 children are affected by the disorder (Bryson, 1996). Even the combined prevalence of autism and other pervasive developmental disorders is extremely low, perhaps 20 out of every 10,000 children (Wing & Gould, 1979).

At one time experts believed that autism was more common among the higher social classes, but research reveals that the apparent relation was created by referral bias (Gillberg & Schaumann, 1982). Parents with fewer resources may accept an initial misdiagnosis of mental retardation, but wealthier and better-educated parents continue to seek opinions from specialized professionals, who eventually recognize the autism (Schopler, Andrews, & Strapp, 1979). This referral bias creates a misleading correlation between social class and autism. The majority of children seen at prestigious specialty clinics have wealthy, educated parents; thus it may seem that the disorder is related to social class. However, no association is found when the general population is examined. This methodological problem is important, because it resulted in some misleading substantive conclusions. The supposed relation between autism and social status has been used as "evidence" to support the false views that children with autism have superior intellects and that the disorder is caused by successful but cold and distant parents.

A more promising epidemiological finding is that the risk for autism increases dramatically among the siblings of children with autistic disorder. The prevalence of autism among

Leo Kanner (1894–1981) was a U.S. psychiatrist who promoted the study of psychological problems among children. Kanner was noted for his identification of autism as a distinct psychological disorder.

TABLE 14–6

DSM-IV Diagnostic Criteria for Autistic Disorder

A. A TOTAL OF SIX (OR MORE) ITEMS FROM (1), (2), AND (3), WITH AT LEAST TWO FROM (1), AND ONE EACH FROM (2) AND (3):

1. Qualitative impairment in social interaction, as manifested by at least two of the following:
   a. marked impairment in the use of multiple nonverbal behaviors such as eye-to-eye gaze, facial expression, body postures, and gestures to regulate social interaction
   b. failure to develop peer relationships appropriate to developmental level
   c. a lack of spontaneous seeking to share enjoyment, interests, or achievements with other people
   d. lack of social or emotional reciprocity
2. Qualitative impairments in communication as manifested by at least one of the following:
   a. delay in, or total lack of, the development of spoken language (not accompanied by an attempt to compensate through alternative modes of communication such as gesture or mime)
   b. in individuals with adequate speech, marked impairment in the ability to initiate or sustain a conversation with others
   c. stereotyped and repetitive use of language or idiosyncratic language
   d. lack of varied, spontaneous make-believe play or social imitative play appropriate to developmental level
3. Restricted repetitive and stereotyped patterns of behavior, interests, and activities, as manifested by at least one of the following:
   a. encompassing preoccupation with one or more stereotyped and restricted patterns of interest that is abnormal either in intensity or focus
   b. apparently inflexible adherence to specific, nonfunctional routines or rituals
   c. stereotyped and repetitive motor mannerisms
   d. persistent preoccupation with parts or objects

B. DELAYS OR ABNORMAL FUNCTIONING IN AT LEAST ONE OF THE FOLLOWING AREAS, WITH ONSET PRIOR TO AGE 3 YEARS: (1) SOCIAL INTERACTION, (2) LANGUAGE AS USED IN SOCIAL COMMUNICATION, OR (3) SYMBOLIC OR IMAGINATIVE PLAY

the overall population is about .05 percent, whereas the prevalence among children with a sibling with autism is 2 to 5 percent, a 50- to 100-fold increase (Smalley, Asarnow, & Spence, 1988; Smalley & Collins, 1996). Although these statistics don't prove that autism has a genetic cause, they have encouraged research in this area. Finally, the fact that autism is 3 to 4 times more common among boys than among girls has prompted a search for a gender-linked etiology.

Etiological Considerations and Research

Autism appears to have multiple causes. Several problems that we have already discussed as causes of mental retardation also appear to cause autism. In addition, recent findings suggest that genetic factors play an important role in the etiology of the disorder. Before discussing evidence on biological etiologies of autism, we first briefly consider—and reject—environmental explanations.

PSYCHOLOGICAL AND SOCIAL FACTORS

For many years after Kanner identified autism, a number of professionals asserted that the disorder was caused by poor parenting. In particular, the disorder was said to be caused by parents who were cold, distant, and subtly rejecting of their children. This view was once so popular that, in 1960, *Time* published an account of these "refrigerator parents." The article claimed that the parents of children with autism "just happened to defrost long enough to produce a child" (Schreibman, 1988).

Evidence to support these speculations either has crumbled or failed to emerge. The observation that many parents of children with autism came from higher socioeconomic backgrounds once formed a major part of the justification for theories about "refrigerator parents." But, as we saw earlier, research has demonstrated that autism is not associated with high parental intelligence and social status. More directly, researchers have found no differences in the child-rearing styles of the parents of children with autism when compared with those of the parents of normal children (Cantwell, Baker, & Rutter, 1979).

The view that "refrigerator parents" cause autism also can be seriously challenged on logical grounds. How could a parent's emotional distance create such an extreme disturbance so early in life? Even the heinous abuse of infants does not cause symptoms that approach the form or severity of the problems found among children with autism. And no one has ever suggested that children with autism suffer anything approaching traumatic abuse. Moreover, if parents are emotionally distant from their disordered children, could this be a reaction to their children's gross disturbances? Attachment behaviors are maintained by reciprocal interaction. If an infant shows no normal interest in cuddling or mimicking, is it surprising if the parent becomes a bit distant?

Speculation that autism is caused by poor parenting can never be completely disproved. However, logic, the lack of empirical support for psychological hypotheses, and mounting research on biological causes suggest with virtual certainty that autism does not have a psychological cause. More basically, the rules of science require scientists to prove their hypotheses and not to force others to disprove them (see Research Methods in Chapter 1). Parents have been unfairly blamed for causing autism, and we greet further assertions that poor parenting causes autism with extreme skepticism.

BIOLOGICAL FACTORS

A number of findings indicate that biological abnormalities play an important role in the etiology of autism. These include the following:

- Nearly half of all children with autistic disorder develop seizure disorders by adolescence or early adult life (Tsai, 1996; Wing, 1988).
- Substantial increases in the prevalence of autism are found among children who have certain known genetic and infectious diseases (Reiss, Feinstein, & Rosenbaum, 1986).
- The prevalence of autism is higher among immediate relatives of individuals with autism than among the general population. Prevalence is particularly high among twin pairs (Bailey et al., 1995; Smalley et al., 1988).
- A disproportionate number of neurological abnormalities have been identified among children with autism by a variety of techniques ranging from evidence of pregnancy and birth complications to abnormal EEGs to findings based on postmortem examination of the brain (Bauman, 1996; Schreibman, 1988).

Autism as a Consequence of Known Biological Disorders   One view of these diverse findings is that autism has several different biological causes (Reiss, Feinstein, & Rosenbaum, 1986). In support of this view, one epidemiological study found that over half the cases of

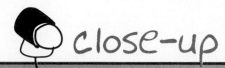

close-up

A Study of Facilitated Communication

Facilitated communication is a technique that has created both excited optimism and deep skepticism concerning the possibilities for treating autism. In facilitated communication, a "facilitator" supports the hand and arm of a disabled individual, thus allowing the child to type on a keyboard. The technique was developed in Australia by the educator Rosemary Crossley, who originally used it with people with motor disabilities such as cerebral palsy (Crossley & McDonald, 1980). It was brought to the United States by the Australian special educator Douglas Biklen, who has used the technique with autism. Biklen (1992) has claimed that the technique allows people with autism to express themselves. He reports that people with autism show insight, awareness, and literary talent. He also maintains that they sometimes report traumatic experiences during facilitated communication.

Many popular media sources, including nationally televised programs, have portrayed facilitated communication enthusiastically and uncritically. Eager for a breakthrough cure, many relatives of people with autism have embraced the technique. Is facilitated communication a legitimate breakthrough?

Whereas Biklen (1992) argues for a case study approach to facilitated communication and invariably finds positive results, independent investigators have conducted more systematic studies of the technique. One such study was carried out by Eberlin, McConnachie, Igel, and Volpe (1993), who investigated facilitated communication in 21 adolescents diagnosed with autism and 10 adult facilitators who were enthusiastic about the technique.

The research study involved four primary procedures. First, in the baseline condition the adolescents with autism were asked a variety of questions and allowed to type or otherwise communicate their answers to the best of their abilities. A special, alphabetically configured keyboard was used for typing in this and all other conditions. Second, in the pretest the adolescents responded to the same questions as in the first condition, but they were encouraged to type their answers with the aid of the facilitator, who was screened from hearing or seeing the questions being asked. Third, in the free response condition the adolescents were asked to respond to questions with the aid of the facilitator after the facilitator had received 20 hours of training in the technique. In this condition, the facilitator could see and hear the questions being asked. Finally, in the posttest the adolescents were asked to respond to the identical questions as in the first and second conditions with the aid of the facilitator. The facilitators were screened again in this last condition.

Test questions included items from an intelligence test and personal questions like "What is your favorite food?" Results indicated that responses to the questions were *worse* during the facilitated communication pretest than they had been during baseline. (Some of the adolescents were able to communicate with words or gestures on their own, at least to a minimal degree.) For example, 14 of 21 subjects were able to answer at least one personal question correctly during the baseline, but only 3 subjects did so with facilitated communication at pretest. (A few subjects could type accurately on their own, thus explaining the correct answers.) Scoring of correct answers was very liberal. For example, a response of "APPXYZ" was judged to be the correct answer "apple" on the pretest.

autism were associated with various known biological difficulties or disorders (Wing, 1988). These illnesses include many established causes of mental retardation, in particular fragile-X syndrome, tuberous sclerosis, PKU, rubella, and encephalitis (Reiss, Feinstein, & Rosenbaum, 1986). Other causes of mental retardation, however, are not associated with an increased prevalence of autism. For example, autism is not related to Down syndrome, the most common biological cause of mental retardation. Thus there are many brain pathologies that cause mental retardation but only a few specific disturbances that may cause both mental retardation and autism.

A Strongly Genetic Disorder?   In recent years a handful of studies have suggested that genetic factors also play an important role in the etiology of many, if not all, cases of autism. In the largest study to date, concordance rates for autism were 60 percent for MZ twins and 0 percent for DZ twins. Concordance rates for a social or cognitive disorder were 92 percent for MZ pairs and 10 percent for DZ pairs. Importantly, all twins in this new study were carefully screened for known heritable conditions (like fragile-X) that may have distorted the results of earlier studies. The fact that only a few conditions were detected by screening suggests that

A teacher attempting facilitated communication with a student with autistic disorder. Evidence indicates that the technique does not allow us to communicate with people with autistic disorder.

know the results of the next phase of study. Responses during the facilitated communication posttest, when facilitators were screened from the questions, were again significantly *worse* than baseline. Only five subjects answered at least one question correctly. Apparently, the facilitators were experiencing something akin to the effect of a Ouija board. Their own thoughts subtly influenced the "response" they "facilitated." In fact, the Science Working Group on Facilitated Communication of the American Psychological Association recently reviewed numerous studies of the technique and concluded that no evidence supports the effectiveness of facilitated communication (Jacobson, Mulick, & Schwartz, 1995).

"Breakthrough" treatments like facilitated communication have a ready audience. Mentally ill people and their relatives, frustrated professionals, and the popular media often are desperate for dramatic advances and therefore are uncritical and susceptible to inadequately documented claims. Although we share the desire for spectacular and successful treatments, once again we urge you to be healthy skeptics. The burden of proof falls upon the shoulders of the proponent of a treatment (see Research Methods in Chapter 1). When a truly effective new treatment is discovered, it will not be difficult to demonstrate its effectiveness using sound scientific methods.

Results obtained from a few subjects during the free response condition contrasted dramatically with the pretest findings. For example, before facilitated communication, one subject was able to communicate only by using two manual signs. When asked to define emotion during free response, however, with the aid of a facilitator this same subject typed "EMOTION ZOME-THIN* FEEL EXPREZ."

This response and other improvements with facilitated communication surely would be more impressive if we did not

most cases of autism are caused by a genetic abnormality that has yet to be detected, not by known genetic or infectious illnesses (Bailey et al., 1995). If so, autism is strongly but not completely genetic.

Treatment

Some controversy exists about the degree to which treatment can alter the prognosis for children with autistic disorder. Some people are optimistic about the possibilities of new or established treatments, whereas others are far more skeptical (see Close-Up, page 418). Everyone acknowledges, however, that there is no cure for autism. Thus the effectiveness of treatment must be compared against the natural course and outcome of the disorder.

COURSE AND OUTCOME

Unfortunately, autism is a lifelong disorder. In one study of 63 children with autism who were followed into adulthood, only 1 was functioning in what could be considered the normal range. Another 22 children achieved fair to good adjustment as adults. Even this group exhibited social isolation and odd behavior, however, and required some form of specialized supervision. The remainder of the people with autism in the study (over 60 percent) were living in institutions or other special settings at the time of follow-up (Rutter, 1970). This gloomy picture is consistent with the findings painted by several similar longitudinal investigations (Schreibman, 1988), although Asperger's disorder has a more optimistic prognosis (Gillberg, 1991).

Two developmental periods are especially important to the course of autism: the early preschool years and early adolescence. Children who have developed language skills by the age of 5 or 6 have a significantly more positive prognosis than do those who have no or severely limited speech at this age. Not surprisingly, higher IQ as measured during the early school years also is a positive prognostic indicator (Schreibman, 1988).

The other key developmental period in autism is early adolescence. During the early teen years, the cognitive and social skills of some children with autism improve notably, whereas those of others decline. Scientists cannot yet predict which path any given child will follow. Adolescence is also important because as many as half of all teenagers with autism develop seizure disorders (Wing, 1988).

MEDICATION

A huge variety of medications have been used to treat autism, including antipsychotics, antidepressants, amphetamines, psychedelics, and megavitamins. Unfortunately, none of these medications is an effective treatment for autism, and few show much promise.

Of all the medications, fenfluramine has generated the most excitement. Fenfluramine was used initially as an experimental treatment for autism based on the hypothesis that some symptoms of autism are caused by excess levels of serotonin (Geller et al., 1982). In several studies by the UCLA group that first experimented with the drug, fenfluramine was reported to reduce blood serotonin levels and to improve the cognitive performance and social behavior of children with autism (Geller et al., 1982; Ritvo et al., 1984).

Some investigators replicated the positive findings of the UCLA group (e.g., Campbell et al., 1986). Unfortunately, other researchers have found few positive benefits and several side effects associated with fenfluramine treatment. Fenfluramine does reduce serotonin blood levels, but several independent researchers have not found improved functioning among children with autism as a result (Ekman et al., 1989; Sherman et al., 1989). In any case, the effects of fenfluramine clearly are not dramatic. This fact, together with side effects that include the possibility of brain damage, has led some experts to recommend against further use of fenfluramine in treating autistic disorder (McDougle, Price, & Volkmar, 1994).

Other medications may help alleviate aspects of some symptoms of autism. Certain antipsychotic medications, particularly haloperidol (Haldol), help the management and education of children with autism. Recently, medications used in treating obsessive–compulsive disorder (e.g., clomipramine; see Chapter 6) have been found to help with some stereotyped behavior in autistic disorder (Lewis, 1996). However, all medications fall far short of "curing" autism (Lewis, 1996; Schreibman, 1988).

PSYCHOTHERAPY: INTENSIVE BEHAVIOR MODIFICATION

Behavior therapists have focused on treating the specific symptoms of autism, including communication deficits, self-care skills, and self-stimulatory or self-destructive behavior. Even within these different symptom areas, behavior modification emphasizes very specific and small goals. In attempting to teach language, for example, the therapist might spend hours, days, or weeks teaching the pronunciation of a specific syllable. Months of intensive effort may be needed to teach a small number of words and phrases. The lack of imitation among many children with autism is one reason why so much effort goes into achieving such modest goals.

If the first goal of behavior modification is to identify very specific target behaviors, the second is to gain control over these behaviors through the use of reinforcement and punishment. Unlike normal children, who are reinforced by social interest and approval, children with autism do not understand ordinary praise, or they may find all social interaction unpleasant. For these reasons, the child's successful efforts must be rewarded repeatedly with primary reinforcers such as a favorite food, at least in the beginning phases of treatment.

Similar detailed strategies are used to teach children with autism other language skills. In the hope of speeding the process, some therapists have used sign language to teach communication to children with autism (Carr, 1982). Unfortunately, this method has not led to a breakthrough. The communication deficits in autism apparently are more basic than receptive or expressive problems with spoken language. Behavior modification remains a painfully slow process that differs greatly from the way in which children normally learn to speak. The intensity and detail of these necessary efforts remind us that normal children come into the world remarkably well equipped to acquire language.

In other areas of intervention, behavior therapists have been fairly successful in teaching self-care skills and less successful in teaching social responsiveness. As Schreibman (1988) noted in her review of attempts to modify the social isolation of children with autistic disorder, "It is perhaps prophetic that the behavior characteristic which most uniquely defines autism, is also the one that has proven the most difficult to understand and treat" (p. 118).

Although behavior therapy often focuses on specific target behaviors, ultimately the important question is: To what extent does treatment improve the entire syndrome of autism? Research has demonstrated that children with autism can learn specific target behaviors, but do intensive training efforts bring about improvements that are clinically significant?

An optimistic answer to this question has been provided by O. Ivar Lovaas, a psychologist at UCLA who is an acknowledged leader in behavior modification for autism. In a comprehensive report on the efforts of his research team, Lovaas (1987) compared the outcomes of three groups of children with autism: 19 children who received intensive behavior modification; 19 children who were referred to the program but who received less intensive treatment due to the unavailability of therapists; and 21 children who were seen elsewhere. In this study, all children received independent diagnoses of autism. Children with extremely low IQ scores were excluded, and treatment began before the children were 4 years of age. The children in the treatment group received the types of interventions described above, including both reinforcement and punishment procedures. In fact, they were treated 40 hours a week for a period of more than 2 years.

No differences among the three groups of children were found before treatment began. Assessments following treatment were conducted between the ages of 6 and 7, at the time when the children ordinarily would have finished the first grade. In the intensive behavior modification group, 9 children (47 percent) completed first grade in a normal school. Eight more children (42 percent) passed first grade in a special class for children who cannot speak. In comparison, only 1 child (2 percent) in the two control groups completed first grade in a normal classroom. In addition, 18 children (45 percent) in the control groups completed first-grade classes for **aphasic** children.

These data provide a reason for some optimism, and we applaud the efforts of Lovaas and others who have used behavior therapy to teach skills to children with autism. Despite the fact that autism seems to be caused by neurological abnormalities, the most effective treatment for the disorder is highly structured and intensive operant behavior therapy (Rutter, 1996; Schreibman, 1988). Still, cautions must be raised. Are the children who passed first grade functioning normally in other respects? Would treatment have been as effective if it had not begun so early in life? Because pretreatment IQ predicted outcome (Lovaas, 1987), does behavior modification produce dramatic changes only with children who are high-functioning? What about the 53 percent of children who received intensive therapy but who were not in normal classrooms? Why have other researchers and clinicians found much more modest benefits following intensive behavior modification?

Perhaps the most important question about the effectiveness of behavior modification is its cost. Remember that the children in the intensive behavior modification group were treated for 40 hours per week for a period of more than 2 years. At the same time, children in the "limited treatment" control group received almost 10 hours of weekly treatment, yet they showed few improvements. The expenses associated with early but effective treatment clearly are far less than those involved in a lifetime of care (Lovaas, 1987). Still, our question is this: How do we, as a society, justify devoting large amounts of resources to the rare problem of autism?

aphasia   The loss or impairment of previously acquired abilities in language comprehension or production that cannot be explained by sensory or motor defects or by diffuse brain dysfunction.

O. Ivar Lovaas, a psychologist at UCLA, is a leader in using behavior modification to treat children with autistic disorder.

getting help

Psychological Disorders of Childhood

Childhood disorders often go unrecognized, even by professionals. One reason for this is that children are limited in their ability to understand their problems and in their motivation to seek treatment. In addition, scientific information about psychological disorders of childhood is less complete than for adult disorders because less research has been done. Perhaps for this reason, self-help books and the Internet contain a lot of dubious "information." However, getting good information is an essential first step toward getting help for an infant, child, or adolescent with a psychological problem.

The National Institute of Child Health and Human Development (NICHD), the primary federal agency charged with improving knowledge about the health of children and families, is one of the best resources for objective information about a variety of problems and disorders among children. Visit the NICHD on the Internet at http://www.nih.gov/nichd/ if you want basic, scientific information on a timely or controversial issue—for example, the use of the new medication secretin in treating autistic disorder. The American Academy of Child and Adolescent Psychiatry, on the Internet at http://www.aacap.org/, also maintains a Web site with good summary information on a variety of disorders and problems that affect children. For more detailed, practical information on externalizing disorders, the most common category of childhood problems, two self-help books that

we recommend are *Taking Charge of ADHD* by Russell Barkley, and *Parenting the Strong-Willed Child* by Rex Forehand and Nicholas Long.

Pediatricians and family physicians may prescribe medications commonly used to treat childhood disorders such as psychostimulants for ADHD or antidepressants. If you are looking for psychotherapy, the child's primary care physician also should be able to provide a referral to a mental health professional. It is best if children are seen by a psychologist or other mental health professional who specializes in treating children and families. Specialists know more about the unique nature of childhood disorders, and they are more experienced in child and family therapy and in relating to children of different ages.

Before the first appointment, the child's parents may want to talk to the mental health professional, and they definitely should talk to the child about why they are going to therapy and what the child can expect to happen. Parents should expect that they, too, will be involved in the treatment process, or at a minimum, that they will be informed about the nature, goals, and progress of treatment. During the first appointment, the mental health professional should make it clear exactly what kind of information will be shared with parents, and what will be kept confidential. Parents have a right to know about their child's treatment, but children also have a right to privacy—more so the older they are. ✹

Summary

Psychological problems that arise more commonly among children than adults are listed in the DSM-IV category "Disorders Usually First Diagnosed in Infancy, Childhood, or Adolescence." The most important disorders in this category are the various **externalizing disorders.** Externalizing disorders create difficulties for the child's external world. They are characterized by children's failure to control their behavior according to the expectations of others. The most familiar externalizing disorder is **attention-deficit/hyperactivity disorder (ADHD),** a prevalent behavior problem that is particularly noticeable in school and is characterized by inattention, overactivity, and impulsivity. ADHD often is contrasted with **oppositional defiant disorder (ODD),** an externalizing disorder characterized by negative, hostile, and defiant behavior that is also prevalent among school-aged children. **Conduct disorder (CD)** is a similar problem to ODD, except the rule violations are much more serious and conduct disorder is more common among adolescents than younger children.

Internalizing disorders are psychological problems that primarily affect the child's internal world, for example, excessive anxiety or sadness. The DSM-IV does not list internalizing disorders as separate psychological disorders of childhood but instead notes that children may qualify for many "adult" diagnoses, such as anxiety or mood disorders. The DSM does include 26 additional childhood disorders, such as **learning disorder** and **separation anxiety disorder.** Some of these additional disorders are relatively rare conditions; other DSM categories are questionable in terms of their status as "mental disorders."

At least 12 percent of the 63 million children living in the United States suffer from a mental disorder. Boys are more likely to be identified as having psychological problems during childhood, but girls are found to have more difficulties in adolescence and early adult life. Family adversity is a particularly important risk factor for externalizing problems, and epidemiological data indicate that suicide has been a growing problem among teens.

Troubled attachments are one of the social factors that may play a role in causing children's emotional problems. Other research indicates that parents are most effective when they are **authoritative:** loving and firm in disciplining their children. **Coercion** is a more specific parenting problem that occurs when parents reinforce children's misbehavior by giving in to their demands. Conflict and inconsistent discipline are other parenting problems that may arise when parents are unhappily married or divorced. Other social factors that contribute to the etiology of internalizing and especially of externalizing problems include television violence, deviant peer groups, poverty, and societal attitudes.

Biological factors are thought to be more critical to attention-deficit/hyperactivity disorder than to oppositional defiant disorder; these include **temperament,** genetics, and neuropsychological abnormalities.

Biological risks and problems in **socialization** may combine to produce psychological factors that cause or maintain children's psychological disorders. Lack of self-control, a tendency to over-attribute aggressive intentions to others, and less developed moral reasoning are some of the psychological characteristics related to externalizing disorders. Insecure working models of attachment or problems with emotion regulation may foreshadow the development of internalizing problems.

Few treatments for anxiety or mood disorders have been developed specifically for children, with the exception of some encouraging research on the combination of family and cognitive-behavior therapy. The most promising treatments for externalizing disorders include **psycho-stimulants** for attention-deficit/hyperactivity disorder, **behavioral family therapy** for oppositional defiant disorder, and multisystemic family therapy for treating conduct disorders and delinquent youth. The difficulty of changing externalizing problems is underscored by the limited success of numerous attempts to treat conduct disorders and **juvenile delinquency** in families, in group homes, and in the juvenile justice system. The **pervasive developmental disorders** involve profound disturbances in relationship, stereotyped activities, and communication difficulties. **Autistic disorder** is the most widely researched pervasive developmental disorder. Social impairments in autism may be relatively mild oddities, but they also may include extreme difficulties in which there is little awareness of the existence of others. About half of all children with autism fail to develop communicative speech, and the remainder have either highly restricted language abilities or striking oddities in speech. Finally, many people with autism spend hours engaging in self-stimulation or compulsively adhere to rigid daily routines.

Other difficulties associated with autism and the pervasive developmental disorders include apparent sensory deficits and self-injurious behavior. **Savant performance** is an exceptional ability at performing mental feats such as rapid mathematical calculations. Despite such unusual abilities, most people with pervasive developmental disorders do not have exceptional intelligence; rather, they have mental retardation. One exception is **Asperger's disorder,** characterized by the same difficulties that are found in autism except that language acquisition is not impaired.

The pervasive developmental disorders are rare conditions, and they almost certainly are caused by biological abnormalities. Several know causes of mental retardation may also cause pervasive developmental disorders (for example, fragile-X syndrome). Recent evidence also suggests that genetics plays an important role. At this time, there is no easy, effective treatment for these conditions. Intensive behavior modification has shown much promise as a treatment, but the expense and effort involved are considerable. Without intensive treatment over a prolonged period of time, the prognosis for the pervasive developmental disorders is a gloomy one. The majority of people with these conditions require intensive, lifelong care, often within an institution.

Critical Thinking

1. Under what circumstances do you think a parent or teacher might be especially biased or inaccurate in assessing a child's problem behavior? Do you think depressed, anxious, or angry parents or teachers sometimes project their own concerns on to children? How could you detect such inaccuracies, either for individual cases or on standardized instruments?

2. Family adversity is a risk factor for various externalizing problems, but many children are resilient in the face of adversity. What factors do you think help to make children resilient in the face of difficult life circumstances?

3. What are your personal thoughts on the use of psychostimulant medication? Do you think it is appropriate to use medication to help children behave in school? How might your feelings change if you had a child with attention-deficit/hyperactivity disorder?

15

Mental Health and the Law

The *insanity defense* may be the most familiar of the intriguing and often controversial issues found at the intersection of abnormal psychology and the law. When judges or juries determine that defendants are insane, perpetrators are not held to be legally responsible for their actions, even though they have committed a crime. Instead of going to jail, insane defendants are likely to be confined in a mental institution. But what is insanity, and how does it differ from mental illness? As we address these and other questions in this chapter, you will learn that the legal system views abnormal behavior very differently from the way it is understood by mental health professionals.

Overview

In addition to the insanity defense and related questions of criminal responsibility, the topics considered in this chapter include several issues related to mental hospitals, especially involuntary commitment, deinstitutionalization, and the rights of mental patients. The confinement of an in-

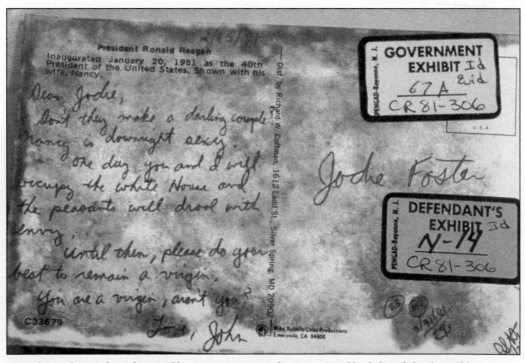

One of several notes that John Hinckley wrote to actress Jodie Foster. Hinckley believed that he could win Foster's love by gaining notoriety, a delusion that apparently motivated him to attempt to assassinate former President Ronald Reagan.

dividual against his or her will is a serious action that must balance broad societal values against the needs and rights of the individual. Recall that many political dissidents in the former Soviet Union were confined to institutions to "treat" their "mental illnesses."

We also discuss legal intervention in families in this chapter, with an emphasis on the issues of child abuse and custody disputes after divorce. Concerns about serious mental illness are the exception, not the rule, in custody and abuse cases. However, predictions about children's emotional well-being often are vital to decisions in these cases—and the legal decisions, in turn, can have far-reaching implications for children's emotional and physical health.

Finally, we consider some of the legal responsibilities of mental health professionals to their clients, especially confidentiality and the limitations on it. Confidentiality and other topics in psychology and the law are not only of interest to legal and mental health professionals, but they also have broad implications for society. The manner in which we treat the most disturbed members of our society often marks the boundaries that define some of our most basic legal rights and responsibilities as citizens.

As a way of introducing the topic of mental health and the law, we consider an infamous and successful use of the insanity defense: the acquittal of John Hinckley. In 1981, Hinckley attempted to assassinate Ronald Reagan, the president of the United States. Our account is based on information in two detailed books on the assassination attempt (Clarke, 1990; Low, Jeffries, & Bonnie, 1986), and it is summarized in the following case study.

case study

John Hinckley and the Insanity Defense

On March 30, 1981, John Hinckley stood outside the Washington Hilton hotel, drew a revolver from his raincoat pocket, and fired six shots at President Ronald Reagan. The president and three other men were wounded. The president rapidly recovered from his potentially fatal wound, but the presidential press secretary, James Brady, was permanently crippled by a shot that struck him just above the left eye. Hinckley was charged with attempted assassination, but his trial resulted in a verdict of "not guilty by reason of insanity."

Hinckley, who came from a wealthy family, had never been convicted of a crime. He had a history of unusual behavior, however, and had expressed violent intentions. Hinckley had read several books on famous assassinations and had joined the American Nazi Party. In fact, he was expelled from the Nazi Party in 1979 because of his continual advocacy of violence. A particular oddity was Hinckley's obsession with the actress Jodie Foster, whom he had seen play the role of a child prostitute in the movie *Taxi Driver*. In an attempt to win her favor, Hinckley adopted much of the style of Foster's movie rescuer, Travis Bickle. This included acquiring weapons similar to those used by the movie character and stalking the president, much as the movie character had stalked a political candidate.

Hinckley repeatedly tried to contact Foster in real life and succeeded a few times, but his approaches were consistently rejected. He came to believe that the only way to win her over was through dramatic action. Less than 2 hours before he shot the president, he completed a letter to Foster, which said:

> Jodie, I would abandon this idea of getting Reagan in a second if I could only win your heart and live out the rest of my life with you, whether it be in total obscurity or whatever.

> I will admit to you that the reason I'm going ahead with this attempt now is because I just cannot wait any longer to impress you. I've got to do something now to make you understand, in no uncertain terms, that I am doing all of this for your sake! By sacrificing my freedom and possibly my life, I hope to change your mind about me. This letter is being written only an hour before I leave for the Hilton Hotel. Jodie, I'm asking you to please look into your heart and at least give me the chance, with this historical deed, to gain your respect and love.

Hinckley's trial centered on the question of his sanity, or as one author put it, whether he was "mad" or merely angry (Clarke, 1990). Both the defense and the prosecution called numerous expert witnesses to determine whether Hinckley was legally sane or insane. According to the federal law that was in effect at the time, the prosecution had to prove "beyond a reasonable doubt" that Hinckley was indeed sane. That is, the prosecution had to establish that mental disease had not either (1) created an irresistible impulse that made it impossible for Hinckley to resist attempting to kill the president, or (2) so impaired Hinckley's thinking that he did not appreciate the

continued

wrongfulness of his actions. (The burden of proof and the definition of insanity in the federal law subsequently were changed because of Hinckley's acquittal, as we discuss later in this chapter.)

All the prosecution's experts concluded that Hinckley was sane; all the defense's experts concluded that Hinckley was insane. The prosecution's experts called attention to the fact that Hinckley's actions were planned in advance and to Hinckley's awareness that his actions would have consequences, including possible imprisonment or death. He chose six deadly "devastator" bullets from an abundance of ammunition, and he fired them all accurately in less than 3 seconds. Defense experts emphasized his erratic behavior, particularly his obsession with Jodie Foster. One psychiatrist suggested, for example, that the president and other victims were merely "bit players" in Hinck-ley's delusion that through his "historic deed" he would be united with Foster in death.

Hinckley was found not guilty by reason of insanity. We don't know what factors influenced the jury to come to this decision or whether they found him insane based on the "irresistible impulse" or the "right from wrong" part of the insanity defense. In any event, the verdict meant that Hinckley received no prison sentence. Instead, he was ordered into a mental hospital to be treated in confinement for an unspecified period of time. As of now, Hinckley remains confined in St. Elizabeth's Hospital outside Washington, D.C. Theoretically, he could be released if he is considered by the hospital staff no longer to be dangerous to himself or to others. On the other hand, Hinckley could remain confined to the hospital for the rest of his life. In fact, he has unsuccessfully petitioned for release on several occasions. ⚟

insanity   A legal term referring to a defendant's state of mind at the time of committing a crime. An insane individual is not held legally responsible for his or her actions because of a mental disease or defect.

John Hinckley obviously was emotionally disturbed, and legally he was determined to be insane when he shot the president. As is illustrated in this case study, however, the insanity defense is an area of conflict between mental health and the law. One conflict involves the unreliability of expert testimony, as different mental health experts often disagree about a given defendant's sanity, thus creating a "battle of the experts" (Low, Jeffries, & Bonnie, 1986). A more basic conflict centers on the difference between the legal concept of sanity and the psychological concept of mental disorder, as we discuss shortly. An even more fundamental conflict involves the opposing assumptions that the legal and mental health systems make about the causes of and responsibility for human behavior—that is, free will versus determinism.

Free Will versus Determinism

Criminal law assumes that human behavior is the product of *free will*, the capacity to make choices and freely act on them. Because behavior is assumed to be a product of free will, in the eyes of the law people are responsible for their own actions. When a person violates the law, the individual is held accountable. This is the legal concept known as *criminal responsibility*.

In contrast, mental health professionals assume that human behavior is determined by biological, psychological, and social forces. This assumption, known as *determinism*, is made by all psychologists (except humanists; see Chapter 2), but it is particularly obvious in the study of abnormal behavior. Mental disorders and the actions that stem from them are not viewed as choices but as conditions that are outside of voluntary control. Just as the concept of responsibility follows from an assumption of free will, a consequence of the deterministic view is that no one is ultimately "responsible" for his or her actions.

The assumption of determinism is not arbitrary. Rather, it is essential if psychology is to be a science. The causes of human behavior cannot be studied without assuming that behavior is determined by factors that can be measured and perhaps controlled. To draw an analogy, if meteorologists assumed that hurricanes were caused by "free will," they would have nothing to study. Imagine a weather forecast in which the meteorologist says, "Well, I wonder where Hurricane Bob will choose to head tonight." If meteorologists wish to have a scientific discipline, they must assume that the path of a hurricane is determined, that it is caused by forces that are potentially knowable. Similarly, free will is a concept that is foreign to psychologists when they are thinking as scientists, because it is an unscientific concept.

Assumptions about free will and determinism come into particular conflict in the case of the insanity defense. In U.S. law, **insanity** is an exception to criminal responsibility. The legally insane individual is assumed *not* to be acting out of free will. As a result, like John Hinckley, the legally insane are held not to be criminally responsible for their actions. Ironically, the insanity defense reaffirms the legal system's view that people are responsible for their actions by calling attention to the rare exceptions when they are not.

Thus debates about the insanity defense involve a broad conflict of philosophies, as well as differences about the specifics of a given case. Is human behavior a product of free will, or is it determined by biological, psychological, and social forces? Are people with mental disorders responsible for their actions, or are they not responsible?

IS MENTAL ILLNESS A MYTH?

The American psychiatrist Thomas Szasz (1963, 1970) abandons the traditional deterministic view held by behavioral scientists and embraces a humanistic philosophy that puts free will at the center of human behavior. In fact, Szasz asserts that the concept of mental illness is a myth. According to Szasz, abnormal behavior must be defined relative to some social or moral standard. Because there is no objective standard, there can be no objective mental disease. Thus Szasz argues that mental disorders are subjective "problems in living," not objective diseases.

The logical conclusion of Szasz's view of free will is that all people—even people with emotional disorders—*are* responsible for their actions. Consistent with this position, Szasz has argued that the insanity defense should be abolished (Szasz, 1963).

The psychiatrist Thomas Szasz has called attention to fundamental conflicts about individual rights and responsibilities in the philosophies of the legal and mental health systems.

RIGHTS AND RESPONSIBILITIES

In arguing for a broader concept of responsibility, Szasz also fights for broader recognition of human dignity and individual rights. In the law, rights and responsibilities go hand in hand. When responsibilities are lost, rights are lost too. When responsibilities are assumed, rights are gained. Thus, while opposing the insanity defense, Szasz simultaneously supports greater recognition of the rights of mental patients who become involved in either the legal or the mental health system. The basic, human rights of mental patients sometimes have been trampled on, and much concern has been raised about their better protection. Szasz argues that the mentally ill should be treated identically to the mentally healthy in terms of both social responsibility and social dignity.

Szasz's concerns about the "myth of mental illness" extend beyond the individual to broad social abuses. He asserts that the concept of mental illness can be invoked to obscure the logic of behavior that runs counter to social standards and to blame social deviance on disease instead of on society. This clearly happened in the former Soviet Union, where some dissidents were judged insane for holding political beliefs that conflicted with those of the Communist Party. Their "diagnosis" justified their confinement to mental hospitals. Szasz asserts that similar, albeit far more subtle abuses of the "myth of mental illness" occur in the United States.

Not surprisingly, Szasz's view that mental illness is a myth is generally seen as an extreme—and inaccurate—position (Appelbaum, 1994). Nevertheless, Szasz has contributed greatly to issues in mental health and the law by cutting to the heart of philosophical assumptions. Many debates about the rights and responsibilities of people with a mental disorder ultimately turn on contrasting views about whether or how much mental illness impairs free will. As we will see in numerous examples in this chapter, the core of the dilemma is how to reconcile concepts of individual rights and responsibilities, which follow from an assumption of free will, with the deterministic view that is at the core of a scientific approach to understanding human behavior.

Mental Health, Criminal Responsibility, and Procedural Rights

Criminal law assumes that mental disorders sometimes may affect an individual's capacity to exercise his or her rights and responsibilities. Defendants who are judged *incompetent to stand trial* are thought to be unable to exercise their right to participate in their own trial defense. Defendants who are found not guilty by reason of insanity are determined not to be criminally responsible for their actions. We consider each of these issues in this section.

The Insanity Defense

The idea that mental disability should limit criminal responsibility dates back to ancient Greek and Hebrew traditions and was evident in early English law. Records indicate cases where English kings pardoned murderers because of "madness," and later judicial decisions similarly excused some criminals who were "madmen" or "idiots" (Reisner & Slobogin, 1990). The emerging rationale underlying many of these insanity acquittals was that the defendant lacked the capacity to distinguish "good from evil" or what eventually became known as the inability to distinguish right from wrong. This ground for the insanity defense was codified in 1843, after Daniel M'Naghten was found not guilty of murder by reason of insanity.

M'NAGHTEN TEST

M'Naghten was a British subject who claimed that the "voice of God" had ordered him to kill Prime Minister Robert Peel, but who mistakenly murdered Peel's private secretary instead. His insanity acquittal raised considerable controversy and caused the House of Lords to devise the following insanity test:

> To establish a defense on the ground of insanity, it must be clearly proved that, at the time of the committing of the act, the party accused was laboring under such a defect of reason, from disease of the mind, as not to know the nature and quality of the act he was doing; or, if he did know it, that he did not know he was doing what was wrong. [*Regina v. M'Naghten,* 8 Eng. Rep. 718, 722 (1843)]

Subsequently known as the *M'Naghten test,* this rule clearly articulated the "right from wrong" principle for determining insanity. If at the time a criminal act is committed a mental disease or defect prevents a criminal from knowing the wrongfulness of his or her actions, the criminal can be found to be *not guilty by reason of insanity (NGRI).* The "right from wrong" ground established in the *M'Naghten* case continues to be the major focus of the insanity defense in U.S. law today. However, subsequent developments first broadened and later narrowed the grounds for determining insanity.

IRRESISTIBLE IMPULSE AND THE PRODUCT TEST

Later in the nineteenth century, the insanity defense was broadened in the United States when a second ground for determining insanity was introduced—the so-called *irresistible impulse test.* The irresistible impulse test determined that defendants also could be found insane if they were unable to control their actions because of mental disease. *Parsons v. State* was one of the first cases in which the irresistible impulse test was adopted [81 Ala. 577, 596, 2 So. 854 (1886)]. In this 1886 case, an Alabama court ruled that defendants could be judged insane if they could not "avoid doing the act in question" because of mental disease. The rationale for the irresistible impulse test was that when people are unable to control their behavior, the law can have no effect on deterring crimes. *Deterrence,* the idea that people will avoid committing crimes because they fear being punished for them, is a major public policy goal of criminal law. In the *Parsons* case, however, the court reasoned that convicting people for acts that they could not control would serve no deterrence purpose. In such cases, a finding of NGRI was justified.

A 1954 ruling by the Washington, D.C., federal circuit court in *Durham v. United States* further broadened the insanity defense [214 F.2d 862 (D.C. Cir. 1954)]. Known as the *product test,* the Durham opinion indicated that an accused is not criminally responsible if his or her unlawful act was the product of mental disease or defect. The ruling made no attempt to define either "product" or "mental disease." In fact, the terms were purposely designed to be very broad. The vague product test was justified as a way of allowing mental health professionals wide discretion in using their expertise in determining insanity and testifying in court.

Problems arose in applying the product test, however, including the fact that some mental health professionals decided to include psychopathy (antisocial personality disorder in DSM-IV) as one of the "mental diseases" that could be used as a basis for an insanity defense. This created a circular problem: Antisocial personality disorder is defined primarily by a pattern of criminal behavior, yet the same criminal behavior could be used to substantiate that the perpetrator was insane (Campbell, 1990). This and other problems with the definition of mental disease under the product test came to a halt when the *Durham* decision was overruled in 1972 (Reisner & Slobogin, 1990).

LEGISLATIVE ACTIONS

In 1955, a year after the original *Durham* decision, the American Law Institute drafted model legislation designed to address various problems with the previous rules for determining insanity. The model legislation is important because it subsequently was adopted by the majority of states. The rule indicates that:

> A person is not responsible for criminal conduct if at the time of such conduct as a result of mental disease or defect he lacks substantial capacity either to appreciate the criminality [wrongfulness] of his conduct or to conform his conduct to the requirements of the law.

This definition of insanity combines the M'Naghten rule and the irresistible impulse test, although it softens the requirements somewhat with the term *substantial capacity*. (Compare this with the language used in the M'Naghten rule.) A second component of the American Law Institute's model legislation, which also has been enacted by many states, excluded a history of criminal behavior from being used to define "mental disease or defect." This eliminates the problem of circularity caused by the antisocial personality disorder diagnosis.

The most recent developments in the law governing the insanity defense occurred as a result of the acquittal of John Hinckley. Following the controversy over this case, both the American Bar Association and the American Psychiatric Association recommended the elimination of the irresistible impulse component of the insanity defense. These organizations judged this strand of the insanity defense to be more controversial and unreliable than the right from wrong standard (Mackay, 1988). Consistent with these recommendations, federal law was changed. The Insanity Defense Reform Act was passed in 1984 and defined the insanity defense as follows:

> It is an affirmative defense to a prosecution under any federal statute that, at the time of the commission of acts constituting the offense, the defendant, as a result of severe mental disease or defect, was unable to appreciate the nature and quality or the wrongfulness of his acts. Mental disease or defect does not otherwise constitute a defense. (Title 18 of the United States Code)

GUILTY BUT MENTALLY ILL

Several states have since echoed this change in federal law by enacting similar legislation. Another change prompted by the Hinckley case was the promotion of the new verdict of *guilty but mentally ill (GBMI),* which has been enacted by 13 states (American Bar Association, 1995). Defendants can be found guilty but mentally ill if it is demonstrated that they are guilty of the crime, were mentally ill at the time it was committed, but were not legally insane at that time. The GBMI verdict was designed as a compromise to NGRI. The GBMI verdict holds defendants criminally responsible for their crimes but acknowledges their mental disorder and helps ensure that they receive treatment (Mackay, 1988). Thus a defendant found GBMI can be sentenced in the same manner as any criminal, but the court can order treatment for the mental disorder as well. Some evidence indicates, however, that rather than replace NGRI verdicts, the GBMI verdict is most often used in cases in which defendants simply would have been found guilty (Smith & Hall, 1982).

Recent developments clearly represent a move toward restricting the insanity defense. The furor surrounding the high-profile Hinckley case was not unlike the controversy that surrounded the high-profile M'Naghten case more than 100 years earlier. Ironically, the Hinckley case also caused the insanity defense to be revised to resemble the original M'Naghten test (Mackay, 1988). As it was for a time after 1843, the most common contemporary standard for determining legal insanity is the inability to distinguish right from wrong.

BURDEN OF PROOF

In addition to the definition of insanity, the *burden of proof* substantially influences the meaning and likely success of the insanity defense. Under U.S. criminal law, the defendant is assumed to be innocent until proven guilty "beyond a reasonable doubt." The burden of proof thus rests with the prosecution, and the *standard of proof* is a very high one—beyond a reasonable doubt. But must the prosecution also prove beyond a reasonable doubt that a defendant is sane?

further thoughts

The Battered Woman Syndrome as a Defense

For centuries large numbers of women have been physically beaten by their husbands or lovers. This fact is easy to document, because wife battering has been institutionalized for much of Western history—and it remains an accepted practice in parts of the world today. For example, the familiar phrase "rule of thumb" refers to the size of the stick, no thicker than a man's thumb, with which men were legitimately allowed to beat their wives according to common law.

Nevertheless, spousal abuse has been recognized as a social problem only in the last few decades. During these years, laws have been passed that for the first time protect wives from their husbands' physical and sexual abuse. Even today, however, in some states a husband cannot be charged with raping his wife no matter what the circumstances of forced sex might be. American laws have protected people from assaults by strangers much more stringently than they have protected people from assault by members of their own family.

The prevalence of spouse abuse in the United States today is a matter of political and scientific debate, in large part because of disagreements about what constitutes abuse. Some startling facts about family violence cannot be disputed, however. For example, FBI statistics indicate that approximately one-third of all female murder victims are killed by a husband or a boyfriend.

Battered women often remain in the abusive relationship for incomprehensibly long periods of time. To outsiders, the battered woman's reluctance to leave the relationship seems foolish, even masochistic. To the battered woman herself, however, leaving the relationship often seems wrong or impossible. She may feel trapped in an abusive relationship by finances or out of concern for her children; chronic abuse may cause her to lose perspective on the extent of her maltreatment; or she simply may see no viable alternative to subjecting herself to repeated abuse. Some women who have been constantly threatened, intimidated, and beaten by their husbands or boyfriends eventually escape the abuse only by killing their tormentors. According to a report of the American Psychological Association (1995), approximately 1,000 women kill their current or former batterer each year. (A similar circumstance arises when an abused child kills a parent or stepparent.) Is this violence in response to violence ever justified?

The killing of an abuser clearly is justified in the U.S. law when the victim's life is in immediate danger. In such a circumstance, the action can easily be construed as self-defense. In other cases, however, the killing of a batterer takes place when the threat of abuse may be looming in the background but is not immediate. In this situation, a woman might still plead self-defense. According to contemporary trial practice, the defense may depend heavily on what has been called the battered woman syndrome.

The **battered woman syndrome** is a term coined by the psychologist Lenore Walker (1979) to describe her observations about the psychological effects of being chronically abused by a husband or lover. Two aspects of the syndrome are especially crucial to its use as a defense. First, Walker discusses what she

---

battered woman syndrome
A controversial classification of the common psychological effects of spousal abuse. Includes a tension-building phase leading up to violence, the battering incident itself, and a stage of loving contrition, during which the batterer apologizes. According to some experts, this induces learned helplessness in battered women.

In fact, about one-third of all states require the prosecution to prove a defendant's sanity beyond a reasonable doubt, and until the Insanity Defense Reform Act was passed in 1984, this also was the practice in federal courts. In the Hinckley trial, the prosecution was obliged to prove that Hinckley was sane beyond a reasonable doubt, a case they failed to make. Changes implemented in federal law following the Hinckley case shifted the burden of proof. In federal courts the defense now must prove defendants' insanity rather than the prosecution having to prove their sanity. Insanity must be proven by the standard of "clear and convincing evidence," a stringent standard but not as exacting as "beyond a reasonable doubt." About two-thirds of states also now place the burden of proof on the defense, but the standard of proof typically is less restrictive than that found in federal law—"the preponderance of the evidence." Thus the insanity defense has been narrowed even further by shifting the burden of proof from the prosecution to the defense in federal law and in many states (American Bar Association, 1995).

DEFINING "MENTAL DISEASE OR DEFECT"

An issue of obvious importance to the mental health professions is the precise meaning of the term *mental disease or defect,* which is used in one form or another in all the legal definitions of insanity. The American Law Institute's proposal specifically excludes antisocial personality disorder, but would any other diagnosis listed in the DSM qualify? The 1984 federal legislation indicates that the mental disease must be "severe," but what does this mean?

The question of which mental disorders qualify for the "mental disease or defect" component of the insanity defense is unresolved, although the legal definition of "mental discalls the "cycle of violence," which includes three stages: (1) a tension-building phase leading up to violence; (2) the battering incident itself; and (3) a stage of loving contrition, during which the batterer apologizes and attempts to make amends for his actions. A second crucial aspect of Walker's battered woman syndrome is her view that the abused woman experiences learned helplessness (see Chapter 5). Walker assumes that learned helplessness makes it impossible for some battered women to leave an abusive relationship. These two assertions are essential to a successful defense, because they imply that the battered woman expects to be beaten repeatedly but becomes immobilized and unable to leave the relationship.

Expert testimony on the battered woman's syndrome apparently has been influential in successfully defending a number of battered women who have killed abusive men. Walker (1989) reported that members of her firm had testified in over 160 cases where a battered woman had killed her abuser. This defense has become controversial, however. A number of courts have determined that expert testimony on the battered woman syndrome is inadmissible on various grounds, although the trend appears to be toward increasing acceptance of such testimony by the legal system (Brown, 1990). Others have questioned the scientific status of the battered woman syndrome, doubting the coherence of the theory and the evidence that supports it (Faigman, 1986). One question that has been asked, for example, is: How can someone who is suffering from learned helplessness bring herself to kill?

Questions like this can make it difficult to plead self-defense based on the battered woman syndrome. A defense of *temporary*

insanity is an alternative that may be more easily proved in court. The legal definition of insanity refers to a defendant's mental state at the time of committing the criminal act; thus it is possible for a defendant to suffer from "temporary insanity." An argument for temporary insanity based on the battered woman syndrome could be made on the basis of either the right from wrong or the irresistible impulse strand of the insanity defense. The essence of such an argument would be that the stress of the physical abuse so impaired the battered woman's thinking that either she was unable to appreciate the consequences of her actions or she was driven to the point where she could no longer control her behavior (Cipparone, 1987).

The questions of whether the woman was imminently threatened and why she did not leave the relationship usually play a lesser role in a temporary insanity defense than in a plea of self-defense. However, in cases where women have killed their batterers, temporary insanity pleas appear to be used less frequently than self-defense. Perhaps this is because the temporary insanity defense is less palatable. This defense carries the stigma of an insanity determination, as well as the possibility of confinement in a mental institution. More broadly, advocates for battered women feel strongly that abused women are in a vulnerable and dangerous situation, and they wish to establish that the victims' actions are legitimate acts of self-defense. A successful insanity defense relieves one woman of criminal responsibility for her actions. In contrast, the successful use of self-defense makes a broader political statement—that women have a right to take extreme actions to protect themselves against chronic battering (Walker, 1989). ♛

---

ease" generally is more restrictive than the mental health definition (Campbell, 1990). Some legal and mental health professionals would allow any disorder listed in the DSM to qualify for the insanity defense, however, provided that the other criteria for the legal definition of insanity also were met. Others have argued that some especially difficult circumstances—for example, being a victim of repeated violence—should qualify defendants for the "mental disease or defect" component of the insanity defense, even if the problems are not listed as DSM diagnoses (see Further Thoughts on p. 432). Still other commentators would sharply restrict the mental diseases or defects that can be used as a part of the insanity defense. One suggestion is to confine the insanity defense to mental retardation, schizophrenia, mood disorders, and cognitive disorders, excluding cognitive disorders induced by substance use or abuse (Appelbaum, 1994). Finally, the American Psychiatric Association has stated that mental diseases or defects are limited to "those severely abnormal mental conditions that grossly and demonstrably impair a person's perception or understanding of reality that are not attributable primarily to the voluntary ingestion of alcohol or other psychoactive substances" (APA, 1983).

MENTAL HEALTH PROFESSIONALS AS EXPERT WITNESSES

Whether testifying about a defendant's sanity or about other mental health matters, mental health experts for the prosecution and the defense often present conflicting testimony. Such a "battle of the experts" can be an embarrassment to the profession and can raise questions about professional

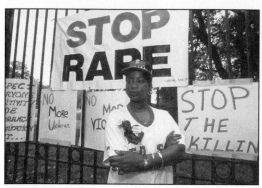

A member of the "Framingham Eight," eight women imprisoned for killing their abusers. The women petitioned for early release from prison, claiming they acted in self-defense.

competence Defendants' ability to understand legal proceedings and act rationally in relation to them. Competence evaluations can take place at different points in the legal process, but competence to stand trial (the ability to participate in one's own defense) is particularly important.

ethics. For example, a commonly asked question is whether an expert's testimony has been "bought" by one side or the other. This possibility sometimes seems feasible to juries when they learn about the fees paid to *expert witnesses,* specialists who are allowed to testify about specific matters of opinion (not just fact) that lie within their area of expertise.

In fact, some psychologists have argued that mental health professionals should not be allowed to offer expert testimony at all. These critics assert that the mental health questions posed by the legal system cannot be answered with adequate reliability or validity. They also deny that mental health experts help judges and juries reach more accurate decisions (Faust & Ziskin, 1988). Reflect for a moment about the many concerns about diagnostic reliability raised throughout this textbook. If mental health professionals often disagree about the presence or absence of a carefully defined mental disorder, is it any wonder that they frequently disagree about the presence or absence of a poorly defined concept like insanity? And if the reliability of the insanity diagnosis is poor, is it unethical for an expert witness to testify about its presence or absence?

In considering these questions, we must recognize that the procedures and goals of the legal system differ from those familiar to psychologists. Expert witnesses are expected to offer informed opinion, not to present the "truth" to the court. Lawyers expect questions to be raised about the credibility of an expert witness's testimony, and they also expect conflicting testimony to be presented by the opposing side's experts (Fitch, Petrella, & Wallace, 1987). The duty of the attorneys for the prosecution and for the defense is to present the most convincing case for their side, which is not the same thing as presenting the most objective case. Although courtroom procedure rules do not excuse inaccurate "expert testimony," they do leave room for testimony even in the face of imperfect empirical evidence. The end product of a trial is a judgment about truth made by a judge or a jury, not the establishment of a scientific fact.

Mental health professionals who act as expert witnesses serve their profession and the legal system best if their testimony adheres closely to their expertise. In insanity cases, for example, the mental health experts' job is to testify about defendants' mental health and state of mind, not to determine their sanity. The determination of a defendant's sanity is a decision to be made by a judge or a jury, not by the expert witness. In fact, the American Psychological Association specifically recommends that "since it is not within the professional competence of psychologists to offer conclusions on matters of law, psychologists should resist pressure to offer such conclusions" (Monahan, 1980).

Competence and Criminal Proceedings

Another important link between mental health and criminal law is the issue of competence. **Competence** concerns defendants' ability to understand the legal proceedings that are taking place against them and to participate in their own defense. If defendants have no such understanding—that is, if they are *incompetent*—the legal proceedings must be suspended until such time as they can be understood by the defendant. Competence has been defined as follows by the U.S. Supreme Court in *Dusky v. United States* [363 U.S. 402, 80 S. Ct. 788, 4 L. Ed.2d. 824 (1960)]:

> The test must be whether he [the defendant] has sufficient present ability to consult with his attorney with a reasonable degree of rational understanding and a rational as well as factual understanding of proceedings against him.

You should note several features of the legal definition of competence. First, competence refers to the defendant's current mental state, whereas the insanity defense refers to the defendant's state of mind at the time of committing a crime. Second, as with insanity, the legal definition of incompetence is not the same as the psychologist's definition of mental illness. Even a psychotic individual may possess enough rational understanding to be deemed competent in the eyes of the law. Third, competence refers to the defendant's ability to understand criminal proceedings, not willingness to participate in them. For example, a defendant who simply refuses to consult with a court-appointed lawyer is not incompetent. Finally, the "reasonable degree" of understanding needed to establish competence is generally acknowledged to be fairly low. That is, only those who suffer from severe emotional disorders are likely to be found incompetent (Melton et al., 1987).

Unlike the various definitions of insanity, the legal definition of incompetence contains no reference to "mental disease or defect." The role of expert witnesses in determining competency is therefore quite different from their role in determining sanity. The evaluation focuses much more on specific behaviors and capacities than on DSM disorders. One listing of the specific capacities that should be considered in a competency evaluation has been compiled by the Group for the Advancement of Psychiatry.

The most common finding of incompetence occurs when defendants are found incompetent to stand trial, but the issue of incompetence may arise at several stages of the criminal process. Defendants must be competent to understand the *Miranda warning* issued during their arrest. (The Miranda warning details the suspect's rights to remain silent and to have an attorney present during police questioning.) Defendants also must be competent at the time of their sentencing, which takes place after they have been convicted of a crime. Finally, recent rulings indicate that defendants sentenced to death must be competent at the time of their execution, or the death sentence cannot be carried out.

Many more people accused of crimes are institutionalized because of findings of incompetence than because of insanity rulings. However, incompetence has received far less attention from both legal and mental health scholars. This may reflect the fact that competence determinations raise few broad social and philosophical issues, unlike the insanity defense.

The goal of ensuring fairness forms the rationale for requiring that defendants are competent before criminal actions can proceed. Unfortunately, determinations of incompetence have sometimes produced what would seem to be very unfair results. Defendants who are judged to be incompetent are confined to mental institutions until they are competent to understand the criminal proceedings, at which time the proceedings resume. In some cases, the length of time that defendants have been confined while awaiting their return to competence has greatly exceeded the time that they would have served if they had been convicted. Although there is little doubt that defendants who are found incompetent have severe mental disorders, people who are hospitalized because of incompetence do not always receive the same protections as people who are hospitalized through civil commitment procedures, the topic we turn to next.

civil commitment   The involuntary hospitalization of the mentally ill; the decision typically is justified based on dangerousness to self or others (or inability to care for self).

Mental Hospitals and the Law

Mental health issues are important in civil law as well as in criminal law. In particular, the involuntary hospitalization of the severely mentally impaired raises questions of major importance in civil law. Three issues are of special relevance: (1) civil commitment, the legal process of sending someone to a mental hospital against his or her will; (2) patients' rights, especially their right to treatment, their right to treatment in the least restrictive alternative environment, and their right to refuse certain treatments; and (3) deinstitutionalization, the movement to treat patients in their communities instead of in mental hospitals.

Libertarianism versus Paternalism in Treating Mental Patients

What are society's legal and philosophical rationales for hospitalizing people against their will? As a general matter, debates about involuntary hospitalization highlight the philosophical tension between *libertarian* views, which emphasize protecting the rights of the individual, and *paternalist* approaches, which emphasize the state's duty to protect its citizens. This tension is evident in contemporary rationales for committing mental patients to institutions. For example, the involuntary hospitalization of someone who appears to be dangerous to others serves a protective, paternalist goal. Yet civil libertarians note that *preventive detention*—confinement before a crime is committed—can lead to substantial abuse. With the exception of **civil commitment**—the involuntary hospitalization of the mentally ill—our laws prohibit the confinement of someone simply on the suspicion that he or she is about to commit a crime, no matter how strong or how realistic this suspicion may be.

Many scholars have become embroiled in the debate between the libertarian and paternalist philosophies. Some of these scholars recognize few justifications for civil commitment (Durham & LaFond, 1988), whereas others argue that many such justifications exist (Torrey, 1988). Despite a recent swing of the pendulum back in the direction of paternalism, the major trend over the past several decades has been a libertarian one, including a closer scrutiny of civil commitment procedures, an increasing recognition of patients' rights, and the deinstitutionalization of patients from mental hospitals (Appelbaum, 1994). Note that this increased concern for the rights of patients has run parallel to the increased emphasis on their criminal responsibility in the insanity defense. Rights and responsibilities do indeed go hand in hand.

Civil Commitment

American law contains two broad rationales for civil commitment. The first rationale is based on the state's *parens patriae* authority, the philosophy that the government has a humanitarian responsibility to care for its weaker members. (The literal translation of the Latin phrase *parens patriae* is the "state as parent.") The concept of *parens patriae* dates back to ancient Rome and has influenced U.S. law through English traditions. Under the state's *parens patriae* authority, civil commitment may be justified when the mentally disturbed are either dangerous to themselves or unable to care for themselves (Myers, 1983–84). In addition to the confinement of the mentally ill, the concept of *parens patriae* is used to justify the state's supervision of minors and physically incapacitated adults.

The second rationale for civil commitment is based on the state's *police power*—its duty to protect the public safety, health, and welfare. Our government restricts individual liberties for the public good in many ways. For the safety of others, we are restricted from yelling "Fire!" in a crowded theater or from driving an automobile at 100 miles an hour. The civil commitment of people who are dangerous to others is justified by similar police power rationales. Civil commitment obviously involves a dramatic restriction in individual liberty, however, as it constitutes confinement without having committed a crime. Thus this severe restriction on individual liberty requires the highest degree of scrutiny.

The police power rationales for civil commitment have been invoked throughout the history of U.S. law, even in colonial times, as the "furiously insane" could be detained in order to prevent them from doing harm to others (Myers, 1983–84). In contrast, commitment under *parens patriae* rationales was virtually unknown in the United States until large mental institutions were built in the 1800s. Some evidence suggests that civil commitment standards were very lax during the same historical period that mental institutions were being built (Appelbaum, 1994). For example, an 1842 New York state statute required the confinement of all "lunatics" irrespective of whether they were dangerous or able to care for themselves. The law commissioned "assessors" to round up lunatics and have them confined for a period of no less than 6 months (Reisner & Slobogin, 1990).

Legislation that more carefully defined the grounds for civil commitment and protected at least some of the rights of the mentally ill was not adopted until the latter part of the nineteenth century; its adoption was due in large part to the efforts of Mrs. E.P.W. Packard (Myers, 1983–84). Mrs. Packard was committed to a mental hospital by her husband under an Illinois law that allowed a man to commit his children or his wife to a mental hospital against their will and without the usual evidence of insanity. The commitment of Mrs. Packard was questionable at best. In presenting evidence in favor of her commitment, for example, one doctor noted that Mrs. Packard was rational but she was a "religious bigot" (Reisner & Slobogin, 1990). Following her release 3 years after being committed, Mrs. Packard campaigned to revise commitment standards to prevent such abuses, and she succeeded in influencing the laws in many states.

Following the reforms begun by Mrs. Packard, civil commitment laws remained largely unchanged from the late 1800s until the 1960s and 1970s. During more recent years, several notable cases set important precedents that have affected civil commitment laws and procedures. These developments are discussed shortly, but first we consider civil commitment procedures and philosophies in more detail.

GROUNDS AND PROCEDURES

Most states provide two types of civil commitment procedures: emergency procedures and formal procedures. *Emergency commitment procedures* allow an acutely disturbed individual to be temporarily confined in a mental hospital, typically for no more than a few days. Various states designate physicians, mental health professionals, or even police officers as being qualified to determine whether an emergency commitment is required. Obviously, such action is taken only when a mental disorder is very serious, and the risk that the patient is dangerous to self or others appears to be very high.

Formal commitment procedures can lead to involuntary hospitalization that lasts for much longer periods of time than an emergency commitment, and it can be ordered only by a court. An adversary hearing must be available to mental patients who object to involuntary hospitalization; all of their usual due process rights must be protected in formal commitment procedures, and the need for hospitalization typically must be demonstrated by "clear and convincing" evidence. Furthermore, once an individual is involuntarily committed to a mental institution through formal procedures, his or her case often is automatically reviewed after a set period of time—for example, every 6 months.

Because civil commitment is a matter of state law, the specific grounds for involuntary hospitalization vary from state to state. Still, three grounds tend to dominate commitment laws: (1) inability to care for self, (2) being dangerous to self, and (3) being dangerous to others. The broadest of these is *inability to care for self*. In some states, mental patients may be hospitalized against their will if they are unable to care for themselves adequately in the community or if they do not have family or friends who will care for them. The intention of this commitment standard is benevolent, but because it has been abused in some cases, newly articulated patient rights have been used to attack the "inability to care for self" ground for civil commitment (Appelbaum, 1994; Durham & LaFond, 1988). Debates continue in courtrooms and in state legislatures. Is it better to be paternalist and sacrifice some individual rights by involuntarily committing mental patients who do not want but who clearly need inpatient treatment? Or is it better to protect civil liberties by not committing patients who obviously are severely disturbed but who manage to survive on their own outside of mental hospitals?

The two other grounds for justifying civil commitment generally have not been attacked on philosophical grounds. Few civil libertarians object to hospitalizing people against their will when they clearly are either *dangerous to self* or *dangerous to others*, provided that the danger is "imminent." Thus a commonly accepted standard for civil commitment is "clear and convincing evidence of imminent danger to oneself or others." Questions have been raised about the ability of mental health professionals to predict dangerousness, however.

PREDICTING DANGEROUSNESS AND SUICIDAL RISK

The first question to ask about civil commitment and the prediction of dangerousness is: Are mentally disturbed people more dangerous than other people? To many laypeople, the obvious answer to this question is yes. Until recently, however, psychological research has suggested the opposite answer. John Monahan (1992), a psychologist and law professor and the leading authority on the prediction of dangerousness, once concluded that there was no evidence that violence and mental illness were related. Recently, he has modified his position.

In addressing the question about the link between violence and mental illness, Monahan examined both the rate of violence among the mentally ill and the rate of mental disorder among criminals. Whichever way the question is asked, evidence supports the conclusion that the two problems are associated (Monahan, 1992). The prevalence of bipolar disorder, major depression, and schizophrenia has been found to be several times as high among prison inmates as among general population. Similarly, the rate of violence is about five times higher among people diagnosed with one of these major mental disorders than among those with no diagnosis. People who abuse alcohol or drugs are even more likely to engage in violent behavior.

John Monahan, a psychologist at the University of Virginia School of Law, is a leader in the study of psychology and the law. Monahan is particularly noted for his work on the prediction of violence.

Research documenting the increased risk of dangerousness to others is important, but for several reasons this evidence does not directly translate into a policy of confining the mentally ill. For one, the data indicate that the risk for violence among the mentally ill is far lower than is publicly perceived. In fact, approximately 90 percent of the mentally disturbed have *no* history of violence (Monahan, 1992). Second, other research indicates that although current psychotic symptoms predict violence, a past history of psychosis is not associated with an increased risk (Link, Cullen, & Andrews, 1990). Third, the presence of a mental illness is unrelated to future arrests for violent crime among jail detainees, although the rate of recidivism is high among this group as a whole (Teplin, Abram, & McClelland, 1994). Finally and most importantly, numerous factors other than mental illness are known to predict an increased risk for violence, but they obviously do not justify involuntary confinement. For example, research has documented that people who live in poverty or who have a history of criminal behavior are more likely to be violent. Would anyone suggest that such a statistical risk justifies involuntary hospitalization?

Identical concerns apply to civil commitment and the assessment of suicide risk as to the assessment of dangerousness to others. As we discussed in Chapter 5, mental disorders, particularly depression, are related to an increased risk of suicide, but the risk of suicide clearly is far too small to justify civil commitment simply because of the presence of a mental disorder. Similarly, evidence on the clinical prediction of suicide risk also indicates very high false-positive rates (Pokony, 1983). These findings again raise concerns about the accuracy of clinical prediction, but we can be reassured by the actual procedures used to evaluate patients for civil commitment under either of the two dangerousness standards. In many cases in which a patient is involuntarily hospitalized, patients freely and directly acknowledge their intention to commit suicide or to physically harm others (Appelbaum, 1994).

The Rights of Mental Patients

Several important court cases have clarified the rights of mental patients following their civil commitment to a mental hospital. These rights include the right to treatment; the right to treatment in the least restrictive alternative environment; and the right to refuse treatment.

THE RIGHT TO TREATMENT

Two of the most significant cases for establishing that hospitalized mental patients have a constitutional right to treatment were *Wyatt v. Stickney* and *O'Connor v. Donaldson*.

Wyatt v. Stickney   *Wyatt v. Stickney* (1972) began as a dispute over the dismissal of 99 employees from Bryce Hospital in Tuscaloosa, Alabama. The state mental hospital had been built in the 1850s and housed nearly 5,000 patients when the much-needed staff members were released due to budget cuts. All accounts indicate that conditions in the hospital were very bad even before the layoffs. The buildings were fire hazards, the food was inedible, sanitation was neglected, avoidable sickness was rampant, abuse of patients was frequent, and confinement of patients with no apparent therapeutic goal occurred regularly.

Litigation was filed on behalf of Ricky Wyatt, a resident in the institution, as part of a class action suit against the Alabama mental health commissioner, Dr. Stickney. The suit argued that institutionalized patients had a right to treatment that Bryce Hospital failed to fulfill. The commissioner was in the somewhat unusual position of being a proponent of a suit against him, as he wanted to improve the care of the mentally ill in the state but was faced with budget problems. The case was tried and appealed several times, and the patients' suit was upheld.

The victory forced the state of Alabama to provide services, but *Wyatt* had a broader impact that influenced mental patients and mental hospitals throughout the country. The judicial rulings clearly established that hospitalized mental patients have a right to treatment. Specifically, a federal district court ruled that at a minimum, public mental institutions must provide (1) a humane psychological and physical environment, (2) qualified staff in numbers sufficient to administer adequate treatment, and (3) individualized treatment plans [334 F. Supp. 1341 (M.D. Ala. 1971) at 1343]. The court also ordered that the implementation of changes needed to fulfill these patients' rights could not be delayed until funding was available.

The *Wyatt* decision helped focus national attention on the treatment of the mentally ill and the mentally retarded and led to the filing of numerous "right to treatment" cases. The threat of litigation impelled the staff of numerous other mental hospitals to improve patient care. *Wyatt* also helped to spur the deinstitutionalization movement, because the level of care required by the ruling is impossible to provide in large, overcrowded institutions (Myers, 1983–84). As we shall see, however, this has meant that some mental patients simply were released to the community without adequate care there either (Appelbaum, 1994; Torrey, 1997).

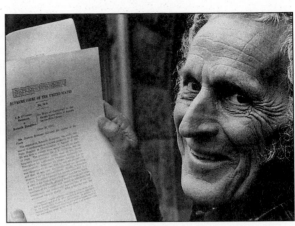

Kenneth Donaldson proudly displays a copy of the U.S. Supreme Court ruling in his case. The Court held that nondangerous mental patients cannot be confined against their will, a decision that freed Donaldson and set an important precedent for other hospitalized mental patients.

O'Connor v. Donaldson   The Supreme Court acknowledged the right of mental patients to treatment in another landmark case, *O'Connor v. Donaldson* [422 U.S. 563 (1975)]. Kenneth Donaldson had been confined in a Florida mental hospital for nearly 15 years, despite his repeated requests for release based on his claims that he was not mentally ill, was not dangerous to himself or others, and was receiving no treatment in the hospital. Eventually, he sued the hospital's superintendent, Dr. J. B. O'Connor, for release, based on the assertion that he had been deprived of his constitutional right to liberty.

The evidence presented at the trial indicated that Donaldson was not and never had been dangerous to himself or others. Testimony also revealed that reliable individuals and agencies in the community had made several offers to care for Donaldson, but superintendent O'Connor had repeatedly rejected them. O'Connor had insisted that Donaldson could be released only to the custody of his parents, who were very old and unable to care for him. O'Connor's position on Donaldson's supposed inability to care for himself was puzzling, because Donaldson was employed and had lived on his own for many years before being committed to the hospital. Other evidence documented that Donaldson had received nothing but custodial care while he was hospitalized.

After a series of trials and appeals, the Supreme Court eventually ruled that Donaldson was not dangerous either to himself or others. It further ruled that a state could not confine him as being in need of treatment and yet fail to provide him with that treatment. Specifically, it ordered that "the State cannot constitutionally confine . . . a non-dangerous individual who is capable of surviving safely in freedom by himself or with the help of willing and responsible family members or friends." Thus *O'Connor* and similar cases not only underscored a patient's right to treatment, but they also set limitations on civil commitment standards. Commitment based on dangerousness to self or others remained unquestioned, but commitment based on inability to care for self became much more controversial, especially if institutionalization offered little treatment or therapeutic benefit.

TREATMENT IN THE LEAST RESTRICTIVE ALTERNATIVE ENVIRONMENT

The patient's right to be treated in the least restrictive alternative environment was first developed in the 1966 case of *Lake v. Cameron* [364 F. 2d 657 (D.C. Cir. 1966)], decided by the Washington, D.C., Circuit Court of Appeals. Catherine Lake was 60 years old when she was committed to St. Elizabeth's Hospital because of "a chronic brain syndrome associated with aging." A particular problem was her tendency to wander away from her home, which posed a threat to her life through exposure to the elements and other dangers.

In contesting the commitment, Mrs. Lake did not object to her need for treatment, but she argued that appropriate treatment was available in a less restrictive setting. The court agreed, suggesting several less restrictive alternatives to institutionalization. These alternatives ranged from having Mrs. Lake carry an identification card to treating her in a public nursing home.

Several additional cases following *Lake* firmly established the doctrine of the least restrictive alternative. Litigation was quickly followed by legislation, as numerous states incorporated the right to treatment in the least restrictive alternative environment into their mental health statutes (Hoffman & Foust, 1977). Although the concept was quickly embraced, no one was or is absolutely certain what the expression "least restrictive alternative" means.

informed consent A legal and ethical safeguard concerning risks in research and in treatment. Includes (a) accurate information about potential risks and benefits, (b) competence on the part of subjects/patients to understand them, and (c) the ability of subjects/patients to participate voluntarily.

Perhaps the most important issue about the least restrictive alternative concerns the problem that developed in the original *Lake* case: Less restrictive alternatives to institutionalization often are not available. No suitable community care was found for Mrs. Lake, who was returned to the institution. If a less restrictive alternative treatment is not available, must such treatment be developed and provided by the community? Some early cases suggested that the courts would mandate such a solution, but this trend quickly faded. Thus *Lake* both established patients' right to treatment in the least restrictive alternative environment and foreshadowed the problem of insufficient alternative treatments in the community. The development of community resources has not kept up with the release of patients from mental hospitals (Hoffman & Foust, 1977). This is especially unfortunate, given that data suggest that community treatment can be more effective than inpatient care (Kiesler, 1982).

THE RIGHT TO REFUSE TREATMENT

The third and most recent development in litigation involving people committed to mental hospitals is the *right to refuse treatment,* particularly the right to refuse psychotropic medication. Several courts and state legislatures have concluded that mental health patients have the right to refuse certain treatments under certain conditions, although this right is on less firm ground than the other two rights we have discussed. In particular, the Supreme Court has yet to establish whether there is a constitutional basis for the right to refuse treatment.

The very concept of a patient refusing treatment is problematic in that involuntary hospitalization itself is treatment against a patient's will. The patient who is committed involuntarily to a mental hospital has refused inpatient treatment but is receiving it anyway. On what grounds can subsequent treatment decisions be refused if the decision about hospitalization already has been taken out of the patient's hands? Many mental health professionals have noted this contradiction, and they argue that patients lose their right to refuse treatment once they are involuntarily hospitalized (Appelbaum, 1994; Gutheil, 1986; Torrey, 1997). After all, a mental health professional is in an awkward position if a patient is committed to a hospital for treatment yet retains the right to refuse medication. How can mental health professionals do their job in such a circumstance?

The question of the right to refuse treatment often turns on the issue of informed consent, one of several legal doctrines that can be used to justify a patient's refusal of mental health (or medical) treatments (Hermann, 1990). **Informed consent** requires that (1) a clinician tell a patient about a procedure and its associated risks, (2) the patient understands the information and freely consents to the treatment, and (3) the patient is competent to give consent. When the patient's competence to provide consent is in question, a common approach is to appoint an independent guardian who offers a *substituted judgment,* deciding not what is best for the patient but what the patient would have been likely to do if he or she were competent (Gutheil, 1986).

The rationales for and parameters of patients' right to refuse treatment are still being debated in litigation and legislation. Several courts have ruled that patients retain their competence to make treatment decisions even if they have been committed through civil procedures. Moreover, half the states have recognized the right to refuse psychotropic medications provided that patients are not dangerous to themselves or others (Hermann, 1990). The Supreme Court first ruled on this topic in the 1990 case of *Washington v. Harper* [110 S. Ct. 1028 (1990)]. This case involved a Washington state prison that overrode a patient's refusal of psychotropic medications. The court decided in favor of the prison, ruling that the prison's review process sufficiently protected the patient's right to refuse treatment. This process stipulated that the patient's wishes could be overruled only after review by a three-member panel consisting of a psychologist, a psychiatrist, and a deputy warden. The Supreme Court's decision may signal a greater willingness on the part of the courts to limit patients' right to refuse treatment.

Almost a Revolution   Overall, the cases and legislation of the 1960s, 1970s, and 1980s served an essential function in articulating and increasing awareness of patients' rights. Recently, however, the swing toward libertarianism has begun to be balanced by important paternalist concerns—the need to protect the public from the violently mentally ill and especially the need to treat severely disturbed patients who lack insight into their condition (Appelbaum, 1994; Torrey, 1997). Serious mental illness is *not* a myth, and mental health professionals—and the state—have a duty to provide care for those who cannot care for themselves. Libertarians help ensure that treatments do not become overly paternalistic, but the paternalist position embraces legitimate and benevolent goals. Thus, in the words of one commentator, the libertarian changes in mental health law have produced "almost a revolution" (Appelbuam, 1994).

Deinstitutionalization

Legal cases have restricted the inpatient treatment of the mentally ill, but a broader influence has been the **deinstitutionalization** movement—the philosophy that many of the mentally ill and mentally retarded can be better cared for in their community than in large mental hospitals. Bertram Brown, a former director of the National Institute for Mental Health, defined the goals of deinstitutionalization as "(1) the prevention of inappropriate mental hospital admissions through the provision of community alternatives for treatment, (2) the release to the community of all institutionalized patients who have been given adequate preparation for such a change, and (3) the establishment and maintenance of community support systems for noninstitutionalized people receiving mental health services in the community" (Braun et al., 1981).

The establishment of mental health centers in communities was part of the effort to achieve these three goals. In 1963, Congress passed the Community Mental Health Centers (CMHCs) Act with the strong support of President John F. Kennedy.[†] The act provided for the creation of community care facilities for the seriously mentally ill as alternatives to institutional care. This law began a broad change in the way mental health services are delivered in the United States. There were no community mental health centers in operation in 1965, but by 1981 nearly 800 were in existence (Torrey, 1988).

Deinstitutionalization has occurred in dramatic fashion. In 1955, more than 500,000 people in the United States were confined to mental hospitals, but by 1994 that number had shrunk to less than 72,000 (Torrey, 1997). The effects of deinstitutionalization are even greater than these numbers suggest, because the overall population grew from 164 million in 1955 to 260 million in 1994. Thus, almost 900,000 people would be in institutions today if the 1955 proportion of inpatients to the total population had remained unchanged (Torrey, 1997). Unfortunately, CMHCs have not achieved many of their goals in helping deinstitutionalized patients. In fact, CMHCs generally have not focused their services on former inpatients with serious mental illness. The percentage of schizophrenic patients served by CMHCs is small and declining, while the percentage of patients with mild problems is larger and growing. In fact, many CMHCs do not even offer services for the seriously mentally ill, despite the fact that they are mandated to do so by legislation (Torrey, 1988, 1997). Other community resources, such as halfway houses, simply have not been implemented in adequate numbers.

Other problems with the deinstitutionalization movement are evident. As public hospitalization has declined, the number of mental patients living in nursing homes and other for-profit institutions has grown (Goldman, Adams, & Taube, 1983; Torrey, 1988). More people with a mental illness also are being confined in jail. In fact, about 10 percent of the prison population suffers from a serious mental illness (Appelbaum, 1994; Torrey, 1997). In addition, a *revolving door* phenomenon has developed in which more patients are admitted to psychiatric hospitals more frequently but for shorter periods of time. For example, one study found that 24 percent of inpatients in New York City had 10 or more previous admissions (Karras & Otis, 1987). Moreover, the deinstitutionalized mentally ill constitute a large part of the homeless population (Fischer & Breakey, 1991; Torrey, 1997). One study found that 31 percent of the

> **deinstitutionalization** The movement to treat the mentally ill and mentally retarded in communities rather than in large mental hospitals.

[†]*President Kennedy had a special interest in mental health because of his sister Rosemary. She was mildly mentally retarded as a child, but she became psychotic as a young adult and underwent a failed lobotomy that left her so impaired that she had to be confined to a nursing home.*

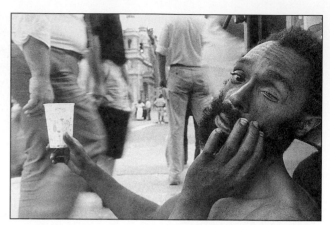

These contrasting photos illustrate how mental patients often are neglected both inside and outside of institutions. The photo on the left, taken several decades ago, shows some of the depressing and dehumanizing conditions that characterized many institutions for the mentally ill. The photo on the right depicts the contemporary problem of homelessness. Many homeless people are deinstitutionalized mental patients.

homeless were in need of mental health services (Roth & Bean, 1986). In his stirring and disturbing book *Nowhere to Go,* the psychiatrist E. Fuller Torrey (1988) notes eight major problems with deinstitutionalization:

1. There are at least twice as many seriously mentally ill individuals living on streets and in shelters as there are in public mental hospitals.
2. There are increasing numbers of seriously mentally ill individuals in the nation's jails and prisons.
3. Seriously mentally ill individuals are regularly released from hospitals with little or no provision for aftercare or follow-up treatment.
4. Violent acts perpetrated by untreated mentally ill individuals are increasing in number.
5. Housing and living conditions for mentally ill individuals in the community are grossly inadequate.
6. Community mental health centers, originally funded to provide community care for the mentally ill so that these individuals would no longer have to go to state mental hospitals, are almost complete failures in this regard.
7. Laws designed to protect the rights of the seriously mentally ill primarily protect their right to remain mentally ill.
8. The majority of mentally ill individuals discharged from hospitals have been officially lost. Nobody knows where they are.

HAS THE PENDULUM SWUNG TOO FAR?

Some advocates for the mentally ill, particularly those in mental health professions, feel that the pendulum between paternalism and libertarianism has swung too far in the direction of patients' rights. Many mental patients who clearly are in need of treatment cannot be committed under existing statutes. Some of the problems of the deinstitutionalized mentally ill are compounded by restrictive civil commitment laws. Torrey (1988) argues, "Freedom to be insane is an illusory freedom, a cruel hoax perpetrated on those who cannot think clearly by those who will not think clearly" (p. 34).

As a means of balancing paternalist and libertarian concerns, some experts have suggested that more paternalism is needed in committing patients, but that commitment should be to involuntary treatment in the least restrictive environment, such as mandatory outpatient care (Myers, 1983–84). Hospitalization would be required only as a last resort. Others call for the involuntary treatment of inpatients but only following careful review.

Mental Health and Family Law

Both the insanity defense and civil commitment primarily involve people who have a serious mental illness. In contrast, mental health professionals who are involved with *family law* issues typically work with people whose problems are less severe, and they often are consulted about issues related to normal development. This is evident in the major issues that form the focus of family law: divorce, spousal abuse, foster care, adoption, juvenile delinquency, child custody disputes, and child abuse and neglect. Any one of these problems can involve serious psychopathology, but they more commonly involve family members who are only mildly disturbed or are functioning normally.

We consider both family law and mental health law issues together in this chapter, because the opinions and advice of mental health professionals are frequently sought by legal professionals working in both areas. However, family and mental health law are distinct in the legal system. The two areas have different roots and practices, and attorneys may specialize in one or the other area but rarely both. In fact, family law cases typically are tried in different courts than are mental health law cases. These separate courts, known variously as "juvenile courts," "domestic relations courts," or "family courts," were first created at the turn of the century and adhere to a different philosophy than other U.S. courts. Much of mental health law is based on the state's police power obligations, but virtually all of family law is premised on the government's *parens patriae* duties.

In theory, the functions of juvenile and family courts are to help and protect children and families. Thus the goals of family courts historically have been more psychological than legal. In fact, the authors of a recent, comprehensive overview of the role of psychologists in the courts concluded, "Perhaps nowhere in the legal system is there as much deference to mental health professionals as in the juvenile court" (Melton et al., 1987, p. 291).

The importance of mental health professionals is particularly evident in the two family law topics considered in this chapter—child custody disputes following divorce and cases of child abuse and neglect. Mental health professionals and psychological findings are of great importance not only because of the family court's philosophy but also because terms like *child abuse* are poorly defined in the law. The laws governing judicial dispositions of these family concerns are similarly vague. In fact, the guiding principle for judicial decision making is the very general directive to make determinations according to what is in the "child's best interest" (Mnookin, 1975). Not surprisingly, family court judges frequently turn to mental health professionals for practical guidance in defining a given child's "best interests."

Balancing the Interests of Children, Parents, and the State

A general dilemma in family law is how to balance the potentially competing interests of children, parents, and the state (Mnookin, 1985). We alluded to this three-sided problem in our earlier discussion of the *Parham* decision on the commitment of minors to mental hospitals. People involved with such cases must address a number of difficult questions: Are children entitled to the same due process rights as adults? Should parental authority be respected above and beyond the wishes of either children or the state? Or should the state's *parens patriae* obligation overrule the desires of both children and parents?

One set of answers to these questions comes from advocates for children who consistently argue that children, or at least adolescents, are entitled to the same basic rights as adults. Advocates for this position were upset by *Parham,* for example, because they want minors to have the same due process rights as adults. Different rationales come from paternalists who believe that children need vigorous protection by the state. Paternalists do not favor *Parham* either, because it limits state supervision by giving parents the power to make decisions about hospitalizing minors. A paternalist might instead advocate for increased government regulation of private mental hospitals. The winners in *Parham* were those people who hold a third position as advocates for parental rights or "family autonomy." Proponents of family autonomy want to minimize the involvement of the state in the family, whether that intrusion comes from state supervision or broader rights for children.

The tension among the rights and responsibilities of children, parents, and the state pervades controversies about child custody and child abuse. Advocates for children's rights want children to have a voice in the outcome of custody disputes and the disposition of abuse cases. Advocates for family autonomy want parents to resolve custody disputes themselves and to narrow the definition of abuse and neglect in order to minimize state intervention in the family. Advocates for state intervention want judges to determine custody arrangements, and they argue for earlier and more vigorous intervention in cases of child abuse.

Child Custody Disputes Following Divorce

Divorce is a common experience for children living in the United States. Every year, approximately 2 percent of U.S. children experience a divorce (SCCYF, 1989), and demographers have estimated that 38 percent of white children and 75 percent of black children born to married parents will experience a parental divorce by the age of 16 (Bumpass, 1984). *Child custody* is one of the issues that must be decided when parents divorce. Although the legal terminology differs from state to state, in effect custody decisions involve two determinations: *physical custody,* or where the children will live at what times; and *legal custody,* or how the parents will make separate or joint decisions about their children's lives. *Sole custody* refers to a situation in which only one parent retains physical or legal custody of the children; in *joint custody* both parents retain custody.

The majority of custody decisions are made outside of court by attorneys who negotiate for the parents. A growing number of custody decisions are being made by parents themselves, however, typically with the help of a *mediator*—a neutral third party who facilitates the parents' discussions. Finally, a small but significant percentage of custody disputes are decided in court by a judge (Maccoby & Mnookin, 1992). Mental health professionals may be involved in providing recommendations during attorney negotiations, they may provide expert testimony in court, or they may act as mediators themselves.

EXPERT WITNESSES IN CUSTODY DETERMINATIONS

Mental health professionals who conduct custody evaluations typically consider a number of factors in evaluating a child's best interests. These include the quality of the child's relationship with each parent, the family environment provided by each parent, each parent's mental health, the relationship between the parents, and the child's expressed wishes, if any (Emery, 1994; Emery & Rogers, 1990). Mental health professionals face a tremendous obstacle in conducting a custody evaluation, however. The law that governs custody disputes, the *child's best interests standard,* is unclear about what a child's future best interests are, how they can be determined, or how they can be achieved.

Because the child's best interests standard is so vague, Mnookin has argued further that it increases the likelihood that custody hearings will be acrimonious. Virtually any information that makes one parent look bad and the other look good may be construed as helping a parent's case— and people who have been married have much private and potentially damaging information about each other. The likelihood that the best interests standard increases acrimony is a particular problem, because a wide range of research indicates that conflict between parents is strongly related to maladjustment among children following divorce (Emery, 1982, 1997; Grych & Fincham, 1990). This raises the sad irony that parents and the legal system may be undermining a child's best interests by fighting for them in a custody battle (Emery & Wyer, 1987). For this reason, many mental health professionals feel that they serve children and the legal system better if they help parents to settle custody disputes outside of court rather than providing testimony in court.

Child Abuse

The legal trend in child custody disputes is toward more family autonomy, but the state's role in regulating child abuse clearly has grown dramatically. Like spousal abuse (see Further Thoughts on battered women, page 432), historically child abuse was common and condoned, and only recently has it been "discovered" to be a problem. The first child protection efforts in the United States did not begin until 1875. A much publicized case of foster parents who physically beat a young girl in their care led to the founding of the New York Society for the Prevention of Cruelty to Children. The society was given the power to police child abuse, and other states rapidly followed New York's example by establishing similar organizations and legislation (Lazoritz, 1990).

Although state governments assumed some jurisdiction over child abuse in the nineteenth century, consistent public attention was not brought to bear on the problem until 1962, when the physician Henry Kempe wrote about the "battered child syndrome." Kempe documented tragic cases of child abuse in which children suffered repeated injuries, fractured bones, and, in a substantial number of cases, death (Kempe et al., 1962). Kempe's influential article prompted legislation that defined child abuse and required physicians to report suspected cases. This reporting requirement continues today, and in most states it extends to include mental health professionals, schoolteachers, and other professionals who have regular contact with children. In fact, mental health professionals not only can but must break the confidentiality of psychotherapy if they suspect child abuse (Melton & Limber, 1989).

Four forms of **child abuse** generally are distinguished by mental health professionals and are treated separately in the law: physical abuse, sexual abuse, neglect, and psychological abuse (American Psychological Association, 1995). *Physical child abuse* involves the intentional use of physically painful and harmful actions. The definition of physical abuse is complicated by the fact that corporal punishments like spanking are widely accepted discipline practices (Emery, 1989; Wolfe, 1987). Only about 10 percent of physically abused children whose caretakers are reported to social service agencies sustain injuries serious enough to require professional care, but the danger to children can be considerable nevertheless. Estimates indicate that 2,000 to 5,000 children die every year because of maltreatment (Zigler & Hall, 1989).

A memorial for Elisa Izquierdo, a 6-year-old girl who was beaten to death by her mother. The child had been repeatedly abused by her mother and stepfather, but overwhelmed social service agencies found at least two reports of her abuse to be "unfounded."

Child sexual abuse involves sexual contact between an adult and a child. Reports of child sexual abuse have increased astronomically in recent years, as this important problem has been fully recognized only since the 1980s (Haugaard & Reppucci, 1988). The sexual abuse of children is now known to be far more prevalent than would have been believed a short time ago. For example, one survey of adult women living in an urban area found that 2.5 percent said that they had been coerced into oral, anal, or genital intercourse with their father, stepfather, or brother before the age of 18 (Russell, 1983).

Child neglect, the most commonly reported form of child abuse, involves placing children at risk for serious physical or psychological harm by failing to provide basic and expected care. Some children are severely neglected, and they experience extreme failure in their growth and development as a result (Wolfe, 1987). Some children also suffer *psychological abuse*—repeated denigration in the absence of physical harm.

The number of reported cases of child abuse has increased dramatically since the 1970s and into the 1990s. As indicated in Figure 15–1, the number of reports of child abuse made to social service agencies climbed from 669,000 in 1976 to 3,111,000 in 1995 (Lang & Daro, 1996). Experts debate the reasons for the increased number of reports. The rate of child abuse could be increasing, but the real increase may be in reports of abuse (Besharov, 1992; Besharov & Laumann, 1996; Finkelhor, 1992). Over half of all reports of abuse are found to be unsubstantiated after an investigation, and some experts have suggested that the percentage of unsubstantiated reports is growing. One reason for this, according to some critics, is that the concept of neglect is applied too broadly (Besharov, 1986, 1988, 1992).

The increasing number of reports of child abuse and the large percentage of less severe cases that are unsubstantiated may create two problems. First, if social service agencies are overwhelmed with more minor cases, they are less able to deal with children who are living in circumstances of clear danger. Second, intervention in less severe cases may actually do more harm than good. Overwhelmed social service agencies may stigmatize and disrupt families that are troubled but coping—and offer them relatively little treatment in return (Besharov, 1986, 1988, 1992).

child abuse   A legal decision that a parent or other responsible adult has inflicted damage or offered inadequate care to a child; may include physical abuse, sexual abuse, neglect, and psychological abuse.

professional responsibilities A professional's obligation to follow the ethical standards of his or her profession and to uphold the laws of the states in which he or she practices, for example, confidentiality.

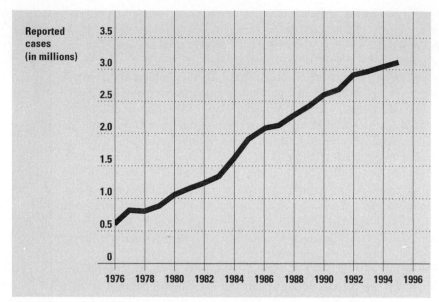

Figure 15–1   Child Abuse Reports: 1976–1995.   Reports of child abuse made to social service agencies have increased sharply. Experts disagree about what has increased—actual abuse or the awareness and reporting of abuse.

Source: Based on data from C. T. Lanf and D. Daro, 1996, *Current Trends in Child Abuse Reporting and Fatalities: The Results of the 1995 Annual State Survey,* Working Paper 808. Washington, DC: National Committee on the Prevention of Child Abuse.

When an allegation of abuse is substantiated, one of the major questions is whether to remove the child from the home. Over 100,000 maltreated children are placed in *foster care* each year. Foster care obviously benefits children who are in physical danger, but as many as half of all children placed in foster care are in no immediate danger of physical injury (Besharov, 1988). Stable foster care can offer children psychological benefits, as well as physical protection (Wald, Carlsmith, & Leiderman, 1988). However, half of the children placed in foster care remain there for at least 2 years, almost one-third are separated from their parents for over 6 years, and a substantial proportion live in many different foster homes during this time (Besharov, 1986).

Professional Responsibilities and the Law

The regulation of the mental health professions is the final area of psychology and the law that we consider in this chapter. Psychiatrists, clinical psychologists, and social workers all have **professional responsibilities** to meet the ethical standards of their profession and to uphold the laws of the states in which they practice. The duties of mental health professionals are numerous and varied, and we focus on only two important and illustrative professional issues: negligence and confidentiality.

Professional Negligence and Malpractice

Negligence occurs when a professional fails to perform in a manner that is consistent with the level of skill exercised by other professionals in the field. Simply put, negligence is substandard professional service. *Malpractice* refers to situations in which professional negligence results in harm to clients or patients. In the law, malpractice is demonstrated when (1) a professional has a duty to conform to a standard of conduct, (2) the professional is negligent in that duty, (3) the professional's client experiences damages or loss, and (4) it is reasonably certain that the negligence caused the damages (Reisner & Slobogin, 1990). When professionals are found to be guilty of malpractice, they are subject to disciplinary action both from their professional organizations and through state licensing boards, as well as to civil suits and possibly to criminal actions.

Whereas medical malpractice claims are common, malpractice claims against mental health professionals are relatively infrequent. For example, one survey found that claims against psychiatrists accounted for only 0.3 percent of all malpractice suits filed in the state of California between 1974 and 1978 (Slawson & Guggenheim, 1984). The inappropriate use of electroconvulsive therapy (ECT) and medication are two of the more common reasons for malpractice claims against mental health professionals. These treatments are clearly defined, research on their appropriate use is more clear-cut than is psychotherapy research, and the treatments can result in physical as well as psychological damages. In other words, malpractice is easier to demonstrate for these treatments.

The existence of a sexual relationship between therapists and their clients is another common ground for successful malpractice suits. Although specific damages can be difficult to prove, it has become commonly accepted that sexual relationships between therapists and their clients are harmful in and of themselves. This is evident in the ethical codes of the American Psychological Association and the American Psychiatric Association, both of which prohibit sexual relationships between therapists and their clients. Other claims of professional negligence stem from the failure to prevent suicide, failure to prevent violence against others, and violations of confidentiality (Leesfield, 1987). Each of these areas of professional negligence is significant, and together they dominate the malpractice claims that have been filed against mental health professionals. As the field continues to evolve, a new area of professional negligence may become important: the failure to offer adequate treatment and to inform clients about treatment alternatives.

INFORMED CONSENT ON THE EFFICACY OF ALTERNATIVE TREATMENTS

Patients may be given a wide range of alternative treatments for the same mental disorder. From the patient's perspective, the choice of treatment hinges, in part, on chance factors such as the profession of the therapist or his or her "theoretical orientation." Only psychiatrists can prescribe medication, and they surely are more likely to recommend this treatment than are psychologists and social workers. Similarly, behavior therapists are likely to offer behavior therapy, and psychoanalysts to offer psychoanalysis.

As we have argued throughout this text, however, the goal of research is to identify specific treatments for specific disorders. This scientific approach has been successful in identifying some approaches that are more effective than others in treating particular disorders. If evidence points to the superiority of one treatment over another, several questions arise. Does the mental health professional have an obligation to offer the more effective treatment, make a referral to another professional who can provide it, or at a minimum, obtain informed consent to pursue an alternative course of therapy?

Osheroff v. Chestnut Lodge   This issue was raised in *Osheroff v. Chestnut Lodge* [62 Md. App. 519, 490 A. 2d. 720 (Md. App. 1985)]. In 1979, Dr. Rafael Osheroff, an internist, admitted himself to Chestnut Lodge, a private psychiatric hospital in Maryland that had long been famous as a center for psychoanalytic psychotherapy. Dr. Osheroff had a history of depression and anxiety, problems that previously had been treated on an outpatient basis with some success using tricyclic antidepressant medication. Apparently, Dr. Osheroff had not been taking his medication prior to his admission to Chestnut Lodge, and his condition had worsened. He was diagnosed by hospital staff as suffering primarily from a narcissistic personality disorder and secondarily from manic–depressive illness (Klerman, 1990b; Malcolm, 1987).

Hospital staff did not offer medication to Dr. Osheroff during his hospitalization because they hoped that he could achieve what they viewed as "more basic" changes in his personality through psychotherapy. As an alternative to medication, Dr. Osheroff was seen in individual psychoanalytic psychotherapy 4 times a week, and he participated in group therapy as well. During Dr. Osheroff's 7 months of hospitalization, his condition did not improve and actually may have deteriorated

confidentiality The ethical obligation not to reveal private communications in psychotherapy and in other professional contacts between mental health professionals and their clients.

somewhat. After this time, his family discharged him from Chestnut Lodge and admitted him to another private psychiatric hospital, Silver Hill in Connecticut. At Silver Hill, Dr. Osheroff was diagnosed as suffering from a psychotic depressive reaction, and he was treated with phenothiazines and tricyclic antidepressants. He began to improve within 3 weeks after treatment began, and he was discharged from the hospital within 3 months. Although he continued to experience some problems, following his discharge Dr. Osheroff was able to resume his medical practice with the help of outpatient psychotherapy and antidepressants (Klerman, 1990; Malcolm, 1987).

In 1982, Dr. Osheroff sued Chestnut Lodge for negligence. His claim stated that Chestnut Lodge had misdiagnosed his condition, failed to offer appropriate treatment, and failed to offer him informed consent about treatment alternatives (Malcolm, 1987). He argued that research available in 1979 provided clear support for the use of medication in the treatment of severe depression but offered no support for the use of psychoanalytic psychotherapy in the treatment of either depression or narcissistic personality disorder. As required by state law in Maryland, the matter was first heard by an arbitration panel. The panel initially awarded Dr. Osheroff $250,000 in damages, but it later reduced the amount of the award. Both sides appealed the decision of the arbitration board, but the matter was eventually settled out of court (Klerman, 1990).

The private settlement of this case limits its precedent-setting value. Nevertheless, it suggests that mental health professionals will be held to increasingly higher standards in offering alternative treatments, or at least in informing patients about the risks and benefits of various treatments. As researchers demonstrate that certain approaches are more or less effective in treating particular disorders, offering informed consent about treatment alternatives is likely to become a routine practice for mental health professionals. Informed consent means providing accurate information about risks and benefits in an understandable and noncoercive manner.

Confidentiality

Confidentiality—the ethical obligation not to reveal private communications—is basic to psychotherapy. The therapist's guarantee of privacy is essential to facilitating the disclosure of important, clinically relevant information, and the maintenance of confidentiality with past clients is essential to gaining the trust of future clients. For these reasons, confidentiality standards are a part of the professional ethics of all of the major mental health professions, and they are frequently addressed in state licensing regulations as well.

Despite the overriding importance of confidentiality, mental health professionals sometimes may be compelled by law to reveal confidential information. For example, all states require mental health professionals to break confidentiality and report suspected cases of child abuse. *Privileged communications* are confidential exchanges that legislation explicitly protects from being revealed. Various state statutes extend some privileged communication to psychologists and psychiatrists, as they do to physicians, lawyers, and the clergy (Morse, 1990), but child abuse must be reported in all states. This requirement can create dilemmas for therapists (Smith & Meyer, 1985). In order to provide fully informed consent, must a therapist make the limits on confidentiality clear before beginning therapy? If therapists tell their clients that their disclosures of child abuse will be reported to social service agencies, does this encourage clients to be something less than honest? Does reporting child abuse undermine the therapeutic relationship that might benefit an abused child?

Confidentiality also must be broken when clients are dangerous to themselves or others, so that civil commitment can proceed. The influential case of *Tarasoff v. Regents of the University of California* [551 P.2d 334 (1976)] identified another obligation that therapists may assume when a client expresses violent intentions: the duty to warn the potential victim.

TARASOFF AND THE DUTY TO PROTECT POTENTIAL VICTIMS

On October 27, 1969, a young woman named Tatiana Tarasoff was killed by Prosenjit Poddar, a foreign student at the University of California at Berkeley. Poddar had pursued a romantic relationship with Tarasoff, but after having been repeatedly rejected by her, he sought treatment at the

getting help

Mental Health and the Law

At a broad social level, getting help for people with emotional disorders involves challenging societal and legal obstacles. Not only must we be good consumers when searching for effective treatments for psychological problems, but we also must be strong advocates for making mental health services available and for the rights of the mentally ill, especially for people with serious mental illnesses.

Advocacy can be a way of giving help as well as insuring that you and those you care for can get help if or when you need it. For serious mental illness, the National Alliance for the Mentally Ill (NAMI) is the largest and most effective national advocacy organization. You can find NAMI on the Internet at http://www.nami.org/. In addition to its national efforts, there may be a local chapter of NAMI in your community. Another advocacy group is the Judge David L. Bazelon Center for Mental Health Law. This group focuses more specifically on legal issues in the treatment of psychological disorders. The Center tracks funding, legislation, and litigation; and it offers legal advice and assistance in selected cases. Their Web site, http://www.bazelon.org/, gives information on a number of their priorities such as improving mental health treatment systems, increasing the availability of services for underserved populations (children, the aged), and addressing homelessness and housing needs. The American Bar Association's Commission on Mental and Physical Disability Law (internet address: http://www.abanet.org/disability/) also collects and offers a wealth of information on mental health law and the rights of people disabled by mental illness.

An excellent book on these topics is *The Rights of People with Mental Disabilities: The Authoritative ACLU Guide to the Rights of People with Mental Illness and Mental Retardation* by Robert Levy, Leonard Rubenstein, Bruce Ennis, and Norman Dorsen.

Of course, mental health advocacy involves individual as well as organized efforts. We encourage you to advocate directly in any number of small ways. You can continue to educate yourself and others about the needs of the mentally ill and our society's failure to meet those needs. Another book (and author) that we highly recommend is E. Fuller Torrey's *Out of the Shadows: Confronting America's Mental Illness Crisis*. In everyday interactions, you can help by standing up for what you believe is right and just in our society's response to the immense problem of mental illness. Even more simply, you can help by being receptive to agencies and individuals in your community. Advocacy, like therapy, begins by recognizing that the person with a psychological disorder is, first and foremost, a person. ♛

Berkeley student health facility. Poddar was diagnosed as suffering from paranoid schizophrenia, and the clinical psychologist who treated Poddar concluded that he was dangerous to himself and others. After consulting with two psychiatrists, the psychologist decided to pursue civil commitment. He notified the campus police of his concerns, and asked them to detain Poddar for the purpose of an emergency commitment. The police concluded that Poddar was not dangerous, however, and released him after he agreed to stay away from Tarasoff. Poddar subsequently discontinued therapy, and no one notified Tarasoff that Poddar posed a threat to her life. Poddar had never mentioned Tatiana Tarasoff by name, but the information he related to the psychologist was sufficient to deduce her identity. Two months after the police had questioned him, Poddar murdered Tarasoff after being rejected by her once more.

Tatiana Tarasoff and Prosenjit Poddar, the man who killed her. The California Supreme Court ruled that Poddar's therapist should have warned Tarasoff that her life might be in danger.

Tarasoff's parents sued the university, the therapists, and the police for negligence. The California Supreme Court ruled that the defendants were liable for failing to warn the woman of the impending danger. Specifically, the court ruled that therapists are liable if (1) they should have known about the dangerousness based on accepted professional standards of conduct, and (2) they failed to exercise reasonable care in warning the potential victim. Subsequent California cases have limited the duty to protect to cases that involve a specific, identifiable target of potential violence. A general statement of intended violence invokes no duty to protect (Goodman, 1985).

The *Tarasoff* case prompted subsequent litigation, and almost 20 states have enacted laws that outline therapists' duty to protect potential victims of violence (Appelbaum, 1994; Geske, 1989). Guidelines for evaluating and documenting assessments of dangerousness to others are rapidly becoming as important as policies for assessing suicide risk (Monahan, 1993). Still, the issues raised by *Tarasoff* are far from resolved. For example, we can easily foresee future cases in which questions will be raised about therapists' duty to protect the unwitting sexual partners of their clients who have AIDS.

Summary

The U.S. legal system assumes that behavior is the product of free will, the capacity to make choices and freely act on them. The law therefore holds people responsible for their own actions. Scientific psychology rejects the notion of free will and instead emphasizes determinism, the idea that behavior is caused by biological, psychological, and social forces. Assumptions about free will and determinism conflict strongly in the **insanity defense.** The legally insane individual is not assumed to be acting out of free will and therefore is not held responsible for his or her actions.

The M'Naghten test is one rule for finding a person not guilty by reason of **insanity.** According to this rule, legal insanity is established if a mental disease or defect prevents a criminal from knowing the wrongfulness of his or her actions. A second major rule, the irresistible impulse test, indicates that defendants are insane if they were unable to control their actions because of mental disease or defect. Controversies about the insanity defense have caused some states to drop the irresistible impulse test, as well as to shift the burden of proof from the prosecution to the defense. Professionals who serve as *expert witnesses* are responsible only for offering opinions about psychological well-being. The court, not the expert witness, is responsible for determining the ultimate issue of insanity.

Competence is the defendant's ability to understand legal proceedings and to participate in his or her own defense. Many more people accused of crimes are institutionalized because of findings of incompetence than because of insanity. Incompetence has received far less attention, perhaps because, unlike the insanity defense, competence determinations raise few broad philosophical issues about responsibility.

The issue of **civil commitment**—hospitalizing people against their will—reflects philosophical tensions within the law. Libertarian views, which emphasize protecting the rights of the individual, often conflict with paternalist approaches, which emphasize the state's duty to protect its citizens. Three grounds dominate commitment laws: (1) inability to care for self, (2) dangerous to self, and (3) dangerous to others. Controversies abound, but a relation between mental illness and "dangerousness" does exist, and mental health professionals can predict dangerousness with some accuracy.

Paternalists and libertarians disagree concerning the commitment of minors who can be hospitalized by their parents. Admissions of adolescents to mental hospitals have increased dramatically, and some critics have suggested that many minors are committed to mental hospitals merely because they are troublesome to their parents and because hospitalization is profitable to private psychiatric hospitals.

The rights of mental patients have received increased attention since the 1970s. The right to treatment indicates that hospitalized patients must receive therapy and not just custodial care. The right to treatment in the least restrictive environment indicates that therapy should be provided in community settings when it is possible and appropriate. The right to refuse treatment indicates that patients cannot be forced to receive certain treatments (for example, taking medications) without **informed consent** or a careful substituted judgment. Concerns about patients' rights also have given impetus to the **deinstitutionalization** movement, the philosophy that many of the mentally ill and mentally retarded can be better cared for in their community than in large mental hospitals. Unfortunately, the lack of follow-up care in the community has undermined this laudable goal.

Family law and mental health law have different roots, and cases involving one are typically tried in different courts than are cases involving the other. A general dilemma in family law is how to balance the potentially competing interests of children, parents, and the state.

Child custody must be decided when parents divorce. These decisions involve determinations about both physical custody—where the children will live—and legal custody—how the parents will make decisions about their children. Custody decisions are based on the child's best interests standard, a vague directive that requires judgments as to what the child's best interests are and what the future will bring. Parents often make determinations about their own children's best interests privately in divorce mediation or elsewhere.

Child abuse may involve physical abuse, sexual abuse, neglect, or psychological abuse. Reports of child abuse have increased greatly in recent years, but neither the law nor mental health professionals have reached consensus on how best to fulfill children's best interests in these cases.

Psychiatrists, clinical psychologists, and social workers all have **professional responsibilities** to meet the ethical standards of their profession and to uphold the laws of the states in which they practice. Key professional issues include obtaining informed consent about alternative treatment procedures, clearly identifying whom the professional is serving, and maintaining **confidentiality.** A relatively new concern is the duty to warn potential victims when a client reveals violent intentions.

Critical Thinking

1. What is your view on the insanity defense? Should we hold mentally ill criminals fully responsible for all of their actions? What about battered women who kill their husbands?

2. What is your position on deinstitutionalization? Has the pendulum swung too far in the direction of releasing mental patients into communities with inadequate services? How would you feel if a group home for the mentally ill was being planned for your neighborhood?

3. What are your own views on the consequences of divorce for children and how the legal system can better serve divorcing families? Do you think laws should make it harder for spouses with children to get divorced?

4. Do you think it is unethical for mental health professionals to offer treatments they prefer even when research indicates that other approaches are more effective?

Glossary

Abnormal psychology The application of psychological science to the study of mental disorders. Includes investigation of the causes and treatment of psychopathological conditions.

Abstinence violation effect The guilt and perceived loss of control that the person feels whenever he or she slips and finds himself or herself returning to drug use after an extended period of abstinence.

Acquired immune deficiency syndrome (AIDS) A disease caused by the human immunodeficiency virus (HIV) that attacks the immune system and leaves the patient susceptible to unusual infections.

Acute stress disorder (ASD) A new category of mental disorder in DSM-IV that is defined as a reaction occurring within 4 weeks following a traumatic experience and is characterized by dissociative symptoms, reexperiencing, avoidance, and marked anxiety or arousal. Contrasts with posttraumatic stress disorder, which either lasts longer or has a delayed onset.

Addiction A term used to describe substance use problems such as alcoholism. Replaced in official terminology by the term *substance dependence,* with which it is synonymous.

Adjustment disorder A DSM-IV classification designating the development of clinically significant symptoms in response to stress in which the symptoms are not severe enough to warrant classification as another mental disorder.

Affect The pattern of observable behaviors that are associated with subjective feelings. People express affect through changes in their facial expressions, the pitch of their voices, and their hand and body movements.

Ageism A number of misconceptions and prejudices about aging and older adults.

Agnosia ("perception without meaning") The inability to identify objects. The person's sensory functions are unimpaired, but he or she is unable to recognize the source of stimulation.

Agoraphobia An exaggerated fear of being in situations from which escape might be difficult. Literally means "fear of the marketplace," and is sometimes described as fear of public spaces.

Alogia A form of speech disturbance found in schizophrenia. Can include reductions in the amount of speech (poverty of speech) or speech that does not convey meaningful information (poverty of content of speech).

Alzheimer's disease A form of dementia in which cognitive impairment appears gradually and deterioration is progressive. A definite diagnosis of Alzheimer's disease requires the observation of two specific types of brain lesions: neurofibrillary tangles and senile plaques.

Amenorrhea The absence of at least three consecutive menstrual cycles; a defining symptom of anorexia nervosa in females.

Amnestic disorder A form of cognitive disorder characterized by memory impairments that are more limited or circumscribed than those seen in dementia or delirium.

Amniocentesis The extraction of fluid from the amniotic sac in order to test for chromosomal and genetic defects in the developing fetus.

Androgyny The possession of both "female" and "male" gender-role characteristics.

Anhedonia The inability to experience pleasure. In contrast to blunted affect, which refers to the lack of outward expression, anhedonia is a lack of positive subjective feelings.

Anorexia nervosa A type of eating disorder characterized by the refusal to maintain a minimally normal body weight along with other symptoms related to eating and body image.

Anterograde amnesia The inability to learn or remember new material after a particular point in time.

Antisocial personality disorder A pervasive and persistent disregard for, and frequent violation of, the rights of other people. Also known as *psychopathy.* In DSM-IV, it is defined in terms of a persistent pattern of irresponsible and antisocial behavior that begins during childhood or adolescence and continues into the adult years.

Anxiety A diffuse emotional reaction that is out of proportion to threats from the environment. Rather than being directed toward the person's present circumstances, anxiety is typically associated with the anticipation of future problems.

Anxious attachment An insecure relationship in which an infant or child shows ambivalence about seeking reassurance or security from an attachment figure.

Aphasia The loss or impairment of previously acquired abilities in language comprehension or production that cannot be explained by sensory or motor defects or by diffuse brain dysfunction.

Apraxia The loss of a previously acquired ability to perform purposeful movements in response to verbal commands. The problem cannot be explained by muscle weakness or simple incoordination.

Asperger's disorder A subtype of pervasive developmental disorder (new in DSM-IV) that is identical to autism (oddities in social interaction, stereotyped behavior), with the exception that there is no clinically significant delay in language.

Assessment The process of gathering and organizing information about a person's behavior.

Attachments Selective bonds that develop between infants and their caregivers, usually their parents, and are theorized to be related to later development. Analogous to the process imprinting which has been observed in many animals.

Attention deficit Inattention characterized by distractibility, frequent shifts from one uncompleted activity to another, careless mistakes, and/or poor organization or effort. A key symptom of attention-deficit/hyperactivity disorder.

Attention-deficit/hyperactivity disorder A psychological disorder of childhood characterized by hyperactivity, inattention, and impulsivity. Typically has an onset by the early school years.

Attribution Perceived causes; people's beliefs about cause–effect relations.

Atypical antipsychotic A type of medication that is beneficial for psychotic patients but does not produce extrapyramidal motor side effects and may not be associated with increased risk of tardive dyskinesia.

Authoritative parenting A style of parenting that is both loving and firm and is often used by parents of well-adjusted children.

Autism Literally, "absorption in one's own mental activity." Formally, a severe pervasive developmental disorder characterized by profound problems in social interaction, communication, and stereotyped behavior, interests, and activities (see also autistic disorder).

Autistic disorder A severe form of pervasive developmental disorder characterized by oddities in social interaction (autistic aloneness), communication impairments, and stereotyped behavior, interests, and activities.

Autonomic nervous system The division of the peripheral nervous system that regulates the functions of various bodily organs such as the heart and stomach. The actions of the autonomic nervous system are largely involuntary, and it has two branches, the sympathetic and parasympathetic nervous systems.

Avoidant personality disorder An enduring pattern of thinking and behavior that is characterized by pervasive social discomfort, fear of negative evaluation, and timidity. People with this disorder tend to be socially isolated outside of family circles. They want to be liked by others, but they are easily hurt by even minimal signs of disapproval from other people.

Avolition (lack of volition or will) A negative symptom of schizophrenia involving a loss of willpower, indecisiveness, and ambivalence. The person becomes apathetic and ceases to engage in purposeful actions.

Axon The trunk of the neuron where messages are transmitted outward toward other cells with which a given neuron communicates.

Balanced placebo design A research design that combines the placebo and antiplacebo methods. It can be used to assess the effect of alcohol, the effect of expectations, and the interaction of alcohol by expectation.

Barbiturates Drugs that depress activities of the central nervous system; mostly for sedation.

Battered woman syndrome A controversial classification of the common psychological effects of spousal abuse. Includes a tension-building phase leading up to violence, the battering incident itself, and a stage of loving contrition, during which the batterer apologizes. According to some experts, this induces learned helplessness in battered women.

Behavioral approach A paradigm that focuses on observable behavior as the subject of psychology. Also emphasizes learning through classical conditioning, operant conditioning, modeling, and perhaps cognitive processes.

Behavioral coding system (also known as a formal observation schedule) An observational assessment procedure that focuses on the frequency of specific behavioral events.

Behavioral family therapy A form of family treatment that may include several variations, but always trains parents to use operant conditioning as a way of improving child discipline.

Behavioral gerontology A subspecialty within behavioral medicine developed specifically for studying and treating the behavioral components of illness among older adults.

Behavioral marital therapy A variation on couples therapy that emphasizes the partners' moment-to-moment interaction, particularly their exchange of positive and negative behaviors, their style of communication, and their strategies for solving problems.

Behavioral medicine A multidisciplinary field concerned with studying and treating the behavioral components of physical illness.

Behavior genetics The study of broad genetic contributions to the development of normal and abnormal behavior.

Behaviorism The belief within scientific psychology that observable behaviors, not unobservable cognitive or emotional states, are the appropriate focus of psychological study.

Behavior therapy An approach to psychotherapy that focuses on behavior change in the present; includes a diverse array of techniques, many of which were developed from basic, psychological research.

Benzodiazepines Group of drugs that have potent hypnotic, sedative, and anxiolytic action (also called antianxiety drugs).

Bereavement Grieving in response to the death of a loved one.

Beta-amyloid Protein material that forms the core of senile plaques, a type of brain lesion found in patients with Alzheimer's disease.

Binge eating Eating an amount of food in a fixed period of time that is clearly larger than most people would eat under similar circumstances. One part of the eating disorder of bulimia nervosa.

Binge eating disorder A controversial diagnosis defined by repeated episodes of binge eating but in the absence of compensatory behavior; included in an appendix of DSM-IV.

Biofeedback Behavioral medicine treatment that uses laboratory equipment to monitor physiological processes (that generally occur outside of conscious awareness) and provide feedback about them. Hypothesized to help patients to gain conscious control over problematic physiological processes such as hypertension.

Biological reductionism The assumption that biological explanations are more useful than psychological explanations because they deal with smaller units—with brain chemistry, for example, instead of emotional experience.

Biomedical approach A paradigm for conceptualizing abnormal behavior that focuses on biological causation and the analogy between physical and psychological illnesses. Sometimes referred to as the "medical model."

Biopsychosocial model A view of the etiology of mental disorders which assumes that disorder can best be understood in terms of the interaction of biological, psychological, and social systems.

Bipolar mood disorder A form of mood disorder in which the person experiences episodes of mania as well as episodes of depression.

Blunted affect A flattening or restriction of the person's nonverbal display of emotional responses. Blunted patients fail to exhibit signs of emotion or feeling.

Body dysmorphic disorder A type of somatoform disorder characterized by constant preoccupation with some imagined defect in physical appearance.

Body image A cognitive and affective evaluation of one's weight and shape, often a critical one.

Borderline personality disorder An enduring pattern of thinking and behavior whose essential feature is a pervasive instability in mood, self-image, and interpersonal relationships. Manifestations of this disorder include frantic efforts to avoid real or imagined abandonment. People who fit this description frequently hold opinions of significant others that vacillate between unrealistically positive and negative extremes.

Boundaries Rules defining a relationship, particularly the rules that separate a third person from an individual or another relationship. For example, the boundary of the marital relationship is defined, in part, by the limited discussion of intimate topics outside the relationship.

Brief psychotic disorder A diagnostic category in DSM-IV that includes people who exhibit psychotic symptoms for at least 1 day but no more than 1 month. After the symptoms are resolved, the person returns to the same level of functioning that had been achieved prior to the psychotic episode.

Bulimia nervosa A type of eating disorder characterized by repeated episodes of binge eating followed by inappropriate compensatory behaviors (such as self-induced vomiting) together with other symptoms related to eating and body image.

Cardiovascular reactivity A measure of the intensity of an individual's cardiovascular reactions to stress in the laboratory; a predictor of future cardiovascular disease.

Case study A careful description and analysis of the problems experienced by one person.

Catatonia Motor symptoms that can include either immobility and marked muscular rigidity or excitement and overactivity.

Catatonic type A subtype of schizophrenia that is characterized by symptoms of motor immobility (including rigidity and posturing) or excessive and purposeless motor activity.

Categorical approach to classification A view of classification based on the assumption that there are qualitative differences between normal and abnormal behavior as well as between one form of abnormal behavior and other forms of abnormal behavior.

Central nervous system The major communication system in the body, which comprises the brain and the spinal cord.

Cerebellum Part of the hindbrain that serves as a control center in helping to coordinate physical movements. The cerebellum receives information on body movements and integrates this feedback with directives about desired actions from higher brain structures.

Cerebral cortex The uneven surface of the brain that lies just underneath the skull, and controls and integrates sophisticated memory, sensory, and motor functions.

Cerebral hemispheres The two major structures of the forebrain and the site of most sensory, emotional, and cognitive processes. The functions of the cerebral hemispheres are lateralized. In general, the left cerebral hemisphere is involved in language and related functions, and the right side is involved in spatial organization and analysis.

Child abuse A legal decision that a parent or other responsible adult has inflicted damage or offered inadequate care to a child; may include physical abuse, sexual abuse, neglect, and psychological abuse.

Chorea Unusual, involuntary muscle movements associated with disorders such as Huntington's disease.

Chromosomes Chainlike structures found in the nucleus of cells that carry genes and information about heredity. Humans normally have 23 pairs of chromosomes.

Civil commitment The involuntary hospitalization of the mentally ill; the decision typically is justified based on dangerousness to self or others (or inability to care for self).

Classical conditioning Pavlov's form of learning through association. A conditioned response eventually is elicited by a conditioned stimulus after repeated pairings with an unconditioned stimulus (which produces an unconditioned response).

Classification system A system for grouping together objects or organisms that share certain properties in common. In psychopathology, the set of categories in DSM-IV that describes mental disorders.

Client-centered therapy Carl Rogers's humanistic therapy that follows the client's lead. Therapists offer warmth, empathy, and genuineness, but clients solve their own problems.

Clinical psychology The profession and academic discipline that is concerned with the application of psychological science to the assessment and treatment of mental disorders.

Coercion A pattern of interaction in which unwitting parents positively reinforce children's misbehavior (by giving in to their demands), and children negatively reinforce parents' capitulation (by ending their obnoxious behavior).

Cognitive behavior therapy The expansion of the scope of behavior therapy to include cognition and research on human information processing. Includes various general techniques, such as Beck's cognitive therapy and Ellis's RET.

Cognitive therapy A psychotherapy technique and important part of cognitive behavior therapy that was developed specifically as a treatment for depression by Aaron Beck. Beck's cognitive therapy involves challenging negative cognitive distortions through a technique called collaborative empiricism.

Cohort A group that shares some feature in common, particularly their date of birth.

Cohort effect Differences that distinguish one cohort from another. Cohorts share some feature in common, especially their date of birth, and cohort effects often distinguish people born in one time period (e.g., the 1960s) from those born in another.

Comorbidity The simultaneous manifestation of more than one disorder.

Competence Defendants' ability to understand legal proceedings and act rationally in relation to them. Competence evaluations can take place at different points in the legal process, but competence to stand trial (the ability to participate in one's own defense) is particularly important.

Compulsion A repetitive, ritualistic behavior that is aimed at the reduction of anxiety and distress or the prevention of some dreaded event. Compulsions are considered by the person to be senseless or irrational. The person feels compelled to perform the compulsion; he or she attempts to resist but cannot.

Conditioned response A response that is elicited by a conditioned stimulus; similar to but weaker than the unconditioned response. Central in classical conditioning.

Conditioned stimulus A neutral stimulus that, when repeatedly paired with an unconditioned stimulus, comes to produce a conditioned response. In Pavlov's experiments, the bell was the conditioned stimulus. Central in classical conditioning.

Conduct disorder (CD) A psychological disorder of childhood that is defined primarily by behavior that is illegal as well as antisocial.

Confidentiality The ethical obligation not to reveal private communications in psychotherapy and in other professional contacts between mental health professionals and their clients.

Construct (or hypothetical construct) A theoretical device that refers to events or states that reside within a person and are proposed to help understand or explain a person's behavior.

Controlled drinking A controversial goal for some alcohol abusers. This concept refers to moderate consumption of alcohol in a pattern that avoids drinking to the point of intoxication.

Conversion disorder A type of somatoform disorder characterized by physical symptoms that often mimic those found in neurological diseases, such as blindness, numbing, or paralysis. The symptoms often make no anatomic sense.

Coronary heart disease (CHD) A group of diseases of the heart that includes angina pectoris (chest pains) and myocardial infarction (heart attack).

Correlational study A scientific research method in which the relation between two factors (their co-relation) is studied in a systematic fashion. Has the advantage of practicality, as correlations between many variables can be studied in the real world, but also has the disadvantage that "correlation does not mean causation."

Correlation coefficient A number that always ranges between -1.00 and $+1.00$ and indicates the strength and direction of the relation between two variables. A higher absolute value indicates a stronger relation, while a correlation coefficient of 0 indicates no relation. The sign indicates the direction of the correlation.

Countertransference The therapist's own feelings toward the client, particularly as described in psychoanalysis.

Couples therapy Partners who are involved in an intimate relationship are seen together in psychotherapy; sometimes called marital therapy or marriage counseling. Improving communication and negotiation are common goals.

Creutzfeldt-Jakob disease A type of dementia caused by a specific viral infection.

Cross-cultural psychology The scientific study of ways that human behavior and mental processes are influenced by social and cultural factors.

Cultural-familial retardation Typically mild mental retardation that runs in families and is linked with poverty. Thought to be the most common cause of mental retardation. There is controversy about the relative roles of genes or psychosocial disadvantage.

Culture The shared way of life of a group or people; a complex system of accumulated knowledge that helps the people in a particular society adapt to their environment.

Cyclothymia A chronic, less severe form of bipolar disorder. The bipolar equivalent of dysthymia.

Defense mechanisms Unconscious processes that service the ego and reduce conscious anxiety by distorting anxiety-producing memories, emotions, and impulses. For example, projection, displacement, or rationalization.

Deinstitutionalization The movement to treat the mentally ill and mentally retarded in communities rather than in large mental hospitals.

Delirium A confusional state that develops over a short period of time and is often associated with agitation and hyperactivity. The primary symptom is clouding of consciousness or reduced awareness of one's surroundings.

Delusion An obviously false and idiosyncratic belief that is rigidly held in spite of its preposterous nature.

Delusional disorder Describes persons who do not meet the full symptomatic criteria for schizophrenia, but they are preoccupied for at least 1 month with delusions that are not bizarre.

Dementia A gradually worsening loss of memory and related cognitive functions, including the use of language as well as reasoning and decision making.

Dementia praecox Kraepelin's original term for the disorder now known as schizophrenia. It referred to psychotic disorders that ended in severe intellectual deterioration (dementia) and that had an early or premature (praecox) onset, usually during adolescence.

Dendrites "Branches" from the soma of the neuron that serve the primary function of receiving messages from other cells.

Dependent personality disorder An enduring pattern of dependent and submissive behavior. These people are exceedingly dependent on other people for advice and reassurance. Often unable to make everyday decisions on their own, they feel anxious and helpless when they are alone.

Dependent variable The outcome that is hypothesized to vary according to manipulations in the independent variable in an experiment.

Depersonalization disorder A type of dissociative disorder characterized by severe and persistent feelings of being detached from oneself (depersonalization experiences). For example, the repeated and profound sensation of floating above your body and observing yourself act.

Depression Can refer to a *symptom* (subjective feelings of sadness), a *mood* (sustained and pervasive feelings of despair), or to a clinical *syndrome* (in which the presence of a depressed mood is accompanied by several additional symptoms, such as fatigue, loss of energy, sleeping difficulties, and appetite changes).

Detoxification The process of short-term medical care (medication, rest, diets, fluids, and so on) during removal of a drug upon which a person has become dependent. The aim is to minimize withdrawal symptoms.

Diagnosis The process of determining the nature of a person's disorder. In the case of psychopathology, deciding that a person fits into a particular diagnostic category, such as schizophrenia or major depressive disorder.

Diathesis A predisposition to disorder. Also known as *vulnerability*. A diathesis only causes abnormal behavior when it is combined with a stress or challenging experience.

Dimensional approach to classification A view of classification based on the assumption that behavior is distributed on a continuum from normal to abnormal. Also includes the assumption that differences between one type of behavior and another are quantitative rather than qualitative in nature.

Disorganization A type of symptom, such as disorganized speech and bizarre behavior, found in schizophrenic disorders that does not fit easily into either the positive or negative category of symptoms.

Disorganized speech (also known as *formal thought disorder*) Severe disruptions of verbal communication, involving the form of the person's speech.

Disorganized type A subtype of schizophrenia (formerly known as hebephrenia) that is characterized by disorganized speech, disorganized behavior, and flat or inappropriate affect. If delusions or hallucinations are present, their content is not well organized.

Dissociation The separation of mental processes such as memory or consciousness that normally are integrated. Normal dissociative experiences include fleeting feelings of unreality and *déjà vu* experiences—the feeling that an event has happened before. Extreme dissociative experiences characterize dissociative disorders.

Dissociative amnesia A type of dissociative disorder characterized by the sudden inability to recall extensive and important personal information. The onset often is sudden and may occur in response to trauma or extreme stress.

Dissociative disorders A category of psychological disorders characterized by persistent, maladaptive disruptions in the integration of memory, consciousness, or identity. Examples include dissociative fugue and dissociative identity disorder (multiple personality).

Dissociative identity disorder An unusual dissociative disorder characterized by the existence of two or more distinct personalities in a single individual (also known as multiple personality disorder). At least two personalities repeatedly take control over the person's behavior, and some personalities have limited or no memory of the other.

Distorted body image A perceptual inaccuracy in evaluating body size and shape that sometimes is found in anorexia nervosa.

Diversion A practice of directing problem youth away from the juvenile justice system and into some alternative treatment or program. For example, a juvenile offender may be referred to counseling instead of having a hearing held in court.

Divorce mediation A procedure in which former partners attempt to resolve child custody or other disputes that arise from a divorce with the help of an impartial third party (a mediator).

Dizygotic (DZ) twins Fraternal twins produced from separate fertilized eggs. Like all siblings, DZ twins share an average of 50 percent of their genes.

Dominance The hierarchical ordering of a social group into more and less powerful members. Dominance rankings are indexed by the availability of uncontested privileges.

Dose-response effects Different treatment responses to different dosages of a medication.

Double blind, placebo-controlled study A study in which neither the therapist nor the patient knows whether the patient receives the real treatment (for example, a medication) or a placebo.

Down syndrome A chromosomal disorder that is the most common known biological cause of mental retardation. It is caused by an extra chromosome (usually on the 21st pair) and associated with a characteristic physical appearance.

Drug of abuse (also called a *psychoactive substance*) A chemical substance that alters a person's mood, level of perception, or brain functioning.

Dyskinesia Involuntary movements, such as tics, chorea, or tremors, that are often associated with certain types of dementia.

Dyspareunia Persistent genital pain during or after sexual intercourse. The problem can occur in either men or women.

Dysphoria Unpleasant mood, often associated with depression.

Dysthymia One of the mood disorders; a form of mild depression characterized by a chronic course (the person is seldom without symptoms).

Eating disorders A category of psychological disorders characterized by severe disturbances in eating behavior, specifically anorexia nervosa and bulimia nervosa.

Eclectic An approach of picking different treatments according to the needs of individual disorders and individual clients.

Ego One of Freud's three central personality structures. In Freudian theory, the ego must deal with reality as it attempts to fulfill id impulses as well as superego demands. The ego operates on the reality principle, and much of the ego resides in conscious awareness.

Ego analysis Originated in the work of different therapists trained in Freudian psychoanalysis, but who focus much more on the ego than on the id. Ego analysts are concerned with the patient's dealings with the external world.

Electra complex Freud's hypothesis of "penis envy," girls yearn for something their fathers have and that they are "missing." In Freudian theory, girls resolve the Electra complex by identifying with their mothers.

Electroconvulsive therapy (ECT) A treatment that involves the deliberate induction of a convulsion by passing electricity through one or both hemispheres of the brain. Modern ECT uses restraints, medication, and carefully controlled electrical stimulation to minimize adverse consequences. Can be an effective treatment for severe depression, especially following the failure of other approaches.

Emotion A state of arousal that is defined by subjective feeling states, such as sadness, anger, and disgust. Emotions are often accompanied by physiological changes, such as in heart rate and respiration rate.

Emotion-focused coping Internally oriented coping in an attempt to alter one's emotional or cognitive responses to a stressor.

Empathy Emotional understanding. Empathy involves understanding others' unique feelings and perspectives. Highlighted by Rogers but basic to most forms of psychotherapy.

Encopresis Inappropriately controlled defecation among children old enough to maintain control of their bowels.

Endorphin The term is a contraction formed from the words *endogenous* (meaning "within") and *morphine*. Endorphins are relatively short chains of amino acids, or neuropeptides, that are naturally synthesized in the brain and are closely related to morphine (an opioid) in terms of their pharmacological properties.

Enmeshed family Families whose members are overly involved in one another's lives.

Enuresis Inappropriately controlled urination (during sleep or while awake) among children old enough to maintain control of their bladder.

Epidemiology The scientific study of the frequency and distribution of disorders within a population.

Erectile dysfunction Difficulty experienced by a man in obtaining an erection that is suffi-

cient to accomplish intercourse or maintaining an erection long enough to satisfy himself or his partner during intercourse.

Estrogen The female sex hormone.

Etiology The causes or origins of a disorder.

Euphoria An exaggerated feeling of physical and emotional well-being, typically associated with manic episodes in bipolar mood disorder.

Exhibitionism One of the paraphilias, characterized by distress over, or acting on, urges to expose one's genitals to an unsuspecting stranger.

Experimental group The group of participants in an experiment that receives a treatment that is hypothesized to cause some measured effect. Participants in the experimental group are compared with untreated participants in a control group.

Experimental hypothesis A new prediction made by an investigator to be tested in an experiment.

Expressed emotion (EE) A concept that refers to a collection of negative or intrusive attitudes sometimes displayed by relatives of patients who are being treated for a disorder. If at least one of a patient's relatives is hostile, critical, or emotionally overinvolved, the family environment typically is considered high in expressed emotion.

Externalizing disorders An empirically derived category of disruptive child behavior problems that create problems for the external world (for example, attention-deficit/hyperactivity disorder).

External validity Whether the findings of an experiment generalize to other people, places and circumstances, particularly real-life situations.

Extinction The gradual elimination of a response when learning conditions change. In classical conditioning, extinction occurs when a conditioned stimulus no longer is paired with an unconditioned stimulus. In operant conditioning, extinction occurs when the contingent is removed between behavior and its consequences.

Extraversion A dimension of personality that describes a person's activity level, especially interest in interacting with other people, and the ease with which the person expresses positive emotions.

Family life cycle The developmental course of family relationships throughout life; most family life-cycle theories mark stages and transitions with major changes in family relationships and membership.

Family therapy Treatment that might include two, three, or more family members in the psychotherapy sessions. Improving communication and negotiation are common goals, although family therapy also may be used to help well members adjust to a family member's illness.

Fear An unpleasant emotional reaction experienced in the face of real, immediate danger. It builds quickly in intensity and helps to organize the person's responses to threats from the environment.

Fetal alcohol syndrome A disorder caused by heavy maternal alcohol consumption and repeated exposure of the developing fetus to alcohol. Infants have retarded physical development, a small head, narrow eyes, cardiac defects, and cognitive impairments. Intellectual functioning ranges from mild mental retardation to normal intelligence with learning disabilities.

Fetishism The use of nonliving objects as a focus of sexual arousal.

Fight or flight response A response to a threat in which psychophysiological reactions mobilize the body to take action against danger.

Fixation The psychodynamic concept that psychological development is arrested at a particular age or stage. The person stops growing emotionally.

Fragile-X syndrome The second most common known biological cause of mental retardation. Transmitted genetically and indicated by a weakening or break on one arm of the X sex chromosome.

Free association A basic technique in Freudian psychoanalysis in which patients are encouraged to speak freely about whatever thoughts cross their mind; presumed to give insight into the unconscious.

Frotteurism One of the paraphilias, characterized by recurrent, intense sexual urges involving touching and rubbing against a nonconsenting person; it often takes place in crowded trains, buses, and elevators.

Gender identity A person's sense of himself or herself as being either male or female.

Gender identity disorder A strong and persistent identification with the opposite sex coupled with a sense of discomfort with one's anatomic sex.

Gender roles Roles associated with social expectations about gendered behavior, for example, "masculine" or "feminine" activities.

General adaptation syndrome (GAS) Selye's three stages in reaction to stress: alarm, resistance, and exhaustion.

General paresis (general paralysis) A set of severe symptoms including dementia, delusions of grandeur, and paralysis caused by the sexually transmitted disease syphilis. Discovery of the cause of general paresis spurred the biological model of mental illness.

Generalization Making accurate statements that extend beyond a specific sample to a larger population.

Generalized anxiety disorder One of the anxiety disorders, which is characterized by excessive and uncontrollable worry about a number of events or activities (such as work or school performance) and associated with symptoms of arousal (such as restlessness, muscle tension, and sleep disturbance).

Genes Ultramicroscopic units of DNA that carry information about heredity. Located on the chromosomes.

Genetic linkage A close association between two genes, typically the genetic locus associated with a disorder or a trait and the locus for a known gene. Two loci are said to be linked when they are sufficiently close together on the same chromosome.

Gerontology The multidisciplinary study of aging and older adults.

Grief The emotional and social process of coping with a separation or a loss, often described as proceeding in stages.

Group therapy The treatment of three or more people in a group setting, often using group relationships as a central part of therapy.

Hallucination A perceptual experience in the absence of external stimulation, such as hearing voices that aren't really there.

Hallucinogens Drugs that produce hallucinations.

Harmful dysfunction A concept used in one approach to the definition of mental disorder. A condition can be considered a mental disorder if it causes some harm to the person and if the condition results from the inability of some mental mechanism to perform its natural function.

Hashish The dried resin from the top of the female cannabis plant. Ingestion of hashish leads to a feeling of being "high" (see marijuana).

Health behavior A wide range of activities that are essential to promoting good health, including positive actions such as proper diet and the avoidance of negative activities such as cigarette smoking.

Heritability The variability in a behavioral characteristic that is accounted for by genetic factors.

Heritability ratio A statistic for computing the proportion of variance in a behavioral characteristic that is accounted for by genetic factors in a given study or series of studies.

Histrionic personality disorder An enduring pattern of thinking and behavior that is characterized by excessive emotionality and attention-seeking behavior. People with this disorder are self-centered, vain, and demanding. Their emotions tend to be shallow and may vacillate erratically.

Holism The assumption that the whole is more than the sum of its parts. A central tenet of systems theory, and counterpoint to reductionism.

Hopelessness theory A theory regarding the role of cognitive events in the etiology of depression; depression is associated with the expectation that very desirable events probably will not occur and that aversive events probably will occur regardless of what the person does.

Humanistic psychology A paradigm for conceptualizing abnormal behavior that rejects determinism and argues that human behavior is the product of free will—how people choose to act. Also adopts an explicitly positive view of human nature.

Humanistic psychotherapy An approach that assumes that the most essential human quality is the ability to make choices and freely act on them (free will). Promoted as a "third force" to counteract the deterministic views of psychodynamic and the behavioral approaches to psychotherapy.

Huntington's disease A primary, differentiated dementia characterized by the presence of unusual involuntary muscle movements. Many Huntington's patients also exhibit a variety of personality changes and symptoms of mental disorders, including primarily depression and anxiety.

Hyperactivity A symptom of attention-deficit/hyperactivity disorder (ADHD), often manifested as squirming, fidgeting, or restless behavior. Found across situations but particularly notable in structured settings.

Hypertension High blood pressure.

Hypoactive sexual desire Diminished desire for sexual activity and reduced frequency of sexual fantasies.

Hypochondriasis A type of somatoform disorder characterized by a person's preoccupying fear or belief that he or she is suffering from a physical illness.

Hypomania An episode of increased energy that is not sufficiently severe to qualify as a full-blown manic episode.

Hypothalamus A part of the limbic system that plays a role in sensation, but more importantly it controls basic biological urges, such as eating, drinking, and sexual activity, as well as much of the functioning of the autonomic nervous system.

Hysteria An outdated but influential diagnostic category that included both somatoform and dissociative disorders. Attempts to treat hysteria had a major effect on Charcot, Freud, and Janet, among others. In Greek, *hysteria* means "uterus," a reflection of ancient speculation that hysteria was restricted to women and caused by frustrated sexual desires.

Iatrogenesis A creation of a disorder by an attempt to treat it.

Id One of Freud's three central personality structures. In Freudian theory, the id is present at birth and is the source of basic drives and motivations. The id houses biological drives (such as hunger), as well as Freud's two key psychological drives, sex and aggression. Operates according to the pleasure principle.

Identity Erikson's term for the broad definition of self; in his view, identity is the product of the adolescent's struggle to answer the question "Who am I?"

Identity crisis Erikson's period of basic uncertainty about self during late adolescence and early adult life. A consequence of the psychosocial stage of identity versus role confusion.

Impulse control disorder A disorder characterized by failure to resist an impulse or a temptation to perform some pleasurable or tension-releasing act that is harmful to oneself or others; examples are pathological gambling, setting fires, and stealing.

Inappropriate affect A form of emotional disturbance seen in schizophrenia. The central features of inappropriate affect are incongruity and lack of adaptability in emotional expression.

Incest Sexual activity between close blood relatives, such as father-daughter, mother-son, or siblings.

Incidence The number of new cases of a disorder that appear in a population during a specific period of time.

Independent variable The variable in an experiment that is controlled and deliberately manipulated by the experimenter (for example, whether or not a subject receives a treatment). Affects the dependent variable.

Infarct The area of dead tissue produced by a stroke.

Informed consent A legal and ethical safeguard concerning risks in research and in treatment. Includes (a) accurate information about potential risks and benefits, (b) competence on the part of subjects/patients to understand them, and (c) the ability of subjects/patients to participate voluntarily.

Inhibited sexual arousal Difficulty experienced by a woman in achieving or maintaining genital responses, such as lubrication and swelling, that are necessary to complete sexual intercourse.

Insanity A legal term referring to a defendant's state of mind at the time of committing a crime. An insane individual is not held legally responsible for his or her actions because of a mental disease or defect.

Insanity defense An attempt to prove that a person with a mental illness did not meet the legal criteria for sanity at the time of committing a crime. The inability to tell right from wrong and an "irresistible impulse" are the two most common contemporary grounds for the defense.

Insight Self-understanding; the extent to which a person recognizes the nature (or understands the potential causes) of his or her disorder. In psychoanalysis, insight is the ultimate goal, specifically, to bring formerly unconscious material into conscious awareness.

Intelligence quotient (IQ) A measure of intellectual ability that typically has a mean of 100 and a standard deviation of 15. An individual's IQ is determined by comparisons with norms for same-aged peers.

Internalizing disorders An empirically derived category of psychological problems of childhood that affect the child more than the external world (for example, depression).

Internal validity Whether changes in the dependent variable can be accurately attributed to changes in the independent variable in an experiment, that is, there are no experimental confounds.

Interpretation A tool in psychotherapy and psychoanalysis in which the therapist suggests new meanings about a client's accounts of his or her past and present life.

Introceptive awareness Recognition of internal cues including various emotional states as well as hunger.

Juvenile delinquency A legal term that refers to a minor who has violated the law and been judged responsible for the lawbreaking.

Korsakoff's syndrome An amnestic disorder sometimes associated with chronic alcoholism. Memory is impaired but other cognitive functions are not.

Labeling theory A perspective on mental disorders that is primarily concerned with the social context in which abnormal behavior occurs. Labeling theory is more interested in social factors that determine whether or not a person will be given a psychiatric diagnosis than in psychological or biological reasons for the behaviors.

Lead poisoning Ingestion of toxic levels of lead (mainly through environmental pollutants) that can cause brain damage and a number of adverse behavioral and cognitive impairments, including mental retardation.

Learned helplessness theory A theory that holds that depressed people do not recognize a contingency between their behavior and outcomes in their environments.

Learning disorders A heterogenous group of educational problems characterized by academic performance that is notably below academic aptitude.

Life-cycle transitions Movements from one social or psychological "stage" of adult development into a new one; often characterized by interpersonal, emotional, and identity conflict.

Life-span development The study of continuities and changes in behavior, affect, and cognition from infancy through the last years of life.

Limbic system A variety of brain structures, including the thalamus and hypothalamus, that are central to the regulation of emotion and basic learning processes.

Linkage A process used to locate the position of a gene on a particular chromosome. Two genetic loci are said to be linked if they are close together on the same chromosome.

Mainstreaming The educational philosophy that mentally retarded children should be taught, as much as possible, in regular classrooms rather than in "special" classes.

Mania A disturbance in mood characterized by such symptoms as elation, inflated self-esteem, hyperactivity, and accelerated speaking and thinking. An exaggerated feeling of physical and emotional well-being.

Marijuana The dried leaves and flowers of the female cannabis plant. "Getting high" on marijuana refers to a pervasive sense of well-being and happiness.

Mean The arithmetic average of a distribution of scores; the sum of scores divided by the number of observations.

Median The midpoint of a frequency distribution; half of all subjects fall above and half fall below the median.

Medulla The part of the hindbrain that controls various body functions involved in sustaining life, including heart rate, blood pressure, and respiration.

Menopause The cessation of menstruation and the associated physical and psychological changes that occur among middle-aged women (the so-called "change of life").

Mental retardation Substantial limitations in present functioning characterized by significantly subaverage intellectual functioning (IQ of 70 to 75 or below), concurrent limitations in adaptive skills, and an onset before age 18.

Midbrain Part of the brain between the hindbrain and forebrain that is involved in the control of some motor activities, especially those related to fighting and sex.

Minimal brain damage (MBD) Damage to the brain too slight to be detected with objective instruments but sometimes inferred from behavior. Was once held to be the cause of attention-deficit/hyperactivity disorder, but now widely rejected.

Mode The most frequent score in a frequency distribution.

Modeling A social learning concept describing the process of learning through imitation. Contrasts with the broader concept of identification.

Monoamine oxidase inhibitors A group of antidepressant drugs that inhibit the enzyme monoamine oxidase (MAO) in the brain and raise the levels of certain neurotransmitters, such as norepinephrine, dopamine, and serotonin.

Monozygotic (MZ) twins Identical twins produced from a single fertilized egg; thus MZ twins have identical genotypes.

Mood A pervasive and sustained emotional response that, in its extreme, can color the person's perception of the world.

Mood disorders A broad category of psychopathology that includes depressive disorders and bipolar disorders. These conditions are defined in terms of episodes in which the person's behavior is dominated by either clinical depression or mania.

Moratorium A period of allowing oneself to be uncertain or confused about identity. Erikson advocated a moratorium as an important step in the formation of an enduring identity.

Multiaxial classification system A classification system in which the person is rated with regard to several separate aspects of behavior or adjustment.

Multiple personality disorder An unusual dissociative disorder characterized by the existence of two or more distinct personalities in a single individual (called dissociative identity disorder in DSM-IV).

Narcissistic personality disorder An enduring pattern of thinking and behavior that is characterized by pervasive grandiosity. Narcissistic people are preoccupied with their own achievements and abilities.

Nature–nurture controversy The debate that pits genetic and biological factors against life experience as causes of abnormal behavior.

Negative reinforcement Occurs when the cessation of a stimulus increases the frequency of behavior (for example, a friend's nagging ends when you give in).

Negative symptoms (of schizophrenia) Include flat or blunted affect, avolition, alogia, and anhedonia.

Neurofibrillary tangles A type of brain lesion found in the cerebral cortex and the hippocampus in patients with Alzheimer's disease. A pattern of disorganized neurofibrils, which provide structural support for the neurons and help transport chemicals that are used in the production of neurotransmitters.

Neuroleptic A type of antipsychotic medication that also induces side effects that resemble the motor symptoms of Parkinson's disease.

Neurologist A physician who deals primarily with diseases of the brain and nervous system.

Neuromodulators Chemicals such as endorphins that may be released from neurons or from endocrine glands. Neuromodulators can influence communication among many neurons, and they often affect regions of the brain that are quite distant from where they were released.

Neuron The nerve cells that form the basic building blocks of the brain. Each neuron is composed of the soma or cell body, the dendrites, the axon, and the terminal buttons.

Neuropsychological assessment Assessment procedures focused on the examination of performance on psychological tests to indicate whether a person has a brain disorder. An example is the Halstead-Reitan Neuropsychological Test Battery.

Neuropsychologist A psychologist who has particular expertise in the assessment of specific types of cognitive impairment, including those associated with dementia and amnestic disorders.

Neurosis A traditional term, often associated with psychoanalytic theory, that describes maladaptive behavior resulting from the ego's failure to control anxiety resulting from unconscious conflicts. In DSM-I and DSM-II, neurotic disorders were defined as those in which anxiety is the chief characteristic. Anxiety presumably could be felt and expressed directly, or it could be controlled unconsciously by defense mechanisms.

Neuroticism A dimension of personality that is concerned with emotional stability, especially the expression of negative emotions, such as anxiety, depression, and anger.

Neurotransmitters Chemical substances that are released into the synapse between two neurons and carry signals from the terminal button of one neuron to the receptors of another.

Normal distribution A frequency distribution represented by a bell-shaped curve—the normal curve—that is important for making statistical inferences. Many psychological characteristics (e.g., intelligence) are assumed to follow the normal distribution.

Normalization The philosophy that mentally retarded or mentally ill people are entitled to live as much as possible like other members of the society. Often associated with deinstitutionalization in providing custodial care and mainstreaming in education.

Null hypothesis The prediction that an experimental hypothesis is not true. Scientists must assume that the null hypothesis holds until research contradicts it.

Obesity Excess body fat, a circumstance that roughly corresponds with a body weight 20 percent above the expected weight.

Obsession A repetitive, unwanted, intrusive cognitive event that may take the form of thoughts, images, or impulses. Obsessions intrude suddenly into consciousness and lead to an increase in subjective anxiety.

Obsessive–compulsive personality disorder An enduring pattern of thinking and behavior that is characterized by perfectionism and inflexibility. These people are preoccupied with rules and efficiency. They are excessively conscientious, moralistic, and judgmental.

Oedipal conflict Freud's view that boys harbor forbidden sexual desires for their mothers, and they typically resolve the dilemma between the ages of 4 and 6 by identifying with their fathers.

Openness to experience A dimension of personality that describes the person's willingness to consider and explore unfamiliar ideas, feelings, and activities.

Operant conditioning A learning theory asserting that behavior is a function of its consequences. Specifically, behavior increases if it is rewarded, and it decreases if it is punished.

Opiates (sometimes called opioids) Drugs that have properties similar to opium. The main active ingredients in opium are morphine and codeine.

Oppositional defiant disorder A psychological disorder of childhood characterized by persistent but relatively minor transgressions, such as refusing to obey adult requests, arguing, and acting angry.

Orgasmic disorder A sexual disorder in which the person has recurrent difficulties reaching orgasm after a normal sexual arousal.

Pain disorder A type of somatoform disorder characterized by preoccupation with pain, and complaints are motivated at least in part by psychological factors.

Panic attack A sudden, overwhelming experience of terror or fright. While anxiety involves a blend of several negative emotions, panic is more focused.

Paradigm A set of assumptions both about the substance of a theory and about how scientists should collect data and test theoretical propositions. The term was applied to the progress of science by Thomas Kuhn, an influential historian and philosopher.

Paranoid personality disorder An enduring pattern of thinking and behavior characterized by a pervasive tendency to be inappropriately suspicious of other people's motives and behaviors. People who fit the description for this disorder expect that other people are trying to harm them, and they

take extraordinary precautions to avoid being exploited or injured.

Paranoid type A subtype of schizophrenia that is characterized by systematic delusions with persecutory or grandiose content. Preoccupation with frequent auditory hallucinations can also be associated with the paranoid type.

Paraphilias Forms of sexual disorder that involve sexual arousal in association with unusual objects and situations, such as inanimate objects, sexual contacts with children, exhibiting their genitals to strangers, and inflicting pain on another person.

Parasympathetic nervous system The branch of the autonomic nervous system that generally controls the slowing of psychophysiological arousal and energy conservation.

Parkinson's disease A disorder of the motor system that is caused by a degeneration of a specific area of the brain stem known as the *substantia nigra* and loss of the neurotransmitter dopamine, which is produced by cells in this area.

Pedophilia One of the paraphilias, characterized by marked distress over, or acting on urges involving, sexual activity with a prepubescent child.

Peer sociometrics A method of assessing children's social relationships and categorizing children's social standing by obtaining information on who is "liked most" and who is "liked least" from a group of children who know each other.

Peripheral nervous system Nerves that stem from the central nervous system and connect to the body's muscles, sensory systems, and organs. Divided into two subdivisions, the somatic and the autonomic nervous systems.

Personality The combination of persistent traits or characteristics that, taken as a whole, describe a person's behavior. In DSM-IV, personality is defined as "enduring patterns of perceiving, relating to, and thinking about the environment and oneself, which are exhibited in a wide range of important social and personal contexts."

Personality disorder Inflexible and maladaptive patterns of personality that begin by early adulthood and result in either social or occupational problems or distress to the individual.

Personality inventory Sometimes called an *objective personality test*, it consists of a series of straightforward statements that the person is

required to rate or endorse as being either true or false in relation to himself or herself.

Pervasive developmental disorders A category of unusual psychological problems that begin early in life and involve severe impairments in a number of areas of functioning. Autistic disorder is one example.

Phenomenology The study of events and symptoms (including subjective experiences) in their own right rather than in terms of inferred causes.

Phenylketonuria (PKU) A cause of mental retardation transmitted by the pairing of recessive genes that results in the deficiency of the enzyme that metabolizes phenylalanine. Infants have normal intelligence at birth, but the ingestion of foods containing phenylalanine causes phenylketonuria and produces brain damage. Can be prevented with a phenylalanine-free diet.

Phobia A persistent and irrational narrowly defined fear that is associated with a specific object or situation.

Pick's disease A form of primary dementia that is associated with atrophy of the frontal and temporal lobes of the brain. Very similar to Alzheimer's disease in terms of both behavioral symptoms and cognitive impairment.

Placebo In medicine, pills that are pharmacologically inert; more broadly, any type of treatment that contains no known "specific ingredients" for treating a given condition.

Placebo control group A group of subjects given a treatment with no known specific ingredients for the purpose of comparison with alternative treatments that are thought to contain specific, therapeutic benefits.

Pons Part of the hindbrain that serves various functions in regulating stages of sleep.

Population The entire group of people about whom a researcher wants to generalize.

Positive reinforcement Occurs when the onset of a stimulus increases the frequency of behavior (for example, you get paid for your work).

Positive symptoms (of schizophrenia) Include hallucinations, delusions, disorganized speech, inappropriate affect, and disorganized behavior.

Posttraumatic stress disorder (PTSD) A psychological disorder characterized by recurring symptoms of numbing, reexperiencing, and hyperarousal following exposure to a traumatic stressor.

Prefrontal lobotomy A psychosurgery technique introduced in 1935 by Egas Moniz in which the two hemispheres of the brain were severed. Moniz won a Nobel Prize for the treatment, which now is discredited.

Premature ejaculation A type of sexual disorder, in which a man is unable to delay ejaculation long enough to accomplish intercourse.

Preparedness theory The notion that organisms are biologically prepared, on the basis of neural pathways in their central nervous systems, to learn certain types of associations (also known as *biological constraints on learning*).

Prevalence An epidemiological term that refers to the total number of cases that are present within a given population during a particular period of time.

Primary sleep disorder A condition where a sleeping difficulty is the principal complaint. In DSM-IV, either a dyssomnia—a difficulty in the amount, quality, or timing of sleep, or a parasomnia—an abnormal event that occurs during sleep; for example, nightmares.

Problem-focused coping Externally oriented coping in an attempt to change or otherwise control a stressor.

Professional responsibilities A professional's obligation to follow the ethical standards of his or her profession and to uphold the laws of the states in which he or she practices, for example, confidentiality.

Projective tests Personality tests, such as the Rorschach inkblot test, in which the person is asked to interpret a series of ambiguous stimuli.

Psychiatry The branch of medicine that is concerned with the study and treatment of mental disorders.

Psychoactive drugs Various drugs—ranging from alcohol, tobacco, and caffeine to controlled substances—that affect the individual's psychological state.

Psychoactive substance A drug that alters a person's mood, level of perception, or brain functioning.

Psychoanalysis Freud's orthodox form of psychotherapy that is practiced rarely today because of its time, expense, and questionable effectiveness in treating mental disorders. Freud viewed the task of psychoanalysis as promoting insight by uncovering the unconscious conflicts and motivations that cause psychological difficulties.

Psychoanalytic theory A paradigm for conceptualizing abnormal behavior based on the concepts and writings of Sigmund Freud. Highlights unconscious processes and conflicts as causing abnormal behavior and emphasizes psychoanalysis as the treatment of choice.

Psychodynamic A variation on the Freudian approach that searches for unconscious conflicts and motivations, but does not adhere to Freud literally as in psychoanalysis.

Psychodynamic psychotherapy An "uncovering" form of psychotherapy in which the therapist typically is more engaged and directive; the process is considerably less lengthy than in psychoanalysis.

Psychological dependence A term used to describe forceful, subjective urges to use drugs, often as a means of relieving negative mood states. Contrasts with the term "physiological dependence," which involves symptoms of tolerance and withdrawal.

Psychology The science, profession, and academic discipline concerned with the study of mental processes and behavior in humans and animals.

Psychometric approach A method of classification that forms diagnostic categories from statistical analysis of symptom checklists. Particularly used in classifying externalizing and internalizing disorders of childhood.

Psychomotor retardation A generalized slowing of physical and emotional reactions. The slowing of movements and speech; frequently seen in depression.

Psychomotor stimulants Drugs such as amphetamine and cocaine that produce their effect by simulating the effects of certain neurotransmitters, specifically epinephrine, norepinephrine, dopamine, and serotonin.

Psychoneuroimmunology (PNI) Research on the effects of stress on the functioning of the immune system.

Psychopathology The manifestations of (and the study of the causes of) mental disorders. Generally used as another term to describe abnormal behavior.

Psychopathy Another term for antisocial personality disorder. Usually associated with Cleckley's definition of that concept, which included features such as disregard for the truth, lack of empathy, and inability to learn from experience.

Psychopharmacology The study of the effects of psychoactive drugs on behavior. Clinical psychopharmacology involves the expert use of drugs in the treatment of mental disorders.

Psychophysiology The study of changes in the functioning of the body that result from psychological experiences.

Psychosis A term that refers to several types of severe mental disorder in which the person is out of contact with reality. Hallucinations and delusions are examples of psychotic symptoms.

Psychosomatic disorder A term indicating that a physical disease is a product both of the psyche (mind) and the soma (body).

Psychostimulants Medications that heighten energy and alertness when taken in small dosages, but lead to restless, even frenetic, behavior when misused. Often used in the treatment of attention-deficit/hyperactivity disorder.

Psychosurgery A controversial treatment that involves the surgical destruction of specific regions of the brain. Modern psychosurgery involves relatively little destruction of brain tissue, unlike the discredited prefrontal lobotomy.

Psychotherapy The use of psychological techniques in an attempt to produce change in the context of a special, helping relationship.

Purging An intentional act designed to eliminate consumed food from the body. Self-induced vomiting is the most common form.

Random selection A method of selecting samples from a larger population that ensures that each subject has a statistically equal chance of being selected.

Rape Acts involving nonconsensual sexual penetration obtained by physical force, by threat of bodily harm, or when the victim is incapable of giving consent by virtue of mental illness, mental retardation, or intoxication.

Rating scale An assessment tool in which the observer is asked to make judgments that place the person somewhere along a dimension.

Rational–emotive therapy (RET) A cognitive behavior therapy technique designed to challenge irrational beliefs about oneself and the world. Developed by Albert Ellis as a treatment for anxiety, depression, and related problems.

Reaction range A behavior genetic concept for conceptualizing the joint influence of genes and environment; specifically, that heredity determines the upper and lower limits of a trait and experience determines the extent to which people fulfill their genetic potential.

Receptors Sites on the dendrites or soma of a neuron that are sensitive to certain neurotransmitters.

Recidivism Repeat offending in violating the law.

Reciprocity The social exchange of cooperation and conflict. Family members with happy relationships reciprocate positive actions; family members with troubled relationships reciprocate negative ones.

Recovered memories Dramatic recollections of long-forgotten traumatic experiences; a controversial topic because the "memories" often are impossible to validate and many such memories may be created rather than recovered.

Regression A return or retreat to an earlier stage or style of coping or behaving.

Reliability The consistency of measurements, including diagnostic decisions. One index of reliability is agreement among clinicians.

Residual type A subtype of schizophrenia that includes patients who no longer meet the criteria for active phase symptoms but nevertheless demonstrate continued signs of negative symptoms or attenuated forms of delusions, hallucinations, or disorganized speech.

Reticular activating system Located in the midbrain, but extending into the pons and medulla as well. Regulates sleeping and waking and sexual behavior.

Retrograde amnesia The loss of memory for events prior to the onset of an illness or the experience of a traumatic event.

Reuptake The process of recapturing some neurotransmitters in the synapse before they reach the receptors of another cell and returning the chemical substances to the terminal button. The neurotransmitter then is reused in subsequent neural transmission.

Reverse causality Indicates that causation could be operating in the opposite direction: *Y* could be causing *X* instead of *X* causing *Y*. A threat to interpretation in correlational studies, and a basic reason why correlation does not mean causation.

Savant performance An exceptional ability in a highly specialized area of functioning typically involving artistic, musical, or mathematical skills.

Schema A general cognitive pattern that guides the way a person perceives and interprets events in his or her environment.

Schizoaffective disorder A disorder defined by a period of disturbance during which the symptoms of schizophrenia partially overlap with a major depressive episode or a manic episode.

Schizoid personality disorder An enduring pattern of thinking and behavior characterized by pervasive indifference to other people, coupled with a diminished range of emotional experience and expression. People who fit this description prefer social isolation to interactions with friends or family.

Schizophrenia A type of (or group of) psychotic disorders characterized by positive and negative symptoms and associated with a deterioration in role functioning. The term was originally coined by Eugen Bleuler to describe the *splitting of mental associations,* which he believed to be the fundamental disturbance in schizophrenia (previously known as *dementia praecox*).

Schizophrenic spectrum A group of disorders that, on the basis of family history and adoption study data, are presumed to be genetically related to schizophrenia. These disorders may include schizotypal personality disorder, schizoaffective disorder, and delusional disorder.

Schizophreniform disorder A condition characterized by the same symptoms as schizophrenia, in which the patient has exhibited symptoms for less than the 6-month period required by DSM-IV for a diagnosis of schizophrenia.

Schizotaxia According to Paul Meehl's theoretical model for schizophrenia, a subtle neurological defect of unknown form that is inherited by all individuals who are predisposed to schizophrenia.

Schizotypal personality disorder
An enduring pattern of discomfort with other people coupled with peculiar thinking and behavior. The latter symptoms take the form of perceptual and cognitive disturbances. Considered by some experts to be part of the schizophrenic spectrum.

School refusal (*school phobia*) Extreme reluctance to go to school, accompanied by various symptoms of anxiety such as stomachaches and headaches. May be a fear of school or an expression of separation anxiety disorder.

Scientist-practitioner model A model of training and professional activity, particularly influential in clinical psychology, that emphasizes the integration of science and practice.

Seasonal affective disorder A type of mood disorder (either unipolar or bipolar) in which there has been a regular temporal relation between onset (or disappearance) of the person's episodes and a particular time of the year. For example, the person might become depressed in the winter.

Selective serotonin reuptake inhibitors (SSRIs) A group of antidepressant drugs that inhibit the reuptake of serotonin into the presynaptic nerve endings and therefore promote neurotransmission in serotonin pathways.

Self-control Appropriate behavior guided by internal (rather than external) rules.

Self-efficacy Albert Bandura's central cognitive concept, the belief that one can achieve desired goals.

Senile plaques A type of brain lesion found in Alzheimer's disease that consists of a central core of homogeneous protein material known as *amyloid* surrounded by clumps of debris left over from destroyed neurons.

Sensate focus A procedure for the treatment of sexual dysfunction that involves a series of simple exercises in which the couple spends time in a quiet, relaxed setting, learning to touch each other.

Separation anxiety disorder A psychological disorder of childhood characterized by persistent and excessive worry for the safety of an attachment figure and related fears such as getting lost, being kidnapped, nightmares, and refusal to be alone. Distinct from normal separation anxiety, which typically develops shortly before an infant's first birthday.

Sex roles Characteristics, behaviors, and skills that are defined within a specific culture as being either masculine or feminine.

Sexual aversion disorder A form of sexual dysfunction in which a person has an extreme aversion to, and avoids, genital sexual contact with a partner.

Sexual dysfunctions Forms of sexual disorder that involve inhibitions of sexual desire or interference with the physiological responses leading to orgasm.

Sexual masochism A form of paraphilia in which sexual arousal is associated with the act of being humiliated, beaten, bound, or otherwise made to suffer.

Sexual sadism A form of paraphilia in which sexual arousal is associated with desires to inflict physical or psychological suffering, including humiliation, on another person.

Socialization The process of shaping children's behavior and attitudes to conform to the expectations of parents, teachers, and society.

Social clocks Age-related goals people set for themselves and later use to evaluate life achievements.

Social phobia A type of phobic disorder in which the person is persistently fearful of social situations that might expose him or her to scrutiny by others, such as fear of public speaking.

Social skills training A behavior therapy technique in which clients are taught new skills that are desirable and likely to be rewarded in the everyday world.

Social support The emotional and practical assistance received from others.

Social work A profession whose primary concern is how human needs can be met within society.

Soma The cell body and largest part of the neuron where most of the neuron's metabolism and maintenance are controlled and performed.

Somatic symptoms Symptoms of mood disorders that are related to basic physiological or bodily functions, including fatigue, aches and pains, and serious changes in appetite and sleep patterns.

Somatization disorder A type of somatoform disorder characterized by multiple, somatic complaints in the absence of organic impairments.

Somatoform disorders A category of psychological disorders characterized by unusual physical symptoms that occur in the absence of a known physical pathology. Examples include hypochondriasis and conversion disorder. Somatoform disorders are somatic in form only, thus their name (note the distinction from psychosomatic disorders, which do involve real physical pathology).

Standard deviation A measure of dispersion of scores around the mean. Technically, the square root of the variance.

Standard scores A standardized frequency distribution in which each score is subtracted from the mean and the difference is divided by the standard deviation.

Stress An event that creates physiological or psychological strain for the individual. Stress has been defined differently by various scientists.

Stress management A treatment used in behavioral medicine and health psychology to teach more effective coping skills, reduce adverse reactions to stress, and improve health behavior.

Substance abuse The less severe form of substance use disorder listed in DSM-IV. Describes a pattern of drug use that is defined in terms of interference with the person's ability to fulfill major role obligations, the recurrent use of a drug in dangerous situations, or the experience of repeated legal difficulties that are associated with drug use.

Substance dependence The more severe form of substance use disorder listed in DSM-IV. Refers to a pattern of repeated self-administration that results in tolerance, withdrawal, or compulsive drug-taking behavior.

Superego One of Freud's three central personality structures, roughly equivalent to the "conscience." In Freudian theory, the superego contains societal standards of behavior, particularly rules that children learn from identifying with their parents. The superego attempts to control id impulses.

Sympathetic nervous system The branch of the autonomic nervous system that generally controls psychophysiological activities associated with increased arousal and energy expenditure.

Synapse A small gap filled with fluid that lies between the axon of one neuron and a dendrite or soma of another neuron.

Syndrome A group of symptoms that appear together and are assumed to represent a specific type of disorder.

Systematic desensitization A treatment for overcoming fears and phobias developed by Joseph Wolpe. Involves learning relaxation skills, developing a fear hierarchy, and systematic exposure to imagined, feared events while simultaneously maintaining relaxation.

Systems theory An innovation in the philosophy of conceptualizing and conducting science that emphasizes interdependence, cybernetics, and especially holism—the idea that the whole is more than the sum of its parts. Often attributed to the biologist and philosopher Ludwig von Bertalanffy.

Temperament Characteristic styles of relating to the world that are often conceptualized as inborn traits. Generally emphasizes the "how" as opposed to the "what" of behavior.

Terminal buttons Buds found on the small branches at the end of the axon where messages are sent from one neuron to other neurons.

Thalamus A part of the limbic system that is involved in receiving and integrating sensory information both from the sense organs and from higher brain structures.

Third variable An unmeasured factor that may account for a correlation observed between any two variables. A threat to interpretation in correlational studies, and a basic reason why correlation does not mean causation.

Threshold model A perspective on etiology that holds that people can exhibit characteristics of a disorder without experiencing any adverse impact on their adjustment until they pass a critical threshold. Beyond that level, there is presumably a dramatic increase in the number of problems that are encountered.

Time-out A discipline technique that involves briefly isolating a child as a punishment for misbehavior.

Token economy A type of contingency management program that has been adopted in many institutional settings. Desired and undesired behaviors are identified, contingencies are defined, behavior is monitored, and rewards or punishments are given according to the rules of the economy.

Tolerance The process through which the nervous system becomes less sensitive to the effects of a psychoactive substance. As a result, the person needs to consume increased quantities of the drug to achieve the same subjective effect.

Transsexualism A severe form of gender identity disorder in adults.

Transvestic fetishism A form of paraphilia in which sexual pleasure is derived from dressing in the clothing of the opposite gender.

Tricyclics A group of antidepressant drugs that block the uptake of neurotransmitters, such as norepinephrine and dopamine, from the synapse.

Type A behavior pattern A characterological response to challenge that is competitive, hostile, urgent, impatient, and achievement-striving. Linked to an increased risk for coronary heart disease.

Unconscious Mental processes or contents that reside outside of awareness. In Freudian theory, the seat of many hidden memories, motivations, and defenses.

Undifferentiated type A subtype of schizophrenia that includes patients who display prominent psychotic symptoms and either meet the criteria for several subtypes or otherwise do not meet the criteria for the catatonic, paranoid, or disorganized types.

Unipolar mood disorder A form of mood disorder in which the person experiences episodes of depression but has never experienced an episode of mania or hypomania.

Vaginismus A form of sexual dysfunction in which the outer muscles of the vagina snap tightly shut when penetration is attempted, thus preventing insertion of any object.

Validity The meaning or systematic importance of a construct or a measurement.

Variance A measure of dispersion of scores around the mean. Technically, the average squared difference from the mean (see also standard deviation).

Vascular dementia (also known as *multi-infarct dementia*) A type of dementia associated with vascular disease. The cognitive symptoms of vascular dementia are the same as those for Alzheimer's disease, but a gradual onset is not required.

Victimization A pattern of responses often observed among victims of violent crimes, particularly rape, that includes fear, guilt, self-blame, powerlessness, and lowered self-esteem.

Voyeurism A form of paraphilia (also known as *peeping*) in which a person becomes sexually aroused by observing unsuspecting people (usually strangers) while they are undressing or engaging in sexual activities.

Weight set point Fixed weights or small ranges of weight around which the body regulates weight, for example, by increasing or decreasing metabolism.

Withdrawal The constellation of symptoms that are experienced shortly after a person stops taking a drug after heavy or prolonged use.

Worry A relatively uncontrollable sequence of negative, emotional thoughts and images that are concerned with possible future threats or danger.

Credits

PHOTOGRAPHS

All portraits illustrated by Van Howell.

Chapter 1: p. 1, Yoav Levy, Phototake NYC; p. 6, Tri-Star Pictures/Everett Collection; p. 16, Dan Habib/Impact Visuals Photo & Graphics, Inc.; portraits: p. 13, based on photo courtesy Lee Robins; p. 19, based on photo from Bettmann.

Chapter 2: p. 28, David Leeson/The Dallas Morning News, The Image Works; p. 43, CNRI/Phototake NYC; p. 46, top, Bob Daemmrich/The Image Works; p. 46, bottom, Art Gingert/Comstock; p. 51, Richard Hutchings/Photo Researchers, Inc.; portraits: p. 32, based on photo from Who/Photo; p. 33, based on photo from Boris of Boston; p. 49, based on photo courtesy Albert Bandura.

Chapter 3: p. 57, Brad Bower, Stock Boston; p. 63, Loren McIntyre/Woodfin Camp & Associates; p. 65, Gary Retherford/Photo Researchers, Inc.; p. 80, Bob Daemmrich/Stock Boston; p. 81, Andy Levin/Photo Researchers, Inc.; portraits: p. 67, based on photo from Bettman; p. 68, based on photo courtesy Joseph Wolpe; p. 72, based on photo from Carl Rogers Memorial Library; p. 75, based on photo from Bettmann.

Chapter 4: p. 85, Laura Dwight, PhotoEdit; p. 89, UPI/Bettmann; p. 97, Faye Ellman Photography; p. 103, Jeff Greenberg/Picture Cube, Inc.; p. 108, Ken Karp/Simon & Schuster/PH College; p. 110, Will & Deni McIntyre/Photo Researchers, Inc.; portraits: p. 90, based on photo from the Archives of the American Psychiatric Association, Washington, DC, copyright 1994; p. 105, based on photo courtesy G.B. Peterson.

Chapter 5: p. 114, Andrew Ward, PhotoDisc, Inc.; p. 118, Mel Digiacomo/The Image Bank; p. 121, Jeffrey Markowitz/Sygma; p. 127, Lester Sloan/Woodfin Camp & Associates; p. 130, Brooks Kraft/Sygma; p. 134, Collins/Monkmeyer Press; p. 143, James D. Wilson/Woodfin Camp & Associates; portraits: p. 126, based on photo courtesy Myrna Weissman; p. 132, based on photo courtesy Peter Lewisohn; p. 139, based on photo courtesy Aaron Beck.

Chapter 6: p. 153, G & M David de Lossy, The Image Bank; p. 156, Rick Friedman/Black Star; p. 159, Schneps/The Image Bank; p. 162, Frederick Ayer/Photo Researchers, Inc.; p. 164, Pamela Frank, Everett Collection; p. 167, Reporters/Chederros/Leo De Wys, Inc.; p. 170, Andrew Lichtenstein/Impact Visuals Photo & Graphics, Inc.; p. 175, Jacques M. Chenet/Woodfin Camp & Associates; portraits: p. 163, based on photo courtesy Donald Klein; p. 172, based on photo courtesy Simon & Schuster/PH College.

Chapter 7: p. 183, Stephen Castagneto, AP/Wide World Photos; p. 195, Rhoda Sidney; p. 200, National Library of Medicine/Mark Marten/Photo Researchers, Inc.; p. 202, Lois Bernstein/Gamma-Liaison, Inc.; p. 209, Photofest; portraits: p. 194, based on photo courtesy Edna Foa; p. 200, based on photo from Bettmann.

Chapter 8: p. 216, Telegraph Colour Library, FPG International LLC; Page 218, left, Elizabeth Crews/The Image Works; p. 218, center, Benelux Press B.V./Photo Researchers, Inc.; p. 218, right, David W. Hamilton/The Image Bank; p. 230, J. Wilson/Woodfin Camp & Associates; p. 231, N. Hashimoto/Sygma; p. 236, Gerd Ludwig/Woodfin Camp & Associates; portraits: p. 222, top, based on photo from Elizabeth Crews/The Image Works; p. 224, based on photo from David W. Hamilton/The Image Bank.

Chapter 9: p. 240, David Stewart, Tony Stone Images; p. 246, Photofest; p. 247, AP/Wide World Photos; p. 250, Super Stock, Inc.; p. 251 left, Everett Collection; p. 251, right, Everett Collection; p. 259, Owen Franken/Stock Boston; portraits: p. 256, based on photo courtesy John Gunderson; p. 262, based on photo courtesy Simon & Schuster/PH College.

Chapter 10: p. 267, John Wong Photography; p. 268, Pat Farley/Monkmeyer Press; p. 273, Kelley Chin/AP/Wide World Photos; p. 281, Jean Auguste Dominique Ingres, Turkish Bath (Bagno Torco), Louvre, Paris, France, Scala/Art Resource; p. 282, Express Newspapers/Archive Photos; portrait: p. 283, based on photo courtesy Simon & Schuster/PH College.

Chapter 11: p. 291, Doug Menuez, PhotoDisc, Inc.; p. 301, Dennis Brack/Black Star; p. 313, R. Lucas/The Image Works; p. 316, Richard Hutchings/Photo Researchers, Inc.; p. 319, Sygma; portrait: p. 308, based on photo courtesy George Vaillant.

Chapter 12: p. 325, Steve Ewert, Workbook Co/Op Stock; p. 328, B. Bachman/The Image Works; p. 333, Suzanne Tenner/Motion Picture & Television Photo Archives; p. 341, Brian Lantelme; p. 349, left & right, UPI/Bettmann; portraits: p. 328, based on photo from UPI/Bettmann; p. 338, based on photo from Bettmann; p. 347, based on photo courtesy Simon & Schuster/PH College.

Chapter 13: p. 352, Jerry Cooke, Photo Researchers, Inc.; p. 356, Mary Ellen Mark Library; p. 358, photo courtesy The New York Academy of Medicine Library, from *Dementia Praecox and Paraphrenia* by Emil Kraeplin, published by E.S. Livingstone, Edinburgh, 1919; p. 363, Mary Ellen Mark Library; p. 377, Focus on Sports; p. 359, Bettmann; portraits: p. 365, based on photo courtesy Dr. I. Gottesman; p. 376, based on photo courtesy Paul Meehl; p. 380, based on photo courtesy Simon & Schuster/PH College.

Chapter 14: p. 384, Howard Sokol, Index Stock Imagery, Inc.; p. 391, Lew Merim/Monkmeyer Press; p. 392, Jeff Greenberg/Picture Cube, Inc.; p. 398, Tom McCarthy/Picture Cube, Inc.; p. 400, Ken Lax/Photo Researchers, Inc.; p. 400, A. Tannenbaum/Sygma; p. 403, Rick Hunter/Sygma; p. 411, Michael A. Schwarz/Gamma Liaison, Inc.; p. 414, Dr. Lorna Selfe; p. 419, Alan Carey/The Image Works; portraits: p. 400, based on photo from Magnum Photos, Inc.; p. 401, based on a photo courtesy Mary Ainsworth; p. 401 based on photo courtesy Mrs. J. Hopkins, The Tavistock Clinic; p. 402, based on photo courtesy G. R. Patterson; p. 415, based on photo from The Alan Mason Chesney Medical Archives of the Johns Hopkins Medical Institution; p. 421, based on photo courtesy O. Ivar Lovaas.

Chapter 15: p. 425, Jim Graham, AP/Wide World Photos; p. 426, R. Mims/Sygma; p. 434, Marilyn Humphries/Impact Visuals Photo & Graphics, Inc.; p. 439, AP/Wide World Photos; p. 442, left, Jerry Cooke/Photo Researchers, Inc.; p. 442, right, Eugene Richards/Magnum Photos, Inc., p. 445, Alex Tehrani/Gamma-Liaison, Inc.; p. 449, left & right, AP/Wide World Photos; portraits: p. 429, based on photo courtesy Thomas Szasz; p. 437, based on photo courtesy John Monahan.

CARTOONS, FIGURES, AND TABLES

Chapter 1: Cartoon 1–2 *Calvin and Hobbes*, "When you're a kid . . ." (March 13, 1993). Copyright © 1993 by Watterson. Distributed by Universal Press Syndicate, and reprinted with their permission. All rights reserved.

Chapter 2: Figure 2–1 "A typical myelinated neuron" adapted from B. Kolb and Ian Q. Whislaw (1985). *Fundamentals of Human neuropsychology* (2nd ed.). New York: W.H. Freeman. Copyright © 1989, 1985 by W.H. Freeman and Company. Reprinted with the permission of the publishers.

Cartoon 2–2 *Calvin and Hobbes*, "Mom! Wake Up!" (March 12, 1993). Copyright

© 1993 by Watterson. Distributed by Universal Press Syndicate, and reprinted with their permission. All rights reserved.

Chapter 3: Table 3–3 "Common Characteristics of Effective Brief Psychotherapies" from M. P. Ross & J. M. Butcher (1986). Research on Brief Therapy. In A. E. Bergin & S. L. Garfield (Eds.), *Handbook of Psychotherapy and Behavior Change* (3rd ed.) (pp. 627–670). Copyright © 1986 by John Wiley & Sons, Inc. Reprinted with the permission of the publishers.

Figure 3–1 "Relation between number of psychotherapy sessions and percentage of clients improved" from K. I. Howard, S. M. Kopta, M. S. Krause, & D. E. Orlinsky (1986). The dose-effect relationship in psychotherapy. *American Psychologist*, 41, 159–164. Copyright © 1986 by American Psychological Association, Inc. Reprinted with the permission of K. I. Howard.

Cartoon 3–1 Leo Cullum, "He's in an H.M.O. . . ." from *The New Yorker* (April 1, 1996). Copyright © 1996 by The New Yorker Magazine, Inc. Reprinted with the permission of *The New Yorker*.

Cartoon 3–2 Mankoff, "So, while extortion . . ." from *The New Yorker* (1991). Copyright © 1991 by The New Yorker Magazine, Inc. Reprinted with the permission of *The New Yorker*.

Chapter 4: Table 4–4 "Sample Items from the Structured Interview for DSM-IV Personality (SUDP-IV)" from Pfohl, B., Blum, N., & Zimmerman, M. (1995). *Structured Interview for DSM-IV Personality*. Iowa City: University of Iowa. Reprinted with the permission of Bruce Pfohl, M.D.

Chapter 5: Table 5–1 From *Mood Disorders: Toward a New Psychobiology*, P. C. Whybrow, H. S. Akiskal, and W. T. McKinney, Jr., 1984. Reproduced with the permission of Plenum Publishing Corporation and Peter C. Whybrow.

Figure 5–1 Adapted with the permission of The Free Press, a Division of Simon & Schuster, Inc. from *Psychiatric Disorders in America: The Epidemiological Catchment Area Study* edited by Lee N. Robins and Darrel A. Regier. Copyright © 1991 by Lee N. Robins and Darrel A. Regier.

Table 5–4 From "Average Morbid Risk . . .," P. Katz and P. McGuffin, 1993 in *Progress in Experimental Personality and Psychopathology Research*, by L. Chapman, Chapman and Fowler, eds. Copyright Springer Publishing Company, Inc., New York 10012. Used by permission.

Chapter 6: Cartoon 6–1 Gary Larson, "Math phobic's nightmare" (July 9, 1990).

Copyright © 1990 by FarWorks, Inc. Distributed by Universal Press Syndicate, and reprinted with their permission. All rights reserved.

Table 6–2 From *The Clinical Management of Anxiety Disorders*, edited by William Coryell and George Winokur. Copyright © 1991 by Oxford University Press, Inc. Used by permission of Oxford University Press, Inc.

Chapter 7: Figure 7–2 "The Detection of Conversion Disorder" adapted from D. M. Kaufman (1985). *Clinical Neurology for Psychiatrists*, 2nd ed. Orlando, FL: Grune and Stratton, p. 28. Copyright © 1985 by Grune & Stratton, Inc. Reprinted with the permission of W. B. Saunders Company.

Chapter 8: Cartoon 8–4 *Calvin and Hobbes*, "Know What I Pray For?" (August 28, 1992). Copyright © 1992 by Watterson. Distributed by Universal Press Syndicate, and reprinted with their permission. All rights reserved.

Figure 8–1 From *Handbook of Psychology and Health-Stress, Vol 5* by A. Baum and J. E. Singer. Reproduced with permission of Lawrence Erlbaum Associates, Inc. and Andrew S. Baum.

Figure 8–2 "Sympathetic and Parasympathetic Divisions of the Automatic Nervous System" from Willis H. Johnson, Louis E. Delanney, Thomas A. Cole, & Austin E. Brooks (1972). *Biology* (4th ed). New York: Holt, Rinehart & Winston. Copyright © 1972 by Holt, Rinehart & Winston, Inc. Reprinted with the permission of the publishers.

Figure 8–5 From R. A. Karasek job strain model, from *The New York Times*, April 3, 1983. Copyright © 1983 by The New York Times. Reprinted by permission.

Chapter 9: Cartoon 9–1 Gary Larson, *The Far Side:* "The four basic personality types" (October 5, 1980). Copyright © 1980 by FarWorks, Inc. Distributed by Universal Press Syndicate, and reprinted with their permission. All rights reserved.

Chapter 10: Figure 10–2 From H. W. Hoek (1995). The distribution of eating disorders. In K. D. Brownell & C. G. Fairburn (Eds.), *Eating disorders and obesity: A comprehensive handbook*, p. 209. Copyright © 1995 by The Guilford Press. Reprinted by permission.

Chapter 11: Table 11–1 Adapted from Marc A. Schuckit in *Drug and Alcohol Abuse: A Clinical Guide to Diagnosis and Treatment (3rd ed.)* 1989. Reprinted by permission of the Plenum Publishing Corporation and the author.

Chapter 12: Cartoon 12–1 Gary Larson, *The Far Side:* "Popeye! No!" (November 21, 1994). Copyright © 1994 by FarWorks, Inc. Distributed by Universal Press Syndicate, and reprinted with their permission. All rights reserved.

Chapter 13: Figure 13–1 From *Schizophrenia Genesis: The Origins of Madness* by Gottesman © 1991 by Irving I. Gottesman. Used with permission by W. H. Freeman and Company.

Chapter 14: Figure 14–1 From A. Blumstein, J. Cohen, and D. P. Farrington; Criminal Career Research: Its Value for Criminology, in *Criminology*, 28. Reproduced with the permission of American Society of Criminology and A. Blumstein.

Cartoon 14–1 *Calvin and Hobbes*, "What Are We Going to Do, Hobbes?" (April 14, 1980). Copyright © 1980 by Watterson. Distributed by Universal Press Syndicate, and reprinted with their permission. All rights reserved.

Cartoon 14–2 *Calvin and Hobbes*, "Are There Any Monsters Under My Bed Tonight?" (December 15, 1989). Copyright © 1989 by Watterson. Distributed by Universal Press Syndicate, and reprinted with their permission. All rights reserved.

Figure 14–2 "The Abbreviated Conners Teaching Rating Scale for Attention-Deficit/Hyperactivity Disorder" from C.K. Conners (1969). A teacher rating scale for use with drug studies with children. *American Journal of Psychiatry*, 126, 884–888. Copyright © 1969 by American Psychiatric Association. Reprinted with the permission of the publishers.

References

Abel, G.G., Becker, J.V., Mittelman, M., Cunningham-Rathner, J., et al. (1987). Self-reported sex crimes of nonincarcerated paraphiliacs. *Journal of Interpersonal Violence*, 2, 3–25.

Abel, G.G., & Gouleau, J.L. (1990). Male sex offenders. In M.E. Thase, B.A. Edelstein, & M. Hersen (Eds.), *Handbook of outpatient treatment of adults: Nonpsychotic mental disorders*, pp. 271–290. New York: Plenum.

Abel, G.G., & Osborn, C. (1992). The paraphilias: The extent and nature of sexually deviant and criminal behavior. *Psychotic Clinics of North America*, 15, 675–687.

Abou-Saleh, M.T. (1992). Lithium. In E.S. Paykel (Ed.), *Handbook of affective disorders*, 2nd ed., pp. 369–386, New York: Guilford.

Abrams, R. (1993). ECT technique: Electrode placement, stimulus type, and treatment frequency. In C.E. Coffey (Ed.), *The clinical science of electroconvulsive therapy*, pp. 17–28. Washington, DC: American Psychiatric Press.

Abramson, L.Y., Metalsky, G.I., & Alloy, L.B. (1989). Hopelessness depression: A theory based-subtype of depression. *Psychological Review*, 96, 358–372.

Achenbach, T.M. (1985). *Assessment and taxonomy of child and adolescent psychopathology*. Beverly Hills, CA: Sage.

Achenbach, T.M., & Edelbrock, C.S. (1981). Behavioral problems and competencies reported by parents of normal and disturbed children aged four through sixteen. *Monographs of the Society for Research in Child Development*, Series No. 188.

Achenbach, T.M., Howell, C.T., Quay, H.C., & Conners, C.K. (1991). National survey of problems and competencies among four- to sixteen-year-olds. *Monographs of the Society for Research in Child Development*, 56, no. 3, Series No. 225.

Achenbach, T.M., McConaughy, S.H., & Howell, C.T. (1987). Child/adolescent behavioral and emotional problems: Implications of cross-information correlations for situational specificity. *Psychological Bulletin*, 101, 213–232.

Ackerman, M.D., & Carey, M.P. (1995). Psychology's role in the assessment of erectile dysfunction: Historical precedents, current knowledge, and methods. *Journal of Consulting and Clinical Psychology*, 63, 862–876.

Adams, G.R., Abraham, K.G., & Markstrom, C.A. (1987). The relation among identity development, self-consciousness and self-focusing during middle and late adolescence. *Developmental Psychology*, 23, 292–297.

Adams, G.R., & Adams, C.M. (1989). Developmental issues. In L.K.G. Hsu & M. Hersen (Eds.), *Recent developments in adolescent psychiatry*, pp. 13–30. New York: Wiley.

Adams, G.R., Ryan, J.H., Hoffman, J.J., Dobson, W.R., & Nielsen, E.C. (1985). Ego identity status, conformity behavior and personality in late adolescence. *Journal of Personality and Social Psychology*, 47, 1091–1104.

Agras, W.S. (1987). *Eating disorders: Management of obesity, bulimia, and anorexia nervosa*. Elmsford, NY: Pergamon.

Agras, W.S. (1993). The diagnosis and treatment of panic disorder. *Annual Review of Medicine*, 44, 39–51.

Ainsworth, M.D.S. (1979). Infant-mother attachment. *American Psychologist*, 34, 932–937.

Ainsworth, M.D.S. (1989). Attachments beyond infancy. *American Psychologist*, 44, 709–716.

Ainsworth, M.D.S., Blehar, M., Waters, E., & Wall, S. (1978). *Patterns of attachment*. Hillsdale, NJ: Erlbaum.

Akiskal, H.S. (1985). Anxiety: Definition, relationship to depression, and proposal for an integrative model. In A.H. Tuma and J.D. Maser (Eds.), *Anxiety and the anxiety disorders*. Hillsdale, NJ: Erlbaum.

Akiskal, H.S. (1992). Borderline: An adjective still in search of a noun. In D. Silver & M. Rosenbluth (Eds.), *Handbook of borderline disorders*, pp. 155–176. Madison, CT: International Universities Press.

Akiskal, H.S. (1994). The temperamental borders of affective disorders. *Acta Psychiatrica Scandinavica*, 89 (suppl. 379), 32–37.

Akiskal, H.S., Chen, S.E., Davis, G.C., Puzantian, V.R., Kashgarian, M., & Bolinger, J.M. (1985). Borderline: An adjective in search of a noun. *Journal of Clinical Psychiatry*, 46, 41–48.

Aldridge-Morris, R. (1989). *Multiple personality: An exercise in deception*. Hillsdale, NJ: Erlbaum.

Alessi, G. (1992). Models of proximate and ultimate causation in psychology. *American Psychologist*, 47, 1359–1370.

Alexander, F. (1950). *Psychosomatic medicine: Its principles and applications*. New York: Norton.

Alexander, F., & French, T.M. (1947). *Psychoanalytic therapy*, New York: Ronald Press. 3–12.

Alexander, J.F., Holtzworth-Munroe, A., & Jameson, P.B. (1994). The process and outcome of marital and family therapy: Research, review, and evaluation. In A.E. Bergin & S.L. Garfield (Eds.), *Handbook of psychotherapy and behavior change*, 4th ed., pp. 595–630. New York: Wiley.

Alexander, J.F., & Parsons, B.V. (1982). *Functional family therapy*. Monterey, CA: Brooks/Cole.

Al-Kubaisy, T., Marks, I.M., Logsdail, S., Marks, M.P., Lovell, K., Sungur, M., & Araya, R. (1992). Role of exposure homework in phobia reduction: A controlled study. *Behavior Therapy*, 23, 599–621.

Allan, C.A., & Cooke, D.J. (1985). Stressful life events and alcohol misuses in women: A critical review. *Journal of Studies on Alcohol*, 46, 147–152.

Allen, A., & Blazer, D.G. (1991). Mood disorders. In J. Sadavoy, L.W. Lazarus, & L.F. Jarvik (Eds.), *Comprehensive review of geriatric psychiatry*, pp. 337–351. Washington, DC: American Psychiatric Press.

Allen, J.P., & Hauser, S.T. (in press). Autonomy and relatedness in adolescent-family interactions as predictors of young adults' states of mind regarding attachment. *Development and Psychopathology*.

Alloy, L.B., Abramson, L.Y., Metalsky, G.I., & Hartlage, S. (1988). The hopelessness theory of depression: Attributional aspects. *British Journal of Clinical Psychology*, 27, 5–21.

Amato, P.R., & Keith, B. (1991a). Parental divorce and the well-being of children: A meta-analysis. *Psychological Bulletin*, 110, 26–46.

Amato, P.R., & Keith, B. (1991b). Parental divorce and adult well-being: A meta-analysis. *Journal of Marriage and the Family*, 53, 43–58.

American Association on Mental Retardation (1992). *Mental retardation: Definition, classification, and systems of support*, 9th ed. Washington, DC.

American Bar Association (1995). *Mental disability law*, 5th ed. Washington, DC.

American Cancer Society (1994). *Cancer facts and figures—1993*. New York.

American Psychiatric Association (1980). *Psychiatric glossary*. Washington, DC: American Psychiatric Press.

American Psychiatric Association (1983). American Psychiatric Association statement on the insanity defense. *American Journal of Psychiatry*, 140, 681–688.

American Psychiatric Association (1994). *Diagnostic and statistical manual of mental disorders*, 1st ed. 1952; 2nd ed. 1968; 3rd ed. 1980; rev. 3rd ed. 1987; 4th ed. 1994. Washington, DC.

American Psychological Association (1991). The definition and description of clinical psychology. *Clinical Psychologist*, 44, 5–11.

American Psychological Association (1995). *Violence in the family*. Washington, DC.

Ames, M.A., & Houston, D.A. (1990). Legal, social, and biological definitions of pedophilia. *Archives of Sexual Behavior*, 19, 333–342.

Anastasi, A. (1986). Evolving concepts of test validation. *Annual Review of Psychology*, 37, 1–15.

Andersen, A.E. (1995). Eating disorders in males. In K.D. Brownell & C.G. Fairburn (Eds.), *Eating disorders and obesity: A comprehensive handbook*, pp. 177–182. New York: Guilford.

Andersen, B.L., & Cyranowski, J.M. (1995). Women's sexuality: Behaviors, responses, and individual differences. *Journal of Consulting and Clinical Psychology, 63,* 891–906.

Anderson, A.A., Russell, C.S., & Schumm, W.R. (1983). Perceived marital quality and family life cycle categories: A further analysis. *Journal of Marriage and the Family, 45,* 127–139.

Anderson, B.L., Kiecolt-Glaser, J.K., & Glaser, R. (1994). A biobehavioral model of cancer stress and disease course. *American Psychologist, 49,* 389–404.

Anderson, N.B., & McNeilly, M. (1991). Age, gender, and ethnicity as variables in psychophysiological assessment: Sociodemographics in context. *Psychological Assessment, 3,* 376–384.

Andreasen, N.C. (1984). *The broken brain: The biological revolution in psychiatry.* New York: Harper & Row.

Andreasen, N.C. (1988). Brain imaging: Applications in psychiatry. *Science, 239,* 1381–1388.

Andreasen, N.C. (Ed.). (1989). *Brain imaging: Applications in psychiatry.* Washington, DC: American Psychiatric Press.

Andreasen, N.C., Arndt, S., Alliger, R., Miller, D., & Flaum, M. (1995). Symptoms of schizophrenia: Methods, meanings, and mechanisms. *Archives of General Psychiatry, 52,* 341–351.

Andreasen, N.C., & Carpenter, W.T., Jr. (1993). Diagnosis and classification of schizophrenia. *Schizophrenia Bulletin, 19,* 199–214.

Andreasen, N.C., Flaum, M., Swayze, V.W.II. Tyrell, G., & Arndt, S. (1990). Positive and negative symptoms in schizophrenia: A critical reappraisal. *Archives of General Psychiatry, 47,* 615–621.

Andreasen, N.C., & Olsen, S. (1982). Negative v. positive schizophrenia: Definition and validation. *Archives of General Psychiatry, 39,* 789–794.

Andrews, G. (1996). Comorbidity in neurotic disorders: The similarities are more important than the differences. In Ronald M. Rapee (Ed.), *Current controversies in the anxiety disorders,* pp. 3–20. New York: Guilford.

Andrews, G., MacMahon, S.W., Austin, A., & Byrne, D.G. (1984). Hypertension: Comparison of drug and non-drug treatments. *British Medical Journal, 284,* 1523–1530.

Anthony, J.C., & Helzer, J.E. (1991). Syndromes of drug abuse and dependence. In L.N. Robins & D.A. Regier (Eds.), *Psychiatric disorders in America: The Epidemiologic Catchment Area Study,* pp. 116–154. New York: Free Press.

Anthony, J.C., & Helzer, J.E. (1995). Epidemiology of drug dependence. In M.T. Tsuang, M. Tohen, & G.E.P. Zahner (Eds.), *Textbook in psychiatric epidemiology,* pp. 361–406. New York: Wiley-Liss.

Anthony, J.C., Warner, L.A., & Kessler, R.C. (1994). Comparative epidemiology of dependence on tobacco, alcohol, controlled substances, and inhalants: Basic findings from the National Comorbidity Survey. *Experimental and Clinical Psychopharmacology, 2,* 1–24.

Appelbaum, P.S. (1994). *Almost a revolution: Mental health law and the limits of change.* New York: Oxford University Press.

Appelbaum, P.S., & Gutheil, T.G. (1979). Rotting with their rights on: Constitutional theory and clinical reality in drug refusal by psychiatric patients. *Bulletin of the American Academy of Psychiatry and Law, 7,* 308–317.

Arato, M., Frecska, E., Tekes, K., MacCrimmon, D.J. (1991). Serotonergic interhemispheric asymmetry: Gender differences in cortex. *Acta Psychiatrica Scandinavica, 84,* 110–111.

Archer, R.P. (1992). Review of the Minnesota Multiphasic Personality Inventory-2. In J.J. Kramer & J.C. Conoley (Eds.), *The eleventh mental measurements yearbook.* Lincoln: University of Nebraska Press.

Aries, P. (1962). *Centuries of childhood: A social history of family life.* New York: Vintage.

Arneric, S.P., Sullivan, J.P., Decker, M.W., Brioni, J.D., et al. (1995). Potential treatment of Alzheimer disease using cholinergic channel activators with cognitive enhancement, anxiolytic-like, and cytoprotective properties. *Alzheimer Disease and Associated Disorders, 9* (suppl. 2), 50–61.

Arno, P.S., Brandt, A.M., Gostin, L.O., & Morgan, J. (1996). Tobacco industry strategies to oppose federal regulation. *Journal of the American Medical Association, 275,* 1258–1263.

Asberg, M. (1994). Monoamine neurotransmitters in human aggressiveness and violence: A selected review. *Criminal Behaviour and Mental Health, 4,* 303–327.

Asher, S.R., & Wheeler, V.A. (1985). Children's loneliness: A comparison of rejected and neglected peer status. *Journal of Consulting and Clinical Psychology, 53,* 500–505.

Asperger, H. (1944/1991). "Autistic psychopathy" in childhood. In U. Frith (Ed. and Trans.), *Autism and Asperger syndrome* (pp. 37–92). Cambridge, UK: Cambridge University Press. (Original published in 1944).

Astin, M.C., Ogland-Hand, S.M., Coleman, E.M., & Foy, D.W. (1995). Posttraumatic stress disorder and childhood abuse in battered women: Comparisons with maritally distressed women. *Journal of Consulting and Clinical Psychology, 63,* 308–312.

Atkinson, D.R., Morten, G., & Sue, D.W. (1993). *Counseling American minorities: A cross-cultural perspective,* 4th ed. Dubuque, IA: William C. Brown.

Attie, I., & Brooks-Gunn, J. (1989). Development of eating problems in adolescent girls: A longitudinal study. *Developmental Psychology, 25,* 70–79.

Babor, T.F. (1992). Cross-cultural research on alcohol: A quoi bon? In J.E. Helzer & G.J. Canino (Eds.), *Alcoholism in North America, Europe, and Asia,* pp. 33–52. New York: Oxford University Press.

Baer, L., Rauch, S.L., Ballantine, T., et al. (1995). Cingulotomy for intractable obsessive-compulsive disorder: Prospective long-term follow-up of 18 patients. *Archives of General Psychiatry, 52,* 384–392.

Bailey, A., Le Couteur, A., Gottesman, I., Bolton, P., Simonoff, E., Yuzda, E., & Rutter, M. (1995). Autism as a strongly genetic disorder: Evidence from a British twin study. *Psychological Medicine, 25,* 63–77.

Baker, C.D., & de Silva, P. (1988). The relationship between male sexual dysfunction and belief in Zilbergeld's myths: An empirical investigation. *Sexual and Marital Therapy, 3,* 229–238.

Baker, T.B., Morse, E., & Sherman, J.E. (1986). The motivation to use drugs: A psychobiological analysis of urges. *Nebraska Symposium on Motivation, 34,* 257–323.

Baker, T.B., & Tiffany, S.T. (1985). Morphine tolerance as habituation. *Psychological Review, 92,* 78–108.

Ballenger, J.C. (1989). Toward an integrated model of panic disorder. *American Journal of Orthopsychiatry, 59,* 284–293.

Ballenger, J.C. (1991). Long-term pharmacologic treatment of panic disorder. *Journal of Clinical Psychiatry, 52* (suppl. 2), 18–23.

Ballenger, J.C., Burrows, G.D., DuPont, R.L., Lesser, I.M., Noyes, R., et al. (1988). Alprazolam in panic disorder and agoraphobia: Results from a multicenter trial. I. Efficacy in short term treatment. *Archives of General Psychiatry, 45,* 413–422.

Baltes, M.M., Kuhl, K.P., & Sowarka, D. (1922). Testing for limits of cognitive reserve capacity: A promising strategy for early diagnosis of dementia? *Journal of Gerontology: Psychological Sciences, 47,* P165–P167.

Baltes, P.B. (1993). The aging mind: Potential and limits. *Gerontologist, 33,* 580–594.

Baltes, P.B., & Kliegl, R. (1992). Further testing of limits of cognitive plasticity: Negative age differences in a mnemonic skill are robust. *Developmental Psychology, 28,* 121–125.

Banazak, D.A. (1996). Difficult dementia: Six steps to control problem behaviors. *Geriatrics, 51,* 36–42.

Bancroft, J. (1989). *Human sexuality and its problems,* 2nd ed. Edinburgh: Churchill Livingstone.

Bancroft, J., Dickerson, M., Fairburn, C.G., Gray, J., Greenwood, J., Stevenson, N., & Warner, P. (1986). Sex therapy outcome research: A reappraisal of methodology. I. A treatment study of male sexual dysfunction. *Psychological Medicine, 16,* 851–863.

Bandura, A. (1973). *Aggression: A social learning analysis.* Englewood Cliffs, NJ: Prentice Hall.

Bandura, A. (1977). Self-efficacy: Toward a unifying theory of behavior change. *Psychological Review, 84,* 191–215.

Bandura, A., & Walters, R.H. (1963). *Social learning and personality development.* New York: Ronald Press.

Banki, C.M. (1995). Prophylactic potential of selective reuptake inhibitors in suicidal patients. *International Clinical Psychopharmacology, 9* (suppl. 4), 61–65.

Barbaree, H.E., & Seto, M.C. (1997). Pedophilia: Assessment and treatment. In D.R. Laws & W.T. O'Donohue (Eds.), *Handbook of sexual deviance: Theory and application.* New York: Guilford.

Barbaree, H.E., Seto, M.C., Serin, R.C., Amos, N.L., & Preston, D.L. (1994). Comparisons between sexual and nonsexual rapist subtypes: Sexual arousal to rape, offense precursors, and offense characteristics. *Criminal Justice and Behavior, 21,* 95–114.

Barkley, R.A. (1988). The effects of methylphenidate on the interactions of preschool ADHD children with their mothers. *Journal of the American Academy of Child and Adolescent Psychiatry, 27,* 336–341.

Barkley, R.A. (1990). *Attention-deficit hyperactivity disorder: A handbook for diagnosis and treatment,* 2nd ed. New York: Guilford.

Barkley, R.A., Karlsson, J., Strzelecki, E., & Murphy, J.V. (1984). Effects of age and Ritalin dosage on the mother-child interactions of hyperactive children. *Journal of Consulting and Clinical Psychology, 52,* 750–758.

Barlow, D.H. (1986). Causes of sexual dysfunction: The role of anxiety and cognitive interference. *Journal of Consulting and Clinical Psychology, 54,* 140–148.

Barlow, D.H. (1988). *Anxiety and its disorders: The nature and treatment of anxiety and panic.* New York: Guilford.

Barlow, D.H. (1991). Disorders of emotion. *Psychological Inquiry, 2,* 58–71.

Barlow, D.H., Brown, T.A., & Craske, M.G. (1994). Definitions of panic attacks and panic disorder in the DSM-IV: Implications for research. *Journal of Abnormal Psychology, 103,* 553–564.

Barlow, D.H., & Cerny, J.A. (1988). *Psychological treatment of panic.* New York: Guilford.

Barlow, D.H., & Craske, M.G. (1988). The phenomenology of panic. In S. Rachman & J.D. Maser (Eds.), *Panic: Psychological perspectives.* Hillsdale, NJ: Erlbaum.

Barlow, D.H., O'Brien, G.T., & Last, C.G. (1984). Couples treatment of agoraphobia. *Behavior Therapy, 15,* 41–58.

Baroff, G.S. (1986). *Mental retardation: Nature, cause, and management,* 2nd ed. Washington, DC: Hemisphere.

Barondes, S.H. (1993). *Molecules and mental illness.* New York: Scientific American.

Barrett, P.M., Dadds, M.R., & Rapee, R.M. (1996). Family treatment of childhood anxiety: A controlled trial. *Journal of Consulting and Clinical Psychology, 64,* 333–342.

Bartak, L., & Rutter, M. (1973). Special educational treatment of autistic children: A comparative study. I. Design of study and characteristics of units. *Journal of Child Psychology and Psychiatry, 14,* 217–222.

Baruth, L.G., & Huber, C.H. (1984). *An introduction to marital theory and therapy.* Monterey, CA: Brooks/Cole.

Basoglu, M., Lax, T., Kasvikis, Y., & Marks, I. (1988). Predictors of improvement in obsessive-compulsive disorder. *Journal of Anxiety Disorders, 2,* 299–317.

Bass, E., & Davis, L. (1988). *The courage to heal.* New York: Harper & Row.

Bastiani, A.M., Rao, R., Weltzin, T., & Kaye, W.H. (1995). Perfectionism in anorexia nervosa. *International Journal of Eating Disorders, 17,* 147–152.

Bates, J.E., Wachs, T.D., & Emde, R.N. (1994). Toward practical uses for biological concepts of temperament. In J.E. Bates & T.D. Wachs (Eds.), *Temperament: Individual differences at the interface of biology and behavior,* pp. 275–306. Washington, DC: American Psychological Association.

Baucom, D.H., & Epstein, N. (1990). *Cognitive-behavioral marital therapy.* New York: Brunner/Mazel.

Baucom, D.H., Notarius, C.I., Burnett, C.K., & Haefner, P. (1990). Gender differences and sex-role identity in marriage. In F.D. Fincham & T.N. Bradbury (Eds.), *The psychology of marriage: Basic issues and applications,* pp. 150–171. New York: Guilford.

Baum, A., Davidson, L.M., Singer, J.E., & Street, S.W. (1987). Stress as a psychophysiological response. In A. Baum & J.E. Singer (Eds.), *Handbook of psychology and health. Stress,* vol. 5, pp. 1–24. Hillsdale, NJ: Erlbaum.

Baum, D. (1996). *Smoke and mirrors: The war on drugs and the politics of failure.* Boston: Little Brown.

Bauman, M.L. (1996). Neuroanatomic observations of the brain in pervasive developmental disorders. *Journal of Autism and Developmental Disorders, 26,* 199–203.

Baumeister, R.F. (1990). Suicide as escape from self. *Psychological Review, 97,* 90–113.

Baumeister, R.F., & Butler, J.L. (1997). Sexual masochism. In D.R. Laws & W.T. O'Donohue (Eds.), *Handbook of sexual deviance: Theory and application.* New York: Guilford.

Baumrind, D. (1971). Current patterns of parental authority. *Developmental Psychology Monograph, 4,* (1, Pt. 2).

Bayer, R. (1981). *Homosexuality and American psychiatry: The politics of diagnosis.* New York: Basic Books.

Beach, S.R.H., Sandeen, E.E., & O'Leary, K.D. (1990). *Depression in marriage: A model for etiology and treatment.* New York: Guilford.

Bean, M.H. (1975). Alcoholics anonymous: AA. *Psychiatric Annals, 5,* 83–91.

Bebbington, P., & Kuipers, L. (1994). The predictive utility of expressed emotion in schizophrenia: An aggregate analysis. *Psychological Medicine, 24,* 707–718.

Bech, P. (1992). Symptoms and assessment of depression. In E.S. Paykel (Ed.), *Handbook of affective disorders,* 2nd ed., pp. 3–14. New York: Guilford.

Beck, A.T. (1967). *Depression: Clinical, experimental, and theoretical aspects.* New York: Harper & Row.

Beck, A.T. (1974). The development of depression. In R.J. Friedman & M.M. Katz (Eds.), *The psychology of depression: Contemporary theory and research,* pp. 3–20. New York: Winston-Wiley.

Beck, A. (1976). *Cognitive therapy and the emotional disorders.* New York: International Universities Press.

Beck, A.T. (1984). Cognition and therapy. *Archives of General Psychiatry, 41,* 1112–1114.

Beck, A.T., & Emery, G. (1985). *Anxiety disorders and phobias: A cognitive perspective.* New York: Basic Books.

Beck, A.T., Rush, A.J., Shaw, B.F., & Emery, G. (1979). *Cognitive therapy of depression.* New York: Guilford.

Beck, A.T., Steer, R.A., & Garbin, M.G. (1988). Psychometric properties of the Beck Depression Inventory: Twenty-five years of evaluation. *Clinical Psychology Review, 8,* 77–100.

Beck, J.G. (1993). Vaginismus. In W. O'Donohue & J.H. Geer (Eds.), *Handbook of sexual dysfunctions: Assessment and treatment,* pp. 381–397. Boston: Allyn & Bacon.

Becker, D., & Lamb, S. (1994). Sex bias in the diagnosis of borderline personality disorder and posttraumatic stress disorder. *Professional Psychology: Research and Practice, 25,* 55–61.

Becker, J.V. (1989). Impact of sexual abuse on sexual functioning. In S.R. Lieblum & R.C. Rosen (Eds.), *Principles and practice of sex therapy,* 2nd ed. New York: Guilford.

Beckson, M., & Cummings, J.L. (1992). Psychosis in basal ganglia disorders. *Neuropsychiatry, Neuropsychology & Behavioral Neurology, 5,* 126–131.

Belar, C.D., & Perry, N.W. (1992). The national conference on scientist-practitioner education and training for the professional practice of psychology. *American Psychologist*, 47, 71–75.

Bell, R.Q. (1968). A reinterpretation of the direction of effects in studies of socialization. *Psychological Review*, 75, 81–95.

Bellack, A.S., & Mueser, K.T. (1993). Psychosocial treatment for schizophrenia. *Schizophrenia Bulletin*, 19, 317–336.

Benet, A.E., & Melman, A. (1995). The epidemiology of erectile dysfunction. *Urologic Clinics of North America*, 22, 699–709.

Benjamin, L.S. (1974). Structural analysis of social behavior. *Psychological Review*, 81, 392–425.

Benjamin, L.S. (1993). *Interpersonal diagnosis and treatment of personality disorders.* 2nd ed. New York: Guilford.

Benson, D.F. (1992). Neuropsychiatric aspects of aphasia and related language impairments. In S.C. Yudofsky & R.E. Hales (Eds.), *Textbook of neuropsychiatry*, 2nd ed., pp. 311–327. Washington, DC: American Psychiatric Press.

Berenbaum, H., & Barch, D. (1995). The categorization of thought disorder. *Journal of Psycholinguistic Research*, 24, 349–376.

Berg, I. (1993). Aspects of school phobia. In C.G. Last (Ed.), *Anxiety across the lifespan: A developmental perspective*, pp. 78–93. New York: Springer.

Berkman, L.F., Seeman, T.E., Albert M., Blazer, D., Kahn, R., Mohs, R., Finch, C., Schneider, E., Cotman, C., McClearn, G., Nesselroade, J., Featherman, D., Garmezy, N., McKhann, G., Brim, G., Praeger, D., & Rowe, J. (1993). High, usual, and impaired functioning in community-dwelling older men and women: Findings from the MacArthur Foundation research network on successful aging. *Journal of Clinical Epidemiology*, 46, 1129–1140.

Berman, A.L., & Jobes, D.A. (1994). Treatment of the suicidal adolescent. In A.A. Leenaars, J.T. Maltsberger, & R.A. Neimeyer (Eds.), *Treatment of suicidal people*, pp. 89–100. Washington, DC: Taylor & Francis.

Bernlef, J. (1988). *Out of mind.* London: Faber.

Bernstein, D.A., & Borkovec, T.D. (1973). *Progressive relaxation training: A manual for the helping professions.* Champaign, IL: Research Press.

Bernstein, D.P., Cohen, P., Velez, C.N., Schwab-Stone, M., Siever, L.J., & Shinsato, L. (1993). Prevalence and stability of the DSM-III-R personality disorders in a community-based survey of adolescents. *American Journal of Psychiatry*, 150, 1237–1243.

Bernstein, D.P., Useda, D., & Siever, L.J. (1995). Paranoid personality disorder. In W.J. Livesley (Ed.), *The DSM-IV personality disorders.* New York: Guilford, pp. 45–57.

Berrettini, W.H. (1993). The molecular genetics of bipolar disease. In J.J. Mann & D.J. Kupfer (Eds.), *Biology of depressive disorders, Part A: A systems perspective*, pp. 189–204. New York: Plenum.

Berrios, G.E. (1989). Obsessive-compulsive disorder: Its conceptual history in France during the 19th century. *Comprehensive Psychiatry*, 30, 283–295.

Berrios, G. (1990). Memory and the cognitive paradigm of dementia during the 19th century: A conceptual history. In R.M. Murray & T.H. Turner (Eds.), *Lectures on the history of psychiatry.* Oxford: Gaskell/Royal College of Psychiatrists.

Berrios, G.E. (1990). Alzheimer's disease: A conceptual history. *International Journal of Geriatric Psychiatry*, 5, 355–365.

Berrios, G.E., & Hauser, R. (1988). The early development of Kraepelin's ideas on classification: A conceptual history. *Psychological Medicine*, 18, 813–821.

Berry, J.W., Poortinga, Y.H., Segall, M.H., & Dasen, P.R. (1992). *Cross-cultural psychology: Research and applications.* New York: Cambridge University Press.

Bertelson, A., Harvald, B., & Hauge, M. (1977). A Danish twin study of manic-depressive disorders. *British Journal of Psychiatry*, 130, 330–351.

Besharov, D.J. (1986). The misuse of foster care: When the desire to help children outruns the ability to improve parental functioning. *Family Law Quarterly*, 20, 213–231.

Besharov, D.J. (1988). How child abuse programs hurt poor children: The misuse of foster care. *Clearinghouse Review*, 20, 219–227.

Besharov, D.J. (1992). A balanced approach to reporting child abuse. *Child, Youth, and Family Services Quarterly*, 15, 5–7.

Besharov, D.J., & Laumann, L.A. (1996). Child abuse reporting: The need to shift priorities from more reports to better reports. In I. Garfinkel, J.L. Hochschild, & S.S. McLanahan (Eds.), *Social policies for children*, pp. 257–274. Washington, DC: Brookings Institution.

Bettelheim, B. (1967). *The empty fortress.* New York: Free Press.

Beumont, P.J.V., Garner, D.M., & Touyz, S.W. (1994). Diagnoses of eating or dieting disorders: What may we learn from past mistakes? *International Journal of Eating Disorders*, 16, 349–362.

Beutler, L.E., Crago, M., & Arizmendi, T.G. (1986). Therapist variables in psychotherapy process and outcome. In S.L. Garfield & A.E. Bergin (Eds.), *Handbook of psychotherapy and behavior change*, 3rd ed., pp. 257–310. New York: Wiley.

Beutler, L.E., Machado, P.P.P., & Neufeldt, S.A. (1994). Therapist variables. In A.E. Bergin & S.L. Garfield, *Handbook of psychotherapy and behavior change*, 4th ed., pp. 229–269. New York: Wiley.

Bianchi, S. (1991). Family disruption and economic hardship: The short-run picture for children. *Current Population Reports* (Series P-70, No. 23). Washington, DC: U.S. Government Printing Office.

Biederman, J., Baldessarini, R.J., Wright, V., Knee, D., & Harmatz, J.S. (1989). A double-blind placebo controlled study of desipramine in the treatment of ADD. I. Efficacy. *Journal of the American Academy of Child and Adolescent Psychiatry*, 28, 903–911.

Biederman, J., Rosenbaum, J.F., Chaloff, J., & Kagan, J. (1995). Behavioral inhibition as a risk factor. In J.S. March (Ed.), *Anxiety Disorders in Children and Adolescents*, pp. 61–81. New York: Guilford.

Biggins, C.A., Boyd, J.L., Harrop, F.M., Madeley, P., Mindham, R.H.S., Randall, J.I., & Spokes, E.G.S. (1992). A controlled, longitudinal study of dementia in Parkinson's disease. *Journal of Neurology, Neurosurgery, and Psychiatry*, 55, 566–571.

Biklen, D. (1992). Autism orthodoxy versus free speech: A reply to Cummins and Prior. *Harvard Educational Review*, 62, 242–256.

Billings, A.G., & Moos, R.H. (1982). Psychosocial theory and research on depression: An integrative framework and review. *Clinical Psychology Review*, 2, 213–237.

Billy, J.O.G., Tanfer, K., Grady, W.R., & Klepinger, D.H. (1993). The sexual behavior of men in the United States. *Family Planning Perspectives*, 25, 52–60.

Bingham, W.V.D., & Moore, B.V. (1924). *How to interview.* New York: Harper & Row.

Binswanger, L. (1963). *Being-in-the-world: Selected papers of Ludwig Binswanger.* New York: Basic Books.

Birtchnell, J. (1991). The measurement of dependence by questionnaire. *Journal of Personality Disorders*, 5, 281–295.

Black, D.W., Noyes, R., Goldstein, R.B., & Blum, N. (1992). A family study of obsessive-compulsive disorder. *Archives of General Psychiatry*, 49, 362–368.

Blackburn, R. (1988). On moral judgments and personality disorders: The myth of psychopathic personality revisited. *British Journal of Psychiatry*, 153, 505–512.

Blader, J.C., & Marshall, W.L. (1989). Is assessment of sexual arousal in rapists worthwhile? A critique of current methods and the development of a response compatibility approach. *Clinical Psychology Review*, 9, 569–587.

Blair, C.D., & Lanyon, R.I. (1981). Exhibitionism: Etiology and treatment. *Psychological Bulletin*, 89, 439–463.

Blanchard, E.B. (Ed.) (1992). Special issue on behavioral medicine. *Journal of Consulting and Clinical Psychology*, 60.

Blanchard, E.B. (1994). Behavioral medicine and health psychology. In A.E. Bergin & S.L. Garfield

(Eds.), *Handbook of psychotherapy and behavior change*, 4th ed., pp. 701–733. New York: Wiley.

Blanchard, R. (1989). The classification and labeling of nonhomosexual gender dysphorias. *Archives of Sexual Behavior, 18,* 315–334.

Blashfield, R.K. (1973). An evaluation of the DSM-II classification of schizophrenia as a nomenclature. *Journal of Abnormal Psychology, 82,* 382–389.

Blashfield, R.K. (1982). Feighner et al., invisible colleges, and the Matthew Effect. *Schizophrenia Bulletin, 8,* 1–6.

Blashfield, R.K. (1984). *The classification of psychopathology: Neo-Kraepelinian and quantitative approaches.* New York: Plenum.

Blashfield, R.K., & Draguns, J.G. (1976). Evaluative criteria for psychiatric classification. *Journal of Abnormal Psychology, 85,* 140–150.

Blashfield, R.K., & McElroy, R.A. (1987). The 1985 literature on the personality disorders. *Comprehensive Psychiatry, 28,* 536–546.

Blashfield, R.K., & McElroy, R.A. (1989). Ontology of personality disorder categories. *Psychiatric Annals, 19,* 126–131.

Blashfield, R.K., Sprock, J., Haymaker, D., & Hodgin, J. (1989). The family resemblance hypothesis applied to psychiatric classification. *Journal of Nervous and Mental Disease, 177,* 492–497.

Blatt, S.J., & Zuroff, D.C. (1992). Interpersonal relatedness and self-definition: Two prototypes for depression. *Clinical Psychology Review, 12,* 527–562.

Blazer, D., Hughes, D., & George, L.K. (1987). Stressful life events and the onset of a generalized anxiety syndrome. *American Journal of Psychiatry, 144,* 1178–1183.

Blehar, M.C., & Rosenthal, N.E. (1989). Seasonal affective disorders and phototherapy: Report of a National Institute of Mental Health–sponsored workshop. *Archives of General Psychiatry, 46,* 469–474.

Bleuler, M. (1978). *The schizophrenic disorders: Long-term patient and family studies.* New Haven, CT: Yale University Press.

Bliss, E.L. (1986). *Multiple personality, allied disorders, and hypnosis.* New York: Oxford University Press.

Bloch, S., & Crouch, E. (1987). *Therapeutic factors in group psychotherapy.* New York: Oxford University Press.

Blum, K., & Payne, J.E. (1991). *Alcohol and the addictive brain: New hope for alcoholics from biogenetic research.* New York: Free Press.

Blume, S.B. (1991). Women, alcohol, and drugs. In N.S. Miller (Ed.), *Comprehensive handbook of drug and alcohol addiction,* pp. 147–177. New York: Marcel Dekker.

Blumenthal, S., Matthews, K., & Weiss, S. (Eds.), *New research frontiers in behavioral medicine: Proceedings of the National Conference.* Washington, DC: NIH Publications.

Blundell, J.E. (1995). The psychobiological approach to appetite and weight control. In K.D. Brownell & C.G. Fairburn (Eds.), *Eating disorders and obesity: A comprehensive handbook,* pp. 13–20. New York: Guilford.

Bodlund, O., & Kullgren, G. (1996). Transsexualism—General outcome and prognostic factors: A five-year follow-up study of nineteen transsexuals in the process of changing sex. *Archives of Sexual Behavior, 25,* 303–317.

Bolger, J.P., Carpenter, B.C., & Strauss, M.E. (1994). Behavior and affect in Alzheimer's disease. *Clinics in Geriatric Medicine, 10,* 315–337.

Booth-Kewley, S., & Friedman, H.S. (1987). Psychological predictors of heart disease: A quantitative review. *Psychological Bulletin, 101,* 343–362.

Borduin, C.M., Mann, B.J., Cone, L.T., Henggeler, S.W., Fucci, B.R., Blaske, D.M., & Williams, R.A. (1995). Multisystemic treatment of serious juvenile offenders: Long-term prevention of criminality and violence. *Journal of Consulting and Clinical Psychology, 63,* 569–578.

Borkovec, T.D. (1994). The nature, functions, and origins of worry. In G.C.L. Davey & F. Tallis (Eds.), *Worrying: Perspectives in theory, assessment and treatment,* pp. 5–33. London: Wiley.

Borkovec, T.D., & Costello, E. (1993). Efficacy of applied relaxation and cognitive-behavioral therapy in the treatment of generalized anxiety disorder. *Journal of Consulting and Clinical Psychology, 61,* 611–619.

Borkovec, T.D., & Inz, J. (1990). The nature of worry in generalized anxiety disorder: A predominance of thought activity. *Behavior Research and Therapy, 28,* 153–158.

Borkovec, T.D., Shadick, R., & Hopkins, M. (1990). The nature of normal versus pathological worry. In R. Rapee & D.H. Barlow (Eds.), *Chronic anxiety and generalized anxiety disorder.* New York: Guilford.

Bornstein, R.F. (1993). *The dependent personality.* New York: Guilford.

Bornstein, R.F. (1996). Dependency. In C.G. Costello (Ed.), *Personality characteristics of the personality disordered,* pp. 120–145. New York: Wiley-Interscience.

Bornstein, R.F., Klein, D.N., Mallon, J.C., & Slater, J.F. (1988). Schizotypal personality disorder in an outpatient population: Incidence and clinical characteristics. *Journal of Clinical Psychology, 44,* 322–325.

Børup, C., Kaiser, A., & Jensen, E. (1992). Long-term Antabuse treatment: Tolerance and reasons for withdrawal. *Acta Psychiatrica Scandinavica, 86,* 47–49.

Boss, M. (1963). *Daseinsanalysis and psychoanalysis.* New York: Basic Books.

Bowers, K.S., & Meichenbaum, D. (Eds.) (1984). *The unconscious reconsidered.* New York: Wiley.

Bowlby, J. (1969). *Attachment.* New York: Basic Books.

Bowlby, J. (1973). *Separation: Anxiety and anger.* New York: Basic Books.

Bowlby, J. (1980). *Loss: Sadness and depression.* New York: Basic Books.

Bowlby, J. (1982). Attachment and loss: Retrospect and prospect. *American Journal of Orthopsychiatry, 52,* 664–678.

Boyer, W.F. (1992). Potential indications for the selective serotonin reuptake inhibitors. *International Clinical Psychopharmacology, 6,* suppl. 5, 5–12.

Bradbury, T.N., & Fincham, F.D. (1990). Attributions in marriage: Review and critique. *Psychological Bulletin, 107,* 3–33.

Bradbury, T.N., & Miller, G.A. (1985). Season of birth in schizophrenia: A review of evidence, methodology, and etiology. *Psychological Bulletin, 98,* 569–594.

Bradford, J. (1997). Medical interventions in sexual deviance. In D.R. Laws & W.T. O'Donohue (Eds.), *Handbook of sexual deviance: Theory and application.* New York: Guilford.

Bradford, J.M.W., Bloomberg, B.A., & Bourget, D. (1988). The heterogeneity/homogeneity of pedophilia. *Psychiatric Journal of the University of Ottawa, 13,* 217–226.

Bradford, J.M.W., Boulet, J., & Pawlak, A. (1992). The paraphilias: A multiplicity of deviant behaviours. *Canadian Journal of Psychiatry, 37,* 104–107.

Bradford, J.M.W., & Pawlak, A. (1993). Double-blind placebo cross-over study of cyproterone acetate in the treatment of paraphilias. *Archives of Sexual Behavior, 22,* 383–402.

Brandon, T.H., Wetter, D.W., & Baker, T.B. (1996). Affect, expectancies, urges, and smoking: Do they conform to models of drug motivation and relapse? *Experimental and Clinical Psychopharmacology, 4,* 29–36.

Braun, B.G. (1989). Psychotherapy of the survivor of incest with a dissociative disorder. *Psychiatric Clinics of North America, 12,* 307–324.

Braun, D.L., Sunday, S.R., & Halmi, K.A. (1994). Psychiatric comorbidity in patients with eating disorders. *Psychological Medicine, 24,* 859–867.

Braun, P., Kochansky, G., Shapiro, R., et al. (1981). Overview: Deinstitutionalization of psychiatric patients: A critical review of outcome studies. *American Journal of Psychiatry, 138,* 736–749.

Brayne, C. (1993). Research and Alzheimer's disease: An epidemiological perspective. *Psychological Medicine*, 23, 287–296.

Brecher, E.M., & the editors of *Consumer Reports*. (1972). *Licit and illicit drugs*. Boston: Little, Brown.

Breggin, P.R. (1994). *Talking back to Prozac*. New York: St. Martin's Press.

Bregman, J.D., Dykens, E., Watson, M., Ort, S.I., & Leckman, J.F. (1987). Fragile-X syndrome: Variability of phenotypic expression. *Journal of the American Academy of Child and Adolescent Psychiatry*, 26, 463–471.

Breier, A., Buchanan, R.W., Irish, D.I., & Carpenter, W.T., Jr. (1993). Clozapine treatment of outpatients with schizophrenia: Outcome and long-term response patterns. *Hospital and Community Psychiatry*, 44, 1145–1149.

Breitner, J.C.S., Gatz, M., Bergem, A.L.M., Christian, J.C., Mortimer, J.A., McClearn, G.E., Heston, L.L., Welsh, K.A., Anthony, J.C., Folstein, M.F., & Radebaugh, T.S. (1993). Use of twin cohorts for research in Alzheimer's disease. *Neurology*, 43, 261–267.

Brenner, D.E., Kukull, W.A., van Belle, G., Bowen, J.D., McCormick, W.C., Teri, L., & Larson, E.B. (1993). Relationship between cigarette smoking and Alzheimer's disease in a population-based case-control study. *Neurology*, 43, 293–300.

Breslau, N., Davis, G.C., & Andreski, P. (1995). Risk factors for PTSD-related traumatic events: A prospective analysis. *American Journal of Psychiatry*, 152, 529–535.

Breslau, N., Davis, G.C., Andreski, P., and Peterson, E. (1991). Traumatic events and posttraumatic stress disorder in an urban population of young adults. *Archives of General Psychiatry*, 48, 216–222.

Bretherton, I. (1985). Attachment theory: Retrospect and prospect. In I. Bretherton & E. Waters (Eds.), *Growing points in attachment theory and research. Monographs of the Society for Research in Child Development*, 56, 1–14.

Brett, E.A., Spitzer, R.L., & Williams, J.B.W. (1988). DSM-III-R criteria for posttraumatic stress disorder. *American Journal of Psychiatry*, 145, 1232–1235.

Brewer, C. (1992). Controlled trials of Antabuse in alcoholism: The importance of supervision and adequate dosage. *Acta Psychiatrica Scandinavica*, 86, 51–58.

Brewerton, T.D., Lydiard, R.B., Herzog, D.B., Brotman, A.W., O'Neil, P.M., & Ballenger, J. (1995). Comorbidity of Axis I psychiatric disorders in bulimia nervosa. *Journal of Clinical Psychiatry*, 56, 77–80.

Brewin, C.R., MacCarthy, B., Duda, K., et al. (1991). Attributions and expressed emotion in the relatives of patients with schizophrenia. *Journal of Abnormal Psychology*, 100, 546–554.

British Medical Research Council (1965). Clinical trial of the treatment of depressive illness. *British Medical Journal*, 1, 881–886.

Brody, E.M. (1989). The family at risk. In E. Light & B.D. Lebowitz (Eds.), *Alzheimer's disease treatment and family stress: Directions for research*. U.S. Department of Health and Human Services, DHHS Publication No. (ADM) 89-1569, pp. 2–49.

Brody, E.M., Saperstein, A.R., & Lawton, M.P. (1989). A multi-service respite program for caregivers of Alzheimer's patients. *Journal of Gerontological Social Work*, 14, 41–75.

Brom, D., Kleber, R.J., & Defares, P.B. (1989). Brief psychotherapy for posttraumatic stress disorders. *Journal of Consulting and Clinical Psychology*, 57, 607–612.

Bromley, D.B. (1990). *Behavioral gerontology: Central issues in the psychology of ageing*. New York: Wiley.

Bronfenbrenner, U. (1979). *The ecology of human development*. Cambridge, MA: Harvard University Press.

Brown, G.W. (1993). Life events and affective disorder: Replications and limitations. *Psychosomatic Medicine*, 55, 248–259.

Brown, G.W., Bifulco, A., & Andrews, B. (1990). Self-esteem and depression. III. Aetiological issues. *Social Psychiatry and Psychiatric Epidemiology*, 25, 235–243.

Brown, G.W., Birley, J.L.T., & Wing, J.K. (1972). Influence of family life on the course of schizophrenic disorders: A replication. *British Journal of Psychiatry*, 121, 241–258.

Brown, G.W., & Harris, T.O. (1978). *Social origins of depression: A study of psychiatric disorder in women*. London: Tavistock.

Brown, G.W., & Harris, T.O. (1993). Aetiology of anxiety and depressive disorders in an inner-city population. 1. Early adversity. *Psychological Medicine*, 23, 143–154.

Brown, L.S. (1992). A feminist critique of the personality disorders. In L.S. Brown & M. Ballou (Eds.), *Personality and psychopathology: Feminist reappraisals*. New York: Guilford.

Brown, P. (1994). Toward a psychobiological model of dissociation and post-traumatic stress disorder. In S.J. Lynn & J.W. Rhue (Eds.), *Dissociation: Clinical and theoretical perspectives*, pp. 94–122. New York: Guilford.

Brown, R. (1990). Limitations on expert testimony on the battered women syndrome in homicide cases: The return of the ultimate issue rule. *Arizona Law Review*, 32, 665–689.

Brown, S.A. (1993). Drug effect expectancies and addictive behavior change. *Experimental and Clinical Psychopharmacology*, 1, 55–67.

Brown, S.A., Goldman, M.S., Inn, A., & Anderson, L. (1980). Expectations of reinforcement from alcohol: Their domain and relation to drinking patterns. *Journal of Consulting and Clinical Psychology*, 48, 419–426.

Brown, T.A. (1996). Validity of the DSM-III-R and DSM-IV classification systems for anxiety disorders. In Ronald M. Rapee (Ed.), *Current controversies in the anxiety disorders*, pp. 21–45. New York: Guilford.

Brown, T.A., & Barlow, D.H. (1992). Comorbidity among anxiety disorders: Implications for treatment and DSM-IV. *Journal of Consulting and Clinical Psychology*, 60, 835–844.

Brown, T.A., Barlow, D.H., & Liebowitz, M.R. (1994). The empirical basis of generalized anxiety disorder. *American Journal of Psychiatry*, 151, 1272–1280.

Brown, W.A. (1990). Is light treatment a placebo? *Psychopharmacology Bulletin*, 26, 527–530.

Brownell, K.D. (1995). Definition and classification of obesity. In K.D. Brownell & C.G. Fairburn (Eds.), *Eating disorders and obesity: A comprehensive handbook*, pp. 386–390. New York: Guilford.

Brownell, K.D., & Fairburn, C.G. (Eds.) (1995). *Eating disorders and obesity: A comprehensive handbook*. New York: Guilford.

Brownell, K.D., Marlatt, G.A., Lichtenstein, E., & Wilson, G.T., (1986). Understanding and preventing relapse. *American Psychologist*, 41, 765–782.

Bruch, H. (1962). Perceptual and conceptual disturbances in anorexia nervosa. *Canadian Journal of Psychiatry*, 26, 187–194.

Bruch, H. (1982). Anorexia nervosa: Therapy and theory. *American Journal of Psychiatry*, 132, 1531–1538.

Bryson, S.E. (1996). Epidemiology of autism. *Journal of Autism and Developmental Disorders*, 26, 165–167.

Buchanan, R.W. (1995). Clozapine: Efficacy and safety. *Schizophrenia Bulletin*, 21, 579–591.

Buchsbaum, M.S., Someya, T., Teng, C.Y., Abel, L., et al. (1996). PET and MRI of the thalamus in never-medicated patients with schizophrenia. *American Journal of Psychiatry*, 153, 191–199.

Buck, R. (1984). *The communication of emotion*. New York: Guilford.

Bulbena, A., & Berrios, G.E. (1986). Pseudodementia: Facts and figures. *British Journal of Psychiatry*, 148, 87–94.

Bulbena, A., & Berrios, G.E. (1991). Cognitive function in the affective disorders: A prospective study. *Psychopathology*, 26, 6–12.

Bullough, V.L. (1976). *Sexual variance in society and history*. New York: Wiley.

Bumpass, L., (1984). Children and marital disruption: A replication and update. *Demography*, 21, 71–82.

Bunney, W.E., & Davis, J.M. (1965). Norepinephrine in depressed reactions. *Archives of General Psychiatry,* 13, 483–494.

Burke, B.L., & McGee, D.P. (1990). Sports deficit disorder. *Pediatrics,* 85, 1118.

Burke, C. (1995). Foreword. In L. Nadel & D. Rosenthal (Eds.), *Down syndrome: Living and learning in the community,* p. ix. New York: Wiley.

Burlingame, M. (1994). *The inner world of Abraham Lincoln.* Urbana and Chicago: University of Illinois Press.

Busby, W.J., Campbell, A.J., Borrie, M.J., & Spears, G.F.S. (1988). Alcohol use in a community-based sample of subjects aged 70 years and older. *Journal of the American Geriatrics Society,* 36, 301–305.

Buss, A. (1991). The EAS theory of temperament. In J. Strelau & A. Angleitner (Eds.), *Explorations in temperament.* New York: Plenum.

Buss, A.H., & Plomin, R. (1986). The EAS approach to temperament. In R. Plomin & J. Dunn (Eds.), *The study of temperament: Changes, continuities, and challenges.* Hillsdale, NJ: Erlbaum.

Buss, D.M. (1992). Mate preference mechanisms: Consequences for partner choice and intrasexual competition. In J.H. Barkow, L. Cosmides, & J. Tooby (Eds.), *The adapted mind: Evolutionary psychology and the generation of culture.* New York: Oxford University Press.

Butler, L.D., & Nolen-Hoeksema, S. (1994). Gender differences in responses to depressed mood in a college sample. *Sex Roles,* 30, 331–346.

Butters, N. (1992). Memory remembered: 1970–1991. *Archives of Clinical Neuropsychology,* 7, 285–295.

Buydens-Branchey, L., Branchey, M.H., Noumair, D., & Lieber, C.S. (1989). Age of alcoholism onset. II. Relationship to susceptibility to serotonin precursor availability. *Archives of General Psychiatry,* 46, 231–236.

Byerley, W.F., Reimherr, F.W., Wood, D.R., & Grosser, B.I. (1988). Fluoxetine, a selective serotonin uptake inhibitor, for the treatment of outpatients with major depression. *Journal of Clinical Psychopharmacology,* 8, 112–115.

Cacioppo, J.T., & Bernston, G.G. (1992). Social psychological contributions to the decade of the brain: Doctrine of multilevel analysis. *American Psychologist,* 47, 1019–1028.

Cado, S., & Leitenberg, H. (1990). Guilt reactions to sexual fantasies during intercourse. *Archives of Sexual Behavior,* 19, 49–63.

Cadoret, R.J., Yates, W.R., Troughton, E., Woodworth, G., & Stewart, M.A. (1995). Genetic-environmental interaction in the genesis of aggressivity and conduct disorders. *Archives of General Psychiatry,* 52, 916–924.

Cairns, R.B., & Green, J.A. (1979). How to assess personality and social patterns: Observations or ratings? In R.B. Cairns (Ed.), *The analysis of social interactions: Methods, issues, and illustrations.* Hillsdale, NJ: Erlbaum.

Caldwell, C., & Gottesman, I.I. (1992). Schizophrenia—A high-risk factor for suicide: Clues to risk reduction. *Suicide and Life-Threatening Behavior,* 2, 479–493.

Caldwell-Smith, G. (1990). First-person account: A mother's view. *Schizophrenia Bulletin,* 16, 687–690.

Cameron, H.M., & McGoogan, E. (1981). A prospective study of 1152 hospital autopsies. II. Analysis of inaccuracies in clinical diagnoses and their significance. *Journal of Pathology,* 133, 285–300.

Cameron, N., & Rychlak, J.F. (1985). *Personality development and psychopathology: A dynamic approach.* Boston: Houghton Mifflin.

Cameron, O.G., & Hill, E.M. (1989). Women and anxiety. *Psychiatric Clinics of North America,* 12, 175–186.

Campbell, E. (1990). The psychopath and the definition of "mental disease of defect" under the Model Penal Code test of insanity: A question of psychology or a question of law? *Nebraska Law Review,* 69, 190–229.

Campbell, M., Green, W.H., & Deutsch, S.I. (1985). *Child and adolescent psychopharmacology.* Beverly Hills, CA: Sage.

Campbell, M., Perry, R., Polonsky, B.B., Deutsch, S.I., Palij, M., & Lukashok, D. (1986). An open study of fenfluramine in hospitalized young autistic children. *Journal of Autism and Developmental Disorders,* 16, 494–505.

Canino, G.L., Bird, H.R., et al. (1987). Prevalence of specific psychiatric disorders in Puerto Rico. *Archives of General Psychiatry,* 44, 727–735.

Cannon, T.D., Mednick, S.A., & Parnas, J. (1990). Antecedents of predominantly negative and predominantly positive-symptom schizophrenia in a high-risk population. *Archives of General Psychiatry,* 47, 622–632.

Cannon, T.D., Mednick, S.A., Parnas, J., Schulsinger, F., Praestholm, J., & Vestergaard, A. (1993). Developmental brain abnormalities in the offspring of schizophrenic mothers. I. Contributions of genetic and perinatal factors. *Archives of General Psychiatry,* 50, 551–564.

Cannon, W.B. (1935). Stress and strains of homeostasis. *American Journal of Medical Science,* 189, 1–14.

Cantwell, D.P. (1988). DSM-III studies. In M. Rutter, A.H. Tuma, & I.S. Lann (Eds.), *Assessment and diagnosis in child psychopathology,* pp. 3–36. New York: Guilford.

Cantwell, D.P., Baker, L., & Rutter, M. (1979). Families of autistic and dysphasic children. I. Family life and interactions patterns. *Archives of General Psychiatry,* 36, 682–687.

Caplan, G. (1964). *Principles of preventive psychiatry.* New York: Basic Books.

Caplan, P.J. (1995). *They say you're crazy: How the world's most powerful psychiatrists decide who's normal.* Reading: MA: Addison-Wesley.

Capron, C., & Duyme, M. (1989). Assessment of effects of socioeconomic status on IQ in a full cross-fostering study. *Nature,* 340, 552–554.

Carey, G., & Gottesman, I.I. (1978). Reliability and validity in binary ratings: Areas of common misunderstanding in diagnosis and symptom rating. *Archives of General Psychiatry,* 35, 1454–1459.

Carey, G., & Gottesman, I.I. (1981). Twin and family studies of anxiety, phobic, and obsessive disorders. In D.F. Klein & J.G. Rabkin (Eds.), *Anxiety: New research and changing concepts.* New York: Raven Press.

Carey, G., & Gottesman, I.I. (1996). Genetics and antisocial behavior: Substance versus sound bytes. *Politics and the Life Sciences,* March, 88–90.

Carlson, E.A., & Sroufe, A. (1995). Contribution of attachment theory to developmental psychopathology. In D. Cicchetti & D.J. Cohen (Eds.), *Developmental psychopathology,* vol. 1, pp. 581–617. New York: Wiley.

Carlsson, A. (1988). The current status of the dopamine hypothesis of schizophrenia. *Neuropsychopharmacology,* 1, 179–186.

Carlsson, A., & Lindqvist, M. (1963). Effect of chlorpromazine and haloperidol on the formation of 3-methoxytyramine and normetanephrine in mouse brain. *Acta Pharmacology,* 20, 140.

Carney, R.M., Freeland, K.E., Rich, M.W., & Jaffe, A.S. (1995). Depression as a risk factor for cardiac events in established coronary heart disease: A review of possible mechanisms. *Annals of Behavioral Medicine,* 17, 142–149.

Carpenter, B.D., Strauss, M.E., & Kennedy, J.S. (1995). Personal history of depression and its appearance in Alzheimer's disease. *International Journal of Geriatric Psychiatry,* 10, 669–678.

Carpenter, W.T., Conley, R.R., Buchanan, R.W., Breier, A., et al. (1995). Patient response and resource management: Another view of clozapine treatment of schizophrenia. *American Journal of Psychiatry,* 152, 827–832.

Carpenter, W.T., & Strauss, J.S. (1991). The prediction of outcome in schizophrenia. IV. Eleven-year follow-up of the Washington IPSS cohort. *Journal of Nervous and Mental Disease,* 179, 517–525.

Carr, E.G. (1977). The motivation of self-injurious behavior: A review of some hypotheses. *Psychological Bulletin,* 84, 800–816.

Carr, E.G. (1982). *How to teach sign language to developmentally disabled children.* Lawrence, KS: H & H Enterprises.

Carroll, M.A., Schneider, H.G., & Wesley, G.R. (1985). *Ethics in the practice of psychology.* Englewood Cliffs, NJ: Prentice Hall.

Casas, J.M. (1995). Counseling and psychotherapy with racial/ethnic minority groups in theory and practice. In B. Bongar & L.E. Beutler (Eds.), *Comprehensive handbook of psychotherapy,* pp. 311–335. New York: Oxford University Press.

Cash, T.F., & Henry, P.E. (1995). Women's body images: The results of a national survey in the U.S.A. *Sex Roles,* 33, 19–28.

Caspi, A., Elder, G.H., & Bem, D.J. (1988). Moving away from the world: Life-course patterns of shy children. *Developmental Psychology,* 24, 824–831.

Caspi, A., & Moffitt, T.E. (1995). The continuity of maladaptive behavior: From description to understanding in the study of antisocial behavior. In D. Cicchetti & D.J. Cohen (Eds.), *Developmental psychopathology,* vol. 1, pp. 472–511. New York: Wiley.

Cassidy, J. (1988). Child-mother attachment and the self in six-year- olds. *Child Development,* 59, 121–134.

Castle, D.J., Abel, K., Takei, N., & Murray, R.M. (1995). Gender differences in schizophrenia: Hormonal effect or subtypes? *Schizophrenia Bulletin,* 21, 1–12.

Cattarin, J.A., & Thompson, J.K. (1994). A three-year longitudinal study of body image, eating disturbance, and general psychological functioning in adolescent females. *Eating Disorders: The Journal of Treatment and Prevention,* 2, 114–125.

Cavanaugh, J.C. (1993). *Adult development and aging,* 2nd ed. Pacific Grove, CA: Brooks/Cole.

Chalfonte, B.L., & Johnson, M.K. (1996). Feature memory and binding in young and older adults. *Memory and Cognition,* 24, 403–417.

Chalkey, A.J., & Powell, G.E. (1983). The clinical description of forty-eight cases of sexual fetishism. *British Journal of Psychiatry,* 142, 292–295.

Chambless, D.L., Cherney, J., Caputo, G.C., & Rheinstein, B.J. (1987). Anxiety disorders and alcoholism: A study with inpatient alcoholics. *Journal of Anxiety Disorders,* 1, 29–40.

Chambless, D.L., & Gillis, M.M. (1993). Cognitive therapy of anxiety disorders. *Journal of Consulting and Clinical Psychology,* 61, 248–260.

Chappel, J.N. (1992). Effective use of Alcoholics Anonymous and Narcotics Anonymous in treating patients. *Psychiatric Annals,* 22, 409–418.

Chappel, J.N. (1993). Long-term recovery from alcoholism. *Psychiatric Clinics of North America,* 16, 177–187.

Charney, D.S., Delgado, P.L., Price, L.H., & Heninger, G.R. (1991). The receptor sensitivity hypothesis of antidepressant action: A review of antidepressant effects on serotonin function. In S. Brown and H.M. van Praag (Eds.), *The role of serotonin in psychiatric disorders.* New York: Brunner/Mazel, pp. 27–56.

Charvat, J., Dell, P.P., Golkow, P., & Folkow, B. (1964). Mental factors in cardiovascular disease. *Cardiology,* 44, 124–141.

Chassin, L. (1984). Adolescent substance use and abuse. In P. Karoly & J.J. Steffen (Eds.), *Adolescent behavior disorders: Foundations and contemporary concerns* [*Advances in Child Behavioral Analysis and Therapy* (vol. 3)]. pp. 99–152.

Chassin, L., Pillow, D.R., Curran, P.J., Molina, B.S.G., & Barrera, M., Jr. (1993). Relation of parental alcoholism to early adolescent substance use: A test of three mediating mechanisms. *Journal of Abnormal Psychology,* 102, 3–19.

Checkley, S. (1992). Neuroendocrine mechanisms and the precipitation of depression by life events. *British Journal of Psychiatry,* 160 (suppl. 15). 7–17.

Chen, C.S. (1972). A further note on studies of acquired behavioral tolerance to alcohol. *Psychopharmacologia,* 27, 265–274.

Cherlin, A.J. (1991). *Marriage, divorce, remarriage,* 2nd ed. Cambridge, MA: Harvard University Press.

Cherlin, A.J. (1996). *Public and private families.* New York: McGraw-Hill.

Chess, S., & Thomas, A. (1984). *Origins and evolution of behavior disorders.* New York: Brunner/Mazel.

Chesselet, M., & Delfs, J.M. (1996). Basal ganglia and movement disorders: An update. *Trends in Neurosciences,* 19, 417–423.

Christensen, A., & Jacobson, N.S. (1994). Who (or what) can do psychotherapy: The status and challenge of nonprofessional therapies. *Psychological Science,* 5, 8–14.

Christiansen, B.A., Smith, G.T., Roehling, P.V., & Goldman, M.S. (1989). Using alcohol expectancies to predict adolescent drinking behavior after one year. *Journal of Consulting and Clinical Psychology,* 57, 93–99.

Ciarnello, R.D., Aimi, J., Dean, R.R., Morilak, D.A., Porteus, M.H., & Cicchetti, D. (1995). Fundamentals of molecular neurobiology. In D. Cicchetti & D. Cohen (Eds.), *Developmental psychopathology* (pp. 109–160). New York: Wiley.

Cicchetti, D., & Beegly, M. (1990). *Children with Down syndrome: A developmental perspective.* New York: Cambridge University Press.

Cicchetti, D., & Cohen, D. (Eds.) (1995). *Developmental psychopathology,* Vols. 1 & 2. New York: Wiley.

Cipparone, R.C. (1987). The defense of battered women who kill. *University of Pennsylvania Law Review,* 135, 427–452.

Clark, D.B., & Sayette, M.A. (1993). Anxiety and the development of alcoholism: Clinical and scientific issues. *American Journal on Addictions,* 2, 59–76.

Clark, D.M. (1986a). A cognitive approach to panic. *Behaviour Research and Therapy,* 24, 461–470.

Clark, D.M. (1986b). Cognitive therapy for anxiety. *Behavioral Psychotherapy,* 14, 283–294.

Clark, D.M., & Ehlers, A. (1993). An overview of the cognitive theory and treatment of panic disorder. *Applied and Preventive Psychology,* 2, 131–139.

Clark, D.M., Salkovskis, P.M., Hackmann, A., Middleton, H., Anastasiades, P., & Gelder, M. (1994). A comparison of cognitive therapy, applied relaxation and imipramine in the treatment of panic disorder. *British Journal of Psychiatry,* 164, 759–769.

Clark, L.A., McEwen, J.L., Collard, L.M., & Hickok, L.G. (1993). Symptoms and traits of personality disorder: Two new methods for their assessment. *Psychological Assessment,* 5, 81–91.

Clark, L.A., Watson, D., & Reynolds, S. (1995). Diagnosis and classification of psychopathology: Challenges to the current system and future directions. *Annual Review of Psychology,* 46, 121–153.

Clarke, J.W. (1990). *On being mad or merely angry.* Princeton, NJ: Princeton University Press.

Clarke-Stewart, A., Perlmutter, M., & Friedman, S. (1988). *Lifelong human development.* New York: Wiley.

Cleckley, H. (1976). *The mask of sanity,* 5th ed. St. Louis: Mosby.

Clementz, B.A., & Iacono, W.G. (1993). Nosology and diagnosis. In A.S. Bellack & M. Hersen (Eds.), *Psychopathology in adulthood,* pp. 3–20. Boston: Allyn & Bacon.

Clementz, B.A., & Sweeney, J.A. (1990). Is eye movement dysfunction a biological marker for schizophrenia? A methodological review. *Psychological Bulletin,* 108, 77–92.

Cloninger, C.R. (1987). Neurogenetic adaptive mechanisms in alcoholism. *Science,* 236, 410–416.

Cloninger, C.R., & Gottesman, I.I. (1987). Genetic and environmental factors in antisocial behavior disorders. In S.A. Mednick, T.E. Moffitt, & S.A. Stack (Eds.), *The causes of crime: New biological approaches,* pp. 92–109. Cambridge: Cambridge University Press.

Cloninger, C.R., Sigvardsson, S., Bohman, M., & von Knorring, A.L. (1982). Predisposition to petty criminality in Swedish adoptees. II. Cross-fostering analysis of gene-environment interaction. *Archives of General Psychiatry,* 39, 1242–1249.

Cohen, C.I. (1993). Poverty and the course of schizophrenia: Implications for research and policy. *Hospital and Community Psychiatry,* 44, 951–958.

Cohen, S. (1988). *The chemical brain: The neurochemistry of addictive disorders.* Irvine, CA: CareInstitute.

Cohen, S., Kaplan, J.R., Cunnick, J.E., Manuck, S.B., & Rabin, B.S. (1992). Chronic social stress, affiliation, and cellular immune response in nonhuman primates. *Psychological Science,* 3, 301–304.

Cohen, S., & Williamson, G.M. (1991). Stress and infectious disease in humans. *Psychological Bulletin*, 109, 5–24.

Cohen, S., & Wills, T.A. (1985). Stress, social support, and the buffering process. *Psychological Bulletin*, 98, 310–357.

Cohler, B.J., & Nakamura, J.E. (1996). In J. Sadavoy, L.W. Lazarus, L.F. Jarvik, & G.T. Grossberg (Eds.), *Comprehensive review of geriatric psychiatry—II*, pp. 153–194. Washington, DC: American Psychiatric Press.

Coie, J., & Kupersmidt, J., (1983). A behavioral analysis of emerging social status in boys' groups. *Child Development*, 54, 1400–1416.

Colby, K.M. (1975). *Artificial paranoia: A computer simulation of paranoid processes*. New York: Pergamon.

Cole, W. (1992). Incest perpetrators: Their assessment and treatment. *Psychiatric Clinics of North America*, 15, 689–701.

Coleman, P. (1993). Overview of substance abuse. *Primary Care: Clinics in Office Practice*, 20, 1–18.

Collaer, M.L., & Hines, M. (1995). Human behavioral sex differences: A role for gonadal hormones during early development. *Psychological Bulletin*, 118, 55–107.

Comfort, A. (1987). Deviation and variation. In G.D. Wilson (Ed.), *Variant sexuality: Research and theory*, pp. 1–20. London: Croom Helm.

Conger, J.J. (1956). Alcoholism: Theory, problem, and challenge. II. Reinforcement theory and the dynamics of alcoholism. *Quarterly Journal of Studies on Alcohol*, 17, 296–305.

Consensus Conference on Electroconvulsive Therapy. (1985). *JAMA*, 254, 103–108.

Consumer Reports (1995, November). Mental health: Does therapy help? pp. 734–739.

Cook, D.R. (1985). Craftsman versus professional: Analysis of the controlled drinking controversy. *Journal of Studies on Alcohol*, 46, 433–442.

Cook, M., & Mineka, S. (1989). Observational conditioning of fear to fear-relevant versus fear-irrelevant stimuli in Rhesus monkeys. *Journal of Abnormal Psychology*, 98, 448–459.

Cook, M., & Mineka, S. (1991). Selective associations in the origins of phobic fears and their implications for behavior therapy. In P.R. Martin (Ed.), *Handbook of behavior therapy and psychological science: An integrative approach*. New York: Pergamon. pp. 413–434.

Cook, W.L., Strachan, A.M., Goldstein, M.J., & Miklowitz, D.J. (1989). Expressed emotion and reciprocal affective relationships in families of disturbed adolescents. *Family Process*, 28, 337–348.

Coons, P. (1986). The prevalence of multiple personality disorder. *Newsletter of the International Society for the Study of Multiple Personality and Dissociation*, 4, 6–8.

Coons, P., & Milstein, V. (1988). Psychogenic amnesia: A clinical investigation of 25 consecutive cases. Unpublished data cited in D. Spiegel & E. Cardena (1991). Disintegrated experience: The dissociative disorders revisited. *Journal of Abnormal Psychology*, 100, 366–378.

Cooper, J.E., Kendell, R.E., Gurland, B.J., Sharpe, L., Copeland, J.R.M., & Simon, R. (1972). *Psychiatric diagnosis in New York and London*. London: Oxford University Press.

Cooper, M.H. (1994). Regulating tobacco: Can the FDA break America's smoking habit? *CQ Researcher*, 4, 843–858.

Cooper, P.J. (1995). Eating disorders and their relationship to mood and anxiety disorders. In K.D. Brownell & C.G. Fairburn (Eds.), *Eating disorders and obesity: A comprehensive handbook*, pp. 159–164. New York: Guilford.

Coovert, D.L., Kinder, B.N., & Thompson, J.K. (1989). The psychosexual aspects of anorexia nervosa and bulimia nervosa: A review of the literature. *Clinical Psychology Review*, 9, 169–180.

Copestake, P. (1993). Aluminum and Alzheimer's disease: An update. *Food and Chemical Toxicology*, 31, 670–683.

Cordova, J.V., Jacobson, N.S., Gottman, J.M., Rushe, R., & Cox, G. (1993). Negative reciprocity and communication in couples with a violent husband. *Journal of Abnormal Psychology*, 102, 559–564.

Corse, C.D., Manuck, S.B., Cantwell, J.D., Giordani, B., & Matthews, K.A. (1982). Coronary-prone behavior pattern and cardiovascular response in persons with and without coronary heart disease. *Psychosomatic Medicine*, 44, 449–459.

Coryell, W., Endicott, J., Andreasen, N., & Keller, M. (1985). Bipolar I, bipolar II, and nonbipolar major depression among the relatives of affectively ill probands. *American Journal of Psychiatry*, 142, 817–821.

Coryell, W., & Winokur, G. (1992). Course and outcome. In E.S. Paykel (Ed.), *Handbook of affective disorders*, 2nd ed., pp. 89–110. New York: Guilford.

Costa, P.T., & McCrea, R.R. (1992). The five-factor model of personality and its relevance to personality disorders. *Journal of Personality Disorders*, 6, 343–359.

Costello, C.G. (1976). *Anxiety and depression: The adaptive emotions*. Montreal: McGill-Queen's University Press.

Costello, C.G. (1982). Fears and phobias in women: A community study. *Journal of Abnormal Psychology*, 91, 280–286.

Costello, C.G. (1992). Problems in recent tests of two cognitive theories of panic. *Behaviour Research and Therapy*, 30, 1–5.

Costello, C.G. (1993). Advantages of the symptom approach to schizophrenia. In C.G. Costello (Ed.), *Symptoms of schizophrenia*, pp. 1–26. New York: Wiley.

Cowan, C.P. & Cowan, P.A. (1992). *When partners become parents*. New York: Basic Books.

Coyne, J. (1976). Toward an interactional description of depression. *Psychiatry*, 39, 28–40.

Coyne, J. (1985). Ambiguity and controversy: An introduction. In J. Coyne (Ed.), *Essential papers on depression*. New York: New York University Press.

Coyne, J.C. (1992). Cognition in depression: A paradigm in crisis. *Psychological Inquiry*, 3, 232–235.

Coyne, J.C., Downey, G., & Boergers, J. (1993). Depression in families: A systems perspective. In D. Cicchetti & S.L. Toth (Eds.), *Rochester Symposium on Developmental Psychopathology*, Vol. 4, *Developmental approaches to the affective disorders*. Rochester, NY: University of Rochester.

Coyne, J.C., & Gotlib, I.H. (1983). The role of cognition in depression: A critical appraisal. *Psychological Bulletin*, 94, 472–505.

Coyne, J.C., & Whiffen, V.E. (1995). Issues in personality as diathesis for depression: The case of sociotropy-dependency and autonomy-self-criticism. *Psychological Bulletin*, 118, 358–378.

Craddock, N., & McGuffin, P. (1993). Approaches to the genetics of affective disorders. *Annals of Medicine*, 317–322.

Cranston-Cuebas, M.A., & Barlow, D.H. (1990). Cognitive and affective contributions to sexual functioning. In J. Bancroft, D.M. Davis, & D. Weinstein (Eds.), *Annual review of sex research*, Vol. 1, *An integrative and interdisciplinary review*, pp. 119–161. Lake Mills, IA: Stoyles Graphic Services.

Cranston-Cuebas, M.A., Barlow, D.H., Mitchell, W., & Athanasiou, R. (1993). Differential effects of a misattribution manipulation on sexually functional and dysfunctional men. *Journal of Abnormal Psychology*, 102, 525–533.

Craske, M.G., Sanderson, W.C., & Barlow, D.H. (1987). The relationships among panic, fear, and avoidance. *Journal of Anxiety Disorders*, 1, 153–160.

Craske, M.G., Rapee, R.M., Jackel, L., & Barlow, D.H. (1989). Qualitative dimensions of worry in DSM-III-R generalized anxiety disorder subjects and nonanxious controls. *Behaviour Research and Therapy*, 27, 397–402.

Creese, I., Burt, D.R., & Snyder, S.H. (1976). Dopamine receptor binding predicts clinical and pharmacological potencies of antischizophrenic drugs. *Science*, 192, 481–483.

Crick, N.R., & Dodge, K.A. (1994). A review and reformulation of social information-processing mechanisms in children's social adjustment. *Psychological Bulletin*, 115, 74–101.

Crocker, J., & Major, B. (1989). Social stigma and self-esteem: The self-protective properties of stigma. *Psychological Review, 96*, 608–630.

Crossley, R., & McDonald, A. (1980). *Annie's coming out*. New York: Penguin.

Cross-National Collaborative Panic Study. Second Phase Investigators. (1992). Drug treatment of panic disorder: Comparative efficacy of alprazolam, imipramine, and placebo. *British Journal of Psychiatry, 160*, 191–202.

Crow, T.J. (1980). Molecular pathology of schizophrenia: More than one disease process? *British Medical Journal, 280*, 66–68.

Crow, T.J. (1985). The two-syndrome concept: Origins and current status. *Schizophrenia Bulletin, 11*, 471–486.

Crowell, J.A., Waters, E., Kring, A., & Riso, L.P. (1993). The psychosocial etiologies of personality disorders: What is the answer like? *Journal of Personality Disorders*, suppl., 118–128.

Csikszentmihalyi, M. & Larson, R. *Being adolescent*. New York: Basic Books.

Cummings, E.M., & Davies, P. (1994). *Children and marital conflict*. New York: Guilford.

Cummings, J.L. (1992). Neuropsychiatric aspects of Alzheimer's disease and other dementing illnesses. In S.C. Yudofsky & R.E. Hales (Eds.), *Textbook of neuropsychiatry*, 2nd ed., pp. 605–620. Washington, DC: American Psychiatric Press.

Cummings, J.L. (1995). Dementia: The failing brain. *Lancet, 345*, 1481–1485.

Cutting, J. (1986). *The psychology of schizophrenia*. London: Churchill Livingstone.

Cutting, J., & McClelland, R. (1986). Psychiatric manifestations of organic illness. In P. Hill, R. Murray, & A. Thorley (Eds.), *Essentials of postgraduate psychiatry*, 2nd ed., pp. 461–493. London: Grune & Stratton.

Dackis, C.A., & Gold, M.S. (1991). Inpatient treatment of drug and alcohol addiction. In N.S. Miller (Ed.), *Comprehensive handbook of drug and alcohol addiction*, pp. 1233–1244. New York: Marcel Dekker.

Dadds, M.R., Schwartz, S., & Sanders, M.R. (1987). Marital discord and treatment outcome in behavioral treatment of child conduct disorders. *Journal of Consulting and Clinical Psychology, 55*, 396–403.

Danforth, J.S., Barkley, R.A., & Stokes, T.F. (1991). Observations of parent-child interactions with hyperactive children: Research and clinical implications. *Clinical Psychology Review, 11*, 703–727.

Daniel, D.G., Zigun, J.R., & Weinberger, D.R. (1994). Brain imaging in neuropsychiatry. In S.C. Yudofsky & R.E. Hales (Eds.), *Synopsis of neuropsychiatry*, pp. 143–156. Washington, DC: American Psychiatric Press.

Darkes, J., & Goldman, M.S. (1993). Expectancy challenge and drinking reduction: Experimental evidence for a mediational process. *Journal of Consulting and Clinical Psychology, 61*, 344–353.

Davey, G.C.L. (1989). UCS revaluation and conditioning models of acquired fears. *Behaviour Research and Therapy, 27*, 521–528.

Davey, G.C.L., de Jong, P.J., & Tallis, F. (1993). UCS inflation in the aetiology of a variety of anxiety disorders: Some case histories. *Behaviour Research and Therapy, 31*, 495–498.

Davidson, J., Kudler, H., Smith, R., Mahorney, S.L., Lipper, S., Hammett, E., Saunders, W.B., & Cavenar, J.O. (1990). Treatment of posttraumatic stress disorder with amitriptyline and placebo. *Archives of General Psychiatry, 47*, 259–266.

Davidson, J.M. (1989). Sexual emotions, hormones and behavior. *Advances* (Institute for the Advancement of Health), 6, 56–58.

Davidson, J.R., & Foa, E.B. (1991). Diagnostic issues in posttraumatic stress disorder: Considerations for the DSM-IV. *Journal of Abnormal Psychology, 100*, 346–355.

Davidson, J.R.T., Tupler, L.A., & Potts, N.L.S. (1994). Treatment of social phobia with benzodiazepines. *Journal of Clinical Psychiatry, 55* (suppl. 6), 28–32.

Davidson, J.R.T., & van der Kolk, B.A. (1996). The psychopharmacological treatment of posttraumatic stress disorder. In B.A. van der Kolk, A.C. McFarlane, & L. Weisaeth (Eds.), *Traumatic stress*, pp. 510–524. New York: Guilford.

Davidson, M. (1982). *Uncommon sense: The life and thought of Ludwig von Bertalanffy (1901–1972), father of general systems theory*. Boston: Houghton Mifflin.

Davidson, W.S., Redner, R., Blakely, C.H., Mitchell, C.M., & Emshoff, J.G. (1987). Diversion of juvenile offenders: An experimental comparison. *Journal of Consulting and Clinical Psychology, 55*, 68–75.

Davis, G.C., & Akiskal, H.S. (1986). Descriptive, biological, and theoretical aspects of borderline personality disorder. *Hospital and Community Psychiatry 37*, 685–692.

Davis, J.P., Chesney, P.J., Wand, P.J., Laventure, M., et al. (1980). Toxic-shock syndrome: Epidemiological features, recurrence, risk factors, and prevention. *New England Journal of Medicine, 303*, 1429–1435.

Davis, K.L., & Haroutunian, V. (1993). Strategies for the treatment of Alzheimer's disease. *Neurology, 4* (suppl. 4), S52–S55.

Davis, K.L., Kahn, R.S., Ko, G., & Davidson, M. (1991). Dopamine in schizophrenia: A review and reconceptualization. *American Journal of Psychiatry, 148*, 1474–1486.

Davis, R.E., Coyle, P.D., Carroll, R.T., Emmerling, M.R., & Jaen, J. (1995). Cholinergic therapies for Alzheimer's disease. Palliative or disease altering? *Arzneimittel-Forschung, 45*, 425–431.

Davis, R.H. (1978). Review of the Rorschach test. In O.K. Burros (Ed.), *Mental measurements yearbook*, 8th ed., p. 1045. Highland Park, NJ: Gryphon Press.

Davis, R.M. (1996). The ledger of tobacco control: Is the cup half empty or half full? *Journal of the American Medical Association, 275*, 1281–1285.

Davis, V.E., & Walsh, M.J. (1970). Alcohol, amines and alkaloids: A possible biochemical basis for alcohol addiction. *Science, 167*, 1005–1007.

Dawes, R.M., Faust, D., & Meehl, P.E. (1989). Clinical versus actuarial judgment. *Science, 243*, 1668–1674.

Day, N.L. (1995). Epidemiology of alcohol use, abuse, and dependence. In M.T. Tsuang, M. Tohen, & G.E.P. Zahner (Eds.), *Textbook in psychiatric epidemiology*, pp. 345–360. New York: Wiley-Liss.

Deblinger, E., McLeer, S.V., Atkins, M.S., Ralphe, D., & Foa, E. (1989). Post-traumatic stress in sexually abused, physically abused, and nonabused children. *Child Abuse and Neglect, 13*, 403–408.

DeLeon, P.H., Sammons, M.T., & Sexton, J.L. (1995). Focusing on society's real needs: Responsibility and prescription privileges. *American Psychologist, 50*, 1022–1032.

Delgado, P.L., Price, L.H., Heninger, G.R., & Charney, D.S. (1992). Neurochemistry. In E.S. Paykel (Ed.), *Handbook of affective disorders*, 2nd ed. New York: Guilford.

Deltito, J.A., & Perugi, G. (1986). A case of social phobia with avoidant personality disorder treated with MAOI. *Comprehensive Psychiatry, 27*, 255–258.

D'Emilio, J., & Freedman, E.B. (1988). *Intimate matters: A history of sexuality in America*. New York: Harper & Row.

Depue, R.A., & Iacono, W.G. (1989). Neurobehavioral aspects of affective disorders. *Annual Review of Psychology, 40*, 457–492.

de Ruiter, C., & van Uzendoorn, M.H. (1992). Agoraphobia and anxious-ambivalent attachment: An integrative review. *Journal of Anxiety Disorders, 6*, 365–381.

de Silva, P. (1988). Phobias and preparedness. Replication and extension. *Behaviour Research and Therapy, 26*, 97–98.

de Silva, P. (1993). Fetishism and sexual dysfunction: Clinical presentation and management. *Sexual and Marital Therapy, 8*, 147–155.

Deutsch, A. (1949). *The mentally ill in America: A history of their care and treatment from colonial times*. New York: Columbia University Press.

Deutsch, M. (1973). *The resolution of conflict*. New Haven, CT: Yale University Press.

Devanand, D.P., & Levy, S.T. (1995). Neuroleptic treatment of gitation and psychosis in dementia.

Journal of Geriatric Psychiatry and Neurology, 8, (suppl. 1), S18–S27.

DeVane, C.L., & Sallee, F.R. (1996). Serotonin selective reuptake inhibitors in child and adolescent psychopharmacology: A review of published evidence. *Journal of Clinical Psychiatry,* 57, 55–66.

Dijkman-Caes, D.I., Kraan, H.F., & DeVries, M.W. (1993). Research on panic disorder and agoraphobia in daily life: A review of current studies. *Journal of Anxiety Disorders,* 7, 235–247.

DiLalla, L.F., & Gottesman, I.I. (1990). Heterogeneity of causes for delinquency and criminality: Lifespan perspectives. *Development and Psychopathology,* 1, 339–349.

DiNardo, P.A., Moras, K., Barlow, D.H., Rapee, R.M., & Brown, T.A. (1993). Reliability of DSM-III-R anxiety disorder categories: Using the Anxiety Disorders Interview Schedule-Revised (ADIS-R). *Archives of General Psychiatry,* 50, 251–256.

DiNardo, P.A., O'Brien, G.T., Barlow, D.H., Waddell, M.T., & Blanchard, E.B. (1988). *Anxiety Disorders Interview Schedule—Revised* (ADIS-R). Albany: State University of New York at Albany, Phobia and Anxiety Disorders Clinic.

Dishion, T.J., French, D.C., & Patterson, G.R. (1995). The development and ecology of antisocial behavior. In D. Cicchetti & D.J. Cohen (Eds.), *Developmental psychopathology,* vol. 1, pp. 421–471. New York: Wiley.

Docherty, N.M., DeRosa, M., & Andreasen, N.C. (1996). Communication disturbances in schizophrenia and mania. *Archives of General Psychiatry,* 53, 358–364.

Dodge, K.A., & Frame, C.L. (1982). Social-cognitive biases and deficits in aggressive boys. *Child Development,* 53, 620–635.

Dohrenwend, B.P., Levav, I., Shrout, P.E., Schwartz, S., Naveh, G., Link, B.G., Skodol, A.E., & Stueve, A. (1992). Socioeconomic status and psychiatric disorders: The causation-selection issue. *Science,* 255, 946–952.

Dolan, B. (1991). Cross-cultural aspects of anorexia nervosa and bulimia: A review. *International Journal of Eating Disorders,* 10, 67–78.

Dolan, B., & Coid, J. (1993). *Psychopathic and antisocial personality disorders: Treatment and research issues.* London: Gaskell/Royal College of Psychiatrists.

Donahey, K.M., & Carroll, R.A. (1993). Gender differences in factors associated with hypoactive sexual desire. *Journal of Sex and Marital Therapy,* 19, 25–40.

Donovan, D.M., & Marlatt, G.A. (1993). Behavioral treatment. In M. Galanter, H. Begleiter, D. Deitrich, et al. (Eds.), *Recent developments in alcoholism,* Vol. 11: *Ten years of progress,* pp. 397–411. New York: Plenum.

Doren, D.M. (1993). Antisocial personality disorder. In R.T. Ammerman & M. Hersen (Eds.), *Handbook of behavior therapy with children and adults: A developmental and longitudinal perspective,* pp. 263–276. Boston: Allyn & Bacon.

Douglas, V.I. (1983). Attention and cognitive problems. In M. Rutter (Ed.), *Developmental neuropsychiatry,* pp. 280–329. New York: Guilford.

Douglas, V.I., & Peters, K.G. (1979). Toward a clearer definition of the attentional deficit of hyperactive children. In G.A. Hale & M. Lewis (Eds.), *Attention and the development of cognitive skills,* pp. 173–248. New York: Plenum.

Draguns, J.G. (1980). Psychological disorders of clinical severity. In H.C. Triandis & J.G. Draguns (Eds.), *Handbook of cross-cultural psychology: Psychopathology,* vol. 6, pp. 99–174. Boston: Allyn & Bacon.

Draguns, J.G. (1994). Pathological and clinical aspects. In L.L. Adler & U.P. Gielen (Eds.), *Cross-cultural topics in psychology,* pp. 165–178. Westport, CT: Praeger.

Drake, R.E., & Vaillant, G.E. (1985). A validity study of Axis II of DSM-III. *American Journal of Psychiatry,* 142, 553–558.

Dreyfuss, R. (1996). Tobacco enemy number 1. *Mother Jones,* 21, 42–48.

Dulcan, M.K. (1986). Comprehensive treatment of children and adolescents with attention deficit disorders: The state of the art. *Clinical Psychology Review,* 6, 539–569.

Durham, M.L., & LaFond, J.Q. (1988). A search for the missing premise of involuntary therapeutic commitment: Effective treatment of the mentally ill. *Rutgers Law Review,* 40, 303–368.

Durham, R.C., & Allan, T. (1993). Psychological treatment of generalized anxiety disorder: A review of the clinical significance of results in outcome studies since 1980. *British Journal of Psychiatry,* 163, 19–26.

Durkheim, E. (1897/1951). *Suicide: A study in sociology.* New York: Free Press.

Dyk, P.H., & Adams, G.R. (1990). Identity and intimacy: An initial investigation of three theoretical models using cross-lag panel correlations. *Journal of Youth and Adolescence,* 19, 91–110.

D'Zurilla, T., & Goldfried, M. (1971). Problem solving and behavior modification. *Journal of Abnormal Psychology,* 78, 107–126.

Eagle, M., & Wolitzky, D.L. (1988). Psychodynamics. In C.G. Last & M. Hersen (Eds.), *Handbook of anxiety disorders.* New York: Pergamon.

Eaton, W.W. (1994). Social facts and the sociological imagination: The contributions of sociology to psychiatric epidemiology. *Acta Psychiatrica Scandinavica,* 90, (suppl. 385), 25–38.

Eaton, W.W., Dryman, A., & Weissman, M.M. (1991). Panic and phobia. In L.N. Robins & D.A. Regier (Eds.), *Psychiatric disorders in America: The epidemiologic Catchment Area Study,* pp. 155–179. New York: Free Press.

Eaton, W.W., Mortensen, P.B., Herrman, H., Freeman, H., et al. (1992). Long-term course of hospitalization for schizophrenia. I. Risk for rehospitalization. *Schizophrenia Bulletin,* 18, 217–228.

Eberlin, M., McConnachie, G., Igel, S., & Volpe, L. (1993). Facilitated communication: A failure to replicate the phenomenon. *Journal of Autism and Developmental Disorders,* 23, 507–530.

Edelbrock, C., & Costello, A.J. (1984). Structured psychiatric interviews for children and adolescents. In G.R. Goldstein & M. Hersen (Eds.), *Handbook of psychological assessment,* pp. 276–290. London: Pergamon.

Edmonstone, Y., Austin, M.P., Prentice, N., Dougall, N., Freeman, C.P.L., Ebmeier, K.P., & Goodwin, G.M. (1994). Uptake of 99mTc-exametazime shown by single photon emission computerized tomography in obsessive-compulsive disorder compared with major depression and normal controls. *Acta Psychiatrica Scandinavica,* 90, 298–303.

Egeland, J.D., & Sussex, J.N. (1985). Suicide and family loading for affective disorders. *Journal of the American Medical Association,* 254, 915–918.

Ehrenfest, H. (1926). Birth injuries of the child. *Gynecological and Obstetrical Monographs.* New York: Appleton.

Ehrman, R., Ternes, J., O'Brien, C.P., & McLellan, A.T. (1992). Conditioned tolerance in human opiate addicts. *Psychopharmacology,* 108, 218–224.

Eisenberg, L. (1995). The social construction of the human brain. *American Journal of Psychiatry,* 152, 1563–1575.

Eklund, P.L.E., Gooren, L.J.G., & Bezemer, P.D. (1988). Prevalence of transsexualism in the Netherlands. *British Journal of Psychiatry,* 152, 638–640.

Ekman, G., Miranda-Linne, F., Gillberg, C., Garle, M., & Wetterberg, L. (1989). *Journal of Autism and Developmental Disorders,* 19, 511–531.

Elkin, I., Gibbons, R.D., Shea, M.T., Sotsky, S.M., Watkins, J.T., Pilkonis, P.A., & Hedeker, D. (1996). Initial severity and differential treatment outcome in the NIMH Treatment of Depression Collaborative Research Program. *Journal of Consulting and Clinical Psychology,* 64.

Elkin, I., Shea, T., Watkins, J.T., Imber, S.D., Sotsky, S.M., Collins, J.F., Glass, D.R., Pikonis, P.A., Leber, W.R., Docherty, J.P., Fiester, S.J., & Parloff, M.B.

(1989). National Institute of Mental Health treatment of depression collaborative research program: General effectiveness of treatments. *Archives of General Psychiatry,* 46, 971–982.

Elliott, G. (1989). Stress and illness. In S. Cheren (Ed.), *Psychosomatic medicine: Theory, physiology, and practice,* Vol. 1, pp. 45–90. Madison, CT: International Universities Press.

Ellis, A. (1962). *Reason and emotion in psychotherapy.* New York: Lyle Stuart.

Ellis, A. (1970). *Reason and emotion in psychotherapy.* New York: Lyle Stuart.

Emery, R.E. (1982). Interparental conflict and the children of discord and divorce. *Psychological Bulletin,* 92, 310–330.

Emery, R.E. (1988). *Marriage, divorce, and children's adjustment.* Newbury Park, CA: Sage.

Emery, R.E. (1989). Family violence. *American Psychologist,* 44, 321–328.

Emery, R.E. (1994). *Renegotiating family relationships: Divorce, child custody, and mediation.* New York: Guilford.

Emery, R.E. (1997). *Marriage, divorce, and children's adjustment* (2nd ed.). Thousand Oaks, CA: Sage.

Emery, R.E., Fincham, F.D., & Cummings, E.M. (1992). Parenting in context: Systemic thinking about parental conflict and its influence on children. *Journal of Consulting and Clinical Psychology,* 60, 909–912.

Emery, R.E., & Marholin, D. (1977). An applied behavior analysis of delinquency: The irrelevancy of relevant behavior. *American Psychologist,* 32, 860–873.

Emery, R.E., & Rogers, K.C. (1990). The role of behavior therapists in child custody cases. In M. Hersen & R.M. Eisler (Eds.), *Progress in behavior modification,* pp. 60–89. Beverly Hills: Sage.

Emery, R.E., & Wyer, M.M. (1987). Divorce mediation. *American Psychologist,* 42, 472–480.

Emmelkamp, P.M.G., & Beens, H. (1991). Cognitive therapy with obsessive-compulsive disorder: A comparative evaluation. *Behaviour Research and Therapy,* 29, 293–300.

Engel, G.L. (1977). The need for a new medical model: A challenge for biomedicine. *Science,* 196, 129–136.

Epstein, S. (1979). The stability of behavior. I. On predicting most of the people much of the time. *Journal of Personality and Social Psychology,* 37, 1097–1126.

Epstein, S. (1980). The stability of behavior. II. Implications for psychological research. *American Psychologist,* 35, 790–806.

Erdelyi, M.H. (1990). Repression, reconstruction, and defense: History and

integration of the psychoanalytic and experimental frameworks. In J.L. Singer (Ed.), *Repression and dissociation,* pp. 1–32. Chicago: University of Chicago Press.

Erikson, E.H. (1959, 1980). *Identity and the life cycle.* New York: Norton.

Erikson, E.H. (1968). *Identity: Youth and crisis.* New York: Norton.

Erlenmeyer-Kimling, L., Squires-Wheeler, E., Adamo, U.H., Bassett, A.S., Cornblatt, B.A., Kestenbaum, C.J., Rock, D., Roberts, S.A., & Gottesman, I.I. (1995). The New York high-risk project: Psychoses and cluster A personality disorders in offspring of schizophrenic parents at 23 years of follow-up. *Archives of General Psychiatry,* 52, 857–865.

Ernst, C., Foldenyi, M., & Angst, J. (1993). The Zurich study. XXI. Sexual dysfunctions and disturbances in young adults. *European Archives of Psychiatry and Clinical Neuroscience,* 243, 179–188.

Eron, L.D. (1982). Parent-child interaction, television violence, and aggression in children. *American Psychologist,* 37, 197–211.

Exner, J.E. (1986). *The Rorschach: A comprehensive system,* vol. 1, 2nd ed. New York: Wiley.

Eysenck, H.J. (1952/1992). The effects of psychotherapy: An evaluation. *Journal of Consulting Psychology,* 16, 319–324.

Eysenck, H.J. (1979). The conditioning model of neurosis. *Behavioral and Brain Sciences,* 2, 155–199.

Fabrega, H. (1991). The culture and history of psychiatric stigma in early modern and modern Western societies: A review of recent literature. *Comprehensive Psychiatry,* 32, 97–119.

Faigman, D.L. (1986). The battered woman syndrome and self-defense: A legal and empirical dissent. *Virginia Law Review,* 72, 619–647.

Fairburn, C.G. (1995). Short-term psychological treatments for bulimia nervosa. In K.D. Brownell & C.G. Fairburn (Eds.), *Eating disorders and obesity: A comprehensive handbook,* pp. 344–348. New York: Guilford.

Fairburn, C.G. (1996). *Overcoming binge eating.* New York: Guilford.

Fairburn, C.G., & Beglin, S.J. (1990). Studies of the epidemiology of bulimia nervosa. *American Journal of Psychiatry,* 147, 401–480.

Fairburn, C.G., Hay, P.J., & Welch, S.L. (1993). Binge eating and bulimia nervosa: Distribution and determinants. In C.G. Fairburn & G.T. Wilson (Eds.), *Binge eating: Nature, assessment, and treatment,* pp. 123–143. New York: Guilford.

Fairburn, C.G., Jones, R., Peveler, R.C., Carr, S.J., Solomon, R.A., O'Connor, M.E., Burton, J., & Hope, R.A. (1991). Three psychological treatments for bulimia nervosa. *Archives of General Psychiatry,* 48, 463–469.

Fairburn, C.G., Jones, R., Peveler, R.C., Hope, R.A., & O'Connor, M. (1993). Psychotherapy and bulimia nervosa: Longer-term effects of interpersonal psychotherapy, behavior therapy, and cognitive behavior therapy. *Archives of General Psychiatry,* 50, 419–428.

Fairburn, C.G., & Wilson, G.T. (Eds.) (1993). *Binge eating: Nature, assessment, and treatment.* New York: Guilford.

Falloon, I., Boyd, J.L., & McGill, C.W. (1985). *Family care of schizophrenia.* New York: Guilford.

Fallon, P., Katzman, M.A., & Wooley, S.C. (1994). *Feminist perspectives on eating disorders.* New York: Guilford.

Farde, L., & Nordstrom, A.L. (1992). PET analysis indicates atypical central dopamine receptor occupancy in clozapine-treated patients. *British Journal of Psychiatry,* 160 (suppl. 17), 30–33.

Farde, L., Nordstrom, A., Karlsson, P., Halldin, C., & Sedvall, G. (1995). Positron emission tomography studies on dopamine receptors in schizophrenia. *Clinical Neuropharmacology,* 18 (suppl. 1), S121–S129.

Faris, R.E.L., & Dunham, H.W. (1939). *Mental disorders in urban areas: An ecological study of schizophrenia and other psychoses.* Chicago: University of Chicago Press.

Farmer, A.E., & Blewett, A. (1993). Drug treatment of resistant schizophrenia: Limitations and recommendations. *Drugs,* 45, 374–383.

Farmer, A.E., & Griffiths, H. (1992). Labeling and illness in primary care: Comparing factors influencing general practitioners' and psychiatrists' decisions regarding patient referral to mental illness services. *Psychological Medicine,* 22, 717–723.

Farmer, A.E., McGuffin, P., & Gottesman, I.I. (1984). Searching for the split in schizophrenia: A twin study perspective. *Psychiatry Research,* 13, 109–118.

Farmer, A.E., McGuffin, P., & Gottesman, I.I. (1987). Twin concordance for DSM-III schizophrenia: Scrutinizing the validity of the definition. *Archives of General Psychiatry,* 44, 634–641.

Farrington, D., Ohlin, L., & Wilson, J.Q. (1986). *Understanding and controlling crime.* New York: Springer.

Faust, D., & Ziskin, J. (1988). The expert witness in psychology and psychiatry. *Science,* 241, 31–35.

Fawcett, J., Clark, D.C., & Busch, K.A. (1993). Assessing and treating the patient at risk for suicide. *Psychiatric Annals,* 23, 244–255.

Fawzy, F.I., Fawzy, N.W., Hyun, C.S., Gutherie, D., Fahey, J.L., & Morton, D. (1993). Malignant melanoma. Effects of an early structured psychiatric intervention, coping, and affective state on recurrence and survival six years later. *Archives of General Psychiatry,* 50, 681–689.

Federal Bureau of Investigation. (1992). *Crime in the United States,* 1992. Washington, DC: U.S. Department of Justice.

Ferreira, L., & Soares da Silva, P. (1991). 5-hydroxy-tryptamine and alcoholism. *Human Psychopharmacology: Clinical and Experimental,* 6 (suppl.), 21–24.

Fichter, M.M., Meller, I., Schroppel, H., & Steinkirchner, R. (1995). Dementia and cognitive impairment in the oldest old in the community: Prevalence and comorbidity. *British Journal of Psychiatry,* 166, 621–629.

Figley, C.R. (1978). *Stress disorders among Vietnam veterans.* New York: Brunner/Mazel.

Fillmore, K.M. (1987). Women's drinking across the adult life course as compared to men's. *British Journal of Addiction,* 82, 801–811.

Fincham, F.D., & Bradbury, T.N. (1987). The impact of attributions in marriage: A longitudinal analysis. *Journal of Personality and Social Psychology,* 53, 510–517.

Fincham, F.D., & Bradbury, T.N. (1990). *The psychology of marriage: Basic issues and applications.* New York: Guilford.

Fingarette, H. (1988). *Heavy drinking: The myth of alcoholism as a disease.* Berkeley: University of California Press.

Fink, M. (1992). Electroconvulsive therapy. In E.S. Paykel (Ed.), *Handbook of affective disorders,* 2nd ed., pp. 359–367. New York: Guilford.

Fink, M. (1993). Who should get ECT? In C.E. Coffey (Ed.), *The clinical science of electroconvulsive therapy,* pp. 3–15. Washington, DC: American Psychiatric Press.

Fink, P.J., & Tasman, A. (Eds.) (1992). *Stigma and mental illness.* Washington, DC: American Psychiatric Press.

Finkelhor, D. (1992). New myths about the child welfare system. *Child, Youth, and Family Services Quarterly,* 15, 3–5.

Finkelhor, D., Hotaling, G., Lewis, I.A., & Smith, C. (1990). Sexual abuse in a national sample of adult men and women: Prevalence, characteristics, and risk factors. *Child Abuse and Neglect,* 14, 19–28.

Finlay-Jones, R., & Brown, G.W. (1981). Types of stressful life events and the onset of anxiety and depressive disorders. *Psychological Medicine,* 11, 803–815.

Finney, J.W., & Moos, R.H. (1991). The long-term course of treated alcoholism. I. Mortality, relapse and remission rates and comparisons with community controls. *Journal of Studies on Alcohol,* 52, 44–54.

Finney, J.W., & Moos, R.H. (1992). The long-term course of treated alcoholism. II. Predictors and correlates of 10-year functioning and mortality. *Journal of Studies on Alcohol,* 53, 142–153.

Fischer, P.J., & Breakey, W.R. (1991). The epidemiology of alcohol, drug, and mental disorders among homeless persons. *American Psychologist,* 46, 1115–1128.

Fitch, S.A., & Adams, G.R. (1983). Ego-identity and intimacy status: Replication and extension. *Developmental Psychology,* 19, 839–845.

Fitch, W.L., Petrella, R.C., & Wallace, J. (1987). Legal ethics and the use of mental health experts in criminal cases. *Behavioral Sciences and the Law,* 5, 105–117.

Flanagan, J.C. (1982). *New insights to improve the quality of life at age 70.* Palo Alto, CA: American Institutes for Research.

Fleming, J.E., & Offord, D.R. (1990). Epidemiology of childhood depressive disorders: A critical review. *Journal of American Academy of Child and Adolescent Psychiatry,* 29, 571–580.

Flint, A.J. (1994). Epidemiology and comorbidity of anxiety disorders in the elderly. *American Journal of Psychiatry,* 151, 640–649.

Flor-Henry, P. (1987). Cerebral aspects of sexual deviation. In G.D. Wilson (Ed.), *Variant sexuality: Research and theory,* pp. 49–83. Baltimore: Johns Hopkins University Press.

Foa, E.B., Rothbaum, B.O., Riggs, D.S., & Murdock, T.B. (1991). Treatment of posttraumatic stress disorder in rape victims: A comparison between cognitive-behavioral procedures and counseling. *Journal of Consulting and Clinical Psychology,* 59, 715–723.

Foa, E.B., & Steketee, G. (1989). Obsessive-compulsive disorder. In C. Lindemann (Ed.), *Handbook of phobia therapy: Rapid symptom relief in anxiety disorders,* pp. 183–206. Northvale, NH: Jason Aronson.

Foa, E.B., Steketee, G., & Rothbaum, B.O. (1989). Behavioral/cognitive conceptualizations of posttraumatic stress disorder. *Behavior Therapy,* 20, 155–176.

Folstein, M.F., & Folstein, S.E. (1977). Clinical, pathological, and genetic heterogeneity of Alzheimer's disease. In L. Heston (Ed.), *Progress in Alzheimer's disease and similar conditions.* Washington, DC: American Psychiatric Press.

Ford, C., & Beach, F. (1951). *Patterns of sexual behavior.* New York: Harper & Row.

Ford, D.H., & Lerner, R.M. (1992). *Developmental systems theory: An integrative approach.* Newbury Park, CA: Sage.

Fordyce, W.E. (1976). *Behavioral methods for chronic pain and illness.* St. Louis: Mosby.

Forehand, R., & McMahon, R.J. (1981). *Helping the noncompliant child: A clinician's guide to parent training.* New York: Guilford.

Forehand, R., Wells, K., & Griest, D. (1980). An examination of the social validity of a parent training program. *Behavior Therapy,* 11, 488–502.

Foster, S.L., & Cone, J.D. (1986). Design and use of direct observation procedures. In A.R. Ciminero, K.S. Calhoun, & H.E. Adams (Eds.), *Handbook of behavioral assessment,* 2nd ed. New York: Wiley.

Foster, S.L., & Cone, J.D. (1995). Validity issues in clinical assessment. *Psychological Assessment,* 7, 248–260.

Fowles, D.C. (1992). Schizophrenia: Diathesis-stress revisited. *Annual Review of Psychology,* 43, 303–336.

Fox, K., Merrill, J.C., Chang, H.H., & Califano, J.A., Jr. (1995). Estimating the costs of substance abuse to the Medicaid hospital care program. *American Journal of Public Health,* 85, 48–54.

Foy, D.W., Resnick, H.S., Sipprelle, R.C., & Carroll, E.M. (1987). Premilitary, military, and post-military factors in the development of combat-related posttraumatic stress disorder. *Behavior Therapist,* 10, 3–9.

Frances, A. (1980). The DSM-III personality disorders section: A commentary. *American Journal of Psychiatry,* 137, 1050–1054.

Frances, A., First, M.B., & Pincus, H.A. (1995). *DSM-IV guidebook.* Washington, DC: American Psychiatric Press.

Frances, A.J., Widiger, T.A., & Pincus, H.A. (1989). The development of DSM-IV. *Archives of General Psychiatry,* 46, 373–375.

Francis, J. (1995). A half-century of delirium research: Time to close the gap. *Journal of the American Geriatrics Society,* 43, 585–586.

Frank, E., Anderson, C., & Rubenstein, D. (1978). Frequency of sexual dysfunction in normal couples. *New England Journal of Medicine,* 299, 111–115.

Frank, E., Turner, S.M., Stewart, B.D., Jacob, M., & West, D. (1981). Past psychiatric symptoms and the response to sexual assault. *Comprehensive Psychiatry,* 22, 479–487.

Frank, J.D. (1961). *Persuasion and healing.* Baltimore: Johns Hopkins University Press.

Frank, J.D. (1973). *Persuasion and healing,* 2nd ed. Baltimore: Johns Hopkins University Press.

Frankel, F.H. (1990). Hypnotizability and dissociation. *American Journal of Psychiatry,* 147, 823–829.

Frankish, C.J. (1994). Crisis centers and their role in treatment: Suicide prevention versus health promotion. In A.A. Leenaars, J.T. Maltsberger, & R.A. Neimeyer (Eds.), *Treatment of suicidal people,* pp. 33–44. Washington, DC: Taylor & Francis.

Franklin, J.A., & Andrews, G. (1989). Stress and the onset of agoraphobia. *Australian Psychologist, 24,* 203–219.

Frasure-Smith, N., & Prince, R. (1985). Long-term follow-up of the ischemic heart disease life stress monitoring program. *Psychosomatic Medicine, 51,* 485–513.

Freeman, H. (1994). Schizophrenia and city residence. *British Journal of Psychiatry, 164* (suppl. 23), 39–50.

Freeman, P.S., & Gunderson, J.G. (1989). Treatment of personality disorders. *Psychiatric Annals, 19,* 147–153.

Freud, S. (1894/1957). On the grounds for detaching a particular syndrome from neurasthenia under the description "anxiety neurosis." In J. Strachey (Ed.), *Standard edition of the complete psychological works of Sigmund Freud,* vol. 1. London: Hogarth Press.

Freud, S. (1917/1955). A difficulty in the path of psychoanalysis. J. Strachey (Ed. & Trans.), *The standard edition of the complete psychological works of Sigmund Freud,* vol. 17. London: Hogarth Press.

Freud, S. (1917/1961). Mourning and melancholia. In J. Strachey (Ed. and Trans.), *The standard edition of the complete psychological works of Sigmund Freud,* vol. 14. London: Hogarth Press.

Freud, S. (1924/1962). The aetiology of hysteria. In J. Strachey (Ed. and Trans.), *The standard edition of the complete psychological works of Sigmund Freud,* vol. 3, pp. 191–221. London: Hogarth Press.

Freud, S. (1926/1959). Inhibitions, symptoms, and anxiety. In J. Strachey (Ed.), *Standard edition of the complete psychological works of Sigmund Freud,* vol. 20. London: Hogarth Press.

Freud, S. (1930/1961). Civilization and its discontents. In J. Strachey (Ed. and Trans.), *The standard edition of the complete psychological works of Sigmund Freud,* vol. 21. London: Hogarth Press.

Freud, S. (1940/1969). *An outline of psycho-analysis.* New York: Norton.

Freund, K., & Blanchard, R. (1986). The concept of courtship disorder. *Journal of Sex and Marital Therapy, 12,* 79–92.

Freund, K., & Blanchard, R. (1993). Erotic target location errors in male gender dysphorics, paedophiles, and fetishists. *British Journal of Psychiatry, 162,* 558–563.

Friedland, R.P. (1993). Epidemiology, education, and the ecology of Alzheimer's disease. *Neurology, 43,* 246–248.

Friedman, M., & Rosenman, R.H. (1959). Association of specific overt behavior pattern with blood and cardiovascular findings: Blood cholesterol level, blood clotting time, incidence of arcus senilis and clinical coronary artery disease.

Journal of the American Medical Association, 169, 1286–1296.

Fries, J.F. (1990). Medical perspectives upon successful aging. In P.B. Baltes & M.M. Baltes (Eds.), *Successful aging: Perspectives from the behavioral sciences* (pp. 35–49). Cambridge, MA: Cambridge University Press.

Frueh, B.C., Turner, S.M., & Beidel, D.C. (1995). Exposure therapy for combat-related PTSD: A critical review. *Clinical Psychology Review, 15,* 799–817.

Fuller, R.K., & Roth, H.P. (1979). Disulfiram for the treatment of alcoholism: An evaluation of 128 men. *Annals of Internal Medicine, 90,* 901–904.

Funder, D.C., & Colvin, C.R. (1991). Explorations in behavioral consistency: Properties of persons, situations, and behaviors. *Journal of Personality and Social Psychology, 60,* 773–794.

Funtowicz, M.N., & Widiger, T.A. (1995). Sex bias in the diagnosis of personality disorders: A different approach. *Journal of Psychopathology and Behavioral Assessment, 17,* 145–165.

Furby, L., Weinrott, M.R., & Blackshaw, L. (1989). Sex offenders recidivism: A review. *Psychological Bulletin, 105,* 3–30.

Fyer, A.J., Mannuzza, S., Chapman, T.F., Liebowitz, M.R., & Klein, D.F. (1993). A direct interview family study of social phobia. *Archives of General Psychiatry, 50,* 286–293.

Gagnon, J.H., & Simon, W. (1973). *Sexual conduct: The social sources of human sexuality.* Chicago: Aldine.

Garber, H.I. (1988). *The Milwaukee project: Preventing mental retardation in children at risk.* Washington, DC: American Association on Mental Retardation.

Garfield, S.L. (1989). *The practice of brief psychotherapy.* New York: Pergamon.

Garfield, S., & Kurtz, R. (1974). A survey of clinical psychologists: Characteristics, activities, and orientations. *Clinical Psychologist, 28,* 7–10.

Garfinkel, P.E., & Garner, D.M. (1982). *Anorexia nervosa: A multidimensional perspective.* New York: Basic Books.

Garfinkel, P.E., Kennedy, S.H., & Kaplan, A.S. (1995). Views on classification and diagnosis of eating disorders. *Canadian Journal of Psychiatry, 40,* 445–456.

Garfinkel, P.E., Lin, B., & Goering, P. (in press). Purging and nonpurging forms of bulimia nervosa in a community sample. *International Journal of Eating Disorders.*

Garland, A.F., & Zigler, E. (1993). Adolescent suicide prevention: Current research and social policy implications. *American Psychologist, 48,* 169–182.

Garmezy, N. (1978). DSM-III: Never mind the psychologists; Is it good for the children? *Clinical Psychologist, 31,* 1–6.

Garner, D.M., & Bemis, K.M. (1982). A cognitive-behavioral approach to anorexia nervosa. *Cognitive Therapy and Research, 6,* 123–150.

Garner, D.M., Garner, M.V., & Rosen, L.W. (1993). Anorexia nervosa "restrictors" who purge: Implications for subtyping anorexia nervosa. *International Journal of Eating Disorders, 13,* 171–185.

Garner, D.M., & Needleman, L.D. (1996). Stepped-care and decision-tree models for treating eating disorders. In J.K. Thompson, *Body image, eating disorders, and obesity,* pp. 225–252. Washington, DC: American Psychological Association.

Garner, D.M., Olmstead, M.P., & Polivy, J. (1983). The Eating Disorder Inventory: A measure of cognitive-behavioral dimensions of anorexia nervosa and bulimia. In P.L. Darby, P.E. Garfinkel, D.M. Garner, & D.V. Coscina (Eds.), *Anorexia nervosa: Recent developments in research,* pp. 173–184. New York: Liss.

Garza-Trevino, E. (1994). Neurobiological factors in aggressive behavior. *Hospital and Community Psychiatry, 45,* 690–699.

Gaylord, S.A., & Zung, W.W.K. (1987). Affective disorders among the aging. In L.L. Carstensen & B.A. Edelstein (Eds.), *Handbook of clinical gerontology.* New York: Plenum.

Geller, B., et al. (1992). Pharmacokinetically designed double-blind placebo-controlled study of nortriptyline in 6- to 12-year-olds with major depressive disorder. *Journal of the American Academy of Child and Adolescent Psychiatry, 31,* 34–44.

Geller, E., Ritvo, E.R., Freeman, B.J., & Yuwiler, A. (1982). Preliminary observations on the effect of fenfluramine on blood serotonin and symptoms in three autistic boys. *New England Journal of Medicine, 307,* 165–169.

Gerner, R.H., & Stanton, A. (1992). Algorithm for patient management of acute manic states: Lithium, valproate, or carbamazepine? *Journal of Clinical Psychopharmacology, 12* (suppl. 1). 57S–63S.

Gerstley, L., McLellan, T., Alterman, A.I., Woody, G.E., Luborsky, L., & Prout, M. (1989). Ability to form an alliance with the therapist: A possible marker of prognosis for patients with antisocial personality disorder. *American Journal of Psychiatry, 146,* 508–512.

Geske, M.R. (1989). Statutes limiting mental health professionals' liability for the violent acts of their patients. *Indiana Law Journal, 64,* 391–422.

Giacobini, E. (1994). Therapy for Alzheimer's disease: Symptomatic or neuroprotective? *Molecular Neurobiology, 9,* 115–118.

Gianoulakis, C. (1993). Endogenous opioids and excessive alcohol-consumption. *Journal of Psychiatry and Neuroscience, 18,* 148–156.

Gibbs, N.A., & Oltmanns, T.F. (1995). The relation between obsessive-compulsive personality traits and subtypes of compulsive behavior. *Journal of Anxiety Disorders*, 9, 397–410.

Gillberg, C. (1991). Outcome in autism and autistic-like conditions. *Journal of the American Academy of Child and Adolescent Psychiatry*, 30, 375–382.

Gillberg, C., Rastam, M., & Gillberg, C. (1995). Anorexia nervosa 6 years after onset. I. Personality disorders. *Comprehensive Psychiatry*, 36, 61–69.

Gillberg, C., & Schaumann, H. (1982). Social class and infantile autism. *Journal of Autism and Developmental Disorders*, 12, 223–228.

Gilbert, D.G., Hagen, R.L., & D'Agostino, J.A. (1986). The effects of cigarette smoking on human sexual potency. *Addictive Behaviors*, 11, 431–434.

Gitlin, M.J. (1993). Pharmacotherapy of personality disorders: Conceptual framework and clinical strategies. *Journal of Clinical Psychopharmacology*, 13, 343–353.

Gittelman-Klein, R. (1988). Questioning the clinical usefulness of projective psychological tests for children. *Developmental and Behavioral Pediatrics*, 7, 378–382.

Glaser, R., Rice, J., Sheridan, J., Fertel, R., Stout, J., Speicher, C.E., Pinsky, D., Kotur, M., Post, A., Beck, M., & Kiecolt-Glaser, J.K. (1987). Stress-related immune suppression: Health implications. *Brain, Behavior, and Immunity*, 1, 7–20.

Gleaves, D.H. (1996). The sociocognitive model of dissociative identity disorder: A reexamination of the evidence. *Psychological Bulletin*, 120, 42–59.

Gleick, J. (1987). *Chaos: Making of a new science.* New York: Viking.

Goldberg, E.M. (1970). *Helping the aged: A field experiment in social work.* London: Allen & Unwin.

Goldberg, J., True, W.R., Eisen, S.A., & Henderson, W.G. (1990). A twin study of the effects of the Vietnam War on posttraumatic stress disorder. *Journal of the American Medical Association*, 263, 2725–2729.

Goldberg, L.R. (1990). An alternative "description of personality": The big five factor structure. *Journal of Personality and Social Psychology*, 59, 1216–1229.

Goldberg, L.R. (1993). The structure of phenotypic personality traits. *American Psychologist*, 48, 26–34.

Goldberg, S. (1991). Recent developments in attachment theory and research. *Canadian Journal of Psychiatry*, 36, 393–400.

Goldberg, S.C., Schulz, S.C., Schulz, P.M., et al. (1986). Borderline and schizotypal personality disorders treated with low-dose thiothixene vs placebo. *Archives of General Psychiatry*, 43, 680–686.

Goldblatt, M.J. (1994). Hospitalization of the suicidal patient. In A.A. Leenaars, J.T. Maltsberger, &
R.A. Neimeyer (Eds.), *Treatment of suicidal people*, pp. 153–165. Washington, DC: Taylor & Francis.

Goldfried, M.R., & Castonguay, L.G. (1993). Behavior therapy: Redefining strengths and limitations. *Behavior Therapy*, 24, 505–526.

Goldman, H.H., Adams, N.H., & Taube, C.A. (1983). Deinstitutionalization: The data demythologized. *Hospital and Community Psychiatry*, 34, 129–134.

Goldman, H.H., Skodol, A.E., & Lave, T.R. (1992). Revising Axis V for DSM-IV: A review of measures of social functioning. *American Journal of Psychiatry*, 149, 1148–1156.

Goldman, M.S. (1994). The alcohol expectancy concept: Applications to assessment, prevention, and treatment of alcohol abuse. *Applied and Preventive Psychology*, 3, 131–144.

Goldman, M.S., Brown, S.A., & Christiansen, B.A. (1987). Expectancy theory: Thinking about drinking. In H.T. Blane & K.E. Leonard (Eds.), *Psychological theories of drinking and alcoholism*, pp. 181–226. New York: Guilford.

Goldman, M.S., Brown, S.A., Christiansen, B.A., & Smith, G.T. (1991). Alcoholism and memory: Broadening the scope of alcohol-expectancy research. *Psychological Bulletin*, 110, 137–146.

Goldman-Rakic, P. (1996). Dissolution of cerebral cortical mechanisms in subjects with schizophrenia. In S.J. Watson (Ed.), *Biology of schizophrenia and affective disease*, pp. 113–127. Washington, DC: American Psychiatric Press.

Goldsmith, H. (1988). Roundtable: What is temperament? Four approaches. *Child Development*, 58, 505–529.

Goldsmith, H.H., Buss, A.H., Plomin, R., Rothbart, M., Klevjord, T., Thomas, A., Chess, S., Hinde, R.A., & McCall, R.B. (1987). Roundtable: What is temperament? Four approaches. *Child Development*, 58, 505–552.

Goldstein, A.J., & Chambless, D.L. (1978). A reanalysis of agoraphobia. *Behavior Therapy*, 9, 47–59.

Goldstein, J.M. (1995a). The impact of gender on understanding the epidemiology of schizophrenia. In M.V. Seeman (Ed.), *Gender and psychopathology*, pp. 159–199. Washington, DC: American Psychiatric Press.

Goldstein, J.M. (1995b). Gender and the familial transmission of schizophrenia. In M.V. Seeman (Ed.), *Gender and psychopathology*, pp. 201–226. Washington, DC: American Psychiatric Press.

Goldstein, M.J. (1994). Psychoeducational and family therapy in relapse prevention. *Acta Psychiatrica Scandinavica*, 89 (suppl. 382), 54–57.

Goldstein, M.J., & Kant, H.S. (1973). *Pornography and sexual deviance.* Berkeley: University of California Press.
Goldstein, M.J., & Miklowitz, D.J. (1994). Family intervention for persons with bipolar disorder. In A. Hatfield (Ed.), *Family interventions in mental illness.* San Francisco: Jossey-Bass.

Golomb, J., de Leon, M.J., Kluger, A., George, A.E., Tarshish, C., & Ferris, S.H. (1993). Hippocampal atrophy in normal aging: An association with recent memory impairment. *Archives of Neurology*, 50, 967–973.

Golub, E.S. (1994). *The limits of medicine: How science shapes our hope for the cure.* New York: Random House.

Golwyn, D.H., & Sevlie, C.P. (1992). Paraphilias, nonparaphilic sexual addictions, and social phobia. *Journal of Clinical Psychiatry*, 53, 330.

Gomberg, E.S.L. (1987). Drug and alcohol problems of elderly persons. In T.D. Nirenberg & S.A. Maisto (Eds.), *Developments in the assessment and treatment of addictive behaviors.* Norwood, NJ: Ablex.

Gomberg, E.S.L. (1988). Alcoholic women in treatment: The question of stigma and age. *Alcohol and Alcoholism*, 23, 507–514.

Gomberg, E.S.L. (1993). Women and alcohol: Use and abuse. *Journal of Nervous and Mental Disease*, 181, 211–219.

Good, B., & Kleinman, A. (1985a). Culture and anxiety: Cross-cultural evidence for the patterning of anxiety disorders. In A.H. Tuma & J. Maser (Eds.), *Anxiety and the anxiety disorders.* Hillsdale, NJ: Erlbaum.

Good, B., & Kleinman, A. (1985b). Culture and depression. In A. Kleinman & B. Good (Eds.), *Culture and depression: Studies in the anthropology and cross-cultural psychiatry of affect and disorder*, pp. 491–506. Berkeley: University of California Press.

Goodman, L.A., Koss, M.P., Fitzgerald, L.F., Russo, N.F., & Keita, G.P. (1993). Male violence against women: Current research and future directions. *American Psychologist*, 48, 1054–1058.

Goodman, L.A., Koss, M.P., & Russo, N.F. (1993a). Violence against women: Physical and mental health effects. Part I. Research findings. *Applied and Preventive Psychology*, 2, 79–89.

Goodman, L.A., Koss, M.P., & Russo, N.F. (1993b). Violence against women: Mental health effects. Part II. Conceptualizations of posttraumatic stress. *Applied and Preventive Psychology*, 2, 123–130.

Goodman, R., & Stevenson, J. (1989). A twin study of hyperactivity. II. The aetiological role of genes, family relationships, and perinatal adversity. *Journal of Child Clinical Psychology and Psychiatry*, 30, 691–709.

Goodman, T.A. (1985). From Tarasoff to Hopper: The evolution of the therapist's duty to protect third parties. *Behavioral Sciences and the Law*, 3, 195–225.

Goodwin, D.W. (1984a). Speculations on the cause(s) of alcoholism. *Journal of Clinical Psychiatry, 45,* 491–493.

Goodwin, D.W. (1984b). Studies of familial alcoholism: A review. *Journal of Clinical Psychiatry, 45,* 14–17.

Goodwin, D.W. (1988). *Alcohol and the writer.* New York: Penguin.

Goodwin, D.W., Knop, J., Jensen, P., Gabrielli, W.F., Schulsinger, F., & Penick, E.C. (1994). Thirty-year follow-up of men at high risk for alcoholism. *Annals of the New York Academy of Sciences, 708,* 97–101.

Goodwin, F.K., & Jamison, K.R. (1990). *Manic-depressive illness.* New York: Oxford University Press.

Gorenstein, E.E. (1992). *The science of mental illness.* San Diego: Academic Press.

Gorton, G., & Akhtar, S. (1990). The literature on personality disorders, 1985–88: Trends, issues, and controversies. *Hospital and Community Psychiatry, 41,* 39–51.

Gosselin, C.C., & Wilson, G.D. (1980). *Sexual variations.* London: Faber & Faber.

Gotlib, I.H., & Colby, C.A. (1987). *Treatment of depression: An interpersonal systems approach.* New York: Pergamon.

Gotlib, I.H., & Hammen, C. (1992). *Psychological aspects of depression: Toward a cognitive-interpersonal integration.* New York: Wiley.

Gotlib, I.H., & McCabe, S.B. (1990). Marriage and psychopathology. In F.D. Fincham & T.N. Bradbury (Eds.), *The psychology of marriage: Basic issues and applications,* pp. 226–257. New York: Guilford.

Gotlib, I.H., & Meltzer, S.J. (1987). Depression and the perception of social skill in dyadic interaction. *Cognitive Therapy and Research, 11,* 41–53.

Gotlib, I.H., & Robinson, L.A. (1982). Responses to depressed individuals: Discrepancies between self-report and observer-rated behavior. *Journal of Abnormal Psychology, 91,* 231–240.

Gotteseman, I.G. (1963). Genetic aspects of intelligent behavior. In N. Ellis (Ed.), *The handbook of mental deficiency: Psychological theory and research,* pp. 253–296. New York: McGraw-Hill.

Gottesman, I.I. (1987). The psychotic hinterlands or, the fringes of lunacy. *British Medical Bulletin, 43,* 1–13.

Gottesman, I.I. (1991). *Schizophrenia genesis: The origins of madness.* New York: Freeman.

Gottesman, I.I., & Goldsmith, H.H. (1994). Developmental psychopathology of antisocial behavior: Inserting genes into its ontogenesis and epigenesis. In C.A. Nelson (Ed.), *Threats to optimal development: Integrating biological,* *psychological, and social risk factors,* pp. 69–104. Hillsdale, NJ: Erlbaum.

Gottesman, I.I., McGuffin, P., & Farmer, A. (1987). Clinical genetics as clues to the "real" genetics of schizophrenia. *Schizophrenia Bulletin, 13,* 23–47.

Gottesman, I.I., & Moldin, S.O. (1997). Genes, experience, and chance in schizophrenia: Positioning for the 21st century. *Schizophrenia Bulletin, 23.*

Gottfries, C.G. (1991). Classifying organic mental disorders and dementia—A review of historical perspectives. *International Psychogeriatrics, 3* (suppl.), 9–17.

Gottman, J.M. (1985). Observational measures of behavior therapy outcome: A reply to Jacobsen. *Behavioral Assessment, 7,* 317–321.

Gottman, J.M. (1994). *Why marriages succeed or fail.* New York: Simon & Schuster.

Gottman, J.M., & Katz, L.F. (1989). Effects of marital discord on young children's peer interaction and health. *Developmental Psychology, 25,* 373–381.

Gottman, J.M., & Levenson, R.W. (1992). Marital processes predictive of later dissolution: Behavior, physiology, and health. *Journal of Personality and Social Psychology, 63,* 221–233.

Gottman, J., Notarius, C., Gonso, J., & Markman, H. (1976). *A couple's guide to communication.* Champaign, IL: Research Press.

Goudie, A.J. (1990). Conditioned opponent processes in the development of tolerance to psychoactive drugs. *Progress in Neuro-Psychopharmacology and Biological Psychiatry, 14,* 675–688.

Gould, M.S. (1990). Suicide clusters and media exposure. In S.J. Blumenthal, and D.J. Kupfer (Eds.), *Suicide over the life cycle: Risk factors, assessment, and treatment of suicidal patients.* Washington, DC: American Psychiatric Press. pp. 517–532.

Gove, W.R. (1970). Societal reaction as an explanation of mental illness: An evaluation. *American Sociological Review, 35,* 873–884.

Gove, W.R. (1990). Labeling theory's explanation of mental illness: An update of recent evidence. In M. Nagler (Ed.), *Perspectives on disability.* Palo Alto, CA: Health Markets Research.

Graham, J.R. (1990). MMPI-2. *Assessing personality and psychopathology.* New York: Oxford University Press.

Grandin, T. (1995). *Thinking in pictures and other reports from my life with autism.* New York: Doubleday.

Grant, William T., Foundation. (1988). *The forgotten half: Pathways to success for America's youth and young families.* Washington, DC: Youth and America's Future, William T. Grant Foundation Commission on Work, Family and Citizenship.

Granville-Grossman, K. (1983). Mind and body. In M.H. Lader (Ed.), *Handbook of psychiatry 2: Mental disorders and somatic illness,* pp. 5–13. London: Cambridge University Press.

Gratzer, T., & Bradford, J.M.W. (1995). Offender and offense characteristics of sexual sadists: A comparative study. *Journal of Forensic Sciences, 40,* 450–455.

Gray, J.A. (1990). Brain systems that mediate both emotion and cognition. *Cognition and Emotion, 4,* 269–288.

Greaves, G.B. (1980). Multiple personality disorder: 165 years after Mary Reynolds. *Journal of Nervous and Mental Disease, 168,* 577–596.

Greenberg, L.S., Elliott, R.K., & Lietaer, G. (1994). In A.E. Bergin & S.L. Garfield, *Handbook of psychotherapy and behavior change,* 4th ed., pp. 509–542. New York: Wiley.

Greenberg, R.P., Bornstein, R.F., Zborowski, M.J., Fisher, S., & Greenberg, M.D. (1994). A meta-analysis of fluoxetine outcome in the treatment of depression. *Journal of Nervous and Mental Disease, 182,* 547–551.

Greene, R.L. (1991). *The MMPI-2/MMPI: An interpretive manual.* Boston: Allyn and Bacon.

Greenough, W.T. (1987). Experience effects on the developing and the mature brain: Dendritic branching and synaptogenesis. In N.A. Krasnegor, E.M. Blass & M.A. Hofer (Eds.), *Perinatal development: A psychobiological perspective,* pp. 195–221. Orlando, FL: Academic Press.

Grenier, G., & Gyers, E.S. (1995). Rapid ejaculation: A review of conceptual, etiological and treatment issues. *Archives of Sexual Behavior, 24,* 447–471.

Griffitt, W. (1987). Females, males, and sexual responses. In K. Kelley (Ed.), *Females, males, and sexuality.* Albany: State University of New York Press.

Grinspoon, L., & Bakalar, J.B. (1993). *Marihuana: The forbidden medicine.* New Haven, CT: Yale University Press.

Grob, G.N. (1994). *The mad among us: A history of the care of America's mentally ill.* Cambridge, MA: Harvard University Press.

Grossman, H.J. (1983). *Classification in mental retardation.* Washington, DC: American Association on Mental Deficiency.

Grotevant, H.D., & Carlson, C.I. (1989). *Family assessment: A guide to methods and measures.* New York: Guilford.

Grove, W.M., & Andreasen, N.C. (1992). Concepts, diagnosis and classification. In E.S. Paykel (Ed.), *Handbook of affective disorders,* 2nd ed., pp. 25–42. New York: Guilford.

Grove, W.M., Andreasen, N.C., McDonald-Scott, P., Keller, M.B., & Shapiro, R.W. (1981). Reliability studies of psychiatric diagnosis. *Archives of General Psychiatry, 38*, 408–413.

Grove, W.M., Andreasen, N.C., Young, M., Endicott, J., Keller, M.B., Hirschfeld, R.M.A., & Reich, T. (1987). Isolation and characterization of a nuclear depressive syndrome. *Psychological Medicine, 17*, 471–484.

Grove, W.M., Clementz, B.A., Iacono, W.G., & Katsanis, J. (1992). Smooth pursuit ocular motor dysfunction in schizophrenia: Evidence for a major gene. *American Journal of Psychiatry, 149*, 1362–1368.

Grove, W.M., & Tellegen, A. (1991). Problems in the classification of personality disorders. *Journal of Personality Disorders, 5*, 31–41.

Growdon, J.H. (1992). Treatment for Alzheimer's disease? *New England Journal of Medicine, 327*, 1306–1308.

Grych, J.H., & Fincham, F.D. (1990). Marital conflict and children's adjustment: A cognitive-contextual framework. *Psychological Bulletin, 101*, 267–290.

Guggenmoos-Holzmann, I. (1993). How reliable are chance-corrected measures of agreement? *Statistics in Medicine, 12*, 2191–2205.

Gunderson, J. (1984). *Borderline personality disorder.* Washington, DC: American Psychiatric Press.

Gunderson, J.G. (1994). Building structure for the borderline construct. *Acta Psychiatrica Scandinavica, 89* (suppl. 379), 12–18.

Gunderson, J., Kolb, J., Austin, V. (1981). The diagnostic interview for borderline patients. *American Journal of Psychiatry, 138*, 896–903.

Gunderson, J.G., & Singer, M.T. (1975). Defining borderline patients: An overview. *American Journal of Psychiatry, 132*, 1–10.

Gupta, S. (1993). Can environmental factors explain the epidemiology of schizophrenia in immigrant groups? *Social Psychiatry and Psychiatric Epidemiology, 28*, 263–266.

Gur, R.E. (1985). Regional cerebral blood flow in schizophrenia. In M. Alpert (Ed.), *Controversies in schizophrenia: Changes and constancies.* New York: Guilford.

Gur, R.E., Mozley, D., Resnick, S.M., Mozley, L.H., et al. (1995). Resting cerebral glucose metabolism in first-episode and previously treated patients with schizophrenia relates to clinical features. *Archives of General Psychiatry, 52*, 657–667.

Gur, R.E., & Pearlson, G.D. (1993). Neuroimaging in schizophrenia research. *Schizophrenia Bulletin, 19*, 337–353.

Gurian, B., & Goisman, R. (1993). Anxiety disorders in the elderly. *Generations, 17*, 39–42.

Gurland, B.J. (1976). The comparative frequency of depression in various adult age groups. *Journal of Gerontology, 31*, 283–392.

Gurland, B. (1996). Epidemiology of psychiatric disorders. In J. Sadavoy, L.W. Lazarus, L.F. Jarvik, & G.T. Grossberg (Eds.), *Comprehensive review of geriatric psychiatry—II,* pp. 3–42. Washington, DC: American Psychiatric Press.

Gurman, A.S., & Kniskern, D.P. (Eds.) (1991). *Handbook of family therapy,* vol. II. New York: Brunner/Mazel.

Gusella, J.F., Wexler, N.S., Conneally, P.M., Naylor, S.L., Anderson, M.A., Tanzi, R.E., Watkins, P.C., Ottina, K., Wallace, M.R., Sakaguchi, A.Y., Young, A.B., et al. (1983). A polymorphic DNA marker genetically linked to Huntington's disease. *Nature, 306*, 234–238.

Gussekloo, J., Heeren, T.J., Izaks, G.J., Ligthart, G.J., et al. (1995). A community based study of the incidence of dementia in subjects aged 85 years and over. *Journal of Neurology, Neurosurgery, & Psychiatry, 59*, 507–510.

Gutheil, T.G. (1986). The right to refuse treatment: Paradox, pendulum and the quality of care. *Behavioral Sciences and the Law, 4*, 265–277.

Guzder, J., Paris, J., Zelkowitz, P., & Marchessault, K. (1996). Risk factors for borderline psychology in children. *Journal of the American Academy of Child and Adolescent Psychiatry, 35*, 26–33.

Guze, S.B., & Robins, E. (1970). Suicide and primary affective disorders. *British Journal of Psychiatry, 117*, 437–438.

Haaga, D.A.F., & Beck, A.T. (1992). Cognitive therapy. In E.S. Paykel (Ed.), *Handbook of affective disorders,* 2nd ed., p. 511–523. New York: Guilford.

Hafner, H. (1990). Primary dementia of Alzheimer's type—Epidemiology and risk factors. *Psychiatria Fennica, 21*, 145–162.

Hafner, H., Maurer, K., Loffler, W., Fatkenheuer, B., an der Heiden, W., Riecher-Rossler, A., Behrens, S., & Gattaz, W.F. (1994). The epidemiology of early schizophrenia: Influence of age and gender on onset and early course. *British Journal of Psychiatry, 164* (suppl. 23), 29–38.

Hage, J.J. (1995). Medical requirements and consequences of sex reassignment surgery. *Medicine, Science and the Law, 35*, 17–24.

Hall, G.C. (1995). Sexual offender recidivism revisited: A meta-analysis of recent treatment studies. *Journal of Consulting and Clinical Psychology, 63*, 802–809.

Hamilton, M. (1982). Symptoms and assessment of depression. In E.S. Paykel (Ed.), *Handbook of affective disorders,* pp. 3–11. New York: Guilford.

Hanson, D.R., Gottesman, I.I., & Heston, L.L. (1976). Some possible childhood indications of adult schizophrenia inferred from children of schizophrenics. *British Journal of Psychiatry, 129*, 142–154.

Hanson, D.R., Gottesman, I.I., & Heston, L.L. (1990). Long range schizophrenia forecasting: Many a slip twixt cup and lip. In J. Rolf, K. Nuechterlein, A. Masten, & D. Cicchetti (Eds.), *Risk and protective factors in the development of schizophrenia,* pp. 424–444. New York: Cambridge University Press.

Harding, C.M. (1988). Course types in schizophrenia: An analysis of European and American studies. *Schizophrenia Bulletin, 14*, 633–643.

Harding, C.M., Zubin, J., & Strauss, J.S. (1992). Chronicity in schizophrenia: Revisited. *British Journal of Psychiatry, 161* (suppl. 18), 27–37.

Hare, R.D. (1983). Diagnosis of antisocial personality disorder in two prison populations. *American Journal of Psychiatry, 140*, 887–890.

Hare, R.D. (1985). Comparison of procedures for the assessment of psychopathy. *Journal of Consulting and Clinical Psychology, 53*, 7–16.

Hare, R.D. (1993). *Without conscience: The disturbing world of the psychopaths among us.* New York: Pocket Books.

Hare, R.D., Hart, S.D., & Harpur, T.J. (1991). Psychopathy and the DSM-IV criteria for antisocial personality disorder. *Journal of Abnormal Psychology, 100*, 391–398.

Harrington, R., Fudge, H., Rutter, M., Pickles, A., & Hill, J. (1990). Adult outcomes of childhood and adolescent depression. I. Psychiatric status. *Archives of General Psychiatry, 47*, 465–473.

Harris, G.T., Rice, M.E., Quinsey, V.L., Chaplin, T.C., et al. (1992). Maximizing the discriminant validity of phallometric assessment data. *Psychological Assessment, 4*, 502–511.

Harris, T., Brown, G.W., & Bifulco, A. (1986). Loss of parent in childhood and adult psychiatric disorder: The role of lack of adequate parental care. *Psychological Medicine, 16*, 641–659.

Harrow, M., Rattenbury, F., & Stoll, F. (1988). Schizophrenic delusions: An analysis of their persistence, of related premorbid ideas, and of three major dimensions. In T.F. Oltmanns & B.A. Maher (Eds.), *Delusional beliefs,* pp. 184–211. New York: Wiley.

Hartmann, H., Kris, E., & Loewenstein, R.W. (1947). Comments on the formation of psychic structure. In A. Freud, et al. (Eds.), *The psychoanalytic study of the child.* New York: International Universities Press.

Harvey, R.J. (1996). Review: Delusions in dementia. *Age and Ageing, 25*, 405–409.

Haskett, R.F. (1993). The HPA axis and depressive disorders. In J. John Mann & David J. Kupfer (Eds.), *Biology of depressive disorders, Part A: A systems perspective,* pp. 171–188. New York: Plenum.

Haugaard, J.J., & Reppucci, N.D. (1988). *The sexual abuse of children.* San Francisco: Jossey-Bass.

Hauser, P., Zametkin, A.J., Martinez, P., Vitiello, B., Matochik, J.A., Mixson, A.J., & Weintraub, B.D. (1993). Attention deficit-hyperactivity disorder in people with generalized resistance to thyroid hormone. *New England Journal of Medicine, 328,* 997–1001.

Havighurst, R.J. (1952). *Developmental tasks and education.* New York: McKay.

Hawley, T.L., & Disney, E.R. (1992). Crack's children: The consequences of maternal cocaine abuse. *Social Policy Report: Society for Research in Child Development, 6,* 1–22.

Hawton, K. (1986). *Suicide and attempted suicide among children and adolescents.* Beverly Hills, CA: Sage.

Hayes, S.C., Nelson, R.O., & Jarrett, R.B. (1987). The treatment utility of assessment: A functional approach to evaluating assessment quality. *American Psychologist, 42,* 963–974.

Haynes, S.G., & Feinleib, M. (1980). Women, work, and coronary heart disease: Prospective findings from the Framingham heart study. *American Journal of Public Health, 70,* 133–141.

Heath, A.C., Jardine, R., & Martin, N.G. (1989). Interactive effects of genotype and social environment on alcohol consumption in female twins. *Journal of Studies on Alcohol, 50,* 38–48.

Heath, D.B. (1991). Uses and misuses of the concept of ethnicity in alcohol studies: An essay in deconstruction. *International Journal of the Addictions, 25,* 607–628.

Heatherton, T.F. & Polivy, J. (1992). Chronic dieting and eating disorders: A spiral model. In J. Crowther, S.E. Hobfall, M.A.P. Stephens, & D.L. Tennenbaum (Eds.), *The etiology of bulimia: The individual and familial context* (pp. 135–155). Washington, DC: Hemisphere.

Heavey, C.L., Christensen, A., & Malamuth, N.M. (1995). The longitudinal impact of demand and withdrawal during marital conflict. *Journal of Consulting and Clinical Psychology, 63,* 797–801.

Heber, R. (1959). A manual on terminology and classification in mental retardation. *American Journal on Mental Deficiency, 64* (Monograph Supplement).

Heiman, J.R. (1980). Female sexual response patterns: Interactions of physiological, affective, and contextual cues. *Archives of General Psychiatry, 37,* 1311–1316.

Heimberg, R.G., Holt, C.S., Schneier, F.R., Spitzer, R.L., & Liebowitz, M.R. (1993). The issue of subtyping in the diagnosis of social phobia. *Journal of Anxiety Disorders, 7,* 249–269.

Heinberg, L.J., Thompson, J.K., & Stormer, S. (1995). Development and validation of the sociocultural attitudes towards appearance questionnaire. *International Journal of Eating Disorders, 17,* 81–89.

Heindel, W.C., Salmon, D.P., Shults, C.W., Walicke, P.A., & Butters, N. (1989). Neuropsychological evidence for multiple implicit memory systems: A comparison of Alzheimer's, Huntington's, and Parkinson's disease patients. *Journal of Neuroscience, 9,* 582–587.

Heitler, S.M. (1992). *From conflict to resolution: Strategies for diagnosis and treatment of distressed individuals, couples, and families.* New York: Norton.

Helmes, E., & Reddon, J.R. (1993). A perspective on developments in assessing psychopathology: A critical review of the MMPI and MMPI-2. *Psychological Bulletin, 113,* 453–471.

Helzer, J.E. (1987). Epidemiology of alcoholism. *Journal of Consulting and Clinical Psychology, 55,* 284–292.

Helzer, J.E., Bucholz, K., & Robins, L.N. (1992). Five communities in the United States: Results of the Epidemiologic Catchment Area Survey. In J.E. Helzer & G.J. Canino (Eds.), *Alcoholism in North America, Europe, and Asia.* pp. 71–95. New York: Oxford University Press.

Helzer, J.E., Burnam, A., & McEvoy, L.T. (1991). Alcohol abuse and dependence. In L.N. Robins & D.A. Regier (Eds.), *Psychiatric disorders in America: The Epidemiologic Catchment Area Study,* pp. 81–115. New York: Free Press.

Helzer, J.E., & Canino, G.J. (Eds.) (1992). *Alcoholism in North America, Europe, and Asia.* New York: Oxford University Press.

Helzer, J.E., Robins, L.N., & McEvoy, L. (1987). Posttraumatic stress disorder in the general population: Findings of the Epidemiologic Catchment Area Survey. *New England Journal of Medicine, 317,* 1630–1634.

Hempel, C.G. (1961). Introduction to problems of taxonomy. In J. Zubin (Ed.), *Field studies in the mental disorders.* New York: Grune & Stratton.

Hendin, H. (1995). *Suicide in America.* New York: Norton.

Hengeveld, M.W. (1994). Serotonin in attempted suicide. *Journal of Psychosomatic Research, 38,* 639–641.

Henggeler, S.W. (1994). *Treatment manual for family preservation using multisystemic therapy.* Charleston: Medical University of South Carolina.

Henggeler, S.W., & Borduin, C.M. (1990). *Family therapy and beyond: A multisystemic approach to treating the behavior problems of children and adolescents.* Pacific Grove, CA: Brooks/Cole.

Henker, B., & Whalen, C.K. (1989). Hyperactivity and attention deficits. *American Psychologist, 44,* 216–223.

Herbert, T.B., & Cohen, S. (1993). Depression and immunity: A meta-analytic review. *Psychological Bulletin, 113,* 472–486.

Herdt, G.H., & Davidson, J. (1988). The Sambia "Turnim-Man": Sociocultural and clinical aspects of gender formation in male pseudohermaphrodites with 5-alpha-reductase deficiency in Papua New Guinea. *Archives of Sexual Behavior, 17,* 33–56.

Herdt, G., & Stoller, R.J. (1990). *Intimate communications: Erotics and the study of culture.* New York: Columbia University Press.

Herman, C.P. & Polivy, J. (1988). Excess and restraint in bulimia. In K. Pirke, W. Vandereycken, & D. Ploog (Eds.), *The psychobiology of bulimia* (pp. 33–41). Munich: Springer-Verlag.

Hermann, D.H.J. (1990). Autonomy, self determination, the right of involuntarily committed persons to refuse treatment, and the use of substituted judgment in medication decisions involving incompetent persons. *International Journal of Law and Psychiatry, 13,* 361–385.

Hernandez, D.J. (1993). *America's children: Resources from family, government, and the economy.* New York: Russell Sage.

Hesselbrock, V., & Hesselbrock, M. (1990). Behavioral/social factors that may enhance or attenuate genetic effects. In C.R. Cloninger & H. Begleiter (Eds.), *Genetics and biology of alcoholism,* pp. 75–86. Cold Spring Harbor, NY: Cold Spring Harbor Laboratory Press.

Heston, L.L. (1966). Psychiatric disorders in foster home reared children of schizophrenic mothers. *British Journal of Psychiatry, 112,* 819–825.

Heston, L.L. (1997). The future is now (provided we recognize it). In L. Heston (Ed.), *Progress in Alzheimer's disease and similar conditions.* Washington, DC: American Psychiatric Press.

Heston, L.L., & White, J.A. (1991). *The vanishing mind: A practical guide to Alzheimer's disease and other dementias.* New York: Freeman.

Hetherington, E.M., & Parke, R.D. (1986). *Child psychology: A contemporary perspective.* New York: McGraw-Hill.

Hill, J., & Holmbeck, G. (1986). Attachment and autonomy during adolescence. In G. Whitehurst (Ed.), *Annals of child development,* Vol. 3, pp. 145–189. Greenwich, CT: JAI.

Hill, M.A. (1992). Light, circadian rhythms, and mood disorders: A review,. *Annals of Clinical Psychiatry, 4,* 131–146.

Hilts, P.J. (1996). *Smoke screen: The truth behind the tobacco industry coverup.* Reading, MA: Addison-Wesley.

Hinde, R.A. (1992). Developmental psychology in the context of other behavioral sciences. *Developmental Psychology, 28,* 1018–1029.

Hinshaw, S.P. (1987). On the distinction between attentional deficits/hyperactivity and conduct problems/aggression in child psychopathology. *Psychological Bulletin, 101,* 443–463.

Hinshaw, S.P. (1994). *Attention deficits and hyperactivity in children.* Thousand Oaks, CA: Sage.

Hirschfeld, R.M.A. (1993). Personality disorders: Definition and diagnosis. *Journal of Personality Disorders,* suppl., 9–17.

Hirchsfeld, R.M.A., Shea, M.T., & Weise, R. (1995). Dependent personality disorder. In W.J. Livesley (Ed.), *The DSM-IV personality disorders,* pp. 239–256. New York: Guilford.

Hite, S. (1976). *The Hite report.* New York: Macmillan.

Ho, D.Y. (1994). Introduction to cross-cultural psychology. In L.L. Adler & U.P. Gielen (Eds.), *Cross-cultural topics in psychology,* pp. 3–14. Westport, CT: Praeger.

Hoch, P.H., & Polatin, P. (1949). Pseudoneurotic forms of schizophrenia. *Psychiatric Quarterly, 23,* 248–276.

Hoehn-Saric, R.,. & McLeod, D.R. (1991). Clinical management of generalized anxiety disorder. In W. Coryell & G. Winokur (Eds.), *The clinical management of anxiety disorders,* pp. 79–100. New York: Oxford University Press.

Hoek, H.W. (1995). The distribution of eating disorders. In K.D. Brownell & C.G. Fairburn (Eds.), *Eating disorders and obesity: A comprehensive handbook,* pp. 207–211. New York: Guilford.

Hoenig, J. (1985). Etiology of transsexualism. In B.W. Steiner (Ed.), *Gender dysphoria: Development, research, management,* pp. 33–74. New York: Plenum.

Hoffman, P.B., & Foust, L.L. (1977). Least restrictive treatment of the mentally ill: A doctrine in search of its senses. *San Diego Law Review, 14,* 1100–1154.

Hogan, D.P., & Lichter, D.T. (1995). Children and youth: Living arrangements and welfare. In R. Farley (Ed.), *State of the union: America in the 1990s.* New York: Russell Sage.

Hogarty, G.E. (1993). Prevention of relapse in chronic schizophrenic patients. *Journal of Clinical Psychiatry, 54* (suppl.), 18–23.

Hogarty, G.E., Anderson, C.M., Reiss, D.J., et al. (1991). Family psychoeducation, social skills training, and maintenance chemotherapy in the aftercare treatment of schizophrenia. II. Two-year effects of a controlled study on relapse and adjustment. *Archives of General Psychiatry, 48,* 340–347.

Hole, J.W., Jr. (1984). *Human anatomy and physiology,* 3rd ed. Dubuque, IA: Wm C. Brown.

Hollin, C.R. (1997). Sexual sadism: Assessment and treatment. In D.R. Laws & W.T. O'Donohue (Eds.), *Handbook of sexual deviance: Theory and application.* New York: Guilford.

Hollon, S.D., & Beck, A.T. (1986). Cognitive and cognitive-behavior therapies. In S.L. Garfield & A.E. Bergin (Eds.), *Handbook of psychotherapy and behavior change: An empirical analysis,* 3rd ed., pp. 443–482. New York: Wiley.

Hollon, S.D., DeRubeis, R.J., & Evans, M.D. (1987). Causal medication of change in treatment for depression: Discriminating between nonspecificity and noncausality. *Psychological Bulletin, 102,* 139–149.

Hollon, S.D., Shelton, R.C., & Davis, D.D. (1993). Cognitive therapy for depression: Conceptual issues and clinical efficacy. *Journal of Consulting and Clinical Psychology, 61,* 270–275.

Holman, J.E., & Caston, R.J. (1987). Interorganizational influences on mental health diagnoses: A macro-level study of labeling processes. *Sociological Perspectives, 30,* 180–200.

Holmes, T.H., & Rahe, R.H. (1967). The Social Readjustment Rating Scale. *Journal of Psychosomatic Research, 11,* 213–218.

Holtzworth-Munroe, A., & Jacobson, N.S. (1991). Behavioral marital therapy. In A.S. Gurman & D.P. Kniskern (Eds.), *Handbook of family therapy,* Vol. II, pp. 96–133. New York: Brunner/Mazel.

Holzman, P.S. (1989). The use of eye movement dysfunctions in exploring the genetic transmission of schizophrenia. *European Archives of Psychiatry and Neurological Sciences, 239,* 43–48.

Hooley, J.M. (1985). Expressed emotion: A review of the critical literature. *Clinical Psychology Review, 5,* 119–139.

Hooley, J.M., & Richters, J.E. (1995). Expressed emotion: A developmental perspective. In D. Cicchetti & S.L. Toth (Eds.), *Emotion, cognition, and representation, Rochester symposium on developmental psychopathology,* Vol. 6, pp. 133–166. Rochester, NY: University of Rochester Press.

Hooley, J.M., & Teasdale, J.D. (1989). Predictors of relapse in unipolar depressives: Expressed emotion, marital distress, and perceived criticism. *Journal of Abnormal Psychology, 98,* 229–235.

Hopps, J.G., & Pinderhughes, E.B. (1987). Profession of social work: Contemporary characteristics. In A. Minehan (Ed.), *Encyclopedia of social work,* 18th ed. Silver Spring, MD: National Association of Social Work.

Horevitz, R., & Loewenstein, R.J. (1994). The rational treatment of multiple personality disorder. In S.J. Lynn & J.W. Rhue (Eds.), *Dissociation: Clinical and theoretical perspectives,* pp. 289–316. New York: Guilford.

Horn, J.M., Loehlin, J.C., & Willerman, L. (1979). Intellectual resemblance among adoptive and biological relatives: The Texas Adoption Project. *Behavior Genetics, 9,* 177–205.

Horney, K. (1939). *New ways in psychoanalysis.* New York: International Universities Press.

Horvath, T.B., Siever, L.J., Mohs, R.C., & Davis, K. (1991). Organic mental syndromes and disorders. In H.I. Kaplan & B.J. Sadock (Eds.), *Comprehensive textbook of psychiatry,* 5th ed., Vol. 1, pp. 599–641. Baltimore, MD: Williams & Wilkins.

Horwath, E., Lish, J.D., Johnson, J., Hornig, C.D., & Weissman, M.M. (1993). Agoraphobia without panic: Clinical reappraisal of an epidemiologic finding. *American Journal of Psychiatry, 150,* 1496–1501.

Hotchner, A.E. (1966). *Papa Hemingway: A personal memoir.* New York: Random House.

Howard, K.I., Cornille, T.A., Lyons, J.S., Vessey, J.T., Lueger, R.J., & Saunders, S.M. (1996). Patterns of mental health service utilization. *Archives of General Psychiatry, 53,* 696–707.

Howard, K.I., Kopta, S.M., Krause, M.S., & Orlinsky, D.E. (1986). The dose-effect relationship in psychotherapy. *American Psychologist, 41,* 159–164.

Hoza, B., Pelham, W.E., Milich, R., Pillow, D., & McBride, K. (1993). The self-perceptions and attributions of attention deficit hyperactivity disordered and nonreferred boys. *Journal of Abnormal Child Psychology, 21,* 271–286.

Hsu, L.K. (1989). The gender gap in eating disorders: Why are the eating disorders more common among women? *Clinical Psychology Review, 9,* 393–407.

Hsu, L.K.G. (1990). *Eating disorders.* New York: Guilford.

Hsu, L.K.G. (1995). Outcome of bulimia nervosa. In K.D. Brownell & C.G. Fairburn (Eds.), *Eating disorders and obesity: A comprehensive handbook,* pp. 238–244. New York: Guilford.

Hucker, S.J. (1997). Sexual sadism: Theory and psychopathology. In D.R. Laws & W.T. O'Donohue (Eds.), *Handbook of sexual deviance: Theory and application.* New York: Guilford.

Hughes, P.H., Canavan, K.P., Jarvis, G., & Aris, A. (1983). Extent of drug use: An international review with implications for health planners. *World Health Statistics Quarterly, 36,* 394–497.

Hughes, P.L., Wells, L.A., Cunningham, C.J., & Ilstrup, D.M. (1986). Treatment of bulimia with desipramine: A double-blind, placebo-controlled study. *Archives of General Psychiatry, 43,* 182–186.

Hull, J.G., & Bond, C.F., Jr. (1986). Social and behavioral consequences of alcohol consumption and expectancy: A meta-analysis. *Psychological Bulletin, 99,* 347–360.

Human Capital Initiative. (1996). *Doing the right thing: A research plan for healthy living.* Washington, DC: American Psychological Society.

Humphrey, L.L. (1987). Comparison of bulimic-anorexic and nondistressed families using structural analysis of social behavior. *Journal of the American Academy of Child and Adolescent Psychiatry*, 26, 248–255.

Huntington's Disease Collaborative Research Group (1993). A novel gene containing a trinucleotide repeat that is expanded and unstable on Huntington's disease chromosomes. *Cell*, 72, 971–983.

Hurt, S.W., Reznikoff, M. & Clarkin, J.F. (1991). *Psychological assessment, psychiatric diagnosis, and treatment planning.* New York: Brunner/Mazel.

Huston, A.C. (1983). Sextyping. In E.M. Hetherington (Ed.), *Socialization, personality, and social development*, Vol. 4, *Handbook of child psychology*, pp. 388–467. New York: Wiley.

Huttunen, M.O., Machon, R.A., & Mednick, S.A. (1994). Prenatal factors in the pathogenesis of schizophrenia. *British Journal of Psychiatry*, 164 (suppl. 23), 15–19.

Huws, R., Shubsachs, A.P.W., & Taylor, P.J. (1991). Hypersexuality, fetishism and multiple sclerosis. *British Journal of Psychiatry*, 158, 280–281.

Hyler, S.E., Williams, J.B.W., & Spitzer, R.L. (1982). Reliability in the DSM-III field trials. *Archives of General Psychiatry*, 39, 1275–1278.

Iacono, W.G. (1985). Psychophysiologic markers of psychopathology: A review. *Canadian Psychology*, 26, 96–112.

Iacono, W.G. (1991). Psychophysiological assessment of psychopathology. *Pyschological Assessment*, 3, 309–320.

Iacono, W.G., & Beiser, M. (1992). Are males more likely than females to develop schizophrenia? *American Journal of Psychiatry*, 149, 1070–1074.

Imperato-McGinley, J., Guerrero, L., Gautier, T., & Peterson, R.E. (1974). Steroid 5a-reductase deficiency in man: An inherited form of male pseudohermaphroditism. *Science*, 186, 1213–1215.

Insel, T.R. (1992). Toward a neuroanatomy of OCD. *Archives of General Psychiatry*, 49, 739–744.

Iqbal, N., & van Praag, H.M. (1995). The role of serotonin in schizophrenia. In J.A. Den Boer, H.G. Westenberg, & H.M. van Praag (Eds.), *Advances in the neurobiology of schizophrenia: Wiley series on clinical and neurobiological advances in psychiatry*, Vol. 1, pp. 221–243. Chichester, England: Wiley.

Jablensky, A. (1985). Approaches to the definition and classification of anxiety and related disorders in European psychiatry. In A.H. Tuma & J. Maser (Eds.), *Anxiety and the anxiety disorders.* Hillsdale, NJ: Erlbaum.

Jablensky, A. (1986). Epidemiology of schizophrenia: A European perspective. *Schizophrenia Bulletin*, 12, 52–73.

Jablensky, A., Sartorius, N., Ernberg, G., Anker, M., Korten, A., Cooper, J.E., Day, R., & Bertelsen, A. (1992). Schizophrenia: Manifestations, incidence and course in different cultures: A World Health Organization ten-country study. *Psychological Medicine*, Monograph Suppl., *20*, 1–97.

Jacobson, E. (1938). *Progressive relaxation.* Chicago: University of Chicago Press.

Jacobson, J.W., Mulick, J.A., & Schwartz, A.A. (1995). A history of facilitated communication: Science, pseudoscience, and antiscience. *American Psychologist*, 50, 750–765.

Jacobson, N.S. (1985). The role of observational measures in behavior therapy outcome research, *Behavioral Assessment*, 7, 297–308.

Jacobson, N.S., & Christensen, A. (1996). *Integrative couple therapy: Promoting acceptance and change.* New York: Norton.

Jacobson, N.S., Follette, W.C., & McDonald, D.W. (1982). Reactivity to positive and negative behavior in distressed and nondistressed married couples. *Journal of Consulting and Clinical Psychology*, 50, 706–714.

Jacobson, N.S., & Hollon, S.D. (1996). Cognitive-behavior therapy versus pharmacotherapy: Now that the jury's returned its verdict, it's time to present the rest of the evidence. *Journal of Consulting and Clinical Psychology*, 64, 74–80.

Jacobson, N.S., Holtzworth-Munroe, A., & Schmaling, K.B. (1989). Marital therapy and spouse involvement in the treatment of depression, agoraphobia, and alcoholism. *Journal of Consulting and Clinical Psychology*, 57, 5–10.

Jacobson, R.R., Acker, C.F., & Lishman, W.A. (1990). Patterns of neuropsychological deficit in alcoholic Korsakoff's syndrome. *Psychological Medicine*, 20, 321–334.

Jacoby, R., & Bergmann, K. (1986). The psychiatry of old age. In P. Hill, R. Murray, & A. Thorley (Eds.), *Essentials of postgraduate psychiatry*, 2nd ed., pp. 495–526. London: Grune & Stratton.

Jacqmin, H., Commenges, D., Letenneur, L., Barbergergateau, P., & Dartigues, J.F. (1994). Components of drinking water and risk of cognitive impairment in the elderly. *American Journal of Epidemiology*, 139, 48–57.

Jaffe, J.H. (1995). Pharmacological treatment of opioid dependence: Current techniques and new findings. *Psychiatric Annals*, 25, 369–375.

Jamison, K.R. (1995). *An unquiet mind: A memoir of moods and madness.* New York: Knopf.

Janet, P. (1914/1915). Psychoanalysis. *Journal of Abnormal Psychology*, 1–35, 187–253.

Jarvis, T.J. (1992). Implications of gender for alcohol treatment research: A quantitative and qualitative review. *British Journal of Addiction*, 87, 1249–1261.

Jellinek, E.M. (1952). Phases of alcohol addiction. *Quarterly Journal of Studies on Alcohol*, 13, 673–684.

Jellinek, E.M. (1960). *The disease concept of alcoholism.* New Haven, CT: Hillhouse Press.

Jenkins, C.D. (1988). Epidemiology of cardiovascular diseases. *Journal of Consulting and Clinical Psychology*, 56, 324–332.

Jeste, D.V., & Caligiuri, M.P. (1993). Tardive dyskinesia. *Schizophrenia Bulletin*, 19, 303–316.

Jiang, W., Babyak, M., Krantz, D.S., Waugh, R.A., et al. (1996). Mental stress-induced myocardial ischemia and cardiac events. *Journal of the American Medical Association*, 275, 1651–1656.

Johansson, B., & Zarit, S.H. (1995). Prevalence and incidence of dementia in the oldest old: A longitudinal study of a population-based sample of 84–90-year-olds in Sweden. *International Journal of Geriatric Psychiatry*, 10, 359–366.

Johnson, D. (1990). Long-term drug treatment of psychosis: Observations on some current issues. *International Review of Psychiatry*, 2, 341–353.

Johnson, P. (1989). Hemingway: Portrait of the artist as an intellectual. *Commentary*, 87, 49–59.

Johnson, S.L., & Roberts, J.E. (1995). Life events and bipolar disorder: Implications from biological theories. *Psychological Bulletin*, 117, 434–449.

Johnston, D.W. (1985). Psychological interventions in cardiovascular disease. *Journal of Psychosomatic Research*, 29, 447–456.

Johnston, D.W. (1989). Prevention of cardiovascular disease by psychological methods. *British Journal of Psychiatry*, 154, 183–194.

Johnstone, E.C., & Geddes, J. (1994). How high is the relapse rate in schizophrenia? *Acta Psychiatrica Scandinavica*, 89 (suppl. 382), 6–10.

Joiner, R.E., & Metalsky, G.I. (1995). A prospective test of an integrative interpersonal theory of depression: A naturalistic study of college roommates. *Journal of Personality and Social Psychology*, 69, 778–788.

Jones, B.M., & Jones, M.K. (1976). Women and alcohol: Intoxication, metabolism, and the menstrual cycle. In M. Greenblatt & M.A. Schuckit (Eds.), *Alcohol problems in women and children*, pp. 103–136. New York, Grune & Stratton.

Jones, D.M. (1985). Bulimia: A false self identity. *Clinical Social Work*, 13, 305–316.

Jones, J.C., & Barlow, D.H. (1990). The etiology of posttraumatic stress disorder. *Clinical Psychology Review*, 10, 299–328.

Jones, M.A., & Krisberg, B. (1994). *Images and reality: Juvenile crime, youth violence, and public policy.* San Francisco: National Council on Crime and Delinquency.

Jones, R.R., Reid, J.B., & Patterson, G.R. (1975). Naturalistic observation in clinical assessment. In P. McReynolds (Ed.), *Advances in psychological assessment*, vol. 3. San Francisco: Jossey-Bass.

Josephs, R.A., & Steele, C.M. (1990). The two faces of alcohol myopia: Attentional mediation of psychological stress. *Journal of Abnormal Psychology,* 99, 115–126.

Junginger, J. (1997). Fetishism. In D.R. Laws and W.T. O'Donohue (Eds), *Handbook of sexual deviance: Theory and application.* New York: Guilford.

Kagan, J. (1958). The concept of identification. *Psychological Review,* 65, 296–305.

Kagan, J., Kearsley, R., & Zelazo, P.R. (1978). *Infancy: Its place in human development.* Cambridge, MA: Harvard University Press.

Kagan, J., Reznick, S., & Snidman, N. (1987). The physiology and psychology of behavioral inhibition in children. *Child Development,* 58, 1459–1473.

Kagan, J., & Snidman, N. (1991). Temperamental factors in human development. *American Psychologist,* 46, 856–862.

Kahn, R.S., & Davidson, M. (1995). Dopamine in schizophrenia. In J.A. Den Boer, H.G. Westenberg, & H.M. van Praag (Eds.). *Advances in the neurobiology of schizophrenia: Wiley series on clinical and neurobiological advances in psychiatry,* Vol. 1, pp. 204–220. Chichester, England: Wiley.

Kamarck, T., & Jennings, J.R. (1991). Biobehavioral factors in sudden cardiac death. *Psychological Bulletin,* 109, 42–75.

Kane, J.M. (1995). Current problems with the pharmacotherapy of schizophrenia. *Clinical Neuropharmacology,* 18 (suppl. 1), S154–S160.

Kane, J.M., & Marder, S.R. (1993). Psychopharmacologic treatment of schizophrenia. *Schizophrenia Bulletin,* 19, 287–302.

Kane, J.M., Woerner, M., & Lieberman, J. (1985). Tardive dyskinesis: Prevalence, incidence and risk factors. In D.E. Casey, T.N. Chase, A.V. Christensen, & J. Gerlach (Eds.), *Dyskinesis: Research and treatment,* pp. 72–78. Berlin: Springer.

Kane, J.M., Woerner, M., Lieberman, J., & Rabiner, C.J. (1984). Studies on the long-term treatment of schizophrenia. *Psychiatric Hospital,* 15, 179–183.

Kanner, L. (1943). Autistic disturbances of affective contact. *Nervous Child,* 2, 217–250.

Kaplan, H.S. (1974). *The new sex therapy: Active treatment of sexual dysfunctions.* New York: Brunner/Mazel.

Kaplan, L.J. (1989). *Female perversions: The temptations of Emma Bovary.* New York: Doubleday.

Kapur, S., & Mann, J.J. (1992). Role of the dopaminergic system in depression. *Biological Psychiatry,* 32, 1–17.

Kapur, S., & Mann, J.J. (1993). Antidepressant action and the neurobiologic effects of ECT: Human studies. In C.E. Coffey (Ed.), *The clinical science of electroconvulsive therapy,* pp. 235–250. Washington, DC: American Psychiatric Press.

Kapur, S., & Remington, G. (1996). Serotonin-dopamine interaction and its relevance to schizophrenia. *American Journal of Psychiatry,* 153, 466–476.

Karasek, R.A., Theorell, T.G., Schwartz, J., Pieper, C., & Alfredsson, L. (1982). Job, psychological factors and coronary heart disease: Swedish prospective findings and U.S. prevalence findings using a new occupational inference method. *Advances in Cardiology,* 29, 62–67.

Karler, R., Calder, L.D., Chaudhry, I.A., & Turkanis, S.A. (1989). Blockade of "reverse tolerance" to cocaine and amphetamine by MK-801. *Life Sciences,* 45, 599–606.

Karno, M., & Golding, J.M. (1991). Obsessive-compulsive disorder. In L.N. Robins & D.A. Regier (Eds.), *Psychiatric disorders in America: The Epidemiologic Catchment Area Study.* New York: Free Press.

Karras, A., & Otis, D.B. (1987). A comparison of inpatients in an urban state hospital in 1975 and 1982. *Hospital and Community Psychiatry,* 38, 963–967.

Kasen, S., Cohen, P., Brook, J.S., & Hartmark, C. (1996). A multiple-risk interaction model: Effects of temperament and divorce on psychiatric disorders in children. *Journal of Abnormal Child Psychology,* 24, 121–150.

Kass, F., Charles, E., Klein, D.F., & Cohen, P. (1983). Discordance between the SCL-90 and therapists' psychopathology ratings: Implications for clinical assessment. *Archives of General Psychiatry,* 40, 389–392.

Kassel, J.D., & Shiffman, S. (1992). What can hunger teach us about drug craving? A comparative analysis of the two constructs. *Advances in Behaviour Research and Therapy,* 14, 141–167.

Kasvikis, Y.G., Tsakiris, F., Marks, I.M., Basogulu, M., & Noshirvani, H.V. (1986). Past history of anorexia nervosa in women with obsessive-compulsive disorders. *International Journal of Eating Disorders,* 5, 1069–1075.

Katon, W., & Roy-Byrne, P.P. (1991). Mixed anxiety and depression. *Journal of Abnormal Psychology,* 100, 337–345.

Katsanis, J., & Iacono, W.G. (1991). Clinical, neuropsychological, and brain structural correlates of smooth-pursuit eye tracking performance in chronic schizophrenia. *Journal of Abnormal Psychology,* 100, 526–534.

Katschnig, H., & Amering, M. (1990). Panic attacks and panic disorder in cross-cultural perspective. In J.C. Ballenger (Ed.), *Clinical aspects of panic disorder.* New York: Wiley.

Katz, R., & McGuffin, P. (1993). The genetics of affective disorders. In D. Fowles (Ed.), *Progress in experimental personality and psychopathology research.* New York: Springer.

Katzman, R. (1976). The prevalence and malignancy of Alzheimer's disease. *Archives of Neurology,* 33, 217–218.

Katzman, R. (1993). Education and the prevalence of dementia and Alzheimer's disease. *Neurology,* 43, 13–20.

Kaul, T.J., & Bednar, R.L. (1986). Experimental group research: Results, questions, and suggestions. In S.L. Garfield & A.E. Bergin (Eds.), *Handbook of psychotherapy and behavior change,* 3rd ed., pp. 671–714. New York: Wiley.

Kaye, D.W.K. (1995). The epidemiology of age-related neurological disease and dementia. *Reviews in Clinical Gerontology,* 5, 39–56.

Kaye, W.H., Weltzin, T.E., Hsu, L.K.G., McConahan, C.W., & Bolton, B. (1993). Amount of calories retained after binge eating and vomiting. *American Journal of Psychiatry,* 150, 969–971.

Kazdin, A.E. (1987). Treatment of antisocial behavior in children: Current status and future directions. *Psychological Bulletin,* 102, 187–203.

Kazdin, A.E. (1989). Identifying depression in children: A comparison of alternative selection criteria. *Journal of Abnormal Child Psychology,* 17, 437–455.

Kazdin, A.E. (1990). Childhood depression. *Journal of Child Psychology and Psychiatry,* 31, 121–160.

Kazdin, A.E. (1994a). Psychotherapy for children and adolescents. In A.E. Bergin & S.L. Garfield (Eds.), *Handbook of psychotherapy and behavior change,* 4th ed., pp. 543–594. New York: Wiley.

Kazdin, A.E. (1994b). Methodology, design, and evaluation in psychotherapy research. In A.E. Bergin and S.L. Garfield (Eds.), *Handbook of psychotherapy and behavior change* (4th ed., pp. 19–71). New York: Wiley.

Kazdin, A.E. (1995). *Conduct disorders in childhood and adolescence,* 2nd ed. Thousand Oaks, CA: Sage.

Kazdin, A.E., French, N.H., & Unis, A.S. (1983). Child, mother, and father evaluations of depression in psychiatric inpatient children. *Journal of Abnormal Child Psychology,* 11, 167–180.

Kazdin, A.E., & Petti, T.A. (1982). Self-report and interview measures of childhood and adolescent depression. *Journal of Child Psychology and Psychiatry,* 23, 437–457.

Keane, T.M., Fairbank, J.A., Caddell, J.M., & Zimering, R.T. (1989). Implosive (flooding) therapy reduces symptoms of PTSD in Vietnam combat veterans. *Behavior Therapy,* 20, 245–260.

Keane, T.M., Zimering, R.T., & Caddell, J.M. (1985). A behavioral formulation of posttraumatic stress disorder in Vietnam veterans. *Behavior Therapist*, 8, 9–12.

Keck, P.E., & McElroy, S.L. (1993). Current perspectives on treatment of bipolar disorder with lithium. *Psychiatric Annals*, 23, 64–69.

Keenan, K., & Shaw, D. (in press). Developmental and social influences on young girls' early problem behavior. *Psychological Bulletin*.

Keesey, R.E. (1995). A set-point model of body weight regulation. In K.D. Brownell & C.G. Fairburn (Eds.), *Eating disorders and obesity: A comprehensive handbook*, pp. 46–50. New York: Guilford.

Keith, S.J., Regier, D.A., & Rae, D.S. (1991). Schizophrenic disorders. In L.N. Robins & D.A. Regier (Eds.), *Psychiatric disorders in America: The Epidemiologic Catchment Area Study*, pp. 33–52. New York: Free Press.

Keller, M. (1970). Tribute to E.M. Jellinek. In R.E. Popham (Ed.), *Alcohol & Alcoholism*, pp. xi–xvi. Toronto: University of Toronto Press.

Keller, M.B. (1987). Differential diagnosis, natural course and epidemiology of bipolar disorder. *American Psychiatric Association Annual Review*, 6.

Keller, M.B. (1988). Diagnostic issues and clinical course of unipolar illness. *American Psychiatric Association Annual Review*, 6.

Keller, M.B. (1994). Depression: A long-term illness. *British Journal of Psychiatry*, 165 (suppl. 26), 9–15.

Keller, M.B., Lavori, P.W., Coryell, W., Endicott, J., & Mueller, T.I. (1993). Bipolar I: A five-year prospective follow-up. *Journal of Nervous and Mental Disease*, 181, 238–245.

Kelly, M.P., Strassberg, D.S., & Kircher, J.R. (1990). Attitudinal and experiential correlates of anorgasmia. *Archives of Sexual Behavior*, 19, 165–177.

Kelly, T.A. (1990). The role of values in psychotherapy: A critical review of process and outcome effects. *Clinical Psychology Review*, 10, 171–186.

Kelly, T., Soloff, P.H., Cornelius, J., George, A., Lis, J.A., & Ulrich, R. (1992). Can we study (treat) borderline patients? Attrition from research and open treatment. *Journal of Personality Disorders*, 6, 417–433.

Kempe, C.H., Silverman, F., Steele, B., Droegueller, W., & Silver, H. (1962). The battered child syndrome. *Journal of the American Medical Association*, 181, 17–24.

Kendall, P.C., & Ingram, R.E. (1989). Cognitive-behavioral perspectives: Theory and research on depression and anxiety. In P.C. Kendall & D. Watson (Eds.), *Anxiety and depression: Distinctive and overlapping features*, pp. 27–53. San Diego, CA: Academic Press.

Kendall, P.C., & Watson, D. (Eds.) (1989). *Anxiety and depression: Distinctive and overlapping features*. San Diego: CA: Academic Press.

Kendall, P.C. (1994). Treating anxiety disorders in children: Results of a randomized clinical trial. *Journal of Consulting and Clinical Psychology*, 62, 100–110.

Kendell, R.E. (1968). *The classification of depressive illnesses*. London: Oxford University Press.

Kendell, R.E. (1975). *The role of diagnosis in psychiatry*. Oxford: Blackwell.

Kendell, R.E. (1976). The classification of depression: A review of contemporary confusion. *British Journal of Psychiatry*, 129, 15–28.

Kendell, R.E. (1981). The present status of electroconvulsive therapy. *British Journal of Psychiatry*, 139, 265–283.

Kendell, R.E. (1984). Reflections on psychiatric classification—For the architects of DSM-IV and ICD-10. *Integrative Psychiatry*, 2, 43–47.

Kendell, R.E. (1989). Clinical validity. *Psychological Medicine*, 19, 45–55.

Kendell, R.E. (1991). Relationship between the DSM-IV and the ICD-10. *Journal of Abnormal Psychology*, 100, 297–301.

Kendler, K.S. (1988). Familial aggregation of schizophrenia and schizophrenia spectrum disorders. *Archives of General Psychiatry*, 45, 377–383.

Kendler, K.S., & Diehl, S.R. (1993). The genetics of schizophrenia: A current, genetic-epidemiologic perspective. *Schizophrenia Bulletin*, 19, 261–285.

Kendler, K.S., Heath, A.C., Neale, M.C., Kessler, R.C., & Eaves, L.J. (1992). A population-based twin study of alcoholism in women. *Journal of the American Medical Association*, 268, 1877–1882.

Kendler, K.S., Kessler, R.C., Neale, M.C., Heath, A.C., & Eaves, L.J. (1993). The prediction of major depression in women: Toward an integrated etiologic model. *American Journal of Psychiatry*, 150, 1139–1148.

Kendler, K.S., Kessler, R.C., Walters, E.E., MacLean, C., Neale, M.C., Heath, A.C., & Eaves, L.J. (1995). Stressful life events, genetic liability, and onset of an episode of major depression in women. *American Journal of Psychiatry*, 152, 833–842.

Kendler, K.S., MacLean, C., Neale, M., Kessler, R., Heath, A., & Eaves, L. (1991). The genetic epidemiology of bulimia nervosa. *American Journal of Psychiatry*, 148, 1627–1637.

Kendler, K.S., McGuire, M., Gruenberg, A.M., O'Hare, A., Spellman, M., & Walsh, D. (1993). The Roscommon Family Study. III. Schizophrenia-related personality disorders in relatives. *Archives of General Psychiatry*, 50, 781–788.

Kendler, K.S., McGuire, M., Gruenberg, A.M., & Walsh, D. (1995). Schizotypal symptoms and signs in the Roscommon Family Study. *Archives of General Psychiatry*, 52, 296–303.

Kendler, K.S., Neale, M.C., Kessler, R.C., Heath, A.C., & Eaves, L.J. (1992a). Generalized anxiety disorder in women: A population-based twin study. *Archives of General Psychiatry*, 49, 267–272.

Kendler, K.S., Neale, M.C., Kessler, R.C., Heath, A.C., & Eaves, L.J. (1992b). The genetic epidemiology of phobias in women: The interrelationship of agoraphobia, social phobia, situational phobia, and simple phobia. *Archives of General Psychiatry*, 49, 273–281.

Kendler, K.S., Neale, M.C., Kessler, R.C., Heath, A.C., & Eaves, L.J. (1993). A longitudinal twin study of 1-year prevalence of major depression in women. *Archives of General Psychiatry*, 50, 843–852.

Kennedy, J.L., Giuffra, L.A., Moises, H.W., Cavalli-Sforza, L.L., Pakstis, A.J., Kidd, J.R., Castiglione, C.M., Sjorgren,B., Wetterberg, L., & Kidd, K.K. (1988). Evidence against linkage of schizophrenia to markers on chromosome 5 in a northern Swedish pedigree. *Nature*, 336, 167–170.

Kenrick, D.T., & Funder, D.C. (1988). Profiting from controversy: Lessons from the person-situation debate. *American Psychologist*, 43, 23–34.

Kent, T.A., Campbell, J.R., & Goodwin, D.W. (1985). Blood platelet uptake of serotonin in men alcoholics. *Journal of Studies on Alcohol*, 46, 357–359.

Kernberg, O.F. (1967). Borderline personality organization. *Journal of the American Psychoanalytic Association*, 15, 641–685.

Kernberg, O.F. (1975). *Borderline conditions and pathological narcissism*. New York: Aronson.

Kernberg, O. (1988). Hysterical and histrionic personality disorders. In A. Cooper, A. Frances, & M. Sacks (Eds.), *The personality disorders and neuroses*. Philadelphia: Lippincott.

Kessel, J.B., & Zimmerman, M. (1993). Reporting errors in studies of the diagnostic performance of self-administered questionnaires. *Psychological Assessment*, 5, 395–399.

Kessler, David A. (1996). Nicotine addiction in young people. *New England Journal of Medicine*, 333(3), 186–189.

Kessler, R.C. (1995). The national comorbidity survey: Preliminary results and future directions. *International Journal of Methods in Psychiatric Research*, 5, 139–151.

Kessler, R.C., McGonagle, K.A., Zhao, S., Nelson, C.R., Highes, M., Eshleman, S., Wittchen, H., & Kendler, K.S. (1994). Lifetime and 12-month prevalence of DSM-III-R psychiatric disorders in the United States: Results from the National Comorbidity Survey. *Archives of General Psychiatry*, 51, 8–19.

Kessler, R.C., & McLeod, J.D. (1984). Sex differences in vulnerability to undesirable life events. *American Sociological Review*, 49, 620–631.

Kessler, R.C., Sonnega, A., Bromet, E., Hughes, M., & Nelson,C.B. (1995). Posttraumatic stress disorder in the National Comorbidity Survey. *Archives of General Psychiatry*, 52, 1048–1060.

Keteyian, A. (1986). The straight-arrow addict: Compulsive gambling of A. Schlichter. *Sports Illustrated*, March 10, 74–77.

Kettl, P.A. (1993). 10 basic rules for managing dementia. *Patient Care*, 27, 79–86.

Kety, S.S. (1987). The significance of genetic factors in the etiology of schizophrenia: Results from the national study of adoptees in Denmark. *Journal of Psychiatric Research*, 21, 423–429.

Kety, S.S., Rosenthal, D., Wender, P.H., Schulsinger, F., & Jacobsen, B. (1975). Mental illness in the biological and adoptive families of adopted individuals who have become schizophrenic: A preliminary report based on psychiatric interviews. In R.R. Fieve, D. Rosenthal, & H. Brill (Eds.), *Genetic research in psychiatry*. Baltimore: Johns Hopkins University Press.

Keys, A., Brozek, J., Henschel, A., Mickelsen, O., & Taylor, H.L. (1950). *The biology of human starvation*, 2 vols. Minneapolis: University of Minnesota Press.

Keys, A., Taylor, H.L., Blackburn, H., Brozek, J., Anderson, H., & Simonson, E. (1971). Mortality and coronary heart disease among men studied for 23 years. *Archives of Internal Medicine*, 128, 201–214.

Kiesler, C. (1982). Mental hospitals and alternative care: Noninstitutionalization as potential public policy for mental patients. *American Psychologist*, 37, 349–360.

Kihlstrom, J.F., Glisky, M.L., & Angiulo, M.J. (1994). Dissociative tendencies and dissociative disorders. *Journal of Abnormal Psychology*, 103, 117–124.

Kihlstrom, J.F., & Hoyt, I.P. (1990). Repression, dissociation, and hypnosis. In J.L. Singer (Ed.), *Repression and dissociation*, pp. 181–208. Chicago: University of Chicago Press.

Kilmann, P.R., et al. (1982). The treatment of sexual paraphilias: A review of the outcome research. *Journal of Sex Research*, 18, 193–252.

Kilpatrick, D.G., Saunders, B.E., Amick-McMullan, A., Best, C.L., Veronen, L.J., & Resnick, H.S. (1989). Victim and crime factors associated with the development of crime-related posttraumatic stress disorder. *Behavior Therapy*, 20, 199–214.

King, B.M. (1996). *Human sexuality today*. Upper Saddle River, NJ: Prentice Hall.

King, D.W., King, L.A., Foy, D.W., & Gudanowski, D.M. (1996). Prewar factors in combat-related posttraumatic stress disorder: Structural equation modeling with a national sample of female and male Vietnam veterans. *Journal of Consulting and Clinical Psychology*, 64, 520–531.

King, N.J., Ollier, K., Iacuone, R., Schuster, S., Bays, K., Gullone, E., & Ollendick, T.H. (1989). Fears of children and adolescents: A cross-sectional Australian study using the Revised-Fear Survey

Schedule for Children. *Journal of Child Psychology and Psychiatry*, 30, 775–784.

King, R.A., Segman, R.H., & Anderson, G.M. (1994). Serotonin and suicidality: The impact of acute fluoxetine administration. I. Serotonin and suicide. *Israel Journal of Psychiatry and Related Sciences*, 31, 271–279.

Kinsey, A.C., Pomeroy, W.B., & Martin, C.E. (1948). *Sexual behavior in the human male*. Philadelphia: Saunders.

Kinsey, A.C., Pomeroy, W., Martin, C., & Gebhard, P. (1953). *Sexual behavior in the human female*. Philadelphia: Saunders.

Kinzl, J.F., Mangweth, B., Traweger, C., & Biebl, W. (1996). Sexual dysfunction in males: Significance of adverse childhood experiences. *Child Abuse and Neglect*, 20, 759–767.

Kirch, D.G. (1993). Infection and autoimmunity as etiologic factors in schizophrenia: A review and reappraisal. *Schizophrenia Bulletin*, 19, 355–370.

Kirk, S.A., & Kutchins, H. (1992). *The selling of DSM: The rhetoric of science in psychiatry*. New York: Aldine.

Kirmayer, L.J. (1984). Culture, affect and somatization. *Transcultural Psychiatric Research Review*, 21, 159–188.

Kirmayer, L.J., Robbins, J.M., & Paris, J. (1994). Somatoform disorders: Personality and the social matrix of somatic distress. *Journal of Abnormal Psychology*, 103, 125–136.

Kivlahan, D.R., Marlatt, G.A., Fromme, K., Coppel, D.B., & Williams, E. (1990). Secondary prevention with college drinkers: Evaluation of an alcohol skills training program. *Journal of Consulting and Clinical Psychology*, 58, 805–810.

Kleiger, J.H. (1992). A conceptual critique of the EA:es comparison in the Comprehensive Rorschach System. *Psychological Assessment*, 4, 288–296.

Klein, D.F. (1981). Anxiety reconceptualized. In D.F. Klein & J. Rabkin (Eds.), *Anxiety: New research and changing concepts*, pp. 235–263. New York: Raven Press.

Klein, D.F. (1995). Psychopharmacological practice and health reform. *Psychiatric Annals*, 25, 79–83.

Klein, D.F., & Klein, H.M. (1989). The definition and psychopharmacology of spontaneous panic and phobia. In P. Tyrer (Ed.), *Psychopharmacology of anxiety*. New York: Oxford University Press.

Klein, D.F., & Ross, D.C. (1993). Reanalysis of the National Institute of Mental Health Treatment of Depression Collaborative Research Program General Effectiveness Report. *Neuropsychopharmacology*, 8, 241–251.

Kleinman, A. (1982). Neurasthenia and depression: A study of somatization and culture in China. *Culture, Medicine, and Psychiatry*, 6, 117–189.

Klerman, G.L. (1984). The advantages of DSM-III. *American Journal of Psychiatry*, 141, 539–545.

Klerman, G.L. (1986). Historical perspectives on contemporary schools of psychopathology. In T. Millon & G. Klerman (Eds.), *Contemporary directions in psychopathology: Toward the DSM-IV*. New York: Guilford.

Klerman, G.L. (1990a). History and development of modern concepts of anxiety and panic. In J. Ballenger (Ed.), *Clinical aspects of panic disorder*, pp. 3–12. New York: Wiley.

Klerman, G. (1990b). The psychiatric patient's right to effective treatment: Implications of Osheroff vs. Chestnut Lodge. *American Journal of Psychiatry*, 147, 409–418.

Klerman, G.L., & Weissman, M.M. (1992). Interpersonal psychotherapy. In E.S. Paykel (Ed.), *Handbook of affective disorders*, 2nd ed., pp. 501–510. New York: Guilford.

Klerman, G.L., Weissman, M.M., Markowitz, J.C., Glick, I., Wilner, P.J., Mason, B., & Shear, M.K. (1994). Medication and psychotherapy. In A.E. Bergin & S.L. Garfield (Eds.), *Handbook of psychotherapy and behavior change*, 4th ed., pp. 734–782. New York: Wiley.

Klerman, G.L., Weissman, M.M., Rounsaville, B.J., & Chevron, E.S. (1984). *Interpersonal psychotherapy of depression*. New York: Basic Books.

Klorman, R., Brumaghim, J.T., Fitzpatrick, P.A., Borgstedt, A.D., & Strauss, J. (1994). Clinical and cognitive effects of methylphenidate on children with attention deficit disorder as a function of aggression/oppositionality and age. *Journal of Abnormal Psychology*, 103, 206–221.

Kluft, R.P. (1987). An update on multiple personality disorder. *Hospital and Community Psychiatry*, 38, 363–373.

Kluznik, J.C., Speed, N., Van Valkenburg, C., & Magraw, R. (1986). Forty-year follow-up of United States prisoners of war. *American Journal of Psychiatry*, 143, 1443–1446.

Koenig, H.G., & Blazer, D.G. (1990). Depression and other affective disorders. In C.K. Cassel, D.E. Riesenberg, L.B. Sorenson, & J.R. Walsh (Eds.), *Geriatric medicine*, 2nd ed., pp. 473–489. New York: Springer.

Kohut, J. (1971). *The analysis of the self*. New York: International Universities Press.

Kohut, J. (1997). *The restoration of the self*. New York: International Universities Press.

Kokmen, E., Beard, C.M., O'Brien, P.C., Offord, K.P., & Kurland, L.T. (1993). Is the incidence of dementing illness changing? A 25-year time trend study in Rochester, Minnesota (1960–1984). *Neurology*, 43, 1887–1993.

Kolb, B., & Whishaw, I.Q. (1990). *Fundamentals of human neuropsychology*, 3rd ed. New York: Freeman.

Koluchova, J. (1972). Severe deprivation in twins: A case study of marked IQ change after age 7. *Journal of Child Psychology and Psychiatry*, 13, 107–114.

Kopta, S.M., Howard, K.I., Lowry, J.L., & Beutler, L.E. (1994). Patterns of symptomatic recovery in psychotherapy. *Journal of Consulting and Clinical Psychology*, 62, 1009–1016.

Koran, L.J. (1975). The reliability of clinical methods, data and judgments. *New England Journal of Medicine*, 293, 642–646, 695–701.

Koranyi, E.K. (1989). Physiology of stress reviewed. In S. Cheren (Ed.), *Psychosomatic medicine: Theory, physiology, and practice*, Vol. 1, pp. 241–278. Madison, CT: International Universities Press.

Kornhuber, J., Riederer, P., et al. (1989). 3H-spiperone binding sites in post-mortem brains from schizophrenic patients: Relationship to neuroleptic drug treatment, abnormal movements, and positive symptoms. *Journal of Neural Transmission*, 75, 1–10.

Koskenvuo, M., Kaprio, J., Rose, R.J., Kesaniemi, A., Sarna, S., Heikkila, K., & Langinvainio, H. (1988). Hostility as a risk factor for mortality and ischemic heart disease in men. *Psychosomatic Medicine*, 50, 330–340.

Koss, M.P. (1992). The underdetection of rape. *Journal of Social Issues*, 48, 63–75.

Koss, M.P. (1993). Rape: Scope, impact, interventions, and public policy responses. *American Psychologist*, 48, 1062–1069.

Koss, M.P., & Butcher, J.M. (1986). Research on brief psychotherapy. In S.L. Garfield & A.E. Bergin (Eds.), *Handbook of psychotherapy and behavior change*, 3rd ed. pp. 627–670. New York: Wiley.

Koss, M.P., Tromp, S., & Tharan, M. (1995). Traumatic memories: Empirical foundations, forensic, and clinical implications. *Clinical Psychology: Science and Practice*, 2, 111–132.

Kosson, D.S., & Newman, J.P. (1986). Psychopathy and the allocation of attentional capacity in a divided-attention situation. *Journal of Abnormal Psychology*, 95, 257–263.

Kotrla, K.J., & Weinberger, D.R. (1995). Brain imaging in schizophrenia. *Annual Review of Medicine*, 46, 113–122.

Kovacs, M., Feinberg, T.L., Crouse-Novak, M.A., Paulaukas, S., Pollock, M., & Finkelstein, R. (1984). Depressive disorders in childhood. II. A longitudinal study of the risk for a subsequent major depression. *Archives of General Psychiatry*, 41, 643–649.

Kovelman, J.A., & Scheibel, A.B. (1986). Biological substrates of schizophrenia. *Acta Neurologica Scandinavica*, 73, 1–32.

Kozel, N.J., & Adams, E.H. (1986). Epidemiology of drug abuse: An overview. *Science*, 234, 970–974.

Krafft-Ebing, R. (1892). *Psychopathia sexualis, with especial reference to contrary sexual instinct: A medico-legal study*. (translation of the 7th edition). Philadelphia: Davies.

Krantz, D.S., Contrada, R.J., Hill, D.R., & Friedler, E. (1988). Environmental stress and biobehavioral antecedents of coronary heart disease. *Journal of Consulting and Clinical Psychology*, 56, 333–341.

Krohn, A. (1980). Some clinical manifestations of structural defects in a borderline personality. *International Journal of Psychoanalytic Psychotherapy*, 8, 337–362.

Kubler-Ross, E. (1969). *On death and dying*. New York: MacMillian. Levinson, D.J. (1986). A conception of adult development. *American Psychologist*, 41, 3–13.

Kuhn, T.S. (1962). *The structure of scientific revolutions*. Chicago: University of Chicago Press.

Kuiper, B., & Cohen -Kettenis, P. (1988). Sex reassignment surgery: A study of 141 Dutch transsexuals. *Archives of Sexual Behavior*, 17, 439–457.

Kuipers, L. (1992). Expressed emotion research in Europe. *British Journal of Clinical Psychology*, 31, 429–443.

Kupfer, D.J., & Thase, M.E. (1989). Laboratory studies and validity of psychiatric diagnosis: Has there been progress? In L.N. Robins & J.E. Barrett (Eds.), *The validity of psychiatric diagnosis*, pp. 177–197. New York: Raven Press.

Kushner, M.B., Sher, K.J., & Beitman, B.D. (1990). The relation between alcohol problems and the anxiety disorders. *American Journal of Psychiatry*, 147, 685–695.

Kutchins, H., & Kirk, S.A. (1986). The reliability of DSM-III: A critical review. *Social Work Research and Abstracts*, 22, 3–12.

L'Abate, L., & Bagarozzi, D.A. (1993). *Sourcebook of marriage and family evaluation*. New York: Brunner/Mazel.

Lacey, J.I. (1967). Somatic response patterning and stress: Some revisions of activation theory. In M.H. Appley & R. Trumball (Eds.), *Psychological stress*. New York: McGraw-Hill.

LaCroix, A.Z., & Haynes, S.G. (1987). Gender differences in the stressfulness of workplace roles: A focus on work and health. In R. Barnett, G. Baruch, & L. Biener (Eds.), *Gender and stress*, pp. 96–121. New York: Free Press.

Lamb, M.E., Thompson, R.A., & Gardner, W.P., et al. (1984). Security of infantile attachment as assessed in the "strange situation": Its study and biological interpretation. *Behavioral and Brain Sciences*, 7, 127–147.

Lambert, M.J., Shapiro, D.A., & Bergin, A.E. (1986). The effectiveness of psychotherapy. In S.L. Garfield & A.E. Bergin (Eds.), *Handbook of psychotherapy and behavior change*, 3rd ed., pp. 157–212. New York: Wiley.

Lancet, Editors of. (1952). *Disabilities and how to live with them*. Cited in C. Landis. (1964). *Varieties of psychopathological experience*, pp. 241–242. New York: Holt, Rinehart, & Winston.

Lancet (1991). Editorial. Phenylketonuria grows up. *337*, 1256–1257.

Landy, F.J. (1986). Stamp collecting versus science: Validation as hypothesis testing. *American Psychologist*, 41, 1183–1192.

Lang, A.R. (1983). Addictive personality: A viable construct? In P. Levison, D. Gerstein, & D. Masloof (Eds.), *Commonalities in substance abuse and habitual behavior*. Lexington, MA: Heath.

Lang, A.R., Pelham, W.E., Johnston, C., & Gelernter, S. (1989). Levels of adult alcohol consumption induced by interaction with child confederate exhibiting normal versus externalizing behaviors. *Journal of Abnormal Psychology*, 98, 294.

Lang, A.R., & Stritzke, W.G.K. (1993). Children and alcohol. In M. Galanter, H. Begleiter, R. Deitrich, et al. (Eds). *Recent developments in alcoholism*. Vol. 11. Ten years of progress. Pp. 73–85. New York: Plenum.

Lang, C.T., & Daro, D. (1996). *Current trends in child abuse reporting and fatalities: The results of the 1995 Annual State Survey*. Working paper 808. Washington, DC: National Committee on the Prevention of Child Abuse.

Lang, F.R., & Carstensen, L.L. (1994). Close emotional relationships in late life: Further support for proactive aging in the social domain. *Psychology and Aging*, 9, 315–324.

Lang, P.J. (1979). A bio-informational theory of emotional imagery. *Psychophysiology*, 16, 495–512.

Lange, A.J., & Jakubowski, P. (1976). *Responsible assertive behavior*. Champaign, IL: Research Press.

Langevin, R. (1992). Biological factors contributing to paraphilic behavior. *Psychiatric Annals*, 22, 307–314.

Langlais, P.J. (1995). Alcohol-related thiamine deficiency. *Alcohol Health and Research World*, 19, 113–122.

Lapouse, R., & Monk, M. (1958). An epidemiologic study of behavior characteristics in children. *American Journal of Public Health*, 48, 1134–1144.

Larsen, J.K. (1991). MAOIs in the treatment of depression: A review. *European Journal of Psychiatry*, 5, 79–88.

Larson, E.W., Olinsky, A., Rummens, T.A., & Morse, R.M. (1992). Disulfiram treatment of patients with both alcohol dependence and other psychiatric disorders: A review. *Alcoholism: Clinical and Experimental Research*, 16, 125–130.

Larson, R., Csikszentmihalyi, M., & Graef, R. (1980). Mood variability and the psychosocial adjustment of adolescents. *Journal of Youth and Adolescence, 9,* 469–490.

Last, C.G., & Strauss, C.C. (1990). School refusal in anxiety-disordered children and adolescents. *Journal of the American Academy of Child and Adolescent Psychiatry, 29,* 31–35.

Laumann, E.O., & Gagnon, J.H. (1995). A sociological perspective on sexual action. In R.G. Parker & J.H. Gagnon (Eds.), *Conceiving sexuality: Approaches to sex research in a postmodern world,* pp. 183–213. New York: Routledge.

Laumann, E.O., Gagnon, J.H., Michael, R.T., & Michaels, S. (1994). *The social organization of sexuality: Sexual practices in the United States.* Chicago: University of Chicago Press.

Lavori, P.W., Klerman, G.L., Keller, M.B., Reich, T., Rice, J., & Endicott, J. (1987). Age-period-cohort analysis of secular trends in onset of major depression: Findings in siblings of patients with major affective disorder. *Journal of Psychiatric Research, 21,* 23–35.

Lawton, M.P. (1989). Environmental approaches to research and treatment of Alzheimer's disease. In E. Light & B.D. Lebowitz (Eds.), *Alzheimer's disease treatment and family stress: Directions for research.* U.S. Department of Health and Human Services, DHHS Publication No. (ADM) 89–1569, pp. 340–362.

Lazarus, A. (1988). Dyspareunia: A multimodal psychotherapeutic perspective. In S. Leiblum & R.C. Rosen (Eds.), *Principles and practice of sex therapy,* 2nd ed. New York: Guilford.

Lazarus, R.S. (1966). *Psychological stress and the coping process.* New York: McGraw-Hill.

Lazarus, R.S., & Folkman, S. (1984). *Stress, appraisal, and coping.* New York: Springer.

Lazoritz, S. (1990). What ever happened to Mary Ellen? *Child Abuse and Neglect, 14,* 143–149.

Leaf, P.J., Berkman, C.S., Weissman, M.M., Holzer, C.E., Tischler, G.L., & Myers, J.K. (1988). The epidemiology of late-life depression. In J.A. Brody & G.L. Maddox (Eds.). *Epidemiology and aging: An international perspective.* New York: Springer.

Lee, S., Ho, T.P., & Hsu, L.K.G. (1993). Fat phobic and non-fat phobic anorexia nervosa: A comparative study of 70 Chinese patients in Hong Kong. *Psychological Medicine, 23,* 999–1017.

Leesfield, I.H. (1987). Negligence of mental health professionals. *Trial, 23,* 57–61.

Leff, J.P. (1988). *Psychiatry around the globe: A transcultural view.* London: Royal College of Psychiatrists.

Leff, J., Sartorius, N., Jablensky, A., Korten, A., & Ernberg, G. (1992). The International Pilot Study of Schizophrenia: Five-year follow-up findings. *Psychological Medicine, 22,* 131–145.

Leff, J., & Vaughn, C. (1985). *Expressed emotion in families: Its significance for mental illness.* New York: Guilford.

Leff, J., Wig, N.N., Bedi, H., et al. (1990). Relatives expressed emotion and the course of schizophrenia in Chandigarh: A two-year follow-up of a first-contact sample. *British Journal of Psychiatry, 156,* 351–356.

Leibel, R.L. (1995). The molecular biology of obesity. In K.D. Brownell & C.G. Fairburn (Eds.), *Eating disorders and obesity: A comprehensive handbook,* pp. 450–456. New York: Guilford.

Leiblum, S.R., & Rosen, R.C. (1989). *Principles and practice of sex therapy: Update for the 1990s.* New York: Guilford.

Leichtman, M. (1989). Evolving concepts of borderline personality disorders. *Bulletin of the Menninger Clinic, 53,* 229–249.

Leigh, B.C. (1989). In search of the seven dwarves: Issues of measurement and meaning in alcohol expectancy research. *Psychological Bulletin, 105,* 361–373.

Leigh, B.C., & Stacy, A.W. (1993). Alcohol outcome expectancies: Scale construction and predictive utility in higher order confirmatory models. *Psychological Assessment, 5,* 216–229.

Leland, J. (1996). The fear of heroin is shooting up. *Newsweek,* August 26, 55–56.

Leon, G., Fulkerson, J.A., Perry, C.L., & Cudeck, R. (1993). Personality and behavioral vulnerabilities associated with risk status for eating disorders in adolescent girls. *Journal of Abnormal Psychology, 102,* 438–444.

Leon, G.R., Fulkerson, J.A., Perry, C.L., & Early-Zald, M.B. (1995). Prospective analysis of personality and behavioral vulnerabilities and gender influences in the later development of disordered eating. *Journal of Abnormal Psychology, 104,* 140–149.

Leonard, H.L., Swedo, S.E., Lenane, M.C., Rettew, D.C., Hamburger, S.D., Bartko, J.J., & Rapoport, J.L. (1993). A 2- to 7-year follow-up study of 54 obsessive-compulsive children and adolescents. *Archives of General Psychiatry, 50,* 429–439.

Leonard, H.L., Swedo, S.E., Rapoport, J.L.,, Koby, E.V., Lenane, M.C., Cheslow, D.L., & Hamburger, S.D. (1989). Treatment of obsessive-compulsive disorder with clomipramine and desipramine in children and adolescents: A double-blind crossover comparison. *Archives of General Psychiatry, 46,* 1088–1092.

Leonhard, K. (1979). *The classification of endogenous psychoses,* 5th ed. New York: Wiley.

Leonhard, K. (1986). Different causative factors in different forms of schizophrenia. *British Journal of Psychiatry, 149,* 1–6.

LeVay, S. (1993). *The sexual brain.* Cambridge, MA: MIT Press.

Levenson, M.R. (1992). Rethinking psychopathy. *Theory and Psychology, 2,* 51–71.

Levenson, R.W., Carstensen, L.L., & Gottman, J.M. (1994). The influence of age and gender on affect, physiology, and their interrelations: A study of long-term marriages. *Journal of Personality and Social Psychology, 67,* 56–68.

Levin, S. (1984). Frontal lobe dysfunction in schizophrenia. I. Eye movement impairments. *Journal of Psychiatric Research, 18,* 27–55.

Levine, H.G. (1978). The discovery of addiction: Changing conceptions of habitual drunkenness in America. *Journal of Studies on Alcohol, 39,* 143–174.

Levine, M., & Perkins, D.V. (1987). *Principles of community psychology: Perspectives and applications.* New York: Oxford University Press.

Levine, S.B. (1987). More on the nature of sexual desire. *Journal of Sex and Marital Therapy, 13,* 35–44.

Levine, S.B., Risen, C.B., & Althof, S.E. (1990). Essay on the diagnosis and nature of paraphilia. *Journal of Sex and Marital Therapy, 16,* 89–102.

Levitt, E.E., Moser, C., & Jamison, K.V. (1994). The prevalence and some attributes of females in the sadomasochistic subculture: A second report. *Archives of Sexual Behavior, 23,* 465–474.

Levy, D.L., Holzman, P.S., Matthysse, S., & Mendell, N.R. (1993). Eye tracking dysfunction and schizophrenia: A critical perspective. *Schizophrenia Bulletin, 19,* 461–537.

Lewander, T. (1992). Differential development of therapeutic drugs for psychosis. *Clinical Neuropharmacology, 15* (suppl. 1), 654–655.

Lewine, R.R.J., & Seeman, M.V. (1995). Gender, brain, and schizophrenia. In M.V. Seeman (Ed.), *Gender and psychopathology,* pp. 131–158. Washington, DC: American Psychiatric Press.

Lewine, R.J., & Sommers, A.A. (1985). Clinical definition of negative symptoms as a reflection of theory and methodology. In Murray Alpert (Ed.), *Controversies in schizophrenia: Changes and constancies.* New York: Guilford.

Lewinsohn, P.M. (1974). A behavioral approach to depression. In R.J. Friedman & M.M. Katz (Eds.), *The psychology of depression: Contemporary theory and research,* pp. 157–178. New York: Winston-Wiley.

Lewinsohn, P.M., Hoberman, H.M., & Rosenbaum, M. (1988). A prospective study of risk factors for unipolar depression. *Journal of Abnormal Psychology, 97,* 251–264.

Lewinsohn, P.M., Hoberman, H.M., Teri, L., & Hautzinger, M. (1985). An integrative theory of depression. In S. Reiss & R.R. Bootzin (Eds.), *Theoretical issues in behavior therapy.* New San Diego: Academic Press.

Lewinsohn, P.M., Mischel, W., Chaplin, W., & Barton, R. (1980). Social competence and depression: The role of illusory self-perceptions. *Journal of Abnormal Psychology*, 89, 203–212.

Lewinsohn, P.M., Roberts, R.E., Seely, J.R., Rohde, P., Gotlib, I.H., & Hops, H. (1994). Adolescent psychopathology, II. Psychosocial risk factors for depression. *Journal of Abnormal Psychology*, 103, 302–315.

Lewinsohn, P.M., Rohde, P., Seeley, J.R., et al. (1993). Age-cohort changes in the lifetime occurrence of depression and other mental disorders. *Journal of Abnormal Psychology*, 102, 110–120.

Lewinsohn, P.M., Steinmetz, J.L., Larson, D.W., & Franklin, J. (1981). Depression-related cognitions: Antecedent or consequence? *Journal of Abnormal Psychology*, 90, 213–219.

Lewis, M., & Michalson, L. (1983). *Children's emotions and moods: Developmental theory and measurement.* New York: Plenum.

Lewis, M.H. (1996). Psychopharmacology of autism spectrum. *Journal of Autism and Developmental Disorders*, 26, 231–235.

Lewis-Fernandez, R., & Kleinman, A. (1994). Culture, personality, and psychopathology. *Journal of Abnormal Psychology*, 103, 67–71.

Liberman, R.P., Cardin, V., McGill, C.W., Falloon, I.R.H., & Evans, C.D. (1987). Behavioral family management of schizophrenia: Clinical outcome and costs. *Psychiatric Annals*, 17, 610–619.

Liberman, R.P., DeRisi, W.J., & Mueser, K.T. (1989). *Social skills training for psychiatric patients.* New York: Pergamon.

Lieberman, J.A. (1994). Clinical biological studies of atypical antipsychotics: Focus on the serotonin/dopamine systems. *Journal of Clinical Psychiatry Monograph Series*, 12, 24–31.

Lieberman, J.A., & Koreen, A.R. (1993). Neurochemistry and neuroendocrinology of schizophrenia: A selective review. *Schizophrenia Bulletin*, 19, 371–429.

Liebowitz, M.R. (1993). Mixed anxiety and depression: Should it be included in DMS-IV? *Journal of Clinical Psychiatry*, 54 (suppl. 5), 4–7.

Liebowitz, M.R., Gorman, J.M., Fyer, A.J., & Klein, D.F. (1985). Social phobia: Review of a neglected anxiety disorder. *Archives of General Psychiatry*, 42, 729–736.

Liebowitz, M.R., Schneier, F.R., Hollander, E., Welkowitz, L.A., et al. (1991). Treatment of social phobia with drugs other than benzodiazepines. *Journal of Clinical Psychiatry*, 52 (suppl.), 10–15.

Liem, J.H. (1974). Effects of verbal communications of parents and children: A comparison of normal and schizophrenic families. *Journal of Consulting and Clinical Psychology*, 42, 438–450.

Light, L.L. (1991). Memory and aging: Four hypotheses in search of data. *Annual Review of Psychology*, 42, 333–376.

Lilienfeld, S.O. (1994). Conceptual problems in the assessment of psychopathy. *Clinical Psychology Review*, 14, 17–38.

Lindenmayer, J.P. (1993). Recent advances in pharmacotherapy of schizophrenia. *Psychiatric Annals*, 23, 201–208.

Linehan, M.M. (1987). Dialectical behavior therapy for borderline personality disorder. *Bulletin of the Meninger Clinic*, 51, 261–276.

Linehan, M.M. (1993). *Cognitive-behavioral treatment of borderline personality disorder.* New York: Guilford.

Linehan, M.M., Heard, H.L., & Armstrong, H.E. (1993). Naturalistic follow-up of a behavioral treatment for chronically parasuicidal borderline patients. *Archives of General Psychiatry*, 50, 971–974.

Linehan, M.M., Hubert, A.E., Suarez, A., Doublas, A., & Heard, H.L. (1991). Cognitive-behavioral treatment of chronically parasuicidal borderline patients. *Archives of General Psychiatry*, 48, 1060–1064.

Linehan, M.M., Tutek, D.A., Heard, H.L., & Armstrong, H.E. (1994). Interpersonal outcome of cognitive-behavioral treatment for chronically suicidal borderline patients. *American Journal of Psychiatry*, 151, 1771–1776.

Link, B., Cullen, F., & Andrews, H. (1990, August). Violent and illegal behavior of current and former mental patients compared to community controls. Paper presented at the meeting of the Society for the Study of Social Problems.

Link, B.G., Cullen, F.T., Struening, E., Shrout, P.E., & Dohrenwend, B.P. (1989). A modified labeling theory approach to mental disorders: An empirical assessment. *American Sociological Review*, 54, 400–423.

Link, B.G., Mirotznik, J., & Cullen, F.T. (1991). The effectiveness of stigma coping orientations: Can negative consequences of mental illness labeling be avoided? *Journal of Health and Social Behavior*, 32, 302–320.

Lipowski, Z.J. (1988). Somatization: The concept and its clinical applications. *American Journal of Psychiatry*, 145, 1358–1368.

Lipowski, Z.J. (1989). Delirium in the elderly patient. *New England Journal of Medicine*, 320, 578–582.

Liptzin, B. (1996). Delirium. In J. Sadavoy, L.W. Lazarus, L.F. Jarvik, & G.T. Grossberg (Eds.), *Comprehensive review of geriatric psychiatry*, 2nd ed., pp. 479–495. Washington, DC: American Psychiatric Press.

Lishman, W.A. (1987). *Organic psychiatry: The psychological consequences of cerebral disorders*, 2nd ed. Oxford: Blackwell.

Litten, R.E., & Allen, E.R. (1991). Pharmacotherapies for alcoholism: Promising agents and clinical issues. *Alcoholism: Clinical and Experimental Research*, 15, 620–633.

Livesley, W.J. (1989). Classifying personality disorders: Ideal types, prototypes, or dimensions? *Psychiatric Clinics of North America*, 12, 531–539.

Livesley, W.J. (1995). Commentary on dependent personality disorder. In W.J. Livesley (Ed.), *The DSM-IV personality disorders.* pp. 257–260. New York: Guilford.

Livesley, W.J., Jang, K.L., Jackson, D.N., & Vernon, P.A. (1993). Genetic and environmental contributions to dimensions of personality disorder. *American Journal of Psychiatry*, 150, 1826–1831.

Livesley, W.J., & West, M. (1986). The DSM-III distinction between schizoid and avoidant personality disorders. *Canadian Journal of Psychiatry*, 31, 59–62.

Lobo, A., Saz, P., Marcos, G., Dia. J., et al. (1995). The prevalence of dementia and depression in the elderly community in a southern European population. *Archives of General Psychiatry*, 52, 497–506.

Loeber, R. (1982). The stability of antisocial and delinquent child behavior: A review. *Psychological Bulletin*, 53, 1431–1446.

Loeber, R. (1988). Natural histories of conduct problems, delinquency, and associated substance use: Evidence for developmental progression. In B.B. Lahey & A.E. Kazdin (Eds.), *Advances in clinical child psychology*, Vol. 11, pp. 73–118. New York: Plenum.

Loeber, R., & Dishion, T.J. (1983). Early predictors of male delinquency: A review. *Psychological Bulletin*, 94, 68–99.

Loeber, R., Lahey, B.B., & Thomas, C .(1991). Diagnostic conundrum of oppositional defiant disorder and conduct disorder. *Journal of Abnormal Psychology*, 100, 379–390.

Loftin, C., McDowall, D., Wiersema, B., & Cottey, T.J. (1991). Effects of restrictive licensing of handguns on homicide and suicide in the District of Columbia. *New England Journal of Medicine*, 325, 1615–1620.

Loftus, E.F. (1993). The reality of repressed memories. *American Psychologist*, 48, 518–537.

Loftus, E.F., Garry, M., & Feldman, J. (1994). Forgetting sexual trauma: What does it mean when 38% forget? *Journal of Consulting and Clinical Psychology*, 62, 1177–1181.

Loftus, E., & Ketcham, K. (1994). *The myth of repressed memory.* New York: St. Martin's Press.

Loftus, E.F., & Klinger, M.R. (1992). Is the unconscious smart or dumb? *American Psychologist*, 47, 761–765.

London, P. (1964). *The modes and morals of psychotherapy.* New York: Holt, Rinehart & Winston.

Longino, C.F., & Mittelmark, M.B. (1996). In J. Sadavoy, L.W. Lazarus, L.F. Jarvik, & G.T. Grossberg (Eds.), *Comprehensive review of geriatric psychiatry—II,* pp. 135–152. Washington, DC: American Psychiatric Press.

LoPiccolo, J. (1985). Diagnosis and treatment of male sexual dysfunction. *Journal of Sex and Marital Therapy,* 11, 215–232.

LoPiccolo, J. (1991). Sexual dysfunction. In Hersen and Bellack (Eds.), *International handbook of behavior modification,* pp. 547–564. New York: Plenum.

LoPiccolo, J., & Stock, W.E. (1986). Treatment of sexual dysfunction. *Journal of Consulting and Clinical Psychology,* 54, 158–167.

Loranger, A.W., Sartorius, N., Andreoli, A., Berger, P., Buchheim, P., Channabasavanna, S.M., Coid, B., Dahl, A., Diekstra, R.F.W., Ferguson, B., Jacobsberg, L.B., Mombour, W., Pull, C., Ono, Y., & Regier, D.A. (1994). The international personality disorder examination: The World Health Organization/Alcohol, Drug Abuse, and Mental Health Administration International Pilot Study of Personality Disorders. *Archives of General Psychiatry,* 51, 215–224.

Lorion, R.P., & Felner, R.D. (1986). Research on psychotherapy with the disadvantaged. In S.L. Garfield & A.E. Bergin (Eds.), *Handbook of psychotherapy and behavior change,* 3rd ed., pp.739–776. New York: Wiley.

Lovaas, O.I. (1987). Behavioral treatment and normal educational and intellectual functioning in young autistic children. *Journal of Consulting and Clinical Psychology,* 55, 3–9.

Lovaas, O.I., Schreibman, L., Koegel, R.L., & Rehm, R. (1971). Selective responding by autistic children to multiple sensory input. *Journal of Abnormal Psychology,* 77, 211–222.

Low, P.W., Jeffries, J.C., & Bonnie, R.J. (1986). *The trial of John W. Hinckley, Jr.: A case study in the insanity defense.* Mineola, NY: Foundation Press.

Luborsky, L. (1984). *Principles of psychoanalytic psychotherapy: A manual for supportive-expressive treatment.* New York: Basic Books.

Luborsky, L., Barber, J.P., & Beutler, L. (1993). Introduction to special section: A briefing on curative factors in dynamic psychotherapy. *Journal of Consulting and Clinical Psychology,* 61, 539–541.

Luborsky, L., Diguer, L., Luborsky, E., McLellan, A.T., Woody, G., & Alexander, L. (1993). Psychological health-sickness (PHS) as a predictor of outcomes in dynamic and other psychotherapies. *Journal of Consulting and Clinical Psychology,* 61, 542–548.

Luborsky, L., Singer, B., & Luborsky, L. (1975). Comparative studies of psychotherapy. *Archives of General Psychiatry,* 32, 995–1008.

Lubs, H.A. (1969). A marker X chromosome. *American Journal of Human Genetics,* 21, 231–244.

Lubs, M., & Maes, J. (1977). Recurrence risk in mental retardation. In P. Mittler (Ed.), *Research to practice in mental retardation,* vol. 3. Baltimore: University Park Press.

Luepnitz, D.A. (1982). *Child custody: A study of families after divorce.* Lexington, MA: Lexington Books.

Lukoff, D., Nuechterlein, K.H., & Ventura, J. (1986). Manual for expanded Brief Psychiatric Rating Scale (BPRS). *Schizophrenia Bulletin,* 12, 594–602.

Lykken, D.T. (1957). A study of anxiety in the sociopathic personality. *Journal of Abnormal and Social Psychology,* 55, 6–10.

Lyness, S.A. (1993). Predictors of differences between Type A and B individuals in heart rate and blood pressure reactivity. *Psychological Bulletin,* 114, 266–295.

Lyon, G.R. (1996). Learning disabilities. *Future of Children,* 6, 54–76.

Lyons, M.J. (1995). Epidemiology of personality disorders. In M.T. Tsuang, M. Tohen, & G.E.P. Zahner (Eds.), *Textbook in psychiatric epidemiology,* pp. 407–436. New York: Wiley.

Lyons, M.J., True, W.R., Eisen, S.A., Goldberg, J., Meyter, J.M., Faraone, S.V., Eaves, L.J., & Tsuang, M.T. (1995). Differential heritability of adult and juvenile antisocial traits. *Archives of General Psychiatry,* 52, 906–915.

Maccoby, E.E. (1992). The role of parents in the socialization of children: An historical overview. *Developmental Psychology,* 28, 1006–1017.

Maccoby, E.E., & Jacklin, C.N. (1974). *The psychology of sex differences.* Stanford: Stanford University Press.

Maccoby, E.E., & Martin, J.A. (1983). Socialization in the context of the family: Parent-child interaction. In E.M. Hetherington (Ed.), *Socialization, personality, and social development,* Vol. 4, *Handbook of child psychology* pp. 1–101. New York: Wiley.

Maccoby, E.E., & Mnookin, R.H. (1992). *Dividing the Child: Social and legal dilemmas of custody.* Cambridge, MA: Harvard University Press.

Mackay, A.V.P., Iversen, L.L., Rossor, M., Spokes, E., Bird, E., Arregui, A., Creese, I., & Snyder, S.H. (1982). Increased brain dopamine and dopamine receptors in schizophrenia. *Archives of General Psychiatry,* 39, 991–997.

Mackay, R.D. (1988). Post-Hinckley insanity in the U.S.A. *Criminal Law Review,* 88–96.

MacMillan, D.L., Gresham, F.M., & Siperstein, G.N. (1995). Heightened concerns over the 1992 AAMR definition: Advocacy versus precision. *American Journal on Mental Retardation,* 100, 87–97.

Maddi, S.R. (1980). *Personality theories: A comparative analysis,* 4th ed. Homewood, IL: Dorsey.

Magenis, R.E., Overton, K.M., Chamberlin, J., Brady, T., & Lovrien, E. (1977). Parental origin of the extra chromosome in Down's syndrome. *Human Genetics,* 37, 7–16.

Mahoney, M.J. (1991). *Human change processes: The scientific foundations of psychotherapy.* New York: Basic Books.

Maier, S.F., Watkins, L.R., & Fleshner, M. (1994). Psychoneuroimmunology: The interface between behavior, brain, and immunity. *American Psychologist,* 49, 1004–1017.

Maier, W., Lichtermann, D., Klingler, T., Heun, R., & Hallmayer, J. (1992). Prevalence of personality disorders (DSM-III-R) in the community. *Journal of Personality Disorders,* 6, 187–196.

Maier, W., Lichtermann, D., Minges, J., Oehrlein, A., & Franke, P. (1993). A controlled family study in panic disorder. *Journal of Psychiatric Research,* 27, (suppl. 1), 79–87.

Major, B., & Crocker, J. (1993). Social stigma: The consequences of attributional ambiguity. In D.M. Mackie & D.L. Hamilton (Eds.), *Affect, cognition, and stereotyping: Interactive processes in group perception,* pp. 345–370. San Diego, CA: Academic Press.

Mäkelä, K. (1986). Attitudes toward drinking and drunkenness in four Scandinavian countries. In T.F. Babor (Ed.), *Alcohol and culture: Comparative perspectives from Europe and America,* Vol. 472, pp. 21–32. New York: New York Academy of Sciences.

Mäkelä, K. (1994). Rates of attrition among the membership of Alcoholics Anonymous in Finland. *Journal of Studies on Alcohol,* 55, 91–95.

Malcolm, J.G. (1987). Treatment choices and informed consent in psychiatry: Implications of the Osheroff case for the profession. *Journal of Psychiatry and the Law,* 15, 9–81.

Maletzky, B.M. (1997). Exhibitionism: Assessment and treatment. In D.R. Laws & W.T. O'Donohue (Eds.), *Handbook of sexual deviance: Theory and application.* New York: Guilford.

Maltzman, I. (1989). A reply to Cook, "Craftsman versus professional: Analysis of the controlled drinking controversy." *Journal of Studies on Alcohol,* 50, 466–472.

Mandler, G. (1975). *Mind and emotion.* New York: Wiley.

Mandler, G. (1966). Anxiety. In D.L. Sills (Ed.), *International encyclopedia of the social sciences.* New York: Macmillan.

Mangone, C.A., Sanguinetti, R.M., Baumann, P.D., Gonzalez, R.C., et al. (1993). Influence of feelings of burden on the caregiver's perception of the patient's functional status. *Dementia, 4,* 287–293.

Mankoo, B., Sherrington, R., Brynjolfsson, J., Kalsi, G., Petursson, J., Sigmundsson, T., Read, T., Murphy, P., Curtis, D., Melmer, G., & Gurling, H. (1991). New microsatellite polymorphisms provide a highly polymorphic map of chromosome 5 bands q11.2-q 13.3 for linkage analysis of Icelandic and English families affected by schizophrenia. *Psychiatric Geriatrics, 2,* 17.

Mann, J.J., & Kupfer, D.J. (Eds.) (1993). *Biology of depressive disorders. Part A: A systems perspective.* New York: Plenum.

Mannuzza, S., Schneier, F.R., Chapman, T.F., Liebowitz, M.R., Klein, D.F., & Fyer, A.J. (1995). Generalized social phobia: Reliability and validity. *Archives of General Psychiatry, 52,* 230–237.

Manschreck, T.C. (1993). Psychomotor abnormalities. In C.G. Costello (Ed.), *Symptoms of schizophrenia,* pp. 261–290. New York: Wiley.

Manson, S.M. (1994). Culture and depression: Discovering variations in the experience of illness. In W.J. Lonner & R.S. Malpass (Eds.), *Psychology and culture,* pp. 285–290. Boston: Allyn & Bacon.

March, J.S., Leonard, H.L., & Swedo, S.E. (1995). Obsessive-compulsive disorder. In J.S. March (Ed.), *Anxiety disorders in children and adolescents,* pp. 251–275. New York: Guilford.

Marcia, J.E. (1966). Development and validation of ego-identity status. *Journal of Personality and Social Psychology, 24,* 551–558.

Marcia, J.E. (1994). The empirical study of ego identity. In H.A. Bosma, T.L.G. Graafsma, H.D. Grotevant, & D.J. de Levita (Eds.), *Identity and development,* pp. 67–80. Thousand Oaks, CA: Sage.

Marder, K., Tang, M., Cote, L., & Stern, Y. (1995). The frequency and associated risk factors for dementia in patients with Parkinson's disease. *Archives of Neurology, 52,* 695–701.

Marder, S.R., Ames, D., Wirshing, W.C., & Van Putten, T. (1993). Schizophrenia. *Psychiatric Clinics of North America, 16,* 567–587.

Marengo, J.T., & Harrow, M. (1993). Thought disorder. In C.G. Costello (Ed.), *Symptoms of schizophrenia,* pp. 27–55. New York: Wiley.

Margolin, G. (1981). Behavior exchange in happy and unhappy marriages: A family cycle perspective. *Behavior Therapy, 12,* 329–343.

Margolin, G. (1987). Marital therapy: A cognitive-behavioral approach. In N.S. Jacobson (Ed.), *Psychotherapists in clinical practice,* pp. 232–285. New York: Guilford.

Margolin, G., Christensen, A., & John, R.S. (1996). The continuance and spillover of everyday tensions in distressed and nondistressed families. *Journal of Family Psychology, 10,* 304–321.

Margraf, J., Barlow, D.H., Clark, D.M., & Telch, M.J. (1993). Psychological treatment of panic: Work in progress on outcome, active ingredients, and follow-up. *Behaviour Research and Therapy, 31,* 1–8.

Margulis, L., & Sagan, D. (1991). *Mystery dance: On the evolution of human sexuality.* New York: Summit.

Markman, H.J., Floyd, F.J., Stanley, S.M., & Storaasli, R.D. (1988). Prevention of marital distress: A longitudinal investigation. *Journal of Consulting and Clinical Psychology, 56,* 210–217.

Markman, H.J., Renick, M.J., Floyd, F.J., Stanley, S.M., & Clements, M. (1993). Preventing marital distress through communication and conflict management training: A 4- and 5-year follow-up. *Journal of Consulting and Clinical Psychology, 61,* 70–77.

Markova, I.S., & Berrios, G.E. (1992). The meaning of insight in clinical psychiatry. *British Journal of Psychiatry, 160,* 850–860.

Markovitz, P.J., Calabrese, J.R., Schulz, C.S., & Meltzer, H.Y. (1991). Fluoxetine in the treatment of borderline and schizotypal personality disorders. *American Journal of Psychiatry, 148,* 1064–1067.

Marks, I.M. (1987). *Fears, phobias, and rituals: Panic, anxiety, and their disorders.* New York: Oxford University Press.

Marks, I.M., & Nesse, R.M. (1994). Fear and fitness: An evolutionary analysis of anxiety disorders. *Ethology and Sociobiology, 15,* 247–261.

Marks, I.M., Swinson, R.P., Basoglu, M., Kuch, K., Noshirvani, H., O'Sullivan, G., Lelliott, P.T., Kirby, M., McNamee, G., Sengun, S., & Wickwire, K. (1993). Alprazolam and exposure alone and combined in panic disorder with agoraphobia: A controlled study in London and Toronto. *British Journal of Psychiatry, 162,* 776–787.

Marlatt, G.A. (1985). Relapse prevention: Theoretical rationale and overview of the model. In G.A. Marlatt & J.R. Gordon (Eds.), *Relapse prevention.* New York: Guilford.

Marlatt, G.A. (1987). Alcohol, the magic elixir: Stress, expectancy, and the transformation of emotional states. In E. Gottheil, K.A. Druley, S. Pashko, & S.P. Weinstein (Eds.), *Stress and addiction,* pp. 302–322. New York: Brunner/Mazel.

Marlatt, G.A. (1996). Models of relapse and relapse prevention: A commentary. *Experimental and Clinical Psychopharmacology, 4,* 55–60.

Marlatt, G.A., & Baer, J.S. (1988). Addictive behaviors: Etiology and treatment. *Annual Review of Psychology, 39,* 223–252.

Marlatt, G.A., Baer, J.S., Donovan, D.M., & Kivlahan, D.R. (1988). Addictive behaviors: Etiology and treatment. *Annual Review of Psychology, 39,* 223–252.

Marlatt, G.A., & Rohsenow, D.J. (1980). Cognitive processes in alcohol use: Expectancy and the balanced placebo design. In N.K. Mello (Ed.), *Advances in substance abuse,* Vol. 1, pp. 159–199. Greenwich, Conn: JAL Press.

Marques, J.K., Day, D.M., Nelson, C., & West, M.A. (1993). Findings and recommendations from California's experimental treatment program. In G.C.N. Hall, R. Hirschman, J.R. Graham, & M.S. Zaragoza (Eds.), *Sexual aggression: Issues in etiology, assessment, and treatment,* pp. 197–214. Washington, DC: Hemisphere.

Marques, J.K., Day, D.M., Nelson, C., & West, M.A. (1994). Effects of cognitive-behavioral treatment on sex offender recidivism: Preliminary results of a longitudinal study. *Criminal Justice and Behavior, 21,* 28–54.

Marsella, A.J., Sartorius, N., Jablensky, A., & Fenton, F.R. (1985). Cross-cultural studies of depressive disorders: An overview. In A. Kleinman & B. Good (Eds.), *Culture and depression: Studies in the anthropology and cross-cultural psychiatry of affect and disorder,* pp. 299–324. Berkeley: University of California.

Marshall, R.D., & Klein, D.F. (1995). Pharmacotherapy in the treatment of posttraumatic stress disorder. *Psychiatric Annals, 25,* 588–597.

Marshall, W.L. (1989). Intimacy, loneliness, and sexual offenders. *Behaviour Research and Therapy, 27,* 491–503.

Marshall, W.L., Bryce, P., Hudson, S.M., Ward, T., & Moth, B. (1996). The enhancement of intimacy and the reduction of loneliness among child molesters. *Journal of Family Violence, 11,* 219–236.

Marshall, W.L., Hudson, S.M., & Ward, T. (1992). Sexual deviance. In P.H. Wilson (Ed.), *Principles and practice of relapse prevention.* New York: Guilford.

Marshall, W.L., Jones, R., Ward, T., et al. (1991). Treatment outcome with sex offenders. *Clinical Psychology Review, 11,* 465–485.

Marshall, W.L., Payne, K., Barbaree, H.E., & Eccles, A. (1991). Exhibitionists: Sexual preferences for exposing. *Behaviour Research and Therapy, 29,* 37–40.

Marshall, W.L., & Pithers, W.D. (1994). A reconsideration of treatment outcome with sex offenders. *Criminal Justice and Behavior, 21,* 10–27.

Martin, C.S., & Sayette, M.A. (1993). Experimental design in alcohol administration research: Limitations and alternatives in the manipulation of dosage-set. *Journal of Studies on Alcohol, 54,* 750–761.

Marwit, S.J. (1996). Reliability of diagnosing complicated grief: A preliminary investigation.

Journal of Consulting and Clinical Psychology, 64, 563–568.

Mash, E.J., & Johnston, C. (1982). A comparison of the mother-child interactions of younger and older hyperactive and normal children. *Child Development, 53,* 1371–1381.

Maslow, A.H. (1970). *Motivation and personality,* 2nd ed. New York: Harper & Row.

Mason, F.L. (1997). Fetishism: Psychopathology and theory. In D.R. Laws & W.T. O'Donohue (Eds.), *Handbook of sexual deviance: Theory and application.* New York: Guilford.

Masters, W.H., & Johnson, V.E. (1966). *Human sexual response.* Boston: Little Brown.

Masters, W.H., & Johnson, V.E. (1970). *Human sexual inadequacy.* Boston: Little Brown.

Masters, W.H., Johnson, V.E., & Kolodny, R.C. (1994). *Heterosexuality.* New York: HarperPerennial.

Matarazzo, J.D. (1983). The reliability of psychiatric and psychological diagnosis. *Clinical Psychology Review, 3,* 103–145.

Mate-Kole, C., Freschi, M., & Robin, A. (1988). Aspects of psychiatric symptoms at different stages in the treatment of transsexualism. *British Journal of Psychiatry, 152,* 550–553.

Mathews, A. (1990). Why worry: The cognitive function of anxiety. *Behaviour Research and Therapy, 28,* 455–468.

Matson, J.L., & Frame, C.L. (1986). *Psychopathology among mentally retarded children and adolescents.* Beverly Hills, CA: Sage.

Matthews, K.A. (1988). Coronary heart disease and Type A behaviors: Update on and alternative to the Booth-Kewley and Friedman (1987) quantitative review. *Psychological Bulletin,* 373–380.

Matthysse, S., & Pope, A. (1986). The neuropathology of psychiatric disorders. In P. Berger & K.H. Brodie (Eds.), *American handbook of psychiatry,* 2nd ed., Vol. 8, pp. 151–159. New York: Basic Books.

Max, W. (1993). The economic impact of Alzheimer's disease. *Neurology, 43,* (suppl. 4), S6–S10.

May, R. (1967). *Psychology and the human dilemma.* New York: Van Nostrand Reinhold.

McBride, W.J., Murphy, J.M., Yoshimoto, K., Lumeng, L., & Li, T.K. (1993). Serotonin mechanisms in alcohol-drinking behavior. *Drug Development Research, 30,* 170–177.

McCabe, M.P., McDonald, E., Deeks, A., Vowels, L.M., & Cobain, M.J. (1996). The impact of multiple sclerosis on sexuality and relationships. *Journal of Sex Research, 33,* 241–249.

McCann, U.D., Rossiter, E.M., King, R.J., & Agras, W.S. (1991). Nonpurging bulimia: A distinct subtype of bulimia nervosa. *International Journal of Eating Disorders, 10,* 679–687.

McCarthy, B.W. (1989). Cognitive-behavioral strategies and techniques in the treatment of early ejaculation. In S.R. Leiblum & R.C. Rosen (Eds.), *Principles and practice of sex therapy,* 2nd ed. New York: Guilford.

McCaul, M.E., Turkkan, J.S., & Stitzer, J.L. (1989). Conditioned opponent responses: Effects of placebo challenge in alcoholic subjects. *Alcoholism: Clinical and Experimental Research, 13,* 631–635.

McConaghy, N. (1990). Sexual deviation. In A.S. Bellack, M. Hersen, & A.E. Kazdin (Eds.), *International handbook of behavior modification and therapy,* 2nd ed. New York: Plenum.

McConaghy, N. (1994). Sexual deviations. In M. Hersen, R.T. Ammerman, & L.A. Sisson (Eds.), *Handbook of aggressive and destructive behavior in psychiatric patients,* pp. 261–286. New York: Plenum.

McDougle, C.J., Price, L.H., & Volkmar, F.R. (1994). Recent advances in the pharmacotherapy of autism and related conditions. *Child and Adolescent Psychiatric Clinics of North America, 3,* 71–89.

McElroy, S.L., Keck, P.E., Pope, H.G., & Hudson, J.I. (1992). Valproate in the treatment of bipolar disorder: Literature review and clinical guidelines. *Journal of Clinical Psychopharmacology, 12* (1, suppl), 42–52.

McElroy, S.L., Pope, H.G., Keck, P.E., & Hudson, J.I. (1995). Disorders of impulse control. In E. Hollander & D.J. Stein (Eds.), *Impulsivity and aggression,* pp. 109–136. Chichester, England: Wiley.

McFall, R.M. (1982). A review and reformulation of the concept of social skills. *Behavioral Assessment, 4,* 1–33.

McFall, R.M. (1990) The enhancement of social skills: An information-processing analysis. In. W.L. Marshall, D.R. Laws, & H.E. Barbaree (Eds.), *Handbook of sexual assault: Issues, theories, and treatment of the offender.* New York: Plenum.

McFall, R.M. (1991). Manifesto for a science of clinical psychology. *Clinical Psychologist, 44,* 75–88.

McFall, R.M. (1995). Models of training and standards of care. In S.C. Hayes, V.M. Folette, R.M. Dawes, & K.E. Grady (Eds.), *Scientific standards of psychological practice: Issues and recommendations,* pp. 125–137. Reno, NV: Context Press.

McFall, R.M., & McDonel, E.C. (1986). The continuing search for units of analysis in psychology: Beyond persons, situations, and their interactions. In R.O. Nelson & S.C. Hayes (Eds.), *Conceptual foundations of behavioral assessment,* pp. 201–241. New York: Guilford.

McGeer, P.L., & McGeer, E.G. (1996). Anti-inflammatory drugs in the fight against Alzheimer's disease. *Annals of the New York Academy of Sciences, 777,* 213–220.

McFarlane, A.C. (1988). The longitudinal course of posttraumatic morbidity. *Journal of Nervous and Mental Disease, 1976,* 30–39.

McGlashan, T. (1986). The Chestnut Lodge follow-up study. III. Long-term outcome of borderline personalities. *Archives of General Psychiatry, 43,* 20–30.

McGowin, D.F. (1993). *Living in the labyrinth: A personal journey through the maze of Alzheimer's.* New York: Delacorte.

McGue, M. (1993). From proteins to cognitions: The behavioral genetics of alcoholism. In R. Plomin & G.E. McClearn (Eds.), *Nature, nurture, and psychology.* Washington, DC: American Psychological Association.

McGue, M., & Lykken, D.T. (1992). Genetic influence on risk of divorce. *Psychological Science, 3,* 368–373.

McGue, M., Pickins, R.W., & Svikis, D.S. (1992). Sex and age effects on the inheritance of alcohol problems: A twin study. *Journal of Abnormal Psychology, 101,* 3–17.

McGuffin, P., Farmer, A.E., & Gottesman, I.I. (1987). Is there really a split in schizophrenia? The genetic evidence, *British Journal of Psychiatry, 150,* 581–592.

McGuffin, P., Farmer, A.E., Gottesman, I.I., Murray, R.M., & Reveley, A.M. (1984). Twin concordance for operationally defined schizophrenia. *Archives of General Psychiatry, 41,* 541–545.

McGuffin, P., & Gottesman, I.I. (1985). Genetic influences on normal and abnormal development. In M. Rutter & L. Hersov (Eds.), *Child and adolescent psychiatry,* pp. 17–33. Oxford: Blackwell.

McGuffin, P., Katz, R., Watkins, S., & Rutherford, J. (1996). A hospital-based twin register of the heritability of DSM-IV unipolar depression. *Archives of General Psychiatry, 53,* 129–136.

McGuffin, P., Owen, M.J., O'Donovan, M.C., Thapar, A., & Gottesman, I.I. (1994). *Seminars in psychiatry genetics.* London: Gaskell.

McGuffin, P., Sargeant, M., Hett, G., Tidmarsh, S., Whatley, S., & Marchbanks, R.M. (1990). Exclusion of a schizophrenia susceptibility gene from the chromosome 5q11-q13 region. New data and a reanalysis of previous reports. *American Journal of Human Genetics, 47,* 524–535.

McKey, R.H., Condelli, L., Granson, H., Barrett, B., McConkey, C., & Plantz, M. (1985, June). *The impact of Head Start on children, families, and communities.* Final Report of the Head Start Evaluation, Synthesis and Utilization Project. Washington, DC: CSR.

McKim, W.A. (1997). *Drugs and behavior,* 3rd ed. Upper Saddle River, NJ: Prentice Hall.

McLellan, A.T., O'Brien, C.P., Metzger, D., Alterman, A.I., Cornish, J., & Urschel, H. (1992). How effective is substance abuse treatment—Compared to what? In C.P. O'Brien & J.H. Jaffe (Eds.), *Addictive states*, pp. 231–251. New York: Raven.

McLellan, A.T., Woody, G.E., & Metzger, D. (1996). Evaluating the effectiveness of addiction treatments: Reasonable expectations, appropriate comparisons. *Milbank Quarterly*, 74, 51.

McLemore, C.W., & Benjamin, L.A. (1979). Whatever happened to interpersonal diagnosis? A psychosocial alternative to DSM-III. *American Psychologist*, 34, 17–34.

McNally, R.J. (1987). Preparedness and phobias: A review. *Psychological Bulletin*, 101, 283–303.

McNally, R.J. (1990). Psychological approaches to panic disorder: A review. *Psychological Bulletin*, 108, 403–419.

McNeal, E.T., & Cimbolic, P. (1986). Antidepressants and biochemical theories of depression. *Psychological Bulletin*, 99, 361–374.

McNeil, T.F., Cantor-Graae, E., Sjostrom, K., et al. (1994). Obstetric complications as antecedents of schizophrenia: Empirical effects of using different obstetric complication scales. *Journal of Psychiatric Research*, 28, 519–530.

McNeil, T.F., Cantor-Graae, E., Torrey, E.F., Sjostrom, K., et al. (1994). Obstetric complications in histories of monozygotic twins discordant and concordant for schizophrenia. *Acta Psychiatrica Scandinavica*, 89, 196–204.

McReynolds, P. (1986). History of assessment in clinical and educational settings. In R.O. Nelson, & S.C. Hayes (Eds.), *Conceptual foundations of behavioral assessment*. New York: Guilford.

Mechanic, D. (1986). The concept of illness behavior: Culture, situation and personal predisposition. *Psychological Medicine*, 16, 1–7.

Mednick, S.A., & McNeil, T. (1968). Current methodology in research on the etiology of schizophrenia. *Psychological Bulletin*, 70, 681–693.

Mednick, S.A., & Schulsinger, F. (1968). Some premorbid characteristics related to breakdown in children with schizophrenic mothers. *Journal of Psychiatric Research* (Suppl. 1), 6, 354–362.

Meehl, P.E. (1962). Schizotaxia, schizotypy, schizophrenia. *American Psychologist*, 17, 827–838.

Meehl, P.E. (1990). Toward an integrated theory of schizotaxia, schizotypy, and schizophrenia. *Journal of Personality Disorders*, 4, 1–99.

Meehl, P.E. (1993). The origins of some of my conjectures concerning schizophrenia. In L.J. Chapman, J.P. Chapman, & D. Fowles (Eds.), *Progress in experimental personality and psychopathology research*, pp. 1–11. New York: Springer.

Melchior, C.L., & Tabakoff, B. (1985). Features of environment-dependent tolerance to ethanol. *Psychopharmacology*, 87, 94–100.

Mellor, C.S. (1982). The present status of first rank symptoms. *British Journal of Psychiatry*, 40, 423–424.

Melman, A., & Tiefer, L. (1992). Surgery for erectile disorders: Operative procedures and psychological issues. In R.C. Rosen and S.R. Leiblum (Eds.), *Erectile disorders: Assessment and treatment*, pp. 255–282. New York: Guilford.

Melton, G.B., & Limber, S. (1989). Psychologists' involvement in cases of child maltreatment: Limits of roles and expertise. *American Psychologist*, 44, 1225–1233.

Melton, G., Petrila, J., Poythress, N., & Slobogin, C. (1987). *Psychological evaluations for the courts*. New York: Guilford.

Meltzer, H.Y. (1985). Dopamine and negative symptoms in schizophrenia: Critique of the Type I-II hypothesis. In M. Alpert (Ed.), *Controversies in schizophrenia: Changes and constancies*, pp. 110–136. New York: Guilford.

Meltzer, H.Y. (1990). Clozapine: Mechanisms of action in relation to its clinical advantages. In A. Kales, C.N. Stefanis, & J. Talbott (Eds.), *Recent advances in schizophrenia*, pp. 237–256. New York: Springer.

Meltzer, H.Y. (1992). The role of dopamine in schizophrenia. In J. Lindenmayer & S.R. Kay (Eds.), *New biological vistas on schizophrenia*. New York: Brunner/Mazel.

Meltzer, H.Y. (1993). Serotonin-dopamine interactions and atypical antipsychotic drugs. *Psychiatric Annals*, 23, 193–200.

Mendelson, J.H., & Mello, N.K. (1989). Studies of alcohol: Past, present and future. *Journal of Studies on Alcohol*, 50, 293–296.

Mendez, M.F., Selwood, A., Mastrie, A.R., & Frey, W.H. (1993). Pick's disease versus Alzheimer's disease: A comparison of clinical characteristics. *Neurology*, 43, 289–292.

Merckelbach, H., de Ruiter, C., van den Hout, M.A., & Hoekstra, R. (1989). Conditioning experiences and phobias. *Behavior Research and Therapy*, 27, 657–662.

Merikangas, K.R. (1990). The genetic epidemiology of alcoholism. *Psychological medicine*, 20, 11–22.

Merikangas, K.R., & Gelernter, C.S. (1990). Comorbidity for alcoholism and depression. *Psychiatric Clinics of North America*, 13, 613–632.

Merikangas, K.R., Risch, N.J., & Weissman, M.M. (1994). Comorbidity and co-transmission of alcoholism, anxiety and depression. *Psychological Medicine*, 24, 69–80.

Merrick, J.C. (1993). Maternal substance abuse during pregnancy: Policy implications in the United States. *Journal of Legal Medicine*, 14, 57–71.

Mersky, H. (1992). The manufacture of personalities: The production of multiple

personality disorder. *British Journal of Psychiatry*, 160, 327–340.

Messick, S. (1989). Validity. In R.L. Linn (Ed.), *Educational measurement*, 3rd ed. New York: American Council on Education/Macmillan.

Mesulam, M. (1981). Dissociative states with abnormal temporal lobe EEG. *Archives of Neurology*, 38, 176–181.

Metalsky, G.I., Joiner, T.E., Hardin, T.S., & Abramson, L.Y. (1993). Depressive reactions to failure in a naturalistic setting: A test of the hopelessness and self-esteem theories of depression. *Journal of Abnormal Psychology*, 102, 101–109.

Migliorelli, R., Teson, A., Sabe, L., Petracchi, M., Leiguarda, R., & Starkstein, S.E. (1995). Prevalence and correlates of dysthymia and major depression among patients with Alzheimer's disease. *American Journal of Psychiatry*, 152, 37–45.

Miklowitz, D.J., Doane, J.A., et al. (1989). Is expressed emotion an index of a transactional process? I. Parents' affective style. *Family Process*, 28, 153–167.

Miklowitz, D.J., Goldstein, M.J., & Nuechterlein, K.H. (1995). Verbal interactions in the families of schizophrenic and bipolar affective patients. *Journal of Abnormal Psychology*, 104, 268–276.

Miklowitz, D.J., Goldstein, M.J., Nuechterlein, K.H., Snyder, K.S., & Mintz, J. (1988). Family factors and the course of bipolar affective disorder. *Archives of General Psychiatry*, 45, 225–231.

Miller, G.A., & Kozak, M.J. (1993). Three-systems assessment and the construct of emotion. In N. Birbaumer & A. Ohman (Eds.), *The structure of emotion: Psychophysiological, cognitive, and clinical aspects*, pp. 31–47. Seattle: Hogrefe & Huber.

Miller, N.S. (1991). *Comprehensive handbook of drug and alcohol addiction*, New York: Marcel Dekker.

Miller, N.S., Belkin, B.M., & Gold, M.S. (1991). Alcohol and drug dependence among the elderly: Epidemiology, diagnosis, and treatment. *Comprehensive Psychiatry*, 32, 153–165.

Miller, P.M. (1987). Commonalities of addictive behaviors. In T.D. Nirenberg & S.A. Maisto (Eds.), *Developments in the assessment and treatment of addictive behaviors*. Norwood, NJ: Ablex.

Miller, T.Q., Smith, T.W., Turner, C.W., Guijarro, M.L., & Hallet, A.J. (1996). A meta-analytic review of research on hostility and physical health. *Psychological Bulletin*, 119, 322–348.

Miller, T.W. (1989). *Stressful life events*. Madison, CT: International Universities Press.

Miller, W.R., & Kurtz, E. (1994). Models of alcoholism used in treatment: Contrasting AA and other perspectives with which it is often confused. *Journal of Studies on Alcohol*, 55, 159–166.

Miller, W.R., & Lief, H.I. (1976). Masturbatory attitudes, knowledge and experience: Data from the

Sex Knowledge and Attitude Test (SKAT): *Archives of Sexual Behavior, 5,* 447–468.

Miller-Johnson, S., Emery, R.E., Marvin, R.S., Clarke, W., Lovinger, R., & Martin, M. (1994). Parent-child relationships and the management of insulin-dependent diabetes mellitus. *Journal of Consulting and Clinical Psychology, 62,* 603–610.

Millon, T. (1981). *Disorders of personality.* New York: Wiley.

Millon, T., & Everly, G.S. (1985). *Personality and its disorders.* New York: Wiley.

Millon, T., & Martinez, A. (1995). Avoidant personality disorder. In W.J. Livesley (Ed.), *The DSM-IV personality disorders,* pp. 218–233. New York: Guilford.

Mindus, P., & Jenike, M.A. (1992). Neurosurgical treatment of malignant obsessive-compulsive disorder. *Psychiatric Clinics of North America, 15,* 921–926.

Mineka, S. (1985). Animal models of anxiety-based disorders: Their usefulness and limitations. In A.H. Tuma & J. Maser (Eds.), *Anxiety and the anxiety disorders,* Hillsdale, NJ: Erlbaum.

Mineka, S., & Cook, M. (1993). Mechanisms involved in the observational conditioning of fear. *Journal of Experimental Psychology: General, 122,* 23–38.

Mineka, S., & Kihlstrom, J.F. (1978). Unpredictable and uncontrollable events: A new perspective on experimental neurosis. *Journal of Abnormal Psychology, 87,* 256–271.

Mineka, S., & Zinbarg, R. (1995). Conditioning and ethological models of social phobia. In R.G. Heimberg, M.R. Liebowitz, D.A. Hope, & F.R. Schneier (Eds.), *Social phobia: Diagnosis, assessment, and treatment,* pp. 134–162. New York: Guilford.

Minthon, L., Edvinsson, L., & Gustafson, L. (1994). Tacrine treatment modifies cerebrospinal fluid neuropeptide levels in Alzheimer's disease. *Dementia, 5,* 295–301.

Minuchin, P. (1985). Families and individual development: Provocations from the field of family therapy. *Child Development, 56,* 289–302.

Minuchin, S. (1974). *Families and family therapy.* Cambridge, MA: Harvard University Press.

Minuchin, S., Rosman, B.L., & Baker, L. (1978). *Psychosomatic families.* Cambridge, MA: Harvard University Press.

Mischel, W. (1968). *Personality and assessment.* New York: Wiley.

Mischel, W. (1983). Delay of gratification as process and as person variable in development. In D. Magnusson & V.L. Allen (Eds.), *Human development: An interactional perspective.* New York: Academic Press.

Mishler, E.G., & Waxler, N.E. (1968). *Interaction in families: An experimental study of family processes and schizophrenia.* New York: Wiley.

Mitchell, J.E., Pyle, R.L., Eckert, E.D., Hatsukami, D., Pomeroy, C., & Zimmerman, R. (1990). A comparison study of antidepressants and structured intensive group psychotherapy in the treatment of bulimia nervosa. *Archives of General Psychiatry, 47,* 149–157.

Mitchell, J.E., Raymond, N., & Specker, S. (1993). A review of controlled trials of pharmacotherapy and psychotherapy in the treatment of bulimia nervosa. *International Journal of Eating Disorders, 14,* 229–247.

Mittelman, M.S., Ferris, S.H., Shulman, E., Steinberg, G., Ambinder, A., & Mackell, J. (1997). Effects of a multicomponent support program on spouse-caregivers of Alzheimer's disease patients: Results of a treatment/control study. In L. Heston (Ed.), *Progress in Alzheimer's disease and similar conditions.* Washington, DC: American Psychiatric Press.

Mitterauer, B. (1990). A contribution to the discussion of the role of the genetic factor in suicide, based on five studies in an epidemiologically defined area. *Comprehensive Psychiatry, 31,* 557–565.

Mnookin, R.H. (1975). Child-custody adjudication: Judicial functions in the face of indeterminancy. *Law and Contemporary Problems, 88,* 226–293.

Mnookin, R.H. (1985). *In the interest of children: Advocacy, law reform, and public policy.* New York: Freeman.

Moffitt, T.E. (1993). Adolescence-limited and life-course-persistent antisocial behavior: A developmental taxonomy. *Psychological Review, 100,* 674–701.

Mohr, D.C., & Beutler, L.E. (1990). Erectile dysfunction: A review of diagnostic and treatment procedures. *Clinical Psychology Review, 10,* 123–150.

Moldin, S.O., Reich, T., & Rice, J.P. (1991). Current perspectives on the genetics of unipolar depression. *Behavior Genetics, 21,* 211–242.

Monahan, J. (1980). *Who is the client? The ethics of psychological intervention in the criminal justice system.* Washington, DC: American Psychological Association.

Monahan, J. (1992). Mental disorder and violent behavior: Perceptions and evidence. *American Psychologist, 47,* 511–521.

Monahan, J. (1993). Limiting therapist exposure to Tarasoff liability: Guidelines for risk containment. *American Psychologist, 48,* 242–250.

Money, J. (1984). Paraphilias: Phenomenology and classification. *American Journal of Psychotherapy, 38,* 164–179.

Money, J. (1987). Masochism: On the childhood origin of paraphilia, opponent-process theory, and antiandrogen therapy. *Journal of Sex Research, 23,* 273–275.

Monroe, S.M., & Simons, A.D. (1991). Diathesis-stress theories in the context of life stress research: Implications for the depressive disorders. *Psychological Bulletin, 110,* 406–425.

Monroe, S.M., & Wade, S.L. (1988). Life events. In C.G. Last & M. Hersen (Eds.), *Handbook of anxiety disorders.* New York: Pergamon.

Montgomery, H.A., Miller, W.R., & Tonigan, J.S. (1993). Differences among AA groups: Implications for research. *Journal of Studies on Alcohol, 54,* 502–504.

Moos, R.H. (1974a). *Family Environment Scale (Form R).* Palo Alto, CA: Consulting Psychologists Press.

Moos, R.H. (1974b). *Evaluating treatment environments: A social ecological approach.* New York: Wiley.

Moos, R.H. (1981). *Work environment scale manual.* Palo Alto, CA: Consulting Psychologists Press.

Morey, L.C. (1988). Personality disorders in DSM-III and DSM-III-R: Convergence, coverage, and internal consistency. *American Journal of Psychiatry, 145,* 573–577.

Morokoff, P.J. (1978). Determinants of female orgasm. In J. LoPiccolo & L. LoPiccolo (Eds.), *Handbook of sex therapy.* New York: Plenum.

Morokoff, P.J. (1989). Sex bias and POD. *American Psychologist,* 73–75.

Morris, J. (1995). Dementia and cognitive changes in Huntington's disease. In W.J. Weiner & A.E. Lang (Eds.), *Behavioral neurology of movement disorders. Advances in neurology,* Vol. 65, pp. 187–200. New York: Raven Press.

Morrow, J., & Nolen-Hoeksema, S. (1990). The effects of responses to depression on the remediation of depressive affect. *Journal of Personality and Social Psychology, 58,* 519–527.

Morse, K.L. (1990). A uniform testimonial privilege for mental health professionals, *Ohio State Law Journal, 51,* 741–757.

Moscicki, E.K. (1995). Epidemiology of suicidal behavior. *Suicide and life-threatening behavior, 25,* 22–35.

Mueser, K.T., Bellack, A.S., Douglas, M.S., & Morrison, R.L. (1991). Prevalence and stability of social skill deficits in schizophrenia. *Schizophrenia Research, 5,* 167–176.

Mulligan, T., Retchin, S.M., Chinchilli, V.M., & Bettinger, C.B. (1988). The role of aging and chronic disease in sexual dysfunction. *Journal of the American Geriatrics Society, 36,* 520–524.

Mumford, D.B., Whitehouse, A.M., & Platts, M. (1991). Sociocultural correlates of eating disorders among Asian schoolgirls in Bradford. *British Journal of Psychiatry, 158,* 222–228.

Munoz, R.F., Hollon, S.D., McGrath, E., Rehm, L.P. et al. (1994). On the AHCPR depression in primary care guidelines: Further considerations for practitioners. *American Psychologist*, 49, 42–61.

Murphy, E., & Macdonald, A. (1992). Affective disorders in old age. In E.S. Paykel (Ed.), *Handbook of affective disorders*, 2nd ed. Pp. 601–618. New York: Guilford.

Murphy, G.E., Simons, A.D., Wetzel, R.D., & Lustman, P.J. (1984). Cognitive therapy and pharmacotherapy, singly and together, in the treatment of depression. *Archives of General Psychiatry*, 41, 33–41.

Murphy, J.M. (1976). Psychiatric labeling in cross-cultural perspective. *Science*, 191, 1019–1028.

Murphy, W.D. (1997). Exhibitionism: Psychopathology and theory. In D.R. Laws & W.T. O'Donohue (Eds.), *Handbook of sexual deviance: Theory and application*, New York: Guilford.

Myers, J.E.B. (1983–84). Involuntary civil commitment of the mentally ill: A system in need of change. *Villanova Law Review*, 29, 367–433.

Myers, J.K., & Weissman, M.M. (1980). Screening for depression in a community sample: The use of a self-report scale to detect the depressive syndrome. *American Journal of Psychiatry*, 137, 1081–1084.

Nasser, M. (1986). Comparative study of the prevalence of abnormal eating attitudes among Arab female students of both London and Cairo universities. *Psychological Medicine*, 16, 621–625.

Nathan, P.E. (1993). Alcoholism: Psychopathology, etiology, and treatment. In P.B. Sutker & H.E. Adams (Eds.), *Comprehensive handbook of psychopathology*, 2nd ed. pp. 451–476. New York: Plenum.

Nathan, S.G. (1986). The epidemiology of the DSM-III psychosexual dysfunctions. *Journal of Sex and Marital Therapy*, 12, 267–281.

National Academy of Sciences, Institute of Medicine (1989). *Research on children & adolescents with mental, behavioral, and developmental disorders.* Washington, DC: National Academy Press.

National Advisory Mental Health Council. (1995). *Basic behavioral science research for mental health: A national investment.* Rockville, MD: National Institute of Mental Health.

National Institute of Mental Health. (1985). *Annual survey of patient characteristics—1985 state and county mental hospital inpatient services.* Rockville, MD.

National Victims Center. (1992). *Crime and victimization in America: Statistical overview.* Arlington, VA.

Neal, A.M., & Turner, S.M. (1991). Anxiety disorders research with African Americans: Current status. *Psychological Bulletin*, 109, 400–410.

Neale, J.M., Cox, D.S., Valdimarsdottir, H., & Stone, A.A. (1988). The relation between immunity and

health: Comment on Pennebaker, Kiecolt-Glaser, and Glaser. *Journal of Consulting and Clinical Psychology*, 56, 636–637.

Neale, J.M., & Oltmanns, T.F. (1980). *Schizophrenia.* New York: Wiley.

Neisser, U., & Harsch, N. (1992). Phantom flashbulbs: False recollections of hearing the news about *Challenger*. In E. Winograd & U. Neisser (Eds.), *Affect and accuracy in recall: Studies of "flashbulb" memories*, pp. 9–31. New York: Cambridge University Press.

Nemeroff, C.B., & Bissette, G. (1986). Neuropeptides in psychiatric disorders. In P. Berger & K.H. Brodie (Eds.), *Biological psychiatry*, pp. 64–110. New York: Basic Books.

Nestadt, G., Romanoski, A.J., Chahal, R., Merchant, A., Folstein, J.F., Gruenberg, E.M., & McHugh, P.R. (1990). An epidemiological study of histrionic personality disorder. *Psychological Medicine*, 20, 413–422.

Newcomb, M.D. (1993). 4 Theories of rape in American society. *Archives of Sexual Behavior*, 22, 373–377.

Newhouse, P.A. (1997). Alzheimer's disease and the cholinergic system: An introduction to clinical pharmacological research. In L. Heston (Ed.), *Progress in Alzheimer's disease and similar conditions.* Washington, DC: American Psychiatric Press.

Newlin, D.B., & Thomson, J.B. (1991). Chronic tolerance and sensitization to alcohol in sons of alcoholics. *Alcoholism: Clinical and Experimental Research*, 15, 399–405.

Newman, J.P., & Kosson, D.S. (1986). Passive avoidance learning in psychopathic and nonpsychopathic offenders. *Journal of Abnormal Psychology*, 95, 257–263.

Newman, J.P., Kosson, D.S., & Patterson, C.M. (1992). Delay of gratification in psychopathic and nonpsychopathic offenders. *Journal of Abnormal Psychology*, 101, 630–636.

Newton, R.D. (1948). The identity of Alzheimer's disease and senile dementia and their relationship to senility. *Journal of Mental Science*, 94, 225–249.

Niebuhr, R. (1951). To be abased and to abound. *Messenger*, February 13, p. 7.

Nietzel, M.T., Bernstein, D.A., & Milich, R. (1994). *Introduction to clinical psychology*, 4th ed. Englewood Cliffs, NJ: Prentice Hall.

Nigg, J.T., & Goldsmith, H.H. (1994). Genetics of personality disorders: Perspectives from personality and psychopathology research. *Psychological Bulletin*, 115, 346–380.

Nisbett, R.E., & Wilson, T.D. (1977). Telling more than we can know: Verbal reports on mental processes. *Psychological Review*, 84, 231–259.

Nolen-Hoeksema, S. (1989). Life-span views on depression. In P.B. Baltes, D.L. Featherman, & R.M. Lerner (Eds.), *Life-span development and behavior*, Vol. 9, pp. 203–241. Hillsdale, NJ: Erlbaum.

Nolen-Hoeksema, S. (1990). *Sex differences in depression.* Stanford, CA: Stanford University Press.

Nolen-Hoeksema, S. (1994). An interactive model for the emergence of gender differences in depression in adolescence. *Journal of Research on Adolescence*, 4, 519–534.

Nolen-Hoeksema, S., Morrow, J., & Fredrickson, B.L. (1993). Response styles and the duration of episodes of depressed mood. *Journal of Abnormal Psychology*, 102, 20–28.

Norden, K.A., Klein, D.N., Donaldson, S.K., Pepper, C.M., et al. (1995). Reports of the early home environment in DSM-III-R personality disorders. *Journal of Personality Disorders*, 9, 213–223.

Nordstrom, A., Farde, L., Eriksson, L., & Halldin, C. (1995). No elevated D-sub-2 dopamine receptors in neuroleptic-naive schizophrenic patients revealed by positron emission tomography and (-sub-1-sup-1C) N-methylspiperone. *Psychiatry Research: Neuroimaging*, 61, 67–83.

Nordstrom, P., Samuelsson, M., Asberg, M., Traskman-Bendz, L., et al. (1994). CSF-5-HIAA predicts suicide risk after attempted suicide. *Suicide and Life Threatening Behavior*, 24, 1–9.

Noyes, R., Jr. (1991). Treatments of choice for anxiety disorders. In W. Coryell & G. Winokur (Eds.). *The clinical management of anxiety disorders*, pp. 140–153. New York: Oxford University Press.

Noyes, R., Jr., Clarkson, C., Crowe, R.R., Yates, W.R., & McChesney, C.M. (1987). A family study of generalized anxiety disorder. *American Journal of Psychiatry*, 144, 1019–1024.

Noyes, R., Garvey, M.J., & Cook, B.L. (1989). Follow-up study of patients with panic disorder and agoraphobia with panic attacks treated with tricyclic antidepressants. *Journal of Affective Disorders*, 16, 249–257.

O'Connor, G.T., Buring, J.E., Yusuf, S., Goldhaber, S.Z., Olmstead, E.M., Paffenbarger, R.S., & Hennekens, C.H. (1989). An overview of randomized trials of rehabilitation with exercise after myocardial infarction. *Circulation*, 80, 234–244.

O'Donohue, W., & Geer, J.H. (1993). *Handbook of sexual dysfunctions: Assessment and treatment.* Boston: Allyn & Bacon.

O'Grady, J.C. (1990). The prevalence and diagnostic significance of Schneiderian first-rank symptoms in a random sample of acute psychiatric in-patients. *British Journal of Psychiatry*, 156, 496–500.

O'Leary, K.D. (1980). Pills or skills for hyperactive children. *Journal of Applied Behavior Analysis*, 13, 191–204.

O'Leary, K.D., & Borkovec, T.D. (1978). Conceptual, methodological, and ethical problems of placebo groups in psychotherapeutic research. *American Psychologist, 33*, 821–830.

O'Shea, B., & Falvey, J. (1988). Huntington's disease: Update of the literature. *British Journal of Psychological Medicine, 5*, 61–70.

O'Sullivan, G., & Marks, I. (1991). Follow-up studies of behavioral treatment of phobic and obsessive-compulsive neuroses. *Psychiatric Annals, 21*, 368–373.

O'Sullivan, G., Noshirvani, H., Marks, I., Monteiro, W., & Lelliott, P. (1991). Six-year follow-up after exposure and clomipramine therapy for obsessive-compulsive disorder. *Journal of Clinical Psychiatry, 52*, 150–155.

Oatley, K., & Bolton, W. (1985). A social-cognitive theory of depression in reaction to life events. *Psychological Review, 92*, 372–388.

Oei, T.P.S., Lim, B., & Hennessy, B. (1990). Psychological dysfunction in battle: Combat stress reactions and posttraumatic stress disorder. *Clinical Psychology Review, 10*, 355–388.

Öhman, A. (1986). Face the beast and fear the face: Animal and social fears as prototypes for evolutionary analyses of emotion. *Psychophysiology, 23*, 123–145.

Öhman, A. (1996). Preferential preattentive processing of threat in anxiety: Preparedness and attentional biases. In R.M. Rapee (Ed.), *Current controversies in the anxiety disorders*, pp. 253–290. New York: Guilford.

Oliver, J.M., & Simmons, M.E. (1984). Depression as measured by the DSM-III and the Beck Depression Inventory in an unselected adult population. *Journal of Consulting and Clinical Psychology, 52*, 892–898.

Olmstead, M.P., Kaplan, A.S., & Rockert, W. (1994). Rate and prediction of relapse in bulimia nervosa. *American Journal of Psychiatry, 151*, 738–743.

Oltmanns, T.F., Neale, J.M., & Davison, G.C. (1995). *Case studies in abnormal psychology*, 4th ed. New York: Wiley.

Onstad, S., Skre, I., Torgersen, S., & Kringlen, E. (1991). Twin concordance for DSM-III-R schizophrenia. *Acta Psychiatrica Scandinavica, 83*, 395–401.

Onstad, S., Skre, I., Torgersen, S., & Kringlen, E. (1994). Family interaction: Parental representation in schizophrenic patients. *Acta Psychiatrica Scandinavica Supplementum, 90* (384 suppl.), 67–70.

Oosterwegel, A., & Wicklund, R.A. (1995). *The self in European and North American culture: Development and processes*. Boston: Kluwer.

Oren, D.A., & Rosenthal, N.E. (1992). Seasonal affective disorders. In E.S., Paykel (Ed.), *Handbook of affective disorders*, 2nd ed., pp. 551–568, New York: Guilford.

O'Shea, B. (1993). Non-lithium pharmacological treatment of manic depression. A review. *Irish Journal of Psychological Medicine, 10*, 114–120.

Öst, L. (1987). Applied relaxation: Description of a coping technique and review of controlled studies. *Behaviour Research and Therapy, 25*, 397–409.

Öst, L.G., & Hugdahl, K. (1981). Acquisition of phobias and anxiety response patterns in clinical patients. *Behaviour Research Therapy, 19*, 439–447.

Overstreet, D.H., Rezvani, A.H., & Janowsky, D.S. (1992). Genetic animal models of depression and ethanol preference provide support for cholinergic and serotonergic involvement in depression and alcoholism. *Biological Psychiatry, 31*, 919–936.

Paikoff, R.L., & Brooks-Gunn, J. (1991). Do parent-child relationships change during puberty? *Psychological Bulletin, 110*, 47–66.

Palmer, R.L. (1995). Sexual abuse and eating disorders. In K.D. Brownell & C.G. Fairburn (Eds.), *Eating disorders and obesity: A comprehensive handbook*, pp. 230–233. New York: Guilford.

Panksepp, J. (1988). Brain emotional circuits and psychopathologies. In M. Clynes & J. Panksepp (Eds.), *Emotions and psychopathology*, pp. 37–76. New York: Plenum.

Paris, J. (1992). Social factors in borderline personality disorder: A review and a hypothesis. *Canadian Journal of Psychiatry, 37*, 480–486.

Paris, J. (1993). Personality disorders: A biopsychosocial model. *Journal of Personality Disorders, 7*, 255–264.

Parloff, M.B., Waskow, I.E., & Wolfe, B.E. (1978). Research on therapist variables in relation to process and outcome. In S.L. Garfield & A.E. Bergin (Eds.), *Handbook of psychotherapy and behavior change*, 2nd ed., pp. 233–282. New York: Wiley.

Parnas, J., Cannon T.D., Jacobsen, B., Schulsinger, H., Schulsinger, F., & Mednick, S.A. (1993). Lifetime DSM-III-R diagnostic outcomes in the offspring of schizophrenic mothers: Results from the Copenhagen high-risk study. *Archives of General Psychiatry, 50*, 707–714.

Parry-Jones, B. (1994). Merycism or rumination disorder: A historical investigation and current assessment. *British Journal of Psychiatry, 165*, 303–314.

Pasupathi, M., Carstensen, L.L., & Tsai, J.L. (1995). Ageism in interpersonal settings. In B. Lott & D. Maluso (Eds.), *The social psychology of interpersonal discrimination*, pp. 160–182. New York: Guilford.

Patrick, C.J. (1994). Emotion and psychopathy. Startling new insights. *Psychophysiology, 31*, 319–330.

Patterson, C.M., & Newman, J.P. (1993). Reflectivity and learning from aversive events: Toward a psychological mechanism for the syndromes of disinhibition. *Psychological Review, 100*, 716–736.

Patterson, G.R. (1982). *Coercive family process*. Eugene, OR: Castalia.

Patterson, G.R., DeBaryshe, B.D., & Ramsey, E. (1989). A developmental perspective on antisocial behavior. *American Psychologist, 44*, 329–325.

Patterson, G.R., & Fleischman, M.J. (1979). Maintenance of treatment effects: Some considerations concerning family systems and follow-up data. *Behavior Therapy, 10*, 168–185.

Patton, J.R., Beirne-Smith, M., & Payne, J.S. (1990). *Mental retardation*, 3rd ed. Columbus, OH: Merrill.

Paul, G.L., & Lentz, R.J. (1977). *Psychosocial treatment of chronic mental patients: Milieu versus social-learning programs*. Cambridge, MA: Harvard University Press.

Pavlov, I.P. (1928). *Lectures on conditioned reflexes*. New York: International Publishers.

Paykel, E.S., & Cooper, Z. (1992). Life events and social stress. In E.S. Paykel (Ed.), *Handbook of affective disorders*, 2nd ed., pp. 149–170. New York: Guilford.

Payne, R.L. (1992). First person account: My schizophrenia. *Schizophrenia Bulletin, 18*, 725–728.

Pedersen, N.L., & Gatz, M. (1991). Twin studies as a tool for bridging the gap between genetics and epidemiology of dementia: The study of dementia in Swedish twins [abstract]. *Gerontologist, 31*, 333.

Peele, S. (1992a). Alcoholism, politics, and bureaucracy: The consensus against controlled drinking therapy in America. *Addictive Behaviors, 17*, 49–62.

Peele, S. (1992b). Why is everybody always pickin' on me? A response to comments. *Addictive Behaviors, 17*, 83–93.

Pelham, W.E., Carlson, C., Sams, S.E., Vallano, G., Dixon, M.J., & Hoza, B. (1993). Separate and combined effects of methylphenidate and behavior modification with attention deficit-hyperactivity disorder in the classroom. *Journal of Consulting and Clinical Psychology, 61*, 506–515.

Pendery, M.L., Maltzman, I.M., & West, L.J. (1982). Controlled drinking by alcoholics? New findings and a reevaluation of a major affirmative study. *Science, 217*, 169–175.

Penn, D.L., & Mueser, K.T. (1996). Research update on the psychosocial treatment of schizophrenia. *American Journal of Psychiatry, 153*, 607–617.

Pennebaker, J.W. (1990). *Opening up: The healing power of confiding in others*. New York: Morrow.

Perani, D., Colombo, C., Bressi, S., Bonfanti, A., Grassi, F., Scarone, S., Bellodi, L., Smeraldi, E., &

Fazio, F. (1995). [18F] FDG PET study in obsessive-compulsive disorder: A clinical/metabolic correlation study after treatment. *British Journal of Psychiatry, 166,* 244–250.

Perilstein, R.D., Lipper, S., & Friedman, L.J. (1991). Three cases of paraphilias responsive to fluoxetine treatment. *Journal of Clinical Psychiatry, 52,* 169–170.

Perris, C. (1992). Bipolar-unipolar distinction. In E.S. Paykel (Ed.), *Handbook of affective disorders,* 2nd ed., pp. 57–75. New York: Guilford.

Perry, C., & Laurence, J. (1984). Mental processing outside of awareness: The contributions of Freud and Janet. In K.S. Bowers & D. Meichenbaum (Eds.), *The unconscious reconsidered,* pp. 9–48. New York: Wiley.

Perry, J.C. (1990). Challenges in validating personality disorders: Beyond description. *Journal of Personality Disorders, 4,* 273–289.

Person, E.S., Terestman, N., Myers, W.A., Goldberg, E.L., & Salvadori, C. (1989). Gender differences in sexual behaviors and fantasies in a college population. *Journal of Sex and Marital Therapy, 15,* 187–198.

Persons, J.B. (1986). The advantages of studying psychological phenomena rather than psychiatric diagnoses. *American Psychologist, 41,* 1252–1260.

Pescosolido, B.A., & Georgianna, S. (1989). Durkheim, suicide, and religion: Toward a network theory of suicide. *American Sociological Review, 54,* 33–48.

Peterson, C., & Seligman, M.E.P. (1984). Causal explanations as a risk factor for depression: Theory and evidence. *Psychological Review, 91,* 347–374.

Petrie, K.J., Booth, R.J., Pennebaker, J.W., Davison, K.P., & Thomas, M.G. (1995). Disclosure of trauma and immune response to a hepatitis B vaccination program. *Journal of Consulting and Clinical Psychology, 63,* 787–792.

Pfohl, B. (1995). Histrionic personality disorder. In W.J. Livesley (Ed.), *The DSM-IV personality disorders.* New York: Guilford, pp. 173–192.

Pfohl, B., Blum, N., & Zimmerman, M. (1995). *Structured interview for DSM-IV Personality (SIDP-IV).* Iowa City: University of Iowa.

Pfohl, B., Coryell, W., Zimmerman, M., & Stangl, D. (1986). DSM-III personality disorders: Diagnostic overlap and internal consistency of individual DSM-III-criteria. *Comprehensive Psychiatry, 27,* 21–34.

Phillips, E.L., Phillips, E.A., Wolf, M.M., & Fixsen, D.L. (1973). Achievement Place: Development of the elected manager system. *Journal of Applied Behavior Analysis, 6,* 541–561.

Phillips, K.A. (1991). Body dysmorphic disorder: The distress of imagined ugliness. *American Journal of Psychiatry, 148,* 1138–1149.

Pickens, R.W., Svikis, D.S., McGue, M., Lykken, D.T., Heston, L.L., & Clayton, P.J. (1991). Heterogeneity in the inheritance of alcoholism: A study of male and female twins. *Archives of General Psychiatry, 48,* 19–28.

Pike, K.M., & Rodin, J. (1991). Mothers, daughters, and disordered eating. *Journal of Abnormal Psychology, 100,* 198–204.

Piper, A. (1994). Multiple personality disorder. *British Journal of Psychiatry, 164,* 600–612.

Pisani, V.C., Fawcett, J., Clark, D.C., & McGuire, M. (1993). The relative contributions of medication adherence and AA meeting attendance to abstinent outcome for chronic alcoholics. *Journal of Studies on Alcohol, 54,* 115–119.

Pitman, R.K. (1984). Janet's obsessions and psychasthenia: A synopsis. *Psychiatric Quarterly, 56,* 291–314.

Pitman, R.K. (1987). Pierre Janet on obsessive-compulsive disorder (1903). Review and commentary. *Archives of General Psychiatry, 44,* 226–232.

Pitman, R.K., van der Kolk, B.A., Orr, S.P., & Greenberg, M. (1990). Naloxone-reversible analgesic response to combat-related stimuli in posttraumatic stress disorder. *Archives of General Psychiatry, 47,* 541–544.

Plomin, R. (1990a). *Nature and nurture: An introduction to human behavioral genetics.* Pacific Grove, CA: Brooks/Cole.

Plomin, R. (1990b). The role of inheritance in behavior. *Science, 248,* 183–188.

Plomin, R. (1994). *Genetics and experience: The interplay between nature and nurture.* Thousand Oaks, CA: Sage.

Plomin, R., & Daniels, D. (1987). Why are children in the same family so different from one another? *Behavioral and Brain Sciences, 10,* 1–60.

Plomin, R., DeFries, J.C., & McClearn, G.E. (1990). *Behavioral genetics,* 2nd ed. New York: Freeman.

Pogue-Geile, M.F., & Harrow, M. (1984). Negative and positive symptoms in schizophrenia and depression: A follow-up. *Schizophrenia Bulletin, 10,* 371–387.

Pokony, A. (1983). Prediction of suicide in psychiatric patients: A prospective study. *Archives of General Psychiatry, 40,* 249–257.

Pollen, D.A. (1993). *Hannah's heirs: The quest for the genetic origins of Alzheimer's disease.* New York: Oxford University Press.

Pomeroy, C. (1996). Anorexia nervosa, bulimia nervosa, and binge eating disorder: The assessment of physical status. In J.K. Thompson, *Body image, eating disorders, and obesity,* pp. 177–204. Washington, DC: American Psychological Association.

Poon, L.W., Kaszniak, A.W., & Dudley, W.N. (1992). Approaches in the experimental neuropsychology of dementia: A methodological and model review. In M. Bergener, K. Hasegawa, S.I. Finkel, & T. Nishimura (Eds.), *Aging and mental disorders: International perspectives.* New York: Springer.

Pope, H.G., & Yurgelun-Todd, D. (1996). The residual cognitive effects of heavy marijuana use in college students. *Journal of the American Medical Association, 275,* 521–527.

Porrino, L.J., Rapoport, J.L., Behar, D., Sceery, W., Ismond, D.R., & Bunney, W.E. (1983). A naturalistic assessment of the motor activity of hyperactive boys. I. Comparisons with normal controls. *Archives of General Psychiatry, 40,* 681–687.

Posner, M.I. (1993). Seeing the mind. *Science, 262,* 673–674.

Potter, W.Z., Grossman, F., & Rudorfer, M.V. (1993). Noradrenergic function in depressive disorders. In J.J. Mann & D.J. Kupfer (Eds.), *Biology of depressive disorders, Part A: A systems perspective,* pp. 1–27. New York: Plenum.

Poulos, C.X., & Cappell, H. (1991). Homeostatic theory of drug tolerance: A general model of physiological adaptation. *Psychological Review, 98,* 390–408.

Power, C. (1979). The time-sample behavior checklist: Observational assessment of patient functioning. *Journal of Behavioral Assessment, 1,* 199–210.

Prescott, C.A., Hewitt, J.K., Heath, A.C., Truett, K.R., Neale, M.C., & Eaves, L.J. (1994). Environmental and genetic influences on alcohol use in a volunteer sample of older twins. *Journal of Studies on Alcohol, 55,* 18–32.

Price, R.A., & Gottesman, I.I. (1991). Body fat in identical twins reared apart: Roles for genes and environment. *Behavior Genetics, 21,* 1–7.

Prochaska, J.O. (1984). *Systems of psychotherapy: A transtheoretical analysis.* Homewood, IL: Dorsey.

Project Match Research Group (1997). Matching alcoholism treatments to client heterogeneity: Project MATCH posttreatment drinking outcomes. *Journal of Studies on Alcohol, 58,* 7–29.

Pruzinsky, T., & Borkovec, T.D. (1990). Cognitive and personality characteristics of worriers. *Behaviour Research and Therapy, 28,* 507–512.

Puig-Antich, J. (1986). Psychobiological markers: Effects of age and puberty. In M. Rutter, C. Izard, & P. Read (Eds.), *Depression in young people,* pp. 341–382. New York: Guilford.

Pulver, A.E., Liang, K., Brown, C.H., Wolyniec, P.S., et al. (1992). Risk factors in schizophrenia: Season of birth, gender, and familial risk. *British Journal of Psychiatry, 160,* 65–71.

Putnam, F.W., Curoff, J.J., et al. (1986). The clinical phenomenology of multiple personality disorder:

Review of 100 recent cases. *Journal of Clinical Psychiatry,* 47, 285–293.

Quality Assurance Project. (1991). Treatment outlines for antisocial personality disorder. *Australian and New Zealand Journal of Psychiatry,* 25, 541–547.

Quay, H.C. (1965). Psychopathic personality as pathological stimulation-seeking. *American Journal of Psychiatry,* 122, 180–183.

Quay, H.C. (1993). The psychobiology and undersocialized aggressive conduct disorder: A theoretical perspective. *Development and Psychopathology,* 5, 165–180.

Quevillon, R.P. (1993). Dyspareunia. In W. O'Donohue & J.H. Geer (Eds.), *Handbook of sexual dysfunctions: Assessment and treatment,* pp. 367–380. Boston: Allyn & Bacon.

Rabins, P.V. (1997). Caring for persons with dementing illnesses: A current perspective. In L. Heston (Ed.), *Progress in Alzheimer's disease and similar conditions.* Washington, DC: American Psychiatric Press.

Rachlin, H. (1992). Teleological behaviorism. *American Psychologist,* 47, 1371–1382.

Rachman, S. (1990). The determinants and treatment of simple phobias. *Advances in Behavior Research and Therapy,* 12, 1–30.

Rachman, S. (1991). *Fear and courage,* 2nd ed. San Francisco: Freeman.

Rachman, S.J., & Hodgson, R.J. (1980). *Obsessions and compulsions.* Englewood Cliffs, NJ: Prentice Hall.

Raichle, M.E. (1994a). Images of the mind: Studies with modern imaging techniques. *Annual Review of Psychology,* 45, 333–356.

Raichle, M.E. (1994b). Images of the human mind. *Neuropsychopharmacology,* 10 (3 suppl part 1): 28S–33S.

Ramey, C.T., & Bryant, D. (1982). Evidence for primary prevention of developmental retardation. *Journal of the Division of Early Childhood,* 5, 73–78.

Rapee, R.M. (1991). Generalized anxiety disorder: A review of clinical features and theoretical concepts. *Clinical Psychology Review,* 11, 419–440.

Raphael, B., Wilson, J., Meldrum L., & McFarlane, A.C. (1996). Acute preventive interventions. In B.A. van der Kolk, A.C. McFarlane, & L. Weisaeth (Eds.), *Traumatic stress,* pp. 463–479. New York: Guilford.

Raskind, M.A., & Peskind, E.R. (1997). Neurotransmitter abnormalities and the psychopharmacology of Alzheimer's disease. In L. Heston (Ed.)., *Progress in Alzheimer's disease and similar conditions.* Washington, DC: American Psychiatric Press.

Rastam, M., Gillberg, C., & Gillberg, C. (1995). Anorexia nervosa 6 years after onset. Part II.

Cormorbid psychiatric problems. *Comprehensive Psychiatry,* 36, 70–76.

Raz, S., & Raz, N. (1990). Structural brain abnormalities in the major psychoses: A quantitative review of the evidence from computerized imaging. *Psychological Bulletin,* 108, 93–108.

Redmond, D.E., Jr. (1985). Neurochemical basis for anxiety and anxiety disorders: Evidence from drugs which decrease human fear of anxiety. In A.H. Tuma and J.D. Maser (Eds.), *Anxiety and the anxiety disorders.* Hillsdale, NJ: Erlbaum.

Regier, D.A., Myers, J.K., Kramer, M., Robins, L.N., Blazer, D.G., Hough, R.L., Eaton, W.W., & Locke, B.Z. (1984). The NIMH Epidemiologic Catchment Area Program: Historical context, major objectives and study population characteristics. *Archives of General Psychiatry,* 41, 934–941.

Reich, J., & Thompson, W.D. (1987). DSM-III personality disorder clusters in three populations. *British Journal of Psychiatry,* 150, 471–475.

Reich, J., Warshaw, M., Peterson, L.G., White, K., Keller, M., Lavori, P., & Yonkers, A. (1993). Comorbidity of panic and major depressive disorder. *Journal of Psychiatric Research,* 27 (suppl. 1), 23–33.

Reich, J., Yates, W., & Nduaguba, M. (1987). Prevalence of DSM-III personality disorders in the community. *Social Psychiatry and Psychiatric Epidemiology,* 24, 12–16.

Reid, J.B., (Ed.) (1978). *A social learning approach to family intervention.* Vol. 2. *Observation in home settings.* Eugene, OR: Castalia.

Reiman, E.M., Raichle, M.E., Robins, E., Mintun, M.A., Fusselman, M.J., Fox, P.T., Price, J.L., & Hackman, K.A. (1989). Neuroanatomical correlates of a lactate-induced anxiety attack. *Archives of General Psychiatry,* 46, 493–500.

Reisman, J.M. (1990). *A history of clinical psychology,* 2nd ed. New York: Hemisphere.

Reisner, R., & Slobogin, C. (1990). *Law and the mental health system,* 2nd ed. St. Paul, MN: West.

Reiss, A.L., Feinstein, C., & Rosenbaum, K.N. (1986). Autism and genetic disorders. *Schizophrenia Bulletin,* 12, 724–738.

Rey, J.M., Stewart, G.W., Plapp, J.M., Bashir, M.R., et al. (1988). DSM-III Axis IV revisited. *American Journal of Psychiatry,* 145, 286–292.

Richardson, S. (1996). The besieged brain: Immune cells in brain may further progression of Alzheimer's disease. *Discover,* 17, 30–32.

Richters, J.E. (1993). Community violence and children's development: Toward a research agenda for the 1990s. *Psychiatry,* 56, 3–6.

Riecher, A., Maurer, K., Loffler, W., Fatkenheuer, B., an der Heiden, W., Munk-Jorgensen P., Stromgren, E., & Hafner, H. (1991). Gender differences in age at

onset and course of schizophrenic disorders. In H. Hafner & W.F. Gattaz (Eds.), *Search for the causes of schizophrenia,* Vol. II, pp. 14–33. Berlin: Springer.

Rifat, S.L. (1994). Aluminum hypothesis lives. *Lancet,* 343, 3–5.

Ritvo, E.R., Freeman, B.J., Yuwiler, A., Geller, E., Yokota, A., Schroth, P., & Novak, P. (1984). Study of fenfluramine in outpatients with the syndrome of autism. *Journal of Pediatrics,* 105, 823–828.

Roberts, J., & Rowland, M. (1981). *Hypertension in adults 25–74 years of age: United States, 1971–75.* Vital and Health Statistics Series 11, No. 221., DHEW Publication No. PHS 81-1671. Washington, DC: U.S. Government Printing Office.

Robin, A.L., Koepke, T., & Nayar, M. (1986). Conceptualizing, assessing, and treating parent-adolescent conflict. In B. Lahey & A. Kazdin (Eds.), *Advances in Clinical Child Psychology,* 9, 87–124.

Robins, E., & Guze, S. (1989). Establishment of diagnostic validity in psychiatric illness. In L.N. Robins & J.E. Barrett (Eds.), *The validity of psychiatric diagnosis,* pp. 177–197. New York: Raven Press.

Robins, L.N. (1966). *Deviant children grown up: A sociological and psychiatric study of sociopathic personality.* Baltimore: Williams & Wilkins.

Robins, L.N., Helzer, J.E., Weissman, M.M., Orvaschel, H., Gruenberg, E., Burke, J.D., & Regier, D.A. (1984). Lifetime prevalence of specific psychiatric disorders in three sites. *Archives of General Psychiatry,* 41, 949–958.

Robins, L.N., & McEvoy, L. (1992). Conduct problems as predictors of substance abuse. In C.P. O'Brien & J.J. Jaffe (Eds.), *Addictive states.* New York: Raven Press.

Robins, L.N., & Regier, D.A. (1991). *Psychiatric disorders in America: The Epidemiologic Catchment Area Study.* New York: Free Press.

Robins, L.N., Tipp, J., & Przybeck, T. (1991). Antisocial personality. In L.N. Robins & D.A. Regier (Eds.), *Psychiatric disorders in America: The Epidemiologic Catchment Area Study,* pp. 258–290. New York: Free Press.

Robinson, P. (1976). *The modernization of sex: Havelock Ellis, Alfred Kinsey, William Masters and Virginia Johnson.* New York: Harper & Row.

Roemer, L., & Borkovec, T.D. (1993). Worry: Unwanted cognitive activity that controls unwanted somatic experience. In D.M. Wegner and J.W. Pennebaker (Eds.), *Handbook of mental control.* Englewood Cliffs, NJ: Prentice Hall.

Rogers, C.R. (1951). *Client-centered therapy.* Boston: Houghton Mifflin.

Rogers, C.R. (1957). The necessary and sufficient conditions of therapeutic personality change. *Journal of Consulting Psychology,* 21, 95–103.

Rogers, C.R. (1961). *On becoming a person: A therapist's view of psychotherapy.* Boston: Houghton Mifflin.

Rogers, M.P. (1989). The interaction between brain, behavior, and immunity. In S. Cheren (Ed.), *Psychosomatic medicine: Theory, physiology, and practice,* Vol. 1, pp. 279–330. Madison, CT: International Universities Press.

Rogers, R., Bloom, M., & Manson, S. (1984). Insanity defenses: Contested or conceded? *American Journal of Psychiatry,* 141, 885–888.

Rohde, P., Lewinsohn, P., & Seeley, J. (1990). Are people changed by the experience of having an episode of depression? A further test of the scar hypothesis. *Journal of Abnormal Psychology,* 99, 264–271.

Roman, P.M., & Blum, T.C. (1987). Notes on the new epidemiology of alcoholism in the USA. *Journal of Drug Issues,* 17, 321–332.

Ronningstam, E., & Gunderson, J. (1991). Differentiating borderline personality disorder from narcissistic personality disorder. *Journal of Personality Disorders,* 5, 225–232.

Rook, K.S., & Dooley, D. (1985). Applying social support research: Theoretical problems and future directions. *Journal of Social Issues,* 41, 5–28.

Room, R. (1987). Alcohol control, addiction and processes of change: Comment on "The limitations of control-of-supply models for explaining and preventing alcoholism and drug addiction." *Journal of Studies on Alcohol,* 48, 78–83.

Rosen, J.C., Reiter, J., & Orosan, P. (1995). Cognitive-behavioral body image therapy for body dysmorphic disorder. *Journal of Consulting and Clinical Psychology,* 63, 263–269.

Rosen, R.C., & Leiblum, S.R. (1995). Treatment of sexual disorders in the 1990s: An integrated approach. *Journal of Consulting and Clinical Psychology,* 63, 877–890.

Rosen, R.C., Taylor, J.F., Leiblum, S.R., & Bachmann, G.A. (1993). Prevalence of sexual dysfunction in women: Results of a survey study of 329 women in an outpatient gynecological clinic. *Journal of Sex and Marital Therapy,* 19, 171–188.

Rosenberg, R. (1993). Drug treatment of panic disorder. *Psychopharmacology and Taxicology,* 72, 344–353.

Rosenthal, D. (Ed.) (1963). *The Genain quadruplets.* New York: Basic Books.

Rosenthal, D., & Quinn, O.W. (1977). Quadruplet hallucinations: Phenotypic variations of a schizophrenic genotype. *Archives of General Psychiatry,* 34, 817–827.

Rosenthal, N.E., Sack, D.A., & Gillin, J.C., et al. (1984). Seasonal affective disorder: A description of the syndrome and preliminary findings with light therapy. *Archives of General Psychiatry,* 41, 72–80.

Rosenthal, R., & Rosnow, R.L. (1969). *Artifact in behavioral science research.* New York: Academic Press.

Rosin, A.J., & Glatt, M.M. (1971). Alcohol excess in the elderly. *Quarterly Journal of Studies on Alcohol,* 32, 53–59.

Ross, C.A., Norton, G.R., & Wozney, K. (1989). Multiple personality disorder: An analysis of 236 cases. *Canadian Journal of Psychiatry,* 34, 413–418.

Ross, D.M., & Ross, S.A. (1982). *Hyperactivity: Current issues, research, and theory.* New York: Wiley.

Ross, H.E. (1989). Alcohol and drug abuse in treated alcoholics: A comparison of men and women. *Alcohol: Clinical and Experimental Research,* 13, 810–816.

Roth, D., & Bean, J. (1986). New perspectives on homelessness: Findings from a statewide epidemiological study. *Hospital and Community Psychiatry,* 37, 712–723.

Roth, M., & Argyle, N. (1988). Anxiety, panic, and phobic disorders: An overview. *Journal of Psychiatric Research,* 22, 33–54.

Rothbaum, B.O., & Foa, E.B. (1996). Cognitive-behavioral therapy for posttraumatic stress disorder. In B.A. van der Kolk, A.C., McFarlane, & L. Weisaeth (Eds.), *Traumatic stress,* pp. 491–509. New York: Guilford.

Rothschild, A.J. (1995). Selective serotonin reputake inhibitor-induced sexual dysfunction. Efficacy of a drug holiday. *American Journal of Psychiatry,* 152, 1514–1517.

Rounsaville, B.J., Spitzer, R.L., & Williams, J.B.W. (1986). Proposed changes in DSM-III substance use disorders: Description and rationale. *American Journal of Psychiatry,* 143, 463–468.

Roy, A. (1992). Are there genetic factors in suicide. *International Review of Psychiatry,* 4, 169–175.

Roy, A., Segal, N.L., Centerwall, B.S., & Robinette, C.D. (1991). Suicide in twins. *Archives of General Psychiatry,* 48, 29–32.

Ruocchio, P.J. (1991). First person account: The schizophrenic inside. *Schizophrenia Bulletin,* 17, 357–359.

Rubonis, A.V., & Bickman, L. (1991). Psychological impairment in the wake of disaster: The disaster-psychopathology relationship. *Psychological Bulletin,* 109, 384–399.

Rush, A.J. (1993). Clinical practice guidelines: Good news, bad news, or no news? *Archives of General Psychiatry,* 50, 483–490.

Rush, A.J., Beck, A.T., Kovacs, M., & Hollon, S.D. (1977). Comparative efficacy of cognitive therapy and pharmacotherapy in the treatment of depressed outpatients. *Cognitive Therapy and Research,* 1, 17–38.

Russell, D.E.H. (1983). The incidence and prevalence of intrafamilial and extrafamilial sexual abuse of female children. *Child Abuse and Neglect,* 7, 133–146.

Russell, D.E.H. (1984). *Sexual exploitation: Rape, child sexual abuse, and workplace harassment.* Beverly Hills, CA: Sage.

Russell, G.F.M. (1979). Bulimia nervosa: An ominous variant of anorexia nervosa. *Psychological Medicine,* 9, 429–448.

Russell, G.F.M., Szmukler, G.I., Dare, C., & Eisler, I. (1987). An evaluation of family therapy in anorexia nervosa and bulimia nervosa. *Archives of General Psychiatry,* 44, 1047–1056.

Rutherford, J., McGuffin, P., Katz, R.J., & Murray, R.M. (1993). Genetic influences on eating attitudes in a normal female twin population. *Psychological Medicine,* 23, 425–436.

Rutter, M. (1970). Autistic children: Infancy to adulthood. *Seminars in Psychiatry,* 2, 435–450.

Rutter, M. (1978a). Diagnosis and definition of child autism. *Journal of Autism and Childhood Schizophrenia,* 8, 139–161.

Rutter, M. (1996). Autism research: Prospects and priorities. *Journal of Autism and Developmental Disorders,* 26, 257–275.

Rutter, M.L. (1978b). Family, area and school influences in the genesis of conduct disorders. In L. Hersov, M. Berger, & D. Shaffer (Eds.), *Aggression and anti-social behavior in childhood and adolescence.* Oxford: Pergamon.

Rutter, M.L. (1978). Isle of Wight revisited: Twenty-five years of child psychiatric epidemiology. *Journal of the American Academy of Child Psychiatry,* 28, 633–653.

Rutter, M.L. (1986). The developmental psychopathology of depression: Issues and perspectives. In M. Rutter, C. Izard, & P. Read (Eds.), *Depression in young people,* pp. 3–32. New York: Guilford.

Rutter, M., & Garmezy, N. (1983). Developmental psychopathology. In E.M. Hetherington (Ed.), *Handbook of child psychology,* Vol. 4, pp. 775–912. New York: Wiley.

Rutter, M., Greenfield, D., & Lockyer, L. (1967). A five- to fifteen-year follow-up study of infantile psychosis. II. Social and behavioral outcome. *British Journal of Psychiatry,* 113, 1187–1199.

Rutter, M., & Rutter, M. (1993). *Developing minds.* New York: Basic Books.

Ryff, C.D. (1995). Psychological well-being in adult life. *Current Directions in Psychological Science,* 4, 99–104.

Sabshin, M. (1990). Turning points in twentieth-century American psychiatry. *American Journal of Psychiatry,* 147, 1267–1274.

Sackett, D. (1992). A primer on the precision and accuracy of the clinical examination. *Journal of the American Medical Association,* 267, 2638–2644.

Sacks, O. (1985). *The man who mistook his wife for a hat and other clinical tales.* New York: Summit.

Safer, D.J., & Krager, J.M. (1988). A survey of medication treatment for hyperactive/inattentive students. *Journal of the American Medical Association, 260,* 2256–2258.

Samuels, J.F., Nestadt, G., Romanoski, A.J., Folstein, M.F., & McHugh, P.R. (1994). DSM-III personality disorders in the community. *American Journal of Psychiatry, 151,* 1055–1062.

Sanders, S.A., Reinisch, J.M., & McWhirter, D.P. (1990). Homosexuality/heterosexuality: An overview. In D.P. McWhirter, S.A. Sanders, & J.M. Reinisch (Eds.), *Homosexuality/heterosexuality: Concepts of sexual orientation.* New York: Oxford University Press.

Sapolsky, R.M. (1992). Neuroendocrinology of the stress response. In J.B. Becker, S.M. Breedlove, & D. Crews (Eds.), *Behavioral endocrinology,* pp. 288–324. Cambridge, MA: MIT Press.

Sargent, T.O. (1988). Fetishism. *Journal of Social Work and Human Sexuality, 7,* 27–42.

Sartorius, N., Jablensky, A., Lorton, A., Ernberg, G., Anker, M., Cooper, J.E., & Day, R. (1986). Early manifestations and first-contact incidence of schizophrenia in different cultures. *Psychological Medicine, 16,* 909–928.

Sartorius, N., Kaelber, C.T., Cooper, J.E., Roper, M.T., Rae, D.S., Gulbinat, W., Ustun, B., & Regier, D.A. (1993). Progress toward achieving a common language in psychiatry: Results from the field trial of the clinical guidelines accompanying the WHO classification of mental and behavioral disorders in ICD 10. *Archives of General Psychiatry, 50,* 115–124.

Sartory, G. (1989). Obsessional-compulsive disorder. In G. Turpin (Ed.), *Handbook of clinical psychophysiology,* pp. 329–356. New York: Wiley.

Sato, M. (1992). A lasting vulnerability to psychosis in patients with previous methamphetamine psychosis. In P.W. Kalivas & H.H. Samson (Eds.), *Neurobiology of drug and alcohol addiction. Annals of the New York Academy of Sciences, 654,* 160–170.

Satterfield, S.B. (1988). Transsexualism. *Journal of Social Work and Human Sexuality, 7,* 77–87.

Sayer, N.A., Sackeim, H.A., Moeller, J.R., Prudic, J., Devanand, D.P., Coleman, E.A., & Kiersky, J.E. (1993). The relations between observer-rating and self-report of depressive symptomatology. *Psychological Assessment, 5,* 350–360.

Scarr, S. (1992). Developmental theories for the 1990s: Development and individual differences. *Child Development, 63,* 1–19.

Scarr, S., & McCartney, K. (1983). How people make their own environments: A theory of genotype-environment effects. *Child Development, 54,* 424–435.

Schacht, T.E. (1985). DSM-III and the politics of truth. *American Psychologist, 40,* 513–521.

Schacht, T., & Nathan, P. (1977). But is it good for psychologists? Appraisal and status of DSM-III. *American Psychologist, 32,* 1017–1025.

Scheerenberger, R.C. (1982). Public residential services, 1981: Status and trends. *Mental Retardation, 20,* 210–215.

Scheff, T.J. (1966). *Being mentally ill: A sociological theory.* Chicago: Aldine.

Scheff, T.J. (1984). *Being mentally ill: A sociological theory,* 2nd ed. Chicago: Aldine.

Schellenberg, G.D., Payami, H., Wijsman, E.M., Orr, H.T., Goddard, K.A.B., Anderson, L., Nemens, E., White, J.A., Alonso, M.E., Ball, M.J., Kaye, J., Morris, J.C., Chui, H., Sadovnick, A.D., Heston, L.L., Martin, G.M., & Bird, T.D. (1993). Chromosome 14 and late-onset familial Alzheimer disease (FAD). *American Journal of Human Genetics, 53,* 619–628.

Schiff, M., Duyme, M., Dumaret, A., & Tomkiewicz, S. (1982). How much could we boost scholastic achievement and IQ scores? A direct answer from a French adoption study. *Cognition, 12,* 165–196.

Schildkraut, J.J. (1965). The catecholamine hypothesis of affective disorders: A review of supporting evidence. *American Journal of Psychiatry, 122,* 509–522.

Schneidman, E.S. (1996). *The suicidal mind.* New York: Oxford University Press.

Schneiderman, N., Chesney, M.A., & Krantz, D.S. (1989). Biobehavioral aspects of cardiovascular disease: Progress and prospects. *Health Psychology, 8,* 649–676.

Schneller, J. (1988). Terror on the A-train: Anatomy of a panic attack. *Mademoiselle, 94,* 148–159.

Schopler, E.M., Andrews, C.E., & Strupp, K. (1979). Do autistic children come from upper-middle-class parents? *Journal of Autism and Developmental Disorders, 9,* 139–152.

Schott, R.L. (1995). The childhood and family dynamics of tranvestites. *Archives of Sexual Behavior, 24,* 309–328.

Schotti, J.R., Evans, I.M., Meyer, L.H., & Walker, P. (1991). A meta-analysis of intervention research with problem behavior: Treatment validity and standards of practice. *American Journal on Mental Retardation, 96,* 233–256.

Schreibman, L. (1988). *Autism.* Beverly Hills, CA: Sage.

Schreiner-Engel, P., & Schiavi, R.C. (1986). Lifetime psychopathology in individuals with low sexual desire. *Journal of Nervous and Mental Disease, 174,* 646–651.

Schuckit, M.A. (1987). Biological vulnerability to alcoholism. *Journal of Consulting and Clinical Psychology, 55,* 301–309.

Schuckit, M.A. (1989). *Drug and alcohol abuse: A clinical guide to diagnosis and treatment,* 3rd ed. New York: Plenum.

Schuckit, M.A. (1994). A clinical model of genetic influences in alcohol dependence. *Journal of Studies on Alcohol, 55,* 5–17.

Schuckit, M.A., & Monteiro, J.G. (1988). Alcoholism, anxiety and depression. *British Journal of Addiction, 83,* 1373–1380.

Schuyler, D. (1991). *A practical guide to cognitive therapy.* New York: Norton.

Schwartz, G.E. (1982). Testing the biopsychosocial model: The ultimate challenge facing behavioral medicine. *Journal of Consulting and Clinical Psychology, 50,* 1040–1053.

Schwartz, G.E. (1989). Dysregulation theory and disease: Toward a general model for psychosomatic medicine. In S. Cheren (Ed.), *Psychosomatic medicine: Theory, physiology, and practice,* Vol. 1, pp. 91–118. Madison, CT: International Universities Press.

Scurfield, R.M. (1985). Posttrauma stress assessment and treatment: Overview and formulations. In C.R. Figley (Ed.), *Trauma and its wake,* pp. 219–259. New York: Brunner/Mazel.

Sedgwick, P. (1981). Illness—Mental and otherwise. In A.L. Caplan, H.T. Engelhardt, Jr., & J.J. McCartney (Eds.), *Concepts of health and disease: Interdisciplinary perspectives,* pp. 119–129. Reading, MA: Addison-Wesley.

Segraves, R.T. (1988). Psychiatric drugs and inhibited female orgasm. *Journal of Sex and Marital Therapy, 14,* 202–206.

Segraves, R.T., & Segraves, K.B. (1990). Categorical and multi-axial diagnosis of male erectile disorder. *Journal of Sex and Marital Therapy, 16,* 208–213.

Segrin, C., & Abramson, L.Y. (1994). Negative reactions to depressive behaviors: A communication theories analysis. *Journal of Abnormal Psychology, 103,* 655–668.

Seidman, B.T., Marshall, W.L., Hudson, S.M., & Robertson, P.J. (1994). An examination of intimacy and loneliness in sex offenders. *Journal of Interpersonal Violence, 9,* 518–534.

Select Committee on Children, Youth, and Families (SCCYF) of the United States House of Representatives. (1989). *U.S. children and their families: Current conditions and recent trends.* Washington, DC: U.S. Government Printing Office.

Selfe, L. (1977). *Nadia: A case of extraordinary drawing ability in an autistic child.* London: Academic Press.

Seligman, M.E.P. (1971). Phobias and preparedness. *Behavior Therapy, 2,* 307–320.

Seligman, M.E.P. (1995). The effectiveness of psychotherapy: The *Consumer Reports* study. *American Psychologist, 50,* 965–974.

Selye, H. (1936). A syndrome produced by diverse nocuous agents. *Nature, 13,* 32.

Selye, H. (1956). *The stress of life.* New York: McGraw-Hill.

Serbin, L.A., & Sprafkin, C.H. (1987). A developmental approach: Sexuality from infancy through adolescence. In J.H. Geer, & W.T. O'Donohue (Eds.), pp. 163–196. *Theories of human sexuality.* New York: Plenum.

Serdula, M.K., Collins, M.E., Williamson, D.F., Anda, R.F., Pamuk, E.R., & Byers, T.E. (1993). Weight control practices of U.S. adolescents and adults. *Annals of Internal Medicine, 119,* 667–671.

Shalev, A.Y. (1996). Stress versus traumatic stress: From acute homeostatic reactions to chronic psychopathology. In B.A. van der Kolk, A.C. McFarlane, & L. Weisaeth (Eds.), *Traumatic stress,* pp. 77–101. New York: Guilford.

Shalev, A., & Munitz, H. (1986). Conversion without hysteria: A case report and review of the literature. *British Journal of Psychiatry, 148,* 198–203.

Shalev, A.Y., Peri, T., Caneti, L., & Schreiber, S. (1996). Predictors of PTSD in injured trauma survivors. *American Journal of Psychiatry, 53,* 219–224.

Shapiro, A.K., & Morris, L.A. (1978). The placebo effect in medical and psychological therapies. In. S.L. Garfield & A.E. Bergin (Eds.), *Handbook of psychotherapy and behavior change,* 2nd ed., pp. 369–410. New York: Wiley.

Shaw, D.S., & Bell, R.Q. (1993). Developmental theories of parental contributors to antisocial behavior. *Journal of Abnormal Child Psychology, 21,* 493–518.

Shaw, D.S., & Emery, R.E. (1988). Chronic family adversity and school-age children's adjustment. *Journal of the American Academy of Child and Adolescent Psychiatry, 27,* 200–206.

Shaw, D.S., Keenan, K., & Vondra, J.I. (1994). Developmental precursors of externalizing behavior: Ages 1 to 3. *Developmental Psychology, 30,* 355–364.

Shaw, D.S., & Vondra, J.I. (1995). Infant attachment security and maternal predictors of early behavior problems: A longitudinal study of low-income families. *Journal of Abnormal Child Psychology, 23,* 335–357.

Shaw, D.S., Vondra, J.I., Hommerding, K.D., Keenan, K., & Dunn, M. (1994). Chronic family adversity and early child behavior problems: A longitudinal study of low income families. *Journal of Child Psychology and Psychiatry, 35,* 1109–1122.

Shea, M.T. (1991). Standardized approaches to individual psychotherapy of patients with borderline personality disorder. *Hospital and Community Psychiatry, 42,* 1034–1038.

Shea, M.T. (1993). Psychosocial treatment of personality disorders. *Journal of Personality Disorders,* supplement, 167–180.

Shea, M.T. (1995). Interrelationships among categories of personality disorders. In W.J. Livesley (Ed.), *The DSM-IV personality disorders,* pp. 397–406. New York: Guilford.

Shearer, D.E., & Shearer, M.S. (1976). The Portage Project: A model for early childhood intervention. In T.D. Tjossem (Ed.), *Intervention strategies for high risk infants and young children.* Baltimore: University Park Press.

Shedler, J., Mayman, M., & Manis, M. (1993). The illusion of mental health. *American Psychologist, 48,* 1117–1131.

Shenton, M.E., Kikinis, R., Jolesz, F.A., Pollak, S.D., et al. (1992). Abnormalities of the left temporal lobe and thought disorder in schizophrenia: A quantitative magnetic resonance imaging study. *New England Journal of Medicine, 327,* 604–612.

Sher, K.J. (1991). *Children of alcoholics: A critical appraisal of theory and research.* Chicago: University of Chicago Press.

Sher, K.J. (1993). Children of alcoholics and the intergenerational transmission of alcoholism: A biopsychosocial perspective. In J.S. Baer, G.A. Marlatt, & R.J. McMahon (Eds.), *Addictive behaviors across the life span: Prevention, treatment, and policy issues,* pp. 3–33. Newbury Park, CA: Sage.

Sher, K.J. (1994). There are two types of alcoholism researchers: Those who believe in two types of alcoholism and those who don't. *Addiction, 89,* 1061–1064.

Sherman, J., Factor, D.C., Swinson, R., & Darjes, R.W. (1989). The effects of fenfluramine (hydrochloride) on the behaviors of fifteen autistic children. *Journal of Autism and Developmental Disorders, 19,* 533–543.

Sherrington, R., Brynjolfsson, J., Petursson, H., Potter, M., Dudleston, K., Barraclough, B., Wasmuth, J., Cobbs, M., & Gurling, H. (1988). Localization of a susceptibility locus for schizophrenia on chromosome 5. *Nature, 336,* 164–170.

Shiffman, S., Kassel, J.D., Paty, J., Gnys, M., et al. (1994). Smoking typology profiles of chippers and regular smokers. *Journal of Substance Abuse, 6,* 21–35.

Shneidman, E.S. (1986). Some essentials of suicide and some implications for response. In A. Roy (Ed.), *Suicide.* Baltimore: Williams & Wilkins.

Shontz, F.C., & Green, P. (1992). Trends in research on the Rorschach: Review and recommendations. *Applied and Preventive Psychology, 1,* 149–156.

Short, A.B., & Schopler, E. (1988). Factors relating to age of onset in autism. *Journal of Autism and Developmental Disorders, 18,* 207–216.

Shorter, E. (1992). *From paralysis to fatigue: A history of psychosomatic illness in the modern era.* New York: Free Press.

Shoulson, I. (1990). Huntington's disease: Cognitive and psychiatric features. *Neuropsychiatry, Neuropsychology, and Behavioral Neurology, 3,* 15–22.

Shover, L.R., Friedman, J.M., Weiler, S.J., Heiman, J.R., & LoPiccolo, J. (1982). Multiaxial problem-oriented system for sexual dysfunctions. *Archives of General Psychiatry, 39,* 614–619.

Siegel, J.M., & Kuykendall, D.H. (1990). Loss, widowhood, and psychological distress among the elderly. *Journal of Consulting and Clinical Psychology, 58,* 519–524.

Siever, L.J., Bernstein, D.P., & Silverman, J.M. (1991). Schizotypal personality disorder: A review of its current status. *Journal of Personality Disorders, 5,* 178–193.

Siever, L.J., Bernstein, D.P., & Silverman, J.M. (1995). Schizotypal personality disorder. In W.J. Livesley, (Ed.), *The DSM-IV personality disorders,* pp. 71–90. New York: Guilford.

Siever, L.J., Coursey, R.D., Alterman, I.S., Zahn, T., et al. (1989). Clinical, psychophysiological, and neurological characteristics of volunteers with impaired smooth pursuit eye movements. *Biological Psychiatry, 26,* 35–51.

Siever, L.J., Friedman, L., Moskowitz, J., Mitropoulou, V., et al. (1994). Eye movement impairment and schizotypal psychopathology. *American Journal of Psychiatry, 151,* 1209–1215.

Siever, L.J., & Klar, H. (1986). A review of DSM-III criteria for the personality disorders. *Annual Review of Psychiatry, 5,* 279–290.

Siever, L., & Trestman, R.L. (1993). The serotonin system and aggressive personality disorder. *International Clinical Psychopharmacology, 8* (suppl. 2). 33–39.

Sifneos, P.E. (1987). *Short-term dynamic psychotherapy: Evaluation and technique.* New York: Plenum.

Signorielli, N. (1989). The stigma of mental illness on television. *Journal of Broadcasting and Electronic Media, 33,* 325–331.

Sigvardsson, S., Bohman, M., & Cloninger, C.R. (1996). Replication of the Stockholm adoption study of alcoholism: Confirmatory cross-fostering analysis. *Archives of General Psychiatry, 53,* 681–687.

Silverstone, T. (1992). New aspects in the treatment of depression. *International Clinical Psychopharmacology, 6* (suppl. 5), 41–44.

Simonoff, E., McGuffin, P., & Gottesman, I.I. (1994). Genetic influences on normal and abnormal development. In M. Rutter, E. Taylor, & L. Hersov (Eds.), *Child and adolescent psychiatry,* 3rd ed. London: Blackwell.

Simons, A.D., Angell, K.L., Monroe, S.M., & Thase, M.E. (1993). Cognition and life stress in depression: Cognitive factors and the definition, rating, and generation of negative life events. *Journal of Abnormal Psychology, 102,* 584–591.

Simons, A.D., Garfield, S.L., & Murphy, G.E. (1984). The process of change in cognitive therapy and pharmacotherapy for depression. *Archives of General Psychiatry, 41,* 45–51.

Singer, J.L. (Ed.) (1990). *Repression and dissociation.* Chicago: University of Chicago Press.

Singer, M.T., & Wynne, L.C. (1965). Thought disorder and family relations of schizophrenics. IV. Results and implications. *Archives of General Psychiatry, 12,* 201–212.

Singh, N.N., Guernsey, T.F., & Ellis, C.R. (1992). Drug therapy for persons with developmental disabilities: Legislation and litigation. *Clinical Psychology Review, 12,* 665–679.

Sizemore, C.C. (1989). *A mind of her own.* New York: Morrow.

Sizemore, C.C., & Pittillo, E.S. (1977). *I'm Eve!* New York: Doubleday.

Skinner, B.F. (1953). *Science and human behavior.* New York: Macmillan.

Skodak, M., & Skeels, H. (1949). A final follow-up study of one hundred adopted children. *Journal of Genetic Psychology, 75,* 85–125.

Skoog, I., Lernfelt, B., Landahl, S., Palmertz, B., Andreasson, L., Nilsson, L., Persson, G., Oden, A., & Svanborg, A. (1996). 15-year longitudinal study of blood pressure and dementia. *Lancet, 347,* 1141–1146.

Slaby, A.E., & Martin, S.D. (1991). Drug and alcohol emergencies. In N.S. Miller (Ed.), *Comprehensive handbook of drug and alcohol addiction,* pp. 1003–1030. New York: Dekker.

Slater, E. (1965). Diagnosis of hysteria. *British Medical Journal, 1,* 1395–1399.

Slawson, G., & Guggenheim, H. (1984). Psychiatric malpractice: A review of the national loss experience. *American Journal of Psychiatry, 141,* 979–981.

Sleator, E.K., & Ullmann, R.K. (1981). Can the physician diagnose hyperactivity in the office? *Pediatrics, 67,* 13–17.

Sloman, L., Gardner, R., & Price, J. (1989). Biology of family systems and mood disorders. *Family Process, 28,* 387–398.

Smalley, S.L. (1996). Genetic, prenatal, and immunologic factors. *Journal of Autism and Developmental Disorders, 26,* 195–197.

Smalley, S.L., Asarnow, R.F., & Spence, M.A. (1988). Autism and genetics: A decade of research. *Archives of General Psychiatry, 45,* 953–961.

Smalley, S.L., & Collins, F. (1996). Brief report: Genetic, prenatal, and immunologic factors. *Journal of Autism and Developmental Disorders, 26,* 195–197.

Smart, R.G., & Mann, R.E. (1993). Recent liver cirrhosis declines: Estimates of the impact of alcohol abuse treatment and alcoholics anonymous. *Addiction, 88,* 193–198.

Smetana, J.G. (1989). Adolescents' and parents' reasoning about actual family conflict. *Child Development, 60,* 1052–1067.

Smith, A.L., & Weissman, M.M. (1992). Epidemiology. In E.S. Paykel (Ed.), *Handbook of affective disorders,* 2nd ed., pp. 111–130. New York: Guilford.

Smith, E. (1991). First person account: Living with schizophrenia. *Schizophrenia Bulletin, 17,* 689–691.

Smith, G., & Hall, M. (1982). Evaluating Michigan's guilty but mentally ill verdict: An empirical study. *University of Michigan Journal of Law Reform, 16,* 77–114.

Smith, G.N., Iacono, W.G., Moreau, M., Tallman, K., Beiser, M., & Flak, B. (1988). Choice of comparison group and findings of computerized tomography in schizophrenia. *British Journal of Psychiatry, 153,* 667–674.

Smith, G.T., & Goldman, M.S. (1994). Alcohol expectancy theory and the identification of high-risk adolescents. *Journal of Research on Adolescence, 4,* 229–248.

Smith, G.T., Goldman, M.S., Greenbaum, P.E., & Christiansen, A. (1995). Expectancy for social facilitation from drinking: The divergent paths of high-expectancy and low-expectancy adolescents. *Journal of Abnormal Psychology, 104,* 32–40.

Smith, S.R., & Meyer, R.G. (1985). Child abuse reporting laws and psychotherapy: A time for reconsideration. *International Journal of Law and Psychiatry, 7,* 351–366.

Snaith, P.T., Michael, J., & Reid, R.W. (1993). Sex reassignment surgery: A study of 141 Dutch transsexuals. *British Journal of Psychiatry, 162,* 681–685.

Snaith, R.P. (1994). Psychosurgery. Controversy and enquiry. *British Journal of Psychiatry, 165,* 582–584.

Snowdon, D., Ostwald, S., & Kane, R. (1989). Education, survival, and independence in elderly Catholic sisters, 1936–1988. *American Journal of Epidemiology, 130,* 999–1012.

Soares, J.C., & Gerson, S. (1995). THA: Historical aspects, review of pharmacological properties and therapeutic effects. *Dementia, 6,* 225–234.

Sobell, L.C., Sobell, M.B., Toneatto, T., & Leo, G.I. (1993). What triggers the resolution of alcohol problems without treatment? *Alcoholism: Clinical and Experimental Research, 17,* 217–224.

Sobell, M.B., & Sobell, L.C. (1973). Alcoholics treated by individualized behavior therapy: One year treatment outcomes. *Behaviour Research and Therapy, 11,* 599–618.

Sobell, M.B., & Sobell, L.C. (1976). Second year treatment outcome of alcoholics treated by individualized behavior therapy: Results, *Behaviour Research and Therapy, 11,* 195–215.

Sobell, M.B., & Sobell, L.C. (1989). Moratorium on Maltzman: An appeal to reason. *Journal of Studies on Alcohol, 50,* 473–480.

Soloff, P.H. (1994). Is there any drug treatment of choice for the borderline patient? *Acta Psychiatrica Scandinavica, 89* (suppl. 379), 50–55.

Solomon, D.A., Keitner, G.I., Miller, I.W., Shea, M.T., et al. (1995). Course of illness and maintenance treatments for patients with bipolar disorder. *Journal of Clinical Psychiatry, 56,* 5–13.

Solstad, K., & Hertoft, P. (1993). Frequency of sexual problems and sexual dysfunction in middle-aged Danish men. *Archives of Sexual Behavior, 22,* 51–58.

Sorensen, D.J., Paul, G.L., & Mariotto, M.J. (1988). Inconsistencies in paranoid functioning, premorbid adjustment, and chronicity: Question of diagnostic criteria. *Schizophrenia Bulletin, 14,* 323–336.

Spaulding, W. (1986). Assessment of adult-onset pervasive behavior disorders. In A.R. Ciminero, K.S. Calhoun, & H.E. Adams (Eds.), *Handbook of behavioral assessment,* 2nd ed., pp. 631–669. New York: Wiley.

Spector, I.P., & Carey, M.P. (1990). Incidence and prevalence of the sexual dysfunctions: A critical review of the empirical literature. *Archives of Sexual Behavior, 19,* 389–408.

Spiegel, D., & Cardena, E. (1991). Disintegrated experience: The dissociative disorders revisited. *Journal of Abnormal Psychology, 100,* 366–378.

Spirito, A., Brown, L., Overholser, J., & Fritz, G. (1989). Attempted suicide in adolescence: A review and critique of the literature. *Clinical Psychology Review, 9,* 335–363.

Spitz, R.A. (1946). Anaclitic depression. *Psychoanalytic Study of the Child, 2,* 53–74.

Spitzer, R.L. (1985). DSM-III and the politics-science dichotomy syndrome. *American Psychologist, 40,* 522–526.

Spitzer, R.L., First, M.B., Williams, J.B.W., Kendler, K., Pincus, H.A., & Tucker, G. (1992). Now is the time to retire the term "organic mental disorders." *American Journal of Psychiatry, 149,* 240–244.

Spitzer, R.L., & Fleiss, J.L. (1974). A re-analysis of the reliability of psychiatric diagnosis. *British Journal of Psychiatry, 125,* 341–347.

Spitzer, R.L., Foreman, J., & Nee, J. (1979). DSM-III field trials. I. Initial interrater diagnostic reliability. *American Journal of Psychiatry, 136,* 815–817.

Spivack, G., & Shure, M.B. (1974). *Social adjustment of young children: A cognitive approach to solving real-life problems.* Washington, DC: Jossey-Bass.

Sprague, R.L., & Sleator, E.K. (1977). Methlphenidate in hyperkinetic children: Differences in doses effects learning and social behavior. *Science*, 198, 1274–1276.

Squire, L.R. (1992). Memory and the hippocampus: A synthesis from findings with rats, monkeys, and humans. *Psychological Review*, 99, 195–231.

Squire, L.R., & Slater, P.C. (1978). Bilateral and unilateral ECT: Effects on verbal and nonverbal memory. *American Journal of Psychiatry*, 135, 1316–1320.

Squires-Wheeler, E., Skodol, A., Bassett, A., & Erlenmeyer-Kimling, L. (1989). DSM-III-R schizotypal personality traits in offspring of schizophrenic disorder, affective disorder, and normal control parents. *Journal of Psychiatric Research*, 23, 229–239.

Sroufe, L.A. (1983). Infant-caregiver attachment and patterns of adaptation in the preschool: The roots of maladaptation and competence. In M. Perlmutter (Ed.), *Minnesota Symposium in Child Psychology*, 16, 41–83.

Sroufe, L.A., & Fleeson, J. (1986). Attachment and the construction of relationships. In W.W. Hartup & Z. Rubin (Eds.), *Relationships and development*, pp. 51–72. Hillsdale, NJ: Erlbaum.

Stacy, A.W., Newcomb, M.D., & Bentler, P.W. (1991). Cognitive motivation and drug use: A 9-year longitudinal study. *Journal of Abnormal Psychology*, 100, 502–515.

Stacy, A.W., Widaman, K.F., & Marlatt, G.A. (1990). Expectancy models of alcohol use. *Journal of Personality and Social Psychology*, 58, 918–928.

Starr, P. (1982). *The social transformation of American medicine*. New York: Basic Books.

Stein, G. (1992). Drug treatment of the personality disorders. *British Journal of Psychiatry*, 161, 167–184.

Stein, L.I. (1995). Persistent and severe mental illness: Its impact, status, and future challenges. In R. Schulz & J.R. Greenley (Eds.), *Innovating in community mental health: International perspectives*, pp. 3–17. Westport, CT: Praeger.

Steinhausen, H. (1996). The course and outcome of anorexia nervosa. In K.D. Brownell & C.G. Fairburn (Eds.), *Eating disorders and obesity: A comprehensive handbook*, pp. 234–237. New York: Guilford.

Steketee, F., & Foa, E.B. (1985). Obsessive-compulsive disorder. In D.H. Barlow (Ed.), *Clinical handbook of psychological disorders*, pp. 69–144. New York: Guilford.

Steketee, G. (1993). Social support and treatment outcome of obsessive-compulsive disorder at 9-month follow-up. *Behavioral Psychotherapy*, 21, 81–95.

Steketee, G., Chambless, D.L., Tran, G.Q., Worden, H., & Gillis, M.M. (1996). Behavioral avoidance test for obsessive-compulsive disorder. *Behaviour Research and Therapy*, 34, 73–83.

Stern, Y., Gurland, B., Tatemichi, T.K., et al. (1994). Influence of education and occupation on the incidence of Alzheimer's disease. *JAMA*, 271, 1004–1010.

Stewart, J.T. (1995). Management of behavior problems in the demented patient. *American Family Physician*, 52, 231–240.

Stice, E., Schupak-Neuberg, E., Shaw, H.E., & Stein, R.I. (1994). Relation of media exposure to eating disorder symptomatology: An examination of mediating mechanisms. *Journal of Abnormal Psychology*, 103, 836–840.

Stiles, W.B., Shapiro, D.A., & Elliott, R. (1986). Are all psychotherapies equivalent? *American Psychologist*, 41, 165–180.

Still, G.F. (1902). The Coulstonian Lectures on some abnormal physical conditions in children. *Lancet*, 1, 1008–1012, 1077–1082, 1163–1168.

Stokes, P. (1993). Fluoxetine: A five-year review. *Clinical Therapeutics*, 15, 216–243.

Stokols, D. (1992). Establishing and maintaining healthy environments: Toward a social ecology of health promotion. *American Psychologist*, 47, 6–22.

Stoller, R.J. (1975). *Perversion: The erotic form of hatred*. New York: Random House.

Stoller, R.J. (1991). *Pain and passion: A psychoanalyst explores the world of S & M*. New York: Plenum.

Stone, M. (1985). Schizotypal personality: Psychotherapeutic aspects. *Schizophrenia Bulletin*, 11, 576–589.

Strauss, J.S. (1969). Hallucinations and delusions as points on continua function: Rating scale evidence. *Archives of General Psychiatry*, 21, 581–586.

Strauss, J.S., & Carpenter, W.T. (1978). The prognosis of schizophrenia: Rationale for a multidimensional concept. *Schizophrenia Bulletin*, 4, 56–67.

Strauss, J.S., & Carpenter, W.T., Jr. (1981). *Schizophrenia*. New York: Plenum.

Strauss, M.E. (1993). Relations of symptoms to cognitive deficits in schizophrenia. *Schizophrenia Bulletin*, 19, 215–231.

Stricker, G., & Healey, B.J. (1990). Projective assessment of object relations: A review of the empirical evidence. *Psychological Assessment*, 2, 219–230.

Striegel-Moore, R.H. (1995). A feminist perspective on the etiology of eating disorders. In K.D. Brownell & C.G. Fairburn (Eds.), *Eating disorders and obesity: A comprehensive handbook*, pp. 224–229. New York: Guilford.

Striegel-Moore, R.H., Silberstein, L.R., Frensch, P., & Rodin, J. (1989). A prospective study of disordered eating among college students. *International Journal of Eating Disorders*, 8, 499–509.

Striegel-Moore, R.H., Silberstein, L.R., & Rodin, J. (1993). The social self in bulimia nervosa: Public self-consciousness, social anxiety, and perceived fraudulence. *Journal of Abnormal Psychology*, 102, 297–303.

Strober, M. (1991). Family-genetic studies of eating disorders. *Journal of Clinical Psychiatry*, 52 (suppl.), 9–12.

Strober, M. (1995). Family-genetic perspectives on anorexia nervosa and bulimia nervosa. In K.D. Brownell & C.G. Fairburn (Eds.), *Eating disorders and obesity: A comprehensive handbook*, pp. 212–218. New York: Guilford.

Strong, S.R. (1978). Social psychological approach to psychotherapy research. In S.L. Garfield & A.E. Bergin (Eds.), *Handbook of psychotherapy and behavior change*, 2nd ed., pp. 101–136. New York: Wiley.

Strupp, H.H. (1971). *Psychotherapy and the modification of abnormal behavior*. New York: McGraw-Hill.

Strupp, H.H. (1986). Psychotherapy: Research, practice, and public policy (how to avoid dead ends). *American Psychologist*, 41, 120–130.

Stuart, F.M., Hammond, D.C., & Pett, M.A. (1987). Inhibited sexual desire in women. *Archives of Sexual Behavior*, 16, 91–106.

Styron, W. (1990). *Darkness visible: A memoir of madness*. New York: Vintage.

Sue, S., Zane, N., & Young, K. (1994). Research on psychotherapy with culturally diverse populations. In A.E. Bergin & S.L. Garfield (Eds.), *Handbook of psychotherapy and behavior change*, 4th ed., pp. 783–820. New York: Wiley.

Sullivan, K.T., & Bradbury, T.N. (1996). Preventing marital dysfunction: The primacy of secondary strategies. *Behavior Therapist*, 19, 33–36.

Sullivan, K.T., & Bradbury, T.N. (in press). Are premarital prevention programs reaching couples at risk for marital dysfunction? *Journal of Consulting and Clinical Psychology*.

Suomi, S.J. (1983). Social development in rhesus monkey: Considerations of individual differences. In A. Oliverio & M. Zapella (Eds.), *The behavior of human infants*. New York: Plenum.

Susser, E., Neugebauer, R., Hoek, H.W., Brown, A.S., et al. (1996). Schizophrenia after prenatal famine: Further evidence. *Archives of General Psychiatry*, 53, 25–31.

Sussman, N., & Chou, J.C.Y. (1988). Current issues in benzodiazepine use for anxiety disorders. *Psychiatric Annals*, 18, 139–145.

Sutker, P.B., Davis, J.M., Uddo, M., & Ditta, S.R. (1995). War zone stress, personal resources, and PTSD in Persian Gulf War returnees. *Journal of Abnormal Psychology*, 104, 444–452.

Swaab, D.F., & Gofman, M.A. (1995). Sexual differentiation of the human hypothalamus in relation to gender and sexual orientation. *Trends in Neurosciences, 18,* 264–270.

Swanson, J., Holzer, C., Ganju, V., & Jono, R. (1990). Violence and psychiatric disorder in the community: Evidence from the Epidemiologic Catchment Area Surveys. *Hospital and Community Psychiatry, 41,* 761–770.

Swartz, M.S., Hughes, D., Blazer, D.G., & George, L.K. (1987). Somatization disorder in the community: A study of diagnostic concordance among three diagnostic systems. *Journal of Nervous and Mental Disorder, 175,* 26–33.

Swayze, V.W. (1995). Frontal leukotomy and related psychosurgical procedures in the era before antipsychotics. *American Journal of Psychiatry, 152,* 505–515.

Swendsen, J., Hammen, C., Heller, T., & Gitlin, M. (1995). Correlates of stress reactivity in patients with bipolar disorder. *American Journal of Psychiatry, 152,* 795–797.

Swinson, R.P., & Kuch, K. (1990). Clinical features of panic and related disorders. In J.C. Ballenger (Ed.), *Clinical aspects of panic disorder.* New York: Wiley.

Szasz, T. (1960). The myth of mental illness. *American Psychologist, 15,* 113–118.

Szasz, T.S. (1961). *The myth of mental illness.* New York: Harper & Row.

Szasz, T. (1963). *Law, liberty, and psychiatry: An inquiry into the social uses of mental health practices.* New York: Macmillan.

Szasz, T. (1970). *Ideology and insanity: Essays on the psychiatric dehumanization of man.* New York: Doubleday.

Szasz, T. (1971). *Psychiatric justice.* New York: Collier.

Tager-Flusberg, H. (1996). Current theory and research on language and communication in autism. *Journal of Autism and Developmental Disorders, 26,* 169–171.

Tanfer, K. (1993). National survey of men: Design and execution. *Family Planning Perspectives, 25,* 83–86.

Tannock, R., Schachar, R., & Logan, G. (1995). Methylphenidate and cognitive flexibility: Dissociated dose effects in hyperactive children. *Journal of Abnormal Child Psychology, 23,* 235–266.

Tarter, R.E., Alterman, A.I., & Edwards, K.L. (1985). Vulnerability to alcoholism in men: A behavior-genetic perspective. *Journal of Studies on Alcohol, 46,* 329–356.

Taylor, S.E. (1990). Health psychology: The science and the field. *American Psychologist, 45,* 40–50.

Taylor, S.E. (1995). *Health psychology,* 3rd ed. New York: McGraw-Hill.

Tearnan, B.H., & Telch, M.J. (1988). Etiology of agoraphobia: An investigation of perceived childhood and parental factors. *Phobia Practice and Research Journal, 1,* 13–24.

Telch, M.J., Brouillard, M., Telch, C.F., Agras, W.S., & Taylor, C.B. (1989). Role of cognitive appraisal in panic-related avoidance. *Behaviour Research and Therapy, 27,* 373–383.

Teplin, L. (1990). The prevalence of severe mental disorder among male urban jail detainees: Comparison with the Epidemiologic Catchment Area Program. *American Journal of Public Health, 80,* 663–669.

Telpin, L.A., Abram, K.M., & McClelland, G.M. (1994). Does psychiatric disorder predict violent crime among released jail detainees? A six-year longitudinal study. *American Psychologist, 49,* 335–342.

Teri, L., & Gallagher-Thompson, D. (1991). Cognitive-behavioral interventions for treatment of depression in Alzheimer's patients. *Gerontologist, 31,* 413–416.

Teri, L., & Wagner, A. (1992). Alzheimer's disease and depression. *Journal of Consulting and Clinical Psychology, 60,* 379–391.

Terman, M., Terman, J.S., Quitkin, F.M., et al. (1989). Light therapy for seasonal affective disorder: A review of efficacy. *Neuropsychopharmacology, 2,* 1–22.

Tesman, J.R., & Hills, A. (1994). Developmental effects of lead exposure in children. *Social Policy Report: Society for Research in Child Development, 8* (3), 1–16.

Test, M.A., Knoedler, W.H., Allness, D.J., Burke, S.S., Brown, R.L., & Wallisch, L.S. (1991). Long-term community care through an assertive continuous treatment team. In C.A. Tammings & S.C. Schulz (Eds.), *Schizophrenia research: Advances in neuropsychiatry and psychopharmacology,* pp. 239–246. New York: Raven Press.

Thangavelu, R., & Martin, R.L. (1995). ICD-10 and DSM-IV: Depiction of the diagnostic elephant. *Psychiatric Annals, 25,* 20–28.

Thapar, A., & McGuffin, P. (1993). Is personality disorder inherited? An overview of the evidence. *Journal of Psychopathology and Behavioral Assessment, 15,* 325–345.

Thase, M. (1988). The relationship between Down syndrome and Alzheimer's disease. In L. Nadel (Ed.), *The psychobiology of Down syndrome.* Cambridge, MA: MIT Press.

Thase, M.E. (1989). Comparison between seasonal affective and other forms of recurrent depression. In N.E. Rosenthal et al. (Eds.), *Seasonal affective disorders and phototherapy,* pp. 64–78. New York: Guilford.

Thigpen, C.H., & Cleckley, H.M. (1957). *The three faces of Eve.* New York: McGraw-Hill.

Thomas, A., & Chess, S. (1977). *Temperament and development.* New York: Brunner/Mazel.

Thompson, J.K. (1996). *Body image, eating disorders, and obesity.* Washington, DC: American Psychological Association.

Thompson, P.A., & Meltzer, H.Y. (1993). Positive, negative, and disorganisation factors from the Schedule for Affective Disorders and Schizophrenia and the Present State Examination: A three-factor solution. *British Journal of Psychiatry, 163,* 344–351.

Thorley, G. (1984). Review of follow-up and follow-back studies of childhood hyperactivity. *Psychological Bulletin, 96,* 116–132.

Thornicroft, G., & Sartorius, N. (1993). The course and outcome of depression in different cultures: 10-year follow-up of the WHO Collaborative Study on the Assessment of Depressive Disorders. *Psychological Medicine, 23,* 1023–1032.

Tiefer, L. (1988). A feminist critique of the sexual dysfunction nomenclature. *Women and Therapy, 7,* 5–21.

Tienari, P., Sorri, A., Lahti, I., et al. (1987). Genetic and psychosocial factors in schizophrenia: The Finnish adoptive family study. *Schizophrenia Bulletin, 13,* 477–484.

Tienari, P., Wynne, L.C., Moring, J., Lahti, I., et al. (1994). The Finnish Adoptive Family Study of Schizophrenia: Implications for family research. *British Journal of Psychiatry, 164* (suppl. 23), 20–26.

Tiffany, S.T., & Baker, T.B. (1986). Tolerance to alcohol: Psychological models and their application to alcoholism. *Annals of Behavioral Medicine, 8,* 7–12.

Tison, F., Dartigues, J.F., Auriacombe, S., Letenneur, L., et al. (1995). Dementia in Parkinson's disease: A population-based study in ambulatory and institutionalized individuals. *Neurology, 45,* 705–708.

Torgersen, S. (1985). Relationship of schizotypal personality disorder to schizophrenia: Genetics. *Schizophrenia Bulletin, 11,* 554–563.

Torgersen, S. (1986). Genetic factors in moderately severe and mild affective disorders. *Archives of General Psychiatry, 43,* 222–226.

Torgersen, S. (1988). Genetics. In C.G. Last & M. Hersen (Eds.), *Handbook of anxiety disorders.* New York: Pergamon.

Torgersen, S. (1994). Genetics in borderline conditions. *Acta Psychiatrica Scandinavica, 89* (suppl. 379), 19–25.

Torgersen, S., Onstad, S., Skre, I., Edvardsen, J., & Kringlen, E. (1993). "True" schizotypal personality disorder: A study of co-twins and relatives of schizophrenic probands. *American Journal of Psychiatry, 150,* 1661–1667.

Torrey, E.F. (1988). *Nowhere to go: The tragic odyssey of the homeless mentally ill.* New York: Harper & Row.

Torrey, E.F. (1997). *Out of the shadows.* New York: Wiley.

Torrey, E.F., Bowler, A.E., Taylor, E.H., & Gottesman, I.I. (1994). *Schizophrenia and manic-*

depressive disorder: The biological roots of mental illness as revealed by the landmark study of identical twins. New York: Basic Books.

Torrey, E.F., & Yolken, R.H. (1995). Could schizophrenia be a viral zoonosis transmitted from house cats? *Schizophrenia Bulletin, 21,* 167–171.

Trachtenberg, M.C., & Blum, K. (1987). Alcohol and opioid peptides: Neuropharmacological rationale for physical craving of alcohol. *American Journal of Drug and Alcohol Abuse, 13,* 365–372.

Tran, G.Q., & Chambless, D.L. (1995). Psychopathology of social phobia: Effects of subtype and of avoidant personality disorder. *Journal of Anxiety Disorders, 9,* 489–501.

Trials of the Hypertension Prevention Collaborative Research Group. (1992). The effects of nonpharmacologic interventions on blood pressure of persons with high normal levels: Results of the Trials of Hypertension Prevention, Phase I, *JAMA, 267,* 1213–1220.

Triandis, H.C. (1994). Culture and social behavior. In W.J. Lonner & R.S. Malpass (Eds.), *Psychology and culture,* pp. 169–174. Boston: Allyn & Bacon.

Truax, C., & Carkhuff, R. (1967). *Toward effective counseling and psychotherapy: Training and practice.* Hawthorne, NY: Aldine.

True, W.R., Rice, J., Eisen, S.A., Heath, A.C., Goldberg, J., Lyons, M.J., & Nowak, J. (1993). A twin study of genetic and environmental contributions to liability for posttraumatic stress symptoms. *Archives of General Psychiatry, 50,* 257–264.

Trull, T.J. (1995). Borderline personality disorder features in nonclinical young adults. 1. Identification and validation. *Psychological Assessment, 7,* 33–41.

Trull, T.J., Widiger, T.A., & Guthrie, P. (1990). Categorical versus dimensional status of borderline personality disorder. *Journal of Abnormal Psychology, 99,* 40–48.

Trzepacz, P.T. (1994). The neuropathogenesis of delirium: A need to focus our research. *Psychosomatics, 35,* 374–391.

Tsai, L.Y. (1996). Comorbid psychiatric disorders of autistic disorder. *Journal of Autism and Developmental Disorders, 26,* 159–163.

Tsuang, M.T., Simpson, J.C., & Fleming, J.A. (1992). Epidemiology of suicide, *International Review of Psychiatry, 4,* 117–129.

Tsuang, M.T., Woolson, R.F., & Fleming, J.A. (1979). Long-term outcome of major psychoses. I. Schizophrenia and affective disorders compared with psychiatrically symptom-free surgical conditions. *Archives of General Psychiatry, 36,* 1295–1301.

Tueth, M.J., & Cheong, J.A. (1993). Delirium: Diagnosis and treatment in the older patient. *Geriatrics, 48,* 75–81.

Turkat, I.D., & Carlson, C.R. (1984). Data-based versus symptomatic formulation of treatment: The case of a dependent personality. *Journal of Behavior Therapy and Experimental Psychiatry, 15,* 153–160.

Turkheimer, E. (1991). Individual and group differences in adoption studies of IQ. *Psychological Bulletin, 110,* 392–405.

Turner, S.M., & Beidel, D.C. (1988). *Treating obsessive-compulsive disorder.* New York: Pergamon.

Turner, S.M., Beidel, D.C., & Stanley, M.A. (1992). Are obsessional thoughts and worry different cognitive phenomena? *Clinical Psychology Review, 12,* 257–270.

Turpin, G. (1991). The psychophysiological assessment of anxiety disorders: Three-systems measurement and beyond. *Psychological Assessment, 3,* 366–375.

Tyrer, P. (1989). Choice of treatment in anxiety. In P. Tyrer (Ed.), *Psychopharmacology of anxiety.* New York: Oxford University Press.

Tyrer, P. (1994). What are the borders of borderline personality disorder? *Acta Psychiatrica Scandinavica, 89* (suppl. 379), 38–44.

Tyrer, P. (1995). Are personality disorders well classified in DSM-IV? In W.J. Livesley (Ed.), *The DSM-IV personality disorders.* New York: Guilford, pp. 29–42.

Tyrer, P., Candy, J., & Kelly, D. (1973). A study of the clinical effects of phenelzine and placebo in the treatment of phobic anxiety. *Psychopharmacology, 32,* 237–254.

Tyrer, P., Casey, P., & Gall, J. (1983). Relationship between neurosis and personality disorder. *British Journal of Psychiatry, 142,* 404–408.

Tyrer, P., & Ferguson, B. (1987). Problems in the classification of personality disorder. *Psychological Medicine, 17,* 15–20.

Tyrer, P., Seivewright, N., Ferguson, B., Murphy, S., Darling, C., Brothwell, J., Kingdon, D., & Johnson, A.L. (1990). The Nottingham Study of Neurotic Disorder: Relationship between personality status and symptoms. *Psychological Medicine, 20,* 423–431.

Uchino, B.N., Cacioppo, J.T., & Kiecolt-Glaser, J.K. (1996). The relationship between social support and physiological processes: A review with emphasis underlying mechanisms and implications for health. *Psychological Bulletin, 119,* 488–531.

Umbricht, D., & Kane, J.M. (1995). Risperidone: Efficacy and safety. *Schizophrenia Bulletin, 21,* 593–606.

U.S. Census Bureau. (1986). Age structure of the U.S. population in the 21st century. *Statistical Brief 1–86.* Washington, DC: U.S. Government Printing Office.

U.S. Census Bureau. (1992). Growth of America's oldest-old population. *Profiles of America's Elderly,*

No. 2. Washington, DC: U.S. Government Printing Office.

U.S. Census Bureau. (1996). Sixty-five plus in the United States. *Current Population Reports.* (P23–190). Washington, DC: U.S. Government Printing Office.

U.S. Department of Health and Human Services. (1993). *AIDS research: An NIMH blueprint for the second decade.* NIH Publication No. 93–3563. Washington, DC: U.S. Government Printing Office.

Vaillant, G.E. (1984). The disadvantages of DSM-III outweigh its advantages. *American Journal of Psychiatry, 141,* 542–545.

Vaillant, G.E. (1992). Is there a natural history of addiction? In C.P. O'Brien & J.H. Jaffe (Eds.), *Addictive states,* pp. 41–58. New York: Raven Press.

Vaillant, G.E. (1994). Evidence that the Type 1/Type 2 dichotomy in alcoholism must be re-examined. *Addiction, 89,* 1049–1057.

Vaillant, G.E. (1995). *The natural history of alcoholism revisited.* Cambridge, MA: Harvard University Press.

Vaillant, G.E. (1996). A long-term follow-up of male alcohol abuse. *Archives of General Psychiatry, 53,* 243–249.

Valenstein, E.S. (1973). *Brain control.* New York: Wiley.

Valenstein, E.S. (1986). *Great and desperate cures.* New York: Basic Books.

Valente, J. (1996). A long road to daylight: Football player's gambling problems. *People Weekly,* January 15, 81+.

Vandereycken, W. (1995). The families of patients with an eating disorder. In K.D. Brownell & C.G. Fairburn (Eds.), *Eating disorders and obesity: A comprehensive handbook* (pp. 219–223). New York: Guilford.

van der Hart, O., & Friedman, B. (1989). A reader's guide to dissociation: A neglected intellectual heritage. *Dissociation, 2,* 13–16.

van der Kolk, B.A. (1996). The psychobiology of PTSD. In B.A. van der Kolk, A.C. McFarlane, & L. Weisaeth (Eds.), *Traumatic stress,* pp. 214–241. New York: Guilford.

van der Kolk, B.A., Boyd, H., Krystal, J., & Greenburg, M. (1984). Posttraumatic stress disorder as a biologically based disorder: Implications of the animal model of inescapable shock. In B.A. van der Kolk (Ed.), *Posttraumatic stress disorder: Psychological and biological sequel,* pp. 124–134. Washington, DC: American Psychiatric Press.

van der Kolk, B.A., & McFarlane, A.C. (1996). The black hole of trauma. In B.A. van der Kolk, A.C. McFarlane, & L. Weisaeth (Eds.), *Traumatic stress,* pp. 3–23. New York: Guilford.

Van der Molen, G.M., Van den Hout, M.A., Van Dieren, A.C., & Griez, E. (1989). Childhood separation anxiety and adult onset panic disorders. *Journal of Anxiety Disorders*, 3, 97–106.

Van Horn, J.D., Berman, K.F., & Weinberger, D.R. (1996). Pathophysiology of schizophrenia: Insights from neuroimagining. In S.J. Watson (Ed)., *Biology of schizophrenia and affective disease*, pp. 393–419. Washington, DC: American Psychiatric Press.

Vasey, M.W., & Borkovec, T.D. (1992). A catastrophizing assessment of worrisome thoughts. *Cognitive Therapy and Research*, 16, 505–520.

Vaughn, C.E., & Leff, J.P. (1976). The influence of family and social factors on the course of psychiatric illness: A comparison of schizophrenic and depressed neurotic patients. *British Journal of Psychiatry*, 129, 125–137.

Verebey, K. (1991). Laboratory methodology for drug and alcohol addiction. In N.S. Miller (Ed.), *Comprehensive handbook of drug and alcohol addiction*, pp. 809–824. New York: Dekker.

Visintainer, M.A., Seligman, M.E.P., & Volpicelli, J.R. (1982). Tumor rejection in rats after inescapable or escapable electric shock. *Science*, 216, 437–439.

Vogel-Sprott, M. (1992). *Alcohol tolerance and social drinking: Learning the consequences*. New York: Guilford.

Vogler, G.P., Gottesman, I.I., McGue, M.K., & Rao, D.C. (1990). Mixed model segregation analysis of schizophrenia in the Lindelius Swedish pedigrees. *Behavior Genetics*, 20, 461–472.

Volkmar, F.R. (1996). Diagnostic issues in autism. Results of the DSM-IV field. *Journal of Autism and Developmental Disorders*, 26, 155–157.

Volkmar, F.R., Klin, A., Siegel, B., et al. (1994). Field trial for autistic disorder in DSM-IV. *American Journal of Psychiatry*, 151, 1361–1367.

von Bertalanffy, L. (1968). *General systems theory.* New York: Braziller.

Von Korff, M., Eaton, W., Keyl, P. (1985). The epidemiology of panic attacks and disorder: Results from three community surveys. *American Journal of Epidemiology*, 122, 970–981.

Vuchinich, S., Emery, R.E., & Cassidy, J. (1988). Family members as third parties in dyadic family conflict: Strategies, alliances, and outcomes. *Child Development*, 59, 1293–1302.

Wagner, W., Zaborny, B.A., & Gray, T.E. (1994). Fluvoxamine: A review of its safety profile in worldwide studies. *International Clinical Psychopharmacology*, 9, 223–227.

Wakefield, J. (1988). Female primary orgasmic dysfunction: Masters and Johnson versus DSM-III-R on diagnosis and incidence. *Journal of Sex Research*, 24, 363–377.

Wakefield, J.C. (1992a). The concept of mental disorder: On the boundary between biological facts and social values. *American Psychologist, 47,* 373–388.

Wakefield, J.C. (1992b). Disorder as harmful dysfunction: A conceptual critique of DSM-III-R's definition of mental disorder. *Psychological Review,* 99, 232–247.

Wald, M.S., Carlsmith, J.M., & Leiderman, P.H. (1988). *Protecting abused and neglected children.* Stanford, CA: Stanford University Press.

Walker, E., Davis, D., & Baum, K. (1993). Social withdrawal. In C.G. Costello (Ed.), *Symptoms of schizophrenia,* pp. 227–260. New York: Wiley.

Walker, L. (1979). *The battered woman.* New York: Harper & Row.

Walker, L. (1989). Psychology and violence against women. *American Psychologist,* 44, 695–702.

Wallis, C.J., Rezazzadeh, S.M., & Lal, H. (1993). Role of serotonin in ethanol abuse. *Drug Development and Research,* 30, 178–188.

Walsh, B.T. (1995). Pharmacotherapy of eating disorders. In K.D. Brownell & C.G. Fairburn (Eds.), *Eating disorders and obesity: A comprehensive handbook,* pp. 313–317. New York: Guilford.

Walsh, D.C., Hingson, R.W., Merrigan, D.M., et al. (1991). A randomized trial of treatment options for alcohol abusing workers. *New England Journal of Medicine,* 325, 775–782.

Walsh, J. (1990). Assessment and treatment of the schizotypal personality disorder. *Journal of Independent Social Work,* 4, 41–59.

Warheight, G.J., & Auth, J.B. (1985). Epidemiology of alcohol abuse in adulthood. In J.O. Cavendar (Ed.), *Psychiatry,* Vol. 3, pp. 1–18. Philadelphia: Lippincott.

Warner, L.A., Kessler, R.C., Hughes, M., Anthony, J.C., & Nelson, C.B. (1995). Prevalence and correlates of drug use and dependence in the United States: Results from the National Comorbidity Survey. *Archives of General Psychiatry,* 52, 219–228.

Warren, S.T,. & Ashley, C.T. (1995). Triplet repeat expansion mutations: The example of fragile X syndrome. *Annual Review of Neuroscience,* 18, 77–99.

Waterman, A.S., & Archer, S. (1990). A life-span perspective on identity formation: Development in form, function, and process. In P.B. Baltes, D.L. Featherman, & R.M. Lerner (Eds.), *Life-span development and behavior,* Vol. 10, pp. 29–57. Hillsdale, NJ: Erlbaum.

Waterman, A.S., & Goldman, J.A. (1976). A longitudinal study of changes in ego identity development at a liberal arts college. *Journal of Youth and Adolescence,* 5, 361–370.

Waterman, G., Geary, P., & Waterman, C. (1974). Longitudinal study of changes in ego identity status from the freshman to the senior year at college. *Developmental Psychology,* 10, 387–392.

Watson, D., & Clark, L.A. (1984). Negative affectivity: The disposition to experience aversive emotional states. *Psychological Bulletin,* 96, 465–490.

Watson, D., & Clark, L.A. (1990). *The Positive and Negative Affect Schedule-Expanded Form.* Unpublished manuscript. Southern Methodist University.

Watson, I.P.B., Hoffman, L., & Wilson, G.V. (1988). The neuropsychiatry of post-traumatic stress disorder. *British Journal of Psychiatry,* 152, 164–173.

Watson, J.B. (1913). Psychology as the behaviorist views it. *Psychological Review,* 20, 158–177.

Watson, J.B., & Rayner, R. (1920). Conditioned emotional reactions. *Journal of Experimental Psychology,* 3, 1–14.

Watt, L.M., & Wong, P.T. (1991). A taxonomy of reminiscence and therapeutic implications. *Journal of Gerontological Social Work,* 16, 37–57.

Watt, N.F. (1984). In a nutshell: The first two decades of high-risk research in schizophrenia. In N.F. Watt, E.J. Anthony, L.C. Wynne, J.E. Rolf (Eds.), *Children at risk for schizophrenia: A longitudinal perspective.* Cambridge: Cambridge University Press.

Watt, N.F., Anthony, E.J., Wynne, L.C., & Rolf, J.E. (Eds.) (1984). *Children at risk for schizophrenia: A longitudinal perspective.* Cambridge: Cambridge University Press.

Weaver, T.L., & Clum, G.A. (1993). Early family environments and traumatic experiences associated with borderline personality disorders. *Journal of Consulting and Clinical Psychology,* 61, 1068–1075.

Weddington, W.W. (1992). Use of pharmacologic agents in the treatment of addiction. *Psychiatric Annals,* 22, 425–429.

Wegner, D.M. (1989). *White bears and other unwanted thoughts: Suppression, obsession, and the psychology of mental control.* New York: Viking.

Wegner, D.M. (1994). Ironic processes of mental control. *Psychological Review,* 101, 34–52.

Wegner, D.M., Shortt, J.W., Blake, A.W., & Page, M.S. (1990). The suppression of exciting thoughts. *Journal of Personality and Social Psychology,* 58, 409–418.

Wehr, T.A. (1989). Seasonal affective disorder: A historical overview. In Rosenthal, N.E. & Blehar, M.C. (Eds.), *Seasonal affective disorders and phototherapy.* New York: Guilford.

Weiden, P.J., & Olfson, M. (1995). Cost of relapse in schizophrenia. *Schizophrenia Bulletin,* 21, 419–429.

Weinberger, D.R. (1987). Implications of normal brain development for the pathogenesis of schizophrenia. *Archives of General Psychiatry*, 44, 660–669.

Weinberger, D.R., Berman, K.F., Suddath, R., & Torrey, E.F. (1992). Evidence of dysfunction of a prefrontal-limbic network in schizophrenia: A magnetic resonance imaging and regional cerebral blood flow study of discordant monozygotic twins. *American Journal of Psychiatry*, 149, 890–897.

Weinberger, D.R., & Lipska, B.K. (1995). Cortical maldevelopment, antipsychotic drugs, and schizophrenia: A search for common ground. *Schizophrenia Research*, 16, 87–110.

Weiner, H., & Fawzy, F.I. (1989). An integrative model of health, disease, and illness. In S. Cheren (Ed.), *Psychosomatic medicine: Theory, physiology, and practice*, Vol. 1, pp. 9–44. Madison, CT: International Universities Press.

Weiner, R.D., & Krystal, A.D. (1994). The present use of electroconvulsive therapy. *Annual Review of Medicine*, 45, 273–281.

Weinstein, R.M. (1983). Labeling theory and the attitudes of mental patients: A review. *Journal of Health and Social Behavior*, 24, 70–84.

Weiss, G., Hechtman, L., Milroy, T., & Perlman, T. (1985). Psychiatric status of hyperactives as adults: A controlled prospective 15-year follow-up of 63 hyperactive children. *Journal of the American Academy of Child Psychiatry*, 24, 211–220.

Weissman, J. (1988). Anxiety and alcoholism. *Journal of Clinical Psychiatry*, 49 (suppl.), 17–19.

Weissman, M.M. (1988). Epidemiology of panic disorder and agoraphobia. In A.J. Francis & R.E. Hales (Eds.), *Annual review of psychiatry*, vol. 7. Washington, DC: American Psychiatric Press.

Weissman, M.M. (1993). The epidemiology of personality disorders: A 1990 update. *Journal of Personality Disorders*, supplement, 44–62.

Weissman, M.M., Bruce, M.L., Leaf, P.J., Florio, L.P., & Holzer, C. (1991). Affective disorders. In L.N. Robins & D.A. Regier (Eds.), *Psychiatric disorders in America: The Epidemiologic Catchment Area Study*, pp. 53–80. New York: Free Press.

Weissman, M., Meyers, J., & Harding, P. (1978). Psychiatric disorders in a U.S. urban community: 1975–1976. *American Journal of Psychiatry*, 135, 459–462.

Welch, S.L., & Fairburn, C.G. (in press). Sexual abuse and bulimia nervosa: Three integrated case control comparisons. *American Journal of Psychiatry*.

Wenzlaff, R.M., Wegner, D.M., & Klein, S.B. (1991). The role of thought suppression in the bonding of thought and mood. *Journal of Personality and Social Psychology*, 60, 500–508.

Werner, E.E., & Smith, R.S. (1992). *Overcoming the odds: High risk children from birth to adulthood.* Ithaca, NY: Cornell.

Werner, J.S., & Smith, R.S. (1982). *Vulnerable but invincible: A longitudinal study of resilient children and youth.* New York: McGraw-Hill.

Wertheimer, J. (1991). Affective disorders and organic mental disorders. *International Psycholgeriatrics*, 3, 19–27.

Westermeyer, J. (1987). Cultural factors in clinical assessment. *Journal of Consulting and Clinical Psychology*, 55, 471–478.

Weston, D., Ludolph, P., Misle, B., Ruffins, S., & Block, J. (1990). Physical and sexual abuse in adolescent girls with borderline personality disorder. *American Journal of Orthopsychiatry*, 60, 55–66.

Whalen, C., Henker, B., Hinshaw, S., Heller, T., & Huber-Dressler, A. (1991). Messages of medication: Effects of actual versus informed medication status on hyperactive boys's expectancies and self-evaluation. *Journal of Consulting and Clinical Psychology*, 59, 602–606.

Whalen, R.E., Geary, D.C., & Johnson, F. (1990). Models of sexuality. In D.P. McWhirter, S.A. Sanders, & J.M. Reinisch (Eds.), *Homosexuality/heterosexuality: Concepts of sexual orientation*, pp. 61–70. New York: Oxford University Press.

Whybrow, P.C., Akiskal, H.S., & McKinney, W.T., Jr. (1984). *Mood disorders: Toward a new psychobiology.* New York: Plenum.

Wicks-Nelson, R., & Israel, A.C. (1991). *Behavior disorders of childhood*, 2nd ed. Englewood Cliffs, NJ: Prentice Hall.

Widiger, T.A., Cadoret, R., Hare, R., Robins, L., et al. (1996). DSM-IV antisocial personality disorder field trial. *Journal of Abnormal Psychology*, 105, 3–16.

Widiger, T.A., & Corbitt, E.M. (1995). Antisocial personality disorder. In W.J. Livesley (Ed.), *The DSM-IV personality disorders*, pp. 103–126. New York: Guilford.

Widiger, T.A., & Frances, A. (1985). The DSM-III personality disorders: Perspectives from psychology. *Archives of General Psychiatry*, 42, 615–623.

Widiger, T.A., & Frances, A. (1987). Interviews and inventories for the measurement of personality disorders. *Clinical Psychology Review*, 7, 49–75.

Widiger, T.A., Frances, A.J., Pincus, H.A., Davis, W.W., & First, M.B. (1991). Toward an empirical classification for the DSM-IV. *Journal of Abnormal Psychology*, 100, 280–288.

Widiger, T.A., Frances, A., Warner, L., & Bluhm, C. (1986). Diagnostic criteria for the borderline and schizotypal personality disorders. *Journal of Abnormal Psychology*, 95, 43–51.

Widiger, T.A., & Rogers, J.H. (1989). Prevalence and comorbidity of personality disorders. *Psychiatric Annals*, 19, 132–136.

Widiger, T.A., & Trull, T.J. (1992). Personality and psychopathology: An application of the five-factor model. *Journal of Personality*, 60, 363–393.

Widiger, T.A., & Trull, T.J. (1993). Borderline and narcissistic personality disorders. In P.B. Sutker & H.E. Adams (Eds.), *Comprehensive handbook of psychopathology*, 2nd ed., pp. 371–394. New York: Plenum.

Wiehe, V.R., & Richards, A.L. (1995). *Intimate betrayal: Understanding and responding to the trauma of acquaintance rape.* Thousand Oaks, CA: Sage.

Wierzbicki, M. (1993). *Issues in clinical psychology: Subjective versus objective approaches.* Boston: Allyn & Bacon.

Wiggins, J.S. (1973). *Personality and prediction: Principles of personality assessment.* Reading, MA: Addison-Wesley.

Wiggins, J.S. (1982). Circumplex models of interpersonal behavior in clinical psychology. In P.C. Kendall & J.N. Butcher (Eds.), *Handbook of research methods in clinical psychology*, pp. 183–221. New York: Wiley.

Wiggins, J.S., & Pincus, A.L. (1992). Personality: Structure and assessment. *Annual Review of Psychology*, 43, 473–504.

Wilfley, D.E., Agras, W.S., Telch, C.F., Rossiter, E.M., Schneider, J.A., Cole, A.G., Sifford, L., & Raeburn, S.D. (1993). Group cognitive-behavioral therapy and group interpersonal psychotherapy for the nonpurging bulimic individual: A controlled comparison. *Journal of Consulting and Clinical Psychology*, 61, 296–305.

Williams, J.B.W. (1985). The multiaxial system of DSM-III: Where did it come from and where should it go? *Archives of General Psychiatry*, 42, 175–180.

Williams, J.B.W., Gibbon, M., First, M.B., Spitzer, R.L., Davies, M., Borus, J., Howes, J.M., Kane, J., Pope, H.G., Rounsaville, B., & Wittchen, H. (1992). The structured clinical interview for DSM-III-R (SCID). II. Multisite test-retest reliability. *Archives of General Psychiatry*, 49, 630–636.

Williams, J.M.B., Mathews, A., & MacLeod, C. (1996). The emotional stroop task and psychopathology. *Psychological Bulletin*, 120, 3–24.

Williams, L.M. (1994). Recall of childhood trauma: A prospective study of women's memories of child sexual abuse. *Journal of Consulting and Clinical Psychology*, 62, 1167–1176.

Williams, L.M., & Finkelhor, D. (1990). The characteristics of incestuous fathers: A review of recent studies. In W.L. Marshall, D.R. Laws, & H.E. Barbaree (Eds.), *Handbook of sexual assault: Issues, theories, and treatment of the offender*, p. 231. New York: Plenum.

Williams, R.B., Barefoot, J.C., Califf, R.M., Haney, T.L., Saunders, W.B., et al. (1992). Prognostic importance of social and economic resources among medically treated patients with angiographically documented coronary artery disease. *Journal of the American Medical Association*, 267, 520–524.

Wilsnack, S.C. (1984). Drinking, sexuality and sexual dysfunction in women. In S.C. Wilsnack & L.J. Beckman (Eds.), *Alcohol problems in women*, pp. 189–227. New York: Guilford.

Wilsnack, S.C., & Wilsnack, R.W. (1991). Epidemiology of women's drinking. *Journal of Substance Abuse*, 3, 133–158.

Wilson, G.D. (1987). An ethological approach to sexual deviation. In G.D. Wilson (Ed.), *Variant sexuality: Research and theory*, pp. 84–115. London: Croom Helm.

Wilson, G.T. (1995). Empirically validated treatments as a basis for clinical practice: Problems and prospects. In S.C. Hayes, V.M. Follette, R.M. Dawes, and K.E. Grady (Eds.), *Scientific standards of psychological practice: Issues and recommendations*. Reno, NV: Context Press, pp. 163–196.

Wilson, M. (1989). The black extended family: An analytical review. *Developmental Psychology*, 22, 246–258.

Wincze, J.P. (1989). Assessment and treatment of atypical sexual behavior. In S.R. Lieblum & R.C. Rosen (Eds.), *Principles and practice of sex therapy*, 2nd ed., pp. 382–404. New York: Guilford.

Wincze, J.P., & Carey, M.P. (1991). *Sexual dysfunction: A guide for assessment and treatment*. New York: Guilford.

Wing, L. (1988). Autism: Possible clues to the underlying pathology. 1. Clinical facts. In L. Wing (Ed.), *Aspects of autism: Biological research*, pp. 11–18. Gaskell: London.

Wing, L., & Gould, H.J. (1979). Severe impairments of social interaction and associate abnormalities in children: Epidemiology and classification. *Journal of Autism and Developmental Disorders*, 9, 11–29.

Winger, G., Hofmann, F.G., & Woods, J.H. (1992). *A handbook on drug and alcohol abuse: The biomedical aspects*, 3rd ed. New York: Oxford University Press.

Winograd, E., & Killinger, W.A. (1983). Relating age at encoding in early childhood to adult recall: Development of flashbulb memories. *Journal of Experimental Psychology: General*, 112, 413–422.

Winokur, G., Coryell, W., Akiskal, H.S., Endicott, J., Keller, M., & Mueller, T. (1994). Manic-depressive (bipolar) disorder: The course in light of a prospective ten-year follow-up of 131 patients. *Acta Psychiatrica Scandinavica*, 89, 102–110.

Winokur, G., Coryell, W., Keller, M., Endicott, J., & Leon, A. (1995). A family study of manic-depressive (bipolar I) disease. *Archives of General Psychiatry*, 52, 367–373.

Winokur, G., Zimmerman, M., & Cadoret, R. (1988). 'Cause the Bible tells me so. *Archives of General Psychiatry*, 45, 683–684.

Wise, M.G., & Gray, K.F. (1996). Delirium, dementia and amnestic disorders. In R.E. Hales & S.C. Yudofsky (Eds.), *The American psychiatric press synopsis of psychiatry*, pp. 305–343. Washington, DC: American Psychiatric Press.

Wise, M.G., & Tierney, J.G. (1994). Impulse control disorders not elsewhere classified. In R.E. Hales, S.C. Yudofsky, & J.A. Talbott (Eds.), *Textbook of psychiatry*, 2nd ed., pp. 681–699. Washington, DC: American Psychiatric Press.

Wittchen, H., Kessler, R.C., Zhao, S., & Abelson, J. (1995). Reliability and clinical validity of UM-CIDI DSM-III-R generalized anxiety disorder. *Journal of Psychiatric Research*, 29, 95–110.

Wittchen, H., Knauper, B., & Kessler, R.C. (1994). Lifetime risk of depression. *British Journal of Psychiatry*, 165 (suppl. 26), 16–22.

Wolf, S., & Chick, J. (1980). Schizoid personality in childhood: A controlled follow-up study. *Psychological Medicine*, 10, 85–100.

Wolfe, D. (1987). *Child abuse: Implications for child development and psychopathology*. Beverly Hills, CA: Sage.

Wolpe, J. (1958). *Psychotherapy and reciprocal inhibition*. Stanford, CA: Stanford University Press.

Wolpe, J., & Rachman, S.J. (1960). Psychoanalytic "evidence." A critique based on Freud's case of Little Hans. *Journal of Nervous and Mental Disease*, 131, 135–147.

Wong, D.F., Wagner, H.N., Jr., Tune, L.E., Dannals, R.F., Pearlson, G.D., Links, J.M., et al. (1986). Positron emission tomography reveals elevated D_2 dopamine receptors in drug-naive schizophrenics. *Science*, 234, 1558–1563.

Wong, P.T., & Watt, L.M. (1991). What types of reminiscence are associated with successful aging? *Psychology and Aging*, 6, 272–279.

Wood, J.M., Nezworski, M.T., & Stejskal, W.J. (1996). The comprehensive system for the Rorschach: A critical examination. *Psychological Science*, 7, 3–17.

Woodside, D.B., & Kennedy, S.H. (1995). Gender differences in eating disorders. In M.V. Seeman (Ed.), *Gender and psychopathology*, pp. 253–268. Washington, DC: American Psychiatric Press.

Woody, G.E., McLellan, A.T., Luborsky, L., & O'Brien, C.P. (1985). Sociopathy and psychotherapy outcome. *Archives of General Psychiatry*, 42, 1081–1086.

Worden, J.W. (1986). *Grief counseling and grief therapy: A handbook for the mental health practitioner*. New York: Springer.

World Health Organization. (1983). *Depressive disorders in different cultures*. Geneva, Switzerland.

World Health Organization. (1992). *The ICD-10 classification of mental and behavioural disorders: Clinical descriptions and diagnostic guidelines*. Geneva, Switzerland.

Wortman, C.B., & Silver, R.C. (1989). The myths of coping with loss. *Journal of Consulting and Clinical Psychology*, 57, 349–357.

Yalom, I.D. (1985). *Theory and practice of group psychotherapy*, 3rd ed. New York: Basic Books.

Yang, B., Stack, S., & Lester, D. (1992). Suicide and unemployment: Predicting the smoothed trend and yearly fluctuations. *Journal of Socio-Economics*, 21, 39–41.

Yates, A. (1989). Current perspectives on the eating disorders. I. History, psychological, and biological aspects. *Journal of the American Academy of Child and Adolescent Psychiatry*, 28, 813–828.

Yates, A. (1990). Current perspectives on the eating disorders. II. Treatment, outcome, and research directions. *Journal of the American Academy of Child and Adolescent Psychiatry*, 29, 1–9.

Yehuda, R., & McFarlane, A.C. (1995). Conflict between current knowledge about posttraumatic stress disorder and its original conceptual basis. *American Journal of Psychiatry*, 152, 1705–1713.

Yi, D. (1991). Alcohol. In N.S. Miller (Ed.), *Comprehensive handbook of drug and alcohol addiction*. New York: Marcel Dekker.

Yonkers, K.A., & Gurguis, G. (1995). Gender differences in the prevalence and expression of anxiety disorders. In Mary V. Seeman (Ed.), *Gender and psychopathology*, pp. 113–130. Washington, DC: American Psychiatric Press.

Zahner, G.E.P., Hsieh, C., & Fleming, J.A. (1995). Introduction to epidemiologic research methods. In M.T. Tsuang, M. Tohen, & Zahner, G.E.P. (Eds.), *Textbook in psychiatric epidemiology*, pp. 23–53. New York: Wiley-Liss.

Zahn-Waxler, C., Kochanska, G., Krupnick, J., & McKnew, D. (1990). Patterns of guilt in children depressed and well mothers. *Developmental Psychology*, 26, 51–59.

Zajecka, J., Fawcett, J., Schaff, M ., Jeffriess, H., & Guy, C. (1991). The role of serotonin in sexual dysfunction: Fluoxetine-associated orgasm dysfunction. *Journal of Clinical Psychiatry*, 52, 66–68.

Zarit, S.H., Zarit, J.M., & Rosenberg-Thompson, S. (1990). A special treatment unit for Alzheimer's disease: Medical, behavioral, and environmental features. *Clinical Gerontologist*, 9, 47–63.

Zatta, P.F. (1993). Controversial aspects of aluminum accumulation and subcompartmentation in Alzheimer's disease. *Trace Elements in Medicine*, 10, 120–128.

Zeiss, A.M., Lewinsohn, P.M., & Munoz, R.F. (1979). Nonspecific improvement effects in depression using interpersonal skills training, pleasant activity schedules, or cognitive training. *Journal of Consulting and Clinical Psychology*, 47, 247–439.

Zigler, E. (1967). Familial mental retardation: A continuing dilemma. *Science*, 155, 292–298.

Zigler, E., & Hall, N.W. (1989). Physical abuse in America: Past, present, and future. In D. Cicchetti, & V. Carlson (Eds.), *Child maltreatment: Theory and research on the causes and consequences of child abuse and neglect*, pp. 38–77. Cambridge: University of Cambridge Press.

Zigler, E., & Hodapp, R.M. (1986). *Understanding mental retardation*. New York: Cambridge University Press.

Zigler, E., & Styfco, S.J. (1993). Using research and theory to justify and inform Head Start expansion. *Social Policy Report for the Society Research in Child Development*, 7(2), 1–20.

Zemishlany, Z., Siever, L.J., & Coccaro, E.F. (1988). Biologic factors in personality disorders. *Israel Journal of Psychiatry and Related Sciences*, 25, 12–23.

Zilbergeld, B. (1978). *Male sexuality*. New York: Bantam.

Zill, N. (1978). *Divorce, marital happiness, and the mental health of children: Findings from the FCD National Survey of Children*. Paper presented at the NIMH workshop on divorce and children. Bethesda, MD.

Zill, N., & Nord, C.W. (1994). *Running in place*. Washington, DC: Child Trends.

Zimmerman, M., & Coryell, W.H. (1989). DSM-III personality disorder diagnoses in a nonpatient sample. *Archives of General Psychiatry*, 46, 682–689.

Zimmerman, M., & Coryell, W.H. (1990). Diagnosing personality disorders in the community: A comparison of self-report and interview measures. *Archives of General Psychiatry*, 47, 527–531.

Zinbarg, R.E., Barlow, D.H., Brown, T.A., & Hertz, R.M. (1992). Cognitive-behavioral approaches to the nature and treatment of anxiety disorders. *Annual Review of Psychology*, 43, 235–267.

Ziskin, J., & Faust, D. (1989). Psychiatric and psychological evidence in child custody cases. *Trial*, 45–49.

Zoccolillo, M., & Cloninger, C.R. (1985). Parental breakdown associated with somatization disorder (hysteria). *British Journal of Psychiatry*, 147, 443–446.

Zola-Morgan, S., Squire, L.R., & Amaral, D.G. (1986). Human amnesia and the medial temporal region: Enduring memory impairment following a bilateral lesion limited to field CA1 of the hippocampus. *Journal of Neuroscience*, 6, 2950–2967.

Zook, A., & Walton, J.M. (1989). Theoretical orientations and work settings of clinical and counseling psychologists: A current perspective. *Professional Psychology*, 20, 23–31.

Zucker, K.J. (1985). Cross-gender-identified children. In B.W. Steiner (Ed.), *Gender dysphoria: Development, research, management*, pp. 75–174. New York: Plenum.

Zuckerman, M. (1990). Some dubious premises in research and theory on racial differences: Scientific, social, and ethical issues. *American Psychologist*, 45, 1297–1303.

Zuckerman, M. (1991). *Psychobiology of personality*. New York: Cambridge University Press.

Name Index

Cade, J., 142
Cado, S., 337
Cadoret, R. J., 263
Cairns, R. B., 103
Caldwell, C., 147
Cameron, H. M., 95
Cameron, N., 47
Cameron, O. G., 165
Campbell, E., 433
Campbell, M., 407, 408, 420
Canino, G. L., 210
Cannon, T. D., 369
Cannon, W. B., 222–224
Cantor-Graae, E., 367
Cantwell, D. P., 417
Caplan, P. J., 10, 19–20, 251
Cardena, E., 184, 201, 202
Carey, G., 263
Carey, M. P., 336, 337
Carkhuff, R., 72
Carlsmith, J. M., 446
Carlson, C. I., 110
Carlson, E. A., 401, 406
Carlsson, A., 371
Carney, R. M., 238
Carpenter, W. T., 379
Carpenter, W. T., Jr., 360, 363
Carr, E. G., 414, 421
Carroll, R. A., 332
Carter, J., 96
Carter, R., 96, 178
Casas, J. M., 75, 76
Cash, T. F., 268, *269*
Caspi, A., 404
Cassidy, J., 401
Castle, D. J., 364
Caston, R. J., 91
Castonguay, L. G., 83
Cattarin, J. A., 283
Cerletti, U., 64
Cerny, J. A., 177
Chaloff, J., 405
Chambless, D. L., 159, 163, 165, 178
Chapman, J. P., *135*
Chapman, L. J., *135*
Chappel, J. N., 319
Charcot, J., 32, 199–200, 207, 212
Charney, D. S., 137, 138
Charvat, J., 224
Chassin, L., 313
Checkley, S., 139
Cherlin, A. J., 51
Chesney, M. A., 233–234, 235
Chess, S., 48, 404
Chou, J. C. Y., 179
Christensen, A., 81
Christiansen, B. A., 316, 317

Ciaranello, R. D., 41
Cicchetti, D., 39
Cimbolic, P., 138
Cipparone, R. C., 433
Clark, D. M., *171*, 172, 178
Clark, L. A., 97
Clarke, J. W., 427
Clarkin, J. F., 108
Cleckley, H. M., 202, 242, 243, 260–262, 264
Clementz, B. A., 88
Cloninger, C. R., 307, 314
Clum, G. A., 258
Cobain, K., 400
Cohen, C. I., 373
Cohen, D., 39
Cohen, J., *389*
Cohen, P., 406
Cohen, S., 51, 224, 226, 227, 315, 318
Coid, J., 264
Coie, J., 51
Cole, T. A., *223*
Cole, W., 344
Coleman, E. M., 189
Collaer, M. L., 345
Collins, F., 416
Cone, J. D., 99, 104
Conger, J. J., 316
Conners, C. K., *390*
Contrada, R. J., *235*
Cook, B. L., 179
Cook, M., 170
Cook, W. L., 376
Coons, P., 201, 203
Cooper, H. M., 301
Cooper, P. J., 273
Cooper, Z., 130
Coovert, D. L., 280
Corbitt, E. M., 262
Cornille, T. A., *25*
Corse, C. D., 234
Coryell, W. H., 125, 250
Costello, C. G., 156
Costello, E., 73, 82, 177
Cottey, T. J., 148
Coyne, J. C., 133
Craddock, N., 137
Crago, M., 77, 78
Cranston-Cuebas, M. A., 338
Craske, M. G., 157
Creese, L., 372
Crick, N. R., 406
Crocker, J., 91
Crossley, R., 418
Crouch, E., 81
Crowell, J. A., 258
Cullen, F., 438

Cummings, E. M., 409
Curoff, J. J., *204*, 204
Cyranowski, J. M., 327, 337

D

Dackis, C. A., 318
Dadds, M. R., 80, 407
Danforth, J. S., 404
Daniel, D. G., 111
Daro, D., 445, *446*
Dasen, P. R., 250
Davidson, J. R. T., 178, 184, 197
Davidson, L. M., *221*
Davidson, M., 36, 371
Davidson, W. S., 410
Davis, D., 359
Davis, D. D., 140
Davis, G. C., 191, *192*, 258
Davis, J. M., 138, 195
Davis, L., 199
Davis, R. H., 108
Davis, R. M., 311
DeBaryshe, B. D., 403
Deblinger, E., 189
Defares, P. B., 197
DeFries, J. C., 44
Delanney, L. E., *223*
DeLeon, P. H., 24
Delgado, P. L., 137
D'Emilio, J., 328
Depue, R. A., 138
DeRisi, W. J., 380
DeRosa, M., 357
deSilva, P., 342
Deutsch, S. I., 407, 408
DeVane, C. L., 407, 408
Diehl, S. R., 367
DiNardo, P. A., 164
Dishion, T. J., 402, 404
Ditta, S. R., 195
Dix, D., 19
Docherty, N. M., 357
Dodd, W. A., 246, *247*
Dodge, K. A., 406
Dolan, B., 14, 264
Donahey, K. M., 332
Donaldson, K., 439, *439*
Donovan, D. M., 321
Dooley, D., 236
Doren, D. M., 265
Dorsen, N., 449
Douglas, V. I., 390–391
Downey, G., 133
Draguns, J. G., 14
Dreyfuss, R., 300
Dulcan, M. K., 408
Dunham, H. W., 372–373
Durham, M. L., 436, 437

Durkheim, E., 147–148
D'Zurrilla, T., 70

E

Eaton, W. W., 145, 381
Eaves, L. J., *137, 280*
Eberlin, M., 418
Edelbrock, C. S., 349, 400
Edmonstone, Y., 112
Egeland, J. D., 146
Ehlers, A., 172
Ehrlich, P., 32
Eisen, S. A., 194
Eisenberg, L., 15
Eklund, P. L., 349
Ekman, G., 420
Elkin, I., 141
Elliott, R. K., 72
Ellis, A., 50, 177
Emde, R. N., 263
Emery, G., 49, 172, 177
Emery, R. E., 51, 70, 79, 403, 409, 410, 444, 445
Ennis, B., 449
Epstein, N., 80
Erdelyi, M. H., 200
Erikson, E. H., 50, 67
Erlenmeyer-Kimling, L., 254
Ernst, C., 335
Eron, L. D., 403
Eshleman, S., *166*
Esquirol, J., 143
Exner, J. E., 108, 109
Eysenck, H. J., 73, 168, 169

F

Fabrega, H., 91
Faigman, D. L., 433
Fairbanks, C. G., *279*
Fairburn, C. G., 274, 275, 277, 279–281, 284, 285, 287–288, *288*
Fallon, P., 286
Falloon, L., 80
Farde, L., 372
Faris, R. E. L., 372–373
Farmer, A. E., 91, 378
Farrington, D. P., 388, *389*
Faust, D., 434
Fawzy, F. I., 218, 229
Fay, J., 196
Feinleib, M., 235
Feinstein, C., 417–418
Feldman, J., 198
Felner, R. D., 74
Ferreira, L., 315
Figley, C. R., 189
Fincham, F. D., 79, 409, 444

Subject Index